as the ship could go. In th[ey] [had]
to stop and tie up to the side sometimes
to let other ships go by.
You would have liked to see the
other ship go by and to see the desert.
The only birds we ~~saw~~ saw were some snipe
and quite a lot of hawks and a few
Cormorants and one old blue Crane.
I miss you, old Mex, and will be glad
to see you again. Will have plenty of good stories
to tell you when we come back.
When you get down to Key West
remember me to captain Bra and Mr. Sully.
Give my best to everybody in Piggott.
Go Easy on the beer and lay off
the hard liquor until I get back.
Dont forget to blow your nose
and turn around three times before you go to
bed.
                    Your affectionate papa,
                              Papa

17th October 81

Tee,

This book you gave
to me once, shortly after I
arrived in England for THE
DARK CRYSTAL.
I now give it to you as
I find it very entertaining &
more interesting as Hemingway
advances in age.
He was an outspoken
man who said exactly what
was on his mind and attempted
to tell his tales truthfully.
Happy Birthday.
Love, Barry

Other books by Carlos Baker

Fiction
THE TALISMANS AND OTHER STORIES
THE GAY HEAD CONSPIRACY
THE LAND OF RUMBELOW
A FRIEND IN POWER

Poetry
A YEAR AND A DAY

Criticism
HEMINGWAY: THE WRITER AS ARTIST
SHELLEY'S MAJOR POETRY

Biography
ERNEST HEMINGWAY: A LIFE STORY

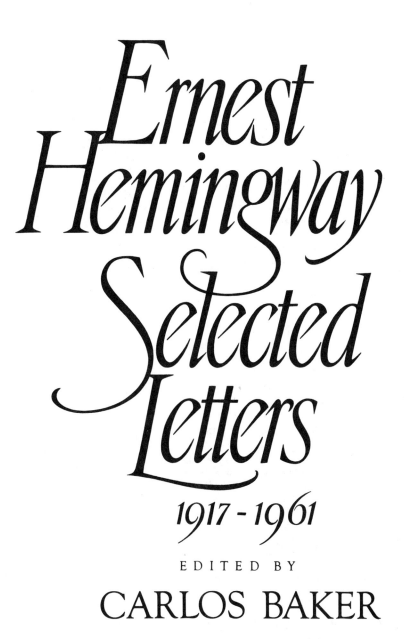

Ernest Hemingway Selected Letters 1917 - 1961

EDITED BY

CARLOS BAKER

First say to yourself what you would be,
and then do what you have to do.

—Epictetus, *Discourses*

GRANADA
London Toronto Sydney New York

Granada Publishing Limited
Frogmore, St Albans, Herts AL2 2NF
and
3 Upper James Street, London W1R 4BP
Suite 405, 4th Floor, 866 United Nations Plaza, New York, NY 10017, USA
117 York Street, Sydney, NSW 2000, Australia
100 Skyway Avenue, Rexdale, Ontario M9W 3A6, Canada
PO Box 84165, Greenside, 2034 Johannesburg, South Africa
61 Beach Road, Auckland, New Zealand

Published by Granada Publishing 1981

ISBN 0 246 11576 9

Printed in the United States of America

Granada ®
Granada Publishing ®

This book is for Charles Scribner, Jr.
Publisher, Editor, Friend

*"Tell Charlie how pleased
and proud I was ... of him
and how he figured things."*
—ERNEST HEMINGWAY,
1959

CONTENTS

Re: DIVORCE FROM HADLEY p 257
Re: FATHER'S DEATH p 291 + 292
                     p 295 + 296

INTRODUCTION

Ernest Hemingway once thanked a friend for a gift copy of the memoirs of the Baron de Marbot, one of Napoleon's generals: "I had never seen that Marbot translation and it is marvellous. It is wonderful what good letters people wrote in those days and miserable how poor our own are." All his life he had sheepishly apologized to friends for the "dullness and stupidity" of his own letters. With rare exceptions, however, the terms were not applicable. For his voluminous correspondence was everywhere diversified with gossip, anecdotes both serious and bawdy, high and low badinage, boasts and self-recriminations, complaints and confessions, instructions and ruminations, passages of wild and witty inventiveness, character sketches of friends and enemies, arresting instances of vilification, memories and predictions, off-the-cuff literary, political, and sociological opinions, information on what he was doing and thinking in what hour of what day and under what climatic conditions, and a thousand other topics that sporadically engaged his teeming and lively mind.

Except on those occasions that required the most precise and carefully honed language, he neither was nor pretended to be a formal letter writer. He knew it, half-heartedly deplored it, and really did not care. "Plenty of times people who write the best write the worst letters," he said in 1929. "It's almost a rule." And in 1957: "This letter is sloppy and full of mistakes but is written in a hurry and is correspondence not an attempt at prose." Despite the frequency of such remarks, he must surely have known what readers can now discover for themselves, that almost every letter from his table or desk or typewriter or clipboard bore the unmistakable impress of one of the most commanding personalities of the age.

All his life after adolescence Hemingway was a confirmed, habitual, and even compulsive correspondent for whom communication was a constant necessity. Including those of his letters that were burned, drowned, nibbled to nothing by rodents or tropical insects, inadvertently or intentionally thrown away (whether by himself or others), or hoarded in trunks and safety deposit boxes or otherwise sequestered from the light of day, he probably wrote six or seven thousand in the fifty years preceding his death in 1961—to say nothing of the flood of cables and telegrams that he sometimes sent in lieu of longer missives.

Had he done fewer, his productivity as a serious writer of fiction might have been greater. This thought often occurred to him. "Any time I can write a good letter it's a sign I'm not working," he once said. Composing letters was "such a swell way to keep from working and yet feel you've done something." He loved to write well enough to be willing to "waste" many words and many hours in turning out the verbal torrents or trickles that flowed from wherever he was to wherever his friends were. "It is only that when you are used to writing it is hard to stop and I like to talk with you even when it is only in letters and the conversation is lamentably stupid and one-sided." So he told Charles Scribner in 1951, out of the midst of an epistolary efflorescence that began about 1949 and extended through 1952. There had been other such periods: 1924 to 1928, for example, when he was rapidly and sometimes ruthlessly ascending the ladder of fame, and 1939 to 1941, during and after the composition of *For Whom the Bell Tolls.*

Even when he was going well as a writer of fiction, he seemed to require the relaxation of letter writing as an antidote to the concentration of creativity. In the letters, he could be as loose, devil-may-care, recklessly copious, and repetitive as he chose, whereas under the discipline of setting down the best words in the best order he seldom exceeded five hundred at a single sitting. So he wrote letters to warm up his brain in the early morning before the day's stint of "serious" composition began, or to "cool out" in the afternoon or evening after he had laid aside the current story or chapter, rather like an athlete jogging once more around the track after the race was done.

Under it all lay his characteristic distinction between work and play. Play was the anodyne that made his serious writing possible by providing periods of relaxation between bouts of the most intensive application. Writing letters was for him one of the forms of play, which was what gave them a kind of dash and spontaneity that they might have lacked if he had taken greater pains with their content or organization. Writing fiction, on the other hand, was work of the most difficult kind. The stories were designed to last, perhaps for centuries. In spite of the time he gave to his correspondence it was only a by-product—a play product—of the always present urge to creativity. Letters were not to be written with the long future in mind. Ford Madox Ford once told him that a man "should always write a letter thinking of posterity." This, said Hemingway in 1950, "made such a bad impression on me that I burned every letter in the flat including Ford's. Should you save the hulls a .50 cal. shucks out for posterity? Have them, O.K. But they should be written or fired not for posterity but for the day and the hour, and posterity will always look after herself."

Although Hemingway rightly boasted that he was a better speller than Scott Fitzgerald, he continued all his life to fall into such obvious errors as *apoligize, responsability, optomistic, its-self, volumne,* and *manoever—*

this last always a problem to one who loved military language. It was a special trademark of his personal style to use *nor* instead of *or* after a previous negative. In easy defiance of the grammarian's rule, he regularly retained the final *e* when adding —*ing* or —*able*, as in *loveing* or *comeing*, or in the phrase immortalized in the title of *A Moveable Feast*. He did not give a damn about the distinctions between *who* and *whom*, *lying* and *laying*. "The last thing I remember about English in High School," he once wrote, "was a big controversy on whether it was *already* or *all ready*. How did it ever come out?" When scribbling hastily—and often illegibly—as he nearly always did in longhand letters, he ignored most apostrophes for contractions or possessive cases, he rarely bothered to cross a *t* or dot an *i*, he believed that the simple plural of a proper name like Murphy was Murphy's, and his spelling of place names was little to be trusted, though he usually knew better than he wrote and commonly excused himself on the grounds that dictionaries were several rooms away. "The spelling and construction of my letters is careless rather than ignorant," he said in 1952. Having learned French, Italian, and Spanish by ear and for the most part without regular recourse to thesauruses, he often committed grammatical mayhem on the foreign language tags with which he spiced up his letters. His position was that one could always hire other people to correct such minor slips. There was also a suspicion that unreined language might just possibly have a life of its own beyond accepted rules. Hemingway would clearly have agreed with the view of Artemus Ward: "Why care for grammar as long as we are good?"

He sometimes leaned over backward to avoid the accusation of pretentiousness in language, a habit that produced what has been called "Hemingway Choctaw." Lillian Ross included some examples in her *New Yorker* profile of the great man on vacation in the great city. On being ushered into a hotel room he said, "Joint looks okay." After a visit to the Metropolitan Museum of Art, he muttered, "Was fun for country boy like me." At lunch, chewing vigorously, he asserted, "Eat good and digest good." The tendency seems to have begun as an attempt to avoid immodest repetition of the first person singular pronoun, moving from there to the elimination of other pronouns, certain verbs, and common articles like *an* and *the*. It was possibly associated with his liking for the language of cables, which had entranced him since his newspaper days. But he seems also to have adopted it as a mode of utterance both in speech and in letters because he thought it down to earth, laconic, and manly. "Difference with us guys," he once wrote William Faulkner, "is I always lived out of country . . . since kid." He often echoed a phrase about the gradual downfall of mankind into modern times, which he said he had picked up from an actual old Indian: "Long time ago good, now heap shit."

In letter after letter he liked to amuse his distant associates with what he called "the dirt." The late Elizabeth Drew, writing of eighteenth-century epistolary effusions, named them *The Literature of Gossip*. Many passages in the epistles of Hemingway richly deserve this title. "Am always a perfectly safe man to tell any dirt to," he wrote John Dos Passos, "as it goes in one ear and out my mouth." The kind of Whitmanesque gab that commonly emerged in his tête-à-tête conversations with close cronies was likely to be duplicated whenever he seized a pen or pencil to communicate with them if they were out of hearing. Gossip flowed from his memory like Spanish wine from an upended *bota*. "I could tell you a funny story about that one," he would write, and the story often followed—funny sometimes, or cantankerous or malicious or vulgar, but very rarely dull. "I write letters because it is fun to get letters back," he said in 1950. He looked forward with demonic relish to the "dirt" they might contain. "Tell me about it," he was always imploring. "I'm lonely. . . . It's boring here. . . . What's the latest?" The letters he longed for, as well as hundreds that he did not want, came to his desk in profusion. He answered them when and if he felt like it, without ever relinquishing his pleasure in dirt given or dirt received.

Because Hemingway was by nature and inclination and profession a spinner of yarns, not all of the stories relayed in his letters can be trusted as true. He believed and often said that writers are liars and took evident delight in living up to his own dictum in conversation and letters. The boundary lines on his personal map of the Kingdoms of Truth and Falsehood were not marked with flapping flags. Many a recipient of his letters, many a listener to his monologues, was convinced by his simulated air of veracity into supposing that a given report was factual, only to discover in due time that it had been mainly fictional. Having spent his life as a narrator who had always mingled invention with reportage, he was little inclined to abandon the habit in the heat of epistolary composition.

Finally, there is plenty of evidence that he used letter writing as a form of occupational therapy, the rough equivalent of the psychiatrist's couch, a way of relieving his mind of some burden that the events of the day had thrown upon it. "I might as well write it out now and maybe get rid of it that way," he told Pauline Pfeiffer in 1926. Twenty-five years later he was saying to his wife Mary, "This letter whines like an air-raid siren. Play it on your pianola and scare the inhabitants. . . . I was just saying I felt a little low today, chucking it off to you to get rid of it." His wives were not his only listeners, though doubtless among the four of them they heard the most. Far back in boyhood he had written Bill

Smith in the odd patois they used to affect: "Havta carp along wit cheerful facial all diurnal and seek relief in a screed." Translated: "You have to move along all day with a cheerful face and then find relief in letter writing."

Such statements suggest the psychology of the confessional booth. Yet they were not so much petitions for absolution—"Bless me, Father, for I have sinned"—as they were pleas for understanding, longing for justification and even admiration in the eyes and minds of others. Speaking out what inwardly plagued him helped to alleviate his red-and-black rages, skimmed his boiling brain of residual feculence, and answered his need for comradely interchange with people he trusted to understand him and to realize what his life was mainly about. "I get lonesome," he once said, "and I like to write to somebody who is literate and knows about what I know about and seems to have a mind." Often, no doubt, he was only explaining himself to himself in the assumed presence of a sympathetic but silent listener. Yet one recurrent note in all the correspondence is the ardent wish that others would see him as he was, would understand how things *really* were with him, rather than how they were widely reputed to be.

Three "letters" that Hemingway wrote at the age of nine have survived to the present day. One went to his father on vacation in New Orleans and the others to his mother and sister on the island of Nantucket. They provide a rough self-portrait of the artist as a very young man.

Dear Papa: Last Friday in our aquarium in School the water was all riley. I looked in a clam that I had brought to school from the [Desplaines] river. Had shut down on one of our big Japanese fantail gold fishes tales. On Saturday Mama and I went across the ford at the river. It was very much higher. I got six clams in the river and some weat six feet tall. Your loving son, Ernest M. Hemingway.

Dear Marc[elline]: Our room won in the field day against Miss Koontz room. Al Bersham knocked two of Chandlers teeth out in a scrap and your dear gentle Miss Hood had Mr. Smith hold him while she lickt him with a raw hide strap. Lovingly, Ernest.

Dear Mom and Marse: I passed to 6 grade so did Marse. Papa and I got some wild roses and wild strawberry. Ursula passed too. The Sundy School picknick is toworow. St. Nicholos [magazine] came and did not have Marces thing in it about the bird. Emily Harding sent you a brass bowl for birthday. We went to Forest Park and went down the grand canon it is like a jiant coaster. Sunny and ted were very scared. Lovingly, Ernest. P.S. Pa gave me 5 *silver dollars* for passing.

These little notes point to some of his future biases: love of nature, interest in physical violence, pleasure in competition, pride in personal fearlessness. Yet they hardly betoken a youthful prodigy. It is not until some years afterward that the Hemingway we think we know best begins to emerge from the chrysalis of boyhood into a far rougher and larger world than the one he knew at the edge of adolescence. We therefore begin with the letter of 1917 when the stalwart eighteen year old, a recent high school graduate, has nearly finished harvesting potatoes and hay in a lakeside field of northern Michigan and pauses to recall with pride the four large trout he has just caught in nearby Horton Bay. When we take leave of him forty-four years later—a world figure, ill and aging, harassed by paranoia and hypertension, standing on the brink of suicide—it is touching to remember the tall young figure in that far-off pastoral terrain, the well-loved scion of a middle-class Christian family, hard-working, responsible, eager for his parents' approbation. He has changed by 1961, but not completely. Two letters written in the final weeks of his life reflect his continuing pleasure in the American landscape and in two of its great rivers, the Mississippi and the Yellowstone, where bass still jump and trout still swim as they have been doing all through his sixty fleeting years.

In the early fall of 1917, Hemingway was about to begin his first adventure outside the family circle, six months as a cub reporter for the *Kansas City Star*. In May 1918 he set off on a far more consequential trip in the opposite direction. The train this time set him down in New York, where he excitedly explored the metropolis, paraded down Fifth Avenue in his brand-new uniform, and gleefully embarked on a troopship to drive ambulances in northern Italy. Less than two months later he became one of the first American casualties on the Piave River front, and one of the earliest patients in the new Red Cross Hospital in Milan.

His letters home from Milan reflect his pride in his military conduct, his courageous behavior under fire, his stoicism during recuperation, and his evident pleasure in having made a contribution to the war that was supposed to end all wars. The boy who came back to Oak Park in January 1919 had changed considerably. The immersion in combat, the severity of his wounds, a love affair with his Red Cross nurse, and association with new comrades in a foreign land had enlarged his horizons, raised him toward adulthood, and sharpened his desire to write other kinds of stories than those he had sweated over two years earlier for the *Star*. He had now learned to drink and smoke, and his interest in the companionship of women had evidently accelerated, though not to the degree of which he was later to boast.

The call of the wilderness was still strong within him, and he spent the better part of the summer and fall among the lakes and streams of northern Michigan, unwilling to surrender to the necessities of job hunting until he had caught and eaten his fill of fat trout. The experiences of Krebs in "Soldier's Home" and of Nick Adams in "Big Two-Hearted River" are the best fictional accounts of Hemingway's first postwar year. But the background for both stories, as well as much else, is vividly represented in his contemporaneous letters, which trace his evolution in his own words, add up to the longest "book" he ever wrote, and constitute the closest approach to an autobiography that he ever did.

Apart from his family, the people he wrote to in these years were Bill Smith, his faithful friend from the boyhood summers in Michigan; Bill Horne, Howell Jenkins, and Larry Barnett, with whom he had driven ambulances in Italy; Grace Quinlan, his fifteen-year-old "Sister Luke" of Petoskey; Isabel Simmons, later Godolphin, his neighbor in Oak Park; and his first-wife-to-be, Elizabeth Hadley Richardson of St. Louis.

As the scene changed, so did the names of the correspondents. Before long he was writing to some of the most famous literary figures of his time: Owen Wister, Ezra Pound, Sherwood Anderson, Gertrude Stein; James Joyce, Dos Passos, Fitzgerald, Archibald Mac Leish. Soon he was engaged with "the publishers" Robert Mc Almon, Ernest Walsh, Harold Loeb, and Horace Liveright, none of whom he really liked; with Edward O'Brien, who helped him to get started; with Maxwell Perkins, the inimitable editor, and subsequently with the Charles Scribners, Senior and Junior, with all of whom he got on famously. In the twenties and thirties he wrote reams to Waldo Peirce and Henry (Mike) Strater, his chief cronies among American painters, and exchanged jocose insults with Guy Hickok of the Paris office of the *Brooklyn Daily Eagle*. Among other journalists with whom he corresponded early and late were Janet Flanner and Lillian Ross of *The New Yorker* and J. Donald Adams, Harvey Breit, and Charles Poore of the *New York Times*. His six-year engagement with *Esquire* magazine led to a friendship with Arnold Gingrich that lasted through the period of the Spanish Civil War. In the course of their successful attempt to free Ezra Pound, Hemingway developed a nodding acquaintance with Robert Frost and T. S. Eliot. The chief literary critics to whom he wrote were Edmund Wilson and Malcolm Cowley, as well as Ivan Kashkeen of the U.S.S.R. Late in life he established an amusing postal relationship with the octogenarian art historian Bernard Berenson. Some of his most candid writing about Fitzgerald was sent to Scott's biographer, Arthur Mizener. His favorite professional soldiers were E. E.

Dorman-Smith, later O'Gowan, a lifelong friend from World War I, and Charles T. Lanham, his chief military hero during and after World War II. In the final decade of his life he wrote often to Adriana and Gianfranco Ivancich, the sister and brother who formed the nucleus of what he called the "Venetian branch" of his family. He blew hot and cold in his estimate of William Faulkner, his acknowledged chief rival in American fiction, usually addressing him through intermediaries, though at least one curious letter from each to the other has survived.

It is both instructive and absorbing to watch this "country boy" as he outgrows the provincialism of his youth and begins to consort with the famous, at first on the level of unknown petitioner, then on terms of socio-literary equality, and finally as recognized master in his chosen field. The letters of the 1920s movingly reflect Hemingway's struggle for recognition. Like many epoch-making writers—Faulkner is another instance—who must create the public taste by which their works are to be judged and accepted, he did not achieve an immediate breakthrough. It was not until the fall of 1925, four years after his postwar move to Paris, that *In Our Time*, the first notable collection of his short stories, began to build him a modest following among American readers. Yet another year would have to pass before the publication of *The Sun Also Rises* stamped him indubitably as a writer to be reckoned with.

In that same year of 1926, a particularly difficult time in his private calendar, he stated that he was "not a saint nor built like one." His unsaintly side had already appeared in some of the earlier letters and would remain visible for years to come. Although he was from the beginning no tyro in the art of backbiting, he was backbitten by many both early and late, and it was characteristic of him to bite back with compound interest. His notoriously short temper was aroused by adverse criticism of whatever kind. His nonliterary grudges sometimes congealed into rejections of people he had formerly loved: his mother for her alleged disloyalty because she had sent him insulting remarks about *The Sun Also Rises*, his older sister because she had scolded him for leaving his first wife, his youngest sister because she had married against his wishes. Praise of his writings always pleased him; pejorative judgments kindled his wrath. His frequent threats to thrash the members of the opposition, though seldom carried out, contain hints of the incipient bully. He modified a line from Kipling's "If" to boast that he could "walk with shits nor lose the common touch." The common touch with him often amounted to anointing the hapless heads of his victims with vinegar and gall, as in his critiques of Robert McAlmon, Max Eastman, Edmund Wilson, Gertrude Stein, and Wyndham Lewis. The almost unbelievable overkill of his attack on James Jones, one of his fellow authors at Scribners, was occasioned by his belief that Jones had not fulfilled his duties as a soldier. Hemingway sporadically purged built-up emotions with vituperation at least as strong as anything in Jonathan Swift. In the large category that he labeled *jerks* were included people as various as Franklin D. Roosevelt, Marshal Bernard Montgomery, General Jacques Leclerc, André Malraux, Cardinal Spellman, and Senator Joseph Mc Carthy, along with dozens of the less famous.

Hemingway defended the retention of a noxious though powerful passage in *For Whom the Bell Tolls* on the ground that removing it would be like "taeking either the bass viol or the oboe" out of his orchestra "because they each make an ugly noise when played alone." The blat of ugly noises is not absent from his letters. His occasional use of terms like *frog*, *wop*, *jig*, and *kike* is regrettable, though we ought to remind ourselves that—like Frost, Pound, and Eliot, to name a few—he was born into a time when such epithets were regrettably commonplace on most levels of American society. Hemingway's anti-Semitism was no more than skin deep; it was mainly a verbal habit rather than a persistent theme like that of Pound. When accused of having pilloried Harold Loeb as Robert Cohn in *The Sun Also Rises*, he rejoined that there was no law against portraying a bounder and a cad as such merely because he happened to be of Jewish extraction. His taste for Grand Guignol, as in the passage from *The Bell* mentioned above, eventuated in several anecdotes, all probably apocryphal, about his surly or murderous misadventures in World War II. On such instances of coarseness there is no need to dwell inordinately. They stand among the flaws in a complex personality structure that under normal circumstances was strong enough and tall. If at times his letters appear to be touched with a boastful pride that approaches megalomania, it was very likely little more than a verbal counterforce to the self-doubts that often assailed him, even when he believed deeply in the work he was doing. His hypochondria, which ran like an elongated groan throughout his life, can be explained, if not explained away, by his recurrent recognition that illness was one of the great enemies of literary productivity.

It is probable that his shortcomings, which were real, undeniable, and in fact not denied even by himself, were balanced by qualities that more than tipped the scale in his favor. Among his virtues must be named his lifelong perseverance and determination in the use and development of his gifts, his integrity as an artist, his unremitting reverence for the craft he practiced, and his persistent love of excellence, whether in his own work or that of others. His literary relationships with Anderson, Pound, Stein, Ford, Fitzgerald, Wilson, Mac Leish, and Faulkner are of compelling interest in showing his competitive spirit, his hatred of cant, his disgust with sloppy workmanship, his proud avoidance of imitation, and the high value he set upon industry, independence, and incorruptibility.

As a man he loved, and ordinarily did his best to follow, the attributes of fortitude, courage, honor, and thoroughgoing honesty in the conduct of his affairs, including the financial. His generosity was wide ranging; he showed a ready sympathy for the ailing, the bereaved, and the downtrodden. He respected form, performance, and endurance wherever he found it among hunters, shooters, fishermen, guides, trackers, skinners, jockeys and race horses, boxers and jai alai champions, military tacticians and historians, pitchers, catchers, and infielders. The concept of fatherhood stood high in his scale of values. He had loved his own father "very much and for a long time" and passed on that love to his three sons, with whom he sought to share all the practical wisdom and experiential knowledge he had acquired in an immensely varied career. He was generally uncomfortable with wet and howling infants, though his affection grew as they matured enough to carry on conversations, and the letters to his boys are full of guiding lights in the best paternal tradition.

His capacity for friendship was a notable trait in this highly gregarious man. The letters reflect his longing to gather his closest male friends around him for hunting, fishing, drinking, or conversational exploits. The formula varied little from his nineteenth to his fifty-ninth year. "Come on up," he urged Howell Jenkins and Jack Pentecost, the object in view being a fishing trip to the Pine Barrens near Vanderbilt, Michigan. He would supply the tackle and the guns; they must bring plenty of grog and cigarettes, along with enough ammunition to take potshots at any deer or bear that might cross their path through the wilderness. "Come on along," he wrote Bill Smith, Dos Passos, Don Stewart, and Harold Loeb as he laid his plans for a week at the annual Pamplona fiesta. "Come on down," he repeatedly cried from Key West to Mike Strater, Waldo Peirce, Archie MacLeish, and Max Perkins in the hope that they would share in his latest assault on the Gulf Stream. The sharing was important; it doubled or tripled his pleasure in manly feats of skill or endurance. "Come on out," he wrote from the Nordquist Ranch in Wyoming, with such warm enthusiasm that he was joined there at various times by Charles Thompson, Dos Passos, Tom Shevlin, Bill Horne, and others. Nothing could exceed his obvious pleasure when they came or his disappointment when they did not. "You know how he was," wrote Agnes von Kurowsky, his Red Cross nurse in Milan. "Men loved him. You know what I mean." What she meant was that his sociable nature steadily required the presence of like-minded men of good will in whose company he could relax, boast, show off, gossip and listen to gossip, tell tall tales, make rough jokes, shoot, fish, drink—often competitively—and share what he had and what he knew with those who were close to him in size, strength, or adventurous disposition.

With all his friends and acquaintances he prided himself as a teacher, the experienced insider who knew many if not all the answers and was eager to transmit them: how to win at roulette or horse racing or poker; how to get from Paris to Montreux, from Chicago to Horton Bay, from New York to Nairobi; how to make a Bloody Mary, outbox an adversary, outfox a customs officer. *Semper paratus* might have been his motto. He was always prepared with what he called "the gen," by which he meant the latest and most trustworthy intelligence, on what hooks and flies to use for steelhead or rainbow trout, what baits for giant marlin, what guns for dangerous game, what vitamins for health. Along with the hows and the whats went his worldly knowledge of the whos, the whens, and the wheres, each one on tap for instant communication.

In another of his guises he was the assiduous statistician, forever setting down weights and measures, dimensions and distances. He kept elaborate charts of the number of words he wrote each day, as well as log books that proved his prowess as a fisherman—the length and weight of each prize he took, the minutes required to bring it to the gaff. On the walls of various bathrooms were the daily readings of his weight and later on of his fluctuating blood pressure. He knew to the penny what his bank balance was, kept abreast of the figures on the sale of his books, the royalties they earned, the horrendous sums he paid in income taxes.

Although we have been examining certain distinctive characteristics of Hemingway as they emerge in the letters, any such survey pales by comparison with the living tissue of the letters themselves. In his salubrious moods, he could be very funny; in damp weather he could erupt into the most savage complaints; by turns he could be tender and tough, fastidious or outrageous, modest or vainglorious. A voracious reader who often gobbled whole volumes in the watches of the night, he was always forthright and sometimes exceedingly shrewd in his literary judgments. Yet he was often blind to virtues—like those of Henry James, Edith Wharton, E. M. Forster, or Virginia Woolf, for example—that fell outside his criteria of taste and performance. In one of his "poems," written in 1928, he says that "the searchers for order will find that there is a certain discipline in the acceptance of experience." The practical empiricist speaks here. Certain of his attitudes gradually solidified into the code of conduct by which he chose to live. Others gradually altered beneath the repeated hammer blows of experience. It is fascinating to watch the shift in his religious views from the cheerful Protestant Christianity of 1918 through the nominal Catholicism of the period 1927 to 1937, and on to the sentimental humanism of the years after World War II. His attitude on patriotism ranged from the exuberant idealism of his youth through the growing cynicism of the Depression years and eventually to the strong resurgence of love for the country of his birth that took shape during his service as observer and participant in the European Theater. If his ideas on marriage and morals became more worldly as he grew older, he yet retained some remnants of respect for the familial ideals and the concepts of ethical restraint that his upbringing had fostered and inculcated. He once said that his experience of foreign and domestic politics left him feeling as though he had been drinking out of spittoons. The so-called statesmen who so crudely mismanaged the world from their seats of power were among his chief villains. Writers, on the other hand, ought to be like gypsies—"outlyers," he called them—dwelling apart, manning the peripheries, defying received opinion, scorning the edicts of the solons in Washington, Paris, Berlin, Rome, or any other seat of the kind of government that intruded unduly into the lives and fortunes of the governed. Always ill at ease with abstract ideas or metaphysical speculation, rejecting the intellectual's vocabulary and the philosopher's stance, he sometimes astonishes us with the expression of ideas and aesthetic pronouncements that could have been learned only from his struggles for mastery of his literary medium.

Any volume of selected letters is perhaps open to the suspicion that only those items have been chosen that might preserve or enhance the reader's liking for the person who wrote them. No such attempt has been made here. A great many letters had of course to be left out in order to represent the vast bulk of the correspondence within a reasonable one-volume compass. The chief criterion for inclusion was the interest and value of the contents. Nearly every letter throws at least some new light on aspects of his professional career, from his early journalism for the *Star* of Kansas City and the *Star* of Toronto to his work on *A Moveable Feast* late in his life. They also reveal in considerable (and welcome) detail his relationships to family, wives, sons, friends, enemies, fellow writers, and sundry world figures. They describe his adventures in some two dozen countries on four continents and bring us close to the course of his life and thought in all his chosen environments.

The author of these letters was primarily a serious writer whose reputation and influence, as he well knew, must depend finally upon his novels and short stories. Like the fiction, though in a far less formal fashion, the letters bear within them the substance of the man he was—imperfect, certainly, cracked and flawed like any other human being, yet vividly alive, an unforgettable force.

"He was," said his friend Archibald Mac Leish, "one of the most human and spiritually powerful creatures I have ever known. The only other man who seemed to me to be as much *present* in a room as Ernest was FDR, and I am not excepting Churchill." Much of this presence is visible—even audible and tangible—in his fiction. It can also be found in the letters, those loose and easy segments of reportage upon his life as it was being lived in all its sorrows and its joys, its triumphs and disasters. His devotion to letter writing was so strong that he kept it up until he died. "Please forgive the long stupid letters," he once asked Bernard Berenson. "I write them instead of stories and they are a luxury that gives me pleasure and I hope they give you some too." For Berenson and many other fortunate recipients, they did that and more. Now that he has been dead for twenty years, they deserve the wider audience that his books have always commanded.

NOTES AND ACKNOWLEDGMENTS

The decision to publish this selection from Hemingway's letters was made in May 1979 by Mary Hemingway and her attorney, Alfred Rice, in consultation with Charles Scribner, Jr. Proceeds are to be devoted to the Ernest Hemingway Foundation, which was incorporated on December 13, 1965, and has since made annual awards in the field of American fiction under the aegis of the P.E.N. Club.

There can be no question about the wisdom and rightness of the decision, which now makes available for the first time a very substantial number of Hemingway's letters exactly as he wrote them over a period of forty-four years. They will not only instruct and entertain the general reader but also provide serious students of literature with the documents necessary to the continuing investigation of the life and achievements of one of the giants of twentieth-century American fiction.

The reason for the long postponement goes back to one hour of one day in 1958 when Hemingway typed out a note to his executors. "It is my wish," he wrote, "that none of the letters written by me during my lifetime shall be published. Accordingly, I hereby request and direct you not to publish or consent to the publication by others, of any such letters." His chief reason for the request was undoubtedly the fact, as he had told Wallace Meyer in 1952, that the letters were "often libelous, always indiscreet, [and] often obscene." While the obscenities did not much matter, the possibility of libel actions and the understandable fear that some of his more indiscreet utterances might hurt people who were still alive were together sufficient to explain his reluctance to move into print with his correspondence.

His last will and testament, dated September 15, 1955, appointed Mary Hemingway executrix of all his property "of whatever kind and nature . . . real, personal, literary, or mixed, absolutely." Upon his death in 1961, she thus became sole owner of the contents of all his letters, even though many individual collectors and institutions had acquired the originals as investments or as historical material for the use of literary scholars. As his heir, Mrs. Hemingway felt that it was incumbent upon her to follow his instructions. During the next fifteen years she therefore sought to prevent publication of the letters whenever such plans or hopes were brought to her attention.

Although the excerpts that she printed in her autobiography, *How It Was* (1976), provided valuable insights and information on the last seventeen years of her husband's life, they obviously could not tell the whole story. The same was true of the more than 230 published quotations from the letters, some of them fairly extensive, which had already been listed by Audre Hanneman in her *Ernest Hemingway: A Comprehensive Bibliography* (Princeton University Press, 1967) and the supplementary volume of 1975. Many of these items had appeared as advertisements in the sales catalogues of various rare book dealers and auctioneers. Still others had been published, sometimes as facsimiles, in literature relating to library exhibitions. The *Mercure de France* (1963) had issued a sequence of his letters to Sylvia Beach, and *American Dialog* (1964) had brought out his correspondence with Milton Wolff.

Even in his lifetime, a considerable number of letters had appeared in print with Hemingway's permission. After brief deletions made at his request, Edmund Wilson included three in *Shores of Light*, and Donald Gallup used four in *The Flowers of Friendship: Letters Written to Gertrude Stein*. Ernst Rowohlt and Arnoldo Mondadori, his German and Italian publishers, had issued in English or in translation certain of his letters to them. More than a dozen of his Letters to the Editor had been printed over his signature in such periodicals as *Hound and Horn, The New Republic, The Saturday Review, Transition, Life, Outdoor Life, The New Yorker*, the *New York Times Book Review, The New York Herald Tribune Books*, and others. He had often yielded to the requests of scholars, bibliographers, journalists, and columnists for the right to print entire paragraphs or shorter extracts from the letters he had written to them, possibly in the hope that at least some of what they were saying about him would bear his personal imprimatur. In short, he had himself departed on many occasions from the letter and spirit of his directive of 1958.

At intervals throughout Hemingway's life he had also toyed with the notion of publishing at least some of his letters to various correspondents. In 1930 he wrote Maxwell Perkins that he would bring out his letters to Ernest Walsh "sometime when we're all broke." A letter to General Charles T. Lanham in 1948 had said, "Mary . . . can get out the letters. (I am thinking about how to feed the troops)." Eight months later he had remarked to Charles Scribner that "we ought to keep copies of our letters like Mr. Lord Byron and [John] Murray [his publisher]. I know some funny things that could write you if wasn't so inhibited. Now I know the copywrite [*sic*] remains with me am liable to write you goddamn near anything. And I don't even have to count the words." But he could not afford the time and energy for such projects as these.

Of the nearly six hundred letters in the present edition, each has been transcribed whole and uncut, and every effort has been made to follow verbatim Hemingway's endearing or exasperating idiosyncrasies of style, spelling, punctuation, and paragraphing. Some few exceptions to this general rule should, however, be mentioned. Occasional brief deletions have been made in order not to hurt the feelings of living persons. These are marked by ellipses in the accepted editorial fashion. Obvious errors in typed letters and slips of the pen in longhand have been silently corrected; punctuation has commonly been altered or added only where the sense of a sentence appeared to require clarification; and inside addresses have been omitted as a space-saving device and to avoid repetition. Each letter is headed with the name of the recipient, place of origin, and date. Inside square brackets in the text, various identifications, dates, places, and translations of foreign language tags have been supplied. Additional information appears in notes, keyed to the text by numbers.

The present location of the original of each letter is indicated by an abbreviation at the lower left of the point where it ends. Whenever such a location could not be determined, usually because an original was in a private collection, two further abbreviations have been used, followed by a key (PH. for photocopy, T.C. for typed copy) to the place where trustworthy copies may be found. For example, PH. PUL means that a photocopy of the original is in Princeton University Library, whereas T.C. JFK means that a typed copy rather than the original is in the Hemingway Collection at the John F. Kennedy Library.

The following abbreviations have been used for locations:

BU: Boston University, Boston, Massachusetts
CHICAGO: University of Chicago Library, Chicago, Illinois
COLBY: Colby College Library, Waterville, Maine
CUL: Cornell University Library, Ithaca, New York
FLA: University of Florida, Gainesville
HAMILTON: Hamilton College Library, Clinton, New York
HUL: Houghton Library, Harvard University, Cambridge, Massachusetts
I TATTI: Berenson Archive, Settignano, Italy
JFK: John F. Kennedy Library, Boston, Massachusetts
KNOX: Seymour Library, Knox College, Galesburg, Illinois
LC: Library of Congress, Washington, D.C.
LHC: Louis Henry Cohn Collection, New York, New York
LILLY: Lilly Library, Indiana University, Bloomington
NEWBERRY: Newberry Library, Chicago, Illinois
OREGON: University of Oregon Library, Eugene
PUL: Princeton University Library, Princeton, New Jersey
SIU: Morris Library, Southern Illinois University, Carbondale

SUNY-B: State University of New York, Buffalo
TEXAS: Humanities Research Center, University of Texas, Austin
UMD: McKeldin Library, University of Maryland, College Park
UVA: Clifton Waller Barrett Library, University of Virginia, Charlottesville
YUL: Beinecke Rare Book and Manuscript Library, Yale University, New Haven, Connecticut

Initials for individual owners who kindly granted permission are HMD (Honoria Murphy Donnelly); WDH (William Dodge Horne); WJ (Waring Jones); HS (Harry Sylvester); and WS (William W. Seward, Jr.).

The editor acknowledges with warm thanks the courteous cooperation of the following librarians and curators: Dr. Cecil Anrep, I Tatti; Jo August, Kennedy Library; Robert L. Beare, McKeldin Library; Edmund Berkeley, Jr., Alderman Library, Virginia; W. H. Bond, Houghton Library; Daniel J. Boorstin, Library of Congress; William R. Cagle, Lilly Library; J. F. Cocks, III, Colby College Library; Kenneth W. Duckett, Oregon; Ellen S. Dunlap, Texas; Donald F. Gallup, Yale; Howard B. Gotlieb, Boston University; Gustave A. Harrer, University of Florida; Diana Haskell, Newberry; Paul T. Heffron, Library of Congress; Donald W. Koepp, Princeton; Frank K. Lorenz, Hamilton; Richard M. Ludwig, Princeton; Charles B. Mc Namara, Cornell; Jean Preston, Princeton; Michael T. Ryan, Chicago; Saundra Taylor, Lilly Library; and Douglas L. Wilson, Seymour Library, Knox College.

For assistance of various kinds, always helpfully given, the editor is indebted to the following: Clifton Waller Barrett; Jacques Barzun; Professors Nina Berberova, James D. Brasch, and Victor Brombert; Helen Brooks, Edward Clohossey, Morrill Cody, Professor and Mrs. David Coffin, Mrs. L. H. Cohn, Earle E. Coleman, Rachel Currivan, Ethel Davis, Elizabeth Dos Passos, Luis Fernandez, Greta Fitzell, Eva Galan, Jonathan Goodwin, Sam Gowan, E. R. and Meyly Hagemann, David R. Hall, Mary Hemingway, Patrick Hemingway, Mary and Andrée Hickok, David Hirst, Dan Hodges, Faith Hostetter, Jeffrie Husband, Professor Samuel Hynes, Marian Johnson; Professors A. W. Litz, John Logan, and Townsend Ludington; Archibald and Ada Mac Leish, Robert Manning, Madelaine Hemingway Miller, Maurice F. Neville, Mardel Pacheco, Joseph M. Quinn, Alfred Rice, John Robben, Charles Scribner, III, Ralph Shadovitz, Marian Smith, Red Smith, Jane Snedeker, Professor Albert Sonnenfeld, Clara Spiegel, Mrs. Walter Stokes, Henry Strater, Professor J. R. Strayer, Professor and Mrs. Edward Sullivan, Mrs. Robert W. Tilney, Jr., Ann F. Van Arsdale, Professor Ira O. Wade, Diane Wagner, Alexander Wainwright, and Dr. Roy Winnick.

Finally, most hearty thanks must go to Dorothy S. Baker for valuable help with proofs and index; to Professor Raymond S. Willis, Jr., un-stumpable Hispanic scholar and linguist; Colonel Lawrence Spellman, whose close knowledge of maps and weapons solved many vexing prob-lems; Helen S. Wright, who cheerfully, promptly, and efficiently typed the entire manuscript; and Charles Scribner, Jr., whose hard work and constant encouragement assisted immeasurably in the preparation of this volume.

To ANSON T. HEMINGWAY, Walloon Lake, Michigan,
6 August 1917

Dear Grandfather:

I have been wanting to write you to thank you for the birthday present and papers but we have been putting in about 12 hours per day haying and working on the farm.[1] We need a rain awfully bad as everything is drying up and we stand to lose our potato crop if it doesn't rain soon. Uncle Geo. and family and Aunt G[race] and Uncle T[yler] are coming over tomorrow to spend the day. All our hay is in now and we can take things easier now. Dad's Ford is running fine now that the cylinders are clean and he wouldn't think of selling it.

The other night I caught three rainbow trout that weighed 6 lb 5½ lb and 3½ lb. respectively. Also a two lb. brook trout in Hortons Bay. That is the largest catch of trout that has ever been made there.

I certainly appreciate your sending me the papers as we have nothing to read up here except the daily paper two days late.

I may stay up here thru October working for [Jim] Dilworth and I am not going to the U. of Illinois this fall. When I get home I am either going out to Uncle Leicester [in California] or try and get a job with the Chicago Tribune. By next year I ought to be fixed so I can go to school.

Much love to Grandma and yourself,

JFK   Ernest

1. Longfield Farm across Walloon Lake from Windemere, the family cottage.

To DR. C. E. HEMINGWAY, Horton Bay, Michigan,
19 September 1917

Dear Dad:

I came in here [to Mrs. J. S. Dilworth's Pinehurst Cottage] last night from Walloon to get the mail and some more clothes. There will be about 60 bushel of marketable potatoes the way it looks now. Those 60 bu. however will be very good. You see there are strips of very good ones and then a lot of little nubbins.

I would advise shipping all the good ones home as Wesley [Dilworth] is only paying 85¢ per bushel. I am digging them all myself as Warren [Sumner] is all crippled up. In his joints.

I expect to finish them all and haul them over to the [Horton] Bay by Sat. night. It is very dry here just like powder and I am afraid our late beans will never get ripe. Our early ones are ready to pull now. Wesley advises shipping the spuds to O. P. [Oak Park]. I dig them, then pick up the good ones and put them in crates and then sack them. Warren comes down for an hour or so in the evening and we put them on the stone boat and haul them in the barn.

Today on the Missouri [lake steamer] go down to you the barrel of apples I spoke about on the card. Also I thot you could use a sack of spuds. That sack shows the general run of the good ones.

Please write your instructions right away so if you want them shipped down I will send them next Wed. on the boat.

I am planning to leave some time during the first week of Oct. I wanted to hire the Polacks to pick up but they wanted 5¢ a bush so I told them nothing doing.

Yours,
Ernie

P.S. Send me a Trib occasionally why not?   EMH

JFK

To HIS FAMILY, Kansas City, Missouri, 19 November 1917

Dear Folks:

This is about the third letter that I have started and had to stop all the others so am writing this right after work about 6:20 and so will try to finish. The last two weeks have been awfully busy with me, doing something every minute. Last Tuesday we all were called out and had drill and maneuvers all day. Yesterday I was up to Uncle Ty's for dinner, in the morning there was a big fire right next door to their new house, a large barn burned and I got there about the same time as the fire dept. and helped chop in the door and carried the hose up on the roof and had a good time generally. Probably I will stay at Miss Haines two weeks longer, I have been there a month today and by two weeks I will be able to get away all right.[1] Glad the Bayley was up last Sunday, I had a good letter from him and from Al Walker, Al sent you all his love. He is at Olivet and they can't get any coal and unless some comes soon they are going to have to close the college. There is no danger of the Star running out of coal. Much obliged for the stamps, they come in handy for mailing letters. This last week I have been handling a murder story, a lot of Police dope and the Y.W.C.A. fund stuff a couple of times so am mixing em up. How is everything going at home? That sure was a bad accident but it was a good job to smash up the Atwood-Rogovsky auto bandits any way. I have ridden in the Ambulance several times and as there is an epidemic of small pox here I think I will get vacinated again tomorrow. Aunt Arrabel[1] is doing lots of Food conservation work and is quite high up in the Food ring. We have been having a swell lot of fun down here with a new fellow named Johnson who is about Baby Dales speed and we have sure pulled some rare ones on him. There is a dandy bunch of fellows down here. I intend to go out to Camp Funston soon and look up Pinckney. He is head of the motor truck unit there. Also I am going down to Oklahoma some time before I go up North. Now if I am going to get any supper I will have to say good bye. The cookies were great try me again. Lots of Love

Ernie.

PS. Got your letter. Much obliged for package sent. It will arrive tomorrow probably.

JFK   EH

1. EH had reached Kansas City by train on 15 October and begun work for the *Star* on 18 October. He had recently joined the Missouri National Guard. EH to his family, 15 November, had said, "I will plan to work here until spring and then get in one more good summer [in Michigan] before enlisting. I couldn't possibly stay out of it any longer time than that under any circumstances. It will be hard enough to stay out till then." (JFK)

To GRACE HALL HEMINGWAY, Kansas City, 16 January 1918

Dear Mother:

I just got your letter today. I was beginning to wonder why I didn't hear from the folks but the trains have all been tied up in bad shape. It was 20° below here too tho not so much snow. In Kansas they had two or three feet in most all the country. No trains got thru at all from the West or East. We were sure cut off for a while. The coal shortage is still pretty bad here. However we should cogittate for it will soon be spring. Now dry those tears Mother and cheer up. You will have to find something better than that to worry about. Don't worry or cry or fret about my not being a good Christian. I am just as much as ever and pray every night and believe just as hard so cheer up! Just because I'm a *cheerful* Christian ought not to bother you.

The reason I don't go to church on Sunday is because always I have to work till 1 a.m. getting out the Sunday Star and every once in a while till 3 and 4 a.m. And I never open my eyes Sunday morning until 12.30

noon anyway. So you see it isn't because I don't want to. You know I don't rave about religion but am as sincere a Christian as I can be. Sunday is the one day in the week that I can get my sleep out. Also Aunt Arabell's church is a very well dressed stylish one with a not to be loved preacher and I feel out of place.

Now Mother I got awfully angry when I read what you wrote about Carl [Edgar] and Bill [Smith].[1] I wanted to write immediately and say everything I thot. But I waited until I got all cooled off. But never having met Carl and knowing Bill only superficially you *were* mighty unjust. Carl is a *Prince* and about the most sincere and real Christian I have ever known and he has had a better influence on me than any one I have ever known. He doesn't drool at the mouth like a Peaslee with religion but is a deep sincere Christian and a gentleman.

I have never asked Bill what church he goes to because that doesn't matter. We both believe in God and Jesus Christ and have hopes for a hereafter and creeds don't matter.

Please don't unjustly criticize my best friends again. Now cheer up because you see I am not drifting like you thought.

With love,
Ernie

Don't read this to anyone and please get back to a cheerful frame of mind!

JFK

1. William B. Smith, Jr., a close friend during EH's boyhood summers in Michigan, was born August 20, 1895, in St. Louis and died in Arlington, Virginia, in January 1972. He and EH began their association about 1916 at Horton Bay, Michigan, where Bill and his sister, Katharine Foster Smith (Kate or Katy, later Mrs. John Dos Passos), spent summers with their aunt, Mrs. Joseph Charles, in a cottage near Pine Lake, later renamed Charlevoix. Carl Edgar, whom EH nicknamed Odgar, was another friend from the north Michigan summers. At this time he lived and worked in Kansas City and was in love with Kate. He appears as Odgar in EH's short story "Summer People," in *The Nick Adams Stories* (New York, 1972), pp. 217–28.

To GRACE HALL HEMINGWAY, Kansas City, 2 March 1918

Dear Mither:

The box came tonight and we just opened it at the Press room the cake sure was great. There were about four of the fellows here and we opened the box and ate the cake. It was a peach, I am going to take the rest of the grub home and Carl and I will finish it up. The fellows all agreed that Mother Hemingstein must be some cook. Your praises were sung in loud and stentorian tones. The cake sure fed a multitude of starving and broke newspaper men tonight. There is not much doing here now except my hospital fight.[1] Things are going great in that. I was officially barred from entering the institution by the Manager yesterday and the Boss and the big political men are sure raising the merry deuce. We are panning the hide offn them for fair. But the boss said to disregard that fact that I am barred and sent me out there any way to get the dope on them. And so we are having all sorts of rows. I have about five conferences with the Managing Ed. per day and am getting along swell. We sure are making them hunt cover. The reason they are trying to keep me out of the joint is because I have enough on them to send them all to the pen pretty near. Any way they sure hate the great Hemingstein and will do any thing they can to frame on him.

But we fight them High wide and handsome.

I'm glad the kids are all better. My love to Dad and I will write him next. Glad the old Ivory [Marcelline] is having such a good time.

Good Luck
Ernie.
Love to everyone
Ernie

JFK

1. "We are making a big fight on the Hospital and Health board. . . . The politicians on the Board have grafted $27,000 since the first of the year. . . . I cover all the Hospital and investigation end of the hospital graft end." (EH to his mother, 23 February 1918.) (JFK)

To HIS PARENTS, Kansas City,[1] 19 April 1918

Dear Folks:

I sure was glad to hear from you both Dad and mother. Everything is going fine down here. It is raining hard now and has been all day. I put my old mackinaw on and turn the collar up and let it rain. All this week I have been handling recruiting. Writing the stories about the Army, Navy, Marines, British-Canadian and lately the new Tank Service. I'm enclosing a couple of the Tank stories. Some of them go pretty good.

I'll hope to see you about the 2nd. I'll let you know when as soon as I find out.[2] How is everything now?

Good night
Ernie

UMD

1. EH was now completing his sixth month of work for the *Star*. 2. He had recently applied for the American Red Cross (ARC) Ambulance Service in Italy.

To HIS FAMILY, New York, 14 May 1918

Dear Folks:

We are quartered here at a very nice Hotel [Earle] in Washington Square. The heart of Greenwich Village. It is just a half block from 5th Ave and the arch and right on the square. The Harvard Bunch left this morning and we leave next Tuesday according to the latest dope. In the meantime we are in New York with all our Hotel bills, meals paid for. We have been given each an officers trunk, regular U.S. officers uniform with full U.S. officers' insignia, my name and unit stencilled on the trunk, officers overcoat, 1 rain coat, 1 cocky field service cap, 1 Dress cap, 4 suits heavy underwear, soft buckskin driving gloves, 1 pair Cordova leather aviators puttees, 2 pair officers shoes, 1 knitted sweater, 6 pair heavy woolen socks, 2 khaki shirts, 1 woolen shirt and a lot of other stuff I cant remember. Well over $200 worth of equipment issued to each man. Our uniforms are regular United States Army officers' and look like a million dollars. Privates and non-coms must salute us. We may wear our uniforms as soon as our pass ports arrive and we get them vized. None of the Chicago passports have come yet. I will get my picture taken as soon as I wear my uniform. Everything is packed in my officers trunk now.

I met Ted [Brumback] all right yesterday and we are rooming together here. We have a bunch of dandy fellows in our unit and are going to have a wonderful time. Ted was very glad that Dad met him and was very sorry he couldnt see you folks.

We have all our time to ourselves and have to report to no one. This morning I had my uniform fitted and then in the aft Ted and How Jenkins, Harve Osterholm, Jerry Flaherty and I rode down to the Battery and went through the aquarium. We bummed around and went up on the top of the Woolworth Tower 796 feet—62 stories high. We could see the camouflaged boats going in and out of the harbor and see way up the

East River to Hell's Gate, and over at Hoboken the "Vaterland" now being used as a transport is docked. She made her last round trip to France in 14 days. I have been all up and down Riverside Drive and seen N.Y. from the Harlem River on North and Grant's Tomb and went to the Libber of Goddesty [Goddess of Liberty] in the South. It is a wonderful sight from the Woolworth Tower. As soon as I don my officers' uniform I have an engagement with the Mrs. and have already investigated the possibility of the Little Church around the Corner. I've always planned to get married if I could ever get to be an officer, you know. It is a new ruling that makes us officers. We are kind of camouflaged 1st Lieuts. We are like aviators in that we have no commands. The war department ruled for the wearing of the uniform in foreign service and just before we sail. 3 or 4 days. Hence the wait for passport vises. Write me here at the Hotel.

Much love,

JFK
Ernie

To DALE WILSON, New York, 19 [18] May 1918

Dear Wilse:

Ha ha! Ha! Ha! Ha! Ha! Tis none other than the greatest of the Hemingsteins that indicts this epistle. Woodrow me lad, comma how are you. Much obliged for your sending ye old Liberty Bond. In the words of Smith ye beamer it was most good of you. And the great Hicks—He of the tortoise shelled disposition and sad lack of anal covering—What of him? Does he still classify the great Chicagoan, Noblest Scion of the Windy City as a well meaning fellow—quotes—Tell him I bury the Hatchet. But also do me this favor. When the story of Brumstein's [Brumback's] and my sad end comes in let not he that is known as Lackpants read copy on it. For it is feared by me that he would cut even the names of the deceased. Not diseased tho sad luck would lead one of your jesting proclivities to infer that.

But to get down the bare, naked, unclothed facts does Tod Ormiston, the journalistic white slaver still take the bi-menstrual stipend from William Moorehead—He that is yclept Broken Will? And does Smith the beamer slip the great Gus the warm palm and tell him Gus, how he Smith, likes to work for the paper he Gus manages? And does Peg Vaughan still fare forth in search of booty and Leo Lovely still be haunted by booty searching for him? And does the G't Fleisler still dog the shadow of the wily Godfrey searching for the pearls of journalistic wisdom which might be cast before the porcine Hebrew? And what does Tannembaumb without the Tasmanian Snobelater, woodsman and Boomerang thrower? Huh? I ask you?[1]

Well they have slipped us our uniforms and we are now Honorary 1st Lieuts. Ye G't Hem's'n stalked down Broadway and returned 367 salutes night before last. Since then he rides on a bus. It's easier on the right arm. Today we paraded down 5th avenue, from 82nd street to 8th street and were reviewed by Woodrow Senior and the Mrs. Also a bunch of large insects. Slang for Big Bugs. Woodrow resembles nothing so much as his pictures. While we all are commissioned yofficers yet we are in an squadron and have non coms. By virtue of his manly form and perfect complexion the one and only Hemsteith has been made Ye Top Cutter and you all should hear his rasping voice. Me duties consist largely of being ye right guide of ye 1st or initial platoon. Today as ye right guide I stalked all alone down the old avenue and felt lonesome as hell. But at eyes right I had a fine look at Woodrow.[2]

This is not for publication, kid, but we are plowing the briny Wednesday. My passport arrived today and I get the French and Italian visas Monday. This also is not for publication but I have been out to see Mae several times and am out there for dinner tomorrow evening. I have spent every damn cent I have too. Miss Marsh no kidding says she loves me. I suggested the little church around the corner but she opined as how ye war widow appealed not to her. So I sank the 150 plunks Pop gave me in a ring so I am engaged anyway. Also broke. Dead. I did have about another 100 but I bought a pair of 30 buck cordovan leather boots, a few sundries and a coupla drinks and now all is gone. Anyway my girl loves me and she believes I am going to be a great newspaper man and says she will wait for me, so What the Hell Bill. And maybe I can win an honest to god commission. Gee she is a wonderful girl, Wilse! Too damn good for me. You can tell Punk Wallace about my being engaged if you want to. But for god's sake don't let it get out amongst the gang and in the sheet.[3]

Well so long old Kid and my love to Hap and remember me to Pete and the Boss and Harry Kohr and John Collins, and Punk and Bill and Harry G. and Swensen and Smith.

Good Luck
Hemingstein

PUL

1. EH's allusions to his former colleagues on the *Kansas City Star* show his bewildering penchant for nicknames. 2. A parade with 75,000 marchers to launch a Red Cross drive was reviewed by President Wilson on 18 May. 3. Mae Marsh (1895–1968) was familiar to EH from her role in D. W. Griffith's *The Birth of a Nation* (1915). In 1966 she said she wished she had known him.

To HIS FAMILY, at sea, *c.* 27 May 1918

Somewhere on les briny

Dear Folks:

Well we are approaching our port of debarkation and are entering the widely known submarine zone so I will get this epistle off so you will be sure and get one any way. Very cheerful thought what aint it? This is the rottenest tub in the world and so it may be revealing a military secret to tell you. But it is absolutely. Now think what the rottenest ship in the world is and you know what I am on.[1] We had two days of glorious weather, warm and calm, just a pleasant breeze! regular waloon lake[2] days. Then we ran into a storm that cleared the dining rooms with great regularity. I would report for a meal and be alright until I would see my next door neighbor clap his hand to his mouth and make a sudden break for the door and then the power of suggestion would be too much and I would break for the rail. However we had two days of regular storm when she pitched, rolled, stood on her ear and swung in wide legubrious circles and I heaved but four times. A record what? How are you all including the massive Ivory and the widely known Dessie.[3] Ted and I and Howell Jenkins are paling together and having the grand time.[4] The storm is over now and for the last two days it has been very pleasant weather.

We are also paling with two polish Lieutenants. Count Galinski and Count Horcinanowitz although it is not spelled that way.[5] And they are dandy fellows. And being with them has taught us that there is a big difference between polacks and Poles. They have invited us to visit them in Paris and we'll put on ze grand party. We are expected to land over seas about four days from now. I will mail this at our port and it will be the only letter that I will send from there so worry not. We had a great time in little old Gotham and are confirmed broadwayites. The Croix Rouge took very good care of us while we were there and we lacked for nothing. The Y.M.C.A. who are just the same here as they are at home and you know what that means, are ever present aboard the ship. also several nigger Y.M.C.Aers. The Knights of Columbus have several representatives aboard and they seem a lot more human. Ted and Jenks and I had our second inoculations day before yesterday and my arm is nearly over the strain by now. We have only one more to take now. And will get that in either France or Italy. Each one has made me sick as a dog. They are triple typhoid and a lot stiffer than those I had while in school. A little while ago a big american cruiser came into sight headed toward home and we heliographed to her and broke out a number of signal flags. She is the first boat we have passed since coming out in the atlant. It is very good to look upon at night when the phosphorescent waves break out from the bow. The wake is also phosphorous and when it is rough the crests of the waves will blow away looking like brands from a camp fire. We have seen several popoises and a number of flying fish. One bunch that got up very early in the morning claim to have glimpsed a whale, but we look upon them with suspicion.

The food aboard is very good but we get only two meals a day. At ten o'clock and at five. You can get coffee and hard bread for breakfast if you want it but it isnt worth getting up for. According to the latest dope we are going right down to our headquarters after we leave Paris and then go right out to the lines. To take the place of the gang whose time is up. Our six months start from the day we start driving and it will probably carry us pretty well into the winter. Address me care the American Consul, Milano, Italy, Italian Ambulance Service, American Red Cross.

Much Love

LILLY

Ernie

1. The *Chicago* sailed for Bordeaux on 21 May. 2. Site of the Hemingways' summer cottage near Petoskey, Michigan. 3. EH's sister Marcelline and his brother Leicester. 4. Theodore Brumback, Jenkins, and EH were to drive ARC ambulances out of Schio, Italy, in June. 5. Jenkins and the Polish officers appear in EH's fragmentary novel *Along with Youth*, begun in June 1925. See *The Nick Adams Stories* (New York, 1972), pp. 137–42, where it has been arbitrarily retitled "Night Before Landing."

This letter and all subsequent letters to EH's family of 1918 are used courtesy of the Lilly Library and EH's sister Sunny, Mrs. Ernest J. Miller.

To RUTH MORRISON [?],[1] Fossalta di Piave, Italy, *c.* 22 June 1918[2]

Dear Ruth:

How is everything in ye olde village? It all seems about a million miles away and to think that this time last year we had just finished graduating. If anybody had told me when I was reading that dam fool prophecy last year that a year from date I would be sitting out in front of a dug out in a nice trench 20 yards from the Piave River and 40 yards from the Austrian lines listening to the little ones whimper way up in the air and the big ones go scheeeeeeeek Boom and every once in a while a machine gun go tick a tack a tock I would have said, "Take another sip." That is some complicated sentence but it all goes to show what a bum prophet I was.

You see I'm ranked a soto Tenente or Second Lieut. in the Italian Army and I left the Croce Rosa Americana Ambulance service a while back, temporarily, to get a little action down here. Don't publish this to the family who fondly picture me chaufing a Ford through Sylvan Glens.

I'm quartered at a nice house about 1-½ miles from the Austrian lines. The n.h. had 4 rooms. 2 down stairs and two up. The other day a shell came through the roof. Now there are three rooms. Two down stairs and 1 up. I was in the other one. The moral is: sleep up stairs. The big Italian guns are all back of us and they roar all night. What I am supposed to be doing is running a posto di ricovero. That is, I dispense chocolate and cigarettes to the wounded and the soldiers in the front line. Each aft and morning I load up a haversack and take my tin lid and gas mask and beat it up to the trenches. I sure have a good time but miss their being no Americans. Gee I have darn near forgot the English language. If Cannon or old Loftbery could hear me speak Italian all day long they would roll over in their graves. Gee but I do get lonesome for the sight of a real Honest to Gawd American girl though I would give my captured Austrian officers automatic pistol, my German helmets, all my junk I've captured and my chances for the war cross for just one dance.

Believe the writer if you want to do some kind deed write me at the address on the envelope and it will be forwarded to me. And Ruth if you know of anybody that I know in Oak Park that by any stretch could be induced to write me brow beat them into it and promise them from me that I will be a prompt answerer. I haven't had a letter from the States yet and have been here[3] since the 4th of June.

I crawled out over the top this afternoon and took some darby pictures of the Piave and the Austrian trenches. If they're any good I'll send you some. The hour of food draws nigh and I am of a great hunger.

So (you know I always used to get fussed when I'd say good bye so I'll sneak out quick, and leave you alone with the letter.)

UMD   Ernie

1. Identification conjectural on the basis of internal evidence. Of the four Ruths who were EH's classmates in Oak Park High School, Class of 1917 (the Misses Bramberg, Glass, Morrison, and Swanson), Miss Morrison, a member of the Girls' Rifle Club, seems the most likely correspondent. He mentions her, as well as Ruth Swanson, in his "Class Prophecy," *Senior Tabula*, pp. 57–62. 2. Dating conjectural on the basis of internal evidence. Commencement at Oak Park High School was 14 June 1917. EH's service record, on a form he filled out himself, states that he "participated in Piave Major Defensive June 15–July 8, 1918." 3. "Here" means Italy, since EH drove ambulances at Schio before going down to the Piave River as canteen officer.

To HIS FAMILY, Milan, 21 July 1918

Dear Folks:

I suppose Brummy has written you all about my getting bunged up.[1] So there isn't anything for me to say. I hope that the cable didn't worry you very much but Capt. Bates thought it was best that you hear from me first rather than the newspapers. You see I'm the first American wounded in Italy and I suppose the papers say something about it.

This is a peach of a hospital here and there are about 18 American nurses to take care of 4 patients. Everything is fine and I'm very comfortable and one of the best surgeons in Milan is looking after my wounds. There are a couple of pieces still in, one bullet in my knee that the X-Ray showed. The surgeon, very wisely, is after consultation, going to wait for the wound in my right knee to become healed cleanly before operating. The bullet will then be rather encysted and he will make a clean cut and go in under the side of the knee cap. By allowing it to be completely healed first he thus avoids any danger of infection and stiff knee. That is wise don't you think Dad? He will also remove a bullet from my right foot at the same time. He will probably operate in about a week as the wound is healing cleanly and there is no infection. I had two shots of anti tetanus immediately at the dressing station. All the other bullets and pieces of shell have been removed and all the wounds on my left leg are healing finely. My fingers are all cleared up and have the bandages off. There will be no permanent effects from any of the wounds as there are no bones shattered. Even in my knees. In both the left and right the bullets did not fracture the patella; one piece of shell about the size of a Tinker's roller bearing was in my left knee but it has been removed and the knee now moves perfectly and the wound is nearly healed. In the right knee the bullet went under the knee cap from the left side and didn't smash it a bit. By the time you get this letter the surgeon will have operated and it will be all healed, and I hope to be back driving in the mountains by the latter part of August. I have some fine photographs of the Piave and many other interesting pictures. Also a wonderful lot of souvenirs. I was all through the big battle and have Austrian carbines and ammunition, German and Austrian medals, officer's automatic pistols, Boche helmets, about a dozen Bayonets, star shell pistols and knives and almost everything you can think of. The only limit to the amount of souvenirs I could have is what I could carry for there were so many dead Austrians and prisoners the ground was almost black with them. It was a great victory and showed the world what wonderful fighters the Italians are.

I'll tell you all about everything when I get home for Christmas. It

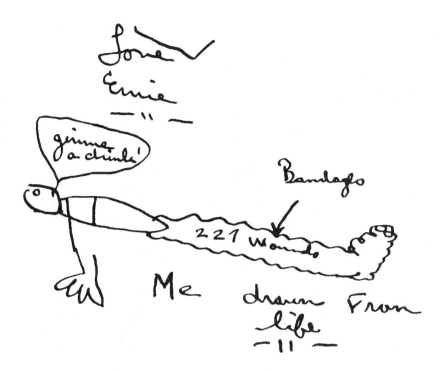

is awfully hot here now. I receive your letters regularly. Give my love to everybody and lots to all of you.

Ernie

LILLY

1. Written on EH's nineteenth birthday, this letter alludes to Ted Brumback's account of EH's wounding which had been sent to the family at home, 14 July 1918. (LILLY)

To HIS FAMILY, Milan, 18 August 1918

Dear Folks:

That includes grandma and grandpa and Aunt Grace. Thanks very much for the 40 lire! It was appreciated very much. Gee, Family, but there certainly has been a lot of burbles about my getting shot up! The Oak Leaves and the opposition came today and I have begun to think, Family, that maybe you didn't appreciate me when I used to reside in the bosom. It's the next best thing to getting killed and reading your own obituary.

You know they say there isn't anything funny about this war. And there isn't. I wouldn't say it was hell, because that's been a bit over-worked since Gen. Sherman's time, but there have been about 8 times when I would have welcomed Hell. Just on a chance that it couldn't come up to the phase of war I was experiencing. F'r example. In the trenches during an attack when a shell makes a direct hit in a group where you're standing. Shells aren't bad except direct hits. You must take chances on the fragments of the bursts. But when there is a direct hit your pals get spattered all over you. Spattered is literal. During the six days I was up in the Front line trenches, only 50 yds from the Austrians, I got the rep. of having a charmed life. The rep of having one doesn't mean much but having one does! I hope I have one. That knocking sound is my knuckles striking the wooden bed tray.

It's too hard to write on two sides of the paper so I'll skip.

Well I can now hold up my hand and say I've been shelled by high explosive, shrapnel and gas. Shot at by trench mortars, snipers and machine guns, and as an added attraction an aeroplane machine gunning the lines. I've never had a hand grenade thrown at me, but a rifle grenade struck rather close. Maybe I'll get a hand grenade later. Now out of all that mess to only be struck by a trench mortar and a machine gun bullet while advancing toward the rear, as the Irish say, was fairly lucky. What, Family?

The 227 wounds I got from the trench mortar didn't hurt a bit at the time, only my feet felt like I had rubber boots full of water on. Hot water. And my knee cap was acting queer. The machine gun bullet just felt like a sharp smack on my leg with an icy snow ball. However it spilled me. But I got up again and got my wounded into the dug out. I kind of collapsed at the dug out. The Italian I had with me had bled all over my coat and my pants looked like somebody had made current jelly in them and then punched holes to let the pulp out. Well the Captain who was a great pal of mine, It was his dug out said "Poor Hem he'll be R.I.P. soon." Rest In Peace, that is. You see they thought I was shot through the chest on account of my bloody coat. But I made them take my coat and shirt off. I wasn't wearing any undershirt, and the old torso was intact. Then they said I'd probably live. That cheered me up any amount. I told him in Italian that I wanted to see my legs, though I was afraid to look at them. So we took off my trousers and the old limbs were still there but gee they were a mess. They couldn't figure out how I had walked 150 yards with a load with both knees shot through and my right shoe punctured two big places. Also over 200 flesh wounds. "Oh," says I, "My Captain, it is of nothing. In America they all do it! It is thought well not to allow the enemy to perceive that they have captured our goats!"

The goat speech required some masterful lingual ability but I got it across and then went to sleep for a couple of minutes. After I came to they carried me on a stretcher three kilometers to a dressing station. The stretcher bearers had to go over lots because the road was having the "entrails" shelled out of it. Whenever a big one would come, Whee - whoosh - Boom - they'd lay me down and get flat. My wounds were now hurting like 227 little devils were driving nails into the raw. The dressing station had been evacuated during the attack so I lay for two hours in a stable, with the roof shot off, waiting for an ambulance. When it came I ordered it down the road to get the soldiers that had been wounded first. It came back with a load and then they lifted me in. The shelling was still pretty thick and our batteries were going off all the time way back of us and the big 250's and 350's going over head for Austria with a noise like a railway train. Then we'd hear the bursts back of the lines. Then there would come a big Austrian shell and then the crash of the burst. But we were giving them more and bigger stuff than they sent. Then a battery of field guns would go off, just back of the shed—boom, boom, boom, boom, and the Seventy-Fives or 149's would go whipping over to the Austrian lines, and the star shells going up all the time and the machines going like rivetters, tat-a-tat, tat-a-tat.

After a ride of a couple of kilometers in an Italian ambulance, they unloaded me at the dressing station where I had a lot of pals among the medical officers. They gave me a shot of morphine and an anti-tetanus injection and shaved my legs and took out about Twenty 8 shell fragments varying from [drawing of fragment] to about [drawing of fragment] in size out of my legs. They did a fine job of bandaging and all shook hands with me and would have kissed me but I kidded them along. Then I stayed 5 days in a field hospital and was then evacuated to the base Hospital here.

I sent you that cable so you wouldn't worry. I've been in the Hospital a month and 12 days and hope to be out in another month. The Italian Surgeon did a peach of a job on my right knee joint and right foot. Took 28 stitches and assures me that I will be able to walk as well as ever. The wounds all healed up clean and there was no infection. He has my right leg in a plaster splint now so that the joint will be all right. I have some snappy souvenirs that he took out at the last operation.

I wouldn't really be comfortable now unless I had some pain. The Surgeon is going to cut the plaster off in a week now and will allow me on crutches in 10 days.

I'll have to learn to walk again.

You ask about Art Newburn. He was in our section but has been trans-ferred to II. Brummy is in our section now. Don't weep if I tell you that back in my youth I learned to play poker. Art Newburn held some delusions that he was a poker player. I won't go into the sad details but I convinced him otherwise. Without holding anything I stood pat. Doubled his openers and bluffed him out of a 50 lire pot. He held three aces and was afraid to call. Tell that to somebody that knows the game Pop. I think Art said in a letter home to the Oak Parkers that he was going to take care of me. Now Pop as man to man was that taking care of me? Nay not so. So you see that while war isn't funny a lot of funny things happen in war. But Art won the championship of Italy pitching horse shoes.

This is the longest letter I've ever written to anybody and it says the least. Give my love to everybody that asked about me and as Ma Pettingill says, "Leave us keep the home fires burning!"

Good night and love to all.

Ernie

P.S. I got a letter today from the Helmles addressed Private Ernest H— what I am is S. Ten. or Soto Tenenente Ernest Hemingway. That is my rank in the Italian Army and it means 2nd Lieut. I hope to be a Tenenente or 1st Lieut. soon.

LILLY

To DR. C. E. HEMINGWAY, Milan, 11 September 1918

Dear Dad:

Your letters of Aug 6th and 11th came today. I'm glad you got that one from Ted and know he will be glad to hear from you. He came in from the front as soon as he knew I was wounded and at the Base here and wrote that letter to you in Milan. It was before my leg had been X-Rayed or operated on and so I don't know just what he told you about it all because I was too sick to give a damn. But I hope it was all right. I had a letter from him from the front a couple of days ago and they are having a good time. Mother wrote me that you and she were going up North and I know you had a good vacation. Write me all about it if you did any fishing. That is what makes me hate this war. Last year this time I was making those wonderful catches of Rainbow at the [Horton] Bay.

I'm in bed today and probably won't leave the hospital for about three weeks more. My legs are coming on wonderfully and will both eventually be O.K. absolutely. The left one is all right now. The right is still stiff but massage and sun cure and passive movements are loosening up the knee. My surgeon Captain Sammarelli, one of the best surgeons in Italy, is always asking me whether I think that you will be entirely satisfied with the operations. He says that his work must be inspected by the great Surgeon Hemingway of Chicago and he wants it to be perfect. And it is too. There is a scar about 8 inches long in the bottom of my foot and a neat little puncture on top. Thats what copper jacketted bullets do when they "key hole" in you. My knee is a beauty also. I'll never be able to wear kilts Pop. My left leg, thigh and side look like some old horse that has been branded and rebranded by about 50 owners. They will all make good identification marks.

I can get around now on the streets for a little while each day with a cane or crutch, but can't put a shoe on my right foot yet. Oh, yes! I have been commissioned a 1st Lieutenant and now wear the two gold stripes on each of my sleeves. It was a surprise to me as I hadn't expected anything of the sort. So now you can address my mail either 1st Lieut. or Tenente as I hold the rank in both the A.R.C. and Italian Army. I guess I'm the youngest 1st Lieut. in the Army. Anyway I feel all dolled up with my insignia and a shoulder strap on my Sam Brown Belt. I also heard that my silver medaglia valore is on the way and I will probably get it as soon as I'm out of the Hospital. Also they brought back word from the Front that I was proposed for the war cross before I was wounded because of general foolish conduct in the trenches, I guess. So maybe I'll be decorated with both medals at once. That would not be bad.

P.S. If it isn't too much I wish you'd subscribe to the Sat. Eve. Post for me and have it sent to my address here. They will forward it to me wherever I am. You need American reading an awful lot when your at the front.

Thanks,
Ernie

I'm awfully glad that Hop [Charles Hopkins][1] and Bill Smith are going to be near where you can be nice to both of them. They are the two best Pals I have about and especially Bill. Do have him out often because I know you will like him and he has done so much for me. I will probably go back to the ambulance for a while when I get out because the gang want me to visit them and they want to put on a big party.

I got a long letter the other day from every fellow in the section. I would like to go back to the ambulance but I wont be much use driving for about six months. I will probably take command of some 1st line post up in the mountains. Anyway don't worry about me because It has been conclusively proved that I can't be killed and I will always go where I can do the most good you know and that's what we're here for. Well, So Long Old Scout,

Your loving son
Ernie

LILLY

1. Hopkins was afternoon assignment editor on the *Kansas City Star* when EH worked there.

To HIS FAMILY, Milan, 18 October 1918[1]

Dear Folks:

Your letter of September 24 with the pictures came today, and, family, I did admire to hear from you. And the pictures were awfully good. I guess everybody in Italy knows that I have a kid brother If you only realized how much we appreciate pictures, pop, you would send 'em often. Of yourselves and the kids and the place and the bay—they are the greatest cheer producers of all, and everybody likes to see everybody else's pictures.

You, dad, spoke about coming home. I wouldn't come home till the war was ended if I could make fifteen thousand a year in the States—nix. Here is the place. All of us Red Cross men here were ordered not to register. It would be foolish for us to come home because the Red Cross is a necessary organization and they would just have to get more men from the States to keep it going. Besides we never came over here until we were all disqualified for military service, you know. It would be criminal for me to come back to the States now. I was disqualified before I left the States because of my eye. I now have a bum leg and foot and there isn't any army in the world that would take me. But I can be of service over here and I will stay here just as long as I can hobble and there is a war to hobble to. And the ambulance is no slacker's job. We lost one man, killed, and one wounded in the last two weeks. And when you are holding down a front line canteen job, you know you have just the same chances as the other men in the trenches and so my conscience doesn't bother me about staying.

I would like to come home and see you all, of course. But I can't until after the war is finished. And that isn't going to be such an awful length of time. There is nothing for you to worry about, because it has been fairly conclusively proved that I can't be bumped off. And wounds don't matter. I wouldn't mind being wounded again so much because I know just what it is like. And you can only suffer so much, you know, and it does give you an awfully satisfactory feeling to be wounded. It's getting beaten up in a good cause. There are no heroes in this war. We all offer our bodies and only a few are chosen, but it shouldn't reflect any special credit on those that are chosen. They are just the lucky ones. I am very proud and happy that mine was chosen, but it shouldn't give me any extra credit. Think of the thousands of other boys that offered. All the heroes are dead. And the real heroes are the parents. Dying is a very simple thing. I've looked at death and really I know. If I should have died it would have been very easy for me. Quite the easiest thing I ever did. But the people at home do not realize that. They suffer a thousand times more. When a mother brings a son into the world she must know that some day the son will die, and the mother of a man that has died for his country should be the proudest woman in the world, and the happiest. And how much better to die in all the happy period of un-disillusioned youth, to go out in a blaze of light, than to have your body worn out and old and illusions shattered.

So, dear old family, don't ever worry about me! It isn't bad to be wounded: I know, because I've experienced it. And if I die, I'm lucky.

Does all that sound like the crazy, wild kid you sent out to learn about the world a year ago? It is a great old world, though, and I've always had a good time and the odds are all in favor of coming back to the old place. But I thought I'd tell you how I felt about it. Now I'll write you a nice, cheery, bunky letter in about a week, so don't get low over this one. I love you all.

LILLY   Ernie

1. This letter was published in *The Oak Parker* (Oak Park, Illinois), 16 November 1918, pp. 6–7.

To WILLIAM B. SMITH, JR., Milan, 13 December 1918

Dear Jaggers:

You do what a man of your bowells should in keeping on with the old air work,[1] and you have my mitt on it Avis. But don't do anything damn foolish! And really, Bird, you can be careful. So be it.

The woodsman sails for the States on the good ship Giuseppe Verdi on January the 4th.[2] And probably will grace Mr. Chicago's city the later part of next month. Where will you be then? Oh plane punisher Oh

potential destroyer of Boche whereinell will you be then? And the officer
and the nee Gub? An reunion must be staged.

But Hark ye. I cannot stall until summer and must resume the battle
for buns shortly. The tussle for tarts or the melee for meringue. One
might even say the combat for cakes. And have no 210 a month. Nothing
but an honorable discharge and 250 lire a year for life from the King.
And 250 lire optimistically translated is $40. And 50 ferrous h[. . .]
are not much to live on.

But listen what kind of a girl I have: Lately I've been hitting it up—
about 18 martinis a day and 4 days ago I left the hospital and hopped
camions 200 miles up to the Front A.W.O.L to visit some pals. Ossifers
in the R.G.A. British outside of Padova. Their batteries are en repose.
They gave me a wonderful time and we used the staff car and I rode to
the hounds on the Colonels charger. Leg and all.

But Bill to continue. We went in the staff car up to TREVISO where
the missus [Agnes von Kurowsky][3] is in a Field Hospital. She had heard
about my hitting the alcohol and did she lecture me? She did not.

She said, "Kid we're going to be partners. So if you are going to drink
I am too. Just the same amount." And she'd gotten some damn whiskey
and poured some of the raw stuff out and she'd never had a drink of anything before except wine and I know what she thinks of booze. And
William that brought me up shortly. Bill this is some girl and I thank
God I got crucked so I met her. Damn it I really honestly can't see what
the devil she can see in the brutal Stein but by some very lucky astigmatism she loves me Bill. So I'm going to hit the States and start working
for the Firm. Ag says we can have a wonderful time being poor together
and having been poor alone for some years and always more or less happy
I think it can be managed.

So now all I have to do is hit the minimum living wage for two and
lay up enough for six weeks or so up North and call on you for service
as a best man. Why man I've only got about 50 more years to live and
I don't want to waste any of them and every minute that I'm away from
that Kid is wasted.

Now try and keep your finger off the trigger cause you may be in the
same fix yourself sometime.

I'll see you soon.

PUL   Ye

1. Following graduation from the University of Missouri in June 1918, Bill Smith
(1895–1972) enlisted in the Marine Aviation Detachment for ground training at the
Massachusetts Institute of Technology in Cambridge, Massachusetts, until discharged
after Armistice in November. 2. EH's return voyage from Genoa to New York City,
4–21 January 1919. 3. Agnes was the American Red Cross nurse with whom EH had
fallen in love at the ARC Hospital in Milan. In the fall and winter of 1918–1919 she

did volunteer work in Florence and Treviso. For a full account of her career, see Michael S. Reynolds, *Hemingway's First War* (Princeton, 1976), pp. 181–219. EH fictionally portrayed her as "Ag" and "Luz" in "A Very Short Story," and (partly) as Catherine Barkley in *A Farewell to Arms*.

This and all subsequent letters to Smith are used courtesy of Princeton University Library.

To JAMES GAMBLE,[1] Oak Park, Illinois, 3 March 1919

Dear Old Chieftain:

Gee you know I'd have written you before. In my day book for over a month you could open it up and find "Write Jim Gamble", scribbled. Every minute of every day I kick myself for not being at Taormina with you. It makes me so damned homesick for Italy and whenever I think that I might be there and with you. Chief, honest I can't write about it. When I think of old Taormina by moonlight and you and me, a little illuminated some times, but always just pleasantly so, strolling through that great old place and the moon path on the sea and Aetna fuming away and the black shadows and the moonlight cutting down the stairway back of the villa. Oh Jim it makes me so damn sick to be there, I go over to the camouflaged book case in my room and pour out a very stiff tall one and add the conventional amount of aqua and set it by my typewriter, slang for mill, battered key board etc., and then I look at it a while and think of us sitting in front of the fire after one of munge uova's dinners and I drink to you Chief. I drink to you.[2]

Don't for the Lord's sake come to this country as long as you can help it. That is from one who knoweth. I'm patriotic and willing to die for this great and glorious nation. But I hate like the deuce to live in it.

The leg is pretty bum, the family are fine, and it was great to see them again. They didn't recognize me by the way when I piled off the train. Had a stormy but pleasant trip home. Three great days at Gib. I borrowed some mufti from a British Officer and went over into Spain. The usual hectic time in New York for a few days. Saw Bill Horne,[3] who thinks a lot of you. They've tried to make a hero out of me here. But you know and I know that all the real heroes are dead. If I had been a really game guy I would have gotten myself killed off. And I know it so it doesn't affect the size of the cranium I hope. But the male youth of this village have either been in the Naval Reserve Force, the Student Army Training Corps or the Q.M.C. All except Al Winslow and myself and a few birds of our old gang who got themselves killed with the Marines.

I've been doing the honors, but Al gets home next week and he brought down several boche and left an arm in a German Field Dressing station so I have announced my retirement from the public eye on his arrival.

I've written some darn good things Jim. That is good for me. And am starting a campaign against your Philedelphia Journal the Sat. Eve. Post. I sent them the first story Monday last. And havent heard any thing yet of course. Tomorrow another one starts toward them. I'm going to send 'em so many and such good ones, no, I haven't really got the big head, that they're going to have to buy them in self defence. Really Chief, I'm so homesick for Italy that when I write about it it has that something that you only get in a love letter. A love letter, not a mash note. One of the Kid sisters just brought up a plate of lobster salad sandwiches, the inference being that fish is brain food I guess. But they need Beer. Did you ever taste the beer at that little Birraria down near the rail way station at Schio? And we might be in Madiera now. Oh Damn it.

Jenks is in town and we foregather pretty often. He sends you his regards as does Art Newburn. The Girl[4] is still up at a God forsaken joint called Torre Di Mosta beyond the Piave. Straight up twenty kilomets from San Dona. She is running a visiting nurse field hospital, and kindergarten and between times acting as mayor of the town. She sent you the colours I guess tho she didn't mention it. Did you get them and the changed American money? I felt bad about not attending to that myself but I was tearing around so when they shifted the sailing of the Verdi that I had to turn it over to her. Did everything come through all right? If you ever get up in the Venezia I'd like to have you look her up. Agnes von Kurowsky, and the pass word is Hemingstein. Had a note from Harry Knapp the other day. He is looking around for something to do. Says Business is very unsettled. His arm is O.K. The cold weather plays hell with my leg and there has been some inflamation of the joint. All clear now though but Dad says to lay off of active work until the middle of the summer anyway.

Coming home with high resolves to start in at once on the battle for buns and expecting to find all finances very low I'm greeted with this from the Dad, "Never better. Everything going great. Why didn't you ask me for some kale and stay over if you wanted to!" That was the last straw. I had everything sized up wrong. And the Dear Uncle, missing believed killed, turns up alive and well in England and beats me home by a week. Damn him.

Dad was talking today about sending me down to the gulf for a while, the race meet closes tomorrow at New Orleans though and I'm working pretty hard with the typewriter so I think I'll stall here for a while. Maybe I'll go down the middle or last of March.

The Girl doesn't know when she will be coming home. I'm saving money. If you can imagine it. I can't. $172 and a fifty buck Liberty Bond in the Bank already. That's what comes from staying away from the ponies and having ones friends over seas. Maybe she won't like me now I've reformed, but then I'm not very seriously reformed.

If you'r still at Taormina, give my regards to Madame Bartlett and the Maggiore and my salutions to the Duke of Bronte. Who, with the exception of your self, is the only real guy in Sicily. Woods and Kitsen are perhaps good workmen but I should judge very fatiguing to Pal around with? Is there anything over here I can send to you? Have you Tobacco? Sure you have Macedonias. Wish I had. Bring some home with you! No, Do you need anything Jim? Really?

You know I wish I were with you,

Hemmy,

As you see I'm a rotten typist. It's one of the privileges of the 4th. Estate.

[drawing of a glass of beer]

The address on the Envelope is your home when you'r in Chicago.
Tel. Oak Park 181

His Mark
—''—

KNOX

1. In 1918 Captain Gamble was a field inspector, Rolling Canteen Service. EH was wounded 8 July 1918 while serving as canteen officer at Fossalta di Piave. 2. After the Armistice Gamble retired to Taormina, Sicily, and on 11 December invited EH to join him. *Munge uova* ("milk and eggs") was perhaps the nickname of Gamble's cook. 3. W. D. Horne, Jr., like Howell Jenkins, Harry H. Knapp, Jr., and Arthur C. Newburn, also mentioned in this letter, were all veterans of ARC Ambulance, 1918. 4. Agnes von Kurowsky; see the letter of 13 December 1918, note 3.

To LAWRENCE T. BARNETT,[1] Oak Park, 30 April 1919

Dear Lawrey:

Come Sta Barney? How's everything? Everything is quiet in the village and there isn't much news of the gang. Bill Horne wrote me the other day from New Haven and I see Jenks pretty often and [Frederick] Spiegel once in a while. Jock Miller, the great Scotch drunkard whom you may remember wrote from Minneapolis the other day. Pease was in town arrayed in purple and fine linen. Feder also blew in. Corp Shaw[2] has been out at Coronado but should be back by now and we're going fishing together pretty soon. I called up your folks and Jerri's when I got home and they told me that you all were at school. That gives me a bone to pick with you too. Do you recall giving K. Meyer, rather good looking and a pretty mean dancer but takes her self too damned seriously, a line of dope about the Great Hemingstein? Well anyway said Kate who lives directly across the street blew into the village of parked oaks and handed out quelque line in regard to me. Had me practically married off and entangled with any amount of femmes. It created some sensation amongst all the nice Oak Park girls to whom I was swearing that I had always been true. You see I hadn't been in Oak Park for over two years and they were ready to believe anything about me. So you owe me something for that and in return I am going to ask a favor. First let me tell you Barney that all bets with any of the women either wild or tame are off definitely. I am a free man! That includes them all up to and including Ag [Agnes von Kurowsky]. My Gawd man you didn't think I was going to marry and settle down did you? Also just got out of the hospital here. Had another operation and everything is going great. And I'm leaving for upper Michigan in about three weeks, or two weeks, to get in two or three months of fishing.

Now here is the dope. My Family, God bless them as always, are wolfing at me to go to college. They want me to settle down for a while and the place that they are pulling for very strongly is Wisconsin. I don't know anything about it except that there is nobody of the male sex from Oak Park that I recall that is worth a damn that goes there except Bob McMasters and perhaps Ruck Jones. And Bob Mac isn't there this year. However I know there are some very priceless femmes go there. And more will next year. So I wondered if you would write me all the dope on it. What kind of a gang there is and most anything you can think of about the place. Frankly I don't know where the hell to go. Wish I could go to Schio instead of any of them. Anyhow write me Barney will you? I stopped with Bill Horne in N.Y. and he asked particularly to be remembered to you.

    CIAOU KID

                                                 Stein

Pardon the bum typing and the pencil but I'm still laid up.
P.S. Yak Harris is in Ft. Worth Tex. getting a divorce from his wife he writes!!!
JFK

1. ARC veteran, Section IV. 2. Probably Carleton Shaw, another ARC ambulance veteran from Section IV.

To HOWELL G. JENKINS,[1] Boyne City, Michigan, 16 June 1919

Dear Fever:

Ciao Kid.

I'm sorry I haven't written before but you know how it is. Anyway here's the dope. First I hope the malaria hasn't been bothering you. Corp Shaw and I were on an enormous party at the Toledo Club. We both lay on the grass out side of the club for some time. Your old pal Hem established the club record. 15 martinis, 3 champagne highballs and I don't know how much champagne then I passed out.

It was a wonderful occasion. The night Toledo went dry. Corp had a wire from Swinnie saying he and you were on a party. Wish I had been along. Corp sends you his best and he'll probably be up here the latter part of July. You and he will get together up here.

We've had darby fishing. See the enclosure of kill. The Buick is running well. We've taken six rainbow trout that would average about 3 lbs. The one in the picture is a four pounder. And gosh, Jenks but they can fight. They are the Arditi [Italian shock troops] of the Lakes. It looks as tho we were going to get a respite from Prohibition. Don't you think? If not I'll send you down some kale to do a little laying in for me.

Had a very sad letter from Ag [Agnes von Kurowsky] from Rome yesterday. She has fallen out with her Major. She is in a hell of a way mentally and says I should feel revenged for what she did to me. Poor damned kid. I'm sorry as hell for her. But there's nothing I can do. I loved her once and then she gypped me. And I don't blame her. But I set out to cauterize out her memory and I burnt it out with a course of booze and other women and now it's gone.

She's all broke up and I wish there was something I could do for her tho. "But that's all shut behind me—long ago and far away and there ain't no busses runnin' from the Bank to Mandalay."

There is a Russian cigarette shop on a cross street between Michigan and Wabash near Monroe. Where they sell Ivanoffs. There are some Russian cigarettes there with a name I can't remember, 10 in a box and they are brown paper, and a square box about the size of Pall Malls. They are kind of slimy looking and the best weeds I've ever smoked. They cost 30¢ a box. I'm enclosing a buck and I wish you'd mail me three boxes up here when you get time. If you don't know where the shop is ask some one. They have fruit and stuff in one window and Russian and imported cigarettes in the other. Perhaps it's Adams Street. I can't remember. There's a shirt shop just beyond it towards Michigan Ave. I sure would appreciate it if you'd get 'em for me when you're over that way. They're the best pills of all.

Bill sends his best and says for you not to forget you're coming up here. We'll have a great old time! Kenley Smith's[2] address is Oak Park Avenue, North. 2 Blocks East and two blocks North of our house. Their number is in the telephone directory under Oliver Marble Gale. They want you to come out. I forgot to give Kenly yours address!

Write me Kid
Your old Pal
Hemmy

PH. PUL

1. Jenkins (1894–1971), nicknamed Jenks, Little Fever, Carper, and Carpative, was a native of Evanston, Illinois, and had driven ambulances with EH in Italy in 1918. Seven of EH's letters to him were sold at auction at Sotheby Parke Bernet, New York, on 9 April 1980. Four others are owned by the University of Texas. Those used here were supplied to the editor by Jenkins in 1962. 2. Yeremya Kenley (Y. K.) Smith (1887–1969) was elder brother to Katharine (Kate) Smith and William B. (Bill) Smith, Jr.

To HOWELL JENKINS, Boyne City, 26 July 1919

Dear Jenks and Barney:[1]

Gee it's priceless that Barney can come up. Your letter just came and I showed it to Bill [Smith] and we're going to send a wire this afternoon from Charlevoix. We'll have a priceless time.

Bill and I have a complete camping outfit for 4 men. Tents blankets cooking utensils, camp grate and so forth. Where we will go will be the Pine Barrens and camp on the Black River.[2] It is wild as the devil and the most wonderful trout fishing you can imagine. All clear— no brush and the trout are in schools. The last time we were over Bill twice caught and landed two at once. Fishing a fly and a grasshopper and there are some hellers[3] too. We can fish all we want and loaf around camp and maybe get a crack at a deer or a bear. Scared a bear out of our last camping place.

We have fishing outfits complete for 4 guys for lake fishing. But we have only 3 complete stream trout fishing outfits. We have 4 stream landing nets.

Barney should go to V.L. and A.'s [Von Lengerke and Antoine's] and buy himself a 10 ft. fly rod. A fly rod and a fly line. That will be all we'll need.

I have a 22 cal. automatic pistol a 22 cal. rifle and my 32 automatic.

Also a 20 guage shot gun. You birds better bring some 22 cal. cartridges.

These are the kind you want. 22 cal "Lesmok" "Long Rifles." *Not* smokeless. Lesmok is *semi* smokeless. Better get about 1000 as they are cheap there and we will do a lot of shooting. Also get a box of 100 No. 4 Carlisle spring steel hooks. That costs about 14¢ a hundred. Better get two boxes.

If you have some old Blankets or canvass bring them up. We have plenty but we can always use more. You want to bring all your old clothes too.

We are about 12 miles out of Charlevoix and on Hortons Bay of Pine Lake. Mrs. Dilworth has a couple of cottages here and takes guests. You and I and Barney will put up there, Jenks. Bill's Farm is about a mile away. We will only be here two or three days to fish for Rainbow in the Bay and then avanti over to the Barrens. It will not cost you anything Jenks as I have arranged for you to share my room. Barney can have a room next door. We'll have a crack at the Rainbow and you see from the Pictures what they are like.

You won't take any chances bringing the grog up as I don't believe that cars are searched at all. The best road to come up is the West Michigan Pike. It is pretty good. You can get the dope on it from any Blue Book. It comes around through Michigan City and up the shore through Muskegon, Ludington, Manistee, Traverse City and then up to Charlevoix. You can drive it in less than three days. Probably in two days. All the roads up here are good. And on the Barrens they are fine. Because theyre not cut up by traffic at all. You can nearly drive across the Pine Barrens without any road just by compass. It is so free from under brush.

Gee but we will have a good time. That Barrens Country is the greatest I've ever been in and you know that Bill and You and Barney and I will have *some* time. There are some great camping places on the Black, and we ought to get some Partridges. I can *guarantee you* and Barney both to catch all the trout you want. And Fever I can sure cook those trout. Bill will like Barney I know and I'll sure be glad to see him and you know what kind of a guy Bill is. Bring a camera and any junk you want to. We'll get some great action pictures.

Now tell Barney we want him and I'll guarantee that you and he both will have a good time. I'll write you again if I think of anything you need. Wire me when you leave. You can telephone me care Mrs. Jas. Dilworth, Hortons Bay, when you get to Charlevoix and we'll come in and meet you. Or anyone in Charlevoix will tell you how to get to Hortons Bay. Its a straight road out and you can easily find it. Like a boulevard all the way.

Gosh Jenks it will be great to have you and Barney here.

Had a letter from the Corp [Shaw] yesterday and he has had to go to Rangeley Lake Maine because of his mothers health and he probably cant make it. He said to give his best to you.

Give my best to Barney and yourself and tear up here. We'll have everything ready for you. Shoot me a letter.

Hemmy

P.S. Bill says to come up Multa Subito and to bring heavy supplies of the grog. Picture us on the Barrens, beside the river with a camp fire and the tent and the full moon and a good meal in our bellies smoking a pill and with a *good bottle* of grog. There will be some good singing.

Hem

I wont say anything to Spiegel.[4]

PH. PUL

1. East of Petoskey near Vanderbilt, Michigan. 2. Larvae of the hellgrammite fly, used as bait. 3. Frederick W. Spiegel, ARC veteran, Section IV.

To HOWELL JENKINS, Petoskey, Michigan, *c.* 15 September 1919

Dear Shittle:

Jock and Al Walker and I just got back from Seney.[1] The Fox is priceless. The big fox is about 4 or five times as large as the Black and has ponds 40 feet across. The little Fox is about the size of the Black and lousy with them. Jock caught one that weighed 2 lbs. 15 and a half of the inches. I got one 15 inches on the fly! Also one 14 inches. We caught about 200 and were gone a week. We were only 15 miles from the Pictured Rocks on Lake Superior. Gad that is great country. I saw several deer and put three shots in one at about 40 yds. with the 22 machine gun. But didn't stop him.

Yesterday Bill and Kate and Jock and I and the Madam[2] went over to the Black and it rained like hell so we only got 23. Jock 8—I *nine* Bill 4—Kate 2. They weren't biting because of the rain. But we had some Darbs. 11-½ of the inches. We were over at the Black once before and rated 40. Bill had one that broke his leader on the stricture. Bill claims he was 3 or 4 of the pounds. A Hooper [grasshopper] is an easy article to lay hold of now that today is the last day of the season. The rainbow have come into the Bay and I expect some super whangleberries. You can see 'em jumping from Dilstein's[3] porch.

Jo heesus an be Guy Mawd [My Gawd] Fever I lost one on the Little Fox below an old dam that was the biggest trout I've ever seen. I was up in some old timbers and it was a case of horse out. I got about half of him out of wasser and my hook broke at the shank! He struck on 4 hoopers. He was as big as any rainbow I've ever caught. I tried for him for 4 different days later but he only struck once and felt like a ton of the Bricks. There are no [illegible] up there and very few flack Blies [Black flies]. Pock is going to get a Ford up next year and you'll be up there. We'll get the Corp [Shaw] and Bill Horne and Yali and the Bird and Jock and Marby[4] and have a peach of a gang. Take in both the Black and the Fox.

Say Shittle you and Marby owe 5 bones apiece on the grub. If you want to, send it to me. I wouldn't mention it only I've only 5 to my name and dont see how I'm going to get out of the country.

These are damned good pictures e vero?

Sua Amico

Hem. Hollow Bone Stein

[Postscript: top corner of first page] Bill sends his best. Jock is home care J. L. Pentecost Jr. Elmhurst, Ill. Call him up.

PH. PUL

1. Seney is in the northern peninsula of Michigan. The Fox River flows through it. This site was used in EH's "Big Two-Hearted River." See Sheridan Baker, *Michigan Alumnus Quarterly Review* 45 (1959): 142–49. The actual Big Two-Hearted is farther north. The present letter describes the trip to the Fox on which EH drew for his story. 2. Jock is John Pentecost, also called Pock and the Ghee; Bill (the Bird) and Kate Smith summered near Horton Bay on Lake Charlevoix; the Madam was their aunt, Mrs. Joseph William Charles of St. Louis. 3. The Dilworths' restaurant at Horton Bay overlooking Lake Charlevoix. EH converts the name on the analogy of his own chosen nickname of Hemingstein. 4. EH's nickname for Larry Barnett became Barney and then Marby.

To HOWELL JENKINS, Petoskey, 20 December 1919

Dear Fever:

I'll bet you've cursed the bird [Bill Smith] and me out for a couple of fine specimens when we havn't written. In every letter he's asked for your address and just the other day I remembered to give it to him. So I suppose by now you may of heard from him. Well how have they been rolling? I had a letter from Pock but he was raving about the Black and the little Fox all the time and it was so full of such terms as Strictures, Whangleberries, Dehooperized, and Peeks, that I couldn't get much news out of it. To avoid my raving along on kindred topics I'd better get down to business. I'm getting home either the 2nd or 3rd of January and will be home for about five days. Then I'm going to Toronto.[1] I'll explain all that when I come down. But the point is that I'll be in the city of sin, and sometimes gin, for about five days at any rate and we want to get together. We'll want to have cognac at the Venice [Café] and take in a show. If you havn't made arangements to go with anyone else I'd like to have us take in the follies together. What do you say. Why don't you get tickets now for some night between the 2nd and 8th and we'll take it in. First getting in the proper state of appreciation through the splitting of a flask of chianti at the Venice and imbibing a couple or three or four Cognaci. How about it? Get the tickets will you and then I'll settle with you when I come. I'd send kale but I'm nearly flat but can tap the banco when I come home. This Toronto thing looks like the original Peruvian Doughnuts. If you want to get in touch with Pock you can call him at John L. Pentecost, Elmhurst Ill. He's in the phone book or just ask central for long distance. Pock is John L/ Jr. Well I've got to ring off. See what you can do and Merry Christmas old cock.

Ciaou,

PH. PUL   Stein

1. EH's plans for Toronto involved serving as hired companion to Ralph Connable, Jr., son of the head of the Canadian branch of F. W. Woolworth.

To GRACE QUINLAN,[1] Oak Park, 1 January 1920

Dear Sister Luke:

Been here since yesterday matin and it seems like a million of the years. Gee up in yon village [Petoskey, Michigan] a day went like a flash —here they're ages long. Gee Luke I do miss you a lot. I wonder if you're at the Elks' Dance tonight? I've had a lot of fun already Luke but I do wish I hadn't left Teposkey.

A gang came down about an hour ago it's 10:30 [P.M.] or so now to get me to go to a dance at the Club but I begged off to write. My gambe went hay wired in pretty hard shape after last nights hoof weilding. Had cramps in both calves of my legs nearly all night. Didn't turn in till after three. By George, Luke, Erion didn't creep in. She galloped in. So I'm off dancage [dancing] for a day or so. The living grandfather [Anson Hemingway] not the dead one [Ernest Hall] he's dead, toted me to luncheon with Harry Lauder [Scottish entertainer] yesterday. 'Arry was in fine shape. He was very bitter about the non-tripage of the Kaiser [Wilhelm] and demanded it in the name of Justice and all that sort of thing.

Himmel but this is a pen of the very foulest, and the writer hates to write on this kind of paper too.

The fudge was priceless, to properly use that much used word. But it wasn't a bit better than your letter which was a darb.

Gee I'm glad you're my Sister Luke.

I told all the family about what a peach you were and how you can ride and dance and swim and do everything just a whole lot better than anybody else and what a good scout you are and how good looking you are, how much of the old think bean you have and oh everything. Then I raved about you when I took tea with Isabel Simmons[2] this aft. Everybody in the middle west will know that Stein Hemingway has a sister up north named Luke that is pretty darned nice.

Foregathered with Tubby Williams yesterday aft and he is the same old bird. Red Pentecost and the Fever called me up and we're lunching Saturday at the Venice Cafe.

There's going to be an ARDITI dinner of 15 of the old gang from all over the country at the North Side Saturday night. Jenks had arranged it and he was going to WIRE me today to come down, called up to see when I'd be here. It'll be quelque occassion. A surmise that the [illegible] of grog will stalk would not be far wrong. 15 of the old gang! Dad has 6 mallards that he's turned over to me to stage a game supper with Sunday night, and Monday I go to Pagliacci to hear Titta Ruffo and Tuesday have to step out Irene Goldsteen [of Petoskey] and Wed. the Follies with the Fever. So it doesn't look like there'll be much time spent studying the S.S. [Sunday School] lesson.

If this letter is too long Luke you can skip whatever you want to, you know. But I miss you so I feel like talking to you so excuse all this raveage about what the screeder is doing etc. Won't it be great to get together again in the Spring? Haven't had any rows. But several girls got a bit miffed because I told 'em they couldn't dance as well as you all. (My best regards to your mother and father).

Maybe I'll not go to Toronto or K.C. either one. Kenley Smith was asked by the Firestone Tyre people to get 'em a publicity man to do some stuff on this "Ship by Truck" campaign and he asked me to do it.

It may be too late as they asked 3–4 days ago. It pays $50 a week and expenses and involves go-age to Cleveland, Toledo, Buffalo, Detroit, etc. If it's still open I'll take it.

Well, I must shut off words.

Good night Luke dear Sister.

Love from your brother,

Stein

Don't stall about inviting. I'll take that swim for you.

[cartoon of full beer stein]

YUL

1. Grace Quinlan, born 30 September 1906 in Petoskey, was a pretty brunette whom EH had befriended, along with Irene Goldstein and Marjorie Bump and her sister, during his stay in the village in the fall of 1919. Grace later married Joseph E. Otis, Jr., Yale, Class of 1916, and until her death lived in South Bend, Indiana. (Information courtesy of Donald F. Gallup.) 2. EH's next-door neighbor in Oak Park. See his letters to her in 1922, 1923, 1925, and 1926.

To DOROTHY CONNABLE,[1] Toronto, 16 February 1920

Dear Dorothy:

Ralph received a letter today from your mother portions of which he retailed to me. According to Ralph you visited the casino with five dollars and returned with seventeen and have taken a great interest in the game.

So I'm stopping work on my magnum opus, "Night Life Of the European Capitols, Or The War As I Seen it" to place at your disposal the results of a mis-spent earlier boy hood.

Paragraph. Roulette is almost invariably honest. It doesn't need to be dishonest because they win anyway. The chances are 38 to 1 against your getting any single number that you select and it only pays 36 to 1 if you win. So in the long run by the law of averages you will go broke.

Paragraph. There are many devices made for croupiers to brake or control a dishonest wheel. But the wheels at Palm Beach are straight so there's no use in going into them.

However there are one or two ways of playing roulette that give you a good chance of making money and you have the satisfaction of knowing that you are playing it well. Gee it makes me feel hungry just to talk about Roulette!

Hunches aren't any good. A hunch may be right once, but it's wrong a lot more times.

One good way to play scientifically is to watch how the wheel is running for a little while and what numbers are winning. The thing to do however is to watch what numbers aren't winning. Then take a number that hasn't been up for a long time, say oo and put a chip on it, if you lose put on two chips, if you lose again four chips and so on until the number comes. You win at that if you stick—but it takes nerve. That's the way the real roulette player does when he is getting down low and wants to get capital to stage a comeback. You see it ought to come once in thirty eight spins and when the wheel has gone twenty or thirty times without a number showing it is a pretty good plan to begin to back it. There's nothing except the law of averages that evens everything up in the long run to prevent it going fifty more times without coming up, and sometimes it does, but the chances are that it won't.

That's a good way to play when the tables are crowded and you can't get in close and get a seat. When you can get a seat this is a pretty good way to do.

[EH here provides a numbered diagram
of a roulette table with suggestions
for the placement of chips for betting.]

The wheel will probably be running, high, medium or low. That is the numbers will be running more often in one of the three thirds of the board. The first twelve, the second twelve or the third twelve. You want to pick which ever third they seem to be coming most often in and play as I have marked. In this way with four chips you are playing twelve numbers. The odds are roughly 1 in three that you will win, two to one against you, that is. But if you win on either of your chips that are covering four numbers it pays nine to one, and if you cash on either of your chips that are covering two numbers you are paid eighteen to one. So in the long run you win if you're lucky you are liable to make quite a lot of kale and at the worst you can play quite a long while at that system before you go broke.

Probably you already know all this and it's comparable to Edwin[2] explaining that English on the right makes the ball go to the right etc. But just on a chance that you didn't I whanged it out. It at least can claim the merit of not being theoretical but was worked out by bitter experience in the very best gambling hells in Yarrup.

Goldwyn Gregory and La Belge were over last night and stayed till after eleven. We played billiards, played the organ yarned around and I committed ghetto french toward Yranne. Spelling very doubtful. Mrs. Dinnink, Dyssique or Derrick, whose name I'd love to spell if I could, called on the phone yesterday for your address. Mr. D----k, D-----e or

D------ck, her husband, has been quite ill. She and I are going to a musicale if there ever is one. She is going to write your mother.

£ are quoted @ three something or other. That remark is made through a desire to use the £ & @ which have never been used heretofore.

Will your mother keep up her bicycling when she returns to Toronto?

Let's see, you don't write letters do you? Neither do I. This is merely a treatise on the evils of gambling. Probably you aren't really interested in roulette any way. But it is the best game in the world, having the advantage over craps that in craps you are winning your friend's money and consequently it is not so much fun. But in roulette you are bucking a wheel and there are no ethics against quitting when you are ahead. You can't do that in craps or poker. It is the loser who has to say when to quit. But in roulette when you get a decent way ahead—quit.

If you should play any along the line I've mentioned I'd like to know how you come out. Arte pour l'arte, or however it is spelled, you know. Wire me collect or something.

My love to Mrs. Connable.

Hoping If luck is a raindrop you is the Mississippi,

PH. PUL   Ernest Hemingway

1. Dorothy (1893–1975), sister of Ralph Connable, Jr., was vacationing with her parents in Palm Beach, Florida. For a fuller account of EH's stay in Toronto, see Carlos Baker, *Ernest Hemingway: A Life Story* (New York, 1969), pp. 66–70; and EH to Charles A. Fenton, 9 October 1952. 2. Edwin ("Dutch") Pailthorp of Petoskey had a job in Toronto while EH was there.

To MRS. HARRIET GRIDLEY CONNABLE, Oak Park, 1 June 1920

Dear Mrs. Connable:

I must apologize for not having written sooner to tell you how much I enjoyed and appreciated being in your home.[1]

You were awfully good to me and I want you to know how much it meant to me to know you all in addition to the priceless time I had.

Bill Smith was delayed getting here—just blew in yesterday, and shot a main bearing in the car so it's in the garage for a couple of days. We expect to shove off Thursday.

Brummy [Brumback] has been out at the house constantly and we've had a good time. He is all set on going in the fall and wants to leave from San Francisco. He says that as ordinary seamen we will make 70 seeds a month and should hit Yokahama with quite a little money, even if we leave San Francisco broke. I am going to try and sign on as a stoker as there is more money in it. He says I only need the fare to Frisco.

Brummy has his passport and I'm getting mine for China, Japan and India.

I stopped in Ann Arbor and saw Jacques Pentecost, and he and Brummy are coming north together about the fifteenth or twentieth of June.

It has been great to get all the gang together again. All the family are jake and are going north the seventh of June. Marcelline, my older sister and I are the best of pals now, so I've no one at all to row with.

I miss Toronto and you and Mr. Connable and Dorothy and Ralph a lot and think of you very often.

It will be very good to see you in Petoskey, and I look forward to having you come out to Walloon.

I've told the family many times that you are the very nicest people I've ever known and I look forward to having them meet you so they will agree with me.

At present the house is pretty badly shot to pieces. Jenny—our last bet in the maid line, couldn't stand the strain and so there is no one.

At Walloon tho it doesn't matter.

Hope you and Dorothy have a darby trip and give my best to Mr. Connable and Ralph.

This letter is too long I know.

Yours very sincerely,
Ernest Hemingway.

PH. PUL

1. The Connables owned a large house at 153 Lyndhurst Street, Toronto, where EH had lived c. 8 January–9 May 1920.

To GRACE QUINLAN, Boyne City, Michigan, 8 August 1920

Dearest G:

Well we were out on the Black and yesterday got back to the [Horton] Bay and your letter was waiting. And I'd rather get a letter from you than anybody else and I sure like to get letters so—

Gosh, G, what a hiker you are. 11 and 15 of the miles! That's real honest to [God] hiking. You must be having a peerless time.

It must be that thee and me are the kind that don't get homesick. Haven't ever been and yours was so far away as not to count.

We had a marvelous time this trip. Brummy [Brumback] and Jacques [Pentecost] and the Fever [Jenkins] and a new guy named Dick Smale.

Brum can play the mandolin wonderfully and in the evening he would play after supper in the dusk and 'side the camp fire.

And before we went to sleep we'd all be curled up around the fire. Often a wonderful moon and the guys would have me read Lord Dunsany's Wonder Tales[1] out loud. He's great.

And Bill [Smith] and Dr. Charles and the Madame [Mrs. Charles] came out one day and we caught about 50 trout and got a wonderful mess for them to take home.

Brummy and Dick were wading down the stream and Brummy was tired and wet and about two miles below camp. Brum's beard was blond and curly and Dick sez, "Gosh, Baugh, you do look like Jesus Christ!"

"Well," the Baugh comes back at him, "If I was I wouldn't wade. I'd get right up on the water and walk back to camp!"

That wasn't such a bad one, Nespah? We rented a car and a trailer for a week. Jock and I took some darby fish.

Came home yesterday and all went into the Voix [Charlevoix] and played Cook's. I had only six seeds to my name and was thinking I'd have to write to the Bank at home for more or work in the cement plant and then I played roulette until 2 A.M. this morning and won 59. Was going strong playing the rouge and noire the way I learned in Algeciras[2] —but the men made me quit as they wanted to go home. Hemingstein luck. 59 of the seeds would be several days at the cement plant.

8 girls must be a lot in one tent, G, we have plenty when we put two guys in one. But then they make you be neat, eh?

Didn't we rate a great moon the first of last week? It was great in camp lying all rolled up in the blankets after the fire had died down to coals and the men were asleep and looking at the moon and thinking long long thoughts. In Sicily they say it makes you queer to sleep with the moon on your face. Moon struck. Maybe that's what ails me.

About the kicking out business. Ursula and Sunny [EH's younger sisters] and young Loomis kid and a girl visiting her got up a midnight supper. They dragged the Baugh (Brummy) and I along. We didn't even want to go on the bludy thing. Pretty much of a bore. And we all went out at 12 bells and had a big feed at Ryan's Point and came in about 3 A.M.

Urse and Sunny and Bob Loomis and his Sister and Jean Reynolds and a boy visiting Bob and Brummy and I went along.

Mrs. Loomis missed the kids and was frantic and went over to our house and raised hell and accused the Baugh and I of getting up the party for the Lord knows what fine purpose! And we dragged along and really acted as chaperones.

So the next morning Brummy and I were kicked out without being allowed to even tell them everything about it!

Mother was glad of an excuse to oust me as she has more or less hated me ever since I opposed her throwing two or three thousand seeds away to build a new cottage for herself when the [jack?] should have sent the kids to college. That's another story. Fambly stuff. All famblys have skeletons in their closets. Maybe not the Quinlans but the Steins have heaps. "Heeps" Red used to spell it.

Grandfather gambled away a fortune, have a great uncle that is a remittance man and can't go back to England and is never unsoused long enough to endorse the checks he gets. His valet has to do it for him. Oh all kinds of fine scandals that we kept from the neighbors. And this is another one.

But isn't that the most ridiculous thing to get kicked out for? Have three or four letters from them that I haven't even opened so don't know what the late dope is. Am so darned disgusted I don't care to have anything more to do with them for a year at least.

The Baugh is all for Wopland and I'm all for workage this winter. Jacques's going to work this winter and we might buy a car in the Spring and then [drive] over all the country next summer. I hate buzzing all over Europe when there is so much of my own country I haven't seen.

But the Wopland gets in the blood and kind of ruins you for anything else. And I'd rather go later. You see I get so darned much fun out of working on a paper and writing and I like this country.

But then—It's all in the lap of the Gods. I'm for a job in New York next winter. But then I'm also for the open road and the long sea swells, and an old tramp steamer hull down on the oily seas.

And waking up in the morning in strange ports. With new delightful smells and a tongue you don't understand. And the rattle of shifting cargo in the hold.

And tall glasses and siphons and rare new stories and old pals in far places. And hot nights on deck with only pyjamas on.

And cold nights when the wind roars out side and the waves smash against the thick glass of the port holes and you walk on deck in the flying scuds and have to shout to make yourself heard. And laying chin down on the grass on a cliff and looking out over the sea. And oh such a lot of things, G.

Anyway I'll bet no one else writes you such damned fool letters as I do.

We're here for about 3 or 4 days of tennis at the Voix. Bill and the Doc—Brummy and I, Jack and the Fever. We get some rare doubles. Also took a 4 lb rainbow this morning.

You played any tennis at camp? We're swimming a lot lately.

Must shoot this off to old dear. What do *you* think about things. And please write. I owe everybody else I know a screed.

                                        Love (all I've got)
                                        Stein

My best to Useless and Evalina. H.T.T. L. for you from Brummy.

YUL

1. *The Book of Wonder* (1915) by Lord Dunsany (1878–1957). **2.** It is possible that EH learned roulette when his homebound ship, the *Giuseppe Verdi*, docked briefly at Algeciras, Spain, in January 1919.

To HOWELL JENKINS, Boyne City, 16 September 1920

Dear Mr. LeFever—The Carper:

Sorry as hell old bean that I haven't written you before—but then the men gave you all the dope up till when they left.

Since they left we have caught a lot of Rainsteins [rainbow trout]. A couple or so pretty near every day we fished for them. Also we have laid hold of a high grade sailing craft and have sailed the ass offn it every day. Yesterday Kate [Smith] and Odgar [Carl Edgar] and I were sailing to the Voix and altho under a double reef we had such a hell of a storm that we had to put in at Ironton. Rain lightning thunder Tidal waves, typhoons and Gawd knows what.

Duck season opens today and we hope for a pogrom of the feathered ones. I expect to stay here until about the middle of October and will then flash down in the car with the Madam and the Bird and Stut [Bill and Kate Smith]. Having been barred from my domicile[1] I know not where I will linger in Chi[cago]. Probably ask Vigano to leave me use a couple of blankets in the Venice [Café]. Will be in Chicago a few days and then allez to either Toronto or K.C. Had a letter from K.C. [*Kansas City Star*] asking me to name my figure! As I can lay hold of fifty of the seeds four times a month in Toronto [*Toronto Star*] I am going to mention those statistics to them. Something tells me that they will come through. In that event I'll have plenty of Jack next summer. They offered the Baugh $175 a month and they always paid me more than the Baugh. Hope I can get some good sized Jack down there because I can clean up a hundred or hundred and fifty a month on the side out of my special correspondence. That's why I think that K.C. is the place cause I'll get a good salary there and supplement it with pertty near as much on the side from Toronto.

Whadda you think?

In regards to Jack and Carp don't let your enthusiasm run away with you.[2]

Remember this. Miske was a set up. He had been sick and was through in the ring and this was really a benefit given for him by Dempsey. They are very good friends and so Jack said. You have to give Miske the first crack at the title. It was ridiculous of course to expect Miske to do anything against Jack.

Now Jack is going up against another good old war horse who is absolutely through, Gunboat Smith. The Gunner was a hell of a good fighter altho a damned wild swinger. But now he is absolutely through. Somebody, some second rater knocked him out in Grand Rapids the other night.

Jack will polish him off in short order and then will knock out Bill Brennan who is one of the poorest fighters of all time.

But what you want to remember Fever is that Geo. [Carpentier] could take these set ups just as easily.

Geo. went twenty rounds against Joe Jeanette, he's fought Billy Papke and Frank Klaus, he's knocked out Wells twice and Beckett in quicker time than Dempsey ever handled any one. He is no bloomer and no morning glory and don't go to think just because Dempsey is koing all the tramps that he is going to make an ass out of Mr. Carp.

If you can get any one to give ten to one or anything like that that Dempsey will put him away in short order I'd snap it up like a shot. Because as soon as they pipe Geo. agin Battling Levinsky the price will tumble right through itself.

Dempsey, Fever, has never had a real fight yet, Geo. has a pile of them under his belt. Dempsey may be just as good as they say he is— but he has never proved that he is anything but a lightning fast puncher who packs a hell of a wallop. What he will do agin a man that is as fast a puncher as he is and that can stay away from him and hand out stuff in return is yet to be seen.

Ponder these things. Dempsey may beat his can off. But on the other hand there is a gaoddam good chance that he won't. And this is the first fight that Jack has ever been in that the result hasn't been determined before they stepped into the ring.

I sure enjoyed seeing Chic Take Francis Ouimet. To hell wit the Harvard Hedgehogs.

What are you doing now? What is Pock doing? Is he going back to school? Do you ever see Dick [Smale]?

How about the liquor problem?

Screed me carper and tell me what you think about my dope on Dempsey-Carp.

We have picked a lot of apples lately and also cut and set up Nine acres of sweet clover for seed. Oh Yes. I tore my gut on a cleat on the boat and had internal hemorrages and yesterday the Doc lanced the navel and took out a lot of puss. Feels better today. They thought I was hay-wired tho for a while though.

We laid hold of some gloves and did a little boxing the other day. I went four rounds wit Honest Will [Bill Smith] without getting a wallop, no only three rounds, and managed to swell Will's face up in nice shape. Will is fast and a hard puncher but don't know enough about the game. He is game though because I rocked him wit right and left hooks to the head and he kept coming in. We played three sets of tennis the other day and Will made me look worse on the courts than I made him wit the gloves.

Well I'll try and catch the official with this.

Screed and my best to your folks and to Dick.

Immer /

PH. PUL   Stein.

1. EH's mother forbade him to stay at Windemere Cottage because of the Ryan's Point episode. See Carlos Baker, *Ernest Hemingway: A Life Story* (New York, 1969), pp. 71–73. 2. After a year's publicity buildup, Jack Dempsey knocked out Georges Carpentier in the fourth round, 3 July 1921.

To GRACE QUINLAN, Boyne City, 30 September 1920

Dearest G:

Your mither told me this morning that it was your birthday and so I at once tore down town to get you something fitting. But haveing only fifty nine centimes in my pocket I was seriously handicapped.

The gift of fifty nine one cent stamps was considered—or a months subscription to the Evening Snewse or a bargain in special cut rate sale of rubbers at Reinhertzes but all were rejected on the grounds that you can borrow stamps, have the paper anyway and probably dont wear rubbers.

So Kate [Smith] and I and the Doc [Dr. Charles] went to Martin's and each had an alleged drink and I requested that they drink to a very estimable lady of my acquaintance whose birthday it was. And we drank and Kate wanted to know how old that lady was an I said that she was approaching Thirty—slowly but surely. And so on the strength of that we drank again and then all the money for your birthday was gone.

But next time old bean I'll try and not go broke until after you celebrate.

This morning in your kitchen we were talking and in came Deggie and a discussion occurred in the course of which I was informed by Deggie that it served me right to lose when I bet on the Sox last fall.[1] Thinking the series was honest. And that he didn't blame the sox for selling it etc. And becoming somewhat wroth, but not showing it I hope, a great and overpowering desire to spank him laid hold of me. But it was conquered because thought I, "Sooth and what will become of the small remnants of my old drag if commit spankage on a dear friend?"

Then Kate and I went to the catholic church and burnt a candle and I prayed for all the things I want and won't ever get and we came out in a very fine mood and very shortly after to reward me the Lord sent me Adventure with a touch of Romance.

It was a very small adventure but it was unexpected and for a moment thrilling and I was glad that I had burned the candle. For the details you'll have to see Liz.

And as we drove home in the rain I thought long long thoughts about how fine it is to be Fifteen and You, and it raining quite hard and Kate going to sleep I made a poem about you being fifteen and then when I got home I remembered how much more sense you have than I have and the rain having stopped and Kate having wakened up I thought that you would think that a poem would be a very foolish thing. And so I didn't send it.

Gee I'm awfully darned sorry that I've been such poor company this summer and so grouchy and I'm darned sorry that you don't like me as well as you did. And because I did like you better than anybody else it hurt when I heard that you were saying things about me behind my back.

But that's not this which is your birthday and I hope it was a darned good one and that maybe if you don't feel too darned old you'll write me a letter.

Good night
Love, old dear,
Stein

P.S. Burned a candle for you. Wonder if you'll rate any results. Told 'em to give you whatever you want.
YUL

---

1. An allusion to the so-called Black Sox scandal in which eight Chicago White Sox players were accused of "throwing" a game against the Cincinnati Reds in the World Series of 1919, which Cincinnati won.

To GRACE HALL HEMINGWAY, Chicago, 22 December 1920

Dearest Mother:

I didn't realize how close it is to Christmas before it is actually upon us.

We'll all miss not having you here. Bill Horne is gone East but Kenley and Doodles [Mrs. Y. K. Smith] are coming out for dinner.

I'm working on this magazine called the Co-operative Commonwealth[1] which is the organ, mouth organ, not pipe organ for the Co-operative movement. If almost any part of what they say about this movement is true it is quelque movement. The mag has 65,000 circulation and this month eighty pages of reading matter and about twenty of ads. Most of the reading was written by myself. Also write editorials and most anything. Will write anything once.

It was nice to get a letter from you and I'm glad Uncle Leicester [Hall] thinks he might like me. I'd try and do the same toward him. Hope you can go swimming in the boiling, bubbling baths—they sound like when we used to swim at Nantucket [1910] and I'd go in with the kelp and the horseshoe crabs and you'd swim in the salt water baths.

Dad lets me read your letters when I'm out at the hoose Sundays and so I keep fairly well informed of your doages [doings]. Can't seem to recall any news that would be news to you. I took Sun [Madelaine] to the foot ball dance and she danced wonderfully well and looked great. Ura [Ursula] was there with Johnny and an apricot and white evening gown slashed like a court jester. She looks terribly well in evening dress because of being a well turned article.

Doodles is going to New York to study with Lawrence the Monday after Christmas, I'm going to live there then. 63 East Division Street. It's a very extra comfortable apartment, seven rooms, and the priceless Della to cook for us. There will be five of us there in batchellor quarters.

Am being frightfully good in pursuit of your instructions. At least you told me to be good didn't you? Being so anyway. Very busy, very good, and very tired. It's fun to be the first but the second and third have a decreasingly stronger appeal. Hash [Hadley Richardson] was up here from Saint Louis for a week end.[2] Came one Saturday night and allezed Monday night. We had a most excellent time. She wants me very badly to come to a big New Years eve dinner and party at the University Club in Sin Louis—but I can't negotiate the grade. Being about as well seeded as the navel orange.

I'm getting a very fair wage but am busily engaged in getting through Christmas, paying off the odd debt and must purchase badly needed clothes, both under and over.

Am giving the kids paper seeds in small denominations for Christmas —haven't had a minute to shop. It would be hardly fitting to send one's wealthy mother luxuriating in California paper seeds—so I'm getting you and Lessie something and will hold it here or forward it out if you decide to stay longer.[3] Give the kid my best love and wish he and Uncle Leicester both Merry Christmas for me. I wish I could see Uncle Leicester.

Had a letter yesterday from the Zist, Doctor Gudakunst, that is, perhaps you recall the fact that he is a physician? He is at Santa Fe New Mex and has been made manager of a Health Resort Ranch at a very good seed basis. He wants to wire me a ticket to come down there claiming that there are horses to burn and a man never has to shave and many other attractions. He is anxious for me to allez down—but I ought not to play the role of the rats deserting the stinking ship yet—the odor from the ship is just beginning to be perceptible. When it becomes a full blown stench I may chase down there. 'Nother words I haven't all the confidence in the world in the [Cooperative] Movement.

Well Merry Christmas to you old dear—won't wish you Happy New Year because New Year is just one lurch nearer the grave and nothing to be happy over.

Hope you have a priceless time.

Love
Ernie

JFK

1. See EH to Bill Smith, 28 April 1921, note 4. **2.** Elizabeth Hadley Richardson (1891–1979) was born in St. Louis. She lost her father by suicide in 1903 and her mother through lingering illness in 1920. A graduate of Mary Institute (1910), she spent one collegiate year at Bryn Mawr. Kate Smith had known her since their days at the Institute and invited her to Chicago. EH first met her at Y. K. Smith's apartment, 1230 North State Street, in early November 1920. **3.** EH's mother, accompanied by her youngest child, Leicester, then nearly six, was visiting her brother, Leicester Hall, in California.

To GRACE HALL HEMINGWAY, Chicago, 10 January 1921

Dear Mother:

I've been very busy lately or I would have written you before. I've moved, guess I told you that, or was going to.

Now at 63 East Division. Haven't been out to the house since New Years I think—now it's the tenth of January so I'll have to allez out soon.

Yesterday I meant to but we had Isaac Don Levine, the Daily News correspondent in Russia at dinner at noon at the apartment and then went to hear Benno Moseiwitch play at orchestra hall in the afternoon. Moseiwitch is the best pianist there is now I think. He's infinitely superior to Levitski or Jeosh Hoffman and I think he has it on Rachmaninoff or Gabrilowitch—he's in the first four anyway.

He played a much better program than he did the last time I heard him, Chopin's B. Minor Concerto and the sunken cathedral Cathedral Engloutie or something like that by DeBussy and then two of Lizst with the Campanella, and some modern stuff that I forget the names of. I'm quoting from memory or I'd be more accurate.

Then Levine took Kenley [Smith] and I to see Lenore Ulric in her new play at Powers. Remember us seeing her in Tiger Rose? This new thing is The Son-Daughter—and it is just as good a melodrama as Tiger Rose— don't know whether it is as well constructed or not—but Lenore is quelque actorine and the thing is filled with notable things like FenCha the illustrious gambler and The Sea Crab—the sea crab is very scary article—I was scared—you might be scared.

Have seen Willie Collier in the Hottentot and Happy Go Lucky and a few other shows and the Ulric twice.

Levine is an excellent fellow and gave us the cold dope on Rooshia. He's just been back for four days and goes to New York tomorrow.

I've been raised ten paper seeds more a week. Ten seeds are ten seeds. That makes me get fifty of the papered seeds every Saturday. Of course that isn't many paper seeds but still it is a few paper seeds.

Horney Bill [Bill Horne] is still in the near East, Yonkers to be exact. The kids are all in good shape I believe. They seem happy. They act well. They look healthy.

I am in good shape. I eat well. I sleep well. I do everything but work well.

Interviewed Mary Bartelme today and she is the genuwind old darticle. An excellent woman and I fell hard for her and wrote a wonderful story.[1] Will send it to you when it comes out.

Did I send you one of the lousy magazines?

How is the Kid Leicester?

Give my love to Uncle Leicester and the same love and any remaining, there is undoubtedly much remaining on account of not being able to love Uncle Leicester except as something abstract like a character of fiction, to yourself.

Always glad to hear offn you.

I'd stay out there as long as you can—we've been having wonderful weather here—which means that we have hells own weather enroute. We always get it sooner or letter and it hasn't come yet.

Love to you, pardon the rotten typer—it's a new one and stiff as a frozen whisker,

JFK   Ernie

1. Mary M. Bartelme (1866–1954), born in Chicago, was a noted helper of delinquent girls. She was known as "Suitcase Mary" because she gave each of her charges a suitcase full of clothes. As a Juvenile Court judge in Chicago from 1923 to 1933, she was the first woman to preside in an Illinois court. One notable character trait of young EH was his admiration for certain older women: Mary Bartelme, Harriet Connable, Mildred Aldrich, and Gertrude Stein, among others.

To JAMES GAMBLE, Chicago, c. 24 February 1921[1]

Rather go to Rome with you than heaven Stop [Not married stop: *these words crossed out*]. Too sad for words stop. Writing and selling it stop [Unmarried: *this word crossed out*] but don't get rich stop all authors poor first then rich stop. me no exception stop Wouldn't we have a great time stop Lord how I envy you

                                            Hemmy.
                                            63 East Division Street
                                            Chicago Illinois.
JFK   care Y.K. Smith

1. Typed copy for use as a telegram, with indicated changes in EH's hand. See EH to James Gamble, 3 March 1919. Gamble's address was now 356 South 16th Street, Philadelphia.

To DR. C. E. HEMINGWAY, Chicago, 15 April 1921

Dear Dad:
    I was very glad to get your two postals—by now you should be having a wonderful time. Things are moving fairly fast here. I'm working very hard at my jawb and have a chanct of promotion and I suppose more seeds—can't go into the details as there is always some one liable to come in and look over your shoulder to see what you're writing. We have a new office in the loop—address room 205 Wells Building—128 North

Wells Street Chicago Illinois will get me. Chance of me being made managing editor of the poiper. That's private and very sub rosa.

Meantime I'm still dickering with [the] Toronto [*Star*] and liable to shove for there any time. The Italian Lira that I've bought around 3.50 and so on have risen to 5.00—I could sell at a good profit—but am buying them because I want the Lira—not as a gamble. Want to go to Italy in November if I've enough Lira. Manfredi was up last night. He's looking well and sent his best to you.

I had Ursula out to dinner one night and am going out to the [Oak Park] house soon. But have been working like a dog. Going up to Wisconsin on a story next Monday.

They hanged Cardinella and Cosmano and some other Wop killer today. Lopez, who was to hang, was reprieved. Cardinella is a good man to swing I guess. Passed the County Jail this morning and there was a big crowd standing outside waiting for the event.[1]

Have you been doing any fishing yet?

Give my love to Grandmother and Grandfather and Aunt Grace and Carol. Hope they are all feeling well.[2]

Get a good rest and some good fishing and go swimming for me—I surely wish I were with you—eat a lot of shrimps too—wish I could rate a vacation—seems as though you work like a dog all week and it's barely Sunday and you get a little sleep and it's back at the treadmill again—I'm going to beat the machine by going to Wopland for a while in the fall.

The sun hasn't shown here for about two weeks. I'm writing you a swell gloomy letter so that you'll appreciate what a fine time you're having. I hate these guys that write to some one that's away on a trip and try and make them feel they would have more fun if they were at home. It's not a bit of fun here—and nothing to look forward to.

With that cheerful prospect I close

Your affct son

JFK   Ernie

1. Sam Cardinella and two others were hanged in Chicago on 15 April 1921. On the 14th, the *New York Times* reported that Cardinella objected to being executed under daylight saving time. See EH, *In Our Time*, chapter 15. 2. Dr. and Mrs. Hemingway with daughter Carol, aged ten, were vacationing at Sanibel Island off the west coast of Florida with Anson and Adelaide Hemingway and their grown daughter Grace.

To WILLIAM B. SMITH, JR., Chicago, 28 April 1921

Gaw Bird you sound in ghastly shape. Far be it from the enditer to count letters on a run down article. You oughta be able to pick up some pretty good jack with this Zelnicker stuff this summer as a side line. You can give the Nicker a good line on the Michigan situation anyway. Does Ben Brown[1] stock our rings?

The enditer is stunned by the shape you sound to be in—the screeds shall flow freely. I'd no idea that you were in such carpy condition—though you looked bad when I was in the village. Laid non hearage from you to some form of displeasure with the Enditer and so after a time stopped screedage on the theory that if a man didn't want to have nathing to do with a man a man ought not to give an imitation of Odgar [Carl Edgar] in epistolary pursuit of Butstein [Kate Smith]. However if you're under the squord, as you obviously sound, the out put will be unrestricted.[2]

Us men are moving to 100 E. Chicago forninst [next?] Saturday.

Doodiles [Mrs. Y. K. Smith] is coming home on the 28th of May. Yen [Y. K. Smith] is in swell shape—172 of the pounds—keeps twixt there and 174. Declares that he has never felt better since first laid by the heels.

Fedith [Edith Foley] is in town and living with her parents at the Virginia Hotel. Stut [Kate Smith] hasn't seen her, to my knowledge, for a week or ten days. Stut has been with Yen or I nearly every night last week—we staged a swell party, She and Yen and the enditer and a fine guy named Krebs [Friend],[3] last saturday nacht at a series of German family resorts that I have never seen rivalled. I doubt if their equal exists in Germany. Moselle wine at 40 centimes the large beaker, regular prewar beer at 40 cents the stein. Man can get a good dinner for 50 cents. Not a word of English spoken. We'll make them when you stop here. Sunday Stut and the men Yen, Horne and Rouse went out to Oak Park, the parentals all being in Michigan. Swell German vaudveel at the places I mentioned, Wurtz n'sepp's, Komicker seppels and two other splendid places.

Fedith being here, she and Stut living apart and not seeing each other would indicate bustage up would it not?

The enditer is not in anyway in the pink hisself. For last two weeks have rated splitting head aches that damn near mort a man. Yesterday at the office rated haywireage of my good optic and had to go home to the domocile. Had to lay off the gloves on account of the headaches—been working like hell at same time as doing regular stuff for Loper.[4] Written more stuff in past two weeks than in preceeding 18 months. Physical doesn't seem to be bucking the mental—feel right up forninst [next] the verge of complete haywireage however. When a man can go swimming here it'll be better. At present come home from the office, feed, shoot a couple or three rubberoids of bridge with the men and then go to bed, sleep a little while and then wake up and can't sleep for nawthing, so start working and keep going till get sleepy in the morning. Pastimed the Veronal but it don't seem to have the wallop. Wish to hell I was going Nort when you men do. Doubt if I get up this summer—Jo Eezus, sometimes get thinking about the Sturgeon and Black during the nocturnal [night] and damn near go cuckoo—Haven't the Odgar attitude on that. May have to give it up for something I want more—but that doesn't keep me from loving it with everything I have. Dats de way tings are. Guy loves a couple or three streams all his life and loves 'em better than anything in the world—falls in love with a girl and the goddam streams can dry up for all he cares. Only the hell of it is that all that country has as bad a hold on me as ever—there's as much of a pull this spring as there ever was—and you know how it's always been—just don't think about it at all daytimes, but at night it comes and ruins me—and I can't go.

Remember that day last summer when we hit the big school at that bend down below Chandler's? That's one of the worst that hits a man. And the day I fished alone with Sam Nickey down on another part of the creek and took all those tremendous ones in that stretch where you and I first butchered them, the day that Hoopkins [Charles Hopkins] and Odgar got their big bunch up the stream. Remember me breaking my rod on that place where you caught your big one and the fight we had before we netted him? Joe Eesus I'll bet there are trout in there a man wouldn't believe. Now I've gotten started thinking about it—ruined for the day.

This is carpy screed—Carper's [Howell Jenkins] making good seeds now—on a basis of strictly commission—making lot more than he ever did before and keeps it right up. Says he's going to take a month up North. Dirty Dick in pretty good shape—had lunch with him this noon. Don't know the Ghee's [Pentecost's] plans yet. What is the dope on Teodore [Brumback]? Had a screed from Theodore—postal rather—didn't give any dope.

Spose one of the principal causes that's haywired you is being too tired at night to take any kind of exercise. Think that's one of the big things that ruins a man. He doesn't realize it till he's a ruint article too. You sure appear to have an air tight drag with Zelnicker. Good thing for a man to have.

Well Waddyoh—shoot you a better screed shortly—couple of screeds of this character would topple a man into the casket.

Immer,

PUL Wemedge

1. Garage owner in Petoskey. Bill worked for the Ever Tight Piston Ring Co., St. Louis. 2. The play-language used here was a staple of the EH-Smith correspondence; the suffix -age was added to common words, food becoming *eatage*, letters *screedage*, death *mortage*, and so on. EH's nickname Wemedge derived from Weminghay = Wemage = Wemedge. 3. Krebs Friend was a crony of EH's in Chicago, and again in Paris in 1924. 4. Richard H. Loper was publisher of *The Cooperative Commonwealth* and Frank Parker Stockbridge was an associate. The firm had recently moved from 1554 Ogden Avenue to the Wells Building, 128 North Wells Street, Chicago.

To MARCELLINE HEMINGWAY,[1] Chicago, 20 May 1921

Dearest Carved Ivory:

Hope the 'domen is feeling in good shape. Gee I was sorry when I heard that you were to go under the knife. There's nothing bothers me like having a dear old friend or relative go under the knife.

Conversation with the male parent however elicited the information that you had come out from under the knife in nice shape.

The men are going to screed you and I will be out shortly to see in what shape you have come out from under the knife.

Tonight the Carper, i.e. Mr. La Fever the Carper [Howell Jenkins] and Yenlaw [Y. K.] Smith and the writer are going to be seated at the ringside while Frankie Schaeffer—of the Stock Yards—and Gene Watson —the Pacific Coast demon—maul ten rounds at 130 lbs. ringside. It should be a good brawl. I look forward to viewing it.

I think that Al [Walker] had a good time with me here. Hope so—I took your tip that he was without seeds and financed the entire entertainment—food drink etc. It must have shocked Al to learn that you were going under the knife.

Does Douglas Wilde know that you have gone under the knife? He ought to come through with something pretty handsome. Think of what you might have rated from him if you had only permitted kissage. Your going under the knife would then have rent him in such bad shape that he would probably have smothered the hospital in onions like a steak is smothered in onions.

All the men were broken up to hear that you had gone under the knife.

Last night Issy Simons [Isabel Simmons] and I had a swell party. Went to four of the best places in the city and while I was saddened at the thought of you being under the knife I managed to assume a certain false Gayety. We had a peach of a time. Issy is a priceless kid. It was a glorious night. We'd come out of some place where we'd been waltzing and into the outer air and it would be warm and almost tropical with a big moon over the tops of the houses. Kind of a warm softness in the air, same way it used to be when we were kids and we'd roller skate or play run sheep run with the Luckocks and Charlotte Bruce.

I'm, and Horney's [Bill Horne], going down to St. Louis next Friday night and stay three days at Hash's domicile. Ought to have a swell time. The new Domicile is a wonder—much larger than the old one—and with an elevator and a view from my front window looking down over the queer angled roofs of the old houses on Rush street down to the big mountain of the Wrigley building, green of the new grass along the street and trees coming out—wonderful view. Bobby's [Rouse] going to New York for good pretty soon—did you know that? Horney's working hard.

We've a fine song—wrote by me about the men—

> Bobby strolls round on La Salle street
> Carper spends money on sin
> Horney'll write ads for a quarter
> My Gawd how the money rolls in!

Gee I'm sorry that you had to go under the knife. But still if a person has to go under the knife they might just as well go right under the knife without struggling. Sleepy as the deuce this aft—hot you know—and I didn't get in till all hours this morning. Gee, had a good time—more fun to go out with Is[abel] than any body I know in this town. Youghta a seen us in the Grottenkeller waltzing round and round and all germans around and a fine beery, smoky, cheerful pound on the table with a stein for more music, atmosphere.

Scuse the rotten typeage and the probably tousands of errati—that's on account of me typing by the touch system—just learned it recently and it's faster but more inaccurate. Kate [Smith] sent you her love and said that you were the last person she would enjoy having go under the knife. Me too I hate to think of you going under the knife—did you have 'em take anything else out too? I'd have had everything out at onc't. Coming out Sunday I think and will cast an optic on you.

Best love to you, dear old swester [sister]—and hope you're comfortable,

ever,

JFK   Ernie

1. Addressed to Marcelline at Oak Park Hospital "(A Patient with the Appendix Out)."

To GRACE QUINLAN, Chicago, 21 July 1921

Dear Old Gee:

You musta thought me all sorts of a dirty bum because of not answering your and Pudges' [Marjorie Bump's] priceless note—but guess the letter to both of you explained that. Woulda written you both together—but can't very well—always been separated in my mind and sides there are things to tell both of you.

Just because you said about my not writing you I'm enclosing letter I wrote you one day last February when I was feeling low—that's so you won't think I just dropped you out of my mind.

Suppose you want to hear all about Hadley—well her nickname is Hash—she's a wonderful tennis player, best pianist I ever heard and a sort of terribly fine article.[1] Spite of the clipping prophecying a big wedding in the fall in St. Louis, we're going to fool them and be married at the [Horton] Bay in that small, trick church there. Then going to kinda bum around for about three weeks and then go back to Chicago— apartment there with Kenley Smith's—stay there through November I guess and then allez to Italy for a year or maybe two years. I've been saving seeds and buying Wop money since came down from Petoskey and I recently had a grant from the King and so I'm setting pretty well thataway. We're going to Naples and stay there till it gets warm in the spring. Living at Capri I guess, and then go up into Abruzzi. Capracotta probably—there's a fine trout stream there—the Sangro River—and tennis courts and it's 1200 meters above sea level—most wonderful place you ever heard of. I've gotten all the dope on prices and so on from my best pal, Nick Neroni, who's just come to this country, we were together in the war, and he's been staying around with me and given me all the dope. He's going back in the fall and will arrange everything for us.

It sounds pretty good? The date hasn't been set for the wedding, but it'll be early in Sept—some time the first week—and you'll be there of course. I can't invite a big lot of people because we're having it up North to get away from all that sort of thing—but you'll come won't you? Invitations and all that sort of thing'll arrive in course of human events.

You don' wanta think, Gee, that I've thrown over all the people I'm fond of up North because I've not been writing this winter. It's been a regular hell of a winter in some ways—been pretty badly sick couple of times—been holding down one jawb days and one nights to get more seeds—been writing stuff on the side all the time and been so busy and tired and done in that I haven't written a line except to Hash [Hadley] all winter.

Have what's really a pretty darned good job now[2]—maybe making a mistake to throw it over to go to Italy—but will have enough seeds to last a couple of years there—and with that time to write in I've a chance to get somewhere.

Irene Goldstein [of Petoskey] was here and we had one good session of tennis and I was going to see her again and then got suddenly ordered east to the [Dempsey-Carpentier] fight and hadda leave in a hurry—packing on the run and didn't even have a chance to call her upwards. Lost 700 and some seeds on the battle—and that didn't help peace of mind any. It was a good bet at 3-1 though—Carp showed that when he nearly got him in the 2nd round. We were out of luck—if he hadn't busted his hand with that first right he landed—but what's the use of Post mortems? I'd rather you didn't say anything bout the seeds loseage—you know—there are too many people like to have a crack at you if you give 'em any chancet.

Well dear old bean I'd better close—must write Useless—I'll be seeing you in September—Irene tells me you're getting beautiful—wouldn't be anything new—you have to be pretty good looking tho to have other girls say so.

Write me will you? And remember me to your Dad and Mother. I'm terribly fond of all of you—you know how fond I am of you—

Always,
Stein

P.S. Maybe your father and mother could bring you and Pudge and who else? Red and Liz? Over to this here wedding. I'm not asking Mrs. Graham—you know why—cause I don't want her. But didn't want Pudge to see this.

Immer
Stein.

Give me all the dope on whats going on—Huh?
YUL

---

1. See EH to his mother, 22 December 1920, note 2. 2. As assistant editor of the *Cooperative Commonwealth*.

To GRACE QUINLAN, Goshen, Indiana, 7 August 1921

Dearest G:

All sorts of things for not having screeded you before of course. But— oh a has the alibis.

Isn't this a lovely place? My boss sent me down East to drive his car through to Chicago and I'm on the last leg of the trip. Get in tomorrow noon I hope to Gawd. Sh——— not meant to be sacrilegious—just prayerful. Is Pudge at camp? Whyn't she answer my letter?

I'm glad your the same my dear, very beautiful, very much older than your years, very unsatisfied (thank Gawd) with Petoskey person that you are. Also you're the best of all sisters. Don't ever tell this, blood or otherwise; and I knew you wouldn't be a [Christian] Scientist.

I'm tired from driving all day, and error has krept into the more bum of my bum legs; so I oughta go and take a long soak in the tub and see if I can't drown error.

Wish you were here to talk to. I'm lonely as the deuce. If you really want it, you can have that snap I sent you with the 'nouncement and picture of Hash [Hadley]. Leave me know if you do. It's at home.

Enclosed is a picture of Hadley in her wedding dress. Very improper to circulate prior to wedding I blieve but your my sister, aren't you? Gee G. I'll be glad to see you at this here wedding. Dearest old Kid. Bet you're having a smashing time at camp.

Know how you feel about my being too young to be married. Felt exactly the same way until Hash and I realized that life would be about as interesting as this splendid hotel (see picture at head of stationery) unless we could have each other to live with. So in circumstances like those you hafta make allowances. I never wanted to be married before, in spite of having faced it on numerous occasions.

Good night old Dearest—I love you a very much.

Always yours Bro.
Stein

YUL

To GRACE QUINLAN, Chicago, 19 August 1921

Dearest G:

Sorry camp is sort of tunking out on you. Maybe it's better now though. Usually things aren't so much fun the second time are they? We oughta do 'em once and then go on to something new—only guess the new things would probably wear all out on us.

Sure I know somebody named Shorney. Two boys Gordon and Herbert. Herbert's older than I am, but Gordon and I were class mates at [Oak Park High] school. He's a very fine article. I just know the sister to speak to.

No, really, did they have me married in France? Gaw. Tell me all about it. Did I desert her, or what? D'ya think I'll be a bigamist? Tell me all about it. I'm frightfully interested.

Why I'm going to leave here the 27th of August and get up North the next morning and probably tear right out to the Sturgeon for the last three days of the fishing season. They close it up on a man the 1st of Sept. and I haven't had any for so long that I'm starved and crazy for it. Then I'll be back and standing by till the 3rd when heavy marriage occurs. Oughta be a fairly high grade occasion, be a pretty good gang there. Not many people, but a lot of people we like. I'll be trying to get into Petorskey to see you before der Tag.

Am enclosing the picture. Look civilizeder than you ever knew me, Huh? Been terrifically civilized for about twelve months now, and it's darned near ruined a man.

Have to go down to interview the president of the U.S. Grain Growers Inc. in a little while, and I'm writing this during lunch hour. Guy I usually eat lunch with is sick. So talking to you instead. You don't mind particularly do you? Hash is somewhere up on the Upper Peninsula having all the fun that is being had in the family. I won't see her again till we're at the [Horton] Bay. Sunny is in Minnesota, Marce in Maine [EH's sisters Madelaine and Marcelline], the Hemingstein's are at Walloon. All the guys I know here are left town, not a soul here, lonely as Boyne Falls. Have to stick out two more weeks of it only though. That's a good thing.

Had a terribly funny dream about you last night. Can't remember it at all now, one of those kind that sort of slither away from you, but it was a very good dream and I wish I could remember it. Foist time I've had you bumming around in my head in a dream in months. Funny that it should come last night and then a letter from you first thing this morning. Maybe the hand of the Maker stalking into the room.

Oh Yes. How about ministers, preachers, priests or prelates. ?? In your wide and diverse acquaintance can you recommend a capable minister to perform this ceremony? Hash says she doesn't care particularly what breed of priest it is, but prefers one that doesn't wear a celluloid collar or chaw tobacco. We thought we could lay hold of Bishop Tuttle from St. Louis that summers at Harbor Point, but he may be gone by then. Remember when selecting this Priest that he's gotta be able to read and be dignified. Dignity's what we're going to pay this here prelate for, we don't want no evangelist that's liable to shout out, 'Praise be the Lord' and start rolling on the floor during a critical part of the ceremony. Presbyterian preferred, or else Episcopal, doesn't make the slightest difference to me. What's the local prelate situation? Give me a brief resume. Huh? Pick me a prelate.

Well I gotta eat something and start after this Grain Grower. We go to press in three days. I've been working like a dawg on account of having to get stuff up for all the time I'm going to be gone. Gradually getting ahead of the line though. Sure am sick of it all though. I'm writing a 100,000 word book for them, being published serially in 5,000 word chunks. Deadly stuff. You won't know me, a wreck, I tell you, a wreck. Slap a lotta thought, or not a lot if it don't take much, don't slap no more thought than you have to, on this here Man of God.

Write me G- I'm lonely as the deuce -

Great amount of love -

YUL
Stein

To Y. K. SMITH, Chicago, 1 October 1921

Dear Y. K.:

I understand from Mother, over the phone, that she mailed you an invitation to a reception at Oak Park tonight.[1]

There is no chance, of course, that you and Doodles would go, but on the chance that you might mis-interpret the bid, I'm taking a couple of minutes to rescind it personally.

Not that I wouldn't be glad to see you, as Doodles says in her often-read-aloud masterpiece, you are "A good-looking young man" but I feel, to quote your wife's universally admired output that "So mote it be."

I'll be over to collect the residue of my clothes and my probably well-thumbed correspondence while you and the good wife are out at the triangular little home in Palos Park.[2]

So mote it be
So mote it be
So hang yourself on a Christmas tree.

> Always,
> [Ernest
> Hemingway]

PH. PUL

1. The twenty-fifth wedding anniversary of Hemingway's parents. 2. Y. K. Smith (1887–1969) replied (*c.* 2 October): "Ernest: Your clothes and things have been gotten together, and are in the Aldis storeroom. You can get the key from the janitress. The items are as follows: 1 box, 2 bundles of clothing, 2 hats, 1 cape, 1 valise. There are some things of Hadley's that I will take the liberty of delivering myself. You can readily understand that your having written me as you have makes your presence in my house quite impossible, at any time, under any circumstances." (PH. PUL) After the wedding at Horton Bay on 3 September, EH and Hadley had honeymooned at Windemere, the family cottage on Walloon Lake, and then moved into a small apartment at 1239 North Dearborn Street, Chicago, having given up the idea of rooming at Y. K. Smith's, owing to the EH-Smith quarrel.

To HIS FAMILY, New York, 8 December 1921

Dear Dad and Mother & children:

We're writing this from the Hotel just before we leave.[1] Everything is very lovely. Fine trip and enjoyed the dates and apples, Mother's check and Nunbone's and Massaweene's [Sunny's and Marcelline's] letters tremendously.

Had dinner with Bobby Rouse and met several other friends here both mine and Hashes [Hadley's] and I've checked all our baggage and seen the boat.

Walter Johnson [a cousin] is going to see us off at the boat. I'll mail this from the pilot.

Everything is very lovely and we're getting off in excellent style. Wish you all a Merry Christmas.

Keep away from the stockyards is my advice until the strike is settled. Keep all the kids away too. They must find a new playground.

Bobby Rouse sends you his love as do

> Ernie and Hash

My dear love to all of yez.

JFK

1. EH and his bride were about to sail to France, where he would write features for the *Toronto Star*.

To HIS FAMILY, at sea, 20 December 1921

Dear Famille:

We've had a fine trip. Stopped at Vigo in Spain and went ashore in a motor launch. Only very rough one day. Then a regular hurricane. Good weather balance of time. It was so warm in Spain I was too hot with only one sweater on. In the harbor were great schools of tuna—some jumped 6 and 8 feet out of water chasing sardines.

Hash is very popular aboard the ship because of playage of the piano. We had a show one night. Took out three tables in the dining room and made a ring and I boxed 3 rounds with Henry Cuddy a middleweight from Salt Lake City who is going over to fight in Paris. We trained together on board and in the 3rd round I had him on the verge of a knockout. Got the decision. Cuddy wants me to fight in Paris. Hash was in my corner and wiped me off with a towel between rounds.

Coming up the coast of Spain off Cape Finisterre we saw a whale. Vigo harbor is almost landlocked and was a great hiding place for German Submarines during the war. I talked my Lingua Franca (International Mediterranean Language) in Vigo and interpreted for all the passengers. Hash (Bones) can talk French so we get along beautifully.

Thank you all for your letters. We were greatly appreciative of all of them and are using dad's rubber bands—Hash is playing the piano now while I'm writing but her fingers are very cold from the English Channel wind. We've been sailing across the Bay of Biscay and up the coast of France all day. Passing many ships that rolled badly but this boat is as steady as a rock.[1]

There are a funny lot of people aboard but a few very nice ones. We land in Havre tomorrow about noon and will be in Paris tomorrow night. Will mail this from Havre [postmarked 25 December]. Hash and I both send love to everyone and all of Grandfather's family.

Love to you all—
Ernie and Hash

Hash is talking French to 3 Argentinians that are in love with her. Also an old Frenchman.

JFK

1. The ship was the S. S. *Leopoldina* of the French Line.

To WILLIAM B. SMITH, JR., at sea, *c.* 20 December 1921

Boid:

Vigo, Spain. That's the place for a male. A harbor almost landlocked about as long as little Traverse Bay with big, brown mountains. A male can buy a lateen-sailed boat for 5 seeds. Cost a seed a day at the Grand Hotel and the bay swarms with *Tuna.*

They behave exactly [like] rainsteins [rainbow trout]—sardines for shiners—chase them the same way and I saw 3 in the air at once—1 easily 8 feet. The biggest one they've taken this year weighed 850 lbs.

Vigo's about 4 times the size of the Voix [Charlevoix, Michigan] and there are three or four little places around the bay to sail to. Gaw what a place.

We're going back there. Trout streams in the mts. Tuna in the bay. Green water to swim in and sandy beaches. Vino is 2 pesetas a qt. for the 3 year old which can be distinguished by a blue label. Cognac is 4 pesetas a litre.

> C'est la vie—
> Immer—
> Wemedge

Why not screed care the American Express Paris *France*?

Hash wielded a towel in my corner for a 3 round session with Young Cuddy—Salt Lake City 158 lber—just grown out of welter ranks—a wop who's going to Paris to fight. Has 3 fights there and 1 in Milan.

We trained daily throughout the voyage. They took up 3 tables in the dining room and made a ring between the posts and we went the 3 stanzas for the benefit of a French woman in the steerage who has a baby and 10 Francs to [last] till France with. A.E.F. husband deserted her.

The passengers claimed it was a good thing to watch.

You'll have to get Hash to tell you about the bout. If I wrote it you'd think it was fiction.

PUL   Wemedge.

To SHERWOOD AND TENNESSEE ANDERSON,[1] Paris,
c. 23 December 1921

Dear Sherwood and Tennessee:

Well here we are. And we sit outside the Dome Cafe, opposite the Rotunde that's being redecorated, warmed up against one of those charcoal brazziers and it's so damned cold outside and the brazier makes it so warm and we drink rum punch, hot, and the rhum enters into us like the Holy Spirit.

And when it's a cold night in the streets of Paris and we're walking home down the Rue Bonaparte we think of the way the wolves used to slink into the city and Francois Villon and the gallows at Montfaucon. What a town.

Bones [Hadley] is out in it now and I've been earning our daily bread on this write machine. In a couple of days we'll be settled and then I'll send out the letters of introduction like launching a flock of ships. So far we haven't sent 'em out because we've been walking the streets, day and night, arm through arm, peering into courts and stopping in front of little shop windows. The pastry'll kill Bones eventually I'm afraid. She's a hound for it. Must have always been a suppressed desire with her I guess.

We had a note from Louis Galantiere this morning and will call on him tomorrow.[2] Sherwood's note was here at Hotel when we got in. It was awfully damned nice of you to send it. We were feeling a little low and it bucked us up terrifically.

The Jacob is clean and cheap.[3] The Restaurant of the Pre aux Clercs at the corner of the Rue Bonaparte and the Rue Jacob is our regular eating place. Two can get a high grade dinner there, with wine, a la carte for 12 francs. We breakfast around. Usually average about 2.50 F. for breakfast. Think things are even cheaper than when you all were here.

We came via Spain and missed all but a day of the big storm. You ought to see the spanish coast. Big brown mountains looking like tired dinosaurs slumped down into the sea. Gulls following behind the ship holding against the air so steadily they look like property birds raised and lowered by wires. Light house looking like a little candle stuck up on the dinosaurs shoulder. The coast of Spain is long and brown and looks very old.

Then coming up on the train through Normandy with villages with smoking manure piles and long fields and woods with the leaves on the ground and the trees trimmed bare of branches way up their trunks and a roll of country and towers up over the edge. Dark stations and tunnels and 3rd class compartments full of boy soldiers and finally everyone asleep in your own compartment leaning against each other and joggling with the sway of the train. There's a deathly, tired silence you can't get anywhere else except a railway compartment at the end of a long ride.

Anyway we're terrible glad we're here and we hope you have a good Christmas and New Year and we wish we were all going out to dinner tonight together.

NEWBERRY   Ernest

1. EH had met Sherwood Anderson (1876–1941) and his wife, Tennessee, at Y. K. Smith's apartment in Chicago in the spring of 1921. See Carlos Baker, *Ernest Hemingway: A Life Story* (New York, 1969), pp. 78–79. 2. Anderson had written letters of introduction to Lewis Galantière, Sylvia Beach, Gertrude Stein, and Ezra Pound. Galantière (1895–1977), of Chicago, was Paris secretary for the International Chamber of Commerce, c. 1921–1928. 3. Hôtel Jacob and D'Angleterre, 44 rue Jacob.

This and all subsequent letters to Anderson are used courtesy of the Anderson Collection, Newberry Library.

To HOWELL JENKINS, Paris, 26 December 1921

Dear Carpative:

Merry Christmas and Multi Grazie for the muffler. Bones and I are located in this hostilery on the Left Bank of the river just back of the Beaux Arts and are in good shape.

Our room looks like a fine Grog shop—Rhum, Asti Spumante and Cinzano Vermouth fill one shelf. I brew a rum punch that'd gaol you.

Living is very cheap. Hotel room is 12 francs and there are 12.61 to the paper one. A meal for two hits a male about 12–14 francs—about 50 cents apiece. Wine is 60 centimes. Good Pinard. I get rum for 14 francs a bottle. Vive La France.

There's nawthing much to write. Paris is cold and damp but crowded, jolly and beautiful. Charcoal braziers in front of all the cafes and everybody in good shape.

Bones and I are going to buy a motor cycle with side car and go all to hell and gone over Yarrup next summer.

Screed a male. My love to the Ghee and Dirty Dick.

Sempre,
Steen.

PH. PUL

To HOWELL JENKINS, Paris, 8 January 1922

Dear Carpative:

Hash [Hadley] and I are moving to an apartment at 74 Rue du Cardinal Lemoine. So you can address us care of the Cardinal. Suppose you have my last screed by now. We've been having a priceless time and I've been working like hell. Written a chunk of my novel and several articles.

Went around to the Florida the other day and often eat [at] a place near the Madeleine. I showed Hash the head that was knocked off while we were there [in 1918].[1] They've left it off.

I'm drinking Rum St. James now with [rare?] success. It is the genu-wind 7 year old rum as smooth as a kitten's chin.

This apt. is a high grade place and we're moving in tomorrow—but not going to keep house till we get back from Chamby Sur Montreaux in Switzerland where we're allezing for a brace of the weeks to shoot some winter sports. It's in the mountains above Geneva and is a place sort of like Dilstein's[2]—but with a better clientele. It would be a para-dise with the men along. Gaw—Can you see us all with unlimited good liquor and skiing, bob sledding and skating. I wish you and the Ghee and the Boid and Dirty were coming.

Must close. Screed a man. The muffler rates daily wear. I laid hold of a suit—made to measure with slacks and knickers—Irish hand made homespun—for 700 francs. As I bought francs at 14 to a paper one that isn't bad. Cook and Co. are a famous London house. You know 'em of course. This was the best stuff they had in the Cile [domicile=shop].

Well screed me Carpative. I miss you like hell and am lonely for the men. This side is the place for a man to live. Love, Steen.

Hash sends you hers also. Screed to the 77 [74] Rue du Cardinal ad-dress. It is just back of the Pantheon and the Ecole Polytechnique. In the best part of the Latin Quarter. Greet Dick for me and tell him I'll write him. Regards to the office.

PH. PUL

1. Stone head knocked off a frieze of the Madeleine during the German bombard-ment, 1918. 2. Dilworths' establishment, Horton Bay, Michigan.

To SHERWOOD ANDERSON, Paris, 9 March 1922

Dear Sherwood:

You sound like a man well beloved of Jesus. Lots of things happen here. Gertrude Stein and me are just like brothers and we see a lot of her.[1] Read the preface you wrote for her new book and like it very much. It made a big hit with Gertrude. Hash says to tell you, quotes, that things have come to a pretty pass between her and Lewy[1]-close quotes. My operatives keep a pretty close eye on the pair of them.

Joyce has a most god-damn wonderful book.[2] It'll probably reach you in time. Meantime the report is that he and all his family are starving but you can find the whole celtic crew of them every night in Michaud's where Binney [Hadley] and I can only afford to go about once a week.

Gertrude Stein says Joyce reminds her of an old woman out in San Francisco. The woman's son struck it rich as hell in the Klondyke and the old woman went around wringing her hands and saying, "Oh my poor Joey! My poor Joey! He's got so much money!" The damned Irish, they have to moan about something or other, but you never heard of an Irishman starving.

Pound took six of my poems and sent them wit a letter to Thayer, Scofield,[3] that is, you've heard of him maybe. Pound thinks I'm a swell poet. He also took a story for the Little Review.[4]

I've been teaching Pound to box wit little success. He habitually leads wit his chin and has the general grace of the crayfish or crawfish. He's willing but short winded. Going over there this afternoon for another session but there aint much job in it as I have to shadow box between rounds to get up a sweat. Pound sweats well, though, I'll say that for him. Besides it's pretty sporting of him to risk his dignity and his critical reputation at something that he don't know nothing about. He's really a good guy, Pound, wit a fine bitter tongue onto him. He's written a good review of Ulysses for April Dial.[5]

I don't know whether he has much drag with Thayer so I don't know whether Thayer will take the poems or not -but I wish to hell he would.

Bones [Hadley] is called Binney now. We both call each other Binney. I'm the male Binney and she is the female Binney. We have a saying -The Male Binney protects the Female - but the Female bears the young.

We've met and liked Le Verrier-he's done a review of the Egg[6] for a french magazine here. I'll get it and send it to you if he hasn't done so already.

Your book[7] sounds swell. Paid you to go to New Orleans -huh? I wish I could work like that. This goddam newspaper stuff is gradually ruining me - but I'm going to cut it all loose pretty soon and work for about three months.

When you've seen Benny Leonard you've seen them all. Hope he was having a good night when you viewed him. I've seen this Pete Herman. He's blind in one eye you know and sometimes blood or sweat gets into the other and they cuff him all over the place - but he must have been seeing well the night you lamped him. He's a fine little wop and can hit to beat hell.

Well this is getting too damned voluminous. Write us again will you? It puts a big kick into the day we get your letter.

Oh Yes. Griffin Barry is still in Vienna and living, they say, with Edna St. Vincent etc.[8] The Rotonde [Café] is cluttered with the various young things, female, she's led astray. Like Lady Lil, she piles her victims up in heaps.

Well, bye-bye and any amount of love to Tennessee[9] and yourself from us -

Ernest

I wrote some pretty good poems lately in Rhyme. We love Gertrude Stein.

NEWBERRY

1. EH had recently met Miss Stein (1874–1946). 2. *Ulysses,* just published by Sylvia Beach. 3. Co-editor of the *Dial.* 4. EH's contributions to the *Little Review* did not begin until volume 9 (Spring 1923). 5. EH and Ezra Pound (1885–1972) had met early in 1922. Pound's eccentric review of *Ulysses* was in the *Dial 72* (June 1922): 623–29. 6. *The Triumph of the Egg* (1921) won the first *Dial* Award. 7. Probably *Many Marriages* (1923). 8. Miss Millay (1892–1950) toured Europe in 1921–1923. 9. Mrs. Sherwood Anderson, whom he divorced in 1924.

To HOWELL JENKINS, Paris, 20 March 1922

Cherished Carpative:

Your screed had dragged me to the mill [typewriter] from a bed of pain and I mill like a wild thing. Jo Eesus but I have been a sick male the last brace of diurnals [two days], the same old throat trouble to the last yencing [fornicating] degree. You give a male a pile of news and it was fine as hell to hear from you Carper.

Lemme see, I don't know what the dope was. Oh yes, I was sitting on the Boulevard Madeliene morting [killing] an Absinthe, they call it by another name, but it is the Genuwind, when I saw Feder[1] going by. I nailed the Duke with a few short ugly words and he and his jewine bride, picture the Duke honeymooning with that mouthful of false fangs, came up to our cile [domicile] for dinner that night. They were Honey-mooning all over Italy and Austria etc. etc and sailed for the states the day after we saw them. Hash and I took them to a couple of dives after we'd chowed and we morted a brace of champagne bottles and a few other things. Feder wouldn't get tight on account of his new respecta-bility, but I, having been married a long time, acted as usual.

Hash sends her love to you and we both send you the picture [of EH in a new tweed suit]. Ogilvey can't cut 'em like that suit, Carpative. It is so homespun that you smell the genuwind peat smoke in the wool.

This damned typer ribbon is about worn out. I've worked like hell. The [Toronto] Star have offered me 75 seeds a week whenever I come home from here—would like to copy the letter, but it is too goddam long, but I hit that and over on space so why the bloody hell ever go back until a male's spring-offs [offspring] are ready to go to cawlegge, except to see youse men, and then why don't youse men come over here? A six pound trout was taken in a stream near Pau day before yesterday, and the guys who fish a wet fly are making some nice catches all along now. Season opens here the first of March.

The enclosed letter came from [Bill] Smith after I'd written him about five in the old vein, this is the first answer I've had.[2] You send it back to me when you're through with it, I want to file it. The temptation of course is to tell him to take his whole damned family and jam them as far as they will go up some elephant's fanny—but I'm still fond of him, so I'm making no answer. Isn't that a goddam hell of a letter from a guy whose been like Smith and I have been? Of course the Madam,[3] damn her soul, has been poisoning him agin me for a couple of years now, but I din't know he would swallow propaganda like that! Christ! Do you think I am so goddam changed for the worse and all that? Didn't we have about the best time bumming around, you and [Bobby] Rouse and I that we ever had? Was I such a leper? Aw hell—It's hell when a male knifes you—especially when you still love him. Show the Ghee [Jack Pentecost] the screed. To Hell wit him if he's that way. I'd written him five letters, the regular old kind you know—I thought he was just too busy to answer.

I'd like to have seen the Ketchell[4] pics—he was a swell battler, but too small for that damned smoke. I haven't seen a fight since I was here on acct no one to go with—but they have very good bouts all the time. I'm going to lay hold of some fight fan and get a season ticket or something.

By the way—do you ever see Butstein [Kate Smith, Bill's sister]? I haven't heard from her since we shived—she wasn't off of me then—and I left about eight hundred dollars worth of wop drafts with her to forward to me as soon as we had an address. She was to keep them in her saving's dep. vault and send them as soon as we wrote. Have written five times and no answer and need the money bad. Perhaps she never got the letters. Meantime the drafts are liable to be outlawed—some of them getting to be over a year old. It's hell of a mess, also I need the money to go to the Genoa [economic] conference. Have to pay my expenses and then they pay me. Will you look her up, either at the Chicago Beach Hotel or at the Co-op [*Cooperative Commonwealth*] 128 N. Wells, and see if she got my screeds, and ask her to please send me the drafts. I'm worried as hell about them. Have them sent registered and insured. To 74 Rue du Cardinal Lemoine or to the American Express Company, 11 Rue Scribe. By the time this screed gets to you the drafts may have come, but as I've heard nothing yet and been writing for two months now, you'd better have a look anyway. Will you please? Thanks ever so much Carp. You can show her Bill's letter if you want. I'm afraid to write her again for fear that she may be sore at me—I wrote Bill five letters and I'm fonder of Stut [Kate] than of Bill, but a man gets a little bit backed about pushing his mush in the dust after a certain length of time. Krebs may know where to lay hold of Kate—he does, I'm pretty sure. Tell her I still feel the same as ever.

We have a hell of a good time. I'm boxing regular with Ezra Pound, and he has developed a terrific wallop. I can usually cross myself though before he lands them and when he gets too tough I dump him on the floor. He is a good game guy and has come along to beat hell wit the gloves—some day I will get careless and he will knock me for a row of latrines. He weighs 180.

My stuff is coming along—I'll look out for a jawb for you over here. Do you speak frawg? Give the Baw [Ted Brumback] my best—I'm going to screed him. I don't screed as much as I ought on account of writing such a gawd awful lot on the mill every day. Day before I got sick four of us went out on a picnic waybout on the Marne to Mildred Aldrich's—she wrote A Hilltop on the Marne—you know—a fine old femme.[5] We saw the woods where the Uhlans were in 1914 and bridges the English blew up and the whole thing. It's a beautiful valley and the trees are all getting into blossom. Aldrich was there during the battle and she told us all about it. Wish you'd been there. I morted a fiasco of wine at lunch on the way out, we had a Ford, and we all were pleasantly lit and I drank a cup full of 3 Star Hennesey to see me homeward on the drive back to Paris. It was near Meaux we went. A lovely place.

Well I goot go back to bed—this bitch of a throat is good for about three days more—two big pus sacs and white patches.

So long old Carper and screed a male.

My regards to John and Dirty Dick—tell him to screed me and I'll screed him, maybe I'll do it before then. Steer clear of women and bad liquor. Hash sends her love to Dick.

Sempre,
Steen

TEXAS

---

1. Walter J. Feder, late of ARC Ambulance, Section IV, Italy. 2. Bill Smith had written EH on 19 February 1922 to say that owing to EH's quarrel with Y. K. Smith, their own friendship had "undergone profound and very unwelcome changes" and that "the 1922 Edition of E.M.H. is so radically different from earlier Editions . . . that I can only hope time will show equal changes in a reverse direction." 3. Mrs. Charles, Bill's aunt. 4. Steve Ketchell, who figures by proxy in EH's story "The Light of the World." 5. A Hilltop on the Marne (1915) by Mildred Aldrich (1853–1928).

To DR. C. E. HEMINGWAY, Paris, 2 May 1922

Dear Dad:

I was very glad to get your last good letter saying that you were going North in May to get some fishing. Hope you are up there now.

Spring has come quite definitely here although it took plenty of time about it. It was a great change getting back here from the warmness of Genoa where I didn't need to wear a coat at all.[1]

Have been laid up in bed for four days with my same old bad throat and it has about run its course and I expect to go out tomorrow. May day was quiet here although the Comrades shot a couple of policemen.[2] I worked very hard at Genoa and wrote some very good stuff. Met L. [Lloyd] George, Chicherin, Litvinoff and many others. [Toronto] Star pays me 75 a week and expenses. Expect to go into Russia for them very soon.[3] Waiting to hear now. I'll let you know as soon as I have details.

It's a rainy rotten day. The country outside of Paris and up into Picardy is beautiful. Fields full of big black and white magpies that walk along the plow furrows like crows do. Lots of larks too. There are lots of common birds I don't know, but I go down to the Zoological gardens that's right near our house[4] and identify them. Saw a crossbill the other day.

The forests are very wild and free of underbrush and cover all the hills and ridges. Hash and I took a forty mile hike through forest nearly all the way. Forests of Chantilly, Chatallate and Compiegne. They have deer and wild boar and foxes and rabbits. I've eaten wild boar twice and it is very good. They cook it up into a pasty with carrots and onions and mushrooms and a fine brown crust. There are lots of pheasants and partridges too. I expect to get some good shooting in the fall.

Krebs [Friend] is down in the south of France wild boar hunting now. They certainly can move fast and look very mean when the dogs are after them.

On Hash's and my hike we went up the Oise river and through the forests and over the hills to where the Aisne comes in. They are working hard rebuilding the towns and are making many of them so ugly with the new, ugly French architecture.

As I'm writing on my Corona in bed I have to stop because it gets so uncomfortable. Mrs. Lewis sent her love to you and spoke very highly of you. We have also seen your old patients the Winslows. Hash has been out with Marjorie Winslow and was at there [their] house to tea while I was in Genoa. Alan has a new diplomatic post in Brazil.

Much love Dad and I hope you have a good trip. I had the two World's Illusion volumes[5] mailed to Mrs. [James] Dilworth before I left Chicago and will trace them up. If she does not, or has not, received them I will send to Kroch's five dollars to send her two new ones, but I am sure she must have gotten them. I left them with Krebs with Postage and Dilworth's address.

Excuse the bum spelling and typographicals.

JFK   Ernie

1. The Conferenza Internationale Economica convened in Genoa in April. 2. See EH's one-sentence May Day sketch in "Paris 1922," in Carlos Baker, *Ernest Hemingway: A Life Story* (New York, 1969), p. 91. 3. EH never got to Russia but was still expecting to go six weeks later. See EH to Harriet Monroe, 16 July 1922. 4. Along the rue Jussieu one block from his flat. 5. *World's Illusion,* by Jacob Wasserman, tr. Ludwig Lewisohn, 2 vols. (New York, 1920).

To DR. C. E. HEMINGWAY, Chamby-sur-Montreux, Switzerland, 24 May 1922

Dear Dad:

Suppose by now you've a letter from me from Paris. The reason you didn't see anything of mine in the Star was because you get only the Star Weekly and my last 16 articles have been in the Daily running from the 24th of April till about the 8th of May. I'm getting some stuff off to the weekly from here now. They've been neglected because the Genoa assignment was a Daily assignment and Mr. Bone, the managing Editor, didn't turn anything over to them.

From the time I came back from Genoa until we came down here I was sick in bed nearly all the time and didn't turn out a thing.

It's great down here. My old pal Major Dorman-Smith[1] has been spending his leave with us and we've been trout fishing and mountain climbing and next week are going to walk over the St. Bernard pass and then down into Italy and take the train back to Paris. I've picked up all the weight I lost and am feeling fine again. My throat still bothers me, but for all Doctors seem able to do for it, I guess it will go on bothering the rest of my life.

Today we climbed Cape au Moine, a very steep and dangerous climb of 7,000 feet and had a great time coasting down the snow fields coming down by simply sitting down and letting go. The fields in the lower valleys are full of narcissus and just below the snow line when we climbed the Dent du Jaman the other day we saw two big martens. They were about as large as a good big skunk but much longer and thinner. I've caught several trout in the stream called Canal du Rhone up the Rhone valley. It is all fly fishing and as the trout have been fished for for over two thousand years or so they are fairly shy. I haven't been skunked on them yet though and have been out four times. The mountain streams are still too full of melted snow and roily to be able to fish, but there is one wonderful stream called the Stockalper over across the Rhone about twelve miles above where it flows into Lake Geneva that I am very keen to fish. It has salmon but is still too roily.

My credentials for Russia from the Star came today and also a good check, 465.00, expenses and three weeks salary at 75 dollars a week.[2] It was quite welcome.

The summer camp sounds hectic. Who are the campers going to be? Hope you got away and got some fishing.

Hadley is very healthy and as red and brown as an Indian. She never looked better. It is nice here where we were in the winter and know the people. We have climbed all the high peaks near here and are about ready to start in on the best ones again.

Hope you are well and that everything is going along in good shape. Give our love to Mother and the kids and all sorts of greetings from Hash and me.

Your loving son,
Ernie

JFK

---

1. See Carlos Baker, *Ernest Hemingway: A Life Story* (New York, 1969), pp. 91–92. EH had first met Eric Edward Dorman-Smith (1895–1969), an Irish officer in the British Army, in 1918. 2. See EH to his father, 2 May 1922, note 3.

To GERTRUDE STEIN AND ALICE B. TOKLAS, Milan, 11 June 1922

Dear Miss Stein and Miss Toklas:

We've been here for about a week playing the races with tremendous success. I get up at dawn and study the dope-sheet and then after my brain has cracked under the strain Mrs. Hemingway, with about three cocktails and an indelible pencil to aid her, picks winners as easy as cracking peanut shucks. With the aid of her alcoholic clairevoyance and an old friend of mine that I think sleeps with the horses we've had 17 winners out of 21 starts.

We walked down here from Suisse over the Grand St. Bernard. Made 57 kilometers in two days with Chink [Dorman-Smith], the Captain, doing the Simon Legree on us. We didn't walk all the way to Milan on account of Mrs. Hemingway's feet swelling on her at Aosta. It was a great trek because the pass wasn't open yet and no one had walked up it this year from the Suisse side. It took the combined efforts of the Captain and Mrs. H. and a shot of cognac every two hundred yards to get me up the last couple of kilometers of snow.[1]

Going from here up to Recoaro and Schio in the Trentino and then down to the Piave and Venice and then back to Paris. Want to be back by about the 18th. It is raining hard today and that will probably mean disaster at the track, I don't think Mrs. H's alcoholic genius could function on a muddy track and I know that once the going gets heavy I can't ever pick them at all. Still it's fun to see them run with their tails all plaited up and the mud scudding.

We had a fine time in Suisse. Climbed a couple of mountains with Chink and then he climbed one himself and nearly got himself killed on Ascension day coming across a torrent that was too deep and fast for him and met us at the Bains des Alliaz and we drank 11 bottles of beer apiece with Mrs. H. sleeping on the grass and walked home in the cool of the evening with our feet feeling very far off and unrelated and yet moving at terrific speed.

Hope to see you both soon.

Your friend,

YUL   Ernest M. Hemingway

1. See Carlos Baker, *Ernest Hemingway: A Life Story* (New York, 1969), pp. 92–94.

To HARRIET MONROE,[1] Paris, 16 July 1922

Dear Miss Monroe:

I am very glad the poems are to appear in Poetry and am sorry not to have written before.[2]

Enclosed are some more you might be able to use.

With very best regards to Henry B. Fuller,[3] and, if you see him, Sherwood Anderson.

Very sincerely,
Ernest M. Hemingway

P.S. I met a boy, Ernest Walsh, here who says he is a friend of yours. He has been quite ill but is much better now.

AUTOBIOGRAPHY

Born in Oak Park, Illinois.

Permanent address 74 Rue du Cardinal Lemoine

Paris V

Occupation - At present in Russia as staff correspondent of the Toronto Star.[4] (passport three weeks over-due now. However, Max Eastman's came yesterday so I might [be able] to get under way shortly. Litvinoff promised me at Genoa there would be no trouble).

Published verse etc. in Double Dealer.[5]

CHICAGO   Ernest M. Hemingway

1. Miss Monroe (1860–1936) founded *Poetry* in 1912 and edited it until 1936. 2. Six poems under the general title "Wanderings" appeared in *Poetry* 21 (January 1923): 193–95. 3. Fuller (1857–1929), Chicago novelist and poet: *The Cliff Dwellers* (1893), *Under the Skylights* (1901), and others. 4. EH never got to Russia. 5. One quatrain, "Ultimately," was published in *Double Dealer* 3 (June 1922): 337.

This letter and that of 16 November 1922 are used courtesy of the University of Chicago Library.

To HIS FAMILY, Triberg, Germany, 25 August 1922

Dear Folks:

Hash and I and Bill Bird of the Consolidated Press and his wife [Sally] have been tramping through the Black Forest having a wonderful time.[1] Because the mark keeps dropping we have more money than when we started two weeks ago and if we stayed long enough could doubtless live on nothing. Economics is a wonderful thing.

Thank you very much Dad and Mother for the birthday greetings and for the lovely handkerchiefs. I appreciated them very much.

We have been trout fishing several times here and Hash caught three nice big ones the first time she fished. We got ten one day and six another and I picked up five in the Elz river with the fly. I am still using my old Mc Gintys and they seem to have a good international flavor.

How did the summer camp go? And what sort of a summer did you all have? We haven't had any news for a long time. I'm enclosing some German money for Dad. Hope everything is going well. I'll shoot you a good letter as soon as I can get a lot of this work cleared up. We go off on a hike for two or three days over the mountains and through the forest and then get back to our typewriters and have our livings to earn.

Love to everybody, belated birthday greetings to Mother in June [15], Carol in July [19] and Pop in September [4]. Not to mention Nunbones [Madelaine] coming on in Thanksgiving time [Nov. 28]. Which reminds me that when we were down in Italy the last time we had a wonderful young turkey in a restaurant in Mestre for 20 cents apiece. But there wasn't any cranberry sauce.

Always
Ernie

The sixty two marks will buy 6 steins of beer. 10 newspapers. Five pounds of eating apples, or a seat at the theater. I'll try and send you some of the good looking money next time. They have some notes that are very beautiful. Saved some for you for a long time and then had to use them.

Ernie

Hash sends her love too. We're going to Frankfurt and take the boat trip down the Rhine to Cologne where Chink [Dorman-Smith] is with his regiment.

JFK

1. See Carlos Baker, *Ernest Hemingway: A Life Story* (New York, 1969), pp. 95–96.

To HARRIET MONROE, Paris, 16 November 1922

Dear Miss Monroe:

I have been wondering when you were going to use the poems, as the Three Mountains Press here, Ezra Pound editing, is bringing out a book of my stuff shortly and I want to use the poems you have if you will give me permission to republish them.[1]

Paris seems fairly quiet now. Dave O'Neil of St. Louis whom you know, I believe, is in town with his family and will probably stay over here a couple of years.[2] He says indefinitely, but that ususally means two years.

Mr. [Ernest] Walsh was in Germany when last heard from. I am just back from Constantinople so I don't know the very latest about Mr. Walsh. I saw Padraic Colum one night but didn't mention the matter to him.

Gertrude Stein is down in St. Remy in Provence and says she won't come back to Paris till after Christmas. We had an enormous candied casaba melon from her in the mail yesterday. It was pretty nearly as big as a pumpkin. She is doing a new book.

I don't know whether you ever knew Lewis Galantiere when he lived in Chicago. He has just undergone a very trying love affair with a girl from Evanston Ill. who is over here getting cultured. She's just left town and we have all cheered up.

Hueffer [Ford Madox Ford] is coming to town tomorrow to stay a month. He's been living on his farm in England. Joyce is sick at Nice. He has a dreadfully hard time with his eyes. Frank Harris has been trying to get Sylvia Beach, who published Ulysses, to publish his autobiography. She doesn't want to although I tell her it will be the finest fiction ever written.

T.S. Eliot's new quarterly The Criterion seems to have inspired the Dial and their last issue was pretty good. But that's American gossip, not Paris.

They say that Gargoyle[3] is going to cease publication. I don't know that gang so I don't know.

The hot rum punch and checker season has come in. It looks like a good winter. Cafes much fuller in the day time now with people that have no heat in their hotel rooms.

This reads like the personal column of the Petoskey Evening Resorter. Perhaps the gossip bores you anyway.

Yours sincerely,

CHICAGO   Ernest M. Hemingway

1. *in our time* (Paris, 1924) contained no poems. **2.** See next letter, note 5. **3.** Little magazine edited by Arthur Moss, August 1921–October 1922.

To HADLEY HEMINGWAY, Lausanne, Switzerland, 28 November 1922

Dearest Wicky — Poor dear little Wicky Poo, I'm so sorry you've felt so frightfully rotten and sick. I've had the same stuff, cough up green stuff with black specks from way down in my chest with a frightful coughing and pain and stuffed up head using millions of handkerchiefs and me with only four. Certainly has been bad for us little tinies. I'm glad Leticia has taken care of you but I feel as though I ought to be doing it and Gee I wish I were with you. Poor dear Poo.

This is the first time I've had to write a letter for days it seems. I never eat till way after two and dinner always leftovers and the three places I have to go back and forth between are about 3 kilometers apart up and down hill and your always afraid you're missing something at one place or the other and they all talk French and the Russians are miles out of the way and I'm only a little tiny wax puppy. Mason[1] has kiked me so on money that I can't afford taxi's and have to take the street car and walk. And they expect me to cover them until midnight every night starting at nine in the morning.

Sunday I layed off and went on a motor trip (free) to Chateau D'oeux or however it's spelled and then from there to Aigle and past the Diablerets and the old Dent and then to Montreux and then I outgot from the car and took the funicular up the hill and had supper with Gang-wisch's.[2] They've heard from Mab and Janet[3] coming the 23rd and Chink [Dorman-Smith] on the Sixteenth and Izzy[4] the 2nd and they are all reserving rooms for and spoke so lovingly of my Poo and it was dark and no snow yet except Rocher du Laye and the Dent but there was snow in the air and Sunday night it snowed. Even Lausanne full of snow now turned slushwards full of gravel and mud here but smooth and lovely looking on all the hills and mountains. Gangwisches think the O'Neil's[5] ought to go to the Grand Hotel at Les Avants because there is good food and people and music etc. and at the Narcissus is bum food and a funereal solemnity and nothing. We'd be Les Avantsward everyday and they'd be down with us. That is undoubtedly the play. Advise Barbara and Dave [O'Neil]. Seems like to me anyway.

I'm so sick of this --- it is so hard. Evrybody else has two men or an assistant, and they expect me to cover everything by myself --- and all for one of Masons little baby kike salaries. It's almost impossible cause they happen at the same time and far apart and evrything.

I've been crazy for you to come and would love so still but if you say you are too miserable for the trip you know what. But please Wickey realise that I want you and wasn't trying to stall. Right now while I'm writing this letter I should be at the Russians. But something like that has happened every time I've started a letter and so hellwards with them. Unless Mason gives me a lot of money I'll upgive the job some time this week, and if he does give me money you've got to come here sick well or anything. You can fly you know. Had you thought of that? Why don't you do it? Then there'll be no Vallorbe or anything. Look up the planes. You can come by way of Bale too. They say that's easy.

There's a Colonel Foster, I think, here from St. Louis, elderly man, knows [knew] your father and everybody, white mustache. Friend of J. Ham Lewis's.

Admiral Bristol's come and they want to meet Mummy. Everybody sends you love. Steffens[6] wrote you a letter. I love you dearest Wicky - you write the very best letters. Anyhow both being laid out with colds we haven't lost so much time on the time of the month because you've probably been too sick. I do so hate for you to miss what is the most comfortable and jolly time for mums. Won't we sleep together though? If I upgive the job this week can you meet me at Dijon on a couple days notice. I'll have to wire you to send me the pissport registered. Deer sweet little feather kitty with the castorated oil and the throwing up, I think it is so pitiful I could just cry.

I'm just your little wax puppy.
Love Pups   to mups—

[along left-hand margin] Dear sweet Mummy!
[upside down at bottom of page] Did you write the Steins?

" " " " Ford Madox Fords

JFK   50 Rue Varen[ne]

1. Frank Mason of Hearst's International News Service. 2. Pension at Chamby-sur-Montreux where EH and Hadley had vacationed in January 1922. 3. Mrs. Percival Phelan and her daughter, of St. Louis. 4. Isabel Simmons, EH's Oak Park neighbor. 5. David O'Neil, retired lumber dealer and amateur poet from St. Louis. The O'Neils' son George appears in EH's story "Cross-Country Snow." 6. Lincoln Steffens (1866–1936), former leader of the muckraking movement in U.S. journalism.

To ISABEL SIMMONS,[1] Lausanne, c. 1 December 1922

[Page 1 is lost]
come yet. I've been hoping and looking for her [Hadley] every day. If she can't come I'll wire the I.N.S. to get somebody else and go on back

to Paris. Poor kid, she's been feeling awfully bum, and it's no fun being sick in Paris.

There are two good trains you can get to go from London to Montreux. You only get a ticket to Montreux. We'll meet you there. The railway from there is a little jerkwater and doesn't sell tickets outside of the country. Both trains leave London at 11 o'clock. One is the Simplon Express which is sleepers only and fairly expensive and the other is a first second and third class train with sleepers from Paris to Montreux. You should book your sleeper ahead if you want one. It gets into the Gare de Lyons in Paris at 7.25 in the evening, that's 19.25 by the continental twenty four hour time, and leaves at 8.35 for Switzerland. You can register your trunk straight through to Montreux, if you are bringing one, and it won't have to be examined at the Swiss frontier. They'll do it at the station in Montreux and we know them there and they'll just pass it. The Simplon Orient gets into Montreux at 6.57 in the morning and the other train at 8.57. The only advantage of the Simplon Orient is that you don't have to get out with your passport and hand baggage at the Swiss frontier at Vallorbe, they do it all in the train. In either event the examination is absolutely perfunctory. They just ask you if you have any gold money, chocolate, tobacco, and you say "rien" and they say, "merci mademoiselle" and that's all.

But as it's the first time you're crossing a frontier, and it happens darned early in the morning, it's easiest if you take the Simplon-Orient. I don't know how much extra it is. Not an awful lot. But the other is perfectly good. And when you can't get a birth [berth] we've often sat up all night and it isn't at all bad. Any way good luck to yez.

You can eat very well in the Gare des Lyons. The restaurant is upstairs.

Wish we were going to be with you coming down. It's lots of fun when about four or three or so people travel together like that cause you dominate the compartment and sit up and talk and get out at Dijon for sandwitches and watch the moonlight on the country going past and open the window as fast as the French close it and one lies down and goes to sleep and the others say "shhh — Malade!" and look very solemn when anybody tries to come in the compartment. It is an easy trip anyway. I've made it about twelve times this last year.

I suppose Hadley's written you about clothes. Mostly girls wear riding breeches for skii-ing and bobbing with a sweater and a tam. If you haven't got mountain shoes you can get very good ones in Montreux. Also skii-ing mitts of canvas with a string to them are cheap there. You know the sort of clothes, Hadley is taking an evening dress too I think for going to a dance or such. We don't dress for dinner in the chalet. It's half the fun eating in your tough clothes. Hadley wears riding breeches, puttees or golf stockings, usually the latter, a white flannel shirt and a sweater or the jacket of her riding habit with a belt. There's nothing formal about the clothes except that everybody wears riding breeks instead of knickers. Knickers are too full for skii-ing and spilling into the snow.

We'll have a wonderful time. I think it's the finest thing ever heard of, you're being in Europe and coming down to Switzerland. World is a funny place. The Seventh of January is the big bob races for the Canton of Vaud on the Col de Sonloup piste - you'll be an intelligent member of a bob crew by that time. Sonloup is a wonderful course when it's right.

Chink [Dorman-Smith] is coming the 16th. You'll like him any amount. And I know you'll love Chamby and Les Avants. I figure it's the finest place in the world. We'll have a lot of stuff to read and if you've any of the new American stuff bring it along. Chink does about a book a day when he's in his stride. I read the Roosians and Joe Conrad pretty near always in the country—because they're so long.

Well this ought to be mailed. I don't know yet why or how you're in Yarrup, but that's a minor part. Point is you're here. That's a fine point.

This [peace] conference is very dull and secretive and everybody follows everyone else around—the Turks today are just like wood chucks when you wanto find them their in their holes and then they pop out as soon as your gone. Well ---- So Long ----

As Ever

PUL
Ernie

1. Isabel Simmons (1901–1964) was next-door neighbor to the Hemingways in Oak Park. She graduated at Oak Park High School (1920), attended the University of Chicago (1920–1922), and sometimes dated EH (1920–1921). In 1922–1923 she toured Europe with friends, spent two weeks with EH and Hadley at Chamby-sur-Montreux, c. 1–14 January 1923, and another at Cortina d'Ampezzo in April.

This and all subsequent letters to Miss Simmons (who married F. R. B. Godolphin in 1925) are used courtesy of Princeton University Library.

To EZRA POUND, Chamby-sur-Montreux, 23 January 1923

Dear Ezra:

We have the intention of joining you. How is it? What do you pay? What is the hotel? Can I, like Northcliffe[1] on the Rhine, preserve my incognito among your fascist pals? Or are they liable to give Hadley castor oil? Mussolini told me at Lausanne, you know, that I couldn't ever live in Italy again. How the hell are you anyway? e sua moglia [moglie = wife]? How long are you going to stay? Answer any of these that seem important.

I suppose you heard about the loss of my Juvenilia? I went up to Paris last week to see what was left and found that Hadley had made the job complete by including all carbons, duplicates etc. All that remains of my complete works are three pencil drafts of a bum poem which was later scrapped, some correspondence between John McClure [editor, *Double Dealer*] and me, and some journalistic carbons.

You, naturally, would say, "Good" etc. But don't say it to me. I ain't yet reached that mood. 3 years on the damn stuff. Some like that Paris 1922 I fancied.[2]

Am now working on new stuff. We have 6 to 8 months grub money ahead. I have laid off the barber in order that I won't be able to take a newspaper job no matter how badly St. Anthonied. The follicles functioning at a high rate of speed I am on the point of being thrown out from all except the society of outliers like yourself. It is several weeks since I would have dared show at the Anglo-American [Press Club in Paris].

The lire appears to be dropping. Evidently Douglas[3] is a greater man than Mussolini. Dave O'Neil the Celto-Kike has just bought two left boots for 18 francs (a mistake at the factory)—the salesman telling him he won't be able to tell the difference after a few weeks. Dave is jubilous. The boots, of course, are very painful.

Hadley sends you and Dorothy Pound her love—as I do—write me—
Immer (as they used to say in the Rhenish Republic)

LILLY   Hem

---

1. A. C. W. Harmsworth, Viscount Northcliffe (1865–1922). 2. EH's manuscripts had been stolen from Hadley in the Gare de Lyon while she was en route to Lausanne. In an undated reply to this letter, Pound called the loss an "act of Gawd" and urged EH to recapture the materials from memory, which he called "the best critic." See also *A Moveable Feast* (New York, 1964), pp. 73–74. The "Paris 1922" sketches had survived the theft. See Carlos Baker, *Ernest Hemingway: A Life Story* (New York, 1969), pp. 90–91. 3. In *A Moveable Feast*, p. 111, EH alludes to "Major Douglas an economist about whose ideas Ezra was very enthusiastic." Major Clifford Hugh Douglas (1879–1952) was the author of *Economic Democracy* and a founder of Social Credit. See Hugh Kenner, *The Pound Era* (Berkeley, Calif., 1971), for a chapter on Douglas, pp. 301–17.

This and all subsequent letters to Pound through 1924 are used courtesy of the Lilly Library, Indiana University.

To EZRA POUND, Chamby-sur-Montreux, 29 January 1923

Carino:

Left Footed Dave [O'Neil] is now taking two French lessons a day. He asked his concierge if this woman he has wasn't a good French teacher and the concierge says, "Oh Yes. But she doesn't know French very well. She's a German."

Dave likes her however. He is also writing a number of new poems. His system is to write a few words about something he doesn't understand. Anything he doesn't understand. The less he understands it the more 'magic' the better the poem. He has re-acted sufficiently from your aroma, I think you were an aroma to him, a 'magic' aroma to tell me that the words in a poem, i.e. cliches, Byronic phrases, Mathew Arnoldania; don't matter. It is the 'magic' that matters. He also says that Rose O'Neil, who draws the cupies, no Kewpies, has written much better poetry than Yeats. It is the O'Neil blood. I suggested that he meant she had drawn better Kewpies than Yeats. This was not well received.

What the hell do you mean you will stay a fortnight longer? Yes I know. Fortnight—two weeks. Lift—elevator. Tram—street car. A shilling in London a quarter here. But why this bloody fortnight? We'd planned to hit there [Rapallo] the last of February. According to that you will be gone. I thought you were staying the hentire hiver.

And Calabria. I would much rather go to Calabria. It is so easy to get to Sicily from. But are you, as it appears, going to Calabria with Nancy [Cunard]. Drop this unbecoming delicacy. I understand you having a gutfull of Rapallo but are you going somewhere else where we would be unobjectionable? Or are you running down the road? The conventional spring running down the road? I aims to cramp no mans stride on the Road but at the same temporal [time] I hates the thought of hitting Rapallo at the Mercy of the Straters. [Henry (Mike)] Strater is all right. I like Strater.

If you all were going somewhere where we wouldn't interfere we'd stay here till along the last part or middle of Feb. and then shake along to where you were. We thought of sticking around Italy till about May. Moving North through the Abbruzzi or something, making wide detours to avoid Rome and other cultural centers and moving sideways through the hills with the Veneto as our final objective. Hadley has never seen Venetzia except with her family and the last time we were at Mestre we didn't have the fare across the viaduct.

If you are shoving off and Dorothy staying at Rappallo for a while we could park down there and get in some tennis and maybe meet up with you later on somewhere.

This high altitude has made me practically sexless. I don't mean that it has removed the sexual superiority of the male but that it has checked the activity of the glands. I would like to discuss the matter with Burman. It could make an interesting contribution to a monograph on the increasing scarcity of prostitutes above 2000 meters u/s and a strange exception to the movement in the Engadine Valley where an annual winter concentration of prostitutes is effected at St. Moritz altitude 2001 meters u/s. I daresay it all could be worked out to the accompaniment of graphs and temperature density charts.

Shoot me the dope. We yearn to see you all. We can't leave here before the fourteenth of February. How can this be co-ordinated?

Love to yourself and Dorothy -----
HEM

I thank you for your advice to a young man on the occassion of the loss by stealing of his complete works. It is very sound. I thank you again. I repeat, I thank you. I will foller your advice.

LILLY

To GERTRUDE STEIN, Rapallo, Italy, c. 18 February 1923

Dear Miss Stein:

Enclosed is the review for the Tribune. You can cut out any or all of it and if you don't like it I'll do another one. That's the liberalest offer I know how to make.

Pounds left here three days after we got here. The weather is good today after seven days muggy. We're going up to Cortina for some more ski-ing last of the month. Hadley is in good shape. There is a nice guy here named [Henry] Mike Strater that I'd planned to box with but he's sprained his ankle. The sea is weak and dull here and doesn't look as though there was much salt in the water. The tide rises and falls about an inch. When the surf breaks it sounds like someone pouring a bucket of ashes over the side of a scow. The place aint much.

I've been working hard and have two things done. I've thought a lot about the things you said about working and am starting that way at the beginning. If you think of anything else I wish you'd write it to me. Am working hard about creating and keep my mind going about it all the time. Mind seems to be working better.

How is Paris? We're coming back in April or thereabouts. Mike is doing a good portrait of Hadley. I had a wonderful time with the book.

Will you give the review to Doctor Johnson?

With love to you all from the two of us,

            Ernest Hemingway

Will you send me a copy of the review when it comes out?

YUL

To EZRA POUND, Milan, 10 March 1923

Dear Ezra:

Your mysterious card received and filed for future reference. I been sick in bed in Milano here. Angina. We put in a little time in Orbitello and were crazy about it. The guy that tried to stop us that night was Della Rossa a millionaire archiologist. McAlmon came and stayed a long time.[1] I read nearly all his new stuff. Some 16–18 stories a novel or so. He wrote seven or nine new stories while at Rappallo. If I was in the tipster business I would whisper into the shell like ear of a friend, "go and make a small bet on McAlmon while you can still get a good long price." The matter needs to be gone into in detail.

We had good tennis. I got so I could just about beat Mike [Strater]. His ankle is all right. He did a corking portrait of Hadley. They've gone to Firenze. Hadley got into shape and played corking tennis. Beating several men around the place. I got some form back and developed a nasty lawford and cross court drive. You probably won't believe it but it's so. We left your rackets at the Splendide to be held by the Mignon for you all. That was the play I believe. Correct me if wrong.

You must either be getting fond of or else have a gutful of Rome by now.

McAlmon has given us the dirt on everybody. It is all most enjoyable.

I may be going on a gold rush in Labrador in June.

I enclose a little piece I did on the Lady poets. With foot notes.[2]

Lucy Stopes[3] or what is her name has announced her engagement to that very pleasant French painter Le Son. That is it isn't announced but they are telling people. We were present at a triumphal lunch.

A Little Review came for you at the Mignon with a very torn wrapper and having nothing to read I pinched it. The flesh, you know, weak. Shall

I forward it or hold it? There is nothing in it. The works of Mr. Stella the fat photographer. That doesn't decrease my Culpa.

Leave us hear from you. Address Poste Restante Cortina D'Ampezzo. (Italia)

Hang onto the lady poets for me.

Immer,

LILLY   HEM

1. This was apparently, though not certainly, EH's first meeting with Robert McAlmon (1896–1956), who was to become his first publisher later in 1923. 2. EH's poem "The Lady Poets with Foot Notes" was published in *Der Querschnitt* 4 (November 1924): 317. Pound to EH, 26 March 1923, said that he could not understand all the footnotes in it. 3. Lucy Holt and Le Son were married in 1924. See EH to Edward J. O'Brien, 2 May 1924.

To DR. C. E. HEMINGWAY, Paris, 26 March 1923

Dear Dad:

Am here enroute for Germany by cabled request of The Star to do a series of 12 articles on the French and the Germans. Mailed the 1st one today should appear in about two weeks. The Daily Star.[1]

When I've finished the trip through Germany I'm going to take my trout tackle and rejoin Hadley in the Tyrol. Cortina D'Ampezzo in the Dolomites.

I hope you have some good fishing this spring. I appreciate your letters so much and am dreadfully sorry I don't write more, but when you make a living writing it is hard to write letters. I've been 38 hours on the train and am awfully tired. I've traveled nearly 10,000 miles by R.R. this past year. Been to Italy 3 times. Back and forth Switzerland-Paris 6 times. Constantinople-Germany-Burgundy-The Vendee. Sure have a belly full of travelling.

I hope Grandfather is well. Excuse this paper. Best love to Mother, yourself and the Kids—

Your loving son

JFK   Ernie

1. EH's first article in this series, "Will France Have a King Again?" was in the *Toronto Daily Star*, 13 April 1923. Ten others followed, five each in April and May. See Carlos Baker, *Hemingway: The Writer as Artist*, 4th ed. (Princeton, 1972), p. 426. List compiled by William White.

To EDWARD J. O'BRIEN,[1] Paris, 21 May 1923

Dear Mr. O'Brien:

The enclosed from Mr. Vance's office has just turned up. It sounds just a little as though Mr. Vance thought I were trying to slip something over on him when I wrote saying you had asked me to send him the story and that you were writing him in regard to it. I suppose it is Mussolini's postal service.[2]

Sure seems as though there is a curse on me, first losing the stuff[3] and then having your letter about this story go astray. When I heard nothing from the Pictorial for two months I thought surely they must have bought it.

Mr. Vance's letter has made me feel pretty low. Got Drunk on the strength of it and feel lower still now. He so obviously was hanging on to it all ready to buy if someone would tell him it was good. Guess it's a hopeless game to buck.[4]

LeSon is here in town now and asked me about you. He and the Holt girl are going to America to be married. He seems cheerful.

[Henry] Strater paints better and better. I showed some of his things to Gertrude Stein the other day and she thinks there's a lot to him. Mrs. Strater's voice gets that rich thick way when she pronounces your name. Everything is unchanged.

I remember sending a story about an Italian gun man to the Red Book, Karl Harriman editor, back four or five years ago and getting a long letter from them written by Kennicott or someone like that name saying that the story lacked heart interest. That if I would make the gun man the sole support of an aged mother and have him reform in the end it would be a corking yarn. So I guess it's not much good sending my old man story to them. This is the first story I've sent out since then.

It is ridiculous, of course, but it frightens me so when storys come back when there are letters like that. Throws me all off and makes it almost impossible to write. Seems to destroy any reason for publishing. Still I do think the readers of a magazine have better sense and taste than the editors.

And yet I want, like hell, to get published.

What do you advise? If anything.

Mrs. Hemingway sends her best regards as I do. Hope the work went well on Allegro and that you got through your job all right. We've thought of you often.

Sincerely,

UMD   Ernest M. Hemingway.

1. Edward J. H. O'Brien (1890–1941) of Boston edited twenty-six volumes of *Best Short Stories*, 1915–1940. **2.** O'Brien was then living in the village of Montallegro, two kilometers north of Rapallo, Italy. **3.** EH refers to the theft of Hadley's suitcase containing his manuscripts at the Gare de Lyon in December 1922. **4.** EH is bemoaning the rejection of "My Old Man" by Arthur T. Vance of the *Pictorial Review*.

To GERTRUDE STEIN, Paris, 20 June 1923

Dear Miss Stein:

Hadley and I will drop over tomorrow (Thursday) after dinner and if you are busy or out we'll go quietly away. We have both cousins and aunts sailed last week. They are due any time. I am very anxious to talk about toros y toreros [bulls and matadors] with you. We will maybe go down to Pampaluna for the 4 days starting the 6th of July. I dont think it would hurt Hadley.[1] In Canada I expect to buy a bull calf to practice veronicas with. It is too late for me of course but we may be able to do something with the kid.

Always your friend,

YUL   Ernest Hemingway

1. Hadley was in the fifth month of pregnancy.

To ISABEL SIMMONS, Paris, 24 June 1923

Dearest Izz:

Well it being Sunday afternoon I can picture you out on the porch [in Oak Park] with seven volumes of philosophy strewn around while you dip into The Nether Ego or The Sublimation of Complexes or one thing or another and long lines of motor cars bearing suitors accumulate on Kenilworth Avenue. Gawd—imagine you living only three doors from Grandma Radcliffe—No by Gosh—it's right next door. And us on the other side. And here summer's just started. Sat night we went to five prize fights—Tiny [Hadley], Ezra Pound, J[ane] H[eap] of the Little Review, Mike Strater, Mac [McAlmon] and I. Swell fights. Warm weather started since yesterday. We're going to sail to Canada sometime the 1st of August.

How are you anyway? Lavinia was over here the other day and asked us to dinner tomorrow night. She is a good kid. Moaning around, not moaning, but sort of talking around about wanting to have a lover etc. As though that would settle things. Thing is not to have a lover so much as a love affair. Must love both ways or the show is no good. She's damned attractive. She had seven volumes of Ibsen carrying around en masse sent by one of your damned English Freds.

Tiny is in good shape. We are going down to Pamplona in Spain for the great bull fighting festa. Wish you were going along. Bull fighting ought to have a stalwart pre-natal influence dont you think? Pamplona is a wild place up in Navarre in the edge of the mountains that run down into the Basque country. Maybe you cant read my writing but remember your own is damn bad.

How are you, what are you doing, thinking about, who in love with etc? Write us. We can get a letter before we go. Hadley sent your jack to Madame Levi. Christ I hate to leave Paris for Toronto the City of Churches. But then all of life is interesting. We have leased an apartment for 1924 in October—Enormous big studio—room for Grand Piano and work room for me—electric light over the bed to read by—garden for puppy and offspring to play in and rent cheap enough so that we can afford to leave it in the winter. I'm never going to be where there isnt snow and mountains.

Remember the first day we went up to the top of the Pleiades in that Gawd awful storm and blizzard?[1]

Steeple chasing tomorrow at Auteuil. Went out last Sunday and bagged 250 splendid francs.

The Feather Cat sends you her love as do I—

always
Ernie

My very best regards to your family, to the Hamiltons, to any other friends I may have.

What's this about you going to N.Y. to go onto the Stage? What in? A fast talking act?

74 Rue du Cardinal Lemoine, Paris, *France*

Thanks for going to see our family.

Tiny says to tell you that Madame Levi got the money she sent and she and Renata[2] both send their love.

PUL

1. On a skiing trip in Switzerland, January 1923. 2. Renata Borgatti, pianist friend of Hadley's, whom Isabel had met in Cortina d'Ampezzo in late March or early April 1923.

To WILLIAM D. HORNE,[1] Paris, 17–18 July 1923

Dear Old Bill:

Weren't you damned sweet to write me such a damn fine wonderful letter after I've kept one from you about this time last year unanswered all the time. I wrote you about seven pages about our trip to Schio and over Dolomite to Trento and back around Garda and down the lake in a boat to Sermione and hike to Verona[2] - remember when we saw the Serbo-Slovaks at the little station at the foot of *Garda* the day we went out to the front from Milan. A hot day in June. Remember when we were going out to the Section and we didn't know what it would be like except that they had a place to swim and all drove Fiats? And Doc Johnson and some other guys met us at Vicenza and what a shit Capt. Bates was and other things and the way the water flowed under this bridge outside the Factory and the baseball field across the way.

Well I wrote all about it and about revisiting - and for Christ's sake dont ever go back Horney - not under any circumstances - because it is all gone. And Italy is all gone and I tore up the letter because it was too doleful and because it had happened to me was no reason to make it happen to you.

Horney we've got to go on. We can't ever go back to old things or try and get the 'old kick' out of something or find things the way we remembered them. We have them as we remember them and they are fine and wonderful and we have to go on and have other things because the old things are nowhere except in our minds now. I suppose this sounds like all sorts of Merde from the good old manure spreader. I'm not meaning to talk moral.

Anyway Hadley and I hiked over the St. Bernard pass with Chink— Dorman-Smith-on leave from his Majesty's Fifth Fusiliers from Cologne, my pal in Milan after the Armistice - we did 38 kilometers the first day from Switzerland and 44 the 2nd and hit Aosta - sleeping the night at the Monastery at the Summit 2000 some meters. Then down into Milan from Aosta - from Milan Hash and I went to Vicenza and the bus to Schio - Sebio over the mountain - Dolomite post (?) is a wop tourist hotel now - to whatayacallit the nice little town the wops didn't shell if the Austriche didn't shell Sebio? And then up to Trento and still in a car around through the Adamello to Riva and down Lago di Garda to Sermione - a beautiful point that runs out into the lake that you can see from Dezenjano - the station where we saw the Czechs remember? Then on to Verona and by train to Mestre and then all through the Piave - saw the silk worm raising house in Monastir where I found the great Horned

article in his pyjamas lying on a stretcher listening to the silk worms
chew[3] - Remember Felice Buongiorno? Fossalta - a brand new ugly
town with nothing to remind you of the war except the scars in the trees
which are growing over and healing. Not a sign of the old trenches. All
the wrecked houses rebuilt and occupied by the people who spent the
war refugeeing in Sicily or Naples. I found where I'd been wounded, it
was a smooth green slope down to the river bank - reminded me of contemporary pictures of the battle of Gettysburg. The Piave was clean and
blue, there'd been no rain, and they were towing a big cement barge
up it with horses working along where the parapet had been.[4]

Oh well,—anyway we came back to Paris—I saw Mussolini in Milan
and had a long interview with him and wrote 3 articles predicting the
Fascist siezing the Govt.[5] And we flew to Strasbourg and hiked all
through the Black Forest and fished for trout and caught lots and lived
in little Inns and loved each other[6] ------- and came down the Rhine
from Frankfurt to Cologne and visited Chink and came back to Paris -
and saw Siki nearly kill Carpentier and I got a cable from the Star to
go to Constantinople and went and was with the Greek Army in the big
retreat - and three weeks in Constant itself - 3 very fine weeks when just
as it was getting light you'd all get into a car and drive out to the Bos-
phorous to see the sun rise and sober up and wonder whether there was
going to be a war that would set the whole world on fire again—and
there damn nearly was. And then came home rode across Thrace in a
car, horseback, and walked and then went through Bulgaria and Serbia
and finally hit Trieste and had a wonderful meal and was damn glad to
talk wop again and got the train straight to Paris and Hadley.[7] She was
more beautiful than ever and we _____ loved each other very
much and went everywhere together, the races at Auteuil with everybody crowded around the big charcoal brazier and a November bright
blue sky and the turf hard and the fields good and we watching each race
from the top of the stands and other things - and then I had to go to
Lausanne to the Conference - and was there till Christmas - and we went
up in the mountains at a Swiss old brown chalet and ski-ed and had a
bob sled and drank hot punch in the evenings and the days were cold
and clear and there was lots of snow. Then we went down to Rapallo
and played tennis - with Pound and Mike Strater - Princeton guy[8] - and
then way up in the Dolomites - Cortina d'Ampezzo and ski-ied until April
when I got a cable to go to the Ruhr and Germany in general and went -
and then after six weeks came back to Cortina and got Hadley and we
came up to Paris.[9]

Your probably tired of the narrative by this time. But I'm trying to
give you the dope and destroy our status as classic myths. /

Second Day ------

Dear Horned article—

So you're in love again. Well, it's the only thing worth a damn to be. No matter how being in love comes out it's sure worth it all while it's going on. Gosh I wish it would come out right Horney. If there is anybody rates it it's you. I wish I could have a series of half hours with your best girls you'd have to fight them off of you after I'd presented them with the true dope.

By the way I've written you cards from all over but always to 45 E. Division. Did nawthing ever hit?

Pinard Baum came up to our apartment here boiled as an owl - in his old section manner, you know,- rather vague and red-eyed and watching how he placed his feet and I pressed him to stay to lunch and he said he would and we each had a drink and were glad as hell to see each other and Hash went out to get some more stuff for lunch for him and then suddenly Pinard laid down the glass, shook hands very solemnly and started right down the stairs. "But Pinard" I says, "You're staying for lunch!" He looked at me very red eyed and solemn and wove back and forth on the stairs, "No, Hemmy," he said, "It wouldn't be fair to your wife!"

Just then Hash came upstairs with the odd head of lettuce and the extra artichoke in her market basket and Pinard grasped her by the hand with both of his and said, "I must go Mrs. Hemingway. It wouldn't be fair to you if I stayed."

Well we hung on to him but he went right on down and we followed him out into the street but he was having this exaltation of renunciation and kept saying "It wouldn't be fair to HER, Hemmy. I just couldn't do it. Not in my condition."

So finally after protesting a block or two I put him in a cab and sent him to his mother or sisters or whoever they were. We entertained the Duke of Feder and his very pert attractive over educated young kike wife to dinner and went out and danced with them afterwards. I saw the Duke passing on the Rue Royale when I was sitting in front of some bocks with some newspaper guys.

No sign of Simmie or his malted Bride.

Spain is damn good in hot weather. Went down there about two months ago to study Bull fighting and lived at a bull fighters pension in the Calle San Jeronimo in Madrid and then travelled all over the country with a crew of toreros—Seville, Ronda, Granada, Toledo, Aranjuez seeing the stuff.[10] Came back and got Hadley and we went to Pamplona, the capitol of Navarre and have just got back from the best week I ever had since

the Section—the big Feria at Pamplona - 5 days of bull fighting dancing all day and all night - wonderful music - drums, reed pipes, fifes -
faces of Velasquez's drinkers (?), Goya and Greco faces, all the men in blue
shirts and red handkerchiefs circling lifting floating dance. We the only
foreigners at the damn fair. Every morning the bulls that are going to
fight that afternoon released from the Corralls on the far side of town
and race through the long main street of the town to the bull ring with
all of the young bucks of Pamplóna running ahead of them! A mile and
a half run - all the side streets barred off with big wooden gates and all
this gang going like hell with the bulls trying to get them.[11]

By God they have bull fights in that town. There were 8 of the best
toreros in Spain and 5 of them got gored! The bulls bagged just one a
day.

You'd be crazy about a really good bullfight, Bill. It isn't just brutal
like they always told us. It's a great tragedy - and the most beautiful
thing I've ever seen and takes more guts and skill and guts again than
anything possibly could. It's just like having a ringside seat at the war
with nothing going to happen to you. I've seen 20 of them. Hash saw 5
at Pamplona and was wild about it.

Well lemme see. This letter sure is stringing out.

On the 17th of August we sail on the *Andania* of the Cunard's for
Montreal should arrive about the 27th - then go to Toronto, and the old,
6-day a week work. In Toronto, as you know, 85% of the inmates attend
a protestant church on Sunday. Official figures. I don't know what the
other 15% do. Probably attend a catholic church.

We are going to have a baby sometime in October. We hope he'll be
a boy and that you'll be his god father.[12] He's spent the first months of
his life on skis and he's seen Battling Siki fight once and Carpentier twice
and 5 bull fights so if prenatal influence can do anything it's been done.
We're both crazy about having the young feller. Hadley hasn't been sick
a minute or even nauseated all the time. She's never felt better and looks
wonderfully, Bill - Doctor says everything is perfect and absolutely
admirable.

Gee, we've had fun, Bill. It doesn't seem possible we're going to leave
it all. But when there were just the two of us it didn't make any difference
how near broke we were - because I always had these assignments from
the Star that brought in good money - but sometimes we'd have to wait
a month from the time I'd send in my expense account till it had got
across and back with the check - and we'd live on ten francs a day and
then be rich as hell when the 5 or six hundred seeds would come. But
I figure I've got to have a steady job during The First Year of the Baby
and expenses etc - anyway. Soon as he gets old enough he can take his
or her chances with the rest of the family.

I have one book being published this month (issued in the fall but I'll try and get an advance copy to you in August.) which I'm reading proof on now and another in the fall.[13] I'll send you both of them. The same gang that published Ulysses are doing the 1st one and the Three Mountains Press the 2nd. I think you'll like some of the yarns. I've worked like hell on them.

Hash sends you her love as I do. Gee, I hope you're having a better time than your letter sounds - and I'll bet you are, too. Banking's undoubtedly probably hell but then any business is hell. [Illegible and partly legible line in fold in original letter, looks to read: "You see Horney, I'm cut out for Romance rather than business"] The only trouble is there isn't any living in Romance. And as long as there are good guys like yourself and Bobby [Rouse?] the world's worth living in no matter what a man has to do.

Go on Horney - Write me a letter that I'll get on board the boat when it gets to Montreal. I never feel as set up as by a letter from you and I sure do feel low as far as I can realize hitting Canada.

Love to you and ——— to the Carper [Jenkins] and if you see him Jack [Pentecost].

PH. PUL   Oin

---

1. William D. Horne, Jr., born 1892, graduate of Princeton, 1913, ARC Ambulance in Schio, Italy, 1918, and EH's roommate in Chicago, 1920–1921. Other veterans of the ARC Ambulance mentioned in the letter are Herbert S. Johnson, Captain Robert W. Bates, Richard T. (Pinard) Baum, and Zalmon G. (Simmie) Simmons, Jr. 2. EH recalls a trip with Hadley in June 1922 and the ARC unit in Schio, June 1918. 3. An incident used fictionally in EH's story "Now I Lay Me," in *First 49* (New York, 1938), p. 461. 4. The visit to Fossalta di Piave with Hadley, June 1922. 5. Two EH articles on Italian fascism appeared in the *Toronto Daily Star*, 24 June 1922, and a third on 27 January 1923. 6. August 1922. 7. EH's Near Eastern trip, 25 September–21 October 1922. 8. Ezra Pound and Henry (Mike) Strater, Princeton, Class of 1919 [see also EH to Henry Strater, c. 24 July 1926], were sojourning in Rapallo with their wives in February 1923. 9. EH telescopes time here. He was in Paris late in March when summoned to the Ruhr assignment and returned to Cortina in mid-April to write "Out of Season." 10. EH's first trip to Spain was with William Bird and Robert McAlmon. See Carlos Baker, *Ernest Hemingway: A Life Story* (New York, 1969), pp. 109–11. 11. See *The Sun Also Rises*, chapter 15. 12. The godfather was in fact Dorman-Smith, the godmother Gertrude Stein. 13. *Three Stories and Ten Poems* and *in our time*; but the latter did not appear until March 1924.

To ROBERT MC ALMON, Paris, 5 August 1923

Dear Mac:

The proofs came this morning. Your letter dated Friday.

The blank page is a printer's error. It was not in the first proof. Why the hell didn't Darantier [printer in Dijon] send the first proof with the second for comparison etc.?

This proof looks very good and clean. I have gone over it twice. Hadley once.

Enclosed a suggested cover. It was Bill [Bird] suggested putting in the titles of the stories and poems. He said they were good titles and would make a good lay out for the cover and at the same time stimulate the purchaser. I like the look of it.

Maybe you don't.

You are the publisher.

If you don't want the titles cross them out and use the

T H R E E   S T O R I E S
&   T E N   P O E M S

spaced so as to come out even as in enclosed cover with the name at the bottom in a size smaller type. Huh? I think the type on the cover should be taller and leaner, but just as black. The type it was set in was too squatty. The & sign for AND makes it much sounder and better balanced and permits of proper spacing as in the enclosed cover. After all, the title is Three Stories *And* Ten Poems.

As for the extra blank pages. Nearly all books have four to eight, counting each side as a page, in the front right after the cover page. I think they would go better there and have as many as are left over at the back after the last story. I think we will find that the added bulk will sell more than we would save by cutting it down to 48, eliminating title pages etc. No body will buy a book if it is too goddam thin.

I've been checking up the blank page stuff on books here in the house. Find in Three Soldiers, Daws Passos, 8 blank pages without a goddam thing on them immediately after cover.

Find in Seven Men, Max Beerbohm, four blank pages but evidence of two having been torn out by owner for can paper.

Find in cheap edition of Madam Bovary by Gus Flaubert four blank pages. etc. etc.

All of them seem to have only one blank page both sides at back after end of story and before cover.

Well that seems to handle things. When are you coming back? They ought to be able to get this out. Today is the fifth. There is about half an hours work on the corrections. They should be able to begin shooting on the cover.

How are things going? I hear you're working. Here too.

If you register this enrote to Dijon it will go faster and no chance of loss.

Will shoot this off to you now. Hope you're getting some good swimming. It's hot as hell here. The Seventeenth we sail [for Canada] from Cherbourg. It is a week [eight days] from this coming Thursday. Mike [Strater] is gone to the States. They've patched up for a year. His grandmother dying.

Let me know right away about getting this and about cover, will you? I'm not registering [the parcel] on acct. it being Sunday. Krebs [Friend] lost all his money. Gone to Brittany with some more. Now contemplating visiting Smith in [place name illegible: Touravil?].[1]

So long,
Hem

P.S. I just took the cover and proof to Gertrude Stein's and she said she thought having the titles all on the cover made it any amount stronger and better looking. She doped it out all sorts of different ways and didn't see how we could beat the heads marked No. I. She said to get a good type for the Titles—good and black but not squatty like the other.
YUL   Hem

1. EH's crony from Chicago, Krebs Friend, had come to France in 1922. The identity of Smith is uncertain; possibly Chard Powers Smith.

To EZRA POUND, Paris, c. 5 August 1923

Dear Ezra:

I will do the hanging. Have redone the death of Maera altogether different and fixed the others.[1] The new death is good. Don't know about Gobar.

They should each one be headed Chapter 1, Chapter 2 etc. When they are read altogether they all hook up. It seems funny but they do. The bulls start, then reappear and then finish off. The war starts clear and noble just like it did, Mons etc., gets close and blurred and finished with the feller who goes home and gets clap. The refugees leave Thrace, due to the Greek ministers, who are shot. The whole thing closes with the talk with the King of Greece and his Queen in their garden, (just written), which shows the king all right. The last sentence in it is ------ Like all Greeks what he really wanted was to get to America. ------- My pal Shorty [Wornall], movie operator with me in Thrace, just brings the dope on the King. Edifying.

The radicals start noble in the young Magyar story and get bitched. America appears in the cops shooting the guys who robbed the cigar store. It has form all right.

The king closes it in swell shape. Oh that king.

I will commence hanging. Then I think she rides. Will try and drop in on you tomorrow a.m.

Immer
Hem.

LILLY

1. EH here attempts to prove that the eighteen miniatures composed for the Paris *in our time* show rough formal patterns. It is clear that he has been consulting Pound about content and order.

To EZRA POUND, Toronto, *c.* 6 September 1923

Dear Ezra:

It couldn't be any worse. You can't imagine it. I'm not going to describe it. But for Christ sake if anybody pulls any more of that stuff about America, Tom Mix, Home and Adventure in search of beauty refer them to me.

Hadley is in good shape. We have come to the right place to have a baby because that is the specialite de ville. They don't do anything else. Jimmy Frise's[1] one pleasure was going deer hunting and every deer hunting season for the last three years he has had a spring off [offspring]. He won't ever go deer hunting again. Deer hunting was the only fun he had. I can hear you, 'but my dear Hem what about the old syringe?' But my dear Ezra I don't know. That's the way they are.

We landed after ten days. It blew a gale all the way. The river was nice. If I'd obeyed the impulse to get off at Quebec and simply live there until our money ran out it would have been much better. I go to work Monday. The Prince gets here on Tuesday. Prince Charming, the Ambassador of Empire, the fair haired buggar.

If I were Strater I would cry. That's what's indicated. As it is I can't sleep just with the horror of the Goddam thing. I have not had a drink for five days. It makes a man understand [Sherwood] Anderson. On my second year here I would run down the road. It's the only thing for a man to do. Thank God we have Dorothy's pictures. I lay awake all last night reading Ulysses to cheer me up. A fine book. You must read it some time.

Have just been talking with the Hon. Raney. Soliciter General for the Province. He is the double of Barthou. He is appalled at the conditions in Europe. He pictures the French starving, the Germans gloating over their victory, the cruel spaniards butchering the poor innocent bulls, the eyetalians slaughtering the armenian orfans of Corfu, which I believe they did, poor man. . . .

Greg Clark tells a good story. Algy, yes poor fellow his regiment's been ordered to India. Poor fellow. Yes Yes Poor Algy. Yes. Yes. You know poor Algy's weakness of course. Yes Yes. Poor Fellow. Poor Algy. Going right out are they. Yes. Sailing next week. Poor Algy. Yes. No women there of course. No, no women. Poor Algy. Yes it will probably be like last time. Yes poor Algy's weakness. Yes you know there were no women and so poor Algy began to flog himself. Yes. Then kept up this flogging himself, flogging himself more and more until he lost his memory.

Then when he lost his memory he forgot to flog himself, now he's quite all right.

Well write to me. You may save a human life. Any news from Kumae as to his probable death in the quake? Poor fellow. Hope the ice plant is still upright. Yes yes Poor Kumae.

Well so long amigo and write to me. Love to Dorothy.

LILLY   Hem.

1. Frise was chief cartoonist for the *Toronto Star*. EH had met him first in 1920.

To GERTRUDE STEIN AND ALICE B. TOKLAS, Toronto, 11 October 1923

Dear Friends:

The free time that I imagined in front of a typewriter in a newspaper office has not been. There hasn't been any time free or otherwise for anything. Young Gallito was born yesterday morning at two o'clock. No trouble. Only took three hours and the doctor used laughing gas and Hadley says the whole childbirth business has been greatly over-rated. Weight seven pounds and five ounces. Which had a good deal to do with making it easy I'll bet. Better to start with Novillos. I am informed he is very good looking but personally detect an extraordinary resemblance to the King of Spain. He is nursing already. Had a good doctor. It is the specialite de ville here. Hadley feels very well and sends you both her love.

Have been very busy. Been almost to Hudsons Bay and all around and last week was in New York to meet L[loyd] George. Travelled with him aboard special train through New York and Canada. Was on the train enroute to Toronto when the baby was born. It was two weeks ahead of schedule. L. George is a cantakerous, mean temperamental and vicious man who never shows it in pooblic. He doesn't have all that long hair for nothing. Every night he cancells all his engagements for the next day and every morning wakes feeling chipper and damns his secretary for cancelling them. I have heard him at his best. He wants to make a fine marriage for [his daughter] Megan and hopes to relaunch himself from this side of the Atlantic. He goes very big in the States but the certain leavening of Canadians who read the British press have apatheticed up his reception here. I am glad to have left him.

Felt dreadfully about Hadley having to go through the show alone. The whole thing here is a sort of nightmare. I work anywhere from 12 to 19 hours a day and am so tired at night that can't sleep. It was a bad move to come back. However we have wall space for Masson, a corking new apt. on a ravine where the town leaves off into country sunny, a stretch of fine country, a hill that you can ski down or rather I can ski down, if the snow comes, and if I come home from the office. But really good for Hadley and the novillero, healthy, cheerful etc. and allowing us to bank all accruing money against the return to Paris while we live off my salary and should be able to save around seven or eight hundred from it beside.

In New York got a Little Review with your Valentine for Sherwood [Anderson]. It is very fine and very mine, couldnt help writing that mean very fine and very Sherwood.

How are you both and where? Contrary to my remembrance the cuisine here is good. They are very fine with a young or fairly young Chicken. I have also found some good Chinee places. We have both been very homesick for Paris. I have understood for the first time how men can commit suicide simply because of too many things in business piling up ahead of them that they can't get through. It is of only doubtful value to have discovered. In New York for four days I could not locate Sherwood or anybody I wanted to see because of being busy. Tried telephoning etc. New York looked very beautiful in the lower part around Broad and Wall streets where there is never any light gets down except streaks and the damndest looking people. All the time I was there I never saw anybody even grin. There was a man drawing on the street in front of the stock exchange with yellow and red chalk and shouting "He sent his only begotten son to do this. He sent his only begotten son to die on the tree. He sent his only begotten son to hang there and die." A big crowd standing around listening. Business men you know. Clerks, messenger boys. "Pretty tough on de boy," said a messenger boy absolutely seriously to another kid. Very fine. There are really some fine buildings. New ones. Not any with names that we've never heard of. Funny shapes. Three hundred years from now people will come over from Europe and tour it in rubber neck wagons. Dead and deserted like Egypt. It'll be Cooks most popular tour.

Wouldn't live in it for anything. I'm going out to the hospital now so will close. With love from Hadley and myself,

YUL   Hemingway

To EZRA POUND, Toronto, 13 October 1923

Dear Ezra:

Yrs. to hand and contents noted. When cabled Bill [Bird] requested he relay the news youwards. All healthy. Practically no trouble. The child bears a remarkable resemblance to the King of Spain but as yet do not contemplate divorce proceedings on that acct.

Who is the man Sandford? He sounds like approximately the genuwind. I feel however that I should be there when you meet any new male friends.

Things get worse here. I am now undertaking the show on a day by day basis. Get through today. Then get through tomorrow tomorrow. Like 1918. It is not, however, the way to spend one of the few remaining years out of ones life. I am at work on a work called OH CANADA which will take the wind out of [B. C.] Windeler. There is no doubt about it being the fistulated asshole of the father of seven among Nations. In every Postoffice, ie. Bureau de Poste there is a big sign, "WRITE OFTEN AND YOU WILL KEEP THE FAMILY TOGETHER." There are also government plans whereby the payment of 25 cents a week from the age of twenty until the age of sixty will give the payer a life annuity of 139. dollars a year from Sixty on. The figures are correct.

On Sunday when I wanted to take a box of Choclate pepruments to Hadley in the hospital I had to buy them from the bootleggers. The Drug Stores cannot sell candy on Sunday.

Withall they are satisfied although nearly all unhappy.

Was in N.Y. to meet L.G. [Lloyd George] and travelled with him on special train etc. here. Was on train at a smut session with correspondents and titled coal barons in the press car while baby was being born. Two o'clock in the morning. Heard about it ten miles out of Toronto and came in intending kill City Editor, [Harry] Hindmarsh. Compromised by telling him would never forgive him of course and that all work done by me from now on would be with the most utter contempt and hatred for him and all his bunch of masturbating mouthed associates. Also offered knockdown if editors trap opened. Consequently position at office highly insecure. Will stick as long as can and then try to borrow enough money from Leticia to get us both over. Have worked steadily from six in the morning till two oclock in the morning and later since came on sheet. Been on four long out of town trips and returned to find stuff piled up that would keep working all nights to catch up. Cant keep food down due to stomach shot from nervous fatigue. Have insomnia. And I was the guy they decoyed home to do a little feature writing and put their cable dept. in order.

Glad Hueffer [Ford Madox Ford] laid hold of Magazine [*Transatlantic Review*]. What Mag. is it or a new One. Will try and get some of Oh Canada in shape for him. Feel that I'm so full of hate and so damned, bitchingly, sickeningly tired that anything I do will be of little value. Still the diseased oyster shits the finest pearl as the palmist says.

For Gawd sake keep on writing me. Yr. letters are life preservers.

I cabled Bill [Bird] to commence firing on the newsprint borders.[1] It all depends how it is done. It is a good hunch. If not well done it will sour quick as hell. That's up to Bill. Christnose he rates a little excitement out of the Press. I tell him to shoot. He is the man to do it.

Give my love to Dorothy. Also Hadleys. She is well and in excellent Etat. She still likes me better than the baby. He is inherently vicious and commenced to nurse the first day with noises like the pig pen. At three days old he bites so badly that Hadley can hardly stand it. She declares, however, that in general the sensation is a pleasant one. Study of the entire problem convinces me that the joys of Motherhood are sung principally by those who are not married to a pukka student of the Ars Amoris. This is not an attempt to hurl the palm at myself. Simply an observation offered for your consideration.

For Christ sake write. Send me a copy of the Rire. Unobtainable here as a lewd magazine. Someday someone will live here and be able to appreciate the feeling with which I launched Ulysses on the States (not a copy lost) from this city.[2]

Write.

Yrs.
Hem.

On the first floor of apt lives an ex guards officer likewise hopeless. Across the hall lives a speedy widow. Extremely contented and eager to lend things. The view from the windows is very fine. While I was at the hospital I left the windows open and the flies are now all inside. The cat is having a good time catching them. From the smell she has moved her shitting place from back of the bath tub and is taking example of this new Freedom. Later in the evening I will track down the piece of Merde by the smell and will carefully wipe it up with the aid of a copy of the Toronto Star.

LILLY

1. Bird was planning a montage of newspaper headlines as the cover for *in our time*. 2. EH had smuggled several copies of Joyce's *Ulysses* into Canada.

To SYLVIA BEACH, Toronto, 6 November 1923

Dear Seelviah:

I've started about five letters to you and always been unable to finish them. Work or accidents or some damn thing. Have just now ripped the beginning of a letter to Lahry Ghains[1] out of the typer. Can't seem to write to him either.

Well the Feather Kcat is well. The baby too. He is well built and looks like his mother. Also like the Roi D'Espagne. Probably he'll be a great attraction in Deauville. We are going to bring him over to France right away and make believe he was born there so he will have to do his military service and thus keep us from haveing to support him during that critical and expensive time. Probably if M. Poincare keeps up by that time the service will be four or five years and we may never have to support him at all.

We will probably see you in January.

It is impossible to live here. I make about the same as in Paris and here an apartment costs 18,000 francs a year and there is nothing to do in it. It is impossible for me to do any writing of my own. The paper wants all day and all night. Much longer and I would never be able to write anymore. Also the people are all merde.

Can you get us an apt?

Thank Gawd we will get back to Paris.

If the baby had been a girl we would have named her Sylvia. Being a boy we could not call him Shakespeare. John Hadley Nicanor is the name.[2] Nicanor Villalta the bull fighter.

How is Adrienne [Monnier]? We both send her our love. We have a new song to sing her.

This is no place to make up songs though. The humane society kills 7,853 feather cats a year. All the humane society does is kill animals. Women call up the humane society to kill woodpeckers that knock on their roofs.

Canadians are all tapettes [gasbags] at heart underneath all the big free open spaces. There are no gigolos because no old women have money. Otherwise they would all be. It is a dreadful country.

O'Brien has taken the story My Old Man for the Best and Worst Short Stories of 1923. He has also asked to dedicate the book to me. Don't say anything about it or he may change his mind. He wants to know if I've got enough stories for a Boni and Liveright book. I'll get on your shelves yet. I think it is fine about putting Shakespurr and Co. on the 3 Mutts [Mountains] Press books if you are good enuff to stand for it.

Have you seen Larry any more? He fights quite often at the Salle Wagram. I am lost without L'Auto. There are no sporting papers here. It is also against the law to sell Candy in the drug stores on sunday. You have to smuggle it out.

We are still as fond of each other as ever and the baby is a good article. We are the only nice people in Canada.

Thank Gawd you will be in Paris when we get back. Tell Adrienne we are going to join her libarary and get so we can read more than about il knock-outa son adversaire par un crochet a la machoire [hook to the jaw].

I would like to swing a crochet on the menton of Canada. I would like to hit all Canada a coup bas [low blow].

Write to us again and our love to yourself and to Adrienne.

Immer,

Hemingways

This letter pretty near went like the others. Just found it at the office. I can write letters but not mail them. No time for anything. Did you know I have not had time to mail out copies of #3 sturries and ten pums to any reviewers. Need a literary manager. Today had a horse in the second race at Pimlico. It ran last. No other news. We are both homesick for Paris and youse people. I think the book will get printed eventually. Boid [William Bird] has had an awful time. Look at the stuff he had to print through first. No wonder he's got discouraged.

This is the longest letter I ever wrote anybody.

Love from Hemingway.

Give my best to [Robert] McAlmon. I am going to write to him. Hadley also sends hers himwards.

PUL

1. Larry Gaines, a black boxer from Toronto. 2. EH's first son was later nicknamed Bumby.

This and all subsequent letters to Miss Beach (1887–1962; owner of Shakespeare and Company, the Paris bookshop) are used courtesy of the Princeton University Library.

To DR. C. E. HEMINGWAY, Toronto, 7 November 1923

Dear Dad:

Hadley had written you to thank you for the check I thought.

I must apologise for our negligence. It was most welcome and very generous of you. We appreciated it tremendously as it came at a very difficult time. It was used on the hospital expenses which amounted to about 150 dollars all together I believe.

I wrote to you and mother on Sunday. Doubtless you have the letter by now.

In regard to the kind of stuff I have been doing I have been up around Cobalt and Sudbury, half way to Hudson's Bay, on different stories. Have interviewed different sorts of people. Count Apponyi, Sir William Lister, Dr. Banting, etc. Handled the Banting business. Travelled with Lloyd George. Handled various out of town assignments and done stuff for the Weekly. Two quite interesting articles on Bull Fighting. I will try and get copies of the Weekly and send you the two. They were both full page articles with pictures on the front page.

All the gang went deer hunting last Friday but not me. The Baby has taken to squawling and is a fine nuisance. I suppose he will yell his head off for the next two or three years. It seems his only form of entertainment. No one gets as much pleasure out of it as he does.

From now until Christmas I will work on the Weekly Star altogether.

Give my best to Mr. Platt. From Mc Daniel[1] I want no congratulations nor anything else. I have no good feelings toward him. Many people who wished me no good I see no reason to feel kindly toward now simply because now they can no longer do me any harm. The people who were my real friends like Fannie Biggs and Miss Dixon have all been injured by that man. Some day I will write a good story about him. Most people like him I have forgotten. They no longer exist for me at all.

It has been raining here for the last three days. Rotten Canadian weather. I wish it would clear up and get cold.

Well I must be getting a [street] car now to ride up home to supper. Thank god we'll be out of this place soon. Is business as bad in the states as it is in Canada? Here there have been bank failures and businesses dropping off right and left. A country with a busted boom is most depressing.

Glad Uncle George got some good shooting. I saw lots of ducks up North. Have not fired a gun except one day last summer when I went out on the Marne shooting crows and shot a couple of big pike in the river with a twenty two automatic.[2] Oh yes. Out in Thrace I shot twenty two quail in one day [October 1922]. Nice open country with sort of sage brush and they seemed easy to hit. I had a borrowed double barrelled twelve gauge. Have had plenty of good trout fishing though and next summer in June when we go down to Spain am going to have some more. Galicia in Spain has the best trout fishing in Europe. All free. You just need a license and the rivers are full of trout. It is great country. Spain, I think, is the best country in Europe. Though almost anywhere you go in Europe is more pleasant to live in than here.

This is a gloomy letter, but lay it to the weather.

I hope you are all well and that everything is going well. We made a mistake to come back here. But the only way to do with mistakes is to pay for them and get out of them as soon as possible.

Best love from your son,

JFK   Ernie

1. M. R. Mc Daniel, known as "Gumshoe," was the Oak Park High School principal. The others named were EH's English teachers, Frank J. Platt, Fannie Biggs, and Margaret Dixon. See Charles A. Fenton, *The Apprenticeship of Ernest Hemingway* (New York, 1954), p. 6. 2. See EH to Howell Jenkins, 20 March 1922.

To GERTRUDE STEIN AND ALICE B. TOKLAS,
Toronto, 9 November 1923

Dear Friends:

We are sorry about [Bill] Bird. I don't understand why he did not get your address from the Botin or somewhere. I would have sent a separate cable but it was at a bad time financially. Not on account of Firpo. Firpo did his best. All I gave him was a chance. Someday I will learn not to bet on those I think have a chance but on those I think will win. It is better to get it than to get so much and not get it.

Hadley is well. Also Mat. She nurses him at six ten two six ten two six ten two six ten two A.M. and P.M. She has lots of milk. He is putting on weight. We have a Canadian Mother's Book which is full of phrases like "Daddy will do it. Won't you Daddy?" It is all about the Canadian Mother being better than all other mothers. We got it free. At six o'clock in the morning I make Hadley get up saying "Daddy will have to push the Canadian Mother out of bed. Won't you Daddy?"

We get along very well still. Hadley is a good article. We have a fine old woman about 89 years old that does things in the house. She is wonderful but has gotten tired. Probably on account of being so old. So she is going away on Tuesday. Then we will try a younger one.

Did I tell you the rent of our apartment is 18,000 francs a year? Beer is 17 francs a bottle. That keeps me from drinking it even if someone offered it to me. I have never had 18,000 francs but I want to go where if I did have them they would do me some good. We are coming back probably in January.

I told you that before I think. If you haven't met Dave O'Neil you have not missed anything. Dave is one of those people that is never so sweet as the first day you meet him.

The paper is full of Hitler and Ludendorff fiasco. It sounds very funny. The early dispatches so far.

It seems there never was a third page. I can't write letters. Not any more. Thanks very much for the review. Bill Bird sent me the Tribune today. It seems very sound to me. I liked it.

What bothers me is why with my fine intelligence I ever came out here.

Mat is in good etat. He can laugh and does laugh. I am getting very fond of him. You will like the look of him.

We are going to settle down somewhere in our quarter back of the Pantheon even if it takes a while to get. We sail in the My Antonia of the Cunard line on January 19 from N.Y. for Cherbourg.

I am going to chuck journalism I think. You ruined me as a journalist last winter. Have been no good since. Like a bull, or a novillo rather, well stuck but taking a long while to go down.

They are turning on you and Sherwood [Anderson] both; the young critical guys and their public. I can feel it in the papers etc. Oh well you will get them back again. Wait till the History of an American Family [*The Making of Americans*] is published.

I have a new god now, young Pancho Villa, too late, however, to name the baby after him. They have got to *have Spanish* in them to really come off.

Now if I dont mail this it may never go. A letter from McAlmon from Antwerpen says he has been working for 3 weeks and has seen no one he knows and is not going to and is going to Norway, Sweden, Finland, Petrograd, Moscow etc. If it is not too much trouble. It may be too much trouble.

Looking at the first part of the letter it was our fault not Bird's.

Excuse the pencil, the dull letter, the delay,—I will try and see Sherwood in N.Y. and bring you the news. Pound has become a great composer. Have you seen Hueffer's [Ford Madox Ford's] new magazine [*Transatlantic Review*]? I have been invited today in a letter by Pound to come home and direct its policy etc. I feel the invitation has been exaggerated. Belmonte is going to fight bulls again next year, making his first appearance at the Easter Feria at Seville. He reserves the right to select his own ganaderos [bull ranchers]. The bull fighter in Geography and Plays who you didn't like was Gaona. He is in Mexico. There are others who do not like him.

We are going to have to save money to go to Pamplona. It will be too late to go to Switzerland this winter, that will save. There is a good Chink restaurant here but the menu is cramped. We eat well.

I'm quitting on January 1. I have some good stories to write—will try not to be turgid.

Love to you both for Christmas.

Your friend
Ernest Hemingway

YUL

To EDMUND WILSON, Toronto, 11 November 1923[1]

Dear Mr. Wilson:

In Burton Rascoe's Social and Literary Notes I saw you had drawn his attention to some writing of mine in the *Little Review*.

I am sending you *Three Stories and Ten Poems*. As far as I know it has not yet been reviewed in the States. Gertrude Stein writes me she has done a review but I don't know whether she has gotten it published yet.

You don't know anything in Canada.

I would like to send out some for review but do not know whether to put a dedication, as compulsory in France, or what. Being an unknown name and the books unimposing they would probably be received as by

Mr. Rascoe who has not yet had time, after three months, to read the copy Galantière sent him. (He could read it all in an hour and a half.)

The Contact Publishing Co. is McAlmon. It has published Wm. Carlos Williams, Mina Loy, Marsden Hartley and McAlmon.

I hope you like the book. If you are interested could you send me the names of four or five people to send it to to get it reviewed? It would be terribly good of you. This address will be good until January when we go back to Paris.

Thanking you very much whether you have the time to do it or not.

Yours sincerely,

YUL
Ernest Hemingway

1. This letter and that of 25 November were published in Wilson's *The Shores of Light* (New York, 1952), pp. 115–18. EH first met Wilson (1895–1972) in New York in January 1924. When preparing his book, Wilson was obliged to edit EH's letters at EH's request. See EH to Wilson, 10 September 1951.

To EDWARD J. O'BRIEN, Toronto, *c.* 20 November 1923

Dear O'Brien:

Your letter couldn't have had any greater effect if it had been to inform me that I'd just been given 1 million dollars, the V.C., a renewable annual pass entitling self and family to the royal suite on the Mauretania —with the promise that I would only have to make one more crossing, and the news that I had been elected to the Academie to replace Anatole France. Yes, you may dedicate the book to me. And to show you how much I appreciate it I will make a very solemn vow to you and God never to think about any readers but you and God when writing stories all the rest of my life—and sometimes not even about you and sometimes not even about God.[1]

We are here in Canada[2] and have had a baby. It is a sort of busted boom country. Pretty much gone to hell. The only places you can live in you cant live in if you are married. I have been up on the Abitibi and around there. There are lots of Bank failures, business failures, newspapers going on the rocks; the boom is busted all right. We are also busted but will have some money the 1st of the year and will go right away to Paris.

I haven't any more books but will have them send you one from Paris and will write in it at Portofino[3] maybe. (No. Will have them send me one here and will re-mail it.) In Our Time (Three Mts. Press) will be out in a month or so. Will have them send it to you. You will like it I think.

I am dreadfully sorry you were sick and overworked and very glad you've got married. There aint anything you can say to anybody that has gotten married that means anything. But out of the two happily married braces that I know both men were people that were extremely happy and quite contented as batchelors. So you have the edge to begin with. Congratulations on Romer Wilson. Hadley joins in congratulations and best luck.

How many stories would I need for a Boni Liveright book?

Have felt pretty low and discouraged here. Working so that you're too tired at night to think let alone write and then in the morning a story starts in your head on the street car and have to choke it off because it was coming so perfectly and easily and clear and right and you know that if you let it go on it will be finished and gone and you'd never be able to write it. I'm all constipated up with stuff to write, that I've got to write before it goes bad in me. And am working 14 to 18 hrs a day to keep the show going until the 1st of the year. Christ we'll be glad to get back to Paris.

Well goodbye and good luck and you've made me feel very proud and happy and I'm very much obliged because there are damn few people can do it. That sounds funny but you know what I mean.

Yours as ever

UMD　　　　　　　　　　　　　　　　　　Ernest Hemingway.

1. O'Brien had asked EH's permission to dedicate to him the forthcoming *Best Short Stories of 1923*. See EH's allusions to this in letters to Sylvia Beach, Edmund Wilson, and James Gamble, 6 November, 25 November, and 12 December 1923. **2.** EH's address in Toronto was 1599 Bathurst Street. 3. Italian village south of Rapallo.

To EDMUND WILSON, Toronto, 25 November 1923

Dear Mr. Wilson:

Thank you ever so much for the letter. It was awfully good of you.

The book is a silly size. McAlmon wanted to get out a series of small books with Mina Loy, W. C. Williams, etc. and wanted me in it. I gave him the stories and poems. I am glad to have it out and once it is published it is back of you.

I am very glad you liked some of it. As far as I can think at the minute yours is the only critical opinion in the States I have any respect for.

Mary Colum is sometimes sound. Rascoe was intelligent about Eliot. There are probably good ones that I don't know.

No I don't think *My Old Man* derives from Anderson. It is about a boy and his father and race-horses. Sherwood has written about boys and horses. But very differently. It derives from boys and horses. Anderson derives from boys and horses. I don't think they're anything alike. I know I wasn't inspired by him.

I know him pretty well but have not seen him for several years. His work seems to have gone to hell, perhaps from people in New York telling him too much how good he was. Functions of criticism. I am very fond of him. He has written good stories.

Would it perhaps be better to postpone the "Briefer Mentions" in the *Dial* until *In Our Time* comes out sometime next month and I will send it to you. You can get from it what I am trying to get at and the two of them together could make one review.

I am awfully glad you liked the *In Our Time* stuff in the *Little Review* and it is where I think I have gotten hold of it.

There is no use trying to explain it without the book.

It is very sporting of you to offer to help me get a book before the publishers. I don't know any of them.

Edward O'Brien wrote me the other day asking formal permission to reprint *My Old Man* in his *Best Short Stories of 1923* and asking if he could dedicate the book to me. As the book isn't out that is confidential. He prints bum ones and good ones. He asked me if I had enough stories for a Boni Liveright book. I don't know whether that means he could get them to publish it. I will write and ask you about it when the time comes if you don't mind.

E. E. Cummings' *Enormous Room* was the best book published last year that I read. Somebody told me it was a flop. Then look at [Willa Cather's] *One of Ours*. Prize, big sale, people taking it seriously. You were in the war weren't you? Wasn't that last scene in the lines wonderful? Do you know where it came from? The battle scene in *Birth of a Nation*. I identified episode after episode, Catherized. Poor woman she had to get her war experience somewhere.

The thing in the L.R. was a joke. I wrote it in the wagon-restaurant going back to Lausanne, had been at a very fine lunch at Gertrude Stein's and talked there all afternoon and read a lot of her new stuff and then drank a big bottle of Beaune myself in the dining car. Facing opening the wire again in the morning I tried to analyse the conference.[1]

Her method is invaluable for analysing anything or making notes on a person or a place. She has a wonderful head. I would like to write a review of an old book of hers sometime. She is where Mencken and Mary Colum fall down and skin their noses.

Please excuse this very long letter and thanks again ever so much for your letter and the good advice. I would like to see you very much when we go through N.Y.

Very sincerely,
Ernest Hemingway.

YUL

---

1. EH's poem "They All Want Peace—What Is Peace?" appeared in the *Little Review* 9 (Spring 1923): 20–21. It dealt satirically with international delegates to the Lausanne Peace Conference.

To JAMES GAMBLE, Toronto, 12 December 1923

Dear Jim:

Your letter was wonderful to get. I've wondered often enough in the last two years if you were not somewhere just around the corner in Europe. Please let's keep track of each other from now on so that we *can* encounter when fate pulls us toward each other. I hope I'll be able to see you in a month or so if you get into New York,

Excuse this typewriter and copy paper, but if I don't write on the machine I don't know when I will get a chance and I've found it to be fatal to delay letters. And I want to write to you bang off.

Here's our news, or a summary. Hadley Richardson and I were married in September of 1921 and went to Europe on a honeymoon. You would like her tremendously, I'm sure of it, won't attempt description, you'll have to take my word for it. However she simply wrapped up the country last year at tennis and plays Ravel, Brahms, or Scriabine equally well. She is a corker Jim and I should know because we have been married over two years and I have practically no friends, as I imagine you have, who are happily married. That's a fine ambiguous sentence.

At any rate we went over to Paris and then down to Switzerland for the winter where I discovered ski-ing which I intend to take up as my life work. Then I covered the Genoa Conference in the spring for a newspaper syndicate, writing cabled articles, and then we went back to Switzerland and climbed for a while and then walked over the St. Bernard Pass into Italy, by way of Aosta. It's a lovely trip. Dorman Smith, who was a young British Officer commanding the troops in Milan and a great pal of mine after I came up from Taormina, hiked with us and then we had a wonderful time in Milan. Boring Hadley stiff with remeniscences and raised ghosts and dining every night at either the

Cova or Campari's in the Galleria and going to the races at San Siro, where they have a new track and grandstand by the way.

Then Chink had to go back to his regiment at Cologne and Hadley and I went down to Vicenza and rode in a bus out to Schio and took a car over the mountains to Rovereto and Trento and then back through the Tonale to Riva at the head of Lago di Garda. At Sirmione, on Garda, we found Ezra Pound and his wife and stayed around there a few days swimming and lying around in the sun.

You remember Sirmione don't you? It's the big point that sticks way up into Garda, you can see it from the train on the way out to Vicenza and Co.

We hiked with our packs from Sirmione in to Dezenzano, where the train used to stop one minute, and then dropped off at Verona and spent the night. Then we went on down to Mestre and hired a car and rode out to the Piave. It is all gone. But it was a lot of fun to see again with Venice way off across the mist of the basso Piave marshes.

This will go on for about forty pages unless it condences. (mis-spelled) At any rate we hiked through the Black Forest in the summer and then in the fall I went out to Constantinople, Anatolia, Smyrna, Thrace etc. as war correspondent for The Toronto Star and the International News Service. Had a wonderful trip and plenty of fun and got back in time to go to Switzerland again for three months of winter sports. Then we were down playing tennis at Rapallo and I did a two months trip through the Rhineland, Germany and the Ruhr for the Star and then we had the pukka spring in Paris. Then last summer Bob McAlmon and I went all over Spain travelling with a cuadrilla of bull fighters, Madrid, Seville, Ronda, Malaga, Granada and ending up in the north.[1]

Spain is the very best country of all. It's unspoiled and unbelievably tough and wonderful.

Finally we came back here in September and John Hadley Nicanor was born on October 10th. He's husky and good looking and we're taking him back to Paris sailing on January 19 from New York on the Antonia, one of the smallest Cunarders extant as far as I can find out.

I wish we could see you in New York. Wouldn't it be excellent? Then we're going to get a big, unfurnished flat in Paris and make that a permanent headquarters. I'm going to chuck newspaper stuff for writing I think. I've two books out, published in Paris, and Edward O'Brien is dedicating his Best Short Stories of 1923 to me for the supposedly best story of the year. He wants me to bring out a book in New York with Boni and Liveright soon.

All this is frightfully full of the perpendicular pro-noun, but I was so excited to hear the small amount of news I got from you that I've run on at great length.

How does your painting go, and what are you going to do, and won't we be able to see you in New York, and when will you get over to Europe again? We're going to get a big barn of a place somewhere around the Luxembourg quarter and will always have a place to put you up. I know an awfully good gang in Paris, Pound, Joyce, Gertrude Stein, and a very good lot of painters. I find that on the whole painters are much better people than writers.

Didn't we have fun in Milan and when I visited you at Taormina? It seems so very long ago and I haven't seen you since. That trip to Milan from the Piave had all the bad part smoothed out by you, I didn't do a thing except let you make me perfectly comfortable.

I've often wondered what became of Det and Esther?[2] I had a wedding announcement from them and cards at Christmas and then I haven't heard anything. Then I wondered again and again about you. I'd have loved to cross over with you that winter, but I was saving to marry Hadley and it couldn't be done. She has some relatives in Philadelphia by the way, the Rosengartens.[3] Where did you go in [Au]stria and when do we see you?

Please write, this is a dull chronicle I know. But there's little inspiration in Canada.

Yours always,
Hemmy

This is a dreadfull sprawling letter—I'm afraid if I re-read it I wouldn't send it—so I wont re-read it but just say Ciaou and stick it in the envelope—

KNOX

1. EH's "facts" are somewhat inaccurate. He did not spend three months of winter sports in Switzerland or two months in the Rhineland and Ruhr. His first trip to Spain was in May 1923, with Mc Almon and Bird. 2. Captain Meade Detweiler, Milan representative, ARC Ambulance, 1918, and his wife. 3. Hadley's late father's sister, Aunt Mary Rosengarten, lived in Rittenhouse Square, Philadelphia.

This and other letters to Gamble are used courtesy of the Hughes Collection, Seymour Library Archives, Knox College.

To JOHN R. BONE, Toronto, c. 26 December 1923

Mr. Bone:

Before I came on the Star staff all my dealings had been with you. Since I joined the staff they have all been with Mr. [Harry] Hindmarsh.[1]

Yesterday in the course of a conversation with me Mr. Hindmarsh proved that he is neither a just man, a wise man, nor a very honest man. I have made every effort to get along with Mr. Hindmarsh. I do my work and have been kept busy with that.

But if work accomplished counts for nothing, nor results, and the only standard is to be at the mercy of any fit of temper or an outraged morbidity of dignity because of fancied slights. If it is a question of Mr. Hindmarsh or myself I of course must go. I was horrified while handling a big story, requiring speed and accuracy above all things, to be made the victim of an exhibition of wounded vanity from a man in a position of Assistant Managing editor on a newspaper of the caliber of the Star because he had himself made a mistake.

There is something morbid about it. For some reason Mr. Hindmarsh *says* that I think I know more about assignments he gives me than he does. I have given him no cause to think this and I cannot be accused of every thot that his inferiority complex suggests to him.

I wrote you a long memorandum several days ago when Mr. Hindmarsh first began to try to force me into a quarrel. But I was so surprised at the way things were going that I could not believe it and put the memorandum away thinking Mr. Hindmarsh must be working under great pressure, and in no case desiring to go over his head.

I of course have the facts on the entire matter at your disposal. It is useless for me to continue to work on the Star under Mr. Hindmarsh.

WJ   [Unsigned. Perhaps not sent.]

PH. PUL

1. Harry Hindmarsh, city editor of the *Toronto Daily Star*; Bone was the managing editor.

To JOHN R. BONE, Toronto, *c.* 27 December 1923

Mr. Bone:

I regret very much the necessity of tendering my resignation from the local staff of the Star. This resignation to take effect January 1st, 1924 if convenient to you.

Please believe there is no rudeness implied through the brevity of this memorandum.

WJ   Ernest

PH. PUL

To EZRA POUND, Paris, 10 February 1924

Dear Prometheus:

We have trouved [found] an appt. at 113 Rue Notre Dame Des Champs semi furnished over a saw mill on a 3 mos to 3 mos to 3 mos etc. basis.

I went around to 70 bis when we got in and the concierge recognized me as yr. beau frere but due to an utter manque of the key, entrance was not effected. I thus discounted [Ford Madox] Ford's report that you were expecting us to occupy until your return.

Its no fun living on your street in your absence so come on home sometime. It is mixing snow with the rain today. Would come down to Rapallo to see you men but cant face any more traveling.

We were ten days on the oshun.[1]

You seem very sound on music in the transatlantic. I am sorry we missed the concert. If you will bring off another one ever I will introduce all of Anastaisies' poulains [colts = young fighters] into the audience and have them attempt to throw each other out when the proper moment comes.

The golden whale of California still waits for you.

This is rotten letter but have been moving and unpacking—still uncompleted.

Henry [Strater] is working hard on the Cantos.[2]

Hadley has been and is sick. She cant sleep and her insides have gone haywired.

                    (have also been sick in bed)

I am going to try and write something for the Transetc.

There is now a tremendous reaction in America against [Sherwood] Anderson, the Broom Boys[3] etc. You are coming back.

I am glad you didnt have to have your gut cut open. All the way over on the boat I thot poor old Ezra out in that goddam Am. hospital [at Neuilly] with his gut cut open by some of those ignorant damn veterinaries like nearly took my adams apple out by mistake for a cyst.

I'm glad you didnt have it done. I'll get a good medical book and study up and take your appendix out sometime if it gets bad.

Please give my love and Hadley's love to Dorothy.

This town is no good without you all.

                                        Immer
                                        Hem.

I have about 7 stories to write. Dont know when or where able to write. The town seems, when you can distinguish faces through the rain and snow, to be full of an enormous number of shits. I however am quite happy eating oysters and drinking the wine of the country.

The Dial have given their 2000 paper ones to Wickham Brooks or Van Wyck Steed or somebody.[4] [Gilbert] Seldes, his sphincter muscle no doubt having lost its attractive tautness, has left the Dial. An aged virgin [Marianne Moore] has his place. There is no doubt a similarity as Montegezza points out.[5]

Write a letter. The Golden Whale inserted an advt. in the N.Y. Herald wanting to meet Buddhists, any age or sex. Just Buddhists. Thats all.

LILLY

1. The voyage aboard the *Antonia* occurred 19–29 January 1924. 2. Henry Strater was preparing decorative initials and motifs for *A Draft of XVI Cantos* (1925). 3. Evidently Harold Loeb, Alfred Kreymborg, Matthew Josephson, Malcolm Cowley, and others, editors and associate editors of *Broom*, which ran from November 1921 to January 1924. 4. The *Dial* award of $2,000 went to Van Wyck Brooks. 5. EH's long-standing prejudice against Gilbert Seldes (1893–1970) apparently dated from his belief that Seldes had rejected one of his stories submitted to the *Dial*. The piece is said to have been "A Very Short Story," Number X in the Paris edition of *in our time*. According to Seldes, the rejection, if made, must have been by Scofield Thayer. (Seldes to Carlos Baker, 20 and 23 March 1962.) See EH to Seldes, 30 December 1929.

To GERTRUDE STEIN, Paris, 17 February 1924

Dear Miss Stein:

Ford alleges he is delighted with the stuff and is going to call on you.[1] I told him it took you 4½ years to write it and that there were 6 volumes.

He is going to publish the 1st installment in the April No. going to press the 1st part of March. He wondered if you would accept 30 francs a page (his magazine page) and I said I thought I could get you to. (Be haughty but not too haughty.) I made it clear it was a remarkable scoop for his magazine obtained only through my obtaining genius. He is under the impression that you get big prices when you consent to publish. I did not give him this impression but did not discourage it. After all it is Quinn's[2] money and the stuff is worth all of their 35,000 f.

Treat him high wide and handsome. I said they could publish as much of the six volumes as they wished and that it got better and better as it went along.

It is really a scoop for them you know. They are going to have Joyce

in the same number. You can't tell, the review might be a success. They'll
never be able to pay 9,000 times 30 francs tho.

Your friend

YUL   Hemingway.

1. EH had helped arrange partial serial publication of *The Making of Americans*
in Ford Madox Ford's *Transatlantic Review*. 2. John Quinn (1870–1924), lawyer,
art collector, and patron of the arts, had funded Ford's magazine. He died in New
York 28 July 1924.

This and all subsequent letters to Miss Stein are used courtesy of the Beinecke
Library, Yale University.

To EZRA POUND, Paris, 17 March 1924

Dear Duce:

No doubt you agree with me that I am a son of a bitch for not having
written before. We have been experimenting with living with a baby etc.
Hadley sick in bed for quite a while, me for a few days, baby hollers etc.
Have tried to write but couldn't bring it off. Have written a few stories in
cafes and one place and another. You were right about a creche reading
room. It needs more room than we will ever be able to afford. I've tried
to figure it so we could live in the studio when youall parti. But afraid
that as Hem minor reached the age of mobile indiscretion it would be
difficult living. Am just now with these words renouncing what we
wanted more than anything else to do. It was so damn good of you to
let us have it and it was exactly and it was what we had always been
looking for that I feel now as though it were a crime to let it go. But I
know the kid would make life hell once it could walk which'll be this
time next year or before.

Hadley has this place under control now and going all right. I aint
been writing badly. Ford has a story in the Transportation Review for
April. Several others he cant publish.

Bunting,[1] they say, is in jail in Genoa. I'll write to anyone you say in
Italy if it will do any good.

We've had good weather for a week. O'Neils got back last night. Have
not and dont give a damn about seeing them.

Henry [Strater] left for America. Father forgive them for they know
not what they do.

His initials and head and tail pieces for your book are god damn good.

Chink [Dorman-Smith] was here for a week. We christened the baby with his aid Sunday.[2] I've got nothing further to worry about him.

MacAlmon in Toulon. Has written 8 or ten novels etc. Thanks me for your message. Hadley doesnt sleep, or says she doesnt sleep. The effect the same.

Fords still looking as through a glass darkly for an apartment. Young Georgio [Joyce] turns down all apartments found for [James] Joyce as he, Georgio, likes hotel life.

He is singing in the Episcopal quior at St. Luke's Chapel.

I will be on hand for any rent, charges or anything else our asquithian policy toward the Studio has let you in for.

[J.P.] Morgan butchered the Shorts. Dollar at 20.15.

I told our feme de menage [Marie Rohrbach] that M. Morgan an American banker had given France a hundred million dollars to help the franc. She did not seem greatly surprised but said "c'est tres gentil cette M. Morgan."

[George] Antheil[3] is reported to be going to Tunis with Barbara and George O'Neil.[4] As this report has been given out every Monday you need take no notice of it.

Joyce is appearing in April Transatlantic. His manuscript started at 7 pages (printed) but by additions to the proof in microscopic handwriting eventually reached about 9 pages.

Bill [Bird] is getting out my book [*in our time*], it was promised by bindery 3 weeks ago—different dates have been set since. After awaiting various set dates by the binder I have lost the fine thrill enjoyed by Benj. Franklin when entering Philadelphia with a roll under each arm. Fuck Literature.

I am writing some damn good stories. I wish you were here to tell me so, so I would believe it or else what is the matter with them. You are the only guy that knows a god damn thing about writing. Ford can explain stuff i.e. Thus to Revisit or Thus to Revise-it, but in private life he is so goddam involved in being the dregs of an English country gentleman that you get no good out of him.

He has never recovered in a literary way from the mirricale, or however you spell it, mirricle maybe, of his having been a soldier. Down with gentlemen. They're hell on themselves in literature.

DeMaupassant, Balzac, the Chartreuse de Parme guy [Stendhal], they all made the war, or didnt they? In any event they just learned from it. They didn't always go on under the social spell of it.

I'm going to start denying I was in the war for fear I will get like Ford to myself about it.

Oh Hell I wish you were here. *And Dorothy.*

Hadley sends her love as do I.

D'Annunzio[5] Principe di Monte Nervosa [Nevoso]. Well he rates it. It's damn late coming. Probably too late for him to get the kick out of it. Chink was sorry to miss you.

Immer,
Hem.

After renouncing Italy and all its works I've gotten all nostalgique about it. I'll bet it's swell now.

LILLY

1. Basil Bunting, poet, who had worked for Ford's *Transatlantic Review*. See Nicholas Joost, *Ernest Hemingway and the Little Magazines* (Barre, Mass., 1968), pp. 70, 72. See also Bunting's *Collected Poems* (New York, 1978). 2. Bumby was christened 10 March at St. Luke's Episcopal Chapel, with Dorman-Smith as godfather and Gertrude Stein as godmother. 3. George Antheil (1900–1959), composer of *Ballet mécanique*, inter alia. Pound's *Antheil and the Treatise on Harmony* was issued by Three Mountains Press (Paris, 1924). See also Antheil's autobiography, *Bad Boy of Music* (New York, 1945). 4. Wife and son of David O'Neil. 5. Gabriele d'Annunzio (1863–1938), whose novel *Flame of Life* (1900) EH had read while staying with the Connables in Toronto in 1920. But see poem 19 in *88 Poems*, ed. Nicholas Gerogiannis (New York, 1979), p. 28. According to Lawrence Spellman, Curator of Maps, Princeton University Library, Monte Nevoso is the former Italian name for a peak now known as Mali [Mount] Sneznik in the Dinaric Alps of northwest Yugoslavia roughly seventy-five miles west-southwest of Zagreb. D'Annunzio saw some military action there in 1917–1918.

To EZRA POUND, Paris, c. 2 May 1924

Dear Ezrah:

Yours to hand.

Re commendation; thanks!

Glad ure able take an interest in disasters of contemporaries. They are plentiful.

E. E. Cummings married to Scofield Buggaring Thayer's first wife [Elaine].[1] That may explain award of Dial prize to Van Wyck Brooks. Abe Linc Steffens gone off to Italy with objectionable 22 year old Bloomsbury Jewine who treats him like Gaugin treated Van Gogh.

George Washington Seldes, the man who discovered Burlesque shows were funny, marrying and enroute to Yarrup. Let us hope the marriage will be consumated.

Ford recently in England. Mrs. Ford, i.e. Stella, confided to Hadley twice in same evening that she had, "you know I caught Ford too late to train him." I don't know whether this means house-break him or what. On the slightest encouragement when dining out she will start on the tale of her 50 hour confinement that produced Julie. I am going to interrupt some time with the story of the time I plugged the can in Kansas City while living at Ed Mayer's so that the plumbers had to be sent for with a turd produced after 5 hours of effort after no peristaltic action over a period of 9 days. If we must go in for recounting these Homeric physical exploits leave us all go in for it.

Sally [Bird] is convalescing at St. Germaine en Lait [Laye].

I have been down in Provence and discovered it ain't no place for a writer. But I wish to hell I could paint. Jeesus Christ what cypress trees. Down there they do always with cypresses what Italy does sometimes. I made a pilgrimage to Van Gogh's whorehouse in Arles and other shrines. A six day trip on 250 francs including railway fares and a seat at the Corrida in Nimes which aint bad in these modern times. Nimes, Arles, Avignon, Le Baux, St. Remy and home.

Galantiere has a big Yahticle in The American Mercury.

John McClure, the double dealer, sets out to prove what poetry is by some pretty good quotations from your works.

Galantiere in the Chi Tribune Sunday mag. sets out to prove that the mantle of Abe Lincoln, Wm. Dean Howells, Hamlin Garland, Sherwood Anderson and yourself is descending upon me. The article takes up some space. In the same week, unknowing he was preparing this blurb, I prove in a squib for Ford that Galantiere is a little Jewish boy and a fool.

Every few days Madam F———— [Ford] comes over in her best Australian manner and while complaining in a high voice of her troubles, all her troubles, sneezes and coughs on our baby. He recovers from these attacks and is doing well. Our old femme de menage [Marie Rohrbach] is learning to handle him so she can take care of him while we go to Spain. Leaving 26th June back 16th July.

I write better I think. Have got 10 stories done.

Hadley and I have a good time. David son of Joshua Son of Isaac son of Abraham O'Neil is in town and kiking everybody with big promises.

Margaret Anderson is in town with Georgette Mangeuse le Blanc.

The ducats came too late to see the Rooshians dance. I just got back from Nimes.

W. C. Williams compares McAlmon with W. H. Hudson in pages of Transatlantic Review.

Well I have given the dirt as it appears. There is more that I cant remember. I wrote you a letter from Nimes. Did you get it?

I suspect Ford of writing in praise of his own work under various pseudonyms in Transatlantic Review.

Hope your gut stays in good shape.

Ford ought to be encouraged, but Jesus Christ. It is like some guy in search of a good money maker digging up Jim Jeffries at the present time as a possible heavy weight contender.

The thing to do with Ford is to kill him. Actually, the thing to do with Mrs. Ford is crucify her.

I am fond of Ford. This aint personal. It's literary.

You see Ford's running whole damn thing as compromise. In other words anything Ford will take and publish can be took and published in Century Harpers etc, except [Tristan] Tzara and such shit in French. That's the hell of it. Goddam it he hasn't any advertizers to offend or any subscribers to discontinue why not shoot the moon?

Don't quote me this way. I wrote him on 1 hour's notice quite a funny N.Y. Paris letter. He changes it, revises it, cuts it, makes it not have sense etc. What the hell.

The only stories I've got that I know the St. Nicholas Mag. wont publish I know damn well Ford wont too. So where the hell do we got off at.

When I asked him if the shares were printed so I could go and see Mrs. Mussolini Cox Mc Cormack he says Goddam it I won't have people ruining our credit. (It seems O'Neil, David, that son of a bitch, is going to get together a syndicate of big business men to run the Mag.) Like hell he will. Don't let any of this get back to Ford because then it would just mean a row with me and no good done. We're on the friendliest basis now and I'm going to do what I can for him right straight along. I dont want any rows.

Give my love to Dorothy. When are youall coming back?

Immer

LILLY   Hem

1. On Cummings's love for Elaine, see Richard Kennedy, *Dreams in the Mirror: A Biography of E. E. Cummings* (New York, 1980), pp. 189 ff.

To EDWARD J. O'BRIEN, Paris, 2 May 1924

Dear O'Brien:

I sent you In Our Time, another copy of Three Stories and Ten Poems and the April Transatlantic review with a story of mine in it to the London address given in the Best Short Stories of 1923. Did they ever arrive?

Now Bill Bird gave me this Rapallo address.

I have ten stories done now and think it might be a good idea to have a literary agent or something peddle them around. Also there is this Harper's Contest. At any rate, I ought to get them moving.

Also I'm about broke and as I have never yet gotten any money except 150 francs from Ford's Transatlantic for anything I've written, it might give me a helpful kick if I did get some money.

In Our Time[1] sold out fast but of course the profits on it went to offset the losses on the others Bill [Bird] published.

What I would like to do would be bring out a good fat book in N.Y. with some good publisher who would tout it and have In Our Time in it and the other stories, My Old Man and about 15 or 20 others. How many would it take?

In the meantime, if I could sell some of the stories it would help out as I have quit newspaper work.

At any rate, I'm enclosing a couple which I think might sell and one (Mr. and Mrs. Smith),[2] which I'm sure wouldn't, but for you to read and keep it as a souvenir or send it back to me as you wish.

Would it be too much to ask you to send the other two to an agent or to somebody you think might take them direct? And what about this Harper's Short Story Contest? Should I fire some to them?

Do you remember me talking one night at the pub up on Montallegro[3] about the necessity for finding some people that by their actual physical conduct gave you a real feeling of admiration like the sealers, and the men off the banks [Georges Bank] up in your country?[4] Well I have got ahold of it in bull fighting. Jesus Christ yes.

I've got something that I really get fun out of again there. It looks as though it would last too. I wish we could go to some together sometimes, I know a lot about them now.

Well, this is a very long letter. Straters have gone to New York. LeSon married Lucy Holt. We see them very often.

I wish you and Mrs. O'Brien would come and see us when you are in Paris.

Yours always,

UMD   Ernest Hemingway.

1. The Paris *in our time*, recently published by William Bird. 2. The *Little Review* 10 (Autumn–Winter 1924–1925) published this story under the title "Mr. and Mrs. Elliot." 3. Village above Rapallo where EH and O'Brien had met in February 1923. 4. O'Brien was a native of Boston. See EH to O'Brien, 21 May 1923, note 1.

To GERTRUDE STEIN, Paris, *c.* 15 May 1924

Dear Miss Stein:

You've probably seen Stearns with the bad news. I saw him and he said Liveright had cabled he was rejecting the book.[1]

I am awfully sorry. It is such a rotten shame to get hopes about anything. I have been feeling awfully badly about it. But there are other publishers and don't you ever get up any hopes and I will keep on plugging and it will go sooner or later. The hell of it is to do anything by mail or cable. Americans can't spend money that way. If Liveright would have been here he would have written a check, let them think it over and they will never spend anything. It is too easy not to.

I feel sick about it but don't you feel bad, because you have written it and that is all that matters a damn. It is up to us, i.e. Alice Toklas, Me, Hadley, John Hadley Nicanor and other good men to get it published. It will all come sooner or later the way you want it. This is not Christian Science.

With love,

YUL Hemingway.

1. Harold Stearns was acting as Paris agent for Horace Liveright. An abridged edition of *The Making of Americans* was published by Harcourt Brace in 1934. The definitive study of the tangled story is that of Donald C. Gallup, "The Making of *The Making of Americans*," in *The New Colophon* (New York, 1950), especially pp. 70–74.

To EZRA POUND, Burguete, Spain, 19 July 1924

Dear Ezra:

Here, at 900 meters above the nivel del mar [sea level] on the Spanish side of the Pyrenees is a good place to observe the ruin of my finances and literary career. Shit. I appeared in the bull ring on 5 different mornings— was cogida 3 times—accomplished 4 veronicas in good form and one natural with the muleta, the last morning, received contusions and abrasions in the pecho [chest] and other places, was drunk twice, saw Bill [Bird] drunk twice, was offered a job as Picador by Algabeno after hanging onto the bulls horns for about 6 minutes and finally getting his nose down on the sand, saw Don[ald Ogden] Stewart cogida twice, saw a man get killed the last day, saw Chink [Dorman-Smith] Mac [Mc Almon], young Geo. O'Neil and Dos Passos start across the Spanish face of the Pyrenees for Andorra—400 kilometers, with nothing but a road map and no roads, no compass and damn little money (most of it mine). Gawd knows what will become of them. We haven't enough pesetas now to pay our hotel bill and dont know how we'll get away from here. You've probably seen Bill by now. He left before the last and best bull fight. Sally did not like them. I think they had a good time however.

I wrote Ford two letters from Pamplona and got no answer. I suppose he is sore at me though Christnose I tried to run his paper the way he would have liked to have it run, except for not printing J. J. Adams and such poets, and have been thoroughly gypped all right.[1] I've tried and tried and can't go on with the thing that was ⅔ done and running smooth when he said I had to run the magazine. Having been bitched financially and in a literary way by my friends I take great and unintellectual pleasure in the immediate triumphs of the bull ring with their reward in ovations, Alcoholism, being pointed out on the street, general respect and the other things Literary guys have to wait until they are 89 years old to get.

The Plaza is the only remaining place where valor and art can combine for success. In all other arts the more meazly and shitty the guy, i.e. Joyce, the greater the success in his art. There is absolutely no comparison in art between Joyce and Maera—Maera by a mile—and then look at the guys. One breeds Georgios the other gets killed or breeds bulls. Then when a guy has a few decent human instincts like yourself what do they do to him? I wish to hell I was 16 and had art and valor.

Burton Rascoe said In Our Time showed the influences of who the hell do you think?—Ring Lardner and Sherwood Anderson!

There it is. Oh well. How did the concert go? I prayed to St. Fermin for you. Not that you needed it but I found myself in Mass with nothing to do and so prayed for my kid, for Hadley, for myself and your concert.

I am going to have to quit writing because we haven't any money. The Transatlantic killed my chances of having a book published this fall and by next spring some son of a bitch will have copied everything I've written and they will simply call me another of his imitators. Now we haven't got any money anymore I am going to have to quit writing and I never will have a book published. I feel cheerful as hell. These god damn bastards.

See you about the 27th of the month.

Love to Dorothy.

Hem

You heard of course of Steffens marriage to a 19 year old Bloomsbury kike intellectual. The last chapter in the book of Revolution.

LILLY

1. Shortly before leaving for Spain, EH had edited the July and August numbers of the *Transatlantic Review* while Ford was absent in the United States. See Carlos Baker, *Ernest Hemingway: A Life Story* (New York, 1969), p. 128.

To GERTRUDE STEIN AND ALICE B. TOKLAS, Paris, 9 August 1924

Dear Friends:

Well the news is that the transatlantic is going on. I have a friend[1] in town who (or whom) I got to guarantee Ford $200 a month for six months with the first check written out and the others the first of each month with an option at the end of 6 mos. of buying Ford out and keeping him on as Editor or continuing the 200 a month for another six months.

That of course was not good enough for Ford, who had hitherto stayed up all night writing pneumatiques and spent 100s of francs on taxis to get 500 francs out of Natalie Barney[2] and that sort of business. Once the grandeur started working Ford insisted on 25,000 francs down in addition and then as the grandeur increased he declared he wanted no money at all till October if Krebs [Friend], this guy, could guarantee him 15,000 francs then! It is a type of reasoning that I cannot follow with any degree of sympathy.

I got Krebs to back the magazine purely on the basis that a good mag. printing yourself and edited by old Ford, a veteran of the world war, etc. should not be allowed to go haywired. Now Ford's attitude is that he is selling Krebs an excellent business proposition and that Krebs is consequently a business man and the foe of all artists of which he—Ford—is the only living example and in duty bound as a representative of the dying race to grind he—Krebs, the natural Foe—into the ground. He's sure to quarrel with Krebs between now and Oct. on that basis and Krebs was ready with the ft. pen and check book. I hope that Bumbie will not grow up and get the megalomania. Anyhow the next number is under weigh.

When Ford told me the day you all left that the next number was in doubt and he was sending no M.S. to the printer in any event, I decided to hang onto your M.S. as he was threatening to bring out a quarterly which was pretty vaporous as he had about decided to use the death of [John] Quinn as an excuse to kill off the magazine.

Jane Heap was trying to fix it up with the Criterion, Major Elliott [T. S. Eliot] and Lady Rothermere's paper,[3] and I didnt want to have to get it away from Ford and then give it back and gum up everything in case he did pull off a Quarterly and the Criterion didnt come through. Jane might have been able to work it at that, but the Major is not an admirer of yours and I dont believe Rothermere could make him print it if he didn't want to. I dont believe Jane's drag would be strong enough to make Rothermere force a fight on the question.

At any rate now there will be regular and continuous publication and after all that is better than embalmed in the heavy, uncut pages of Eliot's Quarterly.

Everything is quiet here. Our Movie of Pamplona Man Ray says is one of the best movies he's ever seen. It's wonderful stuff. I can't wait for you all to see it. We've got the whole thing. Now I have a bull fight every night.

Chink [Dorman-Smith] and Co. got to Andorra 460 kilometers in 14 days exactly. They arrived here loaded with Eidelweiss and bed bugs.

I have been working well. Bumbie has more teeth coming. About 30 to be exact. None appeared yet. Hadley is well and happy and sends you both her love as I do.

> Always
> Ernest Hemingway

It is a fine story about Krebs and his money: he has married millions, literally. He has paid me back the 15 dollars I loaned him in 1920 [in Chicago]—this stuff to Ford is I think the interest on it. Ford claims to have sent a check to Joan Gris. I want to go out there.

Derniere Heure.

[Lincoln] Steffens is in town with his Old Girl. His wife is with child in Germany. He has got the old one over to show her the new one. Its just like in the monkey house at the Zoo. If this one is a boy he wants to have a girl. His Friends all rally round him. Not me.

[Right margin of page 4:] Thanks so much for the 100 francs.
YUL

1. Krebs Friend, EH's acquaintance from Chicago days, had married an heiress who put up the money that temporarily sustained the *Transatlantic Review* from bankruptcy. See Nicholas Joost, *Ernest Hemingway and the Little Magazines* (Barre, Mass., 1968), pp. 92–93. 2. Miss Barney was a wealthy American patron of the arts and among the shareholders in the *Transatlantic*. 3. Jane Heap was co-editor of the *Little Review*; T. S. Eliot, whose name EH consistently misspells, had begun the *Criterion* in October 1922.

To GERTRUDE STEIN AND ALICE B. TOKLAS,
Paris, 15 August 1924

Dear Friends:

I wrote you to the house a few days ago. You've probably gotten it
by now. It is quiet today. The Sawmill isn't running on account of
Assumption.[1]

The able bodied directors of the transatlantic meet today to elect
Krebs [Friend] President. He is going to be president and pay all the
bills. He has breakfast every morning at Ford's and things are going
smoothly. I am so glad it is going on being published with a minimum
of worry now because it was too awfully bad to think of busting off
publishing the long book [*The Making of Americans*] regularly.

Your letter was fine. Goddy[2] is well and has an upper tooth through
and I think another one coming beside it. He is as hard spiritually as a
chunk of carborundum and enjoys himself without anything outside
having any effect or appeal. He is going to be a hard one and the sooner
he gets shoved off into the world the more chance the world will have.
My best hopes for his future are that he will *not* kill his parents some
time because he needs 50 cents.

Mc Almon has gone to England to live among his parents in law [Sir
John and Lady Ellerman]. I understand he is teaching Bryher [his wife]
to drink. That ain't in the Greek tradition is it?

I have had a good cousin here that would like to have shown off to
you. Bill Bird sent you one of his wine books. Did you get it? It is selling very fast.

I have finished two long short stories, one of them not much good and
finished the long one I worked on before I went to Spain ["Big Two-
Hearted River"] where I'm trying to do the country like Cezanne and
having a hell of a time and sometimes getting it a little bit.[3] It is about
100 pages long and nothing happens and the country is swell, I made it
all up, so I see it all and part of it comes out the way it ought to, it is
swell about the fish, but isn't writing a hard job though? It used to be
easy before I met you. Certainly was bad, Gosh, I'm awfully bad now
but it's a different kind of bad.

[Gaston] Doumergue [President of France], you know, is an affi-
cionado—and they are trying to put through corridas for Paris. It will
be an awful time to get it by but there is an Empressa that is backed
from the Elysee and they are going to try and stage one on the first
Sunday in Sept. with Old Gaston himself in the Presidential Palco [box
seat]. Belmonte, [Ignacio] Sanchez Mejias, and Chicuelo with Miura
bulls. What a pipe dream. I dont really think they will be able to get

corridas by here. They've talked about it so often before but now they've got a man in the Elysee that's often been in those Course Libre at Nimes! Did you hear about the ten gold spoons missing at the Elysee, value 8500 francs, after the reception to the American Ad. Men! Its true. I saw the bulletin. The Rotarians would have cleaned them out.

Hadley and Goddy and I all send our love to you both. Don't stay away too long.

YUL   Ernest Hemingway

1. This was the sawmill and lumberyard of Pierre Chautard, EH's landlord at 113 rue Notre Dame des Champs. The Hemingways' flat was upstairs. 2. Bumby had been christened 10 March 1924 in Paris with Gertrude Stein as godmother. She began calling him Goddy for godson. 3. The "Cézanne" story, "Big Two-Hearted River," was published in *This Quarter* 1 (May 1925): 110–28. The other may have been "A Lack of Passion," a bullfight story that gave EH much trouble. He thought of including it in *Men Without Women* (1927) but decided against it.

To EDWARD J. O'BRIEN, Paris, 12 September 1924

Dear O'Brien:

How are you anyway, and how is your family and Rapallo? We are still here and working hard. The baby is nearly a year old and built like Luis Firpo. We might get down to Rapallo sometime this winter.

I have written 14 stories and have a book ready to publish. It is to be called In Our Time and one of the chapters of the In Our Time I sent you comes in between each story. That was what I originally wrote them for, chapter headings. All the stories have a certain unity, the first 5 are in Michigan, starting with the Up In Michigan, which you know and in between each one comes bang! the In Our Time. It should be awfully good, I think. I've tried to do it so you get the close up very quietly but absolutely solid and the real thing but very close, and then through it all between every story comes the rhythm of the in our time chapters.

Some of the stories I think you would like very much. I wish I could show them to you. The last one in the book is called Big Two Hearted River, it is about 12,000 words and goes back after a ski-ing story and My Old Man and finishes up the Michigan scene the book starts with. It is much better than anything I've done. What I've been doing is trying to do country so you don't remember the words after you read it but actually have the Country. It is hard because to do it you have to see the country all complete all the time you write and not just have a romantic feeling about it. It is swell fun.

I edited the July and August numbers of the Transatlantic Review for

Ford while he was in America, and before that read M.S. for him and got him to publish Gertrude Stein's Making of Americans. Have you been reading it? I think it is wonderful stuff, but to get it, really, you have to read it as hard and concentrated as tho you were reading proof on it. Then I've coached young [Nathan] Asch and [Kennon] Jewett and Ivan Beede. They are three kids with plenty of talent—Asch the most— Jewett the least. It is discouraging to try to help people do something in their own way and then just have them imitate.

There is none of that in Asch or Beede, but Jewett is too young and too facile.

You can work like hell on a thing and sweat vinegar, and then somebody reads it and all the places that it was awkward because you couldn't get it any other way, they copy as tricks.

Mc Almon is writing better all the time. He has written a really fine long poem and some really promising prose in a thing called Village.

I've been so busy writing I haven't been able to work to get stuff published—just that one story in the April Transatlantic and one coming out next month that I will send you a proof of.[1]

Dos Passos and Don Stewart and a bunch of us were down in Spain and I got gored in an amateur bull fight at Pamplona. Was in the ring 5 different days. Gotten to know a lot about it. It is what a man needs. Don Stewart was very fine. The men went on and walked across the Spanish face of the Pyrenees to Andorra—469 kilometers in 14 days.

Strater and his family are in N.Y. at 1, Lexington Avenue—Maggie Strater likes it and Mike is working hard.

Pound and his wife [Dorothy] are coming down to Rapallo in November.

Hadley is very well and sends you her best regards.

Did you see the review of the 1923 Book in the Sept. 3 N.Y. Nation and what they said about My Old Man? It was the first comment I'd seen and made me feel very good.[2]

Do please write to me, though I know you're awfully busy. How about my getting this book published? Have you any suggestions? It will run about 300 pages.

Did you ever get the stuff I sent to you? I forget what it was.

With best regards,
Your friend,
Ernest Hemingway.

UMD

1. Probably "Mr. and Mrs. Elliot," *Little Review* 10 (Autumn–Winter 1924–1925): 9–12. 2. *Nation* 119 (3 September 1924): 290, where Johan Smertenko wrote, "Beyond doubt My Old Man by Ernest Hemenway, to whom the volume is dedicated, is the finest story in the collection. . . . A Rembrandt study, rich of color yet subdued, shadowy in background yet clear in outline."

To GERTRUDE STEIN AND ALICE B. TOKLAS,
Paris, 14 September 1924

Dear Friends:

Hadley will write you about the apples. They came last night and are wonderful. The best apples I've ever eaten [in] the states or anywhere. They came while we were eating supper and were talking about you with Jane Heap. They pack them beautifully.

I have spoken to both [Ford Madox] Ford and Krebs [Friend] about your checks and get nothing but promises. If they do not come inside of five days please write to Ford taking a firm and surprised tone. It is important to get them before they start piling up and making too much money for such crooked tight wads to let go of.

Ford of course refused to take a definite sum from Krebs and would accept nothing except Krebs taking over the debts and running it as a business proposition, i.e. a money making proposition, filling him up on fake figures to feed his own ego and kidding himself that it was a money making proposition.

Now Krebs finds all sorts of debts that Ford neglected to mention and that various other things are irregular and where Ford could have had more money than he is getting out of him and no strings now he has every sort of string and every sort of New England tightness through Mrs. Krebs who insisted on making a business woman when he had a chance to get a patron of the arts.

Over three weeks ago both of them promised to send you your checks for July and August and it was just yesterday, the day before rather, that I learned it hadn't been done. Krebs said they were only paying the contributors "that needed it." I bawled him out about that and told him that as far as that went you needed it exactly as much as I did and he promised to send the check yesterday. But do check up on them because it is evidently the old american game of letting a debt mount until you can regard any attempt to collect it with righteous indignation.

The only reason the magazine was saved was to publish your stuff but there is plenty of money there and they have got to come through. If they try to quit publishing it I will make such a row and blackmail that it will blow up the show. So take a firm tone.

I am getting young Bus [Barklie M.] Henry that married Barbara Whitney into shape so that if anything ever happens to Krebs we can throw out Ford and the whole lot of them and make a real magazine out of it. Bus doesn't know it yet so don't say anything.

Dos Passos has gone. There's no news. It is finally good weather now. I'm sick of Ford and his megalomaniac blundering at the way he spoiled the chance he had with the review that it takes a great effort not to row, but I won't.

When are youall coming back? The weather is really good here now. The first decent days since we've been back from Spain.

Oh Yes; I corrected the proof for the October number. It is back in the regular space again, double space, and looks very good. I went over it very carefully with the manuscript. Hope it is all right.

Their September number was a disgrace with typographical errors. Ford had gone completely sloppy.

It is a good thing that you are a stockholder because under the French law you can put them in jail at any time fifty different ways. That's a good thing to have for a coup d'etat.

There was a fellow here from the states with money, cash, to buy some [André] Massons and Galerie Simones was closed and I didn't have Masson's address. He wants me to pick him some out and he will send over the money. So he says.

Goddy [Bumby] is well and has six visible teeth. I haven't been able to go out to Joan Gris's because we are broke.

Did you register for Defence Day? Neither did we.

I am now eating one of the apples and feel much better.

Goddy, Hadley and I all send our love to you both.

If the fish are as big as the apples I will be down there the day the season opens in the Spring.

Always yours
Hemingway

YUL

To GERTRUDE STEIN AND ALICE B. TOKLAS,
Paris, 10 October 1924

Dear Friends:

Well we'll certainly be glad to have you back again. Yes, we expect goddy[1] will soon be giving interviews on how honest he is to the newspapers just like father. Wasn't that wonderful? Didn't it sound like I'd written Marcus O Realius? I suppose any protests on my part that I didn't say any of it except in a general, drunken, denunciatory way wouldn't be accepted.

The next batch of Making of Americans has come and I am correcting it today. Will go down to the office as they did not send the original ms. with it.

By the way did you ever, speaking of honesty, get a letter from Ford marked private and confidential and not consequently to be revealed to me in which he said I had originally told him that the Makings was a short story and he had continued to publish it as such only to have me again tell him after six months that it was not a short story but a novel, in fact several novels?[2] He had a number of other lies in this letter which he hoped I would not see and the gist of it was that he wanted you to make him a flat price on the first book of the novel as serials are paid for at a lower rate than regular contributions like six month long short stories etc.

I don't know whether he ever sent it—if he did you might tell him you will talk it all over on your return.

I have had a constant fight to keep it on being published since Mrs. Friend conceived the bright idea of reducing the expenses of the magazine by trying to drop everything they would have to pay for. She is a priceless one all right, but you can handle her once you meet her. Krebs' latest idea is to have all the young writers contribute their stuff for nothing and show their loyalty to the magazine by chasing ads during the daylight hours. Ford ruined every thing except of course himself, by selling the magazine to the Friends instead of taking money from them and keeping them on the outside as originally arranged. Now the two Friends feel that Krebs must show his mettle by making a Go of the magazine financially and Krebs' business and financial ability and all Mrs. Krebs Friend's instincts and training are that the only way to make a Go is to stop all expenditure. So I believe the magazine is going to Go to hell on or about the first of Jan[3] and in that case I want you to get your money fairly well up to date and to have had the Makings appear regularly straight through the life of the review.

When you consider that the review was dead, that there was never going to be another number and that Ford was returning subscriptions in August (this Ford has forgotten and Krebs never knew) it is something to have it last the year out. There are a good many other angles to it that we can talk about when you all get back. Ford is an absolute liar and crook always motivated by the finest synthetic English gentility.

Tomorrow is Goddy's [first] birthday.[4] I've been down and bought him a bear. Jane Heap and her two kids sail for the states Saturday. Mc Almon is in town. H.D. [Hilda Doolittle] and Mac's wife [Bryher] were and wanted to see you. Ezra goes to Italy for good on Sunday. He has indulged in a small nervous breakdown necessitating him spending two days at the Am. Hospital during the height of the packing. Some good kid writers have appeared in town. Dos Passos has gone to the States. Don Stewart has my book [*In Our Time*] in N.Y. or should by now. We've been going through the usual financial worry of not having had any income since May. Being a capitalist I pray for the election of

Honest Cal and down with the radicals. We have a Manila R.R. bond and Coolidge's is the only platform that advocates hanging on to the Philippines.

Well this had better stop. The weather is fine here now. I've been working hard. Hadley and Goddy also send love to you.

Always yours,
Hemingway

YUL

1. See 15 August 1924, note 2. **2.** EH so exactly describes the contents of Ford's letter to Gertrude Stein of 18 September 1924 that he had clearly seen it, probably in the *Transatlantic Review* office. See *Letters of Ford Madox Ford*, ed. Richard M. Ludwig (Princeton, 1965), pp. 162–63. **3.** The demise of the *Transatlantic* occurred as and when EH here predicts. **4.** EH's letter is clearly dated 10 October 1924, which was Bumby's actual first birthday. The date of this letter may therefore be 9 October.

To EDMUND WILSON, Paris, 18 October 1924

Dear Wilson:

Thank you so much for writing the review in the October *Dial*.[1] I liked it very much. You are very right about the lack of capital letters— which seemed very silly and affected to me—but Bird had put them in and as he was printing the *In Our Time* himself and that was all the fun he was getting out of it I thought he could go ahead and be a damn fool in his own way if it pleased him. So long as he did not fool with the text.

I'm awfully glad you liked it.

How are you anyway? and did you ever get Chaplin for your ballet?

We have lived very quietly, working hard, except for a trip to Spain, Pamplona, where we had a fine time and I learned a lot about bull fighting, the inside the ring scene. We had a lot of minor adventures.

I've worked like hell most of the time and think the stuff gets better. Finished the book of 14 stories with a chapter on [of] *In Our Time* between each story—that is the way they were meant to go—to give the picture of the whole between examining it in detail. Like looking with your eyes at something, say a passing coast line, and then looking at it with 15X binoculars. Or rather, maybe, looking at it and then going in and living in it—and then coming out and looking at it again.

I sent the book to Don Stewart at the Yale Club about three weeks ago. When he was here he offered to try and sell it for me. I think you would like it, it has a pretty good unity. In some of the stories since the *In Our Time* I've gotten across both the people and the scene. It makes you feel good when you can do it. It feels now as though I had gotten on top of it.

Will you get over here this winter do you think? We will probably be in Paris all winter. Not enough money to get out. The baby is very well and husky. Hadley is working on the piano.

She sends her best regards to you and Mrs. Wilson.

Hope everything is going well with you and that you have a good winter. I would like to hear from you and I did appreciate the review. It was cool and clear minded and decent and impersonal and sympathetic. Christ how I hate this terrible personal stuff. Do you remember my writing from Toronto wanting some reviews and publicity? and then got some and it turned me sick.

I think there's nothing more discouraging than unintelligent appreciation. Not really discouraging; but just driving something back inside of you. Some bright guy said *In Our Time* [Paris edition] was a series of thumbnail sketches showing a great deal of talent but obviously under the influence of Ring Lardner. Yeah! That kind of stuff is fine. It doesn't bother. But these wordy, sentimental bastards. You are the only man writing criticism who or whom I can read when the book being criticized is one I've read or know something about. I can read almost anybody when they write on things I don't know about. Intelligence is so damn rare and the people who have it often have such a bad time with it that they get bitter or propagandistic and then it's not much use.

With best wishes to you and to your wife,

Very sincerely,
Ernest Hemingway

Is this *What Price Glory?* really a good play.[2] I don't mean a good *play*—it sounds fine over here.

YUL

1. Wilson's review of *Three Stories and Ten Poems* and *in our time* appeared in the *Dial* 77 (October 1924): 340–41. 2. *What Price Glory?*, a war drama by Maxwell Anderson and Lawrence Stallings (1924).

To HOWELL JENKINS, Paris, 9 November 1924

Dear old Carpative:

Going out to the White Sox Giants ball game yesterday[1] I ran into Don Skene of the Tribune who is just back from Chicago and he brought the news that you were on the turf and in good shape.

How the hell are you Carper you old son of a bitch anyway?

I got the clippings you sent me about Yenla and his love nest and don't remember if I ever answered or not. Reading between the lines in that you could see what a fine part Don Wright played, couldn't you? Jo Eezus. Yen as usual being presented with the soiled end of the stick with no additional compensation. Pity the female Polak lawyer couldn't shoot when she pulled a gun on Doodles.[2]

Look, Carper. The play is for you to come over here next summer. Start saving your seeds now, you can come over for next to nothing, put up with us here in Paris. We have an extra room and we'll all chow together. This is a good place to stay. If you saw Dick Baum he'll tell you about how much fun we have. We have a comfortable place, a swell cook and no love nests. Hadley and I were talking about it today and we decided that you and the Horned Article were the two guys we would rather see and would have the most damned fun with.[3]

How is the article? I hope he is combining social with financial success. He rates it. Everybody ought to have what they want.

What we want is for you to come over here. We have a swell spring off - see enclosure - and all the Month of July our Femme de Menage [Marie Rohrbach] takes him to the country to learn French at the source.

We are going to go to Spain again. Get a Ford for 1,000 francs a month with Insurance and drive down from here. You are going to drive.

There is swell fishing. Like the Black when we first hit it. The wildest damn country in the Spanish Pyrenees in from Roncevaux. The Irati river. We hit it this summer. You leave the car at Burguete and go in fifteen miles by foot. Even the mules pass out on the trail. It is in there where they fought the Carlist wars.[4] We butchered them this summer. Big trout. Hadley caught six in less than an hour out of one whole [hole] where they were jumping a falls. Water ice cold and virgin forests, never seen an ax. Enormous beech forests and high up, Pines. We'll camp in at the headwaters of the Irati for a week and then go back to Burguete, get in the car and drive through the pass down to Pamplona for the big Feria and the bull fights. Six bull fights on six successive days and every morning an amateur fight in which will take part the noted Espadas Howell Griffiths Jenkins and Ernest de la Mancha Hemingway representing the Stock Yards of Chicago.

The godamdest wild time and fun you ever saw. Everybody in the town lit for a week, bulls racing loose through the streets every morning, dancing and fire works all night and this last July us guys practically the guests of the city. If Donald Ogden Stewart[5] comes to Chicago get ahold of him and give him a party and get him to give you the dope. He and Dos Passos were down last year. Don is a swell guy. I've written him to look you up but he may have been there already.

Honest to Gawd Carper there never is anything like it anywhere in the world. Bull fighting is the best damn stuff in the world.

Pamplona is a swell town of about 30,000, on a plateau in the middle of the Mountains of Navarre. Greatest country you ever saw and right on the edge of the only trout fishing that hasn't been ruined by motor cars or railroads. You see in Spain the main roads are like Boulevards - but there are damn few of them - just a few cutting across and linking up the big towns. Swell driving - But the small roads don't exist. Nothing but mule paths. The people have any people in the world skinned. They're all as good guys as Jim Dilworth and as wild as Yak Harris.

We could make the whole Spanish trip from Paris to Paris on $250 apiece. I'm getting mine together now.

Last summer Hadley and I made the whole thing on $300 for the two of us for a month but I'm giving you a big overlapping estimate to cover an additional trip we'd make on down through Spain.

For Christ sake come on. You can only live once, Carper, and this is as good as the best of the best days we ever had on the Black and Sturgeon before the old gang went to pieces. We'd leave Paris on the first of July. You could spend August in Paris with us or we could take a run down to Italy and see the old joints.

But Spain is the only country left that hasn't been shot to pieces. They treat you like shit in Italy now. All post war fascisti, bad food and hysterics. Spain is the real old stuff. And you could have a hell of a good time here and spend hardly any money.

Come on Carper. Dos [Passos] and Don Stewart will probably go down too. They are both great guys. You know, the old stuff. Dos is like Bill [Smith] was before he started to go haywire. The same sort of line in a different way. All the men are drinkers.

Think of Haig in pinch bottles at 2.15 the Q. Imperial Quart.

How is the Ghee [Jack Pentecost]? What is the news of Bill and Butstein [Kate Smith] and Y. K.?

My love to Dirty Dick. He is a rare good guy.

After I was in Chicago the last time and the Ghee was funny about coming around and all that I made up my mind there was no use bellyacheing over the mort of the good old days. We've pulled out of all that now. What is the use of skinning dead horses. Only you never got funny and you never went haywired on a man and there aint any time we have that wouldn't be that much better if the Carper was along. So come on. It's too damn good to miss. And we've got only one time to live and so lets have a hell of a good time together. Start sticking the jack in the bank.

I've been working my ass off. You would like the stuff I think. I have a book in N.Y. now to come out in the spring. Another one about half done. The first one is a long book about 350 pages. Have done some swell fishing stories.

Shoot a screed Carper. Hadley sends her love. We have more fun together all the time. She is the best guy on a trip you ever saw. She is keeping her piano up and runs the house and the baby damned smooth and is always ready to go out and eat oysters at the cafe and drink a bottle of Pouilly before supper. We have good whiskey in the home and a swell lot of books, open fire places and it's comfortable, and a guy can read or lie around and go out when he feels like it. You'll like living here. You got to come.

Write, Carpative. I wish the hell you were here now. It's fall, gray smoky days, good and cold, regular foot ball weather. That's the only thing I miss. But boy we do have some swell fight cards here. I go once a week anywhay. Press ducats [tickets].

If you had the jack up and could come over now we'd all go down to Switzerland for ski-ing and bob racing. We've got a bob and live in a chalet where it costs a little less than Dilsteins [Dilworths'] in the old days. Swell food, featherbeds, big porcelein stoves, so cold outside at night the stars crackle. In the daytime ski-ing you get so tanned you look like an Indian. Ski in shirtsleeves and sometimes no shirts. Bob racing down the mountain roads. Six mile runs. Whiskey in the evening and a big meal and shoot a few hands of bridge.

A lot better than a good dose of piles. A guy can live over here.

Well I've got to cut this short. Will send it to the old Newgard Adress.

Always yours,
Steen

PH. PUL

---

1. John J. Mc Graw (1873–1934), who led the New York Giants to ten pennants (1904–1924) and three World Series victories, conducted the Giants and Chicago White Sox to England and France for a series of exhibition games in October and November 1924. 2. Wanda Elaine Stopa invaded the Palos Park home of her alleged lover, Y. K. Smith; fired three shots at Mrs. Smith (Doodles), who was ill in bed; killed Henry Manning, the caretaker; and escaped to Detroit, where she committed suicide the next day. (*New York Times*, 25–28 April 1924.) 3. Dick Baum, nicknamed Pinard, and William Dodge Horne were ARC Ambulance veterans from 1918.

4. The Carlist Wars were fought intermittently from 1833 to 1876 by partisans of Don Carlos, claimant to the Spanish throne. 5. Stewart (1894–1980): b. Columbus, Ohio; Yale graduate, humorist, parodist, and later Hollywood screenwriter.

To ROBERT MC ALMON, Paris, c. 15 November 1924

Dear Mac:

Enclosed two hundred boules [francs]. I'll send you the other hundred the first of the week. We are all right now. Thanks ever so much.

Have been having a swell time reading the Nansen and Steffenson. The Nansen serves as a sort of a primer for the other. I'd read the Steff in the paper but that was only excerpts.[1] It is wonderful stuff. I want to read his My Life Among the Eskimos now.

It is just about morning, Bumby had a night when he didn't sleep and Hadley and I've been up with him alternately and together. I don't mind a white night so long as the supply of Steffanson holds out. Bumby is getting some new molars through I think.

I have decided that all that mental conversation in the long fishing story is the shit and have cut it all out. The last nine pages. The story was interrupted you know just when I was going good and I could never get back into it and finish it. I got a hell of a shock when I realized how bad it was and that shocked me back into the river again and I've finished it off the way it ought to have been all along. Just the straight fishing [in "Big Two-Hearted River"].

Finished a long 45 page story that I think you would like ["The Undefeated"].

Nothing going on here.

I'd have sent the three hundred francs in one piece but the banks are closed today. Toussaint and I found I'd not taken out quite enough yesterday when paid off other debts.

[Nathan] Ashe [Asch] had a scare that he had the syphyllis and was going around announcing that he was thoroly unmoral and if the test showed he had the syph he would go over to the states and rob a bank to get himself enough money to last on etc. I suggested that if he was so thoroly unmoral as that he'd better return the books he'd borrowed from me. The Wasserman test showed he only had crabs.

[Ralph Cheever] Dunning's poems in the [November] Transatlantic don't look very solid. There is one about "Then put a lily in my hand

And float me out to sea" or something like that that's pretty near the goddamdest poem I've ever read. They're really just as bad as Dunning.

Have had no word from Don Stewart yet about my book. I've got to send him over the change in the Big Two Hearted River story now. Wouldn't it be funny if some publisher had accepted it because of the stuff that I've got to cut? I've got a hunch they've all given it the raz.[2]

Have you heard from Ezra?

Ernest Walsh is here now; he visited Carnevalli in the Hospital outside of Bologna and says he is pretty nearly dead. I tried to get some dope for you on how near dead he was but Walsh, who is supposed to be fairly close to it himself and is beginning to look it, didn't seem to take much interest in discussing it.

Walsh now that he is dying is getting to be a pretty nice guy. I wonder if it would have the same effect on the rest of us. Somehow I think not. I can picture Ezra for instance.

How's the Beer Stube? Have you been having good weather? We never heard anything from Madame Picabia.

If everything goes well we plan to come down to Switzerland about the first part of January.

Hadley sends you her love. See you soon maybe. Have you John Herman's[4] address?

Always yrs.

YUL   Hem

1. EH refers here to the Arctic explorers Fridtjof Nansen and Vilhjalmur Stefansson. 2. EH had finished "Big Two-Hearted River," including the nine-page coda, about mid-August 1924. See EH to Gertrude Stein, 15 August 1924. 3. The In Our Time stories had been sent to Stewart c. 28 September 1924 and were being considered at the George H. Doran Company. They declined to publish. See EH to Gertrude Stein and Alice B. Toklas, 20 January 1925. 4. John Herrmann (1901–1959), best known for his novels What Happens (1927), Big Short Trip, and Summer Is Ended (both 1932).

To ROBERT MC ALMON, Paris, 20 November 1924

Dear Bob:

I'm sorry not to have sent you John Herman's [Herrmann's] address but no one here has it. He left with no address and was going to send one to [Evan] Shipman[1] but hasn't been heard from. I've been waiting to get it.

Your selection of B.A. [British-American] authors sounds swell.[2] I have only two new stories on hand. One is unpublishable I'm afraid as well as too long. The other is a hell of a good one, by far the best I've written but about 10,000 words.[3] I am working now and as soon as I have a good shorter one will shoot it to you. You can have the long one but you say 5000 words. Let me know how things are going and what the time limit is. Naturally I want to get it to you as soon as possible so as to let things get ahead. If the new ones dont turn out so good, what I'm working on now—you could always publish a quite short one 1200 words or so from the book now in U.S.[4]

No word from it [In Our Time] yet. No news here much. [Nathan] Asch and Shipman had a fight and after ½ hour of slugging no one had a mark. Neither packs much of a punch I guess. Shipmans girl has left him and he has gone back to Belgium after her. She left him because he loaned Asch money to get new teeth. Asch hit him out of kike gratitude. Ca va.

It has been cold as hell here. All the fountains frozen. Me too. Am sending you 100 fr. Big time at the Anglo American [Press Club] annual dinner. Got in at seven A.M. this morning. Bill [Bird] is in good shape. Hadley sends her love. Glad you're going well. I'm having a period of not being able to do anything worth a shit after this last story ["The Undefeated"]. Hadley sends her love.

Always yours,
Hem

My best to the Beer Stübe

YUL

1. Evan Biddle Shipman (1904–1957) was an old friend from EH's Paris days. They first met in October 1925, when Shipman, a native of Plainfield, New Hampshire, was serving as European correspondent for the *American Horse Breeder*. EH dedicated *Men Without Women* (1927) to him and discusses his service with the Loyalists in Spain in the introduction to *Men at War* (New York, 1942), pp. xxviii–xxix. He also appears in *A Moveable Feast* (New York, 1964), pp. 131–40. In 1933 Shipman was Bumby's tutor in Key West, and in World War II he was sergeant-major of the 16th Regiment, 16th Armored Division. He was author of a volume of poems, *Mazeppa,* and a racing novel, *Free for All.* 2. For *The Contact Collection of Contemporary Writers,* to be edited by Mc Almon. 3. Probably "A Lack of Passion," never published, and "The Undefeated," which first appeared in *Der Querschnitt* (in German) in summer 1925 and then in *This Quarter* 1 (Autumn–Winter 1925). 4. See EH to Mc Almon, 10 December 1924.

To WILLIAM B. SMITH, JR., Paris, 6 December 1924

Dear Boid:
You could have KO'ed me with the proverbial pinion. I haven't felt
so damned good since we used to pestle them on the Black. I have a
hunch this is going to be a long screed though I feel almost too swell
to write.

Sure I know how you felt when you indited that screed and I had
made a more than offensive bludy ass of myself with Y. K. but Doodles
had my goat and a goatless male aint renowned for sound and noble
actions. To hell with all that. I wish you were here and we could talk.
But screed freely. Gawd I wish you could come over here. Why the hell
cant you? It doesn't take many of the papered ones. . . .

Jo Eezus it has been wild since the Chinese invented gun powder and
all the people want to do is drink with you. We have pastimed it two
summers now and only touched the edge. This summer Chink [Dorman-
Smith] and Dos Passos and George O'Neil (Dave O'Neil's kid from St.
Louis—) started out to walk across the Spanish face of the Pyrenees and
I walked up a ways with them and hit a little town on the Irati and got
a little tight at lunch and a Spaniard offered to show me the biggest
trout in the Irati that had lived in the same hole for 3 years now and
it was where the women wash the clothes in about 10 ft. of water and the
bastard would weigh 16 lbs easy. I tried him with everything and
finally poked him with my rod to see if he was real and he damned
near knocked the rod out of my hand. If you could find what corresponds
to muddlers in the Irati you could get trout up to any size. You get
plenty of the medium sized ones. Hash and I got 7 out of one hole and
they were jumping all the time.

Why don't you come over and we'll go down to Spain in June. We
can rent a Ford with insurance for 1,000 francs a month—about 50
seeds—and drive down all through France and over the Pass of Roland.
Fish the Irati—hiking in from Burguete—and then go to Pamplona for
the big bull fight week. It would be a swell trip. It's healthy as hell. High
and cool nights and swell hot days. No bugs.

What kind of shape are you in? Have you any seeds ahead? You could
live here in Paris in a good room for about 10 francs a day and chow with
us. We feed a man well.

Odgar [Carl Edgar] married! The manufacturer [EH] knows Odgar
rated it in the end. Never did a man try harder to marry. Who and how
did the Gar achieve wedlock with?

I know how damn good all our old stuff was Bird because everything,
almost everything worth a damn I've written has been about that coun-

try. It was the whole damn business inside me and when I think about any country or doing anything it's always that old stuff, the Bay, the farm, rainstein fishing, the swell times we used to have with Auntie [Mrs. Charles] at the farm, the first swell trips out to the Black and the Sturgeon and the wonderful times we had with the men and the storms in the fall and potato digging and the whole damn thing. And we've got them all and we're not going to lose them—and the only way we could ever lose them would be trying to go back and do them all over—but we can go on and get some new ones and some damn fine ones. Like over here and Spain and Austria up in the mts. in the winter time.

It's so god damn swell to know that we will have some of the old genuwind together again. Because Boid the number of genuwind all Caucasian white guys in the world is limited. I should say that maybe there were 5 or 6 at the most. That may be an exaggerated figure. There'd probably be a number more if they didnt marry foecal matter in various forms. There's a guy named Lewis Galantiere over here was a priceless guy and he has been hooked and married by the most absolute copper plated bitch in the world and he aint a good guy any more. And with casualties like that in the thin red line of white guys we have to keep the ranks close together. There is an awful one is damned near married to Dos Passos. He's a guy you'd like.

If all this sounds too much like crap, remember that I aint written a letter in your direction for a long time.

Hash and I have had and have a damn good time. We pastime the fights and the concerts, skiing, bull fights and the finnies. She fishes not with the usual feminine simulation of interest but like one of the men, she's as intelligent about fights as she is about music, she drinks with a male without remorse, and turned out Bumby the boy spring off who is built like Firpo, sleeps all night and is as cheerful as a pup. Gee Boid the way he's built and the way he's coordinated that guy will have a chance to step. The Ghee [Jack Pentecost] is a frail built one along side of him. He's got a headpiece so that when you tell him a thing once he does it. Hash hasnt lost any looks and gets better all the time. She runs the house like a Rolls Royce.

We've been living on about nothing this year while I've written a book that Dos Passos took to N.Y. about 2 mo. ago. Doran are going to publish it I think. We're dickering now. Boni and Liveright want it if they dont come through but I'm all for keeping out of the manuals of the Semites as long as possible. The two years before I was working for the Toronto Star and Hearst and writing the odd story. Not very many and didnt get the breaks there. I was covering the Lausanne conference for Hearst under the name of John Hadley—maybe you lamped that by-line in the American. Probably not. Was in Near East for them

too under the same name. Couldn't use my own on acct contract with
the Star.

Anyway Hash started down to Lausanne to join me after I'd come back
from Constantinople and brought all my stories—carbons and all, everything I'd done for two years—150 pages of a novel included, everything,
because we were going up in the mts after the conference for Xmas
and I was going to send a bunch of stuff out and work on the novel and
she put her bags and the suit case in her compartment and went out the
door to see if her trunk was on and came back and the suitcase full of
Mss. was gone.

She was afraid to tell me for a couple of days and then it took me
awful damn hard. You know that feeling when you feel that you're
facing the Industrialist [Fate?] and he has taped his hands with tin foil.
You feel like you've got about as much chance as you'd have with Harry
Wills.

Only one story left out of the two years work and that was My Old
Man O'Brien published in his book. Then he dedicates the book to me
and misspells the name—so that didnt do me a hell of a lot of good.
I've quit worrying about succeeding as a writer now—putting it all in
on writing and hoping maybe the stuff will hit sooner or later.

Have been pestleing it pretty hard lately. Have you seen any of the
output? If not, I'll send 'em.

How is Yen [Y. K. Smith] making it? The only feeling I have about
the boy is feeling sorry I acted so shitty to him. God it was funny. I was
tight all by myself in Arles last April 25 and read in the Marseilles
paper about the female district attorney of Chicago assassinating with
coups of a revolver the doorkeeper of the Rich publiciste Y. K. Smith of
Chicago in an attempt to kill the wife of same who leaped from the
window etc. It was a funny story in French, especially after it had come
over the cable. In due temporal my family sent the Tribune acct with
suitable moral comments. I seemed to scent the cloven hoof of [Don]
Wright—or am I wrong? I wanted to write Yen and tell him we stood
back of him in every conceivable position but I didnt know how he'd
take hearing from me.

You know how I felt about Auntie. I'm glad you were in St. Louis
when she died. I wanted to write then but I didnt know where to reach
you and there is nothing a man can say. I think she got an awful lot out
of life in spite of the way things broke for her. I cant realize she is dead.

Do you know Don Stewart's stuff? He's a swell guy. Get Mr. and Mrs.
Haddock Abroad. It's got the old Lardeners Stuff. He's never read the
Lardeners either and of course I couldnt get it for him. You and he and
the writer could have a hell of a fine time. I got a hunch that you and

the enditer could do a funny book that would handle us on seeds for some time. A man's got to take a lot of punishment to write a really funny book. Don's taken it. His old male was laid by the heels by the law on acct. temporary shortage in accts, him big banker, City Treas. etc. and bumped himself off while Don was at Yale.

McGraw and Commy were here barnstorming. General impression was that McGraw was keeping his ball team in Europe so nobody would spill any more beans. I don't imagine Cozy [Dolan] and the Boob were the only guys that wanted the Phils not to bear down too hard. Saw Mac at the races, dropping money. They didn't take in enough at the gate here or in England to cover the balls fouled out of the park. Saw two good games here.

We play tennis for exercise. I'm not quite so bad as the old days—still I ain't ever going to be a tennis player. Hash has a damned nice game. I box at Leida's with the pugs—keep in shape keeping out of the way of punches. Swell bouts here. Some really fast boys. Mascart, Ledoux, Brettonell, this damn woodchopper Paolino—when he hits them they never recover—but he can't hit anything but English heavyweights. I think he shuts his eyes when he swings. But when he hits 'em they carry them off in a sack. He's as wide across the shoulders as the Arc de Triomphe and about 5-4 and has little legs like a sandpiper. They have to make the gloves to order for him and he lives on raw fish. He looks bad against everybody he fights and he knocks 'em all cold. Well, it's getting late. Shoot me the dope. And if you're a seeded article come over here. If you're not, save the papered product and come over in June. Hash sends her love.

Immer,

PUL Wemedge.

To ROBERT MC ALMON, Paris, 10 December 1924

Dear Mac:

I've been waiting hoping to have a good new short one but the two stories I've done are about 10 and 12 thousand. This is the best short story I ever wrote so am sending it. It's short enough anyway.[1]

How's everything? We are going to Austria on the 19th—to a place called Schruns—go off the main line from Zurich to Innsbruck at Bludenz —½ hr. on electric tram. Want to get out of Paris and Switzerland's too expensive. We are going to live in Schruns for $18 a week the 3 of us.

Swell skiing—its just across the mountain from Klosters and Davos. I hope Chink [Dorman-Smith] will come down.

Not much news here. I dreamt night before last you were dead. Hope this finds you well. Was careful not to tell dream before breakfast. I dreamt I read it in the papers with a big full page lay out, picture of you and Bryher [Mrs. Mc Almon] and the Ellerman Castle in Scotland etc. Is there one? Watch your step and dont get bumped off by wild adolescent Fascisti. Herman's [John Herrmann's] address not yet arrived.

No more Transatlantic review. Ford is going to start a new review called The Hats Off to France—A Quarterly Journal of Arts and Letters. Did you see Mrs. Conrad's letter to the Times about Ford's "disgusting book about my husband?" Quite a letter.[2]

We've been laid up but are now in good shape. Anxious to get the hell out of here to Austria. Enclose 100 f. I owe you. Thanks. Am crossing it in case letter should miscarry. Hadley sends her best.

Yours always,
Hem

Write here. They will forward it.
YUL

1. "Soldier's Home," in *Contact Collection of Contemporary Writers*, ed. Mc Almon (Paris: Three Mountains Press, June 1925), pp. 77–86. 2. F. M. Ford, *Joseph Conrad: A Personal Remembrance* (Boston, *c.* November 1924). See David Dow Harvey, *Ford Madox Ford: A Bibliography of Works and Criticism* (Princeton, 1962), pp. 63–64. Conrad had died 3 August 1924.

To ARCHIBALD MAC LEISH,[1] Paris, *c.* 11 December 1924

Dear Mac Leish:

I sent word around to Masson asking him to meet me here at twelve o'clock noon on Tuesday to go to lunch at your flat. Hope that date is all right. You can let me know and if it isn't I can fix it up with Andre. Thanks so much for asking me.

Scott [Fitzgerald] has invented that spelling of Hemingway [with two ms and no g]. Why I don't know unless it is that there are two ts in Scott Fitzgerald. He says that he has written a review that will help In Our Time very much. I've never seen it so I imagine that the name is spelled as he gave it to you. It will probably do that Hemminway a lot of good anyway.

We go to Austria a week from tomorrow. Hadley is much better and we look forward to seeing you Saturday.

Yours always,

LC   Ernest Hemingway

1. "I met EH at the [Closerie des] Lilas in the summer of 1924." (Mac Leish to Carlos Baker, 9 August 1963.)

This and all subsequent letters to Mac Leish are used courtesy of the Library of Congress and Mr. Mac Leish.

To HAROLD LOEB,[1] Schruns, Austria, 29 December 1924

Dear Harold:

I sent you a card but to 16 Rue Montessuy so maybe you didnt get it. It's commenced to snow in the high mountains after a week of clear, dry, October weather. Probably be good snow by when you get here.

The grub is excellent and there is good red and white wine and 30 kinds of beer. A bowling alley in the hotel and we all bowl. Hartman[2] and I bowl neck and neck you can probably trim us. It is a swell place. Wonderful town and the people very God fearing and good drinkers.

I'm in such shape already you wouldn't know me. Hard as hematite and at least twice as fast.

Costs practically nothing—85,000 crowns a day for full pension and heat 15 or 20 thou extra. Best looking country you ever saw and swell hikes. Everywhere you hike to there are good crucifixes with Herr Gott in the act of [illegible] any amount of punishment and fine little pubs full of chamois hunters and good [illegible] white wine or red wine from around Bozen.

If you dont come down you are not only a low son of a bitch but also ignorant. It is a pipe to get here as all the customs etc, are made on the train and you only have to get off at Buchs, walk across the tracks, change a little money and buy a ticket to Bludenz.

Bring my book from Fleischmann will you?[3] And a couple of bottles of good whiskey. You can get it at the best price at the Cave Mura—19 Rue D'Antin just off the Avenue de L'Opera.

If you pack it in a rucksack or a musette they wont make you open it. Draw the corks and take a drink out of each bottle. They only open bags and suit cases. 2nd Class is the same as first as the carriages are old pre war Austrian ones—only 3 places each side in each—very comfortable and sinking way back.

How is Kitty [Cannell]? I hope she feels a lot better. Hadley sends her love to Kitty also me. I would like to hear her talk on your new Poppa.

How is he? How is everything? How the hell are you?

Tell Kitty you will be pure because there is only one beautiful girl in the village and she eats garlic for breakfast.

Bumby is in good shape and we have a nurse for him.

Kitty's hat is a K.O. on Hadley.

Well—So Long—and hurry down. Dont forget the MS. and whiskey— get some of yr own stuff copied and bring it down.

Always yrs
Ernest

PUL

1. Harold Loeb (1891–1974), a native of New York, Princeton, Class of 1913, had met EH at Ford's office in the spring of 1924. He edited and published the little magazine *Broom*, wrote three novels, and helped EH with the publication of *In Our Time*. His autobiography, *The Way It Was*, appeared in 1959.

This and all subsequent letters to Loeb are used courtesy of the Princeton University Library.

2. Bertram Hartman, an American painter who had first urged the Hemingways to visit Schruns. 3. Leon Fleischman, a literary scout for Boni and Liveright, was reading EH's stories for possible publication by Horace Liveright, partly at Loeb's instigation.

To HAROLD LOEB, Schruns, 5 January 1925

Dear Harold:

What a lousy business. We're all sad as hell this morning that you're not coming. We'd have had such a hell of a good time. Somehow I had a hunch you would show up.

No, the states in Jan Feb etc. are a hell of a disappointment while they knock you over in the Spring and Fall. I had a hell of a dismal arrival once in Feb. Still you can go to the shows etc. and N.Y. is a damn beautiful place anytime. Maybe you can go to Spain anyway. I should think maybe you would rate that now. Still it aint what we rate but what we get in this life. Hadley claims we get what we rate in the next life. That would probably be just as bad. Here we do beat the gun sometimes.

Don [Stewart] sent a Christmas letter with an enormous check which gave me a chill when I saw it was a check because I thot it was from Doran[1] as there was a letter from Doran enclosed. But it was from Don instead. Christmas present to keep up our morale I think. He's a swell guy. Anyway Doran's letter was to Don and said he would have some idea of how interested that [they] had been in Hemingway MS. on acct length of time they'd taken to reach a decision. Every body had read it 4 times etc. But Mr. Doran felt they couldnt go all the way with me on the matter of sex in a book of Short Stories as Mr. Doran didnt like to "center the shocks in a series of shocks" or some such shit altho he would go all the way with me in a novel and should they write to me suggesting this and then maybe leave the publishing of the short stories as a 2nd volume in abeyance or something like that but that they were all agreed on the power of my stuff and what a great book it was only they didnt want to publish it.

Don said it was all horse cock except they didnt want to lead off with a book of short stories no matter whether good or not. So he has given the book to Menken [H. L. Mencken]—that shit—to recommend to [Alfred] Knopf—well as Menken doesn't like my stuff and [George Jean] Nathan does that will probably end in horsecock too.

Then he is going to take it to [Horace] Liveright.

Don says not to be a horse's ass and starve to death in a place with a name like Schruns.

So Don is functioning well and nothing to worry about there and I never did really worry about him because he is such a hell of a good guy. But I wish you would see him anyway and give him our best and ask him what the late dope is. He's coming back in March.

His address is the Yale Club—Vanderbilt Ave. or else—The Shelton— you know—something and Lexington Ave. Go and see him. He's a swell guy. I'll put him in touch with you too. If you want I'll give you a card to him but cards are such shit.

Wedderkopf[2] writes my bull fight story—which he refers to as an article on Spain—is marvellous and do I "know perhaps stories told by real American flappers with all the utterest insolence of this kind of animals. Or if you dont know it you could tell me perhaps where I could point out this kind of literature."

That is the latest dope on the selling market. All my stuff will appear soon he says.

I will write Fleischmann[3] about the MS. I think that is best.

Hadley sends her love—Hartmans[4] feel miserable you are not coming. We'd all figured on having a swell time with you.

If you want to do something for me will you subscribe to L'Auto—to be sent to this address for 3 mos? You can get the address of L'Auto which is in Faubourg Montmartre out of a copy of that publication available in all the $\begin{cases} \text{better} \\ \text{worst} \end{cases}$ class newsstands.

I will forward you the money.

Write again before you sail unless you dont like to write letters. I havent done any work beyond starting 3 or 4 stories and not being able to go on with them. Need a big town to write in. But what's writing anyway? A hell of a lot as a matter of fact. Haven't had a coat on since we've been down here. Regular September weather.

My best to Kitty[5]—I hope she's having good effects from the treatments.

Yours

PUL   Ernest.

1. George H. Doran, New York publisher. 2. Hans von Wedderkop, Paris scout for *Der Querschnitt* of Frankfurt-am-Main, which published four of EH's poems in English and his story "The Undefeated" in German translation as "Stierkampf." See Nicholas Joost, *Ernest Hemingway and the Little Magazines* (Barre, Mass., 1968). 3. Leon Fleischman was the Paris agent for Boni and Liveright, which published *In Our Time* 5 October 1925. 4. Bertram Hartman, an American artist, then wintering at Schruns with his wife, Gusta. 5. Kitty Cannell, a close friend of Loeb's.

To ERNEST WALSH AND ETHEL MOORHEAD, Schruns, *c.* 12 January 1925

Dear Ernest and Dear Miss Moorhead:

Hurray for the new Review. I think its a fine thing for you both to do, a very fine thing, and I only hope it wont be too much work. We are all very excited about it. It shouldnt be too much work either because the hardest work on a review is to get intelligent reading of the Manuscripts and on a quarterly and you living in Cambo with therefore limited activities that will be easy. Cambo is a metropolis alongside of Schruns.[1]

We decided the best way to carry the gravel [?] Chambertin was in our special gyroscopic action stomachs where it would lose none of its fragrance and quality by being shaken up; but we drank the Chablis on the train. They were two lovely wines.

If there is anything I can do from here about helping you, let me know. I've plenty of time for writing letters and will spread the news.

Yes, I think you're right to attach the tinware to the American Express Co. as you dont want to lose MSS, Exchanges, etc. They're a careless and irresponsible lot.

I'm sending you The Big Two Hearted River which you have already read as it is the best thing I have done by a long shot.

You've heard my ideas about running a review pretty thoro'ly in our Hotel Venezia talk sessions and as you couldnt talk back so well then by Doctors orders I'll be glad to see your ideas practically worked out.

One of the most important things I believe is to get the very best work that people are doing so you do not make the mistake the Double Dealer[2] and such Magazines made of printing 2nd rate stuff by 1st rate writers.

I see by your prospectus that you are paying for MS on acceptance and think that is the absolute secret of getting the first rate stuff. It is not a question of competing with the big money advertizing magazines but of giving the artist a definite return for his work. For the best work can never get into the purely commercially run magazines anyway but he will always hold on to it hoping to get something for it and will only give away stuff that has no value to any magazine or review.

I dont see any reason why you shouldnt publish the best review thats ever been published. Even if you only get out 4 numbers of it - or less - then you have made an achievement that the reviews that live by hand to mouth dragging along to keep alive with no reason for living can never touch. I'm with you both - all the way - and I want to see you get out the finest - the very finest review - ever.

How do you feel about Gertrude Stein? If you want to write her for something you can reach her at 27 Rue de Fleurus Paris VI France. Would you like me to suggest you some people to write for MSS. or have you your number pretty well made up.

And watch proof reading and typography - there is nothing to spoil a persons appreciation of good stuff like typographical errors. Its like sour $\left\{\begin{array}{l}\text{notes}\\\text{chords}\end{array}\right\}$ in a piano concerto.

Well I must get this off. This address will reach us for a couple of months at least and mail to the Paris address will always be forwarded.

Hadley sends her love to you both. We all hope Ernest is feeling well and that you like the Basque country.

Best wishes always,
yours
Ernest Hemingway.

UVA

1. The tubercular Walsh was wintering at Cambo, France, near the Spanish border, with his companion, Ethel Moorhead, a painter. 2. The *Double Dealer* of New Orleans had published EH's fable "A Divine Gesture" and his poem "Ultimately" in May and June 1922.

To SYLVIA BEACH, Schruns, *c.* 15 January 1925

Dear Sylvia:

How are you and how is Adrienne [Monnier] and how is Paris?

We miss you all three. Hadley and Bumby are in great shape and Bumby is running with the kids here and plays tag and is beginning to talk Montafoner.[1]

I've been away on some trips and we've taken some fine overnight skiing tours in the high mountains. You have to climb to get to the snow. Hadley and I ski-ied over the Flexenpasse to Lech in the Arlberg. Bumby has a beautiful nurse [Mathilde Braun] that costs not very much in kronen even.

Haven't seen anything from France except L'auto—wasn't it wonderful about Johnny Dundee? He didn't want to fight for the amount of the Dial prize.

We have read all the books and if you like I'll mail them to Paris or mail any ones you want. Or bring them all later?

What is the dirt in the literary world? Is the Little Review out yet?

Bumby will be able to handle your German trade when we get back.

Mc Almon's Book Village[2] came and is damn good. If anyone asks for it tell them it's recommended by E. M. Hemingway, the famous Austrian skiing authority.

I have gotten such a wonderful beard that every time I get near a frontier am arrested. It looks like a cross between Jo Davidson[3] and Christ. Will curry comb it out and bring it up to Paris sometime in the Spring. They want me to play The Man Moses in the Oberammergau players.

Have done a lot of work besides travelling. Hadley's practiced hard on a good piano.

Am anxiously waiting to hear about Danny Frush and Mascart.[4] That should be worth seeing. Frush hits pretty hard for Mascart but Frush can't take punishment.

I hope Joyce is well and that Adrienne is feeling fine now.

Please write us a letter. We miss you a lot. Hadley sends her love. She says wait till you see Bumby. He sails his boat in the bathtub. He ate the sailor long ago.

Always yours,

PUL   Hemingway.

---

1. Schruns lies in the Montafon Valley of the Vorarlberg, Austria. 2. Robert Mc Almon, *Village* (1924). 3. Jo Davidson (1883–1952), American sculptor. 4. Danny Frush and Edouard Mascart were featherweight boxers.

To GERTRUDE STEIN AND ALICE B. TOKLAS,
Schruns, 20 January 1925

Dear friends:

Goddy came through with a couple of apparently wisdom teeth yesterday or rather they came through Goddy. Maybe wisdom teeth is exaggerating. Call them big molars.

We are all well and Goddy can walk, turn while walking, talk Montafoner, sits beautifully on the pot, never wets any more, is all cleared up, has a beautiful nurse named Mathilda, goes out in a sled, eats cabbage, cries for beer, and is getting very Mittel Europa.

Did you see the Jan. Querschnitt with Juan Gris's famous discourse and lots of Gris reproductions? I got it sent me today. It looks more respectable but still lively. Beautifully gotten up. What have you heard from [Hans von] Wedderkop?

Ernest Walsh wrote me sending the enclosed prospectus—saying he And Miss Moorhead had decided to start a quarterly etc. and I wrote him to write to you. Walsh in the role of an aid to the artist shows how you cant count on things remaining static.

How is Paris and is there any news? Don Stewart sent me Doran's letter saying they had held the book [In Our Time] so long on acct. of everybody in the office reading it 4 times etc. And Mr. Doran did not want to give the public a (with an initial) series of shocks in short stories altho he would be glad to do so in a novel and if I would write a novel they could publish this book as a second book, etc. All of which shows that publishing is a business and books of short stories are believed not to be saleable. Don was next trying Knopf and then Liveright. He seemed cheerful and is coming over in March or April.

We took a 3 day skiing trip over the Mts in the Arlberg getting back yesterday. Bumby produced more teeth while we were away. Mathilda is a wonderful nurse and likes to get up at 5 A.M. She and Goddy have lots of tastes in common.

On skis Dossie Johnston[1] makes up in endurance what she lacks in co-ordination. But she falls more than if it was the other way.

As usual in the country I have an awful time writing. If you run onto any good reading and want to send it down it would be very welcome. I dont get much kick out of the Vorarlberger Tageblatt.

Belmonte is bull fighting again in Peru. Gallo is reported in jail in Caracas in Venezuela for debt. This comes direct from Spain. Harold Stearns is reported in Houston, Texas in much the same situation.

I have grown a fine Jo Davidson beard to break my falls with. Goddy is the king of Schruns in his wooly suit. We are having a good time and saving money. Hadley sends her love as do Goddy and I.

Always yours,
Hemingway

YUL

1. Miss Johnston had been in Schruns since December 1924 with two women friends. She was the daughter of the librarian of the American Library in Paris.

To GEORGE HORACE LORIMER,[1] Schruns, 21 January 1925

Sir:

I have never read a real bull fight story, one written without bunk, from the inside by some one who really knew bull fighting. So I have tried to write this one[2] to show it the way it actually is, as Charles E. Van Loan[3] used to write fight stories.

In Madrid I lived in a bull fighter's boarding house and followed the bull fights all over Spain travelling with a cuadrilla of bull fighters. I'm going back again next summer.

The story may seem technical but all the technicalities, while not obviously explained, are made clear.

I hope very much you will like it.

Very Sincerely,
Ernest Hemingway.

KNOX

1. Lorimer was editor of the *Saturday Evening Post.* 2. "The Undefeated," published in German in *Der Querschnitt* 5 (Summer 1925 and July 1925), in English in *This Quarter* 1 (Autumn–Winter 1925–1926), and in French in *La Navire d'Argent* (March 1926). 3. Charles Emmett Van Loan (1876–1919) wrote novels and short fiction.

This letter is used courtesy of the Seymour Library, Knox College.

To HOWELL JENKINS, Schruns, 2 February 1925

Dear Carpative:

I'm sorry as hell not to have written before but have been all over the Country and had your letter with me. But you know how a man gets once he starts intending to write. Don Skeene is a good fellow. I saw him out at the White Sox Giants Game[1] and he spoke about you. He's a comer and making good in the newspaper game over here. He writes a good funny line too on Sports.

Not long after I heard from you I had a letter from Bill Smith asking if I'd accept an apology from him on all the old Kenley stuff, saying I was right and telling me about the dope on the last couple of years. I wrote back and told him hell yes and then he wrote and told me about some of the hell he's been through. By god he had a hell of a time. He took more punishment than Tommy Gibbons gave to Kid Norfolk. I can see how he got off the way he did on the last elections because he wasn't thinking of Lafollette as we know him but of Wheeler and the farmers. He's had the experience of 60¢ a bu. potatoes while they're hitting 2 bucks and over in the city and apples you cant give away. No, old Bill's had the toughest breaks on family, health, jack and everything else of anybody I ever heard and I dont hold anything against him and want to see him get going. After all he's a hell of a good guy.

When we guys get a little dough we get conservative in politics because we want to protect our jack and quite right. We'd be horses asses if we didn't. But when a male's had the luck Bill's had to take for years it's a wonder he isnt a Bolo.

I hope I'll be in Paris when the Bishop boys are there and would sure consider it a privelege to show them around. From here I go to Italy on business probably about the first of March and then work back North. I'll try like hell to make it. If I miss them maybe I'll see them on their way back. Hadley will get the cook at work a couple of days in advance to turn out something representable as a meal and I'll make sure that they dont overlook anything in the town. There ought to be good fights and in the Spring there are always people in town.

We're sure looking forward to seeing you, Carper. The paternal wrote he'd seen you in the hospital. Glad you've got them out. Piles never helped a man. Dad said he was sending us a swell enlargement of Bumby from you. So far it hasnt come but we're both crazy to see it. I suppose he hung onto it for a while to get it copied. Now we've sent them a big picture of him for Xmas it will probably roll in.

Have had some swell ski ing today. Feel tired. Wish for some good old Scotch. Wish you were here and we could uncork a bottle. You'd have to bring it tho from Paris. No good hootch in Mittel Europa. But great beer - 38 different kinds—Swell Beer from here to Budapest then it gets Bum again until you hit Constantinople. The Boche were there so long that they instituted real German Suds factories—the real Bavarian brand. From here we can ski into Bavaria and back without a visa. I'm going up to Munich to do some work.

Give my very best to good old Soiled Richard. How's everything Dick? Hash sends her best too. I've been working pretty hard lately.

Down about 10 lbs. but am in swell shape. Been the warmest winter they've ever had in Europe while you men have been rating blizzards.

From here I'm going to ski over into Italy - send my baggage on by train and ski down through the Dolomites. Got to see some guys in Milan and Rapallo. By gad Mussolini is running a disgraceful business. Lead pipe government and everybody that squeals gets bumped off. As you wrote the Wops are the tough ones.

Write me another good long letter. It sure is good to hear from you. Bumby has 13 teeth now and plays tag with the kids here, he's got a beautiful Austrian nurse and learns to talk the local German. Then he goes back to France to talk French.

Gee it will be swell to see you. We plan to head for Spain about the 1st of July.

Mascart is the best featherweight in France now. He KO'ed Danny Frush in 2 rounds the other night. If he comes to the states get a bet on him. Not much. It wouldnt be any cinch against boys like Kid Kaplan and Mike Dundee but the little Blonde Bastard is built like a brick slaughter house and hits like a middle weight. He can take any amount of beating and now has learned to box. He's liable to K.O. anybody.

The French may send Lucien Vinez over for the Light weight tourney. There's one to watch. He never Ko's anybody but he has won 734 fights!!! My God what a boxer. Nobody's ever laid a glove on him. He's about Tommy Gibbon's age but still got everything. First he closes one eye of his opponent, then the other eye, very methodical, then busts his nose and then socks him around methodically till the final gong rings. He's like Packey Mc Farland in the old days. All they ever hit is his elbows. He beat Bretonnell and Fritsch (who did well in the States) by about 9,000 punches to 1—If they want to slug he stands still and slugs but nothing ever hits him except his elbows and gloves. He looks easy to hit but try and do it.

This Paolino they talk about is just a big ham that can hit. Just a woodchopper.

Well I've got to get this off. So Long Old Carper, Hash sends her love as do I,

As Ever,
Steen

PH. PUL

1. The New York Giants and Chicago White Sox played exhibition baseball games in England and France in October and November 1924.

To HAROLD LOEB, Schruns, 27 February 1925

Dear Harold:

Hurray for you and the news and Horace Liveright[1] and the whole business. We were up at the Madlener Haus—Alpine Club hut—1987 meters when the two cables came up. One from you and one from Don [Stewart]. I couldn't realize it at first and then couldn't believe it and when I did I got very excited and couldnt sleep. We'd just done a hell of a glacier trip—climb on skis to 3200 meters and such a blizzard my genital organ to wit penis, pecker, cock or tool froze or damn near froze and had to be rubbed with snow. Jesus it was cold. Then ran 5 miles down the face of the glacier in under 12 minutes. Wonderful country. The Silvretta. We went right over the whole chain to Switzerland. Yesterday came 21 kilometers down on skis and then walked 19 kilometers down the valley from Parthenen to Schruns.

Gee I've wished you were on the trips with us. We've flushed ptarmigan, seen lots of fox tracks, big snow hares—saw one fox. 2 marten. But I guess it was better for me you were in N.Y.

What is all the dope on it? Will it be fall publication along with yours? What will I have to cut? How much dough will I get.

It will certainly come handy. The people who sublet our apartment and agreed to stay 3 mos. found an unfurnished one and skipped out in the middle of a month and the son of a bitch in St. Louis paid 2500 on account and the bank statement received today for Feb. 3 shows the check returned 3 times for insufficient funds.[2] So we're worse than broke.

Have to go right back to Paris. I wrote [Leon] Fleischmann to send me the MS. on Jan 10th and have never heard from him.

Thank God for Loeb and Stewart.

I'm sending this to the Princeton Club.

I'm sorry it's not a better letter. God knows I feel wonderful about the book even though simultaneously kicked in the balls.

Hadley sends her love—

Always yours,

Ernest

Hadley had a swell letter from Kitty [Cannell]. All the dirt nourished our under-manured existence.

PUL

1. Since Albert Boni's retirement in 1918, Horace Liveright (1886–1933) had headed Boni and Liveright and had led the fight against Justice John Ford's "Clean Books Bill" in 1924. 2. George Breaker, husband of Hadley's friend Helen, had badly mismanaged Hadley's investments.

To ERNEST WALSH, Schruns, 9 March 1925

Dear Ernest:

Yours of March 5th in this morning but preceded by that damned fine telegram from you and Miss Moorehead. It made us feel great. The Editors of This Quarter are a couple of white men.

Should think you ought to pay [Bertram] Hartman 50–60 francs apiece for the reproductions. Fifty francs would be ample. Sixty generous, may be too much.

As soon as I get this letter off I will write something about Ezra. I wish I was in Paris where I could quote from his stuff, it cant be anything but a personal appreciation from here.

Had a cable from Liveright himself saying he wanted to publish the book in the fall. I accepted by cable. Book is called In Our Time like the little one.[1] 20 short stories, 15 of them, with a chapter of In Our Time between each story. That's what I originally wrote them for. It all hooks up. Think you'd like it.

The Big Two Hearted River is the last story in the book. If you mention it just call it short stories.

The drinks are on me to such an extent that I hope both the Editors of This Quarter and Hadley and the Authors will be able to permanently injure their and our healths thereby when the actual uncorkage takes place.

If you ever wrote a worse sentence than that the 2nd round of drinks are on you. But I know you didnt. So that gives me the 2nd round too. A bottle of Chateauneuf du Pape 1911 let us say to commence. Followed with a Hospice du Beaune 1918 and 1918 was one of the best years since 1896. But why get technical. There wasnt ever any bad Hospice du Beaune.

And look - We'll have a chance to buy them too if we can hook up properly because we'll be in Bayonne the latter part of June on our way to St. Jean Pied du Port and the pass of Roncevalles into Spain and why not open the 1st bottle of the 1st series in Bayonne and the 1st of the 2nd series in St. Jean Pied du Port? If you feel like tooling him down that far.

I'd better get to work on Ezra[2] and close off this letter. Love to the editors from the family

> and good luck yourself.
> Yours
> Ernest.

Just finished the thing on Ezra and Hadley copied it. Hope you like it. Slammed away all day so you'd get it in time. You put on your own title.

UVA

1. *in our time*, published by Three Mountains Press (Paris, 1924). 2. "Homage to Ezra," *This Quarter* 1 (May 1925): 221–25. Omitted here are two further letters in the sequence to Walsh: that of 18 March, detailing EH's struggles with Herbert Clarke, printer in the rue St. Honoré, and that of 27 March, in which EH sent Walsh "The Undefeated," saying that he had worked on it during September, October, and November 1924.

To DR. C. E. HEMINGWAY, Paris, 20 March 1925

Dear Dad:

Thanks for your fine letter enclosing the K.C. Star review. I'm so glad you liked the Doctor story.[1] I put in Dick Boulton and Billy Tabeshaw as real people with their real names because it was pretty sure they would never read the Transatlantic Review. I've written a number of stories about the Michigan country—the country is always true—what happens in the stories is fiction.

This Quarter—a new quarterly review is publishing a long fishing story of mine in 2 parts called Big Two Hearted River.[2] It should be out the first of April. I'll try and get it for you. The river in it is really the Fox above Seney [Michigan]. It is a story I think you will like.

The reason I have not sent you any of my work is because you or Mother sent back the [Paris] In Our Time books. That looked as though you did not want to see any.

You see I'm trying in all my stories to get the feeling of the actual life across—not to just depict life—or criticize it—but to actually make it alive. So that when you have read something by me you actually experience the thing. You can't do this without putting in the bad and the ugly as well as what is beautiful. Because if it is all beautiful you can't believe in it. Things aren't that way. It is only by showing both sides—3 dimensions and if possible 4 that you can write the way I want to.

So when you see anything of mine that you don't like remember that I'm sincere in doing it and that I'm working toward something. If I write an ugly story that might be hateful to you or to Mother the next one might be one that you would like exceedingly.

I appreciate your sending the sporting magazines and the Book Reviews ever so much and though I loan them all to other marooned Sportsmen I see they all come back to the magazine file.

We are hoping to get some good fishing in Spain this summer. It looked for a while as though we would not be able to make it but the $200 advance royalties I am getting from Boni and Liveright will make it possible. I hope that book will sell! My others are all out of print. Someone stole my copy of [the Paris] In Our Time and when I went to the publishers to get another found every copy had been sold some months ago.

There are negociations going on for my book to be published in Germany at the same time as in U.S.A. Many things have been published there already.[3]

Did you never get the big photograph of John [Bumby] Hadley sent you registered just before Xmas?

I'm very glad Mother is painting. I would be awfully interested to see them. If she has any of them photographed I wish she would send me some of the reproductions.

Hope you have had a good winter. It is regular April weather here.

With love and good luck,

JFK   Ernie

1. "The Doctor and the Doctor's Wife," *Transatlantic Review* 2 (December 1924): 497–501. 2. In *This Quarter* 1 (May 1925): 110–28. 3. In *Der Querschnitt*. See Check List, *Hemingway: The Writer as Artist*, 4th ed., Princeton University Press, 1972.

To HORACE LIVERIGHT,[1] Paris, 31 March 1925

Dear Mr. Liveright:

Enclosed is the signed contract and a new story to replace the one you are eliminating as censorable.

As the contract only mentions excisions it is understood of course that no alterations of words shall be made without my approval. This protects you as much as it does me as the stories are written so tight and so hard that the alteration of a word can throw an entire story out of key. I am sure you and Mr. T. R. Smith [Liveright editor] understand this.

There is nothing in the book that has not a definite place in its organization and if I at any time seem to repeat myself I have a good reason for doing so.

As for obscenities you and Mr. Smith being on the spot know what is and what is not unpublishably obscene much better than I do. I understand that it is no longer necessary to eliminate the fine old word son of a bitch. This is indeed good news.

As for the book selling or not selling, I don't look on it in any way as a lost cause. I think, looking at it quite dispassionately, that it has a good gambling chance to sell.

The classic example of a really fine book that could not sell was E. E. Cumming's Enormous Room. But Cumming's book was written in a style that no one who had not read a good deal of "modern" writing could read. That was hard luck for selling purposes. My book will be praised by highbrows and can be read by lowbrows. There is no writing in it that anybody with a high-school education cannot read.

That is why I say it has a good 3/1 chance. And I never bet on Jeffries at Reno nor Carpentier nor other sentimental causes.

If cuts are made outside of possible necessary elimination of obscenities, if there are any, it will be shot to pieces as an organism and nobody will praise it and nobody want to read it. The reason I mention this is that there was a report over here that certain things were to be eliminated because they did not seem to have anything to do with the story. Probably it was without foundation.

The new story makes the book a good deal better. It's about the best I've ever written and gives additional unity to the book as a whole.

You are eliminating the second story—Up In Michigan. The next three stories move up one place each and this new story—The Battler—takes the place at present occupied by—The Three Day Blow.

I do not need to tell you how pleased I am to be published by Boni and Liveright and I hope I *will* become a property. That's up to both of us.

I would like to have the proofs as soon as possible.

With best regards,
Sincerely
Ernest Hemingway

Enclosures   Signed Agreement
New Index showing place of new story
Story entitled
The Battler
~~The Great Little Fighting Machine~~

LHC

1. This is the first of EH's surviving letters to Liveright. Others were sent on 11, 15, and 22 May; 21 June; and 7 December 1925; and 19 January 1926. All but one of these is in the Louis Henry Cohn Collection, with typescript copies at the

University of Virginia. Omitted here are EH to Leon Fleischman, 2 and 5 March 1925. On 2 March EH reports cables from Loeb and Stewart, on 22 and 23 February, saying that *In Our Time* had been accepted; on 5 March he reports a cable of that morning from Liveright offering publication with an advance of $200. EH accepted by cable the same day. The letters to Fleischman appear in facsimile in *In Their Time: 1920–1940* (Bloomfield Hills, Mich., 1977), p. 38.

To MAXWELL PERKINS, Paris, 15 April 1925[1]

Dear Mr. Perkins:

On returning from Austria I received your letter of February 26 inclosing a copy of a previous letter which unfortunately never reached me. About ten days before your letter came I had a cabled offer from Boni and Liveright to bring out a book of my short stories in the fall. They asked me to reply by cable and I accepted.

I was very excited at getting your letter but did not see what I could do until I had seen the contract from Boni and Liveright. According to its terms they are to have an option on my next three books, they agreeing that unless they exercise this option to publish the second book within 60 days of the receipt of the manuscript their option shall lapse, and if they do not publish the second book they relinquish their option on the third book.

So that is how matters stand. I cannot tell you how pleased I was by your letter and you must know how gladly I would have sent Charles Scribner's Sons the manuscript of the book that is to come out this fall. It makes it seem almost worthwhile to get into Who's Who in order to have a known address.

I do want you to know how much I appreciated your letter and if I am ever in a position to send you anything to consider I shall certainly do so.

I hope some day to have a sort of Doughty's Arabia Deserta of the Bull Ring, a very big book with some wonderful pictures.[2] But one has to save all winter to be able to bum in Spain in the summer and writing classics, I've always heard, takes some time. Somehow I don't care about writing a novel and I like to write short stories and I like to work at the bull fight book so I guess I'm a bad prospect for a publisher anyway. Somehow the novel seems to me to be an awfully artificial and worked out form but as some of the short stories now are stretching out to 8,000 to 12,000 words maybe Ill get there yet.

The [Paris] In Our Time is out of print and I've been trying to buy one to have myself now I hear it is valuable; so that probably explains your difficulty in getting it. I'm awfully glad you liked it and thank you again for writing me about a book.

Very Sincerely,

PUL   Ernest Hemingway

1. This is EH's first letter to Maxwell Perkins (1884–1947), who was to become his editor at Charles Scribner's Sons from 1926 onward. See A. Scott Berg, *Max Perkins: Editor of Genius* (New York, 1978). 2. An early version of the idea that became *Death in the Afternoon* (New York, 1932).

To JOHN DOS PASSOS,[1] Paris, 22 April 1925

Dear Dos:

Got a letter from Don [Stewart] giving your address. I'd lost it so I couldnt write. Jesus I wish you were over here so we could get drunk like I am now and have been so often lately. I never knew it was you trying to get the book [*In Our Time*] over and did. You're a good guy, Dos, and I wish to hell you were here. Christ knows I appreciate you and Sherwood [Anderson] jamming it through. I sent back the signed agreement to Liveright on the 1st of April about and they were to send me the $200. but it hasnt come yet. Nor any word from them.

A Mrs. George Kauffman is here and she claims they want to cut it all cut the Indian Camp story. Cut the In Our Time chapters. Jesus I feel all shot to hell about it. Of course they cant do it because the stuff is so tight and hard and every thing hangs on every thing else and it would all just be shot up shit creek.

There is nothing to bother anybody. Not a dam thing.

They made me take out the Up in Michigan story because the girl got yenced and I sent 'em a swell new Nick story about a busted down pug and a coon called The Battler—the next three stories after the Up in Michigan to be moved up one and this to be story no⑤ Its to go like this—Chap (1) Indian Camp. Chap. II The Dr. and the Dr's Wife Chap. III The End of Something Chap IV The Three Day Blow Chap. V The Battler Chap. VI A Very Short Story Chap VII Soldier's Home etc.

This Battler story is a hell of a swell story and better than Up in Mich altho I always liked Up in Mich altho some did not. I suppose if it was called Way Out in Iowa, [H. L.] Mencken would have published it if the fucking would have been changed to a community corn roast.

Oh well. Anyway I've been working like a son of a bitch every morning at 7 A M with gastric remorse and drinking all night and I got a 8 to

12,000 word bull fight story that makes a bum out of everything I ever did and going good on another one and will no doubt finish it if I can drink enough so as to get enough remorse.

It's good summer weather now and I work early so as to be out all day.

Der Querschnitt have translated the bull fight story into German and Picasso is illustrating it for them. The 'Schnitt also publishing a book of my dirty poems to be illustrated by Pascin.[2] Have you got any dirty poems you'd like me to sign. Jeeze I wish you were here to write a few good prurient poems with me because that is now my only source of income. Hadley is showing talent. I think the book ought to be by Mr. and Mrs. C. U. and A. M. Hemingway. Got 650 f. for 2 poems. Got 80 f apiece for 2 4-line poems. Why enter the Nation's poetry contest.

Got an order from the 'Schnitt for something every month and they are making big money now and I got a commission to write a book on bull fighting with Flechtheim—Flechtheim is swell Spanish Jew 25 years an aficionado—knows Dombeta, Vicente Pastor, etc.—for a series theyre getting out.[3] Illustrations by Picasso, Gris, and others and photographs. Theyve already done boxing, and horses.

So that will all help. Thank God for the Junkers. Am thinking of stumping the country for Hindenburg. May[be] if they get the monarchy back I got a good chance to be poet laureate. Understand that's what Eliot's working for in England. Mr. Bridges and Mr. Eliot I want you to meet Mr. Dos Passos and Mr. Hemingway. Mr. Stewart, Gentlemen. Glad to meet you Mr. Stewart. Us laureates have got to stick together. Don wrote he drank you dead. Somebody has got to put that cheap lecturer in his place. He's claiming to be a drinker now. Remember how he vomited all over Pamplona? Drinker? Shit.

Wish you were here to drink. There's a girl named Hadley that's showing a lot of promise as a drinker and she wants to meet you.

Are you coming over? How's the book. Gee I hope Don makes money with the movies and The Crazy Fool.[4] He seemed very bitter about Pity and Irony. What's all this about Pity and Irony. Never heard of them.

Write here. Love from Hadley

Yrs.

Hem

Don't let them cut it. Tell Liveright not to be a damned fool.

UVA

1. EH and Dos Passos (1896–1970) had first met in Italy in 1918 and renewed their friendship in Paris in 1922. 2. "Stierkampf" appeared in *Der Querschnitt* 5 (Summer 1925 and July 1925). 3. On Alfred Flechtheim, founder of *Der Querschnitt*, Berlin, 1920, see Nicholas Joost, *Ernest Hemingway and the Little Magazines* (Barre,

Mass., 1968), pp. 131–32. **4.** Donald Ogden Stewart, *The Crazy Fool* (1925). See the Irony and Pity passage in *The Sun Also Rises*, chapter 12.

This and all subsequent letters to Dos Passos are used courtesy of Elizabeth Dos Passos and the Dos Passos Collection, Manuscripts Department, University of Virginia Library.

To HORACE LIVERIGHT, Paris, 11 May 1925

Dear Mr. Liveright:

On March 31st I mailed you a registered letter enclosing the signed agreement you had mailed me and a new story to replace the story you were eliminating from my book—In Our Time—as censorable. On receipt of this ~~letter~~ agreement you agreed to send me a check for $200.00 as advance on royalties.

I have received no acknowledgement of your receipt of this letter and have not received the check altho you must have received the letter before the 14th of April and I have received New York mail posted May 2.

In the agreement you sent me no mention was made of rights for translation into foreign languages. Mr. Leon Fleischman, your representative here, and Mr. Harold Loeb, who had recently signed a contract with you, assured me there was no need to mention those rights as they all remained my property.

I would like to have a note from you confirming this and stating that all rights of translation into foreign languages of my books are to remain my property in entirety and that I reserve the right to ~~dispose~~ negotiate for them and dispose of them as I see fit. I am sure you will have no objection to doing this. If you send me this in duplicate I will see that one copy is signed and returned to you for your files.

With best regards,
Very sincerely,
Ernest Hemingway

LHC

To HORACE LIVERIGHT, Paris, 15 May 1925

Dear Mr. Liveright:

Thanks so much for your letter of May 1st and for the check. I was worried when I heard nothing from you and wrote the note you doubtless received a few days ago.

It was seeing son-of-a-bitch in the proofs of Harold Loeb's book [*Doodab*] that prompted my original remark about it. Since then I have noticed it in Scott Fitzgerald's last book [*The Great Gatsby*] and imagine it was getting so people did not mind seeing it in print.

I'm awfully glad you like the new story ["The Battler"] and I'm anxious to see the galley proofs. There is no use talking about changes till I see what they are. I don't want it suppressed any more than you do.

I have great admiration and confidence in you as a property builder. That goes without saying but it is nice, every once in a while, to say a few of the things that go without saying. Sherwood Anderson writes me he has gone over to you and I'm very happy about it. He deserves it.

We are going off to Spain the latter part of next month and I would like very much to get the first proof fixed up before then. Stamp collectors in the government service are always liable to steal your letters there. I remember one time finding where the post office had opened up some magazines and cut a lot of the pictures out and pasted them on the walls over the telegraph ticker.

You'll have to go down there with us some time. [Robert] Benchley and Don Stewart and a good gang are going down this year. After I get to be a property I'll take you on a grand tour of Spain to keep down my income tax.

Thanks again for the letter and check.

Yours always,
Ernest Hemingway

PH. PUL

To HORACE LIVERIGHT, Paris, 22 May 1925

Dear Mr. Liveright:

I am mailing the galley proofs back today marked for the Mauretania sailing tomorrow so with this letter they ought to reach you in a few days.

The type the stories are set in is splendid and I am delighted with the way they look and with the few sheets of page proof. I have already written Mr. [Manuel] Komroff about the too black caps in the italics the chapters are set in. They give an entirely false emphasis and jerk that is not intended every time the upper case is used.

As you will see I have revised the Mr. and Mrs. Elliot story and entirely eliminated the obscene image. As the whole story hung again and again on the repetition of the words "they tried very hard to have a baby," I have inserted some stuff about the boat and Paris to pick up the old rhythm and keep it funny. It has to have the repetitions to hold it together.

It is a shame it had to be changed but as you say it would be a very silly play to get an entire first book suppressed for the sake of a few funny cracks in one story. Now that you have cut it and I have smoothed it over again will you make quite sure from various opinions that it is not suppressable? For it would be an even worse business to be suppressed for a story after it has had the dynamite cut out.

Jane Heap ran it in its original form and did not get into any trouble. It is just as funny now, to anyone that did not read the original, and not dangerous. But remember that now that I have agreed to your cuts and made them even milder it's up to you. To me it is not a serious story and I was glad to change it for you.

Whoever did the editing on the whole book was very intelligent and most of the changes of punctuation I agree with. Those I don't I have changed to their original form. My attitude toward punctuation is that it ought to be as conventional as *possible*. The game of golf would lose a good deal if croquet mallets and billiard cues were allowed on the putting green. You ought to be able to show that you can do it a good deal better than anyone else with the regular tools before you have a license to bring in your own improvements. But don't let this inspire whoever went over it for punctuation to any further action because it is all right now. It looks very good.

Reading it over it is even a better book than I remember. That isn't egotistical because every time I read a story after a long time I wonder how the hell did I ever write such a swell story?

I will be anxious to get the page proofs as soon as possible.

With best regards,
Very sincerely,
Ernest Hemingway.

LHC

To SHERWOOD ANDERSON, Paris, 23 May 1925

Dear Sherwood:

I'm sorry not to have written for so long and I certainly do appreciate your having put my book over with Liveright. Dos Passos wrote that you did before I got your letter sent over from Gertrude Stein's.

Sure, probably I was wrong about the Many Marriages.[1] I will read it again some time when I can give it a better break. Reading anything as a serial is awfully hard on it. All criticism is shit anyway. Nobody knows anything about it except yourself. God knows people who are paid to have attitudes toward things, professional critics, make me sick; camp following eunochs of literature. They won't even whore. They're all virtuous and sterile. And how well meaning and high minded. But they're all camp followers.

Ever since we saw you last I've been working like hell at writing and have had a wonderful time. Wait till you and Elizabeth[2] come over and we'll go down to Spain and see bull fights. I get something out of bulls and the men that fight them, I don't know what. Anyhow I've got it all, or a big part of it, into the next book. I'd like to have enough money so I could raise bulls. But I won't ever have. Have to work like hell to have enough money to go down and follow them around in the summer.

I'm terribly glad about you going over to Liveright and I can't write letters and so I can't tell you how grateful I am for your getting my stuff published. It means such a hell of a lot and you have to get it published so you get it back of you and it means a lot other ways.

Hadley is well and we are fond of each other as ever and get along well and have a fine kid that starts to talk now and walks with me to the cafe.

This Making of Americans book of Gertrude Stein's is a wonderful one. Did you see the part of it that was in the Transatlantic Review? Mc Almon is publishing it.[3]

Best to you always and we both want to meet Elizabeth,

Yours

NEWBERRY   Ernest Hemingway.

1. Anderson's novel of 1923. **2.** Elizabeth Prall, Anderson's third wife, whom he married in 1924. **3.** See Donald C. Gallup, "The Making of *The Making of Americans*," in *The New Colophon* (New York, 1950), pp. 54–74.

To MAXWELL PERKINS, Paris, 9 June 1925

Dear Mr. Perkins:

I can't tell you how much I appreciated your sending me the copy of [the Paris] In Our Time. It was one of those very pleasant things that sometimes happen to one and which give a good feeling whenever they are remembered. Thank you ever so much.

Now I have finally gotten hold of another copy and am mailing it to you with this letter. Scott Fitzgerald is living here now and we see quite a lot of him. We had a great trip together driving his car up from Lyon through the Cote D'Or.[1] I've read his Great Gatsby [1925] and think it is an absolutely first rate book. I hope it is going well.

Thanks again for sending me the little book and with very best regards,

Yours sincerely,

PUL   Ernest Hemingway

1. See A Moveable Feast (New York, 1964), pp. 154–76.

To HORACE LIVERIGHT, Paris, 21 June 1925

Dear Mr. Liveright:

I quite agree with you on the anthology question. In the first place I refused permission for two stories and told [Ivan] Beede, who is handling the thing for Ford, that he would have to deal entirely with you.

One story would not hurt my book and might help it. Especially as the story is only 5 pages long. Beede came to me with your letter and said he would write you for permission to use The Doctor and the Doctor's Wife.

Do as you think best about the fee. I dont want to antagonize Ford as he is liable to give me a good 25 dollars worth of review—and has already. You may waive my end of the fee.

We are leaving next week for Spain. Don Stewart is here now and we are meeting Benchley down there. Being a simple country boy from Chicago I dont know anything of the technique of grabbing off authors. So far I've only gotten to the stage of grabbing off a publisher. Next I have to grab off some money so I can dress the part. Then we could have photographs taken—Hemingway—Before and After Being grabbed off By Horace Liveright.—Then with a sample case fitted up with these and similar exhibits I ought to be able to grab off authors as fast as I can get them tight.

Naturally I don't care anything about being published in any anthology. All I want is to have stuff published as I write it and be paid for it. Anthologising out of a magazine like the T.R. is simply giving it to them twice and there is no pleasure for me in the duplication especially by something that calls its-self The Dial Press. But I dont want a row with Ford just now. He dislikes me enough as it is and it is only by a stern effort that he can like my work. I dont want him to stop making that effort.

Yours faithfully

LHC   Ernest Hemingway

To HAROLD LOEB, Paris, 21 June 1925

Dear Harold:

My son of a bitching editor[1] has double Xed me and is arriving to-morrow—i.e. Monday June 22nd—so we cant get off till Wednesday morning or Thursday night.

I'll wire you. Pat and Duff[2] are coming too. Pat has sent off to Scotland for rods and Duff to England for funds. As far as I know Duff is not bringing any fairies with her. You might arrange to have a band of local fairies meet her at the train carrying a daisy chain so that the transition from the Quarter will not be too sudden.

I have been having a swell time with Don Stewart here and feel like a million seeds. Don will be at Pamplona and so will Bob Benchley. Pamplona's going to be damned good. I feel like hell at every day that is lopped off our fishing—but we will get a good week anyway. Hadley and I have been very tight and having a swell time. I havent felt as good since we came back from Austria. See you soon. Hadley sends her love.

Yours,
Ernest.

We'll get your line.

We'll write a note to Pauline [Pfeiffer] about your mail. Is there any-thing else we can do.

Go see Krebs Friend about fishing.

The 1st 15 page installment of my bullfight story are in this mos. Querschnitt.

Yrs.
E.

Bob Mc Almon writes about going to the theater with Kitty [Cannell] in London. I've already written and sent the money for the Pamplona tickets. Paul Fisher may be coming. There is a swell program. No other news I think. I've been having a hell of a swell time and feel like working. Christ I wish this bloody editor wasnt coming. I've had hell getting them rooms during the Grand Semaine.

PUL

---

1. Possibly Leon Fleischman of Boni and Liveright. 2. Duff Twysden and Pat Guthrie, who were to appear in *The Sun Also Rises* as Brett Ashley and Mike Campbell. Duff, born Mary Duff Stirling Byrom in Yorkshire, 1893, died in 1938. Sir Roger William Twysden, Tenth Baronet, was born in 1894 and died in 1934.

To ERNEST WALSH, Paris, 25 June 1925

Dear Ernest:

Joyce sent around last night to find out about This Quarter and where he should send his Ms. It will be finished in 10 days. Will you write him and tell him you are expecting it etc.

You can write him care of Shakespeare and Co. if you lack his address. I sent word through Sylvia [Beach] for him to send it to 338 Rue St. Honore.

Yours always,
Ernest.

We're packing and the cat [Feather Puss] is afraid we're going away and it is very early morning in the courtyard.

UVA

To F. SCOTT FITZGERALD,[1] Burguete, Spain, 1 July 1925

Dear Scott:

We are going in to Pamplona tomorrow. Been trout fishing here. How are you? And how is Zelda?

I am feeling better than I've ever felt—havent drunk anything but wine since I left Paris. God it has been wonderful country. But you hate country. All right omit description of country. I wonder what your idea of heaven would be—A beautiful vacuum filled with wealthy monogamists, all powerful and members of the best families all drinking themselves to death. And hell would probably [be] an ugly vacuum full of poor polygamists unable to obtain booze or with chronic stomach disorders that they called secret sorrows.

To me heaven would be a big bull ring with me holding two barrera seats and a trout stream outside that no one else was allowed to fish in and two lovely houses in the town; one where I would have my wife and children and be monogamous and love them truly and well and the other where I would have my nine beautiful mistresses on 9 different floors and one house would be fitted up with special copies of the Dial printed on soft tissue and kept in the toilets on every floor and in the other house we would use the American Mercury and the New Republic. Then there would be a fine church like in Pamplona where I could go and be confessed on the way from one house to the other and I would get on my horse and ride out with my son to my bull ranch named Hacienda Hadley and toss coins to all my illegitimate children that lived [along] the road. I would write out at the Hacienda and send my son in to lock the chastity belts onto my mistresses because someone had just galloped up with the news that a notorious monogamist named Fitzgerald had been seen riding toward the town at the head of a company of strolling drinkers.

Well anyway we're going into town tomorrow early in the morning. Write me at the /Hotel Quintana
Pamplona
Spain
Or dont you like to write letters. I do because it's such a swell way to keep from working and yet feel you've done something.

So long and love to Zelda from us both,

Yours,
Ernest

PUL

1. Fitzgerald (1896–1940) had first met EH at the Dingo Bar in Paris in May 1925. See *A Moveable Feast* (New York, 1964), pp. 149 ff.
This and all subsequent letters to Fitzgerald are used courtesy of the Princeton University Library.

/

To HAROLD LOEB, Pamplona, Spain, 12 July 1925

Dear Harold:

I was terribly tight and nasty to you last night and I dont want you to go away with that nasty insulting lousiness as the last thing of the fiestas.[1] I wish I could wipe out all the mean-ness and I suppose I cant but this is to let you know that I'm thoroly ashamed of the way I acted and the stinking, unjust uncalled for things I said.

So long and good luck to you and I hope we'll see you soon and well.

Yours,
Ernest.

PUL

1. This is EH's note on the morning after his quarrel with Loeb at Pamplona. See Loeb, *The Way It Was* (New York, 1959), pp. 295–97; Carlos Baker, *Ernest Hemingway: A Life Story* (New York, 1969), pp. 150–51; and *The Sun Also Rises* (New York, 1926), chapter 17.

To GERTRUDE STEIN AND ALICE B. TOKLAS,
Madrid, 15 July 1925

Dear Friends:

We have had a fine time and no bad hot weather and seen Belmonte cogida-ed, and he is not so bad, and had a bull dedicated to us and Hadley got the ear given to her and wrapped it up in a handkerchief which, thank God, was Don Stewart's. I tell her she ought to throw it away or cut it up into pieces and send them in letters to her friends in St. Louis but she won't let it go and it is doing very nicely.

Madrid is nice now and we have good rooms and pensions for 10 pesetas a day. They have re-built and re-hung the Prado—probably on Bob Mc Almon's complaint and it is very fine. Hadley is there now and I'm going down when I finish this. Last night we went to a nocturnal and this afternoon is the big Corrida de la Prensa with Frey-Villaeta, Litri and Niño de la Palma. The last two are the great new phenomenons and Niño mano a mano with Belmonte made Belmonte look cheap. He did everything Belmonte did and did it better—kidding him—all the adornos [decorations] and desplantes [poor stances] and all. Then he stepped out all by himself without any tricks—suave, templando [moderate] with the cape, smooth and slow—splendid banderillos and started with 5 Naturales with the muleta—beautiful complete faena all linked up and then killed perfectly.

He comes from Ronda and everybody in Spain is crazy about him—except of course those that can't stand him. But they were lined up all night before his first appearance in Madrid. We've seen him 4 times and will see him 4 more at Valencia. His giving Hadley his cape to hold etc is quite efficacious at keeping her from worrying about Bumby. He is in great shape Marie [Rohrbach] writes and plays with all the kids and talks more all the time.

How is the proof coming and have you been fishing?

We found our best stream which was full of trout last year ruined by logging and running logs down—all the pools cleaned out—trout killed. We go to Valencia on the 21st and will be there till the 2nd of August at *Poste Restante*. Travelling 3rd class it hasn't been expensive and is very funny. Coming down from Pamplona there was a kid whose father raised wine near Tafalla and he was bringing big sample jugs down to Madrid to sell wine and of course everybody was offering drinks to everybody else and he got inspired and opened jug after jug and 3 compartments including 2 priests and 4 Guardia Civil got very tight including unfortunately myself and I either lost or gave away our tickets and became worried or as worried as I could get as we got near Madrid but the Guardia Civil got us through all right with no tickets at all. It was the best party almost I've ever been on. Spaniards are the only people. Hadley and the priests talked Latin. It was very fine.

Love to you from us both
Always yours
Hemingway.

YUL

To DR. C. E. HEMINGWAY, Paris, 20 August 1925

Dear Dad:

Thanks for the Int. Book Reviews, the Forest and Streams and your good letter. Just got back from Spain yesterday. Splendid trip. Have been swimming nearly every day. Been working day and night and done about 60,000 words on a novel [*The Sun Also Rises*]. About 15,000 more to do. Am going to start in again after writing you.

Boni and Liveright have sent the jacket of my book [*In Our Time*] and it looks very good.

We had no luck fishing this summer. The wonderful stream we got so many out of last summer was ruined by logging. Fish killed, pools destroyed, dams broken down. Made me feel sick.

Saw 24 bull fights and was in the ring several times.

It must have been fun on that trip across the straights [Straits of Mackinac]. The motor car takes the wildness out of the country very quickly.

We would like to come over next summer and Hadley and I take a camping trip to one of the small trout rivers on the north shore of Lake Superior. We could get our equipment and go up from Windemere to the Soo and then around. I was thinking of the Steel River.

Both my legs have begun to bother me quite a bit and I imagine by the time I'm 40 or so if I don't keep them pretty well going and in good shape I'll have quite a bit of trouble.

I'm glad mother is painting if she likes it. I haven't seen any of her work at all. It is fine that Leicester is getting to be a good fisherman. I do not know anything that can give a person more enjoyment through life. I have missed the fishing this year very much.

It's a shame I haven't written oftener but I've been working terribly hard on 2 different jobs and moving around Spain all the time. I started a letter to you and one to Mother in Pamplona but never finished them.

We were at Valencia, Madrid, Saragossa and San Sebastian. Well, good luck and love to all the folks. *Best* always to you,

Yours,
Ernie

Love to Ura [Ursula] and tell her I'll write her. We're going to be forced out of here [113 rue Notre Dame des Champs] maybe but I'll let you know if there's any change of address.

JFK

To ERNEST WALSH, Paris, *c.* 15 September 1925

Dear Ernest:

We used to stop at Bellagio on Como for week ends from Milan during the war but I don't remember names of pubs. Always liked Stresa on Lago Maggiore much better and Sermione on Lago di Garda. Suppose you know those two. Pallanza on Lago Maggiore is nice too. Stresa is a lovely place, at least it was. Don't guarantee Italy any more.

Cortina D'Ampezzo is in the swellest country on earth. The people are good and square too. We spent the end of a winter there once at the hotel Bellevue. Liugie Menarde proprietor. It is the loveliest country I've ever known. We are coming down there this winter on a ski-ing trip if everything goes well.

I've finished my novel—have to go over it all this winter and type it out. Gap sounds like a bad place. I want to go on a walking trip and let my head get normal again. It is tired as hell inside and since I finished the book have been doing good deal drinking again. Can drink hells any amount of whiskey without getting drunk because my head is so tired. Also been swimming every day in the Seine. Colder than the Maine coast. Can't go on the walking trip because tore a ligament in my right foot. Hope it will be all right soon. Hate to waste the autumn in town. Hadley can't go because Bumby's just come back. There are no men in town I'd walk across the street with and am afraid to take any of my girls because I hate complications, illegitimate children and alimony. So will probably go by myself but I feel damned lonesome inside and wish to hell there were somebody to go with. Might walk down over the pass to Aosta and see how Italy is. Would like to be in Venice and get a little romantic fucking and Compari's and get a meal and a real bed to sleep in at the best hotel I know in Vicenza [and] walk out to Schio and Recoaro and spend a night in Bassano and go up to Grappa and Monte Pertica and Asalone and climb—how swell it is that there isn't a war on. But you need to have a girl in Italy. Well to hell with it all. I've buried Italy and why dig it up when there's a chance it still stinks.

Write me the news and your address and our very best to Miss Moorehead.

Yours always
Ernest.

use Guaranty Trust
address as they are liable
to swipe mail here.

UVA

To ETHEL MOORHEAD AND ERNEST WALSH,
Paris, 30 November 1925

Dear Miss Moorhead and Ernest:

I am returning the proof by return mail as you asked. Have only made 4 changes in words and have corrected 61 typographical errors such as no h in had, no h in much, no u in you and various words left out.

So don't think I'm just being like Joyce about the proof and wanting to re-write the whole story every time a proof is sent.

There are many places where, reading the story [*The Undefeated*] over now, I have wanted badly to make changes but have made none except for the numbers in the inscription for the stuffed bull. Those numbers were wrong on the manuscript.

I got Ernest's last letter and haven't answered because Hadley has been sick in bed for a week and I have been working like hell at the same time.[1] Will write a long letter soon. We are going to Austria on December 15. Address then will be HOTEL TAUBE, SCHRUNS, VORARLBERG, AUSTRIA.

Naturally am very excited about This Quarter coming out. It ought to be a great number.

Love to you both,
Ernest

UVA

1. EH had been writing *The Torrents of Spring* (New York, 1926), his satire on Sherwood Anderson. EH's inscription in a copy of the book (n.d.) given to Dr. Don Carlos Guffey says he started it on a Friday and finished the following Thursday, which

was Thanksgiving. This establishes the time of composition as 20–26 November, seven days. EH to Isidor Schneider, 29 June 1926 (not here included), says it took six days and denies it took ten. See Matthew J. Bruccoli and C. E. Frazer-Clark, Jr., eds., *Hemingway at Auction* (Bloomfield Hills, Mich., 1973), pp. 41, 116.

To ISABEL SIMMONS GODOLPHIN, Paris, 3 December 1925

Dearest Izz:

Such a swell letter from you. You have a perfect right to blow our heads off. Hadley and I were too broke in Spain to even send a cable to you and Francis on your wedding.[1] Ever since we've been talking about a present and Hadley has had such swell plans about it that you've never gotten a thing. It is a damned shame but honest to god we will repair it.

I'm terribly glad you and Frisco both liked the book. The clipping bureau has sent me about fifty reviews on it and I guess it is going pretty well. Saw one in Nov. 25 New Republic by [Paul] Rosenfeld, very favourable and etc. but enough to turn your stomach to have to read that sort of crap.

Can't keep it properly remembered that you are a married woman and don't know exactly how to address you as such. Glad you are married to a good guy. Speaking of the harem especially difficult subject now that you married. Since you asked about it must reply your place still open and being held open and will be held open and just let me see anybody try and usurp it. We're going to Austria a week from today. Address there HOTEL TAUBE, SCHRUNS, VORARLBERG AUSTRIA. Also for God's sake write. A letter in Schruns is worth four letters anywhere else and a letter from you worth eight letters from anyone else.

Have written a funny book[2] which am shipping to N.Y. day after tomorrow when it comes back from the re-typist. Gee Izz how I wish you were going down there with us. Swell ski-ing. Fine town about the size of Cortina. Dos Passos is going down. Between Dos and Don Stewart and a few other guys it seems more as though it were Hadley that had the harem so I wish you could come over and help me enforce a little discipline in the old seraglio.

What's Hammy's address?

Heard nothing from the family since the book came out. Have this funny one now. Hope you find it so, and a long novel that I'm re-working over and over and want to be darn good.

We're going to Spain in the spring and stay through May, June and July and come over to Jew S.A. in August. Going to stay all winter up in

Michigan. You'll have to come up. Keeping a place on here. Have an idea will be making quite a little dough soon. Feel it in the bones. Also various propositions from pooblishers.

Think the family are praying over what they should say to me about this last book. They'll have a lot to pray over in the funny one. Think they would be easier off just not to read them. What have your family written to you about it if anything? Oak Park re-actions are swell.

Bumby is husky and built like a pocket sized Firpo. Hadley is in good shape now. She had the grippe and was in bed for a week. She's busy as hell now packing and getting things in shape or she would write. Bumby lost all his English when he was down in Brittany with Marie [Rohrbach] while we were in Spain and talks French all the time. Whenever we go out for a walk he says, "Papa! Cherche un auto!" He has a very deep bass voice and calls his nurse Marie cocotte. He makes about five word sentences now and finds Lions under all the beds which he chases and kills with an old screw driver. After he kills one he says, "Papa, voila le petit lint!" Lint pronounced as in lie or lye. Lynt is about his only English word.

Gee I'm glad you liked the book so much. I know Frisco is a splendid bird. Best to him and love from all three of us,

Love,
Ernie

PUL

1. Isabel had married classics professor Francis R. B. Godolphin, nicknamed Frisco, 25 July 1925. 2. *The Torrents of Spring*, published by Scribners (New York, 1926).

To HORACE LIVERIGHT, Paris, 7 December 1925

Dear Mr. Liveright:

I am sending you, with this letter, on the Mauretania tomorrow the Mss. of my new book The Torrents of Spring. Scott Fitzgerald has read the manuscript and was very excited about it and said he was going to write you about it. I don't know whether he did or not.

This is not the long novel which, so far, I am calling THE SUN ALSO RISES and which I am now re-writing and will be working on all this winter.

As you know in the golden age of the English novel Fielding wrote his satirical novels as an answer to the novels of Richardson. In this way Joseph Andrews was written as a parody on Richardson's Pamela. Now they are both classics. For a long time I've heard various critics bewailing the lack of an American satirist. Maybe when you read this book you will think they haven't so much bewailing to do now.

Louis Bromfield read the mss. also and said he thought it was one of the very funniest books he had ever read and a very perfect American satire.

On the practical side I think the book is the right length for a funny book. You do not want it too long. As it is you can make a full sized book of it by handling it as Doran's handled Don Stewart's books. It is some five thousand words longer than [Stewart's] The Parody Outline of History [1921]. A good sized page with lots of margin and room at the bottom with the breaking up into chapters and the separate chapter headings and Author's notes in different type and spacing will give you plenty of length for a good sized book. Bromfield said he thought it was plenty long enough. I wish you would get Ralph Barton to illustrate it.

As you will see, although a satire it has a moving story, action all the time, never departs into the purely fantastic and mental, and is full of stuff. The humor is not Lardner's, Stewart's or Benchley's either. The book stands by itself.

If you take it you've got to push it. I have made no kick about the In Our Time, the lack of advertising, the massing of all those blurbs on the cover, each one of which would have made, used singly, a valuable piece of publicity but which, grouped together as they were, simply put the reader on the defensive; because I know that you believed you could not sell a book of stories and were simply building for the future. But this book you can sell and it must be given a real play. It should come out in the Spring.

The only reason I can conceive that you might not want to publish it would be for fear of offending Sherwood. I do not think that anybody with any stuff can be hurt by satire. In any event it should be to your interest to differentiate between Sherwood and myself in the eyes of the public and you might as well have us both under the same roof and get it coming and going.

If you take the book I want an advance of $500. as that is the smallest guarantee I can have that the book will be pushed at all. I ought to ask for a thousand dollar advance because you have a book there of which, if you get some one like Ralph Barton to illustrate it, and push it as you know how, you can sell 20,000 copies. I would rather wait for royalties and not have you think I am trying to hold you up. Funny books are not too easy to get hold of. This one has the advantage of starting with all the people who have read Black [Dark] Laughter [1925] to sell to first and when it gets started it will be awfully hard to stop. It does not depend on

Anderson for its appeal, but it has that to start with. It should start plenty of rows too. And anybody who has ever read a word by Anderson will feel strongly about it—one way or the other. My address for the next three months will be

HOTEL TAUBE, SCHRUNS, VORARLBERG, AUSTRIA.

Will you please cable me there, at once, your decision on The Torrents of Spring as in case you do not wish to publish it I have a number of propositions to consider. I want you to publish it, though, because it is a hell of a fine book and it can make us both a lot of money.

With best regards,

yours always,

Ernest Hemingway.

LHC

To GRACE HALL HEMINGWAY, Schruns, Austria,
14 December 1925

Dear Mother:

Congratulations on your success with your paintings! Thank you for sending me the New Republic review.[1] Also the review of [Sherwood] Anderson's Book for the Atlantic Monthly.[2] Archie MacLeish is very intelligent. He voiced my own opinion of Dark Laughter. Except that I regard it as an even more pretensious fake with two or three patches of real writing in it than Archie too politely refrained from calling it. Certainly no one should write who turns out a sentence like that last one.

We sent you a Xmas box with gifts for all the family. Hadley mailed it First Class on Dec 10. One package to Oak Park and one to Marce [Marcelline] in Detroit. Hope they get there by Christmas. I will be delighted to get the book. This address is good till March. The latter part of March we will visit some friends [Gerald and Sara Murphy][3] on the Riviera and sail with them. Go to Spain from there. Come to U.S. in September.

I have a new camera and will send you all some pictures of Bumby. He is out skiing now with his nurse [Mathilde Braun]. We arrived here December 12. 2 feet of snow. 14 below zero. Centigrade of course. I am working very hard. Got run down the last month in Paris. Another book [Torrents of Spring] gone off to the publisher. When I get working so hard that I have no time for exercise I always get run down. Bad cough, lose weight, etc. The mountains will fix all that.

It is lovely country here. Pine trees, green and white plastered houses of the village. We know every one in the town and I play in the weekly poker game and am a member of the ski club. We are the only foreigners in the town. It's the way to learn a language and not be bothered.

Pauline Pfeiffer[4] is coming down to spend Christmas. Dos Passos had to go to Morocco for Harper's Magazine and won't be down till February. We are going up to Munich and fly over the Alps and land at one of the highest mountain plateaus—in the Silvretta—and ski down. It is a new stunt they are getting up this year. We will be the first to do it. Will cost about 75 marks apiece. Five of us are going. Flying with a famous German war flyer. Hadley skied yesterday. I was still too weak. Feel a lot better today.

Best love to you and to Dad from us all and love to all the kinder.

Yours always,
Ernie

What a lot of Blah Blah that N. Republic review was. Still I'm always glad to read them.

JFK

1. Paul Rosenfeld on *In Our Time, New Republic* 45 (25 November 1925). Rosenfeld compared EH's stories to cubist painting and found them influenced by Anderson and Stein. 2. Mac Leish reviewed *Dark Laughter* for the *Atlantic Bookshelf*, December 1925. 3. Gerald (1888–1964) and Sara (1883–1975) Murphy had three children, Honoria (b. 1917), Baoth (1919–1935), and Patrick (1920–1937). The elder Murphys appear, though not by name, in a section of *A Moveable Feast* (New York, 1964), pp. 207–10. See the engaging profile by Calvin Tomkins, *Living Well Is the Best Revenge* (New York, 1971). 4. Pauline, who was to marry EH on 10 May 1927, was born 22 July 1895 in Parkersburg, Iowa. She worked at this time for the Paris edition of *Vogue*. She died suddenly in California, 1 October 1951.

To SYLVIA BEACH, Schruns, c. 14 December 1925

Dear Sylvia:

We were both awfully sorry not to get around on Friday to say good-bye. I was laid up with my damned throat and a fever and the throat's just beginning to go down now. Had a fine trip. Bumby talked all night. He was not sure we would realize we were voyaging in a train and shouted all night, "Papa! Voila le crain!" "Mama! Voila le crain!"

It is cold and nice here and there is about 2 feet of snow already in the town. Hadley skiied yesterday. We will both go tomorrow.

PUL   [Continued by Hadley.]

To F. SCOTT FITZGERALD, Schruns, 15 December 1925

Dear Scott:

I hope you and Zelda are well again. Did Pauline [Pfeiffer] bring the books? I gave her the Ludendorff, Brig. Young and Mr. Farrar's Spot Light.[1] I was pretty sick too with my damned throat and especially so after reading the whole of the Torrents of Spring book out loud to them, the Murphys, as an act of bravado after not being able to talk all day. Jesus Christ some time I'd like to grow up. I've had hell with it now for a week. Suppose it will be all right in a couple of days.

We had a good trip down here. No other foreigners in the town. I've been staying in bed, shooting pool with the natives and ski-ied twice but haven't any strength, consequently no legs, consequently no guts. Hadley and Bumby are in swell shape. I used to give Hadley a handicap of 200 in billiards. Now she beats me level.

It has snowed for two days. About 2½ feet of snow. Cold and the air nice and tight. The mountains are damned nice to see again.

Have read Fathers and Children by Turgenieff and the 1st Vol. of Buddenbrooks by Thomas Mann. Fathers and Ch-en isnt his best stuff by a long way. Some swell stuff in it but it can never be as exciting again as when it was written and that's a hell of a criticism for a book.

You're write about the Murphy's. They're grand people. Nice people are so damned nice.

Buddenbrooks is a pretty damned good book. If he were a great writer it would be swell. When you think a book like that was published in 1902 and unknown in English until last year it makes you have even less respect, if you ever had any, for people getting stirred up over Main Street, Babbit and all the books your boy friend Menken [H. L. Mencken] has gotten excited about just because they happened to deal with the much abused Am. Scene.

Did you ever read [Knut Hamsun's] The Growth of the Soil? And then for Christ sake to read Thom Boyd.[2]

I think you should learn about writing from everybody who has ever written that has anything to teach you. But what all these bastards do is learn certain concrete ideas that are only important as discoveries. Like if I were now, suddenly, to discover the law of gravitation.

Like me to write you a little essay on The Importance of Subject? Well the reason you are so sore you missed the war is because war is the best subject of all. It groups the maximum of material and speeds up the action and brings out all sorts of stuff that normally you have to wait a lifetime to get. What made 3 Soldiers a swell book was the war. What made Streets of Night a lousy book was Boston.[3] One was as well written as the other, I can hear you telling me I'm all wrong. Maybe I am. Love is also a good subject as you might be said to have discovered. Other major subjects are the money from which we get riches and poores. Also avarice. Gentlemen the boy lecturer is tired. A dull subject I should say would be impotence. Murder is a good one so get a swell murder into yr. next book and sit back.

And don't for Christ sake feel bad about missing the war because I didnt see or get anything worth a damn out [of it] as a whole show, not just as touching myself, which is the cheap, romantic viewpoint, because I was too young. Dos, fortunately, went to the war twice and grew up in between. His first book was lousy.

Now dont be a lousy crut and not answer this because letters are worth millions of dollars down here.

Best love to Zelda.
Yrs. always,
Ernest

How did your plan of having Harold Stearns make good in two weeks— after all these years—turn out?
PUL

1. John Farrar edited the *Literary Spotlight* (1924). In 1925 he was an editor at George H. Doran Co. In 1929 he became co-founder of Farrar and Rinehart. 2. Thomas Boyd (1898–1935) wrote *Through the Wheat* (1923) and other novels. 3. *Three Soldiers* (1921) and *Streets of Night* (1923) are novels by John Dos Passos.

To ARCHIBALD MAC LEISH, Schruns, 20 December 1925

Dear Archie:

I was awfully sorry to miss you at the house. Hadley was very happy to get the missing ear ring back and awfully excited about the carnelians (misspelled). The heavier one is especially valuable because hung from the left ear it will correct an unfortunate tendency of Hadley's to carry her head on the right side.

Wish you and Ada were down here. 2½ feet snow. Dry as sand and light as sawdust. Splendid skiing. We have also been shooting a lot of pool with the natives. Are the only foreigners in town. Hadley won 4 straight games of the local form of Kelly pool from the hotel owner, myself, the head of the ski schule and the owner of the hardware store.

I used to give her 200 points at Billiards—shooting 400. Now she beats me at evens. I have come like manna to the local pool players.

My mother sent me your review of Dark Laughter from the Atlantic Monthly. Monthly is correct. It is a damned good review. My mother always sends me everything that shows up Sherwood or when he gets a divorce or anything because she has read that I am much the same thing only not so good and she naturally wants me to know how the Master is getting along. You wrote a good review, intelligent and not to be roused to enthusiasm by exclamation points, mentions of the quatz arts bal or the omission of verbs or other things that at once point a masterpiece to Mr. Lawrence Stallings. Dos [Passos] is very fine about Stallings. It seems Stallings is a great critic because he lost a leg in the war. Dos's theory is that the more you lost in the war the worse critic you are. It doesn't sound very funny. Maybe I haven't gotten it right.

It is Sunday today so there isn't any mail. And by the way, if you ever write letters for god's sake write to us down here. We have a swell time but letters are terribly exciting things in Schruns. I've been in bed for two or three days getting over my damned throat. It's better today.

Big rehearsal for the Kids Christmas play going on in the ball room. The only noise that comes up stairs is the Double-bars.

Thursday we were in town, in Bludenz, and heard Kapitan-Leiutenant Mumm lecture on the Battle of Skaggerack in which he and a few other Germans made bums out of [Admirals] Jellicoe and Beatty and sunk the Warrior, the Indefatigable, Queen Mary, the Warspite etc. etc. suffering themselves only the loss of the Wiesbaden etc. etc. Moving pictures, largely faked, but splendid moving diagrams. Kapitan Leiutenant Mumm was something to see. One of those completely shaved heads where the forehead and bony structure above the eyes sort of juts out solidly above the eyes. Fish eyes. No lips. The Austrian kids got very restless. They didn't follow it any better than we did. Kapt. Leiut. had to bawl them out several times. He was very worked up about the battle but he couldn't get any applause and he couldn't hold their interest and finally it all got sort of mechanical with him too.

Why with Scott's great *gout* for the late war doesn't he go to see it in the movies? There are a number of wonderful films that are always showing somewhere or other. The British Zeebrugge film, German submarine film, British 2nd Ypres, 3 very good French, official Italian in 3 parts—Mountains, Plain and Piave, and Air and Sea. If he wanted to take a little trouble to hunt up the pictures he could see a hell of a lot more war than any of his contemporaries ever saw. The Zeebrugge film was right around the corner from his house on Ave. Wagram.

This is a dull letter. Did you read the Torrents [of Spring] through? How did it go?

I've been reading all the time down here. Turgenieff to me is the greatest writer there ever was. Didn't write the greatest books, but was the greatest writer. That's only for me of course. Did you ever read a short story of his called The Rattle of Wheels? It's in the 2nd vol. of A Sportsman's Sketches. War and Peace is the best book I know but imagine what a book it would have been if Turgenieff had written it. Chekov wrote about 6 good stories. But he was an amateur writer. Tolstoi was a prophet. Maupassant was a professional writer, Balzac was a professional writer, Turgenieff was an artist. I think that would be the awful thing about a success because if you made money on a book or in some way got so that each fall or spring or whenever it was you had to have a book ready then you would be a proffessional writer. It might look just as good. Nobody might know the difference. But there would be a hell of a lot of difference. That's why you ought to have about six years work ahead before you get published. Because they might like the first one.

This is a great lot of crap. It is the conversation of Paris that I always miss so. That and the Luxembourg Gardens and the wine and the newspapers. Imagine Chicago with only 2 morning papers when you read at least 9 in Paris and can go right on reading up until lunch and then start on the afternoon papers and read right through until dinner. If you go in for the Sport Hippique there aren't enough hours in the day to read through Auteuil-Longchamps, Le Jockey, L'Avenir, in the morning and Paris-Sport in the evening. Past performances are terribly concentrated reading.

Just finished Buddenbrooks, Thomas Mann, ½ of it's a pretty good novel. The Moonstone by Wilkie Collins much more enjoyable. Have another fine one by Wilkie Collins to read: Jezebel's Daughter. Also 9 vols. of Trollope. Also 2 Capt. Marryats. Capt. Marryat, Turgenieff and the late Judge [Henry] Fielding are my favourite authors. Schruns is the place to read. Last year ran out of Literature and Kriminal Romanzen and read 21 vols. of Nat Gould. He, at least, wrote much better about horse racing than Sherwood Anderson.

We had a good trip down. Hadley and Bumby are very fit. Hadley sends her love to Ada.

Write me a letter. I won't turn out such a dull mess as this again. Tell me all the dirt. We miss Scandal very much here. Only scandal is that Herr Sten who was shot in the balls on Mount Grappa and who had one of his interstitial glands removed at the time and the other, after many operations, also removed last year. He in the meantime having married, but without children, is much plumper this year. But his voice has not changed. It is as deep as ever. What do you make of that?

Yours always,
Ernest Hemingway

LC

To F. SCOTT FITZGERALD, Schruns, *c.* 24 December 1925

Dear Scott:

Have sent the 400 [dollars] to your concierge. You can keep it your-self or give it to Harold Stearns.[1] You write a swell letter. Glad somebody spells worse than I do.

Sure, I know Hank Wales. He was once a bartender in Goldfields, got to be a newspaper man some way, came over in 1918 when any news-paper man could work anywhere, got all smashed up, in a motorcycle accident I think, taught himself to read, write and speak French and is a hell of a good newspaper man. I used to hate him when I first knew him and now I am fonder of him than any other newspaper man except Bill Bird and Guy Hickock. Hank used to send amazing and beautiful stories during the Peace Conference and one day Col. House said to him, "Wales *where* do you get your facts?" Hank had just given the Yugo Slav oil fields to Japan or something else. "Col. House," Hank says. "What the Chicago Tribune wants isnt facts. It's news."

Why did you ask about Hank? He hasn't got a pleasant manner and he certainly looks and acts like hell. I suppose the reason I like him so much is because he likes me. Any of the dope about him being ex bartender etc. is confidential. He also managed pugs.

Your rating of I.O.T. stories very interesting. The way I like them as it seems now, without re-reading is Grade I (Big 2 Hearted. Indian Camp. 1st ¶ and last ¶ of Out of Season. Soldier's Home) Hell I cant group them. Why did you leave out My Old Man? That's a good story, always seemed to me, though not the thing I'm shooting for. It belongs to another cate-gorie along with the bull fight story and the 50 Grand. The kind that are easy for me to write.

Cat in the Rain wasnt about Hadley. I know that you and Zelda al-ways thought it was. When I wrote that we were at Rapallo but Hadley was 4 months pregnant with Bumby. The Inn Keeper was the one at Cortina D'Ampezzo and the man and the girl were a harvard kid and his wife that I'd met at Genoa. Hadley never made a speech in her life about wanting a baby because she had been told various things by her doctor and I'd—no use going into all that.

The only story in which Hadley figures is Out of Season which was an almost literal transcription of what happened. Your ear is always more acute when you have been upset by a row of any sort, mine I mean, and when I came in from the unproductive fishing trip I wrote that story right off on the typewriter without punctuation. I meant it to be a tragic about the drunk of a guide because I reported him to the hotel owner—

the one who appears in Cat in the Rain—and he fired him and as that was the last job he had in town and he was quite drunk and very desperate, hanged himself in the stable. At that time I was writing the In Our Time chapters and I wanted to write a tragic story *without* violence. So I didnt put in the hanging. Maybe that sounds silly. I didn't think the story needed it.

I'm sorry as hell for H[arold] S[tearns] but there's nothing anybody can do for him except give him money and be nice to him. There's nothing to be achieved. No solution. And again I'm fond of him. Probably as in the case of Hank because he likes me.

There's nothing you can do for him except give him money and you've done that and naturally can't assume the continuance of it as an obligation. He lives altogether in his imagination. The poor old bastard. I always get awfully sorry for people and especially for liars, drunks, homely whores, etc. Never get very sorry for worthy cases. After all, Panhandling is no damned fun. A gent who's drinking himself to death ought not to be constantly having to raise the funds to do it with. I do think Harold had a pretty damned good head. Also think he destroyed it or completely coated it with fuzz by drinking. You've done your part toward him. Just dont give him any more dough. But don't, for Christ sake ever let him think that I don't absolutely believe in him. Because there's nothing to be done about him and therefore it's pretty sad and I couldn't sleep if I hurt his feelings. Christ nose that when I cant sleep I have enough sons of bitching things I've done to look back on without adding any ornamental ones.

The ear that gets pushed is (Referring Battler) the stump.

Mc Almon is a son of a bitch with a mind like an ingrowing toe nail. I'm through defending that one. I still feel sorry for him but damned little. After I called him on you he went around for two nights talking on the subject of what a swine I was, how *he* had done everything for me, started me off etc. (i.e. sold out an edition each of that lousy little book and In Our Time at 15 francs and 40 francs a copy. I not receiving a sou. The only books he ever sold of all the books he's published) and that all I did was exploit people emotionally.

I've defended the lousy little toe nail paring for 3 years against everybody because I knew his horribly unhappy English arrangement etc. But am through now. Am going to write a Mr. and Mrs. Elliot[2] on him. Might as well give his emotional exploitation story some foundation.

Seem to be in a mood of Christ like bitterness this A.M. Have swell piano in her room for Hadley and she's practicing. Played poker last night and drank too much beer. 7 bottles. Won 158,000 Kronen. Makes about $2.35.

No fairies in Vorarlberg anyway.

Will report in full on Dostoevsky.

I think MacLeishes and Murphys are swell. Also Fitzgeralds.

God I hope Zelda gets all right at the bains place.[3] Pain's such an awful thing. It's such a rotten shame for her to be sick. I do think she'll get better down South and you will both be a damned sight better off on the Riviera than in Paris. You both looked so damned well when you came up last fall and Paris is poisonous for you. We'll see you there too.

God I wish I hadn't drunk so much beer. Going to buy Bumby a rocking horse for 80,000 Kronen though. The presents will go swell with it. Please thank Scotty for Bumby.

There was a Chinook yest. and day before and then it rained and now it is bright and cold and the snow ruined.

I am buying you 2 illustrated German war books. The swell illustrated ones are just beginning to come out. One on the mountain fighting Italian Front, and the other the history of the Wurtemburg Artillery. Am sending to Frankfort. Have seen the mountain book it's swell. When you get them if the pictures outweigh the German text I'll get you some more. There's going to be one on the Sturmtruppen. The Mountain pictures are swell.

We went in to Bludenz and heard Herr Kapitan Leutenant Mumm lecture on the battle of Skaggerack with movies. You'd have liked it. Hadley hated the Kapt. Leut. so that she was very thrilled. He was an awful man.

Review of In Our Type from Chicago Post says all of it obviously not fiction but simply descriptive of passages in life of new Chicago author. God what a life I must have led.

Am reading Peter Simple by Capt. Marryat. Havent read it since I was a kid. Great book. He wrote 4 great books. Frank Mildmay or the Naval Officer. Midshipman Easy. Peter Simple and Snarleyow or the Dog Fiend. He wrote a lot of kids books in later life and people get them mixed up. You ought to read Peter Simple.

If you want to read about war read any of those 1st 3.

Pauline Pfeiffer gets here tomorrow to stay for Xmas and New Years.

Know you will be glad to read in N.Y. Herald that 2 men died of cold in Chalons Sur Saone where you nearly did same. Good thing we got out in time. By the way, where the hell is your car?

Hadley, Bumby and I or me send our love and Merry Christmas to Zelda, Scotty and yourself.

This might have been a good letter if it hadnt been for the beer.

Original ending of story had dose of clapp (referring to Very Short Story) instead of gonorreaha but I didn't know whether clap had two ps or one, so changed it to gonoccoci. The hell I did. Try and get it. (This is a piece of slang I invented down here). Hope you have a swell Christmas.

Yrs. always
Yogi Liveright.

Please write even at $400 a letter. Will raise you to $435 but dont get drunk to celebrate.
[In left margin:] You know what Austria (Osterreich) means? The Eastern Kingdom. Isnt that swell? Tell Zelda.
PUL

1. Harold Edmund Stearns (1891–1943), former associate editor of the *Dial*; author of *Liberalism in America* (1919), *America and the Young Intellectual* (1921), and other books; and editor of *Civilization in the United States* (1922). He appears as Harvey Stone in *The Sun Also Rises*. 2. Originally called "Mr. and Mrs. Smith," the story attacked Mr. and Mrs. Chard Powers Smith and appeared in the *Little Review* 10 (Autumn–Winter 1924–1925): 9–12. See EH to Smith, *c.* 21 January 1927. 3. Salies-de-Béarn, France, is in the Pyrenees not far from Bayonne. Zelda was there for her health in January 1926.

To F. SCOTT FITZGERALD, Schruns, 31 December 1925– 1 January 1926

Dear Scott:

Have just received following cable from Liveright—Rejecting Torrents of Spring Patiently awaiting Manuscript Sun Also Rises Writing Fully—

I asked them in the letter I sent with the Ms. to cable me their decision. I have known all along that they could not and would not be able to publish it as it makes a bum out of their present ace and best seller Anderson. Now in 10th printing. I did not, however, have that in mind in any way when I wrote it.

Still I hate to go through the hell of changing publishers etc. Also the book should come out in the late Spring at latest. That would be best. Later would not be bad but Spring would be ideal.

My contract with Liveright—only a letter[1]—reads that in consideration of theyre publishing my first book at their own expense etc. they are to have an option on my first three books. If they do not exercise this option to publish within 60 days of receipt of Ms. it lapses and if they do not exercise their option on the 2nd book it lapses for 3rd book. So I'm loose. No matter what Horace may think up in his letter to say.

As you know I promised Maxwell Perkins that I would give him the first chance at anything if by any chance I should be released from Liveright.

So that is that.

In the meantime I have been approached by Bradley (Wm Aspenwell) for Knopf.

In the meantime I have the following letter from Louis Bromfield.

Dear Ernest—Appropos of "Torrents of Spring" I received a letter today from Alfred Harcourt who replied at once to a line I had written / taking the liberty after talking with you / regarding the chances of your shifting publishers. He is very eager to see the Anderson piece and is thoroly familiar with your stuff—both in the magazines and In Our Time. In this connection he writes—"*Hemingway is his own man and talking off his own bat. I should say, Yea Brother, and we shall try to do the young man as much credit as he'll do us, and that's considerable. I'd like to see his Anderson piece. It's a chance for good fun, if not for too much money for either of us. Hemingway's first novel might rock the country.*["]

He also stands ready to advance money in case you need it, as soon as you like, provided you are free of Liveright and want to go to Harcourt. I was pleased to have so prompt and interested an answer, though of course, it was to be expected. etc.

So that's that.

In any event I am not going to Double Cross you and Max Perkins to whom I have given a promise.

I will wire Liveright tomorrow A.M. to send Manuscript to Don Stewart care of the Yale Club, New York (only address I can think of tonight) and summarize by cable any propositions he may be making me in his letter.

It's up to you how I proceed next. Don I can wire to send Ms. to Max Perkins. You can write Max telling him how Liveright turned it down and why and your own opinion of it. I am re-writing The Sun Also Rises and it is damned good. It will be ready in 2–3 months for late fall or later if they wish.

As you see I am jeopardizing my chances with Harcourt by first sending the Ms. to Scribner and if Scribner turned it down it would be very bad as Harcourt have practically offered to take me unsight unseen. Am turning down a sure thing for delay and a chance but feel no regret because of the impression I have formed of Maxwell Perkins through his letters and what you have told me of him. Also confidence in Scribners and would like to be lined up with you.

You, however, are an important cog in the show and I hate to ask you to write even one letter when I know you are so busy getting away and all.

However there is the situation.

I dont know exactly what to write to Bromfield. Perhaps you will suggest something. In any event say nothing to Bromfield who has been damned decent, nor to anybody else in Paris till you hear from me.

I will wire Liveright in the morning (to send Ms. to Don at Yale Club). Then when I hear from you I can wire Don to send Ms to Maxwell Perkins. Write me Scribners' address.

Today is Thursday. You will get this letter on Saturday (perhaps). The mail boats leaving are the President Roosevelt on Tuesday and the Majestic and Paris on Wednesday. Mark your letter via one of the latter 2 ships and it will go fastest.

Have been on a long trip all day. Tired as hell. Chinook for ten days. Snow all gone to slush. Suppose that I will spend all my advance royalties on cables again this year. Oh yes. That reminds me that the advance I want is $500. The advance I had on the Short Stories was $200.

God it feels good to be out from Liveright with the disturbing reports I have had from Fleischman etc. Liveright supposed to have dropped $50,000 in last theatrical venture. Has sold ½ business, sold Modern Library etc. They ought to get someone like Ralph Barton or [John] Held or [Miguel] Covarrubias to illustrate the torrents. It has 5000 more words than Don's first parody Outline of History [1921].

Well so long. I'm certainly relying on your good nature in a lousy brutal way. Anyway so long again and best love to Zelda and to you both from Hadley and

Ernest

New Years Morning P.S.

Got to worrying last night and couldnt sleep. Do you think I ought to go to N.Y.? Then I would be on the spot and could settle things without a six week lapse between every proposition. Also could be on hand to make or argue any excisions on Torrents. If Liveright wants to hang onto me as his cable indicates could settle that. Also should get In Our Time plates if I change publishers. Etc. Meantime I have to wait at least 2 weeks more for my new passport. Old one ran out Dec. 20. Applied for new one Dec. 8 or 9—takes 5 weeks for it to come.

Well so long anyway. Bumby's very excited about going to get his new jockey cap, whip etc. I'm going down to get them through the Customs today.

Best to you always,
Ernest

PUL

1. The contract, dated 17 March 1925, is reproduced in facsimile in *In Their Time: 1920–1940* (Bloomfield Hills, Mich., 1977), p. 42 recto. (LHC)

To ERNEST WALSH, Schruns, 2 January 1926

Dear Ernest:

I don't write Dear Ernest and Dear Miss Moorhead because you wanted me to write you nothing but the truth and as soon as I start to write the truth in large chunks I always get very profane, not to mention obscene and I have a low middle class upbringing that makes me uncomfortable if addressing such remarks as horse shit to a lady.

This Quarter came this morning. IT IS SPLENDID. Looks fine, comfortable to handle, the right kind of paper, bound right, grand cover, supplement printed separately - as it should be - and mechanically a hell of a fine performance. As for what is in it; it is the first exciting magazine I have read since I was 13 and used to wait for the baseball magazine to come out. That's god's truth. And you know I'm not lying when I tell you I don't get excited about something simply because it is printing stuff of mine or stuff about me.

The poetry is the best bunch of poetry I've ever seen in a review. I wish you had something of Isador Schneider, your last time's Irish poet, and the late Mr. Eliot and you could call it an Anthology and let it go at that. With maybe one [William Carlos] Bill Williams, one by H.D., if she can still write them, and about two lines by Marianne Moore which is about what Marianne rates. And ask her to make the lines her own.

Have not yet read Boyle, Knister prose, Ethel Moorhead prose. Will report on that later.

Joyce is swell. I would always rather know what it is all about but I like Joyce straight, with orange juice, with Liffey water or what have you.

McAlmon I unfortunately read about a year ago. Altho he may make a bum out of Mark Twain, Dickens etc. I have never yet succeeded in re-reading anything by McAlmon. On the other hand I remember all of McAlmon I've ever read. This is the truth, which you asked for.

Rose et noir seemed unimportant if true and if not true what the hell. I hope he likes it in America.

Blue Beard's Last Wife reminded me unpleasantly of all the Italian intellectuals I knew when I was a little boy. However if I saw Linati I would tell him it was a strange and amazing story beautifully told and losing, I am sure, much in the translation. All us wops lie to each other.

Djuna's [Djuna Barnes's] story excellent. Much better than the Perlmutter girls that it is about. Why didn't she make Radiguet a writer in the story? I believe when you are writing stories about actual people, not the best thing to do, you should make them those people in everything except telephone addresses. Think that is only justification for writing stories about actual people. It is what McAlmon always does and then he blurs them to make them unrecognizable and not being an artist he usually blurs them to the reader also. Still Djuna's is a hell of a good story.

I have read my own story twice ("The Undefeated"). Disliked it when I read the proof. I thought it was a great story when I wrote it. Don't think I am getting vacillating or doubtful about my stuff and do not, for instance, think it is a hell of a lot better story than my well known contemporaries can write. But the hell of it is that I am not in competition with my contemporaries but with the clock - which keeps on ticking - and if we figure out some way to stop our own particular clock all the other clocks keep on ticking. For instance, of the two I would much rather have written the story by Morley Callaghan. Though, to him, the Bull fight story will be much the better story. Oh Christ I want to write so well and it makes me sore to think that at one time I thought I *was* writing so well and was evidently in a slump. Callaghan's story is as good as Dubliners.

Have not read Bill Williams yet.

Think you could tell Harriet Monroe to go to hell with fewer words. After all Harriet Monrow is just a faintly sensitized, dried up old bitch who runs a long dead magazine. She never has written a line of poetry and never could. If she wrote the Columbian Ode when the world's Fair opened and she likes to think of herself as having been a beautiful white starched young poetess - what the hell. What the Hell? I only saw her once in my life and that was in Paris and if I hadn't been a little drunk I would have been so sorry for her that I couldn't eat my food.

As for Yeats he and Ezra and Anonymous are my favourite poets. If Yeats hasn't written swell poems then nobody else ever has or ever will. Naturally I think that thing you quoted from him is lousy but that is like judging Walter Johnson by one base on balls. I could never read Yeat's mystic stuff, his plays nor playlets nor any of that stuff. I thought his Memories - that ran in the Dial - were splendid.

When you say you are the greatest living judge of poetry etc. that is just horse-shit. That is the sort of thing we ought to be called on when we say because we all have a tendency to get that way and outsiders don't know we are just getting a little noisy and discount things you really want them to believe. Maybe you are the best judge of poetry alive. But if you are - - - for Christ's sake never say it. As an American he ought to have understood better than this stupidity.

Following out that principle I have to be restrained about yr. review of In Our Time but Christ I thought it was a swell review and I only hope I will be able to write the way you say I write. You are certainly getting to be a hell of a good writer of prose. Hadley wants to know where you found [out] about me and Jewish girls? That has long been a thorn in the family side. You were very interesting on [Emanuel] Carnevali. Too much bag punching at the start of review of Mc Almon's Distinguished Air. Think three of the stories in that book and Village are what Mc will have to show for credentials, with maybe two stories from A Hasty Bunch, if anybody ever reviews his stuff impartially. Trouble with Mac is that he has been so misjudged and slandered and made so many enemies, usually while drunk and vomitty, that he never gets any impartial criticism. Everybody who likes his stuff knows he has had such a lousy deal from the reviewers that they overpraise it, and the others are worse in the opposite direction. Which doesn't do him any good.

When you say Mac is better than Mark Twain you are right in that Mark Twain wrote great, vast quantities of Hog Wash. He also wrote one, and one only very wonderful thing—Huck Finn. And if you will, now, read Huckleberry Finn, honest to God read it as I re-read it only about three months ago, not anything else by Mark Twain, but Huckleberry Finn, and the last few Chapters of it were just tacked on to finish it off by Howells or somebody. The story stops when Jim, the nigger, is captured and Huck finds himself alone and his nigger gone. That's the end.¹ Well you read Huckleberry Finn and if you really, honest to ourselves believe MacAlmon has ever written anything or everything together that deserves to be mentioned in the same room, house, city, continent or magazine with Huckleberry Finn I will stop writing because there will be no damn use to write if such a state of things can be. I am serious about this. I don't mind your making grand and enormous statements to help your friends but between us, privately, I would like to know how you stand on this. Because I feel pretty strongly about Huck Finn and that does not mean I don't consider Mc a very worthy performer, and if he did not have money, worthy of every sort of financial support.

Your list of unrecommended pubs and docs is grand. I'll forward all your mail when you start dodging the libel suits. Forwarded that letter to Clarke day it came. Hope it does the business.

I think comment at foot of Aldington's letter was in bad taste as he was doing his damndest, Brit. Reviewer's Damndest, to write a swell letter about Ezra, being perfectly impartial, for the good it would do. I admired his letter.

[George] Antheil supplement a swell idea. Best thing you can do for any artist. Only two things you can do for an artist. Give him money and show his stuff. These are the only two impersonal needs. Music reproduced beautifully.

Bumby very proud of his picture in magazine. Says, "Vla Petit Jean dans le neige et papa." He hasn't learned about avec yet.

Well I could go on and write like this for a couple of days and don't know what better compliment I could make This Quarter. It is a hell of a fine review. A hell of a fine review.

Although I am catolic have never had much admiration for martyrs or Saints. Mac is being made a martyr of, largely his own fault, no less largely the pressure of the world which is strong, and you are now engaged in making Mac a saint. One of the good things about the church, correct me if I'm wrong, is that they make a definite time limit before we can become Saints. To a real Saint that makes no bloody difference, any more than it makes a difference to a man, if he has really performed the act of valor, whether he is decorated or not. But it keeps out a lot of [Theodore] Roosevelts and [Woodrow] Wilsons. Of course on the other hand it lets in people like Jeanne D'Arc who were the shit of life but developed wonderful publicity organizations after their death. Still it's a good rule. And it seems to me a damned sight more important to give people an impartial square deal in criticism than to try and get them canonized here on earth.

And finally I don't think that good writings or good poetry has anything to do with our age at all - makes no bloody difference.

And this is my idea of Poetry—

> *O western wind, when wilt thou blow*
> *That the small rain down can rain?*
> *Christ, that my love were in my arms*
> *And I in my bed again!*

from somewhere around the 16th century
and Andy Marvell To His Coy Mistress somewhere in 17th century
and this from anonymous written godnose when

> *As I was walking all alane*
> *I heard twa corbies making a mane:*
> *The tane unto the tither did say,*
> *'Whar sall we gang and dine the day?*
>
> *'--- In behint yon fane dyke*
> *I wot there lies a new-slain knight;*
> *and naebody kens that he lies there*
> *But his hawk, his hound, and his lady fair.*
>
> *His hount is to the hunting gane,*
> *His hawk to fetch the wild-fowl hame,*
> *His lady's ta-en anither mate,*
> *Se we may mak our dinner sweet.*[2]

Hell you probably know the rest as well as I do. To me it's not a question of Keats and Shelley having been great and we having changed since then and needing another kind of greatness. I could never read Swinburne, Keats or Shelley. I tried it when I was a kid and simply felt embarrassed by their elaborate falseness. But of real poetry, true poetry, there has always been rymed and unrymed, a very little in all ages and all countries—That's another large statement. I don't know about all countries etc. All I can say is that I believe there has always been good poetry and with a little luck there will always be a little. But there won't be a hell of a lot. And I think you're making hell's own strides as a poet. And I think Ethel Moorhead's portrait of Carnevali is fine. Now I know what Carnevali looks like.

This is too much for now. You've done a damned fine job - both of you. Hadley sends her love and says she is crazy about your new poems.

Best luck.

yrs. always,

Ernest.

[Written on back:] Have been sick again. 5 days in bed. Throat swollen shut. Old stuff. Up tomorrow. Plays hell with my heart. Think will have throat operated on again in N.Y. It is simply a bloody nuisance. You're sick but you never write like it. If I'm in bed 2 days I get funereal as Job.

UVA   Ernest

1. See a similar passage in *Green Hills of Africa* (New York, 1935), p. 22. 2. "The Twa Corbies" (The Two Carrion Crows) was EH's favorite medieval ballad. He thought several times of using "A New-Slain Knight" as a title, but never did.

To HORACE LIVERIGHT, Schruns, 19 January 1926

Dear Mr. Liveright:

I have your letter of December 30 rejecting The Torrents of Spring. About two weeks ago I cabled you to deliver the manuscript of Torrents of Spring to Donald Ogden Stewart at the Yale Club. I hope you have done this.

As The Torrents of Spring is my second completed book and as I submitted it to you and as you did not exercise your option to publish it; according to my contract with you your option on my third book then lapses. This is quite clear. The contract is quite clear that if you do not exercise your option to publish the second book within sixty days of the receipt of the manuscript your option lapses and the contract further states that if your option lapses on the second book it lapses on the third book. There can be no doubt on this point.

There was nothing in the contract about what order books should be submitted in, whether the second book was to be a collection of short stories, a humorous book, or a novel. The contract said one of my next three books must be a full length novel. There was nothing in the contract which said that a full length novel must be the second book which I should submit to you. On the other hand the contract is quite explicit that your option on further books lapses if you reject my second book.

I submitted The Torrents of Spring to you in good faith. I consider it a good book and Scott Fitzgerald, Louis Bromfield, and John Dos Passos, men of widely divergent taste, are enthusiastic about it. You turned it down saying that everyone in your office was opposed to it. I can quite understand that as I remember that everyone in your office, excepting, I believe, Mrs. Kauffman, was opposed to In Our Time and it was quite formally turned down after a discussion. Your office was also quite enthusiastic about a novel by Harold Loeb called Doodab which did not, I believe, prove to be a wow even as a *succes d'estime*. But because it is your *office* that turns down my books, even though you reversed the decision on In Our Time, you can not expect to hold an option on my future books when the option has, by contract, lapsed.

I therefore regard myself as free to give The Torrents of Spring and my future books to the publisher who offers me the best terms.

As you know I expect to go on writing for some time. I know that publishers are not in business for their health but I also know that I will pay my keep to, and eventually make a great deal of money for, any publisher. You surely do not expect me to have given a right to Boni and Liveright to reject my books as they appear while sitting back and waiting to cash in on the appearance of a best seller: surely not all this for $200.

As soon as my new passport, now a week overdue, arrives I am sailing for New York. I look forward to meeting you there and meantime may have an answer to this letter. Will you please address me care of The Guaranty Trust Co. of N.Y., 1, Rue des Italiens, Paris, France.

Yours very truly,
Ernest Hemingway

LHC

To ERNEST WALSH, Paris, 1 February 1926

Dear Ernest:

Have had your grand letter and your small letter. Carry the first around to read. The second, coming today, has worried me greatly. I do hope nothing bad has happened to you. I hope to hell it was just that you were in an Irish black mood.

I didnt mean my note to be uncheerful. Only to tell how much I enjoyed Ethel Moorheads stuff.

Also I have re-discovered that The Undefeated *is* a grand story and I'm very proud I wrote it. Am sending you a long story of which I am very fond as soon as I can get back to Schruns and type it. Sail Wed - 3rd - on Mauretania. (2nd class) Will be in N.Y. 1 week.

Dont worry about me and Mac Almon. I'm really very fond of Mc Almon and besides would never hit any one. Have never hit but 2 gents outside of boxing in my life. Then only because they wanted to hit me. I dont brawl.

Dont let's any of us die of disease. Altho the more I think of it the more I think that any form of dying can be made pretty swell. One of the things that I really look forward to is dying - but want to be at least 85 when it happens. Life is pretty swell and let's only be sore at Shits like the English sometimes are. I see your point about [Richard] Aldington. Also about everything else.

So long and good luck. My best to Ethel Moorhead. I'd have loved to go by Grasse but have to get to N.Y. and <u>back</u>. Especially back. I miss Hadley and Bumby terribly and always drink too much when I'm not with them.

Yours,
Ernest

UVA

To ISABEL SIMMONS GODOLPHIN, New York, 10 February 1926

My Dear Izz:

Am in N.Y. for a week. Got in last night on the Mauretania. Hadley and Bumby are in Austria ski-ing. Hadley sends you all her love. I'm crazy to see you and Frisco [Godolphin]. When you get this will you call me up here at the Brevoort? If I'm out leave your phone number and I'll call as soon as I come in. I was a little tight last night and was all for setting out to call upon you gents at somewhere around midnight but was dissuaded by wise and kind friends.

Best love,
Ernie

PUL

To ISABEL SIMMONS GODOLPHIN, at sea, 25 February 1926

My Dear Izz:

Greater shame hath no man but here are the bare shreds of my alibi. I asked you to eat breakfast. You couldnt or wouldnt. All right. Then a lot of people came in, then I had to be at Ernest Boyds at eleven oclock. Then he and I had three shakers of cocktails. Then I was late to lunch with Jack Cowles and Robby Rouse. Then we drank ale. Went to a show with Robby. Had to stop at O'Neils to get and return stuff and say goodbye. Had to get liquor from Jack Cowles bootlegger from the trip. Had a dinner date at the Merley at 7. Not packed up to that point. Arrived at the Merley and found everybody cockeyed including myself. Marc Connelly wanted us to go to his show but I said I had to pack. Finally left about nine to go and pack. Meantime fell for a girl named Eleanor Wylie.[1] Great love at first sight on both sides. Went to the Brevoort and riding down from 48th street got over Eleanor in the cool evening air. Found your message and while Rouse and I packed I called you up three times between 9.30 and 10. Went up to the theater where we were supposed to meet Connally or Conilly and found everybody coming out. So I didnt see the Wisdom Tooth but everybody says it was swell. Fell back in love with Eleanor Wylie and we stopped at several bootleggers enroute to Hoboken. It now lacking twenty minutes of when the boat was to sail. My head cleared on the Hoboken ferry, not fairy, and decided that what was Wylie to me? Finally the boat left and some of the seeing off party stole all Dorothy Parkers Scotch. It has been a swell trip: grand weather and we've had a swell time. This is the first I've written, letters, cables or anything at all. Now it is Thursday and we are due in Cherbourg on Sunday night. Figure out I had about a quart and a half of Scotch exclusive of champagne and cocktails on Saturday. Also Ale. I wish youse guys had been along. To drink it if for no other reason.

Anyway it was swell swell swell to see you and we'll see you again in the fall. I still love you, in spite of the hamperings of your married state and I think Francis is a grand guy and that you married damned well and on the other hand I only hope Bumby will marry as well as Francis did. Very best of everything to you both and let us have a letter. Hotel Taube, Schruns, Vorarlberg, Austria until the end of March and then Guaranty Trust Co of N.Y. 1 and 3, rue des Italiens, Paris.

Best Love,

Ernie   ~~Ernest~~

P.S. I never did succeed in writing my family nor in cabling. So just deny any rumors that I was in N.Y. It was some impostor.

I left a grand gold mounted waterman fountain pen, large size in my room, No. #344 at the Brevoort. I wonder if you could go over and get it and maybe send it by Hammy before they padlock the Brevoort. Also I may have left other things haven't had the courage to look yet. The pen has a gold band around the part of the cap that screws down, it is a self filler and has a very hard sharp point. Is double size barrel. I know I left it so you might be very nasty to them if they say they haven't got it.

Best always and thanks a lot.

Ernie

PUL

---

1. Elinor Hoyt Wylie (1885–1928), well known for her fixation on the poet Shelley.

To LOUIS AND MARY BROMFIELD,[1] Schruns, c. 8 March 1926

Dear Louis and Mary:

Well what happened in N.Y.—if I've really been to N.Y. and havent just been cockeyed and will wake up to find it's all still to be gone through—was that as soon as I was definitely clear of Mr. Liveright or Horace—because we're Horace and Ernest now—I had a couple of drinks with Horace and told him how sorry I was etc and was up all that night because I couldnt sleep worrying about the Messers. Scribners and Harcourt. I tried to kid myself that I did not have to give Scribners the first look at Torrents but I would have been just a crook if I hadnt because last March I promised Maxwell Perkins that if I was ever free I would turn to them. So there wasnt anything else to do. Max Perkins read it and thought it was grand and not at all censorable as Scott had cabled him and I agreed to let them have Torrents and The Sun Also Rises for a $1500 advance, 15% flat, no split on any outside rights except 2nd serial rights etc. He wrote an awfully swell contract and was very damned nice.

I should have done the business man and tried to see what Harcourt Brace would do in opposition but I think that's all the advance I can expect on any business basis except that they want to back me over a long period of time whether the books sell or not and as they were doing that and never even asked to look at The Sun etc. I just told Perkins I would take it and went over and told Mr. Harcourt the news. I thought he, Alfred Harcourt, was one of the finest. I don't think you could be doing better in any way than going to them. I told him how much I had been sold on Harcourt Brace by you. But altho I could decide for Harcourt with my head I had the obligation to Scribners, not so much an obligation as a promise, if there is a distinction——and I wouldnt have any fun writing the stuff if I did something that made me feel crooked inside.

Anyway Mr. Harcourt said I could always come over there and he seemed to mean it. He said, also, that he admired [Glenway] Wescott's stuff and I told him I thought Wescott's stuff was fundamentally unsound which I suppose I shouldnt have said. I felt sorry as soon as I said it. But I know so well what a literary fake his prose is and I was feeling so cockeyed honest about turning down the chance at Harcourt which my head told me was the thing to do that I said what I thot of Wescott before I thot to keep my mouth shut.

I called up Isabel Patterson twice but missed her. Saw John Farrar at the Coffee House one night. I dont know whether he has always looked exactly like a woman—a woman in sheeps clothing—but he does now. He was very pleasant and we were always going to get together but somehow we never got together. But it was wonderful to have seen him.

Ernest Boyd was grand. I had met Madeleine Boyd before and she was grand too. Madeleine Boyd said she was handicapped in sending you the dirt because her great news source Bernadine Szold is in Paris and I told her I had met her and liked her.

Met hells own amount of people. Bob Benchley came back with me. He couldnt get a sailing and they just gave him a contract saying they'd put him anywhere there was and there wasnt anywhere so he slept in one of the maid's rooms and the 4th day out he said it was funny but he felt just like the time he had crabs and the 6th day out he *had* crabs. Yandel probably sue him. He's cured now anyway. Dotty Parker came over too. She's going South for a while.

This is a rotten letter. Hadley says it's been Spring here all of February.

It looked very beautiful yesterday and now ever since morning it's been snowing. How are you both and how are things going? We'll be in Paris the end of this month or the first of April. I've told Hadley about your apartment—She's wild to see it. She doesn't believe it can be as wonderful as I say but she figures that dividing all that in two it is still worth a trip to Paris. The Gerald Murphys have asked us to Antibes in April but we may not go until August. That way we can see a lot of you in April and May—which can be the best months of the year in Paris. Before the inrush of visiting Elks.

Hadley sends her love to you both. Dont say anything to anybody, will you, about my business arrangements with Scribners. I wanted to give you all the dope but dont want to spread it around.

You and [Ford Madox] Ford seem the most generally admired novelists in N.Y. Manhattan Transfer [by Dos Passos] is in its 4th printing. Gatsby [play] done by Owen Davis pretty darn close to the book—is a hit. I had to pay to get in. Would have paid to get out a couple of times but on the whole it is a good play. Understand it's been turned down by the movies as immoral. Don Stewart is still in Hollywood. Everybody on the boat had at least 3 copies of [Anita Loos's] Gents Prefer Blondes. One of the dullest books I've ever read. It's sweeping the country like the flu in 1918. Maybe it will sweep the world. Well the world needs sweeping. Maybe.

All people talk about in N.Y. is when they are going to come to Paris so I guess we're all not so badly off.

Do write and my very best to you both.

Affectionately,
Ernest Hemingway.

Bumby's talking all German now.
He's wonderfully well and strong.

PH. PUL

1. Bromfield (1896–1956) was known at this time as the author of *The Green Bay Tree* (1924), *Possession* (1925), and *Early Autumn* (1926). EH had met him in Paris in 1925; see his scornful comment on Bromfield, EH to F. Scott Fitzgerald, 31 March 1927.

To MAXWELL PERKINS, Schruns, 10 March 1926

Dear Mr. Perkins:

I was sorry to hear that Colliers did not take the Fifty Grand story but not surprised and I will not be surprised if it comes back from the Post and Liberty. It is quite hard in texture and there is no reason for them to take something that is not absolutely what they want and are used to until the name means something to them.

It was for that reason that it would have meant very much to me in various ways for the story to have been published in Scribners [magazine].

At present I can promise you The Sun Also Rises for fall publication. I have only five more chapters to do over and would then like to have another look through it before sending the Ms. over but I think you will probably have the Ms. some time in May. That should give me plenty of leeway on the proofs. I would perhaps get a better perspective on it that way. Anyway it is sure for fall and you can go ahead on that.

Bob Benchley and I had a grand trip on the Roosevelt. Perfect weather and a very good time. I've been working ever since. Scott and Zelda were in Paris and we had lunch and dinner before they left for Nice. They were looking well and Zelda's cure was very successful.

I am very anxious to see the Torrents proofs and get them back to you. Dos Passos is arriving here tonight or tomorrow and we have planned to go to Munich and fly from there to a place between here and Innsbruck in the Silvretta. Neither the Gerald Murphys nor Dos can ski and that seems the simplest way of getting them up where the ski-ing is good now with the short time they have. All it needs is good weather.

I will be very glad to be through with The Sun etc. and able to think about something else and write some stories.

From now on will you please use my permanent address Care The Guaranty Trust Co. of N.Y., 1, Rue des Italiens, Paris, France, as we will be going to Paris, Antibes, and Spain as soon as I have sent back the Torrents proofs.

With best regards,

Sincerely,

Ernest Hemingway

PUL

To MAXWELL PERKINS, Paris, 1 April 1926

Dear Mr. Perkins:

I have not yet received the proofs but expect them today or tomorrow and will try and get them off on the Aquitania on Sat. April 3. The jacket looks very attractive.

It is quite all right about Maude Adams. We will change Maude Adams to Lenore Ulrich or Ann Pennington which should be funnier and will make the same joke without mentioning Miss Adams' name.[1]

Dos Passos was down in Austria with us and we had a good week of ski-ing. I finished re-writing The Sun Also Rises and felt a desire to let down in a rather larger town than Schruns so we came up to Paris. The people who sub-let our flat are getting out by Easter so we will be moving in tomorrow or the next day.

The Sun Also Rises will go to the typist to be re-typed and then I'll send it to you in a couple of weeks. It is some 330 typewritten pages in my typing which is without margin. Reading it over it seems quite exciting.

We are going to Spain on the 15th of May for 4 months. From now on my permanent address will be Care Guaranty Trust Co. of N.Y., 1, Rue des Italiens, Paris, France. They are very good and accurate.

I am sorry no one wanted the 50 Grand story. You have my authority to make any arrangement with [Paul] Reynolds. I am very anxious to write some stories again—and will try and write the shortest ones first.

I would like to draw $600.00 from the balance of that advance. Could you have it sent to me care of The Guaranty Trust Co. address?

Enclosed are a couple of pictures which may or may not be of use to the Publicity Department. There is also one of my boy for your own information. I will be fooling around with bull fighting during the latter part of June and the first three weeks of July but have no intention of The Sun Also Rises being a posthumous work.

Yours very sincerely,
Ernest Hemingway

Thank you very much for the trouble you took about 50 Grand.
PUL

1. See *Torrents of Spring* (New York, 1926), chapter 5, p. 32.

To F. SCOTT FITZGERALD, Paris, *c.* 20 April 1926

Dear Scott:

Had a letter from Curtis Browne that Jonathan Cape wants to publish In Our Time and will pay 25 pounds advance and (10% and 3 D for a copy) British Empire rights not including Canada. Liveright wouldnt sell them sheets—they are going to set it up themselves.

Curtis Browne is going to be my continental and British agents and say they are dickering with a German publisher that wants I.O.T. [*In Our Time*].

I've returned the proofs of Torrents to Scribners a week or so ago. It looks very good.

Sun Also Rises is all done and back from the typists 1085 francs total typing charges. So I guess I'll send it off. I've cut it to about 90,000 words. May dedicate it like this

TO MY SON
John Hadley Nicanor
This collection of Instructive Anecdotes

I'm hoping to hell you'll like it. You'll see it in August. I think may be it is pretty interesting. Later—you wont like it.

Chink [E. E. Dorman-Smith] is in town for 2 weeks. He and I are going to walk from Saragossa across the Pyrenees by way of Andorra the end of July.

I've had a rotten cold. Been being very social and am god damn tired of it. Do you know anything about the girl [Beatrice Ames] Don's marrying? We go to Spain the 12th of May. Hadley's playing the piano very well. Where are you on your book. Write to me. Rousseau asks about you at the bank. He had us to lunch. We went. Went 5 of the 6 days to the bike race. It was swell [one word illegible] went with Chink and many generals etc. to see Sandhurst play Saint Cyr. Yr. letter just to hand and [Ernest] Walsh's poem or coming in his pants or whatever you want to call it made me vomit again seen on the envelope. But unlike the dog which returns to his vomit I tore up the envelope—just as I tore out the original poem and just as threw away This Quarter after tearing out my story to keep it.

Havent seen Archie MacLeish on acct. his absense in Persia. Seen Bromfield's once. Glad to see you're feeling bitter as understand that stimulates literary production.

Glad to hear you see further than [Booth] Tarkington. Sorry to hear you see not as far as Hemingway. How far do the French women see?

Very glad if you realize criticizm to be horse shit without horse shits pleasant smell nor use as fertilizer. Have not seen Bookman.[1] Nevertheless I thank you for services rendered. Havent seen the New Fiction except Gents Prefer [Blondes] which seemed 2nd rate Lardner and very dull. Perkins sent [John W.] Thomason's book which seemed very juvenile. I'd thought it would be much better. There wasnt that much hand to hand fighting in 100 years of the Crusades. Have not seen Sherwood Anderson's note book[2] though I believe I should in order to get a lot of new ideas.

Fifty Grand is, I believe, in the hands of some agent. I could use the 250 I could have gotten by cutting it for Scribners [magazine]. Am thoroly disgusted with writing but as there is nothing else I care as much for will continue writing.

Paul Nelson would be a good story for you to write if you knew anything about it.

I'm glad as hell you got the money for the movie rights of Gatsby. With that and Gatsby in person at the Ambassador you sh'd be able to write a pretty good novel with the franc around 30. Maybe someday you'll get the Nobel prize. Understand it's not yet been given to an American. Am recommending to Mr. Walsh that he give you This Quarter's $2000 bucks and have just called in my attorney to make you my heir.

So Dont Worry About Money

Chink says he'll leave you Bellamont Forest [3] too if you like. Pauline Pfeiffer says you can have her job on Vogue. I've written Scribner to send all my royalty checks to you.

It makes no difference your telling G[erald] Murphy about bull fighting statement except will be careful about making such statements. Was not referring to guts but to something else. Grace under pressure.[4] Guts never made any money for anybody except violin string manufacturers.

Your friend Ring [Lardner] is hampered by lack of intelligence, lack of any aesthetic appreciation, terrible repressions and bitterness. Any one of those is a terrible load for any writer to carry no matter how talented. He is, of course, 100 times as intelligent as most U.S. writers.

Bumby has the whooping cough. Hadley has had a rotten cough now for over 6 weeks. I expect they give it back and forth to each other.

We go to Spain May 12. If Bumby is not well then I'll go on ahead and Hadley come later. We go to U.S.A. in End of Sept. Antibes in August. I'll have a copy of Sun etc. there and w'd welcome your advising me or anything about it. Nobody's read any amount of it yet. If you are worried it is *not* a series of anecdotes—nor is it written very much like either [Dos Passos's] Manhattan Transfer nor [Anderson's] Dark Laughter. I have tried to follow the outline and spirit of the Great Gatsby but feel I have failed somewhat because of never having been on Long

Island. The hero, like Gatsby, is a Lake Superior Salmon Fisherman. (There are no salmon in Lake Superior). The action all takes place in Newport, R.I. and the heroine is a girl named Sophie Irene Loeb who kills her mother. The scene in which Sophie gives birth to twins in the death house at Sing Sing where she is waiting to be electrocuted for the murder of the father and sister of her, as then, unborn children I got from Dreiser but practically everything else in the book is either my own or yours. I know you'll be glad to see it. The Sun Also Rises comes from Sophie's statement as she is strapped into the chair as the current mounts.

Well why not write?

Regards to all yr. family

PUL   Herbert J. Messkit.

1. Fitzgerald in "How to Waste Material," *Bookman* 63 (May 1926): 262–65, goes out of his way to praise EH. **2.** *Sherwood Anderson's Notebook*, essays and sketches (1926). **3.** Dorman-Smith's ancestral seat at Cootehill, County Cavan, Eire. **4.** The origin of the famous phrase, later given currency in Dorothy Parker's profile of EH, "The Artist's Reward," *New Yorker* 5 (30 November 1929): 28–31.

To MAXWELL PERKINS, Paris, 24 April 1926

Dear Mr. Perkins:

I am mailing you today The Sun Also Rises. It will probably be much better for you to have it so that you can go ahead on it and I can do additional working over in the proofs. There are plenty of small mistakes for the person who reads it in Mss. to catch before it goes to the printer—misspelled words, punctuation etc. I want the Mss. back with the proofs.

The three quotations in the front I'd like to see set up. May cut out the last one.

Jonathan Cape is publishing In Our Time. Setting it up and printing it themselves. Mr. Liveright refused, Curtis Brown write[s] me, to sell them sheets some months ago. I have the contract today. They get the British Empire rights not including Canada and pay me 10% royalty. 25 pounds advance.

Curtis Brown gave them the first refusal of both Torrents and The Sun A.R. Advances and terms for them to be arranged when and if published. This seemed just to me as they are setting up the In Our Time. Torrents would probably be useless in England and it would not seem fair for them to miss a chance at the novel. I believe you said I had the British and foreign rights. I don't think Jonathan Cape is the best publishing house in England but they're not the worst.

I had a long letter from Scott a few days ago saying he'd started his book, was seeing no one, not drinking and working hard. He said he'd gotten $15,000 for some movie rights and this, with other things, would probably see them through until Christmas. I felt very touched by his precarious financial situation and told him that if he was worried about money I would write you to send all my royalties direct to him at the Villa Paquita, Juan les Pins, A.M.

Am working on a couple of stories. La Navire D'Argent published a 15,000 word story of mine translated a couple of months ago and various frenchmen got very excited and made extravagant statements about it so now they all want them and I have a fine french market (in francs). Am supposed to be the re-incarnation of Prosper Merimee whom I've never read but always supposed was pretty bad. The good thing about being a popular French writer like Mr. Merimee and myself, rather than an imported great American Name is that I believe the Great Names have to pay the translator which seems to me, if the law of supply and demand still operates, commercially unsound.

I was awfully sorry to be disappointed in Capt. Thomason's book. There were too many bayonets in it somehow. If you are writing a book that isn't romantic and has that as one of its greatest assets it is a shame to get awfully romantic about bayonets. The bayonet is a fine and romantic thing but the very fact of its being attached to a rifle which is such a fine and practical thing automatically restricts its use in the hands of any practical man also presumably armed with grenades to purely ornamental killing—with which I am not in sympathy. Most of it is fine and the writing is often splendid. There was just that little journalistic something that was disappointing. When you tell so much of the truth you can't afford to have anything not true because it spoils the taste. A little Arthur Guy Empey [author of *Over The Top*] is awfully poisonous. It makes you realize though what an awfully good book [Thomas Boyd's] Through The Wheat was. I hear there is a good new war book called Toward The Flame [by Hervey Allen]. Have you read it? After I read War and Peace I decided there wasn't any need to write a war book and I'm still sticking to that.

This is a long drooling letter but if it arrives at the same time as the Sun A.R. (the pig that you bought in a poke) you'll probably be so busy reading the pig that whatever this letter says will not be very important—nor is it.

Yours very truly,
Ernest Hemingway

PUL

To F. SCOTT FITZGERALD, Paris, 4 May 1926

Dear Scott:

Dont you write any more? How are you going?

I have finished a story—short—and am sending it to Scribners tomorrow. We go to Spain a week from Thursday. Maxwell Perkins writes that Torrents will be out at latest May 21st. I sent them The Sun etc. about 10 or 12 days ago. It's rained here every day for 3 weeks. I feel low as hell. Havent seen Bromfields, Edith Wharton, Comrade Bercovinci [Konrad Bercovici] or any other of the little literary colony for some time. May be there will be a literary colony in Madrid.

Dotty Parker, Les [Mr. and Mrs. Gilbert] Seldes and Seward Collins— you remember the man who shot Lincoln—all went to Spain and of course hated it.

Murphys arrived yest. and it isn't Dos that's marrying. It's Don. If I said Dos it was a slip of the ink. I'll pour that ink out. Oh Jesus it is such foul weather and I feel too low to write. I wish to hell you had come up with Murphys—I've not had one man to talk to or bull shit with for months. In Spain of course I can't talk at all—am in for 3 mos. of listening and reading the papers.

Write to me. I dont ever get letters. How are you feeling? Are you really working on your novel? Is it true that you are swiping my big death house scene? Is it true that you have become blind through alcoholic poisoning and had to have your pancreas removed? I have just given 200,000 francs to save the franc. Harold Stearns is giving the same amount.

I am thinking of going out in a few minutes, and getting very cock eyed drunk.

Love to yr. family,

yrs.

Ernest

(Christ what a name)

To F. SCOTT FITZGERALD, Madrid, *c.* 20 May 1926

Dear Scott:

I was glad to hear from you and glad to note that you were on the "Waggon." Sorry my letter was snooty—I didnt mean it that way. You were saying how little you valued critical articles unless they were favourable for practical purposes and I was just agreeing. That's what all the services rendered was about. Youll be seeing Hadley today. Wish the hell I were. Madrid is fine and cold and dry with a very high sky and lots of dust blowing down your nose—or up my nose. Corrida called off for today by the veterinaries who wouldn't pass the bulls (sic) because they were too small and sick. I was out when they turned them down and it was a collection of animals Harold Stearns could have killed while drunk with a jack knife. Didnt Ford say I was the great writer of English? Tomorrow they have a lad from Seville with a dose of clapp— a local boy (who was admired by Gilbert Seldes if that means anything to you) and one of the lousiest bull fighters on Earth—named Fortuna— and I might just as easily—a damn sight easier be seeing you at Juan les Pins. I missed the big fight on the 13th—of course—todays called off—tomorrow's a lot of cruts and Monday may be a good one.

[H. L.] Mencken is noble all right. I wish to hell I had your letter to answer. Herschel Brickel is in Paris. He read Torrents and was crazy about it. If that means anything. He's a nice guy personally anyway. Seldes is certainly—nothing about Seldes. We met [Seldes] and a lot of other 2nd class passangers at Noel Murphys where we were invited by 2 pneumatiques 2 telegrams and a personal call. I hadnt seen so many 2nd class passengers since I crossed on the Mauretania [February 1926].

I dont want to look up my Spanish friends because then I'll have to be talking Spanish, if I can talk Spanish, and going around and I'd like to work. Yeah you were right about generalities about Ring. All such are the bunk. You were wrong about Paul Nelson—way way wrong. I was referring to a very special exciting and dramatic story that you don't know. No scandal. Neither, however, was it the simple minded uneducated young writer having the wool pulled over his eyes by the smooth Irish chameleon as you suggested. That isnt snooty. Why the hell should we have to pull our punches writing?

I'm glad as hell that your book is going and that it is so swell. That's not kidding. I'll be glad to hear from Max Perkins what they think of Sun etc. It is so obviously *not* a collection of instructive anecdotes and is such a hell of a sad story—and not one at all for a child to read—and the only instruction is how people go to hell- (Doesn't it sound terrible, I can hear you say) that I thought it was rather pleasant to dedicate it to

Bumby—If you're right I wont put in the anecdote part—but I'll dedicate it to him for reasons that will be obvious when you read the book
and also for another reason. I've a carbon with me and you can read it at
Juan les Sapins[1] if there aren't proofs before then.

The 2 bottle men drank *port* and the best were 3 [bottle men] but I
understand the bottles were small. Did you ever read the Encyclopaedia
Brit. on Lawn Tennis in America? There are a hell of a lot more salmon
in Encyclopaedia Brit. than in Lake Superior. Besides it doesnt make any
difference because look at Shakespere and the seacoast of Tchecoslo-
vakia etc. Nouvelle Revue Francaise is going to publish 50 Grand as
Cinquante Grosse Billetes in July or Aug.

No news here. Write me and I swear to God I'll write a good letter
next time. I know this is lousy but I'm lonesome as hell.

Best to Zelda. Hadley will greet you all fully.

Always your co-worker for the Clean Books Bill.[2]

PUL   Ernest M. Shit.

1. Probably a joke. *Sapins* = fir trees. 2. The so-called Clean Book Bill, introduced
at the 1926 winter session of the New York State Legislature by Dr. W. L. Love,
was killed in committee 19 March 1926.

To SHERWOOD ANDERSON, Madrid, 21 May 1926

Dear Sherwood:

Last fall Dos Passos and Hadley and I ate lunch one noon and I had
just loaned Dark Laughter to Dos. He'd read it and we talked about it.
After lunch I went back to the house and started this Torrents of Spring
and wrote it right straight through for seven days.

You said I was all wrong on Many Marriages and I told you what I
thought about the Story Teller's Story. All I think about the Dark
Laughter is in this Torrents book. It is not meant to do any of the things
I see the ad writers say it is, and the great race I had in mind in the subtitle was the white race. It is a joke and it isn't meant to be mean, but
it is absolutely sincere.

You see I feel that if among ourselves we have to pull our punches,
if when a man like yourself who can write very great things writes something that seems to me, (who have never written anything great but am
anyway a fellow craftsman) rotten, I ought to tell you so. Because if we
have to pull our punches and if when somebody starts to slop they just

go on slopping from then on with nothing but encouragement from their contemporaries—why we'll never produce anything but Great American Writers i.e. apprentice allowance claimed.

I guess this is a lousy snooty letter and it will seem like a lousy snooty book. That wasn't the way I wanted this letter to be - nor the book. Though I didn't care so much about the book because the book isn't personal and the tougher it is the better.

It looks, of course, as though I were lining up on the side of the smart jews like Ben Hecht and those other morning glories and that because you had always been swell to me and helped like the devil on the In our time I felt an irresistable need to push you in the face with true writer's gratitude. But what I would like you to know, and of course that sounds like bragging, is - oh hell I can't say that either.

It goes sort of like this: 1. Because you are my friend I would not want to hurt you. 2. Because you are my friend has nothing to do with writing. 3. Because you are my friend I hurt you more. 4. Outside of personal feelings nothing that's any good can be hurt by satire.

Only, of course, it may hurt you at all I.E. make you feel badly. Because nobody likes to be called on anything - but you don't mind being called, it is simply annoying, it doesn't raise any hell with you, if you know the person doesn't know what they are talking about. So that's the way it may turn out. Anyway I think you'll think the book is funny - and that's what it is intended to be -

It is cold and raining here. I'm writing some stories and waiting for Hadley to come here next week. Where are you living now? We are coming over to the states in the fall and live in Piggott, Ark.[1] It's nice country. I haven't seen Gertrude Stein since last fall. Her Making of Americans is one of the very greatest books I've ever read. We were in Austria all winter and I went a week to New York. I work pretty hard all the time and try and write better and sometimes I do and sometimes I don't.

Please let me hear from you whether you're sore or not. My regular adress is care

        The Guaranty Trust Co. of N.Y.

        1, Rue des Italiens,

        Paris. France.

They'll always forward. We are going to be down in Spain all summer. Best always to you and to your wife from Hadley and me,

                      yours always,

NEWBERRY   Ernest Hemingway.

---

1. Family home of Pauline Pfeiffer in northeast Arkansas.

To DR. C. E. HEMINGWAY, Madrid, 23 May 1926

Dear Dad:

I was so glad to hear from you about your splendid Smoky mountain trip and all the news. We are planning to come to the States the end of September or beginning of October and will spend the winter in Piggott, Arkansas. That is the plan at present though nothing is definitely settled.

I made a flying trip to N.Y. while you were in Fla. stayed under seven days—just business—I wanted to come out but had to go back on the President Roosevelt and knew it would just complicate matters if we tried to hook up and make everybody feel bad if we didn't so I didn't let anybody know I was in town.

Shifted to Scribner's as publishers and have an excellent contract with them. They are bringing out a satire of mine The Torrents of Spring—this month—It's out now I believe, and a novel The Sun Also Rises—this fall. I am writing stories now that will be published in Scribner's magazine.

Hadley went with Bumby and his nurse to Antibes on the Riviera when I came down here to Madrid and she was to join me here today.[1] But Bumby has developed the whooping cough and she can't leave him so I am joining her on the Riviera in a few days and when Bumby is all right—we will return to Spain until August—which we are spending with some friends at Antibes.

I've been writing on some stories here. I'm glad you and mother had such a good trip and that everybody is all right. We will come to Chicago when we land and stay three or four days with you in Oak Park if you want us to. Hadley wants to see her people in Saint Louis too but I don't want to get stuck in a lot of entertaining and that sort of stuff so I may stay in Oak Park while she goes down with Bumby and just pick her up for one day of facing the relatives before we shove to Piggott. In Piggott I figure that I will be far enough away from people so they won't come and bother and I can work. I will be working on another novel and some gents when they are working on a novel may be social assetts but I am just about as pleasant to have around as a bear with sore toenails. Pauline Pfeiffer who was down in Austria with us and is going to Spain this summer lives in Piggott when she's in the states and is getting us a house there. I heard that you were upset about my wanting to winter at Windemere so decided not to bother you on that score.

Having been to mass this morning I am now due at the bull fight this afternoon. Wish you were along.

Best love always to you and mother and the kids and Aunt Grace and Grandfather,

                                                                    Ernie

Thanks so much for the *many* fine Sports magazines.

JFK

1. Perhaps EH had heard from Hadley on Saturday 22 May that she could not come. See EH to Sherwood Anderson, 21 May 1926, which says she is due in Madrid "next week."

To MAXWELL PERKINS, Juan-les-Pins, France, 5 June 1926

Dear Mr. Perkins:

I was very glad to get your letter and hear that you liked The Sun a.r. Scott claims to too. We are here temporarily quarantined with whooping cough. I went to Madrid and my wife came down here with the child and nurse expecting to join me in a week in Madrid. Himself developed the whoopings on arriving here so after 3 weeks in Madrid I came on here, and we will be here another 3 weeks and then take up our Spanish trip.

As to addresses: Care Guaranty Trust Co. of N.Y., 1, Rue des Italiens, Paris, is the best permanent address. I will keep them informed by wire of my address in Spain and they have an excellent mail forwarding service.

Between July 6 and July 13—inclusive—I will be at the Hotel Quintana, Pamplona (Navarra), SPAIN if you should want to reach me by cable.

It would be better not to try and hit that address with mail.

That is the only address I am sure of but will keep the Guaranty Trust exactly informed. They will re-wire all cables and re-forward letters with no delay.

I believe that, in the proofs, I will start the book at what is now page 16 in the Mss. There is nothing in those first sixteen pages that does not come out, or is explained, or re-stated in the rest of the book—or is unnecessary to state. I think it will move much faster from the start that way. Scott agrees with me. He suggested various things in it to cut out—in those first chapters—which I have never liked—but I think it is better to just lop that off and he agrees. He will probably write you what he thinks about it—the book in general. He said he was very excited by it.

As for the Henry James thing—I haven't the second part of the Ms.

here—it is over at Scott's—so I can't recall the wording. But I believe that it is a reference to some accident that is generally known to have happened to Henry James in his youth. To me Henry James is as historical a name as Byron, Keats, or any other great writer about whose life, personal and literary, books have been written. I do not believe that the reference is sneering, or if it is, it is not the writer who is sneering as the writer does not appear in this book. Henry James is dead and left no descendants to be hurt, nor any wife, and therefore I feel that he is as dead as he will ever be. I wish I had the ms. here to see exactly what it said. If Henry James never had an accident of that sort I should think it would be libelous to say he had no matter how long he were dead. But if he did I do not see how it can affect him—now he is dead. As I recall Gorton and Barnes are talking humourously around the subject of Barnes' mutilation and to them Henry James is not a man to be insulted or protected from insult but simply an historical example. I remember there was something about an airplane and a bicycle—but that had nothing to do with James and was simply a non-sequitor. Scott said he saw nothing off-color about it.[1]

Until the proofs come I do not want to think about the book as I am trying to write some stories and I want to see the proofs, when they come, from as new and removed a viewpoint as possible.

Up till now I have heard nothing about a story called—An Alpine Idyll—that I mailed to you sometime the first week in May. Did you ever receive it? I have another copy which I will send if you did not. In Madrid I wrote three stories ranging from 1400 to 3,000 words. I haven't had them re-typed and sent on as I was waiting word about The Alpine Idyll.[2]

What is the news about Torrents? Have any copies been mailed to me as yet?

Could you send me a check for $200. in a registered letter to the Guaranty Trust Co. address? It was very pleasant to get your letter and learn that you liked the book.

Yours very sincerely,
Ernest Hemingway

PUL

1. James is called Henry in *The Sun Also Rises*, chapter 12. 2. Refused by *Scribner's Magazine*, "Alpine Idyll" first appeared in *American Caravan*, ed. Van Wyck Brooks (New York, 1927). The stories composed in one day in Madrid were "The Killers," "Ten Indians," and "Today Is Friday." But EH had a start on them before going to Spain.

To SHERWOOD ANDERSON, Pamplona[?], Spain, 1 July 1926

Dear Sherwood Anderson:

Your letter was fine (this is not the Master talking to his pupil) and what a horse's ass I must become as soon as I sit in front of a typewriter if those are the snooty kind of letters I've written you. But anyhow if I did write that way I won't write that way anymore. I won't even try and headslip that one - but will take it on the nose by removing the if and putting in an as. But anyway I think you're quite right in saying the book will do you good (publicity) and I am sure it will hurt me with a lot of people. So what the hell. Because I had a grand time writing it for six days and thought it was funny and got five hundred dollars for it (previous writing earnings 200 dollars and no story ever yet sold in the states) and you being the middle weight champion and as such not having a glass jaw and me not having a glass jaw either - but now having or having had five hundred dollars I feel fine about it.

But I'll counter your lead about the noble reporter in Cleveland by pointing out that I didn't tear up or burn this mss. to "protect" you and all I meant by the letter from Madrid was to say "Mr. Anderson I have read and admired you for a long time and I am now about to attempt to sock you on the jaw and here are my reasons and a copy of my apology which can be read aloud at my funeral."

I'll be awfully glad to see [Ralph] Church. We will be back in Paris in August and will be there until we sail about the middle of September. It would be grand to come through Troutdale [Virginia] and we might do it. I imagine though that we will land in Texas or New Orleans and go straight up to Piggott [Arkansas] from there. We haven't any money and will save the R.R. fare from New York and get a cheaper boat that way. Later in the winter if you've not gone to Paris I'd love to bum up through and see you. It would be grand to see you again and we would love to come to Troutdale. It sounds like lovely country.

Anyway so long and good luck and if you don't go over to Paris I'll see you some time before Christmas - and when I do I'll try and not lead with my chin and forget to duck - like in the last letter. Hadley sends you and your wife her best.

Best to you always,

NEWBERRY   Ernest Hemingway

To MAXWELL PERKINS, Valencia, Spain, 24 July 1926

Dear Mr. Perkins:

Thanks so much for sending me the Adventures of a Younger Son [by E. J. Trelawny]. I haven't received it yet but look forward to it with great anticipation.

I imagine we are in accord about the use of certain *words* and I never use a word without first considering if it is replaceable. But in the proof I will go over it all very carefully. I have thought of one place where Mike when drunk and wanting to insult the bull fighter keeps saying— tell him bulls have no balls. That can be changed—and I believe with no appreciable loss to—bulls have no horns. But in the matter of the use of the word *Bitch* by Brett—I have never once used this word ornamentally nor except when it was absolutely necessary and I believe the few places where it is used must stand. The whole problem is, it seems, that one should never use words which shock altogether out of their own value or connotation—such a word as for instance *fart* would stand out on a page, unless the whole matter were entirely rabelaisian, in such a manner that it would be entirely exaggerated and false and overdone in emphasis. Granted that it is a very old and classic English word for a breaking of wind. But you cannot use it. Altho I can think of a case where it might be used, under sufficiently tragic circumstances, as to be entirely acceptable. In a certain incident in the war of conversation among marching troops under shell fire.

I think that words—and I will cut anything I can—that are used in conversation in The Sun etc. are justified by the tragedy of the story. But of course I haven't seen it for some time and not at all in type.

The reason I haven't sent any more stories to the magazine is because Scott was so sure that it would buy anything that was publishable that my hopes got very high and after I'd tried both a long and a short story— and I suppose the stories aren't pleasant—and both were not publishable it made me feel very discouraged; as I had counted on that as a certain source of income, and I suppose I have been foolish not to copy out more stories and send them. But I will when we get back to Paris the 10th of August. As yet no proofs have arrived.

I plan to go over The Sun etc. in Paris very carefully. By what date should you have the proofs returned?

As for our returning in the fall—the financial situation is so rotten— it being very tenuous and easily affected by whooping cough and the necessity of the Riviera and one thing and another—that I can see no prospect of it although I had hoped and counted on it tremendously. In several ways I have been long enough in Europe.

How did the Torrents go?

The Guaranty Trust is always a permanent address.

I hope you have been having a good summer. Spain is very dusty and hot but much the best country left in Europe.

Yours always,

PUL   Ernest Hemingway

To HENRY STRATER,[1] Valencia, c. 24 July 1926

Dear Mike:

The pictures were swell and thanks for sending them. I am terribly sorry about your mother's death. So is Hadley. She sends her love and her sympathy to you both. There is one thing about dying and that is that the good people do it. I have never yet known a shit to die altho if we live long enough it may happen.

You were awfully swell to me in N.Y. and don't think I don't remember it. We aren't coming through in the fall and if we do will go by Galveston, Texas. Everything is all shot to hell in every direction but in the meantime there are eight bull fights here starting tomorrow. Gallo, Belmonte, Sanchez Mejias, Nino de la Palma and Villalta, Miuras, Villamartas, Concha y Sierras, Murubes, Perez Tabernos, Guadalests and Pablo Romeros. Hadley and I are down here together. Pamplona was grand. We were gypped out of Ondarria by Bumby getting the whoop cough and getting himself and Hadley and eventually me, coming from Madrid, quarantined on the Riviera in a former Villa of Scott Fitzgerald's at Juan les Pins (Alpes Maritimes).

There isn't any news that's fit to print. I'm awfully glad you like the Torrents book and will have the novel fired to you by Scribners this fall just as soon as it's out. We've just been conge-ed [given notice to quit] in Paris and have to go up and get things cleaned out by the 8th of August. Please remember Hadley to the Von Schlegell's and all our love to you and Maggie and the kids.

Write me care of the Guaranty in Paris. I do hope you were able to do something for your father - though it must be an awfully hopeless business to lose someone you've been in love with and made your life with.

It's one of the swell things especially reserved for all of us. So Long, Mike, and write -

Yours always,

PUL   Hem

1. Henry (Mike) Strater, American painter (b. 1896, Louisville, Kentucky), Princeton, Class of 1919, first met EH in Pound's Paris studio in the fall of 1922 and saw much of him in Paris, Rapallo, and later in Key West. In 1979 he compiled "an autobiography in color," *Rocks, Nudes, and Flowers,* which contains his three portraits of EH.

To MAXWELL PERKINS, Paris,[1] 21 August 1926

Dear Mr. Perkins:

The proofs came ten days ago while we were at the Cap D'Antibes on our way home from Spain and I have been over them very carefully with the points you outlined in mind.

1st—I have commenced with Cohn. I believe the book loses by eliminating this first part but it would have been pointless to include it with the Belloc eliminated—and I think that would be altogether pointless with Belloc's name out.

2nd—Roger Prescott is now Roger Prentiss. I believe I went to school with a Roger Prentiss but at least he was not Glenway [Wescott].

3rd—Hergesheimer now changed to something else.

4th—Henry James now called either Henry or Whatsisname—whichever seems best to you.

5th—I do not believe that the blanks left in the Irony and pity song can be objectionable—anybody knowing what words to put in might as well put them in. In case they are offensive the word "pretty" can be inserted.

6th—The bulls now without appendages.

I've tried to reduce profanity but I reduced so much profanity when writing the book that I'm afraid not much could come out. Perhaps we will have to consider it simply as a profane book and hope that the next book will be less profane or perhaps more sacred.

In today's mail there is an invitation to broadcast Torrents of Spring from the Sears Roebuck radio station W L S accompanied by a short talk and the information that "it gives common people a real thrill, to be

remembered always, to hear the voice of a well known, admired author."
(And who do you think that would be?) The other letter was from the
Missouri Historical Society asking for a copy of Torrents to be preserved
along with the most complete collection of the books of all Missouri
authors, which it seems a very strange thing to suddenly be.

In this same mail I am sending you a story—The Killers—which has
been typed by the well known, admired author himself on a six year old
Corona. So if the magazine does not want it you might send it to the
Sears Roebuck broadcasting station care of Mr. John M. Stahl and maybe
he would like to have it to show to a lot of the common people.

I also find, in yesterday's mail, that I owe Henry Romeike, Inc. 220
West 19th Street, N.Y., sixteen dollars for clippings, and as I have no
dollars and Mr. Romeike, who is I believe by his own admittance the
original Romeike, is very lovely about sending clippings, I wonder if you
could have this sixteen dollars sent to him and charged to what must be
rapidly becoming my account. If this were done it might be well to tell
Mr. the original Romeike that the money is coming from me and that
he may continue to send clippings to the same place.

Zelda was looking very well and very lovely when I saw her last week.
Scott was working hard. Don Stewart has arrived with a very new and
awfully nice and good looking wife. I hope you've had a good summer.
We had a grand time in Spain. I'm working very hard now—plan to
mail the proofs the end of the week and will send another story.

With best regards,

PUL   Ernest Hemingway

1. The return address on this letter is 60 rue Froidevaux, Gerald Murphy's studio,
where EH was living alone after the break with Hadley. See EH to F. Scott
Fitzgerald, c. 7 September 1926.

To MAXWELL PERKINS, Paris, 26 August 1926

Dear Mr. Perkins:

I am sending the proofs tomorrow on the Mauretania so you should
have them in a week now.

You did not send a proof of the quotations in the front or of the dedication and I have forgotten exactly what they were. For the quotations I
want the quotation from Gertrude Stein which I believe was "You are
all a lost generation"; there may have been more to it—it's to go as it was
on the Mss. and the quotation from Ecclesiastes. The dedication is to be

THIS BOOK IS FOR HADLEY AND FOR
JOHN HADLEY NICANOR.

I may have changed a few more things and made more cuts before mailing the proofs but you will have seen all that by now. I believe that the book is really better starting as it does now directly with Cohn and omitting any preliminary warming up. After all if I'm trying to write books without any extra words I might as well stick to it. Now that it is finally out of my hands and there is no chance of doing anything to make it any better I feel rather cheerful now about The Sun. Hope you feel the same way.

A letter from Scott today said he was working very hard with the front door barred and all the blinds down and expected to sail for N.Y. on December 10th from Genoa.

If the Irony and pity ditty bothers there are a couple of things you could do—reduce the size of the dashes and omit periods after them. Or just run it all in together. No dashes and no periods. Do whatever you like with it. I don't care what happens to that as long as the words are not changed and nothing inserted.

The other things I believe are all fixed up. We've eliminated Belloc, changed Hergesheimer's name, made Henry James Henry, made Roger Prescott into Roger Prentiss and unfitted the bulls for a reproductive function.

Now I'll get this off so there won't be any further holding up. When do you expect that The Sun will be out? And how did Torrents go? You might send me a check for 200 dollars if you would. It is grand to have The Sun etc. finally off and to be able to start on something else without things to do on the book coming in and smashing up the production of anything else. I'd like to forget it now for a long time. It is a great mistake to put real people in a book and one I'll never make, I hope, again.

With best regards,

Yours very truly,

PUL   Ernest Hemingway

To MAXWELL PERKINS, Paris, 7 September 1926

Dear Mr. Perkins:

The proofs of The Sun etc. went off on the Mauretania almost two weeks ago so I did not answer your cable about sending them in completed galleys. By now you doubtless have them and have gone ahead.

Today I have your letter of August 23 from the country.

As a matter of fact I am not now discouraged, although I may have been when I wrote you from Valencia, and I don't think there is any question about artistic integrities. It has always been much more exciting to write than to be paid for it and if I can keep on writing we may eventually all make some money. In the meantime the thing would seem to be to write, and I am now trying to sell, give away or in some way clear out all the stories I have ahead to clear the way for some more.

O'Brien has written today for permission to publish The Undefeated, a story that I do not know if you ever saw, in his 1926 volume. I suppose that all becomes publicity. It might help The Sun Also Rises as the Undefeated has something to do with bulls and neither of the two mention any of the embarrassing appendages.

Yours always,

PUL   Ernest Hemingway

To F. SCOTT FITZGERALD, Paris, *c.* 7 September 1926

Dear Old Fitz:

Glad to hear again from the Master. How goes the work, Fitz? Glad to hear it. Glad to hear it. Keep it up old boy. I had exactly the same experience myself when I started writing. Then one day I met George Horace Lorimer in the Petit Chaumiere and from then on things simply slipped along.

How the hell are you anyway? I decided to give away all my stories when I got here so as to clear away all the stuff I was counting on selling and that would force me to write some more. So I gave Today Is Friday to some pamphlet organization that had written asking for an essay to be published with a drawing by Cocteau and sent the Alpine Idyll to the New Masses which is the most peurile and shitty house organ I've ever seen - they also having requested a contribution - and just to see what the alibi would be sent The Killers - which I'd just finished to Scribners. So right away back I get a cable from Max Perkins saying Killers grand Bridges writing offer Sun proofs received Perkins.[1]

So even cynical little boys like Ernest get pleasant surprises. Only now I only wait to hear of the sudden death of Bridges, the losing of his job by Perkins and the suspension of Scribner's magazine. Otherwise may get published.

Since then have completed a new story, yest. and am starting another one. Thanks a lot for the letter from [Paul] Reynolds and for your sterling attitude on the censorship question. All France is proud of you.

Don't listen to any of the subversive element of Juan les Pins, exemplified by the police or other bureaucratic classes, that may try to nullify this.

The author of Gatsby le Magnifique will be backed by at least as many people as went to bat for Dreyfuss. Don't let them jail you. Just don't let them. The real France is backing you.

Hadley and I are still living apart.[2] I am thinking of riding down to Marseilles on my bike in Oct. and living in Marseilles for a month or so and working. Will ride over and see you when you get the book finished. Our life is all gone to hell which seems to be the one thing you can count on a good life to do. Needless to say Hadley has been grand and everything has been completely my fault in every way. That's the truth, not a polite gesture. Still having been in hell now since around last Christmas with plenty of insomnia to light the way around so I could study the terrain I get sort of used to it and even fond of it and probably would take pleasure in showing people around. As we make our hell we certainly should like it.

I cut The Sun to start with Cohn - cut all that first part. Made a number of minor cuts and did quite a lot of re-writing and tightening up. Cut and in the proof it read like a good book. Christ knows I want to write them a hell of a lot better but it seemed to move along and to be pretty sound and solid. I hope to hell you'll like it and I think maybe you will.

Have a swell hunch for a new novel. I'm calling it the World's Fair. You'll like the title.

Give my love to Zelda and tell her how sorry we were not to see you when we came around to say goodbye. I haven't been drinking, haven't been in a bar, haven't been at the Dingo, Dome nor Select. Haven't seen anybody. Not going to see anybody. Trying unusual experiment of a writer writing. That also will probably turn out to be vanity. Starting on long semi-permanent bike trip to last as long as the good weather lasts as soon as my present piles go down. Then will get a lot of work done, all the stories I want to write, probably working in Marseilles. Then we'll see.

The world is so full of a number of things I'm sure we should all be as happy as kings. How happy are kings?
Stevenson.

Yrs always,
Ernest

Walsh, author of the Soldier drugfiend bullbaiter poem is attacking me to the extent of several columns in the next This Quarter charging Hemingway has sold out to the vested interests. I wrote him a postcard saying his poem made me vomit when This Q. came out. Now it seems from a flawless knight of LITERATURE I have become a hack writer in the pay of SCRIBNERS earning these vast sums. I saw a copy of this which he is circulating largely in carbons before publication. Gentlemen I give you the Irish.

[Upside down at bottom of letter:] Write if you feel like it. I get lonesome.

PUL

1. "Today Is Friday" was published by As Stable Pamphlets (Englewood, N.J., 1926). Refused by the *New Masses*, "Alpine Idyll" appeared in *American Caravan*, ed. Van Wyck Brooks (New York, 1927), pp. 46–51. "The Killers" was the first of EH's stories to appear in *Scribner's Magazine* 81 (March 1927): 227–33. 2. EH and Hadley had separated after their return from the Riviera in August. The event is handled fictionally in "A Canary for One," *Scribner's Magazine* 81 (April 1927): 357–60.

To SHERWOOD ANDERSON, Paris, *c.* 7 September 1926

Dear Sherwood:

Thanks for the swell letter. Troutdale sounds very fine and I envy you the fall. It must be awfully grand. I am so homesick for America evry fall that I get into awful shape. Piggott is shot to hell now along with a lot of other things. As it was one of the two things that I wanted to do really badly.

Saw the New Masses - Gene Jolas showed it to me with his poems in it - and it seems to be some sort of a house organ. I've sent the proof of my first novel - called The Sun Also Rises off to Scribners. I hope to hell you will like it. It isn't smarty anyway but it's Christ's own distance from the kind of novel I want to write and hope I'll learn how to write. But the only way seems to be to write them and in the end maybe they average up.

You can put enough weight on a horse so he can't have a chance of winning and in America (and Americans are always in America - no matter whether they call it Paris or Paname) we all carry enough weight to kill a horse - let alone have him run under it. I've been living this side of bughouse with the old insomnia for about eight months now. And it's something you can take with you to any country but I'm glad that I was built on the tough side and maybe it will all work out.

I still feel badly about having ever written to you in an ex cathedra or ex-catheter - they have catheters as well as cathedrals over here - manner but I think that is just that the young have to be very sure always, because the show is really very tough and it is winning all the time and unless you know everything when you're twenty five you don't stand a chance of knowing anything at all when it's had time to shake down and you're thirty five. And we've all got to know something. Maybe.

This is a lousy letter but I wish to hell I was in Troutdale. Anyhow we'll be here when you come in November and it will be grand to see you again.

As ever,

NEWBERRY   Ernest

To MAXWELL PERKINS, Paris, 28 September 1926

Dear Mr. Perkins:

It was very pleasant about The Killers and I will surely send you some more stories. All that you say about the arrangement of the title page etc. of The Sun seems very good and I am sure that it will look well as you arrange it.

Unless it is done already, in which case it doesn't matter, there is no need to change Roger to Robert Prentiss. I verified the name of the kid I went to school with and found Prentiss was his first name.

When do you expect The Sun to be out? I had a letter from Curtis Brown saying that were sending copies of Cape's edition of In Our Time and had written Scribners for corrected proofs of The Sun, to show to Cape. It seems to me that he should take it.

Manuel Komroff, who edited the Marco Polo book, and sometimes writes excellent stories read Fifty Grand and when I told him why it had never been published offered to try and cut it 1500 words for me. He's taken it out in the country with him and when it comes back it may be a good magazine story and I could publish it in the original when I have a book of stories out. But if I don't like it I won't send it. I think Mr. Bridges might like to see some of Komroff's stories. Some of his eastern stories are very fine and very short.

I will write Mr. Bridges a letter but am hurrying this off to catch the Majestic.

Yours always,

PUL   Ernest Hemingway

To PAULINE PFEIFFER, Paris, 12 November 1926[1]

Dearest Pfife:

I have not heard anything since your letter October 26 when you were feeling so low except the one cable - communication stopped. When I wrote the last letter, that you will get some time the middle of next week - I did not know that you were in such terrible shape, nor even that you had begun to feel so badly and to worry. So that my letter will probably seem very little understanding and quite heartless. If I had only gotten your letter about how terribly you were feeling I could have written you about that - but it came just after the cable and after I'd sent my last letter.

I've felt absolutely done for and gone to pieces Pfife and I might as well write it out now and maybe get rid of it that way. It was certain that your mother would feel badly about your marrying some one who was divorced, about breaking up a home, about getting into a mess - and it is certain too that silent disapproval is the most deadly and something that you can do nothing about. I was sure that part of it would go badly. Your mother naturally could not feel any other way. Jin[2] showed me a letter she wrote, your mother, on November First saying that when you first came back you were looking well and quite happy and that now all that last week - the week during which I didn't hear from you - you were gone to pieces with nerves and in very bad shape. That you were really quite alone in Piggott with your own thoughts and that your own thoughts were *naturally* not pleasant. So it looks as though you were being put through a fairly complete hell - which may - because you are not strong and very run down, break you. And then we're broken and what good did that do? So I have that to think about all day and all night - and the worry is like a band of some sort across the inside of the top of my head - and there isn't anything else. All I can think is that you that are all I have and that I love more than all that is and have given up everything for and betrayed everything for and killed off everything for are being destroyed and your nerves and your spirit broken all the time day and night and that I can't do anything about it because you won't let me.

I know that when my letter came you had to decide one way or another and I know you took the harder thing and the thing you thought was right and I admire your courage - but I don't know at all that it was what we would have done if we could have talked it over together and all the time day and night I've just felt that it was fatal and that we were being smashed.

You see when you went to Piggott you said that you were going to tell your mother and that if she didn't like it you would leave - or that she would have to come around to it - because it was us against the world and that we had to do our own thing and that you were going to rest and not worry and get healthy and strong and above all not worry - Well and how did all that work out?

Now I can look back on the days when I had just straight lonesomeness and waiting for you - but knowing that everything was all right and that it was just waiting - and they seem unbelievably happy. Because now you have given yourself and your heart as a hostage to your mother too and the whole thing seems so absolutely hopeless. You were always going to cable if you went more than three days without writing - but there wasn't any cable - and your last letter was written the twenty sixth and Jinny got a letter from your mother yesterday that was written November First. And I didn't get anything. So I don't know whether you've given me up - or even then - before you got the letter about the new time - weren't trying to give me up and Pfife the time goes so slowly and so horribly and so flatly that I feel as though I would have to scream out and in the nights it is simply unbelievably terrible.

And all the time when you won't get letters and me instead of us being so happy and having all the world just being made into the figure representing sin and I get the horrors and hear you saying, "I won't go on with it. I won't. I can't do it. I just can't do it any longer."

So that's what I think about. Because if all the other promises were broken how can I rely on that one?

All day long I think of things to say to you and things to tell you and I start to clip things out of the paper and I think how simple it would be and how there was never anything, any difficulties that we got up by ourselves that we could not settle together, - only I'm absolutely tied.

I know that you did the extra three months because you thought that was what Hadley wanted - and also because at the time you were in such a state that sacrifice seemed like the thing to do. And of course all that Hadley wanted was to delay the divorce - anything to delay the divorce - she didn't want to just smash us both up - she won't admit it but she knows we're the same person - sometimes she has admitted it - but instead of giving her the delay that is practically the only thing left in the world that she wants we railroad her toward divorce and smash ourselves both up at the same time.

That makes nice thinking too.

So now no matter how bad it gets, I can't send the wire about *Hurry* because that is automatically shut off because you made the choice - evidently it was better to run a chance of smashing - or smash - than see each other and delay the divorce - So I can't do anything that might ever delay it. And I'm not sure I'm not going to smash, Pfife.

Only I won't of course. Only when you see me maybe think or wonder is this what I went through it all about and that's what it will be.

Because anybody can be smashed and evidently we are to be smashed by choice - our own free choice - in a grievous matter, with deliberation and full consent.

So I know this is a lousy terribly cheap self pitying letter just wallowing in bathos etc. etc. etc. and etc. and so it is. Oh Christ I feel terribly. Just terribly Pfife.

And then where will [we] be at the end when Hadley won't divorce or stalls again on the advice of friends.

As long as I had you I could stand anything and get through anything - and now I haven't got you and you've taken yourself deliberately away and I know you are sick and ill in the head and miserable Pfife and I can't stand it.

Last fall I said perfectly calmly and not bluffingly and during one of the good times that if this wasn't cleared up by christmas I would kill myself - because that would mean it wasn't going to clear up - and I've learned about blowing up from you Pfife and I can't stand it - and evidently all I can do is to remove the sin out of your life and avoid Hadley the necessity of divorce - and compliment Hadley - by killing myself. So then later I promised that I wouldn't do it or think about it under any circumstances until you came back. But now it is getting all out of control again and you have broken your promises and I should think that would let me out. Only nothing ever lets you out. But I'm not a saint, nor built like one, and I'd rather die now while there is still something left of the world than to go on and have every part of it flattened out and destroyed and made hollow before I die.[3]

But I won't and I won't think about it and maybe you'll come back and maybe there will be something left of you and maybe we'll have a little guts and not try self sacrifices in the middle of surgical operations and maybe we'll come through and maybe and maybe and maybe and maybe.

And all I want is you Pfife and oh dear god I want you so. And I'm ashamed of this letter and I hate it. But I had to get this poison out and I've just been stewed in it and not hearing and all the mail boats that get in with nothing on them and then that horrible awful letter from your mother yesterday in which you were getting your just punishment. I'm perfectly willing to go to hell after I'm dead rather than now. But not both. Altho now it looks like both. But it won't be. And please forgive this letter Pfife. It is everything contemptible. But that is the way I get when I'm too long away from you. It's only 84 days more now. And be-

tween now and next Friday I should surely get a letter and Jin has
wired to hear how you are - and I pray for you hours every night and
every morning when I wake up. I pray so for you to sleep and to hold
tight and not to worry and oh Pfife I love you love you love you so - and
I'm your all shot to hell

JFK   Ernest

1. Although the original is clearly dated 12 October, internal evidence indicates
this is an error for 12 November. 2. Pauline's sister, Virginia. 3. See EH to Isidor
Schneider, c. early October 1926: "The world is so tough and can do so many things
to us and break us in so many ways that it seems as though it were cheating when
it uses accidents or disease . . . But all you can do about hell is last through it. If
you can last through it. And you have to. Or at least I always will I guess." EH
adds he is "very prejudiced against suicide" and that "the real reason for not committing suicide is because you always know how swell life gets again after the hell
is over."

To MAXWELL PERKINS, Paris, 16 November 1926

Dear Mr. Perkins:

Thanks so much for sending the reviews and advertisements. The portrait, Bloomshield's drawing, looks much as I had imagined Jake Barnes;
it looks very much like a writer who had been saddened by the loss or
atrophy of certain non replaceable parts. It is a pity it couldn't have been
Barnes instead of Hemingway. Still it is fine to have at last succeeded in
looking like a writer. The ads and the blurb seem excellent.

I wish that I could do as you suggest about inserting some of the
matter about Brett. It doubtless would be of value to anyone reading
the stuff for the first time and there is some very good dope on Brett.
On the other hand any sort of a foreword or preface would seem to me
to break up the unity of the book and altho it does not show there is a
certain rhythm in all that book that if it were broken would be very
much missed. It was a complete unit with all that first stuff including
the Belloc episode—I could cut it where I did and have it stay a unit—
but the hard luck we had with Fifty Grand shows the difficulty of cutting that sort of stuff and further tinkering wouldn't help, I'm afraid.

I am terribly sorry because I would like very much to do it for you
but I think we'll find maybe, in the end, that what I lose by not com-
promising now we may all cash in on later. I know that you would not ask

me to put that back in unless you really liked it and I know it would be good in many ways—but I think in the end perhaps we would both lose by it. You see I would like, if you wanted, to write books for Scribner's to publish, for many years and would like them to be good books—better all the time—sometimes they might not be so good—but as well as I could write and perhaps with luck learning to write better all the time— and learning how things work and what the whole thing is about—and not getting bitter. So if this one doesn't sell maybe sometime one will. I'm very sure one will if they really are good—and if I learn to make them a lot better—but I'll never be able to do that and will just get caught in the machine if I start worrying about that—or considering it the selling. Altho God knows I need the money at this present time and I would so like to see the book really go because you have been so very decent to me.

The other thing is that Brett Ashley is a real person and as long as there were no changes in the way other real people James, Belloc, Her-gesheimer etc. were handled I did not mind what happened to *my* peo-ple—but since they (the others) were protected I might as well leave out that stuff so long as it is not actually necessary. That was the only stuff in the book that was not imaginary—the Brett biography.

I see that Mr. Bill Benet is very disappointed to find me lifting a character from Michael Arland [Arlen] and that is rather funny as I have never read a word of Arland but went around, after the war, with Lady Duff Twisden, Nancy Cunard, Mary Beerbohm who took Arland or Arlen up as a deserving Armenian youth and let him in on a few things and then dropped him as soon as he became annoyingly Armenian and less deserving—but not before he had gotten a little way behind the scenes into various people's lives.

So now it is pretty amusing to have known a girl and drawn her so close to life that it makes me feel very badly—except that I don't imagine she would ever read anything—and watch her go to hell completely— and assist at the depart—and then feeling pretty damned badly about it all learn that you had with boyish enthusiasm lifted a character from the un-read writings of some little Armenian sucker after London names. What do you suppose it is—that Benet imagines that nobody ever really had a title? Was it the title that offended him? Or do people only have titles in books written for servant girls? But as I haven't read Arland I don't know—and now I'm afraid to—because maybe it is like Arland. That would be awfully funny.

Maybe Arland would write a couple of chapters and it would sell millions. Perhaps Benet could get ahold of him for us.

Komroff finally cut only a couple of hundred words out of Fifty Grand. Maybe you could run it some time between serials or if Mr. [William

Lyon] Phelps were sick and copy was short. You might offer Mr. Phelps from me that if he will condense and give me the space I'll pay him whatever it's worth a page where I overlap into him. Or I'll split the price of the story with him. I'd like to have that story published sometime before boxing is abolished. Or magazines abolished.

Everything I publish over here is stolen by Samuel Roth who has never had my permission to publish one word and pirates everything that appears here as fast as it comes out and has never paid me a cent. I've seen the advertisements in the Nation and New Republic of his Two Worlds Monthly.

Joyce is all broken up about it. Roth has stolen his Ulysses without permission, never paid Joyce a cent, is publishing Ulysses in monthly installments and expurgating it. I saw Joyce today and he has just received a copy of an interview Roth gave to some N.Y. paper in which he declares that he is publishing Ulysses with Joyce's consent, that he has a financial arrangement with Joyce greatly to Joyce's advantage which he cannot at present divulge and that Joyce has made large sums selling the book under cover in America. Joyce is in absolute despair. The work of thirteen years of his life being stolen from him by a man who not content with that trys to blacken Joyce's character and not content with stealing a man's life work and lieing about it then garbles it.

Kenneth Simpson who is in the district attorney's office has promised to nail Roth as soon as he gets back to N.Y. Joyce meantime is trying to get an injunction against Roth.[1]

It is a horrible and discouraging business, and does not make one love the Jews any better. I feel badly about his stealing my stories—but that is a small matter compared to his theft of Joyce's entire book—but it does seem as though reputable publications like The Nation should refuse to accept his, Roth's, advertising. Isn't there some national organization that can blacklist the advertising of crooks? Life seems quite complicated today.

Next week I am planning to ride down to the Riviera with a friend who has to take a car down there and I'll see Scott. He's sailing the 12th of December, I believe.

I still have a check for 200 dollars that I haven't cashed because the franc has been too high—but it looks as though it were going to stay there. I hope the Sun will sell so that I may get some more from you when I need it—it seems as though it should—it's pretty interesting and there seems to be a difference of opinion about it—I've always heard that was good. The Times review I had to read to the end before I found whether they really liked it or not. [Conrad] Aiken seemed to like it. Archie MacLeish tells me he's a good critic—Aiken I mean. Maybe that will encourage some of the other boys to like it. It's funny to write a book that seems as tragic as that and have them take it for a jazz superficial story. If you went any deeper inside they couldn't read it because they would be crying all the time. Life's all very funny today—and this type-writer seems to have run away with its-self.

Yours

PUL Ernest Hemingway

1. Roth pirated Joyce's *Ulysses*, continuing through 27 December 1928, when he was enjoined by the New York State Supreme Court from using Joyce's name in any way. See Richard Ellmann, *James Joyce* (New York, 1959), pp. 598–99, 616–17.

To HADLEY HEMINGWAY, Paris, 18 November 1926

My dearest Hadley:

I am terribly sorry that I did not get your letter until after I had seen you—and because I did not know what decisions you had made nor what was in your mind—hurt you again and again by talking about something that you had so wisely concluded we should not discuss but only write about.

I think your letter like everything that you have ever done is very brave and altogether unselfish and generous.

During the past week I found out, and the horror of it was very great, how Pauline and I without meaning to had constantly exerted a pressure on you to divorce me—a pressure that came from a sort of hurried panic fear that we should lose one another—that naturally you were suspicious of and re-acted against as a basis for two people to marry on. Your re-actions have always been right and I have always trusted them and be-lieved in them as well as in your head.

I think that perhaps when Pauline and I realized how cruel we had been to you in that way and that we could not expect to found any basis of happiness on such a continued cruelty—and realized that we could go on any length of time that would suit you without each other rather than have you consent to a divorce that you did not really feel was inevitable, or desireable,—I think that when you felt that, and I hope you believe it was sincere, it maybe [might] have helped to remove your natural and right re-action against setting two people free to marry each other who did not seem to deserve each other or anything else.

Now, if you wish to divorce me, I will start at once finding out the details and about lawyers. I will start that at any rate—as you ask in your letter—and will write you what I learn.

If you don't want to start now or until after Pauline comes back—or later, please do what you wish.

If it is an inevitable step I think we will all feel better and things can start to clear once it is started. That is, please dear Hadley, not me trying to influence you—or speed up my own affairs. It is only that we seem like two boxers who are groggy and floating and staggering around and yet will not put over a knock-out punch: which would terminate the combat and let the process of healing and recovering start.

Another thing—I do not know your plans about America—but I do not think you should be hurried through a divorce in order to get to America which may not be what you want when you get there.

What you could do is start the divorce—and go to America and have a look around and see how you like it and exactly what the situation is in the interval which must elapse between the starting of the divorce and the three or four months which must elapse before it would be necessary for you to appear again in the divorce. I think the process is that a huissier [bailiff] would serve me with demand to return to you—which if I refused would be followed by a second service some months later— then we would both have to appear for a formal refusal to reconcile— ten minutes or five minutes—before a juge d'instruction [magistrate] or something like that and then you would be given a decree of divorce.

If you wished to go to America I am sure you could do it without great expense and it would be a very good way of seeing how things were over there—both on the coast and in N.Y. You might take one of the very comfortable dollar line boats which would take you from Marseilles and land you in California—by the canal. And return to Paris by way of N.Y. which would give you a good chance to see both places. Would change les idees and give you the dope on.

In any event, no matter what you do, I am writing to Scribners that all royalties from The Sun Also Rises should be paid to you. These will not commence until after 3,000 copies have been sold—we spent the advance on that sale together—but from then on will mount rapidly at 30 cents a copy on each book. And from the way Max Perkins writes about future printings etc. and the way they are advertising it might, if it should go, be a very good sum.

In any event you can absolutely count on all the royalties from Cape— I am instructing my agent that these also should be paid to you—Cape has offered to bring the book out between January and March—pay on publication the royalties on all advance sales and a royalty of 10% on the first 3,000 copies, rising to 15% up to 5,000 copies and after that 20%. Which are very generous royalties on a book that might have a great sale in England.

I want you please not to make any objection to this—it is the only thing that I who have done so many things to hurt you can do to help you—and you must let me do it.

There is no question of my suffering from any lack of money as I know that I could borrow money from Scott, Archie [MacLeish], or the Murphies—all of whom are wealthy people—or that I could accept money from Pauline whose Uncle Gus seems always wanting to give it to her. I need in the meantime the financial pressure of starting clean—and the income from those books belongs to you by every right—you supported me while they were being written and helped me write them. I would never have written any of them In Our Time, Torrents or The Sun if I had not married you and had your loyal and self-sacrificing and always stimulating and loving—and actual cash support backing.

I would include In Our Time, and Torrents but I believe the one is on the deficit side still and the other not likely to make money.

But I am making a will and writing to my agents and my publishers that in case of my death the income from all my books, past and future, is to go to Bumby where you can hold it in trust for him.

I must see that you get these Sun royalties Hadley and will you please just take it as a gift without any protestations or bitterness. Because it is really your right and due and it would make [me] terribly happy if instead you would be very generous and take it as a gift.

With that to count on—it cannot be less than several hundred dollars —you can make the American trip and not worry about money. During your absence I would give Bumby the benefit of whatever benefit a papa is. I would also be on my honor that Pauline would not see Bumby in case she should be here any of that time—so you would not have to worry about that. If it would be a thing you would worry about.

Our conversation confused certain phases of your letter. You say the three months absense thing is officially terminated. If it would make any difference to you I am sure Pauline and I would be glad, I am sure, to complete the three months apart from each other. If it makes no differ-ence I imagine she might come back in January or when she wished. Please let me know about this and if you want me to communicate the facts of our letters to Pauline.

I am sorry this is so long and there are doubtless many things I have left out. I'll see a lot of Bumby—and I think perhaps the luckiest thing Bumby will ever have is to have you for a mother. And I won't tell you how I admire your straight thinking, your head, your heart and your very lovely hands and I pray God always that he will make up to you the very great hurt that I have done you—who are the best and truest and loveliest person that I have ever known.

JFK   Ernest

To MAXWELL PERKINS, Paris, 19 November 1926

Dear Mr. Perkins:

I don't know whether the magazine would care for any humorous stuff. Anyway here is a piece[1] and if they should not want it will you use your judgement about turning it over to Edmund Wilson care of The New Republic—who has written saying they will pay me $50 for a page of 1200 words on more or less anything—or perhaps to [Paul] Reynolds who wrote Scott they would like something more of mine—and who might be able to get me some money for it.

Thank you for the Transcript review. They did very nobly by us all. It was refreshing to see someone have some doubts that I took the Gertrude Stein thing very seriously—I meant to play off against that splendid bombast (Gertrude's assumption of prophetic roles). Nobody knows about the generation that follows them and certainly has no right to judge. The quotation from Eccles.—one generation passeth and another generation cometh but the earth abideth forever—The sun also Ariseth. What I would like you to do in any further printings is to lop off the Vanity of vanities, saith the preacher, vanity of vanities; all is vanity—What profit hath a man of all his labour which he taketh under the sun?—delete all that. And start the quotation with and use only the 4th, 5th, 6th and 7th verses of Ecclesiastes. That is starting with One generation passeth away—and finishing with unto the place from whence the rivers come thither they return again.

That makes it much clearer. The point of the book to me was that the earth abideth forever—having a great deal of fondness and admiration for the earth and not a hell of a lot for my generation and caring little about Vanities. I only hesitated at the start to cut the writing of a better writer—but it seems necessary. I didn't mean the book to be a hollow or bitter satire but a damn tragedy with the earth abiding for ever as the hero.

Also have discovered that most people don't think in words—as they do in everybody's writing now—and so in Sun A.R. the critics miss their interior monologues and aren't happy—or disappointed I cut out 40,000 words of the stuff that would have made them happy out of the first Mss—it would have made them happy but it would have rung as false 10 years from now as Bromfield.

The Sun Also rises could have been and should have been a better book—but first Don Stewart was taking a cure for his liver in Vichy while I wrote the first draft of S.A.R. instead—and secondly I figure it is better to write about what you can write about and try and make it come off

than have epoch making canvasses etc.—and you figure what age the
novelists had that wrote the really great novels.

There can be the tour de force by a kid like [Stephen Crane in] The
Red Badge of Courage—but in general they were pretty well along and
they knew a few things—and in the time they were learning and going
through it they learned how to write by writing.

Well I'd better stop before I start getting like a critic myself which
would be pretty bad. I hope you like this funny one anyway.

With best regards
Ernest Hemingway

PUL

1. Probably "My Own Life," *New Yorker* 2 (12 February 1927): 23–24.

To MAXWELL PERKINS, Paris, 23 November 1926

Dear Mr. Perkins:

Yesterday on the Leviathan I sent you a story called—In Another
Country—for the magazine. Enclosed is a letter from College Humor
which Don Stewart tells me pays vast sums. You might send this to [Paul]
Reynolds with the funny thing I sent a week or so ago—unless it has gone
somewhere else or something has happened to it. He could send it to
College Humor.

I am awfully sorry to bother you about this and would not do so if I
had Reynold's address—or if I had not wanted first to give the Magazine
a chance at the funny one.

I wonder if College Humor would buy Fifty Grand. Reynolds might
send them that. I think that's a good hunch.

I am writing on another Italian story.

The letter from Mr. Bridges about the Canary [for One] story has just
come and your two enclosures of ads. They look very handsome.

I took my son, who is three years old, to the café the other afternoon to
get an icecream and while he was eating it and holding his harmonica
in the other hand he looked all around and said, "Ah la vie est beau avec
papa!"

Yours always,
Ernest Hemingway

PUL

To F. SCOTT FITZGERALD, Paris, *c.* 24 November 1926

Dear Scott:

Ive been trying every week to get down to see you before you leave - Mike Ward was getting a car to drive down but first he was sick - then the cars were always full; then the guy who was to take his place in the bank was sick and that brings us to this Wednesday which was today and the last time we were to start.

How are you and how have you been - ? Have you worked and how is the novel. I'll bet it will be a damned good novel once you settled down to writing it - and you must have had plenty of time at Juan les Pins for writing lately.

I've had a grand spell of working; sold another story to Scribners - making two - and have sent them another that I am sure they will buy - a hell of a good story about Milan during the war - and just finished a better one that I should be typing now. Have two other stories that I know can't sell so am not sending them out - but that will go well in a book.

This is a bloody borrowed typewriter - my own busted. I see by an ad in the World that The Sun etc. is in 2nd printing and Heywood Broun in the same paper Nov. 19 a full col. on it etc. Reviews have been good although the boys seem divided as to who or whom I copied the most from you or Michael Arlen so I am very grateful to both of you - and especially you, Scott, because I like you and I don't know Arland and have besides heard that he is an Armenian and it would seem a little premature to be grateful to any Armenian. But I am certainly grateful to you and I am asking Scribners to insert as a subtitle in everything after the eighth printing

THE SUN ALSO RISES (LIKE YOUR COCK IF YOU HAVE ONE)
                    A greater Gatsby
(Written with the friendship of F. Scott Fitzgerald (Prophet of THE JAZZ AGE)

God I wish I could see you. You are the only guy in or out of Europe I can say as much for (or against) but I certainly would like to see you. I haven't enough money to come down on the train and so have been at the mercy of these non leaving free motors. The bad weather has made biking impossible. I started once that way but had a hell of a spill and luxe-ed my epaule. How the hell are you anyway.

What does 2nd printing mean in numbers? Book was published Oct. 22 that was in the ad of Nov. 19. Max Perkins wrote the first of Nov. that the advance orders hadn't been much but that re-orders were coming in. He didn't mention any figures. Has he written to you?

College Humor has written asking me to write them essays, pieces, shit or long fiction and I turned the letter over to Max to give to Reynolds. Sometimes I have funny stuff and I think Reynolds might be willing to sell it as somebody told me Cowedge Humour paid large prices. They said they were reviewing Sun Also etc, in January issue. Hope it goes better at Princeton than the Lampoon.

As for personal life of the noted, noted by who, author, Hadley is divorcing me. Have turned over to her all existing finances and all received and future royalties from Sun. Cape and Heinemann have both made offers for British rights. Do you think Reynolds might sell it to the Movies or some such place. I'm going to take a cut on those if there are any. Have been eating one meal a day and if I get tired enough sleeping - working like hell lately - find starting life poorer than any time since I was 14 with an earning capacity of what stories I sell to Scribners very interesting. I suppose everybody's life goes to hell and anyway have been very healthy and, lately, able to use the head again. If anybody in N.Y. asks about me don't tell them a god damned thing. I would tell you all about things but don't seem able to write about them and am not very good at talking about them. Anyway so many people seem to talk so well about one's affairs that there doesn't seem ever any necessity to speak about them oneself.

Anyway I'm now all through with the general bumping off phase and will only bump off now under certain special circumstances which I don't think will arise. Have refrained from any half turnings on of the gas or slitting of the wrists with sterilized safety razor blades. Am continuing my life in original role of son of a bitch sans peur et sans rapproche. The only thing in life I've ever had any luck being decent about is money so am very splendid and punctilious about that. Also I have been sucked in by ambition to do some very good work now no matter how everything comes out. I think some of the stuff now is good. Have learned a lot.

It is now time to cut this off and mail it.

Write to me and tell me all the dirt. What do you hear from N.Y.? Where are you going to live? How are Zelda? and Scotty? Bumby and Hadley are damned well. I had Bumby for ten days while Hadley was on a trip and one morning I took him to a cafe and got him a glace and a new harmonica and holding the harmonica and eating the glace he said, "La vie est beau avec papa."[1] He is very fond of me and when I ask him what does Papa do, hoping to hear him say Papa is a great writer like the clippings. He says Papa does nothing. So then I taught him to say,

"Bumby will support Papa," so he says that all the time. What will Bumby do? Bumby will support papa en espagne avec les taureaux.

Love to you all

PUL   Ernest.

1. "We agree with Bumby," wrote Fitzgerald in his reply, postmarked 23 December 1926. See *The Letters of F. Scott Fitzgerald*, ed. Andrew Turnbull (New York, 1963), pp. 298–99. He also said: "I can't tell you how much your friendship has meant to me during this year and a half—it is the brightest thing in our trip to Europe."

To HIS FAMILY, Paris, 1 December 1926

Dear Dad and Mother:

Thank you both for your fine letters. I am so glad to hear of mother's success in painting. I felt terribly not to get back this fall and to miss the hunting with Dad but things did not come out. Don't worry about Bumby's health as he lives not in a studio but in a comfortable, light, well heated apartment on the sixth floor with a lovely view and all modern comforts. He recovered completely from his whooping cough, plays in the parc—the Luxembourg Gardens—and is tremendously husky and strong. He talks French and good German and some English and says very intelligent things. It is me that works in the [Murphy] studio where nobody has the address and can't bother me.

The reviews of my novel have been splendid and I see by an ad in the N.Y. World of November 19 that it is in its second printing. The Boston Transcript gave it two columns and the N.Y. Times, World and Tribune all good reviews. It is being published in England shortly. In Our Time has been published there and had very good press. I'll save some of the reviews that Scribner's send me and send them to you if you'd like to see them. Have a story in December Scribner's magazine I believe. Either December or January. One in the following number too. Have read the proof on both of them but am not altogether sure what numbers they are appearing in.[1]

I have a fine new picture of Bumby to send you for Christmas. Man Ray who took the one of me you liked did it. Bumby says he is going to go to Spain with papa next year and sleep with the bulls. He pretended to have drunk some cleaning fluid and when Hadley told him that if he drunk it it would kill him and he would go to heaven with the baby jesus, Bumby said in french that that was true and if the baby Jesus drunk the cleaning fluid it would kill the baby Jesus too. I taught him all his prayers in English. But he doesn't take them very seriously yet and when I took him to church one Sunday he said it was very fine because the church was full of lions. He goes down six flights every morning and brings up the paper all alone. Best love to you both, to Carol, Leicester, Sunny, Marce, and Ura and all their husbands, lovers, and progeny.

JFK   Ernie

1. "The Killers," March 1927; "In Another Country" and "A Canary for One," April 1927.

To PAULINE PFEIFFER, Paris, 3 December 1926

Dearest Pfife:

your letter to me through Jinny and the air mail came last night - Thursday December 2 - and either tonight or tomorrow will send this cable - maybe waiting until tomorrow for the week end rates --- maybe sending tonight from the Bourse. Jinny is coming here at seven. Was to spend yesterday with the lawyer but he put it off until this afternoon.

I've been in pretty terrible shape now for a while and would have wired hurry except I knew you had your Christmas planned and the family and the Macleishes taken rooms and sleeper for me etc. People in the lives.

Doesn't take any particular form outside of the horrors at night and a black depression. You see Pfife I think that when two people love each other terribly much and need each other in every way and then go away from each other it works almost as bad as an abortion. It isn't as though there were a war or it were a whaling voyage or any case of force majeur - where something you could not do anything against ran it --- but where you could buck against that thing; the daily routine of a war or the work of a long trip with nothing to do about it. But the deliberate keeping apart when all you have is each other does something bad to you and lately it has shot me all to hell inside. I know, or anyhow I feel, that I could be faithful to you with my body and my mind and my spirit for as long as I had any of them --- and I know now too that because being the same guy and yet a whole something started with my body that had gotten to be an integral part of everything that being alone and just lonesome all sorts of things seem to damn up and the balance of it all be thrown off and it attacks the spirit and it isn't good for the head either. You lie all night half funny in the head and pray and pray and pray you won't go crazy. And I can't believe it does any good and I do believe it does hell's own amount of harm.

And you had yours too - and I felt so terribly about that - and now you are swell and fine and practical in the head (like we both used to be) and I will be again because I'm not a depressed rat naturally. And I've sense enough to know when I think all the time I want to die that I'm just a fool because what I think about as wanting to die is just to have oblivion until I can have Pfeiffer. But I know it will be swell and to let you know that I am feeling swell and that the world is grand and that I feel good inside and not just dry like a piece of cuttle fish bone like they feed canaries but really fine I'll write you EXCELLENT - and that means that you just read this letter as by somebody else and know that I'm fine in the head and inside.

I love you so Pfife and I want a letter from you - just about loving each other and no facts bulletins nor anything timely --- because it has been a terrible long time since I had a letter like that nor one that wasn't written to catch a mail in ten minutes and what I miss worse is not having any intimacy with you - nor any feeling of us against the others. I knew it was swell and practical and I admired the mechanics and performance of it the air mail in every way but when I got your first letter after the cable - the first time I'd heard from you and was to make contact again - open in a letter from Jinny I just felt like hell. So would you maybe write me a letter like that sometime when [there] isn't anything else to say and ordinarily you wouldn't have been writing a letter - if you should ever feel that way — in which our loving each other will sound like something pleasant and stick in maybe a few references to the future as being something pretty good. All the letters before your bad time sounded as though you loved me more than anything in the world and when one came I used to be just cock-eyed happy. Then since there was just the grand last letter but it seemed as though there wasn't any joy any more - just loyalty and I was afraid maybe you had really given me up as you said you had had to and were just going through with it now ---- and oh everything else bughouse. And I would like a letter like they used to be before you felt so badly.

JFK   [Letter ends here.]

To MAXWELL PERKINS, Paris, 6 December 1926

Dear Mr. Perkins:

Thanks so much for the reviews and the information about the Sun's prospects. As for movie rights please get the best you can i.e. the most money—I do not go to the movies and would not care what changes they made. That is their gain or loss—I don't write movies. Although if they would film Pamplona they could make a wonderful picture. All that racing of the bulls through the streets and the people running ahead and into the ring, amateurs being tossed, the bulls charging into the crowd etc. really happens every morning between the 7th and 12th of July and they could get some wonderful stuff. We made a movie from inside the ring one year with a German portable camera—the sort that takes full size movies; you have only to load it and press down a button to keep it shooting—no cranking—and had the rush of people coming into the ring, coming faster and faster and then finally falling all over themselves and piling up and the bulls jamming over them and right into the camera. It was a wonderful thing but so short that it wasn't of any commercial value. Have another one of Don Stewart being tossed in the amateur fight and one of me bull fighting. When I come over to the states will bring them and we can run them off sometime.

About the stories—I have ten stories now—two long ones The Undefeated—a bull fight story of between 12 and 15,000 words; and Fifty Grand. Eight others will average around three thousand words or so. I don't know whether that is enough for a book. In any event do you think it would be wise to have another book out so soon as Spring—rather than wait until early fall? In Our Time came out last November—Torrents in the early summer—The Sun in Oct. Don't you think we might give them a rest? Or isn't that how it's done?

I will keep the bull fight book going and might do the first part and get it out of the way up to date. It will have illustrations—drawings and photographs—and I think should have some colored reproductions. It is a long one to write because it is not to be just a history and text book or apologia for bull fighting—but instead, if possible, bull fighting its-self. As it's a thing that nobody knows about in English I'd like to take it first from altogether outside—how I happened to be interested in it, how it seemed before I saw it—how it was when I didn't understand it—my own experience with it, how it reacts on others—the gradual finding out about it and try and build it up from the outside and then go all the way inside with chapters on everything. It might be interesting to people because nobody knows anything about it—and it really is terribly interesting—being a matter of life and death—and anything that a young peasant or bootblack can make 80,000 dollars a year in before he is twenty three does something to people. I think a really true book if it were fairly well written about the one thing that has, with the exception of the ritual of the church, come down to us intact from the old days would have a certain permanent value. But it has to be solid and true and have all the dope and be interesting—and it won't be ready for a long time. But you can figure on it for the future if you like.[1]

I think the next thing to figure on is a book of stories—and I think it's very important that it should be awfully good and not hurried. Because if The Sun should have some success there will be a lot of people with the knife out very eager to see me slipping—and the best way to handle that is not to slip. Then I'd like to write another novel when things get straightened out and my head gets tranquil. In the meantime I might as well write stories for a while. I had a note from Scott that he was leaving for Genoa—so I imagine you may see him before you get this letter.

My own typewriter is broken and this borrowed one has so many wretched individual traits that my mind is half occupied all the time I'm writing with the malignancy of the machine and I haven't been able to re-write the other story I was going to send you or do anything new. I'll enclose the proofs of the little canary story with this and perhaps you will turn them over to Mr. Bridges with my compliments.

Yours always,

PUL Ernest Hemingway

1. Another anticipation of *Death in the Afternoon* (1932), which EH had first mentioned to Perkins in 1925.

To MAXWELL PERKINS, Paris, 7 December 1926

Dear Mr. Perkins:

Today your letter of Nov. 26 came. I don't think the book could have been better made nor finer looking.

One thing I would like—four copies only were sent me—and I would like a few more as I had to buy it here at 70 francs a copy to send over to Curtis Brown for his negotiations with Heinemann etc. I have set a trap for [Samuel] Roth by letting a local N.J. printer get out a few hundred copies of a thing of mine called Today Is Friday—which Roth will be very liable to lift for one of his publications. This I have had copyrighted and have just received the certificate of copyright registration from Washington. We may be able to bag him with that.

About the drawing—it really makes no difference. At the time I hated to have my family think that I really looked like that. They feel, I understand, very humiliated because of "the way I write." A copy of The Literary Digest Book Review Magazine from my father has underlined in blue and red pencil the following—The Penn Publishing Company, of Philadelphia, which reports a *constantly increasing sale* for the books of Temple Bailey, wrote in part—"Our feeling is that there is a strong reaction against the sex novel, and even the highbrow realistic novel ---- and that (later on) the clean, romantic, or stirring adventure tale will always *command the wider public.*" But the drawing may have pleased them. And it seems to reproduce very well.

What you say about The Green Hat is quite true. My contact with Arlen was through Scott's talking about him and his stuff when we once drove Scott's car from Lyons to Paris.[1] I remember telling Scott who the people were that had taken Arlen up—and even getting quite irritated about Arlen—Don Stewart talked about him too; I took it for granted that the Green Hat must be a cheap book when I heard that the heroine killed herself—because the one very essential fact about all those people that Arlen knew was that none of them had the guts to kill themselves. So I guess it was really protesting about that sort of twaddle that I made Brett so damned accurate that practically nobody seemed to believe in her. Maybe they do now though. Anyway it was very funny.

There really is, to me anyway, very great glamour in life—and places and all sorts of things and I would like sometime to get it into the stuff. People aren't all as bad as Ring Lardner finds them—or as hollowed out and exhausted emotionally as some of The Sun generation. I've known some very wonderful people who even though they were going directly toward the grave (which is what makes any story a tragedy if carried out until the end) managed to put up a very fine performance enroute. Impotence is a pretty dull subject compared with war or love or the old lucha por la vida [struggle for life]. I do hope though that The Sun will sell a tremendous lot because while the subject is dull the book isn't. Then maybe sometime, and with that impetus to go on, we'll have a novel where the subject won't be dull and try and keep the good qualities of this one. Only, of course, you don't have subjects—Louis Bromfield has subjects—but just write them and if God is good to you they come out well. But it would always be much better to write than to talk about writing.

My son looks forward very much to the Christmas book and told his mother very excitedly—Max Perkins va me donner un jolie cadeau! When she asked him what it was he said it was a very beautiful big book not written by papa.

Yours always

Ernest Hemingway

1. On Fitzgerald and Michael Arlen see *A Moveable Feast* (New York, 1964), pp. 174–75.

To MAXWELL PERKINS, Paris, 21 December 1926

Dear Mr. Perkins:

Thanks for the figures on the Sun. I do hope it will go on again after the New Year and think it may as there seems to be much divergence of opinion etc. which must mean discussion. John Bishop showed me a letter from Edmund Wilson last night in which Wilson was very enthusiastic saying he thought it best novel by any one of my generation— but that plenty of others didn't and what did he, Bishop, think. Maybe Wilson will write something about it. I'm awfully glad he liked it.

I think it is a splendid idea of Bridges about running the three stories together[1]—they are all short—none of them long enough to make much of a row alone—but all 3 complement one another and would make a fine group. And perhaps cheer up Dos, Allen Tate, and the other boys who fear I'm on the toboggan.

I take it for granted then he's buying In Another Country—and if he wants to send it I could use the check.

Thank you ever so much for the Christmas book for Bumby. And a very merry holiday time.

Ernest Hemingway

Dos Passos sent me a carbon of his review. I think it was fine about his not liking the book and wanting it to be better, but a poor criticism that Pamplona in the book wasn't as good as Pamplona in real life— because I think it was maybe pretty exciting to people who'd never been there—and that was who it was written for. It would be easy to write about it for Dos and make it very exciting—because he's been there. But written for him it wouldn't mean anything to the quite abstract reader that one tries to write for.

I suppose by now you have seen Scott. Please give him my best greetings.

I am leaving Paris on Christmas night—perhaps for several months—but letters to the bank will always be forwarded promptly. They relay cables too.

Cape took The Sun with a 50 pound advance—10-15-20-royalties and Spring publication.

I have been writing some more stories. I have given my wife all the Sun royalties—both British and American—and I hope they will be considerable. I don't know when the royalty checks come out. When one does I wish you could consider the advance on Torrents as $500 and that paid on the Sun as $1000 and let the check go on when the earnings commence after the $1000 is paid off.

I don't imagine that Torrents earned $500 but you can deduct the difference from my next book.

When the royalty check comes due you may send it to Hadley R. Hemingway, Guaranty Trust Co. of N.Y., one Rue des Italiens, Paris.

I imagine, now that they seem to be rowing about it that the Sun may go very well. The chief criticism seems to be that the people are so unattractive—which seems very funny as criticism when you consider the attractiveness of the people in, say, Ulysses, the Old Testament, Judge [Henry] Fielding and other people some of the critics like. I wonder where these thoroughly attractive people hang out and how they behave when they're drunk and what do *they* think about nights. Oh hell. There's at least one highly moral hotel keeper [Montoya] in the book. That's my contention and I'll stick to it. And an exemplary Englishman named Harris.

And why not make a Jew a bounder in literature as well as in life? Do jews always have to be so splendid in writing?

I think maybe next book we can save money on the clippings.

Critics, this is still Mr. [Allen] Tate—have a habit of hanging attributes on you themselves—and then when they find you're not that way accusing you of sailing under false colours—Mr. Tate feels so badly that I'm not as hard-boiled as he had publicly announced. As a matter of fact I have not been at all hard boiled since July 8 1918—on the night of which I discovered that that also was Vanity.

PUL

---

1. "In Another Country" and "A Canary for One" were both in *Scribner's Magazine* 81 (April 1927). "The Killers" was in the March number.

To MAXWELL PERKINS, Gstaad, Switzerland, 20 January 1927

Dear Mr. Perkins:

Enclosed are two notes from Rex Lardner and Manuel Komroff. I wrote to Mr. Lardner today telling him I was writing you to please send him Fifty Grand.[1] When they send it back maybe some one in the office could send it to the Editor of the Atlantic Monthly. Then when it comes back from there I think we might put it in dry dock.

Fifty Grand should bring an enormous price to try and get back some of the postage.

I have had letters and now a cable from gents conducting the American Caravan. This it seems is not only a book but a worthy American venture. When they first wrote me last summer I promised Paul Rosenfelt a long bull fight story called A Lack of Passion. I thought it was a very good story but when I came to re-write it decided it was no bloody good at all and that re-writing wouldn't save it. So now I don't know what to send them. Perhaps the Alpine Idyll would do. I may cable you tomorrow to turn it over to Kreymbourg at 77 Irving Place. I would like to send them a longer thing but think we ought to keep the Fifty Grand for the next book and haven't any other long stories on hand.

Sherwood Anderson is in Paris and we had two fine afternoons together. He said a very funny thing about the Editors of the New Masses: they, he said, wanted a revolution because they hoped that under some new system of government they would be men of talent. He was not at all sore about Torrents and we had a fine time. He spoke fondly of Scribner's as having paid him $750 for a story in the Christmas number. If that is exact I will try and get something epoch making for Mr. Bridges for next Christmas. It would be grand sometime to write a story that was neither too long nor too short and full of either the Christmas Spirit or Love Interest. The Nouvelle Revue Francaise wants to bring out The Sun etc. in French but I am stalling them to bring out a book of stories first.

With best regards to yourself and to Scott when you see him,

Yours always,

PUL   Ernest Hemingway

1. "Fifty Grand," *Atlantic Monthly* 140 (July 1927).

To CHARD POWERS SMITH,[1] Gstaad, *c.* 21 January 1927

My dear Smith:

I received your letter several weeks ago but did not wish to answer it hastily. It is very interesting to find you identifying yourself with characters in In Our Time and I hope it may induce you to purchase several copies of the book which, on my next visit to Paris, I will be very glad to inscribe for you or for any of your friends.

Your letter too, in spite of certain defects in construction, seemed a very interesting example of a letter written to some one you were sure was out of town. I noted too, how, unable to rely absolutely on this premise (my absence) you brought in a hope-for-better-things note at the end; very nicely designed to remove the danger from the first part. May I congratulate you on the improvement of your prose style?

Your application of the term "contemptible worm" to myself was very flattering. I feel you must be an authority on anything contemptible and will not attempt to dispute your classification. I remember the feeling of contempt I had for you on meeting you and regreted it intensely as a very cheap emotion and one very bad for literary production. I feel we are in accord on this. However this feeling, contempt, has persisted, greatly to my regret, and has, in fact, increased the more I have heard of you and your adventures in America. I am sure I am a contemptible worm to you, because you have told me, and I feel very humble beside you; because to me, my dear Smith, you are a very contemptible mountain.

It will be a great pleasure to see you again in Paris and somewhat of a pleasure to knock you down a few times, or perhaps once, depending on your talent for getting up; although I am sure I should feel very sorry afterwards. I doubt however if you will still be in Paris in March when I return and if you are I have no doubt you will be carrying numbers of pistols, sword canes or other things commensurate with your truly mountainous character.

You must believe, my dear Smith, that this letter does not end on anything but a note of sincere and hearty contempt for you, your past, your present and your future—and—lest you should have been deceived in an earlier paragraph—for the prose style of your letters.

Your admiring friend,

T.C. PUL   Ernest Hemingway.

1. Chard Powers Smith (1894–1977) was the victim in EH's "Mr. and Mrs. Elliot," originally called "Mr. and Mrs. Smith" and first published in the *Little Review* 10 (Autumn–Winter 1924–1925). The story acidly satirizes the alleged marital problems of the Smiths. Smith wrote EH, *c.* 1 January 1927, to protest the tone and content of the story. For a brief account, see Carlos Baker, *Hemingway: The Writer as Artist* (Princeton, 1972), p. 27.

To GRACE HALL HEMINGWAY, Gstaad, 5 February 1927

Dear Mother:

Thank you very much for sending me the catalogue of the Marshal Field exhibit with the reproduction of your painting of the Blacksmith Shop in it. It looks very lovely and I should have liked to see the original.

I did not answer when you wrote about the Sun etc. book as I could not help being angry and it is very foolish to write angry letters; and more than foolish to do so to one's mother. It is quite natural for you not to like the book and I regret your reading any book that causes you pain or disgust.

On the other hand I am in no way ashamed of the book, except in as I may have failed in accurately portraying the people I wrote of, or in making them really come alive to the reader. I am sure the book is unpleasant. But it is not *all* unpleasant and I am sure is no more unpleasant than the real inner lives of some of our best Oak Park families. You must remember that in such a book all the worst of the people's lives is displayed while at home there is a very lovely side for the public and the sort of thing of which I have had some experience in observing behind closed doors. Besides you, as an artist, know that a writer should not be forced to defend his choice of a subject but should be criticized on how he has treated that subject. The people I wrote of were certainly burned out, hollow and smashed—and that is the way I have attempted to show them. I am only ashamed of the book in whatever way it fails to really give the people I wished to present. I have a long life to write other books and the subjects will not always be the same—except as they will all, I hope, be human beings.

And if the good ladies of the book study club under the guidance of Miss [Fanny] Butcher, who is *not* an intelligent reviewer—I would have felt very silly had she praised the book—agree unanimously that I am prostituting a great talent etc. for the lowest ends—why the good ladies are talking about something of which they know nothing and saying very foolish things.

As for Hadley, Bumby and myself—altho Hadley and I have not been living in the same house for some time (we have lived apart since last Sept. and by now Hadley may have divorced me) we are the very best of friends. She and Bumby are both well, healthy and happy and all the profits and royalties of The Sun Also Rises, by my order, are being paid directly to Hadley, both from America and England. The book has gone into, by the last ads I saw in January, 5 printings (15,000) copies, and is still going strongly. It is published in England in the Spring under the title of Fiesta. Hadley is coming to America in the Spring so you can see Bumby on the profits of Sun Also Rises. I am not taking one cent of the royalties, which are already running into several thousand dollars, have been drinking nothing but my usual wine or beer with meals, have been leading a very monastic life and trying to write as well as I am able. We have different ideas about what constitutes good writing—that is simply a fundamental disagreement—but you really are deceiving yourself if you allow any Fanny Butchers to tell you that I am pandering to sensationalism etc. etc. I get letters from Vanity Fair, Cosmopolitan etc. asking me for stories, articles, and serials, but am publishing nothing for six months or a year (a few stories sold to Scribner's the end of last year and one funny article out) because I know that now is a very crucial time and that it is much more important for me to write in tranquility, trying to write as well as I can, with no eye on any market, nor any thought of what the stuff will bring, or even if it can ever be published—than to fall into the money making trap which handles American writers like the corn-husking machine handled my noted relative's thumb.[1]

I'm sending this letter to both of you[2] because I know you have been worried about me and I am always sorry to cause you worry. But you must not do that—because, although my life may smash up in different ways I will always do all that I can for the people I love (I don't write home a lot because I haven't time and because, writing, I find it very hard to write letters and have to restrict correspondence to the letters I have to write—and my real friends know that I am just as fond of them whether I write or not) that I have never been a drunk nor even a steady drinker (You will hear legends that I am—they are tacked on everyone that ever wrote about people who drink) and that all I want is tranquility and a chance to write. You may never like any thing I write—and then suddenly you might like something very much. But you must believe that I am sincere in what I write. Dad has been very loyal and while you, mother, have not been loyal at all I absolutely understand that it is because you believed you owed it to yourself to correct me in a path which seemed to you disastrous.

So maybe we can drop that all. I am sure that, in the course of my life, you will find much cause to feel that I have disgraced you if you believe everything you hear. On the other hand with a little shot of loyalty as anaesthetic you may be able to get through all my obvious disreputability and find, in the end, that I have not disgraced you at all.

Anyhow, best love to you both,

JFK   Ernie

1. EH's uncle, Dr. Willoughby Hemingway, had been for years a noted medical missionary in Shansi province, China, despite the boyhood accident to his right hand. See Carlos Baker, *Ernest Hemingway: A Life Story* (New York, 1969), p. 13. 2. The first five paragraphs of the letter were written to EH's mother; the rest is to both parents.

To MAXWELL PERKINS, Gstaad, 14 February 1927

Dear Mr. Perkins:

Thank you for the good news about the increasing elevation of the Sun.

I went to the local photographer and had a picture taken which will be ready for tonight to be mailed with this.

As for biographical material—I once at a man named Ernest Walsh's request made out a biography of about 150 words for his magazine and within a year he was using that 150 words as a basis to attack me on in The New Masses for having widely advertised and capitalized my war record (sic).[1] He happily died shortly after. Really though I would rather not have any biography and let the readers and the critics make up their own lies.

As for the book of stories for the fall—I have been working very hard and concentrating on a title etc. Want to call it

Men Without Women

and it will have		
	The Undefeated	15,000
	Fifty Grand	10,000
	The Killers	3,000
	Today Is Friday	2,000
	An Alpine Idyll	1,500
	In Another Country	2,500
	A Pursuit Race	1,800
	Banal Story	1,000
	A Simple Enquiry	1,200
	Up in Michigan	1,600.
etc.		40,000 words.

In all of these, almost, the softening feminine influence through training, discipline, death or other causes, being absent.

The number of words is approximate but fairly accurate I think. Will have some other stories probably. (Please pardon this ribbon.) My head is going well again and I am writing some stories that seem pretty good.

Am staying here and ski-ing and working on alternate days—the best snow in four years—until the snow goes. After that plans are un-made.

The way the stories are listed is not the order they will be in the book. I just wanted to give you an idea of what you would have so they could go ahead with it. You have seen most of the stories so you will know about what it is like. The Undefeated is the long bull fight story from O'Brien's story book. You may have seen it. A Pursuit Race and A Simple Enquiry are two I've just done. One is about the advance man for a burlesque show who is caught up by the show in Kansas City. The other is a little story about the war in Italy. Up In Michigan I'm anxious to print—it is a good story and Liveright cut it out of In Our Time. That was the reason I did not want to stay there. I think it is publisheable and it might set Mr. [Allen] Tate's mind at rest as to my always avoiding any direct relation between men and women because of being afraid to face it or not knowing about it. Anyway when I get to Paris in March I will get them all in shape—you have the Fifty Grand—and send them over. Is that about right for length? Is Scott still Hollywooding?

With best regards,
Ernest Hemingway.

The 5th printing jacket is very handsome. Lacking a Sun I have placed it on G. Moore's Hail and Farewell—the fine 2nd vol.

PUL

1. EH probably means Walsh's sole book review in *New Masses* 1 (October 1926): 28. See EH to Perkins, *c.* 11 April 1930.

To MAXWELL PERKINS, Gstaad, 19 February 1927

Dear Mr. Perkins:

Your letters of the 4th and 7th of February came today.

I wrote about a week ago giving an outline of the stories for the book and a title. Men Without Women may have struck you as a punk title and if it did please cable me and I'll try and work for another one. I don't know anything about titles here in Gstaad. You wrote me you wanted one by March—that was why I hurried it.

Have now had requests for articles stories or serials from New Yorker, Vanity Fair, Harper's Bazaar, Hearst's etc. This all looks so much like the fast smooth flowing shutes that I've watched so many of my ancestors and contemporaries disappear over that I've decided not to sell or send out anything for a year—unless I have to sell a story to eat. In that event I'll send them to you and the magazine can have the first crack. Really I should have an agent, if for no other reason [than] to take this story selling business off your hands. Do you know of one who would try and sell the stuff and yet would not write me letters trying to get me to do serials etc.? It would be fine to have someone who would do that so I would never hear anything about the stuff after I sent it away unless I got a check for it. That way at the end of each two months I could clean the stuff out of my trunk, go over it and send what was good to the agent.

Any arrangement you would make for me with such an agent would be all right. Curtis Brown my London agents take 10 per cent. Has there been any more news about movie rights for the Sun? Am about broke.

As to the biographical material attached to the wood-cut from Hank Strater's portrait—I was attached to the Italian infantry for a time as a very minor sort of camp follower—I was a long way from being a football star at school—and only have one child. I was wounded and have four Italian decorations La Medaglia d'argento al valore militare and Croce di guerra (3) but all of them were given me not for valourous deeds but simply because I was an American attached to the Italian army. At least one of the Croce di Guerra was given me by mistake and the citation mentions an action on Monte Maggio—transport of wounded under heavy bombardment—which I did not participate in—being 300 kilometers away in the hospital at the time. For these reasons anyone reading war record or other personal publicity coming from Scribner's and knowing the facts would think I had furnished you with the information and simply regard me as a liar or a fool.

For instance today I read something by Burton Rascoe in which I earned my way through college as a boxing instructor! As I never went to college and have never told a living person that I went to college that just was amusing as fantasy rascoe. But if Scribner's repeated it, people would think I had put it out and those that knew me would think I was mad.

I know I should have given you some sort of biographical material but the only reason I didn't was because I hate all that so that I thought if I didn't furnish it there would not be any. So it would be a great favor to me if we could lay off the Biography—or if the first paragraph on this sheet could go out in the publicity sheets so it would correct the other. I don't care anything about stories that start out-side; but I feel anything we put out ought to be true. And anytime if I break a leg or have my jewels stolen or get elected to the Academie Francaise or killed in the bull ring or drink myself to death I'll inform you officially. From the way the lies spring up I think they'll handle the other publicity. And anything we don't put out we are not responsible for.

Scribner's have been so very fine to me that I hate to speak about this biography stuff. I know you will understand and realize that it is simply a sensitive point. I'll send all the pictures you want.

Of course the whole thing that is wrong is this damned clipping system. No living person should read as much stuff about themselves as they get through those cursed clippings. I ought to stop them but I don't because they are practically all the mail I get—and living in the country or by ones-self the mail becomes such an event. But I am going to have to stop them. So will you stop them? I think Scribner's are paying for them. They have not sent me a bill in a long time.

Hope Scott gets back safely from the [west] coast. They seem to have absorbed Don Stewart pretty well out there.

Hope the Atlantic does not take Fifty Grand. Don't imagine they will. It will be good to keep it intact for the book. Thanks so much for sending the [Alpine] Idyll to Kreymbourg. I liked the piece in the Scribner Bookstore very much.

With best regards,

Yours always

PUL   Ernest Hemingway

To F. SCOTT FITZGERALD, Paris, 31 March 1927

Dear Scott:

And you are my devoted friend too. You do more and work harder and oh shit I'd get maudlin about how damned swell you are. My god I'd like to see you. I got the two letters from the Roosevelt hotel and the cable about Vanity Fair this week. In principle I'd decided to not write any articles stories to order serials etc. because I don't work very easily and can't throw it off but only throw it out and then it's used up and gone. But you thought up a swell subject that wouldn't be any form of jacking off for me to write on at all. You're a hell of a good guy. Wrote something for them yest. morning in bed. Will look at it tomorrow and then fix it up and send it on. Some crap about bull fights. I think it's interesting maybe.

How the hell have you been? How nearly done is the book really? How do you feel?

Hadley and Bumby are sailing for N.Y. April 16. Bumby was down in Switzerland with me for a while and was grand. I'm to have him vacations according french law and whenever I want him according to Hadley. She is in grand shape, very happy and very much in love. None of this to tell anybody. I told Scribners to turn all the Sun royalties over to her directly. Did the same with Cape. It comes out in England this month. I went over the proofs so they didn't re-write and garble it like In Our Time. Have a couple of stories you'll see in April Scribners. Have written four since. Max Perkins will have told you the Atlantic took fifty grand. Don't know whether they plan to print it on special easily inflammable paper with punctures along the edge so it will detach so that subscribers can detach it and hurl it into the fire without marring their files of the Atlantic.

[Written upside down at bottom of page:] They were too gentlemanly to mention money. As yet I've heard nothing about money for it. Do the Atlantic pay?

Isn't it fine about Mencken. Well well well pitcher that. That last is the Sinclair Lewis influence. That's the way his characters talk. You can write this book you're working on at random without even keeping track or remembering which characters are whom and still not be in danger of any competition from the other boys. Don [Stewart] has taken to automatic writing and his wife assures him it is better and finer than ever. Bloomfield's [Bromfield's] next book is about a preacher. (Unlike Somerset Maugham or S. Lewis) Bloomfield will probably make him a decayed old new england preacher named Cabot Cabot Cabot and naturally he talks only with God - to rhyme with Cod. But sooner or later I can see that the decayed French aristocracy will come into the book and they will all be named the Marquis Deidre de Chanel and will be people whom Louis Bromfield the most brilliant and utterly master of his craft of all the younger generation of decayed french aristocracy novelists will have studied first hand himself at the Ritz and Ciros - doubtless at great expense to his friends. I went out there to dinner one night and they had a lot of vin ordinaire and cats kept jumping on the table and running off with what little fish there was and then shitting on the floor. Bloomfield, in the effort to make me feel at home did everything but put his feet on the table. I thought to show I felt at home perhaps I had better piss in the finger bowls. We talked about what fine books we each wrote and how we did it. Personally I do mine on a Corona Number 4. And when I wash it my dear I simply can't do a thing with it.

Have been broke now for a couple of months. Happily at present it coincides with Lent. I will have piled up so much credit above that will be able to get you, Zelda and Scotty all out of purgatory with no more strain than a bad cold. Pat [Guthrie] has left Duff [Twysden] and taken to living with Lorna Lindsay or Linslay. A guy named [Harold] Loeb was in town and was going to shoot me so I sent word around that I would be found unarmed sitting in front of Lipp's brasserie from two to four on saturday and Sunday afternoon and everybody who wished to shoot me was to come and do it then or else for christ sake to stop talking about it. No bullets whistled. There was a story around that I had gone to switserland to avoid being shot by demented characters out of my books.

Pauline is fine and back from America. I've been in love with her for so damned long that it certainly is fine to see a little something of her.

Haven't been in the [Latin] quarter nor seen anyone—Murphie's came through enroute to Central Europe with the Mac Leish's. Had a card from Gerald from Berlin giving me conge on his studio where I've been living for May 1st. Someone else is going to use it for something else. It was swell of them to let me use it and a hell of a lot better than under, say, the bridges. They have been swell. Also Mac Leishes.

If you don't mind, though, you are the best damn friend I have. And not just-oh hell - I can't write this but I feel very strongly on the subject.

Give my love to Zelda and remember Mr. Hemingway to Scotty.

Yours always,

Ernest

PUL

To MAXWELL PERKINS, Paris, 4 May 1927

Dear Mr. Perkins:

Enclosed is the copy on hand for Men Without Women.

The Stories go in this order

The Undefeated

Today Is Friday

In Another Country

The Killers } You have these

A Canary For One

Pursuit Race

An Alpine Idyll

A Simple Enquiry

Banal Story } will send this week.

Fifty Grand

You better this any way you wish. I've just drawn it up tentatively.

Within three weeks at the latest I plan to send you two more stories—Italy 1927 and After The Fourth—these I am re-writing now. I hope by the middle of June or so to have three more—A Lack of Passion (not *absolutely* sure on this)—a long bull fight story which I am re-writing—and a couple more. Those should make a full sized book I imagine. Will you let me know until what date I can get stories in for the book? I have been unable to decide about the Up In Michigan. Want a little more time to look at the revised version.

I should be going pretty well next month and would like awfully to have a couple of more good ones.

I think there is nothing in the stories to bother any one except a couple of words in Pursuit Race and if I find any way of re-placing those in the proofs I will. You know I never want to shock with a word if another will do—especially if the one word will shock beyond it's context—but if there is nothing to be done sometimes that is all there is to be done.

Any suggestion you would make about the order of the stories I would greatly appreciate. It is not at all finally fixed if you think it can be bettered. I hope you'll like the ones you haven't already read.

I have not sent copies of The Killers, Canary, or In Another Country as you can take them from the March and April Scribner's.

There will probably be quite a good deal more material if there is time to get it in. I want the book to be full 2.00 size but there is no use sending stories that would just be filler. Though I need some quiet ones to come in between the others. Hope to have something good next month.

I am leaving Paris to start working next Tuesday the 10th but the Guaranty Trust will have my address and always forward anything.[1] I'll send anything as soon as it is ready and perhaps you will give me a final date and let me know how the book shapes up on length with what you have. There will be two more stories within the month and can be others. The two will add another 6,000 words.

With very best regards,
Ernest Hemingway

I have another called A Banal Story which appeared in the Little Review[2] and which I had forgotten and have not yet gotten a copy of— (have written) but remember Edmund Wilson writing that he liked it very much. Probably will find others.

This copy of Fifty Grand is the one Komroff cut. I have marked all the cuts *stet* so will you mark it for them to pay no attention to the pencilled cuts and set it up as it was originally typed.

PUL

1. EH and Pauline Pfeiffer were to be married in Paris on 10 May. 2. *Little Review* 12 (Spring–Summer 1926): 22–23.

To MAXWELL PERKINS, Grau-du-Roi, France, 27 May 1927

Dear Mr. Perkins:

Here are two more stories for the book. I didn't get a copy of the Little Review with the Banal Story in it—as I recall it wasn't much but I remember Edmund Wilson writing that he liked it so it might be worth getting hold of in N.Y. It was the number of the L.R. which came out last summer.

Did you see some pieces in the New Republic for, I imagine, the week of May 5? If you think it advisable we could include them at the end of the book. How did it look as to length? They were three sketches called Italy 1927 and were more on the story side than anything else. I would put on a different title in the proofs [retitled "Che Ti Dice La Patria"]. I think they would go rather well.

So that makes three more things to go in and if they are set up (if it's not too late) I can arrange their order in the galleys.

I have your letter with the check for $750. Thank you very much. Dexter was very nice. He is still in Paris and I'll see him when I go up there next week. I'm working pretty well now.

Donald Freide [Friede], who is one of the partners in Boni and Liveright, came to see me in Paris. He was very worked up about getting me to come back to his firm saying that I would never have been allowed to leave if he had been there etc. He said he had made the trip especially to see me etc. and wanted me to sign a contract giving me an advance of $3,000. on any novels, $1,000 on any book of short stories or essays, 15% royalties, no cuts on byproducts and I forget what else. His argument was that Boni and Liveright had published In Our Time when no one else would and that I had only been allowed to leave because he wasn't there.

I told him that I could not discuss the matter as I was absolutely satisfied where I was, that I thought Scribners had advertised the Sun splendidly and had supported it and pushed it through a time before it began to sell when many publishers would have dropped it, and that I had only left Boni and Liveright when they turned down the Torrents which you took without ever having seen the mss. of The Sun. As for the In Our Time, I told him I was sure you would have published it as I found a letter from you, written a long time previously, waiting for me on returning to Paris after accepting Liveright's cabled offer.

Freide also offered to try and buy the Torrents and the Sun from yourselves and bring them all out later in a uniform edition. He said Scribners had offered to buy the In Our Time but that Liveright had no intention of selling it and were now bringing out a new edition. I don't know whether there is anything to that story except the new edition part which I heard some time ago was coming out.

I write you this for your own information so you will not get any garbled versions or think I am dickering with other publishers. The Cosmopolitan people came over here a few weeks ago but I told them before they could talk money that it was useless as I was absolutely satisfied. Freide, however, had his mind made up that he had to make this offer and I could not avoid it.

This is a fine place below Aigues Mortes on the Camargue and the

Mediterranean with a long beach and a fine fishing port. Am going back next week to Paris for a month and then down to Spain until the $750 runs out. Am healthy and working well and it ought to be a good summer.[1]

Hugh Walpole writes me on May 16th that he is saying something in the English Nation of that week which sounds to me extravagant but which, if you encounter the Nation, might make good advertising. I hope you have a fine summer and that these stories are not too late.

Yours always,

PUL
Ernest Hemingway.

1. EH had married Pauline Pfeiffer 10 May 1927 at L'Église de St-Honoré d'Eylau at 9 Place Victor-Hugo in the 16th Arrondissement rather than in the Protestant Temple de Passy, half a mile distant, as Ada Mac Leish remembered and as recorded in Carlos Baker, *Ernest Hemingway: A Life Story* (New York, 1969), p. 185. According to EH to David K. E. Bruce, 27 November 1948 (not here included), Thomas H. (Mike) Ward was EH's best man at the ceremony. The Mac Leishes did not attend.

To WALDO PEIRCE,[1] Valencia, Spain, 22 July 1927

Muy Caballero Mio:

I sweat all over the first sheet and had to start over. You certainly had a hell of a time getting home. It sounded like a fine place though. Thanks for the dough. I feel that I let you in for a lot more expense than you figured on and then Jimmyed you out of more. Will try and make it up sometime.

It has been hell hot now for three days. Wish you were here to sweat. I can out sweat all the big local sweaters and they are going to bring in outside competition and have me sweat derrier grosse motos. I owe you some 50 pesetas on [Harry] Wills. Do I owe you anything on [Jack] Sharkey? Never bet on a Lithuanian if he can talk.

Had three tickets on the evening lottery yesterday, 5 pesetas a decimo and won all three in the evening list, still won on one in the morning paper, but it is the worst printed paper so am waiting for the official list.

Yesterday they disencojconada-ed 58 bulls for the Feria. All in the ring a conida at a time as per the picture. The Pablo Romeros - and Concha and Sienas are the best - 6 of the last bigger than murias [miuras?] when we were boys.

How the hell are you now? I sent Jimmy a wire and he sent over the glasses I'd left in the car.

Mediteranean feels like a pee-ed in bath tub.

Pauline sends her best, and all of mine to you and Ivy. Write anytime you feel like it. We're here until July 31 at Hotel Ingles - then go to Madrid for 3 or 4 days - then La Coruna, 7, 8, 9, August. Then Bilbao 21–24. Then don't know. Let's hear from you. This is a shitty letter but its so damned hot. This is a fine dusty town.

Yours always
Ernest.

The drawings for Bumby were damned lovely. I sent them off, he'll be awfully happy. Thanks like hell.

COLBY

1. EH and Peirce (1884–1970) had recently met in Paris. A native of Bangor, Maine, Peirce was a gifted painter, a Harvard graduate who had driven ambulances in France during the war, and from 1927 onward one of EH's closest friends.

This and all subsequent letters to Peirce are used courtesy of the Colby College Library, Waterville, Maine.

To BARKLIE MC KEE HENRY,[1] La Coruña, Spain, c. 15 August 1927

Dear Buz:

Am here in La Coruna waiting for proof. Sounds like a murder or suspicion of adultery but really only proof from Scribner's - which now ought to be here and I hope to God it comes. Need to read some bloody thing I've written in order to convince myself that ever have written anything in order to eventually write something else. Maybe you know the feeling.

Thanks like hell for the letter that came today. I think it was very damned sporting of Owen Wister - who seems as much of a classic as Homer - except that have never read Homer - not even Homer Croy. It was awfully nice of him to like the stuff. I can quite understand his not liking In Our Time because that was so much on the side of your and my generation that we couldn't expect anybody much older to get it. If there is anything. Anyway I was awfully pleased with what he wrote you. I'd love to meet him.[2]

You're a damned good egg to write me and tell me stuff that is cheerful. I stopped the bloody clippings last winter when they began to get too potent but now without any news I realize that I do like to hear how things go and when people like them. Hearing once in a while is useful and swell - but the clippings coming all the time are poisonous.

This is a grand town as far out in the old Atlantic as Europe can get, fine wide streets with no sidewalks nor gutters and the first good food I've had all summer. The country is a lot like Newfoundland and it only clears between rains but the rain is natural and you don't seem to get wet. Going fishing next week. Somewhere between here and Santiago in the mountains. Am figuring on coming over to the states this fall. Don't say anything about it to anybody. But I hope we can get together. Do you know any place where there would be some sort of fishing - any kind - and some partridges or ducks to shoot - The mosquitoes gone - and pretty good food - within twelve or fifteen hours of New York? I don't know any place in the east at all but would like to go up in the woods for a month or so and then come into town and bum around a while and keep the old ear from going stale and see a few fights and then go back to Paris and work. Do you know a place to go and about what it would cost? I mean board per week if it's a camp. I'm homesick to be back but don't want to see a lot of literary gents.

Anyway write me - it's always grand to hear from you. My very best to Barbara. Bumby now writes he can speak English comme Papa. He's going to spend the winter ski-ing with me. Think I'll meet him in N.Y. in September.

Yours always,
Ernie

PUL

1. Henry (1902–1966) had been educated at Harvard and Oxford, had met EH in Paris in 1924, and in 1927 was assistant to the treasurer of the *Atlantic Monthly*. 2. On 25 July 1927 Henry had sent EH an excerpt from a recent letter of Owen Wister's in which he admitted not having liked *In Our Time* but was high in his praise of *The Sun Also Rises* and "Fifty Grand." "Were I thirty," said Wister, "that's the way I should wish to write." EH and Wister first met in Shell, Wyoming, in 1928. Wister (1860–1938), of Pennsylvania, was best known for his novel *The Virginian* (1902). Wister greatly interested himself in *A Farewell to Arms*. See EH to Maxwell Perkins, 24 June 1929, and EH to Wister, c. 25 July 1929. See also Ben M. Vorpahl, "Hemingway and Wister," *Los Angeles Times Calendar*, 23 February 1969, pp. 8, 11. When *Farewell* appeared Vorpahl wrote to point out that both hero and heroine bore parts of Henry's name. EH to Henry from Paris, 2 December 1929 (not here included), said: "By god I did name all the characters after you didnt I? Mc Kee was the only one left out—I'll get that in next time."

To MAXWELL PERKINS, Santiago de Compostela, Spain,
31 August 1927

Dear Mr. Perkins:
   The proofs were sent off August 17th. Hope you have them by now.
   I had your wire about withholding 50 grand from the O'Brien book
and quite agree with you. I hated like hell for O'Brien to ask for that; he
has been a very good friend to me and done more for my liturary
careeah than anyone except yourself and Ellery Sedgwick who seems
something like Santa Claus in the days when we believed in Santa Claus.
I have just had a note from him asking me to use my influence with
Scribner's to get permission—he had not yet had a refusal from you but
feared one—and I have just answered that I can't do it because I see
your point in not wanting it—one of the only two long stories in the
book—published anywhere else.
   So be very firm and refuse to let it be published no matter what you
hear my public or private attitude is.
   On the other hand I suggested to O'Brien that he ask for either the
Killers or In Another Country if he wanted a story. I don't think printing
either of those would hurt the book any. They are neither as "important"
quotes as 50 Grand but are probably in the long run better stories.
   That is all about O'Brien. Except that I feel badly about turning him
down—but worse about his asking. Although there is no reason why a
person should not ask for a thing, I suppose. O'Brien published a story
called My Old Man of mine when it had never been published in a
magazine, violating all his rules, it had been turned down by every
magazine except Scribner's and The Atlantic, and dedicated the Short
Story book to me. The only reason the dedication did not help more was
that the name was mis-spelled Hemenway—also on the story—and no one
believed I wrote it. He worked on Liveright to make him publish In Our
Time, got Cape to publish it in London, obtained me various offers of
great wealth from Hearst and an invitation to be the distinguished American guest of the Pen Club at London last Spring. Fortunately I was unable to attend due to the presence of the English Channel or some other
valid excuse. So I hate to turn O'Brien down—but at the same time I can't
take the bread out of all our mouths and give it to O'Brien. But if he
asks for anything else in the book I would like him to have it because he
is not only all this but a very good friend too.
   Leave tomorrow morning for Palencia. There is one train leaving at
six a.m. and getting there at five minutes past midnight and another at
3.59 in the afternoon getting there at 3.27 the next morning. A little beyond Palencia a train can be boarded which goes to Hendaye. These are

the only connections for getting north. It is because of the difficulty of facing one or the other of these two trains that I've been so long in Galicia.

Could you tell me what The Sun has done up to date? Mrs. Hemingway [Hadley] will be in New York for three or four days before sailing on the Lancastria Oct. 22 and may wish to draw some of the royalties due. If there are any—and if they have not been paid.

My own experience with the literary life has not as yet included receiving royalties—but I hope by keeping down advances to some day have this take place.

Yours always,
Ernest Hemingway.

I sent the proofs first class registered. It was very hard convincing them in the post office that there was anything in the world worth that many Spanish stamps.

PUL

To DR. C. E. HEMINGWAY, Hendaye, France, 14 September 1927

Dear Dad:

Thanks very much for your letter and for forwarding the letter to Uncle Tyley [Hancock]. I had a good letter from him yesterday. You cannot know how badly I feel about having caused you and Mother so much shame and suffering—but I could not write you about all of my and Hadley's troubles even if it were the thing to do. It takes two weeks for a letter to cross the Atlantic and I have tried not to transfer all the hell I have been through to anyone by letter. I love Hadley and I love Bumby—Hadley and I split up—I did not desert her nor was I committing adultery with anyone. I was living in the apartment with Bumby—looking after him while Hadley was away on a trip and it was when she came back from this trip that she decided she wanted the definite divorce. We arranged everything and there was no scandal and no disgrace. Our trouble had been going on for a long time. It was entirely my fault and it is no one's business. I have nothing but love admiration and respect for Hadley and while we are busted up I have not in any way lost Bumby. He lived with me in Switzerland after the divorce and he is coming back in November and will spend this winter with me in the mountains.

You are fortunate enough to have only been in love with one woman

in your life. For over a year I had been in love with two people and had
been absolutely faithful to Hadley. When Hadley decided that we had
better get a divorce the girl with whom I was in love was in America. I
had not heard from her for almost two months. In her last letter she had
said that we must not think of each other but of Hadley. You refer to
"Love Pirates," "persons who break up your home etc." and you know
that I am hot tempered but I know that it is easy to wish people in Hell
when you know nothing of them. I have seen, suffered, and been through
enough so that I do not wish anyone in Hell. It is because I do not want
you to suffer with ideas of shame and disgrace that I now write all this.
We have not seen much of each other for a long time and in the meantime our lives have been going on and there has been a year of tragedy
in mine and I know you can appreciate how difficult and almost impossible it is for me to write about it.

After we were divorced if Hadley would have wanted me I would have
gone back to her. She said that things were better as they were and that
we were both better off. I will never stop loving Hadley nor Bumby nor
will I cease to look after them. I will never stop loving Pauline Pfeiffer
to whom I am married. I have now responsibility toward three people
instead of one. Please understand this and know that it doesn't make it
easier to write about it. I *do* understand how hard it is for you to have to
make explanations and answer questions and not hear from me. I am a
rotten correspondent and it is almost *impossible* for me to write about
my private affairs. Without seeking it—through the success of my books—
all the profits of which I have turned over to Hadley—both in America,
England, Germany and the Scandinavian countries—because of all this
there is a great deal of talk. I pay no attention to any of it and neither
must you. I have had come back to me stories people have told about me
of every fantastic and scandalous sort—all without foundation. These
sorts of stories spring up about all writers—ball players—popular evan-
gelists or any public performers. But it is through the desire to keep my
own private life to myself—to give no explanations to anybody—and not
to be a public performer personally that I have unwittingly caused you
great anxiety. The only way I could keep my private life to myself was to
keep it to myself—and I did owe you and Mother a statement on it. But
I can't write about it all the time.

I know you don't like the sort of thing I write but that is the difference
in our taste and all the critics are not Fanny Butcher. I *know* that I am
not disgracing you in my writing but rather doing something that some
day you will be proud of. I can't do it all at once. I feel that eventually
my life will not be a disgrace to you either. It also takes a long time to
unfold.

You would be so much happier and I would too if you could have confidence in me. When people ask about me, say that Ernie never tells us anything about his private life or even where he is but only writes that he is working hard. Don't feel responsible for what I write or what I do. I take the responsibility, I make the mistakes and I take the punishment.

You could if you wanted be proud of me sometimes—not for what I do for I have not had much success in doing good—but for my work. My work is much more important to me than anything in the world except the happiness of three people and you cannot know how it makes me feel for Mother to be ashamed of what I know as sure as you know that there is a God in heaven is *not to be ashamed* of.

This seems to go on and on so I'd better stop. Naturally I felt badly about Sunny not coming. I was quite lonely for her and would have given her a fine instructive and pleasant trip and she would have seen many things she won't see with a party.

I'm awfully happy you liked Bumby. He is my very dear and I hope because of my own mistakes and errors to be ever a better and wiser father to him and to help him avoid things. But I doubt if anyone can teach anyone else much. Anyway he is a fine boy and I hope inside of eight years we can all three go fishing together and you'll see that we are not such tragic figures. Leicester sounds like a fine kid. I have sent off the proofs of my new book [*Men Without Women*]. It has 14 stories and will be out this Fall. We are going to Paris next week and I am starting a novel and will work very hard until Christmas vacation.

I love you very much and love Mother too and I'm sorry this is such a long letter—it probably doesn't explain anything but you're the only person I've written six pages to since I learned to use a pen and ink. I remember Mother saying once that she would rather see me in my grave than something—I forget what—smoking cigarettes perhaps. If it's of any interest I don't smoke. Haven't for almost 3 years altho you probably will hear stories that I smoke like a furnace. Many times last winter I would have been very content with anything so simple as being in my grave but there were always enough people who would rather not see me in my grave to whom I owed certain responsibilities to make me keep on going. I just mention this so no one will mention seeing me in my grave. Glad to do anything else to oblige.

I wish you'd let Mother read this letter. She wrote me a fine letter last Spring and I'm afraid I never answered it. The reason I haven't made either of you a confidant was because I was so upset about Mother accusing me of pandering to the lowest tastes etc in my writing that I shut up like a hermit crab. I knew that if we couldn't see eye to eye on the writing which I knew was no pandering, what use was there of going into my life which looked much worse to an outsider.

But anyway I hope you have the dope you both want in this letter—and I'll write often if we can lay off of literary criticism and personalities.

Yours lovingly,
Ernie

JFK

To F. SCOTT FITZGERALD, Hendaye, *c.* 15 September 1927

Dear Scott:

I got your check cashed it like a son of a bitch without writing and never wrote. All of which if you study your bank account I don't have to tell you. But don't think of me as having become a [Ben] Hecht or a [Maxwell] Bodenheim or one of those literary gents that thinks writing books give a gent licence to larceny etc. because I am now writing and I will pay you the one hundred bucks as soon as the new monumental work entitled Men Without Women comes out. Not later than October let us both hope.

How the hell are you? What do you think of Men Without Women as a title? I could get no title, Fitz, run through Ecclesiastics though I did. Perkins, perhaps you've met him, wanted a title for the book. Perkins's an odd chap, I thought, what a quaint conceit! He wants a title for the book. Oddly enough he did. So, I being up in Gstaad at the time went around to all the book stores trying to buy a bible in order to get a title. But all the sons of bitches had to sell were little carved brown wood bears. So for a time I thought of dubbing the book The Little Carved Wood Bear and then listening to the critics explanations. Fortunately there happened to be a church of England clergyman in town who was leaving the next day and Pauline borrowed a bible off him after promising to return it that night because it was the bible he was ordained with. Well, Fitz, I looked all through that bible, it was in very fine print and stumbling on that great book Ecclesiastics, read it aloud to all who would listen. Soon I was alone and began cursing the bloody bible because there were no titles in it - although I found the source of practically every good title you ever heard of. But the boys, principally Kipling, had been there before me and swiped all the good ones so I called the book Men Without Women hoping it would have a large sale among the fairies and old Vassar Girls.

If you think that paragraph is dull, revert to the first paragraph where I promised to pay you back the hundred dollars. There's gold in that paragraph, Fitz.

How is your novel? Have you finished it? When is [it] coming out? I know you will be glad to hear that I am calling my new novel The World's Fair. So is Brommy as I call dear Louis [Bromfield]. Did you see how Fanny Butcher the woman with the Veal Brains called Brommy the American Fielding. Jesus Christ. It was this that moved me to write again. Due to climate, temperature, up-bringing, lack of experience, education, and tripas [guts] there isn't and won't be any American Fielding but I am resolved that son of a bitch - oh hell. It is funny though for a guy to set out to be the American Galsworthy and be dubbed the American Fielding.

I myself, Fitz, have had the splendid experience of being regarded as the tightest man in the world on acct. of never loosening up and spending any of my Sun Also Rises takings while having lived for five months on yr. 100 and $750 I got from Maxwell Perkins in the meantime having turned down large sums of dough from Hearsts including sending back a check for $1000 bucks sent as an advance on a contract for 10 stories at 1000 the first five 1250 the second five - 15,000 for the serial etc. Doubtless it would seem more practical to an impartial observer for me to have taken a thousand off Hearst rather than a hundred off of Fitzgerald and I darsesay it would. The only trouble is that I *cant* absolutely *cant* write a damned thing on contract.

However am now going to write a swell novel - will not talk about it on acct. the greater ease of talking about it than writing it and consequent danger of doing same.

Got a sheet to fill out from Who's Who and my life has been so fuckingly complicated that I was only able to answer two of the questions and did not know but what they might be used against me.

Hadley and Bumby are fine and have been out on the Pacific slopes where you were too so you know what the hell they are like. Hadley plans to sail from N.Y. on the Lancastria Oct. 22 will be in N.Y. for three or four days beforehand—her address is care of the Guaranty Trust N.Y. If you were around town and could see her I know she would be cockeyed pleased and I would appreciate it.

Pauline is fine. We were going to come over to the states this fall but as I am starting working well I better keep on and get the stuff done and then come over in the Spring. Where will you be. Please Scott forgive me for being such a turd about not writing or acknowledging the check. I had a note from Northrup in Santiago enclosing a card of yours - it came just as he was sailing. So I w[rote] him in Chicago.

Love to Zelda and Scotty - write me all the dirt. The Murphies have been in Antibes all summer I think. Have heard nothing from Don Stewart since he left last fall. Nothing from [Bob] Benchley. Lett[ers] from Dos pretty often. Mac Leishes are in America. Pat Guthrie after Duff [Twysden] got her divorce wouldn't marry her because she had lost her looks and now lives with Lorna Lindsley who saved him from jail on a bad check and who can let him go to jail at any time. Duff is on the town. She kidnapped her kid from England and has no money to keep him - all her small amt. of income goes to keep the kid and nurse in south of france in reduced style of titled youngsters. I ran into her one night - she wasn't sore about the Sun - said the only thing was she never had slept with the bloody bull fighter. That was [the] only night I was in the quarter for a year. Been in Spain since first of July - just bumming, went all over Galicia.

What the hell. Please write. I would like to hear all about Literary Affairs - wish I could see you and talk.

Yours
Ernest

PUL

To ARCHIBALD MAC LEISH, Paris, 8 October 1927

Dear Archie:

If I praise your damn poetry any more you'll think I'm a fairy or a critic but I thought your poem in the [American] Caravan (which by the way smelled like a caravan that had been forced to shit in a closed room) was wonderful. It was a grand lovely poem and if you want to make Papa happy write like that and then dedicate to me.[1] I should say, Mac, that you can now write about life and death without getting life and deathy if that means anything to you. You are certainly going bloody good if your published works are any indication of anything and I shd only hope that you continue to be discouraged unappreciated etc. because you are now making a bum out of all the living poets of my perusal and many dead ones. Let us now leave the subject because I am afraid you will think I like you because you are such a fine poet. To hell with your poetry Mac Leish.

Papa has been working like a son of a bitch and has nine—count them but don't read them—chapters done. Is going well, reaping the results of the long layoff.[2]

Been back three weeks or so, haven't been in bed later than 10 o'clock—seen nobody—working all the time. Day before yesterday

Pauline and I rode to Versailles and back without getting off the bikes. This may be hard on Pauline but I am training to surprise Archie. You must promise not to get on a bike until you come back and then I'll say I haven't too and we will go out to ride and I'll say let's ride up the cote du Picardie, Archie, and you'll say no Hem that's too hard. Shit I'll say that's not hard. And then we will start and I hope to kill you off a third of the way up. We rode up the Cote du Behobie this summer four kilometers long and climbing christ nose how many meters without getting off the bikes. First time tried it had to get off 5 times and was dead. Well now you see where I get at training to surprise Archie. Bragging ruins the whole thing. That's what bragging does and then when we start to ride of course you will lever me the same as ever. There is no damn justice. Love to Ada Mimi and Kenny from Papa, Pauline and Jinny.

We certainly will go ski-ing. We'd like to go to Sweizzimen or however you spell it—on the other side of the Saanenmoser.[3] Has a swell bob run down to it—fine little town, closer to the ski-ing, cheaper and more like a village. It's the terminus of the M.O.B. Wonderful food. Pauline and I tried it. It's not quite an hour from Gstaad. Hurry up back. I've got to start work now—Pauline's gone downtown and when she comes back we're going to ride to Versailles for lunch—that's the kind of competition you are going to run into. Or don't you care for competitive sports, Mac. All right we'll have intra-murals.

LC   Papa

1. Mac Leish's poem "Fragment of a Biography," dedicated to EH, in *American Caravan* (New York, 1927), pp. 374–76. EH's "Alpine Idyll" was in the same volume, pp. 46–51. 2. Evidently the abortive Jimmy Breen novel, abandoned six months later in favor of *A Farewell to Arms*. 3. Zweisimmen and Saanenmöser, resorts in southwest-central Switzerland. M.O.B. = Montreux and Bernese Oberland Railway.

To WYNDHAM LEWIS,[1] Paris, 24 October 1927

Dear Mr. Lewis:

I've just received your letter sent to Cape on June 30—and by him forwarded to [Edward] Titus's book shop. The Guaranty Trust Company is my only permanent address and God knows what impelled Cape to address me care of Herr Titus.

At any rate I'm very sorry not to have received the letter. There is not much chance of my getting over to London but if you ever come to Paris I would be very happy if we could meet again. I will be here until Christmas.

I was very glad you liked The Torrents of Spring and thought you destroyed the Red and Black Enthusiasm very finely in Paleface.[2] That terrible shit about the nobility of any gent belonging to another race than our own (whatever it is) was worth checking. [D. H.] Lawrence, you know, was [Sherwood] Anderson's God in the old days—and you can trace his effect all through A's stuff after he commenced reading him. But of course in his autobiography "A Story Teller's Story," he never mentions him. In that, you find, he was formed through contemplation of the cathedral of Chartres! Accompanied, of course, by Jewish gentlemen.

As for my own stuff—I'm sorry there has been so much blood shed. I think it will decrease. The real reason for it (the bloodiness) was, I think, that I have been working for a precision of language and to get it at the start have had to treat of things where simple actions occurred— the simplest—and which I had seen the most of—was one form and another of killing. I imagine, though, that the blood letting will decrease.

Yours always,
Ernest Hemingway

CUL

1. Lewis (1884–1957), American artist and author. 2. Lewis's *Paleface* (1929) was evidently available to EH in an earlier form. His essay "The Dumb Ox" in *Men Without Art* (1934) so infuriated EH that he broke a vase of flowers in Sylvia Beach's bookshop and avenged himself by attacking Lewis in *A Moveable Feast* (New York, 1964).

This letter is used courtesy of the Cornell University Library.

To MAXWELL PERKINS, Paris, *c.* 1 November 1927

Dear Mr. Perkins:

Thanks for your letter and the clipping. I'm very worried about Scott and wish I were over there and could try and get him in some sort of shape. But I won't mention your having written.

About serialization—let's not think about it until the 1st draft is done. Thanks just the same.

The Virginia Woolf review[1] was damned irritating—She belongs to a group of Bloomsbury people who are all over 40 and have taken on themselves the burden of being modern and all very promising and saviours of letters. When they are all busy at it they dislike what they consider the intrusion of anybody much under 40 into the business, though God knows one doesn't wish to intrude. They live for their Literary Reputations and believe the best way to keep them is to try and slur off or impute [impugn] the honesty of anyone coming up.

Of course where they are right is that literary reputations in ones life time are plants that can be nurtured—and blighted and they do their best to nurture theirs and their friends and throw off on the others. Well God be with them though I would have enjoyed taking the clothes off Virginia Woolf this noon and permitting her to walk down the Avenue de l'Opera letting every one, truth, reality, whatever she liked—pass her close each time.

The deliberate twisting of the blurb was what angered me—that and the imputation that I faked and cheated etc. I was glad I did not get it when I was having one of those hellish depressions when you feel you can never write again.

I wonder if you would save the clippings—quite a bunch of them—and then could send them over around Christmas time and I'd read them down in Switzerland—I'm working hard and the damned things are irritating and make you self conscious—especially the ones that misunderstand either on purpose or through dumbness. When a thing is misunderstood you want to explain and that going on in the head is bad for working.

Do you want another picture or pictures? Drawings from imagination or other drawings by gents called Louis Lozowick are too damned much. Where was Louis Lozowick supposed to have drawn that? Its only merit is that it looks a little like John Bishop.

The other critical sportsman misses "Lady Brett that little wanton, so irritatingly childlike in her faith, so engagingly reprehensible in her morals." Well, well.

Did you ever read "that amazing narrative of English and American after-the-war strays running up and down France and Spain in wistful wildness"—that's a book you shouldn't miss.

Yours always,
Ernest Hemingway

The books haven't come but I look forward to them.

PUL

1. Virginia Woolf's essay-review of *The Sun Also Rises* and *Men Without Women*, in the *New York Herald Tribune Books*, 9 October 1927.

To WALDO PEIRCE, Gstaad, Switzerland, *c*. 13 December 1927

Muy senor mio:

That was a fine letter from Spain. Jailed for Judy. Under a dictatorship the only thing that isn't feo [ugly] to kiss in public is the ass of the dictator. Remember that chico when travelling in Italy and the Peninsula. That was a fine thing about Aiken kicking the goal after Joyce made the touchdown-. Let us hope Conrad put the pigskin over the crossbar. Where in hell are you now?

I was in bed for ten days with one thing and another and it snowed all over God's Europe except here in Suisse. Bumby poked his finger in my one good eye and the nail cut the pupil - I'd picked him up at night in Montreux to put him on the pot - Had a hell of a time. Harry Greb stuck his thumb in the other eye at an earlier and more active period of my life. The pupil is all nicely jelled now and during the interval have also vanquished piles and the grippe. Pauline has been fine and has read Henry James (The Awkward Age) out loud - and knowing nothing about James it seems to me to be the shit. He seems to need to bring in a drawing room whenever he is scared he will have to think what the characters do the rest of the time and the men all without any exception talk and think like fairies except a couple of caricatures of brutal "out-siders". You have read more and better ones than this doubtless but he seems an enormous fake in this. What ho? Was he a fake? He had obviously developed a fine very easy way for himself to write and great knowledge of drawing rooms but did he have anything else? Let me hear from you on this.

Why don't you come down here? It is a healthy damn life once the snow comes and if you can keep Bumby's finger out of your eye, and is snowing now outside to beat hell. We are thinking of moving from here to Zweissimen where there are less Bloodies and better beer. This place costs 12 swiss francs a day pension and is the cheapest pub in town with the best food. But for a man with as many families as me that is too much and think Zweissimen will be cheaper and they have good Munich beer and fine ski-ing. Pauline and Jinny have gone over this afternoon to look at rooms.

The Christmas cards were beautiful - the one of Col Baalam the chaste and the lewd and the one for us. They are damned lovely. Would you like me to write anything for you. It is a son of a bitching thing the way you work like a bastard for your friends at your trade and what can they do for you.

Would you like a copy of

The Earnest Liberal's Lament

I know monks masturbate at night
That pet cats screw
That some girls bite
And Yet
Oh Lord What can I do to set things right?

This dedicated to Oswald Garrison Villard and the editors of New Republic.

If Pauline were here she would write something on this letter as she wanted to write you. She and Jinny and I would be happy as hell if you could come down. Also Bumby. He has fought every kid in town and learned German since coming down here. I asked him what he was going to do when he grew up and he said he was going to make whiskey for papa.

Love to Ivy. Do you know Pat and Whitney's address? It is still snowing and looks like the real thing. Come on down. I have a three and a half week's beard and if you came down there would be two of them in town. Bumby is willing to grow a beard but can't make it. I don't know any news - is there any. Best to Saunders.

Best always,
Ernest

COLBY

To F. SCOTT FITZGERALD, Gstaad, *c.* 15 December 1927

Dear Scott:

Always glad to hear from a brother pederast. You ask for the news. Well I have quit the writing game and gone into the pimping game. They have been purifying Paris and running all the former and well known pimps out and it has left a big lack and a fine opportunity both of which I am trying to fill. I have lined up a fine lot of "girls les girls" a french word and when you and the Mrs. come over in the Spring I will be able to offer you some very interesting reductions.

Old Brommy [Bromfield] has certainly swept the women's clubs. It was a sure thing that he would encounter my mother "Mother of Four Takes Up Painting at 52" and he did. He told her he was certain he had recognized her although he couldn't place her because Ernest was his best friend and how wouldn't he know Ernest's mother. Now my mother has a new cause to weep because I don't write [like] Brommy.

Are you keeping little Scotty off of the hop any better? We hear many happy anecdotes over here about how she jammed H. L. Menken

[Mencken] with her own little needle the last time he visited at the Mansions and that that was how the American Mercury came to be written.

Teddy Chandler the boy whom if I am not mistaken once killed your mother is over here. Also Bill Bullitt or Bull Billet a big Jew from Yale and fellow novel writer. Pat Guthrie who once lived with Duff Twizden is now being kept by Lorna Lindsley who is looking even fresher and lovlier. None of these people I ever see but will be glad to look them up for you.

My son Bumby is following in his father's footsteps and makes up stories. Hearsts have offered him 182,000 bits for a serial about Lesbians who were wounded in the war and it was so hard to have children that they all took to drink and running all over Europe and Asia, just a wanton crew of wastrels. I have introduced him to a lot of them and he is writing hard and I am helping him a little now and then with the spelling and Pauline reads aloud to him your stories out of the Post so he will get an idea of the style which is going to be the same as that of the latest poems by Mac Leish only trimmed with Persian Lamb. Bumby is calling the thing

lesbos Lesbos LESBOS

I see few people except Mike Ward the ex Banker who had an amazing adventure the other night in the Club Daunau where he hit a man standing at the bar because he said something about me that he, Mike, did not hear but didn't like the sound of. He asked the man if he was a friend of mine and when the man said no Mike hit him. Later it turned out that the man had not mentioned me at all but Mike said that the man was no friend of mine he could tell.

You ought to have loyal friends like that Fitz.

There was no money in Spanish fly so I gave up the Spanish Fly game. My eye is all right now and we are hoping it will snow. Jinny has been here since the 1st of December hoping it will snow too. We have only been hoping since the 14th of December. I have a sore throat and am in bed. I guess you will agree we got [Charles A.] Lindberg[h] a nice lot of publicity. Would you like me to be publicity man for either Scotty or Zelda. You are right about the Spanish wine skin and I find it very comfortable but it has nothing so unhemanish as a zipper. I have to watch myself that way and deny myself of many of the little comforts like toilet paper, semi-colons, and soles to my shoes. Any time I use any of those people begin to shout that old Hem is just a fairy after all and no He man ha ha.

On acct. being so laid up so long started a fine beard which is now almost rabbinical. May keep it until come to the states but doubt it.

Write me all the news and views. Love to Zelda and little Scotty if you can keep her off of the stuff long enough for her to understand the message. You shouldn't let that child have Heroin Scott. I've thought it over from every angle and it can't be good for her. I know that you have to keep up appearances and I know the way things are nowadays but nobody can convince me that it really does a child of that age any good.

Write again. Now I don't owe you anything besides undying gratitude and say 180 bottles of champagne I can write free-er.

yrs. always,

PUL

Ernest.

To MAXWELL PERKINS, Gstaad, 15 January 1928

Dear Mr. Perkins:

I'm sorry not to have written acknowledging the Illuminated bull and the clippings—thanks ever so much for sending them—especially the bull which has been universally admired. Have you heard anything of the O. Henry people's award? I have not and their letter was so worded that they could avoid actually coming through with the prize if they wanted.

The reason I did not write you, or in fact write anything at all, was a bad cut in the pupil of my right (and only good) eye which is all healed now. The eye still aches though if I read or write. Was quite blind with it for a couple of weeks.

Since the 15th of December there has been 3 days of ski-ing here—the winter completely open. Our only two good snow falls have been followed by rain making breakable crust which is the most dangerous and nastiest thing to ski in there is. Archie Mac Leish and I ski-ied down from the top of the Saanersloch Fluh—ordinarily a beautiful long run—and I took ten of the worst spills imaginable. Even running straight the crust would break and the tip of the ski go under and catch to throw you. I was wearing goggles to protect my eye and once fell so hard and buried my head so deeply that the glass was smashed out of both of them. I have a tin knee and dislike falling intensely and never go in for it—but weighing 208 pounds I was just what the breakable crust was hoping for. Don't know why I write this—except there is nothing to write except the cursed weather.

How I got the eye cut was altogether unromantic—picked up my son out of bed in Montreux in the hotel to have him perform an important function, he put up his hand, one finger went in my eye and the finger nail cut a great half moon in the pupil.

That seems all the news except that we're coming to America in 2 months—but not to N.Y. until the fall.

Hope the Men Without still sells—thought for a while it wd. be last book I'd have. Being blind even for a little while scares you—especially if you don't write just out of yr. head but with all the senses you have on tap. Figured I could probably write by touch on the typewriter—but stuff written on the [typewriter] is not much good—and nothing I write is any good until it's rewritten several times and how would you re-write if you couldn't see? Thought I might get a job hearing for Dexter.

The new Magazine sounds very impressive—what would they pay for pieces? I saw a copy the other day and it looked very handsome but the Swiss wanted a dollar for it so I thought I would have to try and contribute something and get it for nothing.

A gentleman named Burton Emmett sent me a check for $500 to buy some manuscripts of stories The Killers, Fifty G. etc. Have had various other offers. But have given most of these Mss. away during the great tissue towel famine. Don't however tell anyone this as if my eye started to go bad it might be a good provision against the future to start making manuscripts. At present there would seem to be more money in manuscripts than in stories. I should think Scott's original Mss. would bring thousands for the spelling alone. I wonder if Mr. Emmett prefers Mss. of mine before or after I put in the grammar? But I am afraid to joke with these Mss. buyers for fear they won't want them. Think I'll write back and say they are all in the British Museum except The Sun Also Rises which is in the Prado.

Yrs. always,
Ernest Hemingway

What are the sales of The Sun—if it isn't too much trouble.

PUL

To JAMES JOYCE, Gstaad, 30 January 1928

Dear Joyce:

I appreciated very much your writing to Ivan Goll about the Rhein Verlag for me. He wrote me at once but I have had to wait trying to arrange things in Germany—an agent having already signed me up for at least one book with a Berlin publisher. Have written Goll I would see him in Paris next month and I hope by then it will be straightened out.

I hope you and all your family are well. Mac Leish's father died and he left for America to be back late in February. Mrs. Pierce is down here. My family are leaving for Paris tomorrow and I'm taking a trip on skis to Lenk and Adelboden and back and then we'll go up to Paris. Except for two weeks the weather has not been wintry nor dry and we've not had more than ten days of skiing. My little boy, when I picked him up to put him on the pot at night at Montreux coming in here poked his finger in my eye and the nail cut the pupil. For ten days I had a very little taste of how things might be with you.[1] It hurt like hell even with the cocaine wash the doctor gave me to take the pain out, but is all right now.

I hope you are well and that everything goes well with you.

Yours always

SUNY-B Ernest Hemingway

1. Severe iritis had afflicted Joyce for some years.

To MAXWELL PERKINS, Paris, 12 February 1928

Dear Mr. Perkins:

Your letter of Feb. 3 came today. I'm glad the book still goes so well—hope it keeps on steadily. It ought to do something to lay the story about people never buying short stories.

We hit bad weather on the ski trip and had one tough day. Got my new passport and came back to Paris to find all water pipes burst—no heat for a week—caught a cold and grippe in the head. Have been trying to work every morning but all my production seems to be from the nose. In the past twelve months have had the grippe 3 times, nearly passed out from anthrax—cut up my one good eye—etc. This probably due to having led a quiet non-alcoholic non-smoking life.

We leave the end of the month for Florida via Vigo, Canaries, Havana, Key West. I'll need some money pretty soon but will write for it then. Wrote a story a few days ago to warm up to get back into stride before re-starting the book and thought it might do for the Magazine but it is no bloody good.

I read the Roark Bradford story—it was awfully weak and watered beside An Occurrence at Owl Creek Bridge—the [Ambrose] Bierce story you mentioned. He reversed the Bierce story and put on a happy ending. But I could see he got a lot of kick out of writing it—and I'm glad he got the $500. As an award the O'Henry prize is a pretty damned doubtful honor and it ought to go to whom it will make happy.

The best story I've read in a hell of a time was the Owen Wister story in O'Brien's book. It wasn't a story but really part of a novel but part of it was wonderfully good and all very very good and a lesson to our generation in how to write.

The eye seems all right but still aches to read.

Otherwise no news.

Scott sent me an announcement of a debate between the Messrs. [Louis] Bromfield and [Glenway] Wescott—did you hear it? *What* did they debate?

Will you be coming down to Florida in April and May or Arkansas in June or Kansas City in June and July? Or where might we meet? I am going to the Rep. Nat. Convention if they have it in Kansas City. Evan Shipman is going to get married.

Yours always
Hemingway

PUL

To MAXWELL PERKINS, Paris, 17 March 1928

Dear Mr. Perkins:

Guy Hickock showed me a cable today from Scribners asking about my good health and I hope you weren't worried. I was tired of recounting accidents so was not going to mention it. However it was the skylight in the toilet—a friend had pulled the cord that raised it instead of pulling the chain of the toilet and cracked the glass so that when I tried to hook up the cord (going into the bathroom at 2 a.m. and seeing it dangling) the whole thing fell. We stopped the hemmorage with 30 thicknesses of toilet paper (a magnificent absorbent which I've now used twice for that purpose in pretty much emergencies) and a tourniquet of kitchen towel and a stick of kindling wood. The first two tourniquets wouldn't stop it due to being too short—(face towels) and I was rather worried as we had no telephone no chance of getting a doctor at 2 a.m. and there were two little arteries cut. But the third held it very well and we went out to Neuilly to Am[erican] Hospital where they fixed it up, tying the arteries, putting in three stitches underneath and six to close it. No after effects but a damned nuisance.

Maybe this will be the last. Scribner's could have made money this year insuring me. Anyway the purpose of this letter is to tell you that I've finally had some pictures taken by Helen Breaker—who is sending them to you. She is an old friend [of Hadley's] who has lost all her money and started in photography and I thought the pictures being reproduced might help her to get some reputation. I think photography is a lousy thing and that it has gone steadily backward since the daguerrotypes but I promised that whenever her pictures are used they will be credited to her—HELEN BREAKER—Paris. A person would have to be an old friend, stone deaf and to have lost all their money before I would have pictures taken by them. That has nothing to do with it. I think she is probably a very good photographer and that you will like the pictures. I told her I did not know if you paid for the originals or how much—and that if you did pay for them you would pay her at the usual rate—but that in any event you would have them credited to her.

Thank God to be off the subject of photography.

I asked a (Mrs.) Emily Holmes Coleman to send you her novel about an insane asylum. She was in one for a while as a patient and, I think, can write. I have never read it, but she was going to send it to Boni and Liveright (who published a book on psychology by her husband) and I prefferred if it should chance to be good that you see it.

I would like to have finished the novel—but (1) I have been laid up and out a good deal.

(2) It took me 5 years to write all the stories in In Our Time.

(3) It took 5 years to write the ones in Men Without Women.

(4) I wrote Sun Also Rises in 6 weeks but then did not look at it for 3 months—and then rewrote it for another three months. How much time I wasted in drinking around before I wrote it and how badly I busted up my life in one way or another I can't fit exactly in time.

(5) I work *all* the time. But I don't think I can make even an irregular schedule and keep up the quality. I know very well I could turn books out when they should come out (and you have been very damned decent about not even asking me to or putting any pressure on me) but we only want good ones—both of us. You see my whole life and head and everything had a hell of a time for a while and you come back slowly (and must never let anyone know even that you were away or let the pack know you were wounded). But I would like to write a really damned good novel—and if the one I have 22 chaps and 45,000 words of done[1] doesn't go after I get to America I will drop it and put it away and go on with the other one I am writing since two weeks that I thought was only a story but that goes on and goes *wonderfully*.[2]

The first one was supposed to be a sort of modern Tom Jones. (Never mention that because I do not invite comparison but only to name the sort of book.) But there is a *very very* good chance that I don't know enough to write that yet and whatever success I have had has been through writing what I know about.

I know very well that Scott for his own good should have had his novel out a year or two years ago. I don't want you to think that I am falling into that thing or alibi-ing to myself. But this next book *has* to be good. The thing for me to do is write. But it may be better not to publish until I get the right one.

I should have gone to America two years ago when I planned. I was through with Europe and needed to go to America before I could write the book that happened there. But I didn't go—but now have, suddenly, a great kick out of the war and all the things and places and it has been going very well.

My wife says that she will see that I'm bled just as often as I can't write—judging by the way it's been going this last week. Hope to be able to work on the boat. If I find I've any readers in America will change my name.

This letter is long enough to be a bitter test of your friendship to have to read. Also I would appreciate a copy of Men Without Women being sent and charged to my account to W. W. Stigler, Hotel Noble, Jonesboro, Arkansas. I will pay the account any time it reaches $5.00 (five dollars). Thanks very much for the offer of money. I will wire when I need it.

I am glad you are publishing Morley [Callaghan]. I was never off of him but only a poor correspondent.

> Yours always
> Ernest Hemingway

I will write you next from Florida.

What about Foreign Translations? For when I'm back here. I am sure I could have gotten you Luckner's book[3] if I had known you wanted it and that you did not have someone after that sort of thing. Or wouldn't you have wanted it? I thought it a grand book. The Last Privateer it was in the French edition. His early life and the Sea Adler part were wonderful.

Helen Breaker would like to get her pictures published in the magazines. The more expensive (I imagine) the better.

PUL

1. Twenty chapters of a novel tentatively called *Jimmy Breen* (alternate title *A New-Slain Knight*, from the medieval ballad "The Twa Corbies"), set in Chicago and New York. Jimmy and his father, a revolutionist, are on their way to Paris, where Jimmy's mother lives. Item 13 in *The Hemingway Manuscripts: An Inventory*, eds. Philip Young and Charles W. Mann (University Park, Pa., October 1969). 2. This seems to date the start of *A Farewell to Arms* as about 3 March 1928. 3. Probably Lowell Thomas, *Count Luckner, the Sea Devil* (1927), an account of the wartime exploits of Count Felix von Luckner (1881–1966).

To PAULINE HEMINGWAY, at sea,[1] *c.* 28 March 1928

Dear Miss Pfeiffer or may I call you "Mrs. Hemingway"?:

We are five or ten days out on our trip or tripe to Cuba which promises to extend indefinitely into the future. I have often wondered what I should do with the rest of my life and now I know—I shall try and reach Cuba.

It is certainly hell to try and write. You are so handsome and talented and your throat never gets sore and you never say, "Perhaps my husband Mr. Hemingway cant play well enough to interest you."

But you cant stop this bloody ship going up and down. Only Mother-sills could do that and she not for long.

I have been reading about the accomodations on the other liners—the Orcoma, Orita, Oroya, etc. and they all have gymnasiums and beds and double beds and nurseries for the resultant infants but our boat has little cells at $250 a cell and a man might as well have paid 250 to some good monastic order (if they would take that little).

I have discovered what makes our Indian friend look furtive—his neck is so short that he has to turn his shoulders when he looks around. You on the other hand have no defects but this boat is the Royal Mail S Packet and I have no [illegible] except the something that was caught in this pen (one of your eyelashes maybe) and now it's gone and what's a guy to do.

Anyway I love you and if you forgive this bad letter I will write a good one sometime. Only lets hurry and get to Havana and to Key West and then settle down and not get in Royal Male Steam Packets any more. The end is weak but so is Papa.

PUL   Love from Papa.

1. On board R.M.S. *Orita*, westbound from La Rochelle to Havana.

To MAXWELL PERKINS, Key West, 21 April 1928

Dear Mr. Perkins:

I'm terribly sorry to hear about Scott. Could you tell me the name of his ship and I will send him a cable. Perhaps it would be better to wire it, the name of his boat or where he is in a night letter as this place seems to be a long way from New York by mail. I wish he would finish his novel or throw it away and write a new one. I think he has just gotten stuck and does not believe in it any more himself from having fooled with it so long and yet dreads giving it up. So he writes stories and uses any excuse to keep from having to bite on the nail and finish it. But I believe that everybody has had to give them up (novels) at some time and start others. I wish I could talk to him. He believes that this novel is so important because people came out and said such fine things about him after the Gatsby and then he had a rotten book of stories (I mean there were cheap stories in it) and he feels that he must have a GREAT novel to live up to the critics. All that is such (   ) because the thing for Scott to do is WRITE novels and the good will come out with the bad and in the end the whole thing will be fine. But critics like [Gilbert] Seldes etc. are poison for him. He is scared and builds up all sorts of defences like the need for making money with stories etc. all to avoid facing the thing through. He could have written three novels in this length of time—and what if two of them were bad if one of them was a Gatsby. Let him throw away the bad ones. He is prolific as a Gueinea pig (mis-spelled) and instead he has been bamboozled by the critics (who have ruined every writer that reads them) into thinking he lays eggs like the Ostrich or the elephant.

What about the Books—I haven't seen Men Without advertized for a long time.

Glad you saw Waldo Pierce [Peirce]. He wires he is coming down here. I don't just know when but hope it will be soon. Dos Passos is on his way too. I don't know for how long.

Have been going very well. Worked every day and have 10,000 to 15,000 words done on the new book [A Farewell to Arms]. It won't be awfully long and has been going finely. I wish I could have it for Fall because that seems like the only decent time to bring out a book but suppose, with the time necessary to leave it alone before re-writing, that is impossible. I forget when I got the mss. for the Sun to you but think it was sometime pretty early in the Spring. Please tell me if I am wrong. Would like to finish this down here if possible, put it away for a couple or three months and then re-write it. The re-writing doesn't take more than six weeks or two months once it is done. But it is pretty important for me to let it cool off well before re-writing. I would like to stay right here until it is done as I have been going so very well here and it is such a fine healthy life and the fishing keeps my head from worrying in the afternoons when I don't work. But imagine we will have to go someplace for the baby to be born around the end of June. Ought to leave a month before. Still if I keep on going there will be a lot done by then.

It is hot here but there is always a cool breeze and it isn't hot in the shade and you can sleep at night.

After I get the novel done—if it is too late for this fall—I could do quite a lot of stories and that would keep the stuff going until the next fall and then the novel would come out and we would have stories enough for a book of them to follow it.

Have been catching tarpon, barracuda, jack, red snappers, etc. Caught the biggest tarpon they've had down here so far this season. Sixty three pounds. The really big ones are just starting to come in. Also a barracuda on a fly rod. Great quantities of sharks, whip rays and other vermin. We sell the fish we get in the market (the edible ones) and get enough to buy gas and bait. Have been living on fish too. Tonight is a big night (Saturday) although not so cheerful because another cigar factory has closed down. This is a splendid place. Population formerly 26,000—now around ten thousand. There was a pencilled inscription derogatory to our fair city in the toilet at the station and somebody had written under it—'if you don't like this town get out and stay out.' Somebody else had written under that 'Everybody has.'

Would appreciate your asking them to send and charge to me 3 Sun Alsos and 3 Men Without Women (as soon as possible). Nobody believes me when I say I'm a writer. They think I represent Big Northern Bootleggers or Dope Peddlers—especially with this scar.[1] They haven't even heard of Scott. Several of the boys I know have just been moved by first reading of Kipling. A man introducing Robert Service's works would coin money if there was any money to coin—but there isn't.

Yrs. always
Hemingway

Hope I get nothing incriminating as they open my mail.

PUL

1. Scar on forehead from the skylight accident in Paris described in EH to Perkins, 17 March 1928. It developed into a lipoma, a hard protuberance which he carried the rest of his life.

To MAXWELL PERKINS, Piggott, Arkansas, 31 May 1928

Dear Mr. Perkins:

There was no Lady Ashley in Burke's or Debrett's Peerage when I sent you the Sun Mss. and none in either of those stud books when I corrected the proof. A young Ashley married a girl out of musical comedy the summer after the book came out. She might as well try and sue Robinson Crusoe.

You've probably seen Waldo [Peirce]. We had a grand time. I worked every morning too and did 200 pages—200 words or so to a page—in Key West. Am now at the above address—a christ offal place. Hope to get up to Michigan soon. Am delayed by impending childbirth probably to take place at Kansas City or some such great obstetrical center.

Last winter (i.e.) the winter before last—I tried to argue Thornton Wilder out of Boni and Boni. (He was commissioned to argue me into [Boni and Boni] but am afraid he would now have more arguments). I thought Bridge of S.L.R. [San Luis Rey] was a fine book of short stories— 2 splendid ones—The Esteban and I think the other was about a little girl who worked for the Mother Superior. He can write very well. Also a nice boy [aged thirty-one].

I think I will have to get a large advance on my next book to insure to assure it being advertized in florid and gigantic manner in order that Scribners must sell a large number of copies to get the advance back. Glenway Wescott, Thornton Wilder, and Julian Green have all gotten rich in a year in which I have made less than I made as a newspaper correspondent—and I'm the only one with wives and children to support. Something's going to have to be done. I don't want the present royalties until they are due. But I would like to make a chunk of money at one time so I could invest it. This bull market in beautiful letters isn't going to last forever and I do not want to always be one who is supposed to have made large sums and hasn't and doesn't. If I have as many accidents right along as I've had this last year they will be having to give a benefit for me in a couple of years. It did seem as though they laid off advertising Men Without Women when it was still going well just as much as they jumped out with enormous ads for Thornton's book [*The Bridge of San Luis Rey*] the minute it started going. Of course I know nothing about it but after the first of the year—when Men Without was still selling well—it seemed as though they were satisfied with the sale and pretty well laid off.

Anyway am working steadily on the present novel and it seems to go well—and finally—I hope—toward an end. When I get it done I think I will go back to the one I dropped after 60,000 [words] and finish it[1]—it seems now as though it had never been difficult to work but I suppose that time will come again.

I don't think Mrs. Breaker will mind your having removed the scar [from photographs]. It seemed to bother her—the scar—and she wanted to remove it. But I thought that if you give a photographer an inch they will remove an ell.

Yours always,
Ernest Hemingway

Address Piggott, Arkansas for a while. *They will forward.*

PUL

1. The aborted novel *Jimmy Breen (A New-Slain Knight).*

To DR. DON CARLOS GUFFEY,[1] Kansas City, Missouri, *c.* 15? June[?] 1928

Dear Dr. Guffey:

This book was printed and published by Bill Bird who had bought an old hand press and set it up on the Isle Saint Louis in Paris. It came out about a year after it should because I introduced Bill to Ezra Pound and Ezra suggested a series of books—"There'll be me and old Ford and Bill Williams and Eliot and Lewis (Wyndham) and some others," Ezra said, "and we'll call it an inquest into the state of English prose." Eliot didnt include—nor did Lewis and finally Ezra had five titles—Bill said, "What about Hem?"

"Hem's will come sixth," Ezra said. So when they were all printed and this one finally gotten out it was later than the Three Stories and 10 poems although Bill had the manuscript long before Mc Almon had the other set up—

PARKE-BERNET 14 OCTOBER 1958   Ernest

1. Dr. Guffey delivered both of Pauline's sons by Caesarean section. This letter, in the form of an inscription in Dr. Guffey's copy of *in our time*, appears in facsimile in *Hemingway at Auction,* eds. M. J. Bruccoli and C. E. Frazer Clark, Jr. (Bloomfield Hills, Mich., 1973).

To MAXWELL PERKINS, Piggott, Arkansas, 23 July 1928

Dear Mr. Perkins:

I've written you a couple of times but not sent the letters. The child is a boy, Patrick, very big dark and strong seeming. Pauline had a very bad time—cesaerian (can't spell it) and a rocky time afterwards. I was worried enough. Am now on page 486—it must average 180 words to a page—am going out to Wyoming starting the end of this week. Will finish the book there. There will be a lot to cut and I will leave it alone and re-write it when we get back to Paris in Nov. It should be ready to serialize in Feb. anyway. How much $\left\{\begin{array}{l}\text{would}\\\text{will}\end{array}\right\}$ the magazine pay for it?

Am damned sick of the heat. Been over 90° almost every day for nearly a month. Patrick being on a bottle Pauline will be able to leave him here with her family and come out to Wyoming in September for a month if everything goes well.

I hope you are having a good vacation. I have heard nothing from any-one except the Maine fishing news from Waldo [Peirce]. Made some money playing the races.

There seems to be no news.

Yours always,
Hemingway

I wish the boy had been one of your girls.

PUL

To GUY HICKOK,[1] Kansas City, Missouri, c. 27 July 1928

Dear Copernicus:

Whenever I begin to miss Paris there is always some little item in the paper about how Professor Ritchey will be able to see men on Mars (if there are men) with his new telescope. Of course he doesn't think there are men but if it will please the A.P. he will look for them and if they are there he will see them.

Patrick, weighing nine pounds was born in Kansas City. He looks like Count Salm and we hope will show talent along that line as if he keeps on yelling it is a cinch I won't be able to write and support him. They finally had to open Pauline up like a picador's horse to lift out Patrick. It is a different feeling seeing tripas [insides] of a friend rather than those of a horse to whom you have never been introduced. Anyway the thermometer went to 90 the day Patrick was born and stayed there or above for three weeks - Nearly killed Pauline who (to continue the horse motif) blew up with gas like the same rosinante after the tripas removed if left in a hot place. But everything all right finally and no one dead and Patrick back to Piggott on a bottle - on several bottles - His father on page 482 of his monumental opus - leaving tomorrow for Wyoming in the Ford - seeing damerica first. Will find a place where can fish and work and finish the bloody book. Thanks like hell for going around and paying the merchants. You did right to hang ont[o] the receipt. I know how christawful busy you are with the bastardly tourists who would be bad enough in any event but all coming from Brooklyn are therefore the cream and you were damned fine to pay the govt. Also to send the auto and echo. Write to Piggott.

Pauline is coming out to Wyoming in Sept. if all goes well - this typer is not mine and I don't know where the margin release is - am not trying to pull an ezra on you with fancy spellings.

Pauline is o.k. after the cesaerian - scar tight - looks fine and feeling good now but had a near thing - I'm going to find some place in wyoming where it will be comfortable and good fishing in th[e] front yard and then we will come east in oct. stay three weeks maybe and then back to Professor Richeyville where I trust you will have a lot more fascinating dope on telescopes. You certainly had a grand idea that you were not Richey's press agent just because you weren['t] being paid for it. I wish the Swedes would arrest Zappi and try him for murder.[2] I should think they would. That would be a good thing rather than wait for them to get home and let a wop court whitewash the dirty swine. Write. Pauline says your letters were all that made her want to live in the hospital.

I may have written you giving the dope on the operation before. If so pardon repetition. I have been too groggy to recognize my own corner.

Happy touristing to you -

PH. PUL   Ernest

1. In 1922 EH had met Hickok (1888–1951), who ran the Paris bureau of the *Brooklyn Daily Eagle* until 1933. 2. Captain F. Zappi was aboard Umberto Nobile's dirigible *Italia*, which crashed in the Arctic 25 May 1928. Zappi left the site with Captain Mariano to seek help. Roald Amundsen (1872–1928) was killed in the rescue attempt.

To WALDO PEIRCE, Big Horn, Wyoming, 9 August 1928

Dear Mr. Purse:

In your last letters you sound slightly peacock-pecked. By gawd you write a noble letter though; I wish I'd come to Maine instead of out here. It's damned lovely country though. Looks like Spain, Big Horn Mts. [ringers?] for the guadaramas only on a bigger scale, same color, same shape. Drove here in 3 days from K.C. 340, 380, 320. Jack rabbits with us as big as mules. Came to a ranch of a friend where there were 15 girls! Shit. Worked and fished as follows.[1]

1st day - worked four pages, fished with Bill Horne caught 12.
2nd day - worked 4½ pages, fished with two girls caught 2.
3rd day - worked zero, fished by self alone, caught 30 - limit.
Got up at 6 a.m. on morning of 4th day and left without saying goodbye, went into Sheridan where stayed at old hotel and worked. 9 - 6½ - 9 - 11 - then came out to empty ranch and without dudes and did 17½ yesterday - bloody near 2550 words. Probably shite too - I wish to God Pauline would come out and that I would get this book finished before she comes. Am lonely as a bastard, drank too much last night and feel like anything but work now. Eat too much too at this ranch house. Splendid guys. I am glad you are getting such a splendid lot of dough. It will take money to keep us in muttonfish. Pauline wrote Mr. Pfeiffer was delighted with the pictures. It was nice of you to send them. Piggott is the best permanent address altho I'll be here at Big Horn for two weeks more anyway, address Big Horn, Sheridan Wyo. Big Horn is 4 houses and general store. Post office.

Patrick now weighs 12 lbs, looks like chinese woodchuck.

This country around here has been settled too long, when Pauline comes we will go over across the mountains and up around Cody, then through the [Yellowstone] Park maybe after the hotels are closed and out the Southern end through Jackson's Hole. They charge you $50 for a license to shoot an elk. If they paid me $50 to shoot and dress one I would do it but not a cent less.

So far have shot 3 marmots (rock dogs) almost as big as badgers, with the pistol and the head off a water snake. Of the 30 trout caught 26 were eastern brook and 4 rainbows, I was within five of the limit at 3.30 p.m. (7 inches keep) and then slipped back a lot to only keep good ones.

I bought a 12 gage winchester which will come in handy around Key West. I'd like to have seen the hurricane there. By God that's a fine place. We will come to Maine some time. We got to go back to Paris this fall sometime, go to Spain next spring maybe then come to Key West early enough for good monstering the next winter. I've got to see some more toros. By God every Sunday evening this summer at 5 o'clock seems as if my whole life were pointless. I wonder how they were at Pamplona. My bull fight papers haven't come. Valencia is the best 7 bull fights in 7 days starting July 25. Swim in between in the Mediterranean at Grao. Ride out on the tram, dodge turds in the water. Damned good though, eat out there on the beach, or back at Valencia with an ice cold pitcher of beer, good meat melon. Thats where I'd be now instead of here trying to write. To hell with novels, I've written 548 pages, I could write a short story of 12 pages and feel fine and probably it would be better stuff. As it is have been in a state of suspended something or other for 3 or 4 months. Watson has fattened like a calf. Glad to see the pictures of old Kate. Susan, I never cared for, too worthy and noble, nice enough. Always send any clippings. Que le bon Dieu veut

COLBY   Su Amigo Ernesto

1. EH's itinerary included a stay at Folly Ranch (fifteen girls including Bunny, the future Mrs. Horne), Sheridan Inn, and Eleanor Donnelley's Lower Ranch.

To ISABEL SIMMONS GODOLPHIN, Sheridan, Wyoming, c. 12 August 1928

Dearest Izz:

Well that was a *grand* letter - I dont know what an introvert is either but if that is what you are may all my children be them. Patrick weighs 12 pounds and is old enough to stay with his grandparents - Pauline is going to come out here in a week now. Thank God. I was beginning to get sheepherder's madness—Am on Page 574—I hope to get it done soon—It has certainly gone on and on and on but yesterday I read over the Mss. --- It just arrived from Piggott—I was afraid to carry it around - You may recall my losing some Mss. once—Anyway read it and it seemed Swell - cockeyed wonderful - So much so that I (afterwards) drank nearly a gallon of wine and ½ gallon of beer and now have gastric remorse today and cant work at all - but will in a little while anyway. All I do is work and work—never write letters - but love to get them - You certainly presented the town in a masterly way—Those rag rug weavers—

Got to stop - all the juice has to go in the book - Isnt much juice today. Have to get going again—I am *certain* I wrote from Key West—Please write again - give my heartiest to Sim—

Yours always—
PUL   Ernie

To GUY HICKOK, Sheridan, 18 August 1928

Hickock Noble Hickock:

I see the Steffenses have been wedding each other publicly in Am. Magazine. Wait until Pauline and I tell the inside story of our lives.

Patrick now weighs 12½ pounds and is sojourning chez son grand-mere at Piggott—Pauline was due here at 3.20 pm. Its now past 5, train not in yet. I'm on page 600 and only about 2 days from the end—Have been here 1 mo or more—good beer from the brewry—good wine from a wop—a nice French family (bootlegger) where we sit on the vine shaded porch and drink as at the Double Maggots—youth will be served.[1]

Have been doing nothing but work—Book either wonderful or the old shite.

Love to Mary—

Address always Piggott—Write to us you loafer—nothing to do but entertain a few pleasant folk from Brooklyn—and then you complain.

Never mind we'll be back in Nov. We're going up in Big Horn mountains to fish—then over to the [Yellowstone] Park after the season and down in Jackson Hole to shoot ducks and geese—Never travel with less than 3 shotguns now—Love from me and Pauline who I hope is now only about 15 minutes away.

PH. PUL   Ernest

1. Origin of EH's story "Wine of Wyoming."

To WALDO PEIRCE, Sheridan, c. 23 August 1928

Muy Waldo Mio:

Nothing from you in a hell of a while. Hope you're not laid up. Pauline came out and I finished the damn book, first draft - finally. Then we fished, caught 30 apiece everyday, none over 15 inches but damn nice trout. This is a cockeyed wonderful country, looks like Spain, swell people. Every time I go out and see it I wish you were here to paint it.

Saw old Wister,[1] sweet old guy, writes damned well too. Went on a trip, shooting prairie dogs with the pistol from the car, shot and recovered 8. They are like getting planes in wartime, for everyone that is confirmed you lose a bunch down the holes - only unlike the war you go home at night.

We go shooting chickens on the Crow Indian reservation next week then home to Piggott, then east at the end of Oct. then to Key West for all winter, better than trying to keep warm on grogs Americaines. Just decided to go down, you better come too and we will butcher the bloody monsters and swim all winter. Write to Piggott.

Pauline sends her love. She is strong as a goat again. Pat weighs 18 lbs now, parked with his grandparent.

Love to Ivy.

Write, yours in haste

COLBY   Hem.

1. See EH to Barklie Henry, *c.* 15 August 1927, note 2.

To MAXWELL PERKINS, Piggott, Arkansas, 28 September 1928

Dear Mr. Perkins:

I hope the hay fever is over. There's nothing worse and I do hope it is finished now. Arriving at Piggott I found two letters from you and one from Guy Hickock who said, "Sat next to me Scott Fitzgerald very white and equally sober—" So you can add that to your reports though by now Scott may be back. I hope he is in good shape—though I don't know why I should wish him in US for his own good. He wrote the Gatsby in Europe. He drinks no more there and what he does drink is not poisonous. I'm awfully anxious to see him.

Coming back here I am anxious to start re-writing the book. But it is only a month since I finished it and it probably is best to let it lie until we get settled in Florida. I finished the Sun in Sept. and did not start re-writing it until December. This will not take as much re-writing as each day to start with (while I was working on it) I wrote over what I had done the day before. But I want to make sure that I leave it alone long enough so I can find the places where I get the kick when writing it and neglect to convey it to the reader.

I appreciate the offer of the check for $5000 and nothing would please me more. I want to get together about 15000 to buy bonds with when I get to N.Y. in the attempt to add $75.00 a month to our income—$100.00 if possible if I can raise 20,000. Money in the bank does me no good at all—it simply vanishes. That is why I haven't cashed the $3700 royalty check—but if I can save in chunks and invest we can live very well on the income. Pat was very expensive and liveing in U.S. with nurse cook etc. plus travelling is expensive too. So I want to make an investment before I dribble my capital away. With the 3700 and some other I have picked up have about 5000 to invest now and want to get enough more to do some good.

The only drawback to accepting the 5000 advance is that I quite gratuitously promised Ray Long [of *Cosmopolitan*] I would let him have the first look at my next book if I decided to serialize it. I did this to shut them up when they were worrying me with propositions while I was working.

To be completely frank I would greatly prefer to serialize in the [Scribner's] Magazine—I do not care for serializing in Cosmopolitan and the difference of a few thousand—2 or 3—would not make me switch from Scribners to the International Magazine Co. I think it would be a good thing for me to serialize because it is not a good plan to wait *too* long between appearances and as I will not have a book out this fall—nor until next fall—due to working so long on this one—it is good to keep something going.

As I said the money would be very welcome. I would write Ray Long and tell him but am afraid he would think I was trying to bid him up which is the last thing I want. If you can see any way out of this I would be very happy. In the meantime I feel like a damned fool not to take the check. I worry about the whole business and am prevented from writing the stories I wanted to do now in between by worrying about these bloody matters.

Yet I know, and that is what worries me—that so far I have made no money—nor been able to get any ahead—and I have attended enough benefits for people who did make money and did not hang on to it so that I have no idea but that it is an absolute necessity to get some ahead. Also on the other hand it would be no fun if the book was adjudged un-serializable to send the money back.

So that is the situation—if this letter is muddled perhaps it is because the situation seems muddled—Perhaps you can clarify it. If the hay fever season is not over don't try!

Anyway the encouraging thing is that I believe maybe the book is pretty good—and I've 40,000 words on another one to follow it—have never felt better or stronger or healthier in the head or body—nor had better confidence or morale—haven't been sick since I've been in America—knocking on wood—nor had an accident—more knocking. The last few days my good eye that I cut last winter has been bothering me and that and worrying about the money has slowed me up—but today it is all right.

This letter has dragged on long enough. Perhaps on re-reading your letter I would not be breaking my promise to Long by taking the check. Anyway you will know. I don't think I would accept his offer no matter how much it was—there's also a good chance he wouldn't want it. No one may want it. I suppose that's really why I want the cash in hand! Anyway you will know where I stand and what I can and can't do. Your conscience is as $\left\{\begin{array}{l} \text{good} \\ \text{bad} \end{array}\right\}$ as mine.

So good luck anyway and I certainly appreciate the offer.

Yours always
Ernest Hemingway

PUL

To F. SCOTT FITZGERALD, Piggott, *c.* 9 October 1928

Dear Mr. Fizzgeral:

A letter some time ago from Maxwell E Perkins let me in on the little secret that you work eight hours every day - Joyce I believe worked twelve. There was some comparison between how long it took you two great authors to finish your work.

Well Fitz you are certainly a worker. I have never been able to write longer than two hours myself without getting utterly pooped - any longer than that and the stuff begins to become tripe but here is old Fitz whom I once knew working eight hours every day. How does it feel old fellow? What is the secret of your ability to write for eight hours every day. I look forward with some eagerness to seeing the product. Will it be like that other great worker and fellow Celt? Have you gone in for not making sense? If I could only take the slight plunge to going in for not making sense I could work ten and twelve hours a day every day and always be perfectly [word blotted out] like Gertrude Stein who since she has taken up not making sense some eighteen years ago has never known a moments unhappiness with her work.

You dirty lousy liar to say you work (write) eight hours a day.

Send [George Horace] Lorimer a story hell. I'm letting you send Lorimer stories for both of us.

Finished my first draft of the bloody book a month ago - going east now in a couple of weeks. Wanted to write some stories here but laying off writing for a month lost all impetus and now feel too healthy and at the same time mentally pooped. God I worked hard on that book. Want like hell to start re-writing but I know I ought to wait a while still.

Just got back from Montana went there from Wyo. - had a grand time. Pat has doubled his weight in three months - weighed 9 something to begin with. He looks like H [illegible] never cries laughs all the time - sleeps all nights built like a brick shithouse. I am thinking of advertising in the Nation or some suitable medium Are your children Rickety, deformed, in any way unsatisfactory. See E. Hemingway (then pictures of the product - all by different Mothers) Perhaps He can help You. Mr. Hemingway understands your problem. He is the author of Mr. and Mrs. Elliott. He knows what you are up against. His own problem is different. Mr. Hemingway has to avoid children. Since the age of fourteen he has been embarrassed by a succession of perfect Little Ones. Now he has decided to make this great gift available to All. Tear off the enclosed coupon and mail it in a plain stamped envelope and you will receive his booklet Perfect Children for You All.

Just send the coupon and your photo and you will receive a personal answer from Mr. Hemingway himself.

Do not confuse Mr. Hemingway with Mr. FitzGerald. Mr. FitzGerald it is true is the father of a very perfect child with, we must admit, a delightful English accent (a thing Mr. Hemingway cannot guarantee his clients). But Mr. FitzGerald is what is known in the profession as a 'one time performer'. You may take Mr. Fizzgerow if you wish but, in the end, you will be sorry. Mr. Dos Passos, however, we must strongly counsell against. For your best interests do not take Mr. Dos Passos. Mr. Dos Passos is practically 'sterile'. You all know what that means. Mr. D.P. cannot have children. Poor Mr. D.P. It is true Mr. Hemingway sometimes envies Mr. Dos Passos but that is just another proof of Mr. Hemingway's real worth to You.

There has lately been a movement on foot to take Mr. [deleted] Delicacy forbids us to give Mr. [deleted] first name (or last name). We cannot counsel too strongly against this. Do not press us for our reasons. Mr. Donald Ogden Stewart has had a certain amount of publicity lately in this connection but after mature consideration we feel that we cannot conscientiously recommend Mr. Stewart. Mr. Stewart may be a 'one timer.' There is no greater waste of money in modern social hygiene than the employment of a one timer. Then there is the religious issue. Mr. Hemingway has enjoyed success under all religions. Even with no religion at all Mr. Hemingway has not been found wanting. In the matter of Creeds, as in Colours, he is not a Bigot.

You understand, my dear Fitz, that none of this is personal. When I say Hemingway I may mean Perkins or Bridges. When I say FitzGerald I may mean Compton MacKenzie or Stephen St. Vincent Benet the wife of the poet Eleanor Wylie. When I say [deleted] I may mean Horseshit. None of this is even the slightest bit personal or 'mean'. Just good old big hearted Hem speaking. We are on the air tonight through the courtesy of the Kansas City Star and associated newspapers. Oh my this really is a fight. I wish you all could see Tommy Heeney's left eye. Now they are at it again.

Where are you going to be the end of Oct. How's to get stewed together Fitz? How about a little mixed vomiting or should it be a "stag" party.

Write to me Piggott (Arkansas)

Ernest

glad you are friends with Murphy's.

[Partly crossed-out postscript:] I would rather stay friends with, say, Mike Ward than be in and out of being friends with say, Saint Paul or other rich and noble characters. But then the [deleted] aren't Saint Paul nor are they Minneapolis. They are figures in a ballet. A very attractive Ballet. Use that sometime in the Post, Kid.

[In left-hand margin beside the crossed-out portion:] This is crossed-out—Old Hem never speaks nor writes in criticism of his friends and they are my friends. . . .

PUL

To MAXWELL PERKINS, Piggott, 11 October 1928

Dear Mr. Perkins:

Thanks very much for sending the check. I will hang on to it and we or rather you can decide what it is for later. I imagine when I see Ray Long or some of his under Rays I can fix it up with them as you suggest. We will see anyway. I don't see why they shouldn't.

Have a story about ¾ done. Will be leaving here as soon as it is finished to see Chicago and Toronto en route to N.Y. What about Scott? I am awfully anxious to hear.

Is Morley Callaghan in Toronto? Would like to see him.

Nigger To Nigger[1] is very good. I enjoyed it greatly. Thanks very much for sending it and also for the [Conrad] Aiken book [Costumes by Eros, 1928]. His story about the fellow rapping on the wall very funny and the old whore lady quite sad. Haven't read any others yet.

Anyone that would say hay fever was imagination could probably prove that child birth was too. My father had it and I was always grateful to it because it kept us increasingly further north when I was a kid— but I know how hellish it is. I get the same feeling from dust. But it goes away after a couple of days.

Instead of thinking Zelda a possible good influence (what a phrase) for Scott, I think 90% of all the trouble he has comes from her. Almost every bloody fool thing I have ever seen or known him to do has been directly or indirectly Zelda inspired. I'm probably wrong in this. But I often wonder if he would not have been the best writer we've ever had or likely to have if he hadn't been married to some one that would make him waste *Everything*. I know no one that has ever had more talent or wasted it more. I wish to god he'd write a good book and finish it and not poop himself away on those lousy Post stories. I don't blame *Lorimer* I blame Zelda. I would not have Scott imagine I believed this for the world.

Yours always,
Ernest Hemingway

Will leave here in about three days. I'll give you an address in Toronto.

PUL

1. Edward C. L. Adams's account of South Carolina Negroes published by Scribners (New York, 1928).

To F. SCOTT AND ZELDA FITZGERALD, on board *Spirit of St. Louis, c.* 18 November 1928

Dear Scott and Zelda:

The train is bucking and pitching or bitching (but not listing anyway).

We had a wonderful time[1]—you were both grand—I am sorry I made a shall we say nuisance of myself about getting to the train on time—We were there far too early—when you were in the hands of the Cop I called on the phone from our platform and explained you were a great writer—the Cop was very nice—He said you said I was a great writer too but he had never heard of either of us. I told him rapidly the plots of some of your better known stories—He said—this is absolutely literal— "He seems like a Dandy Fellow"—thats the way Cops talk—not as they talk in [Morley] Callaghan's Works.

Anyway we had a grand time and Ellersley Mansion is the most cockeyed beautiful place I've ever seen—Pauline sends her love.

Ernest

I'll write our address in Key West when I know it—Piggott, Ark. will always reach us.

PUL

1. EH and Pauline had stayed overnight with the Fitzgeralds after attending the Princeton–Yale football game at Palmer Stadium on 17 November.

To F. SCOTT FITZGERALD, Oak Park, Illinois, *c.* 9 December 1928

Dear Scott:

You were damned good and also bloody effective to get me that money —I had like a fool only 35–40 bucks with me after Xmas Shopping— plenty for food and tips enroute to Key West.[1]

My Father shot himself as I suppose you may have read in the papers. Will send you the $100 as soon as I reach Key West—or have Max Perkins send it—

Thanks again like hell for your werry admirable *performance* as we say in the automotive game.

I was fond as hell of my father and feel too punk—also sick etc.—to write a letter but wanted to thank you.

Best to Zelda and Scotty— Yrs always Ernest

PUL

1. EH and Bumby were on a Florida-bound train from New York City when a telegram delivered at Trenton, New Jersey, told EH of his father's death. He wired Fitzgerald for a loan, left Bumby in care of the Pullman porter, and at Philadelphia caught a train for Chicago.

To MAXWELL PERKINS, Corinth, Mississippi, 16 December 1928

Dear Mr. Perkins:

Hope to be back at Key West Tuesday morning and at work on the book again. My Father shot himself—Don't know whether it was in N.Y. papers. I didn't see any of the papers. I was very fond of him and feel like hell about it. Got to Oak Park in plenty of time to handle things— Funeral was Sat. aft. Have everything fixed up except they will have damned little money—went over all that too. Realize of course that thing for me to do is not worry but get to work—finish my book properly so I can help them out with the proceeds. What makes me feel the worst is my father is the one I cared about.

You don't have to write any letter of condolence to me—thanks very much for the wire—there was no immediate need for money—when I get the serial money I will try and fix them up.

For your own information (not Scott) there are my Mother and two kids Boy 12 girl 16 still at home—$25,000 insurance—a $15,000 mortgage on the house (house should bring 10 to 15 thousand over the mortgage but sale difficult). Various worthless land in Michigan, Florida etc. with taxes to pay on all of it. No other capital—all gone—my father carried 20–30 yr. Endowment insurance which was paid and lost in Florida. He had angina pectoris and diabetes preventing him from getting any more insurance. Sunk all his savings, my grandfather's estate etc. in Florida. Hadn't been able to sleep with pain etc.—knocked him temporarily out of his head.

I have what I hope won't prove to be the grippe—so excuse such a louzy letter. Thought you might be worrying so wanted to give you the dope.

Yours always,

PUL   [Signature cut away.]

To MAXWELL PERKINS, Key West, 8 January 1929

Dear Mr. Perkins:

Have 20 chapters done and typed—must be around 30,000 words— have been over the whole thing once in pencil and re-read it all. Going good but have been working 6–10 hours every day and will be glad to lay off and take a trip when you come down.

All you need is some old clothes and tennis shoes—better bring tennis things and racket—any sweaters you have—but we have plenty if you haven't any. I must have 15—all sizes.

The Gulf Stream is alive with fish. Now—really—it's like the old wild pigeon and Buffalo days. I've fished every Sunday—we got a 8 ft. 6 inch sailfish a week ago. Last Sunday—day before yesterday—were out salvaging liquor from a boat that went on the reef coming from the Bahamas —got 14 bottles of Chateau Margaux among other things. Boat had about $60,000 worth of liquor on her but everybody else was salvaging too. We got caught in a storm and I was afraid I might Shelley-out on you for a while.[1]

Don't let anyone bluff you out of coming down. It's the only way you can get this Mss. Anytime after next week that you want to come will be fine. I'm getting a carbon made of the Mss. Have about 15 or 20 chapters more to do. But will be glad of some company. I expected Archie

MacLeish down this week but got word he was in some sort of a jam and couldn't come.

Would you send Scott $100.00 I borrowed from him in North Philadelphia. I didn't want to draw it till after the first of the year to hold down my last years income figure.

Have bought a fine 9 x 9 ft. insect proof tent with a sewed in ground cloth so we can camp out at the Marquesas where Waldo caught the big tarpon if you want. There's lots of shooting if you like to shoot—got 9 snipe yesterday after I knocked off work—20 a couple of days before—15 before that. They are very good with the Bordeaux. Have some prewar absinthe too but it makes too crazy dreams so am saving it for you and Waldo.

Best wishes for the New Year.

PUL   Ernest Hemingway

1. An allusion to the poet Shelley's drowning in the Gulf of Spezia in July 1822.

To MAXWELL PERKINS, Key West, 10 January 1929

Dear Mr. Perkins:

After you come down here you will be able to go back and make hash out of all the 15 yr. old boys and 60 yr. old fat men the handball king can find. But seriously handball is a knack too and probably the fat man was a specialist at it as the kid was. It's one of those things like punching the bag that are no criterion of Honest Worth.

Anyway you come down anytime now and we will have a fine time.

My sister [Sunny] and Pauline are both typing on the book today and I will have 29 chapters in type by night. Have finished 413 pages of the hand written Mss.

I will pretty surely have it all ready for you to take back—that is if you come down. If you don't come down you won't ever get it.

I'll try and get a New Republic for the Sonnets. She [Elinor Wylie] always seemed to me personally like a lecherous cat but I'd hoped she would confine herself to staying in love with Shelley and thus give Bill Benet a break.[1] It is awfully tough on him. I'm glad the sonnets are good. I did not know she was dead until I saw some reference to it in the paper last week. What did she die of?

Thanks about the money. I don't need any until I get the book done.

Let me know when to look for you. You can get in a lot of tennis down here. There are good courts and my sister is not much good but plays a strong game and you can get a work out with her anyway. I wrote Waldo and suggested he come too. But it may be too soon for him to leave Bangor.

15 naval planes came down and have scared away all the snipe. But the planes will go and we may get some new snipe who will not be so highly educated as to shotgun ranges. Had 14 for dinner again last night. But they were hard to get.

The boatman we fish with thinks it is a great waste of ammunition to shoot snipe when he says he can take us to a rookery where we can shoot white herons *Right on the nests!* The local ideal of sporting life.

                                    Your always
PUL   Ernest Hemingway

1. See EH to Isabel Simmons Godolphin, 25 February 1926.

To MAXWELL PERKINS, Key West, 22 January 1929

Dear Max:

Finished the book today. The weather is fine—76°—so come on down. Maybe I'll get a letter today or tomorrow from you. Too pooped to write more—but the sooner you come down the better.

                                    Yours always,
                                    Hemingway

The Casa Marina would be a good place to stay maybe. There are very few people there. The Concha is comfortable but in center of town and the Overseas primitive cuban and old fashioned. You don't need to decide where you stay till you look them all over. You can send your mail care of me. It will be fine to see you. Best regards to Wallace Meyer.
PUL

To JOHN DOS PASSOS, Key West, 9 February 1929

Dear Dos:

Enclosed came today. For God's sake come down. The road isn't finished - 45 mile water gap still and the County Treasurer absconded
with all funds and they've closed the schools—let alone build the road.

Tarpon are in and have caught two - lost a big one last night at the
boat - we're here until middle of March - absolutely broke may not be
able to ever leave, but lots of liquor off a wrecked booze boat.

Waldo [Peirce] comes down next week. Come on down. Saw at least
100 tarpon last night out by the jack channel.

Pauline sends her love.

Come on down and we will go to Tortugas - Waldo has some jack.
His mother died. My old man shot himself but it was no help financially—on the contrary!

Come on down kid -

You must have thought me a shite not to write.

HEM

[Postscript upside down:] No eyes dropped out yet.
UVA

To GRACE HALL HEMINGWAY, Key West, 11 March 1929

Dear Mother:

Enclosed please find check for $678.93 - $578.93 for the special assess-
ment taxes and $100 for the month of April. The special assessments were
surely tough luck but I am glad to pay them while I can. If you will send
me the official location and description of *all* property—Pauline's uncle
has a salesman in that territory who is interested in St. Pete[rsburg] real
estate and we will have him look them all up and make a report on them
and we may be able to do something about selling.

I am glad to help all I can as long as I have money. I know you will
do everything to get things going though because I never know when I
may be broke. I can guarantee the $100 a month for this year and next
year too (will put it aside now) but we want to get things going as well
as possible. Never worry because I will always fix things up—can always
borrow money if I haven't it—So don't ever worry, but go ahead with
good confidence and get things going. I am very pleased about the 4
roomers and that you are going to Windermere. Remember you are on

your own but have a powerful backer—To whit me. I will count on Marce and Sterling [Sanford] to do something too. I know Marce is going to have a baby. But we have had one this year too and they are rich and have always been very great friends of the family while I live by my pen and have been more or less of an outcast.

But the main thing is not to worry about money but to go ahead—with courage and confidence. *Make* Uncle George see you sell the house for a good substantial profit or else he must get the mortgage cancelled if he has to pay it himself. He did more than any one to kill Dad and he had better do something in reparation. I know his sanctimonious tightness and he is going to do what he ought to do about that house or I will have his hide—have never written a novel of the H[emingway] family because I have never wanted to hurt anyone's feelings but with the death of the ones I love a period has been put to a great part of it and I may have to undertake it—

This is Saturday. We leave next Thursday. Pauline is down with a septic sore throat—Sunny and Pat fine but Bumby with a bad throat. Imagine they'll all be o.k. by Thursday. Hope so—

Best love to the kids

Yours always
Ernie

You have been *fine* about everything. Remember not to worry and not to hold things back from me but don't bother me with general run of stuff—The more I'm let alone and not worried the better I can function. Have paid Sunny's passage etc so imagine she'll have enough for her trip.

PH. PUL

To MAXWELL PERKINS, Paris, 7 June 1929

Dear Max:

I got the proofs two days ago. They were held up at the Customs because the notation "Proofs for Correction" was made in such small type—without capitals—on the label that the Customs People did not notice it. I cleared them at the Customs and was on them all day yesterday and today.

I am sorry to have made you so much trouble having the corrections made on the original galleys copied.

I find many more suggested—some of them very good, others sad when it makes no difference. I am glad always to make it conventional as to punctuation. About the words—I have made a notation at the side about the bed pan. Originally I had about 2,000 words of that aspect of hospital life. It really *dominates* it. I cut it all out with the exception of the one reference to the bed pan.

It is the same with other words.

You say they have not been in print before—one may not have—but the others are all in Shakespeare.

But more recently you will find them in a book called All Quiet on the Western Front [by Erich Maria Remarque] which Scott gave me and which has sold in the 100s of thousand copies in Germany and is around 50,000 copies in England with the word shit, fart etc. never dragged in for coloring but only used a few times for the thousands of times they are omitted. Please read the statement on page 15 of that book.

The trouble is Max that before my book will be out there will be this All Quiet on the Western Front book and possibly at the same time the second volume of the man [Arnold Zweig] who wrote Sergeant Grischa— who knows his eggs also—and I hate to kill the value of mine by emasculating it. When I looked up in the Quiet on W.F. book to find the words to show you I had a very hard time finding them. They don't stand out.

There has always been first rate writing and then American writing (genteel writing). But you should not go backwards. If a word can be printed and is needed in the text it is a *weakening* to omit it. If it *cannot* be printed without the book being suppressed all right.

No one that has read the Mss. has been shocked by *words*. The words do not stand out unless you put a ring around them.

There is no good my pleading the case in a letter. You know my viewpoint on it. What would have happened if they had cut the Sun also? It would have flopped as a book and I would have written no more for you.

The first place you say you think a word must go is in galley 13. I can consider you leaving that a blank, but in galley 51 where the same word is used by Piani if that is cut out it is pretty ruinous—I don't consent and it's done over my head.

On galley 57 a word is used that is used again at the top of galley 60. If you think this word will cause the suppression of the book make it C——S——R. You see I have kept out all the words that are the constant vocabulary—but have given the sense of them by using once, twice or three times the real words. Using then only the most classic words. You know what General Cambronne said at the battle of Waterloo instead of "the old guard dies but never surrenders." He said *Merde* when they called on him to surrender.

In a purely conversational way in a latin language in an argument one man says to another "Cogar su madre!"

You see there is nothing wrong with any of the words I have used except the last—the one on galley 57—which is used as an expression of supreme insult and contempt. The others are common enough and I dare say will all be in print in U.S.A. before the year is out.

It's unsatisfactory to write this and I hope you don't think I'm getting snooty about it. I wish we could talk and you could tell me just how far you *can* go and what the danger is. I do not want trouble—But want everything that can be had without trouble. I thought you said that if I accepted certain blanks etc. for the serialization the book would be published as it was. I see in the 2nd installment cuts made without my knowledge but am of course in their hands.

Anyway am working all the time on this proof and will get it back to you as soon as possible—By a boat the first of the week.

I hope you got the signed sheets O.K. I mailed them about a week ago. Am enclosing the contract.

Yours always
Ernest Hemingway

P.S.

About the place in galley 38 where F.H. is talking to the hospital matron—I don't know what to do—it is supposed to be the deliberate insult and rout-ing of a person through the use of direct language that she expected by her sex and position never to be exposed to—the final forced conflict between someone from the front and someone of the genteel base. Is the word so impossible of printing? If it is, the incident is killed. It was the one word I remember we omitted from the Sun. Maybe if it had been printed then we'd know now if it was printable.

If you decide that it is unprintable how about b——ls. I think that's the only solution. I suppose on galley 57 C——S——RS and C——ks——r will do for the other too, galley 60. Certainly those letters cannot corrupt anyone who has not heard or does not know the word. There's no proof it isn't cocksure.

PUL

To MAXWELL PERKINS, Paris, 24 June 1929

Dear Max:

Thanks for your letter about the literary guilds etc. I think you have exactly the right dope and that there is no reason to submit. Also received the magazine publicity and one batch of magazine galleys. I hate awfully to have put you to so much trouble.

Am returning the galleys I hope this Tuesday on the Homeric. That should land them in N.Y. about the 2nd of July.

Have worked over and over and have a new and I think much better ending. We leave for Spain July 2nd. Will keep you informed of an address. For Cabling purposes will be at the Hotel Quintana—Pamplona—Spain from July 6 to 14. Will let the bank have my address all the time. We'll settle down in Santiago in August.

Owen Wister was here and we saw him twice and enjoyed it greatly.[1] He agreed there was no change to be made in the last chapter and has read this ending and likes it very much he says. His last words were last night—Don't touch a thing! He is nice and damned kind and generous and I was certainly the last of the wahoos to get angry and write as I did to you. I wish you would destroy the letter. No one knows about it except ourselves and that would wipe it out perhaps and make me feel not quite so lousy about having exploded in such a foul way. The strain of going over and over and living through a thing each time trying to make it better and for two months getting nowhere coupled with other things may have had something to do with me misunderstanding it so completely. But without alibis I wish you would destroy the letter.

Now must go to church at noon mass and then to Auteuil to try and get a winner in the Grand Steeplechase. A damned fine race. Wish you could see it. Jock Whitney's horse Easter Hero is running. The course is not as difficult as the Grand National but bad enough and fine to watch. Scott is working hard he says. I have seen Morley Callaghan several times and boxed with him five times I think. He has not the appearance but is an *excellent* boxer. I have been working hard over the book but have made almost no changes. Write them out, try and better it and then come back to the way it is. Will be awfully glad to see the last of it.

Some one cabled that the June number was banned in Boston.[2] Wister was here at dinner and I told him that and he seemed to think it meant nothing. I hope it causes you no annoyance.

Yours always
Ernest

excuse typographical mistakes.

PUL

---

1. See EH to Barklie Henry, *c.* 15 August 1927, note 2 and EH to Wister, *c.* 25 July 1929. 2. *Scribner's Magazine* paid EH $10,000 for serialization of *A Farewell to Arms* prior to book publication. Sales were banned in Boston.

To ARCHIBALD MAC LEISH, Montroig, Spain,[1] 18 July 1929

Dear Orchie:

For Chrise sake Mac dont drop any more rocks on yr. hands. Heave them at [Lincoln] Kerstein. He says I'm a shit, too and imitate Callaghan!

Visiting [Joan] Miro here.[2] Got your letter at Pamplona. Fine town. I intend to write about it sometime or at least attempt to put it in a book. There was, however, a good deal of drinking going on and so, eventually, we left.

I'm glad as hell you liked the start of the book—if it seems to go shitty later on dont despair because that is emasculation by the magazine authorities—a tiny operation with a great effect. I think you'll like it as a book. If it is still emasculated as a book they are scared now on acct. the Boston business.[3] We'll have the MSS bound and give you that. I am holding out for all the words and everything so will probably end up in the Poorhouse. Let us hope the Poorhouse will prove to be your Turkeyhouse.[4]

It is swell to hear from you, you ignorant rock dropping bastard, so why not write to Hotel Suizo, Santiago de Campostella—Spain.

The bloody book starts to be readable again in about the August No. I hope. I dont think there is much there for the literary gents on the magazine to cut. So if you think you cant write me because it seems so rotten read the Aug. one and we'll be all right again I hope. Anyway write even if it's rotten. I'm all through with it now.

Give our love to Ada Aida and yr. esteemed children. When do we shoot some more ghost partridges?[5] I cant go with Gerald [Murphy] on acct. of proofs. We'll be in U.S. in March. Everybody fine.

Best love,

LC   Pappy

1. Montroig is a village in Tarragona province. A memorable passage on the visit to Montroig appears in *Death in the Afternoon*, chapter 20. 2. EH had known Miró in Paris, where he purchased *The Farm* in 1926. 3. See the preceding letter to Maxwell Perkins. 4. EH addressed the envelope to Mac Leish, "The Laird of Turkpen" in Conway, Massachusetts. 5. "Partridges that weren't there—but Ernest shot a double." (Mac Leish to Carlos Baker, 2 April 1980.)

To OWEN WISTER, Valencia, Spain, *c.* 25 July 1929

Dear O.W.:

I was damned glad to get your letter. Your advice is always good and I will take all I can of it. You must see, having gone through it, that much of the plain speech is from being unable to do it any other way. It is hard as hell for me to write—really—you have always had much greater talent. I will try hard to give the effect—(will you quote me the passage? in your own work) the other (plain speech) is where it seems it must be and that I must stay with. All we can do to restore the old language—as it is spoken it should be written or it dies—is to the good. What if you become an outlaw? I'm afraid we are anyway. We should be maybe. Perhaps not. But really you write for a sort of hidden legal metre (100 centimetres) somewhere within yourself—without pleasure in trying to attain it but only a sense that you must. And it is an added pleasure if one can please yourself too i.e. O.W.

You see too, I know, not like that Harry Hansen, how damned much I try always to do the thing by three cushion shots rather than by words or direct statement. But maybe we must have the direct statement too. It was good in the old days and our life now is very like those days. Especially 1914–1921—and much now in various places. Taste is all that can guide you. Except that I am very grateful when you tell me things.

You are a better writer than Merrimee if you do not mind me saying it. Having read both the gents without benefit of instruction. But the French being more literary than nos otros always speak so skillfully of themselves—where we apologize they imortalize. (misspelled probably)

We came here via Pamplona, Jaca, Huesca, Fraga, Lérida, Tarragona (a lovely place) a good bull fight yesterday, bad one today—the horses wear mattresses on their stomachs now. Here at Hotel Regina until Aug. 3. Then at Hotel Suizo (Santiago de Compostela) until end of Aug. I wish we were to see you again. Have written to send you the *Torrents of Spring*. It seemed funny once maybe it will get a dispensation and seem funny to you. I have been trying to write stories or a story rather and can't a damn bit. This time next year we'll be in Wyoming. Pauline sends her best greetings. I am always yours—(and thank you very much for the dope).

LC   E.H.

To MAXWELL PERKINS, Santiago de Compostela, Spain,
28 August 1929

Dear Max:

Excuse the beautiful edging on the paper. It's Pauline's. I got your two letters of Aug. 14 yesterday. I'm awfully glad you had such a good summer.

You can certainly get drunk on Port and it is bad afterwards too. Those famous 3 and 4 bottle men were living all the time in the open air—hunting, shooting, always on a horse. In that life as in skiing or fishing you can drink any amount.

Am cheerful again—have written 3 pieces—have some more in my head—going to go over them and copy off in Paris. We leave here day after tomorrow—for Madrid—want to see Sidney Franklin of Brooklyn. They say he's good. Be back in Paris Oct 1—maybe before. Glad [Wallace] Meyer likes the book. I hope to God it's better than the Sun. The comparative that way doesn't bother me.

Did I ever write you about seeing Morley Callaghan in Paris—several times—he was working hard. You would not believe it to look at him but he is a *very* good boxer. I boxed with him 3 or 4 times. One time I had a date to box with him at 5 pm—lunched with Scott and John Bishop at Pruniers—ate Homard thermidor—all sorts of stuff—drank several bottles of white burgundy. Knew I would be asleep by 5—so went around with Scott to get Morley to box right away. I couldn't see him hardly— had a couple of whiskeys enroute. Scott was to keep time and we were to box 1 minute rounds with 2 minute rests on acct. of my condition. I knew I could go a minute at a time and went fast and used all my wind —then Morley commenced to pop me and cut my mouth, mushed up my face in general. I was pooped as could be and thought I had never known such a long round but couldn't ask about it or Morley would think I was quitting. Finally Scott called time. Said he was very sorry and ashamed and would I forgive him. He had let the round go three minutes and 45 seconds—so interested to see if I was going to hit the floor! We boxed 5 more rounds and I finally fought myself out of the alcohol and went all right. Can still feel with my tongue the big scar on my lower lip. He is fast, knows a lot and is a pleasure to box with. He can't hit hard—if he could he would have killed me. I slipped and went down once and lit on my arm and put my left shoulder out in that first round and it pulled a tendon so that it was pretty sore afterwards and did not get a chance to box again before we left. Morley had been boxing nearly every day in Toronto for a year. He is fat and looks in bad shape but is really darned good.

What reminded me of this was how you could get rid of alcohol by exercise—after 5 rounds—during which I took a bad beating in the first. I was going well—judgment of distance good—in really good shape and out-pointing (or holding my own) with someone who had been beating me all over the place to sweat it out of me.

PUL   [Ernest Hemingway]

To JOHN DOS PASSOS, Madrid, 4 September 1929

Dear Dos:

Damned glad to hear you men are married. Best love from us to Kate.[1] I'm happy as hell about it!

I wrote you just the other day from Santiago. Pauline is out in the town and as it is raining like hell probably getting wet. Not much news - We came from Santiago to Orense and then down along the Portuguese Border - Verin and a swell town Puebla de Sanabria - (where got drunk) on to Benavento - up to Leon - (a lousy hole) along to Palencia - worst road in Spain 120 Kil of potholes, dust, heat to crack your head open. Two *swell* bull fights in Palencia - me in bed between fights with a busted gut - get up for the bull festival then back to bed - Then here by way of Valladolid and the Guadarramas - Damned nice -

Well it's fine to hear you citizens are married. Let us know where to send 30 or 40 thousand seeds worth of presents -

We're going to come back to U.S. in December or March - Europe is the tripe. I'll bet yr. first vol.[2] is damn good - Trilogies are undoubtedly the thing - Look at the Father, Son and Holy Ghost - Nothing's gone much bigger than that -

I wish the hell we could go to the sailfish side of Mexico on a trip - We could live on game, fish and what tomatoes you brought along - I'd be glad to go anywhere for months on onions alone if we had enough onions and salt - We could take enough stuff though - Lets go winter after next?

The Stewarts were ruined by Don getting that 25 thousand contract and meeting the Whitneys.

Am relying on you to avoid that—Sign nothing. Shoot as soon as you [see] the whites of a Whitney's eye—

Bishop was ruined by Mrs. Bishop's income. Keep money away from Katey.

Eternal youth has sunk the Fitzes - Get old, Passos - Age up Kate -

Old Hem ruined by his father shooting himself - Keep guns away from Katherine's old man—

It certainly will be fine to see you guys - I wish we could shoot you a bottle of absinthe -

Well this letter is tripe—

Yrs always----
Hem

Pauline sends her love -
She's writing too
UVA

1. Dos Passos married Katharine Foster Smith, Bill Smith's sister Katy, in August 1929 in Ellsworth, Maine. They had met at Key West earlier that year. See Townsend Ludington, *John Dos Passos: A Twentieth Century Odyssey* (New York, 1980), pp. 270–80. 2. *The 42nd Parallel* (1930).

To F. SCOTT FITZGERALD,[1] Madrid, 4 September 1929

Dear Scott:

About that "nervous bitterness" you remember my blowing up about the people coming in to look at the Apt while I was working. (I paid 3000 dollars on a promise to have it permanently and considered it our home) but you seem to have damned well forgot my coming around the next day to tell you that I thought Ruth Goldbeck Vallambrosa was a fine girl, had always admired her and told you for gods sake never to let her know that I had cursed about the Apt. *She* did not know I was sore and the only way she would ever find out would be through you. You said you understood perfectly and for me not to worry you would never mention it to her.

I'm damned glad you are going well. There is very small chance of our coming to the Riviera. There was some talk of Gerald and Sara [Murphy] coming here and we going back with them but a wire from Gerald yesterday says Sara has had to go to the mountains with Patrick and a letter following. Havent got the letter yet but believe their Spanish trip off. Would have been damned glad to see them. Havent spoken English to anyone since left Pamplona the 12th July except with Pauline. Havent even heard it. If they aren't coming we will probably go north and see Bumby and Pat. Bumby having good fishing in Brittany he writes.

I cant tell you how glad I am you are getting the book done. Fashionable thing is to deprecate all work and think the only thing is to go to pot gracefully and expensively, but the poor bastards doing this—giving up their writing etc. to compete with people who can do nothing and do nothing but go to pot. Cant finish that Jeremiad without mentioning friends and contemporaries—It sounds pretty bad anyway—Cant write that sort of tripe without a typewriter!

Of course all this may be premature and you may not be finishing your book [*Tender Is the Night*] but only putting me on the list of friends to receive the more glowing reports—

But I hope to God it's true. As far as I read it was better than anything I ever read except the best of Gatsby. You know what part that is.

The good parts of a book may be only something a writer is lucky enough to overhear or it may be the wreck of his whole damn life—and one is as good as the other.

You could write such a damn fine book. What held you up and constipated you more than anything was that review of [Gilbert] Seldes's in the Dial. After that you became self conscious about it and knew you must write a masterpiece. Nobody but Fairies can write Maspertieces or Masterpieces consciously—Anybody else can only write as well as they can going on the system that if this one when it's done isn't a Masterpiece maybe the next one will be. You'd have written two damned good books by now if it hadnt been for that Seldes review.

Of course there are other complications God knows but they are self made. They're not something that's done to you, like using the juice to write for the Post and trying to write masterpieces with the dregs. But now if your using the juice and are desperate enough so you know you have to write one, Seldes or no Seldes, you will write a damned fine book.

This should be enough from Jeremiah Hemingstein the great Jewish Prophet.

If you want some news Dos is married. And if you write a good and unsuperior letter with nothing about my nervous bitterness I'll write and tell you who he's married and all the dope.

On re-reading your letter I find it *Is Not Snooty at all*. And old Hem wrong again. Evidently a prey to his nervous bitterness! (This not sarcastic). But if I dont send this will never send any so throw out the N.B. in it (son of a bitch if I have that!) and write care the Guaranty when your not too tired from work. I know how damned pooping it is and I'm gladder than I can ever let you know that it is going finely—

Yours always affectionately,
Ernest

Best to Zelda and Scotty from us. Are you going to stay down in Cannes? How long. Might come down later when you get the book done. Max

[Perkins] is fine. He'd never let anybody down and I never worry about him.

PUL

1. This is EH's reply to Fitzgerald's letter of 23 August 1929; Fitzgerald replied to it 9 September. See *The Letters of F. Scott Fitzgerald*, ed. Andrew Turnbull (New York, 1963), pp. 304-7.

To F. SCOTT FITZGERALD, Hendaye, France, 13 September 1929

Dear Scott:

That terrible mood of depression of whether it's any good or not is what is known as The Artist's Reward.

I'll bet it's damned good—and when you get these crying drunks and start to tell them you have no friends for Christ sake amend it—it'll be sad enough—if you say no friends but Ernest the stinking serial king. You're not burned out and you know plenty to use—if you think your running out of dope, count on old Hem—I'll tell you all I know—whom slept with who and whom before or after whom was married—Anything you need to know—

Summer's a discouraging time to work—You dont feel death coming on the way it does in the fall when the boys really put pen to paper.

Everybody loses all the bloom—we're not peaches—that doesnt mean you get rotten—a gun is better worn and with bloom off—So is a saddle—People too by God. You lose everything that is fresh and everything that is easy and it always seems as though you could *never* write—But you have more metier and you know more and when you get flashes of the old juice you get more results with them.

Look how it is at the start—all juice and kick to the writer and cant convey anything to the reader—you use up the juice and the kick goes but you learn how to do it and the stuff when you are no longer young is better than the young stuff—

You just have to *go on* when it is worst and most helpless—there is only one thing to do with a novel and that is go straight on through to the end of the damn thing. I wish there was some way that your economic existence would depend on this novel or on novels rather than the damned stories because that is one thing that drives you and gives you an outlet and an excuse too—the damned stories.

Oh Hell. You have more stuff than anyone and you care more about it and for Christ sake just keep on and go through with it now and dont please write anything else until it's finished. It will be damned good—

(They never raise an old whore's price—She may know 850 positions—They cut her price all the same—So either you arent old or not a whore or both) The stories arent whoreing, they're just bad judgement—you could have and can make enough to live on writing novels. You damned fool. Go on and write the novel.

We drove here from Madrid in a day—Hendaye-Plage—Saw our noted contemporary L. Bromfield. Going up to Paris—Have you heard from Max [Perkins] if the Farewell is out? Got a bunch of literary periodicals from Brommy all full of Great German War Books—It was funny how I couldn't get into [Remarque's] All Quiet etc. but once in it it was damned good—Not so great as they think—But awfully good—L. Bromfield is writing a war book. It's bad luck maybe that mine comes out now and after all these that [I] have not had opportunity to profit by them in writing it. In about 2–3 years a man should be able to write a pretty good war book.

Old Dos married Kate Smith—She went to school (college) (not convent) with Pauline—He met her down at Key West last winter—She's a damned nice girl.

We've had letters from Gerald and Sara. It's a damned shame about their Patrick being sick—I think he'll be all right—

Good day today—water nice to swim and the sun the last of summer—

If this is a dull shitty letter it is only because I felt so bad that you were feeling low—am so damned fond of you and whenever you try to tell anybody anything about working or "life" it is always bloody platitudes—

Pauline sends her love to you, Zelda and Scotty—

Yours always—

PUL Ernest

To CAROL HEMINGWAY,[1] Paris, c. 5 October 1929

Dear Carol:

Thanks for the letter. I'm glad you got the piece of underwear. Pauline sent it, not me. The only reason I asked was because thought it might have been lost or custom-confiscated. Your letter doesn't read much as I remember you. Look, if you're trying to write I'd suggest that you avoid the sort of style employed by Sunny[2] in conversation; ie mis-used adjectives as ejaculations to cover a sort of mental ~~vacuity~~ vacancy. For instance I am guilty of using "swell" in writing. But only in dialogue; not as an adjective to replace the word you should use. Try and write straight English; never using slang except in Dialogue and then only when unavoidable. Because all slang goes sour in a short time. I only use swear words, for example, that have lasted at least a thousand years for fear of getting stuff that will be simply timely and then go sour.

I know letters are different from other writing. But this letter didn't sound like you very much. Plenty of times people who write the best write the very worst letters. It's almost a rule. I'm not criticizing your letters.

The worst poverty anyone can have is a poverty of mental interests. Money does not remove it and it does you no good to travel because you take it with you wherever you go. And a person with no interests in their head cannot converse intelligently or even comfortably, and conversation is one of the greatest pleasures—because they only feel at home with people as mentally limited as they are.

When I saw you in Oak Park I thought you were a grand girl and would go a long way. And I hope to God you are not going to be corrupted by the cheapness, flipness, petting instead of love, complete self-absorption and cheap, cheap, petting vacantness that has come to such a perfect flowering in Oak Park.

It doesn't do any good to hope, of course, but you've come to the place where you will go one way or the other and I do hope you will go the one rather than the other. "Don't listen to him. He's just preaching," I I can hear. But anyway good luck to you. We may be back [in the United States] around Christmas. Maybe see you somewhere around then.

Best Love,

PH. PUL   Ernie.

1. EH's youngest sister, born 19 July 1911 at Windemere, the family cottage on Walloon Lake, who in 1929 was a senior at Oak Park High School. 2. EH's sister Madelaine, called Sunny.

To F. SCOTT FITZGERALD, Paris, c. 22 or 29 October 1929

Dear Scott:

Saw Gertrude Stein the other evening and she asked about you. She claims you are the one of all us guys with the most talent etc. and wants to see you again. Anyway she has written me a note asking me to ask you or youse if you would come around Wed. Eve. to her place—after 8:30 or so I fancy—[Allen] Tate or Tates too—A merchant named Bernard Fay or Bernard Fairy to be there too.

Am going—Tate too—Would you or youse like to call by here before 8:30 or then—if not Gertrude's address is 27 rue du Fleurus—But if you come we might go together—

By the way, Gallipoli Memories by Compton MacKenzie (yr. old school fellow) is damned good and the most amusing war book I've read since Repington—Wdnt wonder if it wd go down with G. Moore's Hails and Farewells—

I'll be glad to buy it for you—There are to be 4 more volumes which is best news I've had in a long time—

Yrs. always affect---
Ernest

[Postscript:] No new news from Max [Perkins]. What about yr. suit against McCalls?

PUL

To F. SCOTT FITZGERALD, Paris, *c.* 24 or 31 October 1929

Dear Scott:

Your note just came and am utilizing a good hangover to answer it.

I was not annoyed at anything you said (You surely know by now, I've written it often enough, how much I admire your work). I was only annoyed at your refusal to accept the sincere compliment G. Stein was making to you and instead try and twist it into a slighting remark. She was praising her head off about you to me when you came up she started to repeat it and then at the end of the praise to spare you blushes and not be rude to me she said that our flames (sic) were maybe *not* the same—then you brood on that—

It is O.K. to not accept the compliments if you dont wish (most compliments are horseshit) but there is no need for me to have to re-iterate that they were compliments not slights. I cross myself and swear to God that Gertrude Stein has *never* last night or any other time said anything to me about you but the highest praise. That is absolutely true. The fact that you do not value or accept it does not make it any less sincere.

As for the comparison of our writings she was doing nothing of the kind—only saying that you had a hell of a roaring furnace of talent and I had a small one—implying I had to work a damn sight harder for results obtained—then to avoid praising you to your face and pooping on me she said she wasnt saying the flame was of the same quality. If you would have pressed her she would have told you to a direct question that she believes yours a better quality than mine.

Naturally I do not agree with that—any more than you would—any comparison of such a non existent thing as hypothetical "flames" being pure horseshit—and any comparison between you and me being tripe too—We started along entirely separate lines—would never have met except by accident and as writers have nothing in common except the desire to write well. So why make comparisons and talk about superiority—If you have to have feelings of superiority to me well and good as long as I do not have to have feelings of either superiority or inferiority to you—There can be no such thing between serious writers— They are all in the same boat. Competition within that boat—which is headed toward death—is as silly as deck sports are—The only competition is the original one of making the boat and that all takes place inside yourself. You're on the boat but you're getting touchy because you haven't finished your novel—that's all—I understand it and you could be a hell of a lot more touchy and I wouldn't mind.

This is all bloody rot to write in bed with a bad stomach and if you succeed in finding any slurs slights depreciations or insults in it the morning has been wasted (It's wasted anyway). Gertrude wanted to organize a hare and tortoise race and picked me to tortoise and you to hare and naturally, like a modest man and a classicist, you wanted to be the tortoise—all right tortoise all you want—It's all tripe anyway—

I like to have Gertrude bawl me out because it keeps one['s] opinion of oneself down—way down—She liked the book very much she said— But what I wanted to hear about was what she didnt like and why— She thinks the parts that fail are where I remember visually rather than make up—That was nothing very new—I expected to hear it was all tripe—Would prefer to hear that because it is such a swell spur to work.

Anyway here is page 4 [of this letter]—Will enclose Max's letter—

I'm damn sorry Bromfield started that rumor but it cant hurt Scribners when I nail it by staying with them—I'd be glad to write him a letter he could publish if he wanted—

Look what tripe everything is—In plain talk I learned to write from you—In Town and Country from Joyce - in Chic Trib from Gertrude— not yet reported the authorities on Dos Passos, Pound, Homer, Mc Almon, Aldous Huxley and E. E. Cummings—Then you think I shouldnt worry when some one says I've no vitality—I dont worry—Who has vitality in Paris? People dont write with vitality—they write with their heads— When I'm in perfect shape dont feel like writing—feel too good! G. S. never went with us to Schruns or Key West or Wyoming or any place where you get in shape—If she's never seen me in shape—Why worry? When they bawl you out ride with the punches—

Anyway will write no more of this—I'm sorry you worried - you weren't unpleasant.

Yours always affectionately,

PUL   Ernest

To MAXWELL PERKINS, Paris, 31 October 1929

Dear Max:

I hope to Christ you weren't caught in the market. They're liquidating now so Hoover can have brought us out of this slump by 1932. I've been in bed for the last few days. Grippe. Then my kidneys don't work awfully well and I tore a muscle badly in my groin in Spain this summer and had my trousers full of guts like a picador horse. But that is all healed now altho still bandaged. But can't drink anything without my fingers swelling. Need to get down to Key West if I'm to protect your investment. Been too sick to write for a month and worrying about the book—whether it would keep on so could handle things etc. We want to get away by the last of Dec. maybe but know nothing about this apt yet and have 3000 bucks tied up in improvements, plumbing, heating, fixtures etc.

I saw in the World that some citizen was *lecturing* on Farewell to Arms. God it would be fine to walk in and ask a few questions and then say "Shit, Sir I do believe you are mistaken!"

After I got hurt this summer we stayed 3 days in the hottest room you ever saw 115 in the shade—room on the hot side of the house and no shade—only a small single bed for two and I couldn't move. Hotel full for the bull fights in Palencia. Really hot. Pauline was wonderful.

This letter isn't about anything—sick of reading and can't think enough to write anything except this tripe to you. What about Waldo? How does he look without the beard? It's a loss to the world.

Hope you're all fine and everyone well.

Best luck always
Ernest

I got the two checks for 3000 for Oct. 7–14. One thing you never told me about was whether it would be possible to get the original proofs so I could have one copy without the blanks. When you get this letter will you wire me what the sale is up to the end of whatever week has been completed?

Will you send one of the presentation copies to Owen Wister Esq, Long House, Bryn Mawr, Penn, and one to Mr. and Mrs. Charles Thompson, *c/o Key West Hardware Co.*, opposite *Thompson Fish Co.*, Key West, Florida with my compliments! Thanks ever so much.

That uses up the 4 copies—I want to buy 3 more. Will you have them hold them for me? I'll send a check or they can deduct them.

PUL

To B. C. SCHOENFELD,[1] Paris, 5 November 1929

Dear Mr. Schoenfeld:

Thank you very much for writing. The trouble about the Sun is that I had and still have an idea of trying to make a play out of it myself— There's a lot of stuff I cut out of the book that might help in a play and I thought I should try, maybe, to make a play of it some lean year.

You were awfully good to suggest doing it and I appreciate it very much—After I've made a mess of it I'll be sorry not to have accepted your offer. But I'm afraid I cant accept it now. Although I do appreciate it very much and thank you again for having made it. Please give my best regards to [Conrad] Aiken.

With all best wishes,
Yours always,
Ernest Hemingway

KNOX

1. Mr. Schoenfeld was then a student at Yale University Theater School.

To F. SCOTT FITZGERALD, Paris, 12 December 1929

Dear Scott:

Your letter didnt come until last night—They'd held it at the bank.

I know you are the soul of honor. I mean that. If you remember I made no cracks about your time keeping until after you had told me over my objections for about the fourth time that you were going to deliberately quarrel with me. The first time I thought I had convinced you. You came back to it and I, and Pauline, thought we had convinced you again. On the fourth time after I had also heard how Mc Almon, whom I'd given a letter of introduction to Perkins had lied about me, how Callaghan whom I'd always tried to aid had come to you with preposterous stories I was getting sore.

You'll remember though that I did not, sore as I was about everything in general, accuse you of any such time juggling, I only asked you if you had let the round go on to see what would happen. I was so appalled at the idea of you saying that you were going to deliberately quarrel with me that I didnt know (just having heard this vile stuff from Mc A and C. which I thought I should have heard a long time sooner, if I was to hear it, and it was to go so long unresented) where the hell I stood on anything.

Besides *if you had let the round go on deliberately*—which I *know* you did not—I would not have been sore. I knew when it had gone by the time agreed. It is something that is done *habitually* at amateur bouts often. When two boys are really socking each other around the time keeper gives them an extra ten, fifteen or thirty seconds—sometimes even a minute to see how things come out. You seemed so upset that I thought you had done this and regretted it. But the minute you said you had not I believed you implicitly.

You as I say are a man of the greatest honor. I am not, in boxing at least. When I boxed Jean Prevost here in Paris I proposed Bill Smith as time keeper. I was in bad shape and told Bill to call time (we were supposed to box 2 minute rounds) any time he saw me in trouble. One of the rounds was barely 40 seconds long! Prevost just thought the time went awfully quickly. When I had him going Bill let the rounds go 2 minutes and over.

Having done such things myself you cannot expect me to control my reflexes about what is happening to me. But you can believe me when I say that I at once threw out any such idea and coming home told Pauline you had been interested and forgotten all about time.

You remember too that I put no importance on the incident afterwards and was more pleased than anything. I remember telling it with pleasure at the Deux Magot[s], praising Morley and giving him all credit for knocking me around. I thought, then, he was a friend of mine. It was only when I read his lying boast that I became angry. Then, being sore, I was sore at your carelessness which had given him the opportunity to make such a boast.

I would never have asked you such a thing if you hadnt gotten me nearly cuckoo with this talk about deliberately quarreling with me.

Let me repeat again—I have not the slightest suspicion of you having been disingenuous—I believe you implicitly and did at the time.

I know how valuable your sense of honor is to you, as it is to any man, and I would not wound you in it for anything in the world.

As an attenuating circumstance, though, please look at the different way we each look at sport—You look on it as a gentleman and that is the way it should be. But look how it has been with me—

One of the first times I ever boxed—a fellow named Morty Hellnick—after the bell for the end of the round I dropped my hands. The minute I dropped my hands he hit me with a right swing full to the pit of the stomach. After the fight I was sick for nearly a week. The 2nd time I boxed him I was winning easily—he had lost the fight anyway—so he fouled me deliberately—have never had such pain in my life—one ball swelled up nearly as big as a fist—That is the way boxing is—Look—in so called friendly bouts—you are never trying to knock them out—yet you never know but that they will try to knock you out—you get the complete habit of suspicion—Boxing in the gym with a fellow he let his thumbs stick out beyond his gloves in the infighting—the thumb caught me in the left eye and I was blinded by it—He blinded, in his life, at least 4 other men. Never intentionally—just the by-product of a dirty trick—I mention this only to excuse the reflex of suspicion which I never carried over for a minute.

It was only when you were telling me, against all my arguments and telling you how fond I am of you, that you were going to break etc and that you had a need to smash me as a man etc that I relapsed into the damn old animal suspicion.

But I apoligize to you again. I believe you implicitly and I have always, and I only wish to God you didnt feel so bum when you drink. I know it's no damn fun but I know too everything will be fine when your book is done. . . .

Anyway every kind of luck to you—Did you know Harry Crosby who shot himself yest?[1] He told me about this girl before he went to N.Y. Mac Leishes introduced her to him. He was a hell of a good boy and I feel awfully bad today about him. One of my best friends died two weeks ago and I'll be damned if I'm going to lose you as a friend through some bloody squabble. Best to you always—yr. affectionate friend

PUL   Ernest

1. On Crosby's life and suicide, see Geoffrey Wolff, *Black Sun* (New York, 1976). EH and Crosby had never been particularly close.

To MAXWELL PERKINS, Paris, 15 December 1929

Dear Max:

Your letter of Dec. 3 came yesterday and 2 others written Nov. 30 and Dec. 4 came today—also day before yesterday the wire about letter coming revising contract and the sale. The sale is certainly damned fine. There was no hurry about any revision and no need to do it if it did not seem the thing to you.

I must certainly apologize—I think I have already—for having written that time after Scott got me alarmed about the sale stopping. But came home from Berlin feeling fine and found Scott had been here with some alarm. I went over to see him and he showed me something you had written about the book going well and the only thing to watch was the market slump. I thought there was nothing alarming in what you had written but he knows so much more about the financial side of writing than I do that I imagined, he did not show me the whole letter, but only the part referring to the book that there was some contingencies I did not know about. Also he seemed so alarmed.

Am damned fond of Scott and would do anything for him but he's been a little trying lately. He came over the other day, a little tight, and said "People ought to let you alone. They ought to let you work and not worry you." And then proceeded to tell me the god damndest stories about myself that I've ever heard. He has my interests at heart and wants only to help me but really I have been out in the world making a living for a long time, ordinarily get on with people, have been familiar with slander, jealousy etc. although do not believe it exists as much as people make out and would prefer to ignore things—if they're not true they always die out. But when things are brought to your attention they make you sore as hell. Scott is working hard and well and I know he will be fine when he finally gets his book done.

I wish you would debit my royalty account with the 25^{00} to Waldo. Please do without saying anything to Waldo.

If you are to worry about how you will go down in literary history I will have to write you a series of letters telling you what I really think of you—am no good at that but will do it to remove any such idea from your head.

But the Xian Science business *was* something to worry over I can see— though I don't think *they* will make any trouble for A Farewell. They aren't so smart—they are simply wonderfully organized. If they were more intelligent they wouldn't be Xstian Scientists maybe. Anyway I hope you have luck with the book—the next 2 times that you would in

your plans devote a large space to A Farewell please use ½ the space
and the other ½ for the Eddy Book[1]—I would be damned pleased if
you would.

When I wrote you, angry, about Mc Almon and Callaghan it was only
personal anger. I can and will handle my personal business with them
(only hope I won't have to do any time in jail for making it thorough)
but I do not want you to think I am against them as writers. I want them
to succeed and would do nothing to hurt them as writers—altho it is
dangerous when you have an enemy to do anything but kill him—and
that's too expensive a luxury.

[Owen] Wister is damned nice but all wrong enough. Still there is
this great thing about him—he does, personally, seem to belong to the
same generation as we do. I mean you, me, Mike Strater, Waldo for
instance—all people of quite different ages. He has written about 3 or 4
damned fine stories—A Gift Horse, Pilgrim on the Gila, part of The
Honorable The Strawberries. How writing those he could write such a
thing as Philosophy Four I don't know.[2] Have just read that for the first
time and feel ashamed even to read it. We all write shit but something
should prevent you from publishing it or at least re-publishing it. But I
am very fond of him. If he wants to think of me as a "projection" there's
no harm in it so long as he doesn't try to influence. He could have been
a very great writer and the combination of circumstances that prevent
that are always tragic.

It's 20 minutes to twelve now—Sunday noon—have to shave and get
to mass.

Later—got shaved and to mass and lunch with Pauline, Allen Tate,
and a couple of citizens. Tate is damned intelligent and a very good
fellow. Dos Passos and his wife are due tomorrow.

My throat is bad and full of pus and I can't think or write very well.
I hope I haven't worried or bothered you with letters. I only write when
Scott gets me stirred up. I know he does it only because that is his idea
of the sort of thing that is exciting to a writer. But it's not exciting—only
annoying and when you come to Key West I promise to talk no business
at all. The idea that a writer can write a book then become a business
man, then a writer again is all [- - - -] as we say. The book has stirred up
a hell of a business in England—V. Sackville West broadcasted about it
from the official British Broadcasting and the head of the B.B.C. raised
hell and she, Walpole etc. replied—It's had much better reviews in
England than U.S. Damned funny. I want to get to Key West and away
from it all. Have never been as damn sick of anything as mention of this
book. People write swell letters about it and I am so sick of it that a fan
letter only makes you embarrassed and uneasy and vaguely sick. It's
hard enough to write—and writing prose is a full time job and all the

best of it is done in your subconscious and when that is full of business, reviews, opinions etc. you don't get a damned thing.

Speaking of all such worries the only fear I've ever had about the book was some Italian action to stop it—that may be cuckoo. But how would it be to run in the front matter that statement I wrote that was published in the magazine when the first number of A Farewell appeared? That seems to cover all aspects—the only thing I don't like is that people might think I was trying to compare myself with Shakespeare by making the crack about the Two Gentlemen of Verona. This only to run if you think so.

Must stop—am trying to write an article on bull fighting as an industry for "Fortune."[3] Archy Mac Leish asked me for it—written in journalese full of statistics. It's a romance of business magazine—there's no romance in the article—they probably won't take it—am keeping it as dull as possible. Every aspect I touch on if I could go on and write about would make a long chapter in a book. They wanted something between 5,000 and 20,000 words and I told them it would cost $2500. So they want something over 2500 words for $1000.00 instead. Their magazine came out just at the time of the crash which was hard luck. But if ever a magazine sounded like useless balls this one does. Am doing it for Archy— how he got mixed up with them God knows.

Well if there's anything unanswered in this letter it's only carelessness. Thanks for your fine letters—and Merry Christmas to you and your family.

Best to you always
Ernest

Please debit me with the Waldo business—otherwise I'll have to send a check to you. The debiting is an easy channel! I really want to pay it. But for Waldo not to know.

PUL

1. EH is probably referring to E. F. Dakin's *Mrs. Eddy: The Biography of a Virginal Mind*, published by Scribners (New York, 1930). 2. Between 1896 and 1928 Wister brought out five volumes of short stories, including those that EH admired. *Philosophy* 4 (New York, 1901) is a flat ninety-five-page novella about Harvard sophomores and their tutor. 3. "Bullfighting, Sport and Industry," *Fortune* 1 (March 1930): 83 ff.

To GILBERT SELDES, Montana-Vermala, Switzerland, 30 December 1929

Dear Gilbert:

What would you want from me more convincing than your published denials, Gilbert? What's it all about? You send me the denial but not the accusations. I've never made any.[1] I read D. Parker's piece in N. Yorker and saw no reference or cracks at you.[2] I don't carry the piece with me unfortunately but believe it mentioned the editor of some now defunct magazine of culture. Why should it be you? Aren't all the magazines of culture now defunct? It all sounds like ball room bananas to me.

Best to you always,

PH. PUL   Ernest

1. On EH's long-standing prejudice against Seldes for allegedly having rejected a story submitted to the *Dial*, see EH to Ezra Pound, 10 February 1924, note 5.
2. Dorothy Parker in "The Artist's Reward" (*New Yorker* 5 [30 November 1929]: 30) mentions a "young gentleman who once occupied the editorial chair of a now defunct magazine of culture" and who was once shown some of EH's work, refused it, and said, "I hear he has been a reporter—tell him to go on reporting and not try to write."

To MORLEY CALLAGHAN, Paris, 4 January 1930[1]

Dear Morley:

I traced the story[2] and found that Pierre Loving was responsible for putting it out both in Paris and N.Y. I found out where he lived and sent him this wire to his address, Waverley Place, N.Y.C.

—"Understand you saw Morley Callaghan knock me cold answer Guaranty Trust Paris"—I received no answer.

Scott wired you that he was waiting amicably to read your correction of the story & telling you where the story appeared / *at my request and against his own good judgment.* I did not know whether you had ever seen the story and since over 3 weeks had elapsed since it was first published in N.Y. Post it was up to him to correct it as a witness if you had not seen it and already done so. He, Scott, assured me you would have seen it and did not want to send the wire (which contained his insinuations against you). Since I had not seen the story in 3 weeks I had no way of being sure you had seen it.

It is, however, *entirely my fault* that the wire calling your attention to the story was sent, and since some pretty tough words have been passed around apropos of who sent the wire I want you to know that it was in no way an idea of Scott's. It was *entirely* my fault.

If you wish to transfer to me the epithets you applied to Scott I will be in the States in a few weeks and am at your disposal any place where there is no publicity attached.

Yours always,

PH. PUL
Ernest Hemingway

1. Misdated 1929. 2. This relates to a boxing bout between EH and Callaghan in Paris, June 1929. Fitzgerald as timekeeper mistakenly let one round last four minutes. See Callaghan, *That Summer in Paris* (New York, 1963), pp. 241–51; and Carlos Baker, *Ernest Hemingway: A Life Story* (New York, 1969), pp. 201–2, 206–7. Callaghan (b. 1903) became a leading Canadian novelist. He first met EH in Toronto in 1923. See *A Life Story*, pp. 119–21.

To F. SCOTT FITZGERALD, Paris, *c.* 5 January 1930

Dear Scott:

Your note just came. It's tough luck but there are *no* bullfights in Spain after end of November.

Climate in San Sebastian [from] now on cloudy damp and drisly. Town deserted. Best medium luxe hotel damned good Hotel Biarritz. ARANA—more moderate.

Pamplona, now cold, maybe raining, rain comes from the sea—or melting snow—*nothing* to do. Hotels (1) Grand Deluxe deserted (2) Quintana (the Montoya of Sun Also pretty simple for your tastes perhaps) (3) La Perla—½ way between the two.

In winter Madrid is clear and cold—cold as hell—Hotel Savoy.

Where people go in Spain in winter for good climate is Tarragona—South on the Coast from Barcelona—Hotel de Paris—Lovely old town on a hill above sea.

Malaga further south—good climate—Hotel Regina, and

Ronda—beautiful situation up on R.R. from Gibraltar. Lovely place—nothing much to do but beautiful and romantic—where I would go for a honeymoon for instance if had lots of money—Hotel Maria Christina (maybe called Regina Christina). It's neither, it's Reina Victoria! And also Hotel Royal.

If I can give you any dope let me know. But San Sebastian and Pamplona would be a hell of a disappointment to you in winter![1]

Ernest

P.S. I forgot to tell you to charge the wire to my account. Please forgive me. Glad you liked the books. Hope it (Graves) makes you glad you missed the war! It gives me a hell of a respect for poor Siegfried Sassoon. [Robert] Graves too! Have read [D. H. Lawrence's] Lady Chatt—It didn't hold me.

PUL

1. The Fitzgeralds went instead to Algeria in February. Zelda was then on the brink of a severe nervous breakdown. See Nancy Milford, Zelda (New York, 1970), pp. 157–70.

To MAXWELL PERKINS, Key West, c. 11 April 1930

Dear Max:

Thanks for your two letters and the royalty statement. Haven't received the present but if in your magnificent statement it's in view of bathing beauties, lions and buffaloes it sounds like an indispensability. I feel like before Christmas when we were kids. We had a wonderful trip didn't we?

The In Our Time was advertized on the 3 Stories and 10 pms. because it was announced to appear in 1923 but didn't get out until 1924. It was the last of a series of 6 books the 3 Mts [Press] published. It was an old handpress and they were always months late.

Ernest Walsh was a citizen who had tuberculosis and a very varied career. Edited with Ethel Moorehead This Quarter and died a couple of years ago [1926].

I would like very much to have the letters.[1] Will you please send them to me? I got out the 1st number of his magazine for him when he got hemmorages and had to leave Paris. Did him many favors—was bitched by him in true Irish fashion. He wrote the attack on The Torrents in the New Masses—the cheapest book I Ever Read—after I'd told him I couldn't let him serialize it in This Quarter. Anyway I would like to have the letters. If you cannot sell the 3 Stories and 10 poems for £35 I will pay you the difference between what you paid and what you sell. I do not believe the letters are shameful but they are probably libelous. Send them to me without reading them and if I read them [and] think they wd amuse you will send them to you. Walsh got up a prize The This Quarter Award of $2000.00 to be given to the contributor who printed the best stuff in his Mag. He promised the award to Joyce, to Pound, and to me I found later—He got swell things from all of us on strength of this promise! I have his letter promising it to me. I'd like to keep my letters to him—But there must be more than 6—damn it—and will publish them and his sometime when we're all broke.

Thanks ever so much for getting them for me—always write me about anything like that—there are some I've written to girls I will be prepared to pay a good price for if you ever hear of them coming into the market.

Yours always
Ernest

Ask them to buy any other letters from me to Walsh that come up for sale. I'll trade you something else for them or write you some letters.

Have caught 3 tarpon since you left—now another North Easter blowing like the devil. Have been working hard.

PUL

1. Some of EH's letters to Ernest Walsh written in 1925–1926 had come onto the auction market.

To HENRY STRATER, Key West, 20 May 1930

Dear Mike:

You write a fine letter kid. I haven't answered on acct. being pooped always after working and then cut my bloody forefinger—punching Charles's bag. It suspended by chain and fastened with bolt and nut. 6 stitches to close it and just across knuckle. A bludy nuisance.

Thanks for the caps and for sending the clay. It was for Alzira [Peirce]. Let me know how much it was and I'll add it to my ledger acct. with Waldo. Considerable acct.

Charles [Thompson] is excited as the devil about the trip [to Africa] next fall.[1] I might very well be able to go but won't know until then. I think Charles will go if you bring pressure on him. I'll probably be coming to N.Y. about then with Bumby. But may hunt in Wyo first so long as out there and just come to N.Y. to work. Going to write a play.[2] Don't tell anybody or my creditors will want the dough from it before it's written.

Been working pretty well lately. Excuse orthographic faults in this.

Hot as hell now. Imagine Pat [Morgan] told you about Tortugas. Every damned King gone but a fine trip. I bought a 12 [h]orse johnston [outboard motor]. We broke down off Souwest Key coming home and I brought the Merchants [Pauline and Dos Passos] to K.W. in the Outboard. The 12 orse is very good for fast going and trolling both.

My gun hasn't come yet but is due any minute. We are both anxious as hell to see and try it.

Baker[3] wrote he had lunch with you. He was never what you would call an intimate of mine but has worked hard on this gun racket. Think he knows something about guns altho much of it he may have read in same sporting journals you and me read. The proof of how much he knows will be how my gun turns out. He wanted you to see it before shipping it.

[Guy] Hickock writes the Players have written him about me. He says he gave them a filthy report. Hope I can get in that Cloob. Am having nose straightened.

Looks now as though wouldn't go to N.Y. until fall. Bumby arrives the 24th. I have to drive the damned car to Piggott so guess Jinny [Pfeiffer] will bring him direct to Piggott. Have financed Bra[4] on trip to Bahamas to replace my invitation to him to go to N.Y. Will do that another time. He claims he would rather go to Bahammies anyway.

Lots of tarpon lately. Pauline has caught 10 now. Biggest 74 lbs. Charles largest 100 lbs. Lorine [Thompson] 60 lbs.

Dos lost one that looked like 200. It jumped 7 times. Ran out every bit of line 4 times and we had to chase it. Just at dusk. It was biggest I have ever seen jump. Finally threw it. Kate lost some big ones too. I couldn't fish on acct. of my finger. Dos finally caught one that weighed 54.

Did you see DeadPan [Perkins] again before leaving?

Somebody poisoned Jack Cowles's dog. Rotten hard luck. Everybody is gone even the little Alziras. We would go too but am waiting for Uncle Gus [Pfeiffer].

I have 74 pages done on the book am working on but it gets so damned hot hell to work. Would shove if wasn't waiting for Uncle Gus. His arrival delayed by purchase of 4 million dollar business. I tell him all right to do anything with his cash except spend African Money.[5] He is damned nice. You'd like him. He won't come before 7th of June or so now. Happy brought up 3000 eggs from Tortugas. They are leaving for the Bahams. Braward [Bra] can't sleep nights thinking of the report that they pay a dollar apiece bounty on wild hogs killed. I am loaning them a shotgun to use on the great Saunders Pidgen and Wild Og Scientific Expedition.

Isn't there some way we can make our African trip a Scientific One. We could measure the amount of urine secreted by members of the party when

1. drinking tea 2. drinking schlitz in brown bottles to avoid that skunk taste. 3. when drinking elephant milk. We could measure the amounts by the men being required to urinate their names on the sand. That ought to make it a scientific expedition and then if any of the men are mauled by hippopotamus they will be martyrs to Science.

Write me Kid. Best love to Maggie and all your outfit from us all.

PUL   Hem

1. Postponed until 1933. 2. Possibly based on *The Sun Also Rises*; see EH to B. C. Schoenfeld, 5 November 1929. 3. Milford Baker, a veteran of ARC Ambulance, Section V, Italy, 1918. 4. Bra was Captain Eddie Saunders, Key West charter-boat fisherman. In 1928 he told EH and Waldo Peirce the story of the *Val Banera*, lost with all hands in a hurricane 9 September 1919. See EH's story "After the Storm." 5. Pauline's uncle, Gustavus Adolphus Pfeiffer, had put up $25,000 to underwrite the proposed African trip.

To MAXWELL PERKINS, Key West, 31 May 1930

Dear Max:

Enclosed is the story ["Wine of Wyoming"]. I think you'll like it. It is nearly 6000 words long. Don't let anyone tell you it's not a good story or has too much French in it. Everybody that reads Scribners [Magazine] knows some French or knows somebody that knows some French. The French is necessary in this. I've never given you anything that wasn't good have I? This is a 1st flight story I promise you.[1]

Should have fed all those Doubledays poisonous gum drops the day they came up to the place. After June 7th will you please hold all my mail?

You hold the world's Record for Kingfish all right but by God you should have broken it so far that it would stand for 50 years—it was 58 lbs—yours and Mike's that 1st day would have weighed 80–100. Next year we'll spend all of March there.

Yours always
Ernest

I may go on a trip to the Bahamas—running with Bra [Saunders].

PUL

1. EH had cajoled Lewis Galantière into reading the story and correcting the French. See Carlos Baker, *Ernest Hemingway: A Life Story* (New York, 1969), p. 211.

To HENRY STRATER, Key West, *c.* 20 June 1930

Dear Mike:

The Springfield[1] finally came and you ought to see it kid. Comes up as naturally as pointing your finger—hit about a 6 inch piece of paper 3 times at 100 yards first time tried it—most beautifully made and finished and simple, practical, gun I've ever seen.

But Dr. the telescope sight is the works! Charles [Thompson] said, "Write Mike right away about the telescope." Easier to put on than to shove in a shell—nothing complicated and is the damndest, simple, classy, easy to shoot with thing I've ever seen.

No kick to gun—not as much as a 16 ga—one shot with the 22 grain bullet that went through about a foot and ½ thick palm tree tore out a place the size of your head and shoulders—hell—my head and your shoulders.

Nothing but rain and hurricane weather here for 3 weeks—haven't wet a line in 2 weeks. Before that we were *butchering* them every night. Charles caught on 3 nights (1/92—1/99—1/102 lbs.). Pauline caught on season—only lost 3.

I am going to meet Bumby in N.Y. (he comes in on Lafayette—June 23, expected). (Don't tell *anybody* I'm going to N.Y.) Any chance you being there then? May be there a few days before/2 days after he arrives for sure.

Don't make trip specially. I can see the [Players] Club Kings in the fall. Don't feel any obligation or any such tripe to come down. I only mentioned I'd be there because you said you might be coming and didn't want to miss you. I'll stay at Brevoort or Uncle Gus's. Bra not coming. I gave him the dough instead—he didn't make much jack this year and wanted to go sponging and diving for liquor dumped by chased speed boats near Miami. Swears they've located 100,000 cases.

Happy lost his boat in storm at Bahammys. Later reports he's recovered her though sunk. I had a shot gun aboard (20 ga). Sad end of Saunders Scientific Wild Hog and Pigeon Shooting Expedition.

Write me to Chas Scribners Sons—Fifth Avenue at 48th—I wrote Maxie (Dead-Pan) and asked him if it was true that the publishers were all in the S—T house now. He said in answer that they were in the Place I mentioned. I guess Publishing is a thing of the past. I am offering Maxie a job at sweeping out the fort at Tortugas if he can learn to keep things neat.

Archie [Mac Leish] said the portrait you did of me was swell he said.[2] I tell you I never saw a classier gun in my life than the Griffin and Howe Springfield. I'll bring it to N.Y. in case you sh'd be there. Charles and I are going out to shoot it now. Love to Maggie. So long. What's the sporting news?

Best always
Hem

[Marginal afterthought:] For Christ Sake don't come to N.Y. unless you have to for some reason.
PUL

1. As arranged for by Milford Baker. 2. Strater's third portrait of Hemingway, used on the jacket of Carlos Baker, *Ernest Hemingway: A Life Story* (New York, 1969).

To ARCHIBALD MAC LEISH, Piggott, Arkansas, 30 June 1930

Dear Archie:

I wanted like hell to come to Conway but Jinny and Bumby got in a day and ½ earlier than expected and so it was off until next fall. In N.Y. I started to clip notices of the book [Mac Leish, *New Found Land*, 1930] but there were so many and as good as reviews can be. So I figure H[oughton] Mifflin would send them (which is a long way from anything good—My Christ but reviewers are a shitty folk and Pappa hopes they all will choke). But they were about the best reviews I ever read of a book—i.e. they could tell it was a fine book.

That's the way it is Kid—when you are disgusted with them and expect nothing will happen they make much noise. When you have something you know is the absolute works they never mention it except to, perhaps, point out how you derive from Maurice DeKobra.[1]

You are the best living writing poet. There are a couple of other good poets but not writing or writing tripe and you are living and writing too.

It has been very dry here—bad for crops but wonderful for quail. Have spotted any quantity of coveys and we'll shoot them in Dec. Season opens Dec. 1. Am storing up local wines, moonshine, etc. You'll come and we'll have great shooting.

We leave in 2 days for Wyoming—Bumby, Paulinoes and me—stop at K.C. at my cousins a couple of days.

I am going to read the book in Wyoming.

Saw Galantiere, author of Brushwood Boy at the Front—wanted him to check some french (spelling) in a story I have in August Scribners.[2] He did as much with aid of a dictionary. Maybe you'll like the story. He is a little fellow I trust as long as I'm in the room with him but while he has double-crossed me in mean and petty ways 3 times now I still like him—when I'm with him.

You Mac I feel the same way about when with and away from.

We'll shoot a lot of quail too. Ducks auch [also].

I hope Ada's fine.

Pauline sends her love.

I've had some 40 consecutive hot nights and haven't slept for a long time. It will be fine in the mountains—need like hell to work too.

Good luck to you Andy Marvell[4]—remember when you die it will be a unique experience for the worms to try a good half back, classy diver, lawyer and great poet combined. Become a quail shot this fall Mac and give the worms an extra treat.

LC   Pappy

1. DeKobra (1885–1973) was a prolific novelist in French. 2. "Wine of Wyoming," *Scribner's Magazine* 88 (August 1930): 195–204. For Galantière's version of this incident, see Carlos Baker, *Ernest Hemingway: A Life Story* (New York, 1969), p. 211. 3. A reference to MacLeish's poem "You, Andrew Marvell." EH then plays with the language of Marvell's "To His Coy Mistress," one of his own favorite poems.

To MAXWELL PERKINS, Nordquist Ranch, Wyoming,[1]
12 August 1930

Dear Max:

Have gone over the I.O.T. also the Up In Michigan.[2] I've rewritten it to try and keep it from being libelous but to do so takes all its character away. It clearly refers to two people in a given town, both of them still alive, still living there and easily identified. If I take the town away it loses veracity. But I *can* leave out enough of the first part to eliminate libel. However I *know* you will not publish it with the last part entire and if any of that is cut out there is no story.

I do not feel much like getting into a libel action or being suppressed now for the skin of a dead horse. The Farewell was worth making a fight on and I was willing to make it and take whatever came but this is an old story, one of the first I ever wrote, and I've published it once as I wrote it[3] and do not feel like stirring up trouble with it now when I'm working.

What I would suggest is that you get Edmund Wilson, if he is willing, to write an introduction to the In Our Time. He is, of all critics or people, the one who has understood best what I am working at and I know an introduction by him would be of much value to the book as you are getting it out now. As I understand it you are getting it out somewhat as a new book i.e. you want new material from me and it is not fair to do this without explanation since it is *not* new but my first and earliest book. I'll be damned if I will write a preface but Wilson, if he would, could write what it would need as an introduction. If he wouldn't care to it would be better to have none. Allen Tate might write one. He is a good critic but Wilson knows my stuff very well and writes so damned well and it would be a shame not to have him do it if he were willing.

Please let me know what you think of this.

I know I am not going in for putting out books because there should be something from me on the Scribners list. The In Our Time is, I really believe, a hell of a good book—the stories, when I read them now, are as good as ever—and worth anyone's two dollars but I am not going to jazz it up with anything of another period and try to make it sell as a new book. If you could publish the Up In Michigan without any trouble O.K. But show it to anyone and ask them. I'd like to have it published so people could see Morley's [Callaghan's] source book but it's not worth getting into trouble over when I am still able to write and am writing. What it needs—the In Our Time—is a good introduction. What you are doing is making it really available for the first time to the people who have read the other books. I am too busy, too disinterested, too proud or too stupid or whatever you want to call it to write one for it. If you can get Wilson to it would be excellent. He is a damned fine critic of prose and he writes well. I believe that is the way it should be published —my 1st book, now made generally available with an introduction by Wilson.

Anyway I will return the book to you with a few corrections, the original Mr. and Mrs. Elliott, and with or without a couple of short pieces of the same period depending on how these seem in the book between now and then—not later than the 1st week in September.

However we had better figure out a formula to put in the front about no living persons which will absolutely prevent libel as there are three people who might, if they were in desperate enough straits and the book sufficiently prominent, try a libel action. The reason most of the book seems so true is because most of it is true and I had no skill then, nor have much now, at changing names and circumstances. Regret this very much.

Am going well on the new book [*Death in the Afternoon*]. Have something over 40,000 words done. Have worked well 6 days of every week since got here. Have 6 more cases of beer good for 6 more chapters. If I put in an expense account on this bull fight book it would be something for the accounting Dept to study.

The checks came and your letter with them. Thanks ever so much—
also for the telegram about G. and D. [Grosset and Dunlap] jacket. I
hated like hell to bother you about that—you have enough to worry about
without Grossett and Dunlop. I'm so sorry to hear bad news of Scott.
Please let me know what you hear and let me know <u>anything</u> you think
of that I can do. I'd go over [to France] if you think it would do any
good.

Best to you always. Please if I speak rudely in letters never take it
personally. I'm working damned hard and a letter about some bloody
problem or other is only a damned interruption and curse. Don't let me
get on your nerves. We'll have a good time in March at Tortugas!

Yours always
Ernest

PUL

1. Lawrence and Olive Nordquist owned a dude ranch in Clark's Fork Valley,
Wyoming, twelve miles from Cooke City, Montana. EH had been there since 13 July.
2. For Scribners reprint, 1930. 3. In *Three Stories and Ten Poems* (Paris, 1923).

To HENRY STRATER, Nordquist Ranch, *c*. 10 September 1930

Dear Mike:

I wish to hell you and Charles [Thompson] could come out here to
hunt. Take R.R. to Gardiner Mont. Stage will bring you to Cooke City—
I'll meet you there with horses—if you wire you're coming we'll have
everything set and arranged.

So far I've killed two damned big old cattle eating bear—1 with one
shot at 90 yards—never moved—the other two shots at 35 yards, got up
after 1st one and I nailed him dead.

There are lots of grouse, ducks and geese. *Nobody else will be hunting
here this fall.* Hunting in the mts. is more damned fun than anything you
can imagine. I saw 12 mt. sheep a week ago. I can guaranty you shots at
elk, deer, bear, and Big horn sheep—wonderful rainbow trout fishing—I
caught 28 yest aft between 2:30 and 5:30—all big ones—all on fly.

Am going damned well on my book—page 174—I can shoot the Springfield as well as a shotgun now.

Pauline and Bumby leave the 13th—I stay on through Oct. Hunting
season opens Sept. 16 but from then on all through Oct. is swell. Charles
could get train to Kansas City from there to Gardiner. I wish the hell

you'd come. I've got all trout tackle. All you need is your rifles, heavy old clothes—bring plenty of 220 grain western ammunition.

This is the most beautiful country you ever saw. Grizzlies are best training for Africa—only dangerous animal in North America. I'll pay whatever difference it would cost you between Canada and here.

Wire me as soon as you get this if you can come. Wire Care Laurence Nordquist—Painter—Wyo. Write Care Laurence Nordquist Cooke City—Montana.

You must have had the top in excitement with the big tuna. Wish the hell I'd been there.

I've asked Archie [Mac Leish] to go to Africa too to make a fourth.

Why the hell don't you come out here. It is the best hunting this side of the Upper Peace river country.

License 60 bucks gives you 1 elk, 1 deer, bear, game birds and trout. Mountain sheep 15 bucks extra license. You ought to see the West anyway.

Hope I'll hear you're coming—
Best always, Hem

[Marginal postscript:] Charles can drive back with me in the car as far as Piggott and get train from there—that will save car fare.

PUL

To ARCHIBALD MAC LEISH, Billings, Montana,[1]
22 November 1930

Dear Archie:

It certainly was fine to hear from you, kid, and if this is the worst letter you ever got, it's because Mussolini is the dictator, not old Pappy. But if you want to do a good deed in this Nobel Prize World, sit down and write me again, because nothing happens here except the mail comes, and today it stopped coming.

The arm is coming on fine, but I haven't changed my position for three weeks tomorrow, except to have them set it three times and operate on it once, which took two hours and was very satisfactory, the doctor notching the bone, boring a hole through one side and then tying it together with kangaroo tendons—which ought to help me to land awfully hard on the jaw of Morley Callaghan some day.

It is awfully fine to have you write me what a fine writer I am, and even if it's horseshit it is the stuff to feed the troops when their writing arms are busted. Certainly I can't write anything now, nor for some time, to make you out a liar. There is some kind of numbness that will either clear up or can be relieved by another operation, but in a couple of months I'll know how she's turned out, and whether we shoot 'em in Africa this summer or next summer. I hate like hell to hold up your plans for the summer, but we'll do something anyway.

Don't let Mike [Strater] tell you anything about guns. Every thing he has written me about guns is utter nonsense. As a matter of fact, don't let anybody tell you anything about guns except old Pappy. I will not get onto guns because Pauline is taking this dictation and when I get on guns she gets off me. In other words, you can see I'm getting to be an authority on guns. When I get started on guns we run out of paper, and the little woman's fingers wear out. I wrote Mike a long letter on guns which you might ask him to let you read, if he did not destroy it. I dictated it with the tag end of five days of morphine in me and a pleasant delusion that I had a number of right arms, like the Goddess Siva or whatever the goddesses name is, you may know the goddess, Mac, but I know the principles therein expressed were sound. You see, the thing is that the English have a certain way about guns, and they high tone us always so that the majority of big game hunters get buffaloed by them. Any gun that you're used to, and throws a good heavy bullet that won't go to pieces, ought to be all right. Pauline says she sees we're on guns. But the principle is that foot ball players aren't made by fancy pants, nor baseball players by eight dollar catcher mits, and shots are made by shooting; but a Springfield made to fit you, and heavy enough so it doesn't kick is sure a lovely gun. I got so I thought I couldn't miss with mine because they always fell when I squeezed the trigger, and then I saw a big bull elk at sixty yards it was so easy I just shot it at him like a shotgun. But that isn't what you do in rifle shooting, Mac. There's only one bullet, and it goes wherever you point the gun, and if you point it in the right place, that's the only one you need. Enough about guns.

There is a raddio here, and any time day or night I can get Rudy Valee [Vallee], the somethingless crooner—remember I'm dictating—singing in a thin voice about that Big Blue TEAM. He is the favorite thing they have on the raddio out here, except a phonograph record which is played a good deal by the local broadcasting company and which they call Largo. It's by Handel, I believe.

There is a Russian across the hall who was shot through the thigh at the same time that a Mexican across the hall was shot through the stomach. The Russian groaned a good deal at first but is now very quiet.

The Mexican, on the other hand, has three tubes in him, and drains a good quality of high-grade pus. Two Mexicans came into visit him to-day—one of whom was a lousy crook if I ever saw one, and they also visited me. I gave them a drink of Scotch for [from] a bottle, three drinks from which had nearly killed me two nights ago, and then two drinks of rye, which isn't bad, poisonous, that is, but is pretty lousy and green; and they have promised to come and visit me tomorrow, bringing the finest beer in the city—if they recover from the Scotch, that is.[2]

How is your wife Ada and all your children. Bumbi got back to France safely and Patrick says his father doesn't love him because he never comes to see him. They get these French ideas quick.

This is the Will James[3] country out here. Anybody who comes into see you, outside these two Mexicans, who talked about how many tubes there were in the radio, talks to you about Will James. They feel what you must talk to one writer about is another writer. I have met Will James, one time in Scribner's, and he is a sort of dog-eared moth-eaten, shifty-eyed, fake imitation of old C. W. Russell, who was a real cowboy artist. However, desiring not to speak ill of a local boy, I talk about Will James for hours, but am about through doing it. The next time anybody comes in I'm going to claim to be Will James myself, and present them with an autographed copy of Smoky, that classic for boys.

How are you yourself, Mac? Of course Ezra is an ass, but he has written damned lovely poetry. I don't think he intended any cracks at me because he wrote me how much he thought of my last book and even mentioned it in the same breath as the only other author he's ever read. He just makes a bloody fool of himself 99 times out of 100, when he writes anything but poetry, and 40 times out of 100 when he writes poetry, but the good stuff sentence by sentence certainly deserves a hell of a lot more Nobel prize than Dr. [Sinclair] Lewis.[4] That was a hell of a blow to me because I'd always thought of the Nobel prize as something that you got when your beard was long and white and you needed to put your grandchildren through Devil's Island. But now I know that there's nothing that you get except maybe they operate on you for gallstones, and that the only difference between the Nobel Prize and all the other prizes, is that it's just more money. So maybe we won't get any prizes, Mac, except the grave. And hope they won't give us that until we're so old we can't wipe our own bowels—or even each other's bowels—in case they've segregated all writers by then.

I've finally solved the mystery of why there were fifteen curtain calls the night Farewell to Arms opened, and yet it only ran three weeks. They must have all been by people who wanted to sleep with either Mr. Anders or Miss Landi.

I'll send this to Conway, although you write from Farmington,[5] because I don't know the Farmington address.* My love to Ada, Mimi and yourself

LC   Pappy

1. EH had been in St. Vincent's Hospital, Billings, since an automobile accident on 1 November. 2. Rudy Vallee, the Russian, and the Mexican appear in "The Gambler, the Nun, and the Radio" (*Winner Take Nothing*, 1933), first published in *Scribner's Magazine* 93 (May 1933). 3. James (1892–1942) was a prolific cowboy author and illustrator. 4. Sinclair Lewis had won the Nobel Prize for literature in 1930, and his publisher had held a press conference on 5 November. 5. Farmington, Connecticut, the home of Ada Mac Leish's family.

* *In response to a telegram from Pauline, Mac Leish flew to Billings*, "the most hair raising flight of my life—only to find Ernest in bed with a magnificent black beard, full of suspicion of my motives [in coming] and convinced—or so he said—that I had come out to see him die" (*Mac Leish to Carlos Baker, 9 August 1963*).

To GUY HICKOK, Billings, 5 December 1930

Dear Gros:

Well Gros, it certainly is satisfactory to read of your success at outwitting the French and pitting them the one against the other. I've often thought that if you would have been at 6 rue Ferou instead of us it would have cost de Juvenal over a million francs to take possession, and it would have ended by his not marrying this widow at all but merely turning the hotel over to Hickock as the easiest way out of the whole ghastly business. The French are always bitched in foreign politics and invariably outwitted by any statesman, and you, Gros, have discovered the secret. If you would only operate on a big scale instead of confining yourself to mere domiciliary transactions, you would have been able to drive every Frenchman out of the country by now and we would probably have Ezra Pound back living in Paris. It certainly is a filthy business for them to give the Nobel prize to Mr. [Sinclair] Lewis when they could have given it to Ezra, or to the author of Ulysses. Or is it that the Nobel prize is supposed to represent the best aspects of Swedish life in America, or anywhere, and that is why they give it to Lewis? Well, I suppose we should be thankful they didn't give it to Dr. Henry van Dyke or William Lyon Phelps, both of whom, I'm sure, felt that they were in line for it. Also, it eliminated the Dreiser menace, although of two bad writers Dreiser certainly deserves it a hell of a lot more than Lewis. It has occurred to me that the only difference between the Nobel prize and all other prizes is simply a matter of quantity of money and since all prizes are lousy, what's the difference except in the extent of the sum. Although last year when they gave it to Thomas Mann, and when they gave it to Yeats, it made me damned happy.

If this typing is unusually neat, or if there are any words misspelled that you would expect me to know, or if you detect an understanding feminine touch, it is because it is being typed by Pauline. We have been in ST. VINCENT'S HOSPITAL, Billings, Montana for the last five weeks, and hope to leave next week for Piggott. Coming into Billings with Dos en route to Piggott, had spill brought on by loose gravel and Saturday night drivers and six days later when the doctor operated on my upper arm to fasten the bone together by boring a hole through it and then lashing the ends with kangaroo tendon, the inside of the arm looked like the part of an elk you have to throw away as unfit for human consumption when you butcher it out. So now it is all fine except that it is lousy and has hurt like holy hell ever since it happened, but will be all right in six months or else won't be. The bone is knitting very well and they have it straight and any trouble is in the nerves.

We go from here to Piggott and then to Key West the first of the year and will see you in Paris sometime in the spring, the first of May, maybe. I had my book on bull fighting about three-quarters done and we figured on going to Madrid in May and June to get the illustrations, would have had the first draft of the book done by Christmas. Now it will be done pour Paques [Easter] or le Trinité [Ernest told me how to spell Paques, because he thought I might put down Paques the composer. You can see he has great confidence in me, augmented by being in bed].[1]

An average of 63 banks a day failed in Arkansas. Things are pretty prosperous here in Billings due to the sugar beet racket. Everyone else in America is unemployed including the writer of this letter. If you want to know what kind of car it is that tipped over—it was the same car we put on the boat at Bordeaux and that we used to drive out from Pamplona in. If you're contemplating going into the theatrical business would advise that I received an advance of 750 dollars on A Farewell to Arms, that Mr. [Paul] Reynolds, who obtained this munificent offer, received seventy-five of that, that the lawyer employed to check up on Mr. Reynolds activities, took 102.50, the dramatist Guild took 18 something and several assessments I have refused to pay, and with the rest we bought our Beverly Hills Mansion. The play, according to the producers, Mr. Reynolds who handled the money, and the lawyer employed to check up on Mr. Reynolds, never made the advance. On the other hand, the movie rights sold for 80,000 dollars, of which Mr. Reynolds, who had no part in the negotiations, received 8,000, according to his accounting, the lawyer employed to check up on Mr. Reynolds was content with a modest 200 odd, Mr. Woods, who produced the play just long enough to sell it to the movies, and Mr. Stallings who dramatized it ditto, each received 24,000 and Mr. Hemingway received 24,000 also, which will be good news to all his friends, relatives and dependents, and the Billings hospital.

In case this letter should not seem sweet in tone, it is because it's being dictated. Pen, pencil, or glass in hand I am the sweetest tempered of mortals (Mrs. Hemingway may refuse to type this). But dictating that old Primo de Rivera strain comes up. If you hear any reports that we are backing any Left Bank magazines, will you kindly shoot who-ever brings them to you as an object lesson. We are not backing anything. We are bed panning in the Far West and finding no gold. Several weeks ago, people stopped writing out here because they were all sure that with a simple little thing like a broken arm, we would have shoved off long ago. Even the Billings Gazette sent a reporter up to find out what this fellow Hemingway was still doing in the hospital with nothing more than a fractured arm. The report was at the Billings Gazette that he must have been in frightful shape when he came in, cirrhosis of the liver, probably. Well, Gros, knowing your interest in ghastly details, and the pleasure with which you watch a tumor extracted from anyone, whether you know them or not, let me tell you that the humerus was broken clean off so that my arm was bent back on itself so that the knuckles touched the shoulder, that it was put in place by Mr. Hemingstein himself and held between his knees during a 22 mile drive into Billings. You could see the point of the bone under the skin, but a compound fracture was avoided. It was set three times, and the ends would not hold because the muscle would draw them out of place. The operation took two hours and the incision was nine and one-half inches long, and the kangaroo tendons used came from contented kangaroos. The arm busted is the right one and I believe that we have written you enough and even perhaps a little too much about it. But while the family does not desire either wreaths or couronnes, and I would be glad if you would keep my present condition from the Messrs. Mc Almon, Callaghan, etc., any amount of letters that you may send to Piggott Arkansas, in the heart of the ex-banking belt, would be very well received. And as long as Mrs. Hemingway's hands hold out, would have a good chance of being answered.

Best to you, to Mary, and good luck with your family. I have scrutinized a number of sinister looking former hotel keepers, broken by drink and other excesses, and even whispered Hickok into the ears of several in an effort to surprise them into an admission that they were your father, but so far have been able to get no one in this great Western country to admit to it. However, we are pursuing our searches diligently and will send in an expense account the first of the year. What would you like done with your old man if I could locate him?

So Long Gros. Love to you both from Pauline and me.

PH. PUL   Ernest

1. Pauline inserted this note.

To HENRY STRATER, Billings, *c.* 15 December 1930

Dear Mike:

Enclosed is the check for the Players. Thanks ever so much for paying it. They sent me a receipted bill.

It looks as though it would have to be 1932 [for the African trip] kid. I'll know by the time I get to Key West definitely, but the doctors are talking six months now before the nerve may come back. If it shouldn't come back, it can be relieved by an operation. It may come a lot quicker, of course, but there is still complete paralysis of the wrist and she hasn't stopped hurting like one of those hells that Ezra writes about, but has never been in, since the first of November. What happened technically was that when the ends of the bone were broken off and the arm bent back on itself, the nerve was stretched so that it put it on the bum. Today they fooled with the fleuroscope and took the splint off to look at it and found the bone is coming finely, straight and starting to be solid, but the incision between biceps and triceps was something over nine inches. Oh hell, I'm sick of talking, thinking, writing, or dictating about, but a damn sight more sick of having it.

I hate like the devil to make Pauline pound this typewriter, and I wonder if you'd send this letter to Charles to give him the army dope. I had a swell letter from Bra, who said he must have got hold of some bad liquor because he had fallen outside the door, but thank God he had not broken his arm. He advised us all to be careful as men are dying this year who have never died before.

Well general, there's not much news from here. I hope you saw Mclarnin and Petrolle. I would have given my last hundred bucks to have seen that fight.

We may leave here in a week now for Piggott and go to Key West the first of the year. Hope you and Archie can get some shooting. If he wants double guns let him get them. I don't care what the men shoot as long as they learn to shoot them. I don't think it makes a hell of a lot of difference what you shoot as long as it isn't some freak gun made too light, so that it punishes you so that you can't hold on. We will provide jigs to carry the heavier guns.

I sure appreciate you writing such swell and such long letters because the mail is the only excitement. Do you notice where Hoover is going in for child welfare now and filling the White House with the patter of little feet. They will doubtless run him as a great humanitarian—above mere business problems. I see where his organs are beginning to refer to the unemployed as the idle. Well, your old friend Hem is among the unemployed, or the idle and everybody in the hospital tells me I should just accept this as a good long vacation.

I figure Maxie has double-crossed me pretty badly, but that may just be my diseased condition of mind.

Love to Maggie and best to yourself from Pauline and me. I can't tell you how terribly lousy I feel to have delayed the trip. If dope didn't constipate you I would most certainly become a dope head. I only had five days of it when they got scared that I liked it too much, but it certainly was wonderful, not as an active pleasure but as a means of passing out. What gets you bughouse is to lie awake all night with nothing to think about but how old Max, who you'd trust as far as you would Charles, had double-crossed you. All this is probably a form of bed sores. So long, Mike. Remember me to all the unemployed club mates. I am thinking of taking an hour over the radio at Billings here as the Strater Snuff hour with the Strater Snuff Revellers. This is a great field for snuff as I believe I told you before.[1]

PUL   Hem

1. Strater's grandfather had built the largest snuff mill in the world, and his father operated Strater Brothers Tobacco Co. in Louisville, specializing in chewing tobacco. (Strater to Carlos Baker, 4 April 1980.)

To MAXWELL PERKINS, Piggott, Arkansas, 28 December 1930

Dear Max:

Got here Christmas eve and am still feeling pretty punk, but hope we'll be able to leave for Key West by January third. Thanks ever so much for your letters, wires and the fine books. This is just a note to tell you about Archie Mac Leish, who is leaving Houghton Mifflin of his own accord and who has received offers from Harcourt Brace, Harpers and so forth, but who wants, on my advice, to come to Scribners instead. I think he is without any doubt writing the best poetry written in America, and that he has the biggest future. He's working on a long poem called Conquistador, about Cortez in Mexico, which won't be ready for some time, but which you could make arrangements about publishing when it comes out by writing to him to Archibald Mac Leish, care Fortune magazine, New York, and making an appointment for him to see you. You couldn't get a better name, a better writer, or a better guy for your list of what ever I may call them, and his future is ahead of him instead of behind him. He will be as bashful to talk about money as you will be to offer it to him, and will deprecate any monetary arrangement, but for God's sake offer him as much advance as you can afford because it will cheer him up like hell and you will get it back many, many times over in the end, no matter what you give him. Some poetry that he's written all ready will be good a couple hundred years from now as it is.

You know how I usually write to you recommending somebody, if doing it out of "goodness of heart" or friendship. I usually say to be very polite and not hurt the gentleman's feelings and throw him out as pleasantly as possible. This about Archie is something different. He is the best bet you could have as a poet right now if you had your choice of the whole works, and do not let Edmund Wilson tell you differently. I promise you this before God. He has come on steadily while the others have stood still or gone backwards. It would be a tragedy if he went to any other publisher.

Don't think from this that I'm for God, for Scribner and for Yale, or actuated by patriotic motives, but you yourself have been damn good to me, whether or not your outfit can sell any books, and Archie is the biggest favour I could do you.

This seems to have gotten longer than a note. Did you ever talk to Wilson about the introduction or not. I hope you got my wire in time so that you did not. If I hadn't had a lot of fever and one thing and another I would not have paid any attention except to register it myself for future reference. Oh yes, a fellow named Gregory, a newspaper man in Billings, sent you a novel about which I know nothing. He was a very nice fellow and was damn pleasant to me, and I wish you could give it a good reading and write him a letter about it. I look forward very much to seeing you at Key West in March. If Jonathan Cape comes in and asks you anything about my next book, don't tell him anything. Except that you know it was nearly done when I got hurt. It was, too, by God. I'll let you read some of it when you come down to Key West, if you want to, and are a very good boy in the meantime, and don't shoot any birds on Federal Bird Refuges.

When you get this letter, the forwarding department might start forwarding my mail to Key West. Hope we'll be there to receive it. I'm still in bed most of the time, but count on Key West to fix everything up finely.

Best to you always,
Ernest

PUL

To ARCHIBALD MAC LEISH, Key West, 14 March 1931

Dear Archie:

We just got back from Tortugas—13 days—3 of fine weather the rest blowing a gale—caught about 60 big kings—lots of yellowtail, snappers, grouper etc. I hooked some kings and turned them over to others. Arm getting fine. Writing this with it—all right but still difficult. Can use to catch all small fish.

Didn't write you to Montana because I thought you'd be back before it could reach you. Then found your letter from there and feel like hell not to have a letter at Farmington for you when you got there.

Look—we have a room for you (quiet) in Charles [Thompson's] house (he insists)—or if you dont want it there [another] at Pat Morgans house —or in the house where Chub[1] lives—either Charles or the room where Chub is good bets—Charles free—$5 a week at Chub's place. Henriette (cooking fine). Weather turned fine and warm yesterday. When are you coming and for how long? Swell fishing now—tarpon starting. Lots of fish still in Gulf Stream. I shot 27 out of 30 clay pigeons thrown hard holding gun with left hand against right shoulder, right arm by side— raising gun each time. Also two terns with pistol in left hand. Papa bragging again.

I'd be glad to let Caresse [Crosby] have the Natural History [of the Dead] for the 1500.[2] You can read it when you come. I didnt answer because I couldnt write nor go over the story—will write her soon. Your news of Murphys very good. We had fine wire from them yest. You come down and tell me all about everything. Pauline sends her best love. I am strong and healthy as a pig. Dans la vie il faut d'abord durer [In life one must first last]. Cant write French. Excuse such a rotten letter. Hand still slower than the eye.

Glad Red [Sinclair] Lewis was nice—we'll all be gt men when we're dead and well travaillezed by the ver [worm]. I hope youze know your Baudelaire: Les morts, les pauvres morts ont de grandes douleurs.[3] I wd like to be gt writer but same very difficult. Shooting a shotgun with one hand makes you discoloured all over your chest—may never be a gt. writer but by Christ I am a hell of fine shot with shotgun. Shot one handed against Edgar Stanton shooting regular at 20¢ a target and won twice—lost twice—tied once. Shot 9x10—9x10—7x10—9x10—8x10—6x10. Shoulder too sore finally. Pappy the bragger. Love from Pappy. We leave for Spain in May.

LC

---

1. Chub Weaver of Red Lodge, Montana, was in Key West for a vacation. 2. *In Our*

Time was published by Caresse Crosby's Black Sun Press (Paris, June 1932). 3. From *Les Fleurs du Mal*, "L'Amour du Mensonge" ("The Love of Illusion").

To F. SCOTT FITZGERALD, Key West, 12 April 1931

Dear Scott:

We're both terribly sorry that Zelda had such a rotten time and I would have written long ago. I hope to God she's getting along well now and that you are too. I know you had hell. You have our deepest sympathy.

Outside of this arm have been having a damned fine time and was going well on book until accident on Nov 1—didn't write a line after that until this week. Feel in damned good shape now to go well—nerve in arm has regenerated and paralysis all finished.

We come abroad in May. I'll be working all summer in Spain finishing book [*Death in the Afternoon*], and will look forward like hell to seeing you. If you're still in Switzerland will come down there to see you in the fall. We might take one of those topless motor trips. I havent kept up with Arland [Michael Arlen] or any other of the boys and you could give me cultured synopsis of what the lads have been doing. My operatives in N.Y. report you have become a grave, courageous and serious citizen. This all sounds like horseshit to me and have cut my operatives wage scale accordingly. Give my best to John Bishop when you see him or write him—I would write him but can only write about 400 or so words still before arm poops out and am putting those 400 or so into reducing our national debt to Max—will write him anyway—arm is getting well fast.

Have you become a Communist like Bunny [Edmund] Wilson? In 1919–20–21 when we were all paid up Communists Bunny and all those guys thot it was all tripe—as indeed it proved to be—but suppose everybody has to go through some political or religious faith sooner or later. Personally would rather go through things sooner and get your disillusions behind you instead of ahead of you.

Ah Fitz but we are profound chaps—we word lads.

Enclose latest passport picture showing new alterations in pan [face] caused by last summer's defective horsemanship.

Best always to Zelda. Tell her not to feel any worse than she can feel about dancing. She started it too late anyway. You start it at 6 as in bull fighting to get well up in it. She wouldn't have wanted to start late and be the Sydney Franklin of the Ballet would she? You know us word merchants Fitz—always ready to give comforting advice to others while pewking with the other hand about our own troubles.

By Christ my only trouble now is to have pen and ink (pencil O.K.) and paper and 3 mos. clear to write in. But imagine troubles will be furnished.

So long Scott and our best love to you both.

Ernest (the man who discovered
Curro Carillo)

How does your Ex-Marine write?

I'm sorry you had a trip to U.S. on such sad business. Hope to read your acct. of it between board covers rather than in Post. Remember us writers have only one father and one mother to die. But don't poop away such fine material.

PUL

To WALDO PEIRCE, at sea, 4 May 1931

Dear old Waldo:

Thanks ever so much for the cable Chico—wish the hell you were on this thing[1] and we were going to Spain together.

It looks like a dull voyage—all sacerdotes so far. Hope you and A[lzira] are swell and the twins.

We have bought that old house with the iron rails and balconies opposite the lighthouse in K.W.[2] Alzira will know the one I mean.

I'll write you from Madrid. Guaranty Trust Paris will forward mail. I've been lousy about writing but it was my damned finn. Has only been out of paralysis class for 3 weeks.

Absolutely O.K. now.

Best always
Tu amigo
Ernesto

COLBY

1. S.S. *Volendam* of the Holland-America Line. 2. The house at 907 Whitehead Street, Key West, was purchased with the help of Pauline's uncle, Gus Pfeiffer.

To JOHN DOS PASSOS, Madrid, 26 June 1931

Dos:

Things are pretty well steamed up with the elections day after tomorrow—over 900 candidates but less than 100 of the right—23 different parties—Republican landslide in various colors Red White and Black Republicans.

The govt. has rightly stopped work on the Coruna-Orense R.R. (motor trucks and buses are killing R.R.s) and in consequence the Gallegos are proclaiming the Social Republic of Galicia (until work begins on R.R. again) and are general striking on election day and refraining from voting.

Andalucia is coming to boil but will not probably boil over until after Cortes in order to see what land partition will amount to. The workers committees have gotten all harvesting machinery banned.

(You see it isn't much like Russia.) Navarra has gone for el Cristo Rey in the biggest possible way—and it is no uncommon thing for a prelate to shoot down a good republican from the top of an autobus or for a Carmelite to destroy with kicks an agitator. 23,000 Navarros in Pamplona bull ring 2 weeks ago. Enthusiastic for Don Jaime who has promised to cross the Pireneos [Pyrenees] with the sword in one hand, the cross in the other and the Sacred Heart of Jesus on his chest.[1]

He came into Spain incog and swore an oath as King of Navarre and defender of faith on sacred tree of Don Carlos etc. Is now in Bayonne—all that is being directed from Bayonne.

Catalonia is waiting to do business.

Madrid loves the Republic—which, as soon as any one takes power—Lenoux etc. they shift from left to right faster even than in France.

The King is permanently out.

Ramon Franco etc. are well bughouse and are being read out of the party. Their great ambition is to really bring off an air revolution (cuatros ventos-ism) against *anybody in power*.

Sunday may prove me all wrong on all of this. Am sending big collected bunch of papers for backhouse reading. Have been saving ones with dope. La Libertad is now Le Temps—consequently all my buddies are prosperous. Have been working like hell until it got too hot 42°–46° in shade. Been following politics closely. Seen a few funny things.

Most bull displays lousy. Present republic all for bulls but ganaderos [breeders] have just about ruined the bloody bulls.

How the hell are you? We could have a fine time here now. Communists have *no money at all*—or could make a pretty good show. Except for Andalucia—which had an Arkansas crop season last year—very damned few out of work.

Chances for Marxian revolution nil—may yet have a terror though.

If worst comes to worst history of 1st Republic will repeat.

Pauline and Pat and Bumby all fine—am taking Bumby to Pamplona. Hadley fine too—went up to Paris to see her and Bum.

Write me for <u>anything</u> you want.

We live here damn well on 3.00 a day the two of us. Now is the time to buy anything if anybody had money. Were you ever in Sierra de Gredos? Barco de Avila is wonderful town. Killed a wolf there while we were there. Bear paw nailed to door of church—good trout—River Tormes that flows down to Salamanca—wild goats. Eat better than Botins—same dishes—swell big *clean* rooms—no chinchas [bugs]—damned intelligent—all people nice—old banner of Garibaldi from 1st Republic at Verbena of San Juan—all for 8 pesetas a day.

You are the great writer of Spain—if you would naturalize Katy could be Mrs. Ambassador to any court you name. They all think I am bullshitting because I claim to be a friend of yours. Nobody has read Manhattan [Transfer] less than 4 times. In spite of descriptive introduction you are supposed to be an old man about Unamuno's age—otherwise how did you have time to know the Bajo fondos [basics] so well and have so much experience. I swear to God they think I am one of these guys who claims to know the toreros when I say we are old pals. Send me a book inscribed to me in warm terms or I will be lynchiado-ed as an impostor—they have taken to lynchiaring considerably.

Write the dope. Love to Katy from Pauline and me. Yrs. always, Hem. Arm crooked but serviceable.

UVA

---

1. Pamplona rally: anticlerical action by the second republic (1931–1939) helped revive Carlism, and the Carlists followed Franco in the Civil War.

To CAPTAIN EDDIE SAUNDERS, Madrid, 29 June 1931

Dear Bra:

We are all well and hope you and your wife and Annie [daughter] are the same. Things are very interesting here now. Also everything very cheap. Good wine only 7 *cents* a quart. The kind Pena sells for 3.00 a bottle costs 25¢ here.

It has been very hot but I have been working hard. Lately it has been too hot to do anything but drink beer in the shade and eat shrimps.

Plenty of bull fights but they haven't been very good.

I will send you the money in September so count on it. Look—I wonder if you would grease that outboard engine of mine all over and oil it around plugs so it won't rust? Charles will know where it is.

Hope you have had good luck if you went spongeing. I won a little money at the cockfights in Havana and playing poker and dice on the boat. Didn't get seasick any on the trip—took 12 days from Havana to Vigo—pretty rough the last six.

Met Pauline at the French-Spanish border. Went up to Paris to see Bumby. They are all in fine shape.

There is no chance of the King coming back here but they have plenty of trouble of their own on their hands.

I certainly wish you were here so we could go to the bullfight this afternoon—and show you around afterwards.

Give my best to your wife Julia and to Annie and best luck to you always.

Ernest Hemingway

Pauline sends her love to all. Tell Charles the reason I haven't written is because have been working so bloody hard.

PH. PUL

To WALDO PEIRCE, Kansas City, Missouri, c. 1–12 November 1931

Querido Valdito mio:

?Que tal hombre? lo siento un barbaridad not to see you anymore you bearded twin-begetting bum.[1] Now that you know you have twinmaking cojones for gods sake layoff of domestic life and come down to Key West this winter so we can make a trip out to Tortugas again. We will go there from here as soon as Pauline and the offspring can travel. Sometime before Christmas if the child is timed for Nov. 15. Will stay until May anyway. Come on down in March anyway for the Tortugas trip. You've never been there since we found those damned big kings. It was a shame we didn't get together in N.Y.

The Drs. all say this is another boy so you better hedge in the sweeps. I want a girl very much but so far have never had a legitimate nor illegit daughter so don't know how to go about it. Maybe Max can tell.

You sound in swell shape down to 195. With my damned finn paralysed 8 months or so and not able to get any bloody exercise picked up weight like a hog on cervezeria Alvarez product [beer]. Ran it up to 218 with clothes on. Now down to 211 clothed. Imagine around 200 even stripped. Once we have this baby and get down to K.W. am going to really get in shape again. Working like a bastard now on this book [*Death in the Afternoon*] and must knock off and get back to it. That's why I haven't written.

Best love to Alzira from us both and to you you louzy pere de famille. If you don't leave your damned domestic layout in March once you get things organized and come down for a little of the old life you're a twirp.

Anyway in the meantime best to you both—this damned typer skips like a stammering flannel mouthed nigger.

Spain was damned nice with the revolution. Had a fine time all spring and summer—hated like hell to leave the percebes [goose barnacles: a delicacy] and come back.

Sent Bra some jack to put a new bottom in the old boat. They are all damned fond of you down there. You wouldn't have had any twins if the tarpon that jumped into the boat and hit me in the middle of the back would have hit Alzira in the lap. Well so long Chico—if I don't write it is because I'm so bloody pooped after working all day on this bloody book.

Love from us all

COLBY   Ernesto

1. "My dear Waldo: How's it going, man? It's terrible not to see you," etc. Peirce's third wife, Alzira Boehm, had recently borne twin boys, Mike and Bill.

To PAUL ROMAINE, Kansas City, 9 December 1931

Dear Mr. Romaine:

I cannot recall the poem in question so can't consent.[1] But if you will mail me a copy of it air mail to this address [229 Ward Parkway] will give you yes or no after reading it—provided of course if it is reprinted that mention is made of its place and date of publication. If it is too lousy I will wire no and you will understand my motives.

With best wishes

PH. PUL   Ernest Hemingway

1. Romaine was preparing *Salmagundi* (published January 1932), a reprint of William Faulkner's early work, mostly from the New Orleans *Double Dealer* (1922–1925). EH's minuscule poem was "Ultimately" (*Double Dealer* 3 [June 1922]: 337).

To HENRY STRATER, Kansas City, 10 December 1931

Dear Mike:

Glad you had such a fine trip and I hope Maggie is all right so you can get down to K.W. soon & if everything goes well here we should be there a week or 10 days before Xmas.

Finished my book except some hack work on the appendix. Think you'll like it. Will get it copied in K.W. and send to Max—will have a copy for you to read.

Greg weighs 10½ lbs at a month—no fat—all build—solemn bastard.[1]

Have just been to Piggott shooting quail for a week—swell shooting— killed 3 straight three times—four straight once—the four in the woods— followed them in out of a cornfield—got a double in thick brush—briars and hanging vines from the trees. First one went straight away—couldn't see him fall—turned and swung with second over <u>right</u> shoulder— swinging the gun like a pitchfork—butt down opposite my belly. Dog brought in the first one while I was picking up the second. Pauline's brother [Karl] for a witness—both shots the brush too thick to get the gun to the shoulder even for a snap. Damn but they are fun to shoot— coveys bother me—believe you kill more birds if you only kill one out of a covey—mark him and then mark down all the others. If you shoot more than twice at a covey in high corn or any sort of cover you can't see where they go.

We must hunt there together some fall. You could hunt a new place every day for two months. Lots of peas and beans in the corn for feed. Two years of drought been hard on birds—on account of that I never shot over the limit—12—one day found 7 big coveys—could have killed plenty. Shot my 16 ga Browning.

Listen what did you suffer so getting the buck out for? Why not butcher where you kill—hang up meat and pack out what you can take— that's what we do. Bring in head and scalp and liver and go back for the rest. Why carry a whole buck around? A good bull elk will weigh 1200 lbs. How would you like to tote him to camp?

What about a spring bear hunt in first two weeks of June out at Lawrence's [Nordquist's?]. Bears grow swell hides all winter—come out and shit that plug out and then are fine to hunt—you could try your big gun. Hall Smith has loaned me a 10.5 Mauser that he claims is great Buffalo gun—he killed elephants with it but says it is a little small for that.

Duck season here—30 days—they guessed wrong—it was all over before we got any cold weather—killed 3 one time—8 another. Day after it closed came the first cold and ducks flying all day and all night—lots of geese.

Uncle Gus is back from buying furniture for their new apartment at 770 Park [New York City]. They are moved in there. Why don't you go to see him?

Archie is down on Sullivan Street—get him through Time [magazine].

Caesars form of childbirth dangerous, expensive and difficult. Tough on Pauline to have to go through that every time.

Have been shooting live pigeons out here. Shoot from 30 yards—pigeon sprung from one of 5 traps 12 yards apart on a line. Fly like hell—you have to hit them always shoot both barrels and kill them before they get outside distance—will send you copy of rules. Big shoot here $120 entrance—$2500 sweep—Dec. 12–13.

Best I've shot is 21 x 25. Dead inside enclosure—other four I killed one coming on too late so it fell at my feet and three flew on with shot and went down outside. I average about 20 x 30.

Took Jinny out to try them—she killed 3 quail one day when we hunted but missed 30 live blue rocks straight—from 27 yards. The lead is 6 to 12 feet on the ones that go off fast to either side—only 3 states where you still have it—Penn., Ky. and Mo. Going out this afternoon.

Well hope Maggie is fine and that we'll see you soon!

Best always

PUL   Hem

1. Gregory, EH's third son, was born 12 November 1931 in Kansas City.

To MAXWELL PERKINS, Key West, 26 December 1931

Dear Max:

We've been here a week—in the new house—plumbers, carpenters, nurse sick, and a citizen in the front room typing all day on this manuscript. Hoped to have it done to send you for Xmas but he will certainly have it done for the first of the year. I hate like hell to end it—could write on for another year easily enough—or is it well enough; or maybe just write on for another year handles it.

Started this in bed—bad throat back—this is really going to be the hell of a fine house; the lawn is coming well, figs on the fig tree, coconuts on the trees and plenty of limes. Will plant more limes and coconuts. Wish you could plant a gin tree. Young Patrick filled the mosquito sprayer yesterday with mosquito dope, tooth powder, talcum powder while he was supposed to be taking his nap and sprayed his little brother thoroughly—he woke up and cried loud enough to attract attention before it killed him—Patrick spraying manfully the harder he cried the more spray he received. "Did you want to hurt your little brother?"

"Y e s," said Patrick, very scared.

This rotten throat has filled my head so full of pus that the brain won't work, so enough of this letter. Hope things are going well with you.

Would you ask them i.e. retail department to send one of those monumental quail books to Karl Pfeiffer, 249 Heywood Avenue, Orange, N.J. and one to me here and the last two Will James books Sun Up and Big Enough, I think they are, to Bumby, John H.N. Hemingway, Ecole de Montcel, Chateau de Montcel, Jouy en Josas, France.

Charles and Lorine [Thompson] are fine; both in good shape. There has been no cold weather yet at all. Warm as when we made that trip over to the Cape. Not a Norther yet this season. Steady south east breezes all day and all night.

Bra has a new bottom in his boat and otherwised fixed up that I financed. He is in good shape. Burge hasn't been drinking but came here plenty drunk Christmas eve to tell me how I was his best friend in the world and how it was all John's [Herrmann's] fault they didn't get back to Tortugas that time. John's story is different. Neither of them were too good about that trip but I told Burge if he'd stay sober and prove it by not getting drunk would trust him again. It was as bad as a revival meeting. Of course I can't trust him again but he is a hell of a good man in a boat.

What about Scott?

Write me if you get time. You will be crazy about this place [907 Whitehead Street] when you see it. I haven't heard anything lately from Europe. February is supposed to be the next big wallop.

What did you really think about M. Eastman's book?[1] Don't be so bloody careful in discussing these great writers. When is your World Genius going to publish again? Or is he so worried about living up to his press notices that he'll never be able to put it out? I hope he has a damned fine book. I feel like hell about Archie's poem going to those buzzards.[2]

I have a fine theory about the reason syphylis always speeds up production so with a writer who also likes his bed sports. It isn't that the spiros stimulate the brain so much as that it makes the writer stop his sporting life and that gives him so damned much energy in spite of the old disease that he turns them out with all the over-energy of a [Thomas] Wolfe who's never stood at stud for any length of time. Or am I wrong. And what's become of Bunny Wilson?

Dos has left Harper's for Harcourt Brace or out of the frying pan into the cook's apron because they wouldn't print something about J. P. Morgan the elder[3]—next he says Harcourt will probably refuse to print something about Henry Ford in the next volume and he will end up being published only in Lithuanian. Shall I send him to you? The first I heard about him having trouble was when he wrote he had switched over. He says this new book is a hell of a lot better than the 42nd parallel.

Well so long Max and good luck—we have enough cases that our furniture came in to build on Tortugas—there are some drawings and some other stuff by Roberto to come still.

                                                        Ernest

Has Morley [Callaghan] whelped yet?[4] and what? Wish him luck for me.
PUL

1. Either *Kinds of Love: Poems* or *The Literary Mind*, both published by Scribners in 1931. 2. Mac Leish's *Conquistador*, published by Houghton Mifflin (Boston, 1932). 3. Dos Passos's satiric profile of the elder J. P. Morgan in his novel *1919* led to a contretemps with Harper's, which was indebted to the House of Morgan. 4. Probably a reference to Morley Callaghan's *A Broken Journey*, published by Scribners (New York, 1932).

To MRS. PAUL PFEIFFER, Key West, 5 January 1932

Dear Family:

I have been very remiss in writing but it has not been because I have not thought about you very much and the wonderful time I had in Piggott. It was a splendid trip and I enjoyed every minute of it. You were awfully good to me and I never had a finer time. Once back in Kansas City things were pretty complicated for those few days with Pauline unable to go out and many things to do. Then the trip down here and the new house that Jinny had done miracles to make habitable.

You sent us wonderful christmas presents. Thank you very much. I will have something useful for Pauline's father to show up us younger men with when he comes down. It is grand that we will see you in March. Things should be going well and smoothly by then. The present situation here would offer a wonderful opportunity for a man with real directorial ability to show how creative writing could be done at the same time as running a carry them by hand elevator service, and superintend plumbers, the re-doing of a leaking roof, wiring of house, installation of water system, carpenters etc. while trying to keep someone under doctors orders not to walk upstairs from walking upstairs etc. A wonderful directorial job wasted on someone that doesn't appreciate it. The minute I quit trying to write the rest of it is easy.

Gabrielle [children's nurse] took one look at the house and took to her bed. She hadn't thought Florida was going to be like this. She has been in and out of her bed a good deal since but has done little else. At first she declared she didn't know what it was made her sick since she had never been sick a day in her life. "It must be someding aboud dees house." But after the Dr. had made a thorough examination and found she has been opened up several times and all of her organs not completely essential to eating and sleeping re-moved she said she had been sick just before taking this job and that her Dr. said she probably would be again but that a trip to Florida might do her some good. The Dr. says her present trouble may have been brought on by over-eating.

Have taken every care of her—she has had to do no housework, gets a 2½ hour nap, we have taken nearly all our meals out and she tells the Dr. she feels very badly that she cannot be on her feet or do much work because we have treated her very well but she thinks she had better be near her own Dr. in New York.

For a while were faced with the problem of carrying her upstairs but fortunately the stairs were too narrow so after a good rest in the library and much moaning she was able to regain her bed safely. She was really sick the first two days, threw up and had bad indigestion. But since, in her worst attacks, she has never thrown up nor had a degree of fever. Dr. Warren and Dr. Gayley both examined her for appendicitis and declared she had not one single symptom but had a possibility of adhesions from her old trouble brought on by increasing obesity; but that her principal trouble was homesickness.

So imagine it won't be long now.

Everything else going very well except writing. The house is a grand house and getting better all the time. The two niggers are fine, the gardener, yard man, etc. is excellent and the nigger girl, who has been doing all Gabrielle's work, is splendid.

Went out fishing New Years afternoon with [sister] Carol and found the gulf stream fish starting to come in, tell Jinny. Today there is a norther blowing and that is just what they have needed to bring the migratory fish. The commercial fishermen struck the Kingfish yesterday for the first time and the Spanish mackerel the day before yesterday.

Pauline was in bed a couple of days from doing too much but if I can keep her from over-doing or rather from doing a few forbidden things like hurrying upstairs, lifting etc. through this week believe she will be safe. It is impossible to scare her about the possibility of bringing on a condition that she has never experienced. It is so very important that she take care of herself that I was awfully pleased you wrote about it in your Christmas letter as that had a good effect for a while.

The mechanics of it is that if she hurries up stairs and finds she is still whole at the top of the flight she believes anyone trying to keep her from doing that is an old fogey. There is no way a woman can be more completely and utterly ruined than by not being careful for eight weeks after a baby is born. Until the placental site is healed. They ought all to be shown, in school, or when their minds are at an impressionable age women who have so ruined their bodies so it would be impressed on them.

Well, Mr. Hemingway if you have any other schemes for changing femenine psychology please let us hear them at a later date. I haven't so it is all right.

If this book [*Death in the Afternoon*] is punk it won't do any good to take the readers if there should be any, aside and say, "But you ought to see what a big boy Gregory is and just look at the big scar on my arm and you ought to see our wonderful water-work system and I go to church every sunday and am a good father to my family or as good as I can be." I happen to be in a very tough business where there are no alibis. It is good or it is bad and the thousand reasons that interfere with a book being as good as possible are no excuses if it is not. You have to make it good and a man is a fool if he adds or takes hindrance after hindrance after hindrance to being a writer when that is what he cares about. Taking refuge in domestic successes, being good to your broke friends etc. is merely a form of quitting. All right, you're a fool Mr. Hemingway. What are you going to do about it. Nothing.

Bra and the Thompsons are all in fine shape and everybody sends their love. Gregory weighed 13½ lbs. His great, great uncle Benjamin Tyley Hancock, now 84, my grandmother's brother, sent Greg his pedigree back to 1600 copied out of the family bible so with Uncle Gus's researches into genealogy Greg should be able to trace his ancestry through as many generations as Hoolie anyway.

Thanks very much for sending the children's accounts. Things very slow here. Now the fishermen will get fish they may pick up. Government has slapped a prohibitive duty on Cuban pineapples just after Thompson builds big canning plant. Doubtless at instigation of Hawaaian interests.

Best love to you all and a happy New Year.

PUL   Ernest

To MAXWELL PERKINS, Key West, 5–6 January 1932

Dear Max:

The reason you have not received the Mss. is that the typist sprained his ankle playing basketball—Pauline got sick—or rather overdid and had to rest in bed. The nurse has been laid up practically ever since we've been here—I had ulcerated throat. But he has it all typed now and I have been over ½ of it and you should have it by 1st part of next week if nothing else comes up.

Write this while staying up all night with Patrick who ate as near as we can figure ½ grain of arsenic in form of an ant button. Been vomiting etc. since 6—it's around 11 p.m. now. Done everything that can be done. Hope to Christ he comes out all right. Dr. says he won't be safe for 60 hours.

A great life Max—a great life. But you will get your Mss. Never have any doubts about that. If they should feed me ant buttons you could publish it as it is by having someone check up on spelling and let Mac Leish correct proofs—Dos could go over Spanish. If anything should happen to me by any bad luck get it out with only a few illustrations. No color plates—give Pauline the money they would cost. Pauline could pick the illustrations and write very short captions. Am sending the glossary and 2 appendices with the Mss.—others will follow.

There have been plumbers—roofers—screeners—electricians etc. here to drive you bughouse. Since I started this book have had compound fracture of index finger—bad general smash up in that bear hunt—14 stitches in face inside and out—hole in leg—then that right arm—muscular spiral paralysis—3 fingers in right hand broken—16 stitches in left wrist and hand. Eyes went haywire in Spain—with glasses now. Can't do more than about 4 hours before they go bad. Pauline's 2nd Caeserian etc. etc. etc.

Scott on the other hand had his wife go nutty which is much worse—plenty more worse. During Sun Also plenty happened while during Farewell to Arrums—outside of Patrick being born only incident was my father shooting himself and me acquiring 4 new dependents and mortgages. Then some shitfaced critic writes Mr. Hemingway retires to his comfortable library to write about despair—Is that what I write about? I wonder.

It is blowing like hell outside—from the north-east. First Kings have just come—mackerel too. Charles [Thompson] and I killed 14 big snipe on Sunday. There are a world of cranes this year. Charles and Lorine are fine. Bra too. Burge came drunk on Xmas eve to tell me how he had quit drinking—or did I write you that.

The quail book is monumental, but dull. Eschew the monumental. Shun the Epic. All the guys who can paint great big pictures can paint great small ones.

So Long Max
Ernest

[Postscript dated 6 January, 9 A.M.:] Stayed up with Pat until 4:30. He is much better. Should be all right. Just got your wire about Ann Watkins relaying Metro-Goldwyn-Mayers receptivity. Please thank Miss Watkins and tell her I have had other offers but that I am very busy at present. Too busy to go to coast at present. Do not consider her wire places me under any obligation to deal through her if I ever went out to whore for M.G.M. They have been making offers for a long time. But don't worry— am not going—only want to keep the record straight. EH

PUL

To HENRY STRATER, Key West, 9 February 1932

Dear Mike:

Thanks for good dope. Would send cable but change this much— "Leopard—Nairobi—quote best rates on month and two-month safari buffalo lion possibly elephant for four young men arriving early October stop you and one white hunter wanted no style Clark."

Changed dates and included animals as in his pamphlet Klein says be sure and specify animals wanted other than usual antelope zebra— That determines where they have to go—I would like to see elephants whether we bust them or not—Want to certainly bust buffalo and Lion.

Send cable at my expense—week end rate—

Will govern self on clothes as you suggest—But may carry my woods sleeping roll---We can outfit on clothes—shells—and double express rifles (2nd hand) at Nairobi.

I dont want to fly—Suppose you crack up and miss trip—Everything looks same from air—Think would be swell to go out by Nile etc. Look—Mike if you have time will you look up Messageries Maritime[s] sailings or whatever French sailings and prices from Marseilles to Mombassa. I would like to see Bumby—could land Havre—go to Paris— hoist a few at Lipps—catch Train Bleu from Gare de Lyons for Marseilles—

Save all that water trip from England—make time and still see Bumby and let Charles [Thompson] see Paris—and La Belle France—all get tight together in wagon restaurant—

Boy wont it be a swell trip?

But make sure to get boat that doesnt touch in Italian ports as dont want to go to Lipari—or [get] beaten up—

If no Italian angle we could save time by going on Simplon-Orient Express—Paris—Milan—Trieste—Agreb [Zagreb?]—Sofia—Popodopoulis [Philippopolis?]—Adrianople—Constant—(Out through Sea of Marmora and down coast to Egypt and Suez—Also they say railway runs all way now—across Anatolia—That is a swell trip—I've made it twice to Constantinople—Hell of a good trip—maybe across Anatolia—

Could get Orient Express by Wien and down through Bucharest to Constant too—But I know there are good French boats from Marseilles—English boats of course are on a £ basis but even so it's not a hellish expensive route—Could take Frog vessel to Suez and board lime juicer for [from] there to Mombassa—What say, General---we won't get back until 1st of year.

Not carrying ammunition we will be all right—Les Sportsmen bien connu—

Only thing about Klein is that name—Does Clark say if he's one of those Kleins—Germans are swell—kikes not so good—We dont want him to turn out to be Harold Loeb—but send the wire and lets get a quotation—

I am taking 30.06—10.75 Mauser—12 ga shotgun (pump) and 6.5 Mannlicher—also my Colt 22 cal woodsman—

May take a sword and muleta for buffalo and you carry a kite for us to climb the string of for elephants---

Hope to God Maggie is better—give her all our love and sympathy—See you soon—Hem.

[In left margin:] Have never gone better writing—Am in wonderful shape—3 swell stories done.

[In right margin:] Caught a 44 lb king on Friday—using live yellowtails we should break words [world's] record barracuda—maybe amberjack—

[In right margin, page 1:] Pauline leaves for N.Y. today—to get nurse—2 have gone haywired—She's combed Miami—call her up at Uncle Gus's—770 Park she'll be N.Y. 3-4 days—

PUL

To JOHN DOS PASSOS, Key West, 26 March 1932

Dear old Dos:

The book [*1919*] is bloody splendid—it's 4 times the book the 42nd [Parallel] was—and that was damned good. It comes off all the time and you can write so damned well it spooks me that something might happen to you—wash and peel all the fruit you eat.

Now watch one thing. In the 3rd volume don't let yourself slip and get any perfect characters in—no Stephen Daedeluses—remember it was Bloom and Mrs. Bloom saved Joyce—that is the only thing could ruin the bastard from being a great piece of literature. If you get a noble communist remember the bastard probably masturbates and is jallous [jealous?] as a cat. Keep them people, people, people, and don't let them get to be symbols. Remember the race is older than the economic system—and that the Y.M.C.A. was once a noble movement—as was the Methodist church—the Lutheran church—the French Revolution—the Commune—the Xstian Religion—all badly managed and run by human beings.

Maximilian in Mexico an unworthy business—1st Spanish Republic a worthy business—result the same. Bad management. Good management makes tyranny.

Remember our Lord yellowed out on the cross and was only successful because they killed him. Bunny Wilson has forgotten that Christian religion started as violently anti-capitalist jewish system. It is the management that ruins things and the fact that everything is done by human beings—no unit larger than the village can function justly—what you want is justice—you know damned well it is—and don't let them suck you in on any economic Y.M.C.A.

I should tell you this—Christ you know it all better than I do. But you are in a tough spot because you have a lot of pressure on you that is as bad for you as a writer as the Whitneys. As a writer I say—not as a man—you've got too many cojones for anybody to influence you but remember writing is the toughest thing of all. That is why they all want something or somebody to take the responsibility. You can write the best of any of the bastards writing now and you've been around the most—you write better all the time. For Christ sake don't try to do good. Keep on showing it as it is. If you can show it as it really is you will do good. If you try to do good you'll not do any good nor will you show it. That's where the book is so swell because you get so many shots at it through the camera eye—the news reel—the portraits—but because you have those shots don't take it easy in the straight narrative. Write them as though you didn't have any other chance—don't coast along.

And excuse me for saying all this crap—probably doesn't make sense.

I will work hard on my proofs and try to cut the shit as you say—you were damned good to take so much trouble telling me.[1]

It was grand to see you and Stut [Katy Dos Passos]. Pauline felt terribly. We went to Tortugas 18 days—3 North Westers one right after another. Fine time though.

Your 200 check came back—I took it up. Bank probably trying to knife you. Don't send another. Would like to have a 200 seed stake in the goddamned fine way you are writing. Sold that After the Storm story for plenty.[2]

Everybody fine here. We sent a lot of mail including air mailed check from Brandt and Brandt to Ward Line—Vera Cruz. Will send this to Amexco—Mexico DF—registered with return address—and an envelope full of mail. I wired Brandts I sent on the check—in answer to a wire from them that they were sending it.

I was happy as hell you liked the bull book. Esther [Chambers] says Jack Lawson is leaving Hollywood for East if that makes any difference in your plans. If you should come through here we'll have shellfish and catch tarpon.

Things fairly gloomy at Canby's [Chambers's] seems to me. But why not?

Everybody well here. We shot 15 foot sawfish—caught 49 lb. King—gulf full of sailfish. I wish we could live at Tortugas. Remember to get the weather in your god damned book—weather is very important.

Love to Kate. Everybody sends their best. Christ I'd like to be with you baskets.

We caught all kinds of muttonfish at Tortugas—hit a bunch that followed the boat like amberjacks—caught them out by East Key in shallow water—in a dead calm—ran up to 16 lbs—could see them come to the bait.

The merchants all had a good time.

Well so long—

You've got a damned good book—you ought to have a good time.

UVA   Hem

1. Dos Passos had sent EH a wise critique of *Death in the Afternoon*. This letter is EH's quid pro quo. 2. Published in *Cosmopolitan* 92 (May 1932), for which EH received $2,700.

To JOHN DOS PASSOS, Key West, *c*. 12 April 1932

Dear Dos:

I sent a couple of collections of mail, registered to you care of American Express Co. Mexico DF. and a long letter. Poop on any literary advice in letter. Christ knows you need advice less than anybody in country (or city). But where I was drooling off about not to make any too noble character in the 3rd wolumne for god's sake don't think I was referring to Ben Compton. That is the best narrative in the book to me. Damned wonderful fine story. You don't need any advice.

What about the angel of death? Couldn't the angel of death visit Ward Moorehouse or some of those drawing room bitches?

Esther Andrews got me to write you to Mexico D.F. that Jack (Howard) Lawson had left the Coast. This was dementi-ed [contradicted] shortly after by Mrs. Chambers.

[Canby] Chambers himself in pretty good shape. I tell him my theory is that his paralysis is all a hoax and that you are in the pay of the capitalists. Dos Passos the Lone Wolf of Wall Street.

Listen, Woolf, write us how you are. You sounded, by postcard, as though it were a bloody fine trip.

Esther says why isn't she in any of your books. I tell her I'm not either but that as a fellow Oak Parker I am very happy you made Richard Ellsworth Savage come from the Home of the old Orange and Blue football team.

Am working hard. Cut a ton of crap a day out of the proofs and spread it around the alligator pear trees which are growing to be enormous. Second crop of limes. 3rd crop of Gilbeys.

Writing a fine book about Scott Fitzgerald oddly enough. Very interesting and instructive. Am going to have a camera eye looking up a horse's ass and newsreels of you singing in chinese and give a drink of hot kirsch to every customer. Lieterature has got to be put on its feet or on its what shall we say lads on its -

All fine here. Pauline got a good nurse. Go to Cuban coast on the twentieth, going to run across at night with the full moon if good weather—and come back when there is no moon at all. Stay two weeks.

Sec[retary of the Navy Charles Francis] Adams is shutting up the Navy Yard completely—going to not even have watchmen. Come on down and steal coconuts.

Write to the American Express Co. Mexico D.F. and see the big fine lot of mail you get.

Will send this to Brandt Brandt and Brandt. Brandt Brandt Brandt the Van Dorens are coming. Cheer up Isabel Patterson you can't come and beneath the Bunny Wilson we shall never meet again in the freedom of our old Kentucky Home.

Glenway Wescott, this is no kidding, is issuing a Call To Action. He feels things are in A BAD WAY. To be published in May [*Fear and Trembling*].

It may be well if the South Western Island Republic secedes from the Union at once. I have organized cutting the cables, blowing up Bahia Honda viaduct, burning bridges, destroying all buoys and lighthouses and the seizing of enough tramp steamers to feed the ungry populace. We will be a free port, set up gigantic liquor warehouses and be most PROSPER-OUS ISLAND IN THE WORLD. The PARIS OF THE SOUTH WEST. Sully [J. B. Sullivan] is building a guillotine in his boiler making estab-lishment. Am at work on a project to re-enslave the jigs overnight and am fixing up accommodations in the carferries to run chinamen. Charles [Thompson] guarantees every comrade enough rope to hang himself.

Let us hear from you. The Coup d'etat is planned for the day after the navy and marines go. On the first night we massacre the catholics and the jews. The second the protestants who have been lulled into a false sense of security by the events of the first evening. The third night we butcher the free thinkers, atheists, communists and members of the lighthouse service. The fourth day we fish the gulf and capture another ship to feed our faithful jigs. That evening we knock off a few counter revolutionaries and if things aren't going well we burn the town. The fifth and sixth days are free and members of the party can amuse themselves as they like. On the Seventh day we elect Butstein [Katy] the Goddess of Reason and order Mac Leish to write an Epic Poem about the Movement. Late that evening we shoot Macleish as his poem has turned out Lousy and send for Evan Shipman. You can see how it will be. Just one gay hilarious round with everyone busy and happy. At the end of twelve days we raise wages to beat hell and massacre the poles.

Let me hear if you are with us,

Love from Pauline,

UVA   [Ernest Hemingway]

To WALDO PEIRCE, Key West, 15 April 1932

Dear Old Waldo:

It's a bloody shame you're broke, kid because we counted on seeing you and Alzira down here. It's been a fine winter, not a Norther until the twenty-seventh of February, regular summer weather all during the part when it is usually cold, and now fine and cool during the hot part. Old Dan still holding out. Have to wake him up sometimes to pay him; unlike other general world conditions. Archie and Mike Strater came down with Uncle Gus and we went to Tortugas. Planned to spend the first night at Sou'west Key where we struck the nurse sharks that time with Bill Smith and about three o'clock in the morning it started to blow like hell from the northwest and we had to go into the long beach channel for shelter and were stuck there three days before we could cross the Tortugas. It was very rough going over the quicksands. My bloody eyes are bad (not trying to pull a Joyce on the boys but they give me bad trouble reading and writing and I am dictating this to Pauline). Never could write a good letter, but certainly dictate a foul one. Am getting proofs on this new book now. Have you a good reproduction of the painting of the bulls coming into the ring at Pamplona, or can you get one right away? I want to reproduce it in the illustrations for this book. Let me know about this right away, will you please? Dos read the book in manuscript and claimed he liked it very much. Have some stories, too, one in the May number of that stink Cosmopolitan about down here that you might like if you can read it without looking at the illustrations ["After the Storm"]. You probably remember when Bra [Saunders] told it to us first. Have some other good ones to write and about six done for a book [*Winner Take Nothing*, 1933].

This is a grand house. Do you remember it across from the light house? One that looked like a pretty good Utrillo, somewhere between that and Miro's Farm. Have your two partridges with shotgun, a damn fine picture, over the fireplace in the dining room. Everybody in Paris, that is Miro and Masson and those birds, were crazy about your two pike, pickerel rather, on the platter and the trout. Have you done any more of that kind? What is the chance of bumming or buying some Art from you? Charles and I both bitter about how we were jipped out of the two jacks you painted in the backroom. We are going to run Charles for president to end the depression on the platform of give every man enough rope to hang himself.

Wish you would come down to go on a trip in the boat to the Cuban coast. They have all the giant marlin, both striped and black that Zane Grey goes to Tahiti to catch. We are going to Havana next week to fish out from there, going across in Joe Grunt's [Joe Russell's] boat on the first moonlight night. When you get this why don't you borrow some jack from your old man and buy a round trip ticket to Havana? We will fish out from there for ten days, starting about the twentieth. Remember money will probably be no good anyway as soon as they start inflation so you might as well borrow all you can now and pay it back when it's like

German marks here. We've been too long without seeing you and you've been too bloody domestic. For your own good being a father is only a part time job, remember. And soon all your friends'll be dead and only your old man alive.

Why don't you wire you're coming. Love to Alzira and good luck to the home, but remember home for guys like us is a place that should be left in order to come back to and we're all getting old fast and those giant fish getting no weaker. With your goofy luck we could probably catch one.

Wire that you'll show up. You could come right over on the boat and meet us in Havana. They have special excursion rates round trip to Havana. The thing when you're broke is do some thing like this. L'audace, toujour l'audace, et les round trip cheap excursion rates. Greg weighs twenty and one half pounds. Five months old.

Best love from us all,
tu amigo
Ernesto

COLBY

To JOHN DOS PASSOS, Havana, 30 May 1932

Dear Dos:

Well you played it wrong not to make this trip. Damn I wish you could have made it. Have caught 19 Marlin Swordfish and 3 sailfish (one 8 feet 9 inches). Been feeding the whole water front. It sells for 10 cents a pound even in these times. We've given them all away—cut 'em up and hand 'em out when we come in. But to hell with feeding the water front. You ought to see them strike Dos. Jump more than tarpon and fast as light—one jumped 23 times. Charles fought one 2 hours 5 minutes then hook pulled loose when he went to gaff him. Fish ran out 500 yards of line 3 times. Have to chase them with the boat hooked up—them jumping all the time throwing water like a racing motor boat in a sea. Have had 17 strikes in a day—never less than 3. Biggest we've caught so far a little over nine feet—caught 2 today—Sat. 4—caught 30 lb dolphin.[1]

Have Joe Grunts the bootlegger's boat—going all down coast Mariel—Bahia Honda—everywhere. She only burns 5 gallons to 10 running all day (120 gal tanks). Charles was here—also Bra—Lorine too over a week end—Pauline has been over twice for a week and ten days. Coming back again. She caught 2—one that she caught weighed 75 lbs jumped 19 times. They're so fast they'll jump on one side of boat then the line will go slack and you'll think you've lost them and they'll jump to hell over on the other side. They will come toward the boat jumping—jump 30 feet on a line parallel to the water—stiff as a board.

The fishing boats here have caught them up to 900 lbs—Black Marlin—White—and striped—we have two teasers going (one on each side) one 2½ feet long that Bra made—they rush them sometimes and break them off before you can get them in.

And can't get a son of a bitch down here—am feeling alone now with Joe holding the other rod and an insane night life jig to steer—goes to sleep while steering—goes to sleep minute he hits the boat. Spends the dough he makes every night on night life.

At this hotel—Ambos Mundos—you can get a good clean room with bath right overlooking the harbor and the cathedral—see all the neck of the harbor and the sea for $2.00—2.50 for two people. Write the name down—*Pasajes* closed—went broke.

Have gone over book 7 times and cut out all you objected to (seemed like the best to me God damn you if it really was) cut 4½ galleys of philosophy and telling the boys—cut all of last chapter except the part about Spain—the part saying how it wasn't enough of a book or it would have had these things. That is OK.

Left Old Lady in and the first crack early in book about Waldo Frank's book [*Virgin Spain*]—cut all other references to Frank. Believe old Lady stuff O.K.—or at least necessary as seasoning.

Wish you luck with yours. Don't let a twirp like [Malcolm] Cowley shake your confidence in those damned swell *Camera Eyes*. Remember how nosepicking all those twirps were when we were all out seeing the bloody world. Remember how lousy worried you were about 1919 and it turned out damned bloody fine.

Also none of it makes a god damned bit of difference. I can't be a Communist because I hate tyranny and, I suppose, government. But if you're ever one its swell with me. I can't stand *any* bloody government I suppose. Bunny's book [*The American Jitters*, Scribners, 1932] was *wonderful* reporting—wish he had kept on reporting and not have had to save his soul. Certainly things are in a hell of a shape. But when weren't they? No larger unit than the village can exist without things being impossible. Wilson writing he would send us other writers to write patriotism about some bloody factory—(He knows what's good for people)—Like hell he would. He wouldn't send me anywhere.

If things were like that I would kill him so damned quick—oh hell what's the use of talking like that—could make a living here catching Marlin—really believe. Maybe not. But what the hell—could see them jump anyway.

Love to Katy. Thanks for the presents. They're probably in K.W. now.

[Ernest Hemingway]

1. This marks the start of EH's marlin fishing, which continued through the rest of his life.

To MAXWELL PERKINS, Key West, 28 June 1932

Dear Max:

Wired you yesterday. Have done 233 pages of the page proof and all the captions. Will go right on through it and send it off to you with the list of fixed dates of fights in Spain, Central and South Am[erica] and Mexico. Would prefer not to call these appendices. Limitations of space and costs have aborted any attempt to make the book exhaustive so as it is appendices are only pretentions. So list them in the table of contents by their titles—*removing* the designations Appendix A, B and C.

Am in bed convalescing and probably will be for two or three days more. If the Dr. lets me go will start with [sister] Carol for Piggott on Saturday morning—to go from there to L-T ranch, Cooke City, Montana—being there by July 12. Not going to Africa this year—wouldn't want to miss the literary teas. Had touch of Broncho pneumonia. Didn't recognize it at onset. Steered across from Havana with temperature of 102° (sweating from fighting a big marlin, got caught in rainsquall was what got me sick) was very sick finally.

Will try and find contract and send it to you to protect you against worry in case of any such future contingencies. Know neither you nor I worry about the contract or would have sent it before.

But listen Max could you <u>bawl</u> <u>out</u> please or raise hell with the son of a bitch who slugged all these galleys Hemingway's Death? You know I am superstitious and it is a hell of a damn dirty business to stare at that a thousand times even to haveing it (in this last filthy batch) written in with red and purple ink. If I would have passed out would have said your goddamned lot put the curse on me.

About the combining of pictures—you don't want to open the illustrations with a double page. Also that seed bull and ox are too good to combine. That's why I sent you the wire—the two Villaltas combine much better.

Saw a publicity sheet sent out by Benjamin Hauser presumably rehashing Scribner publicity—mostly ballyhooing stuff I had cut out. What you will do is get everyone disappointed. I put all that stuff in so that anyone buying the book for no matter what reason would get their money's worth. All that story, dialogue, etc. is thrown in extra. The book is worth anybody's 3.50 who has 3.50 as a straight book on bull fighting. If you go to advertizing that it is so many damned other things, all you will do is make people disappointed because it hasn't a cook book and a telephone directory as well.

If you try to sell it as a great classic goddamned book on bull fighting rather than some fucking miscellany you may be able to sell a few. Let the critics claim it has something additional. But suppose all chance of that gone now with that lovely Hauser stuff. If you want to try to find someone to speak well of it ask Dos Passos.

But that's your business—not mine.

About the words—you're the one who has gone into that. If you decide to cut out a letter or two to keep inside the law that is your business—I send the copy and you are supposed to know what will go to jail and what will not. F-ck the whole business—that looks all right. It's legal isn't it.

Max I feel damned sick still but I could break the neck of the punk that slugged those galleys.

Oh yes—what about that Modern Library money? I'm flat broke. What is Mr. Dashiell's budget for stories now? Please answer these last two.

Also will you please have three sets of these *corrected* page proof galleys drawn as want one for Cape, one for Germany and one for myself.

> Best to you always—
> Ernest

If they feel disappointed and still want my "literary credo" in a book on bull fighting they can run an insert saying "F-ck the whole god-damned lousy racket." Hemingway.

If you want some pictures will get some taken but for christ sake no more of those open mouth open collar wonders. Promise me that. And <u>NIX</u> on that one of me lying with the sick steer.

Will send you painting by Luis Quintanilla who did the frescoes in the Casa del Pueblo that you can use.

PUL

To PAUL ROMAINE, Piggott, Arkansas, 6 July 1932

Dear Mr. Romaine:

Thanks for the 15.00. I have not received the book [*Salmagundi*]. Are you sure you sent it to Scribners? They are usually very careful about forwarding—but I have been along the Cuban coast for 65 days and it might have been held up at Havana. When I came in to clear there was notification of a package at Post Office and I filled out a card to have it forwarded. Hope it will be your book and come through safely. Very sorry not to have answered your letters which I enjoyed reading. But I have quit writing letters myself.

As for your hoping the Leftward Swing etc has a very definite significance for me that is so much horseshit. I do not follow the fashions in politics, letters, religion etc. If the boys swing to the left in literature you may make a small bet the next swing will be to the right and some of the same yellow bastards will swing both ways. There is no left and right in writing. There is only good and bad writing.

Dreiser is different. He is an old man and old men all try to save their souls in one way or another.

Dos Passos doesn't swing. He's always been the same. To hell with all your swingers. E. Wilson is a serious and honest bird who discovered life late. Naturally he is shocked and would like to do something about it.

These little punks who have never seen men street fighting, let alone a revolution, writing and saying how can you be indifferent to great political etc. etc. I refer to an outfit in, I believe, Davenport, Iowa. Listen—they never even heard of the events that produced the heat of rage, hatred, indignation, and disillusion that formed or forged what they call indifference.

Now they want you to swallow communism as though it were an elder Boys Y.M.C.A. conference or as though we were all patriots together.

I'm no goddamned patriot nor will I swing to left or right.

Would as soon machine gun left, right, or center any political bastards who do not work for a living—anybody who makes a living by politics or not working.

And if we had a revolution ever and I hadn't been bumped [?] already and had a minute to spare would most certainly see that all limited edition publishers were shot and all their stinking little souls distributed to relieve sanitex shortage. Of all phony rackets that is certainly one of the phoniest. (I know you have to live and my metier is a good metier but when you are street sweeping you don't want to give advice to the horses.)

And you wanted the Leftward swing to have a definite significance for me. Well well well.

Yours always,

PH. PUL   Ernest Hemingway

To MAXWELL PERKINS, Nordquist Ranch, Wyoming, 27 July 1932

Dear Max:

Am sending the proofs that came yesterday airmail with this letter. Did them yest afternoon and last night. Hurrying to get this off on truck.

Will you please erase the two cursings out of the compositors for still setting that Hemingway's Death. On those last galleys of the Dates of fights—I have the proof all wrapped and can't get to it—they are at the top of two of those last galleys. I wish to Christ you wouldn't have sent that slugged Hemingway's Death again after all I'd written and wired. But want those erased as it does no good to slang the compositors—they aren't responsible.

Hope you get these proofs and letter pretty fast—am sending them in to Gardner—64 miles—to get them out today.

When do I get the page proofs? *What did you do to the words*? Why haven't I seen frontispiece or jacket—you haven't even asked what title goes on Frontispiece.

The Torero—By Juan Gris

Will you tell Whitney Darrow I got his very fine letter and will write him. He was very nice to write me.

Am feeling pretty good but don't seem to have a hell of a lot of pep.

The letters you refer to were to Ernest Walsh and Ethel Moorehead—the bastards I helped get out their magazine [*This Quarter*] when he was supposed to be dying of T.B. Did die finally and she sold the letters. Tell the man who wants to sell them that I said for him to stick them up his ass.

The battlefields of the Civil War, last phase, sound fine—especially in the fall—but don't know where I'll be. We drive through Corinth, Shiloh, and have driven through Lookout Mountain and those—going from Piggott to Florida. Would like to see Vicksburg too—would like to go with you.

Poor old Scott. He should have swapped Zelda when she was at her craziest but still saleable back 5 or 6 years ago before she was diagnosed as nutty. He is the great tragedy of talent in our bloody generation.

Well here comes the truck—must stop.

So long Max—good luck

PUL Ernest

To PAUL ROMAINE, Nordquist Ranch, 9 August 1932

Dear Mr. Romaine:

If you had received many letters from me you would not wonder at the heat of the one you wrote of. I was angry at you, a parasite or camp follower of the arts, suggesting smugly to me that you hoped (I forget the words exactly) that I was being influenced by or cognizant of such and such a political or economic movement etc.

What made me angry was not being touched on an exposed nerve, a sore spot, or an Achilles tendon but the god-damned YMCA worker presumption of tone of your politico-literary well wishing.

Your idea that I stay on the right but would like to go left but am restrained by "reasons we both know" is more of the same presumptuous poppycock.

I will not outline my political beliefs to you since I have no need to and since I could be jailed for their publication but if they are not much further left than yours which sound like a sentimental socialism I will move them further over.

As for my childish unwillingness to continue correspondence—let me tell you something. Publishers of limited editions make a practice of selling the personal letters of writers. I know this from experience; dirty experience. If you want to show your sincerity and not have me believe that you are merely practicing your racket in the hope of drawing saleable letters you will return me those letters keeping copies of them if they interest you.

I very much doubt if you will do this but if you do will be willing to continue the correspondence as long as you can stand it.

Am not terrified by the injection of personalities—nor depressed at the prospect of being forgotten if I do not cease to write about "Lost generations and bulls."

I wrote, in six weeks, one book about a few drunks and to show the superiority of the earlier Hebrew writers over the later quoted Ecclesiastes *versus* G. Stein. This was some seven years ago. Since then have not been occupied with this so-called (but not by me) lost generation.

About bulls—for ten years or so—bull fighting was my recreation and amusement as whatever might be yours if you have any need to think about anything but your work. I wrote a book to clear them up and keep them—also something about Spain which I know a little about from having lived there.

I have to live sometime and I have quite a few things to write and my mind is not occupied with lost generations and bulls.

You will do me a considerable favor not to make the very American Jewish mistake of believing that if a man explains something to you he does it from a feeling of being in the wrong or inferiority. I know what I am doing and have never felt a "malajust". I could make my living, without capital, *in these times*, in at least three other ways than by selling what I write and I have never felt myself anything but a part of the world I live in and know how lousily that world is organized and run.

Neither Wilder nor Dos Passos are "good writers." Wilder is a very minor writer who knows his limitations and was over inflated in value by critics and as quickly de-flated.

Dos Passos is often an excellent writer and has been improving in every way with each book he writes.

Both Dos and Wilder come from the same class and neither represents that class—Wilder represents the *Library*—Zola and Hugo were both lousy writers—but Hugo was a grand old man. Did you ever read his *Choses Rue*? Flaubert is a great writer but he only wrote one great book—Bovary—one ½ great book L'Education, one damned lousy book Bouvard et Pecuchet.

Stendhal was a great writer with one good book—Le Rouge et le Noir—some fine parts of La Chartreuse de Parme (wonderful) but much of it tripe and the rest junk.

Well it seems I enjoy writing to you—or perhaps it is that I enjoy writing.

The address here is Cooke, Montana—I have never received a copy of the book of Faulkner's early crap—nor was it the package at Havana, which was forwarded. Was it ever really sent? Since no son of a bitch who has ever asked permission to reprint, promising a copy of the volume, has *ever* sent a volume so pardon my skepticisms.

My wife, just now, says she thinks the Faulkner pamphlet came to Key West. So you may be an honest man, as well as a worker for humanity—in which case accept the necessary apologies on sending the book.

Yours always,
Ernest Hemingway

PH. PUL

To W. C. LENGEL, Nordquist Ranch, *c.* 15 August 1932

Dear Bill:

Here is the story[1]—Pauline had it copied in Key West so am sending it now.

Your goddamned long distance calls get me spooked—each time I think somebody is dead or I'm indicted or what not and then it turns out to be old Bill Lengel. Sorry you had trouble with your eyes. Hope it will clear up. My chest still bothers me after the pneumonia. Was fighting a big fish with no shirt on (neither of us) for an hour and a half, sweating, and got soaked in a rain squall. Was supposed to convalesce there several weeks. But wanted to get out here anyway and get to work. Too hot in Havana—never too hot in Key West. Plenty cold here. Have a lot of work to do.

This is a damned good story—3 stories in one. The amount of dialogue makes it long in space.

[Marginal insertion:] In actual words it is only about 3600 or so words but in length it takes near as much room as a 5000 word story.

It's a new form for a story. The fact that the three parts all open the same way or practically the same is intentional and is supposed to represent Switzerland metaphysically where it all opens in the same way always and where a young man will not marry a young lady until she has had her original teeth out and her store teeth in since that is an eventual expense that the girl's father, not her husband, should bear. But, possibly, Mr. Lengel, you have been in Switzerland yourself.

Anybody will have been there when they read the Homage.

Well, might as well send it off. It is submitted to be published as it is with no changes and no deletions. If unsuitable send it back.

With best regards to you and to Harry Burton,

SIU   Ernest Hemingway

1. The story, "Homage to Switzerland," was rejected by *Cosmopolitan*, published in *Scribner's Magazine* (April 1933), and collected in *Winner Take Nothing*.

This letter is used courtesy of Special Collections, Morris Library, Southern Illinois University.

To THE EDITORS, *HOUND AND HORN*, Nordquist Ranch,
27 August 1932

Sirs:

Referring to Mr. Lawrence Leighton's very interesting and revealing
autopsy[1] on Mr. Dos Passos, Mr. Fitzgerald and myself, may I take exception to one sentence:

"One feels behind Radiguet, Mme. de Lafayette, Benjamin Constant,
Proust, even Racine."

Surely this should read "Radiguet behind Mme. de Lafayette." The
rest of the sentence might stand although it would be more just to place
Cocteau behind Radiguet and give Racine the benefit of the doubt. But
perhaps Mr. Leighton has a feeling for Racine and would not wish to
deprive him of his place.

Yours very truly
Ernest Hemingway

1. EH's reply to Leighton's "An Autopsy and a Prescription," *Hound and Horn* 5
(July–September 1932): 519–39, in which the work of Dos Passos, Fitzgerald, and
EH is called "repulsive, sterile, and dead." EH plays heavily with the closing sen-
tence of the supercilious essay, which celebrates the work of Radiguet.
This letter was printed in *Hound and Horn* 6 (October–December 1932): 135.

To ROBERT M. COATES, Nordquist Ranch, 5 October 1932

Dear Bob:

There weren't any cracks against Faulkner.[1] You read it over and you
will see. Your interpretations, opinions and judgments are naturally none
of my goddamned business-es and would not comment on them. This
only is question of fact. There was a mention, a pretty damned friendly
mention. There was a crack at Cocteau (who is a public character and
perfectly crackable), there was re-buttal to W. Frank, Eliot and [Aldous]
Huxley.

The Eliot thing has been back and forth for a long time. Frank is a
twirp (pen in hand), no matter how admirable politically. Huxley is a
smart fellow, a very smart fellow.

I don't really think of you as a critic—no disparagement, I mean I
think of you as a writer—or would not make any explanations. Certainly,
books should be judged by those who read them—not explained by the
writer.

But I'm damned if I wrote any petulant jibes against Faulkner and the hell with you telling citizens that I did.

All the petulant jibes you like against Waldo Frank (or yourself even, if you're looking for them), or anyone for whom I have no particular respect. But I have plenty of respect for Faulkner and wish him all luck. That does not mean that I would not joke about him. There are no subjects that I would not jest about if the jest was funny enough (just as, liking wing shooting, I would shoot my own mother if she went in coveys and had a good strong flight). If it was not funny to you that is my, or perhaps your, hard luck.

Always,
Your friend
Ernest Hemingway

1. EH's reply to Coates's review of *Death in the Afternoon* in the *New Yorker* 8 (1 October 1932): 61–63. EH's letter was printed in the issue of 5 November, pp. 86–87.

To HENRY STRATER, Nordquist Ranch, 14 October 1932

Dear old Mike:

I wish I could talk to you and I could explain about the African postponement so it would take the hurt out of your feelings. First the letter from Uncle Gus asking if I wanted to postpone—which made me think about postponeing. Then Archie writing he couldn't go. I wrote him I was thinking about the possibility of not going until he could have another chance and would write you to see how you felt and he goes to you before I can write. The goddamned trip *was never postponed until you agreed.* If you would have said you'd rather go I'd have gone and damned glad to. When wouldn't I rather shoot than work? I know you still feel hurt and sore but if you could talk to Charles he would and could make you see how it really was. I couldn't sound everyone at once unless I had a secretary and paid you [the] compliment of thinking your life was more mobile than Archie who is broke and working for a salary and Charles who hasn't a sou and works for his brother.

A man can be a hell of a serious artist and not have to make his living by it—see Flaubert, Cezanne and Co. And it implies no criticism of the seriousness of a guy's work to take it for granted that he would be more willing to knock off work for a trip than a guy who doesn't eat if he loses his job through knocking off.

On the other hand I did bitch your plans and have and do feel god-damned bad about it and feel worse about it all the time.

But I am just as serious about writing as you are about painting and work at least ½ as hard *and lay off plenty* and you can afford to lay off just as much as I can so don't hightone me with any 2 years plan.

We missed you and I *missed you* to beat hell on this trip. You missed a damned good hunt and it was only about half as enjoyable to me as it would have been if you were along.

Charles shot a bull elk, we shot one together, and I killed one alone. He killed 2 damned fine bucks and a bear and I killed an eagle (flying), trapped a coyote and killed a hell of a big bear. Night before last—just at dark, hit him too high in fore shoulder and trailed him (alone) by blood in snow in the dark and killed him at 20 feet. He bawled like a bull. He weighed over 500 lbs. Beautiful hide nearly eight feet spread from paw to paw. The elk we shot together was a six point big bull at nearly 11,000 feet. Charles shot at him head on at 150 yards and missed, hit him broadside (creased him), he went to beat hell and I ran and got a running shot as he crossed an open place in the mountain side. Shot him through both foreshoulders and again a little farther back but too low in lungs. Charles came up as I was shooting. Bull went down in gulch. We started over, Charles watching to see if he got up. ½ way there bull got up and Charles opened on him. I ran back under his fire, got a rest against tree and hit him. He slumped forward and spraddled but still going. Charles shot his hind leg clean off (really) at knee joint and he went down. He was hit five times and when we opened him up found top of his heart shot off—both lungs—Charles first shot was through and through but in his mouth just above back bone.

I killed a 7 point huge bull at 11,000 about one shot, running, (he and I both running!) bullet went in ribs above kidneys took top off lungs. He bled internally—ran 50 yards down hill without a drop of blood and was stone dead.

Goddamn, Mike, in those steep mountains and that altitude it is hell to get on them and damned exciting shooting. Charles killed a 8 point bull yesterday (Ivan Wallace wants the meat to take to Red Lodge on his license and is going out after another one tomorrow that Chub [Weaver] wants for winter meat on his license).

Charles was in bad shape from the strenuous hunting first 10 days. Took an awful beating—game as hell. But is in swell shape now. This damned hunting is work. Four days ago I rode 35 miles to camp in a blizzard—hunted next day all day in Mts. in heavy snow—rode 35 miles back next day. Day after rode 25 miles and killed bear—home at 10.30 pm. Next day 25 miles to skin bear out. Layed off today. We leave day after tomorrow.

We took a beating on sheep. I stalked 8 rams—spooked them all. Charles stalked 11. That sheep hunting was what gave Charles hell. Damndest ledge work you ever saw. I had to take my shoes off on one mt for about 2 miles on a rock slide. Fell 9 times. Never got a shot at a ram—if you're a good climber you could have got a ram. I'm not a good climber. Will send some pictures.

Your bait rig looks O.K. but might spin. In Cuba they troll a mackerel or any long fish so he doesn't spin by passing hook in through mouth and out gill—then cut a slit for shank to fit in and hook the hook sideways through body with ringed end of hook in mouth shank concealed in slit, point projecting. Tie mouth shut with leader projecting—tie around body to hold hook in slit cut—can do all of it in 3 minutes. We trolled all whole fish from 10 to 25 inches long. To keep a bait from spinning you treat it like this:

[EH provides a clear diagram of a rigged bait fish with labels.]

The streamers keep the bait trolling straight in water and keep it from spinning—also give motion—*also give flavor and scent* by cutting the bait. There are 3 different kinds of tuna there and all hit this—also sailfish and Marlin. You can fix them in 3 minutes. We usually had 4 or 5 made up ahead all the time and kept them and the leaders in the ice box.

Trolled mackerel, King fish, barracuda, giant pilchards, goggle eyes— all whole—all without spinning. But must be tied *tight* at head—so they hang straight—the streamers are the works.

Gee Mike I wish I could see you. I can't tell you how we missed your company. It has been a tough trip—starting out with much tough luck and little game—and now game just swarms. I've turned down 3 bull moose—one beauty. It is fine to have old Charles in swell shape and shooting beautifully now. Killed his 2 bucks and last bull with one bullet apiece—one buck huge with a beautiful head—the other head is about like a big white tail buck. I was going out buck hunting this pm but wrote this instead. Hope you are having good pheasant and duck shooting.

Best always
Hem

PUL

To GUY HICKOK, Nordquist Ranch, 14 October 1932

Dear Gros:

Who could scorn such a convenience as that envelope. Here it is with a blizzard sweeping over Idaho, Utah, Montana and your old man turning some poor whore out of his hotel into the streets because he runs a christian place. All them Hickocks is cruel. Like you stopping writing just because I can't write. Well when did I write you last? Let's see we got off on the Isle de France, courtesy of Mary [Hickok] and with her swell flowers - and had a merry drunken crossing. Got glasses in N.Y. Went to K.C. Had baby - 9 lbs 7 ounces or 19 pounds 17 ounces - Hell of a big baby anyway with gigantic sexual equipment and deep bass voice. Went to Keywest. In April went to Cuba for 10 days and stayed 65 - caught 32 *Swordfish* - learned a lot about Cuba.

Coming home I got pneumonia and was sick as hell - Came out here in new Ford V8 - Picked Pauline up at Piggot - (Drove 654 miles one day! Remember our record runs into Italy [1927]) parked kids - been here ever since -

Sent you galleys (as soon as got them) and copy of book. Hope you like it - I worked hard on it - but that isn't enough - Hope I had some luck besides -

Well then where were we - oh yes - here - Well Pauline is cockeyed beautiful - Figure lovely after Greg born - never looked nor felt better - Rode hard here all summer - shot and fished -

She hunted here for first 5 days of season then went down to K.West to work on house - putting in a bathroom in our room - tearing out a partition etc. Bumby landed there day before yesterday -

We've killed 3 big bull elk - 2 bucks - 2 bear - an eagle and a coyote - Grouse all the time - Killed enough meat for the two guides to get married on -

Going to drive to Key West day after tomorrow - Country is all busted - wish it were like this when I was a kid - ½ schools closed - 200,000 guys on the road like the wild kids in Russia - Scribners only printed 10,000 copies of this book - thought that would last until Xmas probably and sold them all out 1st day of publication - When it sells 12,500 the advance is covered - that was done 4th day so you will probably see us toward the end of next summer along with the other tourists - if they still have tourists - I tried to make it completely unsaleable and offend everyone but you see - no bloody luck again -

Who won the Tour de France - and who was 2nd, 3rd, 4th, 5th etc.

We have a big choice this fall between

The Paralytic Demagogue
The Syphylitic Baby
The Sentimental Reformer
The Yes-Man of Moscow -[1]

Why don't you come home and vote?

Everyone thinks it is Roosevelt so Hoover will probably schwozzle him out.

How are you and Mary and the children? This is a lousy letter but will try to write a good one from K.West. Good cotton crop at Piggott - Paulines father held all his cotton over from last year and made plenty of money on it. Jinny is there now. Don't know what her plans are. Well you wanted a letter and this is the sort of crap you get. Poor old Gros - Don't ever come home thinking U.S.A. [is] interesting - It is just the same as ever only now they are all broke where before they were lousy with cash. The scene hasn't changed. Just the condition of the actors -

I got 1.00 a word from Cosmopolitan for a story - last May number - good story too - 2693 words - Think of that in this time of Depression. In a good year should have soaked them about 5 bucks a palabra [word] I suppose - Well well well this depression is hell -

On the other hand we didn't participate in the boom.

So long Guy - write to Key West will you? Did you see them chop Gouryellief?

Best to Mary and thanks to her again for those swell flowers and our luxurious passage -

PH. PUL   Ernest

1. EH apparently means Roosevelt, Hoover, Thomas, and Foster, presidential candidates of the Democratic, Republican, Socialist, and Communist parties, respectively.

To JOHN DOS PASSOS, Nordquist Ranch, 14 October 1932

Dear Dos:

Won't cash the 100 until you say you don't need it right now. Thanks ever so much for sending it. This book looks as though it would sell maybe a grand or two over the advance. Hope the hell it does. I have a story out I will get money on too.

By Christ it made me feel good to get your letter. It certainly did. Was on the way back to Timber Creek—killed two fine bulls—one a seven pointer—hell of a big bear—8 foot spread—shot eagle on wing—trapped a coyote where we killed elk—2 magpies. Grouse every day for a week. Country just as louzy with game as it was empty when you were up. I wish to hell you were here. Saw bull moose and 11 deer one day. Charles [Thompson] killed another bull and 2 bucks and small bear but pretty hide. We've been killing meat for Ivan [Wallace] and Chub [Weaver] to get married on. Rode all way to Timber Creek cabin in a blizzard— read your damned letter over and take a shot of Red Lodge moon to keep warm.

Haven't seen reviews except a lengthy poop-on in Times (a man *should* be pooped on by the Times) and a condescendentious piece of phony intellectuality by Bob Coates in the New Yorker.

God damn but I'm glad you liked it. If Malcolm Cowley or one of those recent converts pans it in New Republic or Nation or New Masses in the name of their newly risen Lord (who shouldn't really have anything to do with the Bull Rings in Spain or at least never, as far as I know, covered the subject) you might write that letter. You see I won't see the review until late or never.

It's damned funny when I used to get the horrors about the way things were going those guys never took the slightest interest nor even followed it. They were all in Europe and got worked up over Tristan Tzara when the god damndest things were happening—then when you've gotten as hot about something or as burned up and finally completely disillusioned on the *working* of anything but intelligent political assassination then they start out and say, "Don't you see the injustice, the Big Things that are happening. Why don't you write about them etc."

If you saw Clemenceau (Père la Victoire and poilu lover) have the Garde Republicain ride down the mutilés, bust wheel chairs, strew the road with legless, armless bastards under horses hoofs, bastards who "knew" that "he" wouldn't hurt his poilus—horseshit—then some guy writes and says what do you think of the President being too busy to receive a delegation of writers, *writers* mind you, a thing (they actually wrote me) that could never happen in an European country. I wrote them how shocked I was at this reception of our writers! You've seen the Garde Republicaine and the Schupes work haven't you? If they (the writers) oppose a guy don't wait on him with memorials. Attack him. Hell if Jaures hadn't been killed France would have had a revolution just as sure as hell—why should a successful politician receive people with no power, no money, and, nothing to trade and representing an un-armed body. Well we are all writers together. Bunny Wilson is damned good. His book (The Jitters) was swell. He is sometimes boreing because, like any convert, he hasn't the necessary elasticity but he is damned good.

But what about the other boys who had no kick against the system as long as it functioned. Did they all see a light like Saint Paul or is it the newest and most necessary religion?

[Marginal comment:] Jaurés, Rosa Luxembourg, Karl Leibnecht, then a different guy but damned good old Rathenau, Stambulisky, as fast as an honest man comes up in Europe he is killed if he must sell out and nobody hangs.

You and Bunny Wilson are the only consistent guys among all the word chaps.

I suppose I am an anarchist—but it takes a while to figure out. They poop on old Ferrer and Malatesta now but their names will sound honester in 20 years than Stalin will. Italia is running the U.S. Grant administration. I don't believe and can't believe in too much government —no matter what good is the end. To hell with the Church when it becomes a State and the hell with the State when it becomes a church. Also it is very possible that tearing down is more important than building up.

Well the hell with this whisker pulling. Chub, Ivan and the Nordquists send you their best as does old Charles.

My love to Kate.

Jesus Christ I wish you luck with the 3rd volume. Don't let a fool like Cowley tell you the Camera Eye isn't swell. We don't have to [illegible] our god damned pasts—we use 'em.

So long Dos. . . .
Hem.

Ranch, Cooke, Montana, Oct. 14. Go to Piggott then Key West day after tomorrow.

UVA

To GUY HICKOK, Key West, 29 October 1932

Dear Gros:

Here at Key West after un-Christly blizzards all across Wyoming and Nebraska—2 bits buys a wonderful meal all thro Nebraska—gas 9¢ a gallon.

Fine letter from you—

Pat and Greg all in great shape at Piggot and Pauline's father (backed by Uncle Gus need I add or would have had to shoot himself long ago like mine) paying farmers more for cotton than he is selling it for at the gin. The farmers, of course, very suspicious and sure they are being gypped some way.

West is Hoovery—Roosevelt a Jesus in Georgia—Alabama and this state—Understand he is weak in East—

Pauline tearing out partitions, plastering, making the house fine—She looks grand (Pauline). Old Bumby here—strong, jolly, good kid—

My damned book *selling*—What do you think of that? I thought of it as a book to end publishers—We'll probably get over late in summer—Go to Spain—lion butchery end of Sept or Oct.

You can still go out to Hollywood when they start making bull pictures and say, "No good. You gotta get more bull in it. Like Hemingway."

Write to us—Love to Mary—

PH. PUL   Ernest

To MAXWELL PERKINS, Key West, 15 November 1932

Dear Max:

Wired you about 750. You can make this payment on the January story or advance whichever you prefer. Thank you for the information about sales etc. on this book.

Pauline had to go to Piggott because Greg and Pat came down with whoop cough. I've been staying here to finish up house, she had plenty of work under way on the interior, and looking after Bumby. Have been working like hell writing. Have four stories ready to be typed. Will send you two. No obligation to take them but they are very good stories. I now have ten ready for a book. Need two, possibly three more. Next fall might be a good time. Have been working until my eyes haywire every day. Gone back to the old system of starting in bed when I wake and working through until toward noon. That way they can't bring things to your attention the way they do if you are up.

Had planned to come to N.Y. Need a dose of town life badly but have been going so well writing that do not want to stop. Then, now, there is the problem of what to do with Bumby in N.Y. He is a good kid and a good companion but I do not want to drag him around speakies too much.

Thanks, too, for sending the books. Could they send me Somerset Moom's [Maugham's] new The Narrow Corner? Zelda I found to be completely and absolutely unreadable. I tried to read it [*Save Me the*

Waltz] but I never could. Scott acknowledged the book so I guess the others must have got theirs too. Thanks for sending Zelda's. I will be glad to forward it to anyone you think might be able to read it.

D. H. Lawrence was—but why write you criticism that you do not request. You must read a lot of literary criticism in a year or don't publishers read it. I always believed only writers and critics read reviews until Alec (Louisa M.) Woolcott wrote about poor old Papa in McCall's. Or perhaps it is that McCall's is such a very widely read periodical here.

Probably, if I ever get a few good unfavourable reviews you will be asking waivers on me or losing all confidence in me so must urge you to expect some unfavourable comment on my works.

The odd thing is that my head is in better shape than it has ever been and I am certain of doing better work than I have ever done. The one thing that I will not do is repeat myself on anything so the new ones are rarely as popular—people always want a story like the last one. Also have so damned much vitality now that I cannot sleep and only knock off writing when my damned eyes get too bad.

Will you answer me this? Did you get a second lot of sheets signed to be bound and mailed from Cody? Mailed about Oct. 15–17. Because I mailed about 14 letters with them (rather left them in the mail bag at the Studebaker garage in Cody in the A.M. before mailman came by for him to mail on the morning we started) and have never had an answer from any of them. Will you answer this by return mail so I can write to Cody. All the letters were important. It was my summer's correspondence which I finally answered before leaving the ranch.

They have suppressed Compton Mackenzies Greek Memories, the 3rd Vol of his reminiscences, that I wanted. Methuen published it I believe. Would there be any chance of getting a copy? He writes louzy fiction but grand reminiscences about that business.

Death in p.m. comes out in England today.

Well it looks as though we wouldn't get to N.Y. now. We've been living on shorebirds, snipe and plover, and doves. Charles and Burge would like to be remembered to you. Bumby would like to thank you for the Two Little Confederates.

So Long, Max
Ernest

P.S. Have you a book on pirates. I remember one that came out serially in St. Nicholas when I was a kid written and illustrated, I believe, by Howard Pyle. I've promised it to Bumby.

If you want to use any of these pictures it is O.K.

PUL

To ARNOLD GINGRICH, Piggott, Arkansas, 4 December 1932

Dear Mr. Gingrich:

If you send the book to Key West when we are there (in January—Feb—March) will be very glad to inscribe it. As for titles I had imagined that I made up A Farewell to Arms until I read in Capt. Cohn's opus where I took it from. Same with In Our Time—which Ezra Pound discovered I lifted from English Book of Common Prayer—after the box office appeal dies out I believe A Farewell to Arms will be a good title. Farewell is about the best word I know in English and To Arms should clang more than the book deserves—that title could handle a book with more and better war in it.

About the Apparel Arts[1]—you do not owe me anything for inscribing a book and I would not like to be in your debt. But I would be glad to have them. Especially since they are as you say.

Am glad you liked the last chapter in the last book [*Death in the Afternoon*]—it is what the book is about but nobody seems to notice that. They think it is just a catalogue of things that were omitted. How would they like them to be put in? Framed in pictures or with a map?

Am getting pretty well rid of a good lot of unsought popularity with this last book and hope to get out a pretty good one next time. Don't get spooked if your editions go down in price.[2] Papa still feels pretty good and hasn't started to write the good ones yet. Thank you for your letter.

Yours always,

PH. PUL   Ernest Hemingway

1. *Apparel Arts* was the predecessor of *Esquire*. 2. Gingrich (1903–1972), a midwesterner from Grand Rapids, Michigan, was collecting Hemingway first editions. He invited EH to contribute to *Esquire*, of which he was editor from 1933 to 1945 and from 1949 to 1951. After the death of his first wife, Helen, in 1955, he married Jane (formerly Mrs. Grant Mason), who survived him.

To MAXWELL PERKINS, Piggott, 7 December 1932

Dear Max:

Will you come out here and meet me at Memphis on December 15 to shoot ducks for a week from the houseboat Walter Adams—anchored in the Arkansas river at Watkins [Watson] Ark. If you can't stay a week stay as long as you can. You don't need to bring anything but some warm clothes. I have everything else and have made the reservation and paid for you in advance. We could talk over everything and have the finest duck shooting in the world. I know how you enjoyed shooting the goldings and these ducks are so plentiful and come in to the decoys so often that you would have a swell time.

I know of course that business and your family affairs absolutely forbid it but I need to see you and you need to get away and we will have the sort of shooting our grandfathers and great grandfathers had. Please wire you are coming because it will be too late to get anyone else and I lose $100 if you don't come. Tried to get Mike [Strater] to come too but he wouldn't. Please come Max and if you don't have a better time than you ever had will push you back to N.Y. in a wheelbarrow. We will meet in Memphis on 15th get to Watson 16th—and start shooting that day. I will be waiting for a wire. From a business etc standpoint you really ought to.

You want to decide about book of stories—when—etc. [*Winner Take Nothing*].

You need to hear about other new book I have under way.[1] You ought to bring me that contract—you need to convince me how hard you work to sell my wolumnes etc.

(I promise not to mention a goddamned one of these topics to you if you will come unless you bring them up for nothing else to talk about.)

Memphis is easy to reach from N.Y. and easy to get back from— through train right from the boat practically to go back on.

Please wire. I have 2300 shells so you can miss 1845 ducks and still kill over your limit.

Thanks for yours of Dec. 3. No I didn't make the statement about waivers seriously. Thanks for the Compton Mackenzie—when it comes will read it and send it back.

Will you give this statement all the publicity you can? You know how I feel about publicity but would like to see you spread this statement around:

> Mr. Ernest Hemingway has asked his publishers to disclaim the romantic and false military and personal career imputed to him in a recent film publicity release. Mr. H., who is a writer of fiction, states that if he was in Italy during a small part of the late war it was only because a man was notoriously less liable to be killed there than in France. He drove, or attempted to drive, an ambulance and engaged in minor camp following activities and was never involved in heroic actions of any sort. Any sane person knows that writers do not knock out middleweight champions; unless the writer's name happens to be Gene Tunney. While Mr. H. appreciates the publicity attempt to build him into a glamorous personality like Floyd Gibbons or Tom Mix's horse Tony he deprecates it and asks the motion picture people to leave his private life alone.

Pauline had 3 of the last stories copied when she had to go to St. Louis. Will send 3 and you can pick what you want. No obligation to take any but the 3 are all excellent stories.[2]

Best to you always—
Ernest

Will you send me [Allen] Tate's address? Will send him a book. He is a damned good fellow. I had nobody's addresses in Montana—that's why I didn't send books. Did you send one to O. Wister? I certainly should have. Christ you ought to look out for me on those—you know who usually gets them.

If you don't come I lose 100 bucks for nothing (appealing to you on *lowest possible basis*).

Come on Max, <u>Please</u>.

Have been asked to lecture at Oxford (England). Do you want the name of the college?

PUL

1. EH's reference is obscure. His next book after *Winner Take Nothing* was to be *Green Hills of Africa*, for which he still lacked materials. Possibly he was thinking of *To Have and Have Not*. See EH to Mac Leish, 27 February 1933. 2. The last three of EH's stories to appear in *Scribner's Magazine* were "A Clean Well-Lighted Place," "Homage to Switzerland," and "Give Us a Prescription, Doctor," all in volume 93 for March, April, and May 1933.

To EVERETT R. PERRY, Key West, *c.* 7 February 1933

Dear Mr. Perry:

Thank you for your letter.[1] The fundamental reason that I used certain words no longer a part of the usual written language is that they are very much a part of the vocabulary of the people I was writing about and there was no way I could avoid using them and still give anything like a complete feeling of what I was trying to convey to the reader. If I wrote any approximation even of the speech of the bullring it would be unpublishable. I had to try to get the feeling by the use of two or three words, not using them directly, but indirectly as I used the Natural History of the Dead to make a point that you may have noticed.

I am trying, always, to convey to the reader a full and complete feeling of the thing I am dealing with; to make the person reading feel it has happened to them. In doing this I have to use many expedients, which, if they fail, seem needlessly shocking. Because it is very hard to do I must sometimes fail. But I might fail with one reader and succeed with another.

My use of words which have been eliminated from writing but which persist in speech has nothing to do with the small boy chalking newly discovered words on fences. I use them for two reasons. 1st as outlined above. 2nd when there is no other word which means exactly the same thing and gives the same effect when spoken.

I always use them spareingly and never to give gratuitous shock—although sometimes to give calculated and what to me seems necessary shock.

Yours very truly,

KNOX
Ernest Hemingway

1. On 28 January, Perry, City Librarian, Los Angeles, tactfully asked EH what he thought was gained by using certain plain words in *Death in the Afternoon*. This letter is used courtesy of the Seymour Library, Knox College.

To ARCHIBALD MAC LEISH, Key West, 27 February 1933

Dear Archie:

Enclosed is Evan's [Shipman's] piece about the trotters. I think it is a damned excellent article. He finished it down here and then re-wrote it. You can write him care of General Delivery—Key West. He's tutoring Bumby mornings—I told him I would send this as am writing you. Called the office just after you left (the day I left) and then wired you at the house.

Havent written because started a novel [*To Have and Have Not*]— have 3½ chapters done and 2 stories finished. Going well. Weather wonderful.

Just got a letter from Sarah [Murphy] that Gerald's been very sick (what a damned shame!) and that you're going to Europe March 20 and not be back until May 5.

What the hell about our Cuban trip? Or will you be coming down in May or June? Any time you want to come is fine. Let me know though, keed, when you know because I told Uncle Gus [Pfeiffer] you were going and I have to work on him very hard to get him to take any sort of a trip and it's really damned important to him that he does. He looked very badly worn and tired last I saw him. If I tell him your going and you cant and Mike [Strater] wont (to snoot me probably because I delayed Africa trip) then Uncle Gus may not go either.

Result old Pappy fishing alone in Cuba again.

I'm going to pay your expenses from N.Y. to N.Y. everything. So dont think about the money end. How are you and zat beautiful Mrs. MacLeish? We are all very well—the children and Pauline are in good shape —me too—a little heavy from sitting on my ass and writing this book (may be very good). I'm going good.

We havent heard from Jinny [Pfeiffer] (that sinvergüenza [rascal]) since she left. Believe she is engaged in bringing [John] Gardner and Carol [Hemingway] together[1]—helpful old daughter.

Write me will you? I didnt write because I thought we were all set— have been getting everything ready. Plan to go over between 10th and 15th of April. Full moon the 10th. Con la luna menguante [with a waning moon]—what the hell—you dont know Spanish and I cant spell it. We'll stay until past middle of June anyway. If don't go Spain for picture will stay all June and July.

I never ate anything better than the ham—it was wonderful. Truly not only best ham but one of the very finest, rarest fine thing we ever ate. Tell Ada. It was wonderful!

So long old Mac—call Gerald at the hospital and tell him how bad we feel to know he's suffered so—will you please. I will write. But I get so hollow when finish on the book that I put it off and you would do me a big favor to call him. Then I wont worry if I cant write today. Hit 96x100 with Sara's and Patrick's gun.

Love to Ada. Love from us all. You should see how beautifully Pauline has fixed the house.

Thought Ada and Sara were coming down? What's happened to them. Of course Gerald being so ill. Damn bad luck. Tell them to come when he's well. This is finest weather (all winter) we've ever had—like Indian Summer. Write me,

Pappy

You know if you wanted to you could run (in a box) with Evan's article his poem about trotting which was in Scribners—it is the best and finest description of it that ever could be written. It would go well that way.

Dont you think the article is good? I think it is damned fine.

You couldnt have more meat or better bones to hang it on.

LC

1. John Gardner married EH's youngest sister in Austria in March 1933. EH opposed the marriage.

To ARNOLD GINGRICH, Key West, 13 March 1933

Dear Mr. Gingrich:

Thanks for your three letters. Enclosed is the one that came back from the St. Moritz. Since I wrote it have written three stories and fifty some pages on a novel. Been going very well due to good weather, no diseases nor accidents (knock on wood) and no more worries than usual. But haven't been able to write letters. Finished a long story yesterday so am laying off today and write this to you.

I didn't think the [Walter] Winchell parody was any good. Too angry and too jealous. You should be a better writer than the man you parody, not just try to establish a moral superiority. [Westbrook] Pegler is a better writer but not 1/100th the newspaper man Winchell is. Winchell is the greatest newspaper man that ever lived. Pegler writes a very funny line about sports. But it is the sort of column that is easy to do. I know I could do one. But this bloody Winchell has to function for six days a week and if on his off days, which are very obviously days of rest, he wants to put in a lot of sentimental crap about his family it is o.k. with me. Look what he does on Mondays. I thought Pegler's thing was in much worst taste than anything Winchell puts in about his wife and remaining child.

About Pound I believe I've read almost every line he ever wrote and still believe the best is in the cantos. Matter of opinion. There is also several stale jokes, and quite a lot of crap in the Cantos but there is some Christwonderful poetry that no one can better.

Now about your projected quarterly. I have two policies about selling stuff. If it is for a non-commercial publication published in the interest of letters, sic, I give the stuff away or take a nominal fee, whatever the man can afford to pay and get his money back. Then, later, usually find the bird has sold the Mss. and my letter asking him to return it as it is only mss I have and then have to tear up the pamphlet to use it as mss. when publishing book of stories (what a sentence) anyway that the pure hearted lover of letters has sold the Mss. for anywhere from 10 to a hundred times what he paid me for the story or article.

The second policy is to make all commercial magazines pay the top rate they have ever paid anybody. This makes them love and appreciate your stuff and realize what a fine writer you are.

There have been several times within last twelve months when I have needed 250 cash badly. But could always have gotten many times that for writing a piece such as you suggest. As for stories the only ones I cannot publish would get your magazine in jail or else I do not wish to publish a story such as the one you mentioned because it is not right.

Also I always try to keep a certain amount of posthumous work around to pay the funeral expenses etc. since carry no insurance of any kind except liability insurance.

So where does that bring us? Oh yes. To the fact that 250 is nice money in the pocket but nothing to negociate about.

I go across to Cuba in small boat April 12 to fish that coast for two months in case go to Spain to make a picture, if not, for four months then to Spain. If I get suddenly flat and need 250 dollars to the extent that knock off and write a piece will wire you if that is agreeable. But do not count on anything. For your information in case I should wire you, I have never accepted an advance on anything without delivering it. Go from Spain to Tanganyika and then to Abyssinia to shoot. Will be back next January or February.

About the book of short stories I have 14 done. Will write one more.

With best regards, and please forgive me for not answering you more promptly.

PH. PUL   Ernest Hemingway

To ARNOLD GINGRICH, Key West, 3 April 1933

Dear Mr. Gingrich:

You write a very good letter.

First about the prospective benefits from the advertisers. The collar size is 17½, 44 in jackets but 46 as good or better. Shoes are wide 11. Trousers 34 by 34. Don't imagine they send many sizes that dimension to photograph. If you ever have anything like that and send it parcel post collect will promise to wear them out.

I don't worship Joyce. I like him very much as a friend and think no one can write better, technically, I learned much from him, from Ezra, in conversation principally, from G. Stein, who was a fine woman until she went professionally patriotically goofily complete lack of judgment and stoppage of all sense lesbian with the old menopause. Until then she was damned smart. Then she started taking herself seriously rather than her work seriously and because she had always been that way began to take that seriously too rather than as an accident of what she happened to be. Then she got the idea that anybody who was any good must be queer, if they did not seem to be they were merely concealing it. But what was worse she got the idea that anybody who was queer must be good. Learned a lot from her before she went haywire. Learned nothing from old Ford except mistakes not to make that he had made. Although he was damned generous about writing things about what I wrote. Learned from Anderson but it didn't last long. Imitated Ring Lardner as a kid but didn't learn from him. Nothing to learn because he doesn't know anything. All he has is a good false ear and has been around. The poor guy really hates everything but Purity. Learned from D. H. Lawrence about how to say what you felt about country. What the hell is this, confession, benedeteme parde porque ha aprendido.[1]

The non-commercial magazines are nearly always run to make a career for the editors or editress-es. The only one that was ever worth a damn was the Little Review. They work out as good things, however, nearly all of them, in the long run. Kids feel they have to publish, and they have to to get the stuff behind them.

It is too cockeyed bloody hot today to write anything else and now it is too hot to write a letter even.

Still must go on and finish about the letters for your quarterly.[2] I'll write the four. First one from Cuba. 2nd from Spain. 3rd and 4th from Africa. If anything should happen to Africa will write 3rd and 4th from somewhere else. Will surely be somewhere if I'm still on tap. You send me the first 250 when I write for it and so on. Getting the money will make me write the piece. If you will have enough money you can send me the advance for two and two ie 500 at a time.

Variety is wrong. Vanity Fair approximately ok on [Lewis] Milestone situation. I was turning down plenty of money in N.Y. to sell title of last book to pictures. Ran into Milestone and we talked over making a picture in Spain using non-professional actors. Could make excellent picture. In case did it this summer would have to be there in June. It is getting late now. Milestone wired me the other day he was writing what situation was from Hollywood. I want to make the picture and use his technical knowledge. If picture is successful he can have credit. Have never worked with him and don't know how we would get on. Can see the picture in my head. We have to get money that is willing to take a chance on being lost. All must be shot in Spain. No Hollywood. No Studio.

About what you say about humor. The bastards don't want you to joke because it disturbs their categories. Most people will not even read the Torrents but Joyce and Ezra like it and so does everybody that knows a damned thing about what I'm trying to do.

This is a very I, me, mine letter but you said you were interested. Capt. [Louis Henry] Cohn after saying 200 copies announced 350. When called by old Papa he wrote the usual sad letter about how he could have made a little money which needed badly out of 350 copies but needed 250 to pay his expenses and would not do anything against my wishes but would I wire him he could print 250. I wired him ok for 300. But why in christ's name not say 350 at the start rather than get it onto that sort of basis?

For christ sake never mention this to him because if wished to offend him would do myself.

Had a card from [Sidney] Franklin last night from London. He must be en-route to Spain.

I wanted to work today but it has been too bloody hot. This letter probably shows it. Working on a title for book of stories now. With enough time you can always get a good title. The hell of it is that you always have a lot that seem good and that it takes time to tell which one is right.

Good luck to you,

yours always,

PH. PUL   Ernest Hemingway

1. In what looks like a combination of Italian and Spanish: "Bless me, father, for I have learned." 2. *Esquire* began as a quarterly, became a monthly in 1934, and published twenty-five articles and six short stories by EH between autumn 1933 and February 1939.

To JANET FLANNER,[1] Key West, 8 April 1933

Dear Jan:

When your letter came we were in Piggott and I felt plenty moved and wrote you a long letter. Tore it up the same night because you wrote me such a damned fine letter and I can't write a good letter. Then felt bad ever since not to have answered.

The Greek place was fine. I remember it as a good time. It was just that I must have had the old Noel Murphy nervousness. I like Noel but she makes me nervous the way cats do some people.

Look, why don't you come to Havana? I'm going over there in three days in a thirty four foot boat fixed up for fishing. We fished along that coast 65 days last year, from this time on. It is wonderful. The gulf stream runs almost black and comes right in to the shore. The marlin swordfish go by, swimming up the stream like cars on a highway. You go in to shore in the boat and look down to see the wrinkles in the white sand through the clear water. It looks as though you would strike bottom and when you drop anchor the rope won't reach bottom. They have beaches miles and miles long, hard white sand and no houses for twenty miles. We go out in the morning and troll the stream, go in to swim and get back somewhere at night. Sometimes sleep on the boat. Sometimes on the town. Fine hotel overlooking the harbor, named Ambos Mundos, good clean room where you can work for $2.00 a day.

Pauline comes over and stays two or three weeks and then goes back to K.W. to check up on the children and the house. Finest life you ever saw. We caught 32 swordfish last year.

We're going to stay there until the middle of June if go to Spain make a picture then. If no go Spain will stay along Cuba until August. Anyway we'll go to Spain then and then after Pauline will stay in France maybe or maybe go back to K.W. and I'm going to Tanganyika and Abysinnia. She says she won't go out there but maybe I can get her to yet. Anyway we ought to see you inside of about three or four months.

It made me very happy that you liked the [bullfight] book that much. I don't know anybody that I would rather have had like it (and I don't think anybody did like it very much). Have a book of stories nearly done. Some good ones. Damned hot today and this is a lousy letter.

We have a fine house here and the kids are all well. Also four coons, a possum, 18 goldfish, three peacocks and a yard with fig tree, lime tree. Very fine the way Pauline has fixed it. We have been (and are) damned happy. I could stay here damned near all the time and have a fine time watching the things grow and be happier than I understand but get homesick for Spain and want to go [to Africa] and see the animals and hear the noises they make at night. Have a good place to come back to. We were out in Wyoming and Montana from early July through November and had a fine time. Good hunting. I like to shoot a rifle and I like to kill and Africa is where you do that. Like to get very tired too with nothing connected with my head and see the animals without them seeing you.

The [Jonathan] Cape edition was foul. I gave him hell but it doesn't do any good. Still it is always better to fight with one publisher than with a series of them. They are our natural enemies.

Nancy [Cunard] I never liked. Gertrude S. I was very fond of and god knows I was loyal too until she had pushed my face in a dozen times. Last time I saw her she told me she had heard an incident, some fag story, which proved me conclusively to be very queer indeed. I said You knew me for four or five years and you believe that? Oh it was very circumstantial, she said. Very circumstantial indeed. She wouldn't tell me what it was. Just how completely credible and circumstantial it was. Poor old Papa. Well I'll probably read it in her autobiography[2] that you had a piece about in N. Yorker. I never cared a damn about what she did in or out of bed and I liked her very damned much and she liked me. But when the menopause hit her she got awfully damned patriotic about sex. The first stage was that nobody was any good that wasn't that way. The second was that anybody that was that way was good. The third was that anybody that was any good must be that way. Patriotism is a hell of a vice. Mabel Dodge is a hell of a rival. America's legendary women sweepstakes.

The only way, I suppose, is to find out what women are going to write memoirs and try to get them with child. The hell of that is that the women that I feel, shall we say, drawn to don't write their memoirs. It is a big mistake to ever meet a legendary woman indoors. Some misinterpretation will be placed on anything you do. Add Maxims for a son— Never encounter a legendary woman anywhere except in the open and then bring your own witnesses.

No one ever got anything out of a legendary woman in the end. I never met a nicer or more flutter brained legendary woman, nor a prettier one in my life than Margaret Anderson and how did it all turn out.[3] Poor old papa was a white rabbit with pink eyes who wandered around his pink rabbit eyes dull with pain saying have you seen so and so where's so and so? While some mysterious woman that I'm sure I hadn't asked refused to give up the best years of her life to me. Who the hell was that? And all my interest in the old bull ring was simulated (merely kicking up his rabbit hind legs). By jeesus I simulated a pretty good book out of it then.

If you didn't love to box and that was all simulation how long would you keep on after you had been dumped on the floor a few times? It's 18 years since I was first knocked down. Last year spent 105 days in the gulf stream. Feigning an interest in the gulfstream now to mask his other pursuits.

By jeesus will write my own memoirs sometime when I can't write anything else. And they will be funny and accurate and not out to prove a bloody thing.

Big promises by Hem. No. By God I will. I wish we could see you, Janet. Anyway will you forgive me for waiting so long to answer your letter and write me when you get this? I'll even put in news to try to get a letter quicker.

Was in N.Y. Benchley has new woman. Terrible. Dotty [Parker] very pretty. Mac Lain out. [Donald Ogden] Stewart back from coast buying everybody mink coats and referring [to] Irving Thalberg as the genius of the age. Dos Passos broke. Hopes go Spain with us. Who else do you know that I know? Phil Barry fat and dumb. Parky died. Mac Gregor that works for Robert had a stroke. Scott become communist (just too late). Came in to N.Y. and told Dos he was in touch with communists in Baltimore. This over phone. I told Dos he will now go back to Baltimore and tell the communists he went to N.Y. and got in touch with Dos Passos. I'm in touch with you I hope Miss Flanner.

Well there is getting to be quantity in this letter even if no bloody quality.

You were very good to me to write me what you did about the book. If now you don't like it anymore don't be embarrassed. That's all right. It was very good that you liked it as much as you liked it when you wrote.

I never read any of your books, Madam, but I like you very much.

PUL   Hem

1. Janet Flanner (1892–1978), born in Indianapolis, spent much of her life in Paris, serving for nearly fifty years as foreign correspondent for the *New Yorker* under the pen name Genêt. In a letter of 27 December 1966 to Carlos Baker she recalled her long friendship with EH as having begun in the early 1920s in Paris. 2. *The Autobiography of Alice B. Toklas* (1933), in which EH is accused of cowardice and other faults. 3. Margaret Anderson, co-editor of the *Little Review* (1922–1929), satirized EH in her autobiography, *My Thirty Years' War* (1930).

To JOHN DOS PASSOS, Havana, *c.* 15 May 1933

Dear Dos:

Damned glad your coming along. That's a hell of a disease and had me spooked—consulted Black's Med. Dictionary at once and would have come up to Baltimore if hadn't heard you were better. Did you run any of that 106° fever?[1]

Enclosed the bludy grand [$1,000]. Listen this G is off the record. Uncle Gus gave me some stock to use to make the African trip. I cashed this out of that. There's plenty to go to Africa still and even come back from Africa. I couldn't make a trip to Coney Island let alone Africa with you, you ignorant Portuguese having some lousy disease that swells the hands and saps the brain. So cash this before I change it into pennies and pelt you publicly as a hypochondriac—this won't keep you from giving the pooblishers hell—nor anything else—just make it simpler to turn around—you can pay a few creditors and re-establish their borrow-ability. Hope to christ I haven't been intrusive. But I was spooked about you. Didn't mean to be [Don] Stewart mink coating a Pal.

Caught 2 damned fine marlin. They bit like grunts. Saw 20 yesterday. We go to Mariel Cabañas Bahia Honda on Tuesday.

Wish to hell you and Katey could come down—come in June and you can still get to Pamplona—a boat from here to Vigo—see Santiago de Compostella—get train Coruña—Madrid—train to Pamplona. Buy your Kilometrico [mileage ticket] in Vigo.

You can get a car cheap to drive to Santiago from Vigo—can drive to Noya too—use the damned $ before it's worthless.

Must close to get this off on the plane.

You are sound on Proust. We should be here another month anyway—
am trying to get title for book of stories—lousy hard. Wish I could show
them to you. Have some good ones.

Will lay off Marlin when moon goes bad and write some more. They
run on the filling moon. Current drops off in declining moon—end of
declining moon makes all fish sick—like women—they won't eat—women
will however.

Learning a lot. Some of it true. Get well Dos. Love to Stut.

Pauline is writing too. Sends much love.

UVA   Hem

1. Dos Passos had been hospitalized in Baltimore with rheumatic fever.

To ARNOLD GINGRICH, Havana, 24 May 1933

Dear Mr. Gingritch:

I'll drop the Mr. if it means anything to you but have a strong tendency
to Mr. anyone that I do not know well personally and prefer to be mis-
tered in turn. This may be a hangover from different times or it may be
a protest against the Ernie, Spike, Ray, Bill etc-ing of Hearst organization
and the Horace, Tommy, Max, Whitney-ing of Publishing. I remember
Max Perkins, of whom I am very fond, asking me, in a letter, when I
would stop calling him Mr. Perkins. I am very fond of him, really, but
wrote him that it would cost me at least $10,000 to stop calling him Mr.
—(it has) and I did. In dealing with anyone in business when you become pals they can always invoke the necessities of business vs. your
own needs while you must do things because you are a friend.

There is no one finer than Max and this anecdote has no point except
to illustrate the professionals' reluctance to become a friend to either
his employer or his audience.

This does not apply to you. You are a damned intelligent (unpaid)
critic. Except that you are an employer since you have bought two pieces
of work from me. You don't have to tell me that title turned out lousily—
the reason it did was them holding forms for the title so they got an
unsuccessful headline instead of a title—it won't be called that in the
book.

If you want to see my correspondence with Cape on that bollixing
will send it to you if I ever get a secretary long enough to copy it. It
might amuse you.

Esquire sounds bad to me (as title). But maybe we will be inflated into a bullshit enough feeling of prosperity for it to go by then. In prosperous times you cannot be too snobbish. Now it sounds very sour.

If you ask if I have anything better—I haven't.

Would have written long ago—especially to thank you for those two damned fine pair of slacks. They are very good and cool as well. Am too damned tired at night to do more than stagger into bed. Later the night picks up and there is a certain amount of very interesting study of politics etc. But no letter writing. I will write you a damned good Cuban Letter though.

Have caught 29 Marlin Swordfish—came 3 weeks too early. They ran late this year—caught 7 last Saturday (believe a record for one rod fishing), 3 Sunday, 3 Monday, 4 Tuesday—stayed in bed today with a hell of a throat. We have a good chance to get a world's record fish—the hell with the record but by God you ought to see what a fish that size is like in the air. They move like a destroyer in the water. I have kept a day by day log book last year and this.

Will be here another month. Mailed your check to my £ account when I saw inflation close. Will spend the £'s in pesetas in Spain. We have booked passage from here on August 7. Dos Passos was very sick. He wrote me he had to return a check to you as he was too sick to do the piece. He sailed for Antibes to convalesce with friends of ours May 25.

You could reach him care Gerald Murphy, Villa America, Cap D'Antibes (A.M.).

We will spend part of August and part of September in Spain together.

I will get you some good pictures. Hard to get any good ones with me in them as I do the camera work with old 4 x 5 Graflex that everyone else buggars up. Will arrange to get some though.

Am down to 185. Feel damned well if I hadn't this throat—sweat in the wind fighting a fish—then ran out of changes of clothes.

I haven't your last two letters here and I know there are things would want to reply to—about the shirt—if you sent it to Key West my wife will bring it over when she comes over here end of next week—will appreciate it. Is there anything you would like from Cuba?

PH. PUL   [Ernest Hemingway]

To HENRY STRATER, Havana, 27 May 1933

Dear Mike:

I felt so damned bad about your news that couldn't write. Then came over here and too dead tired at night to write. That is rotten luck about

Maggie being so ill. I believe you'll be better out of N.Y. though. It will be rotten to lose your shooting club. Still you should have good shooting wherever you go. I wish to Christ you were here. Have been fishing alone 3 weeks. Haven't gone a day for 3 weeks without a Marlin. Have 34 now—caught seven in one day—hooked and fought them alone. Wonderful sport but you feel like hell not to have anyone to share it with—can't take movies even—one jumped 37 times.

We will get a *very* big one yet.

How is Maggie and how are you? I know that sinus is hell. Pauline had it with perfect hell for 3 months but *cured* it by taking quinine. Dries it up—you have to take it in 5 grain doses—all you can take of them.

Will your new plans keep you from going to Africa? You sounded as though you proposed retirement from the world. Plan to sail (have booked passage) on Reina de la Pacifica August 7th from here to Spain— 3 to 5 weeks in Spain and sail for Africa from Marseilles. You are invited and could not be more welcome. Have to go while Dollar still worth something. Hope inflation sells snuff. It will ruin what savings I have made.

However have guns, tackle, good house in K.W., pictures, books—what the hell.

Let me know about Africa will you? I will cable Klein I think. Didn't you think he shaped up as well as any? Charles will go. Haven't heard a word from Archie since he went to Europe. He was coming down here.

In one day saw 100 Marlin—18 strikes—Bumby 3—Josie [Russell] 5— me 10 and I hooked and landed 7—all over 7 feet—current is running like a millrace—about 6½ to 7 miles an hour. Steady East trade wind. Big fish due first and middle of next month—they should run as thick as these 60–90 lb fish.

Dos was awfully sick with rheumatic fever. I was writing to him all the time and that's why didn't write you. He just got out of hospital and sailed 25th to recuperate with the Murphys at Antibes—will see him in Spain.

Feel awfully bad not to have written before—address here at hotel. We all felt frightfully at Key West to hear Maggie was feeling so bad. It's an awful shame. I do hope she is better.

Much love to her—
Best to you always—
Hem

PUL

To ARNOLD GINGRICH, Havana, 7 June 1933

Dear Mr. Gingritch:

Thanks for your letter and for sending the shirt. My wife came over earlier than she expected but she will bring it when she comes again next week. It should be in Key West now.

Have 39 Marlin swordfish now. Have all the dope for the Cuban letter and will write it the first day that the wind is bad for fishing.

We sail from *here* Aug. 7 on Reina de la Pacifica—she doesn't go to N.Y.

Glad you fixed up about Dos. He's been sick as hell.

The title I have for the book is Winner Take Nothing.

"Unlike all other forms of lutte or combat the conditions are that the winner shall take nothing; neither his ease, nor his pleasure, nor any notions of glory; nor, if he win far enough, shall there be any reward within himself."

(This in italics quotation)

If you want to do me a favor will you wire me collect what you think of it as a title—and what you think of the quotation. There are 13 stories. The title is not meant to be tricky—any more than Men Without Women was. It has the same sort of application to the contents.

The stories are—so far—The Light of the World (a very fine story about whores—as good or better a story about whores than Maison Tellier [of Maupassant]); After the Storm (you've read); Sea Change (you've read); The Mother of a Queen (about Ortiz the bullfighter).

What the hell—no need to list them all—you'll see them soon enough. I am going to include Natural History of the Dead as it is a story and some people might not have had 3.50 to read it in the other book [*Death in the Afternoon*].

However I wish you would wire me about title. Have no one to show it to here. Pauline, my wife, likes it but we have both been wrong before. If it isn't cheap it's goddamned good.

PH. PUL   [Ernest Hemingway]

To MAXWELL PERKINS, Havana, 13 June 1933

Dear Max:

Thanks for your wire. Sorry I could not send the title sooner but did not have it any sooner. Now you can make up the dummy with that title.

Would it be any help to you if I sent the 12 stories that I have ready—for you to set up and follow with the other two I am working on. Finished 24 page story yesterday. Have been waking at 3 *am* working early in the cool and going out in the boat in the afternoon. Have had a fine period of working. Yesterday wrote until noon—went out at 12.45 and caught two swordfish in the afternoon. I wish you could come down. Have caught 42—have a world's record of 7 in one day—believe it's record anyway. Having it looked up. Pauline comes over every week. She is fixing up the place where I work in Key West—making it about twice as big and insulating roof etc so it will be cool in hot weather.

Will you please send me a contract for the book, specifying the amount of the advance (one thousand is paid) 6000 dollars. Three on receipt of Mss., three more before publication.

[Max] Eastman has given me a new slant on my so-called friends in N.Y. If he ever gets a solvent publisher to publish that libel between covers it will cost the publisher plenty of money and Eastman will go to jail. Moe Speiser will see to that. I could use some of that dough.[1]

If I ever see him anywhere or anytime, now or in the future I will get my own redress myself.

I am tempted never to publish another damned thing. The swine aren't worth writing for. I swear to christ they're not. Every phase of the whole racket is so disgusting that it makes you feel like vomiting. Every word I wrote about the Spanish fighting bull was absolutely true and result of long and careful and exhaustive observation. Then they pay Eastman, who knows nothing about it, to say I write sentimental nonsense. He *really* knows how bulls are. They are like this—(he explains). I am like this—etc. (he explains). I have seen 50 bulls do what that fool says from his ignorance—no bull can do. It's too disgusting to write about.

And it is a commonplace that I lack confidence that I am a man—what shit. And I'm supposed to go around with your good friends spreading that behind my back away with it. Mr. [Kyle] Crichton—Mr. Eastman etc. why don't you give them space to write it in the magazine? Whenever and wherever I meet any one of them their mouths will make a funny noise when they ever try to say it again after I get through working over them. Mr. Crichton—the brave man who tells everybody things to their faces—we'll see.

They're a nice lot—the professional male beauties of other years—Max Eastman—a groper in sex (with the hands I mean), a traitor in politics and—hell I won't waste it on them.

It certainly is damned fine to have friends. They hear you are out of the country and they open up.

Good. Bring on some more friends. I'll be a long way out of the country and they will all get very brave and say everything they wish were true—then I'll be back and we will see what will happen.

You see what they can't get over is (1) that I *am* a man (2) that I can beat the shit out of any of them (3) that I can write. The last hurts them the worst. But they don't like any of it. But Papa will make them like it.

Best to you

PUL   Ernest

1. EH's response to Eastman's "Bull in the Afternoon," *New Republic* 75 (7 June 1933): 94–97. See Carlos Baker, *Ernest Hemingway: A Life Story* (New York: 1969), pp. 241–42, 606–7.

To MAXWELL PERKINS, Key West, 26 July 1933

Dear Max:

Got back here July 20 and have been cleaning up getting ready to leave, waiting for proof or word from you and winding up affairs. Have everything pretty well cleared now and will start re-writing The Tomb of My Grandfather[1] today.

We leave here August 4th and Havana August 7th on Reina de la Pacifica of Royal Mail line for Santander. Address in Spain will be Hotel Biarritz, Calle Victoria, 2, Madrid, Spain. General european address Guaranty Trust Co. of N.Y., 4 Place de la Concorde, Paris.

Will be in Spain half of August and all of September. Maybe October. Will leave for Africa in November. This gives more time to work before start out again and time to get proofs all fixed up both with you and in England.

Poor old Gertrude Stein. Did you read the August Atlantic?[2] She's finally found a writer she can love and not be jealous of—the real american writer—Bromfield. It's damned wonderful how the story ends. She lost all sense of taste when she had the menopause. Was really an extraordinary business. Suddenly she couldn't tell a good picture from a bad one, a good writer from a bad one, it all went phtt.

Poor old Hem the fragile one. 99 days in the sun on the gulf stream. 54 swordfish. Seven in one day. A 468 pounder in 65 minutes, alone, no help except them holding me around the waist and pouring buckets of water on my head. Two hours and 20 minutes of straight hell with another. A 343 pounder that jumped 44 times, hooked in the bill. I killed him in an hour and forty five minutes. Poor fragile old Hem posing as a fisherman again. Weigh 187 lbs. Down from 211.

I'm going to write damned good memoirs when I write them because I'm jealous of no one, have a rat trap memory and the documents. Have plenty to write first though.

I imagine you are in more or less of a stew about certain words but tell me what you can and can't do and we will work it out. I'm not the little boy writing them on the wall to be smart. If I can make the effect without the word will always do so but sometimes can't. Also it is good for the language to restore its life that they bleed out of it. That is very important.

Anyway would like to hear from you.

Oh yes. Will you please ask that 12 copies of Death In The Afternoon be sent to me at Hotel Biarritz, Calle Victoria 2, Madrid, Spain sending them in four packages of three each, marked books only and open for inspection? I will have to give them away and it will break me to buy them over there. These can be charged to me with postage and garnisheed from my royalties when and if due.

Yours always
Ernest

PUL

1. Retitled "Fathers and Sons," this became the final story in *Winner Take Nothing*. 2. *The Autobiography of Alice B. Toklas* was being serialized in the *Atlantic Monthly*.

To MRS. PAUL PFEIFFER, Madrid, 16 October 1933

Dear Mother and All:

The date at the head of this letter is a shameful time to thank you and Pauline's father for a birthday present received the twenty first of July.

That is why I haven't written. There was so much happening then that I planned to write to thank you from the boat. Then after the boat it was so late that I was ashamed to write.

Yesterday I realized that if I didn't write it would pretty soon be Easter—so here goes.

Thank you very, very much, both you and Pauline's father for the present. I appreciated it very much and am going to spend it in Africa.

Jinny left here not quite a week ago for Paris and the clothes question. It seems you can't get properly clothed in under a month and she plans to leave in just about a month for N.Y. on that paragon of ocean liners the Ilschenstein of the Bernstein line. You may have heard her speak of this vessell. Jin was in good health and spirits when she left but she is worried about those stomach attacks. They come about every ten days now; more often than they used to; but are of shorter duration. She is going to see a doctor in Paris that cured me of both kidney and liver complaints (plenty of complaints). If that one is no good she is going to write out all her symptoms and case history for me to send to Dr. [Logan] Clendenning in K.C. and ask him to recommend a good man in N.Y. or Chicago that she can see on the way home.

Pauline was in fine spirits and very good health and looking splendid. I hope to join her in Paris in a little less than a week. Patrick has gained three pounds and is plump and brown and husky looking Jinny writes. I am going to pick him up at Bordea[u]x and take him on to Paris. A letter from Ada [nurse] says Gregory is very fine and they are happy and contented. Bumby is in school again.

I suppose Pauline and Jinny have written you about their plans so won't go into them.

Have been working at a heavy clip ever since we got here. Found my proofs here, fixed them up. Then edited, cut, and re-wrote dialogue of a 422 page translation of a Spanish novel Sidney Franklin has done for Scribner's. Was a rather hard job as the book is trashy and I had to take attitude that here was a bad book I had written; now go over it and see if you can make it a good one. At same time did not change any of its style. The day I finished that was so sick of trash that decided to write a story to rinse my mouth out and started one that ran to over 100 pages of manuscript.[1] Pauline thought it was a fine story and Jinny wouldn't believe it wasn't true. Must go over it and re-write it when we get to Paris. It is a third as long as the average novel. It may be a very good story. Is almost entirely action and takes place in Cuba and on the sea. Plenty of action. It is exactly the story that this present book needs i.e. Winner Take Nothing. But it will be as well or better in another book. You can't very well put a story that you know will sell like hotcakes in a book called Winner Take Nothing.

I don't expect anybody to like the present book of stories and don't think you have to make an effort to—or even be polite about them. I am trying to make, before I get through, a picture of the whole world—or as much of it as I have seen. Boiling it down always, rather than spreading it out thin. These stories are mostly about things and people that people won't care about—or will actively dislike. All right. Sooner or later as the wheel keeps turning I will have ones that they *will* like.

Will you tell Virginia's father that I have been cashing Virginia's checks for her since she has no account in any bank over here. That is why they are made out to me. I tried to get her not to turn all her dollars into francs at one time but she was worried at seeing the dollar fall and wanted to take what she believed was her loss and stop worrying. Now the dollar is up a little again.

I understand how people who owe money are enthusiastic for inflation. Anyone who has always paid their debts and saved what is supposed to be honest money is not so enthusiastic. Once it starts the thing to do is to owe all you can. I lived through it in three countries over a period of ten years and I know exactly how it works, what the various steps are and what it leads to. So far I have made money on it and anyone having followed my advice would have made a great deal of money. But I hate it for its fundamental dishonesty and for the fact that in the end it does nothing good. It is not just because Pauline has a small fixed income that I hate it.

I hate Hitler because he is working for one thing: war. He says one thing with his mouth and does another with his hands. War is the health of the State and anyone with his conception of the state has to have war or the threat of war to keep it going.

Spain is in what is called a state of confusion. All the idealists now in power have their fingers in the pie and they have gotten down to where the plums are pretty small. When they run out of pie there will be another revolution.

Don't worry about Pauline in Africa. I will take good care of her. Patrick is coming back with Jinny, will meet Ada and Gregory in N.Y. and go down to K.W. with them. My sister Ursula, my best sister, is going to live there with her little girl while we are gone.

Don't know when we will get back exactly.

Tell Karl I will certainly miss the first Mannerhouse Quail season with him this fall. Give him and Matilda my very best regards. I certainly had a fine time with Karl in Havana.

Charles Thompson cabled us that our home was all right after the storm. No damage. But poor old Bra lost his boat. That is pretty tough because a man's boat is his living.

Sidney Franklin, the bull fighter, is out of the hospital here finally after a very serious operation on that three year old horn wound. They had to cut out three inches of his lower intestine. I stayed with him for the operation etc. and he was pretty bad for a while but seems perfectly o.k. now.

What with Mrs. [Jane] Mason breaking her back in that accident with the children along last May and this of Sidney now have seen a lot of hospitals this year. It is amazing though how much easier we put up with the troubles of our friends than our own troubles. I suppose that is how a man can govern a country and still sleep nights.

I know there is a lot I should have written but will stop now and then write oftener.

I'll send you an African address as soon as we know it. You can get a letter out there in eight days from London if you send it by air-mail.

Will you tell Karl and Matilda that this is an off year on Christmas presents. For them not to send us anything. We don't know where we'll be Christmas.

I'm sorry this isn't a better letter, Mother. It's gloomy here this afternoon with Pauline gone but I'll see her the end of the week. Am waiting for my proofs, final ones, that have been sent here so that I can cable an o.k. to Scribner's.

Best love to all and a fine Thanksgiving day to you.

Yours always—

PUL Ernest

1. The first Harry Morgan story, "One Trip Across," *Cosmopolitan* 96 (April 1934).

To MAXWELL PERKINS, Paris, 16 November 1933

Dear Max:

Thanks for your two cables—of a week and two weeks ago and your letter of Nov. 6 enclosing some of the reviews [of *Winner Take Nothing*]. I cabled you yesterday because I had been seeing the N.Y.Times, Herald Tribune and Sat Review of Lit and they all were full of ads of a book of stories by Dotty Parker but nothing about this book. There was an ad in Sunday Times and I believe Daily Times the week the book came out. Then nothing. No follow up at all. Saw no mention of book in Sunday Herald Trib in number it was reviewed in. An ad in with your fall list in the week after. Believe there was an ad in Herald Trib the day it came out. The advertizing is your business—not mine. But if a publisher seems to give no importance to a book and makes no Boom Ha Ha the public takes the cue from the publisher very quickly.

One of the reasons I always stuck by you (in a commercial way) was because you kept on pushing The Sun Also Rises through a terrificly slow start—and one of the things I did not care much about was the way after a wonderful start they dropped Death In The Afternoon absolutely cold. You know yourself.

This happens to be a book *you* have to do a little work to push. But in the end it doesn't do anyone any particular harm to publish literature once in a while. Especially as I have always paid my way.

You mention a review by Soskins in your letter but you didn't send it.

Also I have never had any August royalty reports—nor any accounting since I saw you in N.Y. (May have had a royalty report in the Spring.) Will you please send them.

The bird, when he labelled me as approaching middle age was trying to get rid of me that way—others having failed. So the advertizing department siezes on that to advertize the book by. If I write about *any-body*—automatically they label that character as me. When I write about somebody that can't possibly be me—as in After The Storm, that unfortunate convert to Economics religion Mr. Chamberlain says it is unusually imaginative or more imaginative than anything I've attempted. What shit.

When does middle age commence? That story—Wine of Wyoming is nothing but straight reporting of what [I] heard and saw when was finishing A Farewell To Arms out in Sheridan and Big Horn. How old was I then? That was 1928 and I was just 30 [29] years old while I was out there. Yet that bird says it is about middle aged people because *he himself* is middle-aged. I was 17 [18] when first went to the war. (This for your own information.) I write some stories absolutely as they happen i.e. Wine of Wyoming—the letter one ["One Reader Writes"], A Day's Wait, and another ["After the Storm"] word for word as it happened to Bra, The Mother of a Queen, Gambler, Nun, Radio; After The Storm (Chamberlain found that more imaginative than the others), others I invent completely—Killers, Hills Like White Elephants, The Undefeated, Fifty Grand, Sea Change, A Simple Enquiry. *Nobody* can tell which ones I make up completely.

The point is I *want* them all to sound as though they really happened. Then when I succeed those poor dumb pricks say they are all just skillful reporting.

I invented every word and every incident of A Farewell to Arms except possibly 3 or 4 incidents. All the best part is invented. 95 per cent of The Sun Also was pure imagination. I took real people in that one and I controlled what they did. I made it all up.

A fool like [H. S.] Canby thinks I'm a reporter—I'm a reporter *and an imaginative writer* and I can still imagine plenty and there will be stories to write *as they happened* as long as I live. Also I happen to be 35 [34] years old and the last two stories I wrote in Havana were the best in the book—and this 15,000 word one is better than either of them, several miles better. So if you let all the people who want me over with kid you into believing I'm through—or let the business office start to lay off me as a bad bet—you will be making a very considerable mistake because I haven't started to write yet (won't ever write you this again).

I can't write better stories than some that I have written—what Mr. Fadiman asks for—because you can't write any better stories than those —and nobody else can. But every once in a long while I can write one as good—and *all the time* I can write better stories than anybody else writing. But they want *better* ones and as good as *anyone ever* wrote. God damn it there can't be better ones. The one they pick out as "classic" Hills Like White Elephants not one damn critic thought *anything* of when it came out. I always knew how good it was but I'll be goddamned if I like to have to say how good my stuff is in order to give the business office confidence enough to advertize it after they have read an unfavorable review and think I'm through.

So I won't. Ever again. Will do something else.

Will you please, for God's sake, because this is <u>very</u> <u>important</u> have a statement sent to me of all money paid me in 1933—in any form—and give the income tax people the same amount or total you send me when you report it to them. Please send this on January First or whenever you know everything paid me in 1933—absolutely *as soon as possible.* (I will not ask for any more this year for anything.) Please send this statement to the Guaranty Trust Co. of N.Y., 4 Place de la Concorde, Paris and mark the envelope in large letters—Please Forward By Air Mail. They will send it out to Tanganyika by Imperial Airways and I will be able to prepare my income tax report.

I wanted to have some idea before I left and wrote about it from Spain but have heard nothing.

This seems to be all.

Does it seem of any significance to you that they all say there are 3 really good stories and nearly all pick 3 different ones? That Mr. Harry Hansen who doesn't understand these didn't understand A Farewell To Arms when it came out. Panned it. Now thinks it great novel etc. Oh hell —why go on. Why write as far as that goes? Because I have to.

If Cosmopolitan send this long story ["One Trip Across"] back to you, *Please hold it for my instructions.*

So long, Max. I hope you're fine and haven't too many family worries. We sail on next Wed. This is Friday. Too many things to do.

Yours always,

PUL

Ernest

To PATRICK HEMINGWAY, at sea,[1] 2 December 1933

Dear Old Mex:[2]

Well here we are almost at the southern end of the Red Sea. Tomorrow we will be in the Indian Ocean. The weather is just like Key West on a nice day in winter. Yesterday we saw a big school of big porpoises and many schools of small porpoises.

It was cold and rainy all the way down to Egypt. Then it was hot and fine. Coming through the Suez canal we went right through the desert. We saw lots of Palm trees and Australian pines (like in our yard) whenever there was water. But the rest was mountains and hills and plains of sand. We saw a lot of camels and a soldier riding on a camel made it trot alongside the ship almost as fast as the ship could go. In the canal you have to stop and tie up to the side sometimes to let other ships go by. You would have liked to see the other ship go by and to see the desert. The only birds we saw were some snipe and quite a lot of hawks and a few cormorants and one old blue crane.

I miss you, old Mex, and will be glad to see you again. Will have plenty of good stories to tell you when we come back.

When you get down to Key West remember me to Captain Bra and Mr. Sully [J. B. Sullivan]. Give my best to everybody in Piggott.

Go easy on the beer and lay off the hard liquor until I get back.

Don't forget to blow your nose and turn around three times before you go to bed.

Your affectionate papa,
Papa

PUL

1. On board *General Metzinger*, Messageries Maritimes. 2. Patrick, nicknamed the Mexican Mouse, was then five years old.

To ARNOLD GINGRICH, Nairobi, Kenya, 18 January 1934

Dear Arnold:

That's to show I trust you.

Sorry this is late. Got sick as hell, passed about quart of blood a day. Thought it must be piles because my ass hurt so and didn't really feel bad until the end. But no pep to write. Hunted every day but 2 with it. Will be O.K. in 4 days now but so full of emetine [dysentery remedy] I can't think properly.

One of Gertrude's feathered friends told her Papa was always breaking things, getting sick etc. But wonder what would happen to G. and
friends if they went where papa goes and did what papa does.

Your 2nd No. and letter of [blank] received. I will write you another
letter as soon as get some time at camp and get head in shape.

Will do you 12 [articles] a year if you want. When get back to Key
West will do 3 or 4 so you will have some ahead and not have to worry.
Will try to make up then the difficulty I put you through now.

2nd Number looks damned fine. Keep it up.

I recommended young Alfred Vanderbilt to you because if he *could*
write his name and knowledge (he *really* knows racing and horses)
would be damned valuable to your paper. He is ambitious to do something on his own and is a level headed little squirt. Very tight, I like
him. Lots of people have tried to buy his name or stuff but he no sell.

We go down to an island off Lamu at mouth of Tana river to fish swordfish and giant sailfish (reported to run to 18 feet) and I will have plenty
of good stuff for you. Go there Feb. 20.

I'm sorry I can't give you better service on these letters but believe
I had this damn dysentery when I hit here. Picked it up in Port Said I
believe and tried to write but couldn't make head go. Otherwise would
have written you some to fill in. Started 4. Have 1½ done.

Will write good stuff from Key West.

Killed my 2 buffalo with the 30-06 Springfield—also all lions. Got
some beauties and some wonderful heads. Do you want anything from
here?

I'm sorry if you thought I was unreasonable or double Xing. It was
the cable that confused me.

Slug this enclosed letter anything you like with sub-head of A Tanganyika Letter. Use these pics if you want. The lion ones are damned
good. I took it with 4x5 Graflex at about 8 to 10 yards. 1/50th—stop
No. 8.

Yours always
Ernest Hemingway

No one translates French worse than Ernest Boyd except Lewis Galantiere. Get Malcolm Cowley to translate your French.

Why not write Evan Shipman, 19 Beekman Place, for a story or article.

Your jig cartoonist-artist is <u>damn</u> good. Absolutely first rate.

PH. PUL

To ARNOLD GINGRICH, Key West, 25 May 1934

Dear Mr. G:

Glad you had a good vacation at Bermuda. Would be glad to fish there sometime. Practical way would be to have the Pilar[1] and all equipment put on a steamer for there from Miami. But they would have to arrange everything. Papa is broke—also couldn't do it now. But Bermuda will probably be there for some time.

Better type this to try and make a little on the time. Finished a first draft of the August piece last Sunday. This is Friday. Will re-write it tomorrow and mail it to you tomorrow or Sunday—possibly Monday but not later. That will be the 28th as latest mailing date so you can count on it for June 1st. It seems to be about fish and is I'm afraid a little bit scientific. Will try to ease off on the science and let a good gust of shit blow over it in the re-writing.

Am on the 59th page of a long story in which am very interested. Looks as though it would be considerably longer.

The boat [*Pilar*] is marvelous. Wheeler, 38 footer, cut down to my design. 75 horse Chrystler and a 40 h. Lycoming. Low stern for fishing. Fish well, 300 gal gas tanks. 100 gal water. Sleeps six in cabin and two in cockpit. Can turn on its own tail burns less than three gals an hour trolling and four at cruising speed with the big engine. Will do sixteen with the two motors. The little one will do five hooked up.

And incidentally we caught, day before yest, what I hope is the Atlantic record for sailfish—going out at 2.30 from here after a big morning's work. Weighed 119 ½ lbs. 9 feet and ¾ inch long. 35 inches girth. I've never seen nor heard of a sailfish in the atlantic over 100 lbs. The hell of it is he was hooked by a Jesuit priest who doesn't want his name in the papers as he was supposed to be doing something else here beside fish. He had just fought and lost a sailfish taken by a shark after 14 jumps. He had just put out and hooked this one. His left arm has arthritis and was in bad shape from the first fish so he turned this one over to me after one jump. I had him 44 minutes. I couldn't believe any sailfish could pull and so thought he must be foul hooked. He was so beautifully proportioned he didn't show his weight.

I won't claim him because I didn't hook him so am trying to get Father Mac Grath to claim him. Anyway will enter him for the Atlantic record as a fish. That is a sailfish, Bo. One of fifty pounds is a good one. Seventy five is a hell of a fine one and I've never heard of one that was a hundred. This baby was 119 ½ on tested scales before eight witnesses four hours after he was caught.

Evening is the time to catch the big ones. Just before the sun goes down. We got one 61 the day before after six o'clock. Ordinarily the party boats leave the gulf stream just before the big sailfish start to bite.

Thought I'd let you know there was a piece and that it was a fishy rather than a shooty.

Also you understand that accepting that advance on those pieces does not commit me to accept the same price for any of the articles or release you from the obligation to pay me more as soon as the magazine is making money.

So long Mr. G., Major G., Col. G. Come on down here sometime and we will make you an Admiral.

I'll lay you ten dollars on whatever the odds are at the morning of the fight on Jimmy Mc Larnin to win.

Am working hard. Went to Cuba for May day festivalities with Dos. Fished a couple of days. They're not running yet. I won't go again until July probably—too much work to do here and want them to start then stick with them all July, August etc.

Can't you get any stories from young guys about anything but guys that are supposed to be dead and are and aren't in varying combinations. That has gotten to be a bad formula awfully quickly.

If you ever see E. Simms Campbell [cartoonist] tell him from Papa that he is very very good but any guy as smart as he is knows how good he is.

Yours always

PH. PUL   Ernest Hemingway

1. The cabin cruiser *Pilar*, FOB Miami 9 May 1934, cost $7,500. Gingrich of *Esquire* advanced EH $3,000 against future *Esquire* articles so that he could make the down payment.

To WALDO PEIRCE, Key West, *c*. 26 May 1934

Dear Waldo:

The cuatro tiempos de la corrida de tiburones [four seasons of the running of the sharks][1] were damned fine. Thank you very much bo. They're swell.

How are you now—and all the outfit? It made me feel damned good to see you all so fine in N.Y. And Becky too. She's a lovely kid.

Everything very quiet here now. The visiting fire-women went. Damned nice women. Then A. Mac Leish came down. He's gotten, between ourselves and no to digas a otra gente [not for others] a goddamned bore.

Righteous, fussy, and a bloody bore. Strange mixture of peurility and senility. What the hell do American writers turn into? They write a poem advising poets to stay out of politics then get into politics as fast as they can. It's not as human as writing an epic against picking the nose and then being the great nose picker of all time. It's too bloody pompous. I shouldn't write this. So forget it. But he kept asking for it and asking for it. I only like the people I like. Not the bastards that like me. I wouldn't want to hurt his bloody feelings for anything. So tear this part out and burn it.[2]

Weather has been pleasant. Hot but not too hot and a good breeze. Blowing a hell of a breeze now from the Southwest.

The other evening we caught a sailfish 119 ½ lbs. Right where you and I caught that first one—remember? Must be about the same time of year too. The damned Atlantic record was 108 lbs. and they've been fishing them for a long time so you can see it's a pretty good fish. I'm going to send it to Fred Parke I think. If do, go over and take a look, will you?

The boat is a hell of a lot of fun. Keep every thing on board and don't have to come in from the gulf until [two words illegible].

Been working hard on a long story. Have about sixty pages done. Pauline is going up to Piggott to see her folks for a couple of weeks then coming back. Bumby will be coming down as soon as school is out. Patrick is getting to be a good kid. Fishes out in the boat and brings beer etc. Very serious fisherman. Gregory is too big and dopy yet to tell anything about.

This house is swell and cool. Wish we could have a drink together. Let me know when you run out of segars.

Love to all your outfit.

tu amigo que te quieres
Ernesto

COLBY

1. A picture painted by Peirce, who often made such generous gifts. 2. EH's words were the result of a recent quarrel with Mac Leish, which broke out after an abortive trip to Dry Tortugas with Mike Strater and Uncle Gus Pfeiffer. "He was fed up with the world and I was fed up with him," wrote Mac Leish. "It was my fault as much as his. But . . . it was inevitable: we never could have gone on as close friends." (Mac Leish to Carlos Baker, 31 January 1965.)

To F. SCOTT FITZGERALD, Key West, 28 May 1934

Dear Scott:

I liked it and I didn't like it [*Tender Is the Night*]. It started off with that marvelous description of Sara and Gerald (goddamn it Dos took it with him so I can't refer to it. So if I make any mistakes—). Then you started fooling with them, making them come from things they didn't come from, changing them into other people and you can't do that, Scott. If you take real people and write about them you cannot give them other parents than they have (they are made by their parents and what happens to them) you cannot make them do anything they would not do. You can take you or me or Zelda or Pauline or Hadley or Sara or Gerald but you have to keep them the same and you can only make them do what they would do. You can't make one be another. Invention is the finest thing but you cannot invent anything that would not actually happen.

That is what we are supposed to do when we are at our best—make it all up—but make it up so truly that later it will happen that way.

Goddamn it you took liberties with peoples' pasts and futures that produced not people but damned marvellously faked case histories. You, who can write better than anybody can, who are so lousy with talent that you have to—the hell with it. Scott for gods sake write and write truly no matter who or what it hurts but do not make these silly compromises. You could write a fine book about Gerald and Sara for instance if you knew enough about them and they would not have any feeling, except passing, if it were true.

There were wonderful places and nobody else nor none of the boys can write a good one half as good reading as one that doesn't come out by you, but you cheated too damned much in this one. And you don't need to.

In the first place I've always claimed that you can't think. All right, we'll admit you can think. But say you couldn't think; then you ought to write, invent, out of what you know and keep the people's antecedants straight. Second place, a long time ago you stopped listening except to the answers to your own questions. You had good stuff in too that it didn't need. That's what dries a writer up (we all dry up. That's no insult to you in person) not listening. That is where it all comes from. Seeing, listening. You see well enough. But you stop listening.

It's a lot better than I say. But it's not as good as you can do.

You can study Clausewitz in the field and economics and psychology and nothing else will do you any bloody good once you are writing. We are like lousy damned acrobats but we make some mighty fine jumps, bo, and they have all these other acrobats that won't jump.

For Christ sake write and don't worry about what the boys will say nor whether it will be a masterpiece nor what. I write one page of masterpiece to ninety one pages of shit. I try to put the shit in the wastebasket. You feel you have to publish crap to make money to live and let live. All write [right] but if you write enough and as well as you can there will be the same amount of masterpiece material (as we say at Yale). You can't think well enough to sit down and write a deliberate masterpiece and if you could get rid of [Gilbert] Seldes and those guys that nearly ruined you and turn them out as well as you can and let the spectators yell when it is good and hoot when it is not you would be all right.

Forget your personal tragedy. We are all bitched from the start and you especially have to be hurt like hell before you can write seriously. But when you get the damned hurt use it—don't cheat with it. Be as faithful to it as a scientist—but don't think anything is of any importance because it happens to you or anyone belonging to you.

About this time I wouldn't blame you if you gave me a burst. Jesus it's marvellous to tell other people how to write, live, die etc.

I'd like to see you and talk about things with you sober. You were so damned stinking in N.Y. we didn't get anywhere. You see, Bo, you're not a tragic character. Neither am I. All we are is writers and what we should do is write. Of all people on earth you needed discipline in your work and instead you marry someone who is jealous of your work, wants to compete with you and ruins you. It's not as simple as that and I thought Zelda was crazy the first time I met her and you complicated it even more by being in love with her and, of course you're a rummy. But you're no more of a rummy than Joyce is and most good writers are. But Scott, good writers always come back. Always. You are twice as good now as you were at the time you think you were so marvellous. You know I never thought so much of Gatsby at the time. You can write twice as well now as you ever could. All you need to do is write truly and not care about what the fate of it is.

Go on and write.

Anyway I'm damned fond of you and I'd like to have a chance to talk sometimes. We had good times talking. Remember that guy we went out to see dying in Neuilly? He was down here this winter. Damned nice guy Canby Chambers. Saw a lot of Dos. He's in good shape now and he was plenty sick this time last year. How is Scotty and Zelda? Pauline sends her love. We're all fine. She's going up to Piggott for a couple of weeks with Patrick. Then bring Bumby back. We have a fine boat. Am going good on a very long story. Hard one to write.

Always your friend
Ernest

What about The Sun also and the movies? Any chance?

I dint put in about the good parts. You know how good they are. You're write [right] about the book of stories [*Winner Take Nothing*]. I wanted to hold it for more. That last one I had in Cosmopolitan would have made it.*

PUL

* For Fitzgerald's balanced reply to this letter, dated 1 June 1934, see *The Letters of F. Scott Fitzgerald,* ed. Andrew Turnbull (New York, 1963), pp. 308–10.

To ARNOLD GINGRICH, Key West, 15 July 1934

Dear Arnold:

Thanks for the wire of suggestion but the only guys I knew who were really good and never made any money were either killed in the war, dope-heads, rummies, Ezra and Joyce and now everybody has made it but Ezra. Did you mean for me to write about Ezra? In the meantime almost immediately after writing you what to write about I wrote a piece which Dos and the rest liked but the first two pages of which did not make me laugh when I re-read them. So re-wrote those pages and now like it and send same to you with this letter. Also tell your secretary not to write me any letters signed Arnold while you are gone. Let her sign her own name or desist.

How many pieces do I have to write after this one before I am paid up? The only thing I have had to be proud about this year due to the failure of the cuban marlin season, the arkansas quail season etc. has been the fact that owe-ing you pieces and money I have steadily written you goddamned good or even swell pieces on time or a little ahead of time no matter how badly have needed dough or how easy to make it writing something else. Or perhaps I simply have the braggies. But what I want now is dough in a sufficient sum safe somewhere so I can get out to africa. Because really Mr. G. I do not give a shit for anything except to get out to Africa again and especially on this Sunday afternoon. But no less especially morning, noon and night and to hell with anything else.

As far as I know I have only one life to live and I have worked hard and written good stories, pieces etc. and by Jesus I want to live it where it interests me; and I have no romantic feeling about the American scene. Also pretty soon I will be a long time dead and outside of writing I have two well developed talents; for sea fishing where there is a current and migratory fish and shooting with a rifle on targets at un-known ranges where the vital spots are not marked but have to be under-stood to be hit and for Christ sake why not go where I can use them instead of go out here and play around with chicken shit sailfish that I feel sorry for interrupting when I catch and never put my hand to a rifle from one year's end to the other. Also why not take kids out there and let them die or have fun rather than grow up in this F.E.R.A. Jew administered phony of a town. If I don't give a godamn about America I can't help it.

Well, good evening Mr. G. and if you love America o.k. Pal but it doesn't move me and hasn't moved me for a long time and still I can be moved. It's like trying to imagine Sarah Bernhardt good because she was good once. I say the hell with it. I've been better places and better people (Spain). Here we have the flora and the finest trees and all that but I like the fauna and what the hell.

Yrs

PH. PUL   Ernest

To ARNOLD GINGRICH, Key West, 16 November 1934

Dear Mr. G.:

That's certainly a hell of a damned disease that you have. I looked it up in Black's medical dictionary and couldn't tell a thing about it from what they said. Do you think having your tonsils out will have any effect on it? Here I've been thinking you had too much energy for your own good and you with that lousey angio all the time. I'm damned sorry about it. What'll you do when you get cured, start another magazine? And write two novels simultaneously? Maybe we ought to have a commission appointed to study you.

Thanks for the letter just received and for taking the Belmonte piece. I'll cable Ziff [Lester Ziffren]. I'm sure the price will be all right. Believe you're right about illustrations. I haven't anything that would beat the Death in the Afternoon stuff or I would have used it.

Finished the long book [Green Hills of Africa] this morning, 492 pages of my handwriting. Going to start a story tomorrow. Might as well take advantage of a belle epoque while I'm in one.

Fine norther blowing here. Regular early season football weather. Will try absolutely to get the copy to you for the twenty-first. Don't know what it will be about. Somehow I don't like to write on Gertrude even though it is a sure fire piece. She sounded so God awful over the radio the other night that it's like socking a dummy or a ghost. You'd never believe it and there's no evidence now to prove it, but she was a damned pleasant woman before she had the menopause and it goes against my digestion to take shots at anyone who's ever been a friend no matter how lousey they get to be finally. Besides, I've got the gun and it's loaded and I know where the vital spots are and friendship aside there's a certain damned fine feeling of superiority in knowing you can finish anybody off whenever you want to and still not doing it. Like [Gilbert] Seldes, I've had him worried about that letter for a very long time now and I'm going to keep him worried. Don't say I mentioned it anymore. I've got it locked up with my papers in Paris and no matter how his critical career comes out this makes a bum of him in the end. I've written all the facts about Gertrude so they'll be on tap if anything happens to me but I don't like to slam the old bitch around when she's here [on U.S. tour] having a wonderful time. Your title for it was good, though.

One of my best pals, Luis Quintanilla, is having a show of his etchings at the Pierre Matisse gallery in the Fullar Bldg. in New York opening November twentieth and running for two weeks. The etchings are damned wonderful, the finest dry points I've ever seen by anybody alive. Quintanilla is in jail in Madrid, charged with being on the revolutionary committee of the October revolt. They're trying to give him sixteen years. I've written an introduction for the catalogue and Dos has written another one. I paid to have the prints pulled and [am] paying for the show. This last between ourselves. Do you know anybody you can steam up to go and see it or anybody who buys etchings in New York you could get to go and see these? The stuff is no charity business nor helping out a pal. They're simply bloody marvelous. If you've got twenty bucks to spend you ought to buy one. The money all goes to Quintanilla except twenty per cent to Pierre Matisse as dealer. Pierre is all worked up about them and thinks they're marvelous. I know damned well they are but because I'm his pal I might be supposed to be prejudiced.

This seems to be all. I hope you're feeling a lot better. Will you send the check for the Belmonte piece to Lester Ziffren, Apartado 933, Madrid. It was wonderful to see all those big blowzy ads in the December number. Let me know when we start to get rich.

Yours always,
Ernest Hemingway

PH. PUL

To GERALD AND SARA MURPHY, Key West, 19 March 1935

Dear Sara and Dear Gerald:

You know there is nothing we can ever say or write. If Bumby died we know how you would feel and there would be nothing you could say. Dos and I came in from the Gulf Sunday, and sent a wire. Yesterday I tried to write you and I couldn't.

It is not as bad for Baoth because he had a fine time, always, and he has only done something now that we all must do. He has just gotten it over with. It was terrible that it had to go on for such a long time but if they could keep him from suffering sometimes it is merciful to get very tired before you die when you want to live very much.

About him having to die so young [aged sixteen][1]—Remember that he had a very fine time and having it a thousand times makes it no better. And he is spared from learning what sort of a place the world is.

It is *your* loss: more than it is his, so it is something that you can, legitimately, be brave about. But I can't be brave about it and in all my heart I am sick for you both.

Absolutely truly and coldly in the head, though, I know that anyone who dies young after a happy childhood, and no one ever made a happier childhood than you made for your children, has won a great victory. We all have to look forward to death by defeat, our bodies gone, our world destroyed; but it is the same dying we must do, while he has gotten it all over with, his world all intact and the death only by accident.

You see now we have all come to the part of our lives where we start to lose people of our own age. Baoth was our own age: very few people ever really are alive and those that are never die; no matter if they are gone. No one you love is ever dead.

We must live it, now, a day at a time and be very careful not to hurt each other. It seems as though we were all on a boat now together, a good boat still, that we have made but that we know now will never reach port. There will be all kinds of weather, good and bad, and especially because we know now that there will be no landfall we must keep the boat up very well and be very good to each other. We are fortunate we have good people on the boat.

With all our love to you both and to the Duke of Taxidermy [son Patrick Murphy] and to Honoria [daughter] of the Horses and to old Baoth.

Ernest

TC. PUL

---

1. Baoth, the Murphys' eldest son (1919–1935), had died of tuberculosis after a long illness.

To ARNOLD GINGRICH, Key West, 11 April 1935

Dear Arnold:

Here is the piece. If you can't say fornicate can you say copulate or if not that can you say co-habit? If not that would have to say consummate I suppose. Use your own good taste and judgment.

We are leaving tomorrow morning early. Wound perfectly clean so far and should be healed tight in another couple of days.[1] Very little pain.

Will drop you a line from Bimini. Thought it was safest to write you a piece now as taking three days to get to Bimini would make it too close to your deadline to chance a slip-up.

Best regards.

PH. PUL   Ernest

1. On Sunday, 7 April, on the way to Bimini, EH had accidentally shot himself by ricochet in the calves of both legs. See Carlos Baker, *Ernest Hemingway: A Life Story* (New York, 1969), pp. 271–72; and "On Being Shot Again," *Esquire* 3 (June 1935).

To ARNOLD GINGRICH, Key West, 4 June 1935

Dear Arnold:

Am sending you two copies of a book published in Cuba and apparently a first edition of mine about young [Antonio] Gattorno [Cuban painter].[1] You remember that swell picture of his, the two sisters, both very goofy looking, blue, under the bushbuck head. He is on his ass in Havana having won a gigantic competition which the last revolution buggared up (we lost) so never paid. There are only 460 of these and he sent me fifty. I am paying for ten, making you present of two and keeping the rest to have something to give to my children, and sending 40 to Scribner's telling them to sell them for 5.00 apiece as a starting price and let Capt. Cohn have 10 if he pays cash. All money to be sent to Antonio Gattorno, Villa Estrella, Pogolloti (Marianao), Havana. If Miss Georgia Lilienfeldt wants any she can order them from Scribner's Rare Book dept. By the way thanks very much for the letter about the phony. What a perversion to have. Would it be too much for you to ask her to write me on what date she saw this guy and just what he said? Also describe him? I believe the inerradicable belief that some people have that I am a phony and a buggar can be traced to that boy's operations around the U.S. He has been from coast to coast. Signing books, reading his new stories aloud, staying for 2 months at the Explorers club, taking young men to breakfast etc. I would appreciate any concrete details from her or anyone else that ran into him in Chicago.[2]

Flew here from Cat Cay to see the improvements Pauline has made on the house, see the kids etc. Also clear up the Green Hill Installments [in *Scribner's Magazine*] and try to clean up my mail. We have caught 2 of those big tuna without sharks touching either one and hope for a world's record before yr next issue. Will you please wire me Hemingway, Bimini, the latest date you can handle copy and pics on the next issue. You would be surprised how people follow that stuff. If you want any blurbs from big shots and sportsmen to satisfy your owners that they are not buying shit with their nickels can get them for you; or send them. I think it was a good idea to have these three or four pieces in a sequence. Was sorry I had to write that last one at 3 a.m. but will write you some literature again next winter. Or this fall.

How many do I have to go before I get some more dough? That last paid expenses on about one piece. Am not begging. Just want to know. Took a plane to get it to you on time. The Gattorno piece should be a pretty good collector's item. Hope so. If collector's survive.

Did you see the last edition of Ross and the Mick? It's nothing to bet on any more. Jack Britton and Ted Kid Lewis fought 19 good fights too. Every one on the level.

Would it interest you to know that I knocked cold after cutting up badly one Joe Knapp[3] who afterwards found out owns or is alleged to own Colliers, McCall's etc. It was after dark and with bare hands on the dock at Bimini. Witnesses some 60 including Ben Finney[4] (of 21) Howard Lance, Bill Fagen and plenty others. I think he had read in [Gertrude] Stein that I was a phony and picked the fight. I told him he didn't know what he was getting into and that he was talking so that he could repeat what he had said to me in N.Y. Anyway clipped him three times with left hooks didn't understand why he didn't go down, on the next he fell forward and grabbed, hit him twice hard, clubbing, behind the ear with right, backed away and landed sunday punch making him hit ass and head at almost same time on planks. When he got onto the dock to fight I believe he thought it was going to be one of those where you fade right swings and then some one grabs you. But his crew never made a move. He left at 4 a.m. next day in his yacht the Storm King for Miami for doctorage. In Miami he told Fagen that he was sorry that he had spoken out of turn and had gotten what was coming to him. On the other hand it is called limiting one's market. Still the son of a bitch never touched me once and he started it and weighed 200 lbs, had shoes on and I was barefoot. Lost 2 toenails. If you have any curiosity about this thing it is very easily verified. The nigger band that sings was on the dock, saw it all and have a fine song now that you can hear if you will come to Bimini. I wish to hell you would come. I will be fishing alone there from June 7 to June 25. My wife has to go to St. Louis to get Bumby who is being shipped there from Chicago. I wish to hell you would come down. It is really a fine place and that kind of fishing is a hell of a lot better with two guys than one.

Anyway write me, care Capt. George D. Kreidt, 1437 S.W. 5th Street, Miami, Fla.

For E. Hemingway
Capt. "Pilar" Bimini

He runs the pilot boat and will bring it over, every Tuesday. I go back tomorrow. You can fly from Chicago or N.Y. in no bloody time at all and the Pan American Plane to Nassau from Miami every Monday and Friday leaving at 8 a.m. from Dinner Key Airport brings you to Cat Cay in 28 minutes. Simply wire me meet plane Cat Cay and we will be there. Am getting Carlos [Gutiérrez] over.

We had a marlin at least a third bigger than Mike's [Strater's] whipped and at the boat when the hook pulled out. After the goddamndest fight you ever saw. He made 22 jumps clean out of water and when he had out nearly half mile of line looked like the damned Normandie. I had him at the boat in 28 minutes. He jumped himself to death just as Mike's fish did. But the hook pulled out. Would have beaten the world's record by plenty. Well what the hell. They are there. But you come down when you get this letter and we will put the heat to them. Plenty small ones too but we are using 8 and ten pound tuna trolling. Caught the two tuna in one hour ten and in 48 minutes. All the boats there are had been fishing four years and nobody caught any. Have won 350 bucks betting we would with the rich boys. Plenty rich boys. But now no bets.

So long Arnold. Will try to write you a good piece. If you have any suggestions sing out.

PH. PUL   [Ernest Hemingway]

---

1. *Gattorno* (Havana, April 1935), pp. 11–16, is a comment by EH on the artist's work; reprinted in *Esquire* 5 (May 1936). 2. This impostor, the son of a U.S. Navy admiral, was a psychopath whose activities harassed EH for many years. EH to Carlos Baker, 17 February 1951 (not here included), discusses the problem. 3. Joseph Fairchild Knapp (1892–1952) was associated in magazine publishing with his father, Joseph Palmer Knapp (1864–1951), former board chairman of Crowell-Collier Publishing Co. EH to Gingrich, 31 July 1935 (not here included), wrote: "Since the Knapp thing when anybody is tight here or feels dangerous they ask me to fight. It's a local pastime called 'Trying him.' Have fought 4 times in last 2 weeks—twice with bare fists, twice with gloves. All knock outs . . . Knocked out biggest and toughest jig on island [of Bimini] in less than a minute." (PH. PUL) 4. Finney (b. 1900), a former Marine, had been EH's friend since the 1920s. See his autobiography, *Feet First* (New York, 1971).

To SARA MURPHY, Bimini, British West Indies, 10 July 1935

Dearest Sara:

It's a crime that we had the kids all settled here before we got your letter. It would have been marvellous to be together up there. But they are so crazy about it here that I dont see how we could take them away now. Patrick has gained 2 lbs and is brown as a real Mexican. Gregory is learning to swim and Bumby is out all day in an outboard with his black friends. They have the real ocean and a perfectly safe seven mile long surf bathing clear sand beach at the back door. Have built a cabaña on the beach out of thatched palms. No insects there and the water is absolutely clear Gulf Stream and always cool but never cold. Their house is on a ridge that overlooks the ocean and the lagoon and is only $20.00 a month! It blows a big breeze every day and they swim all morning and fish all afternoon. They are crazy about it and I dont know where in the world we could get such a beach or such water. You'll have to come here. Before we knew you and Patrick had gone to the Adirondacks Pauline and I thought maybe you could come.[1] What you write about the woods makes me want to go there very much. When we come north Pauline and I will come up to see you and Patrick and Honoria. We havent any dates yet. When we finish here I want to go somewhere to write for 3 months.

Lately the fish havent been here. They've gone to Cuba and if they dont show up here in the next 3 weeks they've gone for this year. May go to Cuba for 2 weeks to see. Then north. Have to find some place to put the boat so she will be safe in hurricane months.

You would love this place Sara. It's in the middle of the Gulf Stream and every breeze is a cool one. The water is so clear you think you will strike bottom when you have 10 fathoms under your keel. There is every kind of fish, altho the big marlin and tuna seem to have passed. There is a pretty good hotel [The Compleat Angler: Mrs. Helen Duncombe] and we have a room there now because there have been rain squalls at night lately and so I cant sleep on the roof of the boat. That's not a very nautical term but a fine cool place to sleep. Dos and Katy will tell you about it.

Tell Patrick I have a Thompson Sub Machine gun and we shoot sharks with it. Shot 27 in two weeks. All over ten feet long. As soon as they put their heads out we give them a burst. We caught a Mako shark within 12 lbs of the Worlds Record in 35 minutes. 786 pounds. Dos will tell you about the big tuna and the marlin. We fought one tuna of about 1000 lbs with another man who had him first for 9 hrs and 50 minutes. Then just when we had him whipped and on the surface showing terribly big in the searchlight at 9 o'clock at night 17 miles from where he was hooked the sharks hit him. 5 hit him at once. I shot 3 with the Mannlicher but they cut him up like a log in a planing mill. The head alone weighed 249 lbs. It was a dirty shame. Cook had him 6½ hrs. I had him 3 hrs 20 minutes after Cook's hands gave out.

I dont know any more news. Patrick would love this place. You can catch snappers, tarpon, and 25 kinds of small fish right from the dock here. About 400 people live in the town. Mostly turtling boats and spongers. Bonefish are common as grunts.

We bring our drinking water and ice and fresh vegetables on the pilot boat that comes once a week from Miami. There is no kind of sickness on the island and the average age of people in the cemetery is 85. About ⅔ of population is black. It is under the British flag and there is only one policeman who was gone to Nassau for 2 weeks. We have celebrated the Queen's Birthday, the Jubilee, The Prince of Wales Birthday, the 4th of July, and will celebrate the 14th of July, getting drunk on all of these. We miss you on these occassions as well as all the rest of the time and send you *much* love and hope to see you soon. Best to Patrick and Honoria, much love again from Poor Old Pappa.

How you write here is Capt. George D. Kreidt, 1437 S.W. 5th Street, Miami, Florida, For E. Hemingway, Capt. "Pilar" Bimini, BWI. That way it saves 2 weeks as [it] comes over on the pilot boat every Tuesday.

Ernest.

We got another bunch of wonderful discs from Gerald. Dos and Kate forgot to take your camera. Can I send it?

HMD

1. Patrick Murphy had contracted tuberculosis and was at 29 Church Street, Saranac Lake, New York, with his mother.

To IVAN KASHKIN, Key West, 19 August 1935

Dear Kashkeen:

Thank you for sending the book[1] and the article in *International Literature*. They came, forwarded by [William] Saroyan today. A little while ago the article came forwarded by *Esquire* and I read it.

It is a pleasure to have somebody know what you are writing about. That is all I care about. What I seem to be myself is of no importance. Here criticism is a joke. The bourgeois critics do not know their ass from a hole in the ground and the newly converted communists are like all new converts; they are so anxious to be orthodox that all they are interested in are schisms in their own critical attitudes. None of it has anything to do with literature which is always literature, when it is, no matter who writes it nor what the writer believes. Edmund Wilson is the best critic we have but he no longer reads anything that comes out. Cowley is honest but still very much under the impression of being converted. He is also tending to stop reading. The others are all careerists. I do not know one that I would want with me, or trust with me, if we ever had to fight for anything. I've forgotten Mike Gold. He is honest too.

This is the way most criticism goes. Isidor Schneider will write a piece about me, say. I will read it because I am a professional and so do not care for compliments. Only to see what I can learn. The article will be very stupid and I learn nothing. I am not indignant; only bored. Then some friend of mine (Josephine Herbst) will write to Schneider and say why do you say such and such, what about *A Farewell To Arms,* what about what Hem says in *Death in the Afternoon,* etc. Schneider will write her in answer that he never read anything of mine after *The Sun Also Rises* which seemed to him to be anti-semitic. Yet he will write a serious article on your work. And not read your three last books. It is all balls.

Your article is very interesting. The only trouble, to me, is that it ends with me as Mr. Frazer out in Billings Montana with right arm broken so badly the back of my hand hung down against the back of my shoulder. It takes five months to fix it and then is paralyzed. I try to write with my left hand and can't. Finally the musculo-spiral nerve regenerates and I can lift my wrist after five months. But in the meantime one is discouraged. I remember the study in pain and the discouragement, the people in the hospital and the rest of it and write a story *Gambler, Nun and Radio.* Then I write *Death in the Afternoon.* Then I write the other stories in the last book [*Winner Take Nothing*]. I go to Cuba and there is a little trouble. I go to Spain and write a damned good story about necessity which maybe you did not see called *One Trip Across.* In the meantime I write that stuff in *Esquire* to eat and support my family. They do not know what I am going to write and it gets to them the day before they go to press. Sometimes it is better than others. I write it in one day each time and I try to make it interesting and to tell the truth. It is not pretentious. We go to Africa and have the best time I have ever had. Now have finished a book [*Green Hills of Africa*] and will send it to you. Maybe you will think it is shit and maybe you will like it. Anyway it is the best I can write. If you like it and want any of it for the magazine to translate you can use it. It may be of no interest to you. But I think it will be, perhaps, to yourself if not to the magazine.

Everyone tries to frighten you now by saying or writing that if one does not become a communist or have a Marxian viewpoint one will have no friends and will be alone. They seem to think that to be alone is something dreadful; or that to not have friends is to be feared. I would rather have one honest enemy than most of the friends that I have known. I cannot be a communist now because I believe in only one thing: liberty. First I would look after myself and do my work. Then I would care for my family. Then I would help my neighbor. But the state I care nothing for. All the state has ever meant to me is unjust taxation. I have never asked anything from it. Maybe you have a better state but I would have to see it to believe it. And I would not know then because I do not speak Russian. I believe in the absolute minimum of government.

In whatever time I had been born I could have taken care of myself if I were not killed. A writer is like a Gypsy. He owes no allegiance to any government. If he is a good writer he will never like the government he lives under. His hand should be against it and its hand will always be against him. The minute anyone knows any bureaucracy well enough he will hate it. Because the minute it passes a certain size it must be unjust.

A writer is an outlyer like a Gypsy. He can be class conscious only if his talent is limited. If he has enough talent all classes are his province. He takes from them all and what he gives is everybody's property.

Why should a writer expect reward or the appreciation of any group of people or any state? The only reward is in doing your work well and that is enough reward for any man. There is nothing more obscene to me than a man posing himself as a candidate for the French Academy or any Academy.

Now if you think this attitude leads to sterility and the individual's becoming nothing but human waste I believe you are wrong. The measure of a man's work is not quantity. If you can get as much intensity and as much meaning in a story as some one can get in a novel that story will last as long as it is any good. A true work of art endures forever; no matter what its politics.

If you believe one thing and work at it always, as I believe in the importance of writing, you have no disillusion about that unless you are ambitious. All you have is hatred for the shortness of the time we have to live and get our work done.

A life of action is much easier to me than writing. I have greater faciilty for action than for writing. In action I do not worry any more. Once it is bad enough you get a sort of elation because there is nothing you can do except what you are doing and you have no responsibility. But writing is something that you can never do as well as it can be done. It is a perpetual challenge and it is more difficult than anything else that I have ever done—so I do it. And it makes me happy when I do it well.

I hope this does not bore you. I write it to you because of the care and the accuracy you have used in studying what I write so that you might know something of what I think. Even though it makes you think me a worse shit when you read it. I do not give a damn whether any U.S.A. critic knows what I think because I have no respect for them. But I respect you and I like you because you wished me well.

Yours very truly,
Ernest Hemingway

P.S. Do you ever see Malraux? I thought *La Condition Humaine* was the best book I have read in ten years. If you ever see him I wish that you would tell him so for me. I meant to write to him but I write French with so many misspelled words that I was ashamed to write.

I had a cable signed by him, Gide and Rolland forwarded to me by mail from London asking me to some writers congress. The cable came to me in the Bahama Islands two weeks after the Congress was over. They probably think I was rude not to answer.

This new book is out in October. I'll send it to you then. I can always be reached through Key West, Florida, USA. They forward when we are away.

E.H.

P.P.S. Don't you drink? I notice you speak slightingly of the bottle. I have drunk since I was fifteen and few things have given me more pleasure. When you work hard all day with your head and know you must work again the next day what else can change your ideas and make them run on a different plane like whisky? When you are cold and wet what else can warm you? Before an attack who can say anything that gives you the momentary well being that rum does? I would as soon not eat at night as not to have red wine and water. The only time it isn't good for you is when you write or when you fight. You have to do that cold. But it always helps my shooting. Modern life, too, is often a mechanical oppression and liquor is the only mechanical relief. Let me know if my books make any money and I will come to Moscow and we will find somebody that drinks and drink my royalties up to end the mechanical oppression.

1. *Smert' Posle Poludnya* [*Death in the Afternoon*], ed. and with an introduction by Ivan Kashkin (Moscow, 1934). The introduction appeared separately as an article in *Literaturny Kritik* 9 (September 1934): 121–48. The other article was probably "Ernest Hemingway: The Tragedy of Craftsmanship," *International Literature* 5 (May 1935): 72–90. Kashkin (1899–1963), EH's exact contemporary, graduated from Moscow University in 1924 and followed a career as critic, translator, and teacher. More than anyone else, he was responsible for EH's reputation in the U.S.S.R., be-

ginning in 1934. By 1937, nine out of fifteen Soviet writers named EH their favorite non-Russian writer. See Deming Brown, *Soviet Attitudes Toward American Writing* (Princeton, 1962). EH always spelled the name Kashkeen, except when he borrowed it for use in *For Whom the Bell Tolls,* and was amused by the political joke that Kashkin was red-headed.

This letter was printed in *Soviet Literature* 11 (November 1962): 160–63.

To MAXWELL PERKINS, Key West, 7 September 1935

Dear Max:

I was glad to have your letter and would have answered sooner except for the hurricane which came the same night I received it. We got only the outside edge. It was due for midnight and I went to bed at ten to get a couple of hours sleep if possible having made everything as safe as possible with the boat. Went with the barometer on a chair by the bed and a flashlight to use when the lights should go. At midnight the barometer had fallen to 29.50 and the wind was coming very high and in gusts of great strength tearing down trees, branches etc. Car drowned out and got down to boat afoot and stood by until 5 a.m. when the wind shifting into the west we knew the storm had crossed to the north and was going away. All the next day the winds were too high to get out and there was no communication with the keys. Telephone, cable and telegraph all down, too rough for boats to live. The next day we got across [to Lower Matecumbe Key] and found things in a terrible shape. Imagine you have read it in the papers but nothing could give an idea of the destruction. Between 700 and 1000 dead. Many, today, still unburied. The foliage absolutely stripped as though by fire for forty miles and the land looking like the abandoned bed of a river. Not a building of any sort standing. Over thirty miles of railway washed and blown away. We were the first in to Camp Five of the veterans who were working on the Highway construction. Out of 187 only 8 survived. Saw more dead than I'd seen in one place since the lower Piave in June of 1918.

The veterans in those camps were practically murdered. The Florida East Coast had a train ready for nearly twenty four hours to take them off the Keys. The people in charge are said to have wired Washington for orders. Washington wired Miami Weather Bureau which is said to have replied there was no danger and it would be a useless expense. The train did not start until the storm started. It never got within thirty miles of the two lower camps. The people in charge of the veterans and the weather bureau can split the responsibility between them.

What I know and can swear to is this; that while the storm was at its height on Matecumbe and most of the people already dead the Miami bureau sent a warning of winds of gale strength on the keys from Key Largo to Key West and of Hurricane intensity in the Florida straights [straits] below Key West. They lost the storm completely and did not use the most rudimentary good sense in figuring its progress.

Long Key fishing camp is completely destroyed and so are all the settlements on Matecumbe both upper and lower. There is over thirty miles of the R.R. completely gone and there will probably never be another train in to Key West. Highway is not as badly damaged as the R.R. but would take six months to repair. The R.R. may make a bluff that they will rebuild in order to sell the govt their right of way for the highway. Anyway Key West will be isolated for at least six months except for boat service and plane from Miami.

The Marine Corps plane that is flying some of the 1st class mail just brought two sets of page proof going up to page 130. Do you want me to send this back before the other comes?

To get back to your letter.

But first I wish I could have had with me the bloody poop that has been having his publishers put out publicity matter that he has been staying in Miami because he needs a hurricane in the book he is writing and that it looked as though he wasn't going to have one and him so disappointed.

Max, you can't imagine it, two women, naked, tossed up into trees by the water, swollen and stinking, their breasts as big as balloons, flies between their legs. Then, by figuring, you locate where it is and recognize them as the two very nice girls who ran a sandwich place and filling-station three miles from the ferry. We located sixty nine bodies where no one had been able to get in. Indian Key absolutely swept clean, not a blade of grass, and over the high center of it were scattered live conchs that came in with the sea, craw fish, and dead morays. The whole bottom of the sea blew over it. I would like to have had that little literary bastard that wanted his hurricane along to rub his nose in some of it. Harry Hopkins and Roosevelt who sent those poor bonus march guys down there to get rid of them got rid of them all right. Now they say they should all be buried in Arlington and no bodies to be burned or buried on the spot which meant trying to carry stuff that came apart blown so tight that they burst when you lifted them, rotten, running, putrid, decomposed, absolutely impossible to embalm, carry them out six, eight miles to a boat, on the boat for ten to twenty more to put them into boxes and the whole thing stinking to make you vomit—enroute to arlington. Most of the protests against burning or burying came from the

Miami undertakers that get 100 dollars apiece per veteran. Plain pine boxes called coffins at $50 apiece. They could have been quicklimed right in where they are found, identification made from their pay disks and papers and crosses put up. Later dig up the bones and ship them.

Joe Lowe the original of the Rummy in that story of mine One Trip Across was drowned at the Ferry Slip.

Had just finished a damned good long story and was on another when this started with the warning on saturday night. They had all day Sunday and all day monday to get those vets out and never did it. If they had taken half the precautions with them that we took with our boat not a one would have been lost.

Feel too lousy now to write. Out rained on, sleeping on the deck of the run boat, nothing to drink through all that business so ought to remember it, but damned if I want it for my novel. We made five trips with provisions for survivors to different places and nothing but dead men to eat the grub.

Hope everything all right with Peg. I'll bet it is. Anyway you won't have to worry now she is back.

Imagine a love affair would help Scott if he has anything left to love with and the woman isn't so awful that he has to kid himself too much.

About the Stein thing—I was just trying to be completely honest. I don't mention her name and what proves it is Gertrude? What would you like me to put in place of bitch? Fat bitch? Lousy bitch? Old Bitch? Lesbian Bitch? What is the modifying adjective that would improve it? I don't know what word to replace bitch with. Certainly not whore. If anyone was ever a bitch that woman was a bitch. I'll see if I can change it. (Have just found it and read it over and don't see what the fuss is about.) Unless you think it gives the critics something to burp about. For Christ sake Max don't you see that they have to attack me to believe in themselves. You can't be popular all the time unless you make a career of it like Galsworthy etc. I will survive this unpopularity and with one more good book of stories (only these are going to be with plenty of action so they can understand them) and one good novel you are in a place where they will all have to come around and eat shit again. I don't give a damn whether I am popular or not. You know I never went in for it when I was. The only thing bothers me is that your business office will not have the faith in me that I have and will not see that I am working on a long plan instead of trying to be popular every day like Mr. Roosevelt. I need a certain amount of money too.

All right. Let us take up the word bitch again.

Would you prefer fat female?

That is possible. I'll change it to fat female or just female. That's better. That will make her angrier than bitch, will please you by not calling a lady a bitch, will make it seem that I care less about her lying about me, and will please everyone but me who cares only about honesty.

Well I've fixed it up now. It's all right. Have gotten more how I really feel about her and given it the small degree of importance that it deserves. It's all right now. Don't worry.

Better get this off as no one knows when the mail goes out. Hope your Hay-fever is o.k. now. With the tail end of that storm moving north it may make a sort of false early fall that will kill it off. I appreciate what you wrote about writing. Enclosed is the way the Stein part goes so you can get it reset now for the page proof. This fixes it up all right and puts the emphasis where it belongs. Also betters the end of the chapter I think and avoids the word bitch as applied to a Lady writer [*Green Hills of Africa,* chapter 3].

When you get this letter can you deposit $500 in my account at City Bank Farmers Branch 22 William Street. That will bring the advance up to $4800 I believe.

Will get going on the rest of the proofs now but wanted you to have the revised part to you without delay. Will send this down now.

Good luck, Max.
Yours always,

PUL Ernest

To F. SCOTT FITZGERALD, Key West, 16 December 1935

Dear Scott:

It was good to hear from you but a shame you thought you had to write about the book. I only asked Max whether he'd heard if you ever got it because of your changing addresses and one thing and another. It didn't require any bread and ink letter.

How are you anyway? I hear that you're not drinking and haven't been for months. Then that you're on it. That your insides are on the bum etc. etc. Let me know how you are and what you're doing will you? The line about the body was very good. But I'd rather know really what you have or haven't.

Was delighted from the letter to see you don't know any more about when a book is a good book or what makes a book bad than ever. That means, anyhow, that you're not haveing any sudden flashes of insight or intelligence that would mean The End. The other day going through some stuff found the fifteen some pages you wrote me about what would have to come out and what should go in Farewell To Arms and this letter you have written is just the same.

When did I erroneously think you didn't like Death In The Afternoon? And why? and what about it? You know you are like a brilliant mathematician who loves mathematics truly and always gets the wrong answers to the problems. Of course you're like a hell of a lot of other things too but what the hell. Also you are like nobody but yourself and in spite of the fact that you think when you meet an old friend that you have to get stinking drunk and do every possible thing to humiliate yourself and your friend your friends are still fond of you. I'm damned fond of you. Up in Saranac Sara [Murphy] talked for a whole afternoon about how much she cared about you. She said you wrote her a swell letter.

I started up to see you last September in Asheville [North Carolina]. Then the infantile paralysis was so bad in N. and S. Carolina (had Bumby and Pat with me) that left the car in Columbia S.C. and took them on a train to N.Y. I miss seeing you and haveing a chance to talk. In talk you can winnow out the bullshit which we put out so pontifically when we write literary letters and we get a good sound understanding. I got your wire about coming down two weeks after you sent it when we were cruising in the Bahamas. Tried to get Max and Gingrich both to bring you down.

The more I think back to it the better book Tender Is The Night is. This may irritate you but it's the truth. Why don't you come down here? Am going over to Havana to see the Louis-Gastanaga fight there on Dec. 29th. Come on down and we'll go together. I can get two press seats.

Write here will you—we'll be here all winter. Don't know whether Dos is coming down or not. Have a hell of a lot of things to tell you that don't go in letters. A couple you could get a good story out of.

Best always,
Ernest

PUL

To JOHN DOS PASSOS, Key West, 17 December 1935

Dear Dos:

How are you and Katy and how goes everything. I'm awfully glad you went up to see Sara [Murphy]. I felt bad about putting it the way I did about going up there. I knew you couldn't and shouldn't have gone that time with the car on the bum and in that weather anyway. I know Katy shouldn't go too and I was trying to make it seem that you ought to go anyway (Why the hell should you as far as that goes) and I put it badly. Sara seemed so dismal about nobody coming.

Just had a letter from [Antonio] Gattorno saying that he would like to have "that double page I promised him in Esquire" in the Jan number. I promised him to do my best to promote it with Gingrich. I missed him when he came to N.Y. Trying to get him down here to go to the Louis fight. Have gotten 2 press seats through Dick Armstrong. Or do you suppose Gattorno has fallen for that shit that I now own some of Esquire? He also wanted 100 or 150 for his show. Not if I had it. Just send it. Probably whether have or not. The hell of it is I haven't got it. Will not have any dough until the first of the year. It will take considerable promoting to get Gattorno a single or double page in Esquire but believe I can do it. But can't promise it. As for dough where would I get any? I got paid for three Esquires in Advance and spent it in N.Y. Had spent advance on my book and the critics killed the book. We have about 300 dollars to get through Christmas on and until the first of the year. Will you tell Antonio for me that I can't let him have any money until after Jan first and that this is not a stall but that I am broke. He wouldn't believe it if I told him. I will let him take $100. after the first and I will try to get Gingrich to publish his stuff. Did you take him down to see it? I have to pay $1116.83 before Dec. 31, the interest on that African money. Have raised dough to cover that but that leaves just under 300. I always give my family dough at xmas and they need it as bad or worse than Antonio but I can't explain that to him. He thinks I am a yachtsman millionario y aficionado a la literatura y los toros.

Could you get me or send me the piece Bunny Wilson wrote in the N.R. [*New Republic*].¹ Both Gingrich and Max have written me about it and I haven't seen it. The title sounds pretty dismal. What was the matter—couldn't he stand to have anybody anyplace like my stuff? Still it must have made him feel awful I suppose to go all the way to Russia and find them liking my stuff but he will fix that up won't he? Well it teaches me I ought to come to see people when you ask me to come and see them. Have learned a lot of that sort of thing lately. When do you suppose Bill Smith will write a book attacking me. Certainly expect to be denounced by Quintanilla and Gattorno. It's obvious I am treating Gattorno shabbily. But where did I meet these people and what did I ask them for? After all Bunny Wilson did speak well of me once so he has a right to try to put me out of business. But I don't know what he wrote. Only these bastards writing about it.

It is gloomy as hell here without you. Wish to hell you were here. Weather has been marvellous; norther every day and night for two months. Been too muddy to fish. I've written two stories, had just finished one and saw my next three months clear because it was one of those one out of ten that I can sell when got letter, not telegram *letter* from Gingrich five days on the way here arrived the 9th saying had to have my piece in Chicago on the 12th instead of the 18th or 21st as convenu. I couldn't write a piece in the middle of the story and with only one day so sent him the story and there goes my goddamned capital and the bastards will think there is something wrong with it or I wouldn't have given it to them. Wish you were here to bellyache to. Why in hell couldn't they have *wired* when they knew date moved up?

Just had a very supercilious letter from Scott telling me very pontifically how bad my book was. He'd read it somewhere. Goddamn it that is a *good* book. I'm not a goddamned patriot about my stuff and can tell good from bad and that is a good book.

If nobody can tell when a book is good why the hell write them? If anybody would take on my dependents—aw well what the hell. You can be goddamned sure nobody would. I would like to take the tommy gun and open up at 21 or in the N.R. offices or any place you name and give shitdom a few martyrs and include myself as [word obscure; possibly *tapa*=cover].

Nathaniel's waiting to take this. Let me hear from you will you? And give my message to Antonio will you please? 100 after Jan First. Feel too damned low to undertake a letter in Spanish.

So long Dos, Good luck, hope you're feeling well. Pauline is fine and so are the kids.

Yours always

UVA

Hem

1. Wilson's "Letter to the Russians About Hemingway," *New Republic* 85 (11 December 1935): 135–36, attacks *Green Hills of Africa*, refers favorably to Kashkin's articles on EH and unfavorably to EH's "rubbishy" pieces in *Esquire*.

To F. SCOTT FITZGERALD, Key West, 21 December 1935

Dear Scott:

Well [Joe] Louis must have figured on your necessities because the fight is put off until Feb 2. So come on down then if it's all right to leave Zelda. I'm terribly sorry she was so ill again. And you with a bad liver, lung and heart. That's damned awful. How are you doing now? We all get those livers. Mine was in a hell of a state about six or seven years ago but got it all cleared up. What is the matter with your heart? And your lung?

I mean what does the Doctor say? Non sleeping is a hell of a damned thing too. Have been haveing a big dose of it now lately too. No matter what time I go to sleep wake and hear the clock strike either one or two then lie wide awake and hear three, four and five. But since I have stopped giving a good goddamn about anything in the past it doesn't bother much and I just lie there and keep perfectly still and rest through it and you seem to get almost as much repose as though you slept. This may be no use to you but it works with me.

If I get exercise and go out in the boat sleep like a log right through the night or if I wake on the boat can go right back to sleep. Or if I lay awake on the boat I'm all right. The trouble is that if you start thinking about anything in that wakeing time you go all through it and exhaust it and are pooped in the morning when you have to write. If you can lie still and take it easy and just consider your life and everything else as an outsider and *not give a damn*—it is a hell of a help.

You put so damned much value on youth it seemed to me that you confused growing up with growing old but you have taken so damned much punishment I have no business trying to tell you anything. Would like to see you though. There is a good chance the fight is off because the niggers that own Louis think he is too valuable a piece of property to risk so far away as Havana where there is shooting etc. The next revolution is being financed by money raised through kidnapping, bank robbery etc. It's damned strange the violence that is bred from violence and what a lot of those kids have turned into. Cuba is a hell of an interesting place now and has been for last five years. Probably before too you say. But only know what I've seen. Anyway am writing a story about this next revolution. Come on down any time and I'll take you over there in the boat and you'll get a good story out of it anyway. If you really feel blue enough, get yourself heavily insured and I'll see you can get killed. All you'll have to do is not put your hands up quick enough and some nigger son of a bitch will shoot you and your family will be provided for and you won't have to write any more and I'll write you a fine obituary that Malcolm Cowley will cut the best part out of for the new republic and we can take your liver out and give it to the Princeton Museum, your heart to the Plaza Hotel, one lung to Max Perkins and the other to George Horace Lorimer. If we can still find your balls I will take them via the Ile de France to Paris and down to Antibes and have them cast into the sea off Eden Roc and we will get Mac Leish to write a Mystic Poem to be read at that Catholic School (Newman?) you went to. Would you like me to write the mystic poem now. Let's see. Lines To Be Read At the Casting of Scott FitzGerald's balls into the Sea from Eden Roc (Antibes Alpes Maritimes)

Whence from these gray
Heights unjockstrapped wholly stewed he
Flung
Himself?
No.
Some waiter?
Yes.
Push tenderly oh green shoots of grass
Tickle not our Fitz's nostrils
Pass
The gray moving unbenfinneyed sea deaths deeper than
our debt to Eliot
Fling flang them flung his own his two finally his one
Spherical, colloid, interstitial,
uprising lost to sight
in fright
natural
not artificial
no ripple make as sinking sanking sonking sunk

Aw hell you'll have to get Mac Leish to write the mystic poem. I'll just give a few personal reminiscences of his Paris Period. Get that insurance now, pal. If they won't give you health or life insurance get accident insurance.

So long Scott—

Let me hear from you. Merry Christmas! Pauline sends her love.

Yours always affectionately

Ernest

PUL

To IVAN KASHKIN, Key West, 12 January 1936

Dear Kashkeen:

I was very glad to get your letter and sorry to hear that you have been sick. I hope you will be all right now. What were you ill with? You forgot to put on an address and I have been hunting all through this room, which is a mess, for your other letter and can't find it. So will send this to N.Y. The reason I didn't answer the other letter was because mine was already on the way to you and since I had told you what I believed or didn't believe I thought maybe you would not want to hear from me again. Like my grandfather who would never knowingly sit at table with a Democrat. Only I think you are not as much like my Grandfather as Edmund Wilson is.

Am haveing Scribner's send the Green Hills book. Am also writing to Gingrich to send you copies of the last five Esquires where my "rubbishy articles" are printed that Edmund Wilson criticized so efficiently without bothering to read them. Maybe you saw the piece I wrote in the New Masses about the hurricane. In Esquire there are 3 anti-war pieces, one on writing, one on Baer-Louis fight and a story.

Wilson is really very funny. I'm not sure he really read the Green Hills book even. I think he read the criticisms. Every book I have written I try to purify the party and get rid of all the fools who like you or your writing for what you or it are not and the N.Y. critics now hate what I write very strongly but not very efficiently. If you didn't see Wilson's piece (although I believe it is addressed to you) I enclose the copy that Dos Passos sent me.

I met Ilf and Petrov in N.Y. [September 1935].[1] We had some drinks one evening. They had an interpreter with them that improved what we all said. They seemed very intelligent boys and I felt badly that we had no language in common. I asked them about you and they claimed they did not know you but they wanted to go to Sing Sing penitentiary and I fixed them up to go there with an introduction to the Warden who broadcasts reminiscences of the Death house on a radio program advertizing a mouthwash manufactured and sold by an uncle of my wife's. So you can see what a wonderful country the U.S. is and I hope they did too. We asked them to come down to Key West but their itinerary only took in Florida as far south as Jacksonville. I promised to let them shoot a nigger or to shoot a nigger for them if they had moral scruples and one of them asked if we would have the nigger roasted so he evidently didn't take the offer seriously. Or is he maybe a cannibal. One of them said he liked a story of mine Homage to Switzerland. I was telling him how in Switzerland a man won't marry a girl until she has had her teeth pulled and false ones put in for economic reasons as that expense should be at the charge of the father of the bride and while telling this which took a great deal of interpreting by the more intelligent than any of us interpreter I noticed that either Ilf or Petrov had false teeth which spoiled the story as far as I was concerned. But it was already well on its way to interpretation by the interpreter. Though god knows what he made of it.

I wish you could come down here. The weather is wonderful now like the finest sort of a spring day and it is wonderful out in the Gulf Stream but with Dos in N.Y. there is nobody to talk to at all.

Of the writers you mention I will get the Sholokhov. [Isaak] Babel I know ever since his first stories were translated in French and the Red Cavalry came out. I like his writing very much. He has marvellous stuff and he writes very well. Gorky means nothing to me. But Dos says the Reminiscences are very good and I must read them. His fiction, to me, is not much good. But would like to read the other.

I see you mention Three Stories and Ten Poems but I don't think I can get a copy. It has been out of print for a long time and when I wanted to buy one they asked me $150. for it which, as I wrote it for nothing, would be like the snake eating his own tail to pay. There is only one story in it that you probably haven't read called Up In Michigan. It is an unpublishable story or I would re-print it. It is about a blacksmith who seduces the hired girl at the place where he boards. She is a virgin and it hurts her very much but she knows it is wonderful just the same and by the time she has gotten over some of the pain and would like a little tenderness or something he is asleep. It is a very good story and has been re-written by Morley Callaghan many times in saleable terms but I could never publish it in a collection because if you omitted what she said and what he did there wasn't any sense in publishing it and if you kept them in whoever published it would go to jail. But Scribner's want to bring out all my stories in one book and maybe I can get them to publish it.

I showed your article to Dos and he liked it except that he felt the same way I feel that am not in such bad shape. You see we have, some of us, led a funny life. I've made my living since I was fifteen [eighteen] and there are several things I can do well enough beside writing to make a living at so I do not get that despair personally. When you suffer it is for other people; not for yourself. Being on the sea; the work in catching a very big fish; fighting, fornication, the elation of drinking; a storm; and enjoyment of danger can all make you feel so good physically and give you such a physical enjoyment of life that you can be ashamed of being so happy when most people have no enjoyment. The minute I stop writing for a month or two months and am on a trip I feel absolutely animally happy. But when you are writing and get something the way you want it to be you get a great happiness too—but it is very different; although one is as important as the other to you yourself when you have a feeling of how short your life is. In a way it is like feeling sorry at enjoying a storm in which other people are seasick. You feel sorry for them; you try to make them comfortable and you know how badly they feel; but you yourself are happy except for their distress. But you do not always have to write of a storm from the standpoint of a seasick man although most people are seasick. But it is certainly better to have been seasick in your life so you know what you are talking about.

I don't know how old you are or how much you have been around and remember when you judge other people that you are on the winning side. You have something that you believe in, now, but if things move the way they always have moved you may live to not believe in it. Now maybe I wrote you this before but will run that risk. You write like a patriot and that is your blind spot. I've seen a lot of patriots and they all died just like anybody else if it hurt bad enough and once they were dead their patriotism was only good for legends; it was bad for their prose and made them write bad poetry. If you are going to be a great patriot i.e. loyal to any existing order of government (not one who wishes to destroy the existing for something better) you want to be killed early if your life and works won't stink.

I wish you were over here. Can't you wangle a trip over the way Ilf and Petrov did? Or is it to prevent that sort of thing that they never heard of you? You know more about my writing than anybody but you do not know anything about me and I have very great pride and a hatred of the shit that will be written about me and my stuff after I am dead (I am not so silly but to know that my work will last) and though you may be an enemy of what I believe in I would rather have one setting down by an intelligent enemy who knows you than all the blurry minded, fuzzy brained shit we produce in this country and call criticism.

This is the sort of thing I mean. I am truly, and I say this in all humility, very brave; that is brave enough to sell it as a commodity—and it is the most saleable commodity there is. I have always been very pleased about this but in the war I was frightened, mechanically, enough times to understand fear and to realize its importance in life. But you cannot say you are brave because everyone would think you were a liar and anything that you are awfully good at you are usually modest about. So you will go down as a coward due to malice by one or ignorance by another and by the record thus being false everything is misleading and a lie. Well what the hell. But the immortality I believe in is the immortality of what you write and if your stuff lasts people write about you and if they write the same sort of shit about you when you are dead that they do when you are alive it is very silly. It is all silly as hell anyway but writing isn't silly and neither is the Gulf Stream and I wish you could go out tomorrow and see it. Am going to fish tomorrow and write the next day.

Anyway Good luck. Will send the stuff.

PH. PUL   [Ernest Hemingway]

---

1. Elias Ilf (1897–1937) and Eugene Petrov (1903–1942) were Russian humorists and satirists. Ilf's *One-Story America* (1936) was based on his American tour. Identification courtesy of Nina Berberova.

To JOHN AND KATHARINE DOS PASSOS, Key West, 13 January 1936

Dear Dos and Katy:

Thanks very much for the swell still champagne. The day it came Burris Jenkins was here with three other guys and we drank seven bottles. It was wonderful. Caught six sailfish the last six times out. Been feeling good again since about two weeks. Hope everything going well with youse.

Kick a few pricks for me if you see them around your pent house. Gingrich wired he'd fixed up the thing for Gattorno. Thanks for taking him around.

Thanks again for swell champagne. My god did you read Scott's account of his crackup written under influence of Wm. Seabrook.[1] Once a writer always a fellow writer. Had been writing to Scott trying to cheer him up but no cheer up. See the reason now. He's officially cracked up. That idea about what a crack it would be in Grand Canyon is amazing if you go in for those things. Max says he has many imaginary diseases along with, I imagine, some very real liver trouble.

Have you J. [Ivan] Kashkeen's address in your files? Just had long letter from him but no address to answer it to.

Yrs always
E. Muller Wemedge

Postscript: Pas de coups de pied contre les pricks [No kicks against the pricks].

UVA

1. EH refers to the first of Fitzgerald's three "Crack-Up" articles, which appeared in *Esquire* 5 (February, March, April 1936).

To MRS. PAUL PFEIFFER, Key West, 26 January 1936

Dear Mother:

Every day since Christmas I've meant to write to thank you and Pauline's Father for the check and for the stock. You are both always so generous to us and give us such fine presents and I cannot tell you both how much I appreciated them. We missed being with you at Christmas very much. After Christmas I was in a rush of work (on a new book) and

I was shocked today to realize that it was a month after Christmas and I
had never written to tell you how much I appreciated the presents.

Today I had your fine letter and am hastening to write you but am
afraid this won't be much of a letter. We've just had three day visitor
trouble but so far have had quite a lot of time free this winter for other
pursuits due to the difficulty of getting in and out of here. Still when the
good old visitor comes he has a tendency to stay due to difficulty in leaving. The car ferrys can only take about ten cars a day and the planes,
depending on size, from 4 to 14 passengers. So this great Tourist City
planned by the administration to be purely tourist with all industries
to be discouraged has no way of getting its tourists in or out in enough
numbers to support one good sized hot dog stand. The last act of the local
Jew administrator before he was advanced to a more important position
with the [Rexford Guy] Tugwell outfit to remove him from the juris-
diction when he was being sued in the local courts for an accounting was
to buy those two old condemned ferrys (stern wheelers paddle wheel)
that ran from Cairo across to Kentucky for a reported price of 60,000.
They finally arrived, towed most of the way, in a state of complete dilapi-
dation but will no doubt be fitted up to ferry by early summer and then
Key West, the deserted tourist center, will be even more picturesque
with its picturesque old condemned paddle wheel ferries guaranteed to
give anyone a thrill when the next hurricane hits them.

In the meantime we are all fine. Pauline has been very well and very
happy with her house and her garden, flowers and trees and the place is
looking marvellous. Patrick is the same good companion as always and
we go out shooting together in the afternoons after school and on saturdays. He was delighted with his card from you and the one today from
his grandfather. Yesterday he went out in the boat in the gulf stream and
it was very rough and his stomach was very upset. I was steering and
saw him throwing up over the side and heard him, in the midst of it,
shouting "Papa! Papa!" I jumped to him to see what was the matter and
he said, "There's a sailfish jumping over there. I just saw him while
I was throwing up!" He is getting very tough and was very merry about
throwing up and made up a song that went, "You put the chowder
down. The stomach goes round and round hydeeho hydeehay and it
comes out here." He caught a small sailfish five feet eight inches long in
spite of the rough weather. It was really rough with very big seas. He and
Gregory both love to fish but I have found it is simpler to take them out
one at a time when we go into the gulf. I was never a great child lover
but these kids are really good company and are very funny and I think
(though may be prejudiced) very smart.

Gregory has inherited his grandfather's talent for figures and delights
to add numbers of any size up to the hundreds in his head and to count

by five and by ten—and he is only four. You will say to him "What's 240 and 240, Jew?" and he will put his head on one side and say "I think its about four hundred eighty." He is awfully cute now and has found that he can move at other than a full gallop. The other day we took him out with us fishing while Patrick was in school and there were some friends down here and we harpooned a porpoise and put the harpoon on a rod and reel so the porpoise was making a monkey out of the man who was trying to catch him and when we would shout suggestions to him in the bow Gregory would repeat these all and add new ones of his own showing the same ability to command in an emergency that his grandfather shows when anyone is, say, packing their bags in the back of a car. He is an awfully nice child and very funny and very sweet. They both seem to have a wonderful time all the time and I take great pleasure in taking them out and answering their questions and haveing them around with me. Patrick just came in and said to tell you, in answer to your card, that nothing has happened to the patchwork girl. But that she is still as sassy as ever. I don't know what this refers to.

We haven't heard from Virginia since a letter written on the boat while she was waiting to sail. In that letter she told us about Ward's friend Jay getting a job with Hudnut, and Ward starting off to be a writer. I swear that Ward has no more talent for being a writer than I have for playing the violin and I could not make a nickle playing the violin (even as a blind violinist) if I should work at it 15 hours a day for the next 2000 years. Why couldn't he have picked out something else to fail at without dragging in our old craft? You have to have the talent just as though you would have to have talent to be an acrobat and then work at it the way an acrobat works at his apprenticeship to be a writer and it does seem sort of goofy for Ward to waste time at it. If he were wanting to be a big league ball player say and he came out on the field and couldn't catch a fly or hit a ball out of the infield he could see he couldn't play ball. While Jinny has as much talent or more for writing than I have, only she has no confidence and won't work at it. She really has talent and has been around enough so she has something to write. I wish she would. We miss her very much.

Pauline has the same energy as always and manages to put in a good eight hour day every day and then in the evening is suddenly very tired and goes sound asleep at nine o'clock and sleeps like a child all night. She sees quite a bit of the [Canby and Esther] Chambers and of Mrs. [Lorine] Thompson. She was talking of going up to make a retreat with you but lately she has been reading James Joyce's Ulysses and has taken such an admiration for Mr. Joyce that she may be going to make a retreat with Ulysses instead. She has been in fine shape.

I've been working hard. Had a spell when I was pretty gloomy, that was why I didn't write first, and didn't sleep for about three weeks. Took to getting up about two or so in the morning and going out to the little house to work until daylight because when you're writing on a book and can't sleep your brain races at night and you write all the stuff in your head and in the morning it is gone and you are pooped. But decided that I wasn't getting enough exercise or something so have been going out and driving myself in the boat for a while in any kind of weather and am o.k. now. It is better to produce half as much, get plenty of exercise and not go crazy than to speed up so that your head is hardly normal. Had never had the real old melancholia before and am glad to have had it so I know what people go through. It makes me more tolerant of what happened to my father. But I figure it now that to one who has taken much physical exercise all your life your body and mind for good functioning need this as much as a motor needs oil and grease and being in N.Y. all that time without exercise and then trying to do nothing but headwork when came back was working the one part without greasing it with the other. Anyway am feeling fine now.

Why don't you come down here when you get through with Phoenix [Arizona]? You like the kids and where they are best is in their own home and this place really runs very smoothly and we eat very well and we would love to see you. I'm fonder of you than anybody in the world except Pauline and Jinny and I wish you would come to see us when we are living our regular normal life as well as something like New York. It is only this last year that I have gotten any sort of understanding or feeling about how anyone can feel about their children or what they can mean to them. If you don't come down I'll see that you see however much you want of Pat and Gregory but you would like them here. I've always thought that only one thing mattered, your own career, and like a general in a battle I would sacrifice anything to my work and I would not let my self be fond of anything I could not lose. But now I have learned that you have no success while you are alive; the only success that counts while you live is making money and I refused that. So I am going to work for success after I am dead and I am going to be very careful of the troops and have no casualties that I can help and I am going to take pleasure in the things that I have while I have them. Well, you take care of yourself—and we wish you would come down here. We won't have the Hollywood restaurant but we can have good talk and good food and I'll always have a beer with you at 11:30 in the morning.

We've had lovely weather ever since the first of the year. Like the finest spring days. The last few days the wind has been in the north because of the heavy cold up there but that only makes for good sleeping. This is Sunday afternoon and I've just missed the airmail with this letter so it will have to go tomorrow. Tell Pauline's father we are so pleased you are haveing such fine weather in Phoenix. I would like to see that desert country. We may drive through there next fall. The children all send love.

Much love always,
Ernest

Am looking forward to the belt very much!

PH. PUL

To MAXWELL PERKINS, Key West, 7 February 1936

Dear Max:

Thanks for sending me the dopesheets. Tell the Rand School people they can use the Killers for adaptation as a play and performance by the Experimental Players of the Rand Playhouse, 7 East 15th Street but only there and no where else and that I reserve all rights for any commercial adaptation or performance myself and no performances are to be given outside of the Rand playhouse without my written permission. I also expressly reserve all other rights in the story and grant them only permission to adapt and perform the story as a play in the one place, the Rand Playhouse, 7 East 15th street.

It might be better to have a lawyer state this but that seems to cover it. Just got, now, while writing this, my Feb Royalty statement. There wasn't any mention of the Green Hills. I wrote you some time ago asking about that—what it did—but haven't heard. Could you ask the retail department to send me De Caulaincourt's With Napoleon in Russia, and Inside Europe by John Gunther. Would also like to have a statement from the retail department of the amount of money I spent on books in all of 1935. I need this for my income tax.

Thanks for telling me about Mrs. Flandrau. Perhaps we will run into her. Have been driven nuts by visitors this last ten days. Everything from movie stars up and down and they have cost me a week's work except for one good day. The people all come at once and always in the cool season when I have to get my work done.

Feel awfully about Scott. I tried to write him once (wrote him several times) to cheer him up but he seems to almost take a pride in his shamelessness of defeat. The Esquire pieces seem to me to be so miserable. There is another one comeing too. I always knew he couldn't think—he never could—but he had a marvellous talent and the thing is to use it—not whine in public. Good God, people go through that emptiness many times in life and come out and do work. I always thought, from when I first met him, that if Scott had gone to that war that he always felt so bad about missing, he would have been shot for cowardice. But that has nothing to do with his writing, a writer can be a coward but at least he should be a writer. Hell I can't write about this and it is rotten to speak against Scott after all he had to go through. But I saw all the first part of it and it was so avoidable and self imposed and always from the one source—though the source spread into many channels and some of them you would never believe came from the same spring. Maybe the Church would help him. You can't tell. Work would help him; noncommercial, honest work—a paragraph at a time. But he judged a paragraph by how much money it made him and ditched his juice into that channel because he got an instant satisfaction. While if you don't make so much and somebody said it was no good he would be afraid. It was a terrible thing for him to love youth so much that he jumped straight from youth to senility without going through manhood. The minute he felt youth going he was frightened again and thought there was nothing between youth and age. But it is so damned easy to criticize our friends and I shouldn't write this. I wish we could help him.

Best to Johnny Herrmann when you see him. During the height of the visitors we hooked and landed another triple header on sailfish—caught 7 in 4 days. Waldo [Peirce] and family due here Thursday—good old Waldo.

Best to you always Max

PUL   Ernest

To SARA MURPHY, Key West, c. 27 February 1936

Dearest Sara:

Just got your letter today along with a giant hangover like all the tents of Ringling. So this is letter out of the hangover into the snow [of Saranac Lake, New York]. Hangover came about through visit of my lawyer Mr. [Maurice] Speiser whom I cannot see without the aid and abettment of alcohol plus seeing off in southern farewell the Judge [Arthur Powell] of the Wallace Stevens evening. Remember that Judge and Mr. Stevens? Nice Mr. Stevens. This year he came again sort of pleasant like the cholera and first I knew of it my nice sister Ura [Ursula] was coming into the house crying because she had been at a cocktail party at which Mr. Stevens had made her cry by telling her forcefully what a sap I was, no man, etc. So I said, this was a week ago, "All right, that's the third time we've had enough of Mr. Stevens." So headed out into the rainy past twilight and met Mr. Stevens who was just issuing from the door haveing just said, I learned later, "By God I wish I had that Hemingway here now I'd knock him out with a single punch." So who should show up but poor old Papa and Mr. Stevens swung that same fabled punch but fertunatly missed and I knocked all of him down several times and gave him a good beating. Only trouble was that first three times put him down I still had my glasses on. Then took them off at the insistence of the judge who wanted to see a good clean fight without glasses in it and after I took them off Mr. Stevens hit me flush on the jaw with his Sunday punch bam like that. And this is very funny. Broke his hand in two places. Didn't harm my jaw at all and so put him down again and then fixed him good so he was in his room for five days with a nurse and Dr. working on him. But you mustn't tell this to anybody. Not even Ada [MacLeish]. Because he is very worried about his respectable insurance standing and I have promised not to tell anybody and the official story is that Mr. Stevens fell down a stairs. I agreed to that and said it was o.k. with me if he fell down the lighthouse stairs. So please promise not to tell anybody. But Pauline who hates me to fight was delighted. Ura had never seen a fight before and couldn't sleep for fear Mr. Stevens was going to die. Anyway last night Mr. Stevens comes over to make up and we are made up. But on mature reflection I don't know anybody needed to be hit worse than Mr. S. Was very pleased last night to see how large Mr. Stevens was and am sure that if I had had a good look at him before it all started would not have felt up to hitting him. But can assure you that there is no one like Mr. Stevens to go down in a spectacular fashion especially into a large puddle of water in the street in front of your old waddel street home where all took place. So I shouldn't write you this but news being scarce your way and I know you really won't tell anybody will you really absolutely seriously. Because otherwise I am a bastard to write it. He apologised to Ura very handsomely and has gone up to Pirates Cove to rest his face for another week before going north.[1] I think he is really one of those mirror fighters who swells his muscles and practices lethal punches in the bathroom while he hates his betters. But maybe I am wrong. Anyway I think Gertrude Stein ought to give all these people who pick fights with poor old papa at least their money back. I am getting damned tired of it but not nearly as tired of it as Mr. Stevens got. It was awfully funny to have a man just declaring how he was going to annihilate you and show up just at that moment. Then have him land his awful punch on your jaw and nothing happen except his hand break. You can tell Patrick. It might amuse him. But don't tell anybody else. Tell Patrick for statistics sake Mr. Stevens is 6 feet 2 weighs 225 lbs. and that when he hits the ground it is highly spectaculous. I told the Judge, the day after, to tell Mr. S. I thought he was a damned fine poet but to tell him he couldn't fight. The Judge said, "Oh, but your wrong there. He is a very good fighter. Why, I saw him hit a man once and knock him the length of this room." And I said, "Yes, Judge. But you didn't catch the man's name, did you?" I think it was a waiter. Nice dear good Mr. Stevens. I hope he doesn't brood about this and take up archery or machine gunnery. But you promise you won't tell anybody.

Poor Sara. I'm sorry you had such a bad time. These are the bad times. It is sort of like the retreat from Moscow and Scott [Fitzgerald] is gone the first week of the retreat. But we might as well fight the best god-damned rear guard action in history and God knows you have been fighting it.

Weather has been lousy for fishing the last ten days or so. Put the boat on the ways and scraped and sanded her and repainted. Also copper-painted the bottom with a new paint called murcop that has murcury in it and is supposed to be very good. Have it looking swell. Now must write an Esquire piece, do my income tax, and then get back to my book. Hope to God the people will be gone.

Waldo [Peirce] is here with his kids like untrained hyenas and him as domesticated as a cow. Lives only for the children and with the time he puts on them they should have good manners and be well trained but instead they never obey, destroy everything, don't even answer when spoken to, and he is like an old hen with a litter of apehyenas. I doubt if he will go out in the boat while he is here. Can't leave the children. They have a nurse and a housekeeper too, but he is only really happy when trying to paint with one setting fire to his beard and the other rubbing mashed potato into his canvasses. That represents fatherhood.

HMD   [Rest of letter missing.]

1. Stevens seems to have spent the week of 26 February–4 March at Pirate's Cove. He was back in his Hartford, Connecticut, office on Monday, 9 March. See *Letters of Wallace Stevens*, ed. Holly Stevens (New York, 1966), p. 308. This would place the fight about 19 February and the date of EH's letter to Sara Murphy about 27 February. See Carlos Baker, *Ernest Hemingway: A Life Story* (New York, 1969), pp. 285, 617.

To ARNOLD GINGRICH, Key West, 5 April 1936

Dear Arnold:

I am sending you a story[1] with this as I wrote you I thought I might have to. Pauline is typing it while I write this and I am going in to relieve her while she eats lunch. It is a good story and I think you will like it. Finished it about two months ago. Am on page sixty of another one and in the middle of my book and I can't afford to write an article. But if this story is not suitable for you to publish wire me and I will write an article anyway.

In this you can take out the bolster from between the woman's legs if that is necessary. Also if you think it will be objectionable for the anarcho-syndicalist waiter to refer to the priests as black pigs you can change that to crows. Or remove it. I don't think there is anything else unpublishable. You can use whore for puta or puta for whore. I have a copy of the original mss. for book use.

Harry Burton, ed of Cosmopolitan was down here, leaving yest. He came to get stories and bid on the novel. Offered 7500 for anything the length of One Trip Across and a sliding scale down to 3,000 for the shortest ones. I got either 5500 or 6500, forget which, for One Trip Across. He said he could promise 40,000 for the serialization on novel but asked me not to say anything abut this. I may let him have a couple of good long stories as I need the money and pretty soon if I am not publishing somewhere else your owners will think it is because I cannot publish anywhere else.

As titles for the story I have: Outside The Ring; The Start of the Season; The Capitol of Illusion; A Boy named Paco—too easy; To Empty Stands; The Judgment of Distance?; The Sub-Novice Class. Will try to do better. You may have an idea. I have a carbon.

Will you let me know the deadline for leaving myself off the cover next month in case I am still in this long story which is getting plenty longer? I plan to leave for Cuba the 24th. Am in the novel to where I needed to be over there again for something. Am in sort of a better epoque of working now and just remembered that I always work well in the Spring. Hope everything is well with you. Please wire me as soon as you get the story will you?

In case my name should be on the cover for articles this month you could explain in a note inside that I was too busy on something long to write an article so you got this story out of me. Or whatever. Will wire you today that am sending story and its length as soon as I count the words.

> Best luck always
> Ernest

Sorry about the Fiction Parade mixup—what do I have to do to get my $50.00? Harry Burton told me one, just one, of the editors of reader's digest made $104,000 last year. That was what I was trying to tell you about Ray Long used to get 150,000 a year and a *bonus* of 75,000.

PH. PUL

1. "The Horns of the Bull," *Esquire* 5 (June 1936). In *The Fifth Column and The First Forty-nine Stories* (1938), it was renamed "The Capital of the World."

To MAXWELL PERKINS, Key West, 9 April 1936

Dear Max:

Thanks for your letter of April 6 that came yest. You must have written one that I never got as never had any answer about the stories. This may cross one of yours in answer to my wire but will take a chance.

Here's the story situation.

I have 5 now—One Trip Across runs about 12,000. It is a very good story (I re-read it) and would carry a big part of a book of stories. I also have the one you read in Esquire called The Tradesman's Return which is 4275 words. Another one, one of the best I've ever written called, tentatively, The Capitol which is 4500 which am going to publish in the June Esquire. I was going so well on this long one I've just finished that would not interrupt to write an article so sent them that story at considerable loss. But made plenty by finishing the long one which finished day before yest. It is about 11,000 words and is a very exciting story of Africa which I think can publish in Cosmopolitan. About the length they call a short novel. Their Editor was down here last week and said he would pay me 7,500 for stories as long as the One Trip Across grading down to 3,000 for the really short ones. This last story is tentatively titled A Budding Friendship.[1] Also have another story of Africa called The Happy Ending[2] which is between 7200 and 7500 words long and a major story. Of these five the weakest is the Tradesman's Return and you know it is a long way from lousy. The others all have almost as much action as the One Trip Across and run, I suppose, about sixty percent dialogue. That means we have on hand approximately 39,000 words of new short stories.

Now do you think it best to add these five stories to the 44 stories of In Our Time, Men Without Women, Winner Take Nothing (not counting the chapters between the I.O.T. stories as stories) and bring out the big book as The First Forty-Nine?[3] Or add some more stories to these five and publish as a separate book?

What I was working on was to have some *damned* good ones to end the big book with. That was my first job and I have done that now. But we can always bring out that collection and I have almost enough for a new book now. But I don't want to have a new book without unity and these all have so much action that I need a couple of quiet ones. In Winner Take Nothing they were all quiet ones except the first one. There was damn little for the so-called plain reader. In these new ones only one story is difficult; The Happy Ending and it doesn't seem difficult when reading it because there is so much dialogue. But they are all very good ones because I was shooting all the works figuring on ending with them.

The other problem is when to publish—if I am bringing out a book of stories I want it to be one that is going to knock them over he says, modestly. When is the latest you would have to have title and copy for fall publication? I have two other long stories one with about six thousand words done on it—another with not quite that much which I am going to finish in Cuba. It is always cool there in the mornings and have done some of my best stuff there. Have been working like hell lately and am beginning to get not stale but plenty tired. Any time have a minute is taken up writing to recommend people for the Houghton Mifflin Fellowship. How many of these fellowships are there? If there is only one have written over 1000 dollars worth of letter writing myself. As far as can recall never had any fellowship myself except drunken more or less good fellowship when starting writing but they say times are different now.

You will be delighted to know that I made quite a lot of money gambling which has kept me from hitting you for any since some time. Esquire is also getting prosperous. Sully [J. B. Sullivan] and I are thinking of opening up a high class gambling joint next winter. I hope we can count on your patronage. You will also be delighted to know that I have stopped gambling now and will not be gambling any more until my winnings are gone. Then I want to make enough to go to Africa. Mr. Josie [Russell] is laying off the operation of his highly successful joint because he is getting bartender's foot from standing up all day and all night and the day after the farewell ball of the Fireman's Convention he is going over to Cuba with me and we plan to put in two weeks of intensive recuperation from our arduous winter. Why don't you come down? You could fly down. I will let you read all these stories and we can discuss the book. Havana is a marvellous place especially when you have just made a little money and been going well. I've had a belle epoque of working lately—like the best I've ever had. You have the same juice only now you can handle a wider range and you have more knowledge under your belt. Have been working like a horse and the day finished went out in the aft at 3 p.m. with Patrick and caught two big sailfish 7 feet 8 and 7 feet 11.

Thank you also for the invitation to meet Miss Nancy Hale at your home which I received too late to make the trip up. I would like to get a good idea from her sometime for a story to be called Sea Change and then Dashiel to publish it. Please tell her how sorry I was I could not come.

The other angle about publishing is: if I sell A Budding Friendship to Cosmo they couldn't publish it before July or Aug. Then if they bought The Happy Ending that would carry into Sept. that would be o.k. But if I had another one that was saleable that would be Nov. or Dec. Well we can see and they might not want any of them but A Budding Friendship (I hope to God I can beat that as a title) is a swell story as fool proof as One Trip Across or Fifty Grand, and the guy was down here asking for them. But maybe he was just making conversation.

Gingrich wired me too that Scott seemed better. I wish he would pull out of that shamelessness of defeat. We're all going to die. Isn't it time enough to quit then? What is he doing? What is he going to do? He can't have adopted being through as a career can he? He and Maxie Baer have something in common.

Am going to Cuba April 24. Do you want to join us or go over with us? Have the boat in swell shape and the motors running beautifully. Pauline is fine. She is going up to visit her folks and take Gregory when I go to Cuba. Jinny has just gotten back from Europe and her folks are getting old and miss their children. The kids are all fine. Bumby doing well in school too. Charles has a hell of a time. His brother keeps him down and won't let him make any jack. He gets pretty low sometimes. Burge had a baby. He is doing o.k. for a rummy and working hard. Did you see the pretty girl he married? How is Johnny Herrmann our other rummy? Did you ever see his new girl. You better come to Havana.

So long Max
Ernest

[Marginal postscript:] How is Griswold? Hope he is better. I'll be a son of a bitch if I'll ever be in N.Y. when another book comes out. It took me 2 months to get over it. Being in N.Y., its self, was good though. Don't tell [Whitney] Darrow I need any money. I don't want sales dropped below what he considers the danger mark. Green Hills came out in England April 3—Haven't heard yet. They made a very nice looking book. I took out 7 bloodies, one son of a bitch and 4 or five shits voluntarily to see what difference it would make, to please them and Owen

Wister. See if it will sail as well or as badly with those reefs. A shame I couldn't have removed a cocksucker as a special gift to Jonathan Cape Ltd.

With Up In Michigan to come in 2nd position in the book, that would make 6 stories and probably give the necessary diversification. Then even if I published The Happy Ending in early fall we could come out in the fall.

Am working on a title.

PUL

1. "A Budding Friendship," renamed "The Short Happy Life of Francis Macomber," *Cosmopolitan* 101 (September 1936). 2. "The Happy Ending," renamed "The Snows of Kilimanjaro," *Esquire* 6 (August 1936). 3. *The Fifth Column and The First Forty-nine Stories* (1938).

To JOHN DOS PASSOS, Key West, 12 April 1936

Dear Dos:

Damned glad to hear via Gerald [Murphy] that your book [*The Big Money*] is finished. When I got your letter written on the New Bedford boat wrote you a long letter to your last N.Y. address. But guess you never got it. Next I heard you were at the Lafayette.

We had a good winter in the early part and I got a hell of a lot of work done. Then the visiting shitsmen arrived with their consorts or art editors in overlapping succession. It just quit the last of March.

Waldo was down too, as domesticated as a cow except that they have to buy milk somewhere else. He is like an old bear that had hatched out the Dionne Quintuplets and wanted them saved instead of destroyed. He is as good a guy as ever but it is sort of as though they had taken his cojones out and put in nursing bottles. He will be all right, I guess, when they get off to school but in the meantime with absolutely nothing wrong with the kids nor to worry about them he worries all day and all night and literally, actually, thinks nor ever talks of anything else. Maybe it's on account of haveing children of some sort ever since can remember that am prejudiced against them as a full time occupation for a man—and old Waldo is certainly damned nice.

What are your plans? Pauline is going up to see her family and give them a dose of the jew [Gregory], which they are clamoring for, and I suppose it will be good for Gregory to get whatever disease he hasn't had as that is what a trip to Piggott the disease cultural center of America means. The last trip was whoop cough, before that measles, before that chicken pox etc. Barring children's diseases, which, on form can't be barred she's due back early in may. I'm going to Havana in the boat on the 24th. To stay there a month or so. Then go to Bimini for June. We're going out west somewhere up in the mountains this summer. Might go to Mex. in fall.

If you are ready to tropic up a little why not join me at Havana? You and Katy. I have made a little money gambling and am o.k. to mener [lead] une vie tres large on the boat for a while. Have finished my book of stories and have some very good ones (he says modestly). Pauline says I only write "a fine long letter" and "a hell of a good story." Well at that it is pleasanter than quitting a la irelandais even if more irritating to one's friends. Had to give Gingrich another story rather than interrupt what I was working on to write a piece. Will be in June. Hope you will like. Won't bother to tell you how good it is.

If you and Katy can't come why don't you come? The only friend I have who will go anywhere with me now without his wife is Mr. Josie [Russell]. Of course he has had his wife longer than any of my other friends too. Anyway he is going for two weeks the night after the fare-well ball of the firemen's convention ending here the 23rd of this mo. Mrs. [Jane] Mason, I believe is also crossing with us. Mrs. Mason is almost as apt at going places without her husband as Mr. Josie is without his wife. But then Mrs. Mason has also had her husband for a long time too al-though Mr. Josie I believe there is no doubt has had his much much oftener as well as longer than Mr. Mason.

You ought to meet Gertrude Stein, Passos, it's the wife has a cow in-fluence creeping into the letter.[1]

Could you send me, by return post, the address of J. Kashkeen of Moscow? If you haven't it would you get it from B[unny] Wilson? Tell your wife, Katherine, that I am sad to report after running Mr. Wilson's last pieces through the Haynes Sugar test that I am forced to note heavy deposits of senility. I don't know whether this early senility is a general Princeton complaint and corresponds down there to what we have instead as the old rale but the test tube doesn't lie where a Princeton man is concerned. As a second thought don't say anything about this to Elinor Wylie or Katy either as I have almost enough pals among the critics as it is without winning Wilson's undying gratitude for this inex-pensive analysis.

Do you remember your visitor Mr. [Wallace] Stevens? Have something very funny to tell you about him when see you. I promised Mr. S. not to say anything about it so will have to simply put you in the presence of witnesses. Or if you are in Provincetown and would like to hear about it, as an admirerer of Mr. Stevens, as I am, get hold of Harry Sylvester, a young man high up in the plains clothes jesuits, who was down here on his honey moon at the time.[2]

As I say am always a perfectly safe man to tell any dirt to as it goes in one ear and out my mouth.

Pauline and all the kids are fine. Do you remember that maricon duque de Arcos, twenty sixth Duke, with the swell looking girl he had as front? Well he was killed in a motor car accident just north of Miami running into a swamp jigs old Ford with another Spanish title with him. Was going to wire you in case you needed something good for the last of your book but you can have it for another book, pal.

Canby and Esther [Chambers] have been getting along fine all winter. Jack Coles is here with his new squaw who looks something like one of these new style wrestlers. The hero. Not the villain. You can tell the hero always because he is pimpled. The villain is bearded. The Coles are ideally happy and read aloud from the new collected works of Havelock Ellis.

What else would you care to know, Passos? Kim, they call me, the Little Friend of All the World. Just a sentimentalist at heart and what a heart. Sewer-Heart they call him.

This is nothing Passos to the type of good clean dirt I will put on tap if youse will venture down the carribeans. Let us hear from you, pal, even if it's only a quick maladiction.

Love to Katy.
Yours always,
Hem

We missed you both like hell all winter. I get tired of the four letter folk.

UVA

1. A reference to Gertrude Stein's *A Book Concluding with As a Wife Has a Cow* (Paris, 1926). 2. See EH to Sara Murphy, *c.* 27 February 1936.

To MAXWELL PERKINS, Cat Cay, Bahamas, 11 July 1936

Dear Max:

Gingrich was down here and I showed him the 30,000 words I had done on the Key West-Havana novel of which One Trip Across and The Tradesman's Return were a part.[1] I had taken these for the book of stories and he seemed to think that was crazy. I haven't even looked at

the 30,000 since I left off to finish the book of stories—anyway I've decided to go on and finish that book now when we go out west—that will
only take 2 stories from a book—and you will have plenty of others by
the time you want the stories, and it can come out after this book. The
book contrasts the two places—and shows their inter-relation—also contains what I know about the mechanics of revolution and what it does
to the people engaged in it. There are two themes in it—the decline of
the individual—The Man Harry—who shows up first in One Trip Across—
and then his re-emergence as Key West goes down around him—and the
story of a shipment of dynamite and all of the consequences that happened from it. There is a hell of a lot more that I won't inflict on you.
But with luck it is a good book. Gingrich was very steamed up about
what he read and wanted me to promise not to bring out the stories until
I'd finished this—I got the last stuff I needed for it on my last trip
across—Also have the hurricane and the vets in it.

I owe you as I recall 1100 dollars advance on the book of stories. I
have enough stories for a book but not if I take out One Trip Across and
The Tradesman's Return. I can return you the 1100 if you want—or you
can let that ride on the next book of stories—or let it ride on this new
book. Tell me which you prefer? Have arranged with Gingrich to write
only 6 pieces a year for Esquire instead of what I was doing so as not to
interfere—am to get same amount for six as formerly for 12—but do not
have to have them in if let him know in advance and I refund an advance
so I wouldn't *have* to turn them out if busy on any of this other. Did you
read The Snows of Kilimanjaro and The Short Happy Life of Francis
Macomber? Would have written you this before but had to get it all
straightened out. I stink so to the N.Y. critics that if I bring out a book
of stories no matter how good this fall they will all try to kill it. Well I
will be able to give them both barrels next Spring and Fall with a book
and a book of stories if you want to play it that way. Meantime the stuff
I publish will not hurt my reputation any. All I want to do is get out
west and settled down in a cabin writing. We caught a 514 and a 610
lb tuna. So far have been bitched on marlin—lost one over 700 and one
over 1000. He straightened the hook straight as a pencil! Well what the
hell I really have another trade beside marlin fishing and am very anxious
to get back to work at it. We will stay out west until Oct or so. Then
back to K.W. to work hard before the bloody sons of bitching winter
visitors come.

I hope I've not let you down about the story book.

Please let me know to K.W. Leave here Thursday if catch some decent
weather. It's been blowing a gale for 3 days. Will try to get this off on
plane today. Don't think I'm trying to stall on the story book as have Up
In Michigan; One Trip Across; The Horns of the Capitol [Bull]; Trades-

man's Return; Short Happy Life of Francis Macomber; The Snows of Kilimanjaro; besides what's new and unnamed. But if I can lift those 2 and finish this other then with only a couple more stories I have 2 books instead of one and one of them that thing the pricks all love—a novel.

Best always

PUL   Ernest

1. *To Have and Have Not* (1937).

To MARJORIE KINNAN RAWLINGS,[1] Nordquist Ranch, Wyoming, 16 August 1936

Dear Mrs. Rawlings:

Thank you very much for writing, and for asking us to stop (which we would have done if hadn't got the letter out here) and for writing you liked the Snows story. I couldn't tell much about it. Wrote it last fall just before the Matecumbe hurricane and then put it away and didn't read it until re-wrote it in Cuba this spring. I'm awfully damned glad you liked it. I liked it too but then I always like them or burn them so that doesn't mean anything.

Maybe I could get Max up there sometime. He wants to go I know but he is afraid of women and you according to all accounts and what little I saw of you on Bimini happen to be a woman. You ask what his fear is and damned if I know. I guess he thinks they give you more daughters. I don't know what else there is to be afraid of in them for Max. All the danger they have ever seemed to have is that they can break your bloody heart, marry you, or give you the clap. But am a very simple fellow and maybe they have really dangerous ones somewhere like the Sladang in Indo China where have never been but if went would probably find not very dangerous.

As for being Sportsman being Artist. I always fished and shot since I could carry a canepole or a single barrelled shotgun; not to show off but for great inner pleasure and almost complete satisfaction. Have not been writing as long but get the same pleasure, and you do it alone, only it is a goddamned sight harder to do and if I did nothing else (no fish, no shoot, no drink) would probably go nuts doing it with the difficulty, the times in between when you can't do it, the always being short of what you want to do, the rest of it with all of which you have probably lived some time and various places. Lately I have felt I was going to die in a short time (hope that is nuts and that live to be a wise old man with white beard and chew tobacco) and so I have been haveing more fun maybe than I deserve because in a way I have done my work as well as I could as went along.

Wouldn't care about shoot the bear. Have gotten sort of corrupted and only like to shoot animals any more that run both ways. But shoot anything that flies well any direction or a turkey anywhere. Have you any turkeys around there? Are you liable to be there in end Nov. or early December?

If ever go back to Key West will have to go through Florida and would certainly like to stop. Don't know who we will be or whether kids or not but you won't have to put us up. We can have a drink and go on into Ocala.

Thank you very much again for writing. We caught another tuna of 610 after you left in an hour and a half. But he was a foot and a half shorter than the one that gave me the beating.

Sure all those people are awfully dumb. I like them all and get along all right but [Ben] Finney was the only friend I had there. The one Mrs. Grinnell thought was Wooley Donahue's body guard. Finney is quite a guy. The women who fish seriously are the worthiest but dullest bitches alive. 90 per cent of the men the same with a tendency toward oldmaidism. Most of it until lately was done by boys who couldn't hit a ball out of the infield at school and who wanted to excell in something. Now they are making such mechanical tackle and so many ways of cheating anybody can do it. Still and with all of it I get an awful lot of fun and excitement out of it but the people are plenty dull. My wife says she wishes I would cut it out and go back to shooting and especially live pigeon shooting because the people are so much nicer. She likes the fishing but can't stand the fishermen talking about it all night afterwards. We didn't plan to go to Bimini this year because there were going to be so many people. But its awfully hard for me not to go back anywhere. Probably will be there next year if don't have enough money to get out to Africa again.

As hard to stop a letter as to start one. Good luck and I'll try to bring Max. Am working like hell on a book. Good hunting country was burned out here last fall. Fishing ruined by a road that lets cars in. Now we'll see whether I can still write or whether I can still write. No choice.

Yours always,

Ernest Hemingway

FLA

---

1. Marjorie Kinnan Rawlings (1896–1954) was the author of *South Moon Under* (1933), *Golden Apples* (1935), and *The Yearling* (1938), all published by Scribners. She had a large orange grove at Cross Creek, Hawthorn, Florida.

This letter is used courtesy of the library of the University of Florida, Gainesville.

To ARNOLD GINGRICH, Nordquist Ranch, 16 September 1936

Dear Arnold:

Your wire came though on the forest service telephone pretty well garbled but could make out the sense. Thanks very much. You are a good guy and a good friend.

Now, like vice, it's easier. I'd like to get off from December.

Since we've been out here I've written a little over thirty thousand words. A big part of the time have been in a belle epoque. Have only laid off to go down to hunt antelope for three days and three days up to the granites to fish out of, say, thirty six days. Caught 6 over 16 inch (rainbows) 4 over 18 inch in granites. The book is ¾ through, nearly, and can see the end. Day before yesterday sent [Tom] Shevlin and his wife up to our best elk country and the bear (grizzly) baits have had out for six days to open the season (the first three days are worth the next three weeks) and stayed home to work. Finished the section I'm doing today and am riding up to hunt tomorrow for three days. Maybe five. When come back will be full of juice again but am taking yellow paper and pencil along in case it should snow or had what couldn't wait.

During this time have written you once, answered by wire, Jinny twice, unanswered, and Mac Leish, in response to urgent query once, unanswered.

Antelope hunting got two marvellous bucks one at 600, paced, one at 306 yards paced, both running, dead, one-shot mannlicher. Pauline got a nice buck. Tommy shot a doe and missed seven bucks sitting. His wife is still missing them. He is, as you know, a nice kid but he can't shoot. He has known so many big game hunters he became a big game hunter without ever burning the necessary cartridges—as though I would declare myself a polo player. Don't think I mean I got the bucks with one shot each. I shot five times at the first from 300, where they spooked, to 600 and hit him on the last shot on top of a ridge and when got up there found no blood and crawled on my belly seeing a few does and a buck following them and shot at the buck, standing, and missed and as he ran, faster than a jack rabbit down this grassy, rock filled, slope up next to the timber broke his neck on the third shot and then going on toward him found the first huge buck dead just over the ridge out of sight. Almost like the Kudu. I was not conceited enough to be sure I hit the first buck going over the ridge at 600 although I saw him buck back and if I would have had a drink would have bet a million (wartime marks), that hit him.

Well there is what news there is. You (the magazine) looks very fat and prosperous in Oct. Number. I can see you don't need me and the sound fury emphasizes it. I liked the guy who verified me by Duranty and Seabrook. That was nice. Would have to have a sound and fury party some time and pay transportation to the guys who would like to swing on you etc. Get letters from them and always offer to pay their way to Key West and their doctor bills up to Fifty bucks if they will really come down. Am down to 198 and haven't been over 205 since Bimini. But you don't write a novel with what you weigh though always hope in ten pounds off the body may take one off the brain.

Write me a letter if you get time. The mail here is very dull. Nordquist rode back today and said they have located some grizzlies. I want to shoot one in the belly to see if can make him come. I mean I would shoot him there if close enough so I could get another shot if he ran the wrong way.

Pauline sends her best as do the Shevlins. Tommy thought you were a swell guy. In spite of that am pleased they are leaveing in ten days. They have been here since the First of Sept. and I missed six days, the two trips, work. But had a good time and you fill up with juice.

Bumby has just gone back to Chicago Latin School. He lives about three blocks from you at 1320 of same street. The life out here and lots of horse tightened him up. The mouse [Patrick] is going up with us hunting with his kitty in a saddle bag. I am afraid he will be bow legged. But it is better than knockneed.

So long Arnold. I am a shit not to interrupt and write a piece but you have met other shits so its no surprize.

Best from us all.

Ernest

Will be broke shortly—but can get plenty advance on novel now I see the end O.K. So don't worry.

PH. PUL

To ARCHIBALD MAC LEISH, Nordquist Ranch,
26 September 1936

Dear Archie:

I'm sorry you can't come out, kid. Also I'm sorry your haveing such a damned awful time writing. It must be something to have people like what you write though. Nobody that I know likes what I write anymore but at least it helps them to write the way they write so I hope they like however they write a great deal.

Have been work very hard on this book. She pretty near over. All that remains now is to perform the unperformable miracle you have to always do at the end. Sometimes I think it is hard to write, too. But what the hell so is everything else.

Went on a hunt with young Tom Shevlin who has his old man's hands and feet and a fine frame but a sort of inner fragility and delicacy that will let life gain a number of yards around his end on a very few plays although he can walk very well, has a good sense of country, can't shoot like all the rich boys on account of making a few lucky flukes once so never practiced but a good kid you would like. We got three grizzlies and a couple of good elk. I ran onto three grizzlies in the woods and killed two of them. It was the sort of thing I get something out of they being very beautiful in the woods and unexpected, I'd expected elk when I heard the crashing, and the biggest one stood straight up to look at us. Two days later Tom killed a very big one on a bait. There is a huge one up there in the timberline country and I am going back to try to track him and get him in about ten days. Will work hard these next ten days. We rode home to the ranch yesterday in a blizzard. Galloped the last four miles first me ahead then Shevlin ahead slippery as a bastard on the road, crotted with mud from the hooves of the horse ahead, face solid with mud. We looked like mud statues when got down. Me I like life very much. So much it will be a big disgust when have to shoot myself. Maybe pretty soon I guess although will arrange to be shot in order not have bad effect on kids. Going to finish this book. Got to get to work now. The grizzly hide was very beautiful like a silver fox but thicker and longer and blow beautifully in the wind. Finest hide I'd ever seen. So they just came over from the ranch to say that the fellow who was takeing care of it did not do it properly so the hair has slipped. So there won't be any grizzly hide. And while all our grizzly hides slip I suppose still it is always a disappointment.

Have to get to work, Archie. Give my love to Mimi will you? Tell her to pretend I sent her the most wonderful silver tipped grizzly hide in the world that always she could step on and her feet would never be cold no matter who they were in bed with—but it slipped.

We sent Bumby back to school. Pauline and Patrick are fine. Love to your dependents and something special to Mrs. Mac Leish.

LC

Pappy

To MAXWELL PERKINS, Nordquist Ranch, 26 September 1936

Dear Max:

I'm glad you had such a good trip in Canada. Did you see Pat Morgan and his wife up there? They are at Murray Bay. I've always loved all that Quebec country. That's where we had planned to go last fall instead of New York and then like goddamned fools went to N.Y. instead.

Have worked very hard on this novel ever since out here. Knocked off two days to hunt prong horn antelope and got two very fine heads. Last six days hunted Grizzlies and we got three and two good elk. Tom Shevlin got one and I got two out of three that I ran onto in the last timber up near timberline while hunting elk. It was very exciting. They were beautiful to meet in the timber that way. Tommy got his two days later on a bait. I could have killed the three I think but they were so damned handsome I was sorry I killed more than the one but at the time did not have much time to decide. There is one very huge one that has been killing cattle and that was so big that the govt hunter when he ran onto him was afraid to shoot that am going after in about ten days. Am back to work now. Have never shot better. Hope I can write as well.

Have about 55,000 some words done. It has gone very well lately. Have been working so hard on it that am ashamed not to have written you about the Bahr book.[1] Am delighted to write the introduction of course. Could there be any chance I see them all in type first?

When finish this book hope to go to Spain if all not over there.[2] Will leave the completed Mss. in a vault so you will be covered on it. I can go over it again when I come back. In case anything should happen to me you would always be covered financially even without this novel by the book of stories.

I may have to get some money as advance on the novel soon as have refused again to write for esquire for fifth straight month now. Or is it the sixth? During that time gave them two stories I had on hand. Have no further commitments there until their January Issue. Have not wanted to do any writing that would interfere with this book.

Am down to 198 pounds and have been feeling very fit. Must knock off now to get to work again. If I wire you for money will you please deposit it in the City Bank Farmers Branch, 22 William Street. May not need any for a month or so. Haven't been spending any but haven't seen a bank statement for quite a while and must be sending Pauline and Pat home pretty soon. It is getting very cold out here now.

Hope to finish my first draft this month i.e. October. If I go to Spain will see you in N.Y. on way through. I hate to have missed this Spanish thing worse than anything in the world but have to have this book finished first.

Good bye, Max and good-luck. Thank you and Louise for the invitation to Zippy's[3] wedding. I wish we could have been there and I hope she will be as happy as she deserves. She is a lovely and beautiful girl.

Ernest

Am sorry to have been so poor a correspondent but have been over my eyes in the book.

Am glad you liked the story in Cosmop. Think have some good ones for a book. Did you like the Snows of Kilimanjaro?

PUL

1. EH wrote a preface for *All Good Americans* (1937) by Jerome Bahr, brother-in-law of Waldo Peirce. **2.** The Spanish Civil War had erupted in July. **3.** Elisabeth (Zippy) was the second daughter of Maxwell and Louise Perkins. See A. Scott Berg, *Max Perkins, Editor of Genius* (New York, 1978), p. 310.

To MAXWELL PERKINS, Key West, 15 December 1936

Dear Max:

Thanks for making the deposit. I got what needed in Cuba and am back here now to not move until the book is done.

If you want me to read either of those fishing books for you and advise on their worth would be glad to. I can do anything but write Introductions it seems. I'm sorry as hell about delaying that introduction. Will get it to you soon as can. Is Hay the man who wrote the British book? If so he is an excellent fellow. If not who is it?

Am awfully sorry about that Tom Wolfe libel suit.[1] On this book of mine we will have to put something air tight in the front to make absolutely sure no one identifies themselves with characters. How was Tom caught?

I've *got* to go to Spain. But there's no great hurry. They'll be fighting for a long time and it's cold as hell around Madrid now! I've paid two guys over there to fight (transportation and cash to Spanish Border) already. If I could send seven more could probably be a corporal. But I'm not going there as head of the Hemingstein Legion. Franco is a good general but a son of bitch of the first magnitude and he lost his chance to take Madrid for nothing by being over cautious. Did you know Quintanilla is a general now? I'll bet he's funny. I have some funny things to tell you about Cuba that won't go in a letter.

I had just sense enough never to meet Mabel Dodge. Now know enough never to meet any literate woman. It's really better not to know literate men too, I think sometimes. But what the hell.

Best always,
Ernest

PUL

1. Wolfe was involved in several litigations in 1935–1936. This one was a libel suit initiated in Brooklyn. See *Thomas Wolfe's Letters to His Mother*, ed. J. S. Terry (New York, 1943), p. 318.

To HARRY SYLVESTER,[1] Key West, 5 February 1937

Dear Harry:

The Spanish war is a bad war, Harry, and nobody is right. All I care about is human beings and alleviateing their suffering which is why back ambulances and hospitals. The rebels have plenty of good Italian ambulances. But it's not very catholic or christian to kill the wounded in the hospital in Toledo with handgrenades or to bomb the working quarter of Madrid for no military reason except to kill poor people; whose politics are only the politics of desperation. I know they've shot priests and bishops but why was the church in politics on the side of the oppressors instead of for the people—or instead of not being in politics at all? It's none of my business and I'm not makeing it mine but my sympathies are always for exploited working people against absentee landlords even if I drink around with the landlords and shoot pigeons with them. I would as soon shoot them as the pigeons.

Dos [Passos] doesn't know or understand you nor has he the respect for your faith that I have. That is ignorance. There is no snobbishness like radical snobbishness and when it is working in Dos he is not natural nor much fun. But he is a good fellow just as you are a good fellow. But you can't expect all your friends to like each other. I can like you and Dos and Jim Farrell say. But I can't expect you three guys to like each other. Nor always to like me, I guess.

I'm glad everything is fine with the kid, with you and with Rita. It has blown here now for 65 days straight. Too rough to fish. Muddy as a lye barrell. All east and south east wind. First norther today. Plan to get away to Spain last this month.

My eyes are almost too bad to box now. Am only good for bar and street fights now but think can last in that for a long time maybe if pick my spots. Took off all that fat and am around two hundred. Been feeling pretty good and sort of happy once I knew what I had to do. Good luck, Harry. Hope we see you all soon. Take care of yourself and don't worry about politics nor religion. And *never* mix them if you can help it. I think that's a dirty outfit in Russia now but I don't like any governments. No use to talk about it.

So long,
Ernest

HS

PH. PUL

1. Sylvester (b. 1908), from Brooklyn, New York, a graduate of Notre Dame, 1930, was a novelist and short story writer. He met Hemingway in Key West in the 1930s. EH's "your faith" refers to Sylvester's Catholicism. He later left the Church. See *Twentieth Century Authors*, 1st Suppl. (New York, 1955).

To THE PFEIFFER FAMILY, Key West, 9 February 1937

Dear Family:

This is from the leader of the Ingrates battalion on the wrong side of the Spanish war. When I realize that it is along in February and I have never written to thank you for the grand Christmas presents, the check which I used to pay for putting in new controls on the top deck of the boat (too technical to bore you with describing but exactly what we need for handling really big fish) and the stock, which gives me a stake in all the good actions of both you and The President, and the dividends on the other stock. They were all marvellous and made us very happy and I wanted to write the day after Christmas to tell you how much I appreciated them and instead went back into the novel. Finished that finally and went to N.Y. with it. Got involved in this Spanish business but pulled a contract to write for the North American Newspaper Alliance out of it with checks for $500. per cable to be sent to Pauline and $1000. per mail story (up to 1200 words) and no limit on number I can send.

We are very happy and the place and the kids are fine. I hate to go away but you can't preserve your happiness by trying to take care of it or putting it away in moth balls and for a long time me and my conscience both have known I had to go to Spain. Can usually treat my conscience pretty rough and even make him like it but it catches up with you once in a while. I think, now there are a lot of people down here, that Pauline is as well off here, this time of year, as in Europe. I would sort of worry about her and I have to work fairly hard and wouldn't let her go into Spain in any event. If I have to stay longer than I expect, will have her come over and come out to see her. Sidney Franklin is going with me and he can talk us out of most sort of trouble. At least he's been successful at talking himself out for years.

Saw Jinny in N.Y. looking fine and haveing a good time. Was so busy that I didn't see as much of her as I would have liked. Garfield was there too but didn't see him either. Ward seemed quite a success at doing nothing and I believe has a big future in that ahead of him.

Hope to get back in May. You have to get out of the country to write your uncensored stuff and, if they don't like it, sometimes you can't get back in. We're leaving the end of this month. Have staked the govt to some ambulances etc. The Reds may be as bad as they say but they are the people of the country versus the absentee landlords, the moors, the italians and the Germans. I know the Whites are rotten because I know them very well and I would like to have a look at the others to see how it lines up on a basis of humanity. This is the dress rehearsal for the inevitable European war and I would like to try to write anti-war war correspondence that would help to keep us out of it when it comes. I don't believe in makeing money out of other people's suffering. Hence the ambulances. Well, enough of this.

Good luck and always much love

Ernest

[Along right margin:] I'm very grateful to you both for providing Pauline who's made me happier than I've ever been.
PUL

To WALDO PEIRCE, Cat Cay, Bahamas, 27 July 1937

Dear Waldo:

Found your letter here when got back from the coast and just got the second jacket sketch forwarded from Max's office. It was damned nice of you to want to make a jacket for the book[1] and I appreciate it very much. I wish to hell I could talk to you about it as writing in a letter no bloody good. Been goofy busy re-writing book, making picture, Spanish one you'd like I think, go to see it will you if it ever shows called (named by the great originator Mac Leish) Spanish Earth, and commuting back and forth by plane to N.Y. working on the picture and then flying to coast and back to raise some dough for ambulances. Got jack for twenty cars. Ship first ones next week. Going over again to Madrid in two weeks.[2] So please excuse such a lousy letter as this.

This is Cat Cay by the way. Not the [Hotel] Barclay and it's blowing a bitch of a squall outside.

Anyway about the jacket. The first one was handsome as hell but it was Bra sitting at the tiller of his old boat

COLBY   [Rest of letter lost.]

1. The book was *To Have and Have Not*, published in October 1937. 2. For a fuller account of EH's activities at this time, see Carlos Baker, *Ernest Hemingway: A Life Story* (New York, 1969), pp. 312–16.

To MRS. PAUL PFEIFFER, Cat Cay, 2 August 1937

Dear Mother:

Thank you and Pauline's father very much for the checks for our birthdays. After the flood it must have been pretty dismal sending out $50. pigeons to your wandering children with the only way you can know where the children are is when the checks are cashed. Hope this makes sense to you. The presents were lovely. Thank you both very very much.

We've been here since the end of May with three or four trips to N.Y., the coast and back, Washington thrown in, and this afternoon Ada, Pat and Gregory fly to Miami and tomorrow midnight, Pauline, Bumby and I run the boat to Miami. Then store the boat up the Miami river away from hurricanes. Go to Key West and in a couple of days less than two weeks I go back to Spain where, if you get your politics from direct or indirect, you know I am on the wrong side and should be destroyed along with all the other Reds. After which Hitler and Mussolini can come in and take the minerals they need to make a European war. Well let's wish them all luck because they will need it. I get sort of sick of hearing all this tripe and running against a solid wall of nobody wanting to hear anything true about this war so will be glad, in a way, to be back at it with no necessity for talking about it. I haven't talked about it much. Have my N.A.N.A. [North American Newspaper Alliance] newspaper job back, but if it folds up for any reason have some other jobs to do. We got money for twenty ambulances on the coast and the film should bring in fifty to a hundred more. Which will handle that problem anyway.

Pauline and the children are fine. She looks lovely; is really much prettier than ever. The children are delightful which as you know is something pretty difficult for children to be in hot weather. Gregory will go with Ada to Syracuse when they leave Key West and Pauline is taking the other two boys to a ranch. This time a bull ranch in Mexico where Sidney Franklin is going to look after them all. He did a fine job of looking after me in Spain and now he goes into Reserve for a while. It should be a good variation on a dude ranch.

Virginia was here for a while then went off with Mrs. [Jane] Mason to Havana from where they were both going to Acapulco in Mexico. They seemed to be haveing a very good time.

I like the house in Piggott much better than the White House. Mrs. Roosevelt is enormously tall, very charming, and almost stone deaf. She hears practically nothing that is said to her but is so charming that most people do not notice it. The President is very Harvard charming and sexless and womanly, seems like a great Woman Secretary of Labor, say, he is completely paralyzed from the waist down and there is much skill-ful manoevering of him into the chair and from room to room. The White House, when we were there, was very hot, no air conditioning except in the President's study, and the food was the worst I've ever eaten. (This between us. As a guest cannot criticize.) We had a rainwater soup fol-lowed by rubber squab, a nice wilted salad and a cake some admirer had sent in. An enthusiastic but unskilled admirer. I wished Karl [Pfeiffer] could have been there to eat the meal. They both were very moved by the Spanish Earth picture but both said we should put more propaganda in it.[1]

Am glad to have met them and seen the place, as am glad to have seen Hollywood, but wouldn't care to live there. Harry Hopkins was at the White House dinner. I was very impressed by him and liked him very much.

It was damned nice of the Roosevelts to have us there and to see the picture and I appreciate it. Write you this not as violator of hospitality but only to give inside impression. Not to be circulated. Martha Gellhorn,[2] the girl who fixed it up for Joris Ivens and I to go there, ate three sand-wiches in the Newark airport before we flew to Washington. We thought she was crazy at the time but she said the food was always uneatable and everybody ate before they went there to dinner. She has stayed there a lot. Me, I won't be staying there any more.

Dear Mother I am sorry about going back to Spain and I think what you write about staying here and looking after the boys is very sound. But when I was there I promised them I would be back and while we cannot keep all our promises I do not see how not to keep that one. I would not be able to teach my boys much if I did. Maybe I cannot teach them much anyway but they have a good start, in their varying ways, and no one knows what the goal we aim for is any more. Certainly it is not security; the only thing I was trained to try to achieve.

You have always led such a fine life, giveing such a just proportion to this world and to the next one, that the ones of our generation who have to make our own decisions and mistakes must seem, rightly very often silly. I've temporarily I hope, lost all confidence in the next one. It seems to have no importance at all. On the other hand this last spell of war completely eliminated all fear of death or anything else. It seemed as though the world were in such a bad way and certain things so necessary to do that to think about any personal future was simply very egoistic. After the first two weeks in Madrid had an impersonal feeling of haveing no wife, no children, no house, no boat, nothing. The only way to function. But now have been home just long enough to lose it all; to value all the things again; and now go back knowing I have to put them all away again. So don't point out how much harder it is on them because have a little imagination too. So enough of this lousy talk. But maybe when come back this next time will come up to Piggott to shoot quail and will get all talked out to you.

Good bye and good luck. I feel terribly about the flood. Good old Mother Nature that the boys talk about. If there was such a thing as Mother Nature I'll bet she was as crazy and wicked tempered as Mike Strater's wife. I'd like to see you put in as Mother Nature for a while and let there be a little honest, realistic, gentle reasonableness to the weather. You could blow up once in a while and give us a good moderate cloudburst but none of these insane female tantrums we get from the present occupant.

Must stop this now from lack of paper; the plane leaving and must get out in the boat.

Give my very best to all the family in Piggott. And thank you again for the birthday checks.

Ernest

Finished my novel (re-writing etc.) out in Sept or early October.
PUL

1. See Carlos Baker, *Ernest Hemingway: A Life Story* (New York, 1969), pp. 312–16. The dinner at the White House took place 8 July 1937. 2. Martha Ellis Gellhorn (b. St. Louis, Missouri, 1908), novelist and journalist, educated at John Burroughs School, St. Louis, and Bryn Mawr College, Pennsylvania. Married first to Marquis Bertrand de Jouvenel, French journalist, she brought out her first novel in 1934. She and EH had met in Key West in December 1936.

To HADLEY MOWRER,[1] Key West, 31 January 1938

Dearest Hadley:

Am enclosing two checks just received for Bumby's education fund. Uncle Gus [Pfeiffer] has given each of the children forty more shares of the same stock (par value $100 a share paying a dividend of 4%) and I just today received the notification and the papers to execute and attach to the original trust deed. Will look after it right away.

Hope you and Paul and Bumby are all well and fine and that everything goes well with you.

Just got here day before yesterday and am nine months behind in correspondence business and general pile up. Am also very homesick for Spain. Tell Paul I'd like to tell him about Teruel some time. After I took [Herbert] Mathews and [Sefton] Delmer on my own responsability when they'd been refused passes, had the censor so she was prepared to lose her job to let our stuff through (they were only allowed to send the communique) got the first story of the battle to N.Y. ten hours ahead of Mathews even, went back, made the whole attack with the infantry, entered town behind one company dinamiters and three of infantry, filed that, went back and had most godwonderful housetohouse fighting story ready to put on wire when Nana [N.A.N.A.] cabled they didn't want anymore. Too expensive I guess. So the catholic night desk on the Times threw away all my stuff and cut my name out of Mathews dispatches and just last night in bed read in Time about how Mathews was only newspaperman to actually be in Teruel. But first the Times retook the town for Franco on the strength of a Salamanca communique. They refused to use my stuff so N.A.N.A. would cable me to lay off. Oh well. You certainly learn to eat a ton of it and I've still to learn to like the taste. Mathews is a wonderful guy and I'm glad I could be of any use to him. But when you wait three months for something you know is going to happen and then have your work absolutely and completely sabotaged, add in the papers that printed two columns of things Max Eastman wished he'd said and wished he'd done to me as facts without ever asking me what happened or any of the witnesses what really happened, see them gang up on a book, think maybe I'd better change my name and start over. Or maybe could just get Alexander Woolcott to issue my stuff as reprints collected by him without bothering to publish it separately first.

Tell Paul I saw Richard [Mowrer] when he came to Madrid last time and he was fine.

Give Bumby my love and tell him I will write him. I appreciated his letter very much. Enclose check for him to buy something for Christmas.

Had a rough trip over, gale all the way, then brought the little boat down from Miami in a gale. Am too tired to write. Please excuse. Wrote a play in Madrid [*The Fifth Column*] that think you'd like. Don't know whether it will ever be produced and don't really give a good goddamn about that nor about anything else but on acct setting bad example am going to stick around and make somebody else shoot me. Only they can't hit me anymore the way they could when was a kid. On other hand they can't scare me either which is surprise and relief. Don't pay any attention this. Probably feel cheerful as hell tomorrow. Mr. H. has great elasticity. Excuse lousy gloomy letter. Look at beautiful checks and rejoice. Much love to you and all my best to Paul. I admire you both very much.

PH. PUL   Ernest

1. Hadley, divorced from EH in 1927, had married Paul Scott Mowrer in 1933.

To JOHN DOS PASSOS, Paris, *c.* 26 March 1938

Dear Dos:

I'm sorry I sent you that cable from the boat. It seemed funny when I sent it. Afterwards it seemed only snotty.

But I want to speak to you about something that seems to me to be serious. A war is still being fought in Spain between the people whose side you used to be on and the fascists. If with your hatred of communists you feel justified in attacking, for money, the people who are still fighting that war I think you should at least try to get your facts right. In an article just read in the Red Book you do not mention [Gustavo] Duran's name when it would have been correct and fair to do so. But you do feel you should mention Walter's and you call him a Russian general. You give the impression that it is a communist run war and you name a Russian General you met.

The only trouble about this, Dos, is that Walter is a Pole. Just as Lucacz was a Hungarian, Petrov a Bulgarian, Hans a German, Copic a Yugo-Slav and so on. I'm sorry, Dos, but you didn't meet any Russian generals.[1] The only reason I can see for your attacking, for money, the side that you were always supposed to be on is an unsuppressable desire to tell the truth. Then why not tell the truth? The thing is that you don't find out the truth in ten days or three weeks and this hasn't been a communist run war for a long time. When people read a series of articles running over six months and more from you they do not realize how short a time you were in Spain and how little you saw. That was what made me send the cable but I should have put it in a decent, not a snotty form. Then there is Nin. Do you know where Nin is now? You ought to find that out before you write about his death. But what the hell. There were some good russians in Spain but you didn't meet them and they aren't there now. When [Herbert] Mathews and I went into Teruel in the assault on the fifth day of the fighting behind three companies of Infantry and a company of dinamiters the town people all thought we were Russians. I could tell you some funny stories about it. But in the whole show I saw one Russian tank officer and one Bulgarian officer instructor to the 43rd Brigade. We made the attack with Prieto's Carabinieros who were marvellous fighting troops and about as far to the left in politics as Senator Carter Glass. You know all people are not cowards, many people will fight and not give a damn about dying to save their country from a foreign invasion and war was not invented by either the communists or the fascists and for you to try constantly to make out that the war the government is fighting against the fascist Italian, German Moorish invasion is a communist business imposed on the will of the people is sort of viciously pitiful. Who fought our civil war? Where there wasn't any foreign invasion, even.

Now I am very easy to attack and if you want, instead of trying to get straight on Spain you can simply attack me too. But that won't help you on the road you're going. When people start in being crooked about money they usually end up being crooked about everything. On other hand I suppose me haveing started being crooked about everything can be expected to end up being crooked about money. Will look forward to it anyway.

So this is the end of the letter. If you ever make any money and want to pay me any on what you owe (not the Uncle Gus money when you were ill. I mean others, just small ones, afterwards,) why not send thirty dollars if you make three hundred or twenty or ten or any damn thing. I've got lots of uses for it now. Now I won't send the letter because of why. Because of old friends. Good old friends you know. Knife you in the back for a quarter. Anybody else charge fifty cents.

So long, Dos. Hope you're always happy. Imagine you always will be. Must be a dandy life. Used to be happy myself. Will be again. Good old friends. Always happy with the good old friends. Got them that will knife you in the back for a dime. Regular price two for a quarter. Two for a quarter, hell. Honest Jack Passos'll knife you three times in the back for fifteen cents and sing Giovanezza free. Thanks pal. Gee that feel's good. Any more old friends? Take him away, Doc he's all cut. Tell the editor's secretary to make Mr. Passos out a check for $250. Thank you Mr. Passos that was very very neat. Come around any time. There's always work here for anyone who thinks as you do.

Yrs. always,

UVA Hem

1. EH here emphasizes the international origins of many Loyalist commanders, rebutting Dos Passos's opinion that some general officers were Russian. For an account of the quarrel, see Townsend Ludington, *The Fourteenth Chronicle* (Boston, 1973), pp. 495–98, 600–601; and *Twentieth Century Odyssey: The Life of John Dos Passos* (New York, 1980), pp. 390–91.

To EUGENE JOLAS, Paris [?], *c.* late March [?] 1938

[Dear Eugene:]

Answering your first question[1]—I usually dream about whatever am doing at the time or what I have read in the paper; i.e., run into grizzly with wrong caliber shells for rifle; trigger spring sometimes broken, etc. when shooting; sometimes shoot very large animal of some kind I've never seen; or very detailed fighting around Madrid, house to house fighting, etc., after the paper; or even find myself in bed with Mrs. S . . . (not too good). Have had lovely experiences with Miss Dietrich, Miss Garbo and others in dreams too, they always being awfully nice (in dreams).

2. Second question, don't know much about.

3. I haven't ever felt this as would like to be able to handle day and night with same tools and believe can be done but respect anyone approaching any problem of writing with sincerity and wish them luck.

[Ernest Hemingway]

1. This letter appeared in *transition* 27 (April–May 1938): 237. Jolas, inquiring into "The Spirit and Language of Night," had asked several writers to answer three questions: (1) What was your most recent characteristic dream (or daydream, waking-sleeping hallucination, phantasm)? (2) Have you observed any ancestral myths or symbols in your collective unconscious? (3) Have you ever felt the need for a new language to express the experiences of your night mind?

To MAXWELL PERKINS, Marseilles, 5 May 1938

Dear Max:

Thank you for the letter of April 7 which just have and the cable about the play. Came here from Barcelona yest to get a plane to go up to Castellon and Madrid front and got all my accumulated mail. After this trip, if things look quiet, plan run over to Key West as left on such short notice. We can decide about the stories play etc. then. It was bad luck the producer dying while was on the boat over. Everything up the well known creek now.

Anyway: here's another idea. How would it be to publish the three unpublished stories and the play in one vol? Might be fine. Remember the Gadsbys by Kipling [1889]. Was a vol of plays and stories. One of his best books of stories. Successful too. Would be a good length.

Doubt now if we'll ever have time or whatall to produce it. It reads damned well. With those other three stories would make a fine book. Could lead off with the play and follow it by the three stories. Then when we publish the omnibus we would have them and the new ones I will write. Or I might even have a volume of new ones first. I would write a little introduction.[1] Think this a good idea.

Evan [Shipman] is fine although now marked C3 and unfit to be returned Brigade and am seeing he gets sent home directly. He tried hard to get out to the brigade again but he is really unfit and should go home. Hope you will be seeing him shortly. I saw him day before yest and he sent you his best.

It's been a fuck all of a six weeks. We beat the Italians terribly on the Ebro above Tortosa; above a place called Cherta. Absolutely stopped them. But the left flank went, down by San Mateo, and finally had to give them what they could never take. But there has been no collapse and we hold solidly along the Ebro. I'll tell you about the other side when I get back. Nobody's got any social standing at all now who hasn't swum the Ebro at least once. You should have been with us on Good Friday when the bastards cut the Valencia road. I wrote a good piece about it. You can get it from N.A.N.A. if you're interested, was sent March 18 I think. Fill in with your imagination remembering there was a censorship.

Now have to fly at 4:35 tomorrow morning and today's first day of rest I've had since left U.S.A. and would like to stay in bed for a week and eat and go to sleep and read the papers and have a whiskey and soda (and fuck) and repeat the program like a prayer wheel turning. I'm sorry if I wrote a gloomy letter from the boat. I'm never gloomy, really, when it's close at hand so you can see it and understand. But when you are outside it is so much gloomier than at the front.

Good luck Max and best to everybody. Will probably be seeing you very soon.

The retreat from Mons [Belgium] was chickenshit alongside of this last show. Really will have quite a lot to write when this all over. Am very careful to remember and not waste it in dispatches. When finished am going to settle down and write and the pricks and fakers like [André] Malraux who pulled out in Feb 37 to write gigantic masterpisses before it really started will have a good lesson when write ordinary sized book with the old stuff unfaked in it. What stuff there is. Did you read Frank Tinker's articles in the Post?[2] Satevepost? They were damned good.

So long Max. I hope you like the idea of the play and stories together.

Yours always
Ernest

Best to Charlie [Scribner], [Wallace] Meyer and Bill Weber.
PUL

1. EH finally wrote a preface for *The Fifth Column and The First Forty-nine Stories*, which was published 14 October 1938. **2.** Frank Tinker had flown for the Loyalists and is mentioned in "Night Before Battle." On his suicide, see EH to the Pfeiffer family, 28 July 1939.

To MAXWELL PERKINS, Key West, 12 July 1938

Dear Max:

I have delayed answering your letters because of two things. First the play. The producer failed to have the $25,000 up that was to be in escrow on July first and it has been a question of extending the option to permit him time to raise the money etc. This between ourselves as do not want talk to get out about it which might embarrass him in his efforts to raise the necessary money to produce. Other producers have been after it, too, but everything is getting late. But whether it is produced or not we can figure on publishing in the fall. I have not returned the proofs as there seemed no hurry. Let me know if there is. The preface I would write, if you wanted a preface, would naturally be changed by whether the play was to be produced or not. Can write that in a day or two at the most at any time.

Now about the stories. The Up In Michigan seems to be just the same as it always was. Without that phrase the story is pointless. With it people who are looking for something to jump on have it right there.

The book is supposed to be a definitive collection of all stories up to now. Without Up In Michigan it is not that. If the story is cut it loses all importance.

It is an important story in my work and one that has influenced many people. Callaghan etc. It is not dirty but is very sad. I did not write so well then, especially dialogue. Much of the dialogue is very wooden in that story. But there on the dock it suddenly got absolutely right and it is the point of the whole story and the beginning of all the naturalness I ever got. (Have just re-read the story) was writing from memory before.

Max I don't know what to say about it. If you cut it there's no sense in publishing it.

If you don't want to publish it—o.k. But if it is published I think it should go as it is.

Now here is another idea. Why not publish the play as the first story. Then the forty eight others.

Call it The Fifth Column and the first forty eight short stories of Ernest Hemingway.[1]

You know all there is to strategy is to always be strong—and then always be strong at the right place.

How you get beat is by splitting up your strength.

In these two books we split badly. There is no last story and shows what I've learned since the first 48. And everybody will damn the play alone. Put them all together and no matter how they damn them nor what happens I won't feel bad because I know that there is the work that I have done, there you can see what I have learned, and all the vitality of dialogue and action is there in the play and it comes after all that solid body of work.

It reads damned well you know.

In that event you could leave out the Up In Michigan. I would rather leave it out than cut it. But it does seem a shame not to publish it.

In this book, Max, would like to give them so damned much for their money as well as have the whole business there.

Could write just a short introduction explaining Fifth Column was last thing written. It followed by the other new stories and the other stories in chronological order. Would it make too big a book? I'd like to have a pretty big one for a change.

What do you think about all this?

It was a shame Evan [Shipman] could not get the money to place on that horse. The horse, The Chief, won of course. The second chapter is that Evan got $100. to bet on Fighting Fox last Saturday. He lost but if Evan followed my instructions as to betting for place and show I only lost $25. Have not heard from him yet. Probably will in a day or so. Since the trotting season is comeing on *please do not give anyone any more money to bet on horses unless you have a confirming telegram from me.* Thanks very much for giveing Evan that hundred however.

Will send this off now.

I enclose that story I cabled to Ken the day we evacuated Amposta.

It would make a story for the book I think—An Old Man at a Bridge. What do you think?

Hope everything goes well with you.

Best always
Ernest

The odds are 3–1 the play will *not* be produced this fall.

PUL

1. The forty-ninth story was to be "Old Man at the Bridge," which first appeared in *Ken* 1 (19 May 1938): 36. See the conclusion of this letter.

To MAXWELL PERKINS, Key West, 12 July 1938

Dear Max:

Had the other letter written and sealed and then started going through the galleys on the stories.

I don't like the In Our Time there all by its-self with only numbers and not marked as chapters. They need the breaking apart that separate pages and the heading of chapters give. That would be the only possible way to have it published as one thing.

Then you have two of the chapters listed later as separate stories. No. 10 in the table of contents you sent me A VERY SHORT STORY is also Chapter 10 in In Our Time except that a girl's name in it as A VERY SHORT STORY has been changed from AG to Luz. It should stay as Luz in the book. Ag is libelous. Short for Agnes. Story Number 12 in the table of contents THE REVOLUTIONIST is also Chapter Eleven in IN OUR TIME. So you are short two stories of your 48 in that arrangement. I do not like the look of the In Our Time all run together that way at all. It should either be Chapters each one heading a page separately—or else be the way it was in the Liveright In Our Time and the one published by you in 1931 [1930].

Now Captain [L. H.] Cohns chronological order is all balls.

I wrote My Old Man before Out of Season. I wrote To-day Is Friday and The Killers on the same day in Madrid both of them a couple of years before Hills like White Elephants which was written three or four years after I wrote Fifty Grand. Lots of them I can't remember when I wrote them; but I know that as a chronological order it is all preposterous.

What is the objection to simply running them in the order in which the three books were published? In Our Time, Men Without Women, and Winner Take Nothing, except put the three last stories first i.e. The Short Happy Life of Francis Macomber first, then The Capitol of the World, then The Snows of Kilimanjaro, then, if you are useing it, Up In Michigan and the others just as they were published.

I cannot say just when any given story was written but I can check up on enough of them to know that the Cohn order is simply nonsense.

I was living with Hadley in the rue Notre Dame des Champs over the saw-mill when I wrote Fifty Grand. I was in Madrid in love with Pauline when I wrote the Killers and Today Is Friday. While a Banal story was written in Schruns at least a year before that. In the Chronological order it comes after A Canary For One which was written in Gerald Murphy's studio in Paris in Rue Froidevaux where was living after Hadley and I had busted up. Hills Like White Elephants was written in the rue Ferou in Paris over a year later than that. So I know that the Chronology is nonsense. But if you put me on the witness stand I could not tell exactly when each story was written. Nor do I give a good god-damn. So if they are not to be chronological let's have them in the order they were in the books which was always carefully worked out. The other thing about the In Our Time chapters is that to get the effect I wanted with them (and it was a strange effect, and they made it), I had them set in italics. They need those italics.

I think Max it's best to just have them in the order in which they were published in the three books with the three new stories first, then Up In Michigan (if you decide to publish it). If you don't publish Up In Michigan it is only 47 stories. Change the title of Introduction By The Author to On The Quay At Smyrna. Now what about the Fifth Column starting the whole thing off? Or doesn't that make sense. It would be a fine big lot of reading matter.

Or The Fifth Column and the three new stories. Saveing the collection for later.

I don't like to publish it without Up In Michigan and with them all gunning for you now it gives them something to go on.

Those last three stories are very readable and it would be a good book that way if the other seems too long.

Frankly I don't think the play will be produced. Too much money trouble. Probability of Catholic ban on sale to movies; and movie money has a lot to do with play producing now.

I think published separately they will just jump on them one at a time. Ignore one and pan the other. Together it is too big for them, too damned impressive.

On the other hand might seem sign of weakness to put everything together. I could explain that by saying in introduction that some people had complained that last novel was a little short so had decided that there should be plenty of reading matter in this book.

You want to remember, Max, there was about the biggest gang-up in the reviews on that last novel [*To Have and Have Not*], which was not a bad novel, that you would almost ever see. So I would like to have something so extra good and extra big this time that there wouldn't be any question of that.

I don't think it is persecution mania or egotism if I say that there are a lot of critics who really seem to hate me very much and would like to put me out of business. And don't think I mean it conceitedly when I say that a lot of it is jealousy; I do what they would like to do, and I do what they are afraid to do; and they hate you for it. Now there is politics too. So I think the best thing to do is to make a book with so much good reading, and so obviously good that you have them on quality and bulk anyway.

What do you think?

I could write a modest, straight, and I think interesting introduction about writing the stories and the play. There are some things which are rather impressive if just stated baldly about the play and there are some interesting things about the stories.

If you like I could write it now. Maybe better do that and knock off this letter. Getting pretty long anyway.

I know some of the critic thing too is my fault. I have been very snotty and they hate you for that too.

Well anyway the hell with it.

PUL   Ernest

To ARNOLD GINGRICH, Paris, 22 October 1938

Dear Arnold:

Enclosed is the story.[1]

In the last paragraph I have written—"If you hadn't have known him pretty well and if you hadn't have seen etc."

I guess that is not grammar and Pauline, whose word I take on grammar, is not here.

Still it sounds right. Maybe the have's should come out—but let's leave them in unless you have some objection. In some way they seem to be involved in the rhythm that makes the emotion.

I can't write a story like a piece. The story takes charge of its-self very quickly. So when I started to write you the third Chicote story I got this instead. It's Chicote's all right but plenty else too. I'm not going to pull any punches in a story nor shorten a long one artificially. Twenty rounders have a different pace but when they are good they seem short.

It is as long as two stories or maybe three. So our arrangement being as it is maybe, if you wanted, the best thing would be to pay me a thousand and credit my debit account with another thousand paid. That would make payed up 1200 on that $3000 advance and still oweing $1800. If you wanted, and if you like the story well enough, you could pay me $1000. and say I now only owe $1500 on that $3000. That would make book-keeping easy. You nearly lost that three grand entirely on the day of the night this story is about.

What do you say? This is a swell big story to shoot with in your January issue. I would like to be able to publish with you the best stuff I can write as well as I can write it. It won't do any harm to the magazine to have some major fiction. Anyhow this makes three good ones in a row.[2] Four really, because the last fiction I had with you before was The Snows [of Kilimanjaro].

Christ it is fine to write again and not to have to write pieces. I was really going nuts with that. Everytime I would get going I would have to interrupt. Now I have another swell story done that only need to go over (maybe best ever wrote, anyway one of them) and two chapters done on a novel.[3]

Haven't seen any reviews of the book [*The Fifth Column and The First Forty-nine Stories*] yet nor heard anything. Nor seen the book. Max sent the jacket. I would rather have the book myself but then maybe am prejudiced.

Had a contract with Nana [N.A.N.A.] if there was war and was all set on that Wednesday and also an offer of a staff captain's commission with the French to go with what they were going to move into Spain. Would have been something. (This confidential.) Things here are so foul, now, that if you think about them you go nuts. So am just writing now. You have to climb up in that old tower to do your work every so often even if the flood keeps right on rising until the seat of your pants is wet. A writer has to write and beyond all other things it can make you feel good when it comes out right.

So long Arnold. Best to Dave [Smart]. Don't know just when will be back. Maybe pretty soon.

Won't go into European situation. It's a lot worse even than what you read in the papers.

Ernest

My very best to Helen Mary. I thought she was grand. Have been shooting driven pheasants twice a week with Ben Gallagher (all wild fast birds). Have gotten on to it now. Very tough, they come high like rockets and there is still so much foliage the shots are very hard. We killed 57 last day—45 before—Thing is to get on quickly and never stop your swing. You can't get too far ahead.

PH. PUL

1. "Night Before Battle," *Esquire* 11 (February 1939), EH's final contribution to that magazine. 2. The other two were "The Denunciation" and "The Butterfly and the Tank," *Esquire* 10 (November, December 1938). 3. The story was possibly "Under the Ridge," *Cosmopolitan* 107 (October 1939). The "two chapters of a novel" could mean a start on *For Whom the Bell Tolls*. EH repeated the statement to Perkins on 28 October.

To MAXWELL PERKINS, Paris, 28 October 1938

Dear Max:

I should have written you a long time ago how sorry I was about old Tom [Wolfe].[1] But I knew you would know and it never does any good to discuss casualties. You must have had a hell of a time with it all. That was a good letter he wrote. Everybody writes you fond letters when they think they are going to die. You ought to get quite a collection. Hope I'll write you a lot of them in the next fifty years.

Well we thought we had something pretty unbeatable in that book didn't we? But you can't beat those guys. They can gang up to play it down. You know Max I think I'll still be around and going pretty good when there is a whole new generation of critics. You see those guys all buried me and it is awkward and difficult for them to see you rising like Lazarus. I always thought Lazarus must have been awkward to have around myself. What was it they said "Lord he stinketh" [John 11:39].

I don't give a shit about any of it except the aspect of interfering with my livelihood. When I got the book and saw all those stories I knew I was all right as a sort of lasting business if I kicked off tomorrow. Which, by the way,—oh well let us neither talk nor write balls.

Pauline wrote that on the day the book came out there wasn't a copy visible in the window. But I'm sure there must be a mistake. Is there any connection with the size of the reviews and the size of the ads? I can see how a large ad could *not* get a large review. But a small ad might be used as an indication of size of review. Must be quite a racket.

Think you might emphasize in the advertising that there is 185 pages of hitherto unpublished material. Give the length of the new stories. Mention that Up In Michigan is only obtainable in a book which now sells for $350. a copy, and emphasize the size and number of words in the book.

Those seem to me to be sound points.

There is enough new stuff in the book to make a book a good deal longer than [Steinbeck's] Of Mice and Men say.

Mention that. I think you will have to push it to sell it with those kind of reviews. But I do think, truly, that you offer a very good bargain and that it can be sold if the strong points are emphasized.

I worked like a bastard right up until that Wednesday. Thought maybe it would be last chance ever to write and wrote well. Did two long stories. One was just unfinished when the war was called off. Finished it afterwards. Since, in the mess everything's in, the sort of let down and carnival of treachery and rotten-ness that's going on, coupled with being upset about the damn book (not hearing anything and then everything I hear being bad) it's been hard to work. But I have two Chapters done on the novel.[2] Looks like will be back pretty soon now. Ask Pauline to show you the copy of one of the stories I sent her—Night Before Battle. It is ten thousand some words long.

Will work again on the novel today. Writing is a hard business Max but nothing makes you feel better.

This is confidential. Had a staff captaincy offered me with an outfit French were going to send into Spain. Would have been fine. I had that contract with Jack [John N.] Wheeler [of N.A.N.A.] though and had promised Pauline I would not go to the war. So there were certain conflicting obligations. I am very sick of conflicting obligations which seems to be the product that I have the greatest supply of.

I haven't written the napoleonic story yet. But will. Going to look in on Barcelona next week before comeing home. Max I am a little bit gloomy so I will terminate this.

Remember if anything ever happens to me I think just as much of you as Tom Wolfe even if I can't put it so well.

So long Max.

Ernest

Cable me the sale when you get this: Garritus Paris.

PUL

1. Wolfe died 15 September 1938. Three years earlier, having read that EH had mentioned him in *Green Hills of Africa* (New York, 1935), p. 71, Wolfe wrote Perkins about "the Big Big He Man and Fighter with Words who can't take it." (*The Letters of Thomas Wolfe*, ed. Elizabeth Nowell [New York, 1956], p. 468, letter dated 21 June 1935). 2. See EH to Arnold Gingrich, 22 October 1938.

To MRS. PAUL PFEIFFER, Key West, 6 February 1939

Dear Mother:

It's now a month and six days past the limit for writing a letter after Christmas. So this will have to be just a letter. Please forgive me for not writing at once to thank you for the fine checks from you and Pauline's father and for the lovely robe Jinny sent for you from New York. I needed a robe very badly and you were awfully good to send it.

The trip to N.Y. was an Old Testament nightmare. I re-wrote and then finally wrote two absolutely new acts. The jews[1] had opened the play with the high spots of the third act and had thus made quite an exciting first act but of course had nowhere to go after that and so I had to write two absolutely new acts. It should be called the 4.95 Column marked down from 5 now.

It really is an awful business. Until you have had a success in the theater the entire attitude is that you cannot possibly know what you are doing. And that a good play should be just like the last play that was good or like portions of several other plays that were quite good. Since it costs about 50,000 to put a play on, the one putting up the money feels that the play should be made absolutely fool proof to protect that investment. That [There] is nothing new in it nor anything that hasn't made money before. Since there is no formula for makeing a successful play most of the plays they do are utter flops.

This morning I woke up dreaming that they had obtained new backing from a Vermouth Company and that the play was now to be called Cinzano Express. The first four scenes were to be the same but we should re-write the next to get the proper vermouth angle in. This was a real dream. Their new angle was that the last part of the play take place on an island and they would have a real island on the stage and raise their own exotic plants.

I wish I had never heard of a play but had written a novel instead. Probably a lot of other people do too.

Patrick was confirmed yesterday and was the pride of the Parish since no one could answer the questions the Bishop asked except him. He is terrific on catechism and would make a fine lawyer for the Holy Rota Romana by present showing. Gregory, since he learned that confirmation brings five dollars in its wake, can hardly wait to enter catechism class. I also explained to him about interest when takeing them down to put money in their saveings accounts and Giggy said, "Boy I wish I was the one who thought of that."

Uncle Gus and Aunt Louise had a nice visit. He fished two days in the gulf but the weather was bad: a heavy norther blowing both days so he caught no sailfish but plenty of reef fish. I flew down in a blizzard, six hours late. Uncle Gus was tired. I wish he could have stayed long enough to get rested.

The Italians moved in new troops, artillery and planes while the Spanish government sent away all their foreign volunteers and then had the French border closed against their bringing in artillery and munitions by Chamberlain and Daladier. Oh well there is no use to talk about it. But when I read in the Sunday Visitor about the atrocities of the Reds, the wickedness of the Spanish "Communist" Government, and the humanness of General Franco who could have ended the war months ago if he had not been afraid of harming the civilian population after haveing seen town after town bombed to the ground, the inhabitants killed, the columns of refugees on the roads bombed and machine gunned again and again—well there's no use talking. But that sort of lying kills things inside of you. They take great pains now to prove Franco never bombed Guernica. It was just blown up by the Reds. Harry Sylvester, who was never in Spain in his life, proved it to me in a long letter. Well I was not in Guernica. But I was in Mora del Ebro, Tortosa, Reus, Tarragona, Sagunto, and many other towns when Franco did exactly what he denies haveing done in Guernica. But what's the use now? There is only one thing to do when you have a war and that is win it. When you have been betrayed and sold out a dozen different ways and have lost you shouldn't object to being lied about in addition. The British were the real villains. All the way through from the very start.

Then the Catalans would never fight. They never fought in the whole war. Maybe they are simply too nice people but we have a rhyme in Spanish that translates into English like this:

My face is black
My nose is flat
But still I am a man.
Thank God I am a negro
And not a Catalan.

Mother I should have kept off this subject. I do keep off it all the time but thought Pauline's father would wonder what I thought about how things were going. But am too bitter.

The situation is this. The French frontier has been closed to incoming stuff since last May. They opened up and let a little through when it was too late in January. Central Spain will half [have] to be supplied by water. Italy will put down a blockade probably. The aerial blockade has sunk about half the stuff comeing in. They bomb the ports of Valencia and Alicante every night. This, of course, is legitimate.

It will take Franco from six to eight weeks to organize a large scale offensive against either Madrid or Valencia. If he is smart he will try Valencia.

If he takes Valencia central Spain is doomed. Valencia is the richest part of Spain and feeds Madrid.

The Italians may want an offensive against Madrid to wipe out their defeat at Guadalajara [1937] and it is possible they will organize a simultaneous offensive on the two fronts.

They can very certainly cut the Madrid-Valencia road now with the forces they have at their disposal and the great preponderance of artillery and then they can starve the city. Food has been short for two years all through central Spain.

The best friends I have in Spain are there now and it makes you gloomy to think about it. I slept good and sound every night in Spain through the whole war and I was hungry, really hungry, at least every other day for five months last winter but never felt better. So I guess one's conscience is a strange thing and not controlled either by a sense of security, nor danger of death, nor one's stomach.

In New York I went by the Hollywood Restaurant and wished you were there and we could have another dinner there together. I'd planned on comeing out to Piggott to see you all and pick up the car and drive it down. But they had Otto [Bruce] started before I arrived.

What with war and all last year now find have to pay tax on around 30,000 income. Been figureing that business all day. Fortunately don't have to pay on money earned outside the country because was away over six months so won't have to pay on all that. Sully [J. B. Sullivan] says, "By God Ernest they can say what they like about you. But by God you're a good provider." So will have to get to work hard now to keep that reputation anyway.

Pauline is fine and looking better than ever. The children are all well. I had Bumby in to dinner and spend the night in N.Y. and he is doing well at school. First in his class and second in the school. Gregory and Patrick both husky and in good shape from the northern trip.

Much love to all and thank you again for the presents.

Ernest

My mother due here day after tomorrow for 2 days. Saw Jinny in NY and we had a good time together. She is working *really* hard on her photography. I gave her the first warning she had on the liquor joke business and told her to destroy it all and warn everyone to empty the bottles. It was a good joke but the Revenue people don't joke.

PUL

1. Concerning this reference to the New York play producers, and its echo in the next letter, see EH's later consciousness of possible misconstruction in EH to Edmund Wilson, 10 September 1951.

To MAXWELL PERKINS, Key West, 7 February 1939

Dear Max:

Thank you again for the Peter Scott book.[1] It tells all about wild fowling in all the places I've always wanted to go and never will get to now I guess.

About the lectures. Tell them I am not free to lecture at present. Might as well be polite. Must keep that in reserve in case ever get blind or anything so can't write.

Well we've lost another war. It's bad enough to lose but to have Carney lying and saying the International Brigades have been fighting in this last business is too lousy. The brigade people that Franco took prisoner were men without papers to prove their nationality who were held in camps near the frontier or in towns like Ripoll until the League of Nations commission could arrange for their repatriation. There's only one thing to do with a war and that is win it. But in this one winning was made impossible by many circumstances outside of the control of the military.

When you get this will you please deposit a thousand dollars in my account City Bank Farmers Branch—22 William Street—N.Y.C? Need it to pay income tax. Debit my Fifth Column royalties.

Am going to Cuba next Monday, I think, to work. I know how to work. I think to go next Monday I mean. I ought to have enough new stories for a book in the fall or do you think that is too soon for another book of stories? I have

The Denunciation   Esq
The Butterfly and The Tank   Esq.
Night Before Battle   Esq.
Nobody Ever Dies   Cosmo. *Read it in March No.*
Landscape With Figures—not sent out yet.

And three very long ones I want to write now. One about Teruel called Fatigue. One about the old commercial fisherman who fought the sword-fish all alone in his skiff for 4 days and four nights and the sharks finally eating it after he had it alongside and could not get it into the boat. That's a wonderful story of the Cuban coast. I'm going out with old Carlos [Gutiérrez] in his skiff so as to get it all right. Everything he does and everything he thinks in all that long fight with the boat out of sight of all the other boats all alone on the sea. It's a great story if I can get it right. One that would make the book.[2]

Then I want to write that one of the storming of the Guadarrama pass by the Polish lancers. If I can do those three I'll make enough to support the family for the rest of the year and can then start on the novel again. I have to know how the war comes out to get that right anyway.

Have heard nothing from the play jews since I left. Maybe with the war gone bad they are hedging on the play. Christ how I wish I'd written *that* as a novel. Well I couldnt. There wasn't time when we were waiting for Teruel. Am afraid I insulted them all the night I left anyway. Got to feeling too good with you and Charley [Scribner].

I have bad dreams every night about this retreat. Really awful ones in the greatest detail. It is strange because I never had any *ever* in Spain about anything that happened. Only the always recurring one about getting out of the trucks and haveing to attack without knowing where the objectives were and no one to explain the positions. Last night I was caught in this retreat again in the goddamndest detail. I really must have a hell of an imagination. That's why should *always* make up stories—*not* try to remember what happened.

Well so long Max. Give my best to Charley. Thank you both again for the book.

Yours always,
Ernest

PUL

1. *Morning Flight*, published by Scribners (New York, 1936). 2. Another stage in plans for *The Old Man and the Sea* (1952).

To IVAN KASHKIN, Key West, 23 March 1939[1]

Dear Kashkeen:

Well I'm damned glad to hear from you. Not only just to hear but to know that the translation in the U.S.S.R. is being done by someone who wrote the best and most useful, to me, critique on my stuff I ever read and probably knows more about it than I do. I'm damned happy you are still doing it and I will order Scribner's to send galleys of the books as you suggest. I also hereby authorize you to do the adaptation of the play [*Fifth Column*].

About the order of the stories in the book. Scribner's wanted the three new ones first and since all but those were in the order in which they appeared in books when published it seemed O.K. It would have been better, probably, to have them in the end and keep it all chronological. In future editions I think you would be wise to put them at the end and so authorize you.

There are some new stories finished. Am now writing a novel and have fifteen thousand words done. Wish me luck, pal. Also a story was published in *Cosmopolitan* called *Nobody Ever Dies*. They made some cuts and before you ever publish that one I wish you would let me send you the version that I will publish when I print it in book form. Have no copy or would send it.

For your information in stories about the war I try to show *all* the different sides of it, taking it slowly and honestly and examining it from many ways. So never think one story represents my viewpoint because it is much too complicated for that.

We know war is bad. Yet sometimes it is necessary to fight. But still war is bad and any man who says it is not is a liar. But it is very complicated and difficult to write about truly. For instance to take it on a simply personal basis—in the war in Italy when I was a boy I had much fear. In Spain I had no fear after a couple of weeks and was very happy. Yet for me to not understand fear in others or deny its existence would be bad writing. It is just that now I understand the whole thing better. The only thing about a war, once it has started, is to win it—and that is what we did not do. The hell with war for a while. I want to write.

That piece you translated about the American dead[2] was very hard for me to write because I had to find something I could honestly say about the dead. There is not much to say about the dead except that they are dead. I would like to be able to write understandingly about both deserters and heroes, cowards and brave men, traitors and men who are not capable of being traitors. We learned a lot about all such people.

Well it is all over now but the people like these [who] did nothing about defending the Spanish Republic now feel a great need to attack us who tried to do something in order to make us look foolish and justify themselves in their selfishness and cowardice. And we having fought as well as possible, and without selfishness, and lost, they now say how stupid it was ever to have fought at all.

In Spain it was very funny because the Spaniards where they did not know you always thought we were Russians. When Teruel was taken I had been with the attacking troops all day and went into the town the first night with a company of dynamiters. When the civilians came out of their houses they asked me what they should do and I told them to stay in the houses and not go into the street that night under any circumstances and explained to them what good people we reds were and it was very funny. They all thought I was a Russian and when I told them I was a North American they didn't believe a word of it. During the retreat it was the same. The Catalans all moving steadily away from the war at all times but always very pleased to see us, the Russians, moving through the traffic in the wrong direction—that is toward the front. When the Catalans held a front up in Aragon for so many months and did nothing they had a kilometer between their trenches and the Fascists and on the road, where their front line ran, they had a sign-board that said Frente Peligro. Danger. The Front. I took a nice picture of it.

Well this is enough nonsense. I'd like to see you and I would like to come to U.S.S.R. But what I have to do now is write. As long as there is a war you always think perhaps you will be killed so you have nothing to worry about. But now I am not killed so I have to work. And as you have no doubt discovered living is much more difficult and complicated than dying and it is just as hard as ever to write.

I would be glad to write for nothing but if no one paid you you would starve. I could make much money by going to Hollywood or by writing shit. But I am going to keep on writing as well as I can and as truly as I can until I die. And I hope I never die. Have been working over in Cuba where I could get away from letters, telegrams, appeals etc., and really work. Been going good.

So long, Kashkeen, and good luck. I appreciate your care and integrity in the translations very much. Give my best regards to all the Comrades who work on the stuff. Comrade is a word I know quite a lot more about than when I wrote you first. But you know something funny? The only thing you have to do entirely by yourself and that no one alive can help you with no matter how much they want to (except by leaving you alone) is to write. Very difficult business, my boy. Try it sometimes . . . (joke).

Hemingway

1. Printed in *Soviet Literature* 11 (1962): 163–64. 2. "On the American Dead in Spain," *New Masses* 30 (14 February 1939).

To MAXWELL PERKINS, Key West, 25 March 1939

Dear Max:

Thanks for the good letter and for the enclosure from the Lecture agent. Please be very polite to him and all but we don't have to do that yet. Mustn't ever say what you won't do because usually end up by haveing to do it. But not yet. Be nice to him though.

How has the book sold? What's the sale now?

I don't like to talk about this because it's bad luck but have been going awfully well writing. Got to Cuba intending to write those three stories. Instead wrote one about the war, Pauline thinks among best I've ever written, called Under The Ridge. And then started on another I'd had no intention of writing for a long time and working steadily every day found I had fifteen thousand words done; that it was very exciting; and that it was a novel [For Whom the Bell Tolls]. So I am going to write on on that until it is finished. I wish I could show it to you so far because I am very proud of it but that is bad luck too. So is talking about it. Anyway I have a wonderful place to work in Cuba with no telephone,[1] nobody can possibly bother you, and I start work at 8.30 and work straight through until around two every day. I'm going to keep on doing that until this is finished. I turned down a lot of Hollywood money and other money and I may have to draw on you to keep going. If you want to see the collateral you can—but you don't need to so far. I promise you that. Have worked very slowly reading every word over from the start every day. I hope it will be a good novel. Anyway it will be as good as I can write, being in good shape, putting all worries aside, and writeing as carefully and well as I can. It is 20 times better than that Night Before Battle which was flat where this is rounded and recalled where this is invented.

Am going to stay in one place now and work no matter what. After the way the French treated the Spanish Republic I feel no obligation to fight for the French and anyhow it is more important now for me to write and that is what am doing. To hell with comeing to N.Y. Have figured out that in any personal problems I am no good to anyone if I do not work. So am working where can work and not be interfered with. Bumby is here for his Easter vacation. Then I am going back to Cuba. So it looks like we will have a book of stories and a novel. Have five new stories so far. The Denunciation. The Butterfly and The Tank. Night Before Battle. Nobody Ever Dies. Landscape With Figures. And this new one Hell, that makes six.

Am down to 198 pounds. Have place where can play tennis and swim and am happy and healthy although always that hollow in the middle of yourself daily emptied out feeling you get when working well on a long book. Wish me luck Max. I find I know a lot more than when I used to write and think that is maybe what makes it easier in the end but it is still a very tough business. But working the way I do now I feel as happy and as good as when I was going good on A Farewell to Arms.

So long, Max. Give my best to Bill Webber, to [Wallace] Meyer and best to Charlie [Scribner].

Ernest

I found Scott's Tender Is the Night in Cuba and sent it over. It's amazing how <u>excellent</u> much of it is. If he had integrated it better it would have been a fine novel (as it is) much of it is better than anything else he ever wrote. How I wish he would have kept on writing. Is it really all over or will he write again? If you write him give him my great affection. (I always had a very stupid little boy feeling of superiority about Scott—like a tough little boy sneering at a delicate but talented little boy.) But reading that novel much of it was so good it was frightening.

PUL

1. Hotel Ambos Mundos, Havana. A few weeks later Martha Gellhorn located La Finca Vigia in San Francisco de Paula, twelve kilometers from downtown Havana, and EH soon moved into the house with her.

To THOMAS SHEVLIN,[1] Key West, 4 April 1939

Dear Tommy:

It's so hard to write this that I've been trying to do it for five days and haven't been able to.

Listen, kid I can't come and fish on your team in the tournament. I know that is ratting out and I tell you as soon as possible so that you will be able to get another fisherman.

This is how it is. I went to Cuba intending to write three stories. I wrote the first one and it was good. Then I started on the second one and before I knew it I had fifteen thousands words done and was going better than I have gone since Farewell To Arms and I knew it was a novel. I interrupted it to come back here to K.W. Galaghers were comeing over from France and Bumby was down from school and I've been seeing people every day and being away from the novel and feeling as though I were loseing it has me almost nuts. I'm going back tomorrow and get in it again and I feel like you do before battle. I'm spooked of the necessity to interrupt again sometime the middle of May. If I lost it, and I feel so damned close to loseing it now, I should really be shot because it is the most important thing I've ever done and it is the place in my career as a writer I have to write a real one.

I hope you understand it Tommy. Any guy who says he will do a thing and then rats out is a shit. But it would be a sin against the bloody holy ghost if I buggared up this book and I've got to stick with it until I finish it. In Cuba I worked every morning from eight thirty until two or three in the afternoon and it went as good as the best it ever went in my life. I didn't want to write a novel. I wanted to write three stories and make some jack and fish with you and see Loriney [Mrs. Shevlin] and have a fine time and pull on tunas and stay away from the gambling tables and a lot of other things. But instead I am writing a novel.

So there it is. I can't be a sportsman and write a novel at the same time. If I blow up on it (but I can't you see. That's the one thing you can't envisage. It's like quitting on a fish) I will wire you and fly over and help you with the team anyway I can as a substitute or any damned thing. But you will have to get some one else now and not count on me.

I know you understand about it where most guys think you can jump in and out of your work. Here in K.W. it got so I couldn't work. You see I always had a sort of quarantine about working and people couldn't get in and break it. But being away for around two years naturally it was different and rightly so and Pauline had to have people around and as good a life as possible. Then home comes Papa and you can't run them all out and the swimming pool brings voices up like a sounding board and the road brings in every son of a bitch I ever knew or who ever read a line I wrote. So to write I go back to the old desolation of a hotel bed room I started to write in. Tell everybody you live in one hotel and live in another. When they locate you in the other move to the country. When they locate you in the country move somewhere else. Work everyday till your so pooped about all the exercise you can face is reading the papers. Then eat, play tennis or swim or something in a work daze just to keep your bowells moveing and the next day write again.

We felt like hell not to come for pigeon week. You see Gallaghers were comeing and he shoots better than the pros and then they were supposed to get here the 22nd and finally arrived the 29th with me seething at wanting to work all the time. They were fun though and we finally caught a few fish. Bumby was fine. He is very tall now and weighs 165. He plays football but he is like you and Ferdinand the bull about it. Pauline is fine and prettier all the time. Jinny is down here now and I would not be surprized if she had maybe the makeings of a rummy. What are the makeings of a rummy? Gin and French Vermouth? The jew [Gregory] has all the money of the family and I borrow a little from him from time to time to go to church with. Patrick got a hundred in so many subjects that we have decided it is a lousy school.

You must have had a wonderful shoot in Africa. The elephant sounded wonderful.

Shipwreck Kelly was here yest and we were makeing a deal about a picture to be made from The Short Happy Life of Francis MacComber [*The Macomber Affair*, 1947]. Howard Hawks wants to do it and I could work with them after the novel is done and we could all go to Africa. It sounds like a fine set up and hope the hell it doesn't fall through. I boxed 5 rounds with the Ship. He's fast the way an animal is fast. Fun to box with.

There's not much other news. I have a large hangover and I wish you were here and we could split it. Give my love to Lorrainey and tell her this Tuna tournament is only promise am ratting out on and will try keep all others. I feel like a shit about it and if you feel the same way you don't need to tell me because I feel bad enough already.

Good luck Tommy. I hope you beat hell out of them. Who will probably win the thing will be some unknown broker who has never seen a tuna. I've had such stinko luck on fish that it's probably an asset to you not to have me. But I would have loved to fish with you and with Hugo [Rutherfurd].

Yours always

PH. PUL Papa

1. Shevlin (b. 1914, Minneapolis) left Hill School, Pennsylvania, in 1932 to become associated with family lumber interests in the Northwest. He first met EH at Bimini, in the winter of 1934–1935. An eminent sportsman, he drew up (with others) the first rules for big game fishing adopted by the International Game Fishing Association.

To CHARLES SCRIBNER,[1] Havana, 23 May 1939

Dear Charley:

I was glad to hear from you but sorry that you were laid up. Feel a little dopy myself today with the wind gone into the south. That is the one direction that buggars everything; fish won't bite; muggy and rainy; hard to get to work. It usually only lasts for a day or so though and then the trade wind blows.

Work goes good. Am on page 199 of the Mss. [*For Whom the Bell Tolls*] now. That should be over half through. I was supposed to fish on the Cat Cay team in some silly tuna tournament to start tomorrow, with Tommy Shevlin and Hugo Rutherford, for a pretty big side bet. After I started this book the first of March and saw how it was going I wrote Tommy in early April that I couldn't interrupt the book and to get some one else. Am afraid they are sore at me. But am going to stay in one damned place until I finish this even if go broke and lose all my friends. If book good enough will make some new friends.

For a while it looked as though war were very close. But now I do not believe we will have it this summer. Hope not anyway. I want to shoot abroad again this fall (with a shotgun).

Cosmopolitan are after me about the serializing but am not thinking about that while writing it. After I finish will see if it is serializable and if so we can then figure on what time that will take to know when to publish. If we don't want to serialize can figure then, without worrying about that. So far I should think it would be quite serializable (pretty word) but do not want to think about that; only to write a good novel. Have a good story[2] to sell to Cosmopolitan now that I wrote in February when was warming up before this but so far haven't wanted to take the time out to get it re-written and copied.

Take care of yourself Charley and thanks for the letter. I started to make some crack about that "little dark man" but then thought maybe it would be bad luck.

Best always,
Ernest

PUL

1. Charles Scribner (1890–1952), Princeton, Class of 1913, was born in New York. He was president of Charles Scribner's Sons from 1932 to 1952. He married Vera Gordon Bloodgood in 1915, and they had a daughter and a son: Mrs. Thomas J. Bingham and Charles Scribner, Jr. 2. "Under the Ridge." See EH to Max Perkins, 25 March 1939, and *Cosmopolitan* 107 (October 1939).

To PATRICK HEMINGWAY, Havana, 30 June 1939

Dear Old Mouse:

Many Happy returns of day before yesterday.[1]

I wish I would have flown up for the fight and we could have had a birthday party but got Mother's letter about it same day as fight.

[Tony] Galento certainly came very close to knocking [Joe] Louis out and if he can do that on beer I wonder what he could do on Frozen Daiquiris?

Have now written 53,000 words (280 some pages) and it looks about two thirds done. Anyway it is over half done.

I was getting awfully stale from working so hard and then Mr. Ben Finney (remember the one who christened you "SPEEDY") turned up on Mr. Leed's yacht the Moana. We stayed up late and I drank a few highly frozen Daiquiris just to see what their effect would be (it was moderately terrific and made me feel a friend of all mankind). Then the next day Mr. Finney and Papa went out to fish and were both sound asleep but quite comfortable when a huge marlin took the bait out of the outrigger and hooked himself pulling against the rod in the rod-rest. Gregorio [Fuentes] jumped for the rod and turned loose the drag so that the good old marlin backlashed the reel and broke the line just as I reached the rod and then went off jumping over the ocean throwing spray like a motor boat trying to get rid of the hook. Yesterday we caught a small one makeing 15 for this season.

It's really hot now and they call the place where they play Basque pelot the Horno Verde or the Green Oven because it is painted green inside and get's so hot.

Ben Finney was out in Africa and is absolutely crazy about it and going back soon. He says that your slogan "Papa, if Africa is like you say it is we are fools to be here." is his motto now. He says we ought to all go out there and I think he is probably right.

Reeves continues to be wonderful. The other night he says to me, "Mister Ernest what for you never tell me you're an important man? Why you hide that from Reeves?"

I asked him where he got that idea and he said he met a man in the Cuban telephone company and he ast him who was his boss now. Reeves says Mister Hemingway my boss now. Mister Ernest Hemingway? the man say. You mean who writes all those books? Yes sir, Reeves said Mister Ernest Hemingway as fine a gentleman as ever drew breath or I mixed a drink for but I done know nothing about no books. Yes sir, the man say. He writes books. Fine books and I read every one he ever wrote and my wife she read some too and she say 'They good. They really good.'

What for you never tell Reeves you write books?

Well Reeves, I said, I've asked you a hundred times not to bother me nor let anybody in because I was working on a book.

Oh, said Reeves, "I didn't know you meant that kind of books. I thought you work on books like book-keeper books. I didn't know you just sit in there all by yourself with just pants on and no shirt and write those reading books. Mister Ernest you owe it to Reeves to tell him that you was so important a man. Why I told this man "Come on out and see Mr. Ernest. I guess he lonesome. He sure like to see somebody what read one of his books. He sure be glad to see you if you read books."

So you see he is as wonderful as ever.

How is the old Gregory? I guess we can't call him Jew around there or people will think he is a refugee.

Thank you both very much for the letters. It made Papa very happy that you liked the camp so much and were haveing such a good time.[2]

Now I better stop because I want to write to mother and then have to get to work again. What I would like to be is A Fugitive From a Typewriter.

Haven't any check book and have written Mother to send me some checks. As soon as they come will send the birthday check of ten dollars and also small check to Gregory to encourage him to keep on so he will have a birthday too.

Much love.

Yours in prickly heat,
Papa

For Mouse and for Giggy

| 2nd letter: |—Same style as Giggy's to me!

Dear Giggy:

How are you doing pal? The Mouse will read this other letter to you. Thanks for yours. I'll write you next.

Much love
Papa

KNOX

1. Patrick's eleventh birthday was 28 June. 2. The boys were at Camp Te Whanga, New Preston, Connecticut.

To MAXWELL PERKINS, Havana, 10 July 1939

Dear Max:

Thank you very much for the books. I haven't gotten them yet but expect to clear them through the Customs tomorrow. Look forward to them very much.

Have 56,000 words done now. Fourteen chapters. 342 pages of Mss. Guess it is about ⅔ through.[1] Wish you could read it. Went well yesterday and today.

Pauline is sailing on the Normandie for Europe with the Paul Willerts etc and I guess by the time she hits the Paris coutouriers the EH Federal working reserve will be a thing of the past so I will probably have to start drawing on the book. Will let you know.

It is very hot now and in spite of bragging about how the heat does not affect me I know it is very hot. I got a little stale a week ago so knocked off and spent 3 days at sea. If it gets too hot will go to the [Nordquist] ranch and take the children. But have had the idea of fighting the whole thing through here. And unlike Grant it will certainly take all summer, but a lot of it so far I think would make you very happy.

Best to Charley. Take care of yourself. Give my best to Evan [Shipman]. I'm glad Tom's [Wolfe's] book [*The Web and the Rock*, 1939] has gone so well.

Yours always
Ernest

PUL

1. The final version contains forty-three chapters.

To HADLEY MOWRER, Havana, *c.* 15 July 1939

Dearest Hadley:

I haven't your letter here about going out west so write for you to let me know about the dates. Did you ever get a letter from me in April or early May enclosing a check for $150? I sent it to this same address (Lake Bluff, Ill.). Will register this to make sure.

Anyway here is the point. Have been working so hard on this novel (now have 58,000 words done—340 mss. pages) that could not make any summer plans. First I was trying to jam it through before war should come and have never worked harder nor steadier; but war seemed less and less likely and the book has gotten longer and longer. Now I know I can't finish it before September First and want so much to have part of the summer with Bumby that am going to knock off sometime in August wherever I am and get in some time at the ranch with Bumby and get the other children out there too. They had counted and hoped so for the ranch this summer too.

When your western vacation is over Bumby can go to the L bar T and I will pay for his board there until I come out. Will write Irma Patrick who runs the ranch and she will look after him well if it is any time at all. She has two kids of about the same age and is a good friend of ours and a wise and good woman. I wish I knew when it was that you said you were finishing off out west. But can't remember. My impression was it was sometime in August.

So you can figure on sending Bumby to the L bar T ranch—Cooke City P.O. Montana when you leave. He knows how to get there. Through the [Yellowstone] Park to Cooke City. Or via the new road (don't know if it is finished yet) from Cody up the Clark's Fork. Gregory and Patrick are in a camp in Connecticut and will pick them up and bring them on West.

Will you let me know when Bumby will be going to the ranch so that I can write Irma Patrick and Laurence Nordquist. Will you let me know too what day he has to be in School so I can figure my time according to that. I would like to get out as late in August as possible and still have a good chunk of time together. If it got too awfully hot here might make it earlier. Please write me air-mail to Ambos Mundos Hotel—Havana— Cuba. That will get there very quickly. It's ten cents for each half ounce.

Hope you are all haveing a lovely time.

Not much news from here. Have been working so hard that I am very dull. Don't think the book is though! Pauline had figured on going to Nantucket this week but suddenly decided, (I think after a very good dinner) to go abroad on the Normandie with the Willerts. Brenda and Paul. They are very nice and you would like them. She did not know how long exactly she would be gone nor when get back but was very happy and excited about the trip. Jay Allen was going too, also Negrin and Elliot Paul so they will have a jolly time. Jinny was thinking of going over later.

Has Edgar [Mowrer] come over yet? Give him and Lillian my very best will you please?

Hope you have good fishing. Best to Paul. Much love and love to Bumby. I will bring him a lot of ammunition for his rifle from the case that is at Key West. Ask him if I should order some pistol cartridges too. Oh yes. And I guess he had better write me. Tell him that it finally looks as though he would have to write me.

Best love and luck
Ernest

Please write to *Ambos Mundos*. I put the name of the hotel co. on out-side as hotel letters go to dead letter office if not delivered.

PH. PUL

To MRS. PAUL PFEIFFER, Havana, 21 July 1939

Dear Mother:

I've just re-read your letter and May 30, when you wrote it, is a long time away. It seems as though it had only come the other day. Have never known a summer to go so fast. When am working as hard as have been since the first week in April the days all just blur together. Have 63,000 words done on this novel and am about two thirds through. The Sun Also Rises was only 55,000 so you see there has been plenty of working. Wake about seven thirty, have breakfast and am working by nine and usually work straight through until two p.m. After that it's like living in a vacuum until working time next day.

I don't know whether Pauline had time to write you when she was makeing all her quick decisions so I'll summarize a hundred and sixty dollars worth of long distance calls and give you the latest news of your far flung family as gathered in Cuba.

I don't know what she or Virginia wrote you about her diagnosis trouble. It seems Pauline went up to Nantucket with Ruth Allen (Jay Allen's wife) to look that Island over as a summer prospect. On that trip she had some bleeding from the rectum. She was naturally worried and consulted a doctor in Boston who told her there was a possibility of a malignant tumour. Pauline told no one about this at the time and wrote me nothing about it. I had been writing but not hearing from her for about ten days so got very worried and called up. She had just had an examination that day (that I called) and was to have a final one the next. The first examination had shown no stomach nor rectal trouble. The second was of the intestine. I was to call immediately after examination. Meantime got passage on plane, arranged about boat, packed Mss. etc. for long siege in N.Y. and prospect of immediate operation if there was anything. But thank God there wasn't. She is absolutely and completely o.k. and healthy and there is no tumor of any kind neither malignant nor benign. It was evidently only a small burst vein or something of that sort.

I think in the reaction from such a prospect the jolly trip on the Normandie with the Willerts (Brenda and Paul. He is Am. publisher of the Oxford Press and they have visited us in K.W. two different winters) was a fine thing. A fine crowd was going on the boat and I think practically every one in N.Y. who wasn't going decided to go. I would certainly liked to have been aboard. Have only used the Normandie to go to war on and the feeling is never quite the same. There is plenty of money for a European trip as I had just deposited the proceeds of sale of To Have and Have Not to the pictures. So it all worked out finely. Brenda Willert is a niece of Winston Churchill (the English one) and is really very nice. They ought to have a fine time and this may be the last chance at Europe before it blows up. I expect to see Chamberlain present Dantzig to Hitler in one way or another if he cannot conclude his Russian pact so look for no war this summer. But you can never tell. Hitler knows there is everything to gain by war scares and nothing to gain by war. But if you keep on lighting matches to show how many powder barrels you have open something may ignite.

Bumby is going out west with his mother and Paul Mowrer shortly. The Edgar Mowrers are comeing over from Paris and they are all going to be together. I am going to pick Patrick and Gregory up at camp and have all the boys together at the ranch (L bar T) as soon as Bumby finishes with the Mowrers. Thought you might like to have the boys (Patrick and Gregory) in Piggott end of September or early October. Will you write me if you do? We could bring Ada on from Syracuse to look after them so they would not be a nuisance. It has been, or will be, almost a year since you have seen them. A year is a long time with Gregory. Patrick is always about the same; the best companion that I know. But if someone didn't see Gregory for a couple of years they might find he was Secretary of the Treasury (the Greatest Secretary of the Treasury since Alexander Hamilton).

Anyway have written all this to Pauline. She quite rightly did not want to make any definite plans when she left because if the trip was great fun there would be no need to rush back. If it wasn't fun she could always cut it short. You should have a good time in the last of Europe.

Well here it is my [fortieth] birthday. It seems, somehow, of very little importance. If I can write a good novel that will be much more. Well I *have* to write a good one. And I will. But some days the going is tough. Today for instance.

Much love and thank you for such a fine letter. Mine isn't any good. Best to all in Piggott.

PUL   Ernest

To HADLEY MOWRER, Havana, 26 July 1939

Dearest Kat:

Was certainly fine to hear from you. Tell the Bumby I wrote to Hardys today ordering his rod, worm flies, shrimps, and a reel and fly line sent direct to Crossed Sabers. Hope it gets there promptly. Tell him to write.

It's good discipline! His last letter was very good (also ordered Hardy rod-reel and line for Paul for present but don't say anything about that. When there is two of everything in the shipment it's not a mistake. It's a surprize). There'll be some duty to pay but if Paul will pay that when it comes I will send check for same.

I'm sorry to not have been better about money. It's been sort of complicated lately. I went to the war several times and always when was away lived on average of under $200 a month. Always made plenty. Paid everything I made directly into joint account. But life in New York very expensive. Key West irreducible over-head up to $1000 a month when house open. I sold To Have and Have Not to pictures for derisory amount to have money to finance writing this novel. Doubt if much of it will go into that. I've worked like a galley slave since Jan 1. When came home from abroad last time for Thanksgiving Day in previous almost 3 months we had banked about 4700. I'd spent around 750 outside of that. Money I'd get from British rights etc. But when get home find bank balance of 300 or 400. New York very expensive. Guess everything is very expensive and the best things are all free.

Anyway never mention any of this to anyone. I'm in the wrong of course. But I never do what I shouldn't just to do it; nor from carelessness. Only sort of when you have to. And nobody will ever hear it but in a lot of this if you knew about it you would think I'd done about as well as a man could. Life is quite complicated. And you don't always have luck. Anyway not a thing to write about. Important thing for me to do is not get discouraged and take easy way out like your and my noted ancestors.[1] Because very bad example to children. Also have to finish this book. An uncompleted novel by Tom Wolfe much the same as a completed novel. But an uncompleted novel by your old Waxen obviously an uncompleted novel.

Bury all this. But boy the more I see of all the members of your sex the more I admire you.

Maybe we will all have a fine time in Heaven. Sure and maybe we have already had the hereafter and it was up in the Dolomites, and the Black Forest and the forest of the Irati. Well if that is so it's O.K. with me. Was a fine time.

See if I know any news.

Old Chink [Eric Dorman-Smith] is one of the biggest big shots on the British General Staff now and the author of The Future of Infantry.

George O'Neil got fat as a porpoise and married his grandmother or something. Very complicated.

Bill Bird exactly the same. Better looking than ever. Sally unchanged in temperament. Looks sort of like owneress of Maison Tellier [Maupassant].

Got interrupted at this point so this end of the letter. Best to Paul. Maybe see you all at Crossed Sabers before you leave. Have 63,000 words done. Caught a 525 lb. Marlin Saturday. Plenty of big ones now. Fishing only Saturday afternoons and Sunday have caught 18. Hope Edgar can make it.

Much love, and *good* luck and a fine time at the ranch.

Yours always
Tatie

Enclosed put on your credit for the over-lapping J.H.N.H. [Bumby] expenses.

Also two pics [pictures]—Schatz [Bumby] might want. Weigh 202.

PH. PUL

1. A reference to the suicides of the fathers of Hadley (1903) and EH (1928).

To MR. AND MRS. PAUL PFEIFFER, Havana, 28 July 1939

Dear Father and Mother Pfeiffer:

Thank you very much for the birthday check and for the two good letters. Bumby gets to the ranch about September First. The children's Camp finishes August 27th. So I will have Otto [Bruce] pick them up then and bring them West and we will all come to Piggott on the way home from the ranch.

Had a letter from Pauline from the boat written the day before they were to land. She was haveing a very gay trip. Jay Allen, it seems, did not go at the last minute but they were a big enough and jolly enough party as it was. She has since cabled that she and Brenda Willert were following the big Tour De France bicycle race with Robert Capa the photographer who worked with us in Spain.

Have been working very hard and working steadily toward 70,000 words. Am in the very hardest part to write now. Hope I have good luck with it.

I hope you have a fine visit to the [New York World's] fair and the Homestead. Am so sorry to hear about Uncle Loney's stroke. I liked him more than almost anyone I have ever met. If you write him please send him all my sympathy and wishes for a speedy recovery.

Was sorry I did not see Frank Tinker before he took such a drastic step.[1] Have argued myself out of that so often that I think I could have kicked the idea out of his head. He was a good fellow; very brave and a truly fine flyer.

Am delighted to hear that Pauline is haveing such a fine trip. Feel more and more that this may be the last time there will be to enjoy Europe for a long time. Perhaps ever, in our lifetimes. It is very good that she has the opportunity. If ever get this book done and Europe still in one piece am going to cut me a slice of it myself.

Certainly look forward to seeing you all in Piggott. Best love to all and thank you again for the present.

Ernest

(Have to get back to work now. Am down to 201 lbs. Get plenty of exercise and sleep well but am getting tired of this writing. Been at it every day almost except for the two ocean voyages for about twelve months now. Six long short stories, don't know how many magazine articles, re-written a play twice and now have 67,000 words done on a novel. Machine holding up all right but been going under forced draft for a long time. Think I'd better take it up in the mountains and let it cool off.)

Hope you have a fine trip east.

PUL

1. Tinker, who had flown for the Loyalists in Spain, was a recent suicide.

To PATRICK AND GREGORY HEMINGWAY, Key West, 23 August 1939

Dearest Mouse and Giggy:

Well we got back to Key West all right but it certainly is lonesome with no family. Had to cross in a bad blow and my legs still ache from steering all night. Too rough to sit on the seat and the sea abeam (sideways) so it was all roll.

The place is fine. Six banties still alive. Peacocks killed some. All hen peacocks have chicks. He peacocks have no tails. Jimmy has no tobacco Mr. Ernest.

Mother writes she is haveing a wonderful time. She has been in Germany and Austria too and all over France in a car.

Have to stop now for packing. Everybody from here sends love to you. Either [Otto] Bruce or I will pick you up. Probably Bruce as I do not want to face New York with all business to do as well as the Stork Club to look after when should get out to the ranch.

74,000 words done on the book. I was sitting with prickly heat writing about a snowstorm and it was getting more difficult and more difficult and so I thought, "What the what citizens let's go out west and see a snow-storm."

Be very good with Bruce on the train and not be nuisances because being all by ourselves everybody has to be as good as possible or we will be liable to have the glorious discipline of indiscipline and you remember where that got the Spanish Republic to.

(That well known Creek)

Much love from Papa and see you soonest. Have the Air-rifle and so on. The Bumby caught a big rainbow trout, he writes, in the North Fork of Shoshoni.

wj   Papa

To HADLEY MOWRER, Sun Valley, Idaho, 24 November 1939

Dear Kath. Kat:

I'm dreadfully sorry about the duty. Check enclosed. I'd asked Bumby to let me know about this so I could send it; but never heard. Did he deliver Paul the reel and line? Hope so. Caught the duty on them as they came in. I feel very badly about the other as it is awful to give a person a present and then make him pay for it. Still, Hemingstein *is* a Jewish name.

I wrote Jack [Bumby] about ten days ago. Also wrote today on subject of working better at school trying to treat it in simplest terms.

Have been here ever since Wyoming[1] writing every day on this novel. It is over 100,000 words now. Working so hard I get too pooped to write letters. Have to go out to get some exercise and then before you know it is the next day and am working on novel again. Decided to write as good and big a novel as I can rather than put off to when older which, the way things go what with war and all, could be an epoch that might never come.

What about Bumby's Christmas vacation? Is that to be with you or with me? Whichever you want and as most convenient. But let me know here, will you, so can make plans.

I had planned to be in Key West from about the 10th of December on. But a letter from Pauline this morning seems to alter those plans.[2]

But let me know whether you want Jack with you or whether he is to be with me and I will see that he has a good vacation with plenty of tennis etc. I can open up a place in the country where I sometimes stay in Cuba very easily and it is fine there.

N.A.N.A. wants me to cover the war for them as soon as it gets dangerous enough to justify paying me that kind of money. Am very glad to not waste a winter of my life at the sort of war it has been so far.

I haven't sent any more cash for Bumby's schooling because I have not made a nickel while working on this book since sold that last story to Cosmo at which time sent some. On Jan 1 there will be the income from his Trust. As soon as I get this novel finished will be makeing some money again and in a position to help out. But if you need any please always tell me as I have good credit with Scribner's and can borrow on an advance. Also if for any reason you ever need money please let me know because if I did not have it I could either borrow it or sell securities.

It was lovely meeting the three of you on that trail.[3]

Please don't think that I'm getting sloppy about my obligations nor in my attitude toward Bumby. It is just that I have worked under terrific concentration, trying not to worry, trying only to do this one most important thing well. Have had no help from anyone and you could even say, maybe, quite a little hindrance.

Give Edgar [Mowrer] my love when he comes. I am very fond of him. Tell him Marty Gellhorn is in Finland and Scandinavia for Colliers. She had hoped to see him in Paris. She should be back sometime in January.

Have had fine pheasant and duck shooting here. The book is good, I think. I hope you are both fine and I send much love.

Tatie

Am only inhabitant of this vast glamour house. When the season opens will vacate.

PH. PUL

1. Pauline had been with EH at the Nordquist Ranch in September, but he soon left Wyoming for Sun Valley, Idaho, where Martha Gellhorn joined him before her trip to the Finnish front. 2. Owing to EH's liaison with Martha, Pauline had indicated that he would not be welcome in Key West. 3. See Carlos Baker, *Ernest Hemingway: A Life Story* (New York, 1969), p. 341.

To MAXWELL PERKINS, Sun Valley, 8 December 1939

Dear Max:

Thank you very much for writing the letter and depositing the money. Sorry to keep asking for it but suppose you would rather have it in small doses that way and I have turned down all writing offers since the first of March in order to work on this novel. It goes well and can see the finish.

When you get this letter will you deposit $500. again in my Special Account in First National Bank of Key West, Florida.

Otto [Bruce] has come out to drive with me and is packing now and I hope to get away for Key West early tomorrow morning. Was very sorry you didn't get out here.

Thanks very much for the books, Max. They were fine. The Dorrance Rivers book has truly fine things in it. The Gen Fuller books are extremely interesting.[1] Have read other stuff of his beside the little book on Generalship you sent one time. I think the biggest balls up in history would have resulted from his gigantic tank offensive projected for 1919 as those tanks were no good; still he has more sound military imagination than most British.

That was a shame about Al Bessie not likeing the ideology of that story. What do those guys use for Ideology nowadays? Marty Gellhorn has been in Helsinki and at Finnish front since it started. I imagine it did not take her long to realize that those bi-motored Katuskas were no longer our planes. Don't say anything about this or anything else I say to Bessie. Those poor unfortunate bastards need all the ideology they can get and I would not want to deprive anyone of any anymore than would make cracks about religion to a nun. But Max it is a foul business and it was a foul business plenty of times in Spain too. But if you have a war you have to win it. If you lose you lose everything and your ideology won't save you. He wrote a good, fine straight book.[2] But what was wrong with his outfit was too much ideology and not enough military training, discipline or materiel. The lat[t]er nobody can be blamed for except the Russians, French and British. We only won one battle; Guadalajara. The Professionals won that. We took Teruel too and the ideology boys lost it. Bessie's outfit has been taught to believe they saved the Valencia-Madrid highway but they were pitiful there and uselessly massacred by their incompetent officers. The real fascist attack was way North of them at Arganda. That war could have been won if we had necessary material. But Bessie's outfit had been lousy and awful at the start. Gotten good about the time when Evan [Shipman] was in it and been excellent all that summer and fall and until the end of Teruel. Bessie never saw the war until it was hopelessly lost but he was a fine guy and brave soldier and excellent writer and he certainly wrote a damned good book. Very few books read as true as that book did. Whatever happened that kept it from being pushed I think it was a damned crime it wasn't.

If it's impossible to work in K.W. will go to Cuba and not move until this book is finished. Will certainly be wonderful when it is. I mean I will feel wonderful. It has taken a greater power of concentration than I knew I had not to worry about some things that have gone on.

Best always

PUL   Ernest

1. W. A. Dorrance, *Where the Rivers Meet* (New York, 1939), and Major General J. F. C. Fuller, *Decisive Battles* (New York, 1940), both published by Scribners. 2. Alvah C. Bessie, *Men in Battle* (New York, 1939), also published by Scribners.

To MRS. PAUL PFEIFFER, Sun Valley, 12 December 1939

Dear Mother Pfeiffer: *

I had counted very much on comeing to see you last fall with the children. I wanted to see you both very much and I wanted to ask your advice about some things.

But Pauline came home unexpectedly from Europe, got a terrible chest-grippe cold on landing at the Billings airport and was sick all the time at the [Nordquist] ranch. I cooked her meals etc. and tried to take care of her but conditions were primitive and her cold got worse instead of better. The rest you know more about than I do. Her arrival and her plans changed all my plans so I did not get to Piggott.

If we could have talked I believe you would have found that I have changed less than Pauline and Virginia have. Virginia's version of my life and conduct is a very fantastic one. But she spread it sufficiently and at the right time to break up my home. So am now doing the best I can. I do not mean that I have ever been in the right in *anything* but the true version would be very different from anything you have heard.

Anyway I wanted you to know how badly I felt not to bring the children to Piggott, not to see you then, nor now, and please never worry but that I will look after Pauline's material interests as though they were my own. Will also be very careful about the children and take very good care of them. The children and I get along very well.

This kind of letter is no fun to write and probably less to read. So let's stop it. I miss you very much. Have had a very lonely time working on this book. Hope it will be very good. Anyway it is very long and so far it hasn't a bad word in it. *Extraordinary.*

As always, reading this over, seem to have a lot of *very* trouble. Count them in above paragraphs. I certainly write an almost illiterate letter.

Anyway much love and a good Christmas. If it's not merry it will be sooner or later again. Please tell Karl [Pfeiffer] I'm sorry not to hunt with him this fall.

Yours always
Ernest

PUL

---

* *Mrs. Pfeiffer's undated letter in reply to this one says:* "This is the saddest Christmas I have ever known. A broken family is a tragic thing, particularly so when there are children."

To MAXWELL PERKINS, La Finca Vigia, San Francisco de Paula, Cuba, *c.* 4 or 11 February 1940

Dear Max:

Well here is your regular Sunday hangover letter. We won again at the pelota last night and stayed up till three a.m. So today will have to take Marty to the movies as a present for being drunk Saturday night I guess. Started out on absinthe, drank a bottle of good red wine with dinner, shifted to vodka in town before the pelota game and then battened it down with whiskys and sodas until 3 a.m. Feel good today. But not like working.

Worked good last week. Have averaged over five hundred words a day for last 17 days including saturdays and sundays (haven't worked on them either). Am down to 198 pounds due to terrific tennis with the pelota players.

When you get this will you send me a check for $1500? Please make it out to Manuel Asper. He needs it to buy motor truck in U.S.A. to ship to Spain. If he sends the money out of the country he will have to pay a 4 per cent tax. So he will give me $1500 here and I will use it to pay my income tax and he will save the 4%. Charge it against me. He is the owner of the [Hotel] Ambos Mundos and has always done all my banking for me and I am glad to do anything I can to help him. Gave him money on this same system to buy a truck last summer. But right now I have no money in the bank to draw a check on. So send me the check for $1500 and charge it against my advance on this book.

Am started working on a title. Want a big one. I don't have to worry about over-titling this one. She'll carry quite a lot. I think it is good that it is a long book. You know there are pricks who are impressed by length. I'll never forget Sinclair Lewis calling To Have etc. [*To Have and Have Not*] a "thin screaming of only 67,000 words!" May have the number of words wrong. He himself writes a hoarse scream of never less than 120,000. But if I wrote as sloppily and shitily as that freckled prick I could write five thousand words a day year in and year out. My temptation is always to write too much. I keep it under control so as not to have to cut out crap and re-write. Guys who think they are geniuses because they have never learned how to say no to a typewriter are a common phenomenon. All you have to do is to get a phony style and you can write any amount of words.

Everything went through o.k. with Sweeny.[1] Thanks very much. I always thought you would like him. He wants me very much on his staff. It is a compliment because he is really a very talented soldier. But he has a definite plafond as a soldier. He can't get along with *anybody* in action. He can with me because I love him and understand him and will take anything from him knowing he doesn't mean what he says when he is angry. But he is *always* angry when things are bad. He has one of the most brilliant military brains I have ever known and the French General Staff trust and respect him but I know the sort of thing that will happen when he has a division as he will now and I could prevent some of it maybe. He knows about the plafond too and he knows I get more cheerful the worse things go (this isn't bragging. I wasn't always that way. I think it is part of growing up. You get to be one way or another and I turned out to be one of the cheerful bastards) and I think that is the reason he wants me because God knows I am a very chickenshit military man. The kind of thing I mean is that every time Charley gets angry he wants somebody shot. Well I agree and they are shot. Only I wouldn't shoot them and afterwards it would be o.k.

He made the plans for the Teruel offensive. Rather he corrected them and showed everything that was wrong with the Russian staff work and every goddamned thing came out exactly as he said it would including how we lost the town and why because of not doing one thing which should have been done when it was taken. He and Gen. Armangeau of French Gen Staff came to Madrid as newspaper correspondents and brought me, also a correspondent, six bottles of cognac and three of absinthe. We started to argue (me to explain, Sweeny to denounce) at seven a.m. and it went on all over the front all day, in my room until 2 a.m. with Sweeny calling me all sorts of names, continually insulting me, harping on my lack of military education, my abysmal ignorance, my lack of this, my lack of that, balling me out in front of everybody and everyone there thought we must be bitter enemies. Then at three a.m. they all were very surprised when Charley said, "You old bastard. You're getting a little sense after all. Promise me you won't do silly things."

I said, "So long you old bastard."

Then we embrace, kiss each other on both cheeks and he goes out with both of us as fond of each other and as full of respect for each other as people can be. But everyone who was there was waiting for the guns to be pulled. He's really absolutely goddamned insufferable sometimes but I know he won't shoot me and I'm about the only white man alive that can get along with him all the time. I wish the three of us could have gone out together and I could have got him talking for you. Waldo [Peirce] gets along with him too by takeing what no human would take. Ask Waldo about the time he was painting Charley's portrait and Charley finally started painting it himself. Boy I'd like to have that confidence.

Charley got into the Spanish war late and every time I would go from Paris he would come and help pack the rucksacks, get the tickets, look after everything that had to be done and then come down to the station and buy a supper with champagne. He'd send books and grub and liquor and he acted just like a fire-horse that wasn't allowed to pull the hose-cart anymore. Then the minute he got into it he acted as though all the rest of us were simply criminal lunatics and the minute the war started was when he entered. And the war stopped when he left. He's wonderful. But I would rather listen to him on military things than anybody I have ever known. He thinks I am skunk brave and have no brains while in reality I have good brains and am only temporarily brave again on account of the confidence that grows in you when you go a long time without being hit. I'm a writer anyway. Well this is enough of this. Writing to you on Sunday is getting to be a habit. You don't have to answer.

Everything o.k. here. What would I have to do to get you to come down? Will have the boat over here the end of March. This is the best place you'll ever see.

Good luck Max
Ernest

PUL

1. Colonel Charles Sweeny (1882–1963), born in San Francisco, California, was a brilliant soldier of fortune whom EH had first met in Constantinople in September 1922. He is said to have fought in seven wars with the armed forces of five countries.

To CHARLES SCRIBNER, Havana, 24 February 1940

Dear Charlie:

It will be swell to see you any time you get fed-up on Palm Beach.

Don't worry about the words. I've been doing that since 1921. I always count them when I knock off and am drinking the first whiskey and soda. Guess I got in the habit writing dispatches. Used to send them from some places where they cost a dollar and a quarter a word and you had to make them awful interesting at that price or get fired. Then I kept it up when started writing stories etc. I don't know as many words as a guy like Tom Wolfe and so it is a hell of a thing for me to get anything over five hundred of them down in a day. Then at the end of the week I always add them up so that I can think even if I am a no good son of a bitch I wrote, say, 3500 words this week. It's wonderful to be a writer. You ought to try it.

I always knew Max had some sinister kind of woman trouble but somebody ought to tell him you have to be firm with them. He should say, sure he will take her to Havana. Then at the last minute say Darling, things have come up so that I cannot take you to Havana. No, I cannot explain. It involves issues that are Too Big. Trust me darling as you always have. I am takeing the plane at 8.45.

I wish he would come down though. I never see the bastard any more. Why can't he take an interest in me like he took in Tom Wolfe? I will let him cut out useless bits of what I write if that is what he likes. He can administer my estate. I will send my worst sisters to him with books. I'll do everything for him that Tom Wolfe did except go to Harpers.

Maybe he won't come to see me anymore because I never dedicate any books to him. Tell him I don't do that not because I don't love, admire, respect and cherish him but because whenever one of his authors dedicates a book to him the author usually blows up and isn't any good anymore. I can't afford to blow up and not be any good anymore because I have so many dependents and so many houses and homes. All I can do that geniuses do is not get a haircut. But finally I always have to get a haircut too.

Charlie there is no future in anything. I hope you agree. That is why I like it at a war. Every day and every night there is a strong possibility that you will get killed and not have to write. I have to write to be happy whether I get paid for it or not. But it is a hell of a disease to be born with. I like to do it. Which is even worse. That makes it from a disease into a vice. Then I want to do it better than anybody has ever done it which makes it into an obsession. An obsession is terrible. Hope you haven't gotten any. That's the only one I've got left. Well I better try to do a little of it now instead of talking about it.

Will look forward to seeing you.

Best always,
Ernest

Oh yes. I forgot. I've got one ambition. Not an obsession. Just an ambition to nail that son of a bitch max eastman to the top of a fence post with a twenty penny spike through the base of his you know what and then push him backwards slowly. After that I'd start working on him. No I think I'd rather nail him to Max's desk and leave him there. Maybe every few hours I'd just come in and rock him a little.

PUL

To MAXWELL PERKINS, La Finca Vigia, 21 April 1940

Dear Max:

How about this for a title

For Whom The Bell Tolls

A Novel

By Ernest Hemingway

No man is an *Iland,* intire of itselfe; every man is a peece of the *Continent,* a part of the *maine;* if a *Clod* bee washed away by the *Sea, Europe* is the lesse, as well as if a Promontorie were, as well as if a *Mannor* of thy *friends,* or of thine own were; any man's *death* diminishes me, because I am involved in *Mankinde;* And therefore never send to know for whom the *bell* tolls; It tolls for *thee.*

John Donne[1]

I think it has the magic that a title has to have. Maybe it isn't too easy to say. But maybe the book will make it easy. Anyway I have had thirty some titles and they were all possible but this is the first one that has made the bell toll for me.

Or do you suppose that people think only of tolls as long distance charges and of Bell as the Bell telephone system? If so it is out.

The Tolling of the Bell. No. That's not right. If there is no modern connotation of telephone to throw it off For Whom The Bell Tolls can be a good title I think.

Anyway it is what I want to say. And so if it isn't right we will get it right. Meantime you have your provisional title for April 22.

Let me hear from you. Best to Charley. Going now to the Jai-Alai to try to make it 21 straight.

Best always

PUL Ernest

1. After much effort, EH had located the quotation in *The Oxford Book of English Prose*.

To MAXWELL PERKINS, La Finca Vigia, *c.* 1 May 1940

Dear Max:

Well Winston Churchill has been mixed up in three landings now; Antwerp, Gallipoli and Norway. Have no doubt he will be able to write a magnificently interesting book about this last one too.

Have thought of a new phrase Coitus Britannicus: referring to her allies; translates: F--ked from the back with withdrawal.

Coitus Britannicus; that's the thing. Or appeasement carried even onto the field of battle.

What a degenerate people the English are. Their politics have been suicidal ever since the last war. They gave us the worst bitching anybody did in Spain where we fought both Hitler and Mussolini for them for nothing and could have kept them tied up there indefinitely (exactly as the Peninsular war beat Napoleon) if they had only given any aid at all —any at all.

The British volunteers in the International Brigade were the absolute scum of the Brigades. After the Jarama fight they deserted by whole companies; they were cowards, malingerers, liars and phonies and fairies. They were absolutely panic-ed by the tanks and their officers, when they were brave, were so stupid that their stupidity was absolutely murderous.

Sure plenty of exceptions and some fine ones. But in general the British volunteers were the scum of the Brigades. The bums and clochards [derelicts] of Lyons that Herriot shipped to Spain to get rid of them were twenty times better soldiers than the English.

Well enough of this.

Sent you a wire about the title. Hope to Christ that was the [New York] Times error and not that it has gone out all wrong everywhere.

There's a difference between The Sun Also Rises and Also The Sun Rises. Also between A Farewell To Arms and Goodbye to the Weapons

and there's a hell of a lot of difference between For Whom The Bell Tolls and For Whom Tolls The Bell even if it doesn't show at the time.
Well have to get to work now.

Best always,
Ernest

PUL

To MAXWELL PERKINS, La Finca Vigia, 13 July 1940

Dear Max:

Hope to get up to N.Y. by the end of next week with the Mss. They are copying it all now except the last chapter where am still working on the end. The last chapter is the most exciting in the book. It's almost unbearably exciting during and after the bridge is blown. I finished the part where—what the hell—will not tell you—you can read it—I was as limp and dead as though it had all happened to me. Anyhow it is a hell of a book. I knew I had to write a hell of a last chapter. But have it all now except the very end—the action and the emotion are all done. Been too shot about it all to write yest. or today. (The girl doesn't get killed.) I hated to have that damned Jordan get what he got after living with the son of a bitch for 17 months. Felt worse than if it were me. Wrote 2600 words (all action) on last day. Almost like a genius. The hell of it is they all make sense so no chance of genius-hood.

When you get this will you send a check for $890. to Muhlberg (Muhlberg Motor Co.) Key West—Florida—and charge it against the advance on the book?

I had to get another car. This one had 4 bad wrecks and it wasn't safe any more. Frame too bent etc.

Will be seeing you soon. Give my best to Charlie.

Best always,
Ernest

There is so much panic and hysteria and shit going around now I don't feel like writing any flagwaving stuff. I will fight but I don't want to write that syndicated patriotism. Don't tell them that though. Just tell them I'm doing it and I will never do it.

Did you send the 1st of July money to Pauline's bank?[1]

PUL

1. Pre-divorce "alimony" of $500 a month.

To CHARLES SCRIBNER, La Finca Vigia, *c.* 15 August 1940

Dear Charley:

Thanks very much for the letter of suggestions. Will do what I can about all of them. Value them very much.

Thanks too about the horse. I will make it a wind gall instead. Or will people write to the Field about that? As I understand it a wind gall don't amount to anything and can be easily reduced. Will place it in the fet-lock if that is o.k. with you and the Field and if there is such a place. Let me know about that will you?

I had intended the animal to have knocked the lower part of his knee against a piece of down timber and there to have been a swelling there that didn't amount to nothing either.

It was my impression that the cannon bone ran straight south from the knee until it hit the fetlock, the pastern etc. and that it was bounded on the north by the knee as you explained so clearly.

I have never seen a horse myself so this is all hearsay but I am going to try and get near one sometime and see if I could find such mysterious places as the Hock (which I had always imagined to be inferior white wine as drunk by the English) and the Gaskin which for years I took to be a mis-spelling of the Gasket.

Now take the withers. I had always imagined this to be a mis-spelling of the Whithers or the place the horse had just come from. Don't tell me where they actually are. I want life to hold some mysteries.

My own experience with the horse has been confined to his use as a bear bait. On this I am qualified to write to The Field. I have shot more old, broken-down, beloved horses for bear-baits while their owners, who couldn't bear to do it or to see it, waited a hundred yards or so down the hill than has the combined editorial board or subscribers of The Field. When you write to the Field next tell them the best horse for a bear bait is a big horse, so there will be a lot of him, who is not worth wintering. You want to kill him where the sun will strike him so he will start to get high quickly. If you kill him in shade or if he gets rained on he is liable to simply go sour and not come up at all. To bring him up faster you can build a fire on him. The smell of the burnt hair and charred meat carries a long way on the wind and the bear picks it up. You must be careful not to burn clean through him because then he won't come up and then, also, the ravens and the magpies and the eagles will get into him. Now the reason you want him to come-up (these are all technical terms) as quickly as possible is so he will commence to put-out. Naturally you will always approach with the wind in his favour in order not to spook off

anything that may be feeding on him so you can judge how he is putting
out as you approach.

There is more to this but why should I write such priceless data on the
ultimate phase of horsemanship for nothing?

When you get this wire me where we stand on the Book of The Month.
I need to know in order to organize my scale of living.

Am returning the jacket. It seems o.k. although I know nothing about
them. Except that the bridge should be a thin, high-arching, metal, canti-
lever bridge instead of a stone bridge. It will go in there o.k. Should be
high, thin and spidery looking. Blowing up that stone bridge in the
picture wouldn't hold up anything. If bridge is used it must look to be
distant and to be bridgeing a steep gorge. I think it should be fore-
shortened in the picture as it is to give the impression of a road going up
the far mountain.

Tell this in exactly these words to the artist will you?

The typography looks good. The "spot" looks pleasant and cheerful.
Only thing wrong I see is the bridge. I know it is only lightly symbolocal
and supposed, perhaps, not even to be that. But if there is any bridge it
must be a steel bridge not a wooden one. If he can't make a metal one
like the one in the book then let's have no bridge at all. But no reason
why he can't.

How about makeing that journalist British; not American?

When there are too many obscenities on a page will get in some other
word. Some of those you suggest are o.k. Maybe I can find some others.

The smell of death part [chapter 19] seems to me to be an integral and
valid part of the whole thing. You remember there is a whole dark
business about that from the very start. The man Kashkeen who has
killed himself, the same necessity which faces Jordan, the question about
forebodeings which I know is not phony from haveing seen people walking around with it sitting on their shoulders (this is not being romantic).
There is the balanceing of Jordan's good sense and sound skepticism
against this gypsy crap which isn't all crap. And to make the gypsy thing
valid and not just seeming phony as all that stuff always does I needed
some completely naturalistic thing which gives some of the horror that
is in Madrid.

It isn't dragged in. I haven't just put every goddamned thing I know
or ever heard in. I didn't put in Pilar's husband (really Rafael el Gallo)
being impotent on his wedding night and lying there on the public bed
(it doesn't count unless it is done in public or unless the sheets are produced with Gypsies) and the gypsies makeing incantation and trying to
bring him up and she disgraced and him sobbing.

I omitted that.

I also omitted going one time in the Calle Carmen where a man went upstairs with a leper with her face three quarters gone to do this thing for a duro with the leper and how afterwards when one of the gypsies protested that it was a phony and not real that the leper woman reached down and flicked out with one finger and tossed a long string of it into his face.

No, Charley. There is a goddamned horribleness about part of Madrid like no other place in the world. Goya never half drew it. I need that to make this book whole. But I tried to get it without putting in unpublishables.

There is a lot of soliloquy there somewhere that I am going to cut. I didn't have the original Mss. with me in N.Y. and couldn't see where the part came out and went in there one time and so had them set it all.

About all the other things I will do whatever I can.

Hope I am not just being stubborn about the smell of death part but to make what I was trying to make I need something like that. Afterwards you would miss the effect very much that was made if it was taken out.

About Onan etc. will have to see when I come to it. I start work on it on Monday.

This book is one whole thing; not just a lot of parts. You start takeing out parts put there for a purpose and the next thing you haven't any whole.

Enclose drawing of how that bridge ought to be to show the artist. Also possible improvement on the building. Also a picture of some of that country on acct. of bell arrangement. Also a picture of a bell.

I never interfere in jackets except the time they made the bull a heifer or an androgynous steer—whichever it was—and I had to fix that. Feel the same way about this bridge. Otherwise I think the drawing is pleasant and would lead people on rather than drive them away.

One other thing—Andre Marty is the name of a real person [chapter 42]. He has fled from France to Russia under sentence of death. He is a member of the French Communist Central Committee. He could never come to U.S. under any circumstances. He cannot go back to France unless the Communists come into power. Can he sue? Ask your lawyer. He has been publicly accused of murder in several books and numerous articles in France before he fled the country and he did not sue. He was under investigation by the chamber of deputies when he fled the country when the Communist party was outlawed.

Nick Guillen accused him of murder in Marianne (a large French Weekly) in article after article; each time nameing who Marty had shot. He accused him of the same thing in a book entitled Le Mercenaire published in 1938. I have a copy. Marty took no action against him. He really had the people shot and is in no position to sue. Also he is a fugitive from justice. The book is still on sale or was in January of this year when Martha bought me one in Brussels to take the place of one I gave to Herbert Mathews.

The journalist named Mitchell I spoke of represents a certain American journalist. Would it not make that all cleared up and make no libel if I called him a British Journalist? There is no such British journalist alive or dead. The said Mitchell is a real crook but is still in circulation. His name of course is not Mitchell nor anything like that. I could call him either a British Journalist or a Danish journalist? I'd cut all that out but it is part of the character of Karkov and also shows the necessary relation between Karkov and Jordan that we have to have.

Will you show this letter to Max and I will write him on his points as I take them up.

Martha says she has bit and soaked the ring and it seems to hold up. Beautiful weather here. Am fishing this afternoon.

Best to you always,
Ernest

Wire me about Book of Month. I suppose they won't take it. I am sure from what he said Whitney [Darrow] doesn't like the book. But am also sure he wouldn't have like[d] Grapes of Wrath [Steinbeck] or Native Son [Wright] nor, to mention a slightly better book The Brothers Karamazov nor Madame Bovary either. I don't mean this in that class. I just don't think he would have liked them. They all sold though.

PUL

To CLARA SPIEGEL,¹ La Finca Vigia, 23 August 1940

Dear Clara:

How are you and my wicked boyhood chum Freddy?

I finished the first draft of the book on my birthday July 21 and then it had to be typed and I took it to N.Y. It's 200,000 words long and I had my lawyer Moe Speiser send you a bound up copy of the first un-corrected galleys out to Sun Valley two weeks ago. Only you never got them because yesterday I got a letter from him that he hadn't sent them. I think he thought you were a rival agent (he has metamorphosed from my lawyer into my agent) and he was scared of you. He said he hadn't sent them because they weren't copyrighted yet.

So today I wired him that you wouldn't plagiarize them in a mere two weeks and that you were o.k. and would show them to no one. So you ought to have them around the same time you get this letter.

Bumby, my oldest boy, he is called Jack I guess now and is somewhere around fifteen sixteen or seventeen is enroute to Sun Valley (when he gets letter I sent him today) from Holm Lodge in his own jalopy to get there before the other kids and fish Silver Creek.

He should hit there the 27th or 28th.

I wrote Taylor [Williams] to send somebody with him to Silver Creek once to head him in. If Taylor isn't there would you tell Art or Chape?

Would you also ask Mac [Forrest Mac Mullen] to give them a room in either the Inn or one of those skier places and charge against me?

Patrick and Gregory (the Mouse and Jew) are due to hit Ogden, Utah enroute to Sun Valley from San Francisco on the first of September at 7.05 p.m.

I have written Bumby he is to proceed from Sun Valley to Ogden by train and bus (NOT BY HIS CAR) to meet the two kids. He is to go in plenty of time to get there and meet the train and then is to bring them to Sun Valley by the train that leaves Ogden at 9.20 for Sun Valley getting into Sun Valley the following morning Sept 2 at 6 a.m. Can you see he starts out to do this? He is vague but he speaks English.

If neither Marty nor me are there to meet them would you see they get a room until we get there?

This is a hell of a lot to ask you to do but I will do something for you sometime or make a speech at the grave if we ever have to plant either you and/or Freddy.

I am arrangeing a divorce, doing proofs on 141 galleys, re-writing the end etc. and then have to take boat to K.W. and car to Sun Valley. Marty and I thought we would be married by now but tell Freddy not to ever marry any rich girls next time he gets married because it is much more expensive than marrying the poorest people in the world unless you should run into Peggy Joyce when she was starting as I never did. Anyway everything will be o.k. shortly.

Bumby can stay only until time to get to Chicago on the eleventh. Patrick and Giggy can stay all through September and October.

I can stay till hell freezes over or as long as I can keep Marty out there and away from war, pestilence, carnage and adventure.

There is a chance the book of the month will take the book. If they do they will print a hundred thousand and Scribner's a hundred thousand and we will be off in a cloud of Steinbecks. If they don't it is still close to anybody's two and a half's dollars worth and let us hope people will buy it. It is the best goddamn book I have ever written and you were damned good and helpful to me dureing one of the worst parts of writing it.

Boy it will be wonderful not to work and to have fun.

No matter when the divorce comes through now we naturally won't get married while the children are out in Sun Valley but afterwards it certainly will be fine.

I am awfully tired daughter and maybe I do not make such good sense.

If the bookadamunt takes it then we will go on a pack-trip. Otherwise will go somewhere in the car or something with the kids in early september and then settle into Sun Valley when the season is over.

Hope you likea da book. The corrected galleys are greatly improved and much errors and nonsenses removed but this set will sort of give you the idea. You read it and Freddy and nobody else, huh?

Think you will like the Mouse, Gig and Bumby after papa has kicked some sense into them. They have been at camp and will probably be terrible.

Marty is lovely. We are both fat as pigs from this sitting down and typescript and proof reading lately but in Sun Valley will ride and play tennis and walk and will be thin. I got down to a steady just under 200 for a long time but now am back up to 207. Marty weighs 130 or just under.

Please give my love to Tilly and Lloyd [Arnold] and Nin [Mrs. Gene Van Guilder] and Mac and everybody out there.

It will be swell to see you and old Freddy again and I certainly look forward to it.

I look forward to seeing your new writing too and hope there is a lot of it for me to read.

The show starts on the road in October. The book comes out October 14. It is now getting ready to rain and me back to the proofs again.

Best love to all of you from us guys,

PH. PUL   Ernie

1. Wife of Frederick Spiegel, with whom EH had driven ambulances in Italy in 1918. Mrs. Spiegel was at this time vacationing in Sun Valley, Idaho.

To MAXWELL PERKINS, La Finca Vigia, 26 August 1940

Dear Max:

I am air-mailing you today 123 galleys. I have gone over it all but I thought you might as well get going on these. I also enclose with this letter a style sheet giveing the corrections that must be made throughout all the galleys. All of Meyers queries and suggestions are answered or embodied in this style sheet.

Your suggestions and Charlie's I have taken up as I went along.

I sent Charles a re-write of parts of galleys 21 (the Communist business) and Galley 29 (the over-use of the word obscenity) to be set up and embodied in all galleys sent out. He got these early last week.

I have cut the part about the man Mitchell drastically and removed all libel without, I think, removeing the flavour of Karkov's mind. It does no good to describe a man such as Karkov as witty and intelligent and then have no conversation to prove it [chapter 18].

I have made the thees and the thous as accurately used as possible without giveing the book an archaic-ness that would make it un-readable. When I use you instead of thee etc. I know what I am doing.

Throughout I removed the word unprintable as I thought it gave a literary connotation that was bad. I changed it to un-nameable or some other word.

I do not agree with you on the passage where something is written about Pilar at the end of galley 18. You thought it was o.k. when it was Pablo and the horses. I know it was necessary. It was simply that the first time it was done it would always be a shock to you. The second time o.k.

I got out that about bigotry etc. as you quite rightly suggested. It was confuseing on Jordan's status.

About the smell of death part [chapter 19]. Unless this will impair the sale of the book seriously or cause its suppression I think it is necessary to leave it in. I have to make many effects that do not show at the time and it is like takeing either the bass viol or the oboe out of my orchestra because they each make an ugly noise when played alone.

If you or charley think that is a dangerous or unpublishable passage I could change it to read instead of wrap it around your head and try to breathe through it to ------- You raise this sack to your face and inhale deeply—and use this same phrase in the next sentence down.

Let me know about this. The passage is meant to be horrifying. It is not meant to be gratuitously obscene or unpublishable. But I have to somehow give that quality of Madrid and make the idea of the odour earthily and concretely and vulgarly believable—instead of seeming to be gypsy-cross-my-hand-with-silver-nonsense. Real gypsies are a very strange people and the ones in this book are not book-gypsies anymore than my indians were ever book-indians.

On the Sordo fight galley 94 I agreed with your correction.

I fixed up the Onan so it would not bother Charley I hope. After all Robert Jordan is a man and the idea of holding some girl all night in your arms that you had intercourse with normally, on a night before an attack when he wanted to go to sleep would bring up some sort of a problem. I tried to handle his rejection of one solution of the problem delicately. If it is repulsive to several people to whom you show it I can cut it out. But remember it is by the small things of that sort that the man becomes absolutely credible instead [of] just a Hero.

Be frank about this.

Now here is some more.

What would you think of ending the book as it ends now without the epilogue?[1]

I have written it and re-written it and it is o.k. but it seems sort of like going back into the dressing room after the fight or following Catherine Barclay [Barkley][2] to the cemetery (as I originally did in Farewell to Arms) and explaining what happened to Rinaldi and all.

I have a strong tendency to do that always on account of wanting everything completely knit up and stowed away ship-shape.

I can write it like Tolstoi and make the book seem larger, wiser, and all the rest of it. But then I remember that was what I always skipped in Tolstoi.

What do you think? Is it o.k. as it is? (I have fixed the emotion some and made it better.)

Please write me air-mail on this the day you get this. Ask everybody if they think it ends all right as it is.

I am leaveing here on Thursday to take the boat across and then drive and fly to Sun Valley. Should be there September 4th at latest. Will send you the remaining 18 galleys before I leave.

Re-wrote on them all day yesterday.

You see the epilogue only shows that good generals suffer after an unsuccessful attack (which isn't new); that they get over it (that's a little newer) Golz haveing killed so much that day is forgiveing of Marty because he has that kindliness you get sometimes. I can and do make Karkov see how it will all go. But that seems to me to date it. The part about Andres at the end is very good and very pitiful and very fine.

But it really stops where Jordan is feeling his heart beating against the pine needle floor of the forest.

You see every damned word and action in this book depends on every other word and action. You see he's laying there on the pine needles at the start and that is where he is at the end. He has had his problem and all his life before him at the start and he has all his life in those days and, at the end there is only death there for him and he truly isn't afraid of it at all because he has a chance to finish his mission.

But would that all be clear?

Should I put on the epilogue? Is it needed? Or would it just be grand manner writing and take you away from the emotion that the book ends on?

Please write me when you get this.

There is also a paragraph on galley 127 that I would like your advice on. It is the long paragraph at the top of the galley. I could take out the last sentence which starts Comrade Marty's part is given only because etc.

Or I could take it out and the first part of the First sentence too and start it—Comrade Andre Marty's interference was probably only fortuitous as there was no one etc.

Let the rest of that go as it is and omit the last sentence.

Let me know about this.

I don't like to write like God. It is only because you never do it, though, that the critics think you can't do it.

The whole story of Marty and Karkov would take another entire volumne to tell. But that is no reason for starting something you do not finish. It was for this reason that I wrote that paragraph. It explains why there was no finish.

Well I will send you the complete galleys by Wednesday.

These couple of corrections (there are no question of any before galley 78) should not hold up your manufactureing up to there at once and if you write me by return air-mail I will get it Wednesday or Thursday and have plenty of time to fix all. Will probably work it out and fix it on my own anyway first. But please write at once when you get this and remember it is ten cents for each ½ ounce.

Well so long Max. Best to Charley. Write me about the end. Maybe better wire about that when you get this letter. If that end is o.k. it would save a lot of time to know it and I would just work over and over that last Chapter until I send it.

Should have one proof on it just to make sure all my corrections are o.k. You can have that pulled and sent to me at Sun Valley, Idaho, by air-mail registered and mark it very prominently. *Please hold.* If there are no corrections I will simply wire to go ahead. If there are corrections will make them by air-mail same day. Send my corrected proof with the new proofs so that I can check the additions faster.

Pauline, haveing agreed to accept what Uncle Gus decided was a just settlement now wants more and of course will get it. Deposit the $500. in her account on Sept. 1 and Oct. First. She's been very tricky. Accepts it to Uncle Gus then tells her lawyer to do something else.

Marty and I can't go out west together. So will meet out there. My advice would be to marry as little as possible but never to marry a rich bitch. [Two and a half lines deleted in heavy pencil.] It will all come out o.k. and very shortly too. So nothing to worry about.

Best always,
Ernest

Ernest Hemingway   *Don't lose this for Christ's sake.*
EH

Memorandum on corrections of proof For Whom The Bell Tolls. These corrections may not have been made on this set of galleys due to lack of space. They are uniform and each word and usage should be checked throughout all the galleys.

Throughout the book use Heinkel for planes—never Henkel.

It is Golz—never Goltz

It is Estremadura—never Extremadura.

Rafael is the gypsy—never the Gypsy (except at the beginning of a sentence).

Maria is referred to as guapa—not Guapa (except at the beginning of a sentence).

Maria is referred to as rabbit—not Rabbit (except at beginning of a sentence).

It is viejo (l.c.) never Viejo (except at beginning of a sentence).

It should be *máquina*—never machina

In *Qué va* the accent aigu should be used in every instance.

guerrillero should be in italics throughout the book.

partizan should be italics and l.c. through the book.

It should be Agustín through the book—never Augustín.

In some places the Sierra de Gredos is referred to as the Gredos (Robert Jordan always refers to them thus). Sordo and Pablo would simply say Gredos. Follow my corrected galleys on this without querying them. I have checked all usage carefully.

Since I have cut chapter three into chapters three and four the numeration of all subsequent chapters should be advanced by one. Check this carefully.

Please check with some one who is familiar with Russian names as to whether Kashkeen should be spelled Kashkin. (I do not have my Russians here.) If it should be spelled Kashkin correct the spelling to this throughout the book.

I will wire you the name of a proper cavalry regiment to insert in the blank left in galley 91.

The dedication is to read:

This book is for Martha Gellhorn.

Check carefully my corrections on the passage from Donne. In the galleys it was full of errors which I have corrected from the original.

PUL

1. The epilogue was finally deleted. 2. EH's slip, no doubt owing to his recent stay at the Hotel Barclay in New York.

To MAXWELL PERKINS, Sun Valley, Idaho, c. 12 October 1940

Dear Max:

Please on receipt of this send $1500 of Book of Month money to my special account in First National Bank of Key West. Thanks.

I was mighty pleased to see that Bob Sherwood review. Thanks for sending it. There are some very big money negotiations going on for picture rights and I believe we have turned down 100,000 for the book and may get 150,000.[1] Wouldn't that be bloody wonderful? I have not had any money for so damn long and would know what to do with it pretty well by now even if the government took half or more.

Have been reading Tom's [Wolfe's] book and a lot of that Fox stuff gave me a pain in the ass. I could not recognize the voice and as for Bill Webber Christ I will write a portrait of you two guys in 1000 words sometime and you see if I cannot get you straighter.[2] I think Tom was only truly good about his home town and there he *was wonderful and unsurpassable*. The other stuff is usually over-inflated journalese.

I sent out all of those thirty copies to where they would do the book the most good and would like to have thirty five more sent out here. Have a kid who wraps and mails them and checks the addresses so it was simpler than sending them back to you to do that. So will you send me thirty five more right away. I would also like to buy six more for myself to give to friends and would like to have two of those Sunrise Sets sent here too that I promised to people. Also please send me Scott's address. Also John Peale Bishop's.

Also will you have the retail department send me

The Ox-Bow Incident—By a man named [Walter van Tilburg] Clark
The latest book by Margery Allingham
New England, Indian Summer—VanWyck Brooks
To The Finland Station—Edmund Wilson
The Hill Is Mine—Maurice Walsh
Audubon's America—Donald Peattie
Farewell My Lovely—Donald Chandler

How To Play and Win at Poker (Doubleday Doran)[3]

The divorce business seems all o.k. now. A property settlement, custody settlement etc. haveing been reached. Once Pauline's attorney approves it as to Florida legality and she signs then I just sign and then she gets the divorce.[4]

Thanks very much for the books. Marty is reading Dawn's book and I loaned the Judge book.[5] But will write you about them as soon as I read them.

Dorothy Parker and her husband have come out here and Gary Cooper and his wife are here so there is plenty of company and so we are going to the primitive area of the middle fork of the Salmon river tomorrow although I like the people very much. Cooper is a fine man; as honest and straight and friendly and unspoiled as he looks. We have good times together. He is married to a nice girl too who plays a hell of a game of tennis. She and I can beat Mart and Cooper and this afternoon we will see if Marty and I can beat the two Coopers. I played very badly first starting in this altitude but now am playing o.k. Cooper is a very, very fine rifle shot and a good wing shot. I can shoot a little better than he can with a shotgun but not nearly as good with a rifle due I guess to drinking too much for too many years as much as anything. Can beat him playing tennis. We are going to get some gloves and box. He is a good guy, as nice as Charles Thompson or Sully [J. B. Sullivan] or any of the good guys we know.

Tell Charley I am going to have to ride a horse now for about a week but that I will get off and walk as much as possible and hang onto the horse's tail going up-hill. If I have to look into the horse's ass while doing this I will try to remember the technical term for it. I think it is his crupper but I am not sure. Bob Miles who did all the bad horse stuff for everyone who ever worked for Paramount has suggested that he and I ride a downhill race over country mutually selected and I have agreed to do so but will never do so. He needs the late John Mytton; not honest Ernie Hemingstein. Maybe Charley would come out and ride it for me instead? I will ride it if Charley will. We take the horses up in a ski-lift. You cannot finish without some part of your horse.

So long Max

Wish you would come out

Ernest

PUL

1. The rights to For Whom the Bell Tolls were sold to Paramount Pictures in January 1941, for $100,000. 2. Wolfe's You Can't Go Home Again (1940) contained an editor named Foxhall Edwards, based on Maxwell Perkins. 3. This booklist is marked "Sent" in Perkins's hand. 4. The divorce from Pauline became final 5 November 1940. 5. Two Scribners books of 1940: Dawn Powell, Angels on Toast, and J. C. Knox, The Judge Comes of Age.

To CHARLES SCRIBNER, Sun Valley, *c.* 21 October 1940[1]

Dear Charley:

I was damned sorry to hear from Marty about your brother-in-law. Bad luck for him and for everybody. Please tell Vera [Mrs. Charles Scribner] how truly sorry I am. That's one thing I know about. Tell her I'd write her a letter but letters are no damned good for anything. But she has my true sympathy and understanding about it.

Glad the book got good reviews and that everything looks o.k. I'll let you know how we want to handle the money business once the picture situation is cleared up. May get quite a good piece of money from there and if that comes this year will want to let all other money go over until next year. In the meantime will keep drawing on that Book Club money as I need it.

Since Marty has been around with the Coopers seeing that Gary she wants me to have clothes and be handsome and that sort of thing. But only the t.b. would thin me down to Cooper dimensions and then it would still be the same goddamn face.

We rode up into the Middle Fork of Salmon River country on a pack trip last week. Good but rough trip. 23 miles of trail to get in; some fairly bad precipice to precepice and back to piss again sort of thing.

You helped me a hell of a lot with your suggestions and criticism on the book and don't think I don't appreciate it. Am not the type of bloke who goes dedicating books to their publishers so don't mind that little omission. Have usually found that those dedicators are either in debt (financially) to their publishers, about to leave them and have a bad conscience, on the skids, or promising authors.

Good duck shooting here now. Martha is sick in bed with the grippe. Kids o.k. If I sell the book to the pictures I will buy you a horse and ride him upstairs in the elevator to present him to you. Am dickering now for a very rare palomino hermaphrodite that nobody can catch and that promises to be the horse of the year. He or she has universal attraction.

Have just talked to the coast and told them they are asking too much money. They can sell it for 100,000 and they bloody well better, plus a royalty on every copy sold.

All matters are being fixed up so Martha and I can get married in November.[2] Her idea of fun after that is to go to the Burma Road. I wish to Christ she had written this book and I was marrying her. But I like everything once it starts so I guess I will like the Burma Road and then will probably want to stay out on the Burma road and Martha will want to go to Keokuk Iowa. Well I guess I will like Keokuk Iowa too. They have a nice damn there.

Is there anybody you want me to write in books and send them to or don't you go in for that sort of thing? I don't believe in it much myself but some people do. I am catching a bunch of errors in the book for when your plates wear out.

So long Charley. Don't let anything get you down.

Best always and my love to Vera.

PUL Ernest

1. EH misdates this letter 21 September. 2. EH and Martha Gellhorn were married in Cheyenne, Wyoming, on 21 November.

To HADLEY MOWRER, La Finca Vigia, 26 December 1940

Dearest Kat:

Didn't the Bumby look marvellous? He's working hard in school and concentrating much better all around. I took him out a couple of times in N.Y. and started him learning to box from the great George Brown. Also bought some clothes and a good week end bag.

If there's anything else he needs in N.Y. let me know as I'll be there about January 20th.

Marty goes to Manila and Hongkong on Clipper of Jan. 15. I go on Clipper of Feb. 7.[1] Meet her in Hongkong. We are very happy. After 4 years it's wonderful to be legal and all. Though I have such guerrilla sleeping habits—wake and get out with the dawn—that it's hard to break.

Have made a good will to look after Bumby's and the other children's interests and also for you for disposing of these big due royalties in case we should ever need a will. Best way to avoid needing one. But have such a horror of people leaveing their affairs in sloppy shape due to haveing been through it with my father etc.

Thanks for the Xmas card and the letter beforehand of good wishes to Sun Valley.

We wish plenty good to you and Paul too and you've got it. Have a plan about Bumby for next year if you agree would like to talk over.

Think he'd appreciate college much more if stayed out one year and ½ fished and hunted with me and learned to really box, ½ worked at a job. War comeing so soon to kids that age good life first not wasted. A man might as well catch a steelhead [trout] in this life if there's only one life; if catching a steelhead is what a man wants in life up to that time.

Also he would be much more mature in college and realize it's a serious business.

Anyhow much love and Merry Christmas.

The N.Y. Daily News sent reporters all over St. Louis, Chicago, Albany, Key West to dig stuff for a smear story. It was disgusting and I hope you didn't read it. Lies, half truths and smear. Jinny [Pfeiffer], I understand, collaborated.

However I told Patrick that every time we sold 100,000 copies I would forgive a son of a bitch and when we sold a million I would forgive Max Eastman. But Mouse said, "No Papa I'd greatly prefer you to leave it as it is and let our ancestors fight his ancestors."

Give my love to Bumby. Also the Martys and Mousie and Giggy.

Much love
Tatey

I'll take Bumby as a dependent on my incomely tax. Awful tax this year 62% to Govt. of everything made.[2]

PH. PUL

1. EH had contracted to write about the Sino-Japanese war for the newspaper *PM*, edited by Ralph Ingersoll. 2. On 28 December, however, EH bought La Finca Vigia for $12,500.

To HADLEY MOWRER, New York, 26 January 1941

Dearest Hadley:

Enclosed is the check for Education. The Bumby spent Sat and Sunday with us here [Lombardy Hotel]. He had just finished exams and was rather tired which shows he worked.[1] Did well and came 2nd in his class. Had 86 and better in English and Spanish—76 general average I think. He *is* working. Looked lovely. We boxed twice with George Brown and went to a show. Am in hellish rush getting off to China tomorrow so won't write more.

Marty sends her love too to you and Paul. Write c/o her mother. She will have forwarding addresses. My typhoids made me sick also have a little flu so excuse lousy letter. Book selling like frozen Daiquiris in hell.

PH. PUL Taty

1. Bumby was then a student at the Storm King School on the Hudson.

To SOLITA SOLANO,[1] New York, 26 January 1941

Dearest Solita:

Here is the check for Margaret [Anderson]. I hope so [much that] she has good luck getting over. Greet her for me will you?

Have grippe and so god damned many things to do with no time to do them so please forgive such a lousy note and also me not seeing you which would love to do.

Much love Solita and take good care of yourself and don't ever worry because as long as any of us have any money we all have money.

PUL   Ernest

1. Miss Solano, a close friend of Janet Flanner's, had left France for New York in 1940. Margaret Anderson had stayed behind to care for Georgette Leblanc Maeterlinck, who died of cancer, leaving Miss Anderson stranded and hungry. EH's check was for $400, "a lot then," said Solita.

To MAXWELL PERKINS, Hong Kong, 29 April 1941

Dear Max:

I was glad to get your letters of April 4th and April 11th when flew in here from Rangoon last night. The last leg of the trip from Kunming (Yunnanfu) to here was pretty bad and when we got over Hongkong the static was so bad the telefunken would not work and with a 200 foot ceiling we circled for nearly an hour before we could get down through. Have flown 18,000 some miles since I saw you last and have about 12,000 more to fly before see you again. Wish I was paid by the mile instead of by the word.

I had a wire from Charley, two in fact, in answer to one I sent him from Chungking asking about the sale and another I sent saying I was not happy at haveing no word from any of you nor not too happy about the sale or lack of it.

Probably anyone who is not happy with a sale of half a million is headed for the booby hatch. On the other hand when I left you were announceing a printing of 500,000 and I had imagined that the sale had been pushed on. Regret that it was not.

Am damned tired just now and so do not want to be unjust but I sometimes wonder if you, Charley and company ever worked as hard selling the damned book as I worked writing it what the sale would be—

or rather what it would have been. Not that you didn't work. I know you did. And I know how I worked too when it was impossible.

I hope it is not too late to keep on pushing it. It is bad luck to have gone away and then heard nothing, absolutely nothing when Hongkong is only eight days from Newyork by airmail; and then have heard finally the sort of news I did hear. And have to cable to hear that.

It doesn't make anybody feel good not to have a damned line from their publishers from late January until April 4th. Even if you thought I was comeing back in April that was no reason to let me go all of February and March with no word when air-mail only takes one day over a week. Especially when you look forward like hell to getting mail and make every arrangement to have it forwarded and each time you see a pilot with the letters there was never a damned thing.

I don't know how to put it in terms of horse so that Charley will get at its true meaning but I suppose it might correspond with how the quadraped would feel if you neither fed nor watered it on the day after you have given it a hell of a ride.

Hope Bunny Wilson will not knife Scott in that thing he is going to write.[1] Since they both went to Princeton together and all that I suppose he won't. It is damned hard on Scott to publish something unfinished any way you look at it but I suppose the worms won't mind. Writers are certainly dying like flies. It is a damned shame about old Sherwood.[2] He always liked living very much. I suppose finally no one will be left alive but the Sitwells.

It sounded as though Waldo [Peirce] had a good show. Am very glad.

Will be back now before the end of May. Had a good time at the front with the chinese army. Hard trip but very interesting. Will be glad to be home. I want to write some stories.

Will fly to N.Y. from the coast, go down to Washington and then to Cuba. Martha has one job more to do that will take her about two weeks. I hope we can make the trip back together. If not she will come the second clipper after.[3]

She says she wants to chuck correspondent's work now and stay home. But don't tell that to anyone.

Best always.
Ernest

Please send check for $500 to Pauline on June 1st.

PUL

1. *The Last Tycoon*, the unfinished novel, with *The Great Gatsby*, five stories, and a foreword by Edmund Wilson, was published posthumously by Scribners in 1941. **2.** Sherwood Anderson died 8 March 1941. **3.** For an account of EH and Martha's travels in China, see Martha Gellhorn, *Travels with Myself and Another* (New York, 1979).

To PAULINE HEMINGWAY, La Finca Vigia, 9 June 1941

Dear Pauline:

Thanks for the wire about the kids arriving o.k. And damned sorry if you had any headaches about it. Also sorry not to send any sort of decent wire about Patrick's birthday which I remember much more as a celebration to be honored for you than for the good old Mouse. He had a good birthday though and I was thinking about you and I suppose it all averages up in the grave which and if ever F.O.B. F.D.R. Anyway it is marvellous about his bells and he is a very good fellow and a budding naturalist and good company.

Giggy is better all the time I think. He has the biggest dark side in the family except me and you and I'm not in the family. He keeps it so concealed that you never know about it and maybe that way it will back up on him. But maybe too it will disappear as nearly all talent does along with youth and all the perishable commodities that shape our ends. (Sic)

Because I write such stupid letters and seem like a globe girdling rhinoceros do not think I am that way truly because losing Mr. Josie[1] was no fun for Mr. Josie and I was riding with him somewhere in it all only should have protected him better and truly. Though he always had so much sense and judgment and so I didn't worry. No good to write about. Anyway hope you have good time this summer and *I* had one wonderful sunny unbelievable day in San Francisco comeing in this time and think you have something there pal. Also with all the fights and all that, which I can't remember, only that we fought. I always miss you and good Godly Christly knows the jokes and battery A. and battery B. even when the stations were not speaking so don't ever say regards at end of telegram and I won't add any tenth word either to them but let the telegram carry its own weight so will sign this letter with love if you know what I mean.

PUL   Ernest

1. Joe Russell (Josie Grunts), once owner of Sloppy Joe's Bar in Key West and partly a model for Harry Morgan in *To Have and Have Not*, had died recently.

To PAULINE HEMINGWAY, La Finca Vigia, 19 July 1941

Dear Pauline:

Got your letter of July 16 (mailed that day anyway) yesterday. That's very quick time from the coast.

You ask me for the date when Belmonte died. I didn't know (and don't know yet that he is dead). If he died it must have been while I was in China as have heard nothing about it.

Was it by any chance Joselito or some other bull fighter you want to know about? Joselito died May 16 either '20 or '21. Could it have been Gitanillo de Triana you wanted the date of? I can look that up.

The Altman bill must be either yours or Jinny's. It was for something, a dress I think, bought in March while Marty and I were both out of country. Also she has no Altman account; nor have I.

Haven't heard anything about me and Bumby being in Movie.

In your paragraph about children you say "It is a pity you can't be with them yourself. Can't you arrange that?"

If you'll look at my letter you'll see I wrote you the only reason I had to have the children proceed [precede] me by early part of September was to keep my 6 months non-resident time straight. That was why I had to arrange that.

I have to have a little money of some kind to run things you see. I pay over $15,000 tax on the $6,000 you get tax free. Practically everything I make is confiscated and under the new ruling that all married people must file joint returns what Marty has made by that bastard of a trip will be added on top of all the book earned and three quarters of it confiscated by taxes. That is unless she stays out of country as bonafide non-resident for over six months. Now they make the months be consecutive. Odd times do not count. They have to be solid calendar months from the 20th of February, say, to twentieth of March etc.

There were three solid months in the Orient trip and now is necessary to have the other three months which finish middle September.

If anyone asks the children what their father did in Mr. Rooseveldts war they can say "He paid for it." Practically everything of all that work on the book has gone or will have to go for taxes. Have nearly 100,000 due all of which must go direct into tax account. Hope you have a good Birthday. Enclose a letter I wrote a while back and hadn't sent because was waiting to hear from you. It may work out that I can have [Otto] Bruce pick up the children. If not will have it all worked out to get them to Idaho o.k.

Am awfully glad the bowl and box got there and that you liked them. I felt sick when I thought they were lost on account of that wood being very emotional piece. Moved me anyway. I wanted to get you some good jade to have drinks out of. Will get.

Ernest

Answer all letters day received on my newest new system.

Bought skiff with the $60 for that old man on the water front we called

"Langosta" who, with his dog, has been starving to death since he lost his [skiff].

PUL

To PRUDENCIO DE PEREDA,[1] La Finca Vigia, 14 August 1941

Dear Prudencio:

I was very happy to hear from you and know that you are finishing your book. I will look forward to reading it very much. Please fix it so that I can get an advance copy of it as soon as any are ready.

About the picture [*For Whom the Bell Tolls*]—I know very little more than you do. I have written [Gary] Cooper to find out what the situation is. When I originally sold it to Paramount, it was so Cooper could play in it and through him we would have some voice in the direction, because in his contract with Paramount he can refuse any director. Now, it seems that Sam Goldwyn is making trouble about Cooper playing in the picture. He is trying to tie him up legally so that he cannot do it. I don't know whom Paramount has in mind for the direction as everything that has come out so far that I have seen has been merely publicity releases. They have been giving out stuff that I have discovered a "perfect" Maria down here on the farm and spending day and night testing her with my own camera. After this gets a play in the papers, they cabled to me asking me if I will stay with them and make the story good by sending pictures of any pretty Cuban girl that I can photograph. So you see how serious the advance stuff you read about a picture is. As soon as I know anything definite, or they make me any sort of offer to work on, I will let you know.

I know how very good you were when we did The Spanish Earth together and how much I would love to have you work with me on this one, if I had any voice in it. But don't count on anything, because it is a very good chance that I will be in China again or in Russia when they are turning on this.

Good luck to you, Prudencio, always and best love from Martha and myself.

Your friend and comrade

PH. PUL   Ernesto

1. De Pereda (b. 1912), an American novelist of Spanish ancestry, had befriended EH by mail in 1934. In 1937 he helped materially with the preparation of *The Spanish Earth* film. His later novels include *All the Girls We Loved* (New York, 1948) and *Fiesta* (New York, 1953).

To MAXWELL PERKINS, Sun Valley, Idaho, 15 November 1941

Dear Max:

First, about business. It is o.k. to let Robert [Penn] Warren reprint "The Killers." I agree with you about the importance of having it in the school books, no matter how hard it is on the poor students. Anyhow it is more interesting than "A Dog of Flanders" [Ouida] and the stuff we had to read as short stories when we were kids. I'll never forget how sick I was of "A Piece of String" and "The Necklace" of de Maupassant. But I suppose they couldn't put his good ones in the school books.

I read all of Scott's book [*The Last Tycoon*] and I don't know whether I ought to tell you what I truly think. There are very fine parts in it, but most of it has a deadness that is unbelievable from Scott. I think Bunny Wilson did a very creditable job in explaining, sorting, padding and arranging. But you know Scott would never have finished it with that gigantic, preposterous outline of how it was to be. I thought the part about Stahr was all very good. You can recognize Irving Thalberg, his charm and skill, and grasp of business, and the sentence of death over him. But the women were pretty preposterous. Scott had gotten so far away from any knowledge of people that they are very strange. He still had the technique and the romance of doing anything, but all the dust was off the butterfly's wing for a long time even though the wing would still move up until the butterfly was dead.[1] The best book he ever wrote, I think, is still "Tender Is The Night" with all of its mix-up of who was Scott and Zelda and who was Sara and Gerald Murphy. I read it last year again and it has all the realization of tragedy that Scott ever found. Wonderful atmosphere and magical descriptions and none of the impossible dramatic tricks that he had outlined for the final book.

Scott died inside himself at around the age of thirty to thirty-five and his creative powers died somewhat later. This last book was written long after his creative power was dead, and he was just beginning to find out what things were about.

I read over the stories and I think Bunny Wilson made a very poor selection. "The Rich Boy," if you read it, is really profoundly silly. "The Diamond As Big As the Ritz" is simply trash. When you read in "The Rich Boy" about his gradual decay and suddenly see that Scott has given twenty-eight as the age for this oldness setting in, it is hardly credible that he could write that way.

I am happy the book had such a fine review by J. Donald Adams in the Sunday Times with such a good picture of Scott. I think that should please Scotty very much and be very good for her because she never really knew how good Scott was. But J. Donald Adams is not really a very intelligent man, and to someone who knew Scott truly well and is in the same trade, the book has that deadness, the one quality about which nothing can be done in writing, as though it were a slab of bacon on which mold had grown. You can scrape off the mold, but if it has gone deep into the meat, there is nothing that can keep it from tasting like moldy bacon.

When you wrote Martha, you said that Hollywood had not hurt Scott. I guess perhaps it had not because he was long past being hurt before he went there. His heart died in him in France, and soon after he came back, and the rest of him just went on dying progressively after that. Reading the book was like seeing an old baseball pitcher with nothing left in his arm coming out and working with his intelligence for a few innings before he is knocked out of the box.

I know you're impressed by all the stuff about riding in aeroplanes on account of you not doing that and Scott had done it so recently that it impressed him too and he got something of the old magic into it. But in the things between men and women, the old magic was gone and Scott never really understood life well enough to write a novel that did not need the magic to make it come alive.

This sounds gloomy and critical, but I know you would want me to write what I really thought about it. You've had three guys. Scott, Tom Wolfe and me. Two of them are already dead, and no one can say what will happen to the third one. But I think it is best to criticize strongly so when you get the new ones that will come along afterwards, you can talk to them truly.

I don't know what else there is to write except that we are not coming to New York this fall. I promised Martha that we would go on a trip and we had given up coming to New York before I got the notice about that Gold Medal business.[2] So you and the other guys in the office will have to do the honors. Does that mean that they will publish a limited edition of the book later on? Sinclair Lewis wrote me a damn nice letter and I truly appreciate the honor, but I had promised Marty we would take this trip.

Thank you ever so much for sending me that last batch of books. They were all good. How is everything going? What is the news on Martha's book [The Heart of Another]? We will be here another week anyway, so write here. There are many movie people here now. Robert Taylor is sort of a little miniature man. Everything about him would photograph up into manhood and very handsomely, but the actual model that the lens enlarges is neither very gay nor very impressive. His wife, Barbara Stanwyck, is truly ugly in the flesh, wears grease on her face to

· dinner and is very nice with a good tough Mick intelligence. Cooper is wonderful and fine company to hunt with. Also as tight about money as a hog's ars in flytime. He is being worn out by working too hard and making too many pictures. I hope he will get a rest before and after the next one. There is some chance he will still play in The Bell Picture.

Will you send a copy of Evan's book, "Free For All" to me here to be forwarded to Howard Hawks. He is going to make a trotting picture and I talked about Evan [Shipman] to him for a long time and I think I might get Evan a job as technical adviser for the picture and perhaps to do some of the writing. Hawks was very interested in him and I promised to get him a copy of the book. Hawks is a very intelligent and sensitive man with a lovely girl.

That's all I know about to write now. Please excuse the long letter, and if I sound deprecatory about Scott, remember I know how good he is and was only criticizing Wilson's selections and the posthumous work.

Best to you always,

PUL   Ernest

1. The butterfly image reappears in *A Moveable Feast* (New York, 1964), p. 147.
2. The Limited Editions Club, with Sinclair Lewis as editorial chairman, awarded EH the Gold Medal in a ceremony on 26 November, which EH did not attend. See EH to Perkins, 11 December, and EH to Charles Scribner, 12 December 1941. Yale's Beinecke Library has EH's letter to Lewis of 15 November 1941 explaining why he could not come in person. The two men had met in Key West and Cuba in December 1940. See Mark Schorer, *Sinclair Lewis* (New York, 1961), pp. 671–72.

To CHARLES SCRIBNER, Sun Valley, *c.* 20 November 1941

Dear Charley:

Have never had the letter you were going to send me about your debiting my royalties with Speiser's charges to you on that plagiarism suit you were served with in California.

If I commit any plagiarism, or there is any semblance of plagiarism, or any "deadly parrallels" that would be one thing. But when an obvious psychopathic case sues Scribner's, Twentieth Century Fox and Paramount because For Whom The Bell Tolls, The Cisco Kid, NorthWest Mounted Police were all stolen from an unpublished scenario and then you calmly deduct your legal charges from my royalties exactly as though I had committed plagiarism while, in fact, I have never even seen the man, been in California, nor been served in the suit, then, that is something else.[1]

I cannot understand it, either, when we have both gained largely from mutual work and could be expected to gain in the future, that you should wish me to be saddled with all costs of a baseless attack when you have gained from my work as I have from yours. The only reason I did not hear from you would seem to be that you thought the suit might come to trial and it was wiser not to show any solidarity with me before such an event.

Anyway have waited about three months for your letter and haven't had it yet. That's all on that.

We are going to drive south through Utah to Arizona and then through Texas to the Gulf. Next address for mail until December First is care Mrs. Mathew Baird—Ruby Star Route—Tucson, Arizona. Don't want to come to N.Y. this fall. May have to come after the first of the year on some tax business. I wish you wouldn't pay me any more money the rest of this year if you can help it. Can't you pay it next year? Will have no money next year and am starting work on a book in January.

Will wire Max where to send mail after the Baird address. Hope you are well and have had a good fall. We had fine shooting all fall and now with it around zero there is wonderful duck and goose shooting. Going out now to a pass between two low hills, lowest on a range of mountains along Silver Creek [at Picabo, Idaho] where the flight comes through in bunches, comeing so fast you would think they were going to knock you over. All big northern mallards and pintails.

Children all o.k. Martha is fine and very beautiful and happy. She is anxious to get back to Cuba.

Best to you always,

PUL
Ernest

---

1. A plagiarism suit was brought by John Miguel De Montijo and served on Scribners 2 June 1941. The plaintiff alleged that his film scenario "Viva Madero" had been plagiarized in *For Whom the Bell Tolls*. The suit was resolved in February 1942 in favor of EH and codefendants. EH had been in California in 1937 and 1941, both times very briefly.

To MAXWELL PERKINS, San Antonio, Texas, 11 December 1941

Dear Max:

First about business:

(1) It is o.k. to have John Bishop publish the Killers in Spanish. But as that is a foreign translation and not a reprint the fee should be credited to me rather than divided.

(2) It is o.k. to have that school book republish The Killers.

About the war. Don't take Charley Sweeny seriously when he baits you about the Civil War: when he is angry he always says such wild unjust things. Both he and John Thomason were both completely and fatally wrong about war with Japan when we argued it in Washington as events have proved. Now the myth of our matchless navy has been exploded as badly as the myth of Gamelin the great general. If we are to win this war rather than simply defend and cover up the incompetents who will lose it, Knox should have been relieved as Sec. of Navy within 24 hrs of the Pearl Harbor Debacle and those responsible at Oahu for that disaster shot. The above opinions are not for publication nor circulation.

Lastly, and to leave the war, I cannot tell you how badly I feel about Scribner's failing to get a stenographer to take down [Sinclair] Lewis's speech *after I had wired asking them to please do so*. From your own elementary best interests it would have been a useful thing to publish in pamphlet form. From my own interest it is all that I got out of the book that means anything to me (as a permanent record) and I will never get it to keep *nor ever even see it*.[1]

Scribner's not haveing it taken down as I requested as a favour was the most careless, shiftless and callous action I have ever met in civil life. I would like to present the firm with the gold medal so every time anyone should see it they would remember how I feel about it. I do not ever want to see it. Ever.

Yes I know someone heard a rumour [John] Macy would have a stenographer; or a report, or a promise of that. What I asked was for *Scribner's* to have a stenographer take it down.

Yours always

PUL   Ernest

---

1. Lewis's speech would hardly have pleased EH. It named him as one of six greatest living novelists, the others being Theodore Dreiser, Willa Cather, Somerset Maugham, H. G. Wells, and Jules Romains. Lewis rewrote his speech as a preface to the Limited Editions Club reissue of *For Whom the Bell Tolls*, published by Princeton University Press in October 1942. See Mark Schorer, *Sinclair Lewis* (New York, 1961), p. 680.

To CHARLES SCRIBNER, San Antonio, 12 December 1941

Dear Charley:

Thank you for your two letters which I found at the Baird ranch out from Tucson.

I am sorry I blew up so badly when I found the royalty statement with your legal costs deducted. I sent a wire next morning saying sorry I'd blown up and to disregard what I said. Perhaps Max [Perkins] didn't happen to show it to you. Have no desire to quarrel nor to have misunderstandings. . . . It has taken me since 1926 or 7 to begin to understand the quite straight and honest minds (I mean it—it isn't sarcasm) of Max, you, Webber, and Meyer. Not to mention my fellow clubman Whitney Darrow. Webber and Meyer simplest, Max most complicated, you most delicate and circuitous (can't spell it but it doesn't mean crooked nor devious. It means what the word means if I could spell it).

With the war now will probably not be seeing much of each other for a very long time so we ought to be friendly. Through our (American) laziness, criminal carelessness, and blind arrogance we are fucked in this war as of the first day and we are going to have Christ's own bitter time to win it if, when, and ever. Oh, well, why go into it all at 5:45 a.m.

I wrote Max exactly how I felt about not getting Sinclair Lewis's speech so won't go into that. It is over and I'm fucked on that. Had driven all the way from Idaho to Arizona looking forward, like a dope, to reading it and then from Arizona here. Now know I never will and that something that could have had will never have. It was the only thing connected with writing I ever wanted to keep and the fact that by takeing it down and re-printing it as a pamphlet you could have probably gotten me the Nobel prize is *not* what I mean. Chances are there aren't going to be any Nobel prizes any more and anyhow this was what I wanted instead. I know I give much too much importance to it. People want different things and what I wanted was to read and have, for my kids, that speech. So what? So you don't get it. I really wish you'd keep the medal. I don't want to ever see it.

We go from here to New Orleans to Miami to Cuba. Will probably see you in N.Y. before do or go whatever or wherever have to do or go. No matter how many countries you see fucked and bitched and ruined you never get to take it easily. Having to watch all the steps and know them all so well. Oh hell too gloomy this morning to write. You and Max were impressed by Scott's last because you never ride in airplanes. That's kidding. The Thalberg part was very good. But he wouldn't have finished it in 2000 years. His brain was starting to work O K but his glands wouldn't and he didn't have enough brain to replace the loss of that other stuff he used to get for nothing and not even know where it came from. I re-read Tender Is The Night last summer and that, all balled up so he didn't know who was Gerald and Sara and who Scott and Zelda and all, is still the best and finest thing he ever wrote. Parts of it are really wonderful.

We had a lovely trip through the Indian country. Martha the most beautiful and happiest I've ever seen her. We had good luck to have this fall and this trip before our week-end admirals condemned us all to what we will go and see for the next ten years.

So long Charley. Good luck and take care of yourself.

Ernest

PUL

To MAXWELL PERKINS, La Finca Vigia, 8 July 1942

Dear Max:

Thanks for your letter of July 1.

Yes, I did hear from Evan [Shipman] who is with an armoured unit. He wrote me a long and very good letter all about his work and problems and things in general. He told me too he got $50.00 from you because there was no time to let me know before he left. He seems quite happy and has put on about twelve pounds. I hope he can keep it. His big problem in health comes with the cold weather as that is when it hits his chest. If he can get sent to any warm climate he should be all right. I am writing him tomorrow and will give him your best. The only thing is that he is very lonely without letters. I will put his address on the end of this letter and would you please have Nelson Algren's book, "Never Come Morning", sent to him. I think it very, very good. It is as fine and good stuff to come out of Chicago as James W. [T.] Farrell is flat, repetitious and worthless. The first Farrell book about Studs Lonigan had some marvelous parts in it and gave a fine picture of the utter horror of that district of the South Side. But this man Algren can write the pants off of Farrell, and the North Side of Chicago that he writes about was always about twenty times the place that Farrell's bailiwick was anyway. I am writing Evan about the book so when you get this will you have it sent to him, please. If you have any other really good book, would you send it to him too? I don't mean, "Sea of Memories", or, "The Opinions of Oliver Allston".[1]

In regard to the question of the Garden City Publishing Company reprinting, "The Short Happy Life of Francis Macomber", I am all against giving them permission to reprint it in a 69¢ edition. We, that is Scribner's and I, have never made any money out of those four stories which headed off the last collection of stories that I published [1938]. Sooner or later if we hang on to them they will make some money because the book they were published in never had any sale. I remember myself trying to buy a copy in Scribner's just a couple months after it was published and there not being one in the store. It just occurs to me that where they will have the sale now is in that Modern Library edition. By the way when is the payment for this? Could use it. But still we may be able to get out a book of my stories, a selection, which could still have a good sale. I am against letting a story as long and as big as the Macomber one go out in those cheap pocket reprints when they can just as well publish something else.

As it is [Jonathan] Cape takes only 25% on reprinted stuff while a story like Francis Macomber which Scribner's only acquired title to by printing in a book which was not sold at all, nor even attempted very seriously to be sold, they then can sell again and again and I only get half of what my property brings.

I have been checking up on the [Nat] Wartels business and he has now included all of your selections except, "The Thistle". He sent me John Thomason's letter and also Charley's letter and I am working on every-thing that they have suggested. I have cut out a lot more of his deadwood and put in many other things and also reorganized and re-arranged it. So that I think it could legitimately be called edited by me now. Have the Bagration piece in and it is certainly the most compact account of an action in which the whole is visible through the part that is shown, that you can get. It would have been a big loss not to have included it and I am very grateful for [to] you for taking the time to look it up. I put in the whole thing from the time he first gets there and looks over the positions and meets the artillery officer in the canteen until the very end of the action. The book as it stands now is going to be very good if I can get the stuff grouped properly. It isn't right to group it chronologically and you have to be very careful not to make any divisions tricky. I only wish that you were publishing it and that we were both going to make some money out of it. As it is, I hope it will be a useful publication.[2]

I am awfully happy that you are going to publish Alden Brooks's book.[3] It sounded very good to me when he told me about it in Tucson. I haven't got his, "Fighting Men", here. I wish I had it. Could you send a copy down or see that Wartels gets a look at, "The Odessy of the Three Slavs". I do not trust Wartels' judgment for a dime. He likes very many corny things, but on the other hand he some times shows excellent sense. I think his main trouble is that he is one of those people that always wanted to be a writer, or at least stick his finger into writing. Anyway, he has to do exactly as I say about this book now.

Best always and to Charley,
Ernest

(Martha is off for carribean to write for Colliers. Children are here. I am trying to finish up my work so can get off to war.)
PUL

1. *Sea of Memories*, by Charles Moran, a popular history of the Mediterranean published by Scribners (New York, 1942); *The Opinions of Oliver Allston*, by Van Wyck Brooks (New York, 1941). 2. EH was editing *Men at War* for Crown Publishers (New York, 1942). See EH to Evan Shipman, 25 August 1942. 3. Alden Brooks, *Will Shakespere and the Dyer's Hand* (New York, 1943). His *The Fighting Men* (New York, 1917) contains "The Odyssey of Three Slavs."

To HADLEY MOWRER, La Finca Vigia, 23 July 1942

Dearest Kat:

Thanks for the fine letter from Minesota (insert necessary n's). Got it on my birthday and was very happy to hear from you. Sounds like a grand fishing place.

Marty is on her Carribean trip for Colliers and Mousie and Giggy are here. So it is not as lonesome as it could be but was never much on liveing alone and certainly never liked it. However Winston Guest is flying down for this week end and Tommy Shevlin is in here with some sub chasers and so we divert ourselves as well as work. I don't run around with no women as all I get running around with same is trouble almost instantly so stick with the boys.

About Bumby's car: we talked that all over when he was here. It is impractical to bring it East because he would use up his tires on the trip and rationing is so severe in Eastern States that it would really be of little use. Besides it hasn't got a spare and I doubt if it could survive the transcontinental trip. Better for it to stay out there and he will have a car there when he can ever get out there. The boys club together on going fishing, furnishing gas etc. at Dartmouth. I have been trying to get a good European bicycle that I have up to him and with a little co-operation from Key West will do so. But that is not the headquarters of co-operation.

Have done a few useful things for war and for govt. in past two years and have been turned down on offer to do some much more useful ones. At present my principal war problem is financial. Had to borrow 12,000 bucks to pay my 103,000 income tax last year. I have to pay that back and get enough ahead so I will not be wiped out and broke when come back from war. War will last at least five years, maybe ten, maybe always. Depending on what we have promised as war aims. Pauline gets 500 bucks a month from me every month (tax free) and this year I haven't made it so that is a drain on capital that in ten years would take sixty thousand dollars; i.e. I'd be wiped out in less than five years. So it's not all simple. I went to all the wars that were fought to prevent this one and comported myself o.k. Would just as soon see some of the warmongers who brought on this one but would not fight in or work in the wars fought to prevent this one fight in this before I do. However they never will so that wish is purely platonic. In the meantime I try to bring up my children this summer and if possible get a little money ahead. So I don't think can make Sun Valley this fall; but maybe I can. Marty knows nothing about money, she saves terrifically on pennies and lets large sums go without a thought. She has a brave child's attitude toward it but she doesn't know that when you get older you have to have a steady something to live on between books—books get further apart as you get older if you write only good books.

Gigi is fine this summer. He is a better boy all the time. He is shooting marvellously and so is Patrick. The Local shooting club gave Gigi a gold medal engraved "To Gigi as a token of admiration from his fellow shooters, Club de Cazadores del Cerro." At nine years old he beat 24 grown men, all good shots and many of them very fine shots, shooting live pigeons. He useing a .410 against men useing 12 gauge. And live pigeon shooting isn't just a trick like skeet. Every bird is different. And you don't have to just hit them. You have to kill them dead inside a certain distance. Patrick right now is outshooting Giggy but he does it so modestly and quietly and with no form or style that nobody notices it except the old timers and the book makers but Gigi is known in the papers as el joven fenomeno Americano and day before yesterday an article called him "el popularissimo Gigi." So now we say go down to the post-office and get the mail popularissimo or time for bed, popularissimo. But inside himself he is very happy to be the popularissimo and he shoots like a little angel. Bumby shoots pigeons beautifully too. And they must all shoot pretty well because the shooting critics wrote that there aren't four shots in Cuba that can beat the combination of Bumby, Papa and the two boys. Gigi killed twenty one straight the other day. Patrick shot 19 out of twenty two shoots running. I have an average of 92 x 100 for the season. We shoot in the Championship of Cuba on Sunday. I only wish we could have Bumby here. Because he shoots as coolly as he is nervous playing tennis.

Well I'd better stop this. I hope Paul is well and has good news from his boys. Tell him my Hardy stuff, in which there were some items for you both, has never come through. Bumby's order has. So mine may eventually. Isn't fishing lovely though? I would hate to die, ever, because every year I have a better time fishing and shooting. I like them as much as when I was sixteen and now I've written good enough books so that I don't have to worry about that I would be happy to fish and shoot and let somebody else lug the ball for a while. We carried it plenty and if you don't know how to enjoy life, if it should be only one life we have, you are a disgrace and don't deserve to have it. I happen to have worked hard all my life and made a fortune at a time when whatever you make is confiscated by the govt. That's bad luck. But the good luck is to have had all the wonderful things and times we had. Imagine if we had been born at a time when we could never have had Paris when we were young. Do you remember the races out at Enghien and the first time we went to Pamplona by ourselves and that wonderful boat the Leopoldina and Cortina D'Ampezzo and the Black Forest? Last night I couldn't sleep and so I just remembered all the things we'd ever done and all the songs,

> "A feather kitty's talent lies
> In scratching out the other's eyes.
> A feather kitty never dies
> Oh immortality."

We have three good cats here so I sang them the song and they were very pleased. We have a genuine Wax Puppy too with a tail curled exactly the same way and the cats all like him. The cats are a smoke grey Persian called "Tester" and a black and white cat called Dillinger or Boissy D'Anglas and a half maltese cat called Willy who is just a kitten and has a huge purr-prr. When I can't sleep at night I tell them stories about F. Puss and our great cat Mooky out west who fought the badger. When I say "The BADGER!" Tester has to get under the sheets she is so frightened.

Good bye Miss Katherine Kat. I love you very much. It is all right to do so because it hasn't anything to do with you and that great Paul; it is just untransferable feeling for early and best Gods. But will never mention it if bad. Thought you might just be interested to know.

Your friend Taty
Ernest Hemingway

PH. PUL

To EVAN SHIPMAN, La Finca Vigia, 25 August 1942

Dear Evan:

    I was damned happy to get your letter and I would have written long before this if had not been so busy. Marty wrote you right away and I had Max send a copy of Nelson Algren's Never Come Morning which I thought was very good and about the best book to come out of Chicago. The guy who wrote it is working now as boiler maker's asst. down in East Saint Louis. Has Polish wife which explains good knowledge Polish. We always knew how tough the Poles were in Paris and looks like Chicago even more so.

    Bumby was down here for the ten days he had between end of Spring term and start of the summer term. He has gone into Marine Corps Reserve which means they let him finish college if can do it in 2½ years and then go to Quantico for training as officer. He is as we saw him last time when I got back from China. A little more grown up and was looking very good.

    Pat and Giggie have been down here all summer. They are both fine. Tommy Shevlin is here with subchasers. Good subchaseing here they claim. Marty, my Marty, is down in the Carribean on a thirty foot sloop with a crew of three negro comrades doing some pieces for Colliers. Last heard from by cable from St. Kitts yesterday. If she gets sunk with all hands I think Colliers pay double for the article. Or maybe instead they get me to write a Tribute To Her.

    I have edited an anthology of best writing on War from Caesar Xenophon down. Will send it to you as soon as can get advance copy. It goes over a thousand pages and was godawful job—also Introduction. They insisted on an introduction of ten thousand words and over. I can say anything I want to say in from 200 to 2000 so Introduction probably not so good. It comes back from typist this morning. I am going to cut the shit out of it then. Wish you were here to help. You know what [how] bad I can write when have nobody to show it to. Now hope to have good job that will keep out in open air. Had one good trip to Mexico and saw many old friends there. Cisneros and others. It is a crime that such fine and useful men should not be used in this war. Certainly hope they will be. It's like letting a fine ship rot in harbour in these times.

    John Tsanakas finally got a ship and is afloat again. I just write you personal things because we are at war and anybody who thinks indiscreetly or criticizes in time of war adds to whatever dossiers of photostated letters he has accumulated in a lifetime. Am always reminded of the time in Spain when Malraux asked Walter what he thought on some subject and Walter said "Pense? Moi pense pas. Moi general sovietique. Pense jamais." Me am neither sovietique nor general but I don't ever think either in war except to think and know we must win same. Which will do.

Am sorry I am such a filthy letter writer. I handle all letters now by haveing a secretary in twice a week and dictating everything. Have gotten so can dictate fast and a hell of a lot better than can write a letter but didn't want to dictate a letter to you. I am always proud of you Evan. That may seem odd from anyone who has had to bawl you out as many times as I have or did I always just mean to bawl you out and you understood it and so we omitted it? Anyway, as I said, I am always proud of you. I am going to write a story about you sometime to show you what I mean. Not very good at saying it in letter.

The boys send their best. Is there anything you need or anything can have Max Perkins send you from New York? Let me know if there is. I wish you would write and I will be better about writing.

PH. PUL   Hem

To MAXWELL PERKINS, La Finca Vigia, 27 August 1942

Dear Max:

Thank you very much for sending me the galleys from Alden Brooks's Shakespeare book. I think it is very possible, as he told me last fall in Tucson, that he has really nailed the man at last. He is so enthusiastic, and follows so like a bloodhound and a district attorney with a record for conviction, on the trail of poor Will that he will alienate many people, but as you say he piles up a terrific amount of evidence. Anyway, it is a marvelous job and it would be a crime for it not to be published. He is a good man too and was a fine soldier.

I have finally finished and sent off the introduction to the man Wartels and also finished all the editing.

Will probably be away from here now for some time but will arrange for any communications you send me to be forwarded. Will you please mark anything important, and a good personal letter is probably as important a thing as anyone can receive, "IMPORTANT. PLEASE FORWARD." I will work out a way to get it. But if there is any delay, please understand why you do not receive my answer immediately.

When the money comes in from the Modern Library edition of the collected stories, will you please deposit it in my account in the Guaranty Trust Company of New York, Fifth Avenue Branch. We are about broke again and it will be very welcome. Have less than $500.

It is marvelous that Ingrid Bergman is going to play the Maria in that picture [*For Whom the Bell Tolls*]. I went all over Dudley Nichols' script and suggested an enormous amount of changes and absolutely necessary alterations, excisions, and additions. In the end he rewrote it and incorporated almost everything that I had suggested. But they were still going to make the picture with Zorina who is a lovely dancer but has a face rather like a dashund and unless you can get away from her face and see the rest of her, could not possibly be any good on the films which is a visual medium. She was so terrible in the rushes from the first shots they took in the Sierras where they were filming the picture that they finally got rid of her and brought in the Bergman girl. Unless something awful has happened to her in the last year and a half, she should be marvelous in the role.[1]

You can keep in touch with [Maurice] Speiser as to when the picture will be produced. Please do this, for God's sake, so as not to lose the chance of publishing the cheaper edition when the picture comes out. It would be very, very bad if through some kind of slip-up this publication was missed.

Bumby is still up at Dartmouth. That is, he is there as far as I know. Have written him but have heard nothing lately. Gregory and Patrick are here and Patrick must go north to [Canterbury] school near New Milford, Connecticut, to be at school for the 17th of September. You may see him when he comes through New York. Gregory will be staying down here for some time.

It is a fine feeling to have that Wartels book finally off our hands, but I wish you would have thought of it so that we could have done it together. It would have been a much more pleasant experience and we could have made a pot of money. I don't know whether it could have been a better book because we fought out with them on all questions of taste, but since you have always had much better taste than I have, would have been very happy to let you carry the ball on that.

What do you know about Mike Strater getting married? I had an announcement but know absolutely nothing. I wrote him and his bride, if he has a bride, a letter of congratulations but would give much to know the details. It happened in Maine. Can't you find out something about it from Waldo [Peirce]? If Maggie [Strater] should be triumphed over after all these years, there is hope for our side in the great, unending battle between men and women which Thurber illustrates so beautifully—and why doesn't he do it any more? Have seen nothing of his in the New Yorker for a long time. Being almost blind, can it be that he is now in the Air Corp? Along with Thornton Wilder and Jimmy Sheean. This is not subversive thought; it is a joke, censor.

I sent up for a lot of books and hope that Wilcox can find them and get them down here. Reading matter is hard to get. Did you read Beryl Markham's book, "West With The Night"? I knew her fairly well in Africa and never would have suspected that she could and would put pen to paper except to write in her flyer's log book. As it is, she has written so well, and marvelously well, that I was completely ashamed of myself as a writer. I felt that I was simply a carpenter with words, picking up whatever was furnished on the job and nailing them together and some times making an okay pig pen. But this girl who is, to my knowledge, very unpleasant, . . . can write rings around all of us who consider ourselves as writers. The only parts of it that I know about personally, on account of having been there at the time and heard the other people's stories, are absolutely true. So, you have to take as truth the early stuff about when she was a child which is absolutely superb. She omits some very fantastic stuff which I know about which would destroy much of the character of the heroine; but what is that anyhow in writing? I wish you would get it and read it because it is really a bloody, wonderful book.

I forwarded Charley's letter to Martha. She is at present navigating the Caribbean in a thirty foot sloop with a 4′x5′ cabin with a 4′ 5″ head room, accompanied by three faithful negro followers. I understand that if she is lost at sea, Colliers will pay double for her last article. I expect they will also want me to write a Tribute to their intrepid correspondent. Tell Charley he can start now writing a piece of it. That way we can always have it in the morgue and not so much time will be lost. I might not feel up to writing a tribute myself at the time and Charley could prepare a large part of it now. It will give him something to do in the long fall nights in New Jersey.

Please give my love to everybody in the book publishing business and tell them that down here everything is perfectly dandy or not so dandy.

Best always,

PUL

Ernest

---

1. Vera Zorina, the dancer, cropped her hair and played Maria for three weeks before being replaced in the role by Ingrid Bergman, whose performance in *Casablanca* had prompted rave reviews. (A. Scott Berg to Carlos Baker, 15 May 1980.)

To PATRICK HEMINGWAY, La Finca Vigia, 7 October 1942

Dearest Mousie:

We were awfully glad to get your letter and to hear that you were such a good football player and that school was as good as you had expected. Gigi wrote you about poor Bates dying. It was really awful. He had that same thing that killed Pony, that took so long for him to die, but we gave him all the medicine he should have had and took good care of him and did everything that we could about it. But Gigi felt awful about it and we didn't know how he would stand up under it finally. He took it very well really because he has such good sense and though he loved Bates he knew there was nothing we could do about it. The other thing that helped him out is that Wolfer has got to be such a fine cat and that we have Testor's new baby who is a wonder cat.

He looks just like Boysy except that he is a Persian and has long fur and he is as strong as a bear and is built like a wolverine. Testor is lovely with him and takes such good care of him and has purred almost every minute since he has been born. He is three weeks old yesterday and is now able to make a purr-purr and to walk around and is really a marvelous cat. Gigi plays with his ball team and is really pitching very well. It was a big blow to him to have the Yankees beaten by the Cardinals the way they were and he lost fifteen bucks on the series. He went with Mayito [Menocal] to the Pan American the first day to hear it and the second day went with Juan [Dunabeitia] to the big score board in the park. After that he went with me to listen to it here at the house and we heard it very well on the radio here and kept score. The last game we heard down in the cove on the boat radio and it was a bitter blow to the old man.

Boysy is in fine shape and so is Willy and so is the new cat and Stoopy Wolfer. I found that what was the matter with your catnip was that you planted it too shallow. You needed to drill down the holes and plant it deep because what was coming up as long stalks with you was really the roots of the plant. Once you planted it deep enough the leaves had a chance to develop.

Marty is coming up to New York and will be there on the eleventh. She and Wolfer [Guest] will come out to see you at school if it is possible. If she can't make it out to the school she'll talk to you on the telephone. Anyway, you'll get a chance to get out to Gardiner's Island and shoot there over Thanksgiving holidays. I'll fix it up with Wolfer when he is down here exactly how you are to do that.

If this letter is jerky and doesn't seem to make too good sense, blame it on the dictaphone which Papa is trying out for the first time. It shows at least that we are getting somewhere to have a dictaphone anyway. It's lovely at the finca now and we all certainly miss you and wish you were here. There are plenty of quail in the back country. Every time Marty or Gigi go out they run into at least a couple of big coveys. Gigi hasn't gone out on any big dove shoots or quail shoots yet but he has won about fifty bucks in team shoots and miss and outs. He still is about $65 ahead even with his World Series losses.

There're lots of birds coming through now, all sorts of warblers, orioles, and small birds that I haven't had time to identify. There are also big flights of teal coming across which probably means an early winter.

All the scientific projects[1] are in fine shape and everything will be okay with them. Dearest Mousie we miss you very much, both as a brother, a partner and a joke companion. It isn't the same here without you at all. I'm going to have Marty get the seats on the plane for you for the day after Christmas, so that you will be sure to have them and there will be no excuse for you not getting down here. They have almost finished the picture of "For Whom the Bell Tolls" and talk about sending it to New York and having me come up to see it. I will try and get them to send it down here so we'll have a look at it. Cooper and Bergman ought to be good, no matter how the rest of them are.

Mousy, write about school and tell us all about it. We all want to know how it is. Give my love to the H.Fs. and much love to you from all of us.

Much love from
Papa

Will write often. Gigi wrote yesterday. Max Perkins is sending the big book I wrote about [*Men at War*].

About football—always remember to swing your arms wide when you tackle. Open them *wide* before you make the tackle and then slam them together <u>hard</u>. Like slapping them together across your chest. Try always to fall sideways so as to protect your balls as in boxing. Wear a jockstrap when you play.

PUL   Papa

1. In mid-1942 EH had secretly armed the *Pilar* as a Q-boat and was hunting German submarines in the Caribbean. Owing to necessary secrecy and wartime censorship, he referred to his activities as a scientific expedition. See Carlos Baker, *Ernest Hemingway: A Life Story* (New York, 1969), pp. 374-75.

To ARCHIBALD MAC LEISH, La Finca Vigia, 4 April 1943

Dear Archie:

Could you find out (I ask you because I remember that God wonderful apparatus you have into which you just speak and all knowlege comes right back at you) when and on what wave length our old pal Ezra [Pound] broadcasts? Sooner or later he will have to be tried, of course, and I want to hear him so that I can know what it is all about when such a time should come. I think we both should know as much about it as possible because it is a pathological business in which we might be called upon to testify. I wish I could talk it over with you.

Why dont you come down here sometime? I am in and out but if I were out would get in to be with you or we could meet somewhere. Martha will be going off to the wars after she finishes a book she is on and you could get a good rest in this place which is damned lovely. Why dont you come down here in July? I could take you to some odd places and you could have a change. I will promise absolutely not to be self righteous, no-good and bastardly as in my great 37–38 epoch when [I] alienated all my friends (who I miss like hell) (not to mention my sonofabitching epoch of 1934 when was even worse). How is my lovely Ada and my beautiful Mimi? What is Kenny doing? Bumby is private John Hemingway going to officers school, he hopes, in next couple weeks. He is turning out all right.

What do you know about Sara and Gerald [Murphy]? I would write to Sara if I had her address.

Excuse dull letter. Just got back here and on last trip got to thinking about the Ezra business and that it was something I ought to know about. I know there is no time any more but if you ever have any will you write?

Love to Ada and to Mimi—even if she is happily married.

LC   Pappy

To ARCHIBALD MAC LEISH, La Finca Vigia, c. 5 May 1943

Dear Archie:

After I got your letter from the Library [of Congress][1] I delayed answering because you said you were writing from home. Today I had your letter of April 27th and it made me very happy.

Will you please send the photostats of Ezras broadcasts that you have? Whenever the damned business comes up we will probably be called on,

or should be called on, and I think should know what it is all about. If
Ezra has any sense he should shoot himself. Personally I think he should
have shot himself somewhere along after the twelfth canto although
maybe earlier. He has certainly lived with very little dignity for a man
who gave his allegiance to a government simply because under that
government he was treated seriously. But it is a pathological business all
the way through and he should not be punished on any other basis.

You old bastard. We must both be thinking we are going to die or
something to become so forgiveing. I was *awful* for a whole period of
years. Too awful for anybody to stand. Lately I've been good for almost
a year but I never see any of my old friends so nobody can appreciate
it. That's one reason why I would like you to come down to see how
good, non-righteous, non-bragging, non-boasting, almost non-chickenshit
I have become. Otherwise am liable to die and nobody will ever register
it.

For christ sake don't worry about the war and thee and me in same.
I used to think I had a possible military career but with [Vincent]
Jimmy Sheean a Colonel I prefer to do whatever I do very quietly and
as well as possible with neither the leaves of the oak, the good old fish
eating predator nor the stars of the sky on the shoulders or collar.
Actually have been working hard for a year and never happier. You come
down here and get some sun and a change from Washington. If you get
here in the next two months I will arrange to fly you down to wherever
we are and you can have a change and a rest and see this damned
wonderful island.

After this summer don't know what shall be doing. I think we shall be
at war in the east for ten years or more. Maybe I could be some use in
China. Will have to figure things out. If you come down we could talk
about lots of things. Actually I think we will be at war for the rest of
our lives. That may seem silly but I could argue it at a pinch. Anyway
I want to write one more novel because have found out two or three
more things and usually only had one each new to a book. You know—
Promiscuity no solution 1927 [1926];—a passage you quoted once—
1929; one man alone aint got no bloody etc. 1936; no man is an island
entire of its selfe 1939; and now I know three new ones I think although
often am wrong or is it wrong? Ask Donne, he knows. Papa probably
never could think good with his head but by Jesus he thinks good with
his bones. Maybe write novel in 1945. Put it down on the agenda. Do you
think the Library will be able to give me a grant to write a novel in that
year? Or will writers be abolished by then? I paid 104,000 income tax
in 1942, have made no money this or last year, was overdrawn 104.36 in
one bank and 1732 in another last month and pay $500 a month alimony
to a woman [Pauline] whose father owns 76,000 acres of land and whose

uncle [Gus] is worth, say, 40,000,000. There must be something slightly cockeyed about our financial structure for these conditions to exist but viva la virgen say I and set them up in the next alley for that old man may be rip van winkle and we want it to look as though they were giveing the joint a play. Chantechante chante pour Lydia Pynkham et sa grande amour pour l'humanite and a singer sewing machine in the home of every untouchable. But not from Bermingham unless it is Bermingham alabama. Like the soldier Marty overheard when there was a big broadcast about the four different freedoms, she was down somewhere in the carribean, and nobody said anything while it was on and when it was over and then one guy said, "Just freedom would be all right with us." I think people are just starting to be tired of words and to see how unsuccessfully the words wrap the cynicism. Maybe I need to hear a lot of things from you to straighten me out but I told you I could always think good with my bones and my bones are thinking heavy now. But I wish you could come and tell me a lot of things because the bone thinking racket ne marche pas trop bien today. Maybe it is because it is the broken bones you think with and the barometer is wrong but there are a lot of things that don't taste good any more that used to taste all right.

    Anyway much love to you and Ada,

LC   Pappy

    1. Mac Leish was Librarian of Congress from 1939 to 1944.

To MRS. JASPER JEPSON, La Finca Vigia, 30 July 1943

Dearest Ura:

    It was lovely to get your birthday letter and made me very happy. Especially remembering about the birthday trees and the smell of the cedars.[1] Windemere is still the clearest part of my life, I guess, and I suppose that is why I never go back there. I am going to, though, sometime after the war and take the boys once you can drive a car again. Bumby is finishing his OCS at Fort Custer, Michigan. Will put his address at the end of this letter. He's due to finish there by the 17th and then will come down here with his two weeks leave if he can make it. Patrick and Gigi are here now. Marty is just finished a novel and when I go off on my next trip she will shove off too, to go again for Collier's as a war correspondent. Have just gotten back from a two months trip with lots of hard work and some pretty good luck.

What is the news of our brother [Leicester] the Baron? I haven't heard from him for almost a year. Also how is Mother and the rest of the family? Had a letter from Sunny from Memphis but haven't heard from Beef [Carol] for years.

Excuse this letter being so lousy and being dictated but if I didn't get it off might go another year without writing and I wanted to tell you what there is of our news and how much I love you always. Best to Jap and Gayle and my dearest love to you, Ura.

JFK   [Ernie]

1. EH reminds his sister of the family custom at Windemere: decorated trees for birthdays.

To MAXWELL PERKINS, La Finca Vigia, 2 August 1943

Dear Max:

Thank you very much for your last letter. I was distressed to hear about Harold Stearns' illness but I remember his having gone through so many almost fatal illnesses that it is hard to believe completely in this one although certainly no man's stomach can take the punishment Harold's took in the old days without inaugurating some tendency toward that disease. It reminds me of Winston Guest who has explained to me not so long ago on the boat that one of his father's favorite drinks was gin with Worcestershire sauce and red pepper and that nothing ever made him feel better or more healthy. I asked Winston what his father died of and he said hurriedly "Cancer of the stomach." Harold has a long history behind him in Paris which would certainly predispose him toward a carcinomous condition. I hope, though, that he is feeling better and will be able to get up to the Hambletonian with Evan [Shipman].[1]

Am awfully glad to know that John Thomason is well and OK. He must have had a fine trip and I envy his getting out there. On the other hand, wouldn't trade present job for anybody's.[2]

Martha is working very hard on her title [*Liana*, 1944]. Getting a title is a lot like drawing cards in a poker game. You keep on drawing and they're all worthless but if you can last at it long enough you always get a good hand finally. She's having a tough time, though, because each year there are fewer good titles since the mines have all been worked for a long time. There are still some wonderful ones in John Donne but two people in the same family become selfconscious about digging into that wonderful lode. So many people have robbed the Bible that nobody minds that and I think we ought to start Marty digging into Ecclesiastes or Proverbs where there are still very valuable properties buried.

Since I wrote you that business letter there is nothing new here. I appreciated very much your writing steadily and with so much news when letters were at such a premium. Will be getting off again now I believe in a couple of weeks. Wish you could come down. Why don't you ever break away from that outfit any more? We could make a whole succession of new good old days if you would ever cut loose again. There are no rummies better than John and Burge but you would be surprised how constant the supply of fine rummies and worthless characters remains.

Best always,
Ernest

PUL

1. Harold Edmund Stearns (1891–1943) died of cancer 13 August. 2. EH no doubt means his submarine-hunting activities.

To ARCHIBALD MAC LEISH, La Finca Vigia, 10 August 1943

Dear Archie:

Thanks for sending the [photo]stats of Ezra's rantings. He is obviously crazy. I think you might prove he was crazy as far back as the latter Cantos. He deserves punishment and disgrace but what he really deserves most is ridicule. He should not be hanged and he should not be made a martyr of. He has a long history of generosity and unselfish aid to other artists and he is one of the greatest of liveing poets. It is impossible to believe that anyone in his right mind could utter the vile, absolutely idiotic drivel he has broadcast. His friends who knew him and who watched the warpeing and twisting and decay of his mind and his judgement should defend him and explain him on that basis. It will be a completely unpopular but an absolutely necessary thing to do. I have had no correspondence with him for ten years and the last time I saw him was in 1933 when Joyce asked me to come to make it easier haveing Ezra at his house. Ezra was moderately whacky then. The broadcasts are absolutely balmy. I wish we could talk the whole damned thing over. But you can count on me for anything an honest man should do.

Was plenty worried about Kenny [Mac Leish] about three weeks ago. Is he okay? Give him my best.

Will be here about ten days more and then gone for two three months. If you come down you can use the house and catch yourself a good rest.

Or you might come wherever we were and get a change of scenery and routine.

Whatever you do if you have time keep on writing to me. Feel as though had an old friend back from the dead where, unfortunately, most of old friends now are. What the hell has become of John Peale Bishop by the way? He had such a good, disinterested love of letters and such an horrid wife.

I found the wire about Honoria's [Murphy's] marriage when got back here. Where can I write her? Do you know? What is Sara's address?

Maybe I can get up to N.Y. by late November. Would like to take two months somewhere away from tropics and write something that would like to write. Haven't written a line now for just over a year.

Is there any chance that we might send guys to the war not to write govt. publications or propaganda but so as to have something good written afterwards? Do you think I have enough category to get any such assignment after finish work here? The British are useing both writers and painters that way. If we don't want such people maybe I could get a job with British. I don't want to be a Lt. Col like Jimmy Sheean to whom I have always previously had to point out which end of a battle-field was which, and in the past year or so have discovered the great joy and vice of anonymity which is a fine good snotty vice, but it occurred to me that when finish up working it might be a good sound thing to do something like have outlined above. What do you think? Maybe I could be the accredited correspondent for the Library of Congress.

Write me about it seriously will you?

So long Archie. Love to the children and to Ada.

LC   Pappy

To ALLEN TATE, La Finca Vigia, 31 August 1943

Dear Allen:

Thank you for your letter of August 23. I am glad that Archie [Mac-Leish] wrote you about my letter. What I wrote to Archie [10 August] I stand by absolutely. They must not hang the guy [Ezra Pound] nor must he be made a martyr in any way. He ought to go to the loony bin, which he rates and you can pick out the parts in his cantos at which he starts to rate it. You must read the photostats of the son-of-a-bitch's broadcasts so that you know exactly what he has said. It is a hell of a corvee to read through it all as it is absolutely loony drivel. It is necessary to read it through so you know what you actually think about what he has said.

On the other hand, with our knowledge of how he went nuts, how gradually and steadily he became irresponsible and idiotic, and what a great, sound and fine poet he was, and what a generous and really noble person he was in aiding all those he believed in back in the old days, such as Elliot [T. S. Eliot], Joyce, many many others including the worthless Dunning,[1] I think we have an absolute and complete obligation to oppose any hanging even though we all should have to get up on the scaffold with the rope on our own necks. I would not want to live a day ever if I did not take this stand and the time to take it is now, and not with publicity, but to present the facts to whose who should have them.

I cannot get up there now nor for several months. If Archie wants to come down to talk it over or if you want to come down I can always fix it up so we can meet wherever I am, and will be, as you know, truly happy to see you.

Am about the same as always. Like you say, it is a hell of a long time between bicycle races and it is getting to be a hell of a long time between everything else including literature. I think it is wonderful you being in the Chair of Poetry in the Northeast Pavilion.[2] There are several jokes could make but they all have either musical or flushing in them and I am sure you made them all yourself long since. By the way, how did the civil war ever come out? Am inspired to ask this by a friend of mine, Winston Guest, having recently been reading Renan's Life of Jesus, due to his thinking he ought to have some spiritual influence in his life in these grave times, and I had to warn him not to skip to the end to see how it came out. As a matter of fact it turned out, finally, that they nailed Jesus in the 34th.

Let me know how all this goes along and tell Archie that with me its a serious thing because it is really sort of a test of whether we are all sons of bitches or not (to let it happen I mean without takeing steps in time) and I don't think we are. There are going to be 3 or 4 times when everybody is going to have to bite on the old nail in this case.[3]

They hanged Roger Casement and they hanged, I believe, Erskine Childers. Both of them were in armed revolt against their Government and paid the legal penalty for such revolt. Pound has made, has written, and has broadcast crazy enough statements to be committed in any civilized country. When I last saw him in 1933 at Joyce's, Joyce was convinced that he was crazy then and asked me to come around when Pound was present because he was afraid he might do something mad. He certainly made no sense then and talked as utter rot, nonsense and balls as he had made good sense in 1923. So I think it would be outrageous for us who followed his decline into ridiculous nonsense and idiocy not to constaté that fact and also constaté what a great and fine poet and generous friend he was before he went goofy. It is sort of a historical necessity

and it would be as criminal to hang him as it was to hang Mrs. Suratt.[4] I suppose the last phrase will hang me but what the hell. What was it the old guy said; if this be treason make the most of it [Patrick Henry, 1765].
Best always.

PUL   Ernest

1. Ralph Cheever Dunning. See *A Moveable Feast* (New York, 1964), pp. 143–46. 2. Tate occupied the Chair of Poetry, Library of Congress, 1943–1944. 3. After Pound had made 125 broadcasts on Rome Radio between December 1941 and July 1943, a Federal grand jury in U.S. District Court, Washington, D.C., indicted Pound for treason 26 July 1943. 4. Mary Suratt, hanged in Washington, D.C., as co-conspirator in the murder of Abraham Lincoln.

To PATRICK HEMINGWAY, La Finca Vigia, 30 October 1943

Dearest Moose:
Glad to get your letter and know that the glorious old third team is still rolling them in the alleys. The hell with the other two teams. Me for the third. I hope you set fire to the town after the victory. Evidently you are carrying on the great pig-skin traditions of Papa who was known as Droopy-Drawers the Sagging All American and Bumby who was called The Spavined Mule of the Hudson in his great days not to mention your Grandfather who could run both ways with equal ease when carrying the ball and always had to be accompanied by a man with a Compass to tell him which goal line to cross. He was the greatest Erratic Full Back ever to play in the middle west. No one ever knew whether he would produce a touchdown or a safety when he seized the ball (usually on the wrong signal).
The weather moved straight from a hurricane warning (it went to East of us) into a huge Norther. So here we are ha ha ha ha ha ha. We've been given the well known triple ha ha by the weather all through Oct. But now it is beautiful here. Cool and fresh and the air all washed and summer and heat and the heavy skies of Oct. all over and the air clean washed and wonderful.
The Marty got away last Monday for her destination [London]. Bumby's also evidently over. Great quantities of ducks have come down with the cold wave there's been in Miami and thousands of snipe. We hope get away Tuesday for a while but not where we thought. No fish there now.
Will you find out about vacation? The dates I mean. And let me know so can plan to be here. Looks like going north in November is out for me

because we have had such a long delay. It was really an awful month. Until the last three days not a good day and right now a big brisote but it feels wonderful. Do you remember Floradella? No that is joke. I mean do you remember that Basque captain we call Sinbad [Dunabeitia]? Tall, that played water polo with us once? Have been carrying him instead of Dini. Honest Don [Saxon] is gone too.

Old Moose I certainly miss you. It is lonesomer than Limbo here. Only the cotsies for company. Your Will as fine as ever. Boisie very loveing and good. Friendless has gotten to be a great cat. Thruster mean and distant. Tester nice with me but mean with everybody else. Furhouse and Bro. fine. Fats is as big as a skunk and moves the same way. He is a fine slow friendly good cat. Uncle Wolfer is in beautiful fur and is so anxious to be popular. He never makes messes anymore and will run on a cat race and now I have trained him and Boisie to make a pyramid like lions at the circus on the pillars on the front porch. They walk toward each other along the railing when called. Uncle Wolfie wants to practice it all day long.

Of Negrita's two pups one is a beauty; black and white and very pretty. The other looks like his yellow dog father. Of course the handsome one had to be a bitch but maybe we will have her spayed. She looks sort of like Paxche's dog Chickie.

Wolfie [Winston Guest] is fine. So is Paxche [Ibarlucia] and Don Andres [Untzain]. Everybody sends their best. I have won five of last six shoots. All with correos but two. Wolfie and I ruined Fatty and Thorwald [Sanchez] in a twenty correo match for 100 bucks a corner.

Ermua [Aretio] has never played better. He is over Guillermo like a tent. It's lonesome without the [Robert] Joyces too. Did I tell you they've changed the name of Bobby's dept from the cloak and dagger to the muffled oar. Maybe it will gradually work into the poisoned chalice or the odour of bitter almonds dept.[1]

Must go in town now to meet the lower element for lunch at the Floridita and then face the ferocious correo at a distance of 25 meters. Today is Sat. Always a big day at the Floridita.

Thanks for writing so often and for being so careful with the penmanship. Much love from Papa.

PUL

1. Robert Joyce was stationed in Havana from January 1941 to 25 August 1943, when he left his post as one of the first secretaries at the American Embassy, resigned from the Foreign Service, and entered the OSS. (Joyce to Carlos Baker, 17 November 1963.)

To MAXWELL PERKINS, La Finca Vigia, *c.* 16 November 1943

Dear Max:

Thank you very much for your letters. Have tried to read the Christine Weston book [*Indigo*, 1943] evenings on the water but it has a peculiarly un-readable quality. Her others were the same for me. She is so unreadable that I have little doubt people will finally believe her to be a classic. She sounds much more lively in real life.

Will you call up Dave Randall in the [Scribner Rare Books] office and tell him I wrote that quotation[1] the Library of Congress was asking about, all same I wrote the other fine medaeval one in the front of Martha's Stricken Field. I probably would have written pretty well in those times but unfortunately that's been written and these are these so try to write in these. Is far from easy.

When you get this letter will you deposit $2000 in my account in the Guaranty Trust Co. of N.Y.? Take it out of the 13,000 you said and [Grosset and] Dunlap said was going to be deposited in December on that cheap edition. Charley suddenly cabled asking if I wanted all of some 29,000 now or next year. I want it as it was promised in the contract or agreement between Grosset [and] Dunlap, yourselves and me and not suddenly in a lump sum upsetting my estimate and declaration of expected income according to contracts made. Only thing is I want $2000 now in November instead of in December. Is that perfectly clear?

We got caught in a sonofabitching norther. The kind that beats your brains out. I came in last night and today the second half of the norther is blowing. I'm sick lonesome without Martha and feel gloomy in the big empty house. Would be ok if the kids were here but they're not. Have heard nothing from Bumby for two months and don't even know care what Postmaster is his address. Had word Martha got to London o.k.

So sorry Waldo [Peirce] is haveing woman trouble. That's one thing you have to hand to Charley Sweeny. He doesn't take nothing from them. If they start to make any trouble with Charley he gives them that old tone of command. A man who suffers from women like Evan [Shipman], say, has a more incurable disease than cancer. And penicillin doesn't cure it. The drug I mean. A woman ruined Scott. It wasn't just Scott ruining himself. But why couldn't he have told her to go to hell? Because she was sick. It's being sick makes them act so bloody awful usually and it's because they're sick you can't treat them as you should. The first great gift for a man is to be healthy and the second, maybe greater, is to fall [in] with healthy women. You can always trade one healthy woman in on another. But start with a sick woman and see where you get. Sick in the head or sick anywhere. But sick anywhere and in a little while they are sick in the head. If they locked up all the women who were crazy—but why speculate—I've known goddamned good ones; but take as good a woman as Pauline—a hell of a wonderful woman—and once she turns mean. Although, of course, it is your own actions that turn her mean. Mine I mean. Not yours. Anyway let's leave the subject. If you leave a woman, though, you probably ought to shoot her. It would save enough trouble in the end even if they hanged you. But you can't do it on account of the children and so there isn't any solution actually to anything except to get so nobody can hurt you and by the time you get to that you've usually been dead for some time.

So long Max. Thanks for the letters. Send me any books except by Christine Weston. Always short of books.

How in hell will anybody who has been able to buy a book for $1.45 be expected to go back to paying $2.75 on it? Why don't we ourselves have a proper cheaper edition or a gift edition or something to give more value. Because when something has been 1.45 who the hell will pay 2.75 unless it is, say, good gin. Our only hope of ever selling another copy is that it is good gin. And next move is I suppose you won't even print any copies and it will be as hard to buy as Death In The Afternoon which I can't get a copy of anywhere in the world even when order it from the publishers. Don't tell me there's never going to be any more For Whom The Bells sold anywhere ever just because Marcia Davenport or Goldilocks and the Seven Dwarfs or any other of your list leaders need so much paper. I mean paper to print on.

Best to you always,
Ernest

PUL

1. EH's headnote to *Winner Take Nothing* (New York, 1933).

To HADLEY MOWRER, La Finca Vigia, 25 November 1943

Dearest Hadley:

Bumby wrote me (first letter in almost three months and was sure he had gone over-seas) that you were in the hospital. So hasten to write to hope it doesn't amount to anything and whether it does or not to send much love and that you be fine soon. Poor Cat I hate to think of you as ever ill with anything. Hope *so* you are all right now. This letter brings much, much love and get well quickness.

Enclosed check is for the money you advanced for Bumby to come down here when he had his leave. I felt terribly selfish haveing him but figured you had seen him in Michigan at the Fort and he loves this damned place so much and it represents romance, gayety (mis-spelled) and I always load him up with so much good advice and frozen daiquiris that it is probably good for him. I would have sent the check before but have been in and out and over-busy and so lonesome when would get back here without Marty (she's in London for Colliers. Took job when it looked as though I had to be gone three solid months and then I've been stuck here alone half the time) that when come in have a few drinks with my cats and the next thing am asleep on the floor with the Capeheart still playing and all correspondence just stacked in two big wooden boxes.

In case you are in hospital or in bed and want to be amused or informed, let's say, there are eleven cats here. One cat just leads to another. The mother is Tester a Persian from the Silver Dawn Cattery somewhere in Florida. She had a kitten named Thruster out of Dillinger a black and white cat from Cojimar a coastal fishing village. By the same sire she also bore Furhouse, Fats, Friendless and Friendless's Brother. All in the same litter. Two lovely black Persian appearings and two Black and Whites like Dingie. We also have a grey, sort of snow leopard cat named Uncle Wolfer (Persian) and a Tiger cat from Guanabacoa named Good Will after Nelson Rockerfeller. There are at present two half grown kittens named Blindie (on acct. of Blindness. Born that way) daughter of Thruster and her own father. That shows us eh fat lady? And Nuisance Value also known as Littless Kitty who is the most beautiful of all with a purr-purr that would blast you out of the hospital.

The place is so damned big it doesn't really seem as though there were many cats until you see them all moveing like a mass migration at feeding time.

We also have 5 dogs; one good pointer and the others small mongrels on the style of Wax Puppy.

It is wonderful when Marty and/or the kids are here but it is lonesome as a bastard when I'm here alone. I have taught Uncle Wolfer, Dillinger and Will to walk along the railings to the top of the porch pillars and make a pyramid like lions and have taught Friendless to drink with me (Whisky and milk) but even that doesn't take the place of a wife and family.

I never had so damned much time to think in my life, especially nights on the water and here when I can't sleep from haveing lost the habit, and have thought about you with great pleasure and admiration and how wonderful you were and are. Did you ever see anything handsomer than that Bumby after the army had knocked the college fat off of him?

Since I've spent so much time with my cats and seen everything they have to go through I don't mind so much never haveing had a daughter.

Marry in heat and repent at leisure was one thing thought up on the boat the other day and the other was something about Custody that great proof of chastity. Maybe I'll turn out to be the Henry James of the People or the comic strips.

So long my dearest Katherine Cat. Paul can't mind me still loveing you because knowing you he would know I would be crazy if I didn't and I have been crazy but never stay that way for very long.

When it is really rough on ocean sing old songs like Oh My Gentlemen, If you've Got Any Feather-Cats, and a Feather Kitty's Talent Lies, the Basque crew think these are folk songs of my Pais [country].

So they are. So, My Pais, get well quickly and take care of yourself and of Paul and accept the obedient devotion of your

PH. PUL   Taty

To MAXWELL PERKINS, La Finca Vigia, 25 February 1944

Dear Max:

Was glad to get the letter with the clipping about the noble Scribner's author who returned the advance. Hope it wasn't meant as a hint. You'll get everything back from me in this same month I hope whenever the Dunlop [Grosset and Dunlap] payment comes in. Or if there isn't enough to pay everything and taxes and have some to live on too will stagger the payments. But remember they are not advances really; but loans against money to come in from reprints contracted for and while they pay a low rate of interest they are as good security as Govt. Bonds. They aren't on some future book I am to write but on reprints of a book already written. At least that is way I look at it. As far as I know I owe no one in the world a cent except Scribner's and at the worst you could collect perfectly well out of my estate if I died.

I wish you would keep all the Scott letters for a definitive book instead of letting Bunny Wilson pee them away in his usual malicious driblets. He never asked me for any letters from Scott and I have very many; unfortunately all packed in Key West but available anytime I have something to do besides this war. Have letters from Gatsby period all through the Paris time and all the rest. All of them about writing and showing Scott's great strength and most of his weaknesses. I should suggest you save all of your letters; don't give permission for any of them to be used; until we could get out a good book on Scott and his letters. I know him, through some periods, better than anyone and would be glad to write a long, true, just, detailed (all of those I mean in the measure that anyone can do any such thing) account of the years I knew him. It might be better to wait and write it for my own memoirs[1] but my memoir expectancy has been so slight these last years that might be good to write a good piece about Scott before I get too punchy to remember. Would suggest that John Peale Bishop who knew, loved, and understood Scott much better than Wilson ever did edit the letters. John is unfailably kind, impersonal and disinterested while Wilson is usually twisting the facts to cover some expressed error of critical judgment he has made in the past or some prejudice or lack of knowledge or scholarship. He is also extremely dishonest; both about money and about his friends and other writers. I know no one who works so hard at being honest and [has] less true inner honesty within himself. His criticism is like reading second rate gospels written by some one who is out on parole. He reads most interestingly on all the things one does not know about. On the things one knows about truly he is stupid, inaccurate, uninformative and pretentious. But because he is so pretentious his inaccuracies are accepted by all those with less knowledge of what he is writing about than he has. He is the great false-honest, false-craftsman, falsegreat-critic of our exceedingly sorry times which, if every one was honest in himself and what he writes, have no need to be sorry in any way. You can trace the moral decay of his criticism on a parallel line with the decline in Dos Passos's writing through their increasing dishonesty about money and other things, mostly their being dominated by women. But let us not attack that theme with limited time available. Anyway above is my suggestion with regard to Scott's letters. When I am through with this war will have to get in training and shape again to write and would be glad to help on the Scott book to warm up and get going.

I miss writing very much Max. You see, unlike the people who belaboured it as a dog's life *ce metier de chien* Conrad and old Ford were always suffering about. I loved to write very much and was never happier than doing it. Charlie's [Scribner's] ridiculing of my daily word count was because he did not understand me or writing especially well nor could know how happy one felt to have put down properly 422 words as you wanted them to be. And days of 1200 or 2700 were something that made you happier than you could believe. Since I found that 400 to 600 well done was a pace I could hold much better was always happy with that number. But if I only had 320 I felt good.

Was very disappointed too not to see you. But things have not gone that simply for a long time. Now it looks as though I might be up there in comparatively short time but since I never know what I am going to do please keep on writing here.

Glad to hear Martha's book [*Liana*] moveing so well. The reviews across the country that I have seen are excellent. The first N.Y. reviews,

Times, Herald Trib etc. were not sent me by Romeikes. In fact no N.Y. reviews.

Wish Charlie Sweeny had come down here. But he always liked San Antonio and there are more people there for him to argue with. I gave up argueing with him years ago.

So long Max. Hope I see you soon.[2] But keep on writing and forwarding mail here until I wire.

Best always to Charlie and your local mob,

PUL   Ernest

1. Three sketches of Fitzgerald appear in *A Moveable Feast* (New York, 1965), pp. 147–93. 2. EH saw Perkins in New York in May on the first leg of his trip to London as correspondent for *Collier's*. The transatlantic flight took place on 17 May. See Carlos Baker, *Ernest Hemingway: A Life Story* (New York, 1969), pp. 386–88.

To MARY WELSH, Villebaudon and Hambye, France, 31 July and 1 August 1944

Small Friend: = Lovely Friend:

Got letter and it made me . . . very happy, and thank you very much for putting the story through. You were very good for and to me and I miss you very much. Am ashamed I know so few adjectives and over-use very. Hell, Small Friend, I wish I could talk to you: preferably in bed. More than preferably as you well know. It will be lovely to be back. —Just then people came into the field where we've just set up and they are shelling away up the hill—Quite a lot.

Very hard to write. Since saw you went and stayed with some air pals and got up a little (Not much. But saw well).[1] Then went where I was supposed to and it was dull as hell and nothing to do. So was much too lonely for that so got permission to detach and attach to a division[2] where have been ever since this last business started. We have had a tough, fine time. This is the 8th day we have been attacking all the time. Have been with very good guys. They have so much worse time than flyers do that I know my passion for flying probably just another form of laziness or some damn thing. Anyway been very happy here and had good time with infantry again. I don't like it with armoured on acct. of the dust. But there is plenty of dust everywhere although some of the time we have been in lovely country. Some very beautiful and we higher than the others even. Rare.

We captured a motorcycle with side car and now use it for transport and yest. we captured a big Mercedes Benz staff car. I have just driven it to the motor pool to get painted. Have gotten you some funny, smaller souvenirs too. But sometime we will drive around in the Mercedes. It is a convertible and had a bullet through the steering column and wiring shot up but we got it going OK and are repairing the steering column. The Division has killed a great many *Germans* and we have gotten excellent cognac from the armoured vehicles. The general [R. O. Barton[3]] is an educated, talented and charming man and a fine soldier. He was very gay and pleasant just now when he saw me driving in the Mercedes.

Christ what a dull writer I am. Small friend, think it is probably because am tired. Sometimes we go all day and all night, too. This is a very good Division really and I try *to be useful* and not a nuisance. Have a fine story when I can write it and I will write it. But should take a rest first. Will write it and then another on next phase and then back to [Room] 612 in the Hotel [Ritz]. I hate to think of those people fouling up our fine room.

Mary I cannot write you well because of how many people read it or can read it in transit makeing me shy and so difficult to write. I wish to hell I could talk to you and pretty soon we will be able to. I was very proud about your grasp of the picture and the fine letter they wrote. Over here I heard fine things said of you too and will remember them all and tell you. I miss you so I am hollow and to fill the hollow I put war in day and night. But it is a lousy substitute; like drinking worcester sauce instead of what? Instead of what? Instead of being happy I guess. Am very happy when I see you. I make as good a war as I can and I understand infantry but am hearing *much* new stuff. Am very happy at Front but that is not loveing.

But you are so busy, and impermanent, and always moveing and tired and makeing decisions and sleep dead-tired sleep when you can get it with a division that is fighting that you really have no other life. I have to do this now and for certain reasons can't leave area or I would be there. I mean I would be with you in London Town.[4]

What a dull letter. Am really not dull and would tell you damndest funny things if—not if, when, see you. We are terribly dirty and we get up before daylight and scrub good all over and all over face hard and sound with soap and washcloth and then with daylight look in pocket mirror and the dust still makes your eyes like a beery whore or ginned debutante who has cried into her mascara.

Small friend I love you very much. After I wrote you up to the cross line under stuff on this page I went up for another infantry attack with platoon. You could write it so well and I write nothing. Just put it in the old sausage machine from which we extract .Dr. Swineless's New Pearls.

Mary, there is no being careful in this world we received as our inheritance, our gleaming aluminum, black and white striped, 700 MPH inheritance, but still the same dust, an equal amount of dirt on your face, and—etc. What I mean is You use your head and be unfearing but careful. You means Toi. This would have made sense with daylight to write it.

Mary at this point it got too dark to write so will write tomorrow—we get up at day light for the attack and then have a day ahead and I will write when get back.

Small Friend I will sleep good with you tonight and feel happy as one can be being away from someone as lovely as you. Please write to the address on this and I will get it they say. Am now writing in the complete dark but do that quite well—(Braggart)—you would love much of this. Much of it—or some—I simply turn my heart to non-receptivity. . . .

Please write because I miss you totally—Headaches much better.

Next day—Aug. 1—Now it is only 5:15 (1715) in the afternoon and so have much light to write and an address from Jack Belden of where to write Time and Life. I went over to the big lot I was supposed to be with and asked permission to stay with the Division as long as we are fighting and then catch up with the other people. We are fighting the most important part now and I do not want to leave because timeliness means nothing and like to finish what you start. Also am learning very much that is new to me about our infantry division and do not want to leave this good one now when it is a sticky time. It is not so much sticky as interesting.

Just read this and it sounds so righteous and boreing but will make only good jokes when we are together, or anyway jokes, and never righteous.

I know can write good story once alone and with typewriter after this over and will go some good place for a couple or three days to do it. All notes are in the head. There are some terrific things—Shouldn't waste on Colliers. Could write book now on this last week. . . .

Of correspondents the best here I have met (as guys) are Ken Crawford and Bill Walton.[5] I do not know Bill Walton well but he was so happy *at haveing made* the air-borne show that it was very nice and touching. Also he was kind and loveing. I wish you were here because you are intelligent and brave and then, too, you would be here.

France is fun now. I mean we have liberated great areas without destruction due to useing infantry, air, and armour intelligently.

Have a chance to send this off now—excuse long letter—will write some more tonight. Much love from us all—please write to this address—

Your Big Friend
E. Hemingway
War Correspondent

PH. PUL

1. For EH and the Royal Air Force see Carlos Baker, *Ernest Hemingway: A Life Story* (New York, 1969), pp. 395–400. 2. Fourth Infantry Division. See *A Life Story*, pp. 401–3. 3. Major General Raymond Oscar Barton (1889–1963) was born in Colorado, graduated from West Point, Class of 1912, and was commanding general of the Fourth Infantry Division, 1942–1944. EH first met him July 1944, and he appears in EH's article "The G.I. and the General," *Collier's* 114 (4 November 1944): 11. 4. At this time EH's liaison with Mary Welsh was two months old. Late in May they had met in London, where she worked for *Time-Life-Fortune*. On 25 May, after an all-night party, EH sustained a severe concussion in a motor accident in Lowndes Square. Hospitalized at London Clinic, he was visited by his third wife, Martha Gellhorn, who was angry at his wartime roistering. He consoled himself with Mary, with whom he was reunited at the Ritz after the liberation of Paris. For details, see Mary Hemingway, *How It Was* (New York, 1976), pp. 93–98, 109–18; and *A Life Story*, pp. 389–93, 419. 5. Bill Walton, a *Time-Life* correspondent then aged thirty-five, had first met EH in London on 24 May. He parachuted into Normandy with the Eighty-second Airborne *c.* 1 A.M. 6 June and later saw EH at Cherbourg (27 June), Mont St.-Michel (6 August), Hürtgen Forest (mid-November), and Luxembourg (31 December). His friendship with EH continued through the 1950s.

To MARY WELSH, St.-Pois and Mont-St.-Michel, France, 1 and 6 August 1944

Small Friend:

It is fun to write to you. Just now someone went up to army so I sent the letter I was writing at the point where it was and now, haveing eaten supper, and haveing fine day light write some more. There is a good wind blowing and it has been a clear fine day, summer but not hot and we will have a good fight. Our dog is eating on my feet which are bare. We took him from the Germans and he is small and silly with flop ears and he (she) eats feet preferably but also anything that has ever been tinned. Break to have to play poker—Christ the times have played poker when would rather do something else—Especially on the boat when too dead to sit up and trying to lose quickly enough so I could quit.

Tomorrow we will have a good day I think. Will go with the first attack in the morning and stay through all day I think if can find same outfit we attacked with yesterday since that is the best way to learn: with people you know already. There is a sergeant in this platoon who is Spanish speaking and a good friend of mine and we keep each other company on those slow ploddings.

Mary I hope I do not bore you with such dull letters. Actually we have a very jolly and gay life full of deads, German loot, much shooting, much fighting, hedges, small hills, dusty roads, metalled roads, green country, wheat fields, dead cows, horses, new hills, dead horses, tanks, 88's, Kraftwagens, dead U.S. guys, sometimes don't eat at all, sleep in the rain, on the ground, in barns, on carts, on cots, on one's ass and always moveing, moveing—I would miss nothing if I did not miss you— all the selfish chickenshit prima donnas I have never thought of since we started this attack—Never once ever—Don't think about the children since now know will not see them for long time; only see lovely souvenirs for them like fine technical German things they would like. I pick them up and throw them away a day later. Mostly I talk French and say where they are and whether they have left or not and how it is ahead, sometimes in very quiet whispers.

Mary write to this address because I cannot get back to our lives until I finish this and write it and write the next one. If things are bad in London then, and you have to stay in London, I will stay there as long as they are bad and you have to stay there. If you should come over, there are some fine places as we take them new.

Now the only bad thought I ever have in the night is of landing in London and finding you were gone somewhere. So keep good contact and write.

It is getting dark now and the little machine pistols go trrrrrrut— Trrrrut—like a kittycat purring but hard and metallic.

August 5 or 6—anyway Sunday [6].

We are out of this line now for a few days and so I am going to spend 4 or 5 days writing. Think will write 4 or so short stories on Infantry Division and cable to Colliers. They can use when they please. Have now made 11 infantry attacks in last 12 days—Know Division, Regimental, Battalion, many company commanders and many platoon commanders and guys. Will know more and better later. But better write now.

It turned out fine that on acct of speak French and old soldier could be useful and general [Barton] and I are good friends and we lie on same blanket when he is dead, dust, impossible tired at end of day and I give him the gen [lowdown] on how it actually is at all the places we go by motorcycle. When we shoved off just now he gave me a bottle of

Bourbon and said, "Ernie I will miss you very much. Both personally and officially." Which was nice and like what they said about you in air-force.

All our jolly futures was on the bum yesterday for a while because while ahead of infantry (he calls us his irregular cavalry) I was knocked down by tank shell and then fired on by tank machine gun and two people with machine pistols on each side of road. Had to pretend to be dead until quite a while later and could hear Germans talking on other side of hedge at about 10 feet. They spoke very disrespectfully of your big friend who they considered dead.

Later we retook motor cycle and all equipment but some parts badly shot up and had to tow home. Was German bike so now changed hands 4 times. Some other equipment changed for 5th time.

I hurt back and been urinateing blood but much better this pm and feel OK. Sleep good and all the worst headaches gone.

Will not ever be nuisance and have some very strange and funny stories. Have been cited for something moderately impressive but probably nothing ever come of it because of irregularity of actions. Maybe will though. When I wrote you last had we taken the SS Panzer people prisoner? There was a heavily censored account in Stars and Stripes. I have small iron cross for you from Officer (only unter-offizier) commanding. But have insignia cut from real officer (dead). They had much stuff and figured to fight.

Small Friend I am dead stink tired so excuse bad dull letter. If you were here now at this old hang out of Henry Adams where am going to hole up and write for 4–5 days we could have lovely time. I miss you very much.

Could you go to [Hotel] Dorchester and make my mail into package (if there is any) (Reading it first if it interests you) and send it to this address and tell R.A.F. Teakle that I am definitely committed here (due circumstances) and let us (you and me) meet in France. I want to stay with [Fourth Infantry] Division and fight as long as they fight. But if you cannot get away and it is bad in London will come back to see you there. J'ai deux amours, toi et mon Division. Love you. Other is idea of one's duty. Please let me know. If it is *bad*, really *bad* there I will come there to see you.

Afterwards write good book this winter.

Small friend write me please. If any way to send Vitamin B1 would be good to have. I go about 15–16 hours per day and probably should have to supplement spotty food.

Now say goodbye and kiss you, you good like mine detector.

PH. PUL   Big Friend

To MARY WELSH, Paris, 27 August 1944

Small Friend:

Just got your letter. First letter had since lifentiman [*Life* and *Time* man] brought your other. Been back twice to contact army to get letters but never have but just came in Ritz now and there was letter and am very happy.

Mary we have had very strange life since wrote you last. On nineteenth made contact with group of Maquis who placed themselves under my command. Because so old and ugly looking I guess. Clothed them with clothing of cavalry recon outfit which had been killed at entrance to Rambouillet. Armed them from Div. Took and held Rambouillet after our recon withdrawn. Ran patrols and furnished gen [intelligence] to French when they advanced. They operated on our gen with much success. Entered Paris by Etoile and Concorde. Fought outfit several times. They did very well. Now very tired.[1] Fortunately in phase of advance Rambouillet Paris had official war historian with us.[2] Otherwise everyone would think was damned lie. Most operation chickenshit as to fighting. But could been bad. Now have rejoined division but have to try to write piece tomorrow. Then will put my people under div orders. Very fine peoples. You would like. But temperamental. Seen your friend Sam Boal several times. He is swell guy.

I was very scared twice when we were holding (sic) screening, or simply furnishing contact is word, that town with 15 kraut tanks, and 52 cyclists as opposition. Some of the patrols we made would scare you worse than Grimm's Fairy Tales even if there had been no Krauts. We checked on tanks with bicycles. Would like to drag down but guess will have to let things ride.

Wish could see you. I miss you very much and would like to be in bed and make jokes. I suppose I can't say I love you because I do not know you but I miss you very much and am very lonely for you and for no one else. So will just say I love you anyway since it is a long time we have not been operateing by the book and I threw the book away somewhere the other side of Chartres.

Have been good and quiet, had to take some disciplinary measures when handling town and briefed the guys always on everything and day of entry loaned typewriter to Joe Driscoll so he could write his story and have taken no advantage as correspondent over other correspondents on acct of participating in action. Have written nothing yet but should and will tomorrow.

Have strong feeling my luck has about run out but am going to try to pass a couple of more times with dice. Have been to all the old places I ever lived in Paris and everything is fine. But it is all so improbable that you feel like you have died and it is all a dream. Wish very much you were here as am all fought out and would like to have something loveley and touchable or is it tangible, same thing anyway, not something, you please thank you very much.

Mary please write me again. I couldn't write lately—too busy. Have been very happy. Am not anyway except OK inside [typescript torn] satisfaction but would rather kiss you and not have taken some damn place. Hope soon to get out of woman kissing country into champagne country altho here has flown freely and women very fine.

Why don't you come over here? Should I ask [Charles] Wertenbaker or would that not be discreet. I can't leave now but can give you good quarters whenever and wherever you come.

I love [Bill] Walton very much.

PH. PUL   [Rest of letter lost.]

1. On EH's part in the liberation of Paris, see Carlos Baker, *Ernest Hemingway: A Life Story* (New York, 1969), pp. 409–18. 2. The "official war historian" was Lieutenant Colonel S. L. A. Marshall.

To MARY WELSH, Libin [?], Belgium, 8 September 1944

My dearest Pickle:

We are living in a fine forest today and there is some little fighting and will be more but everything is very good. I love you very much and could not have been happier and am still happy from being with you. Pickle you can write me to this address [PRO HQ Fourth Infantry Division, APO 4] and censor it and post it in an Army Post Office and will get in a day or two. I see no chance of being back for ten days or so. Please write if you have time or maybe if you haven't. It is lovely in the forest country and I am very happy with the Division altho I think not very useful as we will be away from where I know people so am trying to learn hard and have fine stuff to write later. Am takeing time for first time. We slept on a pine needle forest floor last night. It did not rain and the wind was high and heavy and blew the tops of the pines the way it did in Michigan in the second week of September when I was a boy. So I did not feel cheated out of a fall as one often is when living in the city or in strange countries with different climates. Darling I love you exactly as I told you and as we repeated—Loved you last night, this morning and now this noon—There isn't any more to write.

Will you put all my mail in a big envelope and send it to this address until Sept. 13th—or if you get this on 14th on that date? Will write you what will do.

Yesterday it was very cold with the autumn storm and today I am getting some warm clothes. When you have any time get a pair of bedroom shoes size 11—I will get some shirts and am getting an extra pair of boots. Pickle did we not have a lovely time for such a short impermanence? I know you will work well and I wish you good luck with it and I hope I am not in any very bad trouble.[1] There is none that cannot be aired as have done what I should and the hell with shits. Good by dearest beloved until I can write you again.

> Big Friend
> Ernest Hemingway War Correspondent APO 4

Couldn't get any heavy clothes and it has started to rain and it is cold. Maybe get some next time. Have no underwear.

PH. PUL

1. EH's "trouble" was an accusation that he had actually fought between Rambouillet and Paris, 19–25 August 1944. See Carlos Baker, *Ernest Hemingway: A Life Story* (New York, 1969), pp. 427–30. He was ordered to headquarters, Inspector General Third Army (Rear), 4 October 1944 and exonerated.

To MARY WELSH, Houffalize, Belgium, 11 September 1944

My dearest:

Lovely clean blue fall weather the last two days and two fine full happy useful days in Indian Country. We are just about to the limit of where my Ojibway runs. But Pickle this has been the truly happiest month I've ever had in all my life. On account of you it hasn't been desperate happy —it's been straight, good really happy. Know what you fight for and where and why and to what ends. Not lonely. Not disappointed—not disillusioned. No thing phony. No message. See it clear—help it on as much as you can to get it over. Then write as well as can, and better and never lonely any more.

We loved each other very much with no clothes at all, no lies, no secrets, no pretences, (no underwear), and only one shirt apiece and stove, that traitor, sometimes not working—with stove almost our only capital. Stove works so well for Archie [Pelkey].

I'm tired but I wake every morning happy and when I wake in the night and cannot sleep I just think about Tom Welsh's kid. I hope that you are well and fine and above all (no not above all because we can beat anything if you are well and fine). I hope you're still in Paris so I can see you that much sooner.

Stevie [Captain Marcus Stevenson] has gone back to Div. with 2 correspondents, one of whom, Peter Lawless, knows you and Noel [Monks],[1] and made me happy speaking of you and I said yes I'd met you and you were extremely nice and didn't add "And I love her very much and would be glad to show you here on the map how much I love her. But this is only a small map 1–25,000 and I need a Globe and 3 large Atlases to show you how I love Tom Welshes Daughter Mary because otherwise you might not understand."

So am waiting here in this town we took yest. until he comes back and writing to you and have written, in note book, about yest and day before. Had lovely day with Col. [Charles T.] Lanham[2] and he thinks better of yr old man than before. I hope they come because it is too fine a day to be indoors doing anything but write to you. If they don't come in ten minutes will push on and leave word have gone to join advance elements of the --th.

Pickle if you were here we would have such fun. I am keeping a note book because I have such a good time might not remember and one day of Indian Country drives another day of Indian Country out of yr. head.

Am sorry to write so dully. But always write for censorship in letter. John [Jean Décan] has been fine. 2 marvellous exploits and always on the ball. Everyone is useing French now. They even use them in the regular units and they are very fine.

Yesterday we had a really marvellous time. I'll tell you all about it when I see you.

Small Friend—I like to remember us in the dining room at the Ritz with our own world and the others could keep theirs—and in the Ritz Bar with Mac Kriendler, the greeter and mess sutler for Air Force with oak leaves on his shoulders saying, "What are you doing? Following the Boys?" and loveing you sitting on the quai at the Ile St. Louis and the never lonely magic touching in bed—and you, my true own beloved, lovely to touch, lovely to feel, lovely to just be with and to know that you are there. Dearest lovely I love you so.

[Robert] Capa never came with my mail nor my money. People have borrowed most of the money. But about money—I've made at least 15 G (deposited N.Y.). Colliers owes me about 3 G on expenses. Maybe more. I can get all the French money we need from Gallimard in Paris. Can cash checks with Mr. Brown on money in N.Y. There was to be a popular edition of F.W.T.B.T. in N.Y. to pay 25–35 G and I told Scribner's wanted it ½ in 44, ½ in 45. So there is working dough for next year. These pieces [for *Collier's*]—with censored parts put back—could make a book if we were broke. (Maybe better not to do that). I can get 4 to 6 G for short stories. Can write at least 4. But with no whoreing—with no compromise with nothing we will have clear dough ahead to see us through writing a novel—and every day I train good, sleep, hard outdoor life, not drink too much, learn, and feel straight to be able to write one. The cooling out takes a while. But I know about that haveing been in my own corner a long time—and we have good future Pickle. The best I've ever had.

Hope to write very fine, good, grown-up novel of which all I have so far is the dedication

To Mary Welsh

If you don't like novel you can dedicate it to anybody you want as it is your property.

(Dealing in novel futures bad gamble. Let's take our towns one at a time and now let's leave message for Stevie and get onto next one. But I will write a good novel, win, lose, or draw. And if you've left me and are living with the Shaw of Persia will dedicate it to you altho might add F--K her the Persian Harlot in parenthesis.)

Goodbye dearest beloved Pickle.

Your Big Friend,

PH. PUL   E Hemingway

1. A native Australian, Mary's current husband. See Mary Welsh Hemingway, *How It Was* (New York, 1976), pp. 41–43. 2. EH had met Lanham (1902–1978), West Point, Class of 1924, on 28 July at Le Mesnil Herman, where Lanham was commanding the Twenty-second Infantry Regiment, Fourth Infantry Division.

To MARY WELSH, Hemmeres, Germany, 13 September 1944

My Dearest Small Friend:

Yesterday we came into the new Indian Country after a fine wild day of chaseing and shooting and settled down in a deserted farm house for the night. It was a sort of spooky night as we were way ahead of most things but we had a fine chicken dinner from offhead shot pistol chickens and gave a dinner to Col. [Lanham] and a Battn Commander and they did all business at our farmhouse and we drank up everything we had to celebrate the day. It was a fine day, following tank tracks through the woods and flushing them finally. Seeing the artillery catch them when they had to take to the roads. This country is all a succession of wooded hills and rolling country with some bare heights from which you can see everything that moves. You get up on a height and own all that piece.

Then work on to another height that owns the next stretch of country. Sometimes there is thick forest like at home or in Canada and it seems as odd to be killed as it would be in Upper Michigan and makes you feel very confident and at home.

The people all pulled out when we came in but John[Décan] went down and rounded some up to clean and cook and a man to milk the cows so they won't ache and I take care of the cat and the fine, lovely, intelligent, so confused dog who is heartbroken that everyone is gone and all routines broken. Then we will be gone and I guess the people will be back and anyway the place will be clean and dogs have no nationality nor citizenship.

I loved you in the night when I was awake and early in the morning when I was not quite awake and remembered you and how lovely you are . . . and how much fun jokeing and being together. Pickle I miss you very much. I love you as you well know.

We have quite a lot of small problems here and always some big ones still but I hope to be back with you in ten days. Will you write me when you get this?

This isn't much of a letter but wanted to write you. I don't know whether you ever got the other letters nor whether you are still in Paris. But it is logical to be in Paris as all of Life staff would be moveing forward—same as a Divisional HQ. moves I should think. Anyway being on the spot and haveing done well and started other things should be an advantage.

Mary dearest beloved I am sorry to be so dull. We have had a Brazilian here who have dubbed The Pest of the Pampas. I write a letter like my son Gigi. All small direct statements like I love you.

E. Hemingway, War Correspondent.

September 13th after dinner
My Beloved:

This is only a note to tell you how much I love you. We have had dinner and there was nothing spiritous to drink—the celebration haveing out-cleaned us yest. and no new alcoholic centers taken. There are lots of troops around tonight and can sleep without challenging (or throwing one's true love out of bed). Stevie is writing his girl a masterful letter about how American Women Do Not Appreciate What A Soldier—A Man Trained to Kill—goes through and Expects in Return—and reading me excerpts and I am just happy and purring like an old jungle beast because I love you and you love me. I hope you were quite serious Pickle because I am as committed as an armoured column in a narrow defile where no vehicle can turn and without parallel roads. I am committed horse, foot, and guns—so take good care of you for me, and for us and we will fight the best one we, or anyone, could ever fight—for what we spoke about—and against loneliness, chickenshit, death, injustice, ununderstanding sloth (our old enemy), substitutions, all fear, and many other worthless things—and in favour of you sitting up straight in bed lovelier than any figure head on the finest, tallest ship that ever drew on canvas or heeled over to a wind; and in favour of kindness, permanence, loveing each other and fine loveing nights, and days, in bed. Pickle I love you very much and am your partner, friend, and true love.

It is not so cold tonight but the poor dog is so sad. I try to explain about things to him but the dog knows he should handle the cattle and the pigs and loves his master. He knows I'm good but all his world is gone to pieces and he lies out in the barn and is heart-broken. I've had the cows milked so they do not hurt and fed the cat. But it is very sad about the dog. Have had the place all cleaned up (though that will not last)—but I wish the people would come back and take care of their dog. They are worthless and selfish to go away like that and don't deserve such a fine dog. They only had two books—one on Wild Beasts of Germany—a nice book—and one on the Olympic Games in Berlin in 1936. Not a nice book but with some lovely pictures. Have read them both and cursed the Brazilian tonight to his face for a fool and an imposition. He is like a little child who wants to ride in a racing motor car and then wants the car to stop in the race so he can make pee-pee.

Dearest Mary. . . . Please love me very much and always and take care of me Small Friend the way Small Friends take care of Big Friends— high in the sky and shining and beautiful. Oh Mary darling I love you very much.

PH. PUL

To PATRICK HEMINGWAY, Divisional Headquarters near Hemmeres, Germany, 15 September 1944

Dearest Mousie:

It has been about 2 months since Papa came back to France after landing on D Day on Omaha beach.[1] Suppose you saw that piece in Colliers. After that flew with R.A.F. as I wrote you and then came over to France and have been with an Infantry Division ever since except for the time that commanded a French Maquis outfit (while temporarily detached from being a correspondent) that was the best time of all but can't write you about it but will have to tell you. Was under *same* service Bumby is in now [OSS]. It is lovely story and we need never have any long dull winter evenings until you all get sick of hearing it. We entered Paris with outfit, liberated The Travellers Club, the Ritz etc. and had wonderful time. I had to write a couple of pieces and try to get them passed and then rejoined Division. We went way to the north and then East and the Division has done wonderful job and have been very happy to be with them. We have had some tough times and some wonderful times.

Haven't heard from Marty since letter dated in June. Saw all her friends in Paris and she could just as well have been there and through all that wonderful advance and fight if she had not been such a Prima-Donna that she would not wait one week. As it is she may have made the Southern Landing in which event she will have OK story. . . .

Head is all cleared up. Beat the headaches (the skull was hurt etc) and got down to 202 and thin and brown and head working fine. Only thing bad, as I wrote you, are eyes from so much dust etc. but they will be OK with changed glasses.

Mouse I miss you and the Old Man [Gregory] and Bumby all the time and think a lot about our fine times to come. Have not heard from the old Bum since this last business started but his Colonel promised me to find out about him and I left word at the Ritz he could use my room if he turned up. We have had very hard fighting yest and today but that is to be expected and everything goes as it should. Am writing with the noise of the counter attack going on. I can't write you details but once the campaign is over I will. You will be very proud of what the Division has done and I have never been happier nor had a more useful life ever. Am saveing the maps and we will put them up in the trophy room.

Thought I should write you about Marty so you would know what the score is. Am completely disgusted with her attitude in Cuba, in London, and have only had one letter from her since leaving London describing the beauties of Jock Whitney's garden and how lovely it was to walk through a beautiful, quiet un-warlike city like Rome. May be she has written others and I hear Jock is a Prisoner of War. But we would be prisoners several times every day if we didn't use our heads and those two egg shaped glands we had all the trouble getting down. Also since we have been fighting wondered why the hell had stood being bullied so long. Love: Ball room-Bananas.

In Paris I only had two days semi-free but saw old friends like Sylvia Beach and Picasso and had two fine walks. It cost $100 to take six people to lunch at a moderate restaurant so usually we cooked on a gas stove in room at the Ritz.

When I was in such bloody awful shape in London—have to sleep flat on back with tins on each side because head would go if it turned sideways Capa's girl Pinkie was awfully good to me and so was another fine girl named Mary Welsh. I saw her again in Paris and we had fine time. Think you would like. Have nicknamed [her] Papa's Pocket Rubens. If gets any thinner will promote to Pocket Tintoretto. You will have to go to Metropolitan Museum to get the references. Very fine girl. Looked after me in worst time ever had.

Mouse, my boy, if we last through next two weeks we will have a wonderful life.

Right now have lost my Burberry rain-coat (it rains all yest) have a battle jacket with the zipper broken held together by safety pins, wear same two shirts worn last two months, both at once, have head cold, chest cold, trouble on both flanks, shelling the Bejesus behind, shelling the ditto ahead, counter attack on our right, what-all on our left and never felt happier. Except wish had some nosedrops for head cold. Am drinking some kind of strange German Schnapps and it looks like will be fine day tomorrow.

Will you pass on to Giggy any of this he is grown up enough to take —and work hard be good guy (you are) and love Papa and know he loves you and will see you in N.Y. before Christmas and we will all be together. If headmaster asks tell him Papa actually *Did* go abroad and to various countries there. Best love Moose

PUL   Papa

1. EH did not land on Omaha Beach. The seeming implication that he is saying he did is the result of his omission of *the* before the word *landing*. 2. For MG's side of this, see EH to Mary Welsh, 31 July and 1 August 1944, note 4.

To COLONEL CHARLES T. LANHAM,[1] Paris, 8 October 1944

Dear Buck:

Got your letter last night. Had to go to 3rd Army to be interrogated by I.G. on the Rambouillet incident which had become subject of allegations by correspondents and also received protests by neutral powers signatories of Geneva Convention.

Allegations were that commanded troops, removed insignia, defended town, ran patrols, had full Col as chief of staff, and other crap.

I.G. very sound and understanding. Beat rap by explaining that when troops (be damned if they were troops then but they were later) placed themselves under command refused command explaining impossible war correspondent command troops due to Geneva Convention. When, in emergency troops (sic) later insisted command them explained again could not command but would give them benefit of my advice so long as this advice did not contravene the Geneva Convention.

All other raps on same basis. Send you a couple of funny papers on same but do not show to anyone and keep for me.

You know how I feel about not being with you today or any other damned day. But they would have put me in the can if I had not come. See Enclosure.

Now cleaning up and then will be back. Have it beat good. Or beaten well to speak English.

If anything else comes up (one allegation by correspondents was that I acted as a show-off and impeded, repeat *impeded*, forward advance of troops), I could use a letter from you on my general character and conduct as it seems to you. Never strain yourself on this. If you want to send it address is EH War Correspt. APO.887 COMZONE CARE PRO HQ U.S. Army. If you have any time, which you haven't might write it. Excuse shameful address.

I'm sorry your wife has been worried. I can understand it. Mine never is. She thinks we do it with mirrors.

Wrote a fine poem a couple of times wakeing in the night and sitting on the can. Will show you.

Only ameliorateing circumstance about kid [Bumby] jumping with fish rod is jumped in Jura mts. where knows good streams. After job done could fish. Anyway way could fish supposed be German (very blond kid speaks perfect French ok German). Now in Voges his Col likes him very much. In funny racket had good fight kraut patrol last week. If could do what want to do would see him. His Col offered send him Paris see me but we both knew no and I said no. Col complains he so goddamned military. Can't have any contact with him. Unlike his old man. I was once like that too but that was in another country and beside the wench is dead.

Buck I miss you very much. I feel like a swine here while you fight. I only send paper so you see if you had recd that same damned paper you would have had to be here too. Am quite bitter about some things. But that is another piece of baggage we can not afford.

Have some luck and if anything ever happens to us we will all have a fine time with the better element in hell.

PUL   Ernie

1. During the third week in August, EH detached himself from Lanham's regiment and division for service with the OSS command of Colonel David Bruce between Rambouillet and Paris. After Paris was liberated, he rejoined Lanham at Pommereuil, 3 September, returned to Paris for an interlude with Mary Welsh, then moved into southern Belgium with the Twenty-second Infantry Regiment. For details, see Carlos Baker, *Ernest Hemingway: A Life Story* (New York, 1969), pp. 401–26.

To MAXWELL PERKINS, Paris, 15 October 1944

Dear Max:

Will you please send a check for $52.50 to the Philadelphia Gun Club 1807 Fidelity-Philadelphia Trust Building—Philadelphia, Pa. Have no checks here. Left my check book in London.

We've had quite a hell of a time since I wrote you last. I was with the 4th Infantry Division from the breakthrough above St. Lo until they were temporarily in support on Aug. 18 and I got mixed up with a Maquis outfit. After some very interesting times, straight out of [John Singleton] Mosby [Confederate Cavalry], we entered Paris with very first troops. Liberated the Travellers Club and the Ritz the first afternoon. Finest time ever had in my life. Then rejoined Division. Gen. [Barton] had loaned me a jeep for the Paris campaign and we'd picked up the damndest lot of transport (mostly German) you've ever seen. I then made the rat race campaign in which we went way north, then pivoted East and ended up with the assault on the West Wall and then holding what we'd taken.

Have stuff for wonderful book. Have been with every action of the Div. since just before the breakthrough and if have good luck a little longer want to lay off and get to work on the book. Want to write novel —not war book. It should have the sea and the air and the ground in it.[1] Had the sea ready to write when came over. Then had that time with R.A.F. Now have had the rest of this. Have written two long poems[2] so there would be something around to cover what has happened up until now if had any bad luck.

I got sort of cured of Marty [by] flying. Everything sort of took on its proper proportion. Then after we were on the ground I never thought of her at all. Funny how it should take one war [Spanish Civil War] to start a woman in your damn heart and another to finish her. Bad luck. But you find good people in a war. Never fails. Awful lot of things happen to them though.

Would like to talk to you Max but no good writing letters.

Best to Charley and all the guys. If you get me back you've got a very valuable property because we hit very fine pay dirt on this last prospecting trip.

PUL   Ernest

1. EH's earliest allusion to the sea-air-land book which preoccupied him for the next ten years, resulting in *The Old Man and the Sea* (1952) and *Islands in the Stream* (1970). 2. "To Mary in London" and "Second Poem to Mary," *Atlantic Monthly* 216 (August 1965): 94–100.

To HENRY LA COSSITT,[1] Hürtgen Forest, Germany, 16 November 1944

Dear Henry:

You never asked me to name a beneficiary for the insurance Colliers took out for me. I hereby name Mary Welsh of Life and Time Inc., 4 Place de la Concorde as sole beneficiary of this insurance revoking by this letter any previous beneficiaries that may have been named.

My wife Martha Gellhorn Hemingway entered into a mutual property agreement before leaveing New York and she has been fully provided for.

In addition to the money Colliers has advanced me I have spent $3950.00 of my own money on Expenses for Colliers. Will you please send $1500 of this to my wife Martha G. Hemingway since she advanced it to me and deposit the balance in my account in the Guaranty Trust Co. of N.Y., Fifth Avenue Branch N.Y.C.

Yours very truly

PH. PUL   Ernest M. Hemingway

1. Editor, *Collier's* magazine.

To PATRICK HEMINGWAY, Hürtgen Forest, 19 November 1944

Dearest Mouse:

The above [APO 757] is latest permanent address—when you get this write there once and then the next thing I'll be calling up school from N.Y. Get your passports okeyed by Mrs. Shipley so we can take off for Cuba. Please ask Mother [Pauline] to send Gigi's passport to get Mrs. Shipley's OK and as soon as I know when can be there will give her the dates. Write me vacation dates so can apply for PanAm passage.

Mousie I rely on you, *no matter how busy*, to see that the Passports are in order and write me the vacation dates. Soon as I know that and when I know my dates can get a cable relayed to Mother.

Had hoped to get back for Thanksgiving but couldn't swing it. Regret very much as we would have had fine time together.

Couldn't cable you direct but Hank Gorell put my name in a couple of stories last few days so if you saw them in World Telegram or NY Post you would know how we were doing. We are in the middle of a terrific damned battle Mousie—that I hope will finish off the Kraut Army and end the war—and I cannot leave until our phase of it is over. That is why I didn't get back and I couldn't tell you before hand. Then I got in some trouble accused of commanding irregular troops (allegations of various correspondents). These allegations were proved to be false since it would have been impossible for me to command irregular troops since that would have been a violation of the Geneva Convention. I had explained this situation to these troops and when they insisted on placing themselves under my command I again explained it was impossible since it would be a violation of the Geneva Convention but that I would be glad to offer my advice and criticism in-so-far as these did *not* violate the Geneva Convention. Anyway it came out all right.

We've had a tough time Mousler. Very tough. Now tougher than ever.

But after this one am going to drag down, get to Cuba, fix up grounds (trees blown down by hurricane), get in good shape, and write book— have to write book. The Mart [Martha] wants to stay on in Europe. Good chance she will end up a Dutchess I mean Duchess—we don't fight anymore. Once I was gone she wanted back very much. But we want some straight work, not be alone and not have to go to war to see one's wife and then have wife want to be in different war theatre in order that stories not compete. Going to get me somebody who wants to stick around with me and let me be the writer of the family. Since childies have to be in school am not going to be lonely to die and not able work.

Later—Mouse big fight today in Forest. Forest about same as back of ranch in Clark's Fork [Wyoming]—trees as thick as thickest. Plenty big deer that trip the trip flares at night and get shot—haven't seen any boar yet. But many hare, fox and deer. Last C.P. was in a hunting lodge with many good heads. Lots of wild pigeon too. Don't see many other birds as in coniferous there are really only those big black cock and higher there would be ptarmigan. I haven't seen any grouse or wood cock yet. But they would spook off with all the noise. The favourite game is the cow. In the open I watch the fall of the cow with the eye of an eagle. Mark him (her, rather) on the map with co-ordinates and the next day we butcher out the tenderloin. Once the cow is subjected to the fire of artillery my eye never leaves her. Place the cow under the hideous ravages of bombing I never lose sight of her. If our own, or enemy tracers cross the landscape, I look instantly to see if cow is in their path. Today we ate the tenderloin of the tragic cow of the opening of the offensive. She had been hung 4 days in the basement of where we live while house rocked with shelling. I ate 5 steaks garnished by the excellent German raw onion and washed down by Brandwein and water. Then, stomach-happy, I proceeded into the forest where the ferocious Kraut did his best to do away with us. But a man fed on cow cannot lose.

Mousie cannot remember any good advice or sound maxims to send you.

I know shooting in France, except partridge, which is fine but quickly over—will be on the bum for some time. I intend to make a reconnaissance in Kenya and Tanganyika to see how it is and if OK move there. Time is short for all us guys. From Africa, with modern plane service, we can shoot the pigeon circuit in Europe if there is any such. They are racing in France already and pigeon shooting will be next to be re-established altho I don't think, to be any good really, until Tourist movement starts again. Not U.S. Tourists. Internal.

Moose don't know what else to write. Paris beautiful but still bad chow situation. Bicycle racing going on. Very fine new riders. Harry's Bar open—but only at 5 pm and no whiskey nor any but phony gin. Papa still living at Ritz (joint we took) when back in town. Town so lovely but with the exchange 50 to 1 dollar (when really worth about 200 francs to 1 dollar) that very terribly expensive. None of the great pictures on exhibition. Lots of fine new *very* fine pictures by Picasso and other good painters. Under Krauts painters had nothing to do but stay home and paint. Worked out quite well. Made fine pictures. No oysters yet at Prunier's. It will need a year or so at least to straighten out properly.

Mouse excuse worthless letter. Today very busy day up in the woods—awfully sorry to miss Thanksgiving—But lately we've been missing pretty much everything. But we will get it all back with interest. You have the passports fixed—write me vacation dates day you get this.

Much love
Papa—

PUL

To MARY WELSH, Paris, *c.* 6 March 1945

Dearest Pickle:

I love you always and always will. Now go to get our life started. Don't let anything bother you. I'm sorry to be so sticky getting off. Will be wonderful when I see you and will be truly faithful to you every minute I am away. In my heart in my head and in my body.[1]

Your loving husband

PH. PUL Mountain

Love letter to Miss Mary to read with breakfast (it starts to be a love-letter ½ way through)
[EH here drew a large heart with an arrow through it, labeled "Cheyenne valentine."]

1. This is EH's farewell note to Mary before leaving by plane for New York and home.

To COLONEL CHARLES T. LANHAM, La Finca Vigia, 2 April 1945

Dear Buck:

Was fine to hear from you. I had the news from Whitey Gates in Paris day before I left. Had sent you a long letter by hand through same officer who had brought me your note and the carbine and ammo for which am very grateful. I instructed this officer to deliver the letter to you *personally* and it's sure he did not get back before you were gone so maybe you never got it. I left Paris on March 6. Flew the [deleted] in a bomber. Uneventful except for a battle fatigued radio bloke who got the screemies a couple of times. (He'd been in the drink at one time and being over water impressed him). When I explained to him that become-ing excited accomplished nothing good he said, "But you can't understand. *I'm going home to be married.*" I told him I wasn't figureing on going home to be buried myself.

I called Pete [Mrs. Mary Lanham] from the airport but no answer. Also tried her mother's. Proceeded to N.Y. and continued to call from there. When finally got through to her it was wonderful—like talking to someone I had known all my life. She was just as wonderful as you had said. Made me feel as though I were one of her very best and oldest friends.

She was sweating you out bad. Has been for a long time. I told her how absolutely necessary it was at the time for you to have picked up your attack that time when it was breaking down (Schnee Eifel) and how sound and sensible you had been ever since. I also told her you were plenty beat up for a while but that your resiliency always pulled you back again wonderfully. Also told her many fine things about you that won't repeat and how much you loved her and missed her and depended on her.

Transportation very difficult at home. Pat's and mine came through at nine at night to leave for Miami next morning so I couldn't go to Washington to see her. But truly it was very good on the telephone. We'll all be together sometime. And not too far away. That Mss. was in my censor sealed stuff I couldn't break seals on so will mail it or bring it up next time come north.

Am glad you are with the 104th. I know the CG [commanding general] and Jim Eastman, one of his aids, is a good friend of mine.

It is a hell of a thing going away from the 22nd [Infantry Regiment] tho. It probably sounds wet but I was, and am, absolutely homesick for the regiment and I miss you very badly Buck. I don't give a damn about writing. Will have to get over that. I guess I will. Have gotten over everything else.

Certainly have the Black Ass [depression] today. Miss Mary so much it makes me sick. Always before we had our Double Deuce [Twenty-second Infantry Regiment] problems and some sort of fight going on when I was away from her and I had your companionship. Now today the kids are gone back to school. I don't know how long it will be before I see her. (She couldn't get back by air.) So am being black assed and temperamental—and no Grosshau to go to [to] take my mind off things.

I'm sorry you had to defend me against that CS whoever he was. Don't go in for defending me. It's a lifetime job. And when, in nature of my trade, have to deny anything good ever do under oath there's no future in it. You'll hear I'm a phony, a liar, a coward, maybe even a Man of Honor. Just tell them to Eff off. Remember when we would have to keep the door of the trailer open to keep track of the small arms fire around the CP? I was telling a Marine Col. about that Hürtgen fight and I could see him starting to not believe me. So I just shut up. General attitude seems to be, "Well if you *really* were up around where that sort of thing was going on (*which we doubt*) why haven't you any decorations?"

You couldn't stand it away from the front for 2 days. I always liked it in Paris because knew I was always going back and so tried to have as much fun as possible and never had any guilty feeling because knew where we came from and what we did. Now I just feel homesick, lonely and useless. But will pull out of it. *Because have to.*

Also have cut out heavy drinking to make that a present to Mary when she comes and since Liquor is my best friend and severest critic I miss it. Also have explained to my old girls there is nothing doing—and this light drinking, righteous Life isn't comparable to always haveing at least two bottles of Perrier Jouet in the ice bucket and the old Kraut Marlene [Dietrich][1] always ready to come in and sit with you while you shave—and going to see Mary come into the [Ritz] Bar at noon—and the rest of it. OK. Let's stop this Black ass stuff. The son of a bitch is home. He's out of it. He ought to be happy. He isn't. When Mary comes it will be different. I'll just try to use this dull time to get in good shape for her and to work.

Both kids are fine. No new word on Jack [Bumby].[2] But have hunch [he] will be O.K.

Am so glad you are happy where you are. Hope the [general's] star comes through quickly and then that you have a Division. Am very selfish in this because figure once you have a Division there will be that liquor ration and I will come and drink it for you (thus saveing you from any possibility of rummy-hood) and I can run errands and do any odd jobs the Geneva Convention authorizes such as entertaining Gen. Rodwell when he calls (I'll have my own trailer) and all the time will be working on my new Great Book YOU TOO CAN BE A GENERAL with all its exhaustive studies in Rummyhood and Its Effect on the General. Bourbon or Scotch—Their Effect on the General. The Fear of God—Its Effect on the General. The Fear of Death—Its Effect on the General. Psycho-analysis—Its Effect on the General. Map Reading For Generals. Security or Sleep—A Problem In Generalship. Hormones For The General—Their Use and Abuse. All this time I will be giveing you my almost pathetic devotion with one hand and booby trapping your trailer with the other. It is the only career I really look forward to. So don't just bog down in your military career because we ought to get started.

So long Buck. Have to stop this letter somewhere. Wish could see you. When Mary comes down here we can let her kill a Boogie instead of a Kraut. Tell her it's a very dark Kraut from somewhere in the Schwartz-wald—get him now before he gets away. (It will be the Butler.) Give Pete my love. I got cheered up writing to you.

Ernie

Place will be OK. Lost all best mangoes but re-planting. Boat OK.

My best to any of the mob. Pete got the perfume O.K. I made all the calls time permitted.

Now you over-running Krauts could [you] possibly get me 2 P38s[3] for the Kids?

PUL

1. EH and Miss Dietrich, whom he nicknamed the Kraut, had first met in 1934 aboard the *Île de France*, westbound. 2. John (Bumby) Hemingway had joined the OSS in July 1944, parachuted into Occupied France, and was wounded and captured in late October in the Rhône Valley. After being hospitalized in a POW camp near Hammelburg, he was liberated, recaptured, and sent to Stalag Luft III in Nuremberg, from which he was released in May 1945. He came to the Finca early in June. 3. Walther 9-mm (Luger) automatic pistol P-38.

To MARY WELSH, La Finca Vigia, 9 April 1945

Dearest Pickle:

It's a month and three days since I saw you last, my dearest love, and this fine imitation of purgatory and limbo and those other whistle stops is building up on me. Children left a week ago yesterday. Today is an absolutely perfect, cool day; but with fine sun and high clouds and everything looks fresh and new and lovely.

Yesterday there was a fiesta in the village with wonderful music and all the country people in on their horses and riding races in the street and tilting at rings. Lots of rockets and general festivities. They opened the shooting season at the Club but I decided I can't stand those people and that it was bad for me and bad for us and the pigeon is not the kraut—so didn't go. Invited Graciella Sanchez and her daughter out to play tennis and we played 3 sets. Then everybody was gone and I was alone and read the life of Nathan Bedford Forrest and did Infantry problems until went to sleep with the Capeheart on and then woke and took two sleeping tablets (had played the last two nights before without them), and couldn't sleep. So what? So it won't be forever. And we've been in worse places than this and I ought to get so I can be alone. But can't. I never want anyone but you. But I miss you as though they had cut my heart out with one of those things you take the cores out of apples.

Am haveing all mattresses and cushions on the boat re-covered. There's only one material in all of town. So we'll have to like it—or wear special glasses that will make it look good. Anyway have the old green covers and the old white covers so if we can't stahnd it. Can put them back. Have also practically re-built the foreward cock-pit and done a big job on fixing canvas where house joins the wind shield and various places storm and stress hadn't helped. There are some damned interesting things going on in the ocean. A new species of shark has turned up in 600 fathoms in great quantities. They have no fin on their back (dorsal); are black; with a horrible ugly mouth and their stomachs are full of swordfish swords, marlin bills and they eat each other if you don't get them right in. Also one of the Cojimar fishermen caught a Great White Shark that weighed 7,000 (seven thousand) pounds. Now if you should hook into a shark weighing 7,000 pounds the first time we ever go out in the boat daughter I think it would be a terribly unequal contest and that we ought to protest to the Geneva Conventioners. The biggest shark I ever caught weighed 798 pounds and even a tiny fish of that sort offered considerable resistance. I think on a 7,000 pound shark there would be some doubt as to who had hooked who. Really Pickle if you and I should tie into something of that sort believe it would hold your interest. This shark didn't consider himself hooked, and paid no attention for a long time except to come up alongside of the boat and stick his head out of water and click his jaws at people. Hope that little machine Fred was sending will arrive so we can make some fitting response if he goes into that jaw clicking routine. Click right back at him.

Have found a fine place where we can go and fish for sharks and sell them for a good price. Ought to be able to pay our boat expenses that way and actually the shark is as much fun to do away with as the kraut with added advantage can dispose of same afterwards.

Had a letter from Hadley giveing Bumby's address. He should be overrun [rescued from POW camp] by now or very soon. Won't that be wonderful? We mustn't count on it. But it is the logical thing to expect.

My it feels wonderful to have a typewriter again. (That was just an interpolation.) I wrote Hadley a long letter this morning. I told her I'd ask you to call her up and give her the dope on Bumby. You don't have to Pickle if you don't want to. Excuse me if I am stupid. But I couldn't get her on the long distance from N.Y. And she would like to hear about me and about Bumby. Her address is care of Mrs. Elizabeth Heath, 270 S. Western Avenue, Lake Forest, Illinois. Paul [Mowrer] has gotten to Paris and she is selling, packing, giveing away and getting ready to join him. She has been sweating both Bumby and me out. She wanted to know about us and I wrote her. How much I loved you and how I was going to try to be a good husband and a good writer. If I am a good husband will be a good writer. Good writer takes time. Good husband can start. Have started. Haven't heard from Mouse nor Gigi since they left but that is normal.

Wish it would rain a little before you come. I like the brown way it looks, like Africa, but it would bring out all the flowers if it rained. I think you will love this country Pickle. I see it all now with your eyes.

I know the things that gave us both great pleasure to see in Paris. Remember the early fall Paris and the Ile de la Cite and the wonderful snow days in the Tuilleries? The day you made an angel? Of all the cities I have ever seen anywhere I think this is one of the loveliest. And when I have you will see everything fresh and new again.

You know Buck's Infantry book is marvellous. So cold, sound, unprejudiced (except in favour of comman sense) O (how do you spell comman? It looks awfully funny that way.) All my life I've looked at words as though I were seeing them for the first time: Coman, Commen, Comman, Common, (that's got it) sense. He can write a wonderful new one with all that we have learned. I wish I could hire [Ludwig] Bemelmans, [James] Thurber, and Buck (military) to write what I have learned instead of haveing to write it myself. But will have to write by myself finally and make it better than ever for my Pickle.

Did you know that Nathan Bedford Forrest (great cavalry leader of Confeds) had only six months formal schooling in his life and no military experience nor military education until he was 40? That's why they try to keep the lodge so exclusive. Also been re-reading about Mike Ney.[1] You know Pickle—he was not only a terrible fighting man—he was a very good man.

Have gotten you a lot of lovely books and there is a humming bird that lives quite near and comes every day to the bougainvillea. Little house is fixed up so you can have it if you want it. Is very nice. No childnies come until the end of June. By then you'll have the Bohio. Boat should be all fixed by this Thursday. Cook is wonderful. I know what he does good now and he is a great artist and sits in kitchen all day long cutting radishes and onions into artistic compositions. And keeps cleanest kitchen you ever saw. He knows nothing about salad dressings but you can show him that. The fifty year old parrott suddenly got furious about something last Friday when the pelota players were out here and started to shout (in Spanish), "I'm sick of it. I'm going to take the bus to Havana." One of the boys said something rude to him and the parrot said, "Shut up you Fairy." He's a long way away from the pure Polly wants a cracker type of parrott. I think what he wants is sunflower seeds. But probably only knows their name in chinese. The chinaman says he can't understand the parrott's chinese at all. But maybe the parrott speaks Mandarin and the chinaman Cantonese. I let him out now and he flies around the house. He can imitate a cat fight beautifully.

Pickle I hope to God I hear today or tomorrow that you've arrived and then there's a more or less definite time until I see you. In the meantime when you read this know I love you. I must write Woolfie [Guest] now and then write Mousie and Gig. Writing you is a selfish pleasure. Writing other letters is discipline to get back in writing shape. Letters, simple story, complicated story, novel. That's the program. If you want her changed we will change her.

Your

Bear Mountain.

PH. PUL

1. Michel Ney (1769–1815), Napoleon's general and one of EH's heroes. See *A Moveable Feast* (New York, 1964), p. 30.

To MARY WELSH, La Finca Vigia, 14 April 1945

My Dearest:

This morning wrote seven letters and have one for you to mail but am so cockeyed lonely for you write now again. It's twenty five minutes to five.

Wrote Giggy, Buck, Pauline, Max Perkins, and business letters. Also have put a thousand bucks in a saveings account for Tom [Mary's father]. Don't tell him so he won't get nigger rich.

Dr. Jose Luis Herrera who is a fine brain surgeon and did thousands of operations on the head when he was chief surgeon for our old 12th Int. Brigade was out today and we had lunch by the pool. He has been studying my head. What should have been done was open and drain the original hemmorage (from 1st concussion). But that was impossible on acct of me haveing to lie about it and deny the concussion on acct. [of] D. Day. The second one, it seems was very bad for it. A lot of the things we took as just unlovely (and they certainly were unlovely) traits were symptoms. Brandy, for instance, is a definite poison when your head is like that. Champagne does very little harm. Almost none. Wine, unless too heavy, neither. But the slowness, loss of verbal memory, tendency to write backhand and backwards and the headaches, condition Mr. S[crooby] was in and the inertia, headaches and ringing in the ears were all symptoms of what had been done to head. Everything will clear up and be fine but he says have to take it easy, not worry about it at all, and let everything recuperate same way other things did. But remember how it was always either Brandy or the poison gin that made me not myself. He said it was a miracle kept going at all. (He is not a bit romantic and knows me for ten years and all my faults.) Says I should have had three months convalescence after the London incident (had four days in bed and put the blue [RAF] clothes on [on] the fifth) and by all rules would have been liable to bad cerebral hemmorage after the August 5 business.

He says we have it whipped now and I won't have any more headaches and that you and me should just take care of head for a while and train it slow and good. Do some intellectual work each day and not too much and will be better than ever because will know more. But it seems Pickle that it was pretty bad. So that's the Gen as of now. Nothing to be worried about. All up to date. But have had 5 concussions in a little over two years. Which is not the way to treat what you make your liveing with. But we know, from poem, that she is still a fine instrument and we will bring her into form again good. I know that truer than I know anything.

Also we will have a lovely time recuperateing and I cannot wait to share all the fine world with you. Am so much better than have ever been since you've known me that please don't think of me as a hypo-chrondrious or something just because have tackled this to work it out all same as any problem for Buck, say. Really, have gone into it in absolutely impersonal way. No D-Day H-Hour. No favours asked nor given.

Dearest Pickle suppose you were here tonight and instead of me going into town now in a couple of hours to have dinner with Graciella [Sanchez] who is such a nice girl but with all the difference between a battle and manouevers, We, us, you and me, were going to the chinese restaurant and then either to the fights or the Jai-Alai and a good night club afterwards (a bad night club I mean) and then really sleep and tomorrow swim in the pool with the new drink-holding, floating tray and get out on the ocean, or fly somewhere, or play the Capeheart or whatever. Please write when your reservations are. Yest. killed the 13th. Today the 14th. It's thirteen more to the 27th. And we'll kill them too. But I'd much rather be liveing them with my true love.

Old Mountain Man.

PH. PUL   E. Hemingway

To COLONEL CHARLES T. LANHAM, La Finca Vigia,
14 April 1945

Dear Buck:

How are you; you old beat-up worthless general in waiting? Certainly miss the hell out of you.

Mary finally got to the states. Had a hell of a trip. She couldn't tell me why over the phone. So have thirteen more days of Limbo while she finishes N.Y. and sees her family etc. I've been trying to take care of her property and get it in shape. Cut out all drinking in the night; you know. When you wake up in the night and things are unbearable and you take a drink and make them bearable. So all morning drinking. My chest has cleared up and don't spit any blood anymore and haven't had the real headaches now for quite a while.

The old bad thing is I don't give a damn about writing and would rather be back with you. This goddamn boreing civil life is wonderful I know but I am bored right through the marrow of all the old bones. Will have to get over that and with Mary I can and I will.

Wish I knew your news, Buck. Don't quit writing, will you. Am rebuilding the boat for the uses of peace and comfort. Also doing hell of a job on the place. You know that damned storm blew 160 miles an hour (even if they lied it blew over a hundred) for twelve hours. Gregorio [Fuentes] ought to have been put in for something for sticking with the boat and saveing it. Instead just have to discipline him a little more so he won't get the idea we are still operateing on that *storm* basis. Can't have any heroes on a boat or the next thing there will be roaches.

Have re-read your Infantry In Battle. It is extraordinarily sound and good and what a hell of a book you can write along the same lines with the things we learned in this war. It has less bullshit in it than almost any military book have ever read. Most books read as though the Brazilius [a correspondent, 1944] had a hand in them somewhere. When we are old and worthless and have to be carried to the swimming pool by our aged retainers who will place the glass in our hand and wipe the scud out of our eyes let us re-write some of those tomes into English. Only thing I didn't like about the book was that magazine cover citizen with his BAR [Browning Automatic Rifle] on the cover. If you'd have had Kemper on the cover the way he looked above Grosshau nobody would have wanted to jine the infantry. What a trade Buck. What a terrible trade.

They talk about our Lord haveing a bad time on that tree and everyone in mourning for the death of the Chief Executive [FDR] but nobody has ever been anywhere that hasn't been with Infantry. Catch him, men. Sentiment is about to over-come him.

Will stop now as only object was to write you short letter to let you know always lonesome for you and for outfit. Know Mary would send her love if she were here. Soon she will be and I'll have her write and tell you what she thinks of the joint and the boat and how well I'll be behaveing (Let's hope to God). I will, really, because that is the one good fight I want to make. Will make it too. Have been absolutely faithful and have cut drinking by 90%. Only hope won't be snatched up to heaven in a cloud or something on account of being so goddamned good. Old friend of mine wants me to help her open a whorehouse. Have turned that down too in spite of fact would be lovely place to go in afternoons when bored. And imagine being bouncer in your own whorehouse. The better things of life certainly tempt a man.

Best always,
Ernie

Give my best to your general will you please? Also to Jim Eastman if you see him.

Send me a Patch from your Division will you Colonel so I can scare little children with it.

PUL

To MARY WELSH, La Finca Vigia, 16–17 April 1945

Dearest Pickle:

This is just a note so that you'll have some mail anyway. I counted on some sure this morning but none came. Maybe will get some tonight. Guess it is too early for the boat letters so must just be patient. Anyhow have now gotten through the 12th, 13th, 14th, 15th and there are only twelve more days to go. Today I'll get through the 16th.

Have some good news on your mountain property. Sat[urday] night dined with Graciela Sanchez and stayed out till about 2 a.m. at a cafe on the water front, drinking practically nothing, and talking about you. She offered to write you a letter to tell you how good am being. Woke in the morning feeling wonderful and decided would shoot to see how the reflexes were comeing on. Shot fast and very secure. Won 38 bucks. Beat twenty other shooters and was beaten finally in the shoot-off by a bird I killed dead and shot second barrel in so fast after the first one that knocked bird over the fence. Shooting is of no importance and I don't give it any importance and don't want to bore you with accts. of same. But it is a hell of a good sign in the way your property is comeing along. There was a big breeze and the birds fast.

Had Col and Mrs. [John] Hart to dinner and went to bed somewhere around midnight and made it without a sleeping pill.

Am going into town for lunch and Lord it a little tiny bit over the other shooters (with becomeing modesty). It was such good fun to make a comeback because they were all so delighted to see me a year out of practice and shooting so miserably. I know absolutely the writing will work out the same way. Three weeks ago anybody seeing me shoot pigeons would give you odds I'd never, never come back. And yesterday was faster than steel trap. Pickle you'll just have to have confidence in the writing thing. I know you will have.

You know I realize now I've saved 90 percent of this town and all the fun there is to do and have in it all my life for you. I think you will be crazy about it. If only we were liveing these days instead of just killing them waiting for you to get down here.

Tuesday April 17

Stayed in last night instead of going out to dinner because thought there might be mail. But there wasn't. And then was sure there would be some this morning. There had to be. Today was the 17th and you got in on the 12th. But guess what? There wasn't any mail.

So now I'm going out on the boat with Paxthe [Ibarlucia] and Don Andres [Untzain] and Gregorio [Fuentes] and stay out all day and then come in and I'll be sure there will be letters or a letter. And maybe there will be. If there aren't I'll be a sad s.o.a.b. But you know how you handle that of course? You last through until the next morning. I suppose I better figure on there being nothing until tomorrow night and then it won't be so bad tonight.

By now you should be in Chicago. It ought to be getting lovely now with the Spring. I'd like to meet you walking by the Lake.

Please write me Pickle. If it were a job you had to do you'd do it. It's tough as hell without you and I'm doing it straight but I miss you so could die. If anything happened to you I'd die the way an animal will die in the Zoo if something happens to his mate.

Will send this in with Juan. Much love dearest Mary and know I'm not impatient. I'm just desperate.

PH. PUL   E. Hemingway

To COLONEL CHARLES T. LANHAM, La Finca Vigia, 20 April 1945

Dear Buck:

Got your fine letter mailed April 3 two days ago and today the one you sent to APO 887 telling about the new job. What a ride to have missed. I would have given anything to have stayed as you know and did a very poor job of getting away as it was. But there really wasn't any choice. Unless I wanted to end up as a bum, which fine with me as long as I could bum with any outfit of yours, but it would disappoint hell out of Mary and wouldn't be fair to my kids. He done it for the wife and the kiddies. Also listen to the cry of the wounded Alibi Merchant: head was in bad shape.

Had a first class head king and he said three of them were bad. One very bad and should have been opened and drained. He was unable to see how I proceeded with my martial (sic) career but I explained to him that if my brain hadn't been seriously impaired would not of [have] undertaken the guidance of my French Lootwaffians and that my only other activity was sitting around in a trailer with you bullshitting which I could do with my brains in my hand. They found a lot of other things wrong with me too but nothing that you probably couldn't cure with a guillotine.

Anyway have been training good to be in good shape when Mary comes down on the 2nd. She's with her family in Chicago; bored, lonesome; but doing her duty after haveing been away for more than two years. I wrote you I'd cut out all drinking when wake in the night and all morning drinking. Have cut down about 90 percent. Also have been absolutely faithful. The latter is easy when you really love somebody. But not drinking is a goddamned bore. But since it is all I can do for the girl at the moment is what am doing. Love her very much want to be good guy for her.

My command now consists of the 1st, 2nd, 3rd, and 4th gardners, butler, maid, chink cook, and three small boys. I am not armed. However can scare the shit out of all of them by looking at them and the fact that I am not comfortably drinking and at peace with the world but instead up at first light seeing What Hasn't Been Done comes as a blow to all. So far I can't write worth a damn. But I never could after any war so am not worrying.

Am getting the place so you would never know it had been virtually destroyed if you hadn't seen it before. It is so damned lonely Buck without the kids, without Mary and without you and the outfit that it is bad. When Mary comes life can start. As it is am just killing days and wishing I were a soldier instead of a chickenshit writer. Old worthless wish.

Do you have any news from the outfit? If you do please let me know. You would be delighted by the phonies. The other night bellied up against the bar was a darb. He was telling all takers the worst, the absolute worst was the liquid fire. Oh Gawd, he said. Don't ask him to remember it even. I asked him politely what outfit was he in. Turned out to be the 15th airforce, suggested the improbability of him haveing encountered any flammenwerfers and told him his drink was paid for and he could leave the bar. But that is too expensive. Next time am just going to laugh. At the shooting club last Sunday one of the members said, they had evidently been haveing an argument, "Ernesto you were never actually under fire were you?" "Shit no," I said. "Do you think I'm crazy?"

I haven't met anybody been on less than sixty missions and the ground people have all slain more krauts than we ate K rations. Popular opinion seems to be fighting krauts is in the class with self abuse compared to fighting the terrible Nipponese who as I recall we used to slay with well intentioned and firmly disciplined Chinese in large and ill smelling numbers. Doubtless not their elite troops. Honestly, Buck I think you had a regiment, before Hurtgen, that could outfight any regt. in the world.

This is the time to sign off. We don't want to bore people. Take care of yourself and give Shugarth my best and tell him if he doesn't take care of you he better never fucking well run into me. Are his feet cleared up O.K.?

                    Best always Buck
                    Ernie
                         E. Hemingway (Writer and Farmer)

No word yet from my boy Jack. Other kids OK. Any dope on my Bro. [Leicester]?
PH. PUL

To HADLEY MOWRER, La Finca Vigia, 24 April 1945

Dearest Kat:

Thank you very much for the lovely letter. Hope you got hold of Mary and she could give you more gen about Bumby. She and I both knew his C.O. very well and I knew, eventually, most of his pals. I'd been helping his C.O. out on something just before Bumby had the bad luck. Wish could talk to you instead of write. If you get any news please cable me. In meantime only thing I've learned is that worry is absolutely worthless and helps no one. This from old time all weights champion worrier must have some value.

Isn't that old River Forest woman [EH's mother] terrible? Let's just cut her out of our lives and times. I don't know how I could have been whelped by her but evidently was. There must be some decent blood though somewhere because the Baron, kid bro. [Leicester], who or whom (never learned to handle those two) I always considered a violently useless character volunteered for Bumby's outfit and job the day he heard he had the bad luck. He wasn't qualified. So he got himself transferred from a good safe (comparatively) signal corps job to the same Infantry Outfit I'd been with since the breakthrough in July. It is awfully tough to go into your own Bros. outfit (also very stupid) and I pointed out to him all the disadvantages. But he was really only happy that way as long as the krauts had Bum.[1]

Don't worry about Paul and chow in Paris. Now that we have opened up Bordeaux and with transport steadily improveing in France the food problem will be o.k. Last winter was the tough time. If you get over this summer or fall it will be fine. I saw the house o.k. but naturally couldn't tell it had been looted. Passed it in a jeep, looking for a short cut, when we were moveing north from Paris. It must be awful haveing Paul away and breaking up your lovely home. I hate to leave Anywhere and to make a lovely home and then have to leave is awful. Except that you are going to Paris and that is still the loveliest place there is.

Mary and I lived at the Ritz (you might as well do it in style) and Dave Bruce and I had taken the joint shortly after liberating the Travellers Club. You should have seen it the first days with Archie Pelkey, my driver, cooking on a gas stove in front of the fireplace and the toughest looking bunch of bandits you ever saw cleaning their weapons on the nice delicate old furniture. Me, with three secretaries trying to turn out some non incriminateing account of Rambouillet and Capt. Stevie [Stevenson] from the outfit with a message from—well I'd better skip it. It was the wildest, most beautiful, wonderful time ever ever. You know you don't take Paris every day. Actually only a certain number of citizens have ever taken it. But the knowledge that we were historical never broke through the happiness of fighting back into that lovely town that the damned krauts thought they had for good. We liberated Lipps (old man gave me a bottle of martell) and then liberated the Negre de Toulouse. This is really funny. The French press had written us up quite a lot and I got a note from Monsieur Chautard [EH's landlord, 1924–1926] telling me Madame was dead and he had always thought of us with great friendship and would I have lunch with him! Couldn't because had to move on up North. But would have been nice. Think we should have crossed Madame Chautard with the pride of River Forest to produce a winner in any all time Bitchshow.

You were wonderful to write me such a fine letter. Wish I wrote better ones. As a war goes along I get so security minded that first I won't write, then I won't talk then I won't think. Then the next thing I can't write, can't talk, can't think.

Have to get cleaned up now to go into town. This liveing alone is bod. Should only have a week more of it now. I'm so sorry you have to go through such a long lousy time away from your mon. It's not the way people were made to live and how I hate to kill a day when I could live it. When there is only so much of this our one and only life.

Always dearest Katherine Kat get through everything as well as you can and then go to Paris and have a fine life and we will all meet there and eat at some fine restaurant and laugh and make good jokes. All the things wrong with me are getting better (I sound like a hypochrondrious. But really am not). Did I tell you about our 50 year old parrott that used to belong to Mr. Jim Stillman? When I was talking on the long distance he started to scream something and I couldn't make it out clearly then I realized what he was shouting was, "I can't stand to hear another goddam word of it."

Much love always from your old beat-up Tatie

PH. PUL

1. See EH to Col. Charles T. Lanham, 2 April 1945, note 2.

To THOMAS WELSH, La Finca Vigia, 19 June 1945

Dear Mr. Welsh:

Thank you very much for the three books and for the message you wrote on the fly leaf of Moses Creator of Jehova-God. I liked the books very much and welcome your information and study and the invitation to discuss the whole question. Would like to talk about the books when we meet.

If it is any use to you to know how war affects one man's religious faith this may help start our discussion which haveing had a finer time talking to your daughter Mary (talking occasionally) than I have ever had, I look forward to greatly. She also.

In first war (alleged World War) was really scared *after* wounded and very devout at the end. Fear of death. Belief in *personal* salvation or maybe just preservation through prayers for intercession of Our Lady and various saints that prayed to with almost tribal faith.

Spanish war seemed so selfish to pray for self when such things being done to all people by people sponsored by Church that never prayed for self. But missed Ghostly comfort almost the way a man who was accustomed to take a drink would miss it when he was cold and wet.

This war got through without praying once. Times a little bad sometimes too. But felt that haveing forfeited any right to ask for these intercessions would be absolutely crooked to ask for same no matter how scared.

All this could be considerably elaborated. Meantime all I can add is that I love Mary very much. I have been faithful to her since I first told her I loved her and will be until we can be married. My only ambition is to make her a good husband when we can be married and if you need a son around for any purposes ever please remember you have one. I have 3 and you can count on them too.

Who signs himself
Ernest Hemingway

but that you can call by name or initials or nickname.

PH. PUL

To MAXWELL PERKINS, La Finca Vigia, 23 July 1945

Dear Max:

Am afraid I haven't written you since the last accident. If I did then skip this. Had no bad effects on head, wound in forehead was deep but no fracture nor concussion. Left knee pretty badly hurt (cynoveal hemmorage) mis-spelled and still bothers a little (stiffens up). Chest ok now. Four ribs loosened from cartilage. Now o.k.

Was the first day of rain after an eight months drought on a hill where they had been hauling clay and the road as slippery as though it had been soaped. Bad luck. I had the butler tell the reporters etc. that it was nothing and that I had gone out fishing to hold the news down. But it was pretty bad. The wound in the forehead was from the rear view mirror, the metal part, and penetrated the bone without going through. I buckled the steering column with my chest. Was at noon and I was cold sober. Fourth bad smash in a year. Fortunately only two got into print.

Bumby has been here and gone. Is a nice kid. Hope you will see him. He went down to 160 pounds in prison but is back to 185 now. Escaped once. His wounds were bad but in a lucky place. They wanted to amputate his right arm but he argued them out of it and they took a muscle out of his back for drainage. He says only effect is to loosen up his [tennis] serve which was formerly too tight. He is going out again now. After he first jumped in he was six weeks behind the German lines organizeing resistance. Had some good fights. Was wounded and captured a month and a half later while with Third Inf. Div. in the Voges. We all had a lovely time together while he was here. Other kids are fine. Think Patrick will be a good painter.

Max will you please have the retail department pack and ship, shipping each book separately, one copy each of To Have and Have Not, Green Hills of Africa, Collected Short Stories (Modern Library edition smallest and most practical), Sun Also Rises, A Farewell To Arms (modern library edition preferable on acct. weight), also a copy of Dawn Powell's

A Time To Be Born and The Viking Book of Poetry (edited by Aldington) to Brigadier General Charles T. Lanham 015568, Headquarters 26th
Infantry Division, APO 26, care Postmaster, New York City, N.Y.

He is Buck Lanham my pal and partner and former Col of 22nd Inf.
Reg. now a B.G. and stuck all summer in Germany and very lonesome. He
is asst. Divisional commander now in the 26th. We were sort of partners
all through the rat race, the Schnee Eifel, Hurtgen and the defence of
Luxembourg and if anything ever happens to me you could get hold of
him to set straight any misconceptions about just what we were all doing
in this last war that people like Bunny [Wilson] etc. would like to set
going.

Buck thinks I am a much better guy than I am but his opinion, loaded
in one's favour, might go in the balance against Max Eastman and Bunny
W. and those of the guys who never fought and so denied us those simple
stupid virtues that we have. (This subject bores me.) But last year was a
hard year. What we learned from it may not show for a long time. Very
little of it was bought cheaply and really, Max, it probably isn't exactly
what the dr. would order for a good writer 45 [46] years old, with what,
when it is working right, is a good, delicate instrument. But I learned
more while Buck and I were together than I had learned altogether up
until then so I hope we will get some decent writing from it sometime.
Will try very hard.

Will you have them send me Bunny's book on Scott?[1] I feel badly not
to write anything about Scott when I knew him, possibly, the best of any
of them. But you cannot write anything true as long as Zelda is alive anymore than I can write with my bitch of a mother still able to read. When
I was lieveing with Georgie Wertenbaker's P47 group there was a man
named Jonah something or other (a preposterous name) maybe not even
Jonah; who gave me all the Gen on Scott's last time. He was with him
when he died etc. Also at the terrible thing with Sheilah [Graham]. He
never would have finished the book of course. It was more an outline to
draw advances on; a mock-up of a project than a book. That was why the
wonderful grandiloquence of it so impresses those people who are not in
the secret of how writers are. The Epic, as we know, is usually false. And
he pitched that at an Epic note that would be impossible for anyone to
sustain. It wasn't by accident that the Gettysburg address was so short.
The laws of prose writing are as immutable as those of flight, of mathematics, of physics. Scott was almost completely uneducated. He knew
none of the laws. He did everything wrong; and it came out right. But
geometry always catches up with you. I always feel that you and I can talk
truly about Scott because we both loved him and admired him and
understood him. Where other people were dazzled by him we saw the
good, the weakness and the great flaw that was always there. The

cowardice, the dream world that was not a late symptom as (reading the reviews Bunny seems to feel). He always had the dream of football greatness, war (which he knew *nothing* of) (The Sour Science) and when he couldn't walk across Fifth Avenue in traffic he thought, 'With what I *know* now what a great broken field runner I would be.'

Next time I'll write what was good in him. But we take it for granted people should be good. And in a horse, a regiment, a good writer I look for what is wrong. Take it for granted they are good or would not be looking at them.

Forgive long and stupid letter. Things have been a little bit difficult or I would have written sooner. Thanks for depositing the money. What money do I have now accrued? I feel the same about Charley Sweeny and Waldo [Peirce] as ever but this last year was so sort of bad that it just chopped you away from those you did not spend it with. Poor Charley must be very bitter seeing Leahy do what he is doing to Petain. I never liked Petain, neither as a general, a man nor a politician, and to have to remember exactly when you are 86, betrayed by your former accomplices, is a hell of a way to end.

You know Eisenhower has a hell of a good head and is a fine man. Many mistakes last summer and fall but a good man and a fairly good general. [Omar] Bradley a much better General I think probably as good as Sherman. Patton, if not such an impossible histrionic character and an unmitigated liar is an excellent General officer. It will be fun to read the shit that will come out after this war when they all publish their memoirs. It will be fun and it will be not fun too.

Oh well the hell with this nonsense. Please send the books to Buck, Max, and send me Bunny's and will write when get same. Best to you always and hope it is not a bad year for the hay fever.

PUL   Ernest

1. *The Crack-Up, with Other Uncollected Pieces, Notebooks, and Unpublished Letters of F. Scott Fitzgerald,* ed. Edmund Wilson (New York, 1945).

To MARY WELSH, La Finca Vigia, 1 September 1945

Dearest Pickle:

Hope you had a good trip with no off-loading. It was miserable luck to have to make it just when you did.

Thank you for the lovely going away note. Mine was very lousy. The other one holds.

Boisie and I missed you very much. He wouldn't have anything to do with me and just lay very sadly where you had been. He loves you very much and so do I.

One thing I didn't tell you about enough is the fine, wonderful hard work you did in Spanish. That was the main job you had to do and you did it beautifully and well.

I'm so sorry I was gloomy when you came back from town with the children. Could just as well have been gay and jolly and made my dear love happy instead of sad. I love you very much kitten and I want to take care of you and know that I will learn how to do it well.

Enclose a lovely Arturo [Suarez] sentence and a piece by D[orothy] Thompson who is maybe my least favourite columnist but who makes a very good point in favour of the stand you took that noon about the Lend-Lease cancellation. I think the cancellation was necessary but agree with you that the manner was rude and rudeness will lead us into trouble.

Whole house set-up is fairly worthless. Justo has had a sort of moral break-down. We don't really like the chinaman's food and instead of just haveing a sort of table d'hote of chinaman's designing with [which] a good, light, simple cook could knock off menu's for a week with aid of one of those meal-plan books the joint is full of, and have what we wanted and no more than we wanted. I was just useing chinaman as a stopgap and he *was* useful with that sort of chow to feed up the children who were under-fed and under-nourished. They have very good books of sound and pleasant and simple menus and can make them up for a week—or twice a week. (You probably know so much better ones than the books any-way.) But they have studied good pleasant meals in U.S. and it is fun, anyway for a while, to eat what you want and plan it. When you get bored with it we can let the cook work it out. Dureing war very hard to do any sort of meal planning as buying consists in going to the market and seeing what you can get and then makeing a meal of it. But we can sort of channel it. We both love good food and changes in food and we might just as well have fun with it. If you make out the menus we can get Pilar to translate them. All this just a partnership suggestion and if doesn't appeal to you the hell with it.

I get so tired of Viña Pomal and so lonesome for the lovely simple Paris restaurants where you could eat just what you wanted, in the amount you wanted and have the wine with it that you wanted. By next year we will have that I think. The main thing about France is going to be the necessity to adjust the exchange. You know I can write a book just as well in Paris as down here. This was just sort of a war-time thing. Nobody doomed to here. Can work in the Basque country, in Paris, any-where in the hills, in Spain (am only mentioning places where have worked good). The Finca is a lovely place when it's lovely (you've never even seen it in the months when people are supposed to enjoy the tropics rather than draw extra compensation for putting up with them) (they get that in the State Dept.).

For a year, anyway, Europe will be fairly bad. But France is such a rich country that as soon as communications are re-established it will come back very fast. She was really very little harmed. Normandy is dairy products and cider. Cider, of course, is 90 percent of all the alcohol that makes all the aperitifs. But we never drank them anyway. Just as long as the atomic bomb doesn't wipe out the Juniper berry you'll be o.k.

I'd have loved to come to Chicago. When you were talking about it I wouldn't play because I knew I couldn't and from war got bad and quickly useful habit of throwing away what you know you cannot have. I remember always how exciting it was when I was a kid and the Art Institute where I first saw pictures and made feel truly what they tried to make you feel falsely with religion and the old South State Street whore-house district where we used to go and Hinky Dink's the longest bar in the world and the beer cellars and Wurz n' Zepps and the crap games we gambled in on Saturday nights with me or Jack Pentecost handling dice for the money of all our gang and the cold rides in cars to play foot-ball and the feel of the field under your spikes when you came out fast to warm up and the noise of the crowd you never thought of or looked at or heard from then on, and the taste of hot-dogs with mustard and a pickle in a smooth laquered bun up at Northwestern when we would come out from swimming meets, and The Drake, which was Whites, Boodles and all Class its-self then, and further back going with my Grandfather to the theater in the afternoons, and with him and Gen Leonard Wood, and with him and Theodore Roosevelt with the hearty clasp and the high squeeky voice, and hot nights along the lake when I was poor in the summer after the war, and the boarding houses and the tenements we used to live in and when had money able to send out to the chinamen's for lovely food. Then we got tired of liveing dirty and five of us rented Mrs. Aldis's apartment, just off lake, was very nice and we had good cook and lived fine and could walk to work. When came back in 1928 the city was beautifully built up and fine new drives cut but everyone was stinko-rich (crash hadn't come then) and very self conscious about it. I didn't like it so much then but think it was maybe on acct. the boom and haveing lived in Paris a long time which was a civilized town then. Remember how impressed some Chicagoan was out in Wyoming because wore a locomotive engineer's cap and had Vuitton luggage which never seemed incongruous to me because L.E. cap best thing to wear driving in open car and Vuitton then (before air-travel made it too heavy) best and most dust proof and steal proof and smash proof luggage in the world. But they were awfully self conscious then. That was the year Hoover was elected. Never have been back except to bury my Father that same fall. Since, many times, I haven't gone because it would be rude to go and not see my mother and I can't stand to see her. Also have so many friends there that if did not see them all, each non-see-al would be an individual act of rudeness. But we will go sometime because it is a lovely city. Please have a lovely time in it. Wish was with.

Dearest Pickle you always say I write better letters than I talk or act but that is because, in spite of talking so much, I am faintly inarticulate and my conduct always falls behind my intentions or between two stools. This isn't a good letter but it is a long letter and to keep you company.

Mousie, Gigi and, from his actions, Boisie send love and I love you very much.

Your loveing husband

PH. PUL Papa

To MARY WELSH, La Finca Vigia, 4 September 1945

Dearest Kittner:

Juan just brought your telegram from the Ambos Mundos. Am so happy the trip was not bad and thank you for loveing me. I love you very much and miss you terribly.

There is not much news from the local doldrums. We got off on the Puerto Escondido trip and trolled all the way down there and all the way back without a single strike. (Hurricane weather knocking around.) Puerto Escondido was beautiful though, foliage like a [Henri] Rousseau jungle piece, it's a high limestone entrance, same formation and caves as back there in the hills, and we did not have a single insect although we were right in the river mouth. It was blowing hard when we went in but when the wind dropped there were no insects either.

Comeing back it was heavy rain and as cold as the first of fall. Skeins of ducks were flying south over the water and it really seemed the end of summer.

I started my non-night and non-morning drinking and haven't had one yet; nor will I. Boisie has finally adopted me again and sleeps in the same position he does with you. Any movement you make brings little sleepy protests from him.

Pancho is still working on a job in the Vedado but am starting putting in the big gutter that is to catch the rainfall and take it out over the end of the house where my room is and then pipe it to the big well. That well fills enough each day for the house use. Think with the water from the house can make enough reserve for the pool.

Am checking on Justo's financial deals and have instituted a book that everyone must sign whenever they receive any cash from him.

Also checking on the food racket. If could understand what the china-man says it would be simpler. Been paying bills etc.

Am seeing divorce lawyer this pm or tomorrow am. Hope they haven't changed the laws or anything. If had to go to Reno or Mexico it would be a nuisance. But would be glad to do it.

Yesterday was a cold, rainy depressing day and just worked all day so you aren't missing anything.

Had a long letter from Tubby Barton.[1] His squawk against Life was the caption Cherbourg Bastogne under the 4th Patch in that double page spread of patches. He wanted it to read Utah Beach—Cherbourg—Normandy—Paris—Siegfried Line (5 Times)—Schnee-Eifel—Hurtgen—Luxemburg. Haveing handed out injustice for a long time he seems oddly surprised to receive a little. Injustice is the normal state of life. Anybody cahnt learn to live with injustice probably thinks they should have pure oxygen for air. Half the time, too, if they had real justice we'd all be shot. Prefer a little mercy, not care about the records and be cheerful.

Hope you'll have good fun and it not be too gloomy. I know being loveing and nice to the family when they are so much older and so far removed in experience and knowledge of the world and of life is a long strain. But I know you will do it good and fine and make them very happy to have their beautiful, lovely, brilliant, loveing and successful daughter with them.

Some of the things like being humble and upper births are better than lower and anything better than the plane we can't go back to and plenty will irritate my dearest Pickle. But since you're doing it do it good and kindly. If it gets on your nerves and you don't really have any fun in Chicago I think it would be good maybe for you to go to N.Y. and see some shows and see [William] Walton and have some fun there before you come back and would be glad to send check for same. I wish we could have Walton come down here. Maybe he and the Kraut [Marlene Dietrich] would come for big Christmas or Thanksgiving time. Anyhow if no really good fun in Chicago I think you should go to N.Y. and have a good load of the things you can't get here.

God knows will be glahd when can get to see a few things myself. But I spend so much in N.Y. that I've *got* to make some money before I go there. But a girl doesn't spend anywhere near as much as a guy does (unless shopping big) and we have *plenty* of money for you to go to N.Y. before you come down here.

I want to get up there for November though no matter what. And see the shows, and the museums, and the new painters, and old friends with good heads to talk to, and Mr. [Harold] Ross and Mr. [James] Thurber and Mr. [Robert] Benchley, and feel a northern fall again. And look in all the windows.

We had all winter last year and missed fall. Winter started for us guys on the 14th Sept in Schnee Eifel and never stopped. We've got to be in N.Y. together this fall no matter what. But you go and get some first before you come home if you want it, or need it, the least bit.

You know a good suite with an ice-box and caviar in it and everything else and the lights comeing on outside and the air sharp and crisp outside is awfully nice. Nice in bed with the night cold outside. Wonderful town to walk in too.

Very wonderful world and we have already earned big share of common stock for enjoyment in same if just friends and love each other (we always do that) and not destructive about each other. It's only about a year and three days that we had wedding ceremony in Paris when I had to move north for Tubby [Barton] and there were lots of tactical problems. I've always felt as married since then as though it were in Notre Dame. Have been good and bad but all the bads you pointed out have cut out and the others are easily controllable if you want to do it constructively and almost most important is to recognize or remember when anyone does a cutting out job so they don't get to think, "Well they never notice if you *do* do it. Only if you don't." I know how loveing and good and kind and showing affection you were when you decided if you loved somebody you ought to show it and to make them happy. I love you always my dearest kitten.

So that's the lesson for today (religious term). You see when we haveing found the necessity to discard, don't believe in anybody. Not Mrs Mary Glover Baker Eddy, nor God and his beard, nor (me) any liveing politicians, nor (me) in any liveing soldiers except the goodness and soundness of Ike [Eisenhower] and, for the moment, the true good intentions of the Russkis who know atomic bomb promotes necessity for such understanding, nor in many other things that people mold their lives and their actions on, then we need to believe, just to function on, being good and being good to each other and to all other people, and we need to believe in each other. We ought to tell each other small or big things that don't work. But lovingly and carefully and with faith that they will work. Because we can have a lovelier time than anybody in the world and you know it well and it only takes the care a gardner takes with a good garden in good soil.

And much love from your lover and partner
Papa

Known to later dynasties as *The Imperfect.*
PH. PUL

1. See EH to General R. O. Barton, 27 November 1945.

To MARY WELSH, La Finca Vigia, 28 September 1945

Dearest Kitten Pickle:

Going out in the boat today so am writing this very early in the morning to be sure to get something off to you. It's a lovely cool fresh morning but looks as though there would be much brisa. Buck[1] wants to go to Rincon (the goggle fish reef) to try to catch some small fish. So hope it won't get too rough too early in the day. Anyway it will be a trip and we might always catch a big fish; altho towing the Dinghy is not too good.

It rained a good hard, not too long nor heavy, but just fair-sized shower yest aft and am anxious to see what amount of water it produced. Have just been down to the pool and you can see the grass sprouting up already in the brown path the ditch made. Didn't see Mr. and Mrs. Fish nor the childnies altho the water was very clear. It is absolutely clear and if the bottom wasn't brown would be phenomenal. Will keep you company swimming now as like it again and its awfully good exercise and so easy when you get into it. Am sorry was bad about it before.

Yesterday Buck shot awfully well at the special shoot. He had never shot a shotgun and is the opposite of a reflex king. But he could understand everything you told him to do and why and then do it. He is a fine rifle shot. He had a good time and was pleased.

I shot ok and with a day's practice think could have won it. But was a hundredth second slow on the fast birds (they put them in last) and would look at them in just that time without shooting them and when did kill killed them so they went out. Missed two in twelve that way. Mungo Perez had shot 2nd in The Grand American Handicap at Vandalia, Ohio against a thousand or so shooters and shoot was a homage to Mungo. This necessitated an alibi on Mungo's part if he should not shoot in International form and was provided for by a slightly twisted ankle which produced more limping than was ever seen on any stricken field. Mungo comeing back on the cement was a heart rending sight.

Breeze rising plenty just since have been writing this so don't think there will be much goggle fishing; but maybe they can catch something fishing with sardines.

Starting to blow hard now—

Six minutes later:

Started this before mail came. Didn't get any last night but wanted to write anyway because had written such a gloomy letter yest. from not hearing and wanted to take taste out of your mouth.

You wrote such a lovely letter and am so happy with all the house plans and so happy you liked the piece. It wasn't I wanted praise. Was just to know what my partner thought. I hadn't read it to Pete [Mrs. Lanham] nor let her read it. Am not a big piece pusher. I suppose I could have but it never occurred to me.

You know have never yet heard from Colliers (and that's my money they are still not refunding). Not a question of me accounting for how I spent their money. Wish was working for them again. Would sure know how to give it to them. Am not awfully vengeful but would sure like to give it to that outfit.

I'll write tonight and tomorrow and you'll still have time to get it before you leave and have something new to read comeing down. Wonderful about place. Delighted have your friends whenever you want them. If I were working hard or something you could entertain them until I was through with work for the day.

Haveing babys is just a thing about how people take it. I was writing Farewell To Arms all time Mousie was comeing on and being born and went out west afterwards to finish it and Pauline went to her [family's] from the hospital and joined me out west when Baby was ok to leave. If people start makeing their lives revolve around the baby everybody is bitched includeing the child. Main thing with baby is have good nurse and never let them be spoiled. Lots of times will seem ungracious and heartless but have to do it. 13 years since Gigi was born and twenty one since Bum but don't believe the basic problems have changed much. Hope this not sacrilege but baby's often dullest thing can be for first months and sometimes year and I like to keep away from them much as possible. So if this ever happens don't think I don't love or appreciate our baby. Went to Africa after Giggy was born. He born in Oct., went abroad following July and didn't come back until the next year after May or June. Along about April (ten months) Pauline said, "I think I ought to see my Baby."[2]

I love them but learned from haveing to take all care of Bumby that anybody *good* you hire can take better care of them at the start than I can and no reason to have the drudgery wear out husband and wife or split them apart and no sense ever have baby drive you crazy. Put this in now so won't think am mean with them. Nobody puts more time in on them than I do once they are ready for it. Maybe people love their kids more but I love ours plenty. Will love young Tom or Brigit as much or more.

Have to stop Pickle or we won't get off. Esculy [Excuse] poor and hurried letter. Look forward to getting home and reading yours over again and answering good. Good bye blessed Pickle. We are off to the briny.

PH. PUL   I Love You

1. General and Mrs. Charles T. Lanham had come to La Finca Vigia 22 September for a visit. 2. EH errs on the date of Gregory's birth, 12 November 1931, and of his own foreign travel, of which he did none in 1932. Pauline's remark was probably made in 1933 or 1934.

To MALCOLM COWLEY, La Finca Vigia, 17 October and 14 November 1945

Dear Cowley:

It was awfully good to hear from you. A few days after I got the book and liked the introduction very much.[1] See what you mean about the nocturnal thing now. Hope will have some luck writing now to get you some good new specimens to get the old scalpel to work on.

You see it's awfully hard to talk or write about your own stuff because if it is any good you yourself know about how good it is—but if you say so yourself you feel like a shit. My kids are the only people I ever talk to about my stuff or what have always been trying to do. They know Dos and they love to hear about Scott and Jim Joyce and how things truly were instead of the accepted version. There surely is a great difference. They will ask, "Papa what is the *true* gen on so and so or such and such." The gen is RAF slang for intelligence, the hand out at the briefing. The *true* gen is what they know but don't tell you. The true gen very hard to obtain.

Had no idea we had so much early life in common. It was a fine life wasn't it? Feel very bad to hear you are having trouble with deafness. If we have to lose one, though, that is the one to lose. But no fun to lose any of them.

I'd no idea Faulkner was in that bad shape and very happy you are putting together the Portable of him. He has the most talent of anybody and he just needs a sort of conscience that isn't there. Certainly if no nation can exist half free and half slave no man can write half whore and half straight. But he will write absolutely perfectly straight and then go on and on and not be able to end it. I wish the christ I owned him like you'd own a horse and train him like a horse and race him like a horse— only in writing. How beautifully he can write and as simple and as complicated as autumn or as spring.

I'll try and write him and cheer him up.

We'll have to get together and talk when get up to N.Y. Don't know when that will be though. I'm working good now. Work every morning; haven't had a drink in the night nor until after finish work for a couple of months. That's the hardest thing to do when you come back from a war. You get to useing the old Giant Killer and it is able to fix up practically anything. I remember in Spain I'd have to have about two shots before I could even look at the map but after the two shots it didn't look so bad as all that—even when it was awful. Then after it is over you have to boil it all out of your system and only take what is useful to you to relax after working and not lie to yourself nor kid yourself and it is always a tough process.

Wrote Evan [Shipman] care McGraw but haven't heard from him. He sent me two damned good poems last year.

You know I could never read Katherine Ann P[orter]. I just can't read it. Seems so terribly dull. Not phony like that Carson McCullers but just too dull to live.

When Kenneth Burke was writing well I was too uneducated to understand him. Would like to re-read it now. You see when you guys were first writing I had only been through high school. I knew Italian from the war and had kept on with it and knew a little German. Was getting start on education in Paris same time as was learning to write (mostly books from Sylvia Beach's until I learned French) and then, after, Spanish. Every year keep on studying, keep on reading and every year study something new to keep head learning. Learning is a hell of a lot of fun. Don't see why can't keep it up all my life. Certainly plenty to learn.

November 14

Certainly didn't do very well at getting that letter off!

Been working every day and going good. Makes a hell of a dull life too. But it is more fun than anything else. Do you remember how old [Ford Madox] Ford was always writing how [Joseph] Conrad suffered so when he wrote? How it was un metier du chien [a dog's trade] etc. Do you suffer when you write? I don't at all. Suffer like a bastard when don't write, or just before, and feel empty and fucked out afterwards. But never feel as good as while writing.

Sent for the Portable Poe after I had your letter. What an awful bloody life he had. He had more self propelled bad luck than Scott even. If he'd been born in our time he would probably have been one of Oswald Moseley's [Mosley's] gang. They would have put up the money for the magazine and it would have been the only good Fascist magazine. I looked forward to reading Poe. Thought that would be good to do this winter. Then found I'd read it all before ever went to Italy and remembered it so clearly that I couldn't re-read. Had forgotten them all but they were all there—intact. He seems a lot like Evan. Of course he was doing it first too. You know Evan is a hell of a good writer? Don't think anybody realizes how good.

Does Archie [Mac Leish] still write anything except Patriotic? I read some awfully lifeless lines to a Dead Soldier by him in that Free World anthology. I thought good old Allen Tate could write the lifeless-est lines to Dead Soldiers ever read but Archie is going good.[2] You know his bro. Kenny was killed in last war flying and I always felt Archie felt that sort of gave him a controlling interest in all deads.

What is going to be done about Pound? Did he continue to broadcast after we went to war? I think they should shave his head as a collaborator. Any other punishment would be excessive. He was a great poet and the most generous friend and looker-after of people and so flattered at being respected in Italy instead of being made fun of that he swallowed Fascism whole (No one but an idiot with Ezra's type of ego would but he did: as simple as that, and then set out to justify it.) In 1933 Joyce (James) swore to me Ezra was crazy and asked me to come to be with him at something he had invited Ezra to because he said "Ezra's mad now and I don't know what he will do." I don't think his thinking has been normal for a long time. Those broadcasts of his I read were so silly and insane that they, themselves, if presented in entirety would be his best defense.

Do you know what they want to do about him? William (Haw-Haw) Joyce was a very dangerous business. It would be wicked to consider Ezra who was a traitor but a silly, and a crazy and a harmless traitor in the same category.

JFK   [Ernest]

1. *Hemingway*, Viking Portable Ed., ed. Malcolm Cowley (New York, 1944).
2. EH connects Mac Leish's "The Young Dead Soldiers" (in *Collected Poems* [Boston, 1952], pp. 139–40) with Tate's "Ode to the Confederate Dead" (1928). Mac Leish's brother Kenneth (1894–1918) is alluded to in "Memorial Rain" (in *Collected Poems*, pp. 36–37).

To GENERAL R. O. BARTON, La Finca Vigia, 27 November 1945

Dear Tubby:

Thank you very much for your fine letter and the splendid pictures. They are to frame.

Got to feeling so badly at not haveing written you that knocked off work this morning to get this note off.

What happened was that Buck [Lanham] and his wife came down to visit me and I laid off all writing, even letters, then the day he left (we had a really good time and I think he liked it here) I got going on book and have been working so hard that am like a wrung out dish rag when I quit. Every day I was going to write to you but your letter just stayed on the top of ANSWER AT ONCE.

I hope you are feeling better and are doing what you want to. That is not the thing to say because what you want to do is fight. But we've run clean out of fight.

I received the letter and application for the 4th Division Association and will fill it out and send it in. Thank you very much. It made me very happy to feel I belonged in the outfit in peace time too. Think your plan for the association is sound also. Always let me know anything I can do.

About the other things: You know anything I ever did or tried to do was not with any wish for reward. Only hoped to be useful if possible. But appreciate your haveing spoken well of it. What is going to become of the Division now?

What will you be doing with yourself? I hope it won't be too long before I get to see you again. Take good care of yourself and please forgive such a rotten letter. All my juice goes in the damned book. Anytime I can write a good letter Tubby it's a sign I'm not working.

Now when I think how used to take this expensive brain I write these epoch makeing volumnes with out on that motorcycle—and where—I feel the first flush of battle fatigue. Read a book called Men Under Stress and discovered I'd had all the symptoms for 25 years. Only I just thought it was piles.

It was fine to hear from you General. I do hope you are feeling much better and are haveing the fine vacation you deserve.

My very best to Mrs. Barton and your daughter.

Your always,
Ernie

Mary, who (or is it whom. I only know how to use whom in a title) I hope can marry soon, very soon,[1] sends her best.

That poor dope John Groth wrote a silly piece about me, inserting all sorts of stuff after I'd written an introduction.[2] He was up in Schnee Eifel that time you were in Paris. Fortunately I'd said in the Introduction he wrote Fairy Tales.

PH. PUL

1. EH and Mary Welsh were married in Havana, 14 March 1946. 2. John Groth, *Studio Europe* (New York, 1945).

To KONSTANTIN SIMONOV,[1] La Finca Vigía, 20 June 1946

Dear Simonov:

. . . Your book came last night. I am reading it today and will write you to Moscow when I finish it. . . .

I should have read it when it was first translated but I was just back from the war and I could not read anything about it. No matter how good. Am sure you know what I mean. After the first war I was in I could not write about it for almost nine years. After the Spanish war I had to write immediately because I knew the next war was coming so fast and I felt there was no time. After this war I had my head very badly smashed up (three times) and bad headaches. But finally I have gotten writing again all right but my novel, after 800 mss. pages is still a long way from the war. But if I live O.K. it will get there. Hope it can be very good.

All through this war I wanted to be with the army of the U.S.S.R. and see that wonderful fight but I did not feel justified to try to be a war correspondent there since A—I did not speak Russian and B—because I thought I could be more useful in trying to destroy the Krauts (what we call the Germans) in other work. I was at sea for about two years in a difficult job. Then went to England and flew with R.A.F. as a correspondent before the invasion, accompanied the Normandy invasion, and then spent the rest of the time with the 4th Infantry Division. The time with the R.A.F. was wonderful but useless. With the 4th Infantry Division and with the 22nd regiment of Infantry I tried to be useful through knowing French and the country and being able to work ahead with the Maquis. This was a good life and you would have enjoyed it. I remember how after we had come into Paris ahead of the army, and the Army had caught up with us, André Malraux came to see me and asked how many men I had commanded. I told him never more than 200 at the most and usually between 14 and 60. He was very happy and relieved because he had commanded 2,000 men, he said. So there was no question of literary prestige involved.

That summer from Normandy into Germany was the happiest I ever had in spite of it being war. Later in Germany, in the Schnee Eifel, Hurtgen Forest and the Rundstedt offensive it was very bitter fighting also quite cold. Earlier there was much bad fighting but re-taking France and especially Paris made me feel the best I had ever felt. Ever since I had been a boy I had been in retreats, holding attacks, retreats, victories with no reserves to follow them up, etc., and I had never known how winning can make you feel.

Now, since the fall of 1945, I have been writing so hard, and all the time, that the weeks and the months go by so quickly we will all be dead if we do not know it.

I hope you had a good trip in America and Canada. I wish I would have spoken Russian and gone around with you because there are really many wonderful people to meet and fine things to do. But few of those people speak Russian. I would like you to have known our Colonel of the 22nd Infantry (now General Lanham) who is my best friend and the commanders of the 1st, 2nd and 3rd battalions (those that are alive) and many Company and Platoon commanders and many wonderful American soldiers. The 4th Infantry division from D day on Utah Beach until VE Day had 21,205 casualties out of a strength of 14,037. My oldest boy was attached to the 3rd Infantry Division which had 33,547 out of their 14,037. But they were in Sicily and Italy before landing in Southern France. He dropped in ahead as a parachutist and was later wounded very badly and captured in the fall in the Voges. He is a good kid, a Captain, and you would like him. He told the Krauts (he is very blond) he was the son of a ski instructor in Austria and had gone to America after his father had been killed in an avalanche. When the Krauts finally found out who he was they sent him to a Hostage camp. But he was liberated at the end.

It is a damned shame you could not have come down here. Are your poems or the journal translated into English? I would like to read them very much. I know what you are talking about. As you say you know what I am talking about. After all the world has gotten far enough along so that writers should be able to understand one another. There is so much *govno* (probably mis-spelled) that goes on and yet people are so good, and intelligent and well intentioned and would understand each other well if we could have understanding of each other instead of the repeat performance of a Churchill; doing now what he did in 1918–1919 to preserve something that now can only be preserved by war. Excuse me if I talk politics. I know that I am always supposed to be a fool when I do. But I know that nothing stands between the friendship of our countries. . . .

There is a boy (now probably old man) in the U.S.S.R. named

Kashkeen. Red headed (probably greyheaded). He is the best critic and translator I ever had. If still around please give him my best regards. Was *For Whom The Bell Tolls* ever translated? I read a review by [Ilya] Ehrenburg but never heard. It would be easy to publish with small changes of, elimination of, certain names. Wish you could read it. It isn't about war as we knew it the last few years. But about small hill war; it is all right and there is one place where we kill the fascists you would like.

Good luck and have a good trip.

Your friend
Ernest Hemingway

1. Konstantin Simonov (1916–1979) was a Soviet poet, novelist, and playwright. The text of this letter is from *Soviet Literature* 11 (1962): 165–67; it was evidently printed with some omissions.

To GENERAL CHARLES T. LANHAM, Casper, Wyoming, 25 August 1946

Dear Buck:

Came in here a week ago tonight. Casper that is; not the hospital. Monday morning [19 August] while I was packing the car Mary woke 0700 in great pain. To skip details: was a tubular pregnancy and tube had burst. Got best local surgeon and got her to this hospital. Very heavy internal hemmorage. Had to try to get enough fluids and plasma into her so she would be operatable. Finally operated at 2030 Monday night. While Dr. was administering the spinal anaesthetic preparatory to operating M's veins collapsed, there was no pulse and he could not get a needle in to give plasma. Dr. told me was hopeless; impossible operate; she couldn't stand shock; to tell her goodbye (useless manoever since she unconscious). I got asst. to cut for a vein and got plasma going (they were very short handed and the plasma tubeing had bubbles in it and a too tightly plugged air vent and wouldn't flow). I took over the plasma administration, cleared line by milking the tube down and raising and tilting until we got it flowing, and by the latter end of the first pint she was comeing back enough so that insisted they operate.

To skip again: She took 4 bottles of plasma during operation, two blood transfusions after, been under oxygen tent ever since and now today is feeling fine, blood count OK., pulse and temperature normal and will have stitches out next Wed. or Thursday. Ate a good breakfast this am and will have lunch shortly. They removed the ruptured tube and other tube and all other organs are intact and OK.

But Buck it was closest one I've ever seen. Dr. had given her up—and taken off his gloves. Certainly shows never pays to quit.

Conception was on July 4—first period missed was July 15—second was Aug. 15—there had been no soreness, illness, nausea, no signs of a tubular pregnancy. But there it was and it would have had to burst sooner or later so it was lucky it was in Casper instead of up in the hills.

Have been at hospital ever since. Mary will be here at least a week more. Maybe more. I waited to write you because thought might have a letter from you in the mail forwarded to Ketchum Idaho. But that mail reached here last night and there was no letter so write now so you would not worry in case you had read anything in the papers.

The kids were (and are) waiting in KETCHUM and think will bring them down here to arrive this comeing Thursday and stay over the week-end. Can't gen [plan] out yet exactly how or when to take Mary to Ketchum where she can convalesce until see how she shapes this next week.

Meantime live at the Mission Auto Courts and commute back and forth to Hospital. Address here until Sept 2nd (at least) MISSION MOTOR COURT—RAILROAD AND DURBIN STREETS—CASPER WYOMING.

Plans are the same, except for this interruption, as in my last letter. Love to see you any time. Let's work something out. Sort of worried not hearing that maybe you've gone to East or ETO [European Theater of Operations].

Excuse this sort of fact letter. Trip was fine and unhurried. We had a wonderful time and saw some beautiful country and were just comeing to the best of it when tube blew.

Bad luck to have that form of pregnancy. Mary been brave and patient and good as hell. Very impressed on missing Boot Hill last Monday night. Was closest I've ever seen with *anybody.*

Best always Buck

Your pal
PUL   Ernie

To GENERAL CHARLES T. LANHAM, Casper, 28 August 1946

Dear Buck:

Just got wire. Thanks very much for wireing. Wire made Mary very happy.

Mary is fine. Had good night. Blood count is riseing steadily. She hasn't needed another transfusion and is makeing her own blood now o.k. and of good quality. Still sleeps under the oxygen tent to ease ticker strain; but she is out of the woods and up on the high ground.

Thank you very much for offering to come out. I know you meant it. But there is nothing here I can't handle and I would rather have you when you could have more fun. Anyhow will be getting the gen when your letter comes. You know how much would love to see you.

This is just a note to reassure you and Pete [Mrs. Lanham] about Mary. There isn't any news except that good news.

Dr. is going to take out the stitches today. It is nine full days since operation. He says she shouldn't leave hospital until next Tuesday or Wednesday and then not travel for a week. I can't gen moves out too far ahead until see how things shape. Besides they are all easy decisions and many alternatives. There is a very reasonable charter service (air) here with twin motor cessnas and stretcher equipment and might fly her from here to Hailey which is only 12 miles from Ketchum. Have Bumby to drive car if necessary and other kids to do anything needed.

Am faintly fed with the gay life of the Mission Tourist Court or Motor Court because once the clutch is over and nothing can do one way or another feel old urge to work, fight, f---, or drink. Been drinking almost nothing. I love the west and know it fairly well and of all the towns in the west to be stuck in would pick Casper last. But it has a *really* good hospital and we were awfully lucky to hit it. Don't want to start working though because want to really look after Mary good and when start working it comes first and there really isn't anything else nor much left. As it is, not working, and practically not drinking, am kindly and completely patient character and think takeing good care of her.

Hope you didn't think I was trying to make myself out Dr. Hemingstein the Great Emergency Handler in letter. Was only trying to give you the play by play and was still fascinated by how much can be done to f--- fate rather than accept it. But you need somebody that would put up a fight and Mary really made one. Will write again Buck when get your letter. Thanks so much for wireing and for always makeing me feel that have a partner when I need one.

Ernie

Driving to Rawlins to pick up kids tomorrow.
Address when leave here c/o Lloyd Arnold, Sun Valley Idaho.
PUL

*

To GENERAL CHARLES T. LANHAM, Sun Valley, Idaho, 2 November 1946

Dear Buck:
Hope you had a good cruise and that everything repeat everything has been going good.

I wrote Winston [Guest] that we planned to be there [Gardiner's Island, New York] in first week of Dec. and had wire from him he was delighted whenever you could come.[1]

We are going to leave here Nov. 10 for Salt Lake City and shoot with friends there for a few days. Very nice people. They were up here with Charley Sweeny, very old pal and soldier in various armies, Venezuelan, against Castro, Mexican, with Madero, Foreign Legion, U.S., Morrocan, R.A.F. We were together in Near East and in Spain and he is one of very oldest friends. He is staying in Salt Lake with these people, Clarence Bamberger and his sister Didi Allen and they claim to have very high grade shooting with concrete blinds, marsh buggies, motor boats etc. Sort of thing have never done. Seems a lot of apparatus to kill the innocent duck but have often found things that sound silly turn out to be very practical and fun.

No concrete blinds yesterday but we all got our limits in less than an hour with a blizzard blowing and about fifty mile wind out in the old Silver Creek marsh with a stool of a dozen decoys out and the birds flying wild as hell and comeing in like jet propelled kamikazes.

Also been haveing fine pheasant shooting. Been haveing terrific wind every day and the cocks with that in their ass really can travel. Mary getting so she can walk up to about 3/4 of what a good man can do in the field and is really enjoying it. Killed last two pheasants she shot at. Hope goes good today.

Pat (Mousie) killed a beautiful big fat buck with a lovely head that dressed out close to 285. Col. [Taylor] Williams got an even bigger buck almost too fat to travel. Son of a bitch is most wonderful eating ever had. Will try and ship some to you frozen. Fattest deer meat ever seen and eats like prize winning beef at live stock show.

In New York we will be at Sherry Netherlands unless advise you otherwise. Guy from Universal (Mark Hellinger production of Killers) came out here to bring a Killers print. Thought it was good film. This citizen claimed he could absolutely get us into the Sherry-N with ten days notice. So we can meet there. You let me know what date you want to show, whether Nov. 30, Dec 1 or Dec 2.

From Salt Lake we will drive to New Orleans and leave car there. Proceed to Chicago and see Mary's parents and then to N.Y. May send Mousie on ahead to N.Y. so he and Giggy can shoot at Gardiner's Island on Thanksgiveing which falls on the 28th I think. Maybe we will be there by then. Probably. Hope so.

Am really getting in good shape here and can walk any distance. The cold feels wonderful. As sharp and hard as it was in Luxemburg on Xmas day [1944], though not as cold.

Had really close piece of business day before yest. As you know women should never be entrusted with automatic weapons and Mrs. Howard (Slim) Hawks proved this again when we were unloading guns to get into the car and she let her 16 gauge Browning automatic off so close to my head that it (literally) singed the hair at base of skull. I was kneeling down fixing boots. She was adequately horrified and I played it very lightly but explained that the weapon was obviously unsafe (not her fault: shit) and so now have come in possession of the weapon which is a very fine one and which you can shoot at Gardiners. Told her would trade it in on an over and under which will be safe for her. But think after that singeing business will bloody well keep the weapon which is a beautifully made and fine functioning job with two barrels and a cutts compensator with four different tubes. I shot one (a Browning) for 12 years and it is the only good automatic shot gun. So what are a few burned hairs off the back of the top of the neck for a piece of loot like that. With it came 500 shells so we will have shells for it and also to try the German gun. Altho probably we should shoot it first with light loads altho will be able to tell that by the proof marks.

Buck this vacation has been wonderful. Mary so happy and getting to be so strong and well and not an argument ever since we hit Casper (actually since left New Orleans), getting the shooting now that I love so much and missed for so many good years. Sleep fine and the air cold and sharp. And every night eat wonderfully: mountain sheep, elk, venison, the pheasants and the ducks. I make breakfast in the morning, as wrote you I guess, and Mary cooks supper. She can cook like hell. Learned it in England cooking for ex-husband [Noel Monks] who only liked an over-cooked chop (dry) really and is haveing wonderful time with this succulent basic food.

That me haveing kept her out of the Casper Boot Hill when could have let her go has given her lots of confidence. Was never jealous a minute of Slim who was good friend. Just asked me, "Papa I don't have to worry about Slim do I?" I told her no, honestly. And there it was. Am awfully lucky. Out of that f---ing nettle danger (to her) we pluck this good old flower confidence and faith in a guy.

Am looking forward more than can write you to our time on the [Gardiner's] Island. It is a fine old house and the Island has been in same hands since Colonial times. Capt. Kidd, ex-operative of the First National Bank of Boston, worked out of there. Clarence Mackay rented it for a fabulous sum until he died. Winston pays 30 to 35 G a year for it and it was badly punished by the hurricane of 37 or was it 38 (it was one of the Spain years) but is a charming place, half moon shaped (approx) and out in the ocean with great black-duck, pheasant and lots of deer. We will have fine time eating, drinking, talking, shooting and I have looked forward to it since 40 and now that we will have it together it is about ten times as good. All you need is warmest clothes you have and changes for if get wet. I'm sure Lily will like it. I never had any free time down there before—always a rush—at other times was working —and we will have a wonderful time. Make it for as long as you can because Win expects us for as long as want to stay and we will have wonderful time. It is ok to stay there because I have had Win at my place, and his friends, for months. Will try and put ten or twelve pounds on you of bone and sinew with the old hot oyster stew and champagne treatment in the blinds.

Must stop this letter and do my belly exercises and get off to the lower country. Have cut all the remaining cold cuts off a haunch of venison and Mary is makeing the sandwiches with old fashioned cream salad dressing, chutney and lettuce. Chutney on some. Cream salad dressing on others. Also a pheasant breast apiece and the leather wine bottle (two quart size).

So long Buck. If you write when you get this will get it before leaveing here on tenth. Otherwise it will be forwarded to Salt Lake address which is 2600 Walkers Lane, Murray 7, Utah and will reach us there. Or write there.

Please give our love to Pete. Mary sends her very best.

PUL   Ernesto

1. General Lanham was to join EH for shooting at Winston Guest's rented estate on Gardiner's Island off Montauk Point, Long Island.

To ERNST ROWOHLT,[1] La Finca Vigia, 18 December 1946

My dear Ernst:

I was delighted to receive your letter which reached me in translation after some delay and was glad to know that you are well and back in business again. You certainly had a hell of a war and I am delighted that you were not one of the numerous Krauts that we killed in Schnee Eifel or Hurtgen Forest. Do not think that this is the language of the oppressive victor as you certainly killed many more of our boys at both of these places than we killed of you. (Glad we never killed each other.)

Please write to Anne Marie Horschitz for me and tell her I look forward to having her translate my works again. She was the finest translator I ever had in any language.

Please keep in touch with me through my lawyer, Maurice J. Speiser, 630 Fifth Avenue, New York 20, N.Y., and let me know what conditions are and when you think it will be feasible to publish in German again. Then we can discuss making a deal. In the meantime I will not make any other deals with German publishers without getting in touch with you first.

However, please try to dig up a little money so that I will not have to be at the Kaiserhof again waiting while you chase money all over Berlin.

With warmest affection,
Your old counter-comrade,
Ernest Hemingway

T.C. PUL

1. Rowohlt was EH's German publisher. This letter appeared in *Rowohlts Rot-blonder Roman* (Hamburg, 1947), p. 44.

To MAXWELL PERKINS, La Finca Vigia, 5 March 1947

Dear Max:

I have been very remiss about writing you. Please forgive me. It has been a combination of working very hard, then being interrupted, and haveing to work even harder to make up. Haven't been out in the boat in a month and three days and am getting stale so am going out tomorrow no matter what.

First when got here had to do taxes etc. Then [Mark] Hellinger came down on a movie deal which I have decided against. I do not want to be in a motion picture company even though it means plenty of money. Have all the work I can handle writing. I am going to give him an option (first option) on any stories written and to be written (short stories) for a fixed price and a share of the money they make. This way what he will do is entirely up to him and I have no more to do with it than I always have had: nothing. He wanted us to go into a partnership, form a company to acquire the stories, produce etc. Made it very very attractive financially. But I am a writer of novels, stories and an occasional journalist (never I hope to God again) and I do not want to be in picture business in any way. What I should do is to sell my stories, when I do sell them to pictures, in such a way that I participate in the profits instead of selling out-right and haveing taxes take the most of what the story brings and then it gone for good as property. This am trying to work out.

Then came [Maurice] Speiser [EH's lawyer]: increasingly difficult for me to deal with or through. He's gone now.

Last night [Jonathan] Cape got in. I haven't seen him yet as am putting him up at the Hotel. The son of a bitch first wrote from London for me to get him a visa. To do this I had to go to Dept. of Immigration and then to Minister of State and have him cable visa to N.Y. Consulate. Cape couldn't locate it so I had to take all steps again and send him the number of the cable that carried it. He then asked for a visa for his wife and I had to interrupt my work and go through the whole damned thing again. Asking favours and useing up credit with govt. people I could have well kept for myself. He cabled he needed a bed for four nights so have gotten him a room at the Nacional Hotel and told them I would pay for it and for their meals. That will be about $80 a day. So let's hope his limiting it to 4 days is accurate. But worth it not to have him here at the house so I can continue to work mornings. I never have been able to like Cape and it is too late to make a great effort toward that now.

In spite of all that have been working steadily and well. But it leaves no time for anything else. Have been re-writing from the beginning the part I did before I left, and writing much of it new where I did not have it right. I had a hell of a time starting it originally and all that I have now redone so it is about the way it ought to be. Have done 137 typed pages which, with the newly written part that has gone in, brings me to page 156 of the hand-written Mss. There is 907 pages of the hand-written mss altogether. But a lot of it will take very little re-writing as I was going much better after the start and in the middle. I wish these goddamned visiting firemen would not come and bother me as the cool winter days are the best of the year for working.

Well all of that is why I haven't written you. There have been other interruptions of all sorts but I am fairly ruthless about them. Have a big sign on the gate that says in Spanish Mr. H. receives no one without a previous appointment. Save yourself the annoyance of not being received by not comeing to the house. Then if they do come up I have a right to curse them off.

I will write to you in detail about the illustrating problem later.[1] This much I do know: No [John] Groth under any circumstances. I like him very much but not his illustrations. Please do not make any definite commitment with [Luis] Quintanilla. His work has gone down-grade (for me at least) and has degenerated into caricature. He *could* do it well if he would. But I would have to be sure he would. Hell I seem to be going into this in some detail in spite of haveing to get this off. I think Patrick might do a good Farewell To Arms. Will not know for a while. If I can get to Europe think I might be able to get Picasso to do at least one of the books. He can illustrate beautifully you know and is a good friend of mine. I would like to have really good illustrations. The [Reginald] Marsh things in Dos's books were absolutely atrocious I thought. I am not surprized Dos's didn't sell. None of the separate parts did. All of ours did and still do in some form. Am sorry not to be able to present something constructive at this time but I have thought a lot about it and that is what I *know* so far.

Thank you very much for getting me that Ex-algae. At the risk of being a second Jonathan Cape can I ask to have three or four gallons more sent by air-express by the same people? I will be out in three weeks. It makes all the difference between a fine clear pool and an absolutely un-usable one. We haven't enough water here to drain often as in Key West.

Patrick is working hard here. Besides his work he is studying astronomy, navigation and Spanish and I am giveing him Eng. and Am. literature. His navigation prof taught it in Spanish Naval Academy and he gets Spanish from him too. He is fine and very happy. He wants to go to Harvard and gave your name as a reference. Hope that is o.k. He won money both days in the big International shoot here in Feb. I play tennis with him afternoons to keep in shape but still do not get enough exercise. Mary is fine. Very happy.

Today I am cableing you to please deposit $3138.13 the amount the Feb royalty statement showed in the Guaranty Trust. This I'd planned to use for liveing expenses but got cable from Speiser today that he needed $2100 for first installment of taxes. If I don't sell anything to pictures I will have a light income year. Have turned down $50,000 for Fifty Grand, and they would give $75,000, because do not want to sell anything for cash the way taxes are unless I can have some share in the profits.

When you get this letter will you please *loan* me, not advance me, $3000. and deposit it in my account in the Guaranty. Just cable me $3000 deposited and I will know then I can draw on it. Will pay same interest as on other loans.

Am trying to live as economically as I can altho everything is expensive as hell. I think it is better for all of us concerned to borrow from you when I need it than get mixed up in a big movie deal which could not help but distract from my one job which is to write good book. I do not want to ever have any thought of anything I write being made into motion picture.

The Snows of Kilimanjaro would make a wonderful picture and whenever I sell it I can pay back what I borrow if the book isn't done by then. I think I have enough assets and the book is far enough along so it is o.k. to borrow.

Excuse trying to cram so much into a letter. Have to launch cable, deposit a check here against the $3138.13 you will deposit when you get this cable and then get to work and see how much I can get done before that dogfaced Englishman comes out for lunch. And tomorrow I'm going to go out in the boat Cape or no Cape. Not going to ask him either. Think I will tell him I am going to be in conference all day. No can see. All same combined chiefs of staff and Buckingham Palace.

So you please deposit 3138.13 royalties when you get cable today and $3000. when you get this letter.

Best to Charley and take care of yourself and thank you very much.

PUL   Ernest

1. A new illustrated edition of *A Farewell to Arms* was contemplated.

To BERNARD PEYTON,[1] La Finca Vigia, *c.* 5 April 1947

Dear Bernie:

To make a pitcher of Bloody Marys (any smaller amount is worthless) take a good sized pitcher and put in it as big a lump of ice as it will hold. (This to prevent too rapid melting and watering of our product.) Mix a pint of good russian vodka and an equal amount of chilled tomato juice. Add a table spoon full of Worcester Sauce. Lea and Perrins is usual but can use AI or any good beef-steak sauce. Stirr. (with two rs) Then add a jigger of fresh squeezed lime juice. Stirr. Then add small amounts of celery salt, cayenne pepper, black pepper. Keep on stirring and taste it to see how it is doing. If you get it too powerful weaken with more tomato juice. If it lacks authority add more vodka. Some people like more lime than others. For combatting a really terrific hangover increase the amount of Worcester sauce—but don't lose the lovely color. Keep drinking it yourself to see how it is doing. I introduced this drink to HongKong in 1941 and believe it did more than any other single factor except perhaps the Japanese Army to precipitate the Fall of that Crown Colony. After you get the hang of it you can mix it so it will taste as though it [had] absolutely no alcohol of any kind in it and a glass of it will still have as much kick as a really good big martini. Whole trick is to keep it very cold and not let the ice water it down. Use good vodka and good tomato juice. There is a vodka made in N.J. by Russian process that is o.k. Can't remember the name and don't want to tout you onto the wrong one.

It was very fine seeing you and your lovely wife. Wish we could have had more time together. Mary is writing to thank you for all the subversive economic publications and the algae killer. It was very kind and thoughtful of you to send them. Hope we can shoot together some time before too long.

My very best to you both,
Ernest Hemingway

There is a very fine Mexican sauce called Esta Si Pican (sort of mild Tobasco) that is good added to the Bloody Marys, too. Just a few drops. PH. PUL

1. Peyton (1896–1975), a grandson of Eugene DuPont, Princeton, Class of 1917, drove ambulances in France in 1917 and in 1947 was vice-president and treasurer of the New York Air Brake Company.

To WILLIAM W. SEWARD, JR.,[1] La Finca Vigia, 19 June 1947

Dear Mr. Seward:

Thank you very much for your letter. It is always good to hear from you and it makes me happy that you had such a good opinion of the stories on re-reading them.

I read the [Samuel] Putnam book [*Paris Was Our Mistress*, 1947] and found it a strange mixture full of good intention, inaccurate journalism, and personal alibis for some pretty strange things Mr. Putnam did in his time. When we meet sometime I'll tell you the true story about the abject apology he made to his Fascist friends for haveing proposed me as a judge for some sort of literary contest and the aftermath. He later became a communist and attacked me repeatedly in the Communist press for For Whom The Bell Tolls. But you get no idea of that in the book. Mr. Putnam is a very slippery character who, in Paris, had a very fine subject to write on.

The other book I haven't seen and would be very glad to read if you would send it. I will see it gets back to you. Would you like me to make any marginal notes on any parts that don't seem to make sense?

Am glad you are useing Crime and Punishment; what about The Brothers and The Idiot? I always thought The Gambler was a wonderful story too.

My health is good; thank you very much. Hope yours is. My middle boy, Patrick, had a severe and un-attended concussion in a motor car accident in Key West with his younger brother. If he had been put to bed he would have been o.k. but he played 6 sets of tennis with the pro instead and kept up his exercise without takeing any rest until he was in really bad shape when he got back here. Has been very sick for 64 days and we had to feed him rectally for 45 days. Meantime my wife's father was ill in Chicago and had to be operated on. She came back from Chicago and shortly developed flu and a gastro-enteritis and ran a fever of close to 104 for two weeks in spite of treatment with the various sulfas and, for the last week, penicillin every three hours. Is better today.

So I am two months behind on my novel which was going awfully well and on which I have about 130,000 words done. Was re-writing and cutting on the first part and almost ready to get into the new again when Patrick turned up in such bad shape.

As soon as he is o.k. and Mrs. Hemingway is o.k. (a matter of days for her now) will get in good shape again with a few days on the boat and get back to work. Take this chance to write you now as when I am writing I am so damned tired when I finish each day that it's almost impossible to write letters.

Dr. has just come and must go in to interpret for him. So will close. Thanks for your letter again and for the offer to send the book.

Best to you always,
Ernest Hemingway

Please excuse such a lousy letter—things a little rugged here at this moment.

ws

PH. PUL

1. Seward was an English professor at Old Dominion, Norfolk, Virginia. Among his books is *My Friend Ernest Hemingway* (New York, 1969).

To CHARLES SCRIBNER, La Finca Vigia, 28 June 1947

Dear Charlie:

Don't worry about me kid. You have troubles enough without that. I didn't write you after I cabled because what the hell can you say. We don't need to talk wet about Max to each other. The bad was for him to die.[1] I hadn't figured on him dying; I'd just thought he might get so completely damn deaf we'd lose him that way. Anyway for a long time I had been trying to be less of a nuisance to him and have all the fun with him possible. We had a hell of a good time this last time in New York and wasn't it lucky it was that way instead of a lot of problems and arguments. Anyway he doesn't have to worry about Tom Wolfe's chickenshit estate anymore, or handle Louise's business, nor keep those women writers from building nests in his hat. Max had a lot of fun, anyway I know we had a lot of fun together, but useing up all his resistance that way by not takeing some lay offs to build up is a good lesson to us and don't you get to overworking now, at least until young Charlie gets to know the business for quite a long time because I want to be able to see your alcohol ravaged face when I come in the office for at least the next twenty two years to help me feel someone in N.Y. has a worse hang-over than I have.

Charlie don't worry about me at all. I never liked that son of a bitch Darrow but he's out. Wallace [Meyer] and I like and understand each other very well. You and I get along damn well. A lot better than people know and you don't have to worry about writing me letters. I'd have to work and try to write well if I were in jail, or if I had 20 million dollars, or if I was broke and working at something else to keep going, or if I was going to die, or if I had word I was going to live forever. So don't worry about me. I'm not going to succumb to any temptations and I don't flatter easy any more. You've got enough dough to back me to extent that I have to ask for it while I write this book and I will borrow as little as I can and write as good as I can. Have been working out ways for my existant stories to be sold to pictures on a non-whoreing basis to keep me going while write, same as always, with no regard for whether it is to sell; but only on a basis of how well I can write it. At least have been working on that and if [Maurice] Speiser doesn't blow it up by over-extending his negociatory ability should be o.k. within this month. However things go I have dough now to last me until Sept. But if the deal with Hellinger goes through I am set for all the time I will need on the book and some afterwards.

If it would do any good you might let it be known that while Max was my best and oldest friend at Scribners and a great, great editor he never cut a paragraph of my stuff nor asked me to change one. One of my best and most loyal friends and wisest counsellors in life as well as in writing is dead. But Charles Scribners Sons are my publishers and I intend to publish with them for the rest of my life.

Malcolm Cowley can tell you what he and Max and I and later he and Max were lineing up of getting out a three vol. edition of Farewell To Arms, Sun Also Rises, and For Whom The Bell Tolls showing the relationship between the three with illustrations and an introduction by Cowley. That might come after the new edition of A Farewell To Arms you said you and Max were talking about. I think it is good policy to keep these books going in our own editions and the three comeing out together with the Cowley tie-up of them would insure good reviews. Might do better hitting with all three than throwing in piecemeal.

If only the boys hadn't done away with Ben Siegal we might have put him in charge of getting me the Nobel prize. He asked me one time, "Ernie why don't you ever get any of these prizes? I see other writers getting prizes. What's the trouble Ernie? There's certainly some way that can be rigged."

Won't bother you with any more of this with everything you have on your hands. If young Charlie is going good in the advertizing end why not leave him there for a while instead of yanking him?

Been rugged here with Patrick and Mary both so sick. This is the 78th day with Patrick. Mary has gone over to Key West to convalesce at the Key West house with Pauline looking after her. Pauline was wonderful. Came over and helped in every way. Mary held a fever above 102 and reaching 104 every day for nearly three weeks. Treated her with all the sulfas and then Dr.s gave 2 million units of Penicillin. Started with flu she picked up in Chicago I guess when looking after her father who was being operated there. Turned into gastro-enteritis with some sort of tropical bug that they couldn't isolate. Pauline thinks Mary's a wonderful girl and they've made good friends.

We had to feed Patrick rectally for 45 days. He's eating fine now, regaining weight, getting very strong and completely lucid for as many as four and five hours at a time.

I slept in a bed for first time in a couple months night before last and certainly was easy to sleep. It's been a wonderful year for rain and the place is very beautiful. Wish could send you mangoes and alligator pears. Please give my love to your wife.

We have real Gordon's gin at 50 bucks a case and real Noilly Prat and have found a way of makeing ice in the deep-freeze in tennis ball tubes that comes out 15 degrees below zero and with the glasses frozen too makes the coldest martini in the world. Just enough vermouth to cover the bottom of the glass, ounce ¾ of gin, and the spanish cocktail onions very crisp and also 15 degrees below zero when they go in the glass.

This has been rugged as I said but there are better ways of sweating it out than putting your head on the wailing wall.

Did Max get the invitation to the Bronze Star thing?[2] Gen. Lanham who I was with from Normandy on when he was commanding 22nd Inf. Regt. said I should have turned it down but I thought that would be rude and also imply I thought I should have something better which I thought sort of chickenshit. One time in the war got drunk at a dinner because was to get DSC but it got turned down at the top. So thought better take this before it got cancelled.

So long Charlie. Take care of yourself.

Best always
Ernest

Have you heard anything from Martha? I haven't heard from her since Christmas. Have a new house-maid named Martha and certainly is a pleasure to give her orders. Marty was a lovely girl though. I wish she hadn't been quite so ambitious and war crazy. Think it must be sort of lonesome for her without a war.

PUL

1. Maxwell Perkins had died in Stamford, Connecticut, at 5 A.M. on 17 June 1947.
2. EH had received the Bronze Star on 13 June 1947 at the American Embassy in Havana.

To WILLIAM FAULKNER, La Finca Vigia, 23 July 1947

Dear Bill:

Awfully glad to hear from you and glad to have made contact. Your letter came tonight and please throw all the other stuff away, the misunderstanding, or will have to come up and we both trompel on it. There isn't any at all. I was sore and Buck [Lanham] was sore and we were instantly unsore the minute we knew the score.

I know what you mean about T. Wolfe and Dos and still can't agree. I never felt the link-up in Wolfe except with the N.C. stuff. Dos I always liked and respected and thought was a 2nd rate writer on acct. no ear. 2nd rate boxer has no left hand, same as ear to writer, and so gets his brains knocked out and this happened to Dos with every book. Also terrible snob (on acct. of being a bastard) (which I would welcome) and very worried about his negro blood when could have been our best negro writer if would have just been negro as hope *we* would have.

You picked a very cold one of mine to make the comparison on about the great thing we would all like to do. To make it really how it was any really good morning—but I tried to get way past that like when they are fucking comeing back from makeing contact with the other outfit about the bridge, when the Pilar woman knows what the hell it is all about; again where she is talking about her man, before, and Valencia and the fun they had (which think will stand); where she is talking about smell of death (which is no shit) and all the part with her man who was in bull fight business and where we kill the fascists in the village. Probably bore the shit out of you to re-read but as brother would like to know what you think. Anyway is as good as I can write and was takeing all chances (for a pitcher who, when has control, can throw fairly close) could take. (Probably failed.)

Difference with us guys is I always lived out of country (as mercenary or patriot) since kid. My own country gone. Trees cut down. Nothing left but gas stations, sub-divisions where we hunted snipe on the prairie, etc. Found good country outside, learned language as well as know English, and lost it the same way. Most people don't know this. Dos always came to us as a tourist. I was always makeing a liveing, paying my debts and always stayed to fight. Been chickenshit dis-placed person since can remember but fought each time before we lost (and this last time we fought with most stuff and it was the easiest and we lost the worst). Things never been worse than now.

You are a better writer than Fielding or any of those guys and you should just know it and keep on writing. You have things written that come back to me better than any of them and I am not dopy, really. You shouldn't read the shit about liveing writers. You should always write your best against dead writers that we know what stature (not stature: evocative power) that they have and beat them one by one. Why do you want to fight Dostoevsky in your first fight? Beat Turgenieff—which we both did soundly and for time which I hear tick too with a pressure of 205 over 115 (not bad for the way things have run at all). Then nail yourself DeMaupassant (tough boy until he got the old rale. Still dangerous for three rounds). Then try and take Stendhal. (Take him and we're all happy.) But don't fight with the poor pathological characters of our time (we won't name). You and I can both beat Flaubert who is our most respected, honored master. But to do that you have to be able to accept the command of a battalion when it is given (when you are a great company commander), to relinquish it to be second in command of a regiment (walk with shits nor lose the common touch) and then be able to take a regiment when you loathe the takeing of it and were happy where you were (or were unhappy but didn't want to go over Niagara Falls in a barrell) (I can't go up higher in this hierarchy because have no higher experience and anyway probably bore the shit out of you). Anyway I am your Bro. if you want one that writes and I'd like us to keep in touch. My middle kid (Pat) very sick now 4 months. Had to feed rectally 45 days. Now eats and sleeps OK but not out of woods. Please excuse if write stupidly. This most talented boy. Oldest very . . . nice. Capt Paratroops 3 times wounded etc. Prisoner 6 months. We mounted attack to get him out of hock when first taken P.O.W. and accessible (drop) but was cancelled. This boy (sick) good painter, head smashed in auto accident his kid bro. driveing. Excuse chickenshit letter. Have much regard for you. Would like to keep on writing [letters].

JFK   Ernest Hemingway

To MAXWELL GEISMAR,[1] La Finca Vigia, 10 September 1947

Dear Mr. Geismar:

Thank you very much for sending me the new book [*Last of the Provincials: The American Novel, 1921–1925*]. I look forward to it with great interest. If you are writing to Houghton Mifflin would it be too much trouble to ask them to send it to me at Sun Valley, Idaho and mark it please hold? Am leaveing here next week to drive out there and hole up and work there in the in-between season when there is no one out there between Summer and Winter Sports. It is a fine place and a wonderful climate there and I can recommend it to you if you ever take a vacation in the fall.

Are you still teaching? I've thought of you and your wife often and what good talk we had in that early spring of '44. Have not had much chance to talk about writing since except one day when I met Cowley in N.Y. just before Christmas. Max Perkins being dead makes things more lonely too. I wish we could get together sometime.

Wish you luck with the rest of the books. Would hate to have to write about the early characters after [F. O.] Mathiessen (probably misspelled) but maybe you have another angle. Have you read The Gallery by J. H. Burns. I thought it was excellent. Much better than Dos at Dosses's stuff. I thought big parts of The Big Sky by A. B. Guthrie were really good though he blew up a little on part of it. Liked [A. Hayes's] All Thy Conquests very much. Thought Algren was not so good as Never Come Morning in all but two or three of the stories (first one splendid) in The Neon Wilderness. Couple of good small stories in [John] O'Hara's

last book [*Hellbox*] and two or three better ones in [Jerome] Weidman's
[*Captain's Tiger*]. I liked Weidman's book about the Psychopathical
Warfare outfit, Too Early To Tell. I think he may be a hell of a good
writer. He certainly was in the first two books. I don't think things look
bad at all for writing with three as good writers as Burns, Guthrie and
Hayes showing in one year. Read some other stuff but mostly junk.

Trouble with army was that the tests, classifications, screenings according to ability were so thorough that practically no one who was literate
or articulate ever saw combat. They were all made PRO's, Yank correspondents or put into Intelligence, Psycho warfare etc. We were trying
to get a decent regt. history of the 22nd Infantry regt. that I was with
from Normandy through Siegfried, Hurtgen, the Ardennes Bulge fight,
and practically no one who survived can even write a decent letter. All
wonderful guys completely inarticulate and worse with pen or pencil. I
had thought to have the bare bones of it and then each action commented
on truly by those who participated. But it is going to be impossible.

Meantime been working on same book [probably *The Garden of
Eden*] I was on when I saw you. Getting very big but I cut the hell out
of it periodically. Have had the bejesus knocked out of my work for
five months with my middle boy nearly dying and wife's father very sick,
then wife same, but everybody ok now and am going for a change of
climate and start biteing on the nail again.

Thank you for writing and for sending the book. Would you mind
writing in it so I can leave it for my kids. One of them likes books.

Best luck always and my best regards to your wife.

Yours always
BU   Ernest Hemingway

1. Geismar (1909–1979) was an influential American critic.

To CHARLES SCRIBNER, La Finca Vigia, 18 September 1947

Dear Charlie:

Have just written my friend Maurice [Speiser] (when I first knew him
he was Moe. But now he is Maurice while I am still Ernie) and that
brought you to my mind. You were sort of in my mind anyway on acct.
of stareing at me alongside the typewriter for a month in red letters
WRITE CHARLEY ANSWER ABOUT ILLUSTRATIONS.

So here goes. Awfully sorry to have been delayed. But there has been
hell's own balls up here trying to keep people from dying and all that

sort of thing. But now Patrick is fine. Mary is well again and handsome and brown and happy. Pauline is staying on here with Patrick for a few weeks to finish his convalescence. Mary is staying a couple of weeks to supervise some building we are doing and I am off day after tomorrow to drive out west with [Otto] Bruce my old secretary, treasurer, chauffeur, valet and procurer. With him don't have to worry about driveing at night as he is wonderful at it and I will hole up in Idaho and get going good on the book in the same place where worked on FWTBTolls in 1939 and Mary will come out when finishes here. I could write probably a much better book than am writing on haveing a couple of wives around at the same time and a former and present behaveing absolutely marvellously; *really* good. But maybe will get around to that later.

Got your sad royalty report and the catalogue and samples of literature all of which (except the royalty report which slipped from my nerveless hands and dropped down the can) am takeing out west to read at leisure. Address there will be Sun Valley Lodge, Sun Valley, Idaho for next three months, maybe 4.

Had a hell of a time makeing up my mind about the illustrations. Am sending back three that believe should be changed with comments and returning the originals. They are not the way I would do it: any of it. But they are a damned sight better than haveing the book out of print and some are excellent and some have an excellent feeling that comes through. Would like to have talked with the illustrator when he was doing them but since couldn't, please thank him very much for me for his fine work and feeling and give him the comments on the only ones I really object to. The girl in the book actually looked a lot like Marlene [Dietrich] when Marlene was younger. She wasn't the pinched English type. She had a pure featured, lovely face but it was not at all pinched as she is in that sort of Mother Superior face she had in the picture on the bed I objected to. She was sad as hell in that picture but all the girls I have ever known who cried or got close to it when sad sort of swelled around the eyes and lips rather than pinched up. I think a girl with a naturally lovely face never looks as beautiful as when she has cried or is going to cry—after cried even better. Just as a woman with a face built by artistry goes all to hell when she cries.

Anyway with these three corrections they are o.k. with me if you want to go ahead.[1]

How is everything? Have been so preoccupied with the illnesses here that have been very remiss about writing. Thank you very much for the books and the De Guingand book[2] too. He is a great charmer and a soldier of the Montgomery school and much the same caliber. Believes you have an even chance if you have a superiority of 13/1. Otherwise let someone else fight. When I was a boy we used to say three to one is nigger fun. But 13/1 is Montgomery fun. Have no respect and not much patience with these people but they are so articulate and plausible and well entrenched that there is nothing to be done about them. But it certainly would have been simple if we had to fight them instead of the poor beat up old krauts.

Look forward to the [Mark] Aldanov [*Before the Deluge*, 1947]. Thought his Fifth Seal was brilliant and For Thee The Best one of most disappointing books ever read. Maybe it is just a brick in the whole pattern. But he better produce a pretty good building this time.

Evan Shipman, from his communication, needed that money to bet on a horse, which, I gather, lost. There was a terrible connection on the fone and I thought it was a matter of life and death and so bothered you when I shouldn't have. But next time it may be a matter of L[ife] and D[eath] so we will just continue the exercise as before.

Will look forward to reading Josie [Josephine] Herbst's book [*Somewhere the Tempest Fell*, 1947].

You must miss that damned Max. It has been a bad year for deads. Of two of my very best friends one was assassinated in Warsaw a month ago. Another died in Germany. Both Generals, wonderful guys and fine soldiers. Katy Dos Passos was an old girl of mine, had known her since she was 8 years old, and Dos drove her into a parked truck and killed her last Sat.[3] Another good friend lost his wife in childbirth a month ago when the doctor didn't show up in time. And old Taylor Williams, from Idaho, that think I introduced to you in N.Y. (no it was to Max) lost his one boy in this last war and his daughter, a lovely girl, died two weeks ago. Looks as though our Heavenly Father was perhaps dealing off the bottom of the deck which was why got Bruce to drive out with me to protect your investment as I see worse at night all the time and the days are short this time of year.

Will certainly be happy to get out there and get to working good again.

About business: would like to carry the money I owe as a loan and pay same interest on it. If need any more will borrow some on same basis if agreeable until it is time to take an advance on the book. Maybe won't need one. Am trying to straighten my money affairs out o.k. but had to dig into my reserves these last five months pretty badly and the tax situation is really appalling. You know it better than I do but we have so very few deductions and unless you can build up a reserve you have no chance at this trade. I have made more money than many people with considerable fortunes ever made honestly: but what the hell have I been allowed to keep out of it. And I have fought in every war that I have been taxed to pay for. At least when you go into the Embassy you have a feeling that you own a fair interest in the joint and they can be quite civil.

Well so long Charlie. Please give my best to your wife and take care of yourself and don't worry about me at all in any way. Don't worry about haveing to write me either.

Yours always,

PUL

Ernest

1. A new boxed edition of *A Farewell to Arms*, illustrated by Daniel Rasmusson, with an introduction by EH dated 30 June 1948, was published 15 November 1948. 2. Major General Sir Francis De Guingand, *Operation Victory* (New York, 1947). Sir Francis had been Montgomery's chief of staff. 3. Mrs. Dos Passos was instantly killed and Dos Passos lost his right eye in an automobile accident near Wareham, Massachusetts, 12 September 1947. It was a Friday, not a Saturday. See Townsend Ludington, *John Dos Passos: A Twentieth Century Odyssey* (New York, 1980), pp. 431–32.

To CHARLES SCRIBNER, Sun Valley, Idaho, 29 October 1947

Dear Charlie:

Sorry to be late answering your letter of Oct. 8.

The Josie Herbst book came a couple of days ago and will read it. Dipped into it, which is an unfair way to read. The dipping did not excite me but will read it and let you know. Is very hard to read stuff that is just worth-while when you are working.

About Maurice [Speiser]: he has no authority from me at all to discuss permissions, reprints etc. with you. I have always done all my business with you for better or for worse and no third party has any authority to mix in it. I have not discussed reprint rights with him nor has he written me anything about them. I agree with you that any questions about this you should bring up directly with me. If it is re-printing in a text-book which will have a sale over a number of years I think the author should get what would correspond to his share of royalties rather than a simple re-print fee. If any one is to get a substantial royalty out of the book the man whose stuff is reprinted should have his share. It is a racket for some teacher to write an often stupid and almost always uninspired introduction and then offer a collection of good stories to be used as a text book which kids have to buy (or schools have to buy). Don't you agree?

Been working hard out here. Change of climate acts as a super-charger. Work in morning and shoot in pm.

There's one other thing must write about, Charlie. Do you know where the original photographs reproduced in Death In The Afternoon are? Cape wants to reprint and needs them to reproduce from. Is out of print in England and Cape says he can sell as many as he can get paper to print.

Will you try and trace them? If they were returned to me I have not been able to locate them in Key West nor in Cuba. That does not mean that they are not stored somewhere in K.W. but have not been able to locate them. Bruce, my former secretary, searched through a lot of stuff there but it seems Pauline needed a metal filing cabinet in which most of that sort of stuff was stored and so it was re-distributed (or should we say dispersed). Anyway I haven't been able to find them yet if I had them. I don't remember ever haveing them but do remember haveing all those hundreds we did not use. They haven't turned up either.

Will you please see if you had them, or if they were turned over to Reynal and let Cape know direct? Also, if you do not have them, would it be possible to reproduce them photographing from the photographs reproduced in a first edition before they became worn. Are the plates in such shape now that they do not print properly? If they are o.k. could Cape not get them from you, or buy whatever reproductions he needs? Will you let him know about this and also let me know? . . .

Aldanoff [Mark Aldanov] I've not yet read. Will let you know about that too. His Fifth Seal was wonderfully well written. This starts more stodgily. But maybe when I get into it [it] will start to move. Such damned exciting things happen in our own time that it is hard to leave Now, if you have seen the things, to go back into a fictional past unless they project it very wonderfully.

Did I tell you one of Max's womens wrote me and wanted me to be Max to her. Just for an hour a week or so at some of the old haunts. (Mustn't mention this to any one or make fun of her.) But do you think I could get the old hat stretched, clean up my moral precepts, stuff up one ear, and go out with her? Once I think would probably cure her. Poor bloody woman. Max is dead and he won't come back and there isn't any substitute. Especially I would be none. If we would have known Max was going to die should have made sound movies of him and then run them off for all the women and everybody could take turns speaking well of him and get the womens all drunk and then if any of them were still up to it lay them. Hell it might have gotten to be a religion.

Shouldn't have written about that poor woman but too late to take it all out now. Just throw it out.

Don't think there is anything more that haven't answered except about those Mss. Miss [Irma Wyckoff] Wykoff turned up in Max's desk. Will you ask her to hold them for me and when I get down to Cuba she can send them down. If they are worth anything I can keep them for the kids.

Mary's out hunting for a big buck. Left at five this morning. Was out all yest. afternoon and the day before. There are only three days more of the season for deer and she is covering the hills. She loves it. We have a split season on duck this year. In the first one she shot beautifully. Second season starts 2nd Dec. Pheasant Nov. 1. I've been working hard but had some very good shooting in the afternoons.

Hope you are well Charlie and that everything goes well with you.

Best always,

PUL   Ernest.

1. Martha Gellhorn, "Cry Shame," *New Republic* 117 (6 October 1947), on Hanns Eisler and the House Un-American Activities Committee hearings.

To GENERAL CHARLES T. LANHAM, La Finca Vigia, 15 April 1948

Dear Buck:

I was delighted to hear from you although am still worried about your over-work. It is perfectly possible to work yourself to death. I know because I thought I was an iron man and almost literally worked myself to death last Spring, summer, and early fall with Patrick and Mary. So for Christ sake ease up a little.

Thanks for report on Cowley.[1] Sorry he bothered you. I see no reason to give the story of the Paris entry to him when I can always write it myself or use it in a story. I simply gave him the bare movements in a letter. We separated from the 2nd French armoured main column at Clamart, went down the hill to Bas Meudon while they continued on to Montrouge and the Porte D'Orleans. We secured the Pont de Sevres that night and the next morning went on in and up through the Porte de St. Cloud, Auteuil and up to the Etoile. We had reached the Etoile while LeClerc forces were still fighting around the Luxembourg. Not that any of it matters in the slightest. But I see no reason to give it all to Cowley for free. On other hand might as well be straight historically. In the hurried piece I wrote for Colliers I ended when we were looking down on Paris comeing down the old road I used to climb on bicycle when we would ride Paris-Versailles, Rambouillet and return back in the days when learned that country by heart. Paris was actually liberated by its own people and could have been occupied with only the amount of fighting 2nd French armoured had to do between Rambouillet and Clamart (two small fights) at least five days before. 90% of the shooting 2nd French Armoured did was practically feu de joie. The two real fights were small but intense. The fighting in Paris its-self was just knocking out the small amount of stuff left there and mopping up installations they had been unable to evacuate. That was why it was so goddamned much fun.

Hope you will go to Mexico where can fly over and see something of you. Miss seeing you and talking very much. Sorry about the Swiss deal. I'd like to go to Switzerland too.

Buck, can't give you any pressure statistics as have not taken since left Sun Valley. Have kept on bringing the weight down, though and am 217¼ as of today. Highest was 252. Am following doctor's regime and takeing stuff he prescribed. Hard to take off weight when working so hard. But have whittled it down steadily.

In April have written 556, 822, 1266, fished, 631, 0, 966, 725, 0 (4500 words of letters and business), 679, o (Sunday—laid off), 466, 905, 763 in what has run of this month. Hope it isn't all shit.

About that record of testimony taken before the I.G. [Inspector General] of 3rd Army. I know how goddamned busy you are and hate to bother you with it. But think it is possibly fairly simple employing these steps:

A—Ascertain who was I.G. 3rd Army (Rear) on 5th October 1944. Testimony was taken at 3rd Army Headquarters (Rear) at Nancy, France.

B—Ascertain from I.G. if this record is available.

C—If I.G. has no information ascertain who was the stenographer who took down the testimony. This stenographer can then be located through channels and I will write him once he is located. He told me the day the testimony was taken that he was makeing a copy for me. When I went through Verdun en-route to Luxembourg after the Bulge business had started we spent the night there. This stenographer heard I was in town and attempted to locate me to give me this record. But we were already gone.

Through the I.G. we can find out who took down the testimony. Knowing who this man is I can find out if a copy still exists.

Am sorry as hell to bother about this. But sooner or later, especially if I am dead, there will be a lot of rhubarb about this and I think the record is much the best thing to have.

I know various copies exist since if the I.G. had decided charges should be preferred and there had been a court [martial] I would have been entitled to read the record to refresh my memory.

Now that it is no longer restricted I would like to have the damned thing to refresh my memory when I write it.

My memory has been hit enough times with blunt instruments so that any help is welcomed.

Aint going to write any more about politics. Haveing seen a few latin american revolutions and knowing the back ground on this Columbian one a little the idea that it originated in the Kremlin certainly is a pain in the ass. However it at least provided an occasion for Dr. [S. L. A.] Marshall to hear a shot fired in anger, or at least in irritation, and to gauge the calibre of his G2 gen. Though I imagine that by now his mind is so firmly set that all gen must be made to conform to the groove rather than try and give the really true gen on anything.

If I ever get any further fed up with the Cuban Electric Company (highest rates in the world) or the Cotorro Aqueduct (worthless pipes bought at flea markets and charged triple price. Consequent seepage of water which results in no water for our town) and, exhausting all legal resources, lead those of my fellow townspeople who still have a pair of balls in an assault on either of these two institutions hope you won't think it was Kremlin inspired and I was paid by Russki gold.

Some one broke Mr. [James] Forrestall's nose once in the Raquet Club. Us old broken nose characters would have had the nose fixed. Not Mr. F. He is a tough man. A fighting man. Sure. He'll get his fight and my kids will fight it for him. And if I go Lester Armour will get my DSC (that will give him a cluster to it).

I am for my country right or wrong same as S[tephen] Decatur (can't spell him). But I don't like a lot of stuff that is being pulled by the Unsuccessful Haberdasher [President Truman] and Mr. F[orrestal]. So I shut up as of now. Don't ever ask me what I think. I don't think. Reminds me of General Walter, a soviet soldier I knew in Spain who was a good kidder. He was a pole and later war minister for Poland and assassinated last year. [André] Malraux, a phony, kept asking him questions like what do you think, mon general, about all sorts of things, le masturbation parmi le chinoise, le valeur devant le mort de les indigene du classe super-intellectuelle etc. Finally Walter said, "Pour-quoi demande moi penser? *Penser?* Moi Generale sovietique. Moi pense jamais!"

Moi ecrivain de San Francisco de Paula. Moi ecrire bouqins [old books]. Moi pense jamais.

Good luck Buck
Best from all
Ernie

PUL

1. Malcolm Cowley was gathering material for "A Portrait of Mr. Papa," which appeared in *Life* 25 (10 January 1949): 86–101. See EH to Marion Smith, 31 May 1948.

To MARION SMITH,[1] La Finca Vigia, 31 May 1948

Dear Marion:

Thanks for your letter. Please tell Bill not to give Cowley anything he ever would want to use himself. Chances are Cowley won't even get down to Washington. I had a letter from him day before yest. and they were rushing him on the piece and he told me Bill was in Washington same time I got your letter with same info.

I gave Bill's name to Cowley as my best friend in Michigan times. Just so he could check on anything with Bill.

How I happened to get mixed up in the thing at all was that Cowley got a chance of an expense paid vacation with wife and child to Havana contingent on writing a piece about me. I was sickened of the idea of a piece about me after ten minutes and just gave him the names of my friends that he could ask about me instead of getting a lot of crap from me which would nauseate me to give out and to read.

About Provincetown: I think you should go there and not be gloomy at all about Katy [Dos Passos]. She is dead and so will we all be and there is nothing to do about it. So we might as well remember the people we love exactly as they were and still love them. Of course if it made Bill gloomy and there was nothing to do about it then you should pull out.

Am so happy to have news of you both. Our news is ups and downs and arounds and abouts. Had quite a time in the war from 42 through the early Spring of 45.

It's funny that your address should be N. Pershing Drive [Arlington, Virginia] and in the old days can remember a Pershing address of Bill's in St. Louis. And Pershing still [seven words illegible] and Dos talking sort of like the Pres. of the American Manufacturers Association.

When Katy was killed I felt so god-damned awful that I couldn't write Bill anything. But he knows that I loved Katy almost as much as Bill and Dos did. As much as anybody could without being her brother or her husband.

Take good care of Bill for me among other people. We will keep in touch now we have made contact again and if I come to Washington will up-look. You'd like Mary I think. I love her very much and we get along.

Love to you both,
Wemedge

How are you Smith you ghosting fiend?[2]
Above address is permanent. Tel. is Cotorro 17–3.
PUL

1. Wife of William B. Smith, Jr. 2. W. B. Smith, Jr., to Carlos Baker, 1 February 1962: "I began ghosting for Labor Dept. officials in 1941, continued under Maj. Gen. Philip B. Fleming, director of the Federal Works Agency, and in other spots until I retired last July."

To CHARLES SCRIBNER, La Finca Vigia, 2 June 1948

Dear Charlie:

Just a note to enclose check for the $12000 I borrowed to pay taxes plus 100.00 interest = 5 months at 2 percent. Thank you for banking me. I feel almost the same affection toward you as I have for my book maker.

As a matter of fact I suppose you are my book maker. I don't think I'll come up for [Joe] Louis and [Jersey Joe] Walcott—Louis is through.[1] Will bet the dough the trip would have cost on Walcott—altho betting on fights is a mug's game.

You have been getting out some good books lately and I have been buying them all. Last month caught 18 good dolphin, 5 good wahoos, 6 kingfish (one 54 lbs.), a 48-pound snapper, and 7 marlin. The largest a 110 lb. white marlin on 15 thread line and a feather jig. They had elections here yest. and looks like some crooks still in. I refused to join American Academy of etc. Hope this doesn't offend you. On other hand think will join Whites of London if they will let me in. Eased off on the book[2] in May because Dr. said I worked too hard in April, and May fine month to fish and make love to Miss Mary. I have to ease off on makeing love when writing hard as the two things are run by the same motor. Take care of yourself.

                                                          Ernest

PUL

1. Louis knocked out Walcott in the eleventh round, 25 June 1948. 2. The book that later became *Islands in the Stream* (New York, 1970).

To CHARLES SCRIBNER, La Finca Vigia, 3 June 1948

Dear Charlie:

I had your letter of June 1 this morning after writing you yesterday to return that particular piece of money I borrowed from you.

Here's the bad news quickly: the minimum royalty has to be 12½ percent. From my point of view it should be 15%.

Here is why: You have to carry the ball *sometimes*.

Farewell To Arms is out of print. Green Hills is out of print. I can't even get a copy that I have promised to shooting friends since over two months. I don't know the status of the other books but I don't imagine it is too hot.

In the meantime, knowing all this, I gave you my word that I would stick with you and you had no need to worry. I have turned down all sorts of propositions, deals etc. and have kept the product pure. Whatever it is it is as good as I can make it and I have not corrupted it by working for the coast nor doing things I thought were shitty and would hurt me as a writer no matter how much money they brought in. But you have to carry the ball sometimes if we are going to play in the same back field. Unless I am just to be a blocking back. Which I am not.

I do not give one inferior fuck whether Scribners makes a dime on an edition [of *A Farewell to Arms*] such as you describe. All that is is a prestige (for me and you both) and a piece of good will edition and you do not need to make any money out of it.

How many times do you think I go without makeing money to keep what you and I jointly sell straight and okay and better the quality? Many, many times and practically all the time. Day and night.

To return to the book: If I write an introduction automatically all the poor bloody collectors have to buy it. That is worth something to you as a guaranty.

Life is running a story on me by Malcolm Cowley which will more or less co-incide with your publication. The magazine has a considerable circulation (I don't know whether you have ever seen it. But it is supposed to be doing okay). The story is of the proportion of a cover story. They have decided for some obscure reason that I am a good writer. Maybe this was because they have editors who get outside the country. I sold, for instance, in expensive, not cheap editions, 340,000 copies in Denmark of books you allowed to go out of print. (The Life publicity is probably worth $100,000 depending on space and circulation.)

The sale doesn't mean a god-damned thing. Zane Grey or Gertrude Atherton might sell more. Only they don't. And these were books by a serious writer written as well as I could write them.

So remember, or try to think, that you are a publisher and you have to carry the ball sometimes and just not me who goes to fight in all the fucking wars and gets my brains knocked out and never fake and cheat in writing or write crap for all the dough they offer and waste my expensive time and my one and only life helping Cowley to find out facts and sources for a damned piece that disgusts me to do but is probably necessary historically and from which you will profit plenty more than I will in the long run. Sometimes the run seems very god-damned long too when I see good books of mine out of print.

You can make more dough out of kids and women and God bless them all. But I am an old horse like Exterminator that has won for you every time but once. And I won't run for ten percent and you have that right straight from horse's mouth. I'll give you as good a run as I have in me any time on any track sore feet or no sore feet. But I don't start for ten percent and you would be a god damned smart publisher if you even lost ten thousand dollars on that book and made me happy. But you know damned well you will never lose in the end with me and the only thing that makes horses like Exterminator and me sore is when you make a run and the people that start you haven't got the guts to bet.

None of this is supposed to be insulting nor unfriendly. I am very fond of you, and I have a loyalty to Scribners and to Max (loyalty is a commodity which is not on the market) such as I have had at various times, and retained, to the Spanish Republic, the 4th U.S. Infantry Division and the 22nd Infantry Regiment. I have felt much more deeply about the 12th International Brigade and my children and Mary. But you don't need love for Christ sake for a damn book publishing business or a government or a good military unit. All you need is loyalty. You have it.

But this letter is to tell you very explicitly and for re-reading how I feel about the whole deal and the situation. If you want to get it as straight as possible, I will put it in military terms since am thinking and writing in them lately. I can't think well in bigger terms than a Division (can do it. But it isn't what I really know).

As of that: You are commanding a Division and can give or not give what you decide according to what you have. I am a *completely loyal* regimental commander but I do not like the way my General is thinking. I have seen too many attacks when I tried to take something for a dime, under orders, and then had to spend $64. to take what could have been taken for seventy five cents. Also although loyal completely I am a mercenary and I don't fight for ten per cent.

Good luck Charlie. And take this the way it is written: friendly and as straight as I can write it.

Best always
Ernest

If we are going into business relations, I probably buy more books from Scribner's Retail book store than any steady client you have and I don't get a discount on *Scribner* books. Nor has *anybody* sent me a Scribner book as a present since Max died. (And this can be remedied.)

EH

You sent me a couple of worthless ones at the start. But I bought all the good ones.

PUL   EH

To GENERAL R. O. BARTON, La Finca Vigia, 9 June 1948

Dear Tubby:

It was fine to hear from you and my answer has been delayed because I was away on a trip. Have had a photographer here from Holiday making color shots of jumping fish etc. Color is slow slow and needs such exact light conditions that when you start fitting them to tides etc. it gets more balled up than one of Georgie Patton's columns held up by two burp guns before the Great End Run. Think got good stuff though. Watch for it in about four or five months. I am writing a piece to go with it.[1]

Am glad to know where you are and hear of your job. It sounds very good and am glad you are working. I work hard too but writing is dull as hell after what we used to do. I haven't killed a son of a bitch for over four years now and the tatoo-ing is getting faded. Anyway we had a good and fine and honorable war, maybe the best anybody had, and you and I got not a god-damned thing out of it. But you led a great division and you always have that. You led them from the beach into Germany and through Hurtgen and through the Rundstedt thing. After that the Krauts were through and though there was fighting it was circus fighting.

Also Tubby I am eternally grateful to you for turning me loose that time so I could go on and into Paris so I had a chance to have a command, no matter how irregular, and do something useful and fight into the town I love the best in the world. I could not have done any of the things I was happy about in the war without you backing me. And you backed me afterwards when we found out things were illegal, technically, that should not be in war. I still do not understand some of it. How can a correspondent fly co-pilot in a B25, bombing V1 launching sites for the R.A.F.[2] wearing the blue clothes, carrying pistol and escape kit and lose two kites out of the same box on one particular operation and then when on the ground, with an infantry division, be expected to be a little gentleman and not fight his way out if in trouble nor be useful if you can be useful.

You formed more or less an idea of whether I was a reliable character or one that could be of any use when we made the break through in late July. I tried to be as useful as I could, not playing politics nor passing gossip from then on until I said good-bye to you in Luxembourg. I have only two real gifts. I can fight without worrying and I have a gift for loyalty. We were all beat-up after Hurtgen and in different degrees and some behaved different than others. But the way you behaved about Jim Luckett on that awful night was the most exemplary behaviour by a commanding officer that I have ever seen. I thought Buck should have been there and I had given my story to Life instead of Colliers (for free) so the Division would get credit in time and I wasn't feeling too hot. Also I like Jim. But you were damned good. Incidentally Colliers never paid my expenses. They found out about the Life thing (Wertenbaker of Life and Time was offered a Lt. Col. commission on acct. of what a military writer he was on strength of that story) and they found out from squealers that I had fought. I was useing my own money that I had in England and France (had to take France to get the money) so the war cost me around 12 G. in 1944–45. Not good business, General.

O.S.S. got a DSC for work I did about Rambouillet laying out everything so LeClerc (am glad that prick is dead) went in on a dime where it would have cost him at least $8.95. It was made out to me. But since I was hot then on account of Geneva Convention they gave it, since they had it, to Lester Armour of the meat aristocracy who carried messages from me to G2 of 2nd French Armoured, never made a patrol (I went way behind the Kraut MLR [main line of resistance] and checked three possible routes into town) and who never was even in any chicken-shit fire fights we had going in. I used to always break them off if we had no deads. Break them off and move. Big operation. Move fast. Don't let chicken-shit hold you up. The opposing characters will fuck off once the column shows. If you have deads you have to kill somebody to keep irregulars happy. (correct me if I am wrong) Next best thing is let them steal sewing machines. Sewing machines only in enemy country. (Could tell you some awfully funny stories.) You covered me on that too.

Enclosed will show you how far along 22nd Inf. Convention is and impossibility of them changeing plans. I can't come this Sept. as will be in Europe. Hate like hell not to. I would love to come and to see you and the remaining characters. I would like to send a cable if it is ok with you.

Buck hasn't answered my last letter and am damned if will write him. May get letter from him today. In which case will write him. I love Buck because of all we were through together [in] Schnee-Eifel and Hurtgen. But I want to be friends with everybody as I tried to be in the Division but writing today I realize fully and clearly that it was you with your quickly placed confidence and trust in me that made it possible for me to be in any degree useful and to get out of the war whatever I got out of it. I hope to christ I was useful and not just a deluded nuisance.

Best luck always,
Ernie

PH. PUL

1. "The Great Blue River," *Holiday* 6 (July 1949). 2. On EH's flights with the RAF, see Carlos Baker, *Ernest Hemingway: A Life Story* (New York, 1969), pp. 396–400.

To CHARLES SCRIBNER, JR., La Finca Vigia, 29 June 1948

Dear Charlie:

Thank you for the note about sending the book in your father's absence. Will look forward to it.

Enclosed is the preface or introduction to the illustrated edition of A Farewell To Arms. I thought it might be useful to explain how I felt about war since have been engaged in it so much while hateing it. Don't be afraid of publishing the preface for fear of hurting the illustrator's feelings; illustrators like this one rank a little higher than photographers. You can't hurt a photographer's feelings. I guess you can; but really they run with Loggerhead turtles (in my book).

Also please have no feelings that what I write might be regarded as subversive. My folks have been in the country for quite a long time, we always participate in the various wars etc. and Hemingway is not a pen-name. I can also take an oath at any time that I am not nor never have been a member of the C.P. [Communist Party].

Am not being snooty. Just kidding rough the way I kid with your old man; 12½ percent Charlie I think of him as. But by God we beat him up from 10. Hope this introduction is worth his miserable 12½. How happily I would have written it for 15 he says nobly.

Please give him my best when you write him and ask him not to bandy my name around if he gets into White's or Boodles and the next time I am in town will see if I cannot help him along socially.

Best to you. Think you are getting out some very good books. Hope you are keeping the back-log of good stuff to come up and are building a young ball team. That is the most important and hardest to do.

Good luck,

Ernest Hemingway

Please send me proof on preface promptly.

PUL

To LILLIAN ROSS,[1] La Finca Vigia, 2 July 1948

Dear Lillian:

It was fine to get the letter. They returned it for insufficient postage so I sent the note off about Sinsky two days before it arrived. Have tried to drill into the children that an un-mailed letter is as bad as an unwritten one; but an office will bitch you up on air-mail postage. I am awfully glad you wrote. When didn't get any letter I thought, well you are a dope to think that girl likes doing this as much as you do. Was good letter.

(1) On Business: tried to think yesterday who would like to read profiles on. Came out like this: Jimmy Cannon; a lush who cuts it out and becomes best sports writer in NYC. Jimmy very interesting. Has beautiful ear when he hits it right and great reportorial integrity. Think good profile. Good quotes from the good pieces of his.

(2) Short one on Patricia Smith (Satira), American dancer who is still in Guanabacoa woman's prison under a barbarous sentence for shooting her lover, Lester Mee, while her lawyers peddle all syndicate rights etc. and the boy's father, from Chicago, put up dough to get her the jail sentence. It is a terrible story and it ought to be dug. A Cuban would have been acquitted for the same crime or get a very light sentence. There is very grave doubt whether Patricia didn't do it in self defence. If I did not have to finish book would be at bat on it now. As it is pass you the tip. I was approached by original lawyers who wanted to peddle me a piece of the racket so I know how bad it is.

(3) A profile on Trujillo if they have never done one. You will find that is the damndest story you ever hit. Many Americans involved: Miami Herald—people you know in N.Y.

(4) Arturo Suarez the columnist here that rebuilt syntax of American language. This is wonderful story and Arturo's columns do the work. Will clip a few classics if you would like to see them. This is a story that Mary ought to do, though, and I wish the hell [Harold] Ross [of the *New Yorker*] would commission her to do it.

That's the business.

About tennis: used to love it but we have gotten out of the habit of playing it since the Basque pelota players that were my pals went to Mexico D.F. It is hot to play here in the summer and this winter there was the drought and no water to keep the court up. I was a mediocre player as a kid; learned to play pretty well, but ugly, when was up in Canada working in Toronto. Always played people much better than I was and liked doubles. With the Basques we played doubles against trios with the man at the net allowed to cross over and intercept the serve, and other special ground rules. Guillermo, who you may have seen play, and I would play any trio and we did all right. Lots of betting. . . .

I can't play singles anymore but love doubles. But I have to play an awful lot to have any game and when start after long lay-off look so awful you could not believe could play. Wonderful game though. I would rather watch Big Time tennis than almost anything except bicycle raceing and ball. Like to watch Pro-football and fights too of course. Bull fighting (in Spain) of course is best. But it isn't a sport. Pro-football and fights aren't either.

Glad you were a ball player. Could you hit? What did [John] Huston tell you about playing ball down here? I do not want to blow whistle on anyone but he did not play any ball with us. Our old ball team is busted up. We haven't played any hard ball since around VJ Day or so. I told John some funny stories about playing ball down here and he must have then imagined he played with us. He never did. That's a thing people have on the coast. I would rather have done three or four things, quit when you know you are through, and keep the memory of them straight, so they belong to you, than have that romantic prep-school shit. You never meet anybody from the coast that hasn't played at least semi-pro ball, they've all fought bulls, been Olympic boxing champions, etc. There are some athletes out there but they are all in the record books. But do you know Huston actually told me he had been Light Weight Champion of the West Coast. He told Mary too. He had been drinking, of course, but a strange fantasy. The only way he could be a light weight would be if they cut both legs off at the hips unless he was champion when he was nine or ten. Maybe he was champion. I don't say he wasn't. But he looks more like a guy that gets into fights sometimes than like a fighter. [Errol] Flynn claims to have been a fighter but he loses fights even with dames and I think if had been a champion he would win at least one of his non-professional starts.

There is a guy named [Bill] Ching now who has the baritone lead in Allegro. Very nice looking guy, looks like an athlete. . . . He was down here in the Hooligan Navy when we had the boat set-up and he had been a fighter and a semi-pro ball player (could have gone up. But he wanted to sing etc.). We were playing a pick-up team from Luyano one Sunday when there was a big Norther and no craft going out and I put him on third base. I started the game. Am a knuckle ball pitcher in my old age and they really do not hit it solid but you need eight other guys all of whom can field their positions because a large part of the time they hit it. I can maybe throw three fast balls in a game if I have somebody to hold the arm up between innings. Well almost at once in this game I

saw I was not in my greatest form because I could not get the ball as far
as the plate. (This is all true.) The first two pitches did not get to the
plate. Had very carefully not warmed up because I knew I could only
throw so many times and didn't want to waste any. (This is true too. Why
should I leave any throws in le bull pen?) So I waved in Gigi who had
been warming up keeping one eye on me and I went out to right field
knowing I wasn't ever going to pitch again. Gigi pitched a lovely game.
He had nothing but a little boy's fast ball but he could hit Lenny Lyon's
nose with it throwing from center field. He threw his arm away pitching
too young. But the point of this long and boreing story was that the great
Bill Ching, with the most beautiful swing you ever saw, struck out four
times straight against an aged negro pitcher who looked like a dwarf out
of Goya and worked week-days on the garbage truck catching cans and
throwing back the empties. In spite of this rigorous training and
healthy life he had absolutely nothing and I got four for four and this
beautiful, lousy Ching struck out four straight times. Shortly after that he
located a grouper bed in twenty-five fathoms when he thought he was
off the Morillo of Bahia Honda and was actually off the Heradura of
Cabanas (which bears a faint resemblance to it) and depth charged
the shit, or the groupers rather, out of it, sent for more ships, more
charges, re-inforcements of every sort and finally the Cubans announced
that they had *sunk* the submarine. This was one of the greatest feats of
naval arms in all Latin American history. As you say, "Gee."

See what you mean about foot-work. I learned early to walk very
dangerous so people would leave you alone; think the phrase in our
part of the country was not fuck with you. Don't fuck with me, Jack
you say in a toneless voice. But lately find that when I walk dangerous like
that it is more like a spavined bear.

Tell Joe we made a good trip. It was blowing heavy out of the east
which made the currents too strong for bottom fishing. You couldn't get
to the bottom in 20 fathoms where the yellowtail and grouper patches
are with a five pound lead. Mucho corriente [current]. Bloody well
demasiado [excessive]. But we trolled the corners and the different
current junctures and the edge of the 100 fathom curve and worked it out
pretty good (it bears only an incidental resemblance to the chart) and
caught something over 1800 pounds of marlin (small), wahoo, albacore,
grouper, big kingfish, cero mackerel and barracuda. It ran about 3 cudas
to each of the other fish. We also turned three big turtle on their way up
to the beach, iced all our fish and got home in good shape, and Mousie
speared a lot of crawfish goggling. He is very good at it. He is my boy but
he isn't any copy of me delicate or otherwise. He is a much better guy

than I am in every way and the only thing I would ever change about him is to have him not fragile.

The hell with [John] O'Hara. A good title. Will let you know about that story when read it. "The Lottery" I mean.

Miss Mary has something she is going to write you. Moral problem about writing that you posed in next to last ¶ your letter. I always hit the dirt when they throw a moral problem.

Would it bore you too much to write something about you? Where you come from and all that. Where I come from it isn't polite to ask a stranger where comes from. It is supposed to be good form to look away if you see his face on the Post Office wall. (We'll have to sell that to Huston.) I even feel ashamed about writing that about John and the ball playing. Because where I come from, or elect to come from, is very bad form to blow the whistle on anyone in any way or to appeal to the sovereign majesty of the law. If you can't work it out yourself you ought to go play in the league where you belong. Banana boats aren't rigged for turtle, what you win in Boston you lose in Chicago, only suckers worry, cut out the show boat you apple knocking son of a bitch, and the good simple words we are not allowed to use that have always served as qualifying adjectives. (Mr. Papa and his mistyque of the vulgate.) Anyway I am not asking you any questions except that I would *like* to know ie it would make me happy to know.

Am glad you are not doing [a profile of] Bobby Riggs. . . . I have heroes still: Peter Wickham [Wykeham-] Barnes of the RAF who used to take out Gestapo HQs in daylight precision bombeing with Mosquitoes, Miss Mary when she fought on the operating table and wouldn't die, when she didn't know anything about it, long after pit bulls would have quit, and my heroes that are dead like Michel Ney the cooper's son who fought the 200 some rear-guard actions covering the retreat of the army from Moscow (I'm going to write that sometime and Mary will research it for me), my friend Mr. Flaubert, my friend Mr. Jim Thurber and old Mouse if he can stay the course. I saw Mousie, when he was delerious, defying Satan and all fiends and all local devils. He thought Sinsky and Ermua and myself, who are all big, were very big devils and he said in his delerium, "All right. So there are three of you. Three of the biggest. Against one little boy. All right. And do you know what will happen? One little boy will fight you until he dies. But he will not die. He will defeat the three of you and drive you back to hell."

Okay you take St. George and the Dragon and I'll take Mister Mouse. Hell daughter, you should have seen him give it to those devils. And drunk wounded or delerious is when you really know how they are. Also as you say on the courts or anywhere you are [word illegible] and where the heat is on. That was why never re-negged on Sidney [Franklin] because really saw him good and it would be a crime to deny it. So long Lillian. I like writing to you. But like even more getting letters.

Love from all,
Mister Papa

Down to 209¾. Gave a pint to Palestine Blood Bank yest. People a little suspicious at first. Couldnt understand why give blood if not Hebrew. But before that we were friends.

PH. PUL

1. Miss Ross first met EH in Ketchum, Idaho, 24 December 1947, while she was preparing a profile of Sidney Franklin, the American bullfighter. Her profile of EH appeared in *New Yorker* 26 (13 May 1950): 36–62. See her book, *Reporting* (New York, 1964), pp. 187–222, for a reprint of her article with an autobiographical preface.

To LILLIAN ROSS, La Finca Vigia, 28 July 1948

Dear Lillian:

Thanks for the wire and for the letter that just found last night when got home from trip. The old insufficient postage. We had wonderful birthday: Mary, Sinsky, Gigi, Gregorio, mate on boat, Manolito, kid of the man who owns the cafe at Cojimar. Very good kid; loves the water, doesn't get sea-sick, helps Gregorio and worships Gigi. They are both learning the sea together. We had a case of good champagne an old friend here gave for birthday and a half pound of real caviar, present from our wine merchant, and a little Heidsick Brut of our own. Sinsky and I started drinking the champagne at 0600 and we drank it all day and felt wonderful. Got your cable in the morning just as we were leaveing. Mary had wonderful presents with presentation cards from cats and dogs and a beautiful cake and I was so proud and happy to have made 49, I guess if a golfer it is to break 49, I was just stink happy all day.

About unfinished business: that story[1] was a stinker. Faked phony ending. Everything that could be bad. EVEN IF IT HAPPENED IT IS WRONG. You have to write so people believe it. I thought it was worst story ever read in NY'er.

Glad to get Huston's ball playing upcleared. Was worried about that. I don't know anybody that shines on the coast but what the hell was only there once and for two days [1937]. What I meant about Huston as ball player was that would trade him quick while others hadn't seen the defect. I see it and could drive a coach and six through it with Miss Muffet sitting on top of her Tuffet eating her turds and whey. But in general it is not seen yet and so I meant I would trade him while he was still valuable. They unvaluable on you fast.

About baseball: you were quite right to run rather than slide in soft ball. Sliding actually is a threat to cut the man at the bag so he will be out of the game, it also raises dust and if you can really come in you can avoid the tag as far as is possible. What actually happens is when you get blocked off at second or given the hip you say, "The next time I come down I'll cut your fucking legs off." If the short stop or second baseman are tough (and they always are) they will say let me take him the next time comes down. You can't see from the stands what happens in the dust but when they tag you they give you the ball, which is hard, under the ear, on the chin, in the ribs, where you live, and it is all ok. That is what makes those sudden, unexplained fights you see break out at second base.

The dirtiest and most hated guy in probably the baseball you have watched was Dick Bartell. He would give it to you and would cut you. Before him it was [Ty] Cobb. The greatest of ball players and an absolute shit.

Now I have used the two words and if I were a more careful writer I would not have to. You do not have to because they are not natural for you to use. We use them to save time. I never waste them in writing. But I talk bad on account where and how brought up. Can talk properly. But I remember I asked you if you minded and you said no and so I talked naturally.

There is no substitute in English for the phrase "Fuck off, Jack," if you mean it and will make it good. At the battle of Waterloo Gen. Cambronne did not say when called upon to surrender, "The Old Guard dies but never surrenders." He said, "Merde." It is the old fighting word and when working with Maquis etc. we never said Good luck, Bonne chance or any of that shit. We always said, "Merde." That is the mystique if there is any. If you said good luck to a jockey riding a steeple-chase he would cut you across the face if it were permitted. Good luck is the baddest luck thing to say in combat or in danger and is said by YMCA characters.

In a poem about when we hit the Schnee Eifel in Sept 1944 and I was quite sure would be killed and wanted to write what I knew, or, rather, had learned before it would happen in Hurtgen I wrote:

Today no one uses slang because clarity is of the utmost importance. Fucking, alone, is retained, but is only used as an adjective.

Sweating out is retained.

It means that which one must suffer without any possibility of changing the result or the outcome.

Those of us who know walk very slowly, and we look at one another with infinite love and compassion.

This comes only after one hundred days and is one of the final symptoms. There has been irritation, anger, fear, doubt, accusations, denials, misinterpretations, mistakes, cowardice, inability and lack of talent for this work.

All this has been and will be again. To be counter-balanced by firmness, steadiness, courage, quick understanding and the ability both to manoever and to fight.

But now, for a moment, there is only love and compassion. Knowing how to endure. And only love and compassion.

This is a long poem. There is a lot of it. Not all love and compassion.

If that sounds wet anyway it is what I mean about the language. I say fucking when I want people to move; as an adjective. As a verb it is an insult in thieves talk which is what we have written since Villon. You must know that because you write very close to the edge of it. You have a very fine ear and you are naturally repelled when it is too tough or un-necessarily used.

Am very happy to know about where you come from. Gigi was brought up summers in Syracuse and one time when Mousie and I came back from the ranch where Mousie had been along when we killed three grizzlies (I'd hunted nearly six years to get one.) Gigi, whose idol was a boxer named Burt Courage in Syracuse said, "Well Patrick of course if bears are what you are interested in it is all right. But we don't have bears in Syracuse."

Please never believe anything you read about Mr. Papa. It is all sheiss. I never aided it but I may have abetted it by not comeing out everytime and formally denying crap. Your legend grows like the barnacles on the bottom of a ship and is about as useful. Less Usefull.

Am very glad about your Pop and Eugene V. Debs. He is the only presidential candidate I ever voted for. Came back from War (I) and they made me Republican judge of Election (paid $5.00 and my paternal grandfather had never sat at table knowingly with a Democrat in his life so I was a natural.) I cast only vote for Debs in our precinct. Never voted after that. On the death of our candidate retired from giddy political whirl. Was Harding then [1920]. Now is Truman. Fork they.

Tell Brendan Gill that I think To Have etc. [and Have Not] is a good book. Jerry built like a position you fortify quickly and with errors but declare to hold. It is much better than people think and not nearly as good as I hoped. The night with the vets is wonderful but could have been better but that was the year I had the bone spurs in my ankle and hit .296. I was all fucked up when I wrote it and threw away about 100,000 words which was better than most of what left in. It is the most cut book in the world. That may be part of what offends people. It does not have that handy family package size character you get in Dr. Dickens. It says, "Fuck off Jack," too many times. Although I tried not to. Am afraid maybe I learned that when should have learned "Oh Come All ye Faithful." It has a nice part in it where the girl denounces the writer. Tell Brendan can write better than that now. Two weeks ago let Miss Mary read what had been writing on acct. never let anybody read it on acct. it takes off whatever butterflies have on their wings and the arrangement of hawk's feathers if you show it or talk about it. But thought since she had been so loyal all the time when had the pressure and all and you could have ordinarily used a mechanical counter to check the rat exodus (No Lemmings Allowed on Board) ought to show her whether was just jerking off in the tower or trying to hit the ball sharp and solid without trying to pull it for the owners. Anyway she was very pleased and I have had what with politicians would correspond to a wave of popularity ever since.

Lillian I like to write to you very much. If it is ever no good for you or bad for you we will cut it the hell out. Wish we could come to town and meet your mob which is my mob in the head and heart as far as know (except [John] O'Hara who is a cheap while we are all very expensive and never will be paid for) and please give best to same. Will see Janny [Janet] Flanner in Paris where we go from here direct via Funchal, Lisboa, Gib, Algiers and Cannes. Am rigging to fish all the way across. Maybe [Harold] Ross would make me a roveing correspondent.

Please write if you like to. I like to very much.

PH. PUL

Mr. Pappa

1. Shirley Jackson, "The Lottery," *New Yorker* 24 (26 June 1948).

To W. G. ROGERS, La Finca Vigia, 29 July 1948

Dear Mr. Rogers:

It made me very happy to read your book about Gertrude [*When This You See, Remember Me: Gertrude Stein in Person*, 1948]. I always loved her very much and as you said I never counter-punched when she left herself wide open. She had, or Alice [B. Toklas] had, a sort of necessity to break off friendships and she only gave real loyalty to people who were inferior to her. She had to attack me because she learned to write dialogue from me just as I learned the wonderful rhythms in prose from her. I couldn't understand it when she attacked me but I did not give a damn really because you know more or less how you are and what you are worth and I have no ambition except to write well and she had so many ambitions. It makes us all happy to write and she had discovered a way of writing she could do and be happy every day. She could never fail; nor strike out; nor be knocked out of the box because she made the rules and played under her own rules. When I can't write (writing under the strictest rules I know) I write letters; like today. She found a way of writing that was like writing letters all the time.

I had the good luck to see her in Paris when we had come back from the Schnee-Eifel in the fall of '44. There wasn't a hell of a lot of time then and so I just told her I had always loved her and she said she loved me too which was, I think, the truth from both of us.

I liked her better before she cut her hair and that was sort of a turning point in all sorts of things. She used to talk to me about homosexuality and how it was fine in and for women and no good in men[1] and I used to listen and learn and I always wanted to fuck her and she knew it and it was a good healthy feeling and made more sense than some of the talk. I think Alice was sort of jealous of the friends of Gertrude that were of the same category she was. Picasso had the same theory. He thought we all got flung out into outer darkness on acct. of that and that she did not like Gertrude to be with men who ever worked at that part of their trade.

Anyway thanks for seeing how much I learned from her in the A Farewell To Arms passage. It reads good too and I had forgotten all about that. Learned from her, from Ezra [Pound], and from many great deads. Then you have to do it alone and by yourself and keep on learning; only you are alone. Everybody is dead now and it is a lonesome trade and there is no good talk anymore. I am naturally a happy guy so I have a good time and I love my wife and the ocean and my kids and writing and reading and all good painting along with bar life and whores and responsibility and paying my bills and other mixed pleasures. But I certainly hate for Gertrude to be dead[2] and I am very happy that you and your wife wrote such a good book about her. I was truly fond of Alice too and I couldn't realize that she would hate me. But that was a part of my education (which is still in-complete).

Best to you always,
Ernest Hemingway

TEXAS

1. See *A Moveable Feast* (New York, 1964), pp. 18–20. 2. Gertrude Stein died 27 July 1946.

To HELEN KIRKPATRICK,[1] Torcello, Italy, 12 November 1948

Dear Helen:

Thank you very much for the good letter and for helping Jack.

Now what the hell can I say about Buck [Lanham]?

I met him for the first time at Le Mesnil Herman shortly after the break-through. The 4th Inf Division, as you remember, made the actual assault which resulted in the breakthrough (this may be disputed). I had not met Buck, although I knew the other regimental commanders of the 8th and 12th Inf Regts, because he had been fighting his re-inforced regiment on the left and considerably in advance of the rest of the Div. (It is hard to do this without maps.) The rest of the Division could have been much further up if it had not had to wait for First Inf. Div. to take the town of Marigny. (We will skip that because I need to keep a little something for my own book.)

Anyway I met Buck at his CP [Command Post] in Le Mesnil Herman. I had explained, in too low tones, that I was Hemingway of Colliers and the gentleman with me, who felt ok as long as it was a regimental CP and retained all his heartiness of manner (he didn't know Buck's CPs) was [Ira] Wolfert of Everything. I think it was Lum Edwards of Buck's staff who then introduced us to the Colonel, "Colonel this is Colonel Colliers and Mr. Wolfram."

Buck asked us to eat an excellent meal (I had corrected the error and explained I held the permanent rank of Mister and that Mr. Wolfert was indeed *The* Mr. Wolfert). There was roast chicken to eat and a great atmosphere of calmness and no one was nervous. Everyone was very cheerful and gay and efficient without haveing to drink to be gay nor tighten up to be efficient. I was very impressed. Buck talked on literature and after lunch explained the situation. Wolfram asked some idiotic questions which embarrassed me so we left very promptly.

The next time I saw the Colonel was at Ville Dieu de Poelles. I had several bottles of Champagne which had been given me at a place called Percy by an innkeeper and bistro proprietor who had the mis-apprehension I was the personal advance representative of General Patton. He had asked me who my General was and I said General Raymond O. Barton. "Ah General Patton," he said. "How we admire and revere him. Vite allez chercher du champagne, du bon, pour envoyer comme cadeau a General Patton." So after arriveing at Ville Dieux de Poeles, not without incident, I ran into Buck and at once presented him with a bottle from the side car of the Kraut motorcycle we were useing as transport. Buck was tired, gray, slightly whiskery, dead-eyed tired but very gay and cheerful.

I ran into him once after that in Normandy and then in Paris. Everybody was moveing like hell in those days as you remember and I did not see Buck again until Landrecies, or rather a town just outside that old fortress town the name of which cannot remember. His CP was as usual immaculate, cheerful, functioning perfectly and everybody as cheerful as though there was no damn war. They had had a big fight the day before, a real fight, in which Buck had himself fought (it was necessary) and he greeted me with that famous phrase about "Where were you brave Crillon when we fought at" (look up name of the place).[2]

It was always so much fun to be with a man who was literate, articulate, completely brave and of superior intelligence that I took to hanging around him and neglecting other completely worthy but less interesting characters and finally, on the rat race, and in the Schnee Eifel we became very close friends. I do not think I have ever been closer to anyone, as a friend, than to Buck in Hurtgen; nor admired anyone more.

You can get all the gen on Buck's official valor from the citations. What you do not get there is the standing up, complete and unbroken, dead tired, fighting on a twenty four hour basis all through that battle which was like Paschendaele with tree bursts and remaining absolutely intact, intelligent, humorous and the best company in the world.

Hurtgen anecdotes you can get from Willy [Walton]. I think he can still remember Hurtgen even strained through a sieve of beautiful women.

Miss Martha, by the way, was not at Hurtgen. You may have been and I not have known it or forgotten. Lee Carson came up one day to Buck's CP and when they explained the situation to her she said, "Jesus Christ let's get out of here." And, as we all know, Lee was not repeat not a spooky girl.

So if any of this is any good to you use it and you have my complete permission to quote any of it. If you need more will give.

Mary says she wishes she could go to one of the small parties at the small house [Helen's house in Georgetown]. I'd settle to have a drink with you anywhere. It was so much fun seeing you last winter.

Things are good here; in the north at least. Mary is going to make a tour in the car and see Lucy Moorhead in Firenze, see Pisa, see some friends of ours in Milano and Pam Churchill in Torino. . . .

Our best love to Willy. Tell him not to slip on any wet decks. There's a type of shoe Abercrombie and Fitch sell that is practically slip-proof. But have never worn them to bed.

Take care of yourself and good luck with the piece and love to Buck.

PH. PUL   [Ernest]

1. Mrs. Kirkpatrick had written EH from Washington 4 November asking for data on General Lanham for an article for the *Saturday Evening Post*. 2. For background on EH's exploit, see Carlos Baker, *Ernest Hemingway: A Life Story* (New York, 1969), pp. 420–21.

To MARY HEMINGWAY, Torcello, 20 November 1948

Dearest Kittner:

Been working hard and missing you harder. No mails today at all. I wrote you day before yest and forwarded a letter from your family to the Excelsior in Firenze today. Now writing you just at sun-set. Been beautiful fall weather ever since the day you left. I went shooting with Emilio and shot 25 small birds and we might have gotten two ducks as four flashed over us very low but were eating lunch when it happened. Might have missed them too.

Have my correspondence all done except for letter to [Alfred] Rice.[1] Then will do the article.[2] May do the article and then Rice since will have to go into Venice to get Power of Attorney notarized. Wrote Charley Ritz too.

There is a big duck shoot either tomorrow (Sunday) a.m. or else Monday. Emilio is going to let me know tonight. Hope it's Monday as my shoulder is sore from those high, straight up and down shots. I think those are probably quite heavy loads of the light shot. Can really shoot that over and under now. Haven't started learning the double yet.

Believe magazines etc. held up by the dock strike. They say over 50,000 sacks of mail on the docks in NY. But you read the papleys too so won't Kaltenborn the news to you.

Your last pictures (the tower etc.) came out excellently. Got them last night.

Chinese Govt. evidently useing U.S. and British planes to beat hell against the Communists. But don't believe they can stop it the way it has started to roll. Read Steele in the Herald Trib. I know him (you probably do from news). Is 1st rate and accurate man. Think it was funny them sending Rover Boy Bill Bullitt over to back up Chiang. Hope he gets his letter. He'll be in the game about as long as Gig was.

No more word from Childies.

Hope your news was good.

I've been trying to stay awake and read until midnight or one a.m.

Got your wire, garbled, about the rain enroute Bologna and the fine castle at Ferrara. If it is the big one there I know it. Did you run into our crazies in Bologna? How is Florence? I'll bet even you got tired in the Uffizi. That was the gallery that used to really knock me out. I'd think show me one more goddamn Madonna and see how you like it gentlemen. Is Fiesole shot up? It was lovely but a little precious. You'll love Siena. I expect to hear you went to Rome since it was so close etc. So don't mind doing it. That's what there's a car for. See some of the Etruscan stuff if you are in Umbria. They have me mystified still. Good around Orbetello if you go that way. I walked all over that country with Ezra [Pound] explaining him how and why Sigismundo Malatesta would have fought where and for what reasons and how would have worked. Probably mis-led him badly. Would like to do it better now.

Had black-ass for a couple of days about old Bill Smith. How come Marty never used Black-Ass nor hang and rattle or I'll wind your clock in her book. Guess she must have been figureing on shareing the wealth and left that for me.

No local news. Mooky's foot got ok. Ate outdoors in the sun today and he kept his head in my lap all through lunch; clams, sole, white rice plain. Bobby the other dog, Crazy's brother, can sit up to beg and also make a how do you do and a Fancy Meeting You.

There's nobody liveing here now. Today three couples for lunch though; a character who was either a fairy or a cinema star or both with re-conditioned woman (fenders straightened, bad paint job), a sort of Brusadelli type with woman to match and a brace of Belgiums. I can now tell the travelling Belgium as far as can smell them.

Best to all your friends. Love to my kitten. Be good and have good fun. It's dark now and the shooting has started. Been trying to think what a Belgium smells like (the post-war travelling Belgiums) think it is a blend of traitorous King, toe jam, un-washed navels, old bicycle saddles, (sweated), paveing stones, and emminently sound money with a touch of leek soup and cooking parsnips. Vive l'armee blanche.

I love you dearest kittner and miss you very, very very very, very, very much.

PH. PUL

Papa

1. Alfred Rice succeeded Maurice Speiser, who died on 7 August 1948, as EH's attorney and so remained during EH's lifetime and afterward. 2. "The Great Blue River" for *Holiday* magazine (July 1949).

To ALFRED RICE, Venice, 15 December 1948

Dear Alfred:

Sent you a very long cable yesterday. This is supplementary. Am encloseing the power of attorney and the affadavit.

Please excuse me if I am ever brusque. I am short of time, all of this knocks the hell out of my work and I am working against time with very bad high blood-pressure and trying not to crowd too much steam on or worry. *Keep This Confidential.*

NOW HEAR THIS (as the talker used to say on ship-board.)

I do not want you ever to initiate any action for any refunds of taxes[1] without first consulting me and presenting the matter fully to me so that I may judge whether it is an honorable and ethical action to take, not simply legally, but according to my own personal standards. I have been crippled, financially, by taxes but I am as proud of haveing helped my Government in that way as of any aid I was able to give in the field. I do not wish to squawk about being hit financially any more than I would squawk about being hit physically. I need money, badly, but not badly enough to do one dishonorable, shady, borderline, or "fast" thing to get it. I hope this is quite clear.

Now about non-residence. Here are some facts you may not know about 1942–43–44. In 1942–3 I never left Cuba at any time except to go to sea on the most difficult type of mission you could be assigned in counter espionage and anti-submarine work. Maury [Maurice Speiser] has in my papers a copy, or the original of a letter to me written when I left for Europe by Spruille Braden, our Ambassador in Cuba, dureing that period. I would rather pay any assessments rather than have this brought out publicly. But Mr. Braden's letter, written when I gave up the job when the subs were no longer comeing through speaks for its-self. He would be glad to tell anyone from the Bureau about what we were doing at sea and what it cost us to do it. He would also, I am sure, be glad to confirm my residence in Havana. So also, I am sure, would Robert P. Joyce, Consul General of the U.S., address Dept of State, Washington D.C. who has just returned from Trieste where he was Political Adviser to the U.S. and British Army Headquarters there. Any such enquiries should be made in strictest confidence and only deal with the work at sea. Otherwise I would not last a week; well say a month.

In 1944 I was at sea until the subs left; going to sea each time one was signalled in our area. I took the Colliers job as a step to getting some useful job in Europe. I was in NYCity only long enough for my accreditation and orders to come through and the R.A.F. flew me over on a promise to fly with and write about them. I was badly hurt in London and could not fly for a while so got permission to go with the small Navy Landing Craft LCVP's at Omaha Beach. I only wrote five articles for Colliers and they paid less than half my expenses. The articles I wrote were about hitting the beach in the seventh wave on D Day, flying day and night interception on the buzz bombs and bombing the launching sites, the Infantry break-through in Normandy, our takeing of Rambouillet and guerrila actions on the way into Paris, and finally the 22nd Regt. of Infantry's assault on the Siegfried Line on Sept 13th. Colliers so mutilated my copy that I would write nothing further although I prepared another piece which did not send but am incorporateing into my book. From

Sept till the end of 1944 I was makeing myself as useful as possible to the
4th Inf. Division and gathering, as always, material for my book. When
you see that for the first two months I was at sea (the part of my book
I am writing now) and the last four not writing anything for Colliers
the expenses allotted to gathering material are in no way excessive when
you know the amount of money I have been offered for the taxable
motion picture rights to the book.

I wish you would have whoever is checking the 1944 return read this
letter so they get the picture. I was decorated with the Bronze Star
which was the highest piece of junk they could give a civilian and an
irregular and was proposed for various worthwhile things which could
not be given due to my irregular status and the fact they would
contravene the Geneva Convention.

In the course of 1944 I also ruined my health, smashed my head up
badly twice and came home in 1945 stony cold broke. So it would gripe
me just as badly to have to pay extra for those days at sea, hours in the
air, more than a hundred days in combat, Normandy, the Rat Race,
Schnee-Eifel, Hurtgen Forest, the Bulge Fight smashed-up, sick, going
up to the Bulge Fight with a temperature of 104 wearing a sheep-lined
coat as underwear to absorb the sweating and another one over it. Nope.
Any year but 1944. Have the hurricane blow hell out of the farm when
you are up behind the Siegfried Line. My surviveing mangoe trees,
re-propped up, never have gotten over that hurricane.

If they can tell me any of the benefits I was receiveing from my Govt
in 1944 in exchange for what already paid will be glad to pay anything
they think is right. I did have a passport to fly to London but I paid
$10. for it.

About business: I am not going to sell property each year to pay money
borrowed to pay taxes and then pay taxes on that. That is out. Just
because something was sold for a miserable price once when my nuts
were in the nut-cracker after 1944 is no reason to sell something else for
a miserable price. And don't *offer* anything for sale. Simply transmit any
offers to me.

For two bits I would quit writeing if I have to pay dough for what
I did in 1944 and take out parties fishing and live on a subsistence basis
and nobody would make any money; neither the govt., nor agents, nor
anybody and I could fish and not have to knock my brains out writing
and be a hell of a lot better off. Today that seems like a good idea.

Don't make any German translation deals. I don't have that situation
straight yet. Mondadori and Einaudi reported to you what they paid me.
Put it into dollars at 640 lire to the dollar which is what the change is
here on the free market. That is what they are changeing dollars at. If
that money is taxable declare it, of course, and let me know when you

need accounts of what Guaranty, Esquire, Chicago Bank, Cape have paid me so can send cables for them to cable you.

Best always, and Merry Christmas

Ernie

1. The Internal Revenue Service was auditing EH's income tax return for 1944.

To ARTHUR MIZENER, La Finca Vigia, 6 July 1949

Dear Mr. Mizener:

Thank you for your letter about the Fitzgerald biography.[1] I am very sorry that I do not have any of Scott's letters here. Most of them were stored in Key West and were probably eaten by either mice or roaches, since that is not a good latitude for the preservation of important documents. I had everything filed in a cabinet and in pretty good order, but while I was away at one of the wars someone [Pauline] decided to use the cabinet to keep their files while setting up a small antique business and as a consequence, much of my early manuscripts, Scott's letters and other more or less valuable documents became rat and roach food.

If you were ever around and wanted me to give you any true gen on Scott I would be glad to do so. Who you could get the best dope on his end on the Coast would be from a movie critic named Sheila something or other, and a man I met in the Air Force in the last war named either Jonah or Judah or some such fantastic name. He was with Scott when he died and worked up to dying. The movie critic's name, I now remember, is Sheila Graham and she could give you the name of this other character who could give you an enormous amount of really true gen if he is not writing a book himself.

I loved Scott very much but he was extremely difficult with that situation he got himself into and Zelda constantly making him drink because she was jealous of his working well. There are lots of other aspects of it and if you are writing a really good biography of him I would be glad to tell you many things as truly as I can remember them from the first time I met him. [Maxwell] Geismar's stuff on him made me sick. John O'Hara's introduction to THE POTABLE FITZGERALD was wrapped in O'Hara's old coonskin coat that he never wore to Yale. Bunny Wilson and John Bishop were his pals but they never saw much of him when he was at his best, which was over a short time. He had a very steep trajectory and was almost like a guided missile with no one guiding him.

This sort of letter is no good to you if what you need for your book is documentation. The rats ate the documentation. But, if you ever want to talk about him I would be glad to talk any time it was convenient with you. I am very sorry that I cannot be of more practical use to you.

Yours very truly,

Ernest Hemingway

UMD

1. Mizener was at work on *The Far Side of Paradise* (New York, 1951).
This and all subsequent letters to Professor Mizener are used courtesy of the Mc Keldin Library, University of Maryland, College Park.

To CHARLES SCRIBNER, La Finca Vigia, 22 July 1949

Dear Charlie:
Thanks very much for the letter with the Billy Rose material. I have written Mr. Rose that a jerk can get away with a lot and a little jerk can get away with it longer. But, textually, "But if you steal from me again I will wind your clock so you will be able to hear it tick permanently." I believe Mr. Rose will be able to understand this language which is not the same one we speak in the Pallazzo Mocenigo (mis-spelled) [Venice].

The package of books that turned up had that report on [S. A. Stauffer et al.'s] the American Soldier published by Princeton Press. (An excellent and impressive work) and [W. Van T. Clark's] The Track of The Cat and [J. F. Dobie's] The Voice of The Coyote are semi-animal with metaphysics and animal books. Many other books ordered still missing; especially MajGen [J. F. C.] Fuller (the bastard) [The] Second World War. I need this.

The word count is Wed. 577 and yest morning, my birthday, 573 before breakfast. Weight 200 even. To celebrate my fiftieth birthday (in what other god-damn country where you've spent your life writing as well as you can wouldn't you receive one wire from an American when you'd made fifty against considerable odds) I fucked three times, shot ten straight at pigeons (very fast ones) at the club, drank with five friends a case of Piper Heidsick Brut and looked the ocean for big fish all afternoon. There was nothing although the current was strong and the water very dark. Was the first day of the trade wind which seems now to have set in solidly and sometimes fish don't come up until the 2nd or 3rd day. Have big hopes for this week-end.

Think young Charley makes a mistake not to have some of those aged books for door-stops. Anyway they were offered. Felt faintly bad they were turned down. But can understand he might not like them. Actually they are pretty good and he would make no mistake to have a few signed ones if we could find first editions which would be happy to pay [David] Randall[1] for. This corresponds to the snake eating his own tail.

Think will write today as am in a place where can make country which I love to do better than anything.

Had wonderful birthday presents: Juan Dunabeitia who served with me at sea in the war smuggled in a .22 Cal Colt Match Target pistol. Our Priest gave me two bottles of Tequila. Our wine merchant the case of Heidsick Brut 41. [Otto] Bruce who used to be my valet, chauffeur and man of confidence came over from Key West with a fine Navy Clock, a set of signal flags and two rubber ice buckets. Mary gave me a fine silver flask and a dozen small and thoughtful presents. Had a cable from Cape and other cables from abroad.

Must stop and get to work. Incidentally the reason we made no formal answer to the invitation from young Charlie's in-laws[2] was because it was addressed to Mr. Ernest Hemingway rather than to Mr. and Mrs. If these things are done as a matter of form it is better to observe the forms. I didn't show it to Mary. Understand, of course, the confusion of all such occasions. Am not a formal character myself but when anybody wants to play at it I know how it goes. Had four ancestors who went on the Crusades (which did not tell Cowley) and a Cheyenne great-great grandmother (which did not tell Cowley). Both my grandfathers fought all through the civil war (no one who has any money in America had a grandfather who fought). Jack, my oldest kid, my kid brother, and I all fought in this war. We all were hit and we all got various junk without publicity. I sure would love to be summoned sometime by a congressional committee and asked if I was subversive. Would say, to the chairman, "You cocksucker when did you come to this country and where were your people in 1776–9, 1861–5, 1914–18, and 1941–45. That was when we all lost our health and our fortunes. What did your miserable chickenshit grandfather do in those times? He was probably hireing himself a substitute and calling hogs."

Am very snobbish Charley. Always try not to be and hate all false snobs. But the true snobbery of fighting people and gambling people and people who do not give a shit is what makes White's fun and Boodle's faintly chicken shit and all the others just beautifully run imitations of where the gentry go. The gentry has always been those who didn't give a god-damn. It has nothing to do with where you went to school (the poor bastards suffer and sweat that out). Jerks get into White's. But everybody knows they are jerks and they are tolerated, snubbed, or ignored. The real gentry are almost as tough as the really good gangsters. But it has nothing to do with fascism nor any of the easy answers. You know if a man is o.k. when you meet him, instantly, and as accurately as though you had a Geiger counter on him. . . .

If you want more will give you the true gen. But think this is about enough of the distilled wisdom of my fiftieth birthday. It is nice to feel twenty five and have your head have learned a little bit; possibly.

Only hope I have the health to last another 30 years and write well because I swear the head is good and fairly ruthless (always trying to be kind) and there is a certain amount of local knowledge.

You can read this while commuting. I guess going from the country to the city to work is necessary and you can adjust to it. But it must be awful. I know I would not accept the indignity of the subway for all the money that there is.

Good luck, boy, and for Christ sake stick around and don't die on me. Am still sore at Max for dying like a jerk. Why did he have to work himself to death with dear Louise's estate, Tom Wolfe's estate, always makeing that train, never takeing his hat off. His god damned hat alone could kill him. I hope they buried him in it.

Well God bless as our friends say.

Your old stake horse,
Exterminator

PS.

Did I write you about Sinclair Lewis the author? Probably did. He was liveing with the mother of his ex-mistress Marcella Powers. The mother very neat and well washed and always calling him Mister Lewis. They had the regal suite at the Gritti. He would go down to the bar and have three or four double whiskies in the evening and then write. Sometimes he would write in the mornings too. But mostly at night. The rest of the time he would go out with Mrs. Powers and peer at whatever was 3 starred in Baedaker. When I was in the hospital in Padova he nailed Mary on a three hour diatribe, "I love Ernest BUT." It seems the trouble was I would not write a book, or rather publish one every year. Other trouble was I was a snob (correct). Other trouble I had never written a line about his books altho he had delivered gold medal address about me. (How the hell could I write about his books. Only kind thing is silence.) Other gripes: how difficult it must be you poor dear to have to be the wife to a Genius. (Who ever acted like a Genius? Am a writer and shooter and fisherman. Anyone married to me eats regularly, gets fucked when they wish it and have a fairly interesting life. You move around.) Other gripes: He must be awfully difficult isn't he dear? You know how I sympathize with you.

Mary ended up paying for all his drinks. I told the bartender that if he ever showed again to give him a Mickey Finn which he promised to do. The headwaiter and I fought together when we were kids. He really loathed him. Said he was a real jerk. Thought you bought loyalty with a thin dime instead of with understanding, consideration, good taste and good manners. And the poor Baedaker peering bastard with his Mistress's (who left him) mother defiling Venice with his pock-marked curiosity and lack of understanding.[3]

We ought to keep copies of our letters like Mr. Lord Byron and [John] Murray. I know some funny things that could write you if wasn't so inhibited. Now I know the copywrite remains with me am liable to write you god-damn near anything. And I don't even have to count the words.

EH

All the ordered books came through with this morning's mail. So only need the 3 examples of the Penn Warren introduction to A Farewell To Arms volumes. Am sending another order to Wilcox for books tomorrow. Secretary comeing out this pm and will dictate it.

PUL EH

1. Randall headed the Rare Books Department at Scribner's Bookstore. 2. Charles Scribner, Jr., had married Joan Sunderland on 16 July 1949. 3. This attack on Lewis, somewhat modified, was repeated in *Across the River and Into the Trees* (New York, 1950), pp. 87–88, 124. The passage typifies the rough exuberance that reappeared with some frequency in 1949–1950. It may owe something to EH's pride in *Across the River*, his first novel in ten years.

To FRANCIS CARDINAL SPELLMAN, La Finca Vigia, 28 July 1949

My Dear Cardinal:

In every picture that I see of you there is more mealy mouthed arrogance, fatness and over-confidence.

As a strike breaker against catholic workers, as an attacker of Mrs. Roosevelt[1] I feel strongly that you are over-extending yourself. It is very bad for a Prince of the Church to become over-confident.

I know that you lied about the Spanish Republic and I know why you lied. I know who you take your orders from and why such orders are given. You are heading a minority group in the United States, to which I was a dues-paying member, but you are heading it with arrogance, insolence and the fatness of a Prince of the Church.

The word in Europe is that you will be the next, and first, American

Pope. But please disabuse yourself on this and do not keep pressing so hard. You will never be Pope as long as I am alive.

Yours very respectfully,
Ernest Hemingway

[Typed and signed by EH, but perhaps not sent.]
JFK

1. The cardinal to Eleanor Roosevelt: "I shall not again publicly acknowledge you." He accused her of anti-Catholic bias (*New York Times*, 23 July 1949). She disavowed the accusation in a letter published 28 July. See Archibald Mac Leish, "Acknowledgement," in *Collected Poems* (Boston, 1952), p. 164.

To GRACE HALL HEMINGWAY, La Finca Vigia, *c.* 30 July 1949

My dear Mother:

Thank you very much for your letter on my birthday, which only reached me this morning. I am terribly sorry that I did not write to you on your birthday but I was away at the time in the Bahamas and Gregory had to have an operation and in the general mix-up I missed out on sending you the letter that I should have written. Give my love to Ruth Arnold[1] and take good care of yourself. Everyone here sends their love.

Your affectionate son,
[Ernie]

T.C. PUL

1. With Ruth Arnold as companion, Mrs. Hemingway was living in Studio 551, Keystone Avenue, River Forest, Illinois.

To MRS. M. H. MAINLAND,[1] La Finca Vigia, *c.* 15 August 1949

Dear Nun-bones:

Thank you so much for writing such a fine letter about your trip to Windemere and the condition of the place up there. The place sounds just about in the same shape as it was when Otto Bruce and I went through in the fall two years ago.

Thank you so very much for all the work you and Ken [Mainland] and little Uncle Ernie put in on it. Am sending a check for $200 for any expenses you may have had and to contribute toward the expenses you will have when mother arrives. She ought to have plenty of dough with the trust fund I set up for her and I think it is damn hard on you for her to come and visit for such long periods in the way that she does. I appreciate everything you do for her and I know it seems callous for me not to have her for part of the time. But I simply cannot, or could not, stand to have her around. We have never been friends as you know, although I try to support her, and lately I wrote her a letter as loving as I could make it but hope she will not get any ideas from that that we are friends. I simply wanted her, if it meant anything to her, to know that she had a loving son. Actually she hasn't.

Don't worry about me ever selling Windemere. It is where our roots are and where we were all happiest when we were kids. You and Ken are welcome to use it anytime you want. The same as Ura [Ursula] or Les [Leicester]. Marce [Marcelline] I always thought, from when I first knew her, which goes back now half a hundred years, of as a bitch complete with handles, want nothing to do with her ever. Poor old Beefy [Carol]—we busted up and I am sorry for her but want nothing to do with her either.

Much love to you, you old ball player and my very best to Ken and your Uncle Ernie (miniature). Mary sends her very best love too.

Your loving brother

T.C. PUL   [Ernie]

1. EH's sister Madelaine (Sunny), with her husband, Kenneth Mainland, and their son, Ernest, were living at 1771 Linden Avenue, Memphis, Tennessee.

To CHARLES SCRIBNER, La Finca Vigia, 19 August 1949

Dear Charlie:

Received your very amiable letter and was sorry if I could have been too tough in mine. Thought it was better to blow off than to have misunderstandings. . . .

Thank you very much for your information on Dr. [John] Galsworthy. I fear it is too late to take him as a model. He always seemed to me like a jerk in gent's clothing and, besides that, I could not read the stuff he wrote.

Am glad to see my opinion slightly backed up.

In regard to the reprint by the Colophon, it is OK for them to reprint any letters from me to the late Miss Gertrude Stein so long as they are copyrighted in my name.[1] I liked Gertrude Stein very much and never counter-attacked her even when she attacked me in such force after she had learned to write dialogue from me. To learn anything from a fellow-author is evidently an unforgivable sin. But she had wonderful pictures on the walls of her studio and good drinks and good food at a time when both of these were extremely acceptable.

Everything goes well here. We had a good fishing trip over the week-end and Mary is very happy and well and so am I and the various beasts around the finca.

Please ask Vera [Mrs. Charles Scribner] for me to for Christ's sakes not gallop too much as I will then have to be sweating her out all the time. Nearly all of my best friends have broken everything twice and I suppose it is an occupational hazard. But you still sweat them out.

I raced Tommy Shevlin down-hill [in Wyoming, September 1936], and you know what down-hill means, on a muddy road for $500 and had him ruined (the distance was 5½ miles) until we got on to the flat. At that point he, being 45 lbs lighter, moved ahead of me and I could have been taken for some sort of sculpture in mud when the thing was over. The holocaust occurred in the last 400 yards. But it was complete. It took Tommy's wife and Pauline and several other people an hour's work with a trowel to find out who was under that mud because we were quite close at the end.

I know nothing about the horse except as a medium of locomotion. But know a little about the scatter gun and various other forms of dispensing lead. Hunted with the Montello hounds which was the pack brought from Gib which had hunted previously on the Spanish side of Gibraltar. But since at that time I had never ridden in an English, so-called, saddle it was more of an experience than a sporting event. The colonel of the regiment that I hunted with had been ill with flu and he had two horses much higher than any I had ever seen and nobody had topped them off and when I mounted, knowing nothing about what we were going to do, all the officers of the regiment were measuring my stirrup lengths and comparing them with how Todd Sloane and other notorious American characters used to ride. I wanted a very long stirrup. This astounded them all and they were very busy taking measurements. We hunted twice and I thought it was a most terrifying experience but I knew that you were not supposed to over-run the hounds and I knew also that you should not have your neck cut off by the wires that the mulberry trees were garnished with in the way hops are grown sometimes in England. Therefore, when you had to jump I let the horse jump and trusted in the grace of God and it turned out all right. Afterwards there were many comments on the American seat and I had to do it two times over. The second time was much the worse. So, I sympathize with anyone who hunts on purpose having hunted only twice quite casually. Did not fall off horse although horse and I were not in that complete equilibrium which is desirable. The horse's.

Out where we come from, or where we spent the most time in the U.S., when we were drunk coming into town from Red Lodge, Montana, to Billings, I have gone into Pat Connelly's Saddle Shop with Turck Greenough and a couple of other worthless characters and seen Turck ask Pat to let him try a stock saddle. Pat let Turck try the saddle and Turck, holding it between his legs, broke the tree completely. Then he said to Pat, "Let me try another, Pat. These are worthless."—and Pat said to him, "You son of a bitch, get out of here and take all your worthless friends with you." Have always been able, if I could stay aboard of the animal, to impose a certain amount of discipline with a constriction of the thighs, since we were taught to ride like clothes-pins, and I did not have a saddle until one was given me by the keeper of a whore house in Billings, Montana. But riding is riding and fun is fun and as old Blicky [Baron von Blixen] used to say, "It's always so quiet when the goldfish die."[2]

On this solemn thought I leave you and hope that you are well and that everything goes well with the family and the business. I would like sometime to come in for a period of 6 months to be your second in command, unofficially, as I was with Buck Lanham with the 22nd Infantry and put a little discipline into that business. I honest to God think that you lose a great deal of money by straight inefficiency or non-instruction of the characters involved. On the other hand, I would probably find that I knew nothing about the publishing business and had no good suggestions or criticisms to make. Anyway, Charlie, I hope you are well and everything goes good.

Your friend,

PUL
Ernest

1. The letters were to be quoted by Donald F. Gallup in "The Making of *The Making of Americans*," *New Colophon* 3 (1950): 54–74. 2. Von Blixen may have been recalling W. H. Auden, "It's madly ungay when the goldfish die," in *The Sea and the Mirror, Collected Poems* (New York, 1945), p. 365.

To GENERAL J. LAWTON COLLINS, La Finca Vigia, 19 August 1949

My dear General:

May I congratulate you belatedly on your appointment to Chief of Staff.[1] I only learned of this on returning from a fishing trip.

All of us who were with the Seventh Corps and the First Army are happy about your appointment. I personally was afraid that some jerk from SHAEF would receive this appointment. But it is a fine thing to know that a fine soldier who understands the big picture has it rather than a big picture man.

I hope these are not subversive sentiments and I would like to say that I will be happy to serve under you in any capacity (preferably in one which involves writing) at any time, any where, and against any enemies of our country.

Yours very respectfully
Ernest Hemingway

T.C. JFK

1. General Collins was sworn in as chief of staff 17 August 1949.

To BERNARD BERENSON, La Finca Vigia, 25 August 1949

Dear Mr Berenson:

Thank you very much for your last two books which my wife Mary and I have read with great delight. You write very well, General, and it makes me happy to read you. I am not always of the same opinion. But it would be a sad world if we all agreed and could not argue.

Thank you also, very much, for being so kind to my wife Mary.[1] You are more or less her hero and you are one of the liveing people that I respect most. For your private information I respect god-damn few of them.

This is just a letter that you do not have to answer. I do not care for Firenze (you do not mind a heretic I hope) and am an old Veneto boy myself. I love it and know it quite well. Not as well as you but in a different, disorderly way. Mr. Kipling, who when he wrote well, wrote properly, wrote, "A man has only one virginity to lose and there his heart will ever be."[2]

This statement is slightly wet but it expresses how I feel about the Veneto (all parts) even Pordenone.

Please take good care of yourself and maybe we might meet sometime if I take care of myself too and if we both have lots of luck. My wife sends you her love.

Yours, always

Ernest Hemingway

I TATTI

1. Mary had met Berenson (1865–1959) at the I Tatti villa in November 1948. See Carlos Baker, *Ernest Hemingway: A Life Story* (New York, 1969), p. 469; and Mary Hemingway, *How It Was* (New York, 1976), pp. 229–31. With this message EH elbowed his way into the correspondence. 2. Kipling's poem "The Virginity" ends: "We've only one virginity to lose / And where we lost it there our hearts will be."

This and all subsequent letters to Berenson are used courtesy of Dr. Cecil Anrep.

To CHARLES SCRIBNER, La Finca Vigia, 25–26 August 1949

Dear Charlie:

The talk machine came. Thank you very much. Will have an electrician set it up and explain it to me today. I paid $84.70 duty and air-express on it. Think we will get it all back. Have some lovely topics to speak into the talking machine. How do you like The Things That I Know as a title? Have always been able to get a better title than I started out with; so don't worry. It will only be what I *know* and say in extremis. . . .

House count on book is Monday 802, Tuesday 379, Wed. 314, Thursday 688. Today is Friday and I am warming up writing you and then going in to pitch again. When I was a boy a pitcher named Ed Walsh, spit-ball pitcher for the Chicago White Sox, won 40 ball games one year for a team that rarely gave him more than a one run lead. Am working on this precept. Somebody said of him, Walsh, that he was the only man who could strut sitting down. I can strut when on my ass and will.

This is just warming up. In regard to the new medium sized book I want you to get it into the book of Month club and start chopping down trees for the paper now. If it isn't good you can hang me by the neck until dead. I let Mary read 121 pages of it yest. and she hasn't been any good for anything since. Waits on me hand and foot and doesn't give a damn if I have whores or countesses or what as long as I have the luck to write like that. Have a lovely new whore so beautiful she would break your heart and three fine contessas in Venice. Three, I guess, is about the right number. But the finest one writes a lovely letter too. You would like her very much I think. Is an *admirable* woman. All this time I work at being a good and faithful husband to Mary whom I love. Think you will like book. . . .

This is a strange year. We are in August; tailing off; and still have mangoes which should finish in June. The flamboyante trees did not flower until late July and they should flower in May. There are no Avocados and there always were no matter what. My best coco-nut palm is dying and there is no plague. Have had four good crops in the garden (vegetable) when three is all I rate until now. My fighting chickens are moulting; but they don't molt as they should.

It is August 25 and all our cats and dogs (34 cats; 11 dogs) have their winter coats. The marlin run is three months late and warblers that should be here in late September and October have arrived already.

What is it Charlie? You, as a countryman, should have some idea. I do not wish the opinions of Wolfe, Fitz Gerald, Alfred Knopf, any Doubleday nor David Smart. Might take a reading from Winston Churchill if he was sober. Will not receive any opinions from Harry Truman, Harry Vaughan nor any justice of the Supreme Court.

But it is a god-damn funny year. I'm hitting around .430 writing and I am only a consistent .300 hitter. Can fuck better than when I was 25 and write good afterwards which was never true before.

It is a very strange year. But if it is odd we might as well see how many fucking ball games we can win.

Your friend
Ernest

P.S.

Did 388. Plenty for the week. Adds up to 2516. We have a hurricane which has gone north of here and is due to hit Florida coast this pm. Probably between Miami and Palm Beach. Winds with velocity of 100–125 in the center. Third this year. Bad start. Will have to cut out the weekend fishing trip as there will be a heavy confused swell and fish will be down. Will shoot pigeons this morning (with the squalls and bad weather it will be fun) swim and tomorrow go out to Pinar Del Rio province in the car where they have built some new roads and take a long walk with Mary. The country there is timbered and hilly and not like this over-grown thorn-bush country we have around the farm which made such a bad impression on you. There are many pines and cedars and what must correspond to deodars in the limestone hills there and a spring stream that comes cold as you can take it right out of a mountain. It is full of small mouth bass too but I think that instead of fishing we will take four bottles of champagne and go to one of those places where the local rich take their mistresses, and drink the champagne and fuck and listen to the radio and read the accumulated copies of the N.Y. Times. It is a good life Charlie if you can keep it and like to take it. I was never much at being a gent and meeting such stuffy characters as they have in the United States. Will never forget meeting a jerk poseing as a gent named Eugene V. Connett. Only gent I ever met in the publish business outside of yourself and Max and your defunct ancestors was a boy named Gene Raynal. Jimmy whatsisname who plays the guitar so well is mixed up with Farrar and Strauss is a gent. You know who I mean. So is Joe Lippincott who is known here as Leaping-cock. Just got a card from Miss Pauline that the kids arrived in Venice o.k. and are up in the Dolomites now and will shoot with Nanyuki Franchetti this week end and that Miss Martha is in Venice and looking wonderful. If Miss Martha publishes a book about Venice, the Island of Torcello, the Veneto, Mt. Grappa, Pasubio or the defence of the lower Piave before you publish my book I give you straight word that I will turn in my suit. You can really count on this. Seriously. And double seriously.

Miss Pauline says Martha is devoted to the children; probably pumping them for material. Two god-damned ex-wives in Venice now queering my pitch. Hope they look good at least. Probably spreading horrid tales; Miss Martha's inventions are fairly lurid. But doubt if they can do me much harm in that town. That is pretty much my town; or it was. And I loved both of those women. Christ I wish I was there now for this weekend. Must go now and slaughter a few low, blue drivers for our retainers and the deep freeze. We will shoot 25 apiece and I will give Mary 2 birds in twenty five and shoot from 30 meters with her at 23. That is no way to make money. But fuck money. I am so fucked on it that I do not want to even hear it mentioned anymore. Like my one grandfather who never allowed the Civil War to be mentioned in his presence.

Well this is the end of the cool-out after the warm-up and the work. I keep getting letters from people, mostly ex-fighting men, who hate Maxwell Geismar (author of that silly piece in the Times). They write so indignantly that it is almost comic. Maybe should send a few to Geismar to let him know how the barometer reads. We have a good following among the fighting characters. It makes me prouder, I think, and happier than almost anything. These characters are not the American Legion or Veterans of Foreign Wars type. They are like that wicked old man that boy you have in your stable wrote so magnificently about in The History of Rome Hanks [Joseph Stanley Pennell, 1944]. Parts of that were better than anything ever written in America and parts were worse.

The hell with it all. Miss Mary is sore as a saddle gall you have to piss on to cure because she thinks am working myself to death. But she will get over it. You get over everything but death and death is shit too. Leaveing you with this devout sentiment,

PUL   Ernest

To CHARLES SCRIBNER, La Finca Vigia, 27 August 1949

Dear Charlie:

Thanks for your [letter] with enclosures. Will you ask your secretary to write to the woman from McCall's and tell her that I support my mother and I will cut off her support if she gives out any repeat *any* interviews or contributes information to any articles about me.[1] This is absolute.

This for your information:

My mother is very old, her memory is more than spotty and she is addicted to fantastic statements. Lately, because she is so old, I have played the role of a devoted son in case it pleased her. But I hate her guts and she hates mine. She forced my father to suicide and, one time, later, when I ordered her to sell certain worthless properties that were eating her up with taxes, she wrote, "Never threaten me with what to do. Your father tried that once when we were first married and he lived to regret it."

I answered, "My dear mother I am a very different man from my father and I never threaten anyone. I only make promises. If I say that if you do not do certain sound things I will no longer contribute to your support it means factually and exactly that." We never had any trouble after that. Except that I will not see her and she knows that she can never come here.

My secretary is on vacation but would appreciate yours helping me out and writing the woman from McCall's (who sounds like a go-getter of the worst type) that there will be no such article. I will write my mother expressly forbidding her to co-operate in any such procedure.

Let the woman from McCall's write more about Dr. Kinsey and his wife.

Will your secretary also please write the AP man from Jacksonville that I will be happy to see him any afternoon after five o'clock if he will call two or three days before and make an appointment. But not over the week-end as I fish then. I work in the mornings. Would be very happy to see him, but would like to know when he will show as there are lots of fish in October and I do not want to louse either him or me up.

Will you tell the LIFE people that we will let them know well in advance of the book and will co-operate with them fully and that I appreciate the way they have acted in the past and their decency in regard to a working writer. Please tell them that I regret very much not haveing any new wives to sex up the story but that Miss Mary, their former employee, is too god-damn good to leave.

Don't know what further business we have.

What [Where] does that miserable McCall's woman get the idea that she can write about our family and how I differ from less talented bros. and sisters such as my bitch sister Marcelline, my lovely sister Ura and my kid sister Sunny (nicknames) who pitched on the school team (boys) and plays the harp like an angel? Or my sister Carol who was assaulted, knocked out and raped when she was 12 by a sexual pervert or my kid bro. who refused to accept a commission and served as a private in the 22nd Inf Regt. and was well liked, and then built raceing boats in the Grand Caiman islands and is now in the Embassy at Bogota? What right does that bitch have to this knowledge? Doesn't she know that people have private existences and prides and secrets and do not let bitches batten off them like buzzards. So McCall's have left this entirely to her have they. She goes out on her ass with her heels drumming and I want your secretary to quote exactly my first paragraph and phrase the balance of the letter strongly. Do such bitches think I want publicity? I know you have to have some, and I go through with it, but it is as pleasant to eat as cat shit.

Please give that woman such a throw out that she will think twice before she comes down to the whore's end of our bar again.

Am feeling rough again today just on the morning I decided was going to try truly hard to be a christian non-rough talking gent.

Tell the lady to write an article about whether Chastity Is Outmoded for the Woman's Home Companion or interview Miss Martha on her War Experiences. One time, after the Bulge fight was decided, and she came up to make a play to move back in, I, to be pleasant and cheerful said, "Bug you're getting to be terrific. You've seen damn near more war than I have."

"I have seen more," she said, detailing where she had been like Frederic the Great's mule.

"Unless you count Italy," I said.

"Oh if you want to count *that*," she said haughtily and then began to speak French in front of my Colonel so he couldn't understand, being a Col of Infantry only. And he was the guy who translated De Coulaincourt's Memoirs of his trip back with Napoleon from up where the big cold had set in. . . .

And how do you like it *now*, Gentlemen?

That was an expression I always loved along with, Now share it amongst you, you cocksuckers when you put an anti-tank grenade in on lovely german SS's who had decided not to come out when duly summoned.

One time I killed a very snotty SS kraut who, when I told him I would kill him unless he revealed what his escape route signs were said: You will not kill me, the kraut stated. Because you are afraid to and because you are a race of mongrel degenerates. Besides it is against the Geneva Convention.

What a mistake you made, brother, I told him and shot him three times in the belly fast and then, when he went down on his knees, shot him on the topside so his brains came out of his mouth or I guess it was his nose.

The next SS I interrogated talked wonderfully. Clearly and with intelligent military exposition of their situation. He called me Herr Hauptman [Captain] and then decided that was not enough and called me Herr Oberst [Colonel] (I wore no insignia). I would have worked him up to general. But we did not have time. After that we chased them very fast because we knew exactly what the signs they chalked up meant and who and how many they were.

Will now try to go back to being a christian again.

Yours in Christ
Ernest

PUL

1. See EH to his mother, 17 September 1949, and to Scribner, 4 October 1949.

To CHARLES SCRIBNER, La Finca Vigia, 6 and 7 September 1949

Dear Charlie:

Early morning animal situation report on the Finca:

Dogs are trumps but cats are longest suite [suit] we hold.

Re-read your letter in the first light and saw I had not written anything about book clubs. May be wrong but suggest we submit nothing to no-one and split with no one. (May be wrong about this. You tell me.) Maybe we should do the [Literary] Guild.

Would like to play this horse to win and pile it on. If we don't win we are ok because we have a sure winner in the next book and we can lay off a little with the Book Clubs. But this time let's try to hit one on the actual nose. Hope this use of gambling terms does not shock you.

If the critics don't like it (and I have many such old enemies and lumpen-proletariat adversaries who would love to ham-string you only am not a ham) it is more or less their ass because we run the bulldozer over them with the next book. Hope this doesn't sound over-confident. Am a man without any ambition, except to be champion of the world, I wouldn't fight Dr. Tolstoi in a 20 round bout because I know he would knock my ears off. The Dr. had terrific wind and could go forever and then some. But I would take him on for six and he would never hit me and would knock the shit out of him and maybe knock him out. He is easy to hit. But boy how *he* can hit. If I can live to 60 I can beat him. (*MAYBE*)

For your information I started out trying to beat dead writers that I knew how good they were. (Excuse vernacular) I tried for Mr. Turgenieff first and it wasn't too hard. Tried for Mr. Maupassant (won't concede him the de) and it took four of the best stories to beat him. He's beaten and if he was around he would know it. Then I tried for another guy (am getting embarrassed or embare-assed now from bragging; or stateing) and I think I fought a draw with him. This other dead character.

Mr. Henry James I would just thumb him once the first time he grabbed and then hit him once where he had no balls and ask the referee to stop it.

There are some guys nobody could ever beat like Mr. Shakespeare (The Champion) and Mr. Anonymous. But would be glad any time, if in training, to go twenty with Mr. Cervantes in his own home town (Alcala de Henares) and beat the shit out of him. Although Mr. C. very smart and would be learning all the time and would probably beat you in a return match. The *third* fight people would pay to see. Plenty peoples.

But these Brooklyn jerks are so ignorant that they *start off* fighting Mr. Tolstoi. And they announce they have beaten him before the fight starts. They should be hung by the balls until dead for ignorance. I can write good and I would not get into the ring with Mr. T. over the long distance unless I and my family were not eating.

In the big book I hope to take Mr. Melville and Mr. Doestoevsky, they are coupled as a stable entry, and throw lots of mud in their faces because the track isn't fast. But you can only run so many of those kind of races. They take it out of you.

Know this sounds like bragging but Jeezoo Chrise you have to have confidence to be a champion and that is the only thing I ever wished to be. And it was not until I was one half one hundred years old that I realized had never turned the horse loose and let him run. He's going to run now until the son of a bitch breaks something or dies.

With which pious sentiment I leave you and get to work.

Ernest

Later—

P.S. Did 1149 Friday. Skipped Sat–Sun and wrote letters. Did 640 Sept 6.

EH

Didn't mail this by mistake.

PUL

To W. AVERELL HARRIMAN, La Finca Vigia, 9 September 1949

Dear Averell:

I received a letter signed with your name, but since the signature was so formal, I imagined that it was sent by someone else. They were asking me to write a brief dedication for the birthday memorial concert to be held on 30 January in the Waldorf Astoria.[1]

I would be delighted to do that if I get my book done. As you know I am not an oratoric writer nor a master of rhetoric like the previous occupants but please count on me to write the thing if I can. Will let you know, or your designated representative, who forges your signature, in ample time if I can. Best wishes always to you and to Marie and to Kathleen.

Yours always

JFK
Ernest

1. EH had met Harriman at Sun Valley, Idaho. He was now chairman of the FDR Birthday Memorial Committee. EH soon declined the invitation because he was finishing his new novel, but he let his secretary, Nita Jensen, copy and keep the following, composed 11 October 1949 and presumably never sent: "Today we are gathered together to honor a rich and spoiled paralytic who changed our world. As a person I thought he was a bore with endless ill-told anecdotes and his improbable vicarious adventures when such persons as William Bullitt were in his confidence. Later he was flown to many far-off places, had his own adventures, and quite possibly killed himself through being flown about so much and through over-work. There was no need for

him to over-work since the President of a country such as ours, can apportion and delegate his work among responsible subordinates. But this man that we are gathered together to honor today, while he delegated almost all of his work, reserved for himself so many tasks that he was incapable of performing correctly, that he is dead and our country is as we find it now. I do not find it well, gentlemen, and I suggest that, instead of honoring this person who never wrote a speech he made (unlike his eccentric and hard-drinking colleague, Mr. Winston Churchill), we should all rise quietly now and leave this room out of respect for the dead. For certainly one thing we know, for sure, gentlemen, that he is dead. So we respect him as such. EH" (T.C. PUL)

To GRACE HALL HEMINGWAY, La Finca Vigia, 17 September 1949

My dear Mother:

Thank you very much for your letter of 7 September. It made me so happy the other day to receive the books that you made for all of us children. They have been in storage in Key West and I had not seen them for many years. Please let me congratulate you on diligence and your lovingness for all of us kids when we were young and must have been great nuisances to you. Your handwriting in the book was lovely to see and the photos that my father took were almost uniformly excellent. I hope you are getting along well and that everything goes well with you and with Ruth Arnold, to whom I send my best love.

Scribner's have written me that some woman from McCalls magazine, I believe, was contacting them to get in touch with you to write a piece about me when I was a boy. I do not care for this type of publicity and will not permit it. I told Scribners to write the woman, who was a very pushing, and vicious and, I thought, rather a detestable type of journalist, that I contributed to your support and that I would withdraw this contribution in case they published any such article without my consent. Hope this handled that matter.

All of our boys are well and been having a good time in Europe. Bumby is a captain of Infantry in Berlin, and Patrick and Gregory have visited him this summer on their motor bikes and have made a tour of Italy where they have been seeing the pictures and visiting our good friends there. I worked very hard to get Leicester the job that he has in Bogota, but the one who really got it for him was General Buck Lanham with whom I served in the 22nd Infantry Regiment in the last war. Leicester asked to be transferred to the Infantry from the easy job he had with the photographic unit and served very well and Buck went to bat for him all the way. Naturally, I did not want him in the Infantry as I might have to support his wife and two children. I like his two children but care nothing for his wife.

Congratulations on being a great-grandmother 77 years old. I would like to be a great-grandfather and attain that degree of longevity.

Am working very hard now on a book which I think will be very good. Will leave for Europe for a vacation as soon as it is completed. Please forgive me if I miss sending greetings on anniversaries and other things.

With much love,

T.C. PUL   Your son Ernest.

To JOHN DOS PASSOS, La Finca Vigia, 17 September 1949

Dear Dos:

We were delighted to receive your marriage announcement and almost sorry we didn't receive it in time to send you and your wife a telegram.[1] All good luck, kid, and if your wife would like to see the Finca this is the place to see it. We've had a strange season with the migratory birds here. Several weeks in advance of when they should be. And all the cats with their winter coats now. There are big strings of ducks coming in and months earlier than they should be arriving and we have had five hurricanes, none of which did any damage here.

Am working good and maybe better than I ever did. It is a big relief to work without always getting hit on the head with more or less blunt instruments. Never realized until I got a break that that was one of the things that was slowing me up. Seven concussions in one year is probably more than you should give the average writer except perhaps Mr. Andre Gide.

When we finish this am going to Europe and would sure as hell like to have those francs that you spoke about if they are available. Want to buy Mary some clothes in that town and to buy myself a little Tavel. You can have your agent send them to Charley Ritz at the Ritz Hotel to hold for me or they can be deposited in my account at the Guaranty Trust Co. of New York, 4 Place de la Concorde in that fine town. Hope you are well and happy and working well. If you are married to a new wife you ought to be happy. I had a lot of luck the last time I drew cards and I am not trading Miss Mary in on any new models of any kind. But still, a new wife is a good thing for any old Portuguese to have. Please felicitate her for us. If you would like anything for a wedding present please consult with her and we will get it on the far shore as I think the more loathsome shits used to refer to it as.

Since trip to Italy have been studying the life of Dante. Seems to be one of the worst jerks that ever lived, but how well he could write! This may be a lesson to us all.

Am dictating this into my wire recording machine, one of the greatest inventions since penicillin, so excuse this purity of dictation. Best love from us both.

Tu amigo,
Ernesto

T.C. PUL

1. Dos Passos had married Elizabeth Hamlin Holdridge on 6 August 1949 at Ridgecrest Farm, Baltimore County, Maryland.

To MARLENE DIETRICH, La Finca Vigia, 26 September 1949

My dearest Marlene:

Please let us know at this address where you will be at the end of October so that we may get together. How are you, daughter? And how is everything going? I am very jealous at you being a grand-mother and me not being a legal grandfather. But have told Bumby to throw in his armour and try to remedy this situation.

Daughter, please try to keep contact from now on as I am finishing a book and should be through in around three weeks. I think that you will like it very much. Will give you carbon of manuscript if you like. You are in it and nobody else is in it because it is all made up. But it is made up as well as I can make it.

Marlene, Mary and I love you very much and miss you all the time. Please write, even if it is a corvée.

My health is about as well as can be expected; that of a re-built jeep. Mary is fine and has gone up to visit her parents in Chicago. They are very old and fragile and it is good for her to go and see them. I hope these people at the hotel [St. Regis] will forward this letter to you and if you are not in New York when we get there we can meet in Europe. Am going to publish the poems after this book along with a few stories. We might read them together once more in the Ritz Bar.

I hope you are well and that everything goes well with you and all of your family. It will be wonderful to be together again and to have a chance to talk. Maybe I could get a couple of bottles of something Brut

in the morning and you could help me shave. With all my love and
Mary's love too, if she were here.

Papa

P.S.   I know lots of wonderful gossip. Some of it even true. Will promise
to bring no fishing characters when we have dinner. You promise not to
give my carbons to that man [Erich Maria] Remarque.[1]

JFK   E.H.

1. Miss Dietrich's article on EH, "The Most Fascinating Man I Know," *This Week
Magazine*, 13 February 1955, mentions EH and Remarque in contiguous sentences.

To CHARLES SCRIBNER, La Finca Vigia, 4 October 1949

Dear Charlie:

The hell with writing today. The enclosed letter will show you why I
did not want that magazine bitch jumping my mother. Among other
reasons.

So the boys can't tell a story. You know why? They couldn't tell it if
they put them on the stand. If you have a story it is not hard to tell.
Maybe people won't believe it. But you can tell it straight and true.

A writer, of course, has to make up stories for them to be rounded and
not flat like photographs. But he makes them up out of what he knows.

Most of them, that write, never did it, do not know it, and are sort of
devious thieves or presumptuous pricks. I haven't known a writer who was
a good guy since Jim Joyce died. And he was spotty sometimes. But he
did say to me one time when he was drunk, "But Ernest don't you think
what I write is really awfully suburban?"

"Yes, Jim. But that's what you know better than anybody."

"Yes that's what I know," he said. "God pity me." Of Henry James
you would like, I think, Madame des Mauves. It's quite short. There are
a couple of other good ones too. But the greater part of it is rather
snobbish, difficultly written shit.

You can have your boy Tom Wolfe too, and his sainted mother. If
Max hadn't cut ten tons of shit out of Wolfe *everybody* would have
known how bad it is after the first book. Instead only pros like me or
people who drink wine, not labels, know. I guess you know all right.

Then we have Scott borrowing on the outline of a thing he'd never, and never could write, giveing samples here and there like a mineing prospector with a salted mine.

It gives you the creeps. Anyway we are over 44,000 [words] with lots of dialogue and you can go out and *buy* that horse if you like. Tomorrow we get the series. This noon I go into town to see the oldest and best whore I ever knew. She is the same age I am and I knew her when she was a kid, when she [was] the mistress of Primo de Rivera's boy that started Fascism in Spain (good boy but mis-led in his head), and we will tell sad stories of the death of Kings and get the local gossip. She tells me everything about everybody and gives me all the handkerchiefs her boy friends leave. Have initialled handkerchiefs from every sugar king in the Island. That will kill today and Roberto [Herrera] is bringing the young, new, beautiful whore out tonight. Then will work good tomorrow morning and Miss Mary comes on the plane in the evening in her coat on Thursday. . . .

You would like Gig. He is a cold athlete with no nerves at all when the heat is on. I think he will be a wonderful writer if he doesn't go to hell some way. He is a real Indian boy (Northern Cheyenne) with the talents and the defects. Am going to teach him all I know. He takes teaching just like a rope horse. Enclose picture of him when he was eleven. Also score of the championship shoot so you can see it is not craperoo. Please send it back. He can ride anything and doesn't even know it is difficult. He used to have a sort of rope ladder, that he carried in his saddle bags, that he could use to mount and would be gone all day when he was six. When he was seven was makeing money in big shoots and ride anything bare-back with a postal card under his ass and not lose it. When he left here this last time he gave all the money he had made shooting to the servants. Only heard about this yesterday.

He is seventeen now and is going to St. Johns at Annapolis where they teach those 100 Great Books business. But writes he does not like it but will stick out the term. Writes he wants to go some place where he can read the 100 great books without the professors, and fuck and shoot a little bit to make some money. He loved Venice and he has a girl there now. Also a raceing motor bike in Mestre.

At his age I had shot and be-got my man so what can you do except sweat him out? Wish us old Northern Cheyennes were in business still because Gig would go a long way. He loves to drink, too, as you and I do. Neither of the other boys care anything about it. But Gig went on that motor bike and ate and drank in every place I told him was worth eating and drinking in through Italy. It is sort of different from Henry James in a way. But Gig writes, "I looked up the Baronessa as soon as I was settled and telephoned to ask if I might call. She was very lovely and gave me a number of drinks. After what I considered the proper number, in view of the relations between our two families, I left. It is possible that I miscalculated the amount. The Wild Girl was in the country that night so I didn't see her. But from then on Papa—"

On business: Don't let [Herbert] May's do any fouling up of when they and when we publish. That's simple. You hold the cards.

I really trust [A. E.] Hotchner. Dick Berlin, who runs it all for Hearst said, textually, "Tell Ernest that the relation he has with our organization is such that we'd feel better if he just named his own price. He is a good friend and he should be guided by what he needs and what he thinks the property is worth."

Everybody trusting everybody. Somewhere, sometime, I must have been honest to be trusted by you and these other people.

With which cheerful thought I leave you. I wonder how old Casey Stengel is sleeping tonight.

Ernest

P.S.   The other reason some of your clients are not so good is, besides, they don't know anything and couldn't hit the ball out of the infield if you just lobbed it up to them: nobody anymore wants to learn their trade. Nobody will serve an apprentice-ship. All the Brooklyn Tolstoi's want to be champions without ever haveing had a fight. They could not lick Joe Shit let alone Mr. Tolstoi. Please don't show the other enclosed letter to *anybody* and send it back with the piece on Mister Gigi. Call them all Mister when respect them.

3 Enclosures:
   Mother
   Gigi, Joe Collins
PUL

To MALCOLM COWLEY, La Finca Vigia, 11 October 1949

Dear Malcolm:

I hope you will not get into the high jerk-off notch about that portable or potable Hemingway book.[1] I am working and am in to the stretch and honest to God I cannot give it more attention than I have given. It is fine to say if I were not hot on the book, but the sad thing is that I *am* hot. Will see that your work is preserved and that you receive proper and adequate compensation. Charlie Scribner will have to do this and I may have to put on some pressure. It is not for me to interfere between him and Mr. Viking. What Viking, where, and from when?

Your present job sounds quite difficult since you are dealing with people who can write only at times. You could put Lionel Trilling, Saul Bellow, Truman Capote, Jean Stafford and . . . Robert Lowry into one cage and jack them up good and you would find that you have nothing. Eudora Welty can write. The others I think you waste your time discussing unless we want to discuss who is playing for Dallas, Texas. The Texas League is a very good one if you are playing in it but it is quite different from the big time where you actually have to play to perform whatever it is you do absolutely perfectly within the limits of possibility. This may sound very profound but I think I learned it from Mr. Casey Stengel who just won one himself.

Think that Nelson Algren is probably the best writer under 50, and name your own figure, writing today. He has everything that the fading Faulkner ever had except the talent for magic and he makes Mr. Thomas Wolfe the over-bloated Lil Abner of literature look about how he always looked to us professionals. If Max Perkins had not cut one half million words out of Mr. Wolfe everybody would know how he was but except for the first good book, "Look Homeward, Angel," he never had enough on the ball to strike out Miss Billie Burke in her 64th year, and she never ran as a hitter. She was more or less hit and run.

It would be very nice if you could send me "Witch-cult in Western Europe" by Margaret A. Murray, Oxford, 1921. Have never known much about witches and English although there is considerable witch-craft practised in this neighbourhood especially in Guanabacoa. Us old ex-Cheyennes have various things that we believe in but as an Indian said to me one time, "Long time ago, good, now no good."

Please give our love to Muriel [Mrs. Cowley] and send our best to your boy. Gig nearly broke out of St. John's last week to come down here because, he said what you really do is read the 100 books and why do you have to listen to the professors when you could read them at home and make some money shooting? But I advised him to stick out the semester and maybe he would meet wonderful people.

Yours always,

T.C. PUL   Ernest

1. Cowley had edited *The Viking Portable Hemingway* (New York, 1944), re-printed in October 1949.

To CAPTAIN JOHN HEMINGWAY, La Finca Vigia,
c. 16 October 1949

Dear Jack:

Thank you very much for the lovely pictures of your wedding.[1] We have had them framed and they hang in the corner of the wall where the old picture was of you with the citation of the Croix de Guerre. You both look wonderful, hope everything goes well and please, under no circumstances, omit to call on [General] Buck [Lanham] and his wife. Everything is fine here and I am near to the end of the book. Think it will be pretty good and that we will be in los chips.

We are coming over to Europe this fall as soon as the book is finished and would love to see you and Puck. If you have any leave coming up now maybe we could take it in Venice where we could have marvelous shooting. I miss you very much, Jack, all the time. Hope Mouse and Gig had a good time, they've been shooting very well, and I write almost as though possessed by the devil. Started this morning around 4:30 and have just finished now at shortly before 0800. Did 901 words, yesterday 1176, we may have some dough if I can hold the pace and not blow any gaskets.

Anyway, love to you and Puck from all of us and keep your pecker pointed north.

I want you to make good very badly in this sad science that you are in. We never had a member of the family soldiering in peace time but I suppose now there is no peacetime. Had a good letter from "Lightning" Joe [General Collins] and if I make any money will send you some. All main cats and dogs are well and Miss Mary sends you her love. This is a commodity which is not sent lightly. I send my love, such as it is, to Puck and I look forward to when we can all be here at the Finca. I am shooting over 94% on pigeons and this is always a good sign of how things are going. Book is fairly wonderful I think, but I am prejudiced.

Please keep in touch and write us even though you have no time to do it. My health is that of a re-built jeep and sometimes they are very good.

Take care of yourself and of Puck and be a good boy and know that Papa loves you very much. This may be old fashioned crap but is a way we were in this family. Much love from all of us here and from all your loyal partisans in this country.

Mr. Papa

P.S.   Do you want any pictures of the Finca to show to Puck? Roberto [Herrera], El Monstruo, is here now between jobs and he can make some enlargements. It is lovely now and hurricane months when you do not have any hurricanes are very beautiful. Please give all our love to Puck and tell her to throw some good kids so that I can be a grandfather. Feel pretty bad at being a non-grandfather with Marlene being a grandmother.

T.C. PUL   Papa

1. EH's eldest son had married Byra Whittlesey Whitlock, nicknamed Puck, on 25 June 1949 in Paris. See Mary Hemingway, *How It Was* (New York, 1976), p. 241. Their three daughters are Joan (called Muffet), b. 5 May 1950; Margaux, b. 16 February 1955; and Mariel, b. 22 November 1961.

To CHARLES SCRIBNER, Nice, France, 29 December 1949

Dear Charlie:

Thanks very much for Guns Wanted [J. K. Stanford, 1950]. It is a hell of a funny book and shooting parts are excellent. Am on next to last chapter now. I don't mind the snobism on account being a snob myself though not always about the same things.

We drove down here from Paris with Peter and Virginia Viertel and piled in Hotch [A. E. Hotchner] at the last minute. Had Christmas eve at Saulieux after a lunch at Auxerre to end lunches and Christmas dinner below Valence. Then slept the next night at Nimes after seeing Avignon and the Pont du Gard. Went down to Aigues Mortes at the edge of the Camargue and out to Le Grau de Roi and checked on the tuna fishing there. There are two big runs, one in April and the other in August.

The girls had never seen Provence and Aigues Mortes is a hell of a place. The only old fortified town that has remained intact without ever being restored. They never let Violette le Duc get his hands on it. Where Saint Louis took off for the Seventh and Eighth Crusades that you must be familiar with from Froissard's Chronicles. He picked up the old Rale on the first one and probably amaoebic and died on the second; son finished building the town. St. Louis needed it for a port and supply base when the Dukes of Burgundy held Marseilles and Le Grau de Roi was the only port he had and it made by hand. I always love it down there and we had wonderful weather after two days of fog comeing down through Burgundy and along the Rhone.

Afterwards we drove across the Camargue and through Arles to Aix en Provence and spent the night there and yesterday loaded Viertels and Hotch onto evening train from here to Paris.

Hotch to re-join in Venice if office okays. Otherwise to mail Mss. registered that secretary still hadn't finished copying.

Let me know how long I have to stay away from it before I can get it to you. Longer I can stay away before I have to get it to you the better it will be as gives me a whole new chance to see it cold and plug any gaps and amplify where there is any need.

Think can keep out of jams in Venice since everybody will be at Cortina. Hope so anyway. Trouble is that when finish a book don't give a damn about any form of consequences whatever. Virginia was going to fly top cover for me while Mary went down on the deck and strafed the roads and shipping. But Peter put a stop to that brilliant idea. Probably for the best. Who knows? Not me.

Hope you had good holidays.

Must knock off and write the children. Can't make Venice with the bad weather that has shown up this morning in time to shoot this weekend. But will be there fine and rested for next week, staying here for a day and getting my letters caught up.

You can write to the Guaranty Trust and they will forward it or directly to Gritti Palace Hotel, Venice. They are very sound and reliable and will forward it wherever we go.

Mary sends her love. She has been haveing a very good time.

Best always and holiday greetings etc.

Ernest

PUL

To CHARLES SCRIBNER, Venice, 6 January 1950

Dear Charlie:

Thanks for letter and for Ned Calmer's book [*The Strange Land*, 1950]. Book starts very well. For my own information will you tell me what the changes were, exactly, that you asked him to make in it. Book by the other character hasn't come yet. Will look forward to it.

Today is Friday and we go to shoot on Saturday. Hotch [A. E. Hotchner] is due here Monday with the typed and corrected Mss. [*Across the River and Into the Trees*]. He will probably be returning promptly stateswise. Will send copy to re-assure you. But see no need to set up right away. Why not have me re-write on mss. and you set from that? It will save you money and always give me a final shot at seeing it again in proof and the chance to make all my errors permanent.

Please give me dates when you must have (1) corrected Mss. to set from. (2) corrected proof.

Been haveing fun here as always. Last two, three days been in the country. Nanyuki Franchetti that am shooting with broke his leg last week ski-ing at Cortina [d'Ampezzo] but he shot four days later and broke the cast. Very good boy.

At his house we had some very interesting statue shooting with elephant guns after lunch. I had never shot statues before and was a little reluctant to cut loose at them with a .477 but Nanyuki's mother suggested the shoot, as she said she was sick of these particular statues and that she thought they should [be] done away with. Mary shot the big guns beautifully and did not even have a sore shoulder. She also rang the bell over the chapel consistently with a .22. She is very popular in this town and environs except with the very youngest set who view her sort of as an obstacle like Beecher's Brook say.

Nanyuki's mother told me all about Martha and said she was looking very well here and had written two dull but great hearted articles. Got a good check on all former wives who visited this region last summer. A former wife, in Venice, has a status comparable to a favorite who fell at the first jump and broke his neck. Very hardy town.

Also news of the children. Gigi, it seems, according to Nanyuk's mother, turned up out in the country and said, quite simply, "I am Hemingway." She told him that she recognized the bony structure. He shot very well it seems. Didn't ask if they tried him on statues.

We will miss you in Europe I am afraid as we will be going back on the Ile de France either March third or twelfth. I truly can't fly anymore. It gives my head too much hell. I should not have kept on with it in 44. But there [are] a lot of things I should not have done in 44 and thank God I did them all.

Yesterday and night before last we spent with the Kechler's up near Udine. Carlo Kechler has sold or is selling his horses. Times very bad for people who own land instead of factories.

Had lunch with the British General commanding at Trieste at Carlo's. Very charming man with a nice wife. Arie is his name, I think, but do not Guaranty the spelling. Always capitalize Guaranty as in Guaranty Trust.

No statue shooting at Kechlers. Carlo has dug up a really excellent Goya and a better than fair Greco and sold his Alfa Romeo to buy them which, with the horses going, rather grounds him for the moment. They are good pictures though. He should be able to sell them and make some money.

Most people here out of town now and up at Cortina. Very good snow.

Have been checking all the things I need to re-inforce book. Will have it good and solid and 100 proof.

Don't know anything about the Mss. of Peter Viertel. Will check with him when I see him; or write. He and Virginia left with Hotch from Nice for Paris. We all had a fine trip down together as I wrote you.

Big move in local circles to get me to go to Rome since it seems sinners of the worst type are being pardoned like flies. I would miss purgatory completely, it seems, though would probably have to take a quick look at hell. Not going to Rome however. Anyway have my personal priest [Andres Untzain] comeing here on the twelfth. The headwaiter here has located a good tavern where we can drink and sing in the evenings. It is pretty hard on him to keep him away from the track when he has just discovered the wonders of the 23/1 shot but, after all, a priest must make some sacrifices besides that vow of chastity.

Best always

PUL   Ernest

To GENERAL CHARLES T. LANHAM, La Finca Vigia, 15 April 1950

Dear Buck:
What the hell has happened to our channels of communication? Does every letter I write you have to be intercepted by the Vatican or what?

Have sent three that have not heard from. One okay. Accident. Two maybe. Three heap shit to translate from purest Northern Cheyenne I know.

Red O'Hare told me about the Send Lanham Back Where He Came From movement by the local under-orders peasantry.

Maybe they ought to send us both back to Houfallize where I saw the members of the Armee Blanche take off their arm-bands when the little fire fight started when Pelky, Jean, Marcel and I were drinking happily at that roadhouse awaiting the arrival of the armed forces of the United States. The British fixed up Houfallize good. We probably should have been more fore-handed and ordered an air-mission on it before we approached it. I can remember you going around the top, properly, as you should, and we walking down into it happy, wary, and proud and Peter Lawless dead later possibly from the bad habits I got him into. He was a nice man, brave and cheerful and if he had been intelligent probably could have made a good soldier. He was a good boy officer in the first war.

Had a funny thing in NY. After 25 years ran into the guy who was my best friend in the first war.[1] We were boy or child officers together and he went on to be a Lieut. Gen. (British) and Auchinleck's chief of staff in the desert. He was to have the 8th Army but Churchill put in Monty (that Prince among Men). This boy, Chink, now Lieut. Gen. Retired, told me the whole story, not the whole but the basic, of what happened and it was clear, anyway to me, that they had Rommel beaten when he could not take Alexandria and they were just recuperateing and getting ready to run him out on a cheap basis when in comes Monty with his 14/1 or I won't move concept of war.

Chink says when Monty taught tactics at the war college his only conception was to break a hazel nut with a sledge hammer. Sledge hammers are not usually issued to troops and are quite difficult to carry if they are. Chink said that his and my theory had always been to break a hazel nut useing another hasel nut and your thumb and first finger. It is easier to have a good thumb than a sledge hammer and the thumb is self propelled.

We had a wonderful time and he is comeing down here. Wish you could be here. I don't know anything about war because I abandoned it to try to be a writer. But Chink and I used to walk the great fights when he had leave after first war and we would fight each other at any famous or infamous place like playing chess. We used to take and/or defend Pamplona (Pampelune) till it was worse than Fort Benning. I would tell him that I could come through the pass of Roncevaux and he would say, "You can not." And I would do it the same way Rommel did when he fucked us at Longarone.

It is a healthful sport anyway.

He told me had always kept in mind in the desert my basic concept. I had forgotten all about my basic concept and probably had formulated it when I was drunk anyway.

Well this was it, "Any front is diaphanous if you have truly good intelligence, get your attacks off on time and never assault a strong point."

I told him I couldn't have used a word like diaphanous and he said that I had and had backed it up with assertion any front anywhere is as vulnerable as a spider's web. All you have to do is eliminate the spider. There has to be a little fight once always when you wrap him up in his own web.

This is sort of like showing you what wonderful grades I made in kindergarten.

And what a kindergarten it was, Gentlemen. A noisy kindergarten indeed. Every type of delicious noise furnished free to help the children's nerves through life. No psychiatrists. If you go crazy from too many times up the same damned hill you can always look at a fireing squad. It could look like two fireing squads if you had double vision from concussion. But you always saw the fireing squad for others, double vision or not, and sometimes you commanded it.

Certainly was a beautiful kindergarten.

Should have gone to college though so I could have had a career. Certainly do not give a shit for the one I have.

Black ass day for Hemingstein. So long, my general. See you soon some place I hope.

Love to Pete. Love from Mary.

PUL   Ernesto

1. Captain Eric Edward (Chink) Dorman-Smith (later Dorman-O'Gowan), whom EH had befriended in Milan in 1918. He was now a retired lieutenant general of the British Army, had recently occupied his ancestral estate in County Cavan, Ireland, and had come to the United States on a speaking tour for the Irish government. He and EH met by chance in New York in April 1950.

To ARTHUR MIZENER, La Finca Vigia, 18 April 1950

Dear Mr. Mizener:

Have just gotten home and find your letter which my secretary had filed with her idiotic answer under Priority—To Be Answered.

All I can do is apologize and tell you that you have full permission to use the excerpts from the letters to Scott and to you.

I am so sorry about this when you have been workeing hard on something and trying to get it straight.

Send this to you in a hurry and wish you luck. I read the one lift from your book in Partisan Review. Where did those Partisans fight? (The other day an Italian boy who had been in Partigiani[1] saw the review and said to me, "Oh, I never knew Partisans had enough money to publish a review. Does it commemorate their dead?") He said it without irony, and [I] thought it was straight and ok as far as I knew the epoch you dealt with.

Please call on me to straighten out anything I can recall accurately. Have done the final re-write of book (that was the vacation Miss Juanita J. Jensen referred to) and am now waiting for the galley proofs. After that will have some time.

Yours always,

UMD   Ernest Hemingway

1. Gianfranco, elder brother of Adriana Ivancich of Venice (see EH to Adriana Ivancich, 3 June 1950, note 1). On his wartime experiences in the desert under Rommel and his subsequent service with the partisans in the Veneto, see Carlos Baker, *Ernest Hemingway: A Life Story* (New York, 1969), pp. 471–72.

To ARTHUR MIZENER, La Finca Vigia, 22 April 1950

Dear Mr. Mizener:

Am awfully glad the permission was there in time. Beautiful Nita, my Secretary, did a wonderful job when I was away. It is a wonder I have a friend left. Some old boy will write at Christmas saying Dear Ernie you probably don't remember me but I took over such and such a company when so and so was killed and you loaned me your frenchmen that time we had the thing at the cp [command post].

So Miss Nita thinks company commander eh? I guess Papa wouldn't wish to be bothered with someone who only had a company and only got the company because someone was killed. So she answers the letter as follows, "Dear Sir: Mr. Hemingway is away on a short vacation in the European area and your communication will be called to his attention on his return. No date has been set for his return."

And I would have answered the letter the day I received it anywhere and no matter what I was doing. Finishing a book and going over the first draft has never been my idea of a vacation either.

Will help any way I can on Scott if you run into anything I know that you need to know. By then I should be pretty well in the clear on this book. Getting galleys now. But want to have them all before I start as I die every time I read or write the book and I do not want to die peacemeal.

Poor Scott how he would have loved all this big thing about him now. I remember one time in N.Y. we were walking down Fifth Avenue and he said, "If only I could play foot-ball again with everything I know about it now."

I suggested that we walk across Fifth through the traffic since he wanted to be a back-field man (It isn't difficult at all really for anyone who can do it). But he said I was crazy.

Then there was always the war. He was lucky he never was in a war. It was almost like being broken hearted because you had missed the San Francisco earthquake (the fire).

None of this is for quotation. Am only trying to give a brother writer something I know, or think I know, about another brother writer once he is dead. I never say or write anything about him I would not say to his face or write him. I never had any respect for him ever except for his lovely, golden, wasted talent.

If he would have had fewer pompous museings and a little sounder education it would have been better maybe. But any time you got him at all straightened out and takeing his work seriously Zelda would get jealous of him and knock him out of it.

Also alcohol, that we use as the Giant Killer, and that I could not have lived without many times; or at least would not have cared to live without; was a straight poison to Scott instead of a food.

Here's something you should know too; he never slept with another girl except Zelda until Zelda went officially crazy. She was crazy all the time I knew them but not yet net-able. I remember her at Antibes saying, "Don't you think Al Jolson is greater than Jesus?" I said, "No," which was the only answer I knew at the moment.

A boy named Bud Schulberg who is extremely nice and sensitive and straight, but without either talent or much perception, is writing some sort of life story of Scott and yours should be a corrective of sorts. He wrote a novelized life of Primo Carnera full of strange distortion due to the fear of libel and Carnera said to a friend of mine, "I wish so much Mr. Schulberg would have come to me because I could have told so much more interesting things."

Did I write or tell you how Zelda really ruined Scott? Probably I did. Anyway, in case I didn't, she told him A: That he had never given her sexual satisfaction. B: That it was because his sexual organ was too small (am sending this through the mails so employ these high-flung terms).

He told me this at lunch and I told him to come to the lavoratory with me and would give him a reading on it. His sexual organs were perfectly normal. I told him this (the lunch was at Michauds on the rue Jacob). (He wanted to lunch there because Joyce and I used to eat there.) He wouldn't believe me and said that his organ did look small when he looked at it. I explained that that was because he observed it from above and thus he saw it fore-shortened. Nothing would convince him. So you can see he was not designed to take a punch.[1]

He was romantic, ambitious, and Christ, Jesus, God knows how talented. He was also generous without being kind. He was un-educated and refused to educate himself in any way. He would make great studies about foot-ball say and war but it was all bull-shit. He was a charming cheerful companion when he was sober although a little embarrassing from his tendency always to hero-worship. His heros were Tommy Hitchcock, Gerald Murphy and me. He probably had others that I don't know about. But in those three he certainly played the field. Above all he was completely undisciplined and he would quit at the drop of a hat and borrow some-ones hat to drop. He was fragile Irish instead of tough Irish. I wish he were here and I could give him this letter to read so he would not ever think I would say things behind his back.

Good luck with book
Ernest Hemingway

I am happy if you like what you have seen of the book. I would like it [to] be better than Proust if Proust had been to the wars and liked to fuck and was in love.

UMD   EH

1. This anecdote is repeated in *A Moveable Feast* (New York, 1964), pp. 189–91.

To GENERAL E. E. DORMAN–O'GOWAN, La Finca Vigia, 2 May 1950

Chink:

What a bastard you are to decide not to come down here. I respect your decision moderately but still hope for a re-reading. See-ing you again was all I gave a damn about. But am getting to be like the whore who wouldn't give a fuck for nothing. And this is evidently nothing again. Our well beloved nothing and from who's or whom's well?

There is no news here. I did 38 of 86 galley proofs and ran into no trouble until around galley 60 where I must boucher some trous [fill gaps]. They need more combat and, gentlemen, we will give it to them.

Combat we have, Gentlemen, and if we do not have it we will improvise it from some other and subversive war. Hate to miss talking that stupid one [Spanish Civil War] over with you. We were beat when they took Irun but we ran it out for two and a half years into the longest holding attack in history. And, of course, the attack never came.

In this next book I speak rather irreverently of the good Monte [Bernard Law Montgomery] but I had hoped to speak with you so that in the after-next I could breathe down his neck in the first clinch and blind him. Why should one human (?) being rouse the dislike of another human being? I suppose only to kill him. I have it completely accurate and straight now that have killed 122 (armeds not counting possible or necessary shootings) and this Monte still escapes one. There should be a law.

If you start to be a politician maybe I can come in. Think better not though. Would be an embarrassment to the party. No matter what party you belong to.

Chink I feel damned bloody awful about you not comeing down. It was like the old days of Across The Saint Bernard In Street Shoes to see you and all the other fine times we had.[1]

Please promise me one thing: that you will come here. I can't come to our nation's capitol now because I must do these galley proofs and then page proofs. But I can always raise the necessary dollars for the trip for you and Eve and in return you can allow me to be interred at Bellamont instead of whatever local Arlington.

I remember a boy who was going to jump in who asked me to tell him what he should *really* know and I told him: keep your bowells open, drink the wine of the country, and remember there will be some corner of some foreign field that shall be forever England.

Your speaking schedule (pronounced Shedule) sounds appalling. I hope you believe in this Ireland and we are not just takeing revenge on the horrid Sasenachs [English] (mis-spelled) I have always wanted to fight the British all my life. But on a purely sporting basis and because I was sure could beat them any place where you could make them manouever. But I always had reservations on this because you were a Leftenant General and I knew that if I tried to out-manoeuver (it always reminds me of manure) you I would get a lot of D'Americans killed. Maybe even Irish-Americans.

It is 0730 now and so I had better stop this and get to work. I hope you will like this book. Do you know Venice? It is about Venice and it seems very simple unless you know what it is all about. It is really about bitterness, soldiering, honour, love and death. I probably sound pompous in this but wanted to give you the true gen in case you ever had to read it in a hurry. It comes out in August and I will send one to Los O'Gowans. You be careful to keep it out of the hands of servants and childrens under age.

Must truly get to work now.

There are a couple of Irish-Americans here if you ever get lonely. And one of the principal streets is O'Reilly. The light house was built by Gen. O'Donnell. You can see you can actually come as a sort of damned pilgrimage and tell the Irishes you have been visiting these sacred shrines. The best bar in the world is just up O'Reilly and I can have the name changed, temporarily, to St. Patrick's El Catedral de Daiquiri. I'll meet you at the airport or the boat as Shamus O'Popplethwaite[2] (the writer) and no one will know that I am really General von und zu Hemingstein a man so dangerous in history that children are advised not to read history.

Have a good trip, Chink. How do you like those banquets and that salad? I hope the hell they give you something to drink with meals.

It was splendid see-ing you. Mary sends her love. She is only half Irish but we can probably get rid of the rest of her blood with Penicillin or something.

PH. PUL　　　　　　　　　　　　　　　　　　　　Hem

1. EH, Hadley, and Dorman-Smith had hiked over the Pass of St. Bernard into Italy starting 31 May 1922. See Carlos Baker, *Ernest Hemingway: A Life Story* (New York, 1969), p. 92. 2. Dorman-Smith's nickname for EH, 1918–1926.

To SENATOR JOSEPH MC CARTHY, La Finca Vigia, 8 May 1950

Honorable Senator Joe Mc Carthy:

My dear Senator:

Quite a number of people are beginning to get tired of you and you have possibilities of becomeing a complete stranger. If you lost limbs or your head in the action in the Pacific everyone naturally would sympathise with you. But many people are merely bored since they have seen good fighters who had it in their time. Some of us have even seen the deads and counted them and counted the numbers of Mc Carthys. There were quite a lot but you were not one and I have never had the opportunity to count the numbers of your wounds and get any sort of reading on the comparison with how your mouth, repeat moth, get it straight mouth, goes off.

I know you were in a fine force and you must have been wounded really badly but Senator you certainly bore the bejeesus out of some tax-payers and this is an invitation to get it all out of your system. You can come down here and fight for free, without any publicity, with an old character like me who is fifty years old and weighs 209 and thinks you are a shit, Senator, and would knock you on your ass the best day you ever lived. It might be healthy for you and it would certainly be instructive.

So you are always welcome, kid, and in case you have dog blood, which I suspect, don't resort to sopoeanas (mis-spelled) but come on down all expenses paid and if you are a small Marine you can fight any of my kids and get a reputation. I have them that weigh from 152 to 186. You can fight any one. But afterwards me.

Good luck with the good part of your investigations and, if we can take off the part of the uniform you take when you go outside, and fornicate yourself. You would have a nice fight without witnesses and then you could tell it to all.

> Yours always
> Ernest Hemingway

Actually I don't think you have the guts to fight a rabbit; much less a man. Am old but would certainly love to take you quick. Or to see the kids take you slow and careful.

> Yours always, and with great respect for your office
> Ernest Hemingway

[Typed and signed twice by EH but perhaps not sent.]

JFK

To ARTHUR MIZENER, La Finca Vigia, 12 May 1950

Dear Mr. Mizener:

In doing the book it would be good if you would not let yourself be influenced too much by [Edmund] Wilson. He is an excellent critic about many things but he has strange leaks in his integrity and his knowledge; leaks so bad that if he were an aqueduct he would be dry. Probably I am unjust but when they start writing those over-detailed F--k scenes there is a pretty good chance they couldn't f - - k themselves out of even Princeton. If you make love to a girl and are fool enough or shit enough to write about it you write to please her unless she has given you the clap or something. And then it isn't her fault because somebody gave it to her.

I believe that basically you write for two people; yourself to try to make it absolutely perfect; or if not that then wonderful. Then you write for who you love whether she can read or write or not and whether she is alive or dead. I think Scott in his strange mixed-up Irish catholic monogamy wrote for Zelda and when he lost all hope in her and she destroyed his confidence in himself he was through. It was like makeing your God a canoe, say, or an air-plane or anything that will not last, instead of a good graven image.

My God painted many wonderful pictures and wrote some very good books and fought Napoleon's rear-guard actions in the retreat from Moskova and fought on both sides at Gettysburg and did away with yellow fever and taught Picasso how to draw and sired Citation. He is the best god-damned God you ever knew. But I have never met him. I've seen a lot of his pictures though in the Prado and I read his books and his short stories every year. And I know the exact details of how he killed George Armstrong Custer, which nobody else knows, and my God when he played foot-ball was Jim Thorpe and when he pitched he was Walter Johnson and the ball looked as big as a small marble and it would kill you if it hit you. So my God never dusted anybody off ever.

Scott's God, at the end, was Irving Thalberg. A very nice guy. But your God shouldn't die on you so (can't spell fragily).

You don't have to write a book that is okayed by Wilson, Scottie and anybody else do you? Scott and Zelda are dead. Max [Perkins] is dead. John Bishop is dead. Treat me exactly as though I were dead. I've never squawked to the referee yet. I get sick of Bunny Wilson writing about some mysterious thing that changed or formed my life and then dismissing For Whom The Bell Tolls in a foot-note. Why doesn't he say what the mysterious thing is? Could it be that my father shot himself? Could it be that I did not care, overly, for my mother? Could it be that I have been shot twice through the scrotam and through the right hand, left hand, right foot and left foot and through both knees and the head?

I have a beauty picture of him [Wilson] being kicked in the ass by a photographer that Max Perkins sent me and that evens it all up. Or it should. But it doesn't. First: I am sorry he was kicked in the ass or that anybody should be ever. Second: I wish he would write straight instead of occasionally straight.

You picked a tough subject to write about in Scott and I feel that I have let you down because I don't have his letters. I remember [Ford Madox] Ford telling me that a man should always write a letter thinking of how it would read to posterity. This made such a bad impression on me that I burned every letter in the flat includeing Ford's.

Should you save the hulls a .50 cal shucks out for posterity? Save them. o.k. But they should be written or fired not for posterity but for the day and the hour and posterity will always look after herself.

Lately I am lonely quite a lot, not haveing the children around and not likeing the way things go so that picking up the paper is like (we'll skip it). Anyway I write letters because it is fun to get letters back. But not for posterity. What the hell is posterity anyway? It sounds as though it meant you were on your ass.

Scott took LITERATURE so solemnly. He never understood that it was just writing as well as you can and finishing what you start.

The Last Tycoon, after the part that is written, and was as far as he could write, is really only a scheme to borrow money on. For me the best of the books, in spite of any inconsistencies, is Tender Is The Night. He seemed more grown up in it in spite of the starting with Sara and Gerald and then shifting to Zelda. I thought Gatsby was ok with reservations. No one of the stories is a great story but the best are Babylon Revisited and The Rich Boy I guess. I am someone who would like things to be perfect. I thought, when I read it at the time, haveing come home from Italy that This Side Of Paradise was comic. Couldn't read The Beautiful and the Damned. I remember thinking who the hell said they were beautiful and what the hell were they damned by? I thought the people on the Grappa and Pasubio and the Basso Piave were damned and it did not seem to me you were necessarily damned because you made a little money.

You've probably had about enough of this.

Will sign off.

Yours always
Ernest Hemingway

UMD

To ARTHUR MIZENER, La Finca Vigia, 1 June 1950

Dear Mr. Mizener:

Thank you for the letter. I only warned you about Wilson because if he is screwed up about me he might be about Scott too. It was not to squawk about anything about me. If you want to hit a critic hit him with a book and make him wrong.

I think you are right about Wilson's despair and that is what makes him love Scott's despair so much. But Scott's was a sort of chickenshit, ill-arrived at despair; a very complicated one. Actually I have little respect for either of their despairs because they were too easily arrived at. (You tell me if this makes sense.)

Not that any of it matters: I was desperate when I was 19, 45 and 50 and I did not give a shit about anything except writing, which I respect, for at least ten years in between. The local despairs used to bore me. When I was a kid I missed reform school so close it wasn't funny and after first war I missed Penitentiary so close it *was* funny. And always Scott's sort of cavorting and Tom Wolfe's interminable flow and his silly love affairs and Scott's aborted virginity and their thirst for fame bored me. But I thought this is the literary life and that's what you are in, boy.

Jim Joyce was the only alive writer that I ever respected. He had his problems but he could write better than anyone I knew. Ezra was nice and kind and friendly and a beautiful poet and critic. G. Stein was nice until she had the menopause. But who I respected was Mr. Joyce and not from reading his clippings.

Scott always seemed like a child trying to play in the big league. Maybe a child could. But I used to tell him that for an artist "D'abord il faut durer" [First one must last]. You can translate that into correct French. I can speak and read French but cannot write it; nor Italian, nor German. But can write Spanish. English sometimes too, maybe.

I love to write and I love to write well enough to waste it. However Wilson is on me doesn't mean a shit. [Maxwell] Geismar is through. He has had menopause of the brain. He started good too. But he threw his arm away.

Anyway I can help you on the book about Scott always let me know. This was just a letter to pass the time of day after I'd done 42 galleys from 0600 to 1300 and was bored shitless listening to the Cuban election news on the radio. Will put on a mixed program of Fats Waller and Mozart now. They are really very good together.

Best always
Ernest Hemingway

To ARTHUR MIZENER, La Finca Vigia, 2 June 1950

Dear Mr. Mizener:

Yesterday I did 88 galleys on the book working from 0600 to midnight and then read over the last thirty three again. It is around the two hundredth time I read it and now my horse is under the starter's orders for better or for worse. Poor Geismar; I hope he'll understand it. But it is a little deep for him. Maybe he will understand the next one. I'll try to keep the next one easy. Am writing you only to cool out so please forgive me. I don't know why people shouldn't write to each other anyway. They did in the old days. But now I guess all they want is to be on Television.

My sister Ura [Ursula] went to your college [Carleton] and now lives in Hawaia (mis-spelled) and an irrevelant fact. When I came home after the first war she always used to wait, sleeping, on the stairway of the third floor stair-case to my room. She wanted to wake when I came in because she had been told it was bad for a man to drink alone. She would drink something light with me until I went to sleep and then she would sleep with me so I would not be lonely in the night. We always slept with the light on except she would sometimes turn it off if she saw I was asleep and stay awake and turn it on if she saw I was wakeing. At that time I could not sleep without a light on and this shows you how much Wilson and Geismar know and what a fine girl you had at your college.

Hell this love or hate your mother thing is too simple. What if you've been in love with two of your sisters, five dogs, maybe twenty cats, 4 different airplanes, two cities and five towns, three continents, one boat, the oceans, and Christ count them, womens. So it was your mother. That's much too simple any way one plays it. Also I love my children, writing, reading, pictures, shooting, fishing, ski-ing, and various people in Venice. Also love my wife Mary. Also love the 4th Inf. Div. and the 22nd Regt. of Inf.

Get off your couch Hemingstein and give the Professor a rest. I also love Fats Waller who is dead and the Normandie which was burned by idiocy and sold for scrap. Also love Hong Kong and the New Territories. Two girls in Venice and one in Paris. Love them true and good.

[Edmund] Wilson gives a man this shit about hidden wounds [in *The Wound and the Bow*, 1941]. Fine. I have 22 wounds that are visible (probably beside the hidden one) and have killed 122 sures beside the possibles. The last, no not the last, but the one made me feel the worst, was a soldier in German uniform with helmet rideing on a bicycle along their escape route toward Aachen they [that] we had gotten astride of above St. Quentin. I did not want them to fire the fifty's and maybe spook others that would be comeing in vehicles so I said, "Let me take him" and I shot him with an M1. When we went over to search him and re-set the trap he was a boy of about the age of my son Patrick at the time and I had shot him through the spine and the bullet had come out through the liver. There was not any way to get him back and so I laid him out as comfortably as possible and gave him my morphine tablets and a French kid came up and wanted the bicycle because the German's had stolen his and we gave it to him and told him to get the hell into the estaminet at the cross-roads and we re-set the trap.

No; I think how we are is how the world has been and these psychoanalitic versions or interpretations are far from accurate.

About posterity: I only think about writing truly. Posterity can take care of herself or fuck herself.

Anyway the hell of it is that when they start the excavations who will they find that knew me the way things go? There will only be people that claimed they knew you. Or a few long-lived dislikers.

Chink Dorman-Smith will be dead, Gen Lanham will be dead, Howie Blazzard will be dead, Juan Dunabeitia will be dead (he damn near died here six weeks ago but he is ok now and going to sea tomorrow), Taylor Williams will be dead. There will be a few gamblers around Ketchum, Cody and Red Lodge that might be alive. But they are not articulate. Max is dead. Benchley is dead. Of the nine guys we had on the boat [1942] there are four of us now.

No. It will get all fucked up like always and I figure to have all my papers and uncompleted Mss. burned when I am buried. I don't want that sort of shit to go on.

Anyway I have now gotten this crap out of my system and if you didn't read more than the first paragraph you were tolerant.

Best always,
Ernest Hemingway

When you finish a book it knocks the shit out of you. Never really felt tired before. Have tried to write a really good book.

29/8/50

Don't know why I never sent this. Probably thought it was too violent.

UMD

To ADRIANA IVANCICH,[1] La Finca Vigia, 3 June 1950

My dear Adriana:

First, daughter, I think you write beautifully in Italian and I understand it. The style is clean and good and you never get florid (flowery) unless you are angry. I never mind when you are angry because I think when I was twenty I was angry nearly all the time. Also I remember that when we have a chance to see each other neither one is very angry very long.

That is in regard to the last sentence in your letter. (Am certainly writing now like a backward professor.)

About my work: have had to do proofs of the book twice and make corrections and inserts. I did the second correction and re-writing day before yesterday. The whole book from 0600 until after mid-night I changed the end of about a dozen chapters and tried to be as critical and constructive as I could. Now my horse is under the starter's orders and there is no thing more I can do. It nearly kills me every time I read the book and I have read it now about 200 times.

Now am going out on the ocean tomorrow. Gianfranco is not going because he wants to work. I read some more of his book last night and it is very good. I wrote Charley Scribner about it and he wants to see it very much. Also wrote for a good translator from Italian to English. In an English translation I can make any suggestions of things I know about writing; not to make him write as I do; but to write better in his own style.

That is the program for the summer on his work. I have a *long* short story about one time when we were driven in by a storm when we were doing anti-submarine work in this sea dureing the war. It is over 30,000 words and it is just the happenings of one day. I have outlined the end and will finish it. I know I make it sound awfully dull but really it is not.

Am tired of takeing any side or haveing any opinion in the business of Gianfranco and Sidarma [shipping company]. Stanco e doppio stanco [Tired and double tired]. That is not good Italian either. It is only the way I feel. As a practical man and soldier it looks to me as though 1: Cuban office wanted no one from Venice (home office); 2: Ruggero was too light headed and lacking in decision and courage to make a fight on this point; 3: While Gianfranco is between jobs I think it is excellent for him to work hard at something he loves to do and lead a clean, good, healthy and hard-working life out here; 4: If he wants to write, and he can always write whether he is working for any company or being the head of the family, it can be no loss for him to learn what I have to teach.

We always joke you know. But I could give the same course that I give Gianfranco at any University and I have turned down being a Member of the Academy etc. many times. I really do not think he is wasteing his time. I truly, truly do not think so and I would bet my head on it.

I try to make good discipline by precept and that is good for me because I need it too. Now I write egotistical letter because I am lonesome for you and I do not want to say these things to anyone else. Since I was Gianfranco's age I have been head of the family. I paid all my father's debts; sold land; stopped my mother's extravagances as well as I could; provided for her and the other children, fought in all the wars, brought up children, married and un-married, paid all bills and wrote as well as I could. So you please believe I am a semi-serious animal and that I would never encourage anything that was bad for Gianfranco nor Jackie nor for you. Am prejudiced about you because I am in love with you. But in any situation, under any circumstances where it was my happiness or your happiness I would always want your happiness to win and would withdraw mine from the race.

Now I must stop or maybe you have stopped already.

I love you very much.

TEXAS   Mister Papa

1. EH first met Adriana in December 1948 at a shooting preserve near Latisana. She was then nineteen, the age of Renata in *Across the River and Into the Trees*, for whom she served as a partial prototype. For an account of Adriana and her brother Gianfranco, see Carlos Baker, *Ernest Hemingway: A Life Story* (New York, 1969), pp. 469, 471–72, 476–78 ff.

This and all subsequent letters to Adriana are used courtesy of the Humanities Research Center, University of Texas, Austin.

To HARVEY BREIT,[1] La Finca Vigia, 9 July 1950

Dear Harvey:

Couldn't sleep since 0500 on acct. had to let my Black Dog in and couldn't buy the sleep back. He knows writing is in some way connected with sizzling steaks so he spends all his time getting me to the typewriter which is in my bedroom on top of a book case so can write standing up. Writing and travel broaden your ass if not your mind and I like to write standing up.

You sounded sort of faintly beat-up in your letter before last so this is just a letter like the funny papers to build you up in Old Lyme on

Tuesday. I take it you will have the Herald Tribune and the Times for Sunday.

I can't stop writing when I finish a book but know I shouldn't start fixing the stories until I cool out nor get back into the other book yet. So this is Dr. Hemingstein's Weekly Letter on how Shitty everything is. Probably I should be elegant and speak French mit der waiter and say, how *enmerdent* and then mis-spell it.

Usually I write to Miss Lillian Ross, who is a good friend although you might not gather it from that Profile, Gen. C. T. Lanham, Lieut. Gen. E. E. Dorman-O'Gowan, Bellamont Forest, County Cavan, Ireland, Miss Marlene Dietrich, Miss Ingrid [Bergman], Charlie Scribner, and to [Adriana Ivancich in] Venice.

Have no correspondence with Dr. Maxwell Geismar and you are the only critic with whom am in active correspondence (due to Jackson LaMotta and the pride of Trieste). Except I write to a guy [Arthur Mizener] at Carlton College, Northfield, Minnesota who is or has been writing a book on Scott Fitzgerald. I try to give him the straight dope on Scott because he, Scott, was crazy about immortality etc. and I was very fond of him even though he was a horses ass.

(End of literary criticism)

Black Dog has gone to sleep now happy that I am writing. He doesn't know what but he loves to hear those keys go. He is a big Springer and a good retriever. I love him and he loves me and Dr. [Alfred] Kinsey can have that for free.

Shit I hope we don't have to go and fight again. I don't care about me. I don't have to go but I will go. But the poor god-damn kids that haven't even had time to get an education again and who will be fucking their wives while they are away? They have Fathers Day and Mother's Day and all such things but they should have a day for all men with Reserve Commissions.

Well, Gentlemen, let us pursue some literary topic.

Naturally, being a writer, the pitch is my own works: high and inside and see whether you can turn his fucking cap around. Ok he is spooked but he is mean. I give him the nothing ball, with the same motion, and he gets a little piece of it in his anger and desire to knock it out of the ball park, and he is OUT to short.

Well I guess, some of us write and some of us pitch but so far there isn't any law a man has to go and see the Cocktail Party by T. S. Eliot from St. Louis where Yogi Berra comes from "Royalist, Anglo-Catholic and conservative." A damned good poet and a fair critic; but he can kiss my ass as a man and he never hit a ball out of the infield in his life and he would not have existed except for dear old Ezra, the lovely poet and stupid traitor.

Better cut this out. Am beginning to feel strongly about things. Good luck and get a good rest and love your wife and kids.

EH

HUL

1. Breit (1913–1968), poet, novelist, dramatist, editor, and journalist, befriended EH by mail at this time.
This and all subsequent letters to Breit are used by permission of the Houghton Library, Harvard University.

To CHARLES SCRIBNER, La Finca Vigia, 9–10 July 1950

Dear Charlie:
    We all hope you are ok, kid. Gianfranco has written you a letter and Mary is writing one today.
    We are only three down here but we are all with you all the way.
    Am no good at these bedside letters; but follow the doctor's advice, within reason, and take care of your damn ticker. That's one thing that we have only one of. Max died on us like a rabbit. You have to make a little more of an effort. And the effort is relaxing.
    My head is ok one week after I bought it.[1] Can't fish because Pilar is on the ways or would be out today. Two surgeons said it would kill anybody else or a horse or a steer or a bullock, but that I have a very thick skull. This may be literary criticism.
    Had a letter from the Gen. [Dorman-O'Gowan] in Ireland (Bellamont Forest) who has now read it [*Across the River*] three times with his lady wife. He says he now knows it is the best thing I've written and made many sound, or seemingly to me sound, observations which I shall not repeat for modesty. Please don't worry about how a fighting officer talks or does not talk. I've heard it since I was 17 and Chink addresses me as My Dear General and former A.D.C. (jokeing of course. But I *was* his A.D.C. when he was O.C. troops in Milan and I was a walk-out wounded with nothing to do. We went to all the great things together at the Scala etc.) and Chink taught your friend Freddy de Guingand at Camberley.
    The god-damned military life is something I *do* know a little about on acct. brought up by two grandfathers that were soldiers, thrown into it when I was 17 [19], been wounded 22 times and killed 122 sures.
    Enclose the start of a letter from a commanding Gen. in US army [Brigadier General C. T. Lanham]. Do not show it to anyone and please return it to me without haveing it copied.
    This character and I when he was a Col. of regular army and me an

alleged pickpocket Gen. of irregulars breached the Siegfried line together, fought the Schnee-Eifel together (I commanded by that time two repeat two Frenchmen. Both thieves and beauty scouts.) Fought Hurtgen together (all I did was odd jobs but still had two Frenchmen) and we don't give a fuck for nothing. The regimental losses were greater than any regiment at Gettysburg and the regiment took every objective. So try to eat on that and hear how an officer would speak and whether there was Fornaci and Monastier and Fossalta; especially Fossalta.

Yesterday was the 8th July[2] which is engraved on the back of the thing which corresponds to It. VC with Fossalta di Piave. So I told Gianfranco we ought to make an act of celebration. So we went into town and found Leopoldina and Xenaphobia, after work done, and a couple or eight drinks and ran off the Killers which is quite a good motion picture until the very last. I do not imagine this is the type of life which would have agreed with Henry James but fuck all male old women anyway.

He wrote nice but he lived pretty dull I think. Too dull maybe and wrote too nice about too dull.

Wish I could have seen him on a bad horse just once or trying to hit a ball out of the infield. What did he do when he was a boy do you suppose. Just jerk himself off into Fame and now Fortune like T. S. Eliot. Sports don't mean a damned thing and most sporting people can be jerks. But the complete inability to do them or attempt them ie. fear of failure means something. Jack is an athlete and good at everything but baseball. Patrick couldn't be a worse athlete. But he will play anything includeing third base makeing fun of himself all the time although he knows a line drive could kill him. He can't catch it but he'll knock it down; or try to. He played ball with us here for several years in pick-up and scrub games and I should never have even let him be on a ball field. He was about as good an athlete as your pal the Duke of Windsor. Maybe he can learn golf.

Gigi is a champion, or was. Play anything, ride anything (he used to have a rope ladder to mount with when he would go off all day by himself when he was very small) shoot all day at any sort of shooting with the best around when he was 9/10/11 years old and stay with them or lead. Now women are starting to get to him and there's nothing to do about it so far. When he goes to NY I send him to a friend and Gigi is very polite, sends flowers to his hostess and disappears. I guess it [is] simpler to remember I was a bad boy too at his age. But I wish there had never been a divorce [from Pauline] and loss of control and discipline (not harsh as I rebelled against when I was a boy) but just sound control.

Well the hell with all this too. Get well and, if you can't, die good and fix hell up nicely for me. I'd like a suite with a good view of the other circles and the champagne red-hot please. Max will be there waiting;

probably with that hat on and a little deafer and burned to a crisp. Shit, and the other wonderful characters we will meet.

Mary had me read her letter and it seems awfully full of maidens. Gianfranco can't write English although he writes beautiful Italian. Their children learned German as we did in our family. But they stopped the German when Adriana was two. So she doesn't know any. She learned more English than Gianfranco because he had to go to the war. But though she speaks it with that lovely voice it is an effort for her to write it. She writes to me, when and if she writes, in Italian.

Gianfranco and I talk Englisch, Spanish, sometimes Italian and German together. So you may have had something when you said you thought a certain paragraph had a teutonic construction.

Marlene and I always speak English or sometimes French but get into German if we are angry or there are people around and we wish to say it quick and not be understood.

Adriana and I talk English and sometimes Spanish; also French.

With the Contessa Valeria de Lisca I talk French. With Giovanna Tofani I talk English. She talks it much better than I do.

Here, in the house, we talk Spanish always. Mary corrects my grammar altho she had never heard of the language until 1945 and cannot follow it if it gets fast, or rough, or takes her out of her depth. It is the roughest language that there is and we can say anything in front of her because she knows nothing of the dirty part or old gallows language. But if she does understand she will correct the grammar. That is probably enough and to spare on languages. I know how to tell a jerk to: fuck-off Jack, in six different languages and Christ knows how many dialects. This is not a great accomplishment; but they always go when you give them the word.

One of my nicest Persian kittens is dying in considerable pain on the floor here. But I do not shoot her to put her out of her misery (distemper) in order not to wake Mary. These are our local moral problems.

Also that I love A[driana] to die of it and that I love Mary as she should be loved; I hope.

Beautiful situation. See what you can make of it General.

No other news I guess. Wallace [Meyer] writes he received the proofs as he should.

Sometime, Charlie, you ought to hire me at a dollar a year to put your joint on a disciplined basis: fire every son of a bitch who makes these awful errors no matter what his name is or where he comes from. Get rid of every fool in the place and replace him with a man of talent and energy. Make surgery every place it is needed.

The guy who wrote the piece of letter I enclosed said that I was the most ruthless man that he had ever known, and, he added, probably unjustly, the kindest.

You know that on today July 10th 1950 I have still not received the original duplicate page proofs. I would shoot on that anywhere any time.

I know they are not held up here because I have friends in the Douane, the post-office, etc. and everybody was sweating out the arrival of my proofs. All the agencies in Cuba.

It is just something discourageing and I suppose I should be prepared now to just take defeat on the rest of it.

The salesmen won't sell it. The reviewers will have it imperfectly. Afterwards there probably won't be copies if anyone wishes to buy it. People will want to make cover stories and they will be discouraged. Nobody will know what day of the month it is nor what time of day. Book will come out like that edition of A Farewell To Arms did.

I do not give a damn about either fame or fortune. But I owe you money and I want to fucking well re-pay it. I can't if they go as they have gone up to now. Imagine anyone loseing ten days on production on a four hour haul to La Habana.

And a bastard who can do other things waiting around meeting mails, trains, busses, air-planes, Custom houses etc. waiting for his attack to go.

I would never go with any other publishing house; but Jesus Christ I would like to put yours in order. I would like to see it like the 22nd Regt. of Inft. which was commanded by the man who wrote me fraction of letter enclosed. Instead we attack like cows.

Sometimes I get discouraged, Charlie. Today is one of the days. The two girls I love best in all of this world think you are the finest man that ever lived. But for Christ sake straighten up and fly right, good heart or bad heart, (is spelled hart) and don't heed any further counsels from your true friend

Ernest.

How do you like it now, Gentlemen?
PUL

1. EH had had an accident aboard the *Pilar*. 2. The anniversary of EH's wounding in 1918.

To CHARLES SCRIBNER, La Finca Vigia, 19 July 1950

My dear Charlie:

Your fucking page proofs (first series) turned up yesterday. That ought to be almost a record.

I blame no one. It was not my attack.

Mary would not show me your letter; but she always asks me why can't I be a Gentleman like Charles Scribner instead of telling people to get that rag out of their ass and move. Adriana writes about you as a tesoro [treasure]. Which is a pretty good word in Italian. That is what you call who you are really fond of. (I thank you for being it.)

But if you get any more popular I will ask you to find two friends (if you have them) and I will pick up a couple of characters and kill you at ten paces. You've never been killed before and it will be quite an experience.

I hope those poor jerks who are publishing Hemingstein The Man and His Work[1] will loose a million.

Will send them a picture. Have a wonderful one of me hitting one over the left field fence in the biggest ball park in the upper Michigan League. But I suppose they wouldn't like that and besides it might tend to disprove Cowley's theory that I was a painfully, self-taught athlete. I boxed Sam Langford, Jack Blackburn, Eddie McGoorty, etc. in the gym (Forbes and Ferretti's or Kid Howards) before I was 16 and I bucked out any thing there was in the shoots [chutes] with a bear trap saddle when I need[ed] 100 dollars and did not give a what do call it if the back went or not. You probably know what a bear trap saddle is from haveing that phony Will James[2] work for you. On the second buck the horse throws you because of the twist he makes. In a bear-trap saddle he *can't* throw you. You are with him for keeps. But it is 20/1 he breaks your back.

Fuck them and The Man and His Work and that obscene jacket by Cape with the poor bloody Colonel's name mis-spelled. *Please check on that with him.* I checked on the Army List. It is CANTWELL NOT, REPEAT NOT CANTRELL. Tell Cape to straighten up and fly right. (Quantrell shot one of my grandfathers.)

My comic head is ok. The obscure, to you, part of the sketch is now down to about the size of a golf ball. That is the back part of the sketch and what we might have had trouble from. It is the big, not reducible hemmorage from the artery.

The hell with it all.

Please try to publish and sell the book well. There is nothing for me to do now. The horse is under the starter's orders and there is no thing I can do now. But don't let your horde of vacationists, week-enders, non-thinkers amateur-brainlessers and semi-professional (we won't say its) fuck my horse now. All I want is a good, honest and intelligent ride with two balls when they are needed—and a bat. Though I don't think you will ever have to pull a bat on this horse if you just ride him good with the head. And for Christ sake have some confidence.

You are older than me and I should be respectful. But in some things I am older than you and please believe, always, I am not disrespectful when I speak roughly. I am a bad boy, Charlie, and I am not proud of it. I try to win always until I die. But afterwards I am not proud of winning and I try to be a good modest, quiet boy (without success).

We are going fishing today. Gianfranco is working on his book. So he can't go. Mary and I will go in an hour.

Be a good boy and don't work too hard.

All my best to you and to my hero Vera.

PUL   Ernest

1. J. K. M. Mc Caffery, *Ernest Hemingway: The Man and His Work* (New York, 1950). 2. James (1892–1942) was a cowboy author and illustrator whose works were published by Scribners.

To LIEUTENANT GENERAL E. E. DORMAN–O'GOWAN, Puerto Escondido, Cuba, *c.* 27 July 1950

Dear Chink-Maru:

This harbour is a sort of a miniature fjord. You can't see it from the sea until you are within about 400 yards. It has high lime stone walls that condense the dew with the heat of the sun they get in the afternoon, and in the evenings it is like what the poor B. British call a Fridge. Brought a thermometer along this time and from 84° F. at 1700 it fell to 68° F. at 0600 the following day. Makes for wonderful sleeping in hot weather, although with the Trade wind blowing it felt cool at 84° F.

You wouldn't be too bored with place I think. There is society, Diplomatic society, various clubs, Yacht Clubs etc. Racing, Prize fights, ice carnivals, regattas, swimming meets, the Life of the Mind, one good painter and 80 bad ones, the best bar in the world (La Floridita), Jai-alai games, winter visits from the Fast International Sporting House Set, all forms of gambling, one really good whore-house, and I have a couple of thousand books in the house. We also have good shooting from the middle of September through the middle of April and good fishing the year around. I am not trying to tout you onto the place. But it's worth looking at. Also we have fine swimming the year around.

Oh yes, I forgot, we have a Symphony orchestra (usually with a first rate conductor), Eric Kleiber was the last, a visiting opera company, a ballet season etc.

I thought I wrote you about the toss I took. But if I didn't: it was a spill on the flying bridge, deck wet, when I was relieveing my mate at the wheel. Had one leg over the guard rail and my weight on my right (worse) leg when he swung her broadside to enter the channel. Drew a five inch cut (incised) that reached into the bone and severed some artery whose name I never caught. (I fell among the big gaffs and the clamps that hold them.) Also a concussion of about force 5 (Beaufort scale). Cut all healed now and am down here living on the boat and swimming 2 to 2½ hours a day and the scabs are about soaked off.

It wasn't a S.I.W. [self-inflicted wound] General but number 8 up-stairs is a bore.

About the maybe war. Nobody is supposed to refer to it; so I won't. I am not going to it unless they fight in ETO [European Theater of Operations]. Then I will have to go since Bumby is in Berlin and I promised a general [Lanham] who was my best friend in the 44–45 nonsense that I would go with him. He claims they can give civilians any sort of assimilated? (whatever that is) rank as Specialists. He considers me a specialist at something or something awful. I don't know just what. Retreats?

Excuse if paper is soiled. Have been fireing a few rounds at the innocent buzzard who spreads any type of cattle disease.

San Francisco de Paula is 12 kilometers from the center of town.

You come down *any time* and look it over. The only bad luck is that I will have to go West around the 1st to 12th of October. But there is no reason you can't go too.

Anyway good hunting and good Politik.

Hem

My head will be all right or as all right as it ever was.
PH. PUL

To ROBERT CANTWELL,[1] La Finca Vigia, 25 August 1950

Dear Bob:

It was strange to hear from you after so long. I have worried about you and waited for books. There was the Hawthorne, which I liked very much, but there wasn't any fiction. You were the best bet I had in American fiction and I wish the Christ you would write it.

About the unfavorable publicity: think it is quite simple. Accidents happen in 50 years. But I started driveing in a Stanley steamer and get my safe driver certificate and usually a cut back in premium every year. Have driven with T. Otto Bruce, of Piggott Arkansas and Key West Florida from Memphis to Key West in less than 18 hours. But that never gets into the papers because it is a private thing. If we ran over a pig and were pinched it would be in the papers instantly. It was around 976 miles the way we had to drive it.

That is sort of the pattern. In night clubs people will come up to you and say, "So you're Hemingway are you?" and swing on you without further explanation. Or they will paw you, which a man doesn't like or start to paw your wife or some girl you know, and if you admonish them, warn them, and then have to clip them, it gets in the papers. Henry James was not faced with these same problems.

A man can't stay home all the time and when he goes out if anything happens it is in the papers. It is never in the papers that you wake at first light and start working; nor that you serve your country in any way you have ever been asked to; nor that you, your brother and your eldest son were all wounded and decorated in the last one, nor that your two grandfathers both fought and were wounded in the Civil war, nor that you were wounded on 22 different occasions and have been shot through both feet, both legs, both thighs, both hands and had six bad head wounds due to enemy action. Nor that all the ambition you have ever had is to be the best American prose writer and to work at it hard and not fouling anybody. I'll knock them out, if I can, but I won't foul them unless they foul me first. Then I will foul them until they don't know what happened. I never ran as a saint, Bob, and these times are quite a little rougher than the middle ages and I have functioned in them now for half a hundred years plus one. Probably soon Senator McCarthy, God rest his soul in hell, will decide I should be done away with.

Lillian Ross is on the New Yorker staff and is writing an assigned piece about Sidney Franklin. I thought that seeing Franklin washed up and changed she did not understand nor give him credit for what he was in his youth; when he was very good. She wrote me about him and asked many questions and showed up in Ketchum, Idaho on Christmas eve.

Later she wished to write a piece about me for New Yorker. I like her as much as I like anybody and anything she or anyone else writes about me, good or bad, is their own impression and I will not edit it nor correct it. Except for dates or place names. Lillian's piece is ok with me and so is Lillian. She fouled Charley; but let him learn to keep his hands up on the break.

About agents: I deal direct because I will not give ten percent to any son of a bitch to do what I can do better.

About kick-backs: Once, a character went around saying he was going to shoot me on sight. I sent him a registered letter telling him where he could find me at regular times and to either shoot me or wipe his mouth clean. He did not show. I showed up un-armed at the rendezvous at the hours specified for four days and then sent him another registered letter, waited one day and left.

All that attack stuff is funny and sort of infantile. Mostly (and please don't think I am conceited; I'm only as proud as death and I try to be kind, and Christian and gentle, and a lot of the time I make it and when I don't it gets in the papers) I try to be good and write as well as I can.

I don't know about our ancestors nor romanticize them the way Bill Faulkner does. I do know that my Grandfather told me that anytime you could wake Grant you could get a sound answer from him.

Don't know anybody in NY who has any late information or knows me except Marlene Dietrich and George Brown, 225 West 52nd Street. Other friends are dispersed. Ken Crawford, on your paper knows me, and we were together for the break-through (Valhalla Express) and Rambouillet into Paris with one small fire-fight at Toussus le Noble.

I think he would remember me. I remember him well. He was tall and dark and seemed to be liveing something down as though it were a sin and everybody loved him and they used to ask me, hard, to try to keep him from getting killed. He was beauty brave in action and nobody wanted him killed anymore than a saint.

Recent activities are: a book of poems about combat and jumping horse raceing. Thirteen short stories done. 165,000 words done on a long novel that is too hot to handle.

This for your personal information *and never to publish*: I couldn't write well for a long time because I had those true headaches when the head has been broken and they lasted usually all day from when they woke you. Then would cough blood when I woke from the busted tubes; only bronchial. St. Poix July 1944. The children would stand around and I would be filling up the can and I would explain that it was nothing, that it happened to everybody from blast etc. and you could tell it was nothing by the colour (venous; arterial). Then get it again and throw the wrong colour. The bright red one.

Let's skip it.

Book is truly very good. You pan it to hell if you don't like it. That is your right and your duty. But I have read it 206 times to try and make it better and to cut out any mistakes or injustices and on the last reading I loved it very much and it broke my fucking heart for the 206th time. This is only a personal reaction and should be dis-counted as such. But have been around quite a while reading and writing and can tell shit from the other things.

I think this covers all the points, Bob. Cable me on anything and I will give you a prompt and honest answer. It is funny you have the same name as my poor damned Colonel but it makes [me] rather pleased and proud.

A former Lieut. Gen. in the British Army has already formed The Cantwell Society in Ireland from reading it in the magazine. He always signs himself MCS (Member Cantwell Society) although he has other decorations. Perhaps we can obtain membership in the society ourselves. Especially since you are a legitimate Cantwell.

But pan it, ride it, or kill it if you should or if you can. I would like to be a good American writer; but if they understand nothing about that and do not remember you might as well be like John Mosby (mis-spelled) or you might as well be a desperate man like Jack Ketchum. I don't give a shit either way.

Hope everything goes well with you. Get in touch with Ken. He was too punchy (from cause) to remember me maybe. But tell him I was the character went to bring him no matter what he wanted to do, on a strange day in July when Christ couldn't have walked on the water. He did not want to come back to regiment either. The 8th Infantry Regiment of the Army of the United States. Gen Raymond O. Barton commanding the 4th Inf Div of the Army of the United States had told me, not ordered me, to go up and find Ken and bring him back. A tank or SP gun fired a final armour piercing shot and it pierced the wall of the house where the CP was and took the leg off of a staff captain at the knee and continued on through the back wall over the heads of two signallers that were lyeing on bunks. The leg was on the floor and General Barton never changed his voice on the telephone and I went to make contact with Ken as he requested. The Captain's leg was burned by the projectile and hardly bled. He just looked at it funny. Ernie Pyle, the great hero of the last war was outside crying because our bombers had killed some of our men. He could cry dry and he could cry wet. I told him in the former war we had to keep close enough to the barrage to figure on loseing 20 percent of our effectives to take an objective. He said I was heartless. I said go in and gnaw on that leg that must still be on the floor you ignorant sentimental fool. And don't talk newspaper horseshit to me because I am going up to the second battallion.

That was where Ken was. But at least you see how one makes so many friends; if that was the problem, in the career. Ken was brave as jumping off Empire State Building. But Ernie Pyle was a syndicated national hero. . . . I do not like a man who brags when he drinks, but he is better company than a man who cries when he drinks.

Well this is the end of the paper. There is more to say. But why say it? Don't you agree?

Ernest

One of the stud cats sprayed on the main sheet. So throw it away and send you the carbon.

Dear Bob:

Please do *not* repeat do not put in anything about how many times I have been shot or shot at. I asked both Cape and Scribners not to use any publicity about any military service and it is distasteful to me to mention it and destroys any pride I have in it. I want to run as a writer; not as a man who had been to the wars; nor a bar room fighter; nor a shooter; nor a horse-player; nor a drinker. I would like to be a straight writer and be judged as such.

Best always
Ernest

What difference does it make if you live in a picturesque little out house surrounded by 300 feeble minded goats and your faithful dog Black Dog? The question is: can you write?

OREGON   EH

1. Cantwell (b. 1908) had begun writing as a novelist in the 1930s, switching to biography with his *Hawthorne* (1948).

This letter is used courtesy of Special Collections, the University of Oregon Library.

To CHARLES SCRIBNER, La Finca Vigia, 9 September 1950

Dear Charlie:

When [Where] the hell you been, boy? Did you read the Time review and take off for the wilds of Jersey to launch your counter-attack from there? Well everybody has their own way of doing things. But isn't it sort of customary to inform an author about how things go and what people say when a book comes out that he has bet his shirt on and worked his heart out on nor missed a deadline nor failed to keep a promise?

I was pretty sure I would hear something from you this morning. But nothing. Do you think maybe I am not old enough to be told how my horse broke and what he is doing?

Gianfranco hasn't heard from Venice in 22 days now. I heard last 9 days ago. Everyone fine. Hard work getting passports now with all the new restrictions.

Mary went up to Gulfport to find a place to settle her parents. Fairly costly procedure. Parents old and fragile and must be handled with care.

Had a letter from a friend of my brother's that my kid brother was killed. He had the word from my mother who is next of kin and would be informed. But I do not believe it as am sure would have heard. Am instituteing enquiries and sent the necessary cables.

Could you advance me $5,000 on the book and cable me that it has been deposited in the Guaranty Trust Co, Fifth Avenue Branch? I need it before Sept 15. Will pay you back money I borrowed from out of royalties. Want to check with [Alfred] Rice when is the best time to do it. But that money borrowed is secured by the book. That is if it ever came out; which I am sure it must have. I subscribe to Time and have their word for it.

Don't worry about my brother. My mother is quite old and getting a little vague and if she takes Insullin that would account for loss of memory or vagueness.

I'm going to take a dry martini now and the hell with it: Later: Got the Newsweek review which they sent me; also Times daily and Sunday which Juan, the chauffeur bought in town.

I don't think you backed the wrong horse: if you backed him. O'Hara, a man without education nor culture nor military experience naturally can't understand the book nor the girl, nor the Colonel, nor Venice. But he is spooked of it like a man is of a booby trapped house. Naturally the thing about Shakespeare, the undisputed champion, is ridiculous. There have been about twelve or more good writers and they are all behind Dr. Shakespeare and are all in the pack. But they are all good and I am one of the good ones. All really good writers are quite good at writing. Why did he have to say such a thing? But it gives you a good quote if you have anybody who reads reviews and can paste up quotes. I am very grateful to O'Hara. But I would have been 100 times happier if he had understood the book.[1]

You didn't understand it and did not like it and didn't believe there were any such girls as Renata until you met A[driana]. But in later life, if you live, you and O'Hara will both understand it and know the passage about the Veneto from Latisana, where I met A. waiting two hours in the rain to go duck shooting, are not from Baedeker nor Michelin. They are from your heart or something, or something awful as we used to say.

Oh yes, the other cheerful news is that Xenaphobia that kid I sent you the picture of has the old rale at 19 and has to be injected every afternoon at 1600. So it is sort of lonely about this joint. Naturally we will see that Xena is cured properly. I have written to Mary and Rice and sent a silver service to the daughter of some one I know whose daughter was allegedley raped by the Hon. Georgie Patton when she was a child. Gianfranco is over working in the little house. Roberto Herrera is writing checks and Kid Tunero (who fought four times for the middle-weight championship of the world) has just come out to give me a rub-down so maybe can sleep tonight. Maybe we will work out a little.

So long Charley. Give my love to Vera.

PUL   Ernest

1. EH had evidently seen, probably through Harvey Breit, an advance copy of John O'Hara's review of *Across the River and Into the Trees* which appeared in the *New York Times Book Review,* 10 September 1950, pp. 1, 30–31.

To GENERAL CHARLES T. LANHAM, La Finca Vigia, 11 September 1950

Dear Buck:

Book sold 100,000 without any splits with Book Clubs (refused to have it offered to them as this way I get sixty cents on a copy and with B.C.'s about 12½ cents). Scribner's ordered another 25,000 printed after reading the reviews and ordered another car load of paper. Sold 30,000 before publication in England and printed 30 more and ordered paper. So we eat this year anyway. Trouble is I haven't much appetite. But maybe it will be better.

We've had six hurricanes and maybe I feel low with a low barometer. The day book was out I got that lousy Time smack and didn't feel any more emotion than in the conventional counter attack. It came in the morning mail and I left word for Dunabeitia (Sinbad who was staying at the house while his ship was in port) that we lost the first round and I was going into town and get the NY Times and Newsweek when they came in air-mail. As soon as they came I saw we had won ok. Still didn't feel any emotion. A Venice boy [Gianfranco Ivancich] who is writing a novel in the Little House came in to the Floridita to stick with me when Sinbad told him we had lost the first round. He is the brother of a girl I know in Venice (a town I left my heart in and haven't been able to find the son of a bitch since). We had lunch with Leopoldina, the lovely looking old whore and the Venice boy went to take his girl to the movies and I dropped Leo off at her place and came home.

Mary was up Gulfport Miss. looking for a flat to settle her family in. Then she will go up to Chicago and bring them down. They are getting old and Chicago winters pretty tough.

Am sending the Newsweek if I can find it. Will send any others that seem to make sense and will send any really bad ones. The Time, so far, is the worst. But one of their staff cabled apologizing and said they all liked the answer I wrote to their queries. I also did not say 4th Inf. Div. They inserted that.

The Times Sunday book review first paged it as did the Herald Tribune. John O'Hara wrote the Times review. He started off saying I was best writer since Shakespeare which will make me plenty of friends, I imagine. What a statement. All good writers are good and some are better. The good ones are all good in their own ways. There have been at least a dozen since Dr. Shakespeare that were all very good. Then he couldn't understand the book as he has not known the kind of people I have known; nor have I known his kind much. But I do know fighting people of all kinds, painters, diplomats, thieves, gangsters, politicians, jockeys, trainers, bull fighters, many beautiful women, great ladies, the beau monde, the fast International sporting house set, professional killers, every sort of gambler, Madame Chang Kai Chek and both her sisters, the good one and the bad one, rabid anarchists, socialists, democrats, communists and monarchists and so I guess if you are guilty by association I plead guilty on the above counts. Also have more than a battalion of bartenders and at least a platoon of priests and both the B.T.'s and the Priests have loaned me money and been repaid. Also know many fishermen, shooters, ball players, football players, coaches, Georges Clemenceau, Mussolini, the above two *well*, and ex-kings, and when I was 19 Count Greppi who was a contemporary of Metternich and the Duke of Bronte who was a descendant of Nelson, both over ninety, were trying to bring me up so I would have the beautiful manners a Gentleman should have. (A couple of years later I was bouncing in a whore-house and writing day-times.) So really think I have a different background than the people who evaluate you with such facility. They always have the simple son of the country doctor shy and now since Cowley awkward and with bad eye-sight. My brother wore glasses since he was a child. But I had my father's eyes and never wore glasses until I was thirty one, and they got bad from Greb sticking his thumb in one of them when training,[1] from reading too much on my back in a bad light or damn

near no light in hospitals, and from reading by candle light. Then the
sun on the water for those two years, 12 hours a day or make an average
of nine, and useing the big glasses untill they pull your eyes out haven't
helped them.

Oh well. It is all horse-shit anyway. Then that crap about not being
any such women as I put in books. Do you believe that? What they mean
is that they never met any such women. But where could they and how
could they?

Would they believe that the Kraut [Marlene Dietrich] wrote on a
picture not so long ago: Papa—I write this on a picture so that you
can't lose it so easily. I love you unconditionally. That excludes being
angry, offended etc. etc. It includes Plein Pourvoir for you concerning
me. How do you like it now, Gentlemen (signed).

Will try to find the Newsweek if some one hasn't pinched it.

Just found it so will close this.

Un abrazo de tu amigo,

PUL   Ernesto

---

1. The sight of EH's left eye was deficient from birth. Harry Greb had nothing to
do with it.

To ARTHUR MIZENER, La Finca Vigia, 4 January 1951

Dear Mr. Mizener:

Thank you very much for the book and for the dedication. It is a
splendid piece of re-search. There are many errors that I would be willing
to submit you corrections on for any future editions.

Poor Scott; and didn't he know that the man in The Snow's of Kilimanjaro would have spoken of him, or thought of him, exactly as he,
Scott, would have mentioned actual things, cars and places?

For your information the Callaghan thing was pretty bad. Scott, John
Bishop and I had lunched at Pruniers and drunk a great deal of Sancerre. At the end of the lunch I remembered that I had promised to work
out with Callaghan who was a good amateur boxer and promising writer
but who could not hit a lick. I thought I could chance it anyway though
ordinarily you do not box on a full stomach etc. John had an appointment
and Scott went with me to our flat and then to the gym. We agreed on
two minute rounds and at the end of the two minutes I was o.k. I
figured on a minute's rest. Scott let the first round go *thirteen* minutes
and Callaghan after about the fifth minute was hitting me freely and well

for a period of some eight minutes. But he did me no harm and could not knock me down nor put me away. Scott liked the spectacle and was fascinated by it and I don't know why he ever called time at all. I was cut badly in the mouth and swallowed the blood.

At the end of the round, which he had let go thirteen minutes, I said to Scott, "You son of a bitch."

He said "What do you mean? I'm your greatest friend."

I said "Did you like what you let happen to your best friend for eight full minutes when all you had to do was be honest and call time?"

Callaghan had punched himself out on me and I did not have any difficulties with him in the other rounds. I am pretty sure I could have knocked him out. All of the Prunier lunch had been punched out of me and I felt good. Also I knew, *truly*, he couldn't hit. But I did not want to knock him out. He boxed well. He was a promiseing writer; and I liked him. Also no part of it was his fault. It meant a lot to him to knock me out and the only trouble was he could not hit. I just was thankful to him for the regular exercise and I truly wished him well.

You know it is a horrible thing to be somebody's hero and have them attribute all sorts of qualities to you when you are only a man trying to work at it as well as you can. If this is megalomania make the most of it. But I was Scott's bloody hero for a while and Archie's [Mac Leish's] and it was only embarrassing to me. They both got cured of it. One by death and the other—.

The reason I criticized Scott's books, except for kidding, was because I wanted him to write perfectly and straighten up and fly right.

It embarrassed me when Scott wanted to make a hero out of me and I didn't like it when he would get sore, and finally I decided it was not important any more. We had the Spanish war and the China and then all the rest of it and I couldn't be interested when he was so rum-dumb. He always wanted to play foot-ball and wouldn't cross the street through traffic. He had a great fantasy about going to war and asked me how he would have been. I told him that for his actions in civil life as a criterion he would probably have been re-classified or shot for cowardice.

This was too rough; but it was always trying to get him to work and tell the truth at least to himself.

Well the hell with all of it. He's dead and you've buried him for better or for worse and what he wrote that will stand up will stand up.

It was good of you to work so hard on the research. I like Budd Shulberg very much but I felt his book was grave robbing. Your's is good undertakeing. Almost as good as the job they did on my father's face when he shot himself. One remembers the face better as it actually was. But the undertaker pleases those who come to the funeral.

It is good to counter [Maxwell] Geismar and such people though. But

why shouldn't critics have to write a book sometime to become familiar
with the process ie. move out of the dissecting room into the operating
room? Poor Bunny Wilson writes prose and many people like it. (Please
excuse the typewriter which has become very sticky and must be sent in
for complete cleaning. But hate to have it go out when I am working
well.)

The above is unjust about critics as many have written well; not many;
but a few.

We, the writers, like them when we learn something from them. I have
learned much from this book.

Best luck for what looks like as bad a year as we have seen.

UMD   Ernest Hemingway

To ARTHUR MIZENER, La Finca Vigia, 11 January 1951

Dear Mr. Mizener:

Thanks for the letter. Writing is a rough trade et il faut d'abord durer.
Never be sore at me if I make a rough joke nor mis-spell nor do not like
critics when they teach me nothing. I said your book did tell me many
things I did not know and you can see how I would feel to see Scott
laying, or is it lieing or lying, naked and dead in the market place. Not
like the nakeds and deads of [Norman] Mailer; but really naked and
really dead. From the book I learned a lot and I was very grateful; but
I did not learn nearly as much of the true thing as I have never said and
never written. I am sure this will not make you sore because you are a
serious guy working hard and well on a serious subject.

When Scott was in that last period, or next to last, I had given him up
because of his small bickerings and senseless jealousies etc. and Madrid,
Jarama, Teruel, China, and then the other things held my attention and
my hopes. He did not hold any hope for me anymore and I was out of
touch. (You never should be out of touch; but many times you are.)

With you I have tried to be absolutely straight and I don't hate critics.
I only wish they were co-ordinated a little better together with writers.

But maybe that is too pious a wish.

Let it stand though as the hundredth least important wish of the week.

Good luck with the book.

                                                       Ernest Hemingway

I'll give you the corrections when I finish my book. The long one. Have the first third (the sea part) whipped now. I hope it will please you, eventually, more than details of my life which I do not give a shit about. Incidentally I never knew Scott was sore at me except in a drunken fashion. He would write angry letters sometimes and I would try to answer him as you would some one who was not responsible. I always thought he wrote beautifully when he wrote beautifully and stupidly when he wrote stupidly. Thought he was a rummy (for cause) as well as a straight alcoholic. I have a letter in which he told me how to make A Farewell To Arms a successful book which included some fifty suggestions including eliminateing the officer shooting the sergeant, and bringing in, actually and honest to God, the U.S. Marines (Lt. Henry reads of their success at Belleau Woods while in the Cafe when Catherine is dying) at the end. It is one of the worst damned documents I have ever read and I would give it to no one.

UMD   EH

To CHARLES A. FENTON,[1] La Finca Vigia, 12 January 1951

My dear Air Marshall:

Thanks for the two letters and the clipping. Let's file it all under Ad Astra Per Aspera or To The Stars (sic) The Hard Way. I guess old Cranny [Cranston][2] has more right to his inaccuracies than you and I have to our attempts to be accurate. He was as badly treated by the Toronto Star as a man could be and that is almost as far as a man can get in being badly treated. It is sort of like being an old boy from Buchenwald. I understand your view-point though.

Am sorry I can't help out with any copies of The Co-operative Commonwealth. I got the job there as manageing editor by answering a want ad in the Chicago Tribune; worked until I was convinced it was crooked; stayed on a little while thinking I could write and expose it and then decided to just rack it up as experience and the hell with it. I was writing my own stuff all the time.

If you want the true gen on anything else let me know. I am sorry they poached on your preserve; but think of poor old Cowley who has staked out my whole life of which he knows practically fuck-all nothing. Tell me if you have any really wizard ideas about how it will come out in the end. All I know is that I wrote a short story this morning and am tired as hell and am drinking tea before haveing to dress and go out.

Excuse the dull note.

Yours always,

PH. PUL   Ernest Hemingway

1. Charles Fenton of Yale University was gathering material for *The Apprenticeship of Ernest Hemingway: The Early Years* (New York, 1954). He had served four years with the Royal Canadian Air Force during World War II. 2. J. H. Cranston edited the *Toronto Star Weekly* from 1911 to 1932. See Fenton, *Apprenticeship*, especially pp. 76–81. See also Cranston's autobiography, *Ink on My Fingers* (Toronto, 1953).

To CHARLES SCRIBNER, La Finca Vigia, 5 March 1951

Dear Charlie:

It was so much fun to have you here and to be good partners again. I was only sorry that I was ill and could not fish with you and Vera. The fever was around 102–3–4 for a week or more. Then it dried into sort of a sand-paper itch in the bronchial tubes and now it is getting better. I am tired and not strong yet. But I always have some strength to spare and work drives me and quenches my thirst more than any other thing can.

I was very happy you liked what you read of the book [*The Old Man and the Sea*]. (The end.) But I would have thought you a certifiable fool if you had not (he says cheerfully). There is never any doubt when something is right. But it makes you very happy to have someone you like and respect say so. I had been getting good opinions only from my family.

Today I wrote 1578 words on another long section of the Sea book. You wanted to know when we should publish and I think the sea book should come out in the fall of 1952. That will give plenty of time for you to arrange your end and I can write and re-write on it. I can probably live on that painless televisioning of my stories or of stories that I like while I work. It does not seem dishonorable nor silly as Hotch suggests it. If it turns out to be, I will stop it immediately.

[Alfred] Rice says I can pay you off all the money I owe you this year. I have to figure out how I live this year. If it is o.k. with you I will borrow at the usual rate since I have something to borrow on again and work like hell. I will feel all right about borrowing if that is agreeable to you since I have, or will have, paid up anything I borrowed before. If I made the book no better than it is it would cover anything I borrowed. There is also the $2000. from Bantam still to come.

Rice may sell the book (last one) to the cinema. Then I have no problems of money to live and write on. But so far I have turned down all the offers. I only do not want to worry about money while I am working and I want to lead a sound working life and not think of money at all except to not waste it.

About the James [Jones] book [*From Here to Eternity*]: It is not great no matter what they tell you. It has fine qualities and greater faults. It is much too long and much too bitching and his one fight, against the planes, at Pearl Harbour day is almost musical comedy. He has a genius for respecting the terms of a kitchen and he is a K.P. boy for keeps and for always. Things will catch up with him and he will probably commit suicide. Who could announce in his publicity in this year 1951 that "he went over the hill" in 1944. That was a year in which many people were very busy doing their duty and in which many people died. To me he is an enormously skillful fuck-up and his book will do great damage to our country. Probably I should re-read it again to give you a truer answer. But I do not have to eat an entire bowl of scabs to know they are scabs; nor suck a boil to know it is a boil; nor swim through a river of snot to know it is snot. I hope he kills himself as soon as it does not damage his or your sales. If you give him a literary tea you might ask him to drain a bucket of snot and then suck the puss out of a dead nigger's ear. Then present him with one of those women he is asking for and let him show her his portrait and his clippings. How did they ever get a picture of a wide-eared jerk (un-damaged ears) to look that screaming tough. I am glad he makes you money and I would never laugh him off. I would just give him a bigger bucket on the snot detail. He has the psycho's urge to kill himself and he will do it.

Make all the money you can out of him as quickly as you can and hold out enough for Christian Burial.

Wouldn't have brought him up if you hadn't asked me. Now I feel as unclean as when I read his fuck-off book. It has all the charm and trueness of the real and imitation fuck-off. I give you James Jones, Gentlemen, and please take him away before he falls apart or starts screaming.

Must stop now as have to work tomorrow. Hope you feel well. I'll try to keep so and work well. Mary sends her love to you and to Vera.

Best always,

Ernest

To CHARLES SCRIBNER, La Finca Vigia, 11–12 April 1951

Dear Charlie:

Thanks for your good letter. I am sorry when I write crabby letters. I've been working so hard and at such a pitch that when I get through I'm crabby. Then keeping your weight down to keep your blood pressure down is a daily damned job. Eat three rye-crisps for breakfast, then a few carrots, young radishes and green onions from the garden when I finish work. Light lunch and either nothing or a peanut butter sandwich for dinner. I think that is one reason I wake so damned early. I'm probably hungry. Last night I ate a big steak at the little Yacht club and I slept until nine o'clock this morning. Decided not to write on the book today and not think about it. Will swim fifty laps in the pool so that I'll sleep good and hit the book tomorrow. I'll still go over 5000 for the week. (Did 5267 April 12.) Just finished.

We didn't see a fin yesterday afternoon and all conditions were perfect. I can't figure what is holding the marlin run up. You should come down and fish sometime when neither of us has anything to work or worry about. I was so ashamed to be ill when you and Vera were down. After being in wonderful shape all winter I had to get that damned thing the night before you came. I felt about as proud as a man would be if he got pox-ed at his bachelor dinner.

Mary is going out this afternoon to fish with Lee Samuels. She is a hell of a competitor and she fishes every chance she can to train for the tournament which is May 25–26–27. She is in wonderful shape right now and swims an 880 in the pool every day. But there is no substitute for actual fishing as it uses muscles you don't use for anything else. If you are not in training and hook a really big fish the work is really punishing on the fore-arms.

My God it is fun not to be working for a day. I love to write. But it can be really tough too. The toughest I think I ever had was doing the re-write on the For Whom The Bell Tolls when they set the Mss. up in galleys for me to re-write from and I worked straight around the clock on it from the start to the finish in that N.Y. heat wave. But I've been working as hard as that lately—and not to re-write.

The reason the Col. Jones thing got on my nerves was that when I read the book I spotted him for a psycho and not a real soldier. Served time, sure, but not as soldier. Then you saying he was and everybody saying how wonderful he was I thought I must be crazy to see something that I was absolutely sure of and it not be true. Then I saw the article about Jones and Lowny and one or the other's admission that he came back from Guadal "a whimpering neurotic" and went over the hill because the Army would only give him one month leave when he wanted three and I stopped worrying.

This is not to brag but Col. Jones and I are a different breed of cats. I can remember haveing a major concussion and a smashed head that took two hours and a half of surgery to clean up and fifty seven stitches in it. Also had both my knees so badly swollen that I could not bend either one. Six days later they lowered me from the attack transport in the LCVP because nobody, and especially me, thought I could go down the net. That was at 0200 June 6th 1944. After we were in the water we had orders to proceed to the Empire Anvil, another attack transport and I had to climb the net in a more than moderate sea and then go down it again into another LCVP and stay in the landing circle until we went in for the assault on Fox Green beach of Omaha Beach. Charlie, honest to God, nothing Jones suffered in any stockade hurt worse than going up and down those nets. I swear it because it was unbearable; but you kept doing it.

The next time I hurt my head was six weeks later near St. Pois or Poix. Need a map. It was a big concussion and I had double vision etc. (It was St. Pois.) I remember now. I didn't take any time off from that one. A tank shell lifted me up and dropped me on head. Why go on with them. But please try to see why I had a prejudiced attitude toward the damned bitching and suffering and glorification of incorrigibles instead of good soldiers. I remember that they released a group of crimes of violence convicts from Joliet Penitentiary who volunteered for the war. Not one of them was worth a shit in combat and they all (the ones the 4th drew) ended up in the motor pool or the rear echelon.

I can remember sitting against an apple tree in an orchard while they were setting up the cp for the night. I'd been to see the General and told him what I'd seen and, as far as I knew, how things looked (to me anyway) and I was sitting against this apple tree and trying not to think about the next day and all the rest of them and wondering how long my headache would last. It used to come in flashes like battery fire. But there was a main permanent one all the time. I nicknamed it the MLR 2 (main line of resistance) and just accepted that I had it.

Well this convict from the motor pool comes up and said he'd heard there was somebody from Chicago and he was from Chicago and wanted to talk to them. He'd gotten hold of some Calvados somewhere. They used to carry it in jerry cans on their trucks.

So I said I was from Oak Park.

"Lace curtain stuff, eh?" said the convict.

"That's correct. And now you fuck off back to where you came from before I cut your balls off."

"What do you mean you'd cut my balls off?"

"Like I said. And put them in your mouth. You got a nice chin for a pair of balls. What did you do time for? Molesting little girls?"

"I did time for robbery."

"All right, thief. Fuck off while you still got a pair of balls if you got any. Fuck off, Jack."

That's about the mildest little convict story I know from the last war. From the first one, when I was a kid, I know plenty. And lots of the guys became big shots in the Mafia etc. And as far back as the first one I learned that if you are really tough you do not have to talk out of the side of your mouth. All you have to do is mean it and be able to back it up. I was worried about the Jones deal for everybody concerned because I know a lot of psycho stories too. They bloomed in the Schnee-Eifel like crocuses the first time there was ever any real German artillery. The potential psychos had thought all along artillery was something we owned. They had never been under an enemy artillery concentration. It turned out to be something they could not bear. But Col. Jones enlisted in the Army on purpose. He hired out to be tough. He wasn't drafted.

So now that [Life] article has straightened me out on things I will thank Jones to take my name out of his book. It appears on three occasions that I noted. It is a good fighting name back to 1700's in the states and long before that elsewhere. It is borne by my son Jack who was wounded, a prisoner, and a hostage. And I do not want it used or misused between the covers of a book by any whimpering neurotic. It is used sneeringly by a coward and I would like it removed. I am sure if I spoke to Col. Jones himself he would understand.

I look forward to the Cardinal's Book[1] which we will burn without reading. Did it ever occur to that Prince of the Church that he is taking the bread out of the mouths of young writers? He might have thought of it when he led Seminarists as strike-breakers against his under-paid Catholic grave diggers.

I hope he doesn't persuade you to publish ex-mayor O'Dwyer's memoirs with Imprimatur.

Well furbish them all; as politely as one can put it.

If it costs any sizeable amount of money to take my name out of Jones book let it ride until you can take it out without cost. But it gripes me every day to have the jerk use it.

If he had any brains he would have known how many professional soldiers have had syphylis, as he would have known the origin of his title and the name of the man who wrote the ballad he took it from, and also a short story by Kipling called "Love O' Women."[2] I could write from now until the end of next week case histories of soldiers and bull fighters I have known (also boxers) who had what we called the old rale (a name for it that goes back nearly to Chaucer's time). From the time I was a kid I had to distinguish between soft and hard chancres and courageous Jones comes along and says *he* has had the clap and it was horrible. I can remember a certain golfer winning the National and the Open the same year with his cock in a sling and he said all it did was improve his putting because he didn't worry about the putting.

All I hope is that you can make all the money in the world out of him before he takes that over-dose of sleeping pills or whatever other exit he elects or is forced into. In the meantime I wish him no luck at all and hope he goes out and hangs himself as soon as plausible.

All this written by a boy who resolved to be a good Christian all day today anyway before biteing on the nail tomorrow.

When you think what actual people you know have been through without squawking nor heroism and then the public has to read the wish fulfillment dreams of a punk like that.

Better knock off on this. It is only that when you are used to writing it is hard to stop and I like to talk with you even when it is only in letters and the conversation is lamentably stupid and one-sided.

Best always, Charlie. Take good care of yourself and we will make a good fishing trip and not try for the giant beasts but for all the delight fishes. I know two fine places to go where we can have good fun. Puerto Escondido and Megano de Casigua down the coast.

Mary sends her love. She is very fond of you both.

Best always,
Ernest

PUL

1. Francis Joseph Cardinal Spellman, *The Foundling,* published by Scribners (New York, 1951). Proceeds of sales were donated to the New York Foundling Hospital.
2. The refrain of Kipling's ballad "Gentlemen Rankers."

To CHARLES SCRIBNER, La Finca Vigia, 18–19 May 1951

Dear Charlie:

I'm sorry that my letter made you so angry. As far as I know I have never met "Ham" Basso and I cannot help clerical mistakes the banks make. I had around 1200 in my Div. and Int. account and I owed no man on earth a nickel unless it was you to whom I have always payed everything I owed. Any money I owed you was secured, I thought, with over 200,000 words on a new book. I had some 165,000 words when I was last in New York and I thought that this and my loyalty to you and your house was sufficient security for me to tell The Guaranty to call you up in case there was an accidental over-draft. I'm sorry it bothered you. This was not accidental. It was an error in accounting.

I cut the 165,000 as far as I thought it would cut and I have added three sections. Two are very long and one, the end, you have read [*The Old Man and the Sea*]. I am going to re-do and re-cut as soon as I take a rest.

Sometimes I write you when I have finished work and am tired. But I have no malice against the boy Jones, nor his Lowney, nor the Cardinal. When was it not all right to bet on another horse? I'm glad when a plater of yours wins. But because you are the owner I do not have to like them, respect them, nor bet on them. I also reserve the right to say what I think of them without malice.

About my diet: I train myself as well as I can. It would be nicer to have some one else train you the way George Brown used to train me. But I do not have George and I do as well as I can. I always keep my bowells open, assimilate everything I eat too fast probably, and do a day's work.

Mary is the only one here who reads my work and I am sorry if it gives her goose-flesh. I will continue to write as well as I can goose-flesh or not.

Malice is a rough word to use in a letter.

I loved Max very much too and knew him pretty well and he always trusted me even when I was unjust and mean. (Excuse this machine.) Please bury Max's ghost for keeps and cut out this about he, Tom Wolfe and Scott being gods and you etc. It makes me ashamed. Max was Max with five daughters and an idiot wife. Tom Wolfe was a one book boy and a glandular giant with the brains and the guts of three mice. Scott was a rummy and a liar and dishonest about money with the in-bred talent of a dishonest and easily frightened angel.

Why not forget all that shit and be a fine publisher and a brave man as you are and should be?

Mary sends her love and I send my best always to you both.

Ernest

Please don't be offended at any of this and remember I am writing from fondness.

E.H.

Glass OK. with usual pm decline. Hurricane seems to be petering out.

EH

Saturday - next day - May 19 -

Awfully sorry about this machine and the dim ribbon but it is about punched out and needs to go in and be cleaned and freshened up.

Charlie, honest, boy, everybody's metabolism and eating habits are their own and are different. I can't cut out starches and sweets for example because I never do eat them. I get enough sugar from what alcohol I consume my doctor tells me and to counteract any nervous effect from alcohol I take 6 vitamin B1 combex capsules every morning. The Dr. started me doing this when I was writing For Whom The Bell Tolls. I never drink after dinner and I never have hang-overs.

Each day I take two apiece of these capsules. I send you the cover which contains the formula.

New York is the only place I ever dis-sipate or stay up late and George Brown will call me up at eight a.m. even if I got in at six a.m. and I would go up to the gym and box with him six, eight or sometimes ten rounds and sweat all the alcohol out and afterwards get a rub down and drink a quart of milk.

Everybody is built differently and I used to be able to steer twelve hours every day on my feet without leaving the bridge and have many times steered 18 hours. Plenty people know about this and it is not a delusion on my part. I can steer 12 hours now but the sun is bad for my head.

In the war I never took a sleeping pill and I slept well when I had a chance to sleep. Take two sleeping pills a night when I am writing so I won't wake up and start thinking about what I am going to write before it is light. Have never increased the dose. The doctor says I am not nervously constructed so I could [not] become addicted to anything.

This makes me sound terribly noble. I'm not at all nor trying to be. But I am built differently than most people.

When I was a small kid I would only eat meat and fish. They couldn't get me to eat vegetables no matter how much they whipped me. Finally I got constipated from eating only meat and had terrible piles and then to keep from springing the piles would not move my bowels. I think the longest I ever went without moveing them was nine days. Then I had to go because I got bad cramps at a Track Meet (Interscholastic) at the University of Michigan and the result plugged the toilet and a plumber had to be called to clear it. There was some resemblance to the big stick that T. R. Roosevelt was always brandishing over the corporations in cartoons and there was some talk of haveing it preserved for the museum. All this time I was in perfect health and was Capt. of the water polo team etc.

But I knew I had to learn to eat vegetables and to move my bowells regularly. The piles cured themselves and as soon as I learned to eat the different vegetables I had no trouble about constipation.

No, people are funny in the way they are constructed. I only like to eat at sea or in the hills where I get hungry. What I really like is good fresh fish, grilled, good steaks (not these comic steaks they have bred for slobs to eat so they have no taste but only size) but good steaks with the bone and very rare. Good lamb, rare. Elk, mountain sheep, venison and antelope in that order and grouse, young sage-hen, quail and teal, canvasback and mallards in that order. With mashed potatoes and gravy. For vegetables I like celery and artichokes best; artichokes cold with sauce vinagreat (mis-spelled), Brussels sprouts, Swiss chard, broccoli and all fruits.

To eat when you write is just a stupefyeing bore unless they have some of the above.

So don't worry about me down here eating nothing and makeing an ass of myself. I have had strange eating habits since I was a boy. It is nothing to be proud of, ashamed of nor alarmed about. Bears don't eat all winter and Harry Wills fasts a month each year.

Best always,
Ernest

I think Basso was a friend of Martha's. Have tried to recall him but I can't.

(Am going fishing this p.m. Hurricane fizzled out)

PUL   EH

To GENERAL E. E. DORMAN–O'GOWAN, La Finca Vigia, 13 June 1951

Dear Chinko-Maru (Japanese Gaelic):

I can't plead anything except work (over 45,000 words in April and May) and your letter at the top of MUST BE ANSWERED AT ONCE shameing me every day by the typewriter. Count on me for any foreword. Though what my qualifications are I don't know. I'll write what I think. Then I'll write to your orders and I would not write to any other man's.

You sound as though you had worked like hell. It is good to get it out of the system though. I've heard nothing from the Morrow's. Probably your still pouring on the coal. It sounds like something that needs to be written.

Here not much news. I've been on that sea wakeing in the night with the sentences in my head; putting them off and up at daylight to write. Finally have the book whipped and the last two books of the whole book are as they should be. But now I must start the re-writing and cutting of books one and two.

When I finished we fished two marlin Tournaments. In one we did well without luck. In the second, the International, the club I fished for was second although I did nothing to help it. If I had had any luck with a very big foul-hooked fish we would have won. Mary finished Sixth in a field of 44 boats fishing against many Internationals in the Tin-Kid. Smallest boat in the fleet. She fished with Taylor Williams of Sun Valley, Idaho. He is 64 and we call him Colonel because he is from Kentucky but everybody thinks he is a British Col. because he looks like one who has been in India too long and is also deaf. He is a very nice man and you would like him. They had a line squall the last two hours of fishing of the third day of the tournament and Taylor had two broken ribs and a lump on his head like half a baseball and he paid no attention to any of it until the ribs started to get him the next day. He and Mary both fished very well.

The cook shot himself, by error, in the left shoulder while fooling with a point 22 rifle of mine while we were away at the fishing and I had to go to court about it yesterday. Very nice old Spanish court house built in 1860 and remarkably cool for a hot day. Court seemed a big sort of social event for the various criminals and police and I can see why our servants are always delighted to frequent it. But I haven't time and have to get them out and then let everything cool off and get rid of them and train new ones.

It is the mango season now and they are lovely to eat. Mary has been putting up many of them in the deep freeze and that way we will have them for you whenever you and Eve arrive. The garden is doing well too and we have all vegetables for the table and soon the alligator pears will start. They are the great luxury of the N.Y. night spots and here they are the poor man's butter. They make sandwiches with alligator pears and bread.

Shrimp are running again now and as soon as fish start running well I will put 500–600 pounds in the deep freeze.

I wish I could read your damned book for pleasure. Did I tell you [Air Marshal Arthur William] Tedder and his wife were down here and we went out a couple of days on the boat. Nothing was running but they caught a little of one thing or another and I think they had a good time. I worked so bloody hard to show them fish when there were none. It was like showing someone over a completely quiet sector of your front. On the quiet sector you can always shoot a little artillery and get a response and some peoples killed. But fishing on the ocean you can't do that. Now next month, maybe, they may be pulling you out of the boat, and no guests [that] you would like to show a few pheasants.

Please write, Chink, and forgive me for haveing been so bad about it if you can.

I had to write a long part of the book that I hoped I would never need to write and which I dreaded writing. But I wrote it, liveing in it, and I hope you will like it because there is one good fight (I think as valid as the Sordo fight on the hill in the Spanish book) except that in this fight the other people, the enemy, are being pursued and they out-class those who pursue them. But they do not have the necessary to back it up with. I hope you will like it anyway. The people who were pursuing used their stuff intelligently. But they were sucked into one perfect, but under-armed, ambush ["The Sea Chase," Part III of *Islands in the Stream*].

It is fun to try to write as you should. But it is a hell of a responsibility too. I wish they let you live a hundred years with all intact so that you could do it well.

Have luck with book and write here.

Mary sends her love to you both and so do I.

Hem

I am very anxious to see the book and please count on me in every way.

PH. PUL   EH

To CHARLES SCRIBNER, La Finca Vigia, 20 July 1951

Dear Charlie:

Your letter from Far Hills [New Jersey] of July 18th came in tonight's mail. I'd waited to write until our correspondence stopped being crossed and become more or less unscrambled. Am now writing and listening to it rain straight up and down. If there is any wind behind this rain will have to knock off and close the windows.

I'm sorry if I mixed you up about the book. This book is, in total, some 1900 to 2000 pages in Mss. It is the book about the Sea, but there is no sense in arbitrarily labeling it as such. That designation is only for your information.

This book about the sea could be broken up into four books and each one of them published separately.

At present I am engaged in re-writing the first section which I have not re-read since 1947. It consists of 1195 pages of MSS. and in a month of work I have completely re-written and cut 179 pages. Much re-written entirely new.

I would like to have the entire book be around 130,000 or 140,000 to 150,000 words. This means I must cut and re-write very much.

The last two parts need no cutting at all. The third part needs quite a lot but it is very careful scalpel work and would need no cutting if I were dead.

The reason I told you that the four books which make up the whole could be published separately was in case of my death.

Is this all clear?

At present, when I am not re-writing the first part, I work on a list of titles. Have some that are good. But have found it is worthless to talk about titles until you have the right one.

The reason that I wrote you that you could always publish the last three parts separately is because I know you can in case through accidental death or any sort of death I should not be able to get the first part in proper shape to publish. That is the way the book works. If you did not have one you could start with two. If you did not have two you could start with three. If you did not have three you could start with four and finish with it. But I plan the complete book, in one volume, to consist of parts one, two, three and four.

If any of this is confusing or un-clear please let me know. If it seems un-clear please read it over.

My chances of living to complete the book are excellent according to my doctor. However, I have worked so hard in the last six months that I know I need a rest and a change of climate. You can whip your blood pressure, as I have, by training and abstemiousness and then work so hard that you can be worn down so anything can hit you. I do not think there are many writers who ever averaged over 1000 words a day for over four months, at a stretch, of the sort of writing you read when you were down here [*The Old Man and the Sea*]. Maybe there were. But I can tell you I never did. Now I want to get the same tempo into the first part. And please, because I say that, do not think that I think the first part is inferior. It is not.

About how you present the book: DONT WORRY. I will tell you as simply as possible what I think and we can then work it out.

Please hang onto this letter and refer to it when anything comes up as I am too tired to write it again.

It has hit ninety here nearly every day now for a month and I have permanent prickly heat. It is making up for all the droughts we have had for many years and rains heavily every afternoon.

Let us talk the hell about something else if this is sufficient information to go on.

I'm glad you had your family with you and I hope young Charlie doesn't have to stay in uniform all his life. Bumby will probably have to. But soldiering is the only trade he knows. He's just been made Liaison Officer to the First French Army Corps after being security officer in Berlin.

Patrick is in Spain, as I believe I wrote you, after getting a magnum cum laude at Harvard.

The last I heard from Mary was from New Orleans where she was to get a plane for Chicago and Minneapolis after staying with her family at Gulfport. She should be back sometime next week. It will be wonderful to see her.

I put about 250 lbs of dressed dolphin and kingfish into the deep-freeze today after a three day trip down the coast but could not get away from the book. We came into Harbour with a line squall and with rain so that you could not see the bow from the flying bridge. The rain beat on my head so that it felt as though it had been wrapped in fresh raw hide when it started to dry. After that a bunch of letters, all full of bad news, a scrubby meal, and a lonely bed. And then always work at first light.

How does it go? And tomorrow and tomorrow and tomorrow.

Best always,
Ernest

Hope your health is better and that you will pick up the weight again gradually. Have some fun. Tomorrow is my birthday and I am going fishing.

E.H.

PUL

To EDMUND WILSON, La Finca Vigia, 10 September 1951

Dear Wilson:

Please use the three letters if they are of any use to you, and do not take out any of the part that speaks well of yourself or of your criticism. You may be sure they were sincere. There are only two things I wish you would do: change "Jews" to "New York people." I was speaking of Paul Rosenfeld and Waldo Frank but I did not mean to give any derogatory or anti-semitic meaning as it would read today.[1]

The other thing is: could you make a note that the Halliburton I refer to is the author of Sam Slick the clock-maker (a sort of bush league

Peregrine Pickle) and *not* Richard Halliburton the deceased Ladies Home Journal adventurer?[2]

About The Wound and The Bow: I cannot remember why Max [Perkins] told me it was libelous.[3] But he did. There is no use argueing the history of the Spanish Republic now. But it was something I believed in deeply long before it was an American Communist cause. I thought you did not understand that because I only wrote about bull fights but I had believed in the Republic and known the people who worked for it since the early twenties. Much of it is in that last chapter of Death in the Afternoon that you don't like.[4] But you might, truly, not understand it just as I can not understand the part about what my Wound was. I tried to. But it wasn't any of the wounds I knew.

But now everyone is dead or to be dead I think we might try to resolve our mis-understandings and see what good, if any, there is in all of us along with the bad. Even though we would have to have some neutral character like Dean [Christian] Gauss to point it out. Or is he dead?

Hope this all doesn't sound too dull and holy. It's that there is no one any more to talk to and I've finished work and it's the end of the day. Have been working hard all day.

Please make what use of the letters that you wish.

Yours always,
Ernest Hemingway

YUL

1. Wilson wanted to print three letters EH had sent him in 1923–1924 in *The Shores of Light* (New York, 1952). He made the change EH asked for in a paragraph about Sherwood Anderson on p. 117. 2. The allusion to Halliburton was expunged. 3. *The Wound and the Bow* (New York, 1941) has a chapter on EH. 4. Only one "political" passage appears in chapter 20 of *Death in the Afternoon* (New York, 1932), pp. 274–75.

This and the three subsequent letters to Wilson are used courtesy of the Beinecke Library, Yale University. (EH's original letters were evidently tactfully edited before publication in Wilson's book.)

To PATRICK HEMINGWAY, La Finca Vigia, 16 September 1951

Dear Mouse:

I'm afraid you haven't been getting the letters I've written so am makeing a carbon of this and will send it to your new address, if you've moved, when Mother sends it to me. (Straighten that sentence out with a shoe-horn.) Wrote mother for your news and an address. But she just sent word that you had a three months extention from the KW. [draft] board. I've written her again for the new address if you've moved.

German publishers B. Fischer have been authorized to pay Bumby $2400 (10,000 DRM) and I wrote him to get $500 to you. You'll have to arrange how to transfer it. Maybe he will be able to write a check in dollars for deposit in your K.W. bank. Maybe there is some simpler way. Anyway you have $500. comeing from me through Bum and they wrote they are ready to pay the money.

Here is Bum's address: Capt. John H. Hemingway 0–1798575, Secteur Postal 50.330, Par B.P.M. 517, APO 82, New York, NY.

The address is practically a letter in its-self. He is US liaison officer to the French Third Army Corps and is stationed at Frieburg in Briesgau. They have given him a shoot of his own of about 2000 acres and he has stag, wild-boar, pheasant, hare, rabbits, roe deer and pigeons and duck. They are shooting pigeons now, ducks come later and pheasants in No-vember. They can hunt wild boar already and he has shooting rights in other shoots that total more than 20,000 acres.

I had hoped to go over and shoot with him this fall to take a vacation but Mary's father had a return of that old trouble he had in Chicago and Mary had to go over to Gulfport. She only had to stay about a week and he is out of the hospital now. But we never know when he may have to go back in and she have to go over again. So I will have to stand by here. At least through Sept. and October.

Been the hottest August in the history of the Island. Six hurricanes so far. But nothing near here. One really big one hit Jamaica and smashed Kingston badly before going on to Mexico where it did damage from Tampico all the way up into the mountains.

The others hit the windward islands and blew out in the Atlantic. But it looks like a bad hurricane year (typewriter is resting on wood). Barometer has been consistently low since early July and the first hurri-cane came in early June. Fishing absolutely kaputt. Mary has been fine. She had a good vacation up at Bemidji [Minnesota] and at her cousin's place at Eagle Harbour up on Lake Superior.

Gianfranco is fine. They bought a Finca out in that Red earth country past Ranco Boyeros. He has been getting that planted and fixed up and been working at the Steamship Company since the first of June.

I've re-written 76,000 words (cut, revised etc.) and written new of the first part of my book that I stopped on when you were laid up that summer [1947]. The second part is about 35,000 and the third is 44,000 and the last one, that I wrote right after you and Henny left here last New Years is 22,000. The third and the last parts won't have to have any re-writing at all practically. But will have to do quite a lot of the second part. But I'm tired now and stale and I want to take some sort of a rest or vacation and hit the going over fresh.

The pool has been wonderful and clean and cool all summer. Who has had a rough time with the heat is poor Black Dog. But pretty soon we'll get northers again.

I hope your painting is going good old Mouse and that you and Henny[1] didn't have too uncomfortable a summer. Have you ever gotten to the Prado yet? Madrid should be nice after the middle of September. I am so glad you got the extention and I hope you will get another one.

When and if you get this letter let's try and keep good contact because I might still be able to get over while you and Henny are in Europe.

Best love to Henny. Mary sends her love and so does Gianfranco.

Much love,
Papa.
PUL   Kiss

1. On 17 June 1950 Patrick had married Henrietta F. Broyles (1929–1963) of Baltimore, Maryland.

To EDMUND WILSON, La Finca Vigia, 19 September 1951

Dear Wilson:

I read those copies of my letters to you over again when I had more time to read them thoroughly and I am sorry that I must withdraw my permission for you to publish them. When I read them at first I did not realize how anti-Canadian they would seem. I am not anti-Canadian at all and have many close friends there and love much of the country.[1]

So you have permission to publish any extracts referring to your help and criticism and nothing else. Is this quite clear?

With best wishes,
Yours very truly
YUL   Ernest Hemingway

1. The only anti-Canadian sentence that survived Wilson's required editing is in *The Shores of Light*, p. 116: "You don't know anything in Canada."

To EDMUND WILSON, La Finca Vigia, 22 September 1951

Dear Wilson:

Thank you for the review of the Stein book and the letter. I have ordered (rather *am* ordering the book). If you are ever writing about her at length maybe it would be useful to know that A.T. was the dominant one of the two. I know this from many incidents over many years. But the one I remember clearest was this: Gertrude had told me to come in at any time and that I had in her words, "The run of the house." This meant that the servant would admit me if they were out and I could sit in the big studio room and look at the pictures and the servant would bring me a drink.

This day I rang and the servant let me in and took me into the big room and said Mademoiselle Gertrude was busy but she knew she would want me to wait. They were packing to go away on a trip. I said I would stop by on my way home as I was takeing a walk after working. But the servant insisted that I wait as Mademoiselle Gertrude had especially asked that she keep me there if I came in.

The servant went away and I was standing looking at the pictures when I heard Gertrude in a very loud and anguished voice say, "Pussy! Pussy please don't. Oh please don't say you will do that. I'll do anything if you won't. Please Pussy. Please-"

I was out of the door and had shut it by the next words. I didn't want to hear anymore.[1]

If you are interested in this, and you seem to be the only person working out anything about Gertrude sensibly, I can tell you more any time. Gertrude and I became good friends again before she died. She knew that I knew that the malice and some if not all of the lies in her book The Autobiography of A.T. came from Alice. Alice had the ambition of the devil and was very jealous of Gertrude's men and women friends. Gertrude was terribly lazy but she had finally discovered a way of writing that enabled her to write every day and thus have the sense of accomplishment. But then came the necessity to have this prose, which sometimes was not much better than daily automatic writing, recognized officially. After she had change of life she went through a long phase of megolomania which was difficult to take since it co-incided with her patriotic homo-sexual phase. She lost her judgement on painting completely and judged pictures by the sexual habits of those who painted them. Picasso and I used to laugh about it but we always agreed how fond we were of her no matter what she did. But Alice was her evil angel as well as her great friend.

About first reviews of published work: Yours in the Dial was the first review of mine as far as I know.[2]

Am sorry I had to write you withdrawing permission for publishing those letters except for anything concerning your own work. They would only make trouble and mis-understanding in Canada where I had good friends who are dead and have good friends liveing. I also remembered how much I loved many different parts of the country. I also remember what I did not like but I should write that balanced by what I did like. In a letter there is not the time you need to be just.

Now that we live in a time of such violence, false-witness, inaccuracy, calumnies and lies for profit I am going to spend the rest of my life trying to be just. That doesn't mean that there are not people that should be justly hanged though.

Best always
Ernest Hemingway

YUL

1. EH often repeated this anecdote and used it in *A Moveable Feast* (New York, 1964), pp. 117–19. 2. EH had forgotten two earlier reviews.

To CHARLES SCRIBNER, La Finca Vigia, 2 October 1951

Dear Charlie:

The glass is lower; now 29.30 but the sky looks as though the storm were going away. It is a very strange storm. But this has been the strangest year for weather that I have ever known. I certainly would like to see the glass start to rise.

A couple of people who owed me money came through with checks in the afternoon mail so there is no need for you to deposit the $750.00 I asked you to deposit in my Guaranty Trust Co. account and charge to my loan account. Unless you have deposited it please cancell that request.

News from the coast is not good.

The wave of remembering has finally risen so that it has broken over the jetty that I built to protect the open roadstead of my heart and I have the full sorrow of Pauline's death[1] with all the harbour scum of what caused it. I loved her very much for many years and the hell with her faults.

Best always
Ernest

PUL

1. Pauline had died unexpectedly in Los Angeles at 4 A.M. Monday, 1 October.

To CHARLES SCRIBNER, La Finca Vigia, 5 October 1951

Dear Charlie:

Thanks for your letter of October 3rd in answer to my black ass letter of whenever it was I had the bad throat and the letter I wrote in bed the next day to you asking you to disregard anything it said. (Try to write a worse sentence than that!)

Thank you too for your cable of today in regard to Pauline and depositing the 750.00. I had written you there was no need to deposit the money (enclose this letter). But the chauffeur had not mailed it dureing the time I was standing by a non-functioning telephone which the company kept promising to have working any minute. So long as you deposited it, let it remain charged to the Loan account which is secured by royalties and future earnings.

Will try to use this account as little as possible. Since I will have very little taxable income this year—will not need much for next year on tax. If I sell something to pictures or television will have money to pay the tax. Same if I sell the Key West property.

All the news from Mary's father is good. But it will be until it is bad. Imagine haveing a Christian Science G-2 set up. Our storm went north and continued at sea off Hatteras. Hope it keeps out in the Gulf Stream.

As occupational therapy (joke) while waiting around with bad things happening and no communications I counted word by word the Book IV of the Book that you read from the Mss. (The Old Man and The Sea part). It was *exactly* 26,531 words. My previous count was on an incomplete copy. This is the exact count on the part you read in the same Mss. you read it in.

This is the prose that I have been working for all my life that should read easily and simply and seem short and yet have all the dimensions of the visible world and the world of a man's spirit. It is as good prose as I can write as of now.

But I think you would like the third book as well. It is the one about the pursuit and destruction of the crew of a submarine when the objective was to make them prisoners and everything possible was done to accomplish this mission. It has the same quality you may have observed in the book IV (old man) that you read but the action is very fast and the dialogue very exact.

The second book might be too rough for anyone brought up on James Jones. It deals with the life ashore of people on an irregular mission at sea (just after and before a mission) and the death of a man's oldest son and his meeting with the boy's mother. (The third book deals with the mission which follows.)

The first book is Idyllic until the Idyll is destroyed by violence. While it is Idyllic I think you will like it very much. The same people are in books 1, 2, 3. In the end there is only the old man and the boy = (Book 4).[1] I have many titles for it. But will get one finally. (Three are good.) As of today the entire book is 182,231 words long.

It was nice about Lee Samuels[2] because he does not have the same problems you have; I have given him adequate security and you need not be cramped or worried financing me while I write and re-write this book.

Mary is very well and sends you her love.

We have had another record hot day on October Fifth.

It was so hot this morning that when I was working the Mss. was soaked wet with sweat. However did 40 belly exercises, swam 10 laps in the pool, wrote the checks to pay my bills, wrote [Alfred] Rice and worked until the Series started and then later in the afternoon when it was cooler.

Best to you always
Ernest

This has been a rough year. Contents and outline of the book is confidential <u>and</u> <u>for</u> <u>you</u> <u>only</u>.

PUL   EH

1. What EH here calls Part IV appeared as *The Old Man and the Sea* (1952). Parts I–III appeared posthumously as *Islands in the Stream* (1970). 2. Hemingway collector and bibliographer: *A Hemingway Check List* (New York, 1951).

To D. D. PAIGE, La Finca Vigia, 22 October 1951

Dear Mr. Paige:

I received your long letter of October 15 today and hasten to reply.

The initiative of Gabriela Mistral seems a very brave and noble one in requesting an amnesty for Ezra in the name of all Nobel Prize winners or with the signatures. But how many liveing Nobel Prize winners are there and how many of them would sign?[1]

Here are some other practical things to remember: An election year is comeing up and I doubt very much if the head of the Democratic party would sign any amnesty which could be used against himself or the Democratic party by the Republicans. The Democratic administration is being attacked from various sources as favouring Communists or haveing permitted Communist control or pressure in the formation of Foreign policy especially in China. Giveing an amnesty to Ezra, while others convicted under the same charges that he was charged with are still in jail, would raise a great stink and open the government to charges of favouring Fascists as well as Communists; in other words all sorts of totalitarians. I am sure of this.

Remember that as soon as Ezra is declared sane he must stand trial for treason. You have to always remember that Pound the great poet who we respect and Pound the old friend who I care for greatly are legally not the Pound of the treasonable broadcasts. The Pound of the treasonable and anti-semitic broadcasts has been declared insane. That is his protection from the charges against him.

If he were declared sane you can be sure that the people who resent his anti-semitic broadcasts will take up the offensive against him. This is a fact you have to face. Another one is that no administration is going to risk alienating the Jewish vote by freeing Pound at this time.

If Gabriela Mistral wishes to organize the Nobel prize winners in a gesture for Ezra to be amnestied that is her business. It cannot do Ezra any harm. I doubt if it will do him any practical good. I am positive in my opinion that the President would refer it to the Department of Justice. It might well be that the Department of Justice would be pleased to have Ezra declared sane so he could be tried and convicted. On the other hand they might consider it better that Ezra's case be left as it is now.

Please do not think that my heart is cold toward Ezra when I try to make my brain as cold as possible in considering his situation.

This too to remember: Ezra is an American citizen. He cannot travel abroad without a passport. He cannot be deported to Italy as it is not the country of his birth. There is also the question of whether Italy would receive him. Certainly the town of Rapallo, where he was well loved, would receive him. But the question of his entry into Italy is a question between governments.

Why does not Gabriella Mistral offer him asylum in her own country, officially, and make a guaranty that he will not broadcast nor write or utter treasonous sentiments but devote himself to poetry? That would be something practical. I can see a possibility of his being released on that basis.

I do not think [T. S.] Eliot's letter was timid. It seemed sound to me. It is simpler for La Mistral to attack in a valiant way without a knowledge of the strength of the charges against Ezra than for Eliot who should know them. Many people have tried with great valour and little sense to free a prisoner and had the prisoner killed due to their blind zeal.

For an example: when my boy Jack was wounded and a prisoner in a camp of hostages held by the Germans, General George Patton ordered a battalion of tanks to make a raid into Germany to free his son-in-law and other prisoners in the same camp. The Germans threw in road blocks behind the tanks. General Patton's son-in-law was shot by an S.S. officer in the mix-up when the tanks attacked the camp. Jack and the others rode out on the tops of the tanks and they were all eventually shot or re-captured and I believe none of the tanks were able to return to the American lines. Patton always said that he regretted this more than any-thing in his life. All the prisoners would have been released in due course had he been patient.

I will write Dorothy Pound today to try to clarify what it is that they really want. The [Olga] Rudge business is unfortunate and I believe is the basis for much of the hysterical thinking about the case.[2]

Please excuse me not writing you at greater length. I am finishing a novel; have had two deaths in the family and many problems. A letter like this takes a working day (with that to Dorothy) to write.

With all best wishes,

PH. PUL Ernest Hemingway.

1. Ezra Pound had been at St. Elizabeth's Hospital for the Insane in Washington, D.C., since 21 December 1945. 2. Olga Rudge was the mother of Pound's daughter, Mary. She had written EH on 13 March 1950, urging him to do something about securing Pound's release.

To DOROTHY POUND, La Finca Vigia, 22 October 1951

Dear Dorothy:

Enclosed is a letter I have just written to D. D. Paige of Rapallo in answer to a long letter from him about a project the South American poetess G. Mistral has for freeing Ezra. I suppose you know the details of the project and that Eliot had written advising that they proceed cautiously etc. I assume Ezra is in touch with Paige since Paige quoted a letter from him in regard to Eliot, asking him "for the 58th time" to have nothing to do with lawyers.

My letter is self explanatory and I think it is sound. Maybe it is not but it is as cold as I can see the situation.

Could you tell me something about Paige and how much authority he has to speak for or about Ezra? There seem to be some people who make almost a career out of Ezra's trials and misfortunes. Could you let me know who is authorized to speak for him and who is not?

Would you tell me also how you are and how Ezra is and what are your true plans, hopes and objectives? From what I have heard, and from a letter I received from her when I was last in Paris, the person who makes least sense and most hysteria and trouble in all this is Olga Rudge. Unless we count that Prince of the Truth: Bill [William Carlos] Williams.

I always remember him confideing to me that you had not really had a baby. It was all a fake engineered by Ezra and you had worn a pillow under your clothes to simulate pregnancy and then gone away letting Ezra announce the birth of a son [Omar S.]. Remembering the taxi ride out to the hospital in Neuilly and how you finally told me it was time to go I always had great confidence in the good doctor's veracity after that.

Please don't think my letter to Paige is harsh. It is exactly what I think of the situation as of today.

It would help me very much if you would answer the questions I have asked if they are not indiscreet and tell me anything else that you think that I should know.

My love to you and give Ezra good wishes and congratulate him on his prize[1] and tell him how much I admire what he has written since he has been in trouble. I am sure that he would have hanged with as much style as Roger Casement.[2] But I am much happier that he is writing good poetry instead.

PH. PUL   Hem

1. Pound had won the Bollingen Prize in Poetry (1949) for his *Pisan Cantos*.
2. Sir Roger (1864–1916) was an Irish rebel hanged by the British.

To EDMUND WILSON, La Finca Vigia, 28 November 1951

Dear Wilson:

Thank you for your letter of Nov. 22. The letters are quite o.k. to publish in the form you sent them and I am returning the Mss. herewith.

Bird was William Bird who was the publisher of The Three Mountains Press. He printed on a hand press. He was a great friend of Joyce and an old friend of mine. He put up with an awful lot from Ford Madox Ford and from Pound when Pound was being difficult. I always was very fond of him and still am.

The mention of What Price Glory meant that what we heard of it in Paris sounded fine; ie there were good reports on it brought back from N.Y.

Could you make that clear? The Canada sentence is ok.

I never saw What Price Glory. As a matter of fact the only war play I ever saw was Journey's End which, in spite of everything, was quite affecting if you knew the English. I shouldn't care to see it more than once, nor to have to read it, but I remember that was my reaction when I saw it played in Paris.

Will send this off to get your copy back to you.

It was bad luck about Christian Gauss. We were quite good friends in Paris one year when Scott was really trying to straighten out and work. I'm very sorry that he is dead.[1]

Would you mind telling me, sometime when you have time, what you think of the business of putting Tender Is The Night into chronological order rather than the way it was published. I read it all through and it seemed to take the magic out of it. Nothing came as a surprise and the mystery had all been re-moved. I think it was one of those ideas Scott had sometimes, like his titles that Max Perkins kept him from useing, which was not too good. But I would like very much to know what you thought about it. But only when you have plenty of time.

Best always,

YUL   Ernest Hemingway

1. Dean Gauss of Princeton had died suddenly in Pennsylvania Station, New York City, 1 November 1951.

To THOMAS BLEDSOE,[1] La Finca Vigia, 9 December 1951

Dear Mr. Bledsoe:

Thank you for your letter of December third which had been returned for insufficient postage and so arrived only this morning.

Malcolm Cowley's letters to me are available here but I am too busy to look them up this morning. He must have told you, in any event, what he wrote to me. He is a friend of mine and I am fond of him. What I wrote to Charlie Scribner you already know.

I don't know Mr. Young[2] although I certainly sympathise with him in any difficulties I may cause him or have caused him.

This typewriter is pretty well punched out from writing 183,251 words of a novel. So please forgive it any lapses.

If I knew you or Mr. Rinehart or Mr. Young I don't think there would have been any problem about this except the one basic one: I do not want books written about my life nor about any part of it while I am liveing. For one thing too many people are involved in any man's life.

If I had known, in time, that Mr. Young was writing a critical study of my work I would have been happy to provide him with any facts about my work which were not available to him. There are many things that are not available and some [of] them might be interesting.

But there has been too damned much written about my personal life and I am sick of it. It was a very bad thing for me that Malcolm Cowley's article was published in LIFE. But that was not Malcolm's fault and everything he did was well intentioned. Please do not think, though, that the life article was authorized. Malcolm told me he had been commissioned to write it and I gave him a list of people who knew me, or whom I had served under, or been with under various circumstances and he got his facts from them. I never saw the article nor any part of it until I read it in LIFE in Italy.

Lillian Ross wrote a profile of me which I read, in proof, with some horror. But since she was a friend of mine and I knew that she was not writing in malice she had a right to make me seem that way if she wished. I did not believe that I talked like a half-breed choctaw nor that it gave a very sound impression of some one who gets up at first light and works hard at writing most of the days of his life. But I had just finished a book and when you have done that you do not really give a damn for a few weeks. So I did not mind it although I knew it was harmful to me just as the Life piece was. There was no harm intended and much received. But I am still fond of Lillian.

So what then, Dr. Bledsoe? A friend of my wife's from old London newspaper days named Sammy Boal crosses on a boat with us and I talk carelessly, and cheerfully and without the necessary pomposity of the author and it turns out Sammy is or has been commissioned to write a profile on me.[2]

Wonderful. He needs the money too as everybody else has up to this point. I read it with the usual, by now, horror and make one suggestion: that it would have been impossible for any human being to have made one remark attributed to me. I then correct this one remark to show him how people actually talk and that correction gives the piece a touch of dreadful authenticity. Everything is well intentioned and it all comes out very bad.

I am a very serious but not a solemn writer and I like to joke when I am not writing. But by this time I decide that I have had bloody well enough.

So when I hear from Malcolm Cowley that Mr. Young is writing a book which proves that I am all my heroes it occurs to me that it would be as well to dissuade him as early as possible so that he would not have lost his time and his work. That accounts for my first letter to Cowley and my subsequent letters to Charlie Scribner.

Every writer is in much of his work. But it is not as simple as all that. I could have told Mr. Young the whole genesis of The Sun Also Rises for example. It came from a personal experience in that when I had been wounded at one time there had been an infection from pieces of wool cloth being driven into the scrotum. Because of this I got to know other kids who had genito urinary wounds and I wondered what a man's life would have been like after that if his penis had been lost and his testicles and spermatic cord remained intact. I had known a boy that had happened to. So I took him and made him into a foreign correspondent in Paris and, inventing, tried to find out what his problems would be when he was in love with someone who was in love with him and there was nothing that they could do about it.

This was the sort of thing I would have been glad to tell Mr. Young for his own knowledge. But I was not Jake Barnes. My own wound had healed rapidly and well and I was quit for a short session with the catheter. This, I think, could have helped Mr. Young in this thesis. He would *not have had to publish it nor write biography.* He would simply have had information not otherwise available to him to draw his critical conclusions from.

The other thing that seems incongruous in the thesis that I can only write about myself is: Who then is Francis Macomber? Is that me? I know very well it is not.

(Am sorry this letter had to be interrupted at this point.)

Now as I read it over I see that we are back where we started from except that I am trying to make clear to you my position in an informal and I hope not un-pleasant way.

There are a couple of other things: If the book were one that would not be objectionable to me how did it happen that I never heard from you to that effect?

If, as you write, it is a serious critical study of what I have written why does it contain "only infrequent short passages" of quotations from that work. It would seem to me to be quite possible that such a form of taking things out of context might well be only to prove a thesis.

I will send a copy of this to Malcolm Cowley to try to keep the record straight. Certainly I have no wish to embarrass him in any way. When I say his profile or article was harmful to me I mean that it gave inordinate publicity to my personal life. This life is my own business and three times, out of friendship, I have allowed it to be intruded on. Now three different friends' impression of what it consists in has become so widely publicized that my work is criticized from the standpoint of these friends' impression of me and rather than from the work its-self.

You will understand my opposition to haveing my personal life presented as a subject of study for college students. If you do not at least
I have attempted to explain.

If you and Mr. Young like what I write this whole argument must be
both boreing and painful to you and I must seem very difficult and
churlish. It is really boreing and painful to me. But please believe I do
not do it out of churlishness.

Best wishes to both you and to Mr. Young. My position remains the
same as I stated it in the letter to Charlie Scribner; but I have tried to
clarify it for you.

After the New Yorker piece I decided that I would never give another
interview to anyone on any subject and that I would keep away from all
places where I would be likely to be interviewed. If you say nothing it is
difficult for someone to get it wrong. But I have learned that for the
academic critics a writer must not joke. Have you noticed that? I think
it must have been much more fun in the old days when there were more
writers and fewer critics.

Probably soon, at the way things are going, there will be no writers
and only critics. Then the critics can go to the coast to write the way the
writers have done (and none survived). Then the motion pictures will
die from the writings of the critics. What do you want to bet Arthur
Mizener won't be a star on Television within our time? The only thing
we have to do is to get him another Scott Fitzgerald. But you see? These
are the sort of jokes a writer shouldn't make.

Best holiday greetings,
Ernest Hemingway

T.C. PUL

1. An editor at Rinehart. 2. Philip Young, who was writing *Ernest Hemingway*
(New York, 1952). On the contretemps with EH see Young's *Ernest Hemingway: A
Reconsideration* (University Park, Pa., 1966), pp. 5–24. 2. Sam Boal, "I Tell You
True," *Park East* 10–11 (December 1950–January 1951).

To CHARLES SCRIBNER, La Finca Vigia, 8 January 1952

Dear Charlie:

I wrote you a couple of stupid letters but just tore them up on
re-reading them to send. They were mostly recounting oddities and
vagaries about Pauline's estate and the children's financial affairs. When
I read them over I realized how much of family money matters you have
had to handle in your life and realized I might spare you these anecdotes.
Even though some of them might have pleased, horrified, or shocked

you. Anyway the two boys will be well off if they take care of their money. Some things, though, I have to tell you sometime when we are together.

Last night when I woke up and could not sleep being absolutely out of books I read as a last bloody recourse that Anniversary book on Scribners by Roger Burlingame [*Of Making Many Books*, 1946]. Charlie when that book can't make me sleep what do you suggest? Did you ever read anything duller about something that must have been very interesting? Have you any other volumes by Burlingame that I could try?

We had a good norther day before yesterday and yesterday and last night it was cold enough to sleep with wife and blankets both. Then after being happy and loveing Mary truly I had to wake up and read Burlingame. Lee Samuels brought me a new thing called Dormison to take which is a sort of near beer of the barbituates. I took two and had a taste as though a very old sea gull had shit in my mouth and lay wide awake with the taste and my thoughts. If you take the world even faintly seriously it is nothing to spend the night thinking about. Last night with the Churchill visit and the Eastern and European picture and Lodge's announcement of Ike's candidacy was a no good night if you get started trying to think things out.

I better stop this letter now and send it off before it starts to get gloomy. Well Washington was a General Officer and he was a good President. Probably the best way is to think about it like that.

I'm certainly glad, selfishly, that I have a book done before it all starts.

Hope you came though the holidays o.k. Let's have a cheerful year anyway no matter how bloody bad it gets.

Mary sends her love to you both.

PUL   Ernest

To THOMAS BLEDSOE, La Finca Vigia, 17 and 31 January 1952

Dear Mr. Bledsoe:

Thank you for your letter of January 10th which arrived last night. It was again delayed by initial insufficient postage.

Due to pauvresse oblige, or whatever it is that writers sometimes have instead of the tweeds and pipes of publishers and critics, I again answer promptly although I am bored with the whole business.

Why, for instance, if you were too busy to answer the prompt reply I wrote to your letter did I not hear from Mr. [Philip] Young? If Mr. Young is not too busy to be reading papers on my work I should think he would not be too busy to write me a letter and send me a copy of the paper he read. Since it was conceded to be the best of a series read on that subject, I would naturally be interested to read it.

If so much mystery had not been built up about this book I would not have had to write any letters about it nor take any position about it. As it is I decided not to be co-operative for the reasons I gave you in my last letter. I tried to explain the position I had taken in a straight and friendly way. To this letter I received no answer for a month.

This is a short, but prompt, note to say that a letter from Mr. Young himself and a copy of the paper that he read on my work in Detroit might clarify things. I hold, very simply, that a critic has a right to write anything he wishes about your work no matter how wrong he may be. I also hold that a critic has no right to write about your private life while you are alive. I am speaking about moral rights; not legal rights. My lawyer handles legal aspects.

I still think too that if I wanted to write a book about a man's work trying to involve it with his life I would first write the man and ask if he had any objections. If he had I would write about someone else who had no objections; or about a man who was dead.

But a letter from Mr. Young might clear all of this up.

I couldn't go along with you on the statement that a joking remark made to Mr. Earl Wilson was a valid basis for justifying a school of criticism. Public psycho-analyzing of liveing writers is most certainly an invasion of privacy.

January 31, 1952

I held this letter up for two weeks so that I would not be the only one mixed up in this business who answers letters promptly. Is it true Mr. Young is in correspondence with another critic in the Sudan? I shall be interested to read his paper and take it there is nothing un-ethical in this. It might help me in my present work.

Yours very truly,

Ernest Hemingway

T.C. PUL

To MRS. CHARLES SCRIBNER, at sea, 18 February 1952

My dear Vera:

Mary went ashore Saturday afternoon in the launch with Gregorio at a place called La Mulata to get ice and when she came back she told me about Charlie.[1] We were both stunned and sick about it. I loved Charlie very much and we were such good friends. It was very hard to accept. You know all about this and there is nothing we can say that makes it any easier.

Mary asked me if I couldn't tell her something that would help her to reconcile herself or anything to console both of us because it was very bad. I told her the best thing was to think of how you and Charlie loved each other and how kind you were to each other when you were here and how proud he was of his children and his work and of you. How fortunate Charlie was to have the good fortune to be a christian and how you had said your prayers together when you were down here.

I said what I could and what I really believed but words are no good in losses as you know.

Please know we love you and that you and the children have all of our true sympathy.

Mary heard about Charlie from René [Villarreal] the house-boy on a phone call. He said Gianfranco had wired you when the cable came. I had written Charlie we were going down the coast and would be out of touch with mail and cables.

It was a lovely trip from Monday until Saturday evening. Then came this news and a big storm came the same night with thunder and lightning (like in the Bible) and the surf pounding on the reef outside of where we lay and the Norther started to blow at six a.m. Today we will get into La Mulata and send this to you on a truck that goes into Guanajay where there is a post office.

Vera I was worried about Charlie dying ever since the time when you were down here. I could tell then how ill he had been and I tried to write him always so as not to worry him. I tried hard too to keep him from going on that Defence inspection trip where he would fly so much. But with no success.

Now my dear and good friend is gone and there is no one to confide in nor trust nor make rough jokes with and I feel so terribly about Charlie being gone that I can't write any more. When we get back I'll write.

Please forgive such a stupid letter. And please know how we feel for you and the children in your sorrow.

Your devoted friend
Ernest

PUL

1. Charles Scribner died in New York on 11 February 1952.

To WALLACE MEYER, La Finca Vigia, 21 February 1952

Dear Wallace:

Thank you for the letter with the details of how Charlie died. It was at the house when we got home last night. As you say there is nothing we can say. I feel terribly to have been away and out of touch when it happened. We were storm bound down the coast when I first heard the news three days after Charlie had been buried. From there I sent a letter to Vera at Far Hills and then came back here the first day the weather would let us. I hope she received the letter. It had to be sent inland to be posted.

Nearly every time I wrote him I tried to get him to take care of himself and I tried especially not to have him make that damned armed forces inspection trip where he had to fly so much. But it didn't do any good.

Wallace you know it doesn't do any good to talk wet. So I will try not to. But I'm glad he died quick and well like that if he had to die. It would have been nicer in his sleep and I had hoped maybe it was that way until I heard from you.

It is pretty gloomy to think about never hearing from him again. You know I used to write him any damned thing with no regard for caution nor discretion and we used to joke a lot and pretty rough. He would write me anything he thought or felt too. He wrote a lot of things he shouldn't have too and I will take good care that none of his letters ever fall in anybody's hands. I don't know what he did about my personal letters to him. But I think you or the family should take great care that nobody gets hold of them nor that they are ever "consulted" by any of the personal approach critics; or any critics or biographers. The personal letters are often libellous, always indiscreet, often obscene and many of them could make great trouble. We each used to write to the other when we felt bad and I used to write to him when I thought he felt bad and that I might cheer him up.

I know what you mean about Max and Charlie. When Max died I did not think I could stand it. We understood each other so well that it was like haveing a part of yourself die. But it happened so there was nothing to do until I saw that there was something to do about Charlie. He was takeing an awful beating filling in for Max and I thought the only thing I could do to give him confidence was to give him absolute loyalty. We had been friends for a long time (although we made friends fairly reluctantly) but finally we got to be very close friends. I used to get angry sometimes and so did he. But when he came down here and I saw how ill he had been dureing a time when I had thought he had been inefficient I knew I must never hurt him nor worry him if I could help it. I wish to Christ I could have done something for him. But what can you do, Wallace? I loved Charlie very much and I understood him and appreciated him I hope and I feel like hell that he is dead.

Now what is going to happen? Who is going to run what? Does Young Charlie have to stay in the Navy?[1] And for how long? Is it you I keep in contact with now? If it is, please don't be sore ever because I was annoyed about whether there was Fossalta, Fornace and Monastir sometimes spelled Monastier. Just remember Wallace that I have a short temper about things being questioned that I have already verified. It is never personal and it is a hangover from a different sort of life than the life of letters.

What do you think about this Rinehart book [Philip Young's *Ernest Hemingway*] complete with attached mysteries. The only reason I told Charlie not to give any permissions in the first place was because Cowley told me it was a book where the author wanted to prove I was all of my characters and that he had read the book and sent it back for extensive revision. Then there seemed to be some mystery about the whole thing and it seemed it was a psychoanalysis of me etc. There was never any frankness or clarity about the book and I have only just now (last night) received a letter from the author. I didn't want to bother Charlie with the correspondence. What I wish to avoid is giveing the book any publicity or importance by seeming to have held it up. I am sure it will be dull enough to die of its own weight (although, from the mystery there may be something vicious about it) if it is not given publicity. But for reasons which I wrote to Charlie I am opposed to writing about the private lives of liveing authors and psychoanalysing them while they are alive.

Criticism is getting all mixed up with a combination of the Junior F.B.I.-men, discards from Freud and Jung and a sort of Columnist peep-hole and missing laundry list school. Mizener made money and did some pretty atrocious things (to young Scotty and any offspring she might have) with his book on Scott and every young English professor sees gold in them dirty sheets now. Imagine what they can do with the soiled sheets of four legal beds by the same writer and you can see why their tongues are slavering (this may not be the correct word. If not you please supply it).

Will stop now, Wallace, and not bother you further. I was going to take two months vacation or a month and a month before I started going over the book again. But I got six days and then the news of Charlie's death. So for your information I will be here for a week or ten days say, try to put everything in order and then try and get the rest. Slept well every night until I heard about Charlie and felt refreshed and good. Last blood pressure was 125 over 60. Haven't had a cardiograph since Italy when they were all surprized to find my heart was excellent. All I have is over-work and over-worry. But I come back very quickly with a rest. We went to bed every night by nine thirty and woke at six thirty with the sun and usually fished four or five hours and then read and took it easy in the afternoons.

Please let me know anything I should do. Please let me know about Vera.

I will write to young Charlie.

All my best to you and please know how I appreciate your loss and your difficulties. Please write me frankly about anything at all times. My present situation is that after the heavy work and problems of last year I still need some more healthy rest in order to work at my best. My health is the main capital I have and I want to administer it intelligently.

Best always,
Ernest

PUL

1. Charles Scribner, Jr., served in the U.S. Navy from 1943 to 1946 and 1950 to 1952, attaining the rank of lieutenant.

To HARVEY BREIT, La Finca Vigia, 24 February 1952

Dear Harvey:

I was glad to get your note because I was worried, not hearing, that you might have been upset that I was worthless to you on the Burlesque project. Glad it wasn't so.

Listen, kid, vitamins are good for you. They cost money but they are worth it. I'll tell you my own experience. Then at least try Combex which is a composite of the various B1 Vitamins.

When I work I work so hard that I nearly work myself to death. If I am not tired I know I haven't worked as hard as I should have. But I always try to stop while I am going good and know what is going to happen next. That way you can always go on.

But just the same one day when I was writing for Whom The Bell Tolls I was so tired that I could hardly get up out of bed. Dr. Kohly our family physician here told me to stay in bed for two or three days and eat well and quit drinking so much iced tea (I drink tea when I work like rummies drink beer) and he started me on Combex. Also Afaxin (Vitamin A). The combination was just like a shot in the arm. I couldn't get tired no matter how hard I would work.

Then later I found out that Vitamin B1 (Combex) cancels out any effect that drinking may have on your nerves. It can't hurt you and it can help you tremendously. I take four or five capsules every morning. I used to feed it to all the guys on the boat in the war and we called it the morale vitamin.

I don't think this is tampering with nature. You live in a big city and fill your lungs with all kinds of dirt and soot and live un-naturally and drink for relief, not for pleasure, and all this raises hell with you and anything that corrects it is good for you.

The last time Paul De Kruif was down here he brought me some stuff called Vi-Syneral put out by the U.S. Vitamin corporation. There are two capsules; one dark which has all the vitamins you need, and one white which has all the minerals you need. You take one of each each day. I know these couldn't hurt you and they might be good for you in combination with the extra Vitamin B1.

Then if you are really run down and fatigued and gloomy there is no reason why you shouldn't take Methyltestosterone. You don't have to take it as a shot in the ass. And it is not to make you fornicate more. Paul explained to me that it was good for the head and for the whole general system. He gave it to me in the form called Metandren Linguets put out by CIBA Pharmaceutical Products Inc. Summit N.J. They are small tablets and I am supposed to take one a day dissolveing it under the tongue. Actually I forget to take them for several months and then if I start to feel low, or tired or drag ass I start them again. When Paul wanted me to take them I explained to him that I had no need for any sexual stimulation and didn't want to take anything that would get me into any more trouble than I got into already. But he explained that this was something that kept your head in good shape and counter-acted the gloominess everybody gets.

I'm not trying to practice medicine without a license and I'm not advising you to take anything. But I thought I should tell you my experience with Vitamins especially B1 which I have used steadily since Dr. Kohly gave it to me when I was writing FWTBT and all through the war. I know it is good to take after drinking as what alcohol hits is the nerves and Vitamin B1 in large doses absolutely counteracts it. They straighten out people with Dt's now by injections of B1.

You ought to ask a Dr. about Testosterone. But I am sure the Vitamin B1 could do you no harm.

Hope this isn't just a bore to you. But I hate to think of you fatigued, weary and low in your head if there is something simple and not harmful that would relieve the condition.

We have two damned good doctors down here and by following Dr. Jose Luis Herrera's advice and by takeing only these medicines he okayed and keeping my weight down I brought my blood pressure down from 225 over 125 to 135 over 65. I have a lot of luck in that he has known me as a medical and surgical subject since 1937 when he was a surgeon with the 12th Int. Brigade. One of the things medical people are finding out is, finally, that all people are different. This is especially true about alcohol. He says that my tolerance for alcohol is about ten times that of a normal person; or more. But that I shouldn't abuse it. Nor should I abuse my capacity for work.

I've been good about drinking for a long time now. Not because I get tight or feel bad. But to give myself all the edge I can. But I can remember one time in 1942 comeing in when the weather was too bad to stay out and running into Guillermo the great Basque pelota player at the Floridita. It was about ten thirty in the morning and he had played the night before and lost and I was feeling beat-up. We drank seventeen double frozen Daiquiris apiece in the course of the day without leaveing the bar except for an occasional trip to the can. Each double had 4 ounces of rum in it. That makes 68 ounces of rum. But there was no sugar in the drinks and we each ate two steak sandwiches. He left finally because he had to go to the Fronton to be a judge at the Jai-Alai that night. I drank one more double and went home and read all night.

We met the next day at the bar at noon and had a couple of frozen Daiquiris. We both felt good and neither one of us had been drunk and there was no compulsion to go on drinking and neither one of us had a hangover. Guillermo has been playing professional pelota since he was a boy wonder at twelve. He has used cocaine and smoked marijuana for more than fifteen years and can and does quit any day he feels like it and stays away from narcotics for months at a time. Then when he gets with bad companions he will use them again. He's forty five now; still a professional athlete in the fastest ball game in the world. Try and figure that out.

I've never taken dope of any kind nor ever smoked marijuana so I don't know anything about that. But have you ever heard of people who could start and stop on drugs like Guillermo and have them have absolutely no effect on their reflexes? I've known quite a lot of boxers who used narcotics but they were all addicts sooner or later. With ball players it was drinking in the nights; the solitary drinking to keep the nervousness away. Has anybody ever written any stories about that?

Harvey please think about the vitamin stuff I wrote. If I have a constitution like a mule and I need them I don't think you should be ashamed to use what has been provided for us when you work under much greater strain and under vastly less healthy conditions than I do. Please try the B1 COMBEX. It is made by Parke Davis and I know it can't hurt you and might make you feel better.

I saw no sense in [Edmund] Wilson and I quarreling with so many of our friends dead and other people going to pieces in various pompous ways.

Mary and I were on what I hoped was going to be my austerity vacation before I started re-working again. But poor Charlie Scribner died and I had to come back. We were haveing a wonderful time; going to bed at 9 or 9.30, sleeping well, getting up at daylight and fishing until the middle of the day in the Tin Kid and then reading or loafing and reading in the afternoon. Am going to get out again as soon as we can. Mary had a wonderful time and we caught a boatload of fish that filled the deep freeze and paid for the gas and the ice. I'd wanted to go to Paris. But this is sounder. This is the year I am going to try to be good; not speak badly about people; no fights; not commit adultery; not etc. But to carry out the program am going to have to go to sea often and keep out of the way of a lot of shits that I know. Project number one is that we've got to get you to feeling better.

Write because I'll get it sooner or later. Probably won't leave here now until the end of next week. Would write more about Charlie Scribner but there's no use ever discussing casualties.

HUL   Ernest

To CHARLES SCRIBNER, JR., La Finca Vigia, 25 February 1952

Dear Charlie:

It would seem strange to call your father Charlie and then address you as Mr. Scribner. But I can do it if you would prefer and if it makes things any simpler.

Please know how badly I felt to be away and out of touch when your father died. We must have left the harbor about an hour before he felt ill from what Wallace Meyer and [Alfred] Rice wrote me and Mary brought word of his death the following Saturday evening. From down the coast we tried to write your mother how Mary and I felt about him. But I do not even know if she received the letter as it had to be sent inland to be posted.

I won't try to write to you how much he meant to me as a friend and as a publisher. He was the best and closest friend that I had and it seems impossible that I will never have another letter from him. It does not do any good to talk about it and there is nothing to say that makes it any easier. Since he had to die at least he has gotten it over with.

If there is anything practical I can do please let me know. After the

March 15 income tax has been paid I will plan to draw nothing more on my loan account this year except for the four payments of $750 that Rice figures must be made against 1952 tax. Please cancel the monthly payment of $100. a month to Gregory Hemingway as of March First ie. make no payment on March First nor thereafter. As soon as the money is paid me for the cinema rights to Across The River and Into the Trees I will pay something to reduce my loan account. There is $25,000 in escrow as an advance against ten percent of the gross in that picture deal. But the picture people still have to fulfill certain requirements before it is paid. When I talked to Rice on the phone he was optimistic about them raising all their money. This is the first time he has been optimistic and told me this is the type of deal that cannot be hurried. It is a good property and there is no sense in makeing a forced sale when it is possible to wait.

I will try and not worry you about finances nor about anything else. You don't have to write me letters nor have me on your mind in any way. I know what a terribly tough job you have now with Navy, Estate and the House of Scribner to look after. They shouldn't do that to any human being. Please take it as easy as you can and feel free to call on me in any way that I can be of help. If there is anything Mary and I can do for your Mother please let us know. She likes Mary and she likes the sea and to fish and she might like to come down some time and stay with us and get some fishing with Mary.

I plan to pick up the vacation where we left it and not worry about anything nor think of things that can't be helped and keep on getting in the best of shape to hit the book again. On the boat we were getting to bed at nine, sleeping well, getting up at daylight and fishing all forenoon and reading and loafing in the afternoon. I could feel the batteries rechargeing every day. It is not fair to *anyone* not to keep in shape to do your best work and I am going to get in the best shape I can now no matter what other things have to [take] second priority for the necessary time. I've over-worked for 18 months.

This is not a good letter, Charlie. But I still feel too sad to write a good one.

> Your friend
> Ernest Hemingway

Am sorry I don't know your rank so address this as a civilian.

PUL   EH

To WALLACE MEYER, La Finca Vigia, 4 and 7 March, 1952

Dear Wallace:

Thank you very much for your letter. You could not have written one explaining more clearly the whole picture nor one that gave me the details I needed to know about Charlie's death. I've had to write many letters about how people died and how good and well loved they were. But usually you have to be so careful about how they died in the letter that it is worthless. I thank you very much for the letter.

With this letter I am sending you an un-corrected typescript of The Old Man and The Sea. I do not want to correct it nor attempt to retitle it until I have done the two weeks of the second part of the austerity vacation Mary and I are going to under-take next week. But it is [in] such shape that you will know what you think about it. Please do not let anyone outside of the office nor anyone not of your complete confidence read it.

It is 26,531 words in length. It may be impossible to publish a book of this length. But I know that in the history of publishing there have been books of this length which have had an extraordinary and continued sale. I will not try to point out to you what virtues or implicaciones (mis-spelled) it has. But I know that it is the best I can write ever for all of my life I think, and that it destroys good and able work by being placed alongside of it. I'll try to write better but it will be tough. Please do not think that I am haveing a rush of conceit to the head. I am a professional writer and I know something about this piece of work. It is not a short story nor a novella. I would rather have your opinion of it than to try to sound off with what I know about it.

So far I only showed it to Charlie and his wife and to various friends of mine including the boy who edits Cosmopolitan. It had a very strange effect on all of them. It affected all of them in a stronger way than anything that I have ever written. While I was writing it you can more or less imagine the effect it had on me after you have read it. It is the epilogue to my long book. But it is a complete unit in its-self. Actually the book, when properly finished, does not need an epilogue. But this can always be republished as such; or as an epilogue to all my writing and what I have learned, or tried to learn, while writing and trying to live. This sounds grandiose. It will go at the end of the book where it belongs.

Leland Hayward, who has just read it while here in Havana on vacation, suggests that it could be published in a single issue of LIFE. I don't know whether that would be better than publication in a single issue of The New Yorker. Of course neither of them might want it. The editor of Cosmopolitan wanted to publish it in a single number but his budget only allowed him to pay $10,000 for it and I told Charlie that I did not think that was worthwhile compensation for the loss of surprise and shock of anyone comeing on it suddenly in a book.

But now I think it should be a separate book and be published this fall if your schedule permits. It could be moderately priced and would not take too much paper for costs.

You will know what you think of it when you read it. Tactically, publishing it now will get rid of the school of criticism that I am through as a writer. It will destroy the school of criticism that claims I can write about nothing except myself and my own experiences. That would give us, in the long run, a great strategical advantage. These martial terms are extremely tedious. But no more than always hearing Generals talk in terms of foot-ball, a game I always thought you could get very tired of without even playing it.

I am tired of not publishing anything. Other writers publish short books. But I am supposed to always lay back and come in with War and Peace or Crime and Punishment or be considered a bum. This is probably very bad for a writer and I will bet it did more to wreck poor old Scott than anything except Zelda, himself and booze. I know Max would have been happy with a truly good and sound book from Scott. But Scott tried to be a better writer than he was and he threw the ball over the grandstand (where I must throw this typewriter if it isn't over-hauled).

I would like to publish this book now. Publish the next book that I have worked so damned hard on next and keep on like that. This book comes out again with the other as added value. The other one, long, is a hell of a good book and this comes after as a million dollar postscript.

On the practical side books that have had no size and sold in great amounts were (not to make comparisons but only speaking technically) Dicken's Christmas Carol, The Story of the Other Wise Man, Mary Raymond Shipman Andrew's story about the Gettysburg Address (may have author's and characters mixed on this), and The Man Without a Country[1] Your researchers would turn up more and give you the figures on these.

I know that my own dislike of Jones book[2] which was a wonderful selling volume, aside from it being psychopathic and Over-The-Hilly was its weight and length. There is always the certainty that the tide turns. People, possibly, might like to handle a good non-overweight book where a man shows what a human being is capable of and the dignity of the human soul without the word soul being capitalized.

I held this letter up to think it over and to see if Hayward had the same re-action about it as he had originally. They left yesterday and he and his wife felt as strongly about it as when they first read it. She is a very intelligent girl that I have known for many years and is a very tough critic.

Hayward suggested that the Book of the Month club might take it as a selection along with another full sized book. He said that he wanted to have lunch with the editor of LIFE and talk the Mss. over with him. I asked him to wait until after Scribners had read it. In times like these I do not want you or young Charlie to have any impression that I am going over anybody's heads in anything. You will naturally hear the usual false rumours that I am negotiating with other publishers etc. There is no way from [of] stopping those lies. But never believe a word of any movement of mine that you do not hear from me.

Charlie wrote me a couple of times asking me if I did not want to serialize this and to be sure to do so if I wanted to. I hinted to him several times that it would make a book (as any of the four sections of the long book about the sea would) but I did not want to press him or worry him.

If you will send the MSS. back to me after Scribners has read it then I will go over it on my return from this trip that we start on Monday and send it to Hayward. I will pick up mail in a week and be back almost surely in two weeks. It would be better to read it over now and correct it for final form on a time basis. But I want to see it absolutely clear and fresh when I do that. Charlie's death really knocked hell out of me. Hearing of it so long after it happened made it much worse in it's impact. When you are present and can do something, or know you can do nothing, you accept something at once through its actuality. I remember how I could not let my father's death make any impression on me until I had finished re-write on A Farewell To Arms. Then it moved in properly. I wrote another novel then.[3] But it was written with my heart cauterized and I'm glad I knew enough not to publish it.

This you will read I have read about twenty times beside reading all of it from the beginning each day I wrote it. Am sure there is not much I would change, or any, except to correct any errors in Mary's typeing or in my spelling. But there always might be someway I could make it better. But I [am] sure it is in good enough shape to let you form an opinion.

I will stop now Wallace as I must write you a letter on that Rinehart book. What a waste of time all that is. If you have any reactions or ideas on the Mss. I send you that you think justify a cable I will get any cables or letters that arrive here March 13th on the night of the 14th. A boy from here is going to bring them down the coast.

Good luck Wallace. I hope I am bringing you a victory instead of makeing you trouble and worry.

Ernest

1. The short books enumerated, all of which EH probably read in childhood, are Mrs. Andrews's *The Perfect Tribute* (1906); Henry Van Dyke, *The Story of the Other Wise Man* (1896); and Edward Everett Hale, *The Man Without a Country* (first published 1863). 2. James Jones, *From Here to Eternity* (New York, 1951). See EH to Charles Scribner, 5 March 1951. 3. EH probably means the Jimmy Breen book, *A New Slain Knight*, which he had abandoned in favor of *A Farewell to Arms*.

To PHILIP YOUNG, La Finca Vigia, 6 March 1952

Dear Mr. Young:

If you give me your word that the book is not biography disguised as criticism and that it is not a psycho-analytical study of a living writer I have no objection to your quoting from my books if Scribner's has none.

I have written the late Mr. Charles Scribner and Mr. Bledsoe why I am opposed to biography of liveing writers. There is no use going over that again.

But do you know it can be as damageing to a man while he is writing in the middle of his work to tell him that he is suffering from a neurosis as to tell him that he has cancer? The man himself can say "oh shit." But he has been damaged with everyone who reads him. And I have known writers who could be damaged by such statements to such an extent they could no longer write.

Regret *truly* that you have had delay with your book. But your first delay came from [Malcolm] Cowley who advised revisions I understand. I had never heard of the book until he wrote me about it.

If you are going to publish the book it certainly should have the necessary quotations to attempt to prove any theories of legitimate literary criticism you may hold.

But my opposition to public psycho-analyzing of living people and my conception of the damage this may do the people is not merely personal. It is a matter of principle.

I thought your paper, that you so kindly sent me, was very interesting; but fairly shocking in the way the three critics and their critic lightly used serious medical terms without, as far as I knew, being medically qualified to pronounce such judgements even in private. This is not a personal crack nor an attempt to be rude nor smart. I was interested in the paper and in your conclusions but shocked at the ir-responsibility of some of the statements made in public.

Does this letter bring us any closer to an understanding? I am writing with complete good will and frankness.

It seems to me, truly, that there are enough dead writers to deal with to allow the living to work in peace. From my own stand point, as writer, I have so far had worry, annoyance and severe interruption of my work from this book. Worry from Cowley writing me, un-solicited, that he was recommending extensive revisions. Later when I asked him what the hell it was all about he could not tell me because of the ethics involved. Then later I heard that he was washing his hands of it; wanted nothing to do with it and was returning his fee. No part of this is good for some one who is trying to keep his peace of mind and work well with, in one year, the death of his first grand-son in Berlin where his son was stationed as a Capt. of Infantry; the death of his mother; serious illness of his father-in-law with cancer; death of his former wife and mother of two of his sons; suicide of the maid servant of this house (one previous attempt); had kept her on and tried to pull her out of it; then last the death of my last old friend in Africa and then the death of my very dear friend and publisher Charlie Scribner. All this time I have tried to work steadily and well and this mystery about your book and now the neurosis or neuroses charges at Detroit have been of little help.

Hope you are haveing good luck yourself *truly*. Around here the last 12 months have been rough.

With best wishes

Ernest Hemingway

It is hot today and your (i.e. my) forearm sweats onto the paper.

T.C. PUL

To PHILIP YOUNG, La Finca Vigia, 27 May 1952

Dear Mr. Young:

You will have received my cable of this date and you also have my letter to you about your Detroit paper and the objections I made to it and the project of a biographical and psycho-analytical study.

I have made my stand on this thing throughout as a matter of principle and have explained it to you and Mr. Bledsoe at some length. He wants to get a book out and you say that whether you and your wife eat depends on it. I would maintain my stand with Mr. Bledsoe forever. But I feel damned badly at your work, however mistaken I believe it to be, being held up and you yourself being thwarted and your liveing imperilled.

I had written you a six page letter stateing why I did not believe you should publish the book. But since I have given you the rights to use the quotations it could only worry you. I am writing Scribner's to pay to you my share of whatever Mr. Bledsoe pays Scribner's for the rights to quote and I would be happy if you would quote more extensively than you have if economy in quotation has been to hold down costs.

In this way perhaps I can make up to you whatever my six weeks delay in answering your letter has cost you.

I am very sorry, kid, if you are up the creek financially. I can let you have $200. if you need it and you can feel free to call me a son of a bitch if you wish. If you are broke you cannot be sued and collected from. That would be the publishers.

Yours sincerely,

PH. PUL   Ernest Hemingway

To ADRIANA IVANCICH, La Finca Vigia, 31 May 1952

My Dearest Adriana:

I have never been prouder of you and it seems as though I have been proud of you ever since I can remember.[1] Enclosed is the letter I had from Wallace Meyer this morning. The coperto [*copertina* = book jacket] they took is the one of the hill with the fine apartments and of the shacks where you made the sketches of old Anselmo and the bay and the blue gulf behind. It is really splendid. Just what I would have wanted if I had brains enough to ask for it. Gianfranco and Mary both thought it was wonderful too.

At the start they said there was no time and that they must have a cover at once. They sent me down three awful ones and I cabled you the same day and wrote Scribner's that you knew the story and the sea and the houses and the Old Man and that I would guaranty that impossible as it seemed you would have the cover there on time. I knew it was wicked to ask anybody to do anything that fast. But I also knew the kind of Great Black Horse you were and that the more difficult or impossible a thing is the better you can do it. This sounds like compliments I know but it is the honest to God truth.

If I could only have been there to celebrate with you when you had finished. I think we have what triumphs we have at much too great a distance from each other. But the air-mail is fast. But it is not the same as to hold you tight in an abrazo [hug] and tell you how proud I am of you and how wonderful I think you are.

The best thing to me is not the speed nor the reliability but the steady improvement in the quality. The drawing of the fisherman's shacks and the bait-house and the composition is superb and the boats are perfect. Everything that was wrong with the boats is gone. I cannot wait to see the colour of the ocean nor the other copertini. Maybe they can use them in a window exhibition when the book comes out. I will suggest that to Meyer. Could I have them send them down so I can see them and tell you which ones I think about for other publishers? Or do you want them back right away? Let me know.

I don't know how much he means by paying very well. But it should be good. I wrote him I would pay for everything if they were not acceptable but that I was sure they would be. It would have [been] tragic to have a book without your cover. But it was only you and your wonderful speed and promptness and SUFFICIENT POSTAGE that made it possible.

I must send this fast now with nothing else but love from Mary and Gianfranco and congratulations from everybody.

You are wonderful, daughter, and I thank you very much and love you very much and am *so so so* proud of you.

con todos errores [with all mistakes]
Papa

> *Viva El Torre Blanco*[2]
> *Viva!*
> *Viva La Sociadad Anonima (Inc.)*
> *(Un momento de Silencio) Viva!*

TEXAS

1. Adriana had drawn a jacket design for *The Old Man and the Sea*. 2. The White Tower was EH's name for the new tower at La Finca Vigia where he and Adriana had sometimes worked together as the "Anonymous Society," or "Corporation."

To CHARLES A. FENTON, La Finca Vigia, 18 June 1952

Dear Mr. Fenton:

I'm sorry my letter made you sore and that you wrote the letter you sent. Last night I wrote you a three page letter. But I will try now, at first light, to write you cold and straight and not in anger. We will let the stuff about haveing the wind up etc. go by. I have seen enough people blow up to understand it and I know how straight I tried to help you on what you said your project was and I know from many first lights that I am not too windy a character. Dry-mouthed many times; not likeing it; sure. But windy; no and usually cheerful.

Here is the point. I had a wonderful novel to write about Oak Park and would never do it because I did not want to hurt liveing people. I did not think that a man should make money out of his father shooting himself nor out of his mother who drove him to it. . . . Tom Wolfe wrote only of his own life with rhetoric added. I wanted to write about the whole damned world if I could get to know it. When I started I wrote some short stories about actual things and two of them hurt people. I felt bad about it. Later if I used actual people I used only those for whom I had completely lost respect and then I tried to give them a square shake. I know this all sounds very noble but it is not really horse-shit. The man [Harold Loeb] who identifies himself as Cohn in The Sun Also Rises once said to me, "But why did you make me cry all the time?"

I said, "Listen, if that is you then the narrator must be me. Do you think that I had my prick shot off or that if you and I had ever had a fight I would not have knocked the shit out of you? We boxed often enough so you know that. And I'll tell you a secret: you do cry an awful lot for a man."

So now we get back to Oak Park where you feel it your duty as a scholar (when does a writer get to be a scholar and have these obligations?) to dig into my family while I am still alive. . . . Nobody in Oak Park likes me I should suppose. The people that were my good friends are dead or gone. I gave Oak Park a miss and never used it as a target. You wouldn't like to bomb your home town would you? Even if it ceased to be your home town the day you could leave it?

When you go into my family, etc. it is to me an invasion of privacy and I gave you the cease and desist. There are defensible interpretations for any violation of ethics or good taste. But I think you will agree that if I had written about Oak Park you would have a point in studying it. But I did not write about it.

I know it is better to have a straight guy write about your work than a crook. I think of you as a straight guy. But nobody likes to be tailed. That is not a sign that you are windy. It is a sign that you do not like to be tailed, investigated, queried about, by any amateur detective no matter how scholarly or how straight. You ought to be able to see that, Fenton. It was one of the rights that was agreed upon, in principle at least, when our ancestors set up the country.

Then take the [Lionel] Moise thing.[1] I tried to remember if I had ever helped get Moise home when he was stabbed by either a whore or somebody's husband and whether I was present when he threw a typewriter through the window of the press room at police headquarters and I honestly could not. In newspaper work you have to learn to forget every day what happened the day before. Everything was wonderful to me in Kansas City (that sounds like a line from a song) but I was working on a newspaper and so I cannot remember as I should. You might note for your book that newspaper work is valuable up until the point that it forcibly begins to destroy your memory. A writer must leave it before that point. But he will always have the scars from it. Just as any experience of war is invaluable to a writer. But it is destructive if he has too much. You could probably write on this better than I could. If you had not served as well and as long as you did you would probably be writing instead of teaching writing and rideing herd on my childhood.

But I know too bloody well that Hurtgen Forest was much more destructive to me than instructive.

Let's drop Dave Randall [of Scribners' Rare Book Department]. I never should have picked it up in the first place.

Hope you take this in the spirit in which it is written. I trusted you completely on your project. But it was getting out of hand. The proof of that is the extent to which you wrote you had been urged to extend it. Do you agree?

Write me what you think and lay off the words that provoke with guys like ourselves. Maybe I should not include myself in people like us. But I have certain ethical standards about prose in spite of my marriages, my blunders etc. as you list them. Maybe when you are 52 going on 53 you will have some blunders too. There are usually some reasons for the marriages and I hope to Christ I never give them. The writing published in books is what I stand on and I would like people to leave my private life the hell alone. What right has anyone to go into it? I say no right at all.

Best luck *truly* luck

T.C. PUL

Ernest Hemingway

1. On Moise, see Carlos Baker, *Ernest Hemingway: A Life Story* (New York, 1969), p. 35.

To HARVEY BREIT, La Finca Vigia, 21 June 1952

Dear Harvey:

I'm sorry about asking you to send the damn letter back. It was just that I had written you a two page one that I couldn't send because it had too many things that could be violations of Tunero's confidences and then wrote this one and the Pamplona part sounded braggy and self righteous. I knew you wouldn't mind too much and would forgive it. But I didn't have time to write another letter and so instead of tearing it up I said to send it back. I should have said to tear it up. Please excuse me.

Brennan [Gerald Brenan] wrote two other good books; one a definitive book on Spanish literature and the other on a trip to Spain a couple of years ago, travelling around Spain with a visit to Granada looking for where Lorca was buried. Both were reviewed in the Sunday section. I've loaned them both out so I haven't got the titles. But you can get them from the index. They came out last year.

Has Wallace Meyer ever sent you the page proof yet? I hope so.

This will be a dull letter because I got too much sun on my head sitting on my ass on a rock while Eisenstadt from LIFE took colour shots for a cover for them. The sun here is the same as the Sudan (same latitude) and it is June and 92 in the shade and I was sitting bareheaded for two or three hours. You explain it isn't doing you any good etc. and then finally you just say, "Oh shit," and keep on. But it knocked the hell out of my head. The last day Eisenstadt nearly got a sun stroke himself when he forgot his cap. Then he realized what the sun was. On the Pilar in the hot months I always put a couple of thicknesses, or three, of folded paper towells on my head and the tennis eye shade holds them on when I am steering up on the flying bridge. If I have to fight a big fish in the sun any length of time they keep sloshing me with buckets of salt water. That keeps your head cool. But sitting in one place out in the sun in June in these latitudes without a hat is no good. Much less when your head's been hurt bad on the top three or four times.

I read Lillian Ross's last piece[1] in an advance copy day before yesterday and I thought it all added up to a fine and terribly sad story. I think it makes a better story than most novels. I'm glad their new editor has a winner with this thing. He must be a good editor because he was checking on it all along and Lillian wrote me that he liked it. I was spooked about it because she worked on it for so damned long. But it was worth it all right. I don't know about the calling business. The first time I met her was in Ketchum, Ida. I was sitting on the can and I heard Patrick talking to some woman outside. It was the day before

Christmas and I didn't know who the hell it could be. Then Patrick explained that this was a lady he had met in San Francisco who wanted to talk to me about a piece she was writing about Sidney Franklin and he had said of course papa would be delighted to see her but had forgotten to tell me she was comeing. We were liveing in two log cabins and I had invited the guys who had been on the boat with me in the war to spend Christmas and all expenses paid and we were going to spend the money I was going to get from a contract with Mark Hellinger. Unfortunately Mark Hellinger had died a few days before and I had given back the money on the phone because I felt badly about his poor widow who it eventually turned out inherited into the millions. Anyway Lillian had a good Christmas with us and so did the boys and [Juan] Dunabeitia and Roberto Herrera. But everything was financed in a bold but sketchy manner. I think she liked our general gaiety and not giving a damn and was trying to pay a tribute to that in the New Yorker. People got the impression that I was just a stumble bum. But I am sure that her idea was that people knew I was a serious writer and she was showing that I was relaxed when not working.

You know lots of criticism is written by characters who are very academic and think it is a sign you are worthless if you make jokes or kid or even clown. I wouldn't kid Our Lord if he was on the cross. But I would attempt a joke with him if I ran into him chaseing the money changers out of the temple.

This reminds me of my journal two fragments of which I am encloseing. You have to send them back if you don't mind. But if you want to have them copied so you can bind them and keep them on your night table please do so. Charlie [Poore] might like to read them as he is an old friend of Goya. The reason to send them back is I have no copies. Will make copies from now on in.

Probably I better knock off now and write some more on my Journal.

Do you think maybe with the publication of my Journal I will be able to become an *Homme des Lettres?*

It has always been my ambition.

Yours in belle *lettres*
Ernest

Encl. *A Journal*

Fragments from Ernst von Hemingstein's JOURNAL

Friday. — Saw Valery. He looked very poorly. We both agreed Joyce's eyes were bad and that Gide is now impotent. Fargue is dead. A pity.

Saturday. — The Scribners (father and son) are publishing my The Sun Also Rises. It is a treatise on basic loneliness and the inadequacy of promiscuity. Perkins the Scribners editor is enthused. Not as much for the moral content but what he naively calls the dialogue. I must study how to eliminate this as well as the over-long description of the Spanish country side.

Monday. — Lunched at Lipps with two young American writers. [Selden] Rodman and [William H.] Hale. Liked Rodman. Hale a bit over-promising.

Tuesday. — Drunk with Joyce in the literal rather than the figurative sense.

Wednesday. — Learned Fargue is alive not dead. Splendid. Another report on Gide this time from ******. Most depressing. Learned that the young man Hale was not the son of Nathan Hale as I had supposed.

Thursday. — Commenced writing a new novel. It is to be called A Farewell to Arms and treats of war on the Italian front which I visited briefly as a boy after the death of Henry James. A strange coincidence. Some difficulty about deciding how the book will end. Solved it finally.

Friday. — Attended the Crucifixion of our Lord. Tintoretto was there. He took copious notes and appeared to be very moved. Dined with Goya. He asserted the entire spectacle was a fraud. He was his usual irascible self but sound company. He says Joyce drinks too much and confirmed several new anecdotes of Gide. The unfortunate Gide it seemed was refused admission to the Crucifixion as they had decided (officially) to call it. Goya offered me La Alba for the evening. Really charming of him. A well spent evening.

HUL   [The journal continues for four more pages.]

1. "Picture," on the making of M-G-M's *Red Badge of Courage* by John Huston. See Lillian Ross, *Reporting* (New York, 1964), pp. 223–442.

To HARVEY BREIT, La Finca Vigia, 27 June 1952

Dear Harvey:

Thanks for sending me the Faulkner quote.[1] He did not forget what the occasion was that I wrote him that. He remembers it very well. In one of his rummy moments (I hope) he had said, flatly, that I was a coward.[2] The Trib picked it up (the lecture was reprinted) and I sent it to Brig. Gen. C. T. Lanham, former commander of the 22nd Infantry Regt. We had been together a long time in 1944–5 and I let him write

Faulkner. We both received apologies from Faulkner who wrote that I had not the courage to experiment or take a chance in writing etc. (See Requiem for a Nun on how to take a chance when rum dumb). No criticism on personal courage.

I wrote Faulkner a friendly letter which he quotes and now says "resemble the wolves who are wolves only in pack, and singly, are just another Dog."

Figure that one out.

OK to continue with the record. He spoke well of me once, as you wrote me. But that was before he was given the Nobel Prize. When I read he had won that, I sent him as good a cable of congratulations as I know how to write. He never acknowledged it. For years I had built him up in Europe. Any time anyone asked me who was the best American writer I told them Faulkner. Everytime anyone wanted me to talk about me I would talk about him. I thought he had a rotten deal and I did everything I knew to see he got a better shake. I never told people he couldn't go nine innings, nor why, nor what I knew was wrong with him since always.

So he writes to you as though I was asking him a favour to protect me. Me, the dog. I'll be a sad son of a bitch. He made a speech, very good. I knew he could never, now, or ever again write up to his speech. I also knew I could write a book better and straighter than his speech and without tricks nor rhetoric.

Harvey at this point I started to get sore and so I cut the rough part out. The point is that Faulkner in that very strange statement acts as though I had asked him for help (being a dog) and he was kind enough to say I didn't need it really. This is damned nice of him.

You see what happens with Bill Faulkner is that as long as I am alive he has to drink to feel good about haveing the Nobel prize. He does not realize that I have no respect for that institution and was truly happy for him when he got it. I cabled him how pleased I was truly and he would not answer. Now he comes out with this wolves and the dog stuff and the condescension of how he rated what remains, which I take it, must include Death In The Afternoon etc.

He writes this *without* haveing read the book which you asked him if he wanted to review. It adds up to a very strange statement. Maybe I am just a sore-headed, touchy bastard. I know that I am sometimes and I deplore it. But why couldn't he just say he wasn't writing reviews or was disqualified (as I told you I was on Orwell's book). Why the strange statement as though I needed defence and was *not* really a dog? He even got involved in repetition in the second and third paragraphs of that statement.

You asked me what I think of all this. This is how: I don't want any part of Faulkner's statement. He is a good writer when he is good and could be better than anyone if he knew how to finish a book and didn't get that old heat prostration like Honest Sugar Ray at the end. I enjoy reading him when he is good but always feel like hell that he is not better. I wish him luck and he needs it because he has the one great and un-curable defect; you can't re-read him. When you re-read him you are conscious all the time of how he fooled you the first time. In truly good writing no matter how many times you read it you do not know how it is done. That is because there is a mystery in all great writing and that mystery does not dis-sect out. It continues and it is always valid. Each time you re-read you see or learn something new. You do not just see the mechanics of how you were tricked in the first place. Bill had some of this at one time. But it is long gone. A real writer should be able to make this thing which we do not define with a simple declarative sentence.

Criticism class is out.

I am very, very happy that Alice [Mrs. Breit] liked the book. I wrote you how happy I was that you liked it. I hope they hit on somebody of good judgment and without prejudice who does like the book to review it. But if they don't it is just the book's and my bad luck.

Best always
Ernest

P.S. I'm sure I am too hard on Faulkner. But I know I am not as hard on him as I am on myself. I'll be 53 on July 21st and I have been trying to write well since I can remember. I would rather have written this last book with no shit and no compromise and know how many people will read it than anything I know. And I don't have to drink to have the feeling inside about it. What I want to do now is forget it and try and write a better one.

Please do not speak about any of this to Faulkner. I do not want any quarrels. If he had wanted to review the book when he read it that would [be] fine.[3] But to make statements *without* reading it is chicken. But I want no quarrel nor trouble with him and I wish him luck and hope Anomatopeoio [Yoknapatawpha] county will last as long as the Sea. I wouldn't trade him counties. But he picked his. I feel cramped in a county, any county. But he has done a damned good job on his and I hope it always keeps him happy and satisfied. Yesterday got one 176 lbs and saw a son of a bitch as long and big around as a saw log. He couldn't make up his mind that he wanted to eat. Going out now. Mary's folks are ill again and we want to get in one more day together before she has to leave to go and stay with them a while. Am sorry I mentioned

Faulkner. But I promise I wouldn't if you hadn't brought him up. Let's forget him unless he writes when he reads the book.

HUL

1. On 20 June 1952 William Faulkner sent Breit a curious statement in nominal praise of EH. The first paragraph ran as follows: "A few years ago, . . . Hemingway said that writers should stick together just as doctors and lawyers and wolves do. I think there is more wit in that than truth or necessity either, at least in Hemingway's case, since the sort of writers who need to band together willy nilly or perish, resemble the wolves who are wolves only in pack, and, singly, are just another dog." 2. In 1947 Faulkner had told some students that EH lacked courage to go out on a limb of fictional experimentation. EH called on General Lanham to testify as to his personal bravery, which was not the point at issue. Faulkner apologized. See Carlos Baker, *Ernest Hemingway: A Life Story* (New York, 1969), pp. 461, 647. 3. Faulkner reviewed *The Old Man and the Sea* in *Shenandoah* 3 (Autumn 1952): 55, calling the novel EH's "best."

To HARVEY BREIT, La Finca Vigia, 29 June 1952

Dear Harvey:

I read the Faulkner statement over again this morning and it puzzles me more all the time. First he assures you I'm really not a dog and so I don't need to be defended on that charge. Then if what I've written since a certain book is no good he will defend the fact that I tried as well as I could and would have burned it if I didn't think it was good.

What's it all about? It really does sound as though he considered that he had been asked to speak well of something worthless by someone who could no longer write and he was, instead, makeing just as noble a statement about the poor chap as his conscience would allow.

In the first place take the wolf part. Surely he has never seen a wolf in wild state or he would know that he is nothing like a dog. No one would ever mistake him for a dog and the wolf knows he [is] not a dog and he does not have to be in a pack to give him dignity nor confidence. He is hunted by everyone. Everyone is against him and he is on his own as an artist is. My idea [is] that wolves should not, and in the wild state never would, hunt each other. The part about doctor's and lawyers is that there is a *secret professionel* and the good ones do help each other. Gypsies don't steal from other gypsies. They kill each other. But they do not prey on each other.

He just missed what it was all about. He hunts black bear because a black bear is a strange and fearsome animal in that County. I think it is a sin to kill a black bear because he is a fine animal that likes to drink, that likes to dance and that does no harm and understands better than any other animal when you speak to him. They get spoiled and bad sometimes in Yellowstone park. But it is the tourists that spoil them. I have killed enough of them since I was a boy to know it is a sin. It isn't just a sin I invented. But for many years I only killed bear when the stockmen's association would make a protest about some bear that was eating cattle. Then I would kill that bear so they wouldn't send a government hunter in who would kill off all the bears. Usually the bear would have only eaten cattle that had died; not killed them. But sometimes grizzlies will kill cattle. But never the black bear that is Faulkner's idea of an animal to kill. He has never seen a grizzly as he has never seen an old lobo wolf. If he had he would not have mixed wolves up with dogs.

If he would even read this book he probably wouldn't understand it because his fish is the cat-fish and he would probably think that no big channel catfish would do that so A. It isn't true. B. Since it isn't about the County it isn't either interesting or important.

I get fed on that County sometimes. Anything that needs genealogical tables to explain it is a little bit like James Branch Cabell. Then if you need the longest sentence in the world to give a book distinction you might as well hire Bill Veek [Veeck] and have midgets. As a technician I would say that sentence was not a sentence. It was made of many, many sentences. But when he came to the end of a sentence he simply did not put in the period. It would have been much better if properly punctuated. As it was it was damned good but as always I felt the lack of discipline and of character and the boozy courage of corn whiskey. When I read Faulkner I can tell exactly when he gets tired and does it on corn just as I used to be able to tell when Scott would hit it beginning with Tender Is The Night. But that is one of the things I thought writers should not tell out-siders. But he did not understand about writers sticking together against out-siders. It is not a question of log-rolling or speaking well of each other. It is a question of knowing what is wrong with a guy and still sticking with what is good in him and not letting the out-siders in on *secrets proffesionel.*

Maybe that is what he was trying to do in that statement. But it was complicated by so many other things. What got me was that he believed the majority criticism and thought that I was through and that he was being asked to help me out. Maybe because he had won the Nobel prize. It sure was a busher's reaction.

Well the hell with it. Mary got a fish the other day but not big. We raised a huge one just before sun-set after a heavy squall. I was trolling a whale dolphin and the marlin would only take it by the head to smash it. He didn't want to eat it. Gave him all the free line to take it in his mouth he needed but all he would do was crush it. Was probably a male fish cleaning up the ocean before he and the female spawned. Sometimes in the migration there is a wave of these soldier fish that come through ahead of the breeding fish and smash at everything to kill and don't stop to feed. You only hook them by accident. But this one was bigger than the soldier fish. The females just open up their mouth and swallow a bait. I've seen three very big ones this year but they were not feeding. Usually that is because they have had good feed down deep in the ocean before they come up on the surface.

Am going out this afternoon with big baits and try for a large one again. If you can hook into one big one a week you get enough exercise to last you and keep you in good shape. I have lost ten pounds fighting a fish when I was in good shape before I hooked him. You get a work-out from the soles of your feet up through your legs, your belly, your chest, arms and shoulders. Two big fish a week and it flattens your belly like a board. Three a week and it makes the old wash-board ridges in it. Some years we will get a couple of big ones in the afternoons three times a week and I get in wonderful shape and can sleep nights and wake feeling happy as when I was a kid. Am useing the same tackle I used in 1933. None of the modern stuff with changes of gear and winch methods that make it possible for anyone to fight a fish. Those new things are great aids. But you do not get the work-out. I will use them when I get older. Sometimes you will feel like you are getting older fast. But each fish you catch in the season makes you feel better and in better shape. Have 14 now this season, Mary three, and Taylor Williams, who fished with us in a couple of the tournaments, has five.

Have your plans on the vacation advanced any? Our plans for getting to Europe are all up in the air. Mary's father is about due to be ill again and now her Mother is ill. Roberto Herrera was very bad and nearly died and I've had to pay for that one and it has cost so far about one round trip first class on the Ile de France. Have to pay back the money I borrowed for income tax and have set aside other money for this year's income tax. It leaves damned little with the over-head here. If the book goes O.K. in the Scribner edition we will be o.k. Maybe we can get over in September when I see how the book goes. Have been here pretty damned long now and the heat gets you if the trade wind does not blow.

Hope you and the family are fine.

HUL   Ernest

To CHARLES A. FENTON, La Finca Vigia, 29 July 1952

Dear Mr. Fenton:

Thank you for your letter and for sending me your article.

Your article contains many inaccuracies. For example you seem to have fallen hook, line and sinker for the Moise story. If Lionel Moise believes, or states, that he influenced either my way of writing or my character, such as it is, I would never protest if it gave him any pleasure to believe so. But for you to put that out in a serious and scholarly work is something else.

The Moise influence seems, from your article, to rest on the testimony of Wesley Stout and Moise himself. Now if I had been taught or influenced by Moise I would be only too happy to admit it. I wrote you what a good disciplinarian and Teacher Pete Wellington had been and I wrote you about the Star's style sheet and other things.

But there are two things wrong with Moise teaching me to write A: It isn't true. B: My relations with Moise are described by Wesley Stout.

Would you mind checking up and seeing how much of the time Wesley Stout was in Kansas City while I worked for the Star? I remember being introduced to him once. He was never a friend of mine nor a close acquaintance and I believe, though this may be an inaccurate recollection, that he was working in Washington for the Star most of the time I was there. The Stout that I worked for on the Star was Ralph Stout who was the Managing Editor.

There were at least ten men on the Star who were better friends of mine than Lionel Moise who you did not mention in the list of people you sent me that you had been in contact with in regard to the apprenticeship I served on the Star. It was then that I began to become un-easy in regard to this project.

I knew Moise only slightly and what impressed me most in him was his facility, his un-disciplined talent and his enormous vitality which, when he was drinking, and I never saw him when he was not drinking, over-flowed into violence. I never, to my knowledge, heard him discuss writing seriously. His style of journalism as I recall it at that time was flamboyant and rhetorical and what amazed me was the facility with which he turned it out. I saw very little of him because we worked in different parts of town. I always spoke well of him and always will. But I was appalled by the way he wasted his talent and by his violence.

You have been assured by Moise that he helped teach me to write, or maybe you weren't and that is your own conclusion. I think Moise is too much of a man, or was too much of a man, to claim that. It was Wesley Stout, not Moise, that said I was Moise's acolyte.

I always felt that Lionel Moise's morals were his own business and that he was a very picturesque, dynamic, big-hearted, hard-drinking and hard-fighting man and I have always regretted that his talent was not disciplined and canalized into good writing. Maybe he did write something good that I never read.

I truly don't think you make an accurate comparison when you say he was a combination of Richard Harding Davis and The Front Page. I always heard that Davis was a great snob and a first rate war correspondent. Moise was never a snob and I don't believe he was a war correspondent. I remember him as a sort of primitive force, a skillful and extremely facile newspaper man who had his troubles and his pleasures with drink and women. Now I wish I had known him better and I would be interested in knowing how much of the time he was working on the Star during the time I was there.

Mr. Fenton the trouble with a project like yours is that you in-evitably do not arrive at the true gen. You get survivours gen. For instance on your Moise deal Carl Edgar, who is a true and legitimate old friend of mine, could only give you hear-say about Moise. I don't think Carl would ever have met him. He met very few of the other characters I did go around with. You were working on Kansas City and missed all of them. Wesley Stout issues confident pronouncements about things he knows nothing about. Pete Wellington has been too hard working and busy to remember details of things that happened nearly thirty five years ago. How could he be expected to? He and I were not friends when I was on the paper. He was my immediate boss and I respected, admired and liked him. But he did not keep any track of my life outside of the office because he was not that kind of a guy. Working under Pete was like serving under a good officer.

Here is an example of the true gen that you do not get. Carl Edgar was always in love with Kate Smith who was Bill Smith's sister. I had known Katey since I can remember and Bill was my best friend for many years. Honest John Dos Passos met Kate Smith down in Key West around the time I was writing A Farewell To Arms. He had never seen her before nor ever been to Northern Michigan. But he gets to Northern Michigan and he marries Katey and kills her dead finally when he drives into the back of a truck. The windshield cuts her throat and Honest John loses an eye. Many years have passed between when Dos met Katey at Key West and when he drove into the truck. I'm condensing the true gen to the minimum. Dos has heard lots of stories about Michigan at our house and with Katey. In 1951 he brings out a novel called Chosen Country. A big part of it is about Michigan and I am one of the more loathsome characters in it [George Elbert Warner]. He takes badly remembered anecdotes heard at our table when he was a guest and fouls them up a little more. He takes the incident when Bill's brother Y.K., his wife and that toothsome morsel you met or corresponded with named Donald Wright got involved in some sort of a killing out at a place called Palos Park south of Chicago. Some woman who was in love with Y.K. shot a gardener by mistake I believe [1924]. I had been living in Europe for several years and remember reading about it in either a french or spanish newspaper. Dos makes the loathsome character who is supposed to be me in the book then betray Kate, Y.K. et al by publishing a photograph and writing a feature story in some Chicago newspaper accusing them of weird sex cult rites. (I have no hope you are still following this.) The true gen is, of course, that I was in Europe and knew nothing about the case except what I read in the paper. But the picture, a photograph Dos must have found in Katy's pictures, is one of Bill and I and Carl Edgar welcomeing an old friend of mine from the Kansas City Star after the war.

This is an example of the true gen versus what will be handed out to you. I think you ought to drop the entire project. It is impossible to arrive at any truth without the co-operation of the person involved. That co-operation involves very nearly as much effort as for a man to write his autobiography.

It is easy to fall into a plausible trap like the Moise business and it is difficult for me to have to write letters trying to keep you from making mistakes. If you go on into the Toronto Star period of apprentice-ship and the Paris part it is an endless task for me to keep you out of serious trouble. I might much easier write about both those epochs myself (as I have always intended to).

It is important that I should write about the Paris part as no-one knows the truth about it as I do and it is an interesting time in writing. I knew Joyce very well and he was my good friend. I knew F. M. Ford (Hueffer) for a long time and too bloody well. Stein and Pound I knew very well and Leo Stein was a friend of mine as were Picasso, Braque, Masson, and Miro. I knew many of the French writers very well and what I would have to say about them could be interesting and I would be paid for writing it.

I average between fifty cents and a dollar a word for everything that I write and I write you letters between five hundred and fifteen hundred words long which you in-corporate in material which you sell for 2½ cents a word with a royalty deal over 100,000 copies sold. Mr. Fenton I hope you will agree that this is economically unsound.

Your letter and Mss. came yesterday morning but I put off answering you until today and did my own work. By the time I have tried to write you as you asked about your Mss. and attempted to set you straight on the Moise business I will not be able to do any work today. A few weeks ago I wrote you a very long letter explaining all the things that you would never get from anyone about Oak Park and why. But I did not send it when I had your angry letter. I still believe that you should cease and desist on this project or else organize it in such a way that both you and I should profit adequately from the material and criticism which I must supply if it is not to be a failure. Any man's autobiography is his own property. He should have the choice of deciding whether he chooses to write it or not. But he should certainly not feed it piece-meal into letters for another man to use. If you will look over your Mss. you will find that the soundest and the straightest stuff and that which can be verified and elaborated on was that which I wrote you.

Maybe it would be simpler to tell you to just go ahead and publish the Moise thing. It would please Moise and I would be happy about that. But it is not true and it would be bad for your reputation when I would prove it was not true and it would be bad for anybody who read it seeking instruction in how to write.

Reading your Mss. ----

###################

I've just read the Mss. over and to hell with trying to make it perfect or correct. The part about Moise will please Moise and he must be an old man by now. I'd like to please him and I certainly would like to please Pete [Wellington]. I think you could take the Wesley Stout acolyte quote out without damageing the Mss. Let the rest of it go if that is the way you see it. It makes just one faded snap-shot more compared to what truly happened on a given day. I'll get back to work. Thanks very much for refreshing my memory about Kansas City. I could write a good story about Kansas City now.

You have my permission to print the quotations from my letter as they appear in this article.

Imagine that's all. Give my best to Moise if you write him and do not tell him anything I ever wrote that would hurt his feelings. It will make him very happy to read this in New World Writing[1] and I think that is an excellent project.

The basic mis-conception in your approach is that most people can't remember anything accurately. That was what you wanted me to tell you about wasn't it? The other flaw in the approach is that everything is so changed now in America where a prairie is now a sub-division, a bare-assed hill now can be the grassy slope to a monument, buildings are torn down and others put up, green lawns and big trees are gone and apartment houses are in their place, where the speaks were we have Rockerfeller Center, a good man is dead and a garrulous fool speaks for him, and no amount of Mizener makes it come alive. You need local knowledge and to have seen the hill before the bull-dozer hit it. You need to have fished the stream before they put in the dam for the irrigation project. You need many things that you don't have to do this sort of thing well.

I hope you will get them. And I hope you will work on someone else, scholarly and decent as your approach is.

Best always,
E. Hemingway

PH. PUL

1. *New World Writing* 2 (1952): 316–26.

To CHARLES SCRIBNER, JR., La Finca Vigia, 3 September 1952

Dear Charlie:

I told [Alfred] Rice to check with you about the Television offer. It was my first interest to protect your publication of the book [*The Old Man and the Sea*]. From my end it does not seem possible that they could make a television presentation which would be fair to the book without considerable research and I do not want to have anything to do with something, no matter how well intended, which would not be as good as it could possibly be. I believe their dead-line, due to contracts, is much too short. Could use the tax-free money. God knows. But not enough to compromise for it.

After a book I am emotionally exhausted. If you are not you have not transferred the emotion completely to the reader. Anyway that is the way it works with me. I could read the narration much better in six months or a year.

I agree with you that the Western (Dell Books) offer of $17,500 on a 35¢ edition of Across the River and Into the Trees is the best one. Will you check with Alfred Rice when the money (my share) should be paid to me. We will know more about when this is when we see how the book goes.

I certainly hope it goes well. With the friendship I had for your father and with the absolute loyalties we had for each other it makes me feel badly when reviewers write as though I had done a disloyal thing to Scribners. You are familiar with the whole thing so we do not have to go into it.

It would be nice to get past anger I suppose. But reading little Mr. Orville Prescott in the Times saying condescendingly that there were "no phony glamour girls" in this book etc made me wonder again at the terrible complacence of ignorance.

That's no phenomenon. But this business of long distance telephone calls at any hour of the night by people haveing arguments about what something means in the book or by hysterical people, or people comeing up to you to thank you and starting to cry (sober) is new to me. A yacht came in to the club from the Bahamas and a Bahama Negro boy from Abaco had found the Life on board and has now read it five times in two days. His theory is, "There aint no such gentleman alive can write that. Can't know it. Can't write it. Don't try to tell me. Something very strange about this." That's the super-natural approach.

Also too many telephone calls by un-identified newspaper men. If you answer they will twist anything you say. Last night one was trying to trap me on trick questions about religion. I explained to him that I wrote fiction and that any religion in the story was that of the Old Man. Then the son of a bitch asked me if I fished on Sunday. He claimed to be from an Australian paper. I told him I fished on Sunday only when fish were running. Hope that's the proper attitude.

We caught 2 more day before yesterday afternoon bringing it up to 28. If this second hurricane does not disturb the stream too much we might get 8 or 10 more big ones. There is a 4½ knot current now, about twice normal. This next fortnight is the best fishing for the really big fish of the year. But when the barometer falls the fish go deep. Hurricane weather always upsets them too. But they feed well after the hurricane is past shoals of the big black-winged Bahian flying fish.

When the fishing is over I want to get away badly. Too much interference in work and I rate a vacation.

We would like to meet Joan [Mrs. Charles Scribner, Jr.]. Maybe it will be this fall.

What young Charlie is probably trying to do is get the dead wood out of publishing.[1] Make a note of it for his biographers.

Best always

PUL Ernest

1. Charles Scribner III, aged fifteen months, had taken to pulling books out of bookcases.

To BERNARD BERENSON, La Finca Vigia, 13 September 1952

Dear Mr. Berenson:

Thank you very much for the letter and for liking the book. I'm sorry it came to you so sloppily but that was the only way I knew to get it to you quickly. If it had been sent from here it might have been a Christmas present.

I'll be happy to have the book of the war years in English. I liked it in Italian but some Italian friends who were staying with us took it with them when they left. It was the only book they took so I think it is my loss and your compliment.

The reason I haven't written to you more is that it was a bad year for deaths and details and problems. Mary and I are very fond of you and I did not want to bother you with details. Mary is fine and as good an 'άλοχος [wife] as Dr. Homer ever knew. But you, being a wise old man, (my only aim in life), must have had a pretty good idea of that when you saw her.

Is it all right to talk about Moby Dick as though we were talking? It always seemed to me two things; journalism (good) and forced rhetorical epic. Thought you could take the ocean, not as some malignant force, but as the ocean: *la puta mar* that we have loved and that has clapped us all and pox-ed us too. We always call her la puta mar and I suppose you can't love a whore but you can be very fond of her and know her well and keep on going around with her.

Then there is the other secret. There isn't any symbolysm (mis-spelled). The sea is the sea. The old man is an old man. The boy is a boy and the fish is a fish. The shark are all sharks no better and no worse. All the symbolism that people say is shit. What goes beyond is what you see beyond when you know. A writer should know too much.

Since I ever saw pictures I tried to learn from them. Painters, as you know, are much better men than writers. It's bad luck. But it is true. Of course they do sell the contents of their wastebaskets. But we know that, too. Your way of judging is what I had worked out without being articulate and then reading you I found you had stated it completely. This is probably very impertinent. But please know I'm not.

Do you think it would be wrong if I asked you if you wanted, or wished to, or would be pleased to, write 2 or 3 sentences or 1 sentence about this book that could be quoted by Scribners? You are the only critic that I respect and if you really liked the book it would jolt some of the people I do not respect. But please don't do it and try to forget I asked you if it seems an ignoble thing to ask. I feel pretty ignoble for haveing asked it. Probably best to forget it. But, anyway, you know I didn't send it to you for that.

We have had hurricane weather for a week. Mary is going to New York next week I think. Somebody should have some sort of triumph when we win, or seem to, but I don't want to go to town now.

We have a wonderful current in the Gulf still in spite of the changes in weather and we have 29 good fish so far. Now they are all very big and each one is wonderful and different. I think you would like it very much; the leaving of the water and the entering into it of the huge fish moves me as much as the first time I ever saw it. I always told Mary that on the day I did not feel happy when I saw a flying fish leave the water I would quit fishing.

Please forgive such a long letter; forget any request and know you have two people here in Cuba who are very fond of you and hope that you are well and happy. I hope we have luck and see you soon.

Yours always,

I TATTI   Ernest Hemingway

To DONALD C. GALLUP, La Finca Vigia, 22 September 1952

Dear Mr. Gallup:

Thank you very much for your two good letters and for the enclosed letters that I wrote to G.S.[1] I am very happy that you liked the last book.

About Gertrude: I have decided not to let any letters I ever wrote her be published as long as that Toklas ----- is still alive. After she is dead we will sort them out. Don't you think that letters written to people --- Let's leave that.

Anyway, to make this letter a collector's item, I used to have the run of the house at 27 rue de Fleurus. That is Gertrude told me to come in at any time and wait for her if she wasn't there and to make myself comfortable and ask for a drink. "You have the run of the house," was her expression. So one day I came to say good-bye because they were going away. The *bonne* let me in and asked me to please wait and sit down and have a drink because they were packing. She got out a carafe of kirsch and a glass and went away and then I started to hear Toklas talk to G.S. and the terrible things she said and G.S.'s pleading. I went out not listening and trying to forget what I had heard.[2]

So if it is all right with you (or I am afraid whether it is or not) I will not permit publication of any letters of mine to G.S. as long as Toklas is alive. G.S. and I were good friends when she died [1946] and we always would have been good friends if it had not been for Alice Toklas.

I'm awfully sorry but I am afraid that about sums up the situation.

With sincere good wishes

YUL   Ernest Hemingway

1. Gallup of Yale was selecting and editing *The Flowers of Friendship: Letters Written to Gertrude Stein* (New York, 1953). 2. An anecdote elaborated in *A Moveable Feast* (New York, 1964), pp. 117–19.

To WALLACE MEYER, La Finca Vigia, 26 September 1952

Dear Wallace:

Thanks very much for your letter with the dope on the sale. I don't want to be hovering over the sale like a bird of ill omen nor do I want to be breathing down your neck like a hyena (just got these new symbols by reading reviews of The Snows of Kilimanjaro). Just wanted to know how we were doing. There is a big, gusty wind blowing that whipped the second page back over the carriage of the typewriter. Hurricane gone north of us again. It is number 3 of the season and all we are getting is the back wash of its wind. We had it spotted and charted three days before the weather bureau did.

It is o.k. to mention the Cuban thing [Medal of Honor from Cuban government]. They awarded it without asking me and it would have been rude to refuse it so I accepted it in the name of the professional marlin fishermen from Puerto Escondido to Bahia Honda. Then I named some great fishermen; living and dead.

Mary flew up to New York yesterday. I would like to have gone up. But you know how it would be. I can walk with shits nor lose the common touch. But I can't put up with some things without drinking to dull my critical faculties and somebody would set out to provoke me and succeed. Then some perfectly innocent character thinks he bought the right to call you "Papa" by paying 20 cents for the copy of LIFE and you say, "I may be your father but you look like a son of a bitch to me," and the next thing you have hurt somebody's feelings and you have to cool him to put him out of his misery. If you don't cool him he says he cooled you and that is always news. If you do cool him he can sue you or if he falls wrong you are in trouble. I wish they would put out a crash helmet for hecklers that when it hit the floor would automatically deliver a signed legal paper giving you full immunity.

Poor Mr. [Jersey Joe] Walcott. What happened was his legs went; maybe on account of the body punches; maybe from the spring in the last four rounds. When your legs go just the least little bit you start to get hit by what has missed you before and [Rocky] Marciano hits so hard that nobody can trade with him. Walcott might beat him again. But I am afraid he taught Marciano too much in those twelve rounds.

Let me have the news of the sale every week or so unless it is too much bother. Don't bother to dress it up. I just want to know. A lot of book stores have written to me, unsolicited, and said the magazine did not hurt their sale at all. Lots of letters from people who have read it many times already and from people saying they are buying the book to have it on their shelves for their children to read. Big turmoil about it all through Texas. They clip out the reviews and send them. Then out through the west they have rival reviewers on the same papers. Sometimes two at the same time. Sometimes one at one week and then one the next. Have had up to two hundred and fifty a day. It is very bad for a man to read so much shit pleasing or not about himself. But how am I to know if I don't open a letter that it is not from someone I knew and would like to hear from? But this five million (or however many it is) readers at a time is spooky, Wallace. I still think it is less destructive to have read the stuff down here though, than to have gone up to New York and talked about it.

I wish Max and Charlie were alive because they would have had fun seeing some of the boys run for cover. We certainly moved that Sterling North fast. But there will be some sort of a big counter-attack soon. They will probably get somebody like Bunny Wilson to head it. He can say, outright, the book is worthless. That is their best counter-attack. Dull, repetitious, no action, no character, the sea completely falsified, the language un-real etc. I guess we have to wait though for the Quarterlies for them to throw that one in. But I don't think they can do any better with it than the Kraut's did at Avranche nor in the Bulge. But a lot of crockery gets broken in these things. Then, of course, there is always my life and character to attack. That's simple. But it seems simpler than it is because my lousy life goes on over quite a long time and anybody that starts proving things about it or drawing horrid lessons from it is liable to get pretty bogged down in 1942–43–44–45 and they do not know what they are getting into. Would hate to get into it myself. Please excuse such a stupid letter Wallace. Alone in the house with nobody to gossip with.

Best always,

PUL
Ernest

To DONALD C. GALLUP, La Finca Vigia, 28 September 1952

Dear Mr. Gallup:

You have my permission to use the [truncated] letters as you sent them to me in your letter of September 24th. You should check though as to where there is any libel in regard to Mr. and Mrs. Krebs Friend. I give you permission to use the letters *unless they contain anything libellous.*

There is no reason I should louse-up your project that you have worked so hard on because of my personal feelings about Alice Toklas. These selections skip Miss Stein's and my friendship and are just literary and commercial history. I wish you lots of luck with the book.

Please excuse such a short note. It's not meant to be curt. It is that I am truly snowed under with letters about this last book. I love to get mail but it is no life for a man to sit on his ass and read thousands of letters on a single subject; a book you have written and done with. I want to be courteous and decent and appreciative and I hope I am truly appreciative. But I wish Miss Toklas got the letters and had to answer every one.

Best always,
Ernest Hemingway

YUL

To BERNARD BERENSON, La Finca Vigia, 2 October 1952

Dear Mr. B:

Thank you very much for sending the thing about the book.[1] I can't thank you for takeing so much trouble but I will try to write always in a way to make you proud if I can do it.

Mary has gone to New York to see the theater and the town and make the small triumphs that I don't like and that only make me feel bad. The fun is when you have just finished a book and know it is right. I get excited when they come out. But afterwards I would rather think and talk about something else.

We have lovely weather now and the sky is almost like Italy. I ought to be in Italy now but I have to try to run my life so that it does not ruin everyone else's life. But this is when I miss Italy the most. When Mary is here then I love her very much and forget about everything else. But when she is away I get very lonely and many things move in that ordinarily I can keep out.

Your book [*Rumor and Reflection*, 1952] is haveing very big reviews.

All reviews are shit. But I send these anyway air-mail in case you should not have seen them. When I was a boy some one told me that we had to eat a ton of it in our lives and so it was better to eat it fast and get it over with. So I ate it fast but then I found you were expected to eat it all your life. But sometimes I re-act a little and say, "I am very sorry, gentlemen, but I am not hungry today." Confirmed, or patriotic, shit eaters never forgive this deviation.

Why did we have to be born on such separate dates? We could have had a lot of fun. Maybe we will yet. What you wrote about the book made me happier than anything about it except writing it.

Do you ever have the feeling that you lived at all times in many different countries? Or is that crazy. I can smell the horses in the morning and I know exactly how the different types of body armour felt and where you chafed and I know all about Tyburn hill and when I was first in Mantova it was like comeing home at night after a concussion. When I am a little crazy I can remember the damndest things and [Flaubert's] Salaambo always bored me because I remembered how it really was. But everything has been written except those things nobody wrote about. So I write them. It would have been fun though to have lived in the old days when there was better companionship and [to] have written when everyone started from scratch.

Having books published is very destructive to writing. It is even worse than making love too much. Because when you make love too much at least you get a damned clarte that is like no other light. A very clear and hollow light.

Must stop and not bore you any more and send the clippings. Please forgive me for writing dull and stupid letters.

Mary would send her love if she were here. Please take good care.

Your friend,
Ernest Hemingway

The book, in English, has not come yet.

I TATTI   EH

---

1. Berenson's "blurb" for *The Old Man and the Sea*: "An idyll of the sea as sea, as un-Byronic and un-Melvillian as Homer himself, and communicated in a prose as calm and compelling as Homer's verse. No real artist symbolizes or allegorizes—and Hemingway is a real artist—but every real work of art exhales symbols and allegories. So does this short but not small masterpiece."

To CHARLES A. FENTON, La Finca Vigia, 9 October 1952

Dear Mr. Fenton:

Am sorry not to have answered your letter sooner. But load with this. I am 3,814 letters-to-answer behind with my home-work. My secretary married a diplomat and has gone to Japan. Out of the letters I should, absolutely, answer at least a hundred. You can't get a good Secretary here now. I've tried it.

You have that all loaded? In the first page or pages of your Mss. I found so many errors of fact that I could spend the rest of this winter re-writing and giving you the true gen and I would not be able to write anything of my own at all.

For instance: You have me tutoring the two Connable children. There were two Connable children; a boy and a girl. The boy was Ralph named after his father and injured at birth in a high forceps delivery. He was what is known as an exceptional child. You know there are schools for exceptional children.

Dorothy Connable had graduated from Wellesley; had served in France with the Red Cross I believe, was older than I was and while we were very good friends I certainly was not hired as her tutor and it would make you look silly to write that.

Also, as far as I knew or know, the Connables had nothing to do with Chicago. Mrs. Connable was a friend of my Mother's in Upper Michigan. I believe she came from Petoskey originally. Anyway she was a lovely woman; one of the finest, loveliest and most lovely looking I have ever known.

I was living and writing in Upper Michigan when I met her. I was selling nothing and writing pretty good stories. Mrs. Connable asked me if I would come to Toronto and tutor Ralph Jr. also teach him to box etc. She said they had a cabin down behind the house in a ravine where nobody would bother me and I could suit my working hours to whatever work I had to do with Ralph. Vice versa rather. I was beginning to get a little involved with about three girls in the town [Petoskey] where I met Mrs. Connable and I thought I should get the hell out. No, now remembering I was in love with four girls, all really fine girls, and was engaged, or partly so, to one of them and in trouble with a fifth. This sounds stupid and is. But maybe you were nineteen and twenty once yourself and know you can get into trouble without looking for it.

Anyway I went to Toronto. The first thing the Connables did was to go down to Palm Beach and leave me in charge of the house and of Ralph Jr. I had never run a house nor a house of that size nor with that many servants etc. before and it was fun. . . .

But when the Connables came back from Palm Beach I told them I could do nothing with Ralph and that I wanted to shove off. They did not want me to leave because I was supposed to be a good influence on Ralph but I said I could not work on that job and write. Ralph was a full time job. So I said I wanted to do some newspaper work to have some money of my own and a job and I would do my own writing down at the Cabin. Mr. Connable was paying me $20 a week and giving me board and drinks and the use of a car with a chauffeur when I wanted it and I used to go around with Dorothy and friends I had met in Toronto. I said, as soon as I started to write for the Star that I did not want the $20. but Mr. Connable insisted I take it as he had a system for takeing it away from me. He loved to play billiards and he was about 8 points in 100 better than I was and he took the $20 and a little more from me every week. I bet my own money on fights, horses, and gambled a little and got enough ahead to be able to leave in the Spring for Michigan with a stake. After I resigned from the job with Ralph, my only duty was, by Mrs. Connable's request, to sleep in the same room with him. I did this for her because I was truly fond of her. There was no need of it though. Whatever the boy's problems had been his working hard at a job in one of the Woolworth branch stores and his girl had changed them.

So that is about one tenth of the true gen required to correct "He tutored the two Connable children."

Another thing: You have located unsigned pieces by me through pay vouchers. But you do not know which pieces were changed or re-written by the copy desk and which were not. I know nothing worse for a writer than for his early writing which has been re-written and altered to be published without permission as his own.

Actually I know few things worse than for another writer to collect a fellow writer's journalism which his fellow writer has elected not to preserve because it is worthless and publish it.

Mr. Fenton I feel very strongly about this. I have written you so before and I write you now again.

Writing that I do not wish to publish, you have no right to publish. I would no more do a thing like that to you than I would cheat a man at cards or rifle his desk or wastebasket or read his personal letters. I think you should make an examination of conscience before you keep on with something you have been warned to cease and desist on and which will lead you if not to jail at least into plenty of trouble.

Best always,
Ernest Hemingway

JFK

To BERNARD BERENSON, La Finca Vigia, 14 October 1952

Dear Mr. B.:

Here is another cutting. I liked this one very much. It was the only really modest one in the weekly Herald-Tribune which was devoted to writers writing about themselves. Last year I did it too so I was quit for this.

Mary is sunning on the top of the tower and my black dog is lying at my feet and haveing a night-mare. He dreams as much as I do and I wake in the night sometimes and hear him haveing terrible dreams. There is a plague of armed robberies now and he dislikes armed robbery more than anything. When I have to get up with a gun when there is a noise he will pretend to be sound asleep. He is quite brave in the daytime and hates policemen, members of the Salvation Army, and anyone in uniform. But at night he is very prudent and sensible. Sometimes he will get up and make the rounds with me. But I know what it costs him and I don't blame him when he is asleep.

Mary and I met your cousin, strangely enough, about two months ago. It was in the Floridita bar where we go when we come in from the Ocean. Mary was nice to him because he told her he was your cousin. I had no chance to talk to him because I was inside the corner of the bar to keep out of trouble. But I know that I did not believe he was your cousin and thought he was lying because he was so big and hearty and thoroly sure of himself. He has a few people who do not like him here and two or three of them, Basque boys who play pelota (Jai-Alai) had prejudiced me against him before I ever met him. But I will be nice to him the next time I see him. He looked to me, though, to be a man so sure of himself that he did not need to have people like him nor to have friends. But heavy-weights often give that impression without meaning to. Anyway I will be nice to him. Mary has been nice to him already and I should think that would mean more to him.

[Arthur] Koestler I do not think that I have ever met but I might have met him in London when I had a bad concussion and not remembered him. Darkness at Noon was a very good book. I have ordered the Autobiography but it has not come. Neither has the U.S. edition of your book. I remember during the Spanish civil war we were all working very hard to keep Koestler from being shot when he was taken prisoner at Malaga and then to get him released. I had lived in Spain for many years and knew people on both sides as you always do in a civil war and I did all I could for him. I remember a Russian I knew named Michel Koltzov who I put in a book [*For Whom the Bell Tolls*] about that war under the name of Kharkov saying to me, "Ernesto why are you such a damned fool? Don't you know that a man who deliberately allows himself to be taken prisoner once will, if you save him, allow himself to be taken prisoner again and, if you save him, again?"

I didn't know this and maybe it is not true. But it is interesting. Kolzov himself, of course, ended up in Siberia if he is still alive. He knew I was not a Communist and never would be one. But because he believed in me as a writer he tried to show me how everything was run so that I could give a true account of it. I tried to do that when I wrote the book. But I did not start on the book until after the Republic had lost the war and it was over because I would not write anything in the war which could hurt the Republic which I believed in and tried to serve as well as I could.

Hope Martha is well and happy. I understand she talks very bitterly about me. But that is quite natural. I would not believe too much of it. I think no one gets a very accurate or credible account from either party to a broken marriage. Certainly I am not giving one. Anyone confusing a handsome and ambitious girl with the Queen of Heaven should be punished as a fool. Not to mention heresy.

Always remember Joyce saying, "Hemingway, blasphemy's no sin. Heresy is the sin."

Did you know Joyce? He was terrible with his admirers; really insupportable. With idolators: worse. But he was the best companion and finest friend I ever had. I remember one time he was feeling fairly gloomy and he asked me if I didn't think that his books were too suburban. He said that was what got him down sometimes. Mrs. Joyce said, "Ah Jim could do with a spot of that lion hunting." And Joyce said, "The thing we must face is I couldn't see the lion." Mrs. Joyce said, "Hemingway'd describe him to you Jim and afterwards you could go up and touch him and smell of him. That's all you'd need."

Please keep well and write the book. It is only one word after another and once you start you can always do it. Don't write silly stuff about wasting your life. It was in doing what you had to do that you learned what it is worth while to say now. Writers of fiction are only super-liars who if they know enough and are disciplined can make their lies truer than the truth. If you have fought and diced and served at court and gone to the wars and know navigation, sea-manship, the bad world and the great world and the different countries and other things then you have good knowledge to lie out of. That is all a writer of fiction is.

I would like to make a pact with you. You start to write the book now and write it a day at a time and I will write a story as well as I can and for you alone and we will keep at them until they are finished.

Mary sends her love and so do I.

Ernest

I think the pact would be a good short term program. Cable me "pacted" (not impacted) and I'll start. Anything we do will be good. But we have to start.

EH

Dear B.B.:

I did not send you this because I could not find the cutting. Now I have it. But the letter seems too presumptuous to send. But maybe you will forgive it. Your book came finally and I enjoy it even more than in Italian. You were very good to write it in a war. I never can write anything during a war except poetry. One time, in Madrid, I wrote a play. It seemed good when I wrote it but it was probably worthless. Have been reading a strange British book with an extraordinarily bad and yet effective style and like a bloody *lagarto* (couldn't spell chameleon) am imitating it. That is what comes of reading novels before breakfast. Maybe I can stop it now. Ordinarily I never read anything before I write in the morning to try and bite on the old nail with no help, no influence and no one giving you a wonderful example or sitting looking over your shoulder. In Madrid I learned to go to the Prado before I wrote. This was very good and not harmful or pharmaceutical the way reading is. I know it is not your dish but a boy who has not had a formal education can get a pretty good one in the Prado if he goes there every morning and takes his time. The variety and the great and the worthless and the un-known wonderfuls make a range that interests and holds some one who is un-educated. The Spaniards bought some awfully good pictures long before Dr. [Sir Joseph] Duveen took it up and they must have stolen some very fine ones when they were on the prod in Flanders.

I know only a little about stealing pictures but the funniest one I know was a flyer named Whitey Dahl. He was a very good flyer and he came to me one day and said, "Mister Ernest I'd like you to give me an opinion."

"Sure," I said.

"Is Van Dick a good painter?" He pronounced it that way.

"Very good painter, Whitey. Well thought of."

"What would a good Van Dick be worth?"

"I can't tell you Whitey exactly. I'd have to find out. But it would be worth a considerable sum of money."

"Well I'm certainly glad to hear that," Whitey said. "I'm glad to know my judgment is good. I picked up that old Van Dick when we were first out at the castle and I carry it with me everywhere and it hangs over my bed. I love that old Van Dick and I'm certainly glad to hear you confirm that I've got good taste."

It is a shame Whitey never got in touch with Sir Joseph. Whitey promised me he would turn in the picture after the war. But he got shot down instead and captured and sentenced to death in Salamanca. He got out finally. But I don't know who has the picture. All the Prado pictures were taken good care of and none of them was damaged. I was always very proud of how the Republic took care of pictures. I remember a column of trucks going by [with] the Prado pictures on the road from Valencia to Barcelona the day the Franco people cut the road and reached the sea. What was left of one company was holding up the column that was trying to cut the road. Messersmidts and Fiat's were circling round and round strafeing and I was praying for the pictures. That was the worst time they had. After that they went straight on to Switzerland and later were all returned. I guess it was wrong to take the chance of evacuating them by road. But nobody knew what would happen in Valencia and plenty of people got killed who could have been pulled out in the rear guard action that held the road open until they were all safely out. During the fascist bombing and shelling of Madrid the slogan was for the people who could not read and write, "Respect anything you do not understand. It may be a work of art."

Seems like a pretty good basic slogan for any time.

If you are getting awfully tired of this letter just think of it as a bad book and skip.

Your letter came this morning from the Eden Hotel, Roma.

No, one does not care about the reviews. I cared about yours. But reading the others is just a vice. It is very destructive to publish a book and then read the reviews. When they do not understand it you get angry; if they do understand it you only read what you already know and it is no good for you. It is not as bad as drinking Strega but it is a little like it.

I remember in the first war a British Tommy came into a bar at Thiene [near Schio] or Marostica or some place behind the Siete Communi and said "What's that bloody stuff?" They told him it was Strega and he said, "Give me a bottle of it. Here's your bloody Liri." He then drank the bottle down as though it were beer and promptly died.

With me it was necessary to establish, in the face of very bad criticism of the last book, that this book was good. You did that. After that the hell with the rats returning to the non-sinking ship. They are never well received. Not even by the ship's cat. What I needed you for was a compass and a sextant. If you can be a friend of your compass and your sextant then it [is] wonderful. B.B. I need much discipline and training like a difficult but very good horse. I have to make the damned discipline myself and my mistakes the same way. But I can never tell you what it meant to me for you to really like The Old Man and The Sea and write what you did about it. I thought what you said but I could never say it and certainly not say it as clearly. Now it is said and I never have to explain the book nor talk about it any more to anybody ever.

It was the book that made me happiest to write of any. If you read the others: these detalles may be funny to you. I started The Sun Also Rises in Valencia on my birthday because I had never completed a novel and everyone else my age had and I felt ashamed. So I wrote it in 6 weeks. I wrote it in Valencia, Madrid, St. Sebastian, Hendaye and Paris. Toward the last it was like a fever. Toward the last I was sprinting, like in a bicycle race, and I did not want to lose my speed making love or anything else and so had my wife go on a trip with two friends of hers [Pauline and Virginia Pfeiffer] down to the Loire. Then I finished and was hollow and lonely and needed a girl very badly. So I was in bed with a no good girl when my wife came home and had to get the girl out onto the roof of the saw mill (to cut lumber for picture frames) and change the sheets and come down to open the door of the court. Everybody happy at the surprise return except the girl on the roof of the sawmill. All small tactical problems you have to work out. But I had written too fast and the excitement was all in me and almost nothing in the book. So I fornicate into that terrible, dreadful state of absolute clear-headed-ness that is non-believer's limbo and then we go down to Schruns in the Vorarlberg and have a wonderful, healthy, happy life and I re-write. Then you re-write again. Then you have a book. With all sorts of various dreadful things happening all the time.

The next novel, A Farewell To Arms, was more accidentado. It is almost too rough to remember. I had the first draft written and was ready to re-write when my father shot himself and I was the head of a large family with many problems and debts. It was necessary to put these completely out of my mind and think only of the re-writing and at the same time attend to all problems and debts meticulously. This is the training that makes people who run into you later in your life think that you are taking pleasure when you are ruthless.

Better to stop now before comeing to the circumstances of other novels.

About projects I do not know. My middle boy, Patrick, is out in Kenya. He loves Africa as though Africa were a girl. She has never poxed him yet and I know I loved her the same way and still do; and she poxed me good. Africa and the Sea are the two loveliest whores I know. If we have money at the first of the year and I owe no money to anyone I think Mary and I should go to Africa. Have worked here now two and a half years hard and should get up in the hills and I might be some help to Patrick out there. We could try to get to Italy and see you comeing back. You would be disappointed in me but you would see Mary and out of

Africa there is always something new and I could try to bring it if nothing else.

This letter is like a three feature cinema. Basta [Enough].

Your friend

I TATTI   Ernesto

To EDMUND WILSON, La Finca Vigia, 8 November 1952

Dear Edmund Wilson:

Thank you very much for sending me the book [*The Shores of Light*] and for writing in it as you did. I wanted to send you the Old Man and The Sea book very much but because we had exchanged a few civilized and friendly letters I thought you might think I was sending it hoping for a favorable notice. You know I was thinking about actual sharks when I wrote the book and had nothing to do with the theory that they represented critics. I don't know who thought that up. I have always hoped for sound, intelligent criticism all my life as writing is the loneliest of all trades. But I have had little of it except from Kashkin and from you. Some of yours I disagreed with very much and others were illuminating and helpful.

It made me very happy to see how your journalism stands up as prose and I read the book until three o'clock in the morning. That was the mystic hour that haunted Scott. It always seemed to me the best hour of the night once you had accepted insomnia and no longer worried about your sins. Now I have about three good night's reading on the book left and I am saving it carefully. One of the best things was to read how you felt about things at the time. Your review of Scott's book, the early one, was very sound. Dos fooled us all I think. But he fooled himself the most. The last book, Chosen Country [1951] made me sick to read. My only hope for him as a writer was that it was a re-write of something dear Katy had written for a Woman's Magazine. But that is not a very fine hope. Have you ever seen the possession of money corrupt a man as it has Dos? When Eisenhower received his tax free money from the Democrats for his book he became a Republican. His political development, and that of Dos, have very strange parallels.

It was comic to read how you were robbed of your good books by the Russians and that strange and funny story. I knew them only through Kashkeen who I had never met but who wrote excellent letters and I thought, within his doctrinaire straight-jacket, was a wonderful critic. I thought that he knew what I was trying to do better than I did. It was like having a wonderful catcher if you are a pitcher. Then I met them in Spain and Koltzov seemed to want me to know the truth about how things were. He let me have the run of Gaylord's and concealed nothing and let me know how things really were. They were not good. But he wanted me to know how things really were whether they were good or not. So while you had those awful and chicken experiences with them I was seeing them behaving at their best. I watched Konieff learning tank tactics by trial and error; mostly error. I saw Walter at a bridge with nothing to blow it and the fascists tanks on the other side thinking it was mined and four of us watching them. Under these circumstances Walter could make jokes. Lucasz was killed. Heilbrun was killed. Hans and I rowed across a river, the Ebro, under bad enough circumstances. Now all of these people are dead. But this was not a Stalinist experience. These were episodes in the defence of the Spanish Republic. The Russians pulled out and were gone, giving Spain up as a hopeless problem for them, by October of 1937 (would have to check the exact date). But they decided to pull out after the failure of the attack on Fuentes del Ebro. They left a few people but pulled out their effort.

All the history of that war is written by people who care nothing about the truth but are only proving their theories and beliefs.

I read, in the Times, a good piece about you by Harvey Breit.[1] He wrote something about you wishing to learn Spanish and know Spanish literature. The language is easy to learn superficially. But there are so many meanings to each word that, spoken, it is almost double talk. In addition to the known meanings of a word there are many secret meanings from the talk of thieves, pick-pockets, pimps and whores, etc. This occurs in all languages and most of the secret language is very ancient. If you want to start on it I would think that the best book to head in with is Gerald Brenan's The Literature of The Spanish People published by the Cambridge press. It is a sound book. His book The Spanish Labrynth (probably mis-spelled) is the best book I know on Spain politically. If you really want to learn the language you can skip a lot and start in with Quevedo. It is tough to cut your teeth on. But the fashionable thing of learning Lorca is completely stupid. His poetry is based on Andalusian music. If you do not know the disonnances of that music, or if you do not know Arabic, it is almost meaningless. (If I mis-spell please do not think I am basically illiterate as Scott was. I know each time I mis-spell a word. But how would you finish a hand typed letter if you worked with a dictionary? I use a dictionary or dictionery to check on spelling when I write for keeps. Sometimes the dictionary, in English, is wrong. I accept it in languages I was not born to.)

In the matter of the homo-sexuality in Stein I wish you had maintained your position rather than qualified it. I will give you all the material you will ever need on that if you wish to back up the position you took in the review of the early book. She talked to me once for three hours telling me why she was a lesbian, the mechanics of it, why the act did not disgust those who performed it (she was at this time against male homosexuality but changed later out of patriotism) and why it was not degrading to either participant. Three hours is a long time with Gertrude crowding you and I was so sold on her theory that I went out that night and fucked a lesbian with magnificent results; ie we slept well afterwards. It was this knowledge, gained from G.S., that enabled me to write A Sea Change, which is a good story, with authority. This conversation, in which Toklas left the room, was one of the reasons for her later malice. At one time it reached the proportions of, "You give up the friendship of Hemingstein or you give up me." Toklas used to be quite wicked to Gertrude but Gertrude's ego grew vaster than that thing Andrew Marvell described[2] and finally it was all she needed. But her whole attitude toward life and toward the practice of letters changed with the menopause. It was the year she had the menopause that she broke with all her old and good friends.

This only for your information.

Thank you again for the book and for the dedication. Keep well and keep on writing.

Your friend

YUL Ernest Hemingway

1. Interview with Wilson in the *New York Times Book Review*, 2 November 1952. Reprinted in Breit, *Writer Observed* (Cleveland, 1956), pp. 267–69. 2. "To His Coy Mistress," lines 23–24: "And yonder all before us lie / Deserts of vast eternity."

To CHARLES SCRIBNER, JR., La Finca Vigia, 20 November 1952

Dear Charlie:

Thank you very much for the beautifully bound and arranged book that you sent with the photostats of the press cuttings and other notices. It is very beautiful and Mary and I are delighted with it. She is going to put some of the letters about the book in those transparent loose leaf containers. They are very handsome and practical.

We had a difficult time getting the album out of the Cuban Post Office and Customs because it was marked value $100. and they demanded a Consular Invoice or they would not release it. At one time they were going to send it back. But on the third day of negotiations they gave in and released it with no charges. I would have been glad to pay the duty but they couldn't undertake that paper work without their consular invoice etc. But it took six letters and three visits to Post Office and Customs. But it was well worth it.

Thank you too for being nice to Mary in N.Y. She liked Joan and you very much. I haven't yet heard all about her trip there. But she had a fine time.

Sending anything out of here, even an autographed book, is a matter of permissions and paper work still hung over from wartime regulations. So I planned to send back those Ernest Walsh/Ethel Morehead letters and the book autographed to them by Lee Samuels. He comes down here every two weeks or so on his tobacco business. But he is off today and Mary wanted to read the letters. So I will send all but four that I am holding out with him the next time. There is no reason why [David] Randall should not sell them to any serious collector or Museum. If you want to we can split the profits any way you say. The Rare Book Dept. should not work for nothing.

It is a disillusioning thing to see the letters you wrote to someone while you were doing their work (editing their magazine for nothing) while the man Walsh was ill with T.B. kept and sold callously for cash. I was working very hard at writing at this time and it was an awful job to put a magazine through a French press with no English proof-readers and look after every detail of printing, cuts etc. When it was impossible for me to give it the time it needed and not destroy my own work I suggested someone they could get to do the bulk of the work for 1000 francs a month. I would still help on anything important. The idea of spending any money, as I later learned, always outraged the Morehead woman and my wishing to continue my own work was regarded as treachery by Walsh. He was a very strange character.

I met him first at Ezra Pound's studio one afternoon when I had gone there for Ezra's boxing lesson. Walsh had just come in on the Aquitania I believe and had two blondes in mink coats with him. They were all staying at Claridge's and one of the blondes told me in confidence that Walsh was the highest paid poet in the world. I asked what he wrote for and she showed me: Harriet Monroe's Poetry a Magazine of Verse published in Chicago. It was then paying either $5.00 or $12.00 a page for verse.

"Mr. Walsh got twenty two thousand four hundred and fifty dollars for these poems," the Blonde told me. "Don't you think he's Divine?"

Claridge's threw him out at the end of the week, of course, but he was picked up by this Moorehead woman who was middle-aged, seemed sound and serious and came of a very decent family. She wanted to start a magazine, literary, and pay for contributions. They were also going to give a prize each year of $2000. (Like the Dial of those days) for the best contribution published. At three different intimate little dinners she told me, Jim Joyce, and Ezra Pound that we were going to get the prize for the first year. To me she said I was getting it the first year, Pound the next and Joyce the third. To the others she said Pound 1, Joyce 2, Me 3 and Joyce 1, Pound 2, Me, 3.

As soon as they started their magazine, made the promises, got their contributions, made their contracts, etc. Walsh had a hemmorage and left all work on getting out the magazine in my hands. He could throw a hemmorage in any kind of emergency. I believe first he sucked his gums to get blood and then coughed it up. But finally he could cough up blood from lower down in the bronchials. Finally he could cough up the genuine scarlet product. He looked sort of like those pictures you see of Stevie Crane and I knew he was both a malingerer *and sick*. I knew he was crooked from the blondes incident. But he was sort of a poet and he seemed genuinely to want to help all writers getting started and besides he had promised along with the seemingly steady Moorehead $2000 to Joyce, Pound and myself.[1]

Well to cut this charming histoire short I wrote The Sun Also Rises and he wanted to serialize it in his quarterly which was appearing irregularly when I had a contract with Scribners to publish it in the fall. He had written me a terrific letter about how good it was and had picked out, very intelligently, those things that were good about it. He had also seen what I was trying to do and I was pleased. But I explained to him that I was publishing it with Scribners and it was impossible to give it to him as a serial $2000. prize or no $2000 prize. So, on its publication, he wrote a review of it titled The Cheapest Book I Ever Read.

Later Joyce told me about the $2000. So did Pound. Nobody ever got the $2000.

I suppose it was quite valuable for my education but I filed it under not trusting Irishmen as poets and beware of all hemmoraged characters. But my next lovely surprise was to come from Gertrude Stein who was not Irish and had no t.b. at all.

It was funny to remember all this reading the letters. The ones I retired from circulation simply had personal things or references that I do not want kicking around. The ones that are left tell the story and this letter, and the one I wrote to Wallace [Meyer], are the key to them.

I have written to Wallace again about the sale as I was worried by the David Dempsey story in last Sunday's Times entitled The Verdict.

If you want to use them I have some of the damndest letters you ever read. One from Aksel Wickfeld who holds the Blue Marlin record for instance. One from a Brooklyn Housewife. One from a very old lady. Any number you want to pick from from children. Also from guys in the service, etc. It would be possible to make a striking presentation, if you wished, useing a cross section of American opinion, or American and foreign, useing these letters.

Please let me know about this. I do not want to mix up with your end of things at all. Maybe everything is going o.k.

Best always,
Ernest

PUL

1. See "The Man Who Was Marked for Death," in A *Moveable Feast* (New York, 1964), pp. 123–29.

To CHARLES POORE,[1] La Finca Vigia, 23 January 1953

Dear Charlie:

Thanks for your letter of 19th inst.

I wrote Wallace [Meyer] to okay the first part i.e. open with Big Two Hearted; Torrents of Spring complete, Sun Also Rises complete. He agreed that it was to be a reader; not a teaser and agreed to making the stress part of A Farewell to Arms a unit by using chapter XXXV as well as XXXVI and XXXVII and the first Five chapters of To Have and Have Not.

He didn't mention cutting any stories. So let's not cut any. We always went for broke before. Why not go for broke once again.

You keep the poems for a present if you want them. I trust you and then I'll know where they are if they ever burn this place down or it gets robbed again.

I can't tell you when Big Two Hearted River was written exactly but it was before The Sun Also Rises when we still lived at Rue Notre Dame des Champs over the saw mill. I used to write it there and at the Closerie de Lilas mornings and at another café in the Place St. Michel where I didn't know anybody and would go to work.

I suppose you know it; but it is a story about a boy who has come back from the war. The war is never mentioned though as far as I can remember. This may be one of the things that helps it.

The Sun Also Rises I wrote the first draft of in six weeks starting on my birthday July 21 in Valencia just before the Feria and writing through the Feria (6 corridas) and then in Madrid, San Sebastian, Hendaye, and finishing in Paris on Sept. 6. I couldn't cool out and wrote The Torrents of Spring in the week before Thanksgiving Day of that year. Right after that we went to Schruns (SCHRUNS) in the VORARLBERG to ski and for me to re-write on The Sun Also Rises. You can check on what year this was [1926] through Scribners. I left Schruns and went to N.Y. with the Mss of The Torrents of Spring and I don't know whether I took the part I had finished on the re-write of The Sun Also Rises with me or not.

Anyway Liveright turned down The Torrents and Scribners accepted it. I hoped he would turn it down because I did not like him nor trust him. But I did not write it to be turned down. I wrote it to be published.

You can find out from Scribners when they accepted it and when they published it. In the meantime I went back to Europe on a boat with Bob Benchley and Dotty Parker and from Paris went down to Schruns to ski and finish the re-write on The Sun Also Rises. I don't know whether Scribners brought it out the fall of that year [1926] or the next year.

But I remember going down to Madrid that May [1926] and the corridas of San Isidro being snowed out 15th–16th–17th and I stayed in the room of the Pension ALVAREZ in the Carreterra San Jeronimo and I wrote The Killers, Today Is Friday and Ten Indians in one day. Morning, afternoon, and evening.

After the corrida at ARANJUEZ MAY 30 I went on the train to join Hadley and Pauline who was staying with her at Juan les Pins at a house Scott had found for us.

That July we took the Gerald Murphy's, Pauline, I think, and Dos to the Feria of St. Fermin at Pamplona. Hadley and I went down to the Feria at Valencia (my birthday again. So a year must have elapsed. I was always working so hard and in so much trouble I couldn't keep track) and then after that I remember doing galley proofs on The Sun Also Rises at Antibes where we stayed with the Murphys. Scribners will know when the book came out.

Next I did Men Without Women as a book but I wrote the stories all over in different places; Paris mostly. I wish I could tell you where I wrote The Light of the World. But it was either Key West or Havana. It probably was in Key West. I know I wrote A Way You'll Never Be there and A Natural History of the Dead.

I wrote Death In The Afternoon in Key West, the ranch near Cooke City, Montana all one summer, Havana, Madrid, Hendaye and Key West. It took about two years. The glossary I remember I wrote at Hendaye. It was a bastard to do. Max's correspondence will show when it was finished and Scribners will know when it was published.

I wrote A Farewell To Arms starting in Paris, then in Havana, Key West, Piggott, Arkansas, Kansas City, Mo. (during the convention that nominated Hoover) then in Sheridan, Wyoming and finished it in Big Horn, Wyoming. Returned to Key West. My father shot himself just before Christmas of that year (Hoover year) and I was in the middle of the

re-write at the time. You can find out from Scribners when it was serialized and published. I did the last of the re-write in Paris I'm pretty sure.
Or maybe the proofs there. I rewrote the last chapter over 40 times but
I hope it does not read that way. Now I remember; I am sure the last
re-write was done in Paris. Because I had a long letter sent over by F.
Scott Fitzgerald in which among other things he said I must *not* under
any circumstance let Lt. Henry shoot the sergeant and suggesting that
after Catherine dies Frederick Henry should go to the café and pick up
a paper and read that the Marines were holding in Chateau Thierry.
This, Scott said, would make the American public understand the book
better. He also did not like the scene in the old Hotel Cavour in Milano
and wanted changes to be made in many other places "to make it more
acceptable." Not one suggestion made sense or was useful. He never saw
the Mss until it was completed as published. (This comes under being
lonely when you have the point.) I had learned not to show them to him
a long time before. Will tell you about that some day; too long to write
now when am trying to give you the gen you said you needed.

For Whom The Bell Tolls was written here and in Sun Valley Idaho
then here. Scribner's files will show the dates.

As you know I was out of business as a writer except for 6 Colliers
pieces and the poems (where I tried to distill what I never knew if
[whether] I would get to write) from early 1942 through 1945.

Then I started, or continued rather, on the long book and interrupted
with Across The River when it looked as though I would never get to
finish the long book. That was what the doctors fed me anyway. Started
in Cortina D'Ampezzo then wrote here and finished it writing on the can
(my best place of composition in the Ritz in winter); at 0500 you can
shut the bathroom door and be warm with the window of the room still
open in the bedroom and no light on so Mary can sleep.

Does that round up where they were written?

Remember Charlie in the first war all I did mostly was hear guys talk;
especially in hospital and convalescing. Their experiences get to be more
vivid than your own. You invent from your own and from all of theirs.
The country you know, also the weather. Then you have a map 1/50,000
for the whole front or sector; 1/5000 if you can get one for close. Then
you invent from other people's experience and knowledge and what you
know yourself.

Then some son of a bitch will come along and prove you were not
at that particular fight. Fine. Dr. Tolstoi was at Sevastopol. But not at
Borodino. He wasn't in business in those days. But he could invent from
knowledge we all were at some damned Sevastopol.

Hope some of this will be useful.

There's no rule on how it is to write. Sometimes it comes easily and perfectly. Sometimes it is like drilling rock and then blasting it out with charges.

Best always,
Ernest

Mary sends her best.

UMD

1. Poore of the *New York Times* was gathering data for an introduction and notes to his edition of *The Hemingway Reader* (New York, 1953).

To BERNARD BERENSON, La Finca Vigia, 24 January 1953

Dear Mr. B:

Lillian Ross wrote me yesterday that you had not heard from me. I wrote a long letter when I had your last. So either it went astray or I never received another that you sent. Enclose a clipping from this week's Newsweek on how the mail has been. Also there are difficulties here.

I never keep copies of letters to people that I trust or I would send you the last one.

How did you like Lillian's book? I thought it was a very sad story. She doesn't know about joking except what I have taught her. But I thought her detail and ear for what those people said was very good. She is a strange girl and I like her very much and we are good friends. It is like being good friends with a circular saw. But I have been there too. She has the real devil of work that drives her. But I have it too. But I always thought it was not the devil but my trustee or Liege Lord that I had sworn to serve and would serve always until I die. That does not mean that I do not call my master (writing) that old shit, nor blaspheme about him. But I serve him as well as I know how and I know better all the time. My master does not interfere nor ever change a decision that I make. He is dead, as a matter of fact, but I have not told anyone and I serve him as though he were alive. This is probably stupid. But we all need some discipline and I need more than most. So I take it from writing. Women provide the local discipline.

How are you? It sounds like a bad winter. My news always comes from Venice. It is two years now that I have not been there and that is twenty years too long. Today is a gloomy wet day and that makes me more homesick. I wish there were no rules and I could send you a letter I had from there. You never thought Across The River etc. was "contrived" as the critics said and that there could not be such a human being as the girl Renata did you? I hope not.

The critics' wives all look like Mrs. Alger Hiss or Mrs. Whitaker Chambers and *worse*. Maybe I wrote you this.

How did you like the letters between Gide and Claudel? And Gide's posthumous catty-ness to his Madelaine?

Si le grain ne meurt [Gide] was a good book and some of the others too. But I always felt about him the way some stupid people felt about cats. He made me feel the same way Alice Toklas did. Gertrude I always loved in spite of everything, and she loved me too and that made Alice murderous jealous. I was very fond of Leo [Stein] too. Did you like him?

Sherwood Anderson was a slob. Un-truthful (not just inventing un-truthful; all fiction is a form of lying) but untruthful in the way you *never* could be about a picture. Also he was wet and sort of mushy. He had very beautiful bastard Italian eyes and if you had been brought up in Italy (with very beautiful Italian eyes) you always knew when he was lying. From the first time I met him I thought he was a sort of retarded character. The sort that gets to be Minister of Culture in a new chicken-shit Republic where there are no standards except charm. You know we boys who are bad, I mean brought up roughly, never trust a man with a Southern accent nor a man with beautiful eyes.

How you can tell a man who has killed men (armed) is that usually his eyes do not blink at all. A liar's eyes blink all the time. Meet [André] Malraux sometime. How bored are you getting? You can always stop and always throw it away.

But I felt so badly that you thought I had not written.

If you like I can write you quite funny stories about Malraux and al-most anybody of my time. We have no great news. Waiting still to clear up the contract and plan for making a picture (good) of The Old Man and The Sea and some other things before we go to Africa. Mary is well and very happy. There was another armed robbery but this time I heard them and there was much shooting in the dark and I think no more robbery. Hope so anyway.

I can't write with things pending and movements pending. But as soon as the picture business is contracted I will try to make the combat shots—sharks and fish jumping—and then go to Africa after the spring rains.

This last book sells steadily and well. I hope you are steady and well. We have to get through one winter at a time now.

Mary sends her love. She wrote a thing about me in which she quoted you (from yr. next to last book) on how we'd like to be. She'd like to send it if it wouldn't nauseate you.

I have hell living up to how you are with her. But I tell her give me 35 years.

Love from Cuba

Ernest

I TATTI

To BERNARD BERENSON, La Finca Vigia, 17 February 1953

Dear B.B.:

You know we have to give them marks for some things. Your letter of Feb. 12 came this morning and gave me indecipherable joy.

I CAN WRITE ESTILO MILITAR if it is any more legible but I hate to write on the typewriter and especially to you. You are one of my few heroes.

Biographies at 53 are shit. They don't know. You are too proud to tell them. And they could not understand.

You (ie. me) are ignorant, make mistakes, wish to forget them, having learned from them, and to keep or working and haveing fun. They want laundry lists and dirty linen. They think maybe the secret is contained in the discarded jock strap. Maybe it is. Pero tengo dudas [But I have doubts]. In valid myths the truth is always more interesting than the published (journalistic) myth. Except by an affectionate wife.

[André] Malraux is a jerk of his own invention. Carried in his own image by a shaky hand with a tic in the left eyebrow.

True example: In Paris after the entry into the town, three days after, we (French irregulars) were preparing to move north ahead of the 4th Inf. Division going via Compiegne to cross the Aisne at LaFere, take St. Quentin and then cut sideways in two columns to get astride the German escape route to Aächen. We made two big slaughters before St. Quentin and later it was necessary to cut my way to Le Cateau where my best friend and Col. [Lanham] of the 22nd Infantry greeted me, "Go hang yourself brave Crillon. We fought at chickenshit and you were not there."[1] They had made a great slaughter at Montrecies.

Well Mr. B.B. before we set out on this chase, intercept and slaughter I was in the Ritz Hotel Paris with my worthless characters cleaning their weapons and stripping them and busy trading people and getting rid of those who were content in Paris and would not fight going away from the stable when A.M. appeared. He had 5 galons [gold braids]—polished cavalry boots—decorations etc. I had one of two shirts I owned.

I said "Bonjour André," he said

"Bonjour Ernest. How many have you commanded?"

I said, "Dix aux douze. Au plus deux cent."

He said, "Moi: deux mille."

I said, "What a shame my colonel that we did not have the assistance of your force when we took this small town (a patelin [village])."

Then we went on working and let him preen, and jerk, and twitch until he left.

One of my characters asked me into the bathroom and said, "Papa on peut fusiller ce con? [Should this phony be shot?]" (I can't spell French)

I said, "No. Offer him a drink and he will go by himself."

This is the 3rd best Malraux story I know. The other two are better but they are in Spain. In Spain he surpassed himself.

Gide stories are a dime a dozen. Valery stories are all nice. Joyce stories as good as Joyce. Very good. Very strange. Afraid of God and of lightning and thunder above all. I'm awfully happy always, boy, that you weren't brought up in the church.

Later 1145

The canasta players are at it. If you are not a snob about cards I suppose it is defensible. But as long as there is one good book to read or a friend to write to I will not play it. Nor will I ever play it. Bridge is a lovely game when you are snowed in in an Alpen Club hutte with nothing to read but canasta is the game of the un-properly fucked wife which I suppose is wives' fate. An ill wife is the sign of a worthless husband.

But a canasta playing wife is the sign of a husband whose mind, or something, has wandered. Will try to keep my mind on the subject.

Christopher La Farge is here house-guesting. He says he visited you, or called on you, in 1924. He is a declared poet and a good wing shot.

You didn't read those books about Hemingstein the tentative uncanonized Saint of Letters did you? There are three now. They are a vice to read. They made me feel unclean for about a week but am over it now.

It is a very beautiful winter here. I wish you were here whenever we read about the bad weather in Europe or when I hear directly from Venezia. Good night and sleep well, which is about the best thing we get. Pity the poor people who believe in any other life (San Ernesto El Profundo). If they really had any such dirty trick we will be together and have a fine time. You classify and I will make a running comment and we'll disturb the circles. Poor Dante. Maybe we can find him a job as concierge. Another great man has left Firenze. You know the old lovely story of the man who clothed the dead.

Best love from Cuba

I TATTI   Ernest

---

1. Parodying King Henry IV to the Duke of Crillon after Arques. See Carlos Baker, *Ernest Hemingway: A Life Story* (New York, 1969), p. 420.

To DOROTHY CONNABLE, La Finca Vigia, 17 February 1953

Dear Dorothy:

Thank you for the letter and the loyalty *and* the valentine. Maybe it was not a valentine but it made me feel like one. It gives me a fine feeling to know where you are and that I can write you and you will get the letter. We must all be together sometime soon. You are always welcome here. I felt awfully when I found that I had missed you at Petoskey.

The man [Charles] Fenton is one of those who think that literary history, or the secret of creative writing, lies in old laundry lists. Thank you for warning him off and please do not co-operate with him in any way. He has been invading my privacy for two years now. He has a pleasant approach, a plausible story and then when he obtains some private information about your life it might as well be in the hands of Arthur Mizener the man the friends of Scott Fitzgerald all trusted.

He is now writing about the Toronto period of my life, and what I have seen of it is completely inaccurate and silly—last year I spent uncounted hours trying to help him on his study of my apprenticeship on Kansas City Star. I could have written three good stories in the time he cost me. But I thought it might be useful to kids starting writing—in the end though, when he published it, he retained all his mis-information and gossip. I have warned him to cease and desist and have copy-righted my signed journalism in the Toronto Star so that he cannot use it. (He doesn't know this yet.)

Dorothy it is a miserable thing to have people writing about your private life while you are alive. I have tried to stop it all that I could but there have been many abuses by people I trusted. You cannot stop trusting people in life but I have learned to be a little bit careful. The way to make people trust-worthy is to trust them. But this man is not a person that works with that system.

Anything about Toronto is yours, your mother's, your father's, Ralph's and my business and is private and no concern of Fenton's. But the only way to stop those buzzards is to tell them *absolutely nothing.* If you tell them the truth about anything they reject it for anything more sensational or that fits the theory into which they try to cram your life.

We had such a fine time in Toronto, and I loved and admired your lovely mother so much and learned from your father and liked Ralph and was useless to him, that I hate to have the Fentons of this world put their dirty hands on it.

I think I can stop Fenton from publishing anything about me after the Kansas City piece which appeared in New World Writing. It may take a little doing—must warn Hadley now.

Bumby is an instructor in a special intelligence course at Ft. Bragg, N.C. Is still a captain but having superior efficiency reports. He did very well in the war and was the only person I ever knew to parachute into occupied France with his fly rod. He was wounded quite badly and taken prisoner in November of 1944. At one time I was doing the same work with the 4th Inf. Div. that he was doing with the 3rd. and he sent his commanding officer to me to get some good Frenchmen. We sent him some that were very good—a little rough. When I was in France last I found a good part of my people were in jail because they kept on practising the things we taught them.

Thank you very much for liking The Old Man and the Sea. I had a lot of luck writing it. Hope the other books to come will be good. Would you like to have all those that Scribners have published for the Michigan place? If you would I could write in them when we get to New York and send them. If there are any you don't like tell me and I will not send them.

Please skate once for me. And how is your tennis?

Ever since your letter came I've felt the wonderful dry cold of the Toronto winter and how nice you were to someone as stupid as me and how much fun it used to be to talk in your lovely room when we were both such very young old soldiers. I would like to write about Toronto sometime instead of having Mr. Fenton do it and try to put in all the delicacies and my stupidity and the wonderful worthless servants. We ought to get Henry James to write it. But possibly I will get so I can write delicately. But then I was a guest and I never write about when I was a guest.

Mary claims she never was in Toronto but remembers you in New York. She sends her very best in any case and we both look forward to when we will meet. We would love to see you here.

Ernest

This letter is stupid. But I was very moved to hear from you. More than I thought I ever could be about almost anything. Good, fine, lovely, beautiful Dorothy.

T.C. PUL   February 14, 1953

To LILLIAN ROSS, La Finca Vigia, 20 February 1953

Dear Lillian:

Thanks very much for your letter and the news about Mr. Faulkner the writer. What's he doing in N.Y. again? Thought he never left that little old Homestead in Mississippi.

I cannot help out very much with the true dope on God as I have never played footy-footy with him; nor been a cane brake God hopper; nor won the Nobel prize. It would be best to get the true word on God from Mr. Faulkner.

I know the same amount about God as you do. Have not been vouchsafed any revelations. It is quite possible that Mr. Faulkner sits at table with him each night and that the deity comforts him if he has a bad dream and wipes his mouth and helps him eat his corn pone or hominy grits or wheaties in the morning.

I hope Mr. Faulkner never forgets himself and gives it to the deity with his corn cob. It is nice to know he has good taste and judgement but, as one of my oldest friends, remember never to trust a man with a southern accent and never trust a God-hopper either North or South of the Macy-Dixie line.

You ask if I know what he means. What he means is that he is spooked to die and he is moving in on the side of the strongest battalions. We will fight it out here and if there are no reserves it is too Faulking bad and they will find what is left of Dog company on that hill.

Please do not quote me on any of the above as it is controversial.

Lillian I cannot help but think that people who talk about God as though they knew him intimately and had received The Word etc. are frauds. Faulkner has always been fairly fraudulent but it is only recently that he has introduced God when he is conning people.

The Old Man in the story was born a catholic in the island of Lanza Rota in the Canary Islands. But he certainly believed in something more than the church and I do not think Mr. Faulkner understands it very well. He talks like a convert or a man afraid to die. Because I always joke do not take me seriously on this and please do not quote me in any way. I am going to make no statements about The Old Man and the Sea now or ever. Everybody can bring to that story what they have as baggage. But there are going to be no explanations.

I have no message to give to Mr. Faulkner except to tell him I wish him the grace of a happy death and I hope he will not continue to write after he has lost his talent. Don't give him that message either. But that is what I would really tell him.

The shirt was beautiful. Thank you very much Lillian. Some day I'll give you something good. All I can give you now is my love.

H. von H.

JFK   [Huck von Hemingstein]

To BERNARD BERENSON, La Finca Vigia, 20–22 March 1953

Dear B.B.:

Thank you very much for writing me about [George] Santayana. Now I think I understand it. When I finished the book I felt very differently than I felt in the part about the elder Russell and his problems. I have never envied anyone and it is late to start. But if you like I will envy Santayana as a spiritual exercise.

Please don't get mixed up about LIFE. That is only a picture magazine. I always joke and much of it is gallow's humor. You must truly know that no matter how stupid people act, in order not to argue with fools, any writer that you respect at all, or that has given you pleasure, can think a little bit.

The violence is the violence of our time. It is my heritage, not yours. I feel terribly that you should have been exposed to its idiocy. You came from a good time. Any time must be a good time to me and we make each day a day. I cannot write beautifully but I can write with great accuracy (sometimes; I hope) and the accuracy makes a sort of beauty. (Not like the camera.) I know how to make country so that you, when you wish, can walk into it and I understand tactile values, I hope. Sometimes I can make people because, as a writer, I have almost a perfect ear. That sounds like bragging but it is only telling you about a horse that I might be advising you to buy if you were buying a horse; which you are not. I am not buying him either. I own him for better or for worse. Caveat etc.

You speak about being drunk. I think it is wonderful that you have never been drunk. I think I can say that I have never been drunk when I had any duty, and in so-called civil life I am never drunk unless I am very bored. Because I am very shy I drink sometimes to make people bearable. But I do not know why the wines you love should be so expensive. If I had all the money in the world I would drink Cahors and water, Tavel (very cold), Valpollicello (mis-spelled), your local product once a week, and I could go on for pages. But none of them are expensive. The only wine I drink that is expensive is good Brut champagne.

It and really good caviar are the only things I know that are costly that are worth what they cost. I mean perishable things.

Please never think because someone has an over-large body that they are gross. (No dictionary handy and I am writing this early in the morning before going out on the Gulf Stream which is the poor man's Arno.)

Actually if a writer needs a dictionary he should not write. He should have read the dictionary at least three times from beginning to end and then have loaned it to someone who needs it. There are only certain words which are valid and similies (bring me my dictionary) are like defective ammunition (the lowest thing I can think of at this time).

Next morning—March 21   0630

[Paul] Claudel always seemed ridiculous. When I first started to be published in French he thought I was a wonderful writer and it made me very uneasy and I thought, "There must be something wrong with this stuff that I do not see. If Claudel likes it there has to be something wrong." Gide had that awful lascivious protestant coldness; like the pastor of the Fourth Presbyterian church who is caught by the janitor interfering with little boys behind the church organ. He is usually apprehended by the janitor. Of those people that I knew when I was twenty through twenty five in Paris I liked Fargue (maybe mis-spelled) the best (Leon Paul), Valery Larbaud was stupid but kind and pleasant, I liked a man named St. Leger Leger who had some other name, Perse I think, who worked in the Foreign Office and wrote very good poems. Valery was a nice man. We were quite good friends but just before he died he expressed a wish to meet me and Sylvia Beach and Adrienne Monnier wanted to make a party for the event. I suppose I should have gone. But I was hurt, I suppose, that he did not remember me when I was a very quiet boy whose name nobody knew. Then most of the older people thought I was a boxer because I used to have to work in the morning in the gym on the rue Pontoise as a sparring partner before I would write. Then I would go to Sylvia Beach's book shop in the afternoon to get books and sometimes I would meet people at her place.

Usually, then, I did not have enough money to go to the cafe except the Closerie de Lilas and the Select where I had personal credit with two waiters. One I used to work with in his vegetable garden outside the Porte D'Orleans and he would make me a whole whisky (all whisky to the top of a *fine a l'eau* glass) and then I would take a little sip and put siphon in it for the rest of the evening. He used to come to the gymn to watch me box (we trained very good heavyweights and for ten francs a round they tried to knock you out every morning. You were polite, like a servant, but you were supposed to fight. But not too much or you would have to take the punishment from the ego of the fighter). My friend at the cafe knew I was a writer and he worried all the time. Nobody but me knew I was a good writer and the only places I could get published in was Der Frankfurter Zeitung and Der Querschnitt and money was very difficult. My friend at the Closerie de Lilas (we lived around the corner) worried all the time that I would hurt my brains in boxing. But he had never read anything of mine in French and, you know, unless it is in French it means nothing.

This is getting to be a long and involved story and I will spare you the rest of it. The end is that I became a good writer; even in French. In the meantime, when I needed more credit, I would dump some heavyweight on his ass when we were training and my friend, who had seen it, could borrow money if I needed it. But B.B. we all have different lives and he-man is a rude thing to say. We are all men with all the faults of men. Love, as you say, is not fornication. One time when Mary was afraid something dreadful had happened to her I told her never to worry ever. That when we slept together if we only touched our feet it was the same as making love.

You know that if you love someone, truly, it is only in their pleasure that you are happy.

About the business of fighting and bleeding etc. You must know that none of us bled on purpose. I have had it so many times. You see the color and whether it is jetting or not. By the color you know whether it is arterial or from a vein. You make the thing to stop it accordingly. There is no mystery or romance about it. It is like an industrial accident. When I see it bright red and pulsing strong I say, "Shit," which is an old word used by [Pierre] Cambronne and still valid. These things have nothing to do with writing. A writer, who loves to write, should not be shot nor shot at too much. When wounded he takes care of himself; but he gives no mystical importance to the industrial accident.

You see there is the problem of our up-bringing. When I was your age, when we both were boys, you had freedom to move around in Europe as you wished and your problems were self imposed. So were Santayana's. When I was the same age the problems were imposed by other people and they were the Adamello, Riva, Pasubio, the Siete Communi, (Altipiano de Asiago) Monte Grappa, the Montello, and the Basso Piave. I loved pictures very much but I looked at them on crutches or with a leg in a cast. I loved the Italians and thought the war was stupid but when we would come back from treatment at the Ospedale Maggiore (Padiglione Zonda) in Milano the drunkards and the lumpen-proletariat would knock us down and break our crutches and say abasso gli ufficialli (Milanese) I hope I still understood it and their problem and all of it. But we had not bought that on purpose. We would have to check the dates but I think I was wounded badly before Henry James received the O.M. for his patriotic sentiments. One of my grandfathers [Ernest Hall] always told me that patriotism is the last refuge of thieves and scoundrels. He probably mis-quoted it from some one else.[1] But he was a very fine man and had been badly wounded in our Civil war and never allowed the war to be mentioned in his presence. My other grandfather [Anson Hemingway] was a hero and when I was a little boy I went with him to see Annette Kellerman and The Birth of a Nation and to bury all members of the Grand Army of The Republic. He always made the speech at the funeral and coming home we would stop at some saloon and he would say, "Ern, don't believe a damned word of what I said about that son of a bitch today. A son of a bitch alive is a son of a bitch dead. But I have to have toujours le fucking politesse."

I am sorry about the Mistering. We call everyone by some title. Mary is Miss Mary. We have a legendary character in the family who is known as the Snicketesnee. When things are bad we make songs about him. They have a very broken rhythm which allows the inclusion of any number of words which the voice will carry. The Snicjketeesgny (polish spelling) is supposed to be sort of like Santayana (the man we envy except that he is dead).

A typical verse is:

> George Armstrong Custer
> And the seventh Cavalry
> Never killed as many Indians
> As the Snicketeesnee.

If you are familiar with the battle of the Little Big Horn you will see this is ironical.

Another verse dealing with His Lordship goes:

> Jesus Christ Almighty and the Holy Trinity
> Were considered simply converts
> By the Snicketeesnee.

Another:

Will omit, because they get worse. They are only good with the tune. It is the tune of Doing What Comes Naturally.

If there is any point that I would try to make it is that if you come from Avila there is no mystery about Avila. I never knew Saint Teresa because she was before my time. If we had been contemporaries, I am quite sure we would have been good friends. The same with Juan de la Cruz. Quevedo I feel I know better than my brother. Santayana to me is a different business. Because he comes from a walled town he thinks that makes a difference. It makes no difference in the heart. Anyone who has lived in a walled town knows how much human shit there is on the ramparts and under the towers. We know who fought for it and helped build it and who did not. And we think the son of the owner of the Bodega is ridiculous when he is confused in his thinking. You know that what ruined, and what made Spain, was the Inquisition. They missed Santayana's family and he became a beautifully writing apologist for it. This is very unjust but you be patient with me too. Everyone loves something and I love Spain and know it, in a small way, as you know pictures.

About dying: We must do it but there is no reason we should give it importance.

You have done a good job and have left things in order. If it is of any use to you, two people here love you very much; Mary and I.

Lately we have had the curious juxtaposition of Venus, Jupiter, Mars and Mercury in the sky. I have never seen Venus so wonderful in my life and no one will again for a long time. Then, now, all the migratory birds are coming through and there are ten pairs of mocking birds nested here on the place. I play Bach on the phonograph to one and he learns it very well. We have a pure black lizard at the pool and I have learned to whistle to him soundlessly so that he comes to me any time I call him. I do not know what the magic is in the calling. I learned it from a man who learned it from someone else. You whistle without making any sound but the lizard hears it perfectly and it is evidently a password. I have tried different tunes. But the tune is not important. It is the frequency modulation. Do you like *largartos*? I love them very much for their wonderful speed and elegance. It was strange to learn they had a weakness and could be called as you call birds or animals.

Thank you very much for the Preface which has just come. I have bought the book and hoped it would be here to take on a trip Mary and I are going on the day after tomorrow down the coast. The boy [Harvey Breit] who had the review copy for the N.Y. Times wanted to give it to me but I preferred to buy it. Anyway I can read the Preface on the trip. (Have read it now and like it very much. It is so clear that they probably will not understand it.) You know that when we write the straightest and simplest that we know how we write quite a lot alike. I hope this does not make you angry. It is said very respectfully.

It is now 0700 on Palm Sunday. I just read this letter and never read so many mis-spelled words and the sentiments expressed sound like printed mottos on the wall of the house of illiterates.

Communication between human beings is not very good. When I write to you it is to amuse you and because I am lonesome. One thing Santayana said that was good was that he never had a French friend. It was a terrible critique. Imagine living in France and having no friends; not even Robert Desnos nor Jacques Prevert nor your doctor nor your concierge nor your concierge's wife nor any whore nor anybody where you had credit nor Cricri du Boisrouvray who you would have married if you had not been a fool nor Henriette who came up from Bordeaux when it was impossible to do in the war because she heard you were in Paris and you never saw her because you had gone North nor all the people you fought with in the different wars.

"Ecoute, Boursier. Il faut retirer."

"Merde. Je me trouve tres bien ici. Ma flanc gauche est proteger par une colline. Jai le mittrailleuse bien place. Je me trouve ennormement bien ici et je reste."

Never a french friend. I can think of no more unenviable poverty.

When we were fighting to come into Paris we had a fine song. It went,

> *"Dix bis Avenue des Gobelins*
> *Dix bis Avenue des Gobelins*
> *Dix bis Avenue des Gobelins*
> *That's where my Bumby lives."*

It was the song we made up for my oldest boy to sing when he was a little boy so he would remember where he lived. These French were bad boys and crazies and they thought it was a great American fighting song. Red Pelkey, who had served seven years in the regular army, and never spoken a word of French in his life until we had landed in Normandy, now, since we had been commanding French, spoke only French and had forgotten English. He was under the impression that his name was Jim because the French all called him Jim. Actually his name was Archie and he was my driver and a private; not first class. I think he was a legitimate crazy anyway. But there had been a fight outside of Rambouillet and we had dressed all our Frenchmen in the clothes of the deads and Pelkey had become a sergeant through inheriting clothes and stayed a sergeant for months. The French all called Paris "Paname." That is the argot name for it if you love it. It comes from Devil's Island slang I think. Since we were figuring on taking this place and reaching a mystic point known as Dix Bis Avenue des Gobelins Pelkey got sort of confused by it being always referred to as Panama. His vocabulary, with me, was now reduced to saying, "Oui, Papa. Jenay pah vue, Papa. Eel son pahs encore arrivay, Papa. Sa gazhe bien, Papa. Too lemond cohntent, papa, but un peu trow de tanks."

I used to say, "Archie can't you truly speak English any more?"

He would say, "No, Papa. Too say jelly perdu. Toolemong parle francay ay moi jay pense on francay."

I would say, "You still can read a map in English and understand co-ordinates?"

"Oui, Papa. Nayeh jamais purr sur moi. *Dix bis Avenue des Gobelins*. Pah deh problemme. Ohn battre. May pah pour patrie. Patrie foutu."

This went on for quite a long time and Santayana might have detected something wrong. But Pelkey had many French friends and I had a few and we were doing what we were supposed to do. Sometimes Pelkey would have spiritual problems like this, "Papa, tchay dee jamay fussillay le john avahnt que papa inteeerogay. Bon?"

"C'est un ordre."

"Merci, Papa. Ohn ah fussilay troe without raisons. Le boys sohn trop enthusiasteeque. Eels ohnt voolu fussilay oon faim."

"On fait ca jamais."

"Merci, Papa. Say mon avee ossie. Jemmay foosillay day faim. Respectay leh faim. May too say le patree footoo."

"We'll fix that up."

"Le boys dit jamais Une fois foutu jamais le meme. Faim, motociclette, jeep, toos con ah."

"Faut pas etre defaitiste, Pelkey."

"Jamais defaitiste, Papa. Mais le boys mah expliquay."

You are probably justifiably tired of Archie by now. But he *did* have French friends and the night before we moved into Paris he was very worried about "Paname." He said, "Papa jeh vais con toi. Tu sais. Ohn va attackay comme toujours. tulemond content. Dix bis Avenue de Gobelins. Mais tu sais tray purr de john pour attackay la canal."

After we secured a bridge-head at the Porte de Saint Cloud he did not have to worry about the canal and Paname was Paris. When they broke up the irregulars and they sent Pelkey back to the motor pool he had despair and went by himself and cried all the time like someone when their heart is broken. He would not work nor obey orders nor salute nor say sir nor do anything. They called in the Divisional psychiatrist and it did not do any good. Archie said his life had been changed by being with irregulars and if he could not be with Papa he wanted to die. There was no punishment they could inflict on him that would impress him in any way. So they sent him back up to me.

This all started with the business about life and me having spoken ill of Santayana. You should never speak ill of anyone. But if you are a snob how can you avoid it? Do you remember what a dull and conceited man Unamuno was? But often he was right. I used to sit around by the hour listening and waiting for him to be right. It would have been more fun with Pascin and you always had a good time with Joyce because he was never conceited with his equals. I liked Pound very much. He had this great pretence to universal knowledge and he got to be un-bearable. But the things he did know about he knew very well and he had a lovely heart until he turned bitter. Fascism is always made by disappointed people. Mussolini I knew fairly well. When you had known a wicked old man like Clemenceau, Mussolini was not very interesting. Then, too, it was impossible not to remember him as a coward in the war and as a crooked journalist. I hate things like Dongo [where Mussolini was murdered by partisans]. But he did not come to too bad an end when you think of his cheap cynicism and how he really hated Italians. He was not much of a specimen to have come from Forli. No one would wish to live in the Romagna. But it is a great asset to have been born there. I come from Barco de Avila, Cooke City, Montana, Oak Park, Illinois, Key West, Florida, here, the Veneto, Mantova, Madrid. Too many places. But you are a local boy in all of them. This has its advantages and dis-advantages.

Tomorrow we leave at 0400 from the harbour. Mary and I will sleep on board tonight and we will go down the coast for a week or ten days and look at the stars at night and not worry about stupid things. Bed is my fatherland and the sea is my true fatherland and we can combine them both and I will try to be a kind and gentle, and I hope, good hus-band. Please forgive the long stupid letters. I write them instead of stories and they are a luxury that gives me pleasure and I hope they give you some too. If they do not I can always stop writing you and would under-stand completely if you were tired of it. Maybe because you have com-plicated blood, as I have, you would understand this. One time when I was out at the Wind River reservation a very old Indian spoke to me and said, "You Indian Boy?" I said, "Sure." He said, "Cheyenne?" I said, "Sure." He said, "Long time ago good. Now no good."

Pues nada mas; yo te quiero y soy a sus ordenes [So nothing more; I salute you and am at your service].

I TATTI   Ernesto

1. Misquoted ("Patriotism is the last refuge of a scoundrel.") from Dr. Samuel Johnson; in James Boswell, *Life of Johnson*, vol. 2, ed. G. B. Hill, rev. L. F. Powell (Oxford, 1934–1950), p. 348, 7 April 1775.

To ALFRED RICE, La Finca Vigia, 26–27 April 1953

Dear Alfred:

Your letter of April 23rd arrived this morning with the deposit slips. I enclose my check for $2500. for your 10% of the non-personal services check for $25,000.

I'm sorry you felt I had not expressed appreciation for your loyal, efficient and arduous work. Please consider the circumstances under which my manners were evidently bad.

Three contracts had arrived of 14 pages each to be read, compared, initialled and signed. They were late through being mis-sent to San Francisco, California. Your addressing was technically correct but several times communications from you had been mis-sent by the mails due to CUBA not being emphasized in the address. My first duty was to correct this without rancor and with a clear explanation to you to avoid it's re-occurence.

Then I must read the contracts which I think you will agree could give a head-ache to anyone who is not a lawyer and is not familiar with the motion picture business and it's financing. The contracts had come to me without any explanation of any part of them. So I had to work them out as well as I could by myself.

The first thing to do was to check the part in which I was obligated to perform certain things. I found that you had protected me expertly and well in this and that the contract said exactly what had been agreed on. The rest of the contract was rough to understand in some of the paragraphs but I wrote you that I relied on you to explain to me anything that looked like a joker in case it was simply a question of legal verbiage. The one I called your attention to seemed to give a right on foreign monies which I would not have given. So I called your attention to it.

When I have to do something fast and in a hurry and without a Secretary please and thank-you are implied. You get your citation after the fight. I know you take a beating because I take one most days of my life. The only times I don't take one is when we go on the Pilar down the coast and Mary is feeling cheerful.

I'm sorry that I cost you cash money by making concessions so the deal would be closed. Am also pretty sure that if I had not firmed-up bad it would have dragged on forever. You are in on a very big thing now where you will have to do lots of work for your participation. So far your work has been exemplary as far as I can judge. Hell Alfred you don't want me to write out one of those, "Alone in New York, surrounded by superior numbers of enemy legal forces he assumed command of his platoon after all other lawyers were dead and/or dis-honored and single handedly with only a part time Secretary defended Suite 1959, 630 Fifth Avenue etc. [Rice's office]."

We are in a big fight from now on in and can make a terrific killing if we make a great picture. But there won't be any great picture nor nothing unless [Spencer] Tracy and I carry the ball most of the time. He knows it and I know it. Everybody is going to have to work like hell and we are going to have to do the miracle stuff. I appreciate everything you do but in a fight I expect it of you.

We had all the ice and grub on the boat and were ready to shove tonight at midnight when I got a letter of the imminent arrival of Leland [Hayward] and [his wife] Slim on Monday qualified by maybe. So I will be on the telephone at noon. Tried to locate them last night. No locate. So if you take a beating on the staff, Alfred, remember the troops get shooted at too.

I need to train hard to be in shape for Africa and to write what I have to write before I work on this picture. Came into form quickly with the training the last time. But you have to build up a back-log of lots of exercise and little drinking and not frittering away your time on useless people. Alfred it is hard to estimate the damage to my working and resting time that LIFE publication of The Old Man and The Sea has done. In the old days I could go into the Floridita in the corner and drink a frozen Daiquiri and read the paper. Now I cannot be there three minutes before some absolutely sincere son of a bitch comes up to you and asks if you will have a drink with him and his wife and they have been waiting 5 days going in every day for you to come in etc. And I am polite as hell. About half of the U.S. read that story and you are going to cash in on that if it is a good picture. But never think that part of it is any fun for somebody who is shy if people speak well of him.

Then since they started to write all these phony books and articles psychos come from everywhere and bother you. It seems that you have the same problems they have and they come to you because you must know The Secret. They don't pay any attention to the sign on the gate and they come in the house if the screen door is unlocked and come in the forenoons. I have had to beat two bad who wouldn't leave the house. You can't throw them out as you should or beat them outside because it is a stone steps, stone approach, and another stone steps and you drop some son of a bitch just once there wrong and you have another manslaughter rap.

I'm polite and polite and polite until they won't go. Then I cool them. But they bleed all over everything and Miss Mary gets sore forgetting she asked me to cool them. I told her she had no idea how that looked.

Roberto [Herrera] can't fight anymore at Floridita for six months on acct. of the Judge of the first district warning him that he would have trouble right or wrong. The Floridita has no bouncer and no one who can bounce and we inherit all the trouble. Now that it is an air-conditioned place with only two slow opening doors instead of all the old free-swing exits it is a very bad place for trouble. There is a window opposite the Tobacco Counter where anybody outside can see who is inside and people looking for trouble or to put the bite on you case it from there and then it is your own responsibility to see they get out once they get in. Everytime anybody reads in the paper or hears on the radio that I have made any money some gangster out of office tries to shake me down. Sometimes it is not too funny but I try and maintain the humorous or stick that gun up etc. approach. Twice it has been a little rougher than rough.

So when I don't give you the old Lord Chesterfield touch when you have done well and don't sing out, "Oh well played. Well played." or the great curler's cry of "Oh good shot. Good shot. Almost a perfect shot." Just look forward to how beautifully I will write you up post-humously.

But when I have to get something back to you in a hurry, politeness and praise is implied if you have done well. Did you ever hear a short stop and a second baseman speaking beautifully to each other *during* a double play?

Now the fire fight has died down temporarily and I say, "Thanks very much Alfred. It must have been pretty fucking rough out your way. Now this is what I figure to do to break down the counter-attack."

Just talked on the telephone. They have put in a new phone and you can actually hear what people say and do not have to shout. Slim sounded fine. Arrival is postponed to Tuesday to meet Mary Martin to do business on Wednesday. Have staffed out how they can reach us Thursday. Slim (Nan) may stay down a few days. We will sail at midnight tonight or a little after.

Alfred in the letter I tried to tell you not to be sore because I was in a hurry and I have spent this Sunday morning telling you something else. I hope to Christ I haven't hurted you again.

Enclosed is my last correspondence with Charles A. Fenton. Will you please write him to his University address as follows. "My client, Mr. Ernest Hemingway has asked me to write you to ascertain why he has not received an answer to his registered letter to you of February 18th 1953. In the future, since Mr. Hemingway is travelling, will you address all communications to him through me. Yours etc."

Please send it registered and if no answer in a week please send a registered letter to Yale University, Department of English, New Haven, Conn. enclosing a copy of your letter to Mr. Fenton and asking them if they will be certain that it is delivered to Mr. Fenton.

This man Fenton, who I spoke to you about, is engaged in being an amateur FBI operative and pin-pointing (mostly in-accurately) every-thing in my life from 1915 through 1925. By naming actual people with their real names he makes it impossible for me to write fiction and by saying that so and so was such and such real person he exposes me to any amount of libel suits. He has also interfered with my privacy to an unbelievable extent. I do not know how much of the shit in articles like WHY and PAGEANT comes from him or from his colleague Philip Young.

I have all our correspondence filed including many letters from him that would not go down well with his University. He is the son of a head master at Hill school, served in the RAF, published an unsuccessful novel and teaches creative writing at YALE. As an un-successful writer he hates fiction and wants to confound it constantly with fact.

Some of his letters come very close to black-mail and a number of them are obscene. I warned him many months ago to cease and desist but he goes on and, as you see, he has not answered my registered letter of February 18th on today, which is the 26th of April.

A typical sentence of his in regard to a piece I wrote on shop-lifting in the Toronto Star Weekly is this sort of thing, "There is no actual proof that Hemingway was ever at any time a shop-lifter but-" I had the dope for the article from the manager of Eaton's Department store and from a store detective. But that is his style.

It is quite easy to prove that I went around with some fairly tough characters when I was a reporter in Kansas City and when I lived in Chicago and some other places. But as a reporter, covering police, it is necessary. As a writer if you don't know the boys how would you be expected to write about them? If you were around with fighters how could you not know the mob?

But I know all this stuff that he does not know such as for example who the fighter was in The Killers and why he was killed (different from the Hellinger version) and I know quite a lot of things that there is no statute of limitations on. My father did most of the surgery for the boys in Maywood and Cicero and Harlem (our Harlem; not yours) and I was a good friend of Jim Colosimo when I was a kid and the Union wanted to run me for Alderman in the 19th Ward after the war against Tom Connors. I had sense enough not to be mixed up in that and they ran and elected Tony D'Andrea who was killed inside a year. When I went away from Chicago I wanted to go just about as far away from there as I could go. Kansas City the same.

Now I've never written but one story even about the start of prohibi-tion days; none about the old days practically except about Michigan. I was writing a wonderful story about Michigan where I was in some very bad and interesting trouble[1] and this Fenton moved in on Michigan and started pin-pointing it. Most of the people in this story are alive and I was writing it very carefully to not have anybody identifiable. In comes Fenton and starts working out who everybody was I knew in Michigan. It worried me and threw me off and I held up on the story which is a hell of a story.[2]

I want to drop a good road block in on him; ahead of him and behind him.

***** Monday a.m.

It started to blow heavy out of the South with torrential rains at six thirty pm and then went into the Northwest and blew sixty mph. Had to get out three anchors and put the trip off twenty four hours. Barometer still way down this morning.

Thinking over the Fenton business: Hold up any letter to the English Department at Yale until after I get back from this trip. Please send the registered letter to Fenton at his Yale address (630 Berkely College). I do not want to go to law in this since you remember the old ruling in the Federal League case that you cannot enter a court of equity without clean hands. Anyway you are sticking out your neck if you do. But I want him worried, off balance, and I want his publisher [Farrar, Straus, and Young] too worried to touch the book. I don't think he is a spooky guy but he goes into almost psycho rages [if you] call him. Both times I called him he blew his top. I have an idea that he got in some trouble in the RAF from something he wrote me once. But will have to check that.

In blocking this sort of publication I believe it is a question of who bluffs who out. Most of the issues have not been tested and testing them is expensive. I believe you can threaten an injunction or Invasion of Privacy. But that comes later. The thing now is to request his answer by registered mail. Just the sight of a legal letter-head spooks most people.

Just talked with Gregorio [Fuentes] and it is still pretty rough outside. It seems it blew over 80 mph in the gusts and one of the finest and biggest Yachts in Cuba the "Jaguar" was lost coming back from Varadero. Much damage in the harbour. We o.k.

Hope Philip is well and doing o.k.

Mary sends her best. Sinsky was here in exceptionally fine shape last week when I sent off the contracts. But Don Andres has a really bad cardiac condition. Can't make it up the hill any more. Roberto has a job as manager of the photo and camera dept. at Sears. He gets a salary that isn't much but gets 10% on the gross. Also a six months contract and full benefits.

He is almost finished with the filing and is working 3 nights a week here now. No more mau-maus [burglars] since the last shootly-maru.

We certainly had a break, though, not to be at sea when that thing broke last night. But it brought the rain we needed so badly.

The way things shape now we hope to be in Europe by the end of June. Want to get in and out of N.Y. without any publicity.

Will you let me know the dates and sums on which Tax Money must be paid?

Best always and many thanks,
Ernie

Enclosures = 1 check
                Fenton letter and answer—
                receipt for registered letter sent.

JFK

1. The heron-shooting episode of July 1915. See Carlos Baker, *Ernest Hemingway: A Life Story* (New York, 1969), pp. 20–21. 2. EH may mean "The Last Good Country" or "Summer People," both of which appeared in *The Nick Adams Stories,* published by Scribners (New York, 1972).

To WALLACE MEYER, off Mégano de Casigua, Cuba, 6 May 1953

Dear Wallace:

We heard on the radio May 4 that The Old Man and the Sea won the Pulitzer prize along with "Picnic" [by William M. Inge], some reporting by Don Whitehead, and Archie's [MacLeish's] collected poems. Hope this is some good to Scribners and to the book. Never having had one of these I don't know what difference it makes to a book. Can't hurt it I guess. Certainly was lucky I was at sea and away from the telephone so I would not say I was sorry my black dog didn't get it or that I was sure a lot of people would have been more happy and better off if Native Dancer had won the Derby.

Actually Mary was very pleased and I was pleased too although I don't take it very seriously after the A Farewell to Arms business and For Whom the Bell Tolls. Wasn't it that year [1941] that they refused to give a prize at all? I remember Max [Perkins] writing me about it. There was some kind of monkey business too about *A Farewell to Arms.* But I've forgotten what it was. Anyway somebody must have dug up something about it because they spoke about me winning this one on the news cast again yesterday morning and on Lowell Thomas last night. That's a hell of a long time to keep a simple piece of news like that on the radio.

Am sure my old whore Leopoldina whose favourite book is the one she calls Too Many Short Stories by Ernest Hemingway celebrated the award with my other friends at the Floridita. It was on the Cuban radio too at 15 minute intervals all day. Leopoldina and Co. probably think it is the Nobel prize and they are waiting for me to come back and spend the money.

In case anybody is worried that I would pull that [Sinclair] Lewis publicity stunt and not accept the prize (don't say I said this nor mention Lewis), you can tell the committee or whoever gives it that quotes Mr. Hemingway heard that The Old Man and the Sea had won the Pulitzer Prize while he was at sea with his wife on the Pilar which is not equipped with radio telephone. He thanks the committee very much (end quotes). There isn't anything more I should do about it is there? Let me know. Am sending this off to you this afternoon by Juan the chauffeur who brings Taylor Williams down to the fishing port of La Mulatta at 1500 today. We'll be getting back to the Finca by the end of this week or first of next.

Best to everybody Wallace. I'll buy you a drink on it when I get to town. Mary has to go to see her family. They are taking our getting off to Africa OK. Hope the Christ nothing happens when we get out there so Mary would have to come back. Must close this up. Mary is out fishing and I am going to take the Tin Kid when she comes in and try to get in an hour or so before the Tin goes in to pick up Taylor.

Best always
Ernest

PUL

To PATRICK HEMINGWAY, Pamplona, Spain, 11 July 1953

Dear Mouse:

Thanks for your letter with the gen on how to reach your farm. We will arrive at Mombassa on Fernand de Lesseps Aug 27th and proceed to Potha-Machakos. Philip [Percival] is going out with us and he will have another character to do the work. Mayito [Menocal] is coming. He's very excited. We won't hit you until late in Sept. I think. We'll write you when Philip and I staff it out. Am shipping guns etc, arms etc out to [O. M.] Rees in Nairobi.

Having a fine trip here getting the gen for an appendix to Death In The Afternoon on the evolution and decline of the modern bull fight. One marvellous matador though—Nino de la Palmas boy, Antonio Ordoñez. Better than his father was on his father's best day.

Much love to you and Henny. Address c/o Guaranty Trust Co. of N.Y., 4 Place de la Concorde, Paris, France / cable address (GARRITOS). They will forward.

Papa

Am bringing all the word on Key West. It's all good.

PUL
Papa

To BERNARD BERENSON, at sea, 11 August 1953

Dear B.B.:

With the French strike, and all, God knows (if he follows it) what has become of our letters. I'm a couple ahead I think. Anyway there has been no word from you since we left Cuba.

When I found that a U.S. citizen needed no visa for Spain (Tourisme is an industry now) I told Mary I would take her to see the Prado and other sights. It was a little spooky at the border, but only for a moment. Afterward they seemed rather proud and pleased that one had the cojones to come. It really took very little as they would not harm Mary who had never been there and it was late to shoot me. They treated us very well and when journalists asked, hopefully, if I would not want to change any of F.W.T.B. Tolls now I told them that whatever I'd written I'd written and that anything I had signed I was responsible for.

We stayed at the Hotel Florida where I had lived with Martha during the siege of the town and there were no ghosts. The Prado was wonderful and I was very proud of the care the Republic had taken of the pictures. Someone should write about that properly some time. Now I have all the good pictures again in my head and in my heart, much more secure than if they were in my dining room. They had never gone, of course, but it was lovely to give them to Mary though it was no gift since she could have had all Spain, and freely, if she had not the taint of being married to me. As it was the noise of the trams bothered her and the plateau was arid and my friends were repetitious. But she liked the pictures and the bull fights, she has a true feeling for both just as she has a lovely place, but God deliver us all from women's brains and from the lack of mercy of the brave ones. Really I don't think any of them are brave. They have a lack of imagination and when anything hits them they think they are the first person it has ever happened to. Sometimes it is as hard to trust a woman who has never born a child, being of the age for it, as it is to trust a banker or a high priced surgeon. I think whores are nicer in many ways and more trustworthy emotionally and, probably, about money. But you've probably known better women than I have or treated them better. Spain is really no country for a woman unless she is Spanish. So it's not a fair course to put them over.

We were to go to Africa on a French ship sailing August 14th which would have made time to drive to Firenze. But it was cancelled in Madrid and we had to sail on this ship from Marseilles on Aug. 6. We had a Lancia and a good racing driver from Udine (arranged through Venice and Friuli and with what Mondadori money left over after the Prix Hemingstein) but even with racing driving it was a little brusque. Then the damned ship stopped at Genova with Settignani just out of range and so again I was like the stupid one who never did see Carcasonne. (Have seen Carc. etc and the Aigues Mortes is much better if you like fortified towns.)

Christ I wish I could paint. I was painting that town in my head with the crusaders off loading their baggage and their piss-pots to leave from Le Grau de Roi. I remember that Crusade so well that I always have to be careful not to say I made it. But I didn't make it and I'll never see you. It is all part of the same thing though. Now that I know how it is it is much simpler and more acceptable.

This afternoon we will arrive off Port Said for the miserable passage of our chicken-shit crusade. Yesterday there was a great North wind off the mountains until we came into the lee of Crete. Now it is a following sea. But it was a clean cold wind, the brother of the Bora, and with everything of winter on the 11th day of August.

If it is even of comic interest I prayed for you sincerely and straight in Chartres, Burgos, Segovia and two minor places. It is sort of cheerful for a non believing ⅛ Northern Cheyenne[1] to pray for a Jew but if they have it to sell I am a buyer. Sorry not to have made the home office of Santiago de Compostella. But we have tickets in the 3 sweepstakes above which could not be better spread.

Much love,
Ernest

I TATTI

1. See EH to Harvey Breit, 23 July 1956.

To BERNARD BERENSON, Kajiado, Tanganyika–Kenya border, 15 September 1953

Dear B.B.:

Are you all right? It has been a long time since I have heard.

This is a fine trip. We have been killing cattle-killing lions for the Masai. The Masai are all very rich in cattle and there is no reason for the lions not to kill a few. But like most rich people they are very avare and we only kill one for every ten they want killed. Yesterday we ran with a lot of Morani spearmen. They threw very spectacular epileptic type fits when I shot the lion but if you did not watch them they quieted down. They weren't as nice as the Masai we had been with on the other side of the desert nor could they run as well and they were very reluctant about closing with the lion.

Mary is very well and has finally found a country that is as tough as she is. The rains have failed for two years and it is desert and oasis country now. But the Masai hire natives from Tanganyika to dig wonderful wells in the dry river beds. For the price of one cow they get a well dug that will water 500 head of cattle.

We get up at 5 a.m. and hunt in the early morning light. The birds are very beautiful and we usually see elephant and rhino every day beside the animals we need for meat. Lion is very good to eat. The tenderloin tastes like wiener schnizel when it is breaded.

Please write and let me know you are well.

Much love,
Ernest

I TATTI

To HARVEY BREIT, near Magadi, Kenya, 3 January 1954

Dear Harvey:

How are you kid and how is everything? We're camped here on the Kenya-Tanganyika border. I've been in this area now about seven weeks. Got made an Honorary Game Warden and due to the emergency [Mau-Mau rebellion] been acting game ranger here. It is a first class life. Problems all day and every night. Like yest. 21 elephants hit a shamba [village] belonging to my Wakamba Fiancée's family. They are travelling and nine go through the corn which is nearly 15 feet high now after the rain. But they are not really bad we figure because they just go through and eat a swathe as they move. One group of seven and one of five go by outside. Track them up in the hills and then leave Arab Minor the game scout with another man to spook them off if they come back that night. Check the buffalo herd (82) and they are OK. Find the lioness that had the cubs day before Christmas; she is OK. She killed a water buck out of a herd of 11. He was a friend of mine since September but there are six young bucks coming up and one will take over the herd. But I feel bad about him. Go to bed and get up in the night and take a walk with my spear. Study the noises and the different ones the game make at night. Don't use any flash light and go by myself in soft shoes. In the morning tea at 5:30 and Miss Mary and I go out with her gun bearer Charo who must be around 80 and is shorter than she is, and mine, N'Gui, who is the son of M'Cola who was my gun bearer when I wrote TGHOA [*The Green Hills of Africa*]. N'Gui is a *very* tough boy— served 7 years in K.A.R. [King's African Rifles] Abyssinia, Burma, etc. He speaks some Italian from Abyssinia. He and I are in love with 2 girls here in the Wakamba Shamba. It is a beautiful shamba on a creek with anyway 15 acres of corn and small crops and our girls are heiresses, sort of like Brenda Frazier in the old days only black and very beautiful. Every day they bring us presents; sweet corn and beer they make (very good) and today I gave them a pound of lard and the haunch of a warthog Miss Mary shot. Also some salt and a copy of Life. Yesterday I met my girl's mother and her brother and two sisters. Her father is not awfully distinguished altho he is very well off. Her mother is very nice and has a new baby. Miss Mary just stays the hell away from it and is understanding and wonderful. I got to know my fiancée while she [Mary] was away when we killed a leopard in an awful dog fight and everybody came to celebrate in a big N'Goma sort of an Epworth League meeting only a little different. I have to kill the beasts that kill their stock or molest and destroy their crops. So as long as I go OK on that I have a certain popularity. The beasts are no dopes by the time they take up marauding. Harvey really I think you would be interested. It is like knowing *every* day you are going to pitch in big league ball. Pitching you have to do with your arm so you could never start every day but I am a relief pitcher in this. You never come on until it's no good. Have gone back to chewing tobacco to have confidence.

It's like this. You sit down to write like Flaubert, H. James (not Jesse) etc. and two characters with spears come and stand easy outside the tent. I am trying to write and Miss Mary says, "There are two of your friends to see you. I don't know whether they are from your girl's family or if they have a problem." "They must have a problem," I say. So they have. They live 25 miles away. There are no young warriors. (Young warriors have all taken to drink.) The lion came into the boma and killed 2 cows. He is outside the boma now eating one of the cows and growling. It is 25 miles away. ¾ of it passable by moto-cah. So you go, view the remains of the cows, ascertain where the water is, follow (track) the lion out of the fucking country. The exercise will be repeated in 3 to 4 days. I tracked one lion *down* Kilimanjaro with N'Gui and the other hunting dogs and then (sweating) had to go back up in the rain.

Now weigh 186. Was steady at 190–192 for a long time. Have my head shaved because that is how my fiancée likes it. She likes to feel all the holes in my head and the wealts. It is sort of fun too. I never knew about it before. I thought they were a kind of disgrace. But not here. Harvey, African girls, Kamba and Masai anyway, are really wonderful and all that nonsense about that they can't love you is not true. It is just that they are more cheerful than girls at home. My girl is completely impudent, her face is impudent in repose, but absolutely loving and delicate rough. I better quit writing about it because I want to write it really and I mustn't spoil it. Anyway it gives me too bad a hardon.

N'Gui is about 30 he thinks and he has five wives and with the money from this trip he will get maybe 2 more. Maybe only one, the sister of my girl. Maybe he will marry my girl because he and I are brothers so it is OK. But my girl wants to go to N.Y. where she will see me kill all those animals in that prehistoric animal number of Life. She thinks they have all those brontosauruses and Pterodactyls where I live along with the Mammoth, the Sabertoothed tigers and Irish Elk and the Giant Sloth because she saw the pictures.

At night I tell them how we killed George Armstrong Custer and the 7th Cavalry and they think we are wasting our time here and should get the hell to America. It's a lovely country, Harvey.

Much love and happy New Year

HUL Papa

To BERNARD BERENSON, Shimoni, Kenya, 2 February 1954

Dear B.B.:

Thank you very much for the cable.[1] It made Mary and me both very happy. You were so nice to send it and send it properly. We leave Mombasa (old spelling Mombassa) on March 10 (Si Dios y la Puta Hostia quieren) [If God and the Whore Host grant it] and arrive Venice [March] 26 (Si Dios y la Puta Hostia quieren) and after we see the Venetian branch of the family will drive down and make a small pilgrimage to you. Will write you from Venezia, address there Gritti Palace Hotel. From March 26 on.

I have many funny things to tell you and you alone. How you say that in W'Kamba is with one word *Tu*. This means you alone, you only, you who I love, you who I see again, you with who I share a tribal secret. In Kamba (M'Wakamba is just an affected way of talking by Proffessors (misspelled) who say Kiswahili) etc. you say all that with Tu. It is strange that you should say it the same way in Spanish the only language I really know. If I had been born in Spain like your defunct friend [George] Santayana I would have written in Spanish and been a fine writer I hope. As it is I must write in English, a bastard tongue but fairly manoeuverable. Spanish is a language Tu.

This is a funny thing. Maybe—concussion is very strange—and I have been studying it: Double vision; hearing comes and goes, your capacity for scenting (smelling something) can became acute beyond belief.

I want to write to Adriana in Venice and I write quite a good and a truly loving letter and I read it over to see if it is OK and it is wonderfully OK except that half is in Spanish and ½ in Kamba. That is when you know things are perhaps not too good.

Tu. So today I write to you Tu and see if I connect the hand a little better with the brain.

Miss Mary is fine and her ribs about healed. She never had broken ribs before and did not know there is nothing to do for them except not breathe deeply. This is easy; but hard to teach a woman.

B.B. (Brother, Tu) I must write too much because am working at not being Kivisha. You know you tell the press you were never better etc. That is in order not to tell any secrets of our metier which is to ride it out or *durer* (probably mis-spelled). But what your true friend has now and in the hour of our Puta Muerte is: Ruptured kidney (much blood and pieces of kidney in urine). The hell with the rest of it. It goes on from there. It is all much better but it hurts and people aren't indestructible even if the journalists say so.

I declare to win on this one though it would be easier not to get up. Death is just shit as we both know. But I want to see my lovely Adriana and I want to make the small pilgrimage to see you. B.B. I hope such a long letter will not Bore you too much.

Remember if you wish to do so (and don't do it if it isn't good) that in some ways I am your pup from being educated, a little, by you through the books, the god-damned beautifully worked out lovely books. I was a Bergamo boy before I ever heard your name, and I had not heard it only because I had grievously neglected being brought up properly. But I am sort of your pup. You never have to acknowledge me and can always denounce me with impunity.

But B.B. (my brother and father) if you ever wanted to father a really bad repeat bad (Give no quarter-Take no quarter) boy then you have this worthless object who will make the small pilgrimage but I promise will not embarrass you. Specially with Miss Mary who is under the impression that she (SHE) keeps the discipline in the column.

Please forgive me for continuing writing. It is only because I am lonely. You with your lovely achieved age are, in a way, or without any stupid compliments my *HERO*. Also Miss Mary's. Also Patrick's. This my only existing father only if it [is] any fun for you (Tu).

Anyway (get out Big Glass) and read it. We all love you very much and let us all go to (I wasn't brave) gether and have fun. God (Gott) BLESS You and our love my true love

Ernesto
Hemingway (taking off)

[In left margin:] Written but not re-read. If silly burn it.

I TATTI   E.H.

1. Like many others, Berenson had cabled congratulations on the Hemingways' survival after two plane crashes on 22 and 23 January at Murchison Falls and Butiaba, Uganda. The Shimoni visit followed. See Carlos Baker, *Ernest Hemingway: A Life Story* (New York, 1969), pp. 518-22.

To HARVEY BREIT, Shimoni, 4 February 1954

Dear Harvey:

Have established some communication between the right arm and the head so can write you by hand. If I did it before please forget it. Wrote a lovely letter to [Adriana in] Venice and then found, when I read it before mailing, it was about half in Wakamba.

For your information the 2nd kite [plane] that pranged [crashed] was a little bit bad. We always say, "You never hit me you son of a bitch" but I ruptured the kidneys, or maybe only one, the liver, the spleen (whoever she is) had the brain fluid ooze out to soak the pillow every night, burnt the top of the scalp off, etc. Also (also you see how you can get with a big concussion) had to take two breathes in the fire which is something that never really helped anybody except of course Joan of Arc the reincarnation (admitted) of Gen. Charles De Gaulle. Also lost sight of left eye (was never very good anyway).

Harvey it was a little more rugged than Nobel Prize winners corncob by FAULKNER.

Miss Mary OK but nerves a little spotty. Was very brave and lovely.

It was more and less indecisive for a time but now have stopped
bleeding from all the orifices and always had declared to win. But it was
comic to read Billy Rose that cheap cancer that Israel must wear. If you
know any Puerto Ricans please give them my love.

Harvey, kid, things are no good at the moment. I had a good chance to
think them out in the hour of my death (2). Know only one thing well.
How to boot off the counter-attack. Have kicked it off.

Be a good boy and some time I would like to see you. Would you do
me a great favour and call up George Jean Nathan and give him and
Miss ------ my love? And if not too much bother call George Brown—
225 West 57th Street and give him love from Miss Mary and regards
from me.

Yours always,

HUL   ~~Papa~~ Ernest.

To ADRIANA IVANCICH, Nice, France, 9 May 1954

0515

Dearest Adriana:

Last night I wrote you but I just read it and tore it up. It was a late at
night letter. Worthless.

Yesterday was a very beautiful trip from Torino down to Cuneo with
the lovely green of the valley and the snow mountains not too close and
not too far away. Then the pass and the close mountains, the tunnel, the
other passes and then Nice. Very Nice.

It started to get light about 4 o'clock. Spring is closer here.

Daughter you know how I miss you and leaving was like an amputa-
tion. Thank you for being so good and lovely to me.

I look at all the things for both of us but it is only a thing you do
instead of living.

Pretty soon I will have to throw this away so I better try to be a calm
like Henry James the writer. Did you ever read Henry James? He was
a great American writer who came to Venice and looked out of the
window and smoked his cigar and thought. He was born too early and
never saw you.

Venice-Milano en auto-strade is the most vulgar and awful. Finally
there are so many signs you can't see the signs for the signs. Only [Lago
di] Garda beautiful.

Ingrid [Bergman] is the same. Sweet and good and honest and married to the 22 pound rat [Roberto Rossellini]. This not jealousy. Maybe he is the undiscovered 42 pound rat. He makes good children anyway.

The first day travel hurt the back enough to make nausea. Did not know you could hurt so completely. Yesterday hardly hurt at all. Today will be fine. We go to see Cezanne and Van Gogh country: Aix en Provence, St. Remy, Les Baux, then Avignon and Nimes may be on to Montpellier and beyond.

Daughter I love you and miss you so much. You know we were pretty good maybe and with things bad we *never* fought.

Darling (Hotch) [A. E. Hotchner] is very good. I am not as good a companion as I should be because I have death lonesomeness for you. But we make jokes and he has such a loveing and learning mind.

Please give my love to Miss Dora [Adriana's mother] and to Jackie and Francesca. I was very happy to be with a family. Hope not too much nuisance to the family.

Today I'll try to be better company to Hotch.

I love you so very much and always. The sun is up now and it is a lovely day.

Will write you things, daughter.

Papa

I love you (calm).

Maybe can hear your voice (quietly) or see you con la calma consiguente [with the resulting stillness]. How are you?

Love

TEXAS
Papa

To ALFRED RICE, La Finca Vigia, 12 July 1954

Dear Alfred:
About Income in 1953:
You can get from Scribner's amount paid me in 1953, and total of books bought, to deduct.

Movie rights to Old Man and The Sea—you have record of these.

Income from Div. and Interest—get from Guaranty Trust Co. of N.Y.

I also received direct—$400 from W. R. Warner Co.

Income from Jonathan Cape paid in 1953, get from Cape. Cable address, CAPAJON, London.

Foreign income, radio, television, other rights—you have records of these.

Anything paid me direct by Esquire, get from Esquire.

J. Cape will reply to a cable to London, Esquire to a wire. Cables and
wires are much cheaper from New York than here.
LOOK paid $15,000 in June or July, 1953—advance on Expenses. The
other $10,000 was paid in January, 1954.

Mary got $270 from VOGUE, $90 from Modern Woman, London, and
$150 in dividends from International Cellucotton.
Her money from Look came in 1954.
    I do not think there was any money from endorsements. All I ever
endorsed anyway was Parker Fountain Pen and Ballantines Ale and this
was some years ago.
    For your and the Bureau's information all 1953 expenses for aircraft
charter were absolutely necessary for the expedition. Most safaris use
aircraft much more extensively than we did. In 1953 we were on safari
from August 22nd until December 31 in 1953. Philip Percival met us with
transport in Mombassa. I paid for gas, car hire, expenses and for his time
in recruiting the outfit. I can promise you that our safari expenses were
more reasonable than for any other made for that length of time.
    I hope you will point out to the Internal Revenue people that it is
necessary to spend money to make money. They know this of course.
But it would be interesting for them to figure how much taxable income
was produced by my last trip to Africa. It produced The Snows of
Kilimanjaro which was one of the really big money making pictures. I
paid tax on, I believe, $125,000 from that myself and I do not know how
much money 20th Century Fox paid the government on it. There was
also as a result of that trip Green Hills of Africa and The Short Happy
Life of Francis Macomber which made plenty of money for the Government as a picture. My last trip to Africa must have made the Internal
Revenue a sum which I have no idea how to figure.
    Would you please point out to them that getting that sort of material
is extremely expensive and extremely dangerous. If I had not been using
an airplane and very near dead [from amebic dysentery] there would
not have been any Snows of Kilimanjaro. What money I can make for
them out of this last trip depends entirely on how good shape I can get
in and sit on my ass and write without worrying about taxes.
    They do not allow any depreciation to a writer for busting his head
and his back and his insides to get material that no one else can get and
that pays off as no one else's stuff does. This time I have really wonderful
stuff to write but now when I should be writing I am chasing receipts
and writing letters like this. About the expenses doing the field work of
research for making The Old Man and The Sea picture: all those expenses
were legitimate. I had many more expenses than that but when I am

working really hard and concentrated on what I am doing I don't think about book keeping. Then since I use cash a lot when I am working all I have to justify expenses is when I write checks. You can't go along the Cuban coast writing checks and checks don't get you very far in Africa where people will not even take paper money. They want hard money and you carry it in a tin box. After a lion spearing when you come to pay off the spearmen who are so worked up that they would as soon spear you as anything else and are throwing themselves around in the thorn bushes and frothing at the mouth from the stuff they brew to get brave on you don't get receipts from the spear characters. The chief can't read and can't write. Maybe you could try to take their thumb prints. But I was always a little tired myself and lacked the necessary equipment. So for many times when I had to bring the money sack out and really lighten it there haven't been any charges made.

Alfred this was a very rough year even before we smashed up in the air-craft. But I have a diamond mine if people will let me alone and let me dig the stones out of the blue mud and then cut and polish them. If I can do it I will make more money for the Government than any Texas oilman that get's his depreciation. But I have been beat-up worse than you can be and still be around and I should be working steadily on getting better and then write and not think nor worry about anything else.

If I have forgotten any income will check it in if it ever turns up. It is all checked through you are the sources I have indicated. Sorry to bother you to send the check up wires but it is a big saving and we have tried to make up for causing you that trouble by getting this data to you promptly. Since I am not familiar with the new Revenue laws Mary has listed things and left it up to you to decide whether they are deductible.

You know what the problem is of entertaining here. You have to do a lot of it when there is a big deal on and this year (1953) took a lot of it. I do not think Mary's estimates are excessive but you know better about this than I do. I know that you cannot make big deals without spending money and that this place is as important in big money deals as having a good office in New York. Juan, the chauffeur, is not excessive at $50. a month when you consider that that is the only communication with town. I probably have as small a payroll for a business of anybody that files a return. But I pay them in other ways that I never claim on such as doctor bills, hospital expenses, build them houses, loan money when they have the perpetual problems etc.

I hope your wife and Philip are well and that everything goes well with you.

Best always,
Ernie

JFK

To HARVEY BREIT, La Finca Vigia, 18 August 1954

Dear Harvey:

Glad you are taking the vacation the way you are and working well.

I see nothing wrong with you doing a play about Scott. He is in the public domain now. I did not like many aspects of the Mizener. What you will have to watch in Budd's [Schulberg's] novel as I remember it is that it is not a very good novel and the woman wasn't very convincing. I would not be tied too closely to the book if I were either of you. You can draw on Mizener's book which supposed to be history and common knowledge is certainly in the public domain now as much as Scott is.

If it is any use to you as basic background: When I knew Scott in Paris and on the Riviera he had never slept with another woman than Zelda. This is the straight gen.

She was unfaithful to him first with a young French naval flying officer.

That was the first thing that busted Scott up. Then she was crazy (Scyzophrenic; you look up the spelling. I've mis-spelled and it is too far to the dictionary in Mary's room) for a long time and nobody knew it. She was insanely jealous of Scott's work and any time he would work hard she would bust it up. This wasn't difficult as he was a much more than potential rummy. What saved him was that he couldnt drink. He had no tolerance then for alcohol and would pass out cold at the number of drinks that would just make you feel good. He enjoyed passing out cold too because it made him the center of attention. Without meaning to be he was a terrific exhibitionist and as time went on he became a nastier and nastier drunk. Budd knows him from one trip and I don't know how much in Holywood (Insert an l). I knew him for a long time and under all sorts of circumstances and was his hero which is a job you can have any time.

He had all the smugness of the rummy combined with the self abasement of the Irish rummy. He also had wonderful talent, almost no education and he lost his confidence when Zelda told him that his penis was smaller than that of a normal man and that he had never satisfied her. He told me this dreadful secret in Michaud's restaurant and I asked him to step into the John where I took a good look at how he was built. He was quite normal in build. I explained to him that he had been looking at his prick from the top which always made it seem fore-shortened. He thought I was taking a great sorrow flippantly. I explained that it was the angle of erection and the ability to stay erect and a few other basic things such as thinking about your partner's pleasure that made a man good or bad in bed. But he had siezed on this excuse for defeat and nothing would cheer him up. I offered to take him over to the Louvre and show him how people were built in the old days but he didn't want to cheer up. Zelda had told him this so it was true. Zelda at this time was completely crazy.

This stuff may be no good to you but it might be. Scott after he got to be a really nasty drunk used to be very bad. I would go out to dinner with him and he would insult people and I would have to square it to keep him from being beaten up. He could never fight a lick on the best day he ever lived and he got so he liked to hit people and I would have to take over. This is one small sample of how it was in Paris. I lived over a saw-mill on the second floor of a Pavillion. My landlord lived on the first floor. Coming up to see us with young Scotty he had her make pe-pee on the floor at the foot of the stairs just outside the landlord's door. It ran in under the door and the landlord came out and very nicely told Scott there was a toilet under the stairs. He thought the child had been caught short.

"I know there is you son of a bitch," Scott said. "And I'll take you and shove your head in it."

There were hundreds and hundreds like that. But when, after one awful night when I had to give a large sum to the doorman at the Plaza to square something really awful Scott had done, I told him I couldn't ever go out and eat with him any more unless he would promise not to be horrible to people, or make an effort not to be anyway, he was able to write that thing about how he spoke with the authority of failure and I with the authority of etc. and so we would never be able to sit at table together again. A fairly smug version.

Zelda ruined him all right because every time he would get straightened out she would get him on the booze. But Harvey he used to seem to love to be humiliated and, of course, to humiliate whoever he was with. I've seen him do things you could hardly forgive a legitimate crazy for doing. At the start he used to be terribly contrite afterwards. Finally he didn't remember. He was always generous and he could be so damned nice sober.

If this gen is no use to you or is confusing throw it away. I never saw him in his Hollywood days and the play is about a guy then. So this sort of gen is probably no good to you. This is about the six years or so after he wrote Gatsby maybe ten I guess [c. 1925–1935]. If any of it is in any way bad for your conception of the character you are writing about forget it. I'm sure he must have been very different in Hollywood and that is where Budd knew him.

When I first knew him he was very good looking in a too pretty way and every time he took a drink his face would change a little and after four drinks the skin would be drawn and it would look like a death's head. I guess you could do that in a play with lighting. But maybe he wasn't that way when Budd knew him. He was nice when he drank wine then or just a couple of aperatifs.

Hope you have luck with the play and with the book.

Would like to have seen that [Ezzard] Charles–[Rocky] Marciano fight. Right now I don't have any feeling for the fights. But when I see a good one again will get it back.

Have to write another letter now to Philip Percival who is very ill in London. Then have to swim a 440. Very hot here now and heavy rains nearly every afternoon.

Have finished one short story and have twenty some pages done on another. Guess I wrote you that before.

If I can be any use to you and help you out on mid twenty stuff with Scott am glad to. It isn't all sour as this letter sounds. Sometimes it was funny. But it never was sound. I knew him better than anybody did then, I guess. Gerald and Sara Murphy (Gerald is head of Mark Cross) knew him very well and saw him oftener than I did. They could help you. So could Archie Mac Leish. I think everybody though is a little reluctant about helping on anything after what Mizener did. Pauline would have been good to talk to. But she's dead.

Best always,

HUL   Hemmingstein

To BERNARD BERENSON, La Finca Vigia, 24 September 1954

Dear B.B.:

It was good to hear from you and to know that you are well. You are very right about how we never achieve what we set out to do. We do make it come off sometimes as we know when we re-read it after a long time. It always reads to me, then, when it's very good as though I must have stolen it from somebody else and then I think and remember that nobody else knew about it and that it never really happened and so I must have invented it and I feel very happy. One always has the illusion about the last thing that has been written and so I have an exaggerated confidence in the Old Man book. Each day I wrote I marvelled at how wonderfully it was going and I hoped that on the next day I would be able to invent truly as I had done the day before. When I had finished, there were only 3 or 4 corrections to be made and I thought there must be something wrong, but each time I read it, it made the same effect on me as a reader, not as one who had written it, that it made before.

I still can't read it without emotion and I know that you will believe that this is not the emotion of someone admiring what he has done, because he did it, but because I was reading it as completely detached as though it were written by someone who was dead for a long time.

We are old enough to try to talk truly and I tell you this only as a curiosity. A few other things which I invented completely such as the story in "For Whom the Bell Tolls" of Pablo and Pilar and their doing away with the fascists in the village. I read, when by chance I have to do it, with complete astonishment that I could have invented as I did. You know that fiction, prose rather, is possibly the roughest trade of all in writing. You do not have the reference, the old important reference. You have the sheet of blank paper, the pencil, and the obligation to invent truer than things can be true. You have to take what is not palpable and make it completely palpable and also have it seem normal and so that it can become a part of the experience of the person who reads it. Obviously, this is impossible and that is probably why it is considered to be valuable when you are able to do it. But it is impossible to hire out or contract to be able to do it, as to hire out to be an alchemist.

But B.B. I think we should never be too pessimistic about what we know we have done well because we should have some reward and the only reward is that which is within ourselves. I would be very proud, that is an understatement, if I had as good a *hoja de servicio* [service record] as you have. The unobtainable is something else. The mountains have all been climbed, most countries worth visiting have been explored long ago and in old places like Africa you learn that many many people had seen everything long before they were financed by missionary money or James Gordon Bennett [American journalist].

Publicity, admiration, adulation, or simply being fashionable are all worthless and are extremely harmful if one is susceptible to them. You must forgive me for presuming that we are the same age but I had the experience of the destruction of vital organs which ordinarily would take a long time to achieve. Also the indelicacies that accompany these destructions and our life expectancy is more or less the same. This does not give me the right to *tutearte* [to use *tu* instead of *usted*] because I have only the brain of 55 but in the Wakamba tribe to which I belong you are an elder at 55 and once you are an elder you are outranked by older elders but you are considered to have reached a certain age, if not of discretion, of experience.

At present I work at about ½ the capacity that I should have but everything is better all the time and, by someone susceptible as good animals to the weather, I can be depressed by it when it is rainy, muggy and with constant barometric changes which change also the pressure

of the vertebra on the spinal cord. There's only 6 weeks more of bad
weather to get through and then we will have the type of weather that
makes you want to write rather than force yourself to write. I am such
a simple writer that in my books the temperature and the weather of
the day is nearly almost that of the weather outside. The type of weather
we have had this summer I would not wish to inflict on anyone reading
what I write and so I'm working in an air-conditioned room which is as
false a way to work as to try to write in the pressurized cabin of a plane.
You get the writing done but it's as false as though it were done in the
reverse of a greenhouse. Probably I will throw it all away, but maybe
when the mornings are alive again I can use the skeleton of what I have
written and fill it in with the smells and the early noises of the birds and
all the lovely things of this finca which are in the cold months very much
like Africa.

But B.B. there is nothing like Africa as there is nothing like youth and
nothing like loving who you love or waking each day not knowing what
the day will bring, but knowing that it will bring something. Here now
things are quite dull except for annoyances and the occasional presence
of people that you like or care for. I think you are better off at Settignano
and you are always better off than me because you have more books.
Thank God for books. I wish that we could contribute to something
which would make people write ones which were worth reading. Mary
would send her love but she is taking a sun bath. I think I may send it,
safely, without consulting her.

> Our best to you always,
> Ernest

I dictated this in the process of breaking in a new secretary. Reading
it over and correcting her errors (too late to correct my own) it reads
a little like a bloody speech.

I TATTI   E.H.

To GENERAL CHARLES T. LANHAM, La Finca Vigia,
10 November 1954

Dear Buck:

Your letter just came about the Time researcher. Christ Buck you
certainly wrote me up. I'll have to stay alive now cuestan lo que cuestan
[whatever the cost] just to speak adequately over your grave. We won't
call it log-rolling. By God it will be coffin rolling.

That Time story was just a straight double cross. You could spot that. I didn't summon the press. They'd been calling up for a week. When the news came through on the radio I made that short statement and then said, "Are there any questions, Gentlemen?" Then they asked what I was going to do with the money and I tried to answer honestly. Then I spoke of Isak Dinesen, Berensen and Sandburg.[1]

You know I know more or less what category of writer I am but that's no reason to act swelled headed. Or tell anybody. And I learned a long time ago not to ever speak frankly or detached about it. Between us I was thinking like this: Sandburg is an old man and he will appreciate it. (He did.) Blickie's wife (Dinesen) is a damn sight better writer than any Swede they ever gave it to and Blickie (Baron Bror Von Blixen-Finecke) is in hell and he would be pleased if I spoke well of his wife. Berenson I thought deserved it (no more than me) but I would have been happy to see him get it. Or any of the three. That's the way your brain is working.

But I sure as hell did not bring their names out as I staggered around drinking Tom Collinses or was it Gin and Tonic?

When I said I was breaking training I meant I was taking a drink before noon which is when I try to knock off work. I drank a gin and tonic and then switched to coco-nut water. Naturally I never said I was going to live only five years. Who is going to put his own mouth on himself? I think I said that I would settle for five more good working years. As I get a good working year out of every three or four that's fair enough. How much writing did I get to do in 1942-3-4-5? None of it matters.

The day they announced the prize was a nice cool windy day and I saw this character Henry Wallace of Time sweating all the time. So I figured he was going to knife me. So sure enough he did. But when you notice things like that, which is how guys like you and me stay alive, there's nothing you can do under the circumstances. I remarked on it to Mary at the time. But she knew better and told me not to be suspicious. (Wallace says all those cracks were put in at Time. EH.)

Buck you should have been around when I was being responsible for Miss Mary in Africa and her with the valour of ignorance. But she was awfully good though most of the time. And a lot of the time she was exemplary. Then too she's brave on the ocean when things are bad and most women aren't. And she knows about the ocean too. She's over in K.W. now getting that house fixed up to rent.

Buck I can't come up. Wish I could. I'm in a belle epoque writing[2] if they leave me alone. I've gotten back into the country and I live in it every day and some of the stuff I think you'll like unless you have too strong views on mis-cegenation. There's quite a few things beside that though. But everyday people don't come in and fuck me up I go awfully good. Mustn't put my mouth on it.

You know when I called up I was trying to decide whether I ought to accept the thing or not. There were a lot of good reasons not to. But nobody would understand them except your friends and other people would think you were trying to show boat or letting your country down by not taking it etc. But I wanted you to sort of handle me either way. But you were laid up and I didn't want to worry you. So I handled it the best I could and then no matter how you do it Time spoils it with a bunch of slanted untruths.

I'm very grateful for you saying you approved of me when we were together. They'll probably twist it all around or throw it out in favor of the testimony of someone I kicked the ass of in High School. It's always easy for somebody to prove I was a phony since I've had to deny everything I was ever proud of under oath and under orders. Not everything. But plenty and keep on denying plenty and would do it again tomorrow. I was horrified they were going to have Time cover story. If they put some stuff [in] I will have to move. Mr. [Spruille] Braden did some talking while we were in Africa that wasn't good for man or beast.

But I guess will just have to sweat it out like everything else. I didn't give them your name. I think they must have got it, in relation to me, from their research which would naturally include the Cowley piece. I've seen Dave Bruce a couple of times, last time in Venice this trip, and he said Cowley used practically nothing of what he gave him. Maybe it was because Cowley is sort of deaf. Maybe he was saving it for a book. You never know.

I wonder who else they got hold of? No use wondering. Nothing I can do. Maybe your testimony will save me yet, General. Anyway I did not write A Fable by William Faulkner. I can swear to that with a clean heart.

Old Mousie is coming along really good hunting. If he gets through 1955 without being killed he will be about through with his apprenticeship. I wrote you, I guess, that we got him old Mumu a very famous old elephant tracker from around VOI, also poacher First Class, and he is breaking Mousie in. No White Hunter. The hard way. His last trip with Mumu Mouse shot a very fine buffalo exactly as he should and a fine black maned lion. This kind of hunting on foot with nobody to back you up is rugged. He loves it and he is shooting very well now. He writes me a complete sort of after action report (he never lies) and then I write him a critique. He is a natural hunter and he learned very fast last year. At first he was nervous but he is never spooked. This is dangerous, of course, but he makes up for it in being able to shoot absolutely cold. He is shooting a .357 Magnum. He is painting well too so I guess he has about as good a life as anyone. In a couple of years he should be able to get a job with the Game Department. Maybe he won't want to. But I think he will. It is a fine job because you only shoot animals that are more or less criminals and you decide whether they are or not. There is a certain amount of control work which is not of criminals of course and no animal is a criminal probably by his standards. But some can get a little bit bad although it is nearly always because they get old and their natural wild food is too fast for them to kill. Then there are always the animals that have been wounded and are dangerous to everyone that have to be done away with.

An outfit wants me to go to Africa to make a picture. But I would much rather go and hunt with Mouse and teach him what I can and work for the Game Dept. in the emergency. They are very short of people and even with my defects I can be useful.

Too many people know we live here and we have had too much publicity and people come like to see the elephant in the zoo. I'm very sick of it and would like to get somewhere that they don't have white peoples. The sea is still a fine place but the weather has been horrible and now, when I could get out, Gregorio [Fuentes] has to go to Miami to see his daughter who has some sort of trouble. Have not been on the boat in six weeks. We were not hit by any of the hurricanes but had to take the precautions and had all the rain and nasty weather.

Interrupted by arrival of the people who wanted to make pictures. I insisted preliminary recon be made in Jan. as by my gen it is not feasible now. Whole thing pending. Make nothing nor sign nothing for 1956 until after recon.

If you had to make a Nobel speech what would you say? That's an easy one for you maybe. Looks impossible to me. Excuse worthless letter. Been swamped. Tu amigo de siempre.

Ernesto

Hope so much the operated hernia OK. Let me know. Forgive egotistical letter. Was getting to you when was interrupted. Will write.

PUL   EH.

1. On EH's Nobel Prize award see Carlos Baker, *Ernest Hemingway: A Life Story* (New York, 1969), pp. 526–29. 2. EH was working on a book about his recent African safari. Some 55,000 words of the approximately 200,000 words in the manuscript were excerpted and posthumously published as "African Journal" in *Sports Illustrated* 35 (20 December 1971) and 36 (3 and 10 January 1972).

To GEORGE M. ABBOTT,[1] La Finca Vigia, 30 November 1954

Dear Mr. Abbott:

Thank you very much for your letter. I have waited to reply until I could compose the statement which the Ambassador would read on my behalf at the banquet. It is enclosed with this letter and I hope it will be O.K. It runs a little under the usual speech length, but perhaps this is a virtue.

This afternoon the Public Affairs Officer of the Embassy cut a recording of it which will go forward to you tomorrow to be turned over in due course to the Swedish Radio. I did this because I was not approached by the Swedish Radio on this subject. The Swedish Honorary Consul General had recorded a broadcast here for the Swedish Radio which I believe was delivered several days ago.

Will you please give my very best regards to the Ambassador if he is there and tell him I am sorry to burden him with delivering an address but that I have tried to keep it as short as possible.

I remember our meeting in Marseille and I hope you are enjoying yourself in Stockholm. I am very sorry not to see you there and wish that my doctors would have allowed me to make the trip. Perhaps we may meet there another time.

Sincerely yours,
Ernest Hemingway

Enclosure

P.S. If there should be any changes in protocol as to the manner of the address, will you please check on them and insert the proper salutation. Thank you.

JFK

1. Abbott was chargé d'affaires at the American Embassy in Stockholm.

To GENERAL E. E. DORMAN–O'GOWAN, La Finca Vigia, 23 December 1954

Dear Chink:

Am very ashamed not to have written. Was over-run by journalists, photographers and plain and fancy crazies. Was in the middle of writing a book and it is a little like being interrupted in fornication.

I had no idea how bad that whole business was that ended up with you the O'Gowan. It is shocking and awful. You'd joked about it but I never knew it was that devilish.

Hope this Larry Solon character won't do you the dirty too. My own experience has been that any time you ever talk it is a mistake. Enclose a carbon of what was finally said at Stockholm. It was probably a mistake to talk there too. But anyway I kept it short. Think you will see a few things in it though that only you and I know about.

Can see how you feel even about the Mau-Mau. That is a strange business though that it is better to talk than write about.

Chink please remember one thing. You are always welcome here; anytime and as long as you want to stay. Please know that and that I always have the necessary to handle your transport and expenses. I'd love to come to you but right now must stay put and have it out with this book.

This has been a sort of rough year. You know we never discuss casualties but I would not have minded going for a shit at Murchison or Butiaba except I had to look after Mary and there is always the obligation to survive, that mis-understood obligation. But I believe I would have stayed in the kite that burned at Butiaba, once Mary was out, if I could have seen the rest of 1954 as she would be and as she'd feel. We call this "black-ass" and one should never have it. But I get tired of pain sometimes even if that is an ignoble feeling.

You know I was always a fairly cheerful character but have no pleasure nor fun of any kind out of this Swedish gong at all. It is nice money to pay taxes with but otherwise it only furnishes people with some sort of a license to intrude on your privacy. Yesterday was cutting up green turtle and fish we'd acquired on a trip down the coast to get away from the telephone and packaging them for the deep freeze and the representative of the defunct Basque Govt. called; also the Portuguese Consul General and the Chinese ditto. The water supply and the electricity had both cut out and so I took what pleasure there was in shaking them by the hand with a turtle smeared hand and wishing them God Speed.

Better not count on me to fight the local opposition. Unlike the Scottish

I cannot run either forwards nor backwards. And certainly not like hell both ways. I take it your type of war is not that on which back-broken ex-generals of irregs. (not gaelic speaking) can be carried out to think at on a litter. It will be fun though in hell to sit quietly [on] a cooling pile of cinders and listen to Maurice de Saxe.

I'm glad you've flown over Murchison [Falls]. Makes it seem more homey. You should have been there that night. It was really comic. Have lots of comic things to tell you when we get together. Don't know anybody it would be more cheering to see. If you can't come here Chink I'll really come to Eire.

Please try and forgive such a stupid letter. We came back home in a big N.W. blow; beam sea and I steered a 5½ hour watch on the flying bridge to show myself I could and then three hours more below and the net results were that I did it but I can't do it. I used to be able to steer 15 hrs. on the flying bridge and have steered 18 without being relieved. Now am not worth a damn. More worthless than when I had the bowell trouble that time on across the St. Bernard in Street shoes. Wasn't it lovely coming down the Italian side and what fun we had in Aosta and then in Milano in the old Galleria.

We always had a lot of fun Chink. Do you remember beer drinking at Aigle and the horse-chestnuts "like waxen candelabras" and our Bob Racing team at Les Avants? We had fun in Paris and at the saw-mill too. Paris was a lovely town then.[1] We'll have some good fun yet. I know I'll get over the worthless way I feel because it takes time for things to clear up.

Don't you be any more bitter than you have to be. Remember we all should have been quite dead before we were twenty and so we are as ancient and as little understood as people can be. We overstayed our welcome and you having brains and being a fighting man would always be suspect in your Army. I have never known a fighting man with a good brain to ever come to any good end.

If you were a writer you'd have it bad too. I'm always suspect because I'm not particularly a coward. That shows bravado or insensibility. If you do not cry out under torture you must, automatically, not be hurt.

But all that is just the usual ton of shit that we were born to eat. You and all your family have a good Christmas and we'll fight again in 1955 and we won't lose touch anymore.

Mary sends her love to all.

                                          Best always, Chink.
PH. PUL   O'Hem

---

1. See *The Green Hills of Africa* (New York, 1935), pp. 70–71, 279–80.

To PHILIP PERCIVAL,[1] La Finca Vigia, 4 September 1955

Dear Pop:

Thank you for your letter and for sending word of the boys. Patrick wrote me about his job. He is out on a 42 day Safari with a hunter named Russel Douglas. They had been out two weeks and were doing ok; nothing special so far. He told me about Henny's job which seemed an o.k. idea as she did not want to stay at John's Corner alone with Pat hunting. She could never run a house or a farm and it is better for her to keep busy at something.

Pat wrote Gregory was behaving well and that Africa was doing him a world of good. There is no sense me worrying about them since there is nothing I can do. But would appreciate any gen you have any time.

We are filming the actual fishing for The Old Man. Got a 472 and 422 marlin on the first day and some very good shots. Have to get up at 4 and we fish till dark. Steered 7 hours on the flying bridge yest without coming down, ten each day before. Have four local boats rigged as in the story and with two motor boats we ride herd on them and close with the cameras when a fish is hooked. Have big Cinemascope cameras in each boat and a combat camera extra. They shoot from the shoulder and are very fast and accurate to use. When the boats pick up and hoist their sails for home we two boats troll to try to hook one for jumping shots. Mary brings out hot chow at noon for the fishermen and the camera men; in containers for the fishermen in the small boats and in big covered caseroles for the two camera boats. We feed them good; choice of broiled lobster; broiled chicken or broiled steak, black beans and rice as a vegetable and a good salad and fruits; papaya or/and oranges. We have this chow made up by the restaurant at Cojimar the fishing port. In addition I supply ice, bait, gear and keep the characters happy, steer and keep watch on the boats until about 1430 or 1600 and then get down in the fighting chair and troll sixteen to 18 miles home. Mary likes it because she says it is just like running a Safari on the ocean and she is very proud to be in her own boat and happy to be so popular. It is very good for their morale to see a girl coming out in any weather with hot chow. Have camera crew of fourteen men and eight fishermen in the small boats. So with Gregorio, my mate, me and Mary and Elicin [Arguëlles] (cousin of Mayito [Menocal] and his mate and apprentice) on the 2nd boat it is nearly the size of a small safari. We carry a doctor too who doubles as a bar-tender. So far have kept them all happy and keen and we are ahead on the work to be done. It is easy when all you have to do is talk Spanish and easy. But have only three days under our belts and there are twelve to go. Very strong good current though and the fishing should get better as this full moon wanes. If we can't get a big enough fish here will go to Cabo Blanco in Peru where 1000 pounders are common. But they [are] over-grown sluggish fish made oversize because they feed on squid and the squid there weigh 40 pounds; while here they weigh around a pound. But if we could get a few good jumps out of one huge bloody fish then the rest of it would be up to the actors.

Today is Sunday and we layed off for the day so took the rest to write you. Appreciate very much you letting me know about the boys. Pat is good about writing but never writes if he is in any trouble nor if Gigi is in trouble. So I worry when I don't hear from them. Everybody is waiting to hear from Mayito. I saw his oldest boy and he said everything was going fine on the place, all cattle in good shape, feed good, and he figured to be able to ship 200 hogs a month to market, sugar mill and rice o.k. and that Mayito could stay out and hunt as long as he wanted to. His kid is turning out absolutely first rate. And Mayito gave up on him once so maybe Gregory will turn out—had to interrupt this when people came in last Sunday. Been fishing ten–12 hours a day all week. It has been going o.k. but terrible weather. Five more days to go. It is Sunday again and must write some business letters. Resting the two photographic outfits today. Out at daylight tomorrow. Mary sends her love to you and your family and to Mama [Flora Percival].

Best always,

PH. PUL   Papa

1. On Philip and Flora Percival of Potha Hill, Machakos, Kenya, see Carlos Baker, *Ernest Hemingway: A Life Story* (New York, 1969), pp. 248–50, 609.

To BERNARD BERENSON, La Finca Vigia, 18 September 1955

Dear B.B.:

On your [90th] birthday [26 June] I wrote you two letters. One I started by the pool in Key West in the very early morning and the other in the afternoon. But they were no good and I did not send them. The trouble was, I think, that I was envious that you had lived so long and had a chance to do your work so well. We all have a chance to work well but few to be as old and wise and love things as you do. Then the letters were too loving to someone that you've never seen. But this is a loving letter to thank you for your birthday and for the beautiful bibliografia.

Now let us cheer up and neither of us be ninety. I had a very good sign the other day. There was some sort of politics here and someone said, "But remember you have the authority of the premio Nobel." And I can swear to you truly, truly that I had absolutely and completly (misspelled) forgotten that I had received that Swedish prize. So that is a good sign.

Am writing large and clear if you can read it then it is a help to me because I hate the typewriter (my new one) and I must not write letters on any old one because it has page 594 of the [African] book in it, covered over with the dust cover, and it is unlucky to take the pages out.

Do you think I should write for Corriere de la Sera? They asked me to and I saw in the Bibliografia that you did. The problem is that I have so little time left to work and the writing for them, sometimes, would be a pleasure but it is wastage. I would rather write a letter to you.

Beside the book I only write to my children usually and people I know in Veneto and Friuli and Africa. Two of the boys are in Tanganyika now. The one who is a good painter [Patrick] has apprenticed himself as a White Hunter and finished his first 42 day probationary safari September 15. He had been hunting by himself with an Old Ivory poacher named Mumu and had done very well. I buy his paintings so much a month and when he has a show, finally, if the beasts do not kill him he can buy them back at the rate I pay him if he sells them. Naturally I do not tell him that I will take no money then.

I wish he could have met you. He is sort of an angel; not Botticelli angel; Northern Cheyenne Indian angel where they have very good angels too.

Good bye B.B.

I have to see the carpenter.

Mary sends her love and I send mine.

> Ernesto Hemingway y de Las Vegas (Nevada)

Please have a lovely end of September in Italy for me too.

I TATTI

To BERNARD BERENSON, La Finca Vigia, 24 October 1955

Dear B.B.:

We are both terribly sorry to hear that you were ill and hope you are well again. It was lovely that you had such a good time in the town.

I could make out all the news but all the rest was illegible. I only have a very few correspondents now and one of them, old Ezra Pound, who is often a fool and who can so disgust me sometimes with his anti-semitism and childish fascism that I cannot write to him; but was never a knave and often an excellent poet with all his pretensions now writes me excusively in what I can describe as Unknown Tongue. U.T. is hard reading but if *you* my most intelligent friend become illegible even to a cryptographer I get discouraged.

Have been up writing since 0600. The light comes late now and every day is one less that you have to work in. The weather is wild but good for working. Am passed 650 pages typed on the book. Am trying to write now like a good sorcer's apprentice. (sorcerer mis-spelled) I know they really had sorcerers and I can do it quite well but always start to write as an apprentice. By the end of a book you are a master but if you commence as a master, in writing anyway, you end as a bloody bore.

When I get tired sometimes I imitate Faulkner a little bit just to show him how it should be done. It is like loosening up with five finger exercises. Anyone not a musician could mistake them for music.

Sometimes I wonder how much advantage and how much dis-advantage it is to have had a sound musical education. Certainly it is an advantage if you had no great illusions about it and accepted counter-point as Euclid's small brother in the club of my meager learning; but it is probably better not to mention it or practically anything else.

Best love from Mary and from me. Let's both try to make this winter which might be a bad one. We have lost so many people lately that it is to be taken comically; and lost them not through dissipation nor stupidly but just by the conditions we have had to live under catching up with them.

This seems to be getting very solemn for the hour which is 0930 but then I have heard Mass at that hour in Santiago de Campostella (do you like the Portico de la Gloria?). I stayed there three summers trying to learn when I was working on my education, as do each day, and what I learned mostly was how hawks fly; different sorts of Hawks but mostly small cathedral falcons. I remember in the cathedral one morning a peasant woman coming up to me, I think she believed I worked there, and asking me, "Where do you go to eat the body of Jesus?" Esta en Gallego, and I answered her, "Right this way, Lady."

Life has been a lot of fun and I have no complaints.

I TATTI   EH

To HARVEY BREIT, La Finca Vigia, 27 October 1955

Dear Harvey:

Will gladly pay tribute to Ezra but what I would like to do is get him the hell out of St. Elizabeth's; have him given a passport and allow him to return to Italy where he is justly valued as a poet. I believe he made bad mistakes in the war in continuing to broadcast for that sod Mussolini after we were fighting him. But I also believe he has paid for them in full and his continued confinement is a cruel and unusual punishment.

If [James] Laughlin wants to help Ezra, rather than exploit his confinement, he could spend some of his Steel earned money and his time and get him free.

You may send this letter to Laughlin and I would appreciate it if you would send a copy to Ezra at St. Elizabeth's Hospital, Washington D.C. This would be a great favour to me, kid, as am in the position of a rider comeing out of the chutes (rider of bad horses) on the book and I forgot to put a sheet of carbon paper in this. Anyway Ezra will enjoy it being sent by you. You can afford the risk as you are doing too damned good a job to get fired.

Best to Miss Pat.

Yours always,
Hem.

PS/ NOT TO SEND TO ANYONE AND PRIVATE
AND CONFIDENTIAL

Cut it off the letter.

Ezra is a great poet subject to certain aberrations. He should not be confined for any of them. Or there should be a term to his confinement as there was to Paul Verlaine. (Ezra's occasional aberrations and confusions have nothing in common with poor Lillianes.) I have always pitied his political views and his stupid conduct in support of them and have respected him as a poet and critic and loved him as a generous friend and fine companion. Have tried in every way to help him from the day I heard he was in trouble *in practical ways*. I detest the Laughlin procedure of a tribute to "Old Ez" with a list of his books in print published by Laughlin, naturally.

Will stop before I get sore.

HUL   EH

To HARVEY BREIT, La Finca Vigia, 14 November 1955

Dear Harvey:

Please tell Miss Pat that what we have to learn is walk with shits nor lose the common touch. She is now one of my favourite of peoples and tell her for me, please, that it was bad luck to marry into writers. A single writer is ok, maybe, but two are a disaster and three are a farce.

Mr. Faulkner has sent me, or maybe it is only his agents, The Hunting Stories of W/F [*Big Woods*, 1955]. They are not dedicated so I do not have to answer. But when you see him, which is inevitable, please tell him that I found them very well written and delicately perceived but that I would be a little more moved if he hunted animals that ran both ways.

File this under Snobhood: 1st Grade.

About Laughlin he wrote a good and instructive letter. It is hard for me to communicate with Ezra since he has abandoned the English language for Unknown Tongue. I can speak unknown tongue fairly well in African dialects with which I am not familiar. But Ezra could write me if he wished in English, Latin, French, Spanish or Italian and I would understand him to the best of my ability. But I cannot speak Mandarin nor Cantonese nor what they talk in Sechuan correctly and cannot read them and my Tibetan is spotty and I can only interrogate or ski or pass the time of day or, at the extreme pinch, command a platoon in Kraut and when Ezra goes into the complete mixture I am dung for.

So I guess Mr. Laughlin has his problems too. . . . Have been tempted to write to Ezra in Friulano, a border tongue that nobody who is not from Friuli can speak or understand. But figured things were bad enough at St. Elizabeth's the way they are.

Am sorry about [Francis] Brown. But you see why I don't write for him or whatever the other character is that runs the excellent Sunday supplement. Been working very hard and with much luck; too much so that it spooks me. On the 0600 radio this morning we lose Bernie De Voto and Sherwood bad.[1] You can chronicle these losses. The most comical thing I remember about the late De Voto (a jack Mormon) and ballistics expert is that writing about The West one time he told what clothing people wore in a way that showed he had never spent a winter there in his life. Blue jeans etc. He never, in the east, as a professional Westerner and historian had to save up the money he could have made coming out of the chutes on Midnight or any ordinary bucking horse to buy the heavy Pendletons you wear in winter; nor had he ever seen a blizzard nor broke tracks for his horse in waist high snow across a pass. He was a summer historian and a son of a bitch alive is a son of a bitch dead. And who sits now in what easy chair when we write happily and easy on our feet before first light. The late De Voto was a pistol instructor who was never shot at and he wrote three quite good books and about six books of shit and I hope he joins John O'Hara in Valhalla where they never would have had it so good until someone won't drink with them at the bar.

Well we must not be social nor any other type of criticals and I made two short and formal prayers for the soul of Mr. De Voto while I was sitting on the toilet seat and let anyone bury him that can.

So long Harvey. Am on page 689 and wish me luck kid. I have it won good but the last innings are all innings. Need to take a break and will go down to Caracas with Miss Mary to see Luis Miguel [Dominguin] fight and Antonio Ordonez. Nov 27 Dec 4. If anything funny happens you will read about it in the papers.

Best love to both,

HUL   Hem

1. Bernard DeVoto died 13 November and Robert E. Sherwood 14 November.

To WALLACE MEYER, La Finca Vigia, 5 December 1955

Dear Wallace:

Thank you very much for your letter of December 2—and for any others I may not have answered nor acted on. On Nov. 17 I had to go to a stupid decoration ceremony in the local Madison Square Gdns which is very badly ventilated, and remain, waiting our turn, for 2 hrs under the TV lights.[1] Sweated through all my clothes so that at the end you could wring water out of the coat of the dark suit I was wearing. I changed shirt and coat in one of the unheated dressing rooms but had thoughtlessly brought no alcohol to rub down with nor any reserve trousers. So ended up catching a bad cold in the right kidney which ruptured in the air crash. It cut out on me and then the other kidney and the liver were affected. The first I knew it was bad was when my right foot swelled like a football and the pressure brought blood out at the base of the toenails. This was rather impressive but I had caught a cold in the kidneys once in Spain while wading waist deep all day in the river Tambre without waders when I had reached the river from Santiago de Campostella and found I had brought Pauline's waders rather than my own and I knew there was nothing to do but go to bed and ride it out.

The foot swelling occurred on Nov. 19 and the doctor has had me in

bed since Nov. 20. I was not able to get him until late that night. He
and two other doctors were very spooked by the analyses (will not
bother you with details) but for 3 days now the analyses are excellent
and they are all very happy about it but want me to stay in bed another
ten days for everything to heal up normally. The kidney thing was acute
nephritis. The liver business the same that killed G[ertrude] Lawrence
[1952] brought on by the cold and a virus infection. This all bores me as
it must bore you. We have had lovely weather and I started writing on
the [African] book on this writing board Nov. 30 and have been doing
300 to 400 words a day. Am on page 703. I love the book and luckily
had accumulated a good back log of good books to read. The best two so
far are (with their faults) Heritage by Anthony West and The Picnic
at Saccara [Sakkara]—[P. H.] Newby. In The Deer Park [Norman]
Mailer really blows the whistle on himself. Mary McCarty [McCarthy]
[in *A Charmed Life*] writes like the most intelligent trained flea that
ever lay between Fortune's Favors. She wrote nicely about the country
though and her courtroom scene was good. . . . I hope it is never my mis-
fortune to meet her nor any of her characters. An excellent book you
might be interested in is The People of the Sierra—by J. A. Pitts-River
published by Wiedenfeld Nicholson, London. It follows in the tradition
of Gerald Brennan [Brenan] who wrote that splendid book The Spanish
Labyrinth [1943]. I don't know the author [personally]. It was sent me
by an ex test pilot and amateur matador of White's London who knows
and loves Spain [Rupert Belleville].

Otherwise have read two books of trash—Man in Gray Flannel Suit
[Sloan Wilson] and The Great Man [Albert Morgan] and two fine books
on the Zulu War and the 2nd volume of [J. F. C.] Fuller's Military
History [of the Western World]. You are probably bored shitless by now.

About the payment: Will you please deposit it as follows: (Excuse
changing pencils) $8585 to my Special Tax Account, Fifth Avenue
Branch, Guaranty Trust Co of NY; $10,000 to my Savings Account in the
First National Bank of Florida at Key West, Key West, Florida c/o
Jerry J. Trevor—President.

You know Wallace there is a damned funny thing. The only good Dr.
I saw in Kenya [1954] was a RAF MD and he told me, "You can have
6 months (with those internal injuries) if you take care of yourself and
you can live 2 years if you make it a career." (Later I heard he thought
I would not make Venice.) Well I took care of myself for a long time.
But I never made it a career and I over-worked to hell because the time
was short. Before I got the cold I was getting up at 4 and 5 and it still
dark at six.

So it's a good thing now to put in a few weeks of complete rest and
if that's how I'm to take my vacation that's how I'll take it.

Show this letter to Charlie please but don't say anything about my having had hard luck to anyone.

Best always,

PUL   Ernest

1. To receive the Order of San Cristobal at the Havana Sports Palace.

To ALFRED RICE, La Finca Vigia, 24 January 1956

Dear Alfred:

This is the [second] anniversary when we crashed for the second time at Butiaba and burned and I think if that piece of business could have been omitted I would be able to recall the events of the first six months of 1953 much more clearly.

However to the best of my recollection this is how it goes.

Leland Hayward and his wife had come down in December of 1952 to make a deal. In January, February, March and April I worked out and studied the various fishermen's ports along the Northern Marlin fishing coast of Cuba to find one that could be better than Cojimar or could substitute for Cojimar if it were ruined as a location by the steadily increasing urbanization of Havana to the East. This urbanization, unless the picture keeps ahead of it, is liable to be a great danger to the picture.

I also investigated the suitability of these ports as to fishermen and boats and how these people could fit into the original story. The only ports that were in any way suited, and they all had great disadvantages, were ones which had no practicable communication at that time with Havana.

However I checked them all, worked out the fishing situation and the locales and their advantages and disadvantages. Cojimar, unless it was ruined, was obviously where the film should be made and in April and May I worked out in my head how it could be made, [and what] the big problems were that we would have to solve. I also went into the shark problem and figured out how it could be done and where. We had a place called Punta Purgatorio which was alive with sharks in the old days. But the sharks had now deserted it and the shark problem changes with the unusual weather we have had since 1952 and the erratic movements of the Gulf Stream. It is still a problem and I have had to work it out with trial and error.

[Spencer] Tracy and the Haywards were expected several times and did not show up. Tracy was here on the days around April 6th. He and

Hayward and I had made a verbal contract which was to be worked out by the lawyers and after Hayward, Tracy and I had been to Cojimar to show Tracy the situation, Tracy stayed behind a day to have me show him things further and talk over the whole matter of the film and how I thought it should be done.

In March and in April I made a ten day and a sixteen day trip down the North coast to the westward limit of the Marlin fishing getting my idea of the film straight in my head and doing research work on it. I had abandoned all my other projects and was concentrating on this. The longest trip was undertaken on April 27th. I believe you had already closed the deal with Hayward's and Tracy's lawyers before that and received payment.

I wish I could write you all the work and the planning I did on the film and all the research but you can be sure that I lived with it day and night in my head until I went to Africa. It is not a thing that you put down like inter-office memorandum. It goes this way.

The director or Hayward might ask, "Why can't we work out of Puerto Escondido?" And you can answer, "Because there is a big dredge and a sand dump to haul sand for construction put in at the mouth of the harbour and there are barges loading day and night."

You puzzle and figure out how to have the small bird that is crossing the Gulf Stream light on the Old Man's line while he is fighting the fish and you work that one all out with the aid of a country bird trapper who can trap the small birds as they come across and rest here in the bushes and then train them so they will sit on a line if the thing has to be made indoors or out.

There are so many things in the script that I have had to investigate including, and then rule out. Also remember, Alfred, that Hayward had no director until this October and in September of this year we were engaged in photography where I had to train the fishermen and show them what to do and run a boat with cinerama camera in awful weather conditions still trying for the stuff I had worked out as necessary in 1953.

Am enclosing the revocation and the power of attorney for tax matters you asked for.

Have been getting up a few more hours each day and the Drs. were very pleased with the last blood tests and my blood pressure which was 132 over 66 last evening. There is a million and a half defficiency in the blood count, though, and they think this may be something I picked up in Africa. This is the first blood count I've had since I can remember so it may not be anything new. Mary has had over a million defficiency that has not yielded to treatment in six months although she has been taking daily liver injections. So the combination of us both having it might be more than a coincidence. But they have eliminated Filiarsis, Amoeba and think now it is just the regular tropical anemia. I noticed I felt wonderful in Africa as soon as I got up in the high country. Anyway nothing to worry about. And we are doing everything you can do. Will be glad when this picture is over and can get a vacation. Have been working steadily on the African book with a writing board while I was in bed and only missed ten days work out of sixty in bed. Am on page 810.

Best always,
Ernie

This is not a very powerful document but what it boils down to is that I earned that money researching for the picture, scrapping what was worthless, saving what was good and studying the sea and the problems we would have with it. The present script, except for some wording, is almost identical with what I worked out in my head.

JFK   E/H/

To GARY COOPER, La Finca Vigia, 9 March 1956

Dear Coops:

Glad to hear from you and hurry to answer on my gift Swedish typewriter before have to go to the kitchen [telephone] and hear somebody in the Picture business cancel something or change some date.

Coops the picture business is not for me and no matter how much dough we could make how would we spend it if we were dead from dealing with the characters we would have to deal with. After The Old Man and The Sea is finished I will not ever have anything to do with pictures again so Help Me God. God is Capitalized.

You made a good buy picking that old LEOPARD WOMAN up for peanuts (and probably the first time anybody has ever got a LEOPARD WOMAN with peanuts since the British launched their Ground Nut scheme in Southern Tanganyika) but when I get finished on this I am through and am going back up on the slopes of Kibo and get the taste of a lot of things out of my mouth.

I appreciate like hell your wanting me to make some monies but I can picture that one necessary little bit they would want me to do without a double when I crash the Leopard Woman herself into the snow covered crater of Mt. Kilimanjaro (Kibo) and then carry her (personally) into Abyssinia with nobody to help with the stolen ivory but Stewart Granger who is bleeding bad.

Can hear myself being conned, "Ernie, boy, you owe this to The Picture. We're just one happy team working together toward success. We know what she (the LW) means to you and our plane crasher is down with Blackwater. Here's a sample of his urine Ernie. It's like the river Styx isn't it? We know you'll do it to come through for the Team, Papa. We trust you. You're our only hope. Please crash it Papa. It doesn't hurt a bit. You say so yourself and you can't burn in the snow. We've got new gadgets that handle all that. We're getting them from the Navy if the Navy has them and will give them to us. It will be greater than Mister Roberts and we're shooting everything off colour so you can't tell where you are. How can it hurt you, Papa? And besides you love the LEOPARD WOMAN. You've loved her for years and she thought it up just to make you the money. Come on, Papa. Crash her. Just a little preliminary crash this afternoon so we can know whether to shoot in Cinerama, Todd PO or 1/8000. Come on out and crash her Papa and don't be temperamental. We've got dozens of spare planes and the new rubber plane you'll be crazy about. You can inflate it with your mouth just like an air mattress. . . ."

Coops I'm afraid you better deal around me in this one. I know it means I will never have any dough but I know I shouldn't work in pictures when I go well enough in books.

So in Swahili HAPANA CHUI MANAMOUKI or No Leopard for poor old Papa.

It was swell to see you even with those buzzards around. The papers announced that I had given you a dozen guayaberas [Cuban shirts]. So I owe you twelve.

The nail I have to bite on is that if I turned my name in on a Leopard Woman picture everybody would say I had sold out and everybody would be right. So no Leopard Womens.

Best love from Mary and me to you and Rocks and Maria.

                                                                Papa

PS. Now tell everybody that you were born in 1902 (am prepared to make it 1904) and that I helped deliver you and rode eighty miles through the blizzard of any year you name to record the birth. Returning from the same ride sixteen years later I found Miss Mary in a snowbank near what is now Walker, Minnesota and resolved as soon as I could to make her my child bride. There were slight legal difficulties that kept us the one from the other while I had to dispose of Miss Pauline whom I had found huddled under the desk of the President in Morgan's Bank in Wall Street and Miss Martha who was born day before yesterday prematurely in St. Luis Potosi (Missouri). But those things all straighten themselves out.

Best always, kid,

JFK (Papa)

To WALLACE MEYER, La Finca Vigia, 31 March and 2 April 1956

Dear Wallace:

Thank you for the letter and for the list of books sent. They are all in now and let's forget any duplications. Some may have been books sent by the publishers. Please thank Wilcox for me for the three books he sent as a gift. I would also like to thank Charlie and tell him that his Etruscan book [Edward Hutton, *Siena and Southern Tuscany*, 1956] is really excellent. I walked over a lot of that country on foot and the book was a delight to me.

The film people are having what I hope are only their usual troubles. As plans are now, we are to leave for Cabo Blanco, Peru April 15th and come back May 15. Will fly by way of Miami.

April 2

Film characters seem to have gotten over their temperamental squabbles and everything is set now. I bitterly regret ever having participated in the film in any way but it seemed best for all of us that an attempt be made to make a decent picture of the book. Will never have anything to do with motion pictures again. Have trained very hard for the fishing and am down to 209 lbs. Weighed 231 last September having trained down from 242. When I was sick from November 20 to Jan 10th went down to 222 and since I have been training now am down as low as I have ever been except in Africa just before the plane crashes. The fishing has been lousy at Cabo Blanco but we have enough footage from there [here?] to get by (big fish jumps) even if we do not get the stuff we should have. But have to try for it. Mary is going down with me and Gregorio, my mate, and Elicio Arguelles, a very fine fisherman and good friend from here, to spell me on the fishing in case anything goes wrong or breaks in me.

Address there will be Cabo Blanco Club, Cabo Blanco, Peru.

When you get this letter could C. W. Wilcox ship me in the usual way here to the Finca: Wingless Victory, Frances Winwar—Harper and

Bros.; A Night to Remember (story of Titanic); Red, Black, Blond and Olive, Edmund Wilson—Oxford; Lucy Crown, Irwin Shaw—Random House; The Quiet American, Graham Greene.

Please excuse this hurried note.

Best always

Ernest

PUL

To GIANFRANCO IVANCICH, La Finca Vigia, 25 May 1956

Dear Gianfranco:

We were so sorry to miss the wedding, but Roberto sent all the clippings and I was glad to see that I was a witness even if I could not be the best man. Hope everything is going good and give our very best to Cristina [née Sandoval].

Thanks for your good letters. They were really fine and it was like being back in Venice. We had a letter from Joe and Nancy from Rome saying that they were going up to Venice to see you. That will be fun anyway. It will be nice to get out in the country too and give my love to the country and all the peoples.

We miss you very much and it is lonesome to have somebody around as you were and have them like a brother and have them go away. Now I have no brother and no good drinking friend nor hard-working banana grower. Everybody remembers you with so much affection and sends very best wishes. Thank you very much for the Mont St. Michel book.

We had a good time in Peru. It was very rough most of the time on the ocean, but the ocean was interesting and I got in wonderful shape and the back is now as strong as it ever was. Send you a picture that you can show to the Greek sometime.

Here we have had very little rain but just enough to save the mangos that I was irrigating, and by the end of the month we will have very good mangos. That awful storm that blew them all off the trees served one good purpose. The mangos that were left were evidently made by a process of selection and they will be fine and we will think about you when we eat them.

Boise died while we were away. I was very sorry not to be with him when he died. He died in the night and did not suffer at all. It was a heart attack and we buried him alongside of Willie. Blackie will not live very long either I don't think, but he still has fun and we go on walks over the property early in the morning when I wake up.

Gianfranco, it is hard to write a letter about your going away without being sentimental and it is very hard to write a letter to Venice without mentioning Adriana, but I am doing it just the same. Please give my love to all friends there and to all Kechler's and to your family. As soon as we get everything squared away after getting back will write a good letter and tell you all the news. Letters about the death of animals are not the best kind to send.

Mary was wonderful in Peru. She worked like a goat and did the translating for the camera boat and was really happy and had a fine time. We all had a good time because it was rough enough so it was better to have a good time than not. I don't know about the picture because I have just come back. As you knew there was some difficulty with the artist [Spencer Tracy], but they say that is all straightened and we have a docile artist now, but to me in the stills I saw last night he still looked very fat for a fisherman and the boy looks very tiny. There is nothing that a rubber fish cannot fix. In later stills he looks much better and he is such a good actor he can probably surmount most things.

I suppose Cipriani's [Harry's Bar, Venice] is too crowded with the tourists and all, but will you go there and have a drink for me anyway? If anything happens and we should get the money that is coming from Einaudi [publisher], let me know please because I would certainly like to pay something to Dr. Cameroni.

We have no plans yet for anything because I must stay around with the nonsense. There are some shark things that have to be done too. The Colonel [Taylor Williams] is down and has been out fishing twice with Gregorio. He caught four big dolphin yesterday, a sailfish and three marlin strikes. I sent him out again today with Gregorio. It is a little rough on Gregorio to not have his rest after putting in all that time in Peru, but he has been wonderful about it. He was great in Peru and was fast as a tiger and always cheerful.

If we get a break, we will see each other again sooner than we expected. Please keep in touch and please let me know how everything goes with Adriana, to whom I wish all the luck.[1] Must not say more. Be a good boy and thank you very much for the letters.

Best always,
Papa.

PH. PUL

1. Adriana was now married.

To PHILIP PERCIVAL, La Finca Vigia, 25 May 1956

Dear Pop:

Thanks very much for your letter and glad if the rod sockets got there in time. I asked Charles [Thompson] to send some other gear, feathers, rod and reel to replace the one I gave you that was broken on the trip, also the line. Hope they arrive. Please let me know if they don't.

Am sorry about the big elephant and sorrier that we could not be hunting together. We all miss you very much and am so glad to hear that you licked the damn cancer and are fishing and can get around. The fishing there is really wonderful, Pop, as you saw when we were out. I don't think the people there do it very well. . . . Maybe you and I can fish together there next year. I had hoped to make enough money to buy a boat and send it out there, but it doesn't look like now it will ever happen, but maybe I can get some money someplace else.

You would have liked the Peru trip except that the ocean was very rough. Send you a few pictures that will show you the kind of fish we had.

My back is strong again, just as good as it was before the crash. My head is okay too, no headaches and all inside organs are okay. You and I weren't born to die very easy (knock on wood) and we must always remember all the animals that were shot in Tenganika by native hunters and lived many, many years. I have decided (again knocking on wood) now to live for a long time and have plenty of fun and I hope that some of it will be with us together. It's the best fun I have.

Thank you for proposing Patrick to the Association. I think he will make a good hunter because he shoots very well and is not afraid of anything and has good ability with the language and has a decent personality. Young Gregory's wife is leaving him, I understand through him, and he has written me for advice. The same goes forward to him in this mail and doubt whether it will be of any use. If there is anything about either of the boys that I should know please tell me because it is not a question of gossip, but since you are my oldest surviving friend and one of my very best friends, it is all right to trade even between ourselves, and since Gregory never writes unless he is in trouble, I naturally have to worry about him a little bit. Have cut that worry to the minimum in late years but the obligation still exists no matter how they turn out.

Mary sends her love. She is fine and we both send our very best to Mama. I wrote Dennis [Zaphiro] about the rifles (having them cleaned) and sent it registered to his Kajiado address before we left for Peru, but have not heard from him yet. I could not write to Patrick to look after it since he was on his leave in the Greek Islands. I suppose Henny picked Cyprus as an ideal vacation spot.

Will get this off now and hope you have really good fishing.

Best always

Pop II

To HARVEY BREIT, La Finca Vigia, 3 July 1956

Dear Harvey:

It was and is wonderful for you to offer us the use of the house but kid it is completely unfair for us to come there or for Pat to have to think of us comeing there when you are going to have a baby and should not have anything interfere with that. It sounds like a wonderful place and I know how happy we would be. But then I don't figure on getting into heaven either.

Anyway we would not be coming before the middle of August. I want terribly badly to be in NY once without the interviews and photographs that have gotten on my nerves so that I take no pleasure in going anywhere. It would be wonderful to stay up at your house and I love to think about it but I would rather go through the hell Hotel routine than be one shadow of a worry or a nuisance to you.

So let's leave it that we accept with the greatest of pleasure but will not show if we would make any sort of difficulty and tell Pat that we are not the sort of people, whatever you read in Lillian Ross, that Dylan Thomas up a place.

Having people stay with you is funny. The nicest house guests we have ever had were Kipper LaFarge and Bill Walton. They would stay for weeks or months and seemed like days; always cheerful; always respecting work and doing it themselves, like to eat and to drink and fine talk. Gianfranco, of the Venetian branch of the family once came until he could find a room and stayed three years or so living in the tack room on the second floor of the tower; he preferred sleeping on the floor to a bed for some old Italian reason. Since Winston Guest quit drinking he makes me a little nervous but in the old days when he did drink, and very well, he used to live here for weeks and months. Tommy Shevlin is another good guest. . . .

Would welcome the Rhodes book.[1] I never knew him but I knew the country. I think outside of Jim Joyce and an old writer in Chicago named Henry B. Fuller (the Cliff Dwellers etc.) and a man named Edwin Balmer who wrote pot boilers and helped me when I was a kid the only writers I ever liked, really, were Dos when he was still straight in early days, Scott when he was sober (but it was always full of pity as though you had a butterfly or a moth for a friend), Sholem Asch, old Berenson in letters, dear good, kind crazy Ezra, Archie Mac Leish when he would be funny and not noble (never has so few suffered so much from the deaths of so many others), Christ it is getting to be quite a list and John Peale Bishop who was a distracted gentleman; and Owen Wister. He was the most unselfish and most dis-interested and the most loving. When my father shot himself and things were not good at all and I was making trust funds and having to discipline my bitch mother and put it all out of my head and do the re-write on A Farewell To Arms as though no aircraft had crashed nor anyboody been run over by this or that street car he wrote me and sent me a very huge check and said for me not to have any money worries and he would back me all the way and Harvey he did not know anything about the book nor had I shown him the Mss. He just thought I was a good writer and he loved The Sun Also Rises and I think he had seen me ride a horse or something like that.

Sherwood [Anderson] was like a jolly but tortured bowl of puss turning into a woman in front of your eyes. Stein was a nice woman until she had change of life and opted for fags and fags alone. I like young Nelson [Algren]. He is a rough boy but has not learned that if you are really bad you do not have to talk out of the side of your mouth nor that it is only with alchemy that you combine poetry and prose. Faulkner gives me the creeps. Harvey remember that Papa's last words were Never trust a man with a Southern Accent. They could talk reasonable English as we talk it if they were not phony.[2]

I guess our President chooses them by seniority which is one place he could feel at home in letters. This one Harvey you must never tell anybody. Maybe I wrote it to you before. Miss Mary at the time of June 6 1944 had in love with her a Gen who was heading up Psycho-pathological warfare. He taught her to shoot a .45 colt issue pistol and naturally no woman can hit anything with that peculiar device. I don't know about the Gen. This same Gen. had given up the command of a Division to Fight in France for love of Miss Mary he told her. I told her that any son of a bitch who would give up the chance of commanding a Division for any god-damn woman on earth expressly including Miss Mary should be shot. Well relations between me and the then unknown general were deteriorating or, at any rate, not flourishing. There was also an admiral involved. I never asked what he had given up. So to make a long story pointless on my return from the June 6 operation on Fox Green and Easy Red beaches Miss Mary asked me what I had thought of Dr. Eisenhower's speech to all concerned, I told her it was the least inspiring pre-assault shit I had ever been unprivileged to listen to. It was later reported to me that Miss Mary had authored or helped author this epoch marking discourse. So you see that the early days of my courtship of Miss Mary was not all downhill running in powder snow.

I suppose this was reminded back to me by thinking that if Nelson is as tough a boy inside as he thinks he is how could he have devoted more than one evening to Simone de [Beauvoir] etc.? Riddle me that?

Please let us not make Edmund Wilson the only critic or the master critic. There are always good kids come along. The thing is that one should from time to time break up their concentrations by firing for effect.

Understand how you feel about air-craft. If you felt bad about frying those Venezuelans into the drink (I did too. But they shouldn't fly such long over-water flights making necessary the terrific load of gas. Let's not talk about it).[3] How would you feel to have some son of a bitch come up into you at 21,000 feet over the grand canyon because the air-lines are too tight to put radar on the planes. But it is still less dangerous than the highway, and Le Mans, and Labor Day or July 4th, and I will be happy to be back in a Cessna 180 with Roy Marsh again. I wish I could write well enough to write about air-craft. Faulkner did it very well in Pylon but you cannot do something some one else has done though you might have done it if they hadn't. He must have felt pretty strongly about them at one time. I got scared of them very early. Then got over it. Got scared of them again in the first war and took a long time to get over it. Got slug nutty happy about them around 1933 and then in China purged out all the fear for good. In the last war had a wonderful time with them and then started to get punchy from the various concussions in 1943, 44, 45 and was advised to keep out of them as much as I could. Then all the loveliness of it came back with Roy in Africa and it was one of the main things I cared about. Now I still have some credit to use up with Pan-Am. I would not take cash for endorsing their air-line but would take it out in flying time. There is some rule against this but they hold the dough and that is how I spend it. But it is stupid to cross the Atlantic in a plane when you can go on a boat and have fun. No airplane can take you to France as quickly as you can make it by walking up the gangplank onto a good French ship where you know most of the people that work, have the fine food and the gym and pool and blague [gab] with people you have known for thirty years. I've had more fun on French line boats than almost anywhere. Very different from big air-craft.

Can remember one time on a TWA out of Los Angeles for N.Y. the hostess looked at me quite suspiciously because I needed a shave and was drinking a chinese sort of vodka out of a flat pint flask. Then she brought the Captain back to look at me like I was a character in a Budd Shulberg story about Scott Fitzgerald. What made the worst impression on her was that my head was shaved.

"You old son of a bitch," the Capt. said. "Where you flown from?"

"Kunming," I said.

"See Pottsmith?"

"We flew to HongKong."

"Did you come across with Steve?"

"From Wake. We were stuck in Guam. Had to haul ass back twice on reaching the point (of no return)."

"See any of the other friends?"

"Berndt Balchen and Clyde Pangborn flew from Manila to Honolulu."

"They still ferrying PBYs?"

I looked at the air-hostess and skipped that.

"They met their wives in Honolulu."

"Would you like to come up forward, Ernie?"

"No. Kid. I'm tired and I'm going to get some sleep."

"This is Miss so and so," the Captain said. "Miss so and so this will be helpful for you in the future to enable you to distinguish a tired man from a rummy. If you want her to bring anything to mix that stuff with ask Miss So and So for it."

Am afraid I am over-lettering you, Harvey, so will stop. Love and good luck to Miss Pat. Miss Mary is in town at the dentist. I have to take Black Dog down to the pool now. He can't see any more and can't hear and looks very bad. But 3 dollars will get you two he outstays Eisenhower.

HUL   Hem

1. *Bar Cross Man: Life and Personal Writings of Eugene Manlove Rhodes*, ed. W. H. Hutchinson (New York, 1956), about cow country and people of New Mexico. 2. EH to a Mr. Rider, 29 July, called Faulkner "a no good son of a bitch," but recommended *Sanctuary* (1931) and *Pylon* (1935) as "the most readable" of his books and also praised "The Bear." But he compared *A Fable* (1954) to "the night soil [human excrement] from Chungking." 3. EH alludes to the crash of a Super-Constellation in the sea off Asbury Park, New Jersey, on 20 June with the loss of seventy-four lives. Twenty-four victims were Venezuelan children returning to Caracas from U.S. schools.

To EZRA POUND, La Finca Vigia, 19 July 1956

Dear E.:

Tomorrow being the Fifty Seventh year of my age I hope you will accept my Nobel prize medal which is following through channels.[1] I send it on the old Chinese principle, with which you are familiar, that no one possesses anything until they have given it to another.

I also send it because you are our greatest living poet; a small distinction but your own.

It also goes to my old tennis opponent, to the man who founded *Bel Esprit*,[2] and the man who taught me, gently, to be merciful and tried to teach me to be kind when all I had was *omerta*.[3]

It would be possible to cite at great length but I would rather skip it and send you and D[orothy] my love. I cannot bear for you to be confined while others who worked against their country in England have been freed. To you what you did was no sin since you believed in it. To me it was a grave sin. But you have paid for it many thousand times.

In the war I had the monitored broadcasts and sometimes when I had listening duty I would hear you. I did not like them at all and some of them I liked less. But I wrote Allen Tate when it became obvious that we were winning that we would have to all decide what to do when you were over-run. I wrote Tate that if you were to be hanged I would get up onto the scaffold and be hanged too. Tate said that he would do the same.

Well skip all that and skip politics and, if you can, accept the medal and this check [$1,000] which is about the end of the Nobel money which I said I would use as intelligently as I could.

Will write a less formal letter on a less formal occassion. (mis-spelled)

If you win the Swedish prize, as you should, keep mine and dispose of yours as you see fit.

Yours always,

PH. PUL   Hem

1. But EH seems instead to have given his medal to the Shrine of the Virgen del Cobre in Cuba. His speech on this occasion is listed in Philip Young and Charles W. Mann, comps., *The Hemingway Manuscripts: An Inventory* (University Park, Pa., 1969), item 120. 2. See *A Moveable Feast* (New York, 1964), pp. 110–13. 3. The Mafia law of silence: never squeal.

To HARVEY BREIT, La Finca Vigia, 23 July 1956

Dear Harvey:

I am so happy and excited that we are coming to stay at your place [116 East 64th Street, New York City] and to be in a big town again. Mary thought we should not stay with anyone we had not met but I talked her out of that. If we haven't met who the hell ever has met?

Besides we will meet like Diplomats at the station. Will give you the Gen. Not before Aug 15th or any date you say.

Anyway it is wonderful. But I worry about Pat and the baby. Probably I shouldn't worry about that any more than Archie Moore vs. Parker. But I worry, slightly, about that. But nothing to do about either event.

Since I quit the cinema have written two short stories for discipline and purge and to bite on the nail. They are about the old days with the [Free French] irregulars which was a very complicated time in my life and the happiest and worst I ever have had. Will write maybe 3 or 4 more to have changes in the weather. Have too many to write. Three of the stories are too awful to write but am trying to write very simply and gentle but with the real words. I wasn't ever going to write them but now I think it would be wrong not to. It will make up for the time I wasted trying to make a true picture.[1]

Thank you and Pat for the birthday cable. I explained the reference to the cement bull to Mary and my sister [Ursula] who was here for a week with her fine good husband. She is the one who had the 3 cancer operations last year. She is brave as a goat and since she had never seen S[outh] A[merica] her husband decided to take two months off from his very important job and they went to Panama, Lima, Chile, B.A., Paraguay, Rio, San Juan, Haiti, back to Jamaica then here. When she first knew she was starting the run on the black she went to Bangkok, Singapore and Hong Kong. When I was a kid we loved each other very much and we still do. She and her husband both drink wonderfully and never get drunk and never quarrel. They were both wonderful athletes and you could not tell anything was wrong with either one if you didn't see Jep's pallor and the easy way he swims. Have never seen less morbid nor more interested, brave and natural fine people. After seeing Ursula I know why the family nick-named my kid brother Dregs. It is cruel and when I came home after the 1st war I put a stop to it. But girls are more merciless than we are and the sister that invented the name was no good.

After he wrote the book no one in the family will keep track of him even. It is though a Sicilian boy had violated "omerta."

That frustrated F.B.I. character Charlie Fenton ran into the old "omerta" in Oak Park and that is why no one would give him any Hemingstein gen except jerks. You know when my father shot himself there were two local weekly papers the Oak Leaves and The Oak Parker. They both carried the story on the front page and it ran about eight–twelve columns in each. Neither paper mentioned the cause of his death. My father was not an advertizee in the papers and he died broke. But his grandfather had traded swampy land where Marshal Field's store now is in the Loop for high good rolling land with oak trees on it and the North Prairie on the North and the South Prairie on the south and fine prairie chicken shooting. Now a big part of the South Prairie is Cicero.

Dr. Fenton F.B.Iing around didn't find out about this nor that my father had Indian blood on the Edmonds side. Nor that Lewis and Clark ran into a man named Hancock who had been out there for years nor that members of our family ran the Rosebud agency nor that my Uncle Bill [Willoughby Hemingway] was physician to the Dali Lama nor about several things that there was something behind my writing besides the Kansas City Star which I always thought was a step in education. But all these guys have theories and try to fit you into the theory. Malcolm [Cowley] thot I was like him because my father was a Dr. and I went to Michigan when I was 2 weeks old where they had Hemlock trees. P. Young: It's all trauma. Sure plenty trauma in 1918 but symptoms absent by 1928—none in Spain –37–38—none in China 40–41—None at sea, none in air, none in 155 days of combat. I suppose when Archie Moore loses his legs P. Young will diagnose him as a victim of trauma. Carlos Baker really baffles me. Do you suppose he can con himself into thinking I would put a symbol into anything on purpose. It's hard enough just to make a paragraph. What sort of a symbol is Debba, my Wakamba fiancée? She must be a dark symbol. N'gui my rough bad brother. He must be a very dark symbol indeed.

What a National League race. Wish I could have seen Gomez being run by Adcock even on television.

What ball clubs will be at home in last ½ August?

We have to go out a couple of times together. I get too lonesome at a ball game by myself, and I don't want to go with those bums I know in N.Y. Leland Hayward really loves ball games but he is awfully nervous. Jimmy [Cannon] pontificates too much.

Must send this as Mary is going into town.

Best always, Harvey. Luck to Miss Pat.

HUL   Hem

---

1. Among EH's unpublished short stories relating to World War II are "A Room on the Garden Side" (14 pp. longhand); "The Monument" (14 pp. typescript); "The Cross Roads," also called "Black Ass at the Cross Roads" (26 pp. typescript); and "Indian Country and the White Army" (19 pp. typescript). Untitled stories include "The day we drove back from Nancy to Paris" (12 pp. typescript), "It was very cold in England" (17 pp. typescript), "The buzzing was as thin as the night sounds" (19 pp. longhand and ½ page typed), and a fragment in longhand, numbered pp. 22–38, beginning "make you stop flying and get your head well." Five of these are listed in Philip Young and Charles W. Mann, comps., *The Hemingway Manuscripts: An Inventory* (University Park, Pa., 1969), items 34, 35, 56, 68, 79. In all cases their report of page length differs from that given above. See EH to Charles Scribner, Jr., 14 August 1956, following.

To CHARLES SCRIBNER, JR., La Finca Vigia, 14 August 1956

Dear Charlie:

Thank you for your letter and for the report on the books. I am awfully glad they hold up so well and deeply appreciate the action you took to bring them all under one roof.

After I stopped working on the film I found it impossible to resume work on the Africa book without some disciplinary writing so I started writing short stories which is the hardest thing for me to do. Have written 5 which Mary has copied. This with one I wrote to get going after Africa makes six unpublished.

The titles are: Get Yourself a Seeing-eyed Dog; A Room on The Garden Side; The Cross Roads; Indian Country and The White Army; The Monument; The Bubble Reputation.[1]

The last five stories run around 1200 to 4500 words apiece and I suppose they are a little shocking since they deal with irregular troops and combat and with people who actually kill other people. There are no shocking revelations about barrack troops who never fought and no patrols where some one carries a dead man back and the writer does not become a psycho and go over the hill to meet a publisher. Nothing is copied from Tom Wolfe nor Faulkner and when one man calls another a cocksucker he calls him a cocksucker. I did not have to put on my Rabbi suit to write and all I needed was a map. So they are probably very dull stories but some are very funny I think. Anyway you can always publish them after I'm dead. I have five more that I am going to write now.

The main problem we have now is Mary's health. She has a very stubborn anemia that has not yielded to any treatment. The red corp. blood count a week ago was down to 3,200,000. She had a transfusion last week and we get another blood count tomorrow. I must get her to a different latitude and altitude the Dr's say. She is not strong enough yet to go to Africa but maybe she will be.

I think, now, I can arrange the shipping of the shotgun shells you have so kindly given storage space to. Joe Lippincott has gone to shoot grouse. Whenever I get to N.Y. will let you know about these. I've shot shells 20 years old but I cannot recommend them to anyone else without knowing they are OK. And I can't gamble on a mis-fire in Africa where I use a shot gun for backing up on all cats. A load of 7 or 7½ or 8 is much more deadly at five yards on any thin skinned game than buck shot, solid ball or any rifle cartridge. A lion or a leopard comes faster than a tennis ball and who wants to shoot tennis balls with a rifle?

Sorry to bother you with this nonsense. But since your father died I have no one to joke with nor to damn the Egyptians nor be snobs with so ask you to put up with me as much as possible.

Best to you and your wife and we hope you are having a good summer. Please give Mary's and my love to your mother.

Yours always
Ernest

PUL

1. "Get a Seeing-Eyed Dog," *Atlantic* 200 (November 1957). The others, as of 1981, remain unpublished.

To HARVEY BREIT, Paris, 16 September 1956

Dear Harvey:

Mary wrote you both and I mailed it yesterday morning. This is only to tell you how much we miss Pat's beauty and loveliness and your great kindness and charm and how much fun we had living in your house. Hope we did not do it too much damage and that Alan Sebastian [infant son] is doing well and that you had good weather and fun in the country.

There were nice people on the boat and we had perfect weather. People may like to ride in aircraft (and I do) but nothing is as much fun as a good French Line crossing; the healthy work in the gym; the bars and the lovely food and wines and always at least one lovely girl. There were no professional gamblers on this voyage. The characters in the bar told me they almost never make the boats anymore. . . . But the moral tolerance still exists and it is very different from the airplanes that have made the columnists authorities on all the world and the wonders thereof.

From the writing or literary aspect it was very interesting. Ships doctors, of course, are great readers. Ours had all of my books in French and English and knew them better than I pretend to remember them. But I signed about 60 for members of the crew. All the ones the crew bought I paid for afterward in the Library and had them returned the money they spent. It was different from the autograph people outside the theatres. One steward told me that in his village in Brittany two boys had named their dogs Santiago because they had such fine and noble qualities. That must be a strange book. Probably I would do better to never publish anything else. Simpler to leave stuff for when I'm dead.

Mary is much better I think. She's getting a little meaner and not so noble about me other womens which is a good sign.

They had no summer here at all. We've had two good days in a week. Go down to Spain tomorrow. The Lancia is a good one and the driver [Mario Casamassima] gives you the confidence a racing driver does and still scares the shit out of you in the traffic which is very congested. A really fast car gives more intimations of mortality than a sack full of certified cancers. We now have in our little group of literary folk one new big Mercedes Benz, one Porsche, and the Lancia and you can take your choice of riding with Rupert Belleville in the Mercedes, he is an ex great test pilot; Peter Viertel who is careful but fast in the Porsche or Mario Casamassima the pride of Udine. We rendezvous at the Chantaco in St. Jean de Luz on Tuesday. Am going to take Mary down in 2 easy laps. Once drove it easily in a day in the old days when the roads were not as good. But then Otto Bruce and I once drove from Memphis Tennessee to Key West (976 miles) in a single drive. But we spelled each other every 2 or 3 hours and also had a lovely dinner at the home of friends in Ormond Beach. I am a very good boy with cars now. But Pauline and I once drove from Madrid to San Sebastian arriving in plenty of time for the bull fight.

Ah que cet cor a long haleine.[1]

Must get dressed now and go down and comfort Bertin who has the duty this Sunday in the Bar when he would be fishing.

Best love to you both. Will write when we are settled at Escorial. See Antonio Ordoñez fight at Logroño enroute.

Hem.

Please give my very best regards to Sylvia and to May. They were very good to us.

HUL

1. How this handsome line came into EH's possession is not clear, although he had long been interested in the exploits of Roland and alluded to the monastery of Roncesvalles in *The Sun Also Rises*, chapter 11. The original line comes from *La Chanson de Roland*, Oxford Version, ed. T. A. Jenkins (Boston, 1924), p. 136, line 1,789: "cil corz at longe aleine." The words are spoken by King Karl, "That horn is long of breath," upon hearing Roland sound the horn "in anguish drear." I thank my learned colleagues Victor H. Brombert and John Logan for this identification.

To J. DONALD ADAMS,[1] El Escorial, Spain, 30 September 1956

Dear Mr. Adams:

I wish that I might serve on your committee since you wrote me so fully and intelligently about it; but I cannot. The reasons are these. President Eisenhower does not seem to me physically qualified to serve 4 years as President. If Chris Herter was the Vice Presidential nominee I could serve on your committee. I do not want to vote for Nixon, not because of his useful role in the Hiss case, but on his record.

It is impossible for me to vote for Stephenson [Adlai Stevenson] or [Estes] Kefauver.

Actually I have not been in as bad a spot politically since as Republican Judge of Elections I could not vote for Cox and finally voted for Eugene V. Debs since he was an honest man and in jail.

Dont give a thought to not sending the book. When we are back at the Finca I would love to have it for our Library. But will be happy to buy it and have you inscribe it.

About the West: Guthrie's Big Sky was a fine book. I love the country very much; too much. There was a Hancock out there doing quite well when Lewis and Clark arrived. I remember being in hospital in Billings once [1930] and had given, on the entry sheet, my occupation as Writer. The nurse had transcribed it as Rider and the next day the delegate of the association came up to see me and said, "Ernie who the hell ever said you were a rider?" "Not me Turk," I said. "I put it down writer like books in stiff covers."

"How'd you put it down with your arm hanging down your back?"

"I had the arm turned around good with the hand between my legs holding it."

"Alice and Babe sent their best," Turk told me. "Pat Connally's still sore at us."

I tried to remember what that was about. But Bernie DeVoto wasn't there to explain. It probably was difficult for him being a Jack Mormon and never having wintered in the hills. But I still hear from Mon and Johnny Wogoman who are despersed and Chub Weaver in Red Lodge.[2] Mon Wogoman and I were at one time the only guys our age who had killed 3 grown grizzlies by ourselves running onto them alone in the high country and nothing [has] ever happened to me since that gave the same feeling and Swedish prizes do not move you in that way.

I'm very sorry about the committee (mis-spelled) and I hope you will understand.

If you are a betting man 1 dollar will get you 4 that my dog Blackie at least 14, hearing gone, tough for him to get up hill from the pool no vision in one eye but with a good appetite and loves to be alive and to smell me work will outlive Mr. Eisenhower. You can get this up to 100 for 400.

Maybe it's an attractive investment.[3]

With sincere good wishes,

Ernest Hemingway.

1. Adams, editor of the *New York Times Book Review,* was chairman of a committee of writers and artists seeking Eisenhower's reelection. **2.** The brothers Munroe (Mon or Mun) and John Wogoman and Leland Stanford Weaver, called Chub, worked on the Nordquist Ranch in Wyoming when EH was there in 1930. Chub appears by name in *For Whom the Bell Tolls.* **3.** Black Dog died before President Eisenhower.

To HARVEY BREIT, El Escorial, 5 November 1956

Dear Harvey:

Just got yours of Oct 26. I wrote you a couple of long letters, kid. Did you never hear anything? What ungrateful animals you must think us. We have talked so many times of how happy we were at 116 [East 64th Street]—and what wonderful thoughtful hosts and good friends you are.

Mary is better. 4,060,000 without transfusions or boosters. She had grippe a couple of times and I had it once. But the doctor [Juan Madina-veitia] is curing the spasmodic gastritis she had and her colitis. This is slow but coming along well.

He found the usual wrong with me and some interesting new things but I went on a strict regime of everything and in a general examination 2 days ago he said I was better in every way. He had forbidden me to go to Africa but I explained I would go anyway. So now it's settled that if I follow his regime, which is not too easy, I can go. Would go anyway but might as well follow the regime and training is a bore. But have had to do a lot of it and can do it again.

Won't comment on national or international affairs as would be out of date by the time you got it. Communications were very bad on the [World] Series here. Half the time I couldn't hear [Toots] Shor. Still waiting to hear from him.

I asked my son Jack (Bumby) to call on you and Pat. He is at the Training School of Merrill Lynch, Pierce, Benner etc 70 Pine Street. His name is John H. N. Hemingway.

Why should I be angry? *Me* angry at *you?* That would be really crazy. I explained once when we were trying to qualify as friends that we were no relation to the Dylan Thomas's.

Going to Africa in January. Am very happy and excited. Fraiche et Rose comme au jour du battaille.[1] (mis-spelled).

We saw some good bulls fought beautifully and some very bad bulls. I wrote you about Antonio. We have this Limited Company, Hemingway y Ordonez S.A. and we sell shares to no one. The last bull he dedicated to me in Zaragoza he came over and said, "Ernesto we both know this bull is worthless. But let's see what we can do with him and if I can kill him the way you'd like."

He is coming out to join us in Africa. Then the Maharajah of Cooch Behar has wanted us to shoot with him in India. But Antonio has to fight first in Mexico end of Nov. and Dec. Wish you and Pat could see him. All the old real aficionados think he is one of the 4 great fighters of our time. That is from Joselito and Belmonte until now. He fought 66 times in formal corridas this year and was gored 3 times once very badly. Now we have to sweat out Mexico.

If you guys can go to Mexico I'll write Antonio. Had lunch with Belmonte Saturday and we are driving with him tomorrow, Tuesday. Wish you were along. He talks better and tells funnier stories than anyone. A very great man.

I wrote you how strange things are here. In spite of having been on the Republican side am considered a Spanish author who happened to be born in America. Would rather tell you about it than write about it.

We buried Don Pio Baroja [novelist] last Tuesday. It was very moving and beautiful. I'll tell you about it. Thought Dos Passos or *some* Americans could have sent some word. The Time thing[2] was quite false about [my] visiting him. He was a hell of a good writer you know. Knopf dropped him, of course, when he did not sell. The day was misty with the sun breaking through and burning off over the bare hills and on the way out to the un-consecrated ground cemetery the side of the streets were jammed solid with flowers, the flower sellers stands for Nov 2— All Souls day, and we rode out to the cemetery through the country he wrote about in Hierba Mala [*Mala Hierba = The Weed*, 1918], La Busca [*The Search*, 1917], and Aurora Roja [*Red Dawn*, 1910]. There were not too many of us. He was buried in a plain pine coffin, newly painted black so that the paint came off on the faces and the hands of the pall bearers and on their coats.

Much love to you and Pat and to Sylvia,

HUL   Ernest

1. Phrase of the nineteenth-century historian Edgar Quinet about the survival of wild flowers through the ages. EH had picked it up from James Joyce in Paris in the fall of 1933 and modified it in his memory. The original words were "fraîches et riantes comme aux jours des batailles." See Richard Ellmann, *James Joyce* (New York, 1959), p. 676; and Carlos Baker, *Ernest Hemingway: A Life Story* (New York, 1969), pp. 247, 608. 2. *Time* 68 (29 October 1956): 47.

To GEORGE A. PLIMPTON,[1] La Finca Vigia, 4 March 1957

Dear George:

Your questionaire got here the day after I did Feb. 16. So far have done 21 pages of the 32 pages sent.

It came at a very rough time Kid. Found over 400 letters that Monstruo [Roberto Herrera] hadn't forwarded nor even sorted except as to size! Also I have to do income tax. Also, like a bloody fool, I had expected to sit down and go right to work on book.

I'll have the questions done by first week in April or the 2nd. Maybe before. But when I think I could have done them when we were at Escorial and had fun doing it instead of taking the top off each day here. This morning started at 0700 and to 1030 and I've done 3 questions.

Main trouble is that I'm so profoundly un-interested in them and I can feel you are too. We are both way past this question and answer thing and I have none of the exhibitionist's love of being in the book and there are so many more things more important to do with what time I dispose of.

Please don't bother to come over. We always love to see you. But I honest to Christ won't have the time.

Will knock this off now and get back to the interrogation.

Best always,

Papa

Mary sends her very best

If I can get the framework of the questions done then I can take the top of the day for my own work and be happy. I know you know how this is.

PH. PUL   EH

1. Plimpton was preparing the interview with EH that was to appear in *Paris Review* 5 (Spring 1958): 60–89.

To WALLACE MEYER, La Finca Vigia, 24 May 1957

Dear Wallace:

Thanks for your prompt letter. I shouldn't let B[arnaby] Conrad anger me but just now with 2 pictures being made over which I have no control (and receive nothing) and with that bastard [David] Selznick sabotageing A Farewell to Arms (he's rewritten the love story with Ben Hecht) he told [John] Huston it was no good. *His* is a real love story. Selznick would never permit Rock Hunter to approach a girl in such a gauche way. They have rewritten it all etc. My temper is a little rough. Selznick he says has written a love story that is a love story not just followed slavishly some screwy thing by me. It makes you pretty sick, Wallace. But in the first picture version Lt. Henry deserted because he didn't get any mail and then the whole Italian Army went along it seems to keep him company.

Thanks for giveing me Igor Kropotkin's name again. Hope your hand is OK.

Best always
PUL   Ernest

To CHARLES SCRIBNER, JR., La Finca Vigia, 24 May 1957

Dear Charlie:

Wallace wrote me about your third son [John]. Congratulations to you both and to him too. I'm glad to see C.S.S. with all that depth.

Thank you very much for the piece that you wrote about the firm.[1] There were many things that I did not know and it was very interesting.

This is the second letter I wrote you about it. In the first one I got started on Tom Wolfe's letters[2] and had to throw the letter away after 2 typewritten pages. Did you ever know him? I only met him once with Max for a drink at the Waldorf. If I'd read those letters I think I could have found a way not to turn up. Better stop before I have to throw this letter away too.

Hope everything goes well and that you don't work too hard and get a good vacation. We've had foul weather here for nearly 3 months.

Best to you and Joan and please remember Mary and me to your mother.

As ever

PUL   Ernest

1. Charles Scribner, Jr., had written a short history of Charles Scribner's Sons, which appeared in the *American Library Association Bulletin*, March 1957. **2.** *The Letters of Thomas Wolfe*, ed. Elizabeth Nowell (New York, 1956).

To ARCHIBALD MAC LEISH, La Finca Vigia, 28 June 1957

Dear Archie:

Thanks very much for your letter.[1] Ever since I had it, have been working on the letter to [Robert] Frost. Mary is typing it this morning and will mail it with this.

Am afraid it is not as good as it should be as I have tried to keep it simple and the subject is very complicated.

All Ezra's friends were put into the hole with that [John] Kasper business. But it is his megalomania that makes him receive dangerous fawning jerks as Kasper. That is why I wanted him to give an undertaking on no politics as I cabled you. But doubtless he would not and I would lose whatever influence I might have with him by suggesting it. He would not mind taking a martyr's role on all the things we hate and that is what, I believe, everyone should avoid.

If he would go to his daughter's [in Italy] it would be fine. I had heard all sorts of stories from different people about the [Olga] Rudge etc. None of that is our business. We want to see him free to write poetry and practice any of the arts. Personally I think his hunting licence should be restricted for him not to write on or indulge in politics. Otherwise his enemies will get him to say damned fool things that will get him into trouble again. They will do this as soon as he is free of restraint in order to get him into bad trouble. He would be protected from this sort of baiting on subjects which he is not sound about, if he would agree not to discuss politics at all. Otherwise I see nothing but trouble with the type of journalists who will be after him to provoke him into the role of the "Anti-semitic, race-ist mad Poet." The first thing he would probably want to do would be to go on the Mike Wallace show. This sort of thing should be avoided.

Maybe I am borrowing trouble. Certainly Ezra should be released.[2] But he should be released under such conditions that he will not be encouraged and provoked into saying such things that his mind is not sound on that he will be picked up and put inside again.

I wanted to write you this before I started on the letter to Frost. But then I thought I was delaying and maybe saw things too blackly as an abstainer and that if this were in the letter, perhaps there would never be any action, but only the waiting and putting it off. Anyway these are my private thoughts for what they are worth.

On the corporal front the last examinations didn't turn out as we'd hoped after cutting all consumption to two glasses of light red wine per lunch and dinner the Hanger was still positive 2 x. So am now cut to one wine glass with the evening meal. Must cut it out entirely it seems but they do not want to treat the nervous system too violently. After all been drinking wine with meals since I was 17 or before. Anyway let's not talk about it. Makes you plenty nervous and very difficult to be with people you don't know. Would rather not write about it and if it's a dull life for me it must be even duller to read about. The good thing is that if I go through with it (haven't had a real drink for four months when we reach July 4th) and use no wine at all for three more then I will be able to drink wine again and test along to see how much can drink without damage.

Keeping religiously on the diet and to the exercise and weigh 206 and look very good. Going to Key Sal end of next week to fight through the cold turkey nothing to drink part. Trouble was all my life when things were really bad I could always take a drink and right away they were much better. When you can't take the drink is different. Wine I never thought anybody could take away from you. But they can. Anyway in about ten hours now I am going to have a nice good lovely glass of Marques de Riscal with supper.

Hope you and Ada and everybody fine. Mary sends her love. Wish we all could have got together this year.

Please give my best to Mr. Frost and thank him. I'm glad he got so

many honours and seemed to be so happy with them. Me I'd trade all
the honours in this world for two good bottles of claret a day and to have
my Black Dog back again young and well and not buried down at the
pool alongside the tennis court.

Un abrazo

LC   Pappy

1. MacLeish, Robert Frost, T. S. Eliot, and EH were trying to secure Pound's
release from St. Elizabeth's Hospital, Washington, D.C. **2.** Pound wrote EH from
Washington on 16 April, 13 June, 15 July, and 13 and 20 September 1957. On 22
September, Dorothy Pound wrote EH to deny a published report that Pound had
called EH dishonest. Pound himself publicly denied it in *London Times Literary
Supplement*, 6 December 1957.

EH made an insertion after paragraph six of this letter: "Maybe I worry too much
about it but I can see so clearly the type of job the journalists would do. If he
would agree to say 'I will not discuss politics' and then hold to it he would be okay."

To ROBERT FROST, La Finca Vigia, 28 June 1957

Dear Mr. Frost:

This is, as simply as I can state it, my re-action to Ezra Pound's continued confinement in St. Elizabeth's hospital.

Pound must have been confined now since his arrest for more than
twelve years for treason committed while he was of unsound mind. I
could never regard his actions as anything but treasonable, nor could I
ever believe he would have committed them if he were sound in the
head. I have never regarded him however as a dangerous traitor, and
his influence was no more than that of a crack pot. I have understood for
some time that medical authorities say Pound can never be brought to
trial.

What is the problem? The problem is that Pound, while incompetent
on various subjects, is still one of our greatest poets and one of the
greatest poets of the world. While confined he has written poetry that
has been acclaimed all over the world and been given the highest honors
in poetry in his own country. So what happens?

Other countries to whom we send cultural missions do not understand
this situation. They see one of our greatest living poets with an international reputation still confined in an asylum because he can not be
brought to trial for acts committed during the war, while many impor-

tant known war criminals have served their sentences and been released. They get the impression that a country with the power and responsibility of the United States is afraid of Pound. Or else they get the impression that the Government of the United States has no pity nor any mercy toward Pound and plans to hold him in confinement until he dies. If Pound were to die in confinement after eleven years in St. Elizabeth's, it would make an impression in all of the civilized world that cultural missions and programs would not undo.

Mr. Frost because you are a great poet and an honorable man you can tell the Department of Justice about the great poets who have had great trouble in their political and personal lives but whose work has lived on to be a glory to their countries. Dante had plenty of trouble. So did Byron all the way. Verlaine did time. Baudelaire had trouble and I do not have the time to look up all the poets who were killed in tavern brawls. Certainly if Walt Whitman were alive today, *Confidential* would have been framing him.

No one says poets are not to be punished like any other people, but great poets are very rare and they should be extended a measure of understanding and mercy. Ezra Pound has been confined now in St. Elizabeth's for eleven years and eleven years is a long time to confine a poet or anybody else.

If the Department of Justice could nol pros the indictment against Pound and the medical authorities found him fit for release, I understand that his daughter, Mary de Rachlewiltz, can take care of him in Italy. I would be glad to contribute fifteen hundred dollars toward getting him settled with his daughter.

It may be that the Department of Justice will feel that to nol pros the indictment against Pound would be a very unpopular move because of his anti-semitism, race-ism and his crack-pot views and contacts. I detest Pound's politics, his anti-semitism and his race-ism. But I truly feel it would do more harm to our country for Pound to die in confinement, than for him to be freed and sent to live with his daughter in Italy. He loves Italy and has written great poetry there. It was the way that Italy treated him and honored and respected him as a poet that turned his head and made him think that the government of Mussolini which honored him was therefore a good government.

The whole business is a very complicated one and I have probably tried to simplify it too much, but I have sought to present to you, and through you to the Attorney General, what I believe in the matter.[1]

A. Mac Leish will tell you why my doctor is keeping me down here now. I will be available here for any questions that should come up. They can always be sent down here to my home or through the Embassy and I can answer them direct or through one of the Legal Attachés of the U.S. Embassy here.

Please let me know if I can serve you in any way.

Yours very truly,
Ernest Hemingway

T.C. PUL

1. On Frost's part in freeing Pound, see Lawrance Thompson and R. H. Winnick, *Robert Frost: The Later Years 1938–1963* (New York, 1977), pp. 248–58.

To EDWARD WEEKS, La Finca Vigia, 20 August 1957

Dear Mr. Weeks:

Thank you very much for your letter of August 16th about the two stories I sent for the anniversary number of The Atlantic.[1]

When Miss Adams was down she told me that you could only pay one thousand dollars for a story. But, she told me, The Atlantic would very much like to have two stories if it were possible and would be glad to pay for two.

I am therefore enclosing your check. The price for the two stories to you for this special number because The Atlantic first published Fifty Grand so long ago is $2000. It is embarrassing to me to have to tell you how much of a financial sacrifice it is for me to give you the stories at this price.

Writers have agents who handle the selling of their stories. No agent would permit me to sell two stories for this price when I receive one dollar to two dollars a word for stories and have been receiving that since 1933. I could sell these two stories I sent you for at least four times the price I was giving them to you to help with your 100 anniversary number. It was a pleasure to take the monetary loss in what I regarded as something worth doing.

Yours very truly
Ernest Hemingway.

P.S. You will have noted that I sent the stories marked U.S. First Serial rights only. The letter accompanying your check says payment for all rights. I am glad to grant the 1st Canadian Serial rights but must refer your next letter to my attorney to have it clear that no other rights are granted or sold. Also have the two stories referred to by their titles and have them copyrighted separately. I grouped them under "Two Tales of Darkness" only for publication in The Atlantic.

PH. PUL   Ernest Hemingway

1. "A Man of the World" and "Get a Seeing-Eyed Dog," *Atlantic* 200 (November 1957): 64–68.

To GIANFRANCO IVANCICH, La Finca Vigia, 31 January 1958

Dear Gianfranco:

From the business letter you can see we are back in the bastardly income tax epoch that comes to interrupt and bitch work just at the best working time.

This has been the damndest winter there has ever been though. The whole climate has changed and arctic air circulation has broken through and is only contained by violent storms from the south so that there is one norther after another. There has been strange wild weather since early December. Three times it has been below freezing in Miami and once they had snow as far as Tampa. Real snow. The citrus crop ruined and many young trees killed. The cold and wild weather has been so continuous that the big hotels in Miami are being ruined. Here we have had temperatures in the 40s and 50s and three winter storms where the winds were over 70 miles per hour. There have been three storms as bad or worse than the one we had at Escondido that time with your mother and A[driana] [November 1950].

There has never been such a winter in anyone's memory nor by the statistics. All the Florida frutas menores [smaller fruits] killed and then killed again.

There is a depression started in the states that may be as bad as the one of 1929 too. The rich are more prosperous than ever here so far but there is much unemployment and hunger here in the pueblo.

We miss you very much. I have worked very hard and written many things I wish I could show you. Until the cold weather came I swam everyday thirty to forty laps in the pool and was in very good shape. But now it has been too cold for my kidneys. But you would like it. The pool is still lovely. The place is sort of an ilot de resistance in the middle of the spreading slums of repartos [real estate developments].

Mary's mother died on New Year's eve. She heard about it in the evening and went by plane to Minneapolis for the funeral at the start of one of the biggest storms.

Afdera [Franchetti] is in the social columns of the papers or in Vogue or Harper's Bazaar all the time. She has as good a publicity organization as Leland [Hayward] used to give to Slim. Soon she should be in the 10 Best Dressed Women. It is inevitable.

I tried to write you three letters when you wrote about the civil marriage finally but I could not place the words correctly. I hope you have good news from Adriana.

In November we stopped at that hotel at Mariel for lunch one day and I remembered us talking together. The hotel is the same.

Fish have disappeared from the ocean and the fishermen in Cojimar are desperate with the fish never comeing and the unbelievable weather. Gregorio [Fuentes] saved a man from drowning in a big storm. Monstruo [Roberto Herrera] caught a pickpocket and saved a purse with $500. Neither received a reward nor were in the papers like Afdera. They did not use Gregorio's name although he swam far out into the storm in the night and brought in the body of one man and saved another in a sea nobody could live in. They referred to him as "an old man."

This is the first sunny day for a long time and is beautiful the way winter should be and as you remember it.

I wish I could write good letters the way you do. Maybe it is because I write myself out in the other writing.

Will try to remember news. The tunnel is finished and will be opened in February they say. They are now talking of filling in the bar from the Maine Monument to the Castillo de La Punta to make more land to build Hotels on. The present Malecon to be an inside street. I'm sure Cristina will have heard all about it and have told you. Havana is more like Miami Beach all the time. I do not know where to go. Do you?

Everyone always speaks of you. I told Rene [Villarréal] I was writing you and he asked to be remembered. He is the same fine good boy. Mary says she wishes you were here to see her new roses.

Please give our very best to your family and to Cristina and you much love

tu amigo
Ernesto

PH. PUL

To EZRA POUND, La Finca Vigia, 26 June 1958

Muy Querido Maestro Ex Lunacy:

On the day [18 April 1958] you were sprung or spranged to our great happiness I cabled you to St. E's [St. Elizabeth's Hospital] trying to convey that and asking for an address so could send the enclosed [check for $1,500] which I had guaranteed in a letter through R. Frost to the Attorney General for expenses for you to Italy. This letter written June 28 1957.

Have waited to have any reply but without one yesterday cabled Mac Leish for an address and the name of ship you were sailing on since heard on the radio you were leaving July First. Mac Leish has just now given me this address this goes to and says he thinks you are sailing in middle of July.

From the time the Rev'd. [T. S.] Eliot, the prompt Frost, and self signed the letter to the then Att'ny Gen, I thought it wiser to break off communication so my carefully expressed sentiments aimed toward your release could not be interpreted as friendship but rather as National Policy. That may have done no good but I kept the sentiments on a stern and vehement basis and anyway you are out and I sent you an abrazo by cable on the day it was made firm.

Send another with this and for Christ sake cash the check. During the P. Harbor to A. Bomb war which I actively participated in I wrote A. Tate the Poet that if there should arrive any question of you being hanged I would get up onto the gallows and make clear that I should be hanged with you. He said he would do the same but afterwards I never heard from him and perhaps it was not a practical project anyway due to logistics. But I stayed with you within the limits of my ability and intelligence as well as I could and all [two words illegible] always.

Please count on me for anything that I can do ever. I am so ashamed of how you were kept in such a way and so proud of how entire and fine you looked in the pictures we saw the day you left it. Hope you have a good trip and everything goes well. My love to Dorothy.

Your friend,
Hem

Am registering this in case it has to follow you. Saludos

JFK   E.H.

To MR. AND MRS. WILLIAM D. HORNE, La Finca Vigia, 1 July 1958

Dear Bunny and Bill:

It was so fine to see you and have meant to write every day since I got Bill's letter with all the gen and the fine maps [of the K-L Ranch]. But was racing with this book and never knew what we could do or when. Now it looks like stay here and work all this month. But we have the maps and all the gen against another year and Boy do they come around fast now.

Thanks so much for sending it all. The place sounds like the good early L-T [Nordquist Ranch] days.

Mary has written about all the news. Kidnappings are the latest local sport. They now have mining engineers, sugar mill technicians, consular officials, seamen (all ratings) and Marines—I called the Embassy to ask when they were going to start picking up the F.B.I.—the latest gag is that F[idel] Castro will entertain more Americans on July 4 than Ambassador Smith.

Best love to you both and my best to the boys

Ernie

God I wish we were heading out west together again the way we did that year when we first met Bunny![1]

WDH

PH. PUL

1. Late in July 1928 EH and Bill Horne had driven to Folly Ranch near Sheridan, Wyoming, where Horne first met his future wife, Bunny. They were married in 1929. See EH to Waldo Peirce, 9 August 1928.

To ARCHIBALD MAC LEISH, Ketchum, Idaho, 15 October 1958

Dear Archie:

I was awfully glad to get your letter out here but sorry there was something loused up in the [Paris Review] interview. All I could do was try to answer the questions as they were put. Am sure you told it straight and that they got it wrong. Everybody gets everything wrong.

About knowing writers it was older writers they meant and I never thought of you as an older writer. Also think they were asking about when we first hit Paris in the old Rue de Cardinal Lemoine-Place

Contrescarpe days. Maybe I knew you then but I dont think it was until we had gone back to Canada and then come back to live at 113 rue Notre Dame des Champs. I remember very clearly comeing to the Rue du Bac the first time and stealing a cork screw which I remember returning. Anyway George [Plimpton] was asking about the first days in Paris and that was what I was talking about and writing about at the time. When we used to go around together was afterwards when I did not see very much of G. Stein any more and Ezra went to Rapallo and Joyce had finished Ulysses and the fun time between that and going to work on the blind stuff. You correct me if I am wrong because I can remember most things word for word that were important but other times I would forget automatically.

You dope. Did you think I had forgotten Rue du Bac, Juan les Pins, Zaragoza, Chartres, that place of Peter Hamiltons you lived, our bicycles, Ada and the Six Jours [bike races], rue Froidevaux, and a million things, Gstaad,—dont ask me to name them all. Bassano and A Pursuit Race. How many better stories has she published than that turn down—they all write about those people and about the junk now.

But Archie I am a slow writer about the past and I cant put you in before I knew you but I was very fond of you and am and I loved Ada and I do.

Poor Sara and Gerald—let's not write about it. I loved Sara and I never could stand Gerald but I did.

Ezra is something that you behaved magnificently about and now it's over. So good.

When I wrote you then [1954] I was in bad shape. It is not easy to eat 12 bad eggs nor to regenerate smashed insides etc. nor take off weight when you cant exercise. But you can do anything with discipline (so far) and by the time I saw George P[limpton] I was in pretty good shape weight 206—pressure 150/68—Hangar finally almost negative etc. Worked ten months straight after that—swam an 880 every day and sometimes an extra 440 and sometimes two—got down to 205 steady—pressure 136/66—Hangar negative—all liver tests O.K. Colesterol down almost normal. Still had a month to go on this book[1] so Mary suggested we come out here as Cuba weather was getting me down. (Her too) I hadnt taken any time out from working since the end of last October. So [Otto] Bruce from Key West and I drove up here from Key West via Chicago where we picked up Mary. Was nice to see the country in the fall. Bruce and his wife [Betty] now going back to Key West. We'll go out this afternoon and shoot some ducks for them to take.

Sorry about Dick Meyers [Richard E. Myers, composer] and the funeral. Hope you have a good time and good luck with the J.B. [MacLeish play, 1958]. Everything I have heard about it sounds very good.

I do not know about the theater. I mean not understand about it. It must be wonderful if you like it and I hope I will not discover it too late the way I did aircraft.

Dont know what to say about teaching. I still do it quite a lot and enjoy it but don't get paid for it. If you get paid for it and like it probably you better keep it up as anything you really like you will do anyway and the bastards will pay more attention if they have to pay.

Mary is fine but had a bad virus infection (flu) that now is bothering her head. This is the best climate for it though.

Hope you and Ada are well and that the kids are fine.

Bumby is in San Francisco working for Merrill, Lynch. Patrick (Mouse) has his own spread in Africa and is doing very well as a White Hunter. His address Patrick Hemingway, Private Bag, Arusha, Tanganyika Territory. He is very well thought of and is a good hunter. If you know anybody thinking of a safari I can honestly recommend him. He can handle any sort of safari—hunting or photographic.

. . . Gigi . . . is in his 3rd year of pre-med now at University of Miami-Florida or was when I heard from him in September.

Hope you have a fine winter, Archie, and that everything goes the way you want it to.

Best love always
Pappy.

It was so fine seeing you when you both came through with the Cowles. Mary sends her love.

My dearest love to Ada

LC   Pappy.

1. The Paris sketches published posthumously as *A Moveable Feast*.

To BRONISLAW ZIELINSKI,[1] Ketchum, 5 November 1958

Dear Mr. Zielinski:

As I cabled to L.A. your plane for Salt Lake City is Flight 72 *Western Airlines* leaving San Francisco 1205 pm arriving Salt Lake 430 p.m. (1630). Larry Johnston of Hailey Idaho will meet you with a Beechcraft which is a very good air-craft and fly you to Hailey where we will meet you at the field. Johnston is a fine and very experienced pilot. He will be in a hurry to get off to get in while there is still daylight. But can land even if it gets dark so do not worry. The air strip is good.

They tell me the fare by Western to Salt Lake from S.F. is $48.80. I am enclosing a check for $100.00. We will figure out how you want to go back whether by rail or however. You are our guest and will not need money for fares or expenses.

When we first set up this flight from S.F. the daylight was longer than it is now. But have just re-checked with Johnston and by using the faster plane instead of the Tri Pacer it is absolutely OK.

If there is bad weather so Johnston can't fly call me from Salt Lake here at Ketchum 3762 and we will have an alternative way of getting you up here.

Johnston will have you paged when your plane comes in.

There is a good middleweight fight at Salt Lake City Monday night if you have to stay overnight there.

There will be details in the papers—Joe Micelli vs Gene Fulmer.

Have a good time and we look forward to seeing you soon. Good hunting here still.

Best always
Your friend
Ernest Hemingway

UVA

1. Zielinski was EH's Polish translator. Between 1955 and 1957 he had done *The Old Man and the Sea*, *A Farewell to Arms*, *For Whom the Bell Tolls*, *The Sun Also Rises*, and twenty-three short stories. In 1959 he did *Green Hills of Africa*, in 1961 *Across the River and Into the Trees* and twenty-five more stories, and in 1966 *A Moveable Feast*.

To PATRICK HEMINGWAY, Ketchum, 24 November 1958

Dear Mouse:

Your letter came today and was so happy to hear from you and Henny.

It has been wonderful here since we drove out October 6. Drove from K.W. with [Otto] Bruce like in the old days—up to Perry, Florida (now a big highway junction with fine motels) formerly the chain gang capital of the resin country—then by Mobile north through Mississippi to some place in Tennessee and then up through Illinois to Chicago. Picked up Mary there and drove through Northern Illinois—from Rockford to Galena really beautiful—rolling and looking like the Dordogne in France and sometimes like Bucks in England across Mississippi to Dubuque— Galena a wonderful beautiful town—you could see why Gen. Grant was nobody there. Drove across Iowa on N. 210 now a good road and then through Northern Nebraska very fine sand hill prairie chicken country with the Sioux reservations Rosebud etc. just north so town full of Indians at evening and good steaks—many cars with bucks on top—shot opening of season in Western Wyoming. Lot of flighting ducks and saw many pheasants. Drove north of Scott's Bluff and Torrington which are on U.S. N. 30 and into Casper then north through Buffalo and Sheridan and over the Big Horns to Cody. Next day through [Yellowstone] Park and down new Superhighway to Blackfoot and into Ketchum hitting Picabo around 5 p.m. We slept; out from Chicago at noon, one night in Iowa in the Pfeiffer country (went through Parkersburg where Mother [Pauline] was born) and Dyersville where my great grandfather Hancock settled when he sold the barque Elizabeth at Callas and brought his children to U.S., walking across Isthmus of Panama to settle in Iowa when still over run with Indians with [where] the other Hancocks had settled and one gone into Yellowstone country as mountain man before Lewis and Clark. Was very interesting to see the small English town and then the rich German Pfeiffer country towns. I had driven Uncle Gus [Pfeiffer] there once and we only went through accidently. What I wanted Mary to see was the beautiful part of Northern Illinois which I hadn't seen since used to go prairie chicken hunting with my father with a wagon and two pair of dogs.

Then we slept one night in Nebraska just south of the Rosebud Agency and the next in Cody. It was a lovely drive. Everybody in Cody the same except, as always, many rummies passed away or been called or summoned as Hailey Times puts it.

Here it was that wonderful fall—things not much changed—many ducks (local). Northerns did not come down until the first snow that was a blizzard ten days ago. But main Northern flight still to come. Mary has been shooting very well—on driven pheasant—partridges and ducks.

I have been shooting OK. Have weight at 204 to 206. Sprained ankle day before yest. which accounts for letter instead of valid intention of writing letter.

Write 4 days a week—hunt 3 and sometimes afternoons if go well. Pappy and Tilly[1] are fine and send their best. We are living in a cabin near the creek but have to shift to another Dec 20th—can shoot ducks till Jan 6th—I want to finish book [A Moveable Feast] here—go back to Finca—straighten up various things, situations and manuscripts there, do income tax and then go to Spain for San Isidro and stay there during the summer. Then would like to go out to Africa in the fall.

Cuba is really bad now, Mouse. I am not a big fear danger pussy but living in a country where no one is right—both sides atrocious—knowing what sort of stuff and murder will go on when the new ones come in—seeing the abuses of those in now—I am fed on it. We are always treated OK as in all countries and have fine good friends. But things aren't good and the overhead is murder. This is confidential completely. Might pull out of there. Future looks very bad and there has been no fishing in Gulf for 2 years—and will be eventually no freedom coastwise and all the old places ruined.

I've written you from time to time about Key West. Will send you a full report on it anytime you want or need it. Have been holding on to it for you because land worth money—money is on skids—stocks boom—but earnings fall—we have a first speed inflation—when it goes into high it will be too late to put out a first anchor let alone a 2nd. Your common stocks, if good, will be O.K. and go up with it. The institutions and people that are buying them for anchors and shifting from Bonds are what make this market. . . .

Bum is finally doing very well in Merril Lynch in San Francisco. He had a lousy deal in Cuba but made a fine fight last year there and his boss wrote me, unsolicited, how well he is doing in California. His address is Merril Lynch 301 Montgomery Street, S.F. 4, Calif. But you are probably in touch with him.

Mr. [Charles] Thompson is very anxious to hunt with you. He has the money to do it and wants to do it before he dies. Mrs. T. would be along as a non-shooter. I talked with him about it and advised him to book far enough ahead and for a good time. Couldn't give him much gen as you had written me you were booked until next October. I did advise him not to book for rainy season as what they want more than trophies (those kudu, buff, rhino he has are hard to beat) is a fine hunt in Africa when it is good (*where it is good*) before he kicks off. Will give you exact details on his condition and what he wants if you want them. Will see them when we go through on way to Cuba.

Mr. Sully [J. B. Sullivan] is fine but lonely. If you could send him a card for Christmas he would like it. We just had a letter from Denis.[2] He is OK but sort of gloomy. He really had a good time with us I think in spite of worthless fishing. Good eating and reading.

Thanks for sending the African Life piece. The guy meant well certainly. . . . Old Jimmy Robinson is your pal. I might be able to work out a deal with Look that could do you some good but am always shy about burdening you with any tie up with me. It could be a natural of a photo story. But would respect your no or your yes.

Much love, Mr. Moose. Mary will be writing Henny.

[Cartoon of owl head.] Unsuccessful great horned owl Küss. (Have one in barn). Ketchum Idaho until Jan. 15 1959—Finca thereafter until end April. Weigh 205.

PUL   Papa

1. Lloyd R. Arnold (1906–1970) and his wife, Tillie. He was chief photographer for Sun Valley from 1939 to 1959 and author of *Hemingway: High on the Wild* (New York, 1977, rev. from 1st ed. 1968). **2.** Denis Zaphiro (b. 1926), game ranger, Kajiado, Kenya; British Army veteran. EH first met him near Machakos in August 1953.

To GIANFRANCO IVANCICH, Ketchum, 7 January 1959

Caro Gianfranco:

Thank you very much for your Christmas cable and for the letter and the check. I hope you got a good price for the [Gianfranco's] Finca. It was a lovely piece of ground and I remember how happy you were there—like Gaugin [Henri Gauguin] without the big needle. It was a fine place and I remember all the different greens. Speaking of the big needle poor Sinsky [Juan Dunabeitia] was cogida again by his old enemy [coronary]. For the 4th time at 60. A record even for a Basque. Con la izquierda y facil [With the left hand and easy]. But [Drs.] Cucu [Kohly] and Jose Luis [Herrera] have him cured and he is navigating again.

Three nights ago I talked with René [Villarréal] on the phone and everything was OK except short of food. But the huelga general [general strike] is now over. I told him to butcher one of the male calves and to loan the pisycorre [station wagon] to responsible local revolutionaries in any emergency.

The sergeant (the bisco [*bizco* = squint-eye?] from Cottorro who came on the robberies) who killed Machakos our dog and tortured several boys of the village was hanged a couple of months ago by the boys of Cottorro with the usual mutilation. Cosas de Abysinnia. I will cut out the despatches of Herbert Mathews etc. in the N.Y. Times that have just come and send them with this letter. The papers (AP and UP) were announcing the defeat of the rebels with [Fulgencio] Batista in pursuit across Camaguey while Batista was leaving the airport for Cuidad Trujillo [Dominican Republic] with his chief murderers and thieves. The Mauritania and Gripsholm were in the port with New Years Eve in Havana parties in all the Casinos when B. was leaving the country. They all sailed as soon as they could round up the revellers. Wish we had been there together. Very funny. You and Liugino saw him come in, remember. I wish we might have seen him go. Remember how we went to Cayo Paraiso on that 10th of March—Mary and Gregorio and I—Sic transit hijo de puta [So passes the son of a whore].

They had no snow here until 4 days ago. Now 2 feet has fallen—good snow and the ground prepared to hold it by a week of −20°−2F. With good cold ground there won't be avalanches even if the snow keeps up.

Duck shooting finished yesterday. It was really superb this year. We had very good partridges and pheasants too as well as quail. The country was beautiful all fall and no rain until this snow finally came.

You would love the high open valleys at 1600–2000 meters—beautiful streams with trout and some with salmon in the spring. There are ducks and geese along all the streams and yesterday in the deep snow we hunted along small streams in the lava rock with water cress in them. The ducks (Misurini [?]) jumping up high and fast. I shot 3 doubles of big green heads in the snow. Mary shot steadily and well all season. Yesterday and the day before there were many snipe too in spite of the snow.

We hope to get to Europe in May. I hope we can be together in Pamplona and Madrid.

Please forgive me for not writing more often nor better letters. Will write some more on this tomorrow. Must go to bed to try to write well on the book [*A Moveable Feast*] tomorrow.

Very nice people live here in these valleys. The farmers and ranchers. We shoot together and have fun. Mary made a party for 40 people two days after Christmas at Trail Creek cabin and it was very good. An S.S. zither player but very good pianist and Basque food. You and Cristina would have liked it. Now I will not go out again until the book is done.

Gianfranco I worry about A[driana] and wish you could give me any news of her: good or bad. We were very happy to hear from your mother. I will send this and the cuttings from the papers later when Mary has finished reading them altho you will probably have much better news from Cuba.

Excuse my always poor letters and give my love to all good friends in Veneto. I heard from Federico [Kechler] they are at Codroipo—not Percotta. What about this?

Our kitten (Big Boy Peterson) has gotten onto the paper. So I do not have so much left. It has stopped snowing now.

Bumby is doing very well in San Francisco. Mousie is too in Africa. He has his own Safari Outfitting Company now. . . . Mary is fine and very well. Our love to your family. Un abrazo muy fuerte.

PH. PUL   Papa

To L. H. BRAGUE, JR., Ketchum, 24 January 1959[1]

Dear Harry[2]:

Sorry this was delayed. The word on the statements, interviews, books etc. is: you're doing OK. Have an unlisted phone here Ketchum 45–92 if you or Charlie ever have to call me. Don't give it to anyone.

Am hammering on here to get this stage of work done before returning to Cuba which is over-run by every type of character and visiting fireman who put your writing out of business. Since it was published that I was working here get quite a lot of visits and calls from work-killers but I am getting in 5 good days of work a week and keeping in shape. With shooting season over am up to 207 this morning but will bring it down again.

Thanks for the report on the R. [Rowland] Ward elephant book [*Records of Big Game*, 1892]. It is cheap at that price and I hope we get it soon. Advise the rare book dept to get any copies that they can.

Things are OK with us in Cuba. A friend I was in Spain with is one of the new govt. He called me up here to say everything OK. Had been out at the Finca. Officer commanding Havana Garrison is an old S.F. de Paula boy who used to play ball on local team I used to pitch for. Jaime Bofils who called me said they were waiting to give us big welcome. With all the vested U.S. interests they will be bucking to try to give the Cubans a square shake for the first time ever. It will be a very rough time. I knew Phil Bonsal the new Ambassador when he used to work for I.T.T. before he went into the State Dept. He and Pauline and her sister Jinny and I went to the Feria in Salamanca together in 1953 [1933]. He is a very sound able guy but will naturally be working for our interests some of which are run OK (like United Fruit) and some very un-OK with terrific deals made with [Fulgencio] Batista. [Fidel] Castro is up against a hell of a lot of money. The Island is so rich and has always been stolen blind. If he could run a straight government it would be wonderful. Batista looted it naked when he left. He must have 600 to 800 millions and that will buy a lot of newspapermen—and has.

Must stop this and get it off. Excuse me not writing letters. I write each day until I'm dead pooped and then force myself to walk and climb to keep in shape so as to be healthy and sleep. But we had a big magpie shoot last Sunday 105 and another one this Sunday. I wish the hell I could still ski but the Drs. say too dangerous with the back.

Is snowing now. Please give my best to Charlie. Will write on other things another time.

Best always,
Ernest

PUL

1. EH misdated the letter 1958, a common January problem. 2. Brague was an editor in the Trade Department at Scribners.

To L. H. BRAGUE, JR., Ketchum, 22 February 1959

Dear Harry:

Thank you very much for sending me the royalty report and for the books. If you haven't sent the books will you send them to the Finca, please, as we will be leaving here in 2 weeks.

Am delighted you have some good new ones. A great friend of mine of whom I was very fond died last week and we buried him yesterday [Taylor Williams, 18 February]. It is getting to where I have very little depth on the bench in friends.

Worked 4 days out of the week but have no heart to work today. Had hoped to finish the 1st draft here (am on Chap. 45) but lost ground badly this week and will probably have to finish in Cuba or in Spain. Am over-due in Cuba now the way things are going and when I get there must do my income tax. I wish the bastards in addition to taking all your money (or only 90%) did not have to take two weeks to a month out of your working life. . . .

Tell Charlie how pleased and proud I was of the royalty report and of him and how he figured things. I hope to have plenty more good books for him. Can really work well out here and plan to come out and work in a shack and put everything in shape I have cached in the safe deposit vaults. So tell Charlie never to worry. We have plenty of stuff ahead. Some wonderful and I will cut out the shit.

I think probably the next book to publish is the Paris stuff I showed to George Plimpton. I have that all typed and will take it to Europe with me and go over it all and maybe do a couple more of the pieces. It is a hell of a good book—really.

All these people dying makes me feel I should work harder on account of time so short. But honest to Christ I really cannot work any harder, I have to pace my work and also keep in shape. Week before last I wrote 4000 words—last week 2950. But I'm now where I have to read over and re-write so much each day before I start—and we had casualties. Not losing somebody—but how you lose them.

I love to write. But it has never gotten any easier to do and you can't expect it to if you keep trying for something better than you can do.

Just had a telephone call from Charly Sweeny from Salt Lake. He had another stroke after visiting here. But waited to let me know until he was well enough to call. Says he is fine. Strokes don't mean anything any more etc. This one paralysed him slightly on one side etc.

Show this letter to Charlie please. I could give him a book every year like [John] Steinbeck composed of my toenail parings (i.e. reprint of war correspondence), little fantasies about King Poo Poo or other author toe jam.[1] But that is all shit and just the byproducts of egotism or avarice or both. Charlie doesn't need that stuff from me and doesn't want it and neither of us would do it anyway.

Thanks for the Rowland Ward elephant book. When I read it [1954], loaned by one of the authors, I had a fracture (skull) and had to read it in a hurry on acct. we were going to go down to the coast and I was not too good in my head. Thought it was much better than it was. Glad to have it—but it is not as good as I remembered it. Worth what we paid but not to buy as an investment for Scribners I mean.

Best investment I can make is writing manuscripts. Since Dr. [Don Carlos] Guffey in K.C. got 23,000 for the stuff I gave him or signed for him I hate to write letters even. I thought of writing him and asking if he would not like to send me a case of Scotch out of his loot. May yet.

Glad [Jonathan] Cape was in good shape. We always got along well after the first time we had a row more than thirty years ago probably. Quite a bit more. He keeps his word and isn't a bit wet and all his faults are obvious. Don't trust and never could trust his partner. You can trust, within his limits, a gent and also someone who is really *not* a gent in England. The mixture is awful. In America it is more complicated.

Excuse such a dull and vacuous letter. I seem to be shucking off my grief with platitudes and the result resembles hominy; only it needs lye to make hominy. Maybe there is a little lye in my platitudes.

Hope everything goes well with you. We will leave here sometime between the 7th and 12th March. Want to go up to see Yellowstone and the geyser basin and the game with the great cold and deep snow in a snow plane or snow-mobile. (Prop driven ski shod outfit.) Have seen it as late as Nov. but never with the 25 below and the deep snow. Coming home want to see Las Vegas and also the Grand Canyon in winter. Maybe Antonio Ordonez, matador and great friend, will join us. We talked together yest on phone. He is fighting at Bogota. Has 5 fights at 30 G in S.A. and wanted to come here between fights but connections (plane) unsure with winter weather. Now he thinks maybe he can make it after his last fight before he has to return for Spanish season. Maybe you saw piece about him in Sports Illustrated by K. Tynan.

Best to Charlie,
Yours always
Ernest

A guy named Dave Morin who knew Charlie in Navy and thinks very highly of him asked me to send him his best.

PUL   EH

---

1. EH means Steinbeck's *The Short Reign of Pippin IV* (New York, 1957).

To PATRICK HEMINGWAY, Málaga, Spain, 5 August 1959

Dear Mouse:

Awfully sorry to be so late answering your fine letter but you know how Spain is and this has been a very rough temporada. First must tell you that we met the character you hunted with from Valencia who came up to Madrid with his wife. If half he says about how wonderful you are is true it will be quite something to meet you sometime. Another character named Andres B. Zala was even more violent in his praise but I couldn't decide whether he had really hunted with you or not. Hope he did. You have a very good cartel in Spain and I think it would be a good idea for us to be here together sometime. We'd have fun anyway. You could help me out signing copies of 'For Whom the Bell Tolls' in the callejon.

Antonio [Ordóñez] is wonderful, brave, consistent and unbelieveable with both the cape and muleta. His killing is rapid but is still defectuous [faulty] except recibiendo.[1] But he does kill them decently and get them out of the way. I have learned more about bulls and the whole trade every day and it is wonderful to be back with it and have a chance to move around over Spain and make the same roads many times in the different seasons. This place[2] where we stay is really lovely. Bill Davis is an old friend that you met at Sun Valley and we hunted jackrabbit together one time. Have been to your place along the coast going back and forth to Antonio's ranch which is north of Tarifa and this side of Cadiz within sight of Chiclana. That is a country that I never knew and you would love it very much. We are buying some land at a place on the coast in that area called Conil. It is like everything was in the old days before they spoiled everything. Wonderful beach, fine people, real Arab town and good fishermen like [as in] Cojimar. Being around Antonio is like being with you or with Bum except for having to sweat him out all the time. He has had one bad one on May 30th and another that could have been bad but missed the femoral by about a quarter of an inch deflected by the scar tissue of an old cornada. He has thirteen cornadas altogether and not one of them has spooked him. He is spooked sometimes in the night the way we all are and prefers to sleep in the daytime which is smart but he loves his work truly and he loves bulls too. We have a lot of fun together, really fun and he trusts me very much and I hope that I am good for him. There are a lot of worthless people around him some very bad but we are sifting most of them out. We have run into wonderful people on this trip and I have had the best time I ever had and have excellent stuff for new appendix to Death in the Afternoon which Scribner's say will have the effect of a whole new book. Enclose a few family pictures.

I met Tony who worked for you he said and is opening up in Sudan. He seemed o.k. and had quite a good piece on Sudan in Caza Pesca. He gave me the bad news about rhino and lion and yesterday a letter from Philip Percival confirmed it. Please give me any new gen and let me know how this will affect you. Moose have dictated this letter because we are just back from two long ferias and have had to make extra trips on account of Antonio's goring and mail had piled up the way you remember it.

Hope you had a good safari and please let me know your plans when you have a chance to write. Certainly there must be a country where there are bad rhino that you can get permission to take out, when we think of the thousands that Jock Hunter destroyed for Ritchie it is pretty sad. Philip wrote me that I would never want to come back the way things are now but I think there always must be pockets of good country that one can get into and hunt if we were not on the 'big five' basis.

Love to you and to Henny. Will try to write more details about Spain another time. Never saw so many storks as this spring. Mille fois merde.

PUL   Papa

1. "*Recibir*: to kill the bull from in front awaiting his charge with the sword without moving the feet once the charge has started. . . . Most difficult, dangerous and emotional way to kill bulls; rarely seen in modern times . . ." (*Death in the Afternoon* [New York, 1932], p. 472). 2. La Consula, a large estate between Málaga and Torremolinos, where the Hemingways were houseguests of Nathan (Bill or Negro) and Annie Davis from May to October 1959. It was the site of EH's elaborate sixtieth birthday party on 21 July. EH and Davis, a wealthy American expatriate, had known each other since 1940. See Carlos Baker, *Ernest Hemingway: A Life Story* (New York, 1969), pp. 545–47 ff.; and Mary Hemingway, *How It Was* (New York, 1976), pp. 462–76.

To ANDREW TURNBULL, at sea, 1 November 1959[1]

Dear Mr. Turnbull:

Been laid up with grippe or flu. Got up to come down and see you but you were not in your cabin and am sweating too much to hunt the deck etc.

Nothing to say about Scott. Am trying to write a little about him when I knew him. Good luck. I enjoyed your stuff on him in New Yorker very much.

Am going up to the bar at 1st Salon—near bow—known as Jeans, to pay out etc. Will check with Dr and see if can stay up. Otherwise at [stateroom] 48 packing and writing some notes.

Yours

PH. PUL

E. Hemingway

1. Note delivered to Turnbull aboard the *Liberté* westbound shortly before landing. Turnbull had been in Paris gathering material for his life of Fitzgerald, *Scott Fitzgerald* (New York, 1962). EH was carrying the typescript of *A Moveable Feast* for delivery to Scribners on 3 November and was not disposed to reveal his trade secrets to a stranger. Turnbull was saddened by EH's evident physical debility at age sixty. See his article "Perkins's Three Generals," *New York Times Book Review,* 16 July 1967.

To CHARLES SCRIBNER, JR., New York, 3 November 1959

Dear Charlie:

There is one chapter missing[1]—a very good one. But Hotch [A. E. Hotchner] has a photostat of it and will send it in. When you finish reading this please mail it to me c/o C.E. Atkinson, Shopping Center, Ketchum, Idaho.

Best always,

PUL

Ernest

1. In the typescript of *A Moveable Feast,* which EH submitted with this note attached.

To NATHAN DAVIS, Ketchum, Idaho, 7 January 1960

Dear Negro:

Hope you and Annie had good holidays and Teo has a good school and likes it.

We were to leave here day after tomorrow but Mary's arm[1] needs some more whirlpool bath and manipulation and leaveing has been put off one week to 16th. I will go on to Cuba from Chicago but Mary wants to stop to see her cousin [Beatrice Guck] there 2 days. She will be at the Finca by or before the 25th.

Her arm is comeing along OK. The piece about the size of a walnut (English) that was broken off the end of the humerus and was sewed back on seems solid now. She is getting better movement in the joint each day—lateral as well as up and down and under anaesthesia they bent it all the way up. There is one place that is not right and George[2] has sent some special films off for consultation and opinion. But it is so much better than anyone expected it would be and with patience and fortitude she will have a useful arm with which she can both shoot and fish as well as write, use typewriter etc. But it has been very rough although any place else it would have been rougher. She could not have had better people to work on it, nor better facilities and I have been able to devote myself full time to her care, comfort etc. Will not molest you with details nor timetables. Shortly we'll be back in Cuba where there are servants trained to these various duties and can get back to work.

Wanted to phone you at Christmas but we had a big storm with all wires out for 3 days. Since have had —20° —25° weather. But very beautiful. I try and walk enough to keep in shape and have held weight down to 202–203. Had some fair shooting for a while but the hours have been bad for it lately. Days very short and the mornings taken up with the hospital and errands. Been makeing up by really working with the hand trap—beautiful place to throw here with a grove of cottonwoods, the [Big Wood] river, and some fine willow thickets and have shot at a few thousand targets and made some good runs several 50 straights —a 98, a 103–105 etc. George throws very well as do a couple of other friends here. Hotch [A. E. Hotchner] shot well on targets but disasterously in the field on his last day and felt very badly. I felt worse as I thought he had really learned to shoot. But the hell of it was that he had learned to shoot targets that were falling and the damn ducks just towered. Haven't heard from him since he went to N.Y. from the coast for Christmas. May have been on acct. of the wires being down.

I wrote Val[3] the gen on getting to Cuba and our plans and when they were delayed day before yest cabled her we would be there absolutely by the 25th.

She needs a tourist visa for U.S. Needs a ticket to Havana and *return Havana to Miami or Key West* or N.Y. to be given Tourist Card and Tourist Entry for and to Cuba.

Will get this off to you now on way to Hospital and find your other letters and send check for Pembroke coral. Please let me know other expenses.

Best love to you both.

PH. PUL   Ernest

1. EH had driven to Ketchum with Ordóñez and his wife, Carmen, in November. On the 27th, after the Spaniards had left, Mary shattered her left elbow while hunting. See Mary Hemingway, *How It Was* (New York, 1976), pp. 479–80. 2. Dr. George Saviers, EH's personal physician in Ketchum and Sun Valley. 3. Valerie Danby-Smith, a young Irish girl whom the Hemingways had met in Spain in July 1959. See *How It Was*, pp. 470–71.

To GENERAL CHARLES T. LANHAM, Ketchum, 12 January 1960

Dear Buck:

Thank you very much for your good letters and for writing to Mary. I must apologize for not haveing written for so long. Mary really shattered her left elbow Nov 27 and have been looking after her through operation, various manipulations and subsequent therapy plus doing the chores normally performed at the Finca by Juan and René. We have had storms and blizzards and two weeks of 15° to 25° below weather mixed in. Beautiful and healthy but burns lots of oil and Mary got a bronchitis last week and been in bed 4 days etc. Plan to leave here on the 0146 train 4 days from now. That is if her temp is normal today. Been one thing after another all fall and up to now. Some people are better handling pain than others. Anyway let's put it that pain hurts Mary bad and is hard on her nerves. Under those circumstances people sometimes blame whoever is nearest and whoever they know the best receives the smallest ration of their heroism.

So my writing has been limited to paying bills.

Should have set your mind at rest about quotes attributed to me (Yanqui) but figured you knew me well enough not to believe what you'd read in the papers. I sent the message to Lenny [Leonard Lyons, gossip columnist] so my friends that I hadn't been able to write to would have the gen. Also Lenny was publishing rumors as were papers and I thought my message to him would straighten things out.

That Yanqui thing was something taken out of context from a local paper by old pal Edward Scott and published in Havana Post to make me trouble.

To say you are not a Yanqui Imperialist but an old San Francisco de Paula boy (in a village where you've lived 20 years through all sorts of times) is not a renouncing of your citizenship. I am a good American and have been to bat for my country as often as most—without pay and without ambition. But I believe completely in the historical necessity of the Cuban revolution. I do not mix in Cuban politics but I take a long view of this [Castro] revolution and the day by day and the personalities do not interest me. I keep my mouth shut about it and have not given an interview to an American newspaper man since I came in on the "Liberté" Nov. 4 [1].

In the present situation there is nothing I can say that would not be misinterpreted or twisted. I have a terrible amount of work to do and want to be let alone to do it.

This place[1] is a good rental property in the ski-ing season and in Summer and was a wonderful buy. I plan to live here in the shooting months which correspond to the hurricane months and the early northers in Cuba. The place should pay all taxes and expenses and maybe be a source of income. My health and Mary's needs a change of climate from the sub tropics for part of each year. My pressure is bad now from worry and all the contretemps of this fall. Will skip all atrocity stories or bitching.

We may have a hide out in N.Y. [1 East 62nd Street] to use the way we used Harvey's [Breit's] old place that summer. Mary was holding out for one. But it won't be a hideout in that town if anyone knows about it. It would just be a trap. But if I am ever in N.Y. (which don't think I will be before middle of June) I'll call you. I hate N.Y. But Mary loves it. Nobody can afford it. Last time was there only 2 days and one of them election day and was tied up with Scribner's, Hotch [A. E. Hotchner], [Alfred] Rice and Bank. Didn't see Harvey Breit, Lenny, nobody.

Have kept weight below 205 for a year now. 203 this morning. Can't sleep good. Maybe not enough walking and running all the damned errands with the car.

Wish there was better job news from you and that Pete [Mrs. Lanham] didn't have such high pressure. Please tell her how badly I feel for her. Has she used Serpasil? It is very good. Also DIURIL. If the Serpasil depresses her she can counter-act it with RITALIN. Have her ask her doctor about these. George Saviers has been useing DIURIL very successfully for 2 years to control high blood pressure without any bad effects.

Mary is awake now and she has no fever. It is a beautiful bright day and she is cheerful.

I'd better knock this off or you'll never hear from me.

Thanks for being so patient. Best always

un abrazo
Ernesto

When you write to Cuba skip local politics but don't pull any other punches.

Funny piece in Argosy by a real jerk we wouldn't let crash party to celebrate end of bull fight season. He weighed about 240 and was 25 years younger than me and boy did he chicken out when I called him. You should always break those guys jaws though. Although I suppose they would sue you.

PUL

1. EH had bought a two-story concrete chalet built by Henry J. (Bob) Topping on a hillside overlooking Big Wood River just west of Ketchum, on 6 April 1959. He mailed a check for $50,000 in full payment to C. E. Atkinson of Ketchum, who represented him in the purchase.

To CHARLES SCRIBNER, JR., Ketchum, 16 January 1960

Dear Charlie:

Packing and sorting mail & preparing to leave here for Cuba tonight I found your letter of Dec. 21 which had never been opened. It had evidently been brought over from the Shopping Center in the confusion of Christmas.

Mary shattered her left elbow Nov. 27th and has been in and out of the hospital. She will get a useful arm out of it but it has been rough on her. I have been looking after her and it has been a fairly full time business. But have tried to keep in shape to go back to work in Cuba where hope to be by middle of next week. Will stay there working until at least middle of June. Should be able to rent this place for ski-ing season and the summer.

This is just to [a] hurried note to explain why you have had no answer to your letter and why we sent no cards at Christmas.

The school edition sounds OK. Have you ever thought about bringing out the illustrated one Cape has? The drawings are excellent and I have bought many for friends who are always very pleased with them. They were made at Cojimar and are authentic and good.

Please write to the Finca. Best always to you and Joan.

PUL   Ernest

To CHARLES SCRIBNER, JR., La Finca Vigia, 31 March–
1 April 1960

Dear Charlie:

Thank you very much for your letter of March 23rd. You had better scratch the book from the fall list. The enclosed schedule of the work I have been doing on the bullfight thing for Life[1] will explain why. I still have a month's hard work to do on it and then the typing, correcting and retyping. I had no idea that it would run to this length when I started it and had hoped to finish it in 15,000 words. It is not a loss for us however as it can all go in the appendix to Death in the Afternoon or make a separate volume with the additional material I will add to it. We can work that out together later. The thing now is to get the damn thing finished. I sprinted on it very hard as you will see in the statistics, which are moderately spooky. Am no Tom Wolfe, all the words have to make sense; which can be tiring. So please do not feel badly as this is a property too.

As you said the Paris book should be good whenever it comes out but I am very sorry not to have it for this fall as we had planned. But tomorrow is the first of April and I could not possibly get into it before the end of May or middle of June and it is stupid to work yourself to death. Excuse me using a five-letter word but we have both had them in the family and I think it is the stupidest way to bring it about even though it makes you feel righteous.

Plenty of people will probably think that we have no book and that it is like all the outlines that Scott had and borrowed money on that he never could have finished but you know that if I did not want the chance to make it even better it could be published exactly as you saw it with a few corrections of Mary's typing.

I hope that you and Joan are well. We are finally getting some decent weather here and I am going to try to fish two days a week to get some juice back. The pool is good for swimming and Mary's arm is getting much better with that and the massage. It has been a tiresome thing for her but I think that it will turn out all right.

If you want to make any explanations for why the book is delayed after having been announced you might say that I wanted to add three more chapters which I had debated with myself about writing. That is very true and can do no harm I think.

Best always,
Ernest

Best to Harry [Brague]. I did not mean to write him brusquely. Thought he was an old army character and would realize I was in the middle of something. When he sees the word count will know I was. This morning is April First and have just finished paying off. Feel terribly about postponing book but if I do not rest a little as I work the Dr. says I will blow a gasket. Haven't been able to sleep more than 2½ to 3 hrs at a time. Get about 4 a night—five at most. Weigh 200 this morning which is good and what keeps the [blood] pressure down.

PUL   E.H.

1. EH appended a five-page longhand set of worksheets on which he had listed his daily output of words for *The Dangerous Summer* from its start at Nathan Davis's La Consula near Málaga (10 October 1959) through 30 March 1960 in Cuba. He computed 8,693 words done at La Consula and 54,869 at La Finca Vigia, for a total of 63,562.

To GIANFRANCO IVANCICH, La Finca Vigia, 30 May 1960

Dear Gianfranco:

I am so happy whenever we get a letter with news of you and so glad you are writing again. It is raining here today. The first all day rain of the year. There has been a very big current for two months and plenty of fish. The Finca is green and fine now and swimming wonderful not too cold nor too warm. It was a strange winter—Northers one after another. They never had such a winter in America before and there was heavy snow down into Georgia and a big snow storm in Chicago in middle of May. Sinsky [Juan Dunabeitia] went back to Spain so it is possible to work more. I wrote you about Mary's arm I think. She shattered the left elbow falling on frozen ground when shooting in November. The bone broke like a grenata [*granata* = grenade]. Bad operations (good but difficult) and then therapy that goes on still. That was why we sent no cards or letters at Christmas (please tell all friends). She came down here in January (end) and the cold winter was bad for it of course. I have worked very hard on it with massage (the machine) and she has done good therapia but it has been awful for her now for six months. It will be OK though even though she does not have faith; only seeing the daily and not the weekly and monthly progress. Valerie [Danby-Smith] came over to help and has been very good and cheerful.

I have worked terribly hard—written over 100,000 words since end of January and every day when finish too tired to write letters. Have the first draft of this about the bulls that comes after Death In The Afternoon done now.[1] But must have it copied and re-write of course. May have to, probably, come to Europe to get what I need for the end. Life will publish 30 or 40 thousand words of what I contracted to do for them about Luis Miguel [Dominguin] and Antonio [Ordóñez]. I hope you will like it. Since I finished the first draft day before yesterday have worked all yesterday and today on income tax. This year have extension until June 15. You remember what those times are.

When you get this will you write me air-mail here what you paid for the Lancia from the funds we leave in Venice (I have paid income tax on all of them) so that I will be able to put in the price paid in order to take depreciation. The bills you can send later just so I have them when they have to be checked. Also any expenses in Italy on Insurance, piezas [rooms] etc. Put them all in Lira and translate them into dollars. I cannot deduct the price of the car naturally, but only the expenses of the damage I believe and yearly depreciation. I have all the bills for the repairs in Madrid and maybe parts are included. Will check but only started this business yesterday. I had meant to write long ago but the work has been continuous and difficult and all the news sad.[2] Mary's arm will be OK though. As good as my right arm and my back—if she is patient. It has been very difficult for her.

Am very glad you shot well and had good bob racing. I shot well last fall but could not shoot in the field so much with Mary in bad shape. Everyone here is fine and sends very best to you. We always miss you. Wish you were here now on this rainy day and we were all going to have lunch. Yesterday (Sunday) afternoon we won a very big cockfight with Pichilo [Finca head gardener] at Cotorro. He has trained wonderfully this year. René [Villarréal] is fine and sends his best. Mundo [cat] still alive and with the animals. Lots of good grass on the finca and wonderful mangoes starting.

Our very best to Cristina and to your family

un abrazo muy fuerte

PH. PUL   Papa.

1. *The Dangerous Summer*, excerpted in *Life* 49 (5, 12, 19 September 1960), dealt with the rivalry between the matadors Ordóñez and Dominguin. 2. Between the lines of this letter, in the emphasis on sadness, the worrisome preoccupation with details, and the allusion to his "terribly hard" work on the bullfight book, may be detected the imminent onset of EH's mental illness. Mary Hemingway hints that the problems began as early as January 1960. See Mary Hemingway, *How It Was* (New York, 1976), p. 481.

To DR. GEORGE SAVIERS, La Finca Vigia, 14 June 1960

Dear George:

Just a note to answer your letter of May 20 before it gets to be June 20.

Finished first draft of bull thing end of May—over 110,000 words. Been doing Income Tax-copying and re-writing since. Mary in a big bind with the Income Tax. It is always tough and tough on her. Val [Danby-Smith] doing very good job copying. Think you'll like the piece. There is a good part about you at Pamplona and Valencia [July 1959].[1]

Mary's arm is going on OK. The extension is very good and she can reach her fingers to her mouth now. Swimming in the warm water helps it a lot and she is very faithful about the exercises. I give it 20–30 minutes a day massage and have the adhesions broken down pretty well I think. It goes down as far as my right arm does now. The Medicines never came. Everything very slow now. Books ordered from Scribner's in April still drifting in.

Hope Pat and the kids are fine. Please give our love. Sorry poor old Don [Anderson] has had such a rotten time. Give him and the Duke [Forrest Mac Mullen] my best. Haven't written any letters as have been jamming really to hell working.

We'll have to go to Spain to check some stuff on end of piece and book. But will give you the word on that. Antonio fighting wonderfully. But had bad liver trouble probably didn't follow diet in South America.

Best to all friends
Take good care.
Papa

Fishing been lousy due heavy rains from two tropical depressions. Haven't been in boat since May 19.

PH. PUL

1. Dr. Saviers and his wife, Pat, had attended EH's sixtieth birthday party at La Consula.

To CHARLES SCRIBNER, JR., La Finca Vigia, 6 July 1960

Dear Charlie:

Thank you for your letters of June 20, which came June 29th, and July first, which reached here yesterday. I'm terribly sorry Harry [Brague] has been having such a bad time and is in the hospital again. Please give him my very best. At least they have very good stuff for pneumonia now. But it is still plenty tough and the aftereffects are not good.

This typeing is not so good either but have been writing so long in longhand or dictating letters that am rusty. Maybe it will pick up as it goes along.

Thanks for letting me know about the Canadian edition of The Old Man and The Sea. It sounds fine.

We can talk about the bullfight book when we meet. The part I wrote, with the re-write, came to something over 120,000 words. Life originally wanted 4,500 then it went up to 15,000 and on up to 30 and 40. Ed Hotchner came down last week to see if he could help me cut the Life material to 30 or 40 thousand but the best we could do and have it be any good was around 70. My stuff does not cut well, or even excerpt, as I cut as I write and everything depends on everything else and taking the country and the people out is like taking them out of The Sun Also Rises.

But there is so much that I don't use that it should, with the other material to come, and for the appendix, be a good book I think whenever we publish it. Hotch called up last night. He had seen Ed Thompson, the manageing editor who did not seem surprised or upset over the length. They are going to read it over the week-end and Hotch will call me Monday night. They may not want it, of course. In that event I will have wasted five months on the article but no time on the book. In any event I think we should publish the Paris pieces first.

I went over all the ones I had here and arranged them in their proper order and they read very well. I corrected them so they are in shape. I tried to go on and write some more but was so stale from over-work (had not had a day off from work nor been out in the boat from May 19 to July 4) and thought that I had better get some juice back in before writing any others as do not want to lower the quality. If we had only those that you have read it would be o.k. for a book.

Since early April have been haveing bad trouble with my eyes. There is nothing wrong with them that is operable and the lack of vision and the astigmatism can be corrected to 20/20 and has been. They were in very good shape when I came back from Ketchum but were very badly strained working on this book as I worked and read without glasses. The best man here says there is a progressive deterioration of the vitreous (humor) (matter) caused by much former high blood pressure etc. and the astigmatism, strain, reading without glasses etc. Will get another reading on all this in N.Y. Would appreciate your not saying anything about it to anyone. Not knowing how bad they were going to be caused me to jam ahead too hard on the bull fight thing. But now I know that I will not be laid up with them and can continue to work. This man here is supposed to be very good. He was out of the country for a while and I had to wait for him to get back as did not want some enthusiast fooling with them. It is perfectly possible that they have been bad this way before and they seem much better with the new glasses.

Jury duty must have been pretty bad. As you will have read, news is not pleasant here today. Have had the radio on each half hour since six this morning and all news bad.

Going down and swim in the pool now. Our very best to you and Joan and please tell Harry how badly I feel that he is having such a miserable time. We had planned to be leaving here in a couple of weeks. Very hot now and the trades are not blowing and it rains heavily each afternoon. The big fish have not come yet but are over-due and I would like to pull on a couple of big ones before I leave. Down to 194 lbs. this a.m.

Best always
Ernest

PUL

To MARY HEMINGWAY, Madrid, 25 September 1960

Dearest Kittner:

After I wrote you from the Consula same day as you wrote the last letter I got here we came up to Madrid[1] and resumed the nightmare of telephone operations with Hotch [A. E. Hotchner] on that picture deal. The United Nations diplomats and correspondents had the lines tied up and calls were sometimes 4 to 6 hrs behind schedule and cables that should take an hour straight would take 5 hours or more. Night letters up to 36–48 hours. You certainly must have been having a big show and it made what was going on at this end seem very unimportant and trivial. But the telephoning was something. Hotch probably told you. One time was on phone or scheduled and waiting for phone from 6 when woke to 6 that night, then all night until 4 AM—without clothes off nor sleeping so as not to make stupy. Then finally got through at 11 next day. Looked impossible to make Logroño but made it under 5 hrs. Was awake finally 44 hrs and then could not sleep. What we saw at Logrono (wonderful) and what happened with Luis Miguel [Dominguin] in Madrid gave me an ending [for the *Life* articles] so I figured did not have to make Nimes—an additional two days of driving (plus 2½ back) and only a French corrida—plus Paris scandal sheets—plus possible incidents with Luis Miguel (he will make any sort of trouble now for publicity) so headed back here to clean up on various things especially the pictures for book plus still checking same plus other stuff I need, and be here for the Hotch negotiations (also the correction of the Life pictures for Life En Espanol). I see my way through the book now although Luis Miguel's ups and downs keep complicating it. He really worked at a come-back but failed in Madrid the same day Antonio was so very great at Logroño. He [Antonio] made terribly long and moving dedication to me in the callejon and then went out and risked his life worse than I have ever seen him do it—killed him for me in his new wonderful way. High up and beautiful—won't try to write it all as don't want to lose it. He said it was the last bull he'd kill this year in Spain in the dedication. But there is big pressure on him to fight with Luis Miguel on the 12th of Oct at Puerto de Santa Maria —to make an exploitable rivalry—otherwise Miguel may kill 6 but I won't stay for it. Must get out of this and back to you and healthy life in Ketchum and get head in shape to write well. I can say that they went on and did this, whatever it turns out, but that I had to get back to Ketchum —can see how to do it—in the writing I mean. But the pictures are the difficult part now and clearing up some other ends now. Hope you've been having fun. Hotch said you were having wonderful time. Your last letter sounded fine. We can't tell here from the papers what really happens. I opened a letter from Playboy that awful magazine that is planning a new frame-up on my big mistake. It was addressed to you asking you to intercede with me. I just saw the Playboy and slit it open by mistake. But it is something I have to take up with [Alfred] Rice. There are hells own amount of problems in this last mail. Cabled Hotch would call him Monday if he was ready—otherwise Tuesday. Went to Prado this morning—everything disordered replacing the wooden floors with marble and pictures scattered as the pages of a torn book. But as wonderful as ever when you found them. Light perfect. I love you my dearest kitten and as soon as I know what date in October (early) can leave will cable. Lots of problems but we will solve them all. Not sleeping, tricky memory etc bad —any drinking bad for me except lightest claret. Plenty others [problems] but we will work them out and I'll get healthy and write fine. Hope everything fine in N.Y. and that when I come I can get in without press trouble. Would have loved to come in the middle of UN thing[2] when everybody busy. It must have been something. Excuse this being so hurried and such a bad letter. It carries love and high hopes for a lucky fall and the others in the pool.

Your Big Kitten

Hope the Hotch Deal works out. Many angles. It's the Nick Adams story for pictures. But involves ten stories—and I don't know how experienced Hotch is dealing with Picture people. Cabled Coops [Gary Cooper] why [I] couldn't make it to France. Did [two words illegible] ever send the tickets?

PH. PUL

1. EH was now near the end of his ill-starred trip to Spain, August–October 1960. He and Mary had left the Finca on 25 July. After a week in their New York apartment at 1 East 62nd Street, he flew off alone to Madrid to follow again the fortunes of Antonio Ordóñez and to work on pictures for the excerpts from *The Dangerous Summer* that were to appear in *Life*. Mary Hemingway, in *How It Was* (New York, 1976), pp. 485–91, has covered this dangerous autumn and included extensive excerpts from EH's letters of 15 and 26 August and 3, 7, 18, and 23 September. He feared a "complete physical and nervous crack-up from deadly overwork" (15 August), complained of his "worn out head—not to mention body" (26 August), and of recurrent nightmares despite dosages of Doriden (3 September). On 7 September he wrote of feeling much better, though "still not good in the head." On the 18th he exclaimed, "Christ I'll be glad to be out of all this mess and in Ketchum with you and a chance to be well and do good work I can believe in and be happy doing," adding that he was "sick of the whole [bullfight] racket." On 23 September he wrote, "I wish you were here to look after me and help me out and keep from cracking up. Feel terrible and am just going to lie quiet now and try to rest." He reached New York on 8 October, outwardly cheerful, inwardly a turmoil of fears, suspicions, and obsessions. *How It Was*, pp. 491–93, describes his subsequent behavior in New York

and Ketchum. It was not the "lucky fall" he had hoped for but a fall of another kind. On 30 November he entered St. Mary's Hospital of the Mayo Clinic in Rochester, Minnesota, for medical and psychiatric treatment, registering as George Saviers to avoid publicity. He had been there six weeks and three days before his presence was discovered and announced. **2.** The lively fifteenth UN session had opened 1 September. It included speeches by Eisenhower and Castro (four and a half hours) and rostrum-pounding by Khrushchev.

To WHOM IT MAY CONCERN,[1] Rochester, Minnesota, 4 December 1960

To Whom it may concern:

My wife Mary at no time believed or considered that I had ever committed any illegal act of any kind. She had no guilty knowledge of any of my finances nor relations with anyone and was assured by Dr. George Saviers that I was suffering from high blood pressure of a dangerous kind and degree and that she was being booked [at the Kahler Hotel, Rochester] under his name to avoid being bothered by the press. She knew nothing of any misdeeds nor illegal acts and had only the sketchiest outline of my finances and only helped me in preparing my [tax] returns on material I furnished her. The bags that I carried had her labels on them but she always believed from the time I met her in New York that the only reason I traveled as I did was to avoid the press a practice I had followed for years. She was never an accomplice nor in any sense a fugitive and only followed the advice of a doctor friend [Saviers] that she trusted.

JFK   Ernest M. Hemingway

1. This was evidently an unsolicited memorandum designed to free Mary from accusations of complicity in supposed illegal acts in the event that the FBI or the IRS should ever decide to prosecute, as of course they never did, having no cause. The letter was first printed in Mary Hemingway, *How It Was* (New York, 1976), p. 494.

To L. H. BRAGUE, JR., Rochester, 8 January 1961

Dear Harry:

Thank you very much for your letter of Dec 1 that has been forwarded to me here. Am awfully sorry not to have answered sooner but there was some confusion as I had to get out here in a hurry with a blood pressure of 225/125 and am registered here under the name of my Dr. in Sun Valley—George M. Saviers—to keep from being bothered by reporters etc while they knocked the blood pressure down. It was 118/80 this A.M. (which is the worst time of day) and my weight 175. Don't let that weight spook you. They found an incipient diabetes among other minor things that can be controlled by diet without medication (Don't have to have insulin) and hope to be out of here shortly. Please don't mention me being here or under the name Saviers to *anyone* except Charlie and on no account to let it get into the press or be told in confidence to anyone. There is no security any more no matter how well we were all brought up.[1]

Am awfully sorry you cracked the two ribs in Paris and hope you and Charlie are both fit. Sorry about poor Alan Paton too.

About the money due on December 1 ($19,244.10). It has to be reported in 1960 Income (see Taylor Caldwell case) and past procedure. I trust you did report it and that it went into my account in the Morgan Guaranty 5th Avenue Branch before Dec. 31. If it wasn't deposited yet but simply declared to the govt will you have deposited in my checking account $6000 and the balance in my Special Tax account. If they have not been made out can the checks be dated Dec. 31 if that is legal. Imagine will be broke when I pay out of here and the perpetual tax problem coming up.

Have been here since the end of Oct. [30 November] and was pretty damn sick at first. Mary has been staying at the Hotel Kahler here under the name of Mrs. George M. Saviers. Got in a couple of hours walking and dined last night with my Dr [at his] house and had Sancerre, Muscadet and Haut Brion so things are perking up. I had to knock off working on the Paris stories in Nov. So will you give me a MSS. deadline on that for guidance as soon as I can work. Also thanks for the gen on the photographs for the eventual publication of The Dangerous Summer which I see has been criticized, damned and disposed of by Harry Golden without ever having been published. Antonio Ordonez sent some wonderful pictures too.

Could you also have copies of A Farewell to Arms, Across the River and Into the Trees, Death in the Afternoon, For Whom the Bell Tolls, Green Hills of Africa, The Hemingway Reader, The Short Stories of

E.H., The Sun Also Rises, To Have and Have Not, Torrents of Spring sent in that OK edition (not the cheap school one) *one copy each* to Dr. Hugh R. Butt, 1014 SW 7th Street, Rochester, Minn., and Dr. Howard P. Rome, 622 SW 5th Street. Also *two copies of the same books* to me (George M. Saviers—St. Mary's Hospital, Rochester, Minn.) (marked please hold for Mr. Saviers—Do not forward—).

Also please send to Box 555 Ketchum Idaho *to my own name* marked please hold for Mr. Hemingway—Who Killed Society, Clifton Amory; Trumpets from the Steep, Diana Cooper; Ezra Pound, Charles Norman (Macmillan); Set This House on Fire, William Styron; the last book (not title), Herbert Gold; Shadows in the Grass, Isak Dinesen; The Waste Makers, [Vance] Packard, Random House. And please send me here air-mail to George M. Saviers—St. Mary's Hospital, Rochester, Minn.—the December numbers of N.Y. Times Literary Section and Sat Review of Literature, *all numbers of both* so I may order some books. Have Jan. 1 Times and Jan 7 Sat Review and will get this Sundays Times tomorrow.[1]

Please excuse hurried letter and me being in too bad shape to write sooner.[2] You can write me here directly for a day or so when you get this to George M. Saviers—St. Mary's Hospital Rochester or enclose a letter from yourself or one from Charlie to Mrs. George M. Saviers—Kahler Hotel, Room 1006—Rochester Minnesota. Please write air-mail special delivery. Would welcome any news.

Hope to get back to Ketchum from here.

Best always and very best to Charlie.

PUL   Ernest

1. EH's book orders continued. In letters to Brague on 19 and 20 January he ordered thirty-three more books—a total of forty within two weeks. **2.** Signs of EH's mental condition appear in his frequent reiteration of the same addresses, his extreme preoccupation with details, his worry over income taxes, his error on the date of his admission to St. Mary's, and his fear of "security" leaks.

To PATRICK HEMINGWAY, Rochester, 16 January 1961

Dear Mouse:

Thank you very much for your letter of early December. I am so sorry Henny has been having kidney trouble and the dropsy. It is tough for her to have that with the diabetes too and we send her our best love and sympathy. Mary and I stood by here for the call on December 30th and 31st but it didn't come through. Must have been caught up in the New Years telephone overcrowding.

The child you adopted[1] looks marvelous in the pictures and you and Henny too. This is just a short note so you won't worry about me being up here. Had a 250/125 blood pressure which they have knocked down to as low as 126/84 and believe can be controlled by holding the weight at 175 pounds. Was 173 pounds this morning and figure we will be out of here about the end of the week. Will write another letter from Ketchum.

Cuba I imagine you follow in the papers, but it is much more complicated than what you read.

I didn't think the Life pieces were very good but they were part of a long book which might be. Working on another book about early days in Paris which is very good I think or hope anyway, and want to get that finished now. Have plenty of other stuff ahead as you know.

We will be at Ketchum for awhile. Plans uncertain after that. If it wasn't so close to the rainy season would love to get out to Africa. I thought of that last night and haven't had a chance to talk it over with Mary yet. Hard to find any place to work now where people don't bother you and will let you work.

I am enclosing the Trust Company check. Excuse this short letter. You write such good ones and I am ashamed to write a lousy one but I am hurrying so Mary and I can get off on a walk that is part of the weight reduction program. Address Ketchum and mark it hold and let me know anything we can do to help or anything you want to know about.

Best love. Mary sends best love to you both and to the new member of the family. Tina is a good name. Edwina too.

Love to you both

PUL   Papa

1. Patrick and his wife, Henrietta, had adopted a baby daughter immediately after her birth on 31 July 1960 and named her Edwina.

To GEORGE A. PLIMPTON, Rochester, 17 January 1961

Dear George:

Thank you so much for sending me a letter about [Norman] Mailer and his last completely free evening. Feeling that through the last book, remember the one we bought of his together, the sort of ragtag assembly of his rewrites, second thoughts and ramblings shot through with occasional brilliance [*Advertisements for Myself*, 1960], I was awfully glad I missed the party although they say you should see everything.

The Castro piece was very interesting too and I appreciate your sending it. Shame he didn't get that one off. "I would not run if nominated, I would not serve if elected." May have the quotation wrong but you wrote a hell of a fine letter about him and I can see why he would interest you.

Hotch brought out the book [Plimpton's *Out of My League*, 1961] in galleys and it is harder to write about it. A big part of it is magnificent and although you were cramped by not being able to use the actual language and have to say cuss words instead. But a large part of it is splendid. The book seems to get tired as you got tired from the ordeal of having to throw to those batters and let them pick out a pitch to their liking. It was certainly a dreadful thing to have to do and you make that all clear and the tiredness of the ending and the flatness that it achieves is excellent. But for a book I hoped to have at least the Moore fight too, but then I always want too much from my pals anyway and from you more than anyone. Maybe it will go and I will be wrong. Anyway, I hope so. If a quote from me would be any good, I can figure a good one out. Write to Ketchum and let me know in time.

About Peter Matthiessen and his trip to B.E.A., he can write to my boy, Patrick, P.O. Box 504, Arusha, Tanganyika, East Africa, and tell him what the object of his trip is and see what Patrick might suggest. Peter might send Patrick a copy of his book [*Wildlife in America*, 1960], explain all circumstances and say that I asked him to write to Patrick. Patrick might be out on Safari but I am sure he would answer as soon as he got back. I wrote him yesterday in a hurry and unfortunately, didn't mention Peter coming out. But if he says I told him to write, it will be just the same as though I had written to him. To save time, he could send the book and write the same letter to Denis Zaphiro, c/o Game Department, Kadjiado, Kenya, B.E.A. and explain his situation and tell Den that I asked him to write. I have to write a letter to Denis and will mention Peter's trip to him too. Don't promise that anything will come of either of these but it is the best I can do in a hurry.

I can't remember the address of other characters to put him in touch with as do not have my address book here but he certainly should get in touch with the authors [Bernhard and Michael Grzimek] of a book called, "The Serengetti Shall Not Die [1961]," who made a game count of the Serengetti plain and the devastation caused by the Masai cattle and the poachers in that area which is scandalous. I am sure that Den can put him in touch with the right people but he will really need to spend some money of some kind and everybody is very busy and Kenya torn up with the elections and his best sure bet would be to throw in with the Museum of Natural History group and then use the other leads that I have given. The basic trouble out there is the price of gas and transport is very expensive. The whole Safari business is a racket but once he gets to Nairobi, he can make good contacts there. Both with the Game Dept. and the Director of National Parks. There is also a big outfit backing the Save the Serengetti movement and the book will give him the necessary gen.

Excuse this all being late but came out here the end of November with a blood pressure of 250/125. They believe the whole blood pressure problem can be controlled by holding my weight at 175 pounds. By being a writer which requires a certain amount of standing still even if you do not do it sedentary, this is a rough weight for me to maintain. Archie Moore makes it but you know how he bloats in between times of training. I must not bloat at all and it is going to be very rough but will give it a good honest try.

I am writing this in a hurry so please excuse it and let me know anything practical that I can do *ever* when you write to Ketchum. Main problem now is to get back to work and find someplace where you can do it without being bothered.

Mary is fine and sends her best and please do not be thrown off by anything I wrote about the book as it is damned good, but I only wish there was more of it.

Best always,
Papa

That ordeal of pitching with no umpire and the arm out of shape is still a nightmare to me who knows the value of the nothing ball. You handled that part beautifully.

PH. PUL

To GENERAL CHARLES T. LANHAM, Rochester, 19 January 1961

Dear Buck:

Thanks for yours of the 17th which came yesterday. We could have left here the end of last week. Weight down to 173 pounds this morning and blood pressure 140/82 this morning. But they wanted to complete checks of the liver, all favorable, and now I am stuck with a bad cold in the head and we are waiting for flying weather.

Awfully sorry to hear about Pete and that it is the real thing this time. Please tell her for Mary and myself how sorry we are that she is ill.

Talked to my best sister, Ura, on the phone to Honolulu the day before yesterday. She had just come out of the hospital after her third session with throat cancer; the first was three years ago and she was feeling pretty good.

Old Phil Percival at 76 killed two cattle-killing lions up at Machakos three years after they had given him less than six months in London, after the Big Machine. Three years is a long time these times as we both know.

Glad you didn't take the Veterans Administration [position]. It is a worthy one but you have bigger talents than bucking that unbeatable set up. Am glad to hear that Omar [Bradley] did such a good job. I hadn't followed it as have been away so much. We were very happy to see the J.F.K. invitation to the Inaugural and sent off a telegram explaining why we could not attend and yesterday, the local evening rag here carried a phoney story that when asked if I were going to the Inaugural, I had simply said "No comment." They are an irresponsible outfit and never contacted me in any way at all any more than the Newsweek people did that put out that beautiful story [23 January] you probably read yesterday.

Certainly hope David [Bruce] will get the Ambassadorship to the court of St. James. He is good wherever he goes and my only regret is that he will be somewhere where we probably won't be seeing him.

Don't sweat me out at all. Only sweat out flying weather and the common head cold.

Believe Val [Danby-Smith] is living with some friends of hers on Long Island but have not heard from her and do not know whether Mary has their address. Will ask her when she comes in today. She was in Minneapolis yesterday and had a good time there and bought some slip covers for the Ketchum place.

Best always,
Ernesto

It is a Dr. Dunne on L.I. where Val is staying. But Mary has only the phone no. not the address which will send from Ketchum.

PUL

To PRESIDENT JOHN F. KENNEDY,[1] Ketchum, Idaho, *c.* 24 January 1961

[Dear Mr. President]:

Watching the inauguration from Rochester there was the happiness and the hope and the pride and how beautiful we thought Mrs. Kennedy was and then how deeply moving the inaugural address was. Watching on the screen I was sure our President would stand any of the heat to come as he had taken the cold of that day. Each day since I have renewed my faith and tried to understand the practical difficulties of governing he must face as they arise and admire the true courage he brings to them. It is a good thing to have a brave man as our President in times as tough as these are for our country and the world.

JFK   [Ernest Hemingway]

1. Transcribed from an undated handwritten draft in the John F. Kennedy Library. EH and Mary had been invited to the inauguration ceremony but had declined. This message followed some days after the event, which they watched on television in Rochester, Minnesota. They flew back to Ketchum on 22 January. See Mary Hemingway, *How It Was* (New York, 1976), p. 495.

To L. H. BRAGUE, JR., Ketchum, 6 February 1961

Dear Harry:

Can't remember having the subscriptions asked for as I marked various ones in copies of the Times and one of the Drs. Secretaries (Miss McQuarrie) did the ordering. It is of no immediate importance—will look them up.

Here's gen to date: Have material arranged as chapters [in *A Moveable Feast*]—they come to 18—and am working on the last one—No *19*—also working on title. This is very difficult. (Have my usual long list—something wrong with all of them but am working toward it—Paris has been used so often it blights anything.) In pages typed they run 7, 14, 5, 6, 9½, 6, 11, 9, 8, 9, 4½, 3½, 8, 10½, 14½, 38½, 10, 3, 3: 177 pages + 5½ pages + 1¼ pages.

Averaging words (5 pages):
3 pages all type no conversation   209
                                      266
                                      335
             conversation   222
all conversation   171

$$5\overline{)1203}$$
              240

So figure it is about 42,000 to 45,000.

It is a bastard to be here without my library, reference etc. I get up at 7 when it is daylight, make the breakfasts, get to work by 8:30 or before—am dead tired by 1 pm. Lunch doesn't show till 2 pm or so—Dinner at 8 pm or so. Have to walk at least 2 miles to keep in shape and sleep. Weight 170 this AM (too low). But food has not been what the Drs ordered for some time.

Have no secretary but have sent out an experimental chapter to Mary's idea of who I should have for a secretary and we should see by tomorrow I hope.

Have tried to strengthen book by ruthless elimination of much I wrote (Not the parts you saw—none of that). But anything should be judged by the man who writes it by the quality of the material he can eliminate. All the truth and magic in but we need a better title than *The Paris Stories.*

Deal came up for certain of Nick Adams stories for pictures. To check any tendencies toward identification and bad results made necessary name changes. But need

      1. Carlos Baker book -
      2. Fenton Book -
      3. P. Young Book   To know anything
      4. 2nd book by Englishman they compromised
         Forget his name. John Adkin[1]

Also need for title-ing—one copy Oxford Book of English verse, one King James version Bible (clear print). This is the minimum and there is nothing here.

Try to only think from day to day and work the same but things have been rough and are rough all over. Cuba situation—lack of library to work from—etc. Will not bitch on but thought you would like a situation report. Certainly hope this girl Mary took the MSS to can read my hand-writing. Had to copy all corrections on pages in large school boy hand.

This is all being done under difficulty but it is being done. Thank Charlie for his note and for his Faut d'abord Durer letter [first one must last]. Have sure tried. Drs fixed my allowed alcohol intake as 1 liter of claret a day. Have not drunk ⅗ths of this any day but one and not had a drink of hard liquor. My liver was OK when checked in and when checked out of Rochester. Hangar negative. Cholesterol normal. You, Max and Charlie Scribner are accustomed to the lies of Scott [Fitz-gerald]—But this is the true gen.

About ⅓ of books have come through so far.

Best always,

PUL   Ernest

1. Carlos Baker, *Hemingway: The Writer as Artist* (Princeton, 1952); Charles A. Fenton, *The Apprenticeship of Ernest Hemingway: The Early Years* (New York, 1954); Philip Young, *Ernest Hemingway* (New York, 1952); and John Atkins, *The Art of Ernest Hemingway* (London, 1952).

To GEORGE PLIMPTON, Ketchum, *c.* 25 February 1961

Dear George:

Last night found the number of the Paris Review with the interview I wrote the answers to your questions for you at an old friend's house (no source material here) and saw some stuff I might want to quote in the book about Paris early days that I am checking on now—I mean quote directly from the interview as such not stuff I have already written which I told you in another form.

Don't know when you had planned to publish this interview but noticed it was copyrighted so ask permission to quote. The first interviews were collected, I believe, by Viking.

Could you give this permission through the Review formally to Harry Brague of Charles Scribners Sons or should he obtain it from the Review or Viking? Will you please call him at Scribners and also write me the gen here to above address? Count on you to do this first.

Hope the stuff I wrote for your Out of My League was OK. You know the problems—you being deprived of the actual language (I think that was the toughest) and having to refer to cuss-words and the no umpire business. I can't wait for the Archie Moore stuff. That should be wonderful.

Am sending a copy of this letter to Harry Brague today. Hope things are fine with you. Weighed 170 yesterday and oddly enough am getting strong at the weight. Working hard but temporarily held up checking.

Best always

PH. PUL   Papa

To L. H. BRAGUE, JR., Ketchum, 26 February 1961

Dear Harry:

The enclosed letter is self explanatory. George Plimpton's address is 541 E. 72nd Street NYC. The number of the Paris [Review] is Spring 1958. Fifth anniversary issue. Other references are to a foreword or blurb I wrote for a book of his Harper's are bringing out next month. I have done many things for him we are good friends and I believe he would do this for me gladly.

Naturally this morning I do not know exactly what parts [of the *Paris Review* interview] I would wish to quote but they would not be extensive and I would probably use them in the forward matter or at the end.

Am getting this off in a hurry to get back to work—the Post Office will be open tomorrow. The best I can hope for today would be notice of parcel arrived in the P.O. Box.

Best always to you and Charlie

Ernest

Am a little worried about my weight which holds lower than it should be.

PUL   EH

To PATRICK HEMINGWAY, Ketchum, 22 March 1961

Dearest Moose:

Hasten to send this. Have not heard from [Otto] Bruce to write you details from K[ey] W[est] nor anything new. But saw wonderful pictures of you and Henny and the baby that Bud Purdy[1] brought back. Thanks for being so nice to them. N.Y. deal went through but had to deposit 70% against possible taxes and may be worse but wanted to get this off to you. Trying to finish book and things sound so lousy in Africa wanted to do something immediate.

Things not good here nor about the Finca and am not feeling good but mailing this may make feel better.[2]

R⫿ Küss.

Papa

Everyone sends love.

PUL

1. Purdy was a rancher at Picabo, south of Ketchum, who had been hunting in Africa. **2.** EH's two suicide threats within a few weeks of this letter made it imperative for him to return to Mayo's, from which he had been released late in January. He was flown from Hailey, Idaho, to Rochester, Minnesota, on 25 April.

To CHARLES SCRIBNER, JR., Rochester, Minnesota, 10 June 1961

Dear Charlie:

Thank you very much for your letter and for the Guide to the waters of the Yellowstone area by Wellington. It is the best guide to that fishing that I have ever read—and he is wrong in saying that it would have been un-necessary if the old book were in print—as the earthquake has changed things so completely. One big mud-slide in that country when we fished it used to be able to change a river for years and your friend's guide is really marvellous. If you printed it for him, or could buy one and charge it to my account, I would appreciate it very much if you could send it to my oldest boy Jack—John H. N. Hemingway care of Merrill Lynch, Pierce, Fenner and Smith, San Francisco, California. He is about as advanced a fisherman as Herbert Wellington and I started him on those waters years ago. It would be impossible to give him a better present as he feels as strongly about them as anyone I ever knew until you introduced me to Wellington's Guide.

I'm awfully happy the books are selling so well. Thank you for what you say about them. It made me feel very good.

Hope to be out of here [St. Mary's Hospital] as fit as ever before too long. My very best always to you and to Joan—as ever—

PUL   Ernest

To FREDERICK G. SAVIERS,[1] Rochester, 15 June 1961

Dear Fritz:

I was terribly sorry to hear this morning in a note from your father that you were laid up in Denver for a few days more and speed off this note to tell you how much I hope you'll be feeling better.

It has been very hot and muggy here in Rochester but the last two days it has turned cool and lovely with the nights wonderful for sleeping. The country is beautiful around here and I've had a chance to see some wonderful country along the Mississippi where they used to drive the logs in the old lumbering days and the trails where the pioneers came north. Saw some good bass jump in the river. I never knew anything about the upper Mississippi before and it is really a very beautiful country and there are plenty of pheasants and ducks in the fall.

But not as many as in Idaho and I hope we'll both be back there shortly and can joke about our hospital experiences together.

Best always to you, old timer from your good friend who misses you very much

(Mister) Papa

Best to all the family. Am feeling fine and very cheerful about things in general and hope to see you all soon.

PH. PUL

Papa

1. Fritz, the nine-year-old son of Dr. and Mrs. George Saviers of Sun Valley, was hospitalized with viral heart disease. He died 11 March 1967. This letter was published in facsimile in *Life* 51 (25 August 1961): 7.

POSTSCRIPT

Although Hemingway seemed to his doctors to be well enough to be discharged from St. Mary's Hospital, he died by his own hand less than three weeks after he wrote the letter to Fritz Saviers. With his wife, Mary, he left Rochester on 26 June in a rented car driven by his old friend George Brown of New York. They reached Ketchum on Friday, 30 June. The next morning Brown drove Hemingway to the Mollie Scott Clinic in Sun Valley for a conference with Dr. George Saviers, who brought Fritz around for a short visit with Hemingway late that afternoon. On Saturday evening the Hemingways and George Brown dined at the Christiania Restaurant in Ketchum and afterward retired early. On Sunday morning, Hemingway rose before seven, unlocked the basement storeroom, chose a double-barreled Boss shotgun from the rack, carried it upstairs to the front foyer, slipped in two cartridges, lowered the gun butt to the floor, pressed his forehead against the barrels, and blew away the entire cranial vault. It was 2 July 1961. Burial was in Ketchum Cemetery on 5 July. The news of his death had meanwhile spread around the world.

INDEX

MESSAGERIES
MARITIMES

Dear Bed Mex:

Well here we are almost at the southern end of the Red Sea Tomorrow we will be in the Indian ocean. The weather is just like Keywest on a nice day in winter. Yesterday we saw a big school of big porposes and today many schools of small porpoises.

It was coed and rainy all the way down to Egypt. Then it was hot and fine. Coming through the Suez canal we went right through the desert. We saw lots of Palm trees and Australian pines (like in our yard) whenever there was water. But the rest was mountains and hills and plains of sand. We saw a lot of camels and a soldier riding on a camel made it trot alongside the ship almost as fast